Music Finders
Series Editor: David Daniels

Designed with working musicians, conductors, program directors, and librarians in mind, these practical reference books put the music you need at your fingertips: title, publisher, duration, instrumentation, and appendixes for cross-referencing are all provided in these carefully researched volumes. Using the orchestral repertoire as a starting point, this series will also encompass chamber music, ballet, opera, thematic music, and repertoire of individual instruments.

The Music Finders series is based on the Scarecrow titles *Orchestral Music: A Handbook*, by David Daniels (2005) and *Orchestral "Pops" Music: A Handbook*, by Lucy Manning (2008).

Chamber Orchestra and Ensemble Repertoire: A Catalog of Modern Music, by Dirk Meyer. 2011.

The Canon of Violin Literature: A Performer's Resource, by Jo Nardolillo. 2011.

Arias, Ensembles, and Choruses: An Excerpt Finder for Orchestras, by John Yaffé and David Daniels. 2012.

Orchestral "Pops" Music: A Handbook, 2nd edition, by Lucy Manning. 2013.

Orchestral "Pops" Music

A Handbook

Second Edition

Lucy Manning

THE SCARECROW PRESS, INC.
Lanham • Toronto • Plymouth, UK
2013

Published by Scarecrow Press, Inc.
A wholly owned subsidiary of The Rowman & Littlefield Publishing Group, Inc.
4501 Forbes Boulevard, Suite 200, Lanham, Maryland 20706
www.rowman.com

10 Thornbury Road, Plymouth PL6 7PP, United Kingdom

Copyright © 2013 by Lucy Manning

All rights reserved. No part of this book may be reproduced in any form or by any electronic or mechanical means, including information storage and retrieval systems, without written permission from the publisher, except by a reviewer who may quote passages in a review.

British Library Cataloguing in Publication Information Available

Library of Congress Cataloging-in-Publication Data
Manning, Lucy, 1948–
 Orchestral "pops" music : a handbook / Lucy Manning.
   pages cm. – (Music finders)
 Includes bibliographical references.
 ISBN 978-0-8108-8422-9 (hardcover : alk. paper) – ISBN 978-0-8108-8423-6 (ebook) 1. Orchestral music--Bibliography. 2. Popular music–Bibliography. I. Title.
 ML128.O5M36 2013
 016.7842–dc23   2013019516

∞™ The paper used in this publication meets the minimum requirements of American National Standard for Information Sciences—Permanence of Paper for Printed Library Materials, ANSI/NISO Z39.48-1992. Printed in the United States of America.

Dedicated to
my daughters

AMY MANNING JOSEPH
JENNIFER ERIN JOSEPH PERRY

CONTENTS

Preface vii
Abbreviations xi
Alphabetical Listing by Composer 1
Appendices
    A. Works Listed by Instrumentation 283
    B. Works Listed by Duration 329
    C. Works Listed by Themes 373

Americana	374
Animals	375
Black History Month	376
Broadway Musicals	377
Celebration	378
Circus	378
Dance	378
Ecology	381
Fanfare	381
Films	382
Holidays	387
Instrumental Pops	393
International	395
Jazz	398
Novelty	399
Patriotic	399
Popular Classics	401
Popular Songs	404
Seasons	406
Space	406
Sports	407
Travel	407
TV	408
Video Games	409
Weather	409

    D. Works Listed by Title 411
    E. Publishers and Sources 435
About the Author 461

PREFACE

This new edition of *Orchestra "Pops" Music* uses the same convenient cross-referencing format as the 2009 edition which mirrored the well-established and honorable model of David Daniels' *Orchestral Music* tomes. New with this publication are over 1000 additional entries, needed corrections to some of the original entries, expanded information for many of the works, and a much more user-friendly appendix format.

Locating and ordering "pops" works in particular continues to be a daunting job for orchestral librarians, conductors, and music directors. Publishers often change agents or go out of business and original material is discontinued or no longer available. Finding the agents that sell or rent the music is challenging with our mercurial publishing market. This handbook is an attempt to alleviate some of this time-consuming work by creating a comprehensive and informative repertoire list for orchestral "pops" concerts. There are missing titles and certainly many new titles were available before the ink was dry for this book, but an attempt was made to include all publishers and resources so other listings can be found.

Clarity and accuracy were the primary goals for each entry. This book is intended as a useful tool in the search for music suitable for "pops" concerts while addressing the music director's needs of style, instrumentation, duration, and availability. Since this is an on-going and ever-changing endeavor, readers are encouraged to bring any errors to my attention so that appropriate corrections are made.

Procedure

The first hurdle in originally creating this list was defining "pops" music. "Pops" implies a great array of music genres: from country, rock, jazz, and Broadway musicals to familiar classical music and it can mean different things to different people. Therefore, this handbook must be as inclusive as possible to satisfy everyone's desires.

Using the 2009 *Orchestral "Pops" Music* as a base; catalogs from publishing firms and distributors were first reviewed for recent additions. Suggestions from colleagues, conductors, and composers were then reviewed and included. Direct conversations and/or visits with publishers and/or composers confirmed the accuracy of new entries, corrections to previous works listed, and allowed for additional performance comments. A 2011 summer grant from Old Dominion University allowed me to spend a week viewing music distributed by Luck's Music. Only currently available works were ultimately included from these sources, where I could verify all the information needed for performances.

I viewed over half the scores and for many others the details were confirmed with various publishers and/or composers answering directly. For the remainder I relied on listings from catalogs and web site databases which unfortunately are not always correct.

Musicians will question some inclusions and omissions, but I attempted to avoid any judgment calls on the entries, with the goal of providing a starting point in the search for "pops" repertoire. All current publisher sources are included, and the reader is encouraged to visit their constant new offerings.

Instrumentation Formula

The listed instrumentation incorporates the same format used in David Daniels' fourth edition of *Orchestral Music: A Handbook*.[1] The wind instruments are arranged in this order: flute, oboe, clarinet, bassoon – horn, trumpet, trombone, tuba. Percussion follow, identifying the number of players needed for the performance when available. Additional instruments and/or explanations are included within brackets. A dot (.) separates each player and a slash (/) indicates doubling. Items in parentheses are optional. For example:

$$2[1.2/\text{pic}]\ 2[1.2/\text{Eh}]\ 2\ 2 - 4\ 3\ 3\ 1 - \text{tmp}+4 - \text{hp} - \text{str}$$

translates as:
- 2 flutes where the 2nd flute doubles on piccolo
- 2 oboes where the 2nd oboe doubles on English horn
- 2 clarinets and 2 bassoons
- 4 horns, 3 trumpets, 3 trombones, and 1 tuba
- 1 timpanist and 4 additional percussionists
- 1 harp
- String section including the usual violin 1, violin 2, viola, cello, and double bass sections.

- When I could not determine which player was doubling in the wind section, I listed the auxiliary instrument in brackets such as 3[incl bcl] implying that one or more of the clarinetists will either double or play bass clarinet.
- Many entries use various combinations of saxophones and I chose to list them in their own category between the woodwinds and brass. Whenever possible, the specific number and type of saxophones needed are listed. In this example 2 alto saxophones and 1 tenor saxophone are optional for the performance:

$$2[\text{incl pic}]\ 2\ 2\ 2 - (2\text{asx, tsx}) - 4\ 3\ 3\ 1 - \text{tmp}+\text{perc} - \text{str}$$

- Lists of percussion instruments needed are included when available.
- Keyboard, harp and auxiliary strummed instruments such as guitar are given their own position between the percussion and string listings. In this example 4 additional musicians are needed for harp, celesta (doubling on piano), guitar, and banjo:

$$1[\text{pic}]\ 1\ 3\ 1 - 2\ 3\ 2\ 0 - 3\text{perc} - \text{hp, cel/pf, gtr, bnjo} - \text{str}$$

Durations

Performance conditions, including musical discretions, dictate the duration of a work. Thus the durations listed in this document are only an approximation. Generally I included the durations listed by the publisher or composer. The duration of individual movements or sections is given in parentheses when possible.

Themes

Often a "pops" concert is theme-based in its programming, so I have suggested possible categories for each listing. An appendix with suggested themes and titles is included.

---

[1] David Daniels, *Orchestral Music: A Handbook*, fourth edition (Lanham, Maryland: The Scarecrow Press, Inc., 2005).

Titles

All titles are alphabetized disregarding any opening article. Titles in other languages are followed with translations in parentheses when appropriate. For example:

Cenerentola (Cinderella) Overture - Rossini
Central Park in the Dark - Ives
Chaconne for String Orchestra - Pachelbel
Chairman Dances: Foxtrot for Orchestra - Adams, John

Publishers

At the bottom of each entry's description is the original publisher in italics. If permanently out of print (POP), then possible sources for renting the music are listed. Referring to the appendix of publishers and sources will give you the contact information for the publishers and their agents.

Acknowledgments

Many people are responsible for the completion of this work, but foremost is David Daniels. He continues to be an incredible mentor with constant encouragement and advice when needed. In this case I am honored this book is now included in his Music Finders Series. Daniels' *Orchestral Music: A Handbook, 4th Edition,* a reference staple in the hands of conductors and librarians everywhere, remains a model which I try to emulate.

Clinton F. Nieweg, principal librarian (ret.) for The Philadelphia Orchestra voluntarily researched details, suggested entries, and answered many questions. Following his sage advice, a more reliable source was created.

The sales staff at Educational Music Service provided valuable and frequent research with the Publishers and Sources Appendix. Gratitude is expressed to Bennett Graff, Senior Acquisitions Editor of Rowman & Littlefield/ Scarecrow Press, for his patient, yet helpful, prodding in completing this work.

The staff at Luck's Music was exceptionally helpful during my week's visit to peruse their huge library. I deeply appreciate their generous use of space, computers, time and expertise. John Waxman was especially helpful with many email communications confirming details of his many fine offerings through Theme and Variations. Eric Swanson, Assistant Manager of the Music Library, JoAnn Kane Music Service, was equally helpful researching details of their outstanding offerings. Gary Rautenberg, rental manager for Alfred Music Publishing, was an incredible source of efficient information. Alice LaSota, retired music cataloger with the University of Maryland Libraries and former cellist with the National Symphony Orchestra, helped with research and proofing details.

My amazing daughters Amy Joseph and Jennifer Perry, to whom this edition is dedicated, were always supportive and a continual source of rejuvenation. My mother, Martha Lewis Manning, until her recent passing, always had time to listen to my trials, no matter how trivial. My husband Rolf Kramer was a constant source of encouragement and patiently salvaged my computer glitches with his extraordinary technical skills.

Finally I must thank my cat Jam and newly adopted beagle, Maggie, for periodically demanding my attention and reminding me of what is really important in life.

ABBREVIATIONS

/	doubling [1 player, but 2 instruments]
#	number
( )	optional instrument or voice
[ ]	included instrument or voice

A	alto voice		**harm**	harmonium
acl	alto clarinet		**heckl**	heckelphone
afl	alto flute		**hi-hat**	high-hat cymbal
ampd	amplified		**hn**	horn
arr	arranger		**hp**	harp
asx	alto saxophone		**hpsd**	harpsichord
Bs	bass voice		**incl**	including
Bar	baritone voice		**kybd**	keyboard
bar hn	baritone horn		**lg**	large
bcl	bass clarinet		**mand**	mandolin
bd	bass drum		**marac**	maracas
bn	bassoon		**marim**	marimba
bnjo	banjo		**mvt**	movement
brake dr	brake drum		**mx**	mixed
bsx	baritone saxophone		**Ms**	mezzo-soprano voice
btbn	bass trombone		**ob**	oboe
cast	castanets		**opt**	optional
cbn	contrabassoon		**orch**	orchestra, orchestrator
cel	celesta		**org**	organ
cemb	cembalo		**perc**	percussion
Ch	chamber		**pf**	piano
chor	chorus		**pic**	piccolo
cimb	cimbalom		**POP**	permanently out of print
cl	clarinet		**ratch**	ratchet
cnt	continuo		**rec**	recorder
crt	cornet		**S**	soprano voice
crot	crotales		**sandblks**	sandblocks
cym	cymbals		**sarr**	sarrusophone
db	double bass		**scl**	soprano clarinet
dr	drum		**sd**	snare drum
dulc	dulcimer		**slgh-bells**	sleigh bells
Ebcl	E-flat clarinet		**sm**	small
ed	edited, editor		**ssx**	soprano saxophone
Eh	English horn		**str**	strings
elec	electric		**sus cym**	suspended cymbal
Ens	ensemble		**sx**	saxophone
euph	euphonium		**synth**	synthesizer
field dr	field drum		**szl cym**	sizzle cymbal
fl	flute		**T**	tenor voice
flug	flugelhorn		**tambn**	tambourine
glock	glockenspiel		**tbn**	trombone
gtr	guitar		**td**	tenor drum

tmp	timpani
tp	trumpet
tri	triangle
tsx	tenor saxophone
va	viola
vc	cello
vib	vibraphone
vn	violin
w/	with
woodblk	woodblock
xyl	xylophone

A

Abreu, Zequinha de   1880-1935

Tico Tico   3.5'
Tico-Tico no Fubá (Tico-tico in the Maize Flour)
2 2 2 2 – 4 2 2 1 – tmp+2 – str
Tico-Tico no Fubá was recorded and made popular internationally by Carmen Miranda (who performed it onscreen in Copacabana in 1947).
Tico Tico is a bird similar to the sparrow that inhabits most of Brazil. The rhythm of the melody suggests the jumps of the bird when pecking maize flour grains.
Velásquez, arr.

    International (Brazil)
Filarmonika

Adam, Adolphe Charles   1803-1856

Christmas with Renata Scotto: 2'
5. Christmas Song (Cantique de Noël)
2 2 2 2 – 4 2 2 0 – tmp – hp – str
Solo Soprano; SATB Chorus.
John Grady, arr.

    Christmas
AMP (rental)

Cantique de Noël (O Holy Night)   4'
3[1.2.pic] 2 3[1.2.bcl] 3[1.2.cbn] – 4 3 3 1 – tmp+perc – hp – str
Mixed Chorus. Also available for voice and orchestra in the key of Eb and C.

    Christmas
Kalmus

O Holy Night (Cantique de Noël)   4'
2 2 2 2 – 4 2 3 1 – tmp – perc – hp – str

    Christmas
Luck's

Cantique de Noël (O Holy Night)   5'
2 2 2 2 – 4 2 2 0 – tmp – hp – str
Solo Voice; Male Choir. Key of E flat. Although written with choir, it is possible to perform this with only solo voice. The second verse (choir only) can be omitted. No vocal materials are available for this work.
H.W. Pierce, arr.

    Christmas
Novello

Cantique de Noël (O Holy Night)   4.5'
2 2 2 2 – 2 2 2 0 – hp – str
Currently unavailable according to website. This is a new arrangement created in 2011.
Craig Leon, arr.

    Christmas
Novello (rental)

Adams, A. Emmett   1890-1938

Bells of St. Mary's   5'
2[incl pic] 2 2 2 – (2asx, tsx) – 4 3 3 1 – tmp+perc – str
Broege, arr.

    Films
Kalmus

Adams, John   1947-

The Chairman Dances: 12'
Foxtrot for Orchestra
2[1/pic.2/pic] 2 2[1.2/bcl] 2[incl cbn] – 4 2[tp in C] 2 1 – tmp+3 – hp, pf – str

    Dance
Schirmer (rental)

Short Ride in a Fast Machine   4'
4[1.2.pic1.pic2] 3[1.2.Eh] 4[1.2.opt3.opt4] 4[1.2.3.cbn] – 4 4 3 1 – tmp+3 – (synth) – str
perc: bd, bd w/pedal, sus cym, szl cym, sd, tri, tambn, tamtam, glock, xyl, crot, 2woodblk.

    Travel
Boosey (rental)

Adamson, Harold (See: Daniel, Eliot)

Addinsell, Richard   1904-1977

A Christmas Carol (Suite: Scrooge)   13'
    3 3 3 3 – 4 3 3 1 – tmp+perc – hp, cel/pf – str
    Steve Bernstein, arr.

                                                     Christmas
Novello (rental)

Ades, Hawley   1908-2008

Twentiana   7'
    3[1.2.3/pic] 1 3[1.2.(bcl)] 2 – 4 3 3 1 – tmp+3
    – str
    perc: chimes, bells, sd, bd, sandblks, hi hat, tri, cym.
    Optional SATB or SAB Chorus.
    Medley of hits from the Twenties. Includes: I Want
    to be Happy, I'm Looking Over a Four Leaf Clover,
    Carolina in the Morning, Bye-Bye Blackbird,
    Charleston, Tea for Two, Hallelujah!

                                              Popular Song
Shawnee

Adler, Samuel   1928-

The Feast of Lights   4'
    2[incl pic] 2 2 2 – 2 2 2 1 – tmp+perc – hp – str
    SATB Chorus.

                                                 Hanukkah
Schirmer (rental)

Judah's Song of Praise   5'
    2 2 2 2 – 0 0 0 0 – 1perc – str
    SATB Chorus.

                                                 Hanukkah
Schirmer (rental)

Show an Affirming Flame (2001)   7'
    2[incl pic] 2 2 2 – 2 2 0 0 – tmp+perc – str
    Dedicated to the victims on Septmeber 11, 2001.

                                                 Patriotic
Presser (rental)

A Song of Hanukkah   4'
    2[incl pic] 2 2 2 – 2 2 2 0 – tmp+perc – hp – str
    SATB Chorus.

                                                 Hanukkah
Schirmer (rental)

Summer Stock: A Short Merry Overture   5'
    2 2 2 2 – 2 2 3 0 – tmp+2 – str

                                                 Seasons
AMP (rental)

Adolphe, Bruce   1955-

I'm Inclined to New Music: A Comic Parody of   8'
Mozart's Eine Kleine Nachtmusik
    Strings

                                             Instrumental Pops
MMB

Adomian, Lan   1905-1979

Cantata de la revolución Mexicana   15'
    4[incl pic] 3[incl Eh] 4[incl bcl] 4[incl cbn] –
    4 4 4 1 – tmp+3 – str
    SATB Chorus.

                                                 International
Schirmer (rental)

Aguila, Miguel del   1957-

Conga   11'
    2[incl pic] 2 2 2 – 3 2 2 1 – 5perc – hp,pf – str
    Also available with smaller instrumentation using
    solo percussion:
    1 1 1 1 – 1 1 1 1 – perc – hp, pf – str
    Formerly titled *Conga-Line in Hell*.

                                                 Dance
Peer (rental)

Albert, Morris   1951-

Feelings   5'
    2 1 2 1 – 4 3 3 1 – 2perc – elec bs, elec pf, gtr – str
    perc: drumset[with cabasa, bell tree, tambn], glock,(vib).
    Richard Stephan, arr.

                                                 Popular Song
Editora Agusta (rental from Luck's)

Alford, Kenneth J. [pseudonym]   1881-1945
Ricketts, Frederick Joseph

Colonel Bogey March   4'
    3[1.2.pic] 2 3[1.2.bcl] 2 – 4 2 3 1 – tmp+2 – str
      perc: sd, bd
    Theme song of the Three Stooges.
    Clark McAlister, arr.
                                  Films/Patriotic/TV
Kalmus

Hexen (Witches)   13'
    Solo Bassoon and Strings
                                  Halloween
Peer (rental)

Alfvén, Hugo   1872-1960

Dalarapsodi: 18'
  Swedish Rhapsody No. 3, Op. 47
    2[incl pic] 3[incl Eh] 2[incl bcl] 3[incl cbn] – (ssx) –
    4 2 3 1 – tmp+perc – hp, cel – str
                                  International
Hansen

Midsommarvaka: 12'
  Swedish Rhapsody No. 1, Op. 19
    3[1.2.3/pic] 3[1.2.3/Eh] 3[1.2/Ebcl.bcl]
    4[1.2.3.cbn] – 4 2 3 1 – tmp+2 – 2hp – str
      perc: cym, tri, glock
                                  International
Hansen; Kalmus

Allen, Brett Lensley   1958-

Nativity Scenes   28'
    Strings
    Optional Narrator. Without narration the work is
    22'.
                                  Christmas
Oxford

Allen, Robert (See: Stillman, Al)

Alter, Louis   1902-1980

Manhattan Serenade   4'
    1 1 2 1 – asx, tsx – 2 2 1 0 – tmp+2 – str
      perc: cym, sd, bd, glock, sus cym.
    C. Paul Herfurth, arr.
                            Americana/Instrumental Pops
Robbins (POP); Luck's (rental)

Manhattan Serenade   5'
    1 1 2 1 – asx, tsx – 2 2 1 0 – tmp+2 – str
      perc: cym, sd, bd, glock, sus cym.
    Earl Sheldon, arr.
                            Americana/Instrumental Pops
Robbins (POP); Luck's (rental)

Álvarez, Teófilo   1915-1991

Marinera Trujillana (Sailor Trujillana)   4'
    2 2 2 2 – 2 2 3 0 – 2perc – str
    Marinera is the national dance of Peru. Since the
    1960s, the city of Trujillo hosts a Marinera
    competition in January.
                           Dance/International (Peru)
Filarmonika

Alwyn, William   1905-1975

Elizabethan Dances   16'
    2 2 2 2 – 4 3 3 0 – tmp+perc – hp – str
                                        Dance
Schirmer (rental)

Alzedo, José Bernardo   1788-1878

Himno Nacional del Perú (National Anthem   3'
of Peru)
    3[incl pic] 2 2 2 – 2asx – 4 3 3 1– 2perc – str
    Supporting the mission of Caminos del Inka, Inc. to
    discover, preserve and disseminate the musical
    legacy of the Americas.
                                International (Peru)
Filarmonika

Amram, David — 1930-

Three Songs for America — 8.5'
1 1 1 1 – 1 0 0 0 – str
Solo Bass, Wind Quintet, String Quartet.
Patriotic
Peters (rental)

Amundson, Steven — 1955-

Angels' Dance — 5'
3[1.2.pic] 3[1.2.Eh] 2 2 – 4 3 3 1 – tmp+3 – cel – str
perc: tri, tambn, glock, xyl, marim, chimes
Christmas
MMB (rental)

Three's Company — 7'
0 0 0 3 – 0 0 0 0 – 3 perc or drumset – str
perc: bd, sus cym, sd
TV
Tempo

Anderson, Leroy — 1908-1975

Alma Mater — 6'
3[incl pic] 2 2 2 – (2sax) – 4 3 3 1 – perc – (pf) – str
Four short humorous scenes describing life at Harvard University.
Instrumental Pops
Kalmus

Arietta for Orchestra — 3'
3[1.2.pic] 2 2 2 – (3sx) – 4 3 3(1) – tmp+2 – pf – str
perc: sd, slap stick, cowbell, cuckoo, woodblk, 2 elec auto horns.
Also available for strings.
Instrumental Pops
Kalmus

Balladette for Orchestra — 3'
3[1.2.pic] 2 2 2 – (asx, 2tsx) – tmp+1 – str
perc: glock.
Also available for strings.
Instrumental Pops
Kalmus

Belle of the Ball — 3'
3[1.2.pic] 2 2 2 – (2asx, tsx) – 4 3 3 1 – 3perc [incl bells] – pf – str
Dance
EMI (rental); Kalmus; Woodbury

Birthday Party — 2.5'
3 2 2 2 – 4 3 3 1 – 3perc – str
Optional Chorus.
Celebration
Presser (rental); Woodbury

The Bluebells of Scotland — 2'
3 2 2 2 – (asx, 2tsx) – 4 3 3 0 tmp+perc[incl bells, chimes] – str
International
Woodbury

Blue Tango — 3'
3[1.2.pic] 2 2 2 – (2asx, tsx) – 4 3 3 1 – perc – str
perc: sd, bd, cym, glock.
Dance
Kalmus; Warner

Bonnie Dundee — 2.5'
3[incl pic] 2[incl Eh] 2[incl bcl] 2[incl cbn] – 4 3 2 1 – tmp+perc – hp – str
Instrumental Pops
Presser

Bugler's Holiday — 2.5'
3[1.2.pic] 2 2 2 – (2asx, tsx) – 4 3 3 1 – 3perc – str
perc: sd, bd, cym.
Christmas

The Campbells Are Coming — 3'
3 2[incl Eh] 2[incl bcl] 2[incl cbn] – 4 3 3 1 – tmp+2 – hp – str
Instrumental Pops
Presser

Captains and the Kings — 3'
3[1.2.pic] 2 2 2 – (2asx, tsx) – 4 3 3 1 – tmp+2 – str
perc: sd, bd, cym, tri.
Instrumental Pops
Kalmus

Chicken Reel — 3'
3[1.2.pic] 2 2 2 – (2asx, tsx) – 4 3 3 1 – 3perc – str
perc: sd, bd, cym, xyl, cowbell.
Dance
EMI (rental); Kalmus

China Doll   2'
   3[1.2.pic] 2 2 2 – (2asx, tsx) – 4 3 3 1 – tmp+2 – str
   perc: glock, sd, bd, cym, woodblk, 4 temple blks, bells.
                                    Instrumental Pops
EMI (rental); Kalmus

A Christmas Festival (1952)   4'
   3[1.2.pic] 2 2 2 – (2asx, tsx) – 4 3 3 1 – tmp+2 – (hp, org) – str
   perc: sd, bd, chimes, slgh bells, glock, cym.
   The EMI rental is the original publication from 1950. SATB choral settings by Russ Robinson can be used in the performance.
                                           Christmas
EMI (rental); Warner

A Christmas Festival   7.5'
   3[1.2.pic] 2 2 2 – (2asx, tsx) – 4 3 3 1 – tmp+2 – (hp, org) – str
   perc: sd, bd, chimes, slgh bells, glock, cym.
   This is a longer, original concert version as performed/recorded by the Boston Pops. Many selections include additional measures extending the traditional songs. Some sections are in different keys than the shorter version. Includes: Joy to the World; Deck the Halls; God Rest Ye Merry, Gentlemen; Good King Wenceslas; Hark the Herald Angels Sing; First Noel; Silent Night; Jingle Bells; O Come All Ye Faithful.
                                         Christmas
Warner

Clarinet Candy   3'
   3[1.2.pic] 2 2 2 – (2asx, tsx) – 4 3 3 1 – tmp+2 – str
   perc: sd, bd, cym, tri, chimes, slgh-bells, bells.
                                    Instrumental Pops
Kalmus

Classical Jukebox   3'
   3[incl pic] 3[incl Eh] 3[incl bcl] 3[incl cbn] – 4 3 3 1 – tmp+3 – hp, (pf) – str
   Based on "Music! Music! Music!" by Weiss & Baum.
                                    Instrumental Pops
Wendel; Woodbury (rental)

Fiddle-Faddle   3'
   3[1.2.pic] 2 2 2 – (2asx, tsx) – 4 3 3 0 – 2perc – str
   perc: sd, bd.
   Also available for strings
                            Americana/Instrumental Pops
Kalmus

The First Day of Spring   3'
   2 2 2 2 – (2asx, tsx) – 4 3 3 1 – tmp – str
                                        Seasons
Kalmus

Forgotten Dreams   2.5'
   2 2 2 2 – (2asx, tsx) – 4 3 3 0 – bells – str
                                  Instrumental Pops
EMI (rental); Kalmus

The Girl in Satin   3'
   3[1.2.pic] 2 2 2 – (2asx, tsx) – 4 3 3 1 – 1perc – str
   perc: cast.
                                  Instrumental Pops
Kalmus

The Golden Years for Orchestra   3'
   3[1.2.pic] 2 2 2 – (2asx, tsx) – 4 3 3 1 – tmp+1 – (hp), pf – str
   perc: glock.
                                  Instrumental Pops
Kalmus

Goldilocks: 3'
I Never Know When
   3[1.2.pic] 2 2 2 – 4 3 3 0 – 1perc – hp – str
   perc: glock.
                                Broadway Musicals
Presser; Wendel (rental)

Goldilocks: 5'
Lady in Waiting - Ballet Music
   3[1.2.pic] 2 2 2 – 4 3 3 1 – tmp+perc – str
                           Broadway Musicals/Dance
Wendel (rental)

Goldilocks: 3.5'
Lady in Waiting - Waltz
   3[1.2.pic] 2 2 2 – (2asx, tsx) – 4 3 3 1 – tmp+perc – hp – str
                           Broadway Musicals/Dance
Presser; Wendel (rental)

Goldilocks: 2'
Lazy Moon
   3[1.2.pic] 2 2 2 – 4 3 3 0 – tmp+2 – str
                           Broadway Musicals/Space
Presser

Goldilocks:
  Overture — 4.5'
  3[1.2.pic] 2 2 2 – 4 3 2 1 – tmp+2[drumset] – (hp) – str
  This edition includes a concert ending by the editor approved by the Anderson family.
  Robert Wendel, editor
  Broadway Musicals
  Wendel (rental)

Goldilocks:
  Pirate Dance — 2'
  3[1.2.pic] 2 2 2 – (2asx, tsx) – 4 3 3 1 – 3perc – str
  perc: sd, bd, cym, xyl.
  Optional SATB Chorus.
  Halloween/Dance
  Kalmus

Goldilocks:
  Pussyfoot — 3'
  3[1.2.pic] 2 2 2 – 3 2 2 1 – tmp+perc – str
  perc: sd, bd, wind whistle, cym, woodblks, glock, xyl.
  Broadway Musicals
  Presser; Wendel (rental)

Goldilocks:
  Pyramid Dance — 3'
  3[1.2.pic] 2 2 2 – (2asx, tsx) – 4 3 3 1 – tmp+2 – str
  perc: gong, xyl, sd, bd, cym, schellenbaum [or tambns].
  Optional SATB Chorus.
  Broadway Musicals/Dance
  Kalmus

Goldilocks:
  Save a Kiss — 2.5'
  3[1.2.pic] 2 2 2 – 4 3 3 1 – tmp+2 – hp – str
  perc: cym, glock.
  Solo Soprano and Baritone. Range from B - e'.
  Broadway Musicals/Valentine
  Presser; Wendel (rental)

Goldilocks:
  Shall I Take My Heart — 2.5'
  3[1.2.pic] 2 2 2 – 4 3 3 0 – 2perc – str
  perc: glock, cym.
  Solo Baritone version is also available. Range from D - e'.
  Broadway Musicals
  Presser; Wendel (rental)

Goldilocks:
  Town House Maxixe — 3'
  3[1.2.pic] 2 2 2 – 4 3 3 1 – perc – str
  Broadway Musicals
  Wendel (rental)

Goldilocks:
  Who's Been Sitting in My Chair? — 2.5'
  3[1.2.pic] 2 2 2 – 4 3 3 1 – perc – hp – str
  perc: sd, bd, glock, cym, woodblks, tambn.
  Solo Soprano. Range from C - f'.
  Broadway Musicals
  Presser; Wendel (rental)

Governor Bradford March — 3'
  3[1.2.pic] 2 2 2 – 4 3 3 1 – tmp+perc – pf – str
  Patriotic
  Kalmus

Home Stretch — 2.5'
  3[1.2.pic] 2 2 2 – (2asx, tsx) – 4 3 3 1 – tmp+3 – str
  perc: sd, bd, cym, hoof beats.
  Instrumental Pops/Sports
  Kalmus

Horse and Buggy — 3'
  3 2 2 2 – (2asx, tsx) – 4 3 3 1 – 3perc – str
  perc: temple blks, whip, xyl.
  Travel
  EMI (rental); *Kalmus*

Irish Suite — 20'
  (3' 4' 3' 3' 4' 3')
  3[1.2.pic] 2 2 2 – 4 3 3 1 – tmp+4 – hp, pf – str
  perc: sd, bd, cym.
  Includes: The Irish Washerwoman; The Minstrel Boy; The Rakes of Mallow; The Wearing of the Green; The Last Rose of Summer; The Girl I Left Behind Me.
  Movements are available separately.
  St. Patrick/International
  EMI (rental)

Jazz Legato — 2'
  2 2 2 2 – (2asx, tsx) – 4 3 3 0 – perc – str
  Also available for string orchestra.
  Jazz
  Kalmus

Jazz Pizzicato — 2'
  2 2 2 2 – (2asx, tsx) – 4 3 3 0 – drumset – str
  Also available for string orchestra.
  Jazz
  Kalmus

Leroy Anderson Favorites   8'
  Strings
  Optional piano accompaniment or with
  the addition of winds.
  Includes: Syncopated Clock; Sleigh Ride; Blue
  Tango; Plink, Plank, Plunk!; Serenata.
  Jack Bullock, arr.
                                               Instrumental Pops
Warner

Leroy Anderson Favorites   8'
  3[1.2.pic] 2 2 2 – 4 3 3 1 – tmp+perc – pf – str
  Includes: Blue Tango; Belle of the Ball; The
  Syncopated Clock; Serenata.
  Calvin Custer, arr.
                                               Instrumental Pops
Warner

Leroy Anderson for Strings   Folio
  Strings   Collection
  Includes: Belle of the Ball; Blue Tango; Fiddle-
  Faddle; Jazz Pizzicato; Plink, Plank, Plunk;
  Serenata; Sleigh Ride; The Syncopated Clock; A
  Trumpeter's Lullaby; The Typewriter and more.
  William Zinn, arr.
                                               Instrumental Pops
Warner

Lullaby of the Drums for Orchestra   3.5'
  3[1.2.pic] 2 2 2 – 4 3 3 1 – tmp+3 – str
  perc: sd, marim, xyl, bongos.
                                               Instrumental Pops
Kalmus

March of the Two Left Feet   2'
  3[1.2.pic] 2 2 2 – 4 3 3 1 – tmp+2 – str
  perc: optional tmp and xyl.
                                             Instrumental Pops
Kalmus

Mother's Whistler   3'
  3 3[1.2.Eh] 2 3 – 4 3 3 0 – perc – str
                                                        Americana
Kalmus

Old MacDonald Had a Farm   3'
  3[(#3)] 3[1.2.Eh] 3[1.2.bcl] 3[1.2.cbn] –
  4 4 [(3&4)] 3 1 – tmp+2 – str
  perc: cow-moo, duck quack, auto horn, bird whistle,
  cuckoo.
                                                Americana/Animals/
                                                              Popular Song
Kalmus; Presser

The Penny Whistle Song   3'
  3 2 2 2 – (2asx, tsx) – 4 3 3 0 – 1perc – str
  perc: cym, glock.
  Three flutes are featured.
                                             Instrumental Pops
EMI (rental); Kalmus

The Phantom Regiment   3.5'
  2 2 2 2 – (2asx, tsx) – 4 3 3 1 – perc – str
                                                       Halloween
Kalmus

Plink Plank Plunk!   2.5'
  (pf) – strings
  A full orchestra version arranged by
  Tomlinson is available from *Woodbury*.
                                             Instrumental Pops
Warner; Woodbury

Promenade   3'
  3[1.2.pic] 2 2 2 – (2asx, tsx) – 4 3 3 1 – 3perc – pf –
  str
  perc: sd, bd, cym.
                                             Instrumental Pops
Kalmus

Sandpaper Ballet   3'
  3[1.2.pic] 2 2 2 – (2asx, tsx) – 4 3 3 1 – 3perc – str
  perc: 3 sandpaper blks [1 fine & 2 coarse], slide whistle,
  conga or sd.
                                                           Dance
EMI (rental); Kalmus

Saraband   3.5'
  3[1.2.pic] 2 2 2 – (2asx, tsx) – 4 3 3 1 – tmp+2 –
  (hp) – str
  perc: cym, glock.
                                             Instrumental Pops
EMI (rental); Kalmus

Second Regiment Connecticut   2.5'
National Guard March
  3[incl pic] 2 2 2 – 4 3 3 0 – perc – str
                                                        Patriotic
Woodbury (rental)

Serenata   4'
  3[1.2.pic] 2 2 2 – (2asx, tsx) – 4 3 3 1 – 5perc – pf –
  str
  perc: gourd, maracas, claves, temple blks, gong.
                                             Instrumental Pops
EMI (rental); Kalmus

Sleigh Ride   3'
    3[1.2.pic] 2 2 2 – (2asx, tsx) – 4 3 3 1 – 3perc – str
    perc: slgh-bells, whip, temple blks, xyl.
                                                 Christmas
Warner

Song of the Bells-Waltz   3'
    3[1.2.3/pic] 2 2 2 – (2asx, tsx) – 4 3 3 1 – 3perc – str
    perc: chimes, bells, gong, sd, bd, cym.
                                                        Dance
Kalmus

Suite of Carols for String Orchestra   11.5'
    Strings
    Includes: Pastores a Belen; It Came Upon the Midnight Clear; O Little Town of Bethlehem; Bring a Torch Jeanette, Isabella; Away in a Manger; Wassail Song.
                                                 Christmas
Warner

Summer Skies   2'
    2 2 2 2 – (2asx, tsx) – 4 3 3 1 – 1perc – str
    perc: glock.
                                                         Seasons
EMI (rental); Kalmus

The Syncopated Clock   2.5'
    2 2 2 2 – (2asx, tsx) – 4 3 2 0 – 2perc – str
    perc: woodblk, alarm clock, cowbell, wind whistle.
                                                    New Year
Kalmus; Warner

The Syncopated Clock   2.5'
    Strings
    Samuel Applebaum, arr.
                                                    New Year
EMS (rental)

A Trumpeter's Lullaby   3'
    2 2 2 2 – (2asx, tsx) – 4 3 3 0 – 2perc – str
    perc: sd, bd.
                                           Instrumental Pops
Warner

The Typewriter   3'
    3[1.2.pic] 2 2 2 – (2asx, tsx) – 4 3 3 0 – 2perc – str
    perc: glock, typewriter [woodblk and gourd can be used instead].
                             Instrumental Pops/Novelty
Belwin

The Waltzing Cat   3'
    3[1.2.pic] 2 2 2 – (2asx, tsx) – 4 3 3 0 – 1perc – str
    perc: bells, sd, bd, cym, slide whistle, wood blk
                                      Animals/Dance
EMI (rental); Kalmus

Andriessen, Louis   1939-

Workers' Union   20'
    Any loud-sounding group of instruments!
                                          Labor Day
Presser (rental)

Antheil, George   1900-1959

Accordion Dance   5'
    2[incl pic] 2 2 2 – 4 3 3 1 – tmp+perc – accordion (harm) – str
                                          Dance
Schirmer (rental)

Archipelago "Rhumba"   10'
    2[incl pic] 2 2 2 – 4 3 2 1 – 4perc – hp, pf – str
                                          Dance
Schirmer (rental)

Cabeza de vaca   52'
    1 1 3[incl bcl] 1 – 0 0 0 0 – tmp+3 – hpsd, pf – str
    Solo Tenor, Baritone, and Boy Soprano; SATB Chorus.
    Ernest Gold, arr.
                                        Americana
Schirmer (rental)

Hot-Time Dance   5'
    2[incl pic] 4 2 3 1 – tmp+perc – hp, pf – str
                                          Dance
Schirmer (rental)

Jazz Sonata   2'
    1[incl pic] 1 1 0 – ssx – 0 2 2 1 – 2pf, bnjo, harmonica – str[no va]
    Werner Herbers, arr.
                                          Jazz
Schirmer (rental)

A Jazz Symphony (1925 version)   12'
    0 2 2 0 – ssx, asx, tsx – 0 3 3 1 – 2perc –
    2bnjo[(gtr)], 3pf – str
    Solo Piano. Originally written for Paul Whiteman.
                                                                            Jazz

Weintraub (rental)

A Jazz Symphony (1955 version)   6.5'
    1 0 3 0 – 0 3 3 0 – 1perc – pf – str
    Solo Piano.
                                                                            Jazz

Weintraub (rental)

A Jazz Symphony (1999 version)   12'
    1[incl pic] 1 1 1 – ssx – 1 1 1 0 – 2perc – bnjo – db
    Solo Piano.
    Milton Phibbs, arr.
                                                                            Jazz

Weintraub (rental)

Lithuanian Night   4'
    Strings
                                                                     International

Schirmer (rental)

Music to a World's Fair Film (1939)   11'
    1[incl pic] 1 1 1 – 1 2 1 0 – perc – pf – str
    Optional Narrator.
                                                                       Films

Schirmer (rental)

Tom Sawyer Overture: 7'
    California Overture
    3[incl pic] 3[incl Eh] 3[incl bcl] 3[incl cbn] –
    4 3 3 1 – tmp+3 – pf – str
                                                                   Americana

Schirmer

Water Music for 4th of July Evening
    Strings
                                                                     Patriotic

Schirmer (rental)

Antonini, Alfredo   1901-1983

Nursery Rhymes: Fantasy Miniature   2'
    2[1/pic.2] 2 2 2 – 2asx, tsx – 4 3 3 0 – tmp+ 1 – pf
    – str
    perc: glock, ratchet, sd, bd, xyl, sus cym.
    Includes: The Farmer in the Dell; Mary Had a Little
    Lamb; This is the Way We Wash Our Clothes; Row
    Row Row Your Boat.
                                                                Popular Song

Mills (rental)

Arban, Jean Baptiste   1825-1889

The Carnival of Venice: for Trumpet   7'
    and Strings
    Strings
    Solo Trumpet.
    Mikhail Nakariakov, arr.
                                                           Popular Classics

EMR

Arditi, Luigi   1822-1903

Kiss: Il Bacio   4'
    1 0 2 2 – 2 2 1 0 – perc – str
    Waltz.
    Seredy, arr.
                                                                       Valentine

Kalmus

Arias, Clotilde   1901-1959

Huiracocha for voice and orchestra   4'
    2 0 0 0 – 2 0 0 0 – tmp – hp – str
    Solo Voice. Available in Key of E and F. Score is
    available for purchase.
                                                    International (Peru)

Filarmonika (rental)

Arlen, Harold   1905-1986

Blues in the Night   3'
2 2 2 2 – 4 3 3 1 – str
Jazz Vocal.

Warner (rental)

Jazz

It's Only a Paper Moon   3.5'
3[1.2.pic] 2 2 1 – 4 3 3 1 – perc – pf, elec bass – str
Chuck Sayre, arr.

Warner (POP); EMS or Luck's (rental)

Space

Stormy Weather   3'
hp, cel – str
Key of Ab.
Morton Gould, arr.

Popular Song/Weather

Kalmus

Wizard of Oz Choral Review   10'
3[incl pic] 1 1 1 – 2 3 3 0 – tmp+4 – hp, pf – str
SATB or SAB or 2-pt Chorus. Includes:
Munchkinland; Ding Dong! The Witch Is Dead;
The Lullaby League; We're Off to See the Wizard;
If I Only Had a Brain; The Merry Old Land of Oz;
Over the Rainbow.
Greg Gilpin, arr.; Peter Schmutte, orch.

Films

Warner

Wizard of Oz: Munchkin Land   8'
1[incl pic] 1[incl Eh] 3[incl bcl] 0 – (tsx, bsx) –
2 2 1 0 – 4perc – hp, pf, (cel) – str
Solo Voices; Chorus. Royal Shakespeare
Company Version.

Films

EMI (rental)

Wizard of Oz Orchestral Suite: 11'
"Wizard of Oz Medley"
3[incl pic] 2 2[incl bcl] 2 – 4 3 3 1 – tmp+3 –
hp, pf – str
Includes: Over the Rainbow, If I Only Had a Brain,
Ding-Dong the Witch is Dead, Jitterbug, Merry Old
Land of Oz, We're Off to See the Wizard, Miss
Gultch.
Jeff Tyzik, arr.

Films

EMI (rental)

Wizard of Oz: Over the Rainbow   3'
2 1 2 1 – 2 3 2 1 – tmp+perc – pf – str
perc: drumset, vib, glock.
Marty Gold, arr.

Films/Weather

Warner (POP); Luck's (rental)

Wizard of Oz: Over the Rainbow   5'
1 1 3[incl bcl] 0 – 2 0 1 0 – perc – hp, (cel), pf – str
Solo Voice in B flat Major. Royal Shakespeare
Company Version.

Films/Weather

EMI (rental)

Wizard of Oz: Over the Rainbow   5'
2 2 2 2 – 4 2 3 0 – tmp+drumset – str
Solo Piano.
Mario Lombardo, arr.

Films

EMI (rental)

The Wizard of Oz Selections   6'
3[1.2.pic] 2 2 1 – 4 3 3 1 – tmp+3 – str
Chuck Sayre, arr.

Films

Warner (POP); EMS or Luck's (rental)

Wizard of Oz: Yellow Brick Road   5'
1[incl pic] 1 3 0 – 1 2 1 0 – 3perc – hp, pf – str
Solo Voice; Unison Chorus.

Films

EMI (rental)

Armand, Charles, arr.   1849-1905
(pseudonym for Charles Puerner)

Neapolitan Songs for Orchestra   5'
1 1 2 1 – 2 2 1 0 – tmp+perc – str

International

Kalmus

Armstrong, Billie Joe & Green Day

Best of Green Day 4.5'
  1 1 3[1.2.(bcl)] 1 – 1 2 1 1 – tmp+3 – (pf) – str
  Includes: American Idiot; Wake Me Up When
  September Ends; Boulevard of Broken Dreams.
  Green Day is a rock band formed in 1989.
  Douglas E. Wagner, arr.
                                      Instrumental Pops
  Belwin

Arnaud, Leo   1904-1991

Bugler's Dream (ABC Olympic Theme), 4'
Fanfare to the Olympic
  0 0 0 0 – 4 4 3 1 – tmp+3
  Divertissement for Brass and Percussion. Also
  called *Charge*. Listed for sale under *Bugler's
  Dream*.
                                      Fanfare/Sports
  Shawnee

Arnold, Alan   1932-

Cartoon Sketches of the Baroque Suite 10'
  Strings
  Narrator.
                                      Instrumental Pops
  Presser

A Gershwin Portrait 14'
  2 2 2 2 – 4 3 3 1 – tmp+2 – hp – str
  Solo Piano.
                                      Broadway Musicals
  Bosworth

Israeli Work Song 10'
  2 2 2 2 – 4 3 3 1 – tmp+2 – hp – str
  A concert setting of *Hora* dance.
                                      International
  Viola World

Three Colombian Songs 12'
  Strings and Latin percussion
                                      International
  Presser

Three Crazy Pieces 6'
  2 2 2 2 – 4 3 3 1 – tmp+2 – hp – str
  The composer describes this as a "humorous
  treatment of contemporary styles."
                                      Instrumental Pops
  Viola World

Variations for Orchestra 17'
  2 2 2 2 – 4 3 3 1 – tmp+2 – hp – str
  A symphonic treatment of *Greensleeves*.
                                      Instrumental Pops
  Presser

Arnold, David   1962-

Independence Day: Highlights
  3[1.2.3/pic] 2 4[1.2.3.bcl] 2 – asx, tsx, bsx –
  4 3 3 2 – tmp+perc – hp, pf, org, synth – string bass
  Tony Smallwood, arr.
                                      Films
  Kane (rental)

Independence Day Suite 11'
  3[1.2.3/pic] 3[1.oboe d'amore.Eh] 3[1.2.bcl]
  3[1.2.3/cbn] – asx, tsx, bsx – 4 3 4 1 – tmp+perc –
  hp, pf, cel/org – string bass
  SATB Chorus. A 5' version is available with no
  chorus.
  Nicholas Dodd, arr.
                                      Films
  Kane (rental)

Independence Day Suite: End Tags 9'
  3[1.2.3/pic] 3[1.2/oboe d'amore.Eh] 3[1.2.bcl]
  3[1.2.3/cbn] – 4 3[1.pic.pic] 4 1 – tmp+perc –
  hp, pf, cel/org – str
  SATB Chorus.
  Nicholas Dodd, arr.
                                      Films
  Kane (rental)

Arnold, Malcolm   1921-2006

Anniversary Overture, Op. 99   4'
  2 2 2 2 – 4 2 3 0 – tmp+1 – str
  perc: cym, glock, tam, td
  Commissioned in 1968 as a twenty-first birthday piece for Hong Kong Philharmonic Society.
                              Celebration
  Faber (rental)

The Belles of St. Trinians: 8'
  Comedy Suite
  2[incl 2pic] 1 2 1 – 0 2 1 1 – 4 perc – pf[4hand] – str
  Christopher Palmer, arr.
                              Instrumental Pops
  Novello (rental)

The Bridge on the River Kwai: 24'
  Concert Suite
  3[1/pic.2/pic.3pic] 3[incl Eh] 4[incl Ebcl,bcl] 3[incl cbn] – 4 3 3 1 – tmp+6 – hp, pf – str
  Oscar winning score. Includes the Colonel Bogey March by Kenneth Alford.
  Christopher Palmer, arr.
                              Films
  Novello (rental)

Bridge on the River Kwai: March   5'
  3[incl 3pic] 3 4[incl Ebcl bcl) 2[incl cbn] – 4 3 3 1 – tmp+6 – 2hp, 2pf – str
  Christopher Palmer, arr.
                              Films
  Novello (rental)

Comedy Overture: 9'
  Beckus the Dandipratt
  3 2 2 2 – 4 3 3 1 – tmp+perc – str
  Solo Clarinet part.
                              Instrumental Pops
  Lengnick (rental)

Commonwealth Christmas Overture,   19'
  Op. 64
  3 2 2 2 – 4 3 3 1 – tmp+4 – hp, cel – str
                              Christmas
  Lengnick (rental)

English Dances: Set I, Op. 27   8'
  3[incl pic] 2 2 2 – 4 3 3 1 – tmp+perc – hp – str
                              Dance/International
  Lengnick (rental)

English Dances: Set II, Op. 33   9'
  3 2 2 2 – 4 3 3 1 – tmp+2 – hp, cel – str
                              Dance/International
  Lengnick (rental)

Four Cornish Dances, Op. 91   8'
                              (2' 2' 2' 2')
  3[1.2.3/pic] 2 2 2 – 4 3 3 1 – tmp+2 – hp – str
  perc: tubular bells, cym, tam tam, vib, bd, sus. cym, tambn, sd, td.
                              Dance
  Faber (rental)

Four Irish Dances, Op. 126   11'
  3[1.2.pic] 2 2 2 – 4 3 3 1 – tmp+2 – hp – str
  perc: td, bd, cym.
                              Dance/International
  Faber (rental)

Four Scottish Dances, Op. 59   10'
                              (3' 2' 4' 1')
  2[incl pic] 2 2 2 – 4 2 3 0 – tmp+1 – hp – str
                              Dance/International
  Novello (rental)

A Grand, Grand Overture, Op. 57   8'
  3[incl pic] 2 2 2 – 4 3 3 1 – tmp+3 – hp, org – str
  perc: chimes, tamtam, sd, sus cym, bd, 4 rifles
  Solo 3 Vacuum Cleaners, 1 Floor Polisher.
                              Instrumental Pops/Novelty
  Novello (rental)

Hobson's Choice   17'
  2[incl pic] 2 2 2 – 4 2 2 1 – tmp+3 – cel/pf – hp – str
  Christopher Palmer, arr.
                              Films
  Novello (rental)

The Holly and the Ivy: 6'
  Fantasy on Christmas Carols
  3[1.2.3/pic] 2 2 2 – 4 3 3 1 – tmp+3 – 2hp,cel/pf – str
  This suite is derived from the composer's soundtrack for "The Holly and the Ivy," Christmas Round-Up (a BBC documentary), and carols written for the Save the Children Fund. Includes: The Holly and the Ivy; Away in a Manger; I Saw Three Ships; and The First Noel.
  Christopher Palmer, arr.
                              Christmas
  Novello (rental)

The Inn of the Sixth Happiness: 14'
  Suite
    3[incl pic] 2 3[incl bcl] 2 – 4 3 3 1 – tmp+4 –
    2hp, cel/pf – str
    Includes: London Prelude; Romantic Interlude;
    Happy Ending (Mountain Crossing – The Children).
    Christopher Palmer, arr.
                                                            Films

Novello (rental)

Solitaire, Op. 141:   8'
  Sarabande and Polka
    2[incl pic] 2 2 2 – 4 3 3 1 – tmp+2 – hp, cel – str
    Alternate: 2 1 2 1 – 2 2 2 0 – perc – cel, hp – str
                                                             Dance

Novello (rental)

The Sound Barrier Rhapsody, Op. 38   7'
  3[1/pic.2/pic.3/pic] 2 2 2 – 4 3 3 1 – tmp+2 –
  hp, cel – str
  The story is about jet planes.
                                                  Films/Travel

Novello (rental)

Sweeney Todd Concert Suite, Op. 68a   23'
  2[1.pic] 1 2 1 – 2 2 2 0 – tmp+2 – hp, cel/pf – str
  perc: sus.cym, bd, tam tam, sd, glock, woodblck, tubular
  bells, nightingale.
  Not to be confused with the Sondheim
  Broadway show.
                                                Dance (Ballet)

Faber (rental)

Symphonic Study: 6'
  Machines, Op. 30
    0 0 0 0 – 4 3 3 1 – tmp+2 – str
    perc: xyl, sd, cym, bd, tamtam.
                         Labor Day/Instrumental Pops

Faber

Tam O'Shanter: Overture, Op. 51   8'
  3[1.2/pic.pic] 2 2 2 – 4 3 3 1 – tmp+2 – str
  perc: bd, cym, sus cym, sd, td, tamtam, chimes, whip.
                                                  Halloween

Novello (rental)

Toy Symphony, Op. 62   10'
  12 toy instruments – pf – strings
                           Instrumental Pops/Novelty

Novello (rental)

Whistle Down the Wind   9'
  2[pic] 1 2 0 – 2 0 0 0 – 2perc – hp, cel/pf, gtr – str
  Christopher Palmer, arr.
                                             Films/Weather

Novello (rental)

Ashman, Howard (See: Menken, Alan)

Auber, Daniel-François   1782-1871

Fra diavolo: Overture   9'
  2[1.pic] 2 2 2 – 4 2 3 0 – tmp+3 – str
                                                     Halloween

Kalmus

Auric, George (See: Young, Victor)

Austin, Frederic   1872-1952

Twelve Days of Christmas   3'
  2 2 2 2 – 2 2 3 0 – tmp+perc – str
                                                     Christmas

Novello (rental)

Autry, Gene   1907-1998

Here Comes Santa Claus (Right Down Santa   2'
* Claus Lane)*
    1 1 3[1.2.(bcl)]1 – (asx, tsx) – 2 2 2 1 – tmp+2 –
    pf – str
    perc: sd, bd, slgh-bells.
    James D. Ployhar, arr.
                                                      Christmas

Leonard (rental)

Ayars, Bo   1941-

American Fanfare   4'
  1[incl pic] 2 2 2 – 4 3 3 1– tmp+3 – hp – str
                              Americana
  Presser (rental)

Christmas Medley   24.5'
  3 3 3 2 – 4 3 3 1 – tmp+2 – hp – str
        (4' 4.5' 3.6' 3.5' 3' 3.5' 2.5')
  Includes: I Saw Three Ships; The Twelve Days of Christmas [with chorus]; Bring a Torch Jeannette Isabella; I Wonder as I Wander; Il est né le divin enfant; O Come, O Come Emmanuel; Away in a Manger. Carols can be performed separately.
                              Christmas
  Presser (rental)

Cowboy Medley: Cielito lindo   2'
  3[incl pic] 3[incl Eh] 3[incl bcl] 2 – 4 3 3 1 – tmp+2 – hp – str
  Also known as *Western/South of the Border Medley*. Can be played as a suite or separately.
                      Americana/International
  Presser (rental)

Cowboy Medley: Mexican Hat Dance   4'
  3[incl pic] 3[incl Eh] 3[incl bcl] 2 – 4 3 3 1 – tmp+2 – hp – str
  Also known as *Western/South of the Border Medley*. Can be played as a suite or separately.
                  Americana/Dance/International
  Presser (rental)

Cowboy Medley: She'll Be Comin'   2'
Round the Mountain
  3[incl pic] 3[incl Eh] 3[incl bcl] 2 – 4 3 3 1 – tmp+2 – hp – str
  Also known as *Western/South of the Border Medley*. Can be played as a suite or separately.
                              Americana
  Presser (rental)

Cowboy Medley: Shenandoah   4'
  3[incl pic] 3[incl Eh] 3[incl bcl] 2 – 4 3 3 1 – tmp+2 – hp – str
  Also known as *Western/South of the Border Medley*. Can be played as a suite or separately.
                              Americana
  Presser (rental)

Cowboy Medley: Sweet Betsy   4.5'
from Pike
  3[incl pic] 3[incl Eh] 3[incl bcl] 2 – 4 3 3 1 – tmp+2 – hp – str
  Also known as *Western/South of the Border Medley*. Can be played as a suite or separately.
                              Americana
  Presser (rental)

Cowboy Medley: The Yellow Rose   3'
of Texas
  3[incl pic] 3[incl Eh] 3[incl bcl] 2 – 4 3 3 1 – tmp+2 – hp – str
  Also known as *Western/South of the Border Medley*. Can be played as a suite or separately.
  Presser (rental)

Shave and a Haircut March   2.5'
  3[incl pic] 3[incl Eh] 3[incl bcl] 2 – 4 3 3 1 – tmp+2 – hp – str
                              Americana
  Presser (rental)

Ayer, Nathaniel (Nat) Davis   1887-1952

If You Were the Only Girl in the World   3'
  2[1.2/pic] 2 2 2 – 2asx, tsx – 4 3 3 1 – tmp+2 – str
  perc: cym, xyl, sd.
  Timothy Broege, arr.
                          Popular Song/Valentine
  Kalmus

B

Bach, Johann Sebastian   1685-1750

Arioso   7.5'
    2 0 3[incl bcl] 2 – 2 0 0 0 – 2hp – str
    Leopold Stokowski, arr.
                                     Popular Classics
Stokowski (rental)

Chaconne   18'
    4 4[incl Eh] 4[incl bcl] 4[incl cbn] – 6 4 4 2 – tmp – hp – str
    Leopold Stokowski, arr.
                                     Popular Classics
Stokowski (rental)

Fantasia & Fugue in G minor   12.5'
    4[incl pic] 4[incl heck, Eh] 4[incl Ebcl, bcl, cbcl, asx] 4[incl cbn] – 6 4 3 2[incl tenor tuba] – tmp+perc – str
    perc: bd, tam-tam.
    Leopold Stokowski, arr.
                                     Popular Classics
Stokowski (rental)

Fugue in C minor   2'
    4[incl pic] 4[incl Eh] 4[incl bcl, cbcl] 4[incl cbn] – 6 4 4 1 – tmp – elec bass – str
    Leopold Stokowski, arr.
                                     Popular Classics
Stokowski (rental)

Jesu, Joy of Man's Desiring   3'
    (from Cantata No. 147)
    2 2 2 2 – 4 3 3 1 – str
    Chorus may substitute for brass.
    Arthur Luck, arr.
                                     Christmas
Luck's

Jesu, Joy of Man's Desiring   3'
    (from Cantata No. 147)
    3 3[1.2.Eh] 3[1.2.bcl] 3[1.2.cbn] – 4 3 3 1 – tmp – hp – str
    Alfred Reed, arr.
                                     Christmas
Kalmus

Jesu, Joy of Man's Desiring   5'
    (from Cantata No. 147)
    1 2[incl Eh] 0 3[incl cbn] – 3 1 0 1 – str
    Leopold Stokowski, arr.
                                     Christmas
Stokowski (rental)

Jesu, Joy of Man's Desiring   4'
    (from Cantata No.147)
    1 2[1.Eh] 2 2 – 4 3 3 1 – tmp+2 – hp – str
    SATB Chorus.
    Jeff Tyzik, arr.
                                     Christmas
Schirmer (rental)

Prelude in E flat minor   5'
    0 0 0 4[incl cbn] – 3 0 3 0 – perc – 2hp – str
    perc: glock, tam-tam.
    Leopold Stokowski, arr.
                                     Popular Classics
Stokowski (rental)

Prelude from Partita in E Major   4'
    1 1 0 0 – 0 0 0 0 – str
    Leopold Stokowski, arr.
                                     Popular Classics
Stokowski (rental)

Sheep May Safely Graze   4'
    (from Cantata No. 208)
    2 2 0 0 – 0 0 0 0 – str
    Leopold Stokowski, arr.
                               Christmas/Popular Classics
Peters

Sheep May Safely Graze   5'
    (from Cantata No. 208)
    3[1.2.pic] 3[1.2.(Eh)] 3[1.2.(bcl)] 3[1.2.(cbn)] – 4 3 3 1 – tmp – (hp) – str
    Lucien Cailliet, arr.
                               Christmas/Popular Classics
Boosey

Sleepers Awake (Wachet Auf)   4'
    2 2 2 2 – 4 3 3 1 – tmp+1 – str
    Eugene Ormandy, arr.
                                     Popular Classics
Boosey

Three Choral Preludes 9.5'
   Strings (2.5' 4' 3')
   Includes: Jesu, Joy of Man's Desiring; O Man Thy Grievous Sin Bemoan; In Thee Is Joy. Preludes are available separately also.
   Eugene Ormandy, arr.
Popular Classics

Boosey

Toccata and Fugue in C for Organ: Adagio 3.5'
   3 3[1.2.Eh] 2[1.bcl] 3[1.2.cbn] – 4 4 4 1 – tmp+2 – hp – str
   Solo Organ.
   Leopold Stokowski, arr.
Popular Classics

Broude Bros.; Kalmus

Toccata & Fugue in D minor, BWV 565 9'
   4[1.2.3/pic 1.4/pic 2] 4[1.2.3.Eh] 4[1.2.3.bcl] 4[1.2.3.cbn] – 6 3 4 1 – tmp – 2hp, cel – str
   Alternate winds: 4 3[incl Eh] 3[incl bcl] 3[incl cbn]
   Leopold Stokowski, arr.
Popular Classics

Broude Bros.

Bach, P.D.Q.   1807-1742?

1712 Overture 11'
   3 3 3 3 – 4 4 3 1 – tmp+4 – org – str
Instrumental Pops

Presser (rental)

A Bach Portrait 15'
   2 2 2 2 – 2 2 3 1 – tmp+2 – pf – str
   Narrator.
Instrumental Pops

Presser (rental)

Birthday Ode to "Big Daddy" Bach 8'
   0 0 0 0 – 0 3[all pic] 0 0 – tmp – hpsd – str
   Solo Narrator; Soprano, Mezzo, Tenor, Baritone; Mixed Chorus.
Celebrations

Presser (rental)

Broadway Boogie 5'
   1 1 0 0 – 0 0 0 0 – hp, pf – str
   Solo Dog.
Animals/Novelty

Presser (rental)

Canine Cantata "Wachet Arf!" 9'
   0 0 0 2 – 2 2 0 0 – tmp – str
   Solo Dog.
Animals/Novelty

Presser (rental)

Classical Rap 9'
   0 0 0 0 – 0 2 0 0 – hpsd – str
   Narrator [rapper].
Instrumental Pops

Presser (rental)

Prelude to Einstein on the Fritz, S.E=mc2 7'
   2 2 2 2 – 2 2 3 1 – 2perc – str
   Solo Piano, Foghorn, Bell, Kazoo, Balloon with Pitchpipes.
Instrumental Pops/Novelty

Presser (rental)

Requiem Mantras 15'
   3 2 2 2 – 4 3 3 1 – 3perc – cel, pf – str
   Rock group.
Instrumental Pops

Presser (rental)

Bacharach, Burt   1928-

Close to You 4'
   1 1 3[1.2.bcl] 1 – (sxs) – 2 2 2 1 – tmp+perc – pf – str
   James D. Ployhar, arr.
Popular Song

Leonard (rental)

Back, B & Davis, B & Cook, R. & Greenway, R.

I'd Like to Teach the World to Sing 3'
   (in Perfect Harmony)
   2 1 3[1.2.(bcl)] 1 – (asx, tsx) – 2 2 21 – tmp+3 – pf – str
   perc: sd, bd, tambn, vibraslap, glock, xyl.
   Willis Schaefer, arr.
Popular Song

Leonard (rental)

Bacon, Ernst   1898-1990

Christmas Fantasia for Strings   3'
   Strings

                                     Christmas

   Luck's (rental)

From These States, Suite: 20'
   Gathered Along Unpaved Roads
   3 3 3 3 – 4 3 3 1 – perc – str

                                     Americana

   Schirmer (rental)

Badelt, Klaus   1968-

Pirates of the Caribbean: Curse of the   6'
   Black Pearl   Medley
   2 1 3[1.2.bcl] 1 – 4 3 3 1 – tmp+6[2opt] – (pf)
   – str
   perc: tri, sus cym, sd, bd, gong, cym, hi hat, (glock, chimes, marim).
   Includes: Fog Bound; The Medallion Calls; To the Pirates Cave: The Black Pearl; One Last Shot; He's a Pirate.
   Ted Ricketts, arr.

                                     Films

   Leonard

Baerwald, David   1960-

Moulin Rouge: Come What May   5'
   2[1.2/pic] 2 2 2 – 4 3 3 1 – tmp+perc[drumset] –
   hp, pf, synth, 2gtr, elec bass – str
   Solo Male and Female Voices.

                                     Films

   Kane (rental)

Bagley, Edwin Eugene   1857-1922

National Emblem March   3'
   2[1.pic] 2 3 2 – 4 3 3 1 – 3 perc – str
   perc: sd, bd, cym.

                                     Patriotic

   Luck's

National Emblem March   4'
   Strings
   Samuel Adler, arr.

                                     Patriotic

   Presser (rental)

National Emblem March   3'
   3[1.2.pic] 2 3[incl (bcl)] 2 – 4 3 3 1 – tmp+perc
   – str
   Clark McAlister, arr.

                                     Patriotic

   Kalmus

Baker, David   1931-

Le chat qui pêche   33'
   3[1.2.pic] 3[1.2.Eh] 3[1.2.bcl] 3[1.2.cbn] – 4 3 3 1 –
   tmp+3 – hp – str   (6' 7' 9' 5' 6')
   Jazz Quartet: asx, tsx – drumset – elec pf/pf –
   elec db/db
   Solo Soprano (textless). Includes: Soleil d'altamira;
   L'odeur du blues; Sons voiles; Guadeloupe calypso;
   Le miroir noir.

                                     Animals/Jazz

   AMP (rental)

Concertino for Cellular Phones and   14'
   Symphony Orchestra (2006)
   3[1.2.pic] 2 2 3[1.2.cbn] – 4 3 3 1 – tmp+1 – str
   Solo Cell Phone Player. Cell phones also in the
   orchestra, and balcony and floor phones in the
   audience. Includes performance instructions by the
   composer.

                                     Novelty

   LKMP (rental)

Concerto for Cello   15'
   1 1 1 1 – 2 0 0 0 – tmp+1 – str (no vc)
   Solo Cello.

                                 Instrumental Pops

   AMP (rental)

Kosbro   13'
   3[incl pic] 3[incl Eh] 3[incl bcl] 3[incl cbn] –
   4 3 3 1 – tmp+4[xyl] – pf – str

                                     Jazz

   AMP (rental)

Two Improvisations   *8'*
    3[1.2.pic] 3[1.2.Eh] 3[1.2.bcl] 3[1.2.cbn] – 4 3 3 1
    – tmp+perc – str
    Jazz combo: drumset – pf – db
    Includes: Harlem Pipes; Sangre Negro.
                          Black History Month/Jazz
AMP (rental)

Balada, Leonardo   1933-

Homage to Sarasate   *8'*
    2[pic] 2 2[incl bcl] 2 – 3 3 3 1 – tmp+3 – hp, pf
    – str
                                 Popular Classic
EMI

Sinfonia en negro   *19'*
   (*Homage to Martin Luther King*)
    2 2 2 2 – 2 3 2 1 – 3perc – pf – str
                                 Martin Luther King
Schirmer (rental)

Balakirev, Mily   1837-1910

Overture on Russian Folk Themes   *8'*
    2 2 2 2 – 2 2 3 0 – tmp – str
    2 optional perc: bd, cym.
                                        International
Kalmus; Russian (rental)

Ball, Ernest R.   1878-1927

When Irish Eyes Are Smiling   *3'*
    2[incl pic] 2 2 2 – (2asx, tsx) – 4 3 3 1 – tmp+perc
    – str
    Timothy Broege, arr.
                              International/St. Patrick
Kalmus

Bantock, Granville   1868-1946

Old English Suite   *20'*
    2 2 2 2 – 4 2 0 0 – tmp – str
                                   Popular Classics
Novello (rental)

Barab, Seymour   1921-

G.A.G.E., A Christmas Story   *20'*
    2 2 2 2 – 2 2 2 0 – tmp+2 – hp, pf – str
    Narrator.
                                          Christmas
Schirmer (rental)

Barber, Samuel   1910-1981

Adagio for Strings, Op. 11   *8'*
    Strings
                                   Popular Classics
Schirmer

Capricorn Concerto   *14'*
    1 1 0 0 – 0 1 0 0 – str   *(6' 3' 5')*
    Solo Flute, Oboe, Trumpet.
                                              Space
Schirmer (rental)

Commando March for Orchestra   *4'*
    3[1.2.pic] 3[1.2.Eh] 4[1.2.Ebcl.bcl] 3[1.2.cbn] –
    4 3 3 1 – tmp+2 – pf – str
    perc: bd/cym, sd, tri, woodblk, xyl.
                                  Popular Classics
Schirmer (rental)

The Lovers, Op. 43   *31'*
    3[incl pic,afl] 3[incl Eh] 3[incl bcl] 2 – 4 3 3 1 –
    tmp+perc – hp, cel, pf – str
    Solo Baritone; SATB Chorus.
                                           Valentine
Schirmer (rental)

Die natali (*Chorale Preludes for*   *16'*
   Christmas), Op. 37
    3[1.2.3/pic] 3[1.2.Eh] 3[1.2.bcl] 2 – 4 3 3 1 –
    tmp+4 – hp, cel – str
    perc: bd, cym, td, tri, tamtam, glock, xyl, crot.
                                          Christmas
Schirmer (rental)

Die natali (*Chorale Preludes for*   *3'*
   Christmas), Op. 37: *Silent Night*
    1 2[1.Eh] 3[1.2.bcl] 0 – 4 0 3 1 – hp, cel – str
    Alternate winds (as cues): 1 1 2 1 – 2 0 1 0
                                          Christmas
Schirmer (rental)

The School for Scandal: Overture   8'
     3[1.2.pic] 3[1.2.Eh] 3[1.2.bcl] 2 – 4 3 3 1 – tmp+3 – hp, cel – str
     perc: bd, cym, tb, glock.
                                           Popular Classics

Schirmer (rental)

Barroso, Ary   1903-1964

Brazil (Aquarela do Brasil)   3'
     2 2 2 2 – 4 2 3 1 – tmp+2 – (hp) – str
                                           International (Brazil)

Filarmonika

Brazil   3'
     2 2 2 2 – 4 3 2 1 – tmp+2 – pf – str
     Marty Gold, arr.
                                                      International

Warner (POP); EMS or Luck's (rental)

Barry, John   1933-
(Also See: Elfman, Danny)

The Best of Bond   15'
     2[incl pic] 2 2 2 – 4 3 3 1 – tmp+2[incl drumset] – synth, hp, elec bass – str
     Includes: James Bond Theme: Nobody Does It Better; Live and Let Die; For Your Eyes Only; The Look of Love; 007 Theme; Thunderball.
     Jeff Tyzik, arr.
                                                                   Films

Schirmer (rental)

Born Free Theme (1966)   5'
     2 2 2 2 – 4 4 4 1 – tmp – hp – str
     Music from the Oscar winning score.
                                                             Films

T&V (rental)

The Cotton Club (1984)   4'
     2 0 1 0 – asx – 0 0 0 0 – 1perc [vib] – pf – str
                                                            Films

T&V (rental)

Dances with Wolves Suite (1990)   18'
     2 2[incl Eh] 2 2 – 8 1 4 1 – tmp+2 – hp – str
     perc: bd, sd, Pawnee Indian Dr, gong.
     Includes: Pawnee Attack, Kicking Bird's Gift, Journey To Fort Sedgewick, Two Socks: The Wolf Theme, Farewell & Finale. Music from the Oscar winning score.
                                                      Animals/Films

T&V (rental)

Dances with Wolves: Concert Suite   2.5'
     2 1 3[1.2.bcl] 2[(2)] – 4[(3&4)] 3 3 1 – tmp+perc – hp or pf – str
     Includes: Looks Like a Suicide; John Dunbar Theme; Journey to Fort Sedgwick; Pawnee Attack; Love Theme; Two Socks at Play; Farewell; End Title.
     John Rosenhaus, arr.
                                                      Animals/Films

Leonard

Dances with Wolves: Suite for Flute and Orchestra   8'
     1 1 1 1 – 1 0 0 0 – tmp+perc – hp, pf – str
     perc: orch bells, vib (opt 2nd orch bells).
     Includes: Main Title; The John Dunbar Theme; Two Socks - The Wolf Theme; Journey to Fort Sedgwick; The Love Theme; End Title.
                                                      Animals/Films

T&V (rental)

Dances with Wolves: The John Dunbar Theme (1990)   2.5'
     1 0 1 2 – 8 0 4 1 – hp [pf cue] – str
                                                      Animals/Films

T&V (rental)

Goldfinger Theme (1964)   2.5'
     2 2 2 2 – 4 4 5 1 – tmp+3 – hp, pf – str
     perc: cyms, tamb, vib, tri.
                                                             Films

T&V (rental)

King Kong Theme (1976)   2.5'
     2 2[1.Eh] 2 2 – 3 0 0 0 – tmp – hp – str
                                                     Animals/Films

T&V (rental)

Out of Africa: Main Title   3'
    4[1.2.3.4] 2[1.2/Eh] 0 0 – 8 2 5 1 – 2perc –
    2 hp – str
    The work can be played with: 2[1.pic] 1 0 0 –
    1 1 3 1 – 2perc – hp – str
        perc: bd, gong, vib.
    Al Woodbury, orchestrator

                                                        Films
MCA

Robin and Marian (1976)   5'
    2[1.afl] 2[1.Eh] 2 2 – 4 2 3 1 – tmp+2 – hp – str
        perc: chimes, sus cym.
    Includes: John Bursts In, The End.
                                      Films/Valentine
T&V (rental)

Somewhere in Time   3.5'
    2 2 3[1.2.bcl] 2 – 4 3 3 1 – tmp+3 – synth/pf – str
    Calvin Custer, arr.
                                        Films/New Year
MCA

Somewhere in Time (1980)   9'
    2[1.afl] 2[1.Eh] 2 2 – 4 0 0 1– tmp+1[vib] – hp, pf
    – str
                                        Films/New Year
T&V (rental)

Bart, Lionel   1930-1999

Oliver! Selections   8.5'
    3[1.2.pic] 3[1.2.Eh] 3[1.2.bcl] 2 – 4 3 3 1 – tmp+4
    – hp – str
        perc: cym, sd, bd, xyl, glock, sus cym.
    Includes: Oliver; I'd Do Anything; Where Is Love;
    As Long As He Needs Me; Consider Yourself
    Arthur Reed, arr.
                                    Broadway Musicals
TRO

Oliver! for Orchestra   10.5'
    3[1/(afl)/pic.2/(afl)/pic.3/pic] 3[1.2.3/Eh]
    3[1.2/Ebcl.3/bcl] 3[1.2.3/cbn] – 4 3 3 1 – tmp+4
    – pf, (cel), 2hp – str
        perc: sus cym, glock, xyl, marim, vib, chimes, pic sd,
        cym, bd.
    Includes: Overture; As Long as He Needs Me;
    Where is Love?; Be Back Soon.
    John Green, arr.
                                    Broadway Musicals
Lakeview (rental)

Bartók, Béla   1881-1945

Dance Suite   17'
                        (4'   2'   3'   3'   1'   4')
    2[1/pic.2/pic] 2[1.2/Eh] 2[1.2/bcl] 2[1.2/cbn] –
    4 2 2 1 – tmp+3 – hp, cel, pf – str
        perc: bd, cym, sd, td, tri, tamtam, glock.
    Brief passage needs pf 4-hands
                                              Dance
Boosey (rental)

Hungarian Sketches   11'
                        (3'   2'   2'   2'   2')
    2[1.2/pic] 2 2[1.2/bcl] 2[1.2/cbn] – 2 2 2 1 –
    tmp+2 – hp – str
    Includes: An Evening in the Village; Bear Dance;
    Melody; Slightly Tipsy; Swineherd's Dance.
                                PopularClassics/International
Boosey (rental)

Rumanian Folk Dances   6'
    2[1.2/pic] 0 2 2 – 2 0 0 0 – str
                                      Dance/International
Boosey (rental)

Rumanian Folk Dances   6'
    Strings
    Arthur Willner, arr.
                                      Dance/International
Boosey (rental)

Bassman, George (See: Washington, Ned)

Bavil, Zamir   1929-

David and the Ark of the Covenant   15'
    3[1.2.3/pic] 3[1.2.Eh] 3[1.2.bcl] 3[1.2.(cbn)] –
    4 3 3 1 – tmp+ 5to8 – hp, pf/cel – str
        perc: wind chimes, mark tree/bell tree, tri, crotales,
        tambn/cast, slgh bells/conga dr, sus[reg. and sizzle],cym,
        gong/bongo dr.,woodblk/templeblk, glock, xyl, chimes,
        sd, tam, sd, woodblk, cym, tambn, tri, toms, bd.
                                              Holidays
ZB (rental)

Hanukkah Fantasy   12'
   3[1.2.afl/pic] 3[1.2.Eh] 3[1.2.bcl] 3[1.2.cbn] –
   4 4 3 1 – tmp+6 – pf, hp, cel – str
      perc: 12 roto toms, tamtam, bd, slgh-bells, chimes, sistrum, whip, sd, cym, tambn, woodblks, temple blks, xyl, marim, glock.
   Optional SATB Chorus.
   Includes: Y'Malell, Ma'Oz Tsur, Y'May Hanukkah, My Dreidle, Hanukkah Hanukkah, S'Vivon Sov Sov Sov, End of 3rd Blessing, Hanukkah Candles.
                                                                  Holidays
ZB (rental)

Hanukkah Light (1998)   5'
   3[1.2.pic/afl] 3[1.2.Eh] 3[1.2.bcl] 3[1.2.cbn] –
   4 4[1/pic.2.3.4] 3 1 – tmp+3[as many as 8 parts available] – hp, pf/cel – str
      perc: 10 roto toms, tamtam, bd, slgh-bells, chimes, sistrum, whip, sd, cym, tambn, woodblks, temple blks, xyl, marim, glock.
   Optional SATB Chorus. This is an abbreviated version of his Hannukah Fantasy.
                                                                  Holidays
ZB (rental)

Hanukkah Rhapsody (2001)   9'
   3[1.2.pic/afl]3[1.2.Eh] 3[1.2.bcl] 3[1.2.(cbn)] –
   4 4[1/pic. 2.3.(4)] 3 1 – tmp+ 8[as few as 3 can be used] – hp, pf/cel – str
      perc: 12 roto toms, tamtam, bd, slgh-bells, chime, sistrum, whip, sd, cym, tambn, woodblks, temple blks, xyl, marim, glock.
   Optional high school level SATB Chorus. This is a version of *Hannukah Fantasy* with Christmas tunes deleted and Hebrew lyrics provided.
                                                                  Holidays
ZB (rental)

Israeli Rhapsody (1959, 2000)   20'
   3[1.2.pic]3[1.2.Eh] 3[1.2.bcl] 3[1.2.(cbn)] – 4 3 3 1
   – tmp+ 4 – hp – str
      perc: xyl/glock, tam-tam, sd, woodblk, cym, tambn, tri.
                                              International (Israel)
ZB (rental)

Bax, Arnold   1883-1953

A Christmas Carol   4'
   2 2 2 2 – 4 0 0 0 – str
   Solo Medium Voice.
                                                                  Christmas
Chester (rental)

Bazelon, Irwin   1922-1995

Early American Suite   15'
   1 1 1 1 – 1 0 0 0 – hpsd [(pf)]
                                                        Americana
Presser (rental)

Fairy Tale   15'
   1[incl pic] 0 2[incl bcl] 0 – 1 1 0 0 – perc – pf – vc, db
                                                        Halloween
Presser (rental)

Spirits of the Night   15'
   3 3 4 3 – 4 3 3 1 – tmp+4 – pf – str
                                                        Halloween
Presser (rental)

The Beatles

Abbey Road Suite   20'
   3[incl pic] 3[1.2.Eh] 3[1.2.bcl] 3[incl cbn] – 4 3 3 1
   – tmp+3 – hp, pf[(cel)] – str
                                                    Popular Song
ATV (rental)

Beatles!!!: A Medley of   12'
  Lennon and McCartney Favorites
   3 2 3 2 – 4 3 3 1 – tmp+2 – hp, cel, pf, elec gtr, elec bass – str
   Includes: Sgt. Pepper's Lonely Hearts Club Band; Good Day Sunshine; I Want to Hold Your Hand; Golden Slumbers; Ticket to Ride; A Day in the Life; Get Back; Penny Lane; Let It Be; Got to Get You Into My Life; A Hard Day's Night; All My Lovin'; Can't Buy Me Love.
   Bruce Healey, arr.
                                                    Popular Song
ATV (rental)

Beatles Medley   5.5'
   2[1/pic.2] 1 3[1.2.bcl] 1 – (ssx, asx, tsx, bsx) –
   2 3 3 1 – tmp+perc[incl drumset] – pf, (hp), elec bass – str
   Includes: Eleanor Rigby; When I'm 64; Sgt. Pepper's Lonely Hearts Club Band; Yesterday.
   Mendelson, arr.
                                                    Popular Song
Kendor

Beatles Hits Medley   12'
    2 2 2 2 – 4 3 3 1 – tmp+2 – hp, pf, elec bass – str
    Includes: I Want to Hold Your Hand; She Loves You; Yesterday; Eleanor Rigby; Hey, Jude; Get Back; Yellow Submarine.
    Jeff Tyzik, arr.
                                Popular Song
ATV (rental)

Classic Beatles: A Medley   11'
    3 3 3 3 – 4 3 3 1 – tmp+3 – cel/pf – str
    Includes: The Long and Winding Road; Here, There and Everywhere; And I Love Her; When I'm 64; I've Just Seen A Face; A Hard Day's Night; Norwegian Wood; Hey, Jude.
    Peter Mansfield, arr.
                                Popular Song
ATV (rental)

The Great Beatles Singles Suite I: 18'
Strawberry Fields Forever
    3[incl pic] 3[1.2.Eh] 3[1.2.bcl] 3[incl cbn] – 4 3 3 1 – tmp+3 – hp, pf[(cel)] – str
    Andrew Jackman, arr.
                                Popular Song
ATV (rental)

The Great Beatles Singles Suite II: 18'
All You Need Is Love
    3[incl pic] 3[1.2.Eh] 3[1.2.bcl] 3[incl cbn] – 4 3 3 1 – tmp+3 – hp, pf[(cel)] – str
    Andrew Jackman, arr.
                                Valentine
ATV (rental)

A Long and Winding Road   25'
    3 3 3 3 – 4 4 3 1 – tmp+4 – pf – str
    Includes: Sgt. Pepper's Lonely Hearts Club Band; Norwegian Wood; Eleanor Rigby; Here, There and Everywhere; When I'm 64; She's Leaving Home; Yellow Submarine; Yesterday; Can't Buy Me Love; The Long and Winding Road.
    Eric Knight, arr.
                                Popular Song
ATV (rental)

Love is All You Need   19'
(A Tribute to the Beatles)
    3[1.2.pic] 3[1.2.Eh] 3[1.2.bcl] 3[1.2.cbn] – 4 3[1/pic/Eb.2.3/flug] 3[1/alto.2.3.] 1 – tmp+3 – hp, pf/cel – str
    perc: tamtam, sd, bd, 2 sus cym, cym, tambn, tri, chimes, crotales, 2 Bodhrans[bones], 2 mark trees, glock, temple blks, vibraslap, whip, xyl, jingle sticks, sandpaper blks[cabasa], Brazilian tambn, headless tambn.
    Includes: All My Loving; All You Need is Love; Blackbird; Can't Buy Me Love; Come Together; Day Tripper; Here Comes the Sun; If I Fell; Lady Madonna; Let It Be; Ob-La-Di Ob-La-Da; Something; Yesterday. 2 cut options are provided reducing the duration to 15' and 12' respectively.
    Bruce Healey, arr.
                              Popular Song/Rock
Leonard

Sergeant Pepper's Lonely Hearts   18'
Club Band
    3[incl pic] 3[incl Eh] 3[incl bcl] 3[incl cbn] – 4 3 3 1 – tmp+3 – hp, cel, pf – str
    Francis Shaw, arr.
                              Popular Song/Rock
ATV (rental)

Songs from the White Album   16'
    3[incl pic] 3[1.2.Eh] 3[incl bcl] 3[1.2.cbn] – 4 3 3 1 – tmp+3 – hp, pf[(cel)] – str
    Includes: Martha My Dear; Ob-La-Di, Ob-La-Da; Yer Blues; Mother Nature's Son; Back in the USSR.
    Andrew Jackman, arr.
                                Popular Song
ATV (rental)

Beck, Christophe   1972-

Under the Tuscan Sun (2003): Suite
    2[1/afl.2/pic] 2[1.Eh] 2 2 – 4 0 0 0 – tmp+perc – hp, pf, gtr/mandolin – str
                                       Films
Kane (rental)

Beethoven, Ludwig van   1770-1827

Egmont: Overture   9'
                                  Popular Classics
Breitkopf; Kalmus

König Stephan: Overture, Op. 117   8'
     2 2 2 3[1.2.cbn] – 4 2 0 0 – tmp – str
                                 Popular Classics
Breitkopf; Kalmus

Moonlight Sonata (1st movement)   6'
     3 3[incl Eh] 3[incl bcl] 2[incl cbn] – 4 3 3 1 –
     tmp+perc – hp – str
     Leopold Stokowski, arr
                             Popular Classics/Space
Stokowski (rental)

Romance No. 1 in G Major, Op.40   8'
     1 2 0 2 – 2 0 0 0 – str
     Solo Violin.
                           Popular Classics/Valentine
Breitkopf; Henle; Kalmus

Romance No. 2 in F Minor, Op. 50   9'
     1 2 0 2 – 2 0 0 0 – str
     Solo Violin.
                           Popular Classics/Valentine
Breitkopf; Henle; Kalmus

Die Ruinen von Athen (The Ruins of Athens)   6'
     Op.113: Turkish March and Chorus
     2[1.2/pic] 2 2 2 – 2 2 3 0 – tmp – str
     Solo Triangle; Chorus.
                                 Popular Classics
Breitkopf; Kalmus

Bellini, Vincenzo   1801-1835

Romeo and Juliet: Overture   5'
     1 2 2 2 – 4 2 3 1+euph – tmp+perc – str
                                           Valentine
Schirmer (rental)

Bembo, Baldan

Melody (Aria)   9'
     2 1 3[1.2.bcl] 0 – asx – 4perc – pf, elec gtr, elec bs
     – str
     perc: vib, chimes, glock, tambn, tamtam, conga, drumset.
     Richard Stephan, arr.
                                   Instrumental Pops
Warner (available from Luck's)

Bendix, Victor   1851-1926

Grand American Fantasia: Tone Pictures   4'
     of the North and South (1902)
     1 1 2 1 – 2 2 1 0 – 2perc – pf – str
     perc: sd, bd, glock.
     Includes: Keller's American Hymn, Maryland My
     Maryland, Old Zip Coon, Bonny Eloise,
     Reveille/Tenting Tonight, Dixey, Carry Me Back to
     Old Virginny, Old Dan Tucker, Arkansas Traveler,
     Star Spangled Banner.
                           Americana/Patriotic
Luck's

Benjamin, Arthur   1893-1960

Two Jamaican Pieces: 5'
     Jamaican Song; Jamaican Rhumba   (2'   3')
     1 1 (2) 1 – (asx) – 2 1 0 0 – (tmp+2) – pf – str
                                       International
Boosey (rental)

Bennett, Richard Rodney   1936-2012

Celebration   5'
     3[incl pic] 2 2 2 – 4 3 3 1 – tmp+3 – str
                                         Celebration
Novello (rental)

Concerto for Stan Getz   24'
     tmp – str
     Solo Tenor Saxophone.
                                              Jazz
Novello (rental)

Diversions   20'
     2[incl pic] 2 2 2 – 2 2 0 0 – tmp+2 – pf – str
                                 Instrumental Pops
Novello (rental)

Four Weddings and a Funeral: 3.5'
     First Love Scene (1994)
     1[afl] 1 0 0 – 2 0 0 0 – hp, pf, synth [DX7] – str
                                     Films/Valentine
T&V (rental)

London Pastoral 14'
   2[incl pic] 1 1 1 – 1 1 1 0 – perc – hp – str
   Solo Tenor.
                                                International
   EMI (rental)

Lovesongs 22'
   2[incl pic] 2 2 1 – 2 2 2 1 – tmp+2 – hp, cel/pf,
   gtr(ampd) – str
   Solo Tenor. Text by E.E. Cummings.
                                                Valentine
   Novello (rental)

Love Spells 14'
   3[incl pic] 3[incl Eh] 3[incl bcl] 3[incl cbn] –
   4 3 3 1 – tmp+3 – hp, pf[(cel)] – str
   Solo Soprano.
                                                Valentine
   Novello (rental)

Murder on the Orient Express Theme: 4'
   Foxtrot Theme
   2 1[Eh] 2 2 – 4 3 3 1 – tmp+perc[incl drumset] –
   hp, gtr – str
   Solo Piano.
                                                Dance/Films
   EMI (rental)

Murder on the Orient Express Suite 12'
   2[incl pic] 2 2[incl bcl] 2 – 4 3 3 1 –
   tmp+3[incl drumset] – hp, pf, gtr – str
   David Lindup, arr.
                                                Films
   EMI (rental)

Murder on the Orient Express: Suite 7.5'
   2[1.pic] 2[1.Eh] 2[1.bcl] 2 – 4 3 3 1 –
   tmp+4 – 2 hps – pf[cel], gtr, bass gtr – str
   perc: drumset, cym, sus cym, med sus cym, glock, xyl, sd,
   tubular bells, steam effect, bongos, tri.
   Includes: Overture, Waltz & Finale.
                                                Films
   T&V (rental)

Murder on the Orient Express Waltz 4'
   2[incl pic] 2[incl Eh] 2[incl bcl] 2 – 4 3 3 1 –
   tmp+perc – pf – str
                                                Dance/Films
   EMI (rental)

Nocturnes - for Chamber Orchestra 12'
   1 1 1 1 – 1 0 0 0 – hp – str
                                                Instrumental Pops
   EMI (rental)

Partita for Orchestra 17'
   2[incl pic] 2[incl Eh] 2 2 – 2 0 0 0 – tmp – hp – str
   *"I responded to this exciting but rather daunting
   commission by writing a very lively and I hope very
   accessible piece, which, I decided before I started
   composing, should be full of tunes. I wrote it in
   memory of my dear friend Sheila MacCrindle, who
   died in 1993 . . . although this partita is in her
   memory, it never occurred to me to make it gloomy
   or dirge-like . . ."* (Richard Rodney Bennett quote)
   Commissioned by British Telecommunications in
   co-operation with the Association of British
   Orchestra's 95/96 season.
                                                Instrumental Pops
   Novello (rental)

Suite française (1970) 7'
   2[incl pic] 1 2 1 – 2 1 1 0 – tmp+2 – hp – str
   perc: bells, xyl.
                                                International
   EMI (rental)

Variations on a Nursery Tune 15'
   2[incl pic] 2[incl Eh] 2 2 – 4 2 3 1 – tmp+2 –
   hp, cel/pf – str
                                                Popular Song
   Novello (rental)

Bennett, Robert Russell   1894-1981

Columbia, the Gem of the Ocean 4'
   2[1/pic.2/pic] 2 3[1.2.bcl] 2 – 4 3 3 1 –
   tmp+perc[bells] – hp, pf – str
   A patriotic song which was popular during the mid-
   19th and early 20th centuries, especially during the
   Civil War era.
                                                Patriotic
   Lawson-Gould (rental)

A Commemoration Symphony: Stephen 24'
   Collins Foster   (6.5'   5.5'   4.5'   7.5')
   3[1.2.pic] 2[incl Eh] 2[incl bcl] 2 – 4 3 3 1 – 4perc
   – cel, hp – str
   Vocal Soloists; SATB Chorus. Includes: Quasi
   Adagio; Cantabile; Allegretto; Allegro Quasi
   Recitativo. The chorus only sings during the 4th
   movement.
                                                Patriotic
   Warner/Chappell Music (rental)

The Four Freedoms   *20'*
    2[1.2/pic] 2[1.2/Eh] 3[1.2.3/bcl] 2 – 4 3 3 1 – tmp+3 – str
    perc: bd, cym, sus cym, sd, field dr, tri, 2tomtoms. Based on four paintings by Norman Rockwell after a speech by Franklin D. Roosevelt: Freedom from Want; Freedom from Fear; Freedom to Worship; Freedom of Speech.
                                                    Patriotic

Schirmer (rental)

Hollywood   *15'*
    3[1.2.pic] 3[1.2.Eh] 3[1.2.bcl] 2 – 4 3 3 1 – tmp+perc – hp, 2pf[1/cel.2] – str
    Commissioned by the League of Composers in 1936 by the National Broadcasting Company Symphony Orchestra, Dr. Frank Black, conductor.
                                                      Films

Fleisher

The Many Moods of Christmas: Suite 1   *12'*
    3[1.pic.pic] 3[1.2.Eh] 3[1.2.bcl] 3[1.2.cbn] – 4 3 3 1 – tmp+perc – str
    Mixed Chorus. Includes: Christian Men, Rejoice; Silent Night; Patapan; O Come, All Ye Faithful.
                                                      Christmas

Lawson-Gould (rental)

The Many Moods of Christmas: Suite 2   *11'*
    3 3 3 3 – 4 3 3 1 – tmp+perc – hp – str
    Mixed Chorus. Includes: O Sanctissimia; Joy To The World; Away In A Manger; Fum Fum Fum; March of the Kings.
                                                      Christmas

Lawson-Gould (rental)

The Many Moods of Christmas: Suite 3   *12.5'*
    3[1.2.pic] 3[1.2.Eh] 3[1.2.bcl] 3[1.2.cbn] – 4 3 3 1 – tmp+perc – hp, lute, viola d'amore – str
    Choir. Includes: What Child Is This?; Hark! The Herald Angels Sing; Bring a Torch, Jeanette, Isabella; Angels We Have Heard on High.
                                                      Christmas

Lawson-Gould (rental)

The Many Moods of Christmas: Suite 4   *12'*
    3[1.2.pic] 3[1.2.Eh] 3[1.2.bcl] 3[1.2.cbn] – 4 3 3 1– tmp+perc – hp, org, cel – str
    Choir. Includes: Break Forth, O Beauteous Heavenly Light; The First Nowell; O Little Town of Bethlehem; I Saw Three Ships; Deck the Halls with Boughs of Holly.
                                                      Christmas

Lawson-Gould (rental)

Overture to the Mississippi   *10'*
    3[incl pic] 2[1.Eh] 3[1.2.bcl] 2 – 4 3 3 1 – tmp+perc – hp – banjo – str
                                                  Americana/Travel

Warner/Chappell Music (rental)

Suite of Old American Dances   *16'*
    2[1.2/pic] 2[1.2/Eh] 3[1.2.bcl] 2 – 4 3 3 1 – tmp+3 – hp – str
    perc: sd, bd, cym, tri, xyl, glock.
    Includes: Cake Walk; Schottische; Western One-Step; Wall-Flower Waltz ; and Rag.
                                                      Dance

Chappell (rental)

Benzecry, Esteban   1970-

Colores de la Cruz del Sur (Colors of the   *15'*
   Southern Cross)
    3 3 3 3 – 4 3 3 1 – tmp+4 – pf, hp – str
    Commissioned by Radio France.
                                          International (Argentina)

Filarmonika

Berezovsky, Nicolai   1900-1953

Christmas Festival Overture: *8'*
   Ukrainian Noel
    3 3 3 2 – 4 4 3 1 – perc – pf – str
                                                     Christmas

Schirmer (rental)

Berkeley, Lennox   1903-1989

Fanfare for the Royal Academy   *1'*
   of Music Banquet
    8 Trumpets
                                                     Fanfare

Schirmer (rental)

Palm Court Music, Op. 81, No. 2   *7'*
    2[incl pic] 2 2 2 – 4 2 3 1 – tmp+perc – hp – str
                                             Instrumental Pops

Schirmer (rental)

Voices of the Night, Op. 86   10'
    2 2 2 3[incl cbn] – 4 3 3 1 – tmp+perc – hp – str

                                        Halloween

Schirmer (rental)

Berlin, Irving   1888-1989

Alexander's Ragtime Band   2'
    pf – strings
    McLeod, arr.

                                           Jazz

Kendor

Annie Get Your Gun: Overture   5'
    2[incl pic] 1 2 1 – 0 3 3 0 – perc – hp, gtr – str
    Includes: The Girl that I Marry, I Got the Sun in the Morning, There's No Business Like Show Business, They Say It's Wonderful.

                         Broadway Musical

R&H (rental)

Berlin Patriotic Overture   8.5'
    2[incl pic] 2[incl Eh] 2[incl bcl] 2[incl cbn] – 4 3 3 1 – perc – hp, cel, pf – str
    Includes: Give Me Your Poor, Your Tired; God Bless America; Oh, How I Hate to Get Up in the Morning; This Is the Army.
    Sid Ramon, orchestrator.

                                   Patriotic

R&H (rental)

Easter Parade   4'
    2[incl pic] 2[incl Eh] 2[incl bcl] 2 – 2asx, tsx, bsx – 4 3 3 1 – tmp+perc – hp – str
    perc: woodblocks, bells, bd, sd.
    Originally written for the film *As Thousands Cheer*.
    Robert Russell Bennett, orchestrator

                               Films/Holidays

R&H (rental)

God Bless America   5'
    3[incl pic] 3[1.2.Eh] 3[1.2.bcl] 3[1.2.cbn] – 4 3 3 1 – tmp+3 – hp, pf – str
    Solo Mezzo Soprano; optional Chorus and Narrator.
    Bruce Healy, arr.

                                       Patriotic

Leonard

God Bless America   3'
    2[1.2/pic] 2 2 2 – 4 3 3 1 – tmp – str
    Helmy Kresa, arr.

                                       Patriotic

Berlin Music (rental)

God Bless America   3'
    2 (1) 2 1 – 4 3[(3&4)] 2 1 – tmp+perc – pf – str
    Kerr, arr.

                                       Patriotic

Luck's (rental)

God Bless America   3'
    2[1.pic] 1 4[1.2.3.bcl] 2 – 4 3[crt] 3 1 – tmp+3 – str
    perc: cym, sd, bd.
    SATB, SAB, 2-part, Men or Women's Chorus (Festival Edition).
    Roy Ringwald, arr.

                                       Patriotic

Shawnee

Irving Berlin in Hollywood Overture   5.5'
    3[1.2.3/pic] 3[1.2.3/Rh] 3 3 – 2sx, tsx, bsx – 4 3 3 1 – tmp+perc – hp, gtr – str
    perc: glock, cym, sd, sus cym, xyl.
    Includes: Blue Skies; Let Me Sing and I'm Happy; Puttin' on the Ritz.
    Larry Wilcox, orchestrator

                                           Films

R&H (rental)

Irving Berlin - A Symphonic Portrait for   6'
   Chorus & Orchestra
    2 1 2 2[(2bcl)] – 4 3 3 1 – tmp+4 – str
    perc: chimes, bells, sd, woodblk, bd, hi hat cym, cym, sand blks.
    Optional SATB Chorus.
    Includes: There's No Business Like Show Business; Say it with Music; Alexander's Ragtime Band; Easter Parade; White Christmas; God Bless America.
    Hawley Ades, arr.

                               Jazz/Popular Songs

Shawnee

A Pretty Girl Is Like a Melody   3'
    2 1 2 (1) – 4 3 4 0 – tmp+perc – hp, cel, gtr – str
    Mandell, arr.

                                   Popular Songs

Kalmus

A Tribute to Irving Berlin   14'
    3[1.2.3/pic] 3[1.2.Eh] 3[1.2.3/bcl] 3[1.2.cbn] – 4 3 3 1 – tmp+3 – hp, pf/cel – str
    perc: drumset, cym, bd, tri, mark tree, woodblk, bones[or spoons], Acme siren whistle, tambn, shaker, sus cym, glock, xyl, marim.
    Includes: "There's No Business Like Show Business" from *Annie Get Your Gun* (1946); "Alexander's Ragtime Band" from *The Whirl of the World* (1911); "Always" from *The Coconuts* (1925) and a wedding gift to his wife; "Anything You Can Do" from *Annie Get Your Gun*; "How Deep is the Ocean" (1932); "Puttin' On the Ritz" from *Puttin' On the Ritz* (1930), *Idiot's Delight* (1936), *Blue Skies* (1946), and *Young Frankenstein* (1974).
                                          Popular Song
Leonard

When I Lost You   3'
    2 1 2 (1) – 2 3 3 0 – tmp+perc – hp, cel, gtr – str
    Mandell, arr.
                                         Popular Songs
Kalmus

White Christmas   5.5'
    3 2 3[1.2.bcl] 2 – 4 3 3 1 – 2perc – hp, cel – str
    Solo Voice. Key of Bb.
    John Moss, arr.
                                               Christmas
Leonard

White Christmas   4'
    3[1.2.pic] 3[1.2.Eh] 3[1.2.bcl] 2 – (4sx) – 4 3 2 1 – tmp+perc – hp – str
    SATB Chorus.
    Robert Russell Bennett, arr.
                                               Christmas
Leonard

White Christmas   4'
    1 1 2[incl bcl] 1 – 1 3 2 0 – perc – hp, pf, (gtr) – str
    Solo Soprano, Alto, Tenor, and Bass; Duet; or Solo Tenor. Key of Db.
                                               Christmas
Dragon (rental)

White Christmas   4'
    3[incl pic] 2 4[incl bcl] 2 – 4 3 3 1 – 2perc – str
    SATB, SSA, SAB, SA, or TTBB Chorus.
    Roy Ringwald-Hawley Ades, arr.
                                               Christmas
Shawnee

Berlioz, Hector   1803-1869

Béatrice et Bénédict: Overture   8'
    2[1.pic] 2 2 2 – 4 3 3 0 – tmp – str
                                            Popular Classics
Bote & Bock (rental); Breitkopf (rental); Kalmus

Carnaval romain (Roman Carnival)   8'
    2[1.2/pic] 2[1.2/Eh] 2 2 – 4 4 3 0 – tmp+4 – str
    perc: 2tambn, cym, tri.
                                            Popular Classics
Breitkopf; Kalmus

La damnation de Faust: 5'
    (Rákóczy) Hungarian March
    3[1.2.pic] 2 2 2 – 4 4 3 1 – tmp+4 – str
    perc: bd, cym, sd, tri.
                                            Popular Classics
Breitkopf; Kalmus

La damnation de Faust: 4'
    (Rákóczy) Hungarian March
    3[1.2.pic] 2 2 2 – 4 3 3 1 – tmp+perc – str
    Clark McAlister, arr.
    Arranged for youth and community orchestras.
                                            Popular Classics
Masters

The Novello Book of Carols: 3'
    The Shepherds' Farewell (Thou Must Leave)
    0 2 2 0 – 0 0 0 0 – str
    Solo Voice.
    For sale from Kalmus with chorus (from *L'enfance du Christ*).
                                               Christmas
Kalmus; Novello

Roméo and Juliette: 18'
    Scene d'amour, Op. 17
    2 2[1.Eh] 2 4 – 4 0 0 0 – str
    Mixed Chorus.
                                   Popular Classics/Valentine
Breitkopf (rental); Kalmus

Bernard, Felix   1897-1944

Winter Wonderland
    2 2 3[incl bcl] 2 – 4 3 3 1 – tmp+3 – pf – str
    Calvin Custer, arr.
                                               Christmas
Warner

Berners, Lord   1883-1950

The Triumph of Neptune: 5'
   Adagio, Variations and Hornpipe
   Strings

Space/Weather

Schirmer (rental)

Bernstein, Elmer   1922-2004

Airplane!: Suite (1980)   8.5'
   3[pic.2.3.] 3 3 2 – 4 3 3 1 – tmp+3 – hp, pf[cel]
   – str
   perc: bells, sd, bd, sus cym, cym, tamtam, tri, xyl.
   SA Chorus.
   Richard Kaufman, arr.

Films/Travel

American Werewolf in London (1981)   5'
   3[1.pic.pic] 2 3[1.2.Efl] 3[1.2.cbn] – 4 3 3 1 –
   tmp+3 – hp, 2 pf [I#2 = Yamaha org] – str
   perc: 2 vib, glock, sd, field drum, bd, cym, sus cym,
   tamtam, chimes.
   Includes: Metamorphosis and Vascov.
   Christopher Palmer, arr.

Films/Halloween

T&V (rental)

The Babe: End Credits (1992)   5.5'
   3[1.2.pic] 3[1.2.Eh] 3[1.2.bcl] 2 – 4 4 3 1 – tmp+3
   – hp, pf[cel] – str
   perc: glock, sus cym, bd, tamtam, tri, td, drumset, cyms.
   Emilie Bernstein and Patrick Russ, arr.

Films/Sports

T&V (rental)

The Birdman of Alcatraz: Finale (1962)   3'
   2[1.pic] 2[1.Eh] 2 2 – 4 3 3 1 – tmp+2 – hp, pf
   – str
   perc: chimes, slgh-bells, cyms, tri.
   Patrick Russ, arr.

Films

T&V (rental)

Ghostbusters: Theme (1984)   4'
   3[1.2.pic] 2 2 2 – 3 2 2 1 – tmp+3 –
   hp, pf, DX synth – str
   perc: vib, xyl, bell tree, woodblk, sd, sm tri.

Films/Halloween

T&V (rental)

Great Escape March   2'
   3[incl pic] 2 2 1 – 4 3 3 1 – tmp+3 – str
   Chuck Sayre, arr.

Instrumental Pops

Warner (POP); EMS or Luck's (rental)

The Magnificent Seven: Suite   5'
   3 3[1.2.3/Eh] 3[1.2.bcl] 3[1.2.3/cbn] –
   4 4[(#4)] 4[(#4)] 1 – tmp+4 – hp, pf – str
   perc: xyl, tom toms, sd, bd, cym, wdblktambn, claves,
   bongos, big guiro.

Films

T&V (rental)

The Man with the Golden Arm: Suite (1955)   4'
   3 3[1.2.Eh] 3[1.2.bcl] 3[1.2.cbn] – 4 4 4 1 –
   tmp+3 – pf, gtr – str
   perc: sd, bd, hi hat, glock, cowbell, tambn, sus cym, cym.
   Christopher Palmer, arr.

Films/Jazz

My Left Foot: Suite (1989)   7'
   2 2[Eh] 1 1 – 1 0 0 0 – tmp+1 – hp, pf[cel], ondes
   – str
   perc: lg bd, vib, glock.

Films

T&V (rental)

The Sweet Smell of Success: Main Title (1957)   3'
   2 2 2 2 – 2asx, 2tsx, bsx – 4 4 4 1 – tmp+2 –
   hp, rhythm bs [elec or acoustic] – str
   perc: drumset, bd, xyl.

Films/Jazz

T&V (rental)

The Ten Commandments: Suite (1956)   8'
   3[1.2.pic] 3[1.2.Eh] 3 3[1.2.cbn] – 4 3 3 1 –
   tmp+4 – 2 hp, pf – str
   perc: glock, chimes, sd, td, tamtam, cym, lg cym, tambn,
   xyl, field drum, tri, bd, sus cym.
   Christopher Palmer, arr.

Films

T&V (rental)

Thoroughly Modern Millie: 4'
   Sky-Hi Waltz (1967)
   3[1.pic.pic] 3[1.2.Eh] 3 3[1.2.cbn] – 4 3 3 1 –
   tmp+3 – hp, pf – str
   perc: sd, bd, cym, sus cym, tri, bells.
   Oscar winning score.
   Patrick Russ, arr.

Dance/Films

   T&V (rental)

To Kill a Mockingbird: Suite (1962)   *8.5'*
    2[1.pic] 2[1.Eh] 2[1.bcl] 2[1.cbn] – 4 2 3 0 – tmp+2 – hp, pf, cel, accordion – str
      perc: glock, vib, sd, bd, bongos, cym, sus cym.
    Christopher Palmer, arr.
                                                     Films
T&V (rental)

True Grit: Concert Suite (1969)   *5.5'*
    3[1.2.pic] 2[1.Eh] 3[1.2.bcl] 2[1.cbn] – 4 3 3 1 – tmp+3 – hp, pf[cel], 2 gtr – str
      perc: sd, 2 toms, vib, bells, cyms, sus cym.
    Includes: Main Title, Rooster and Runaway, Warm Wrap-up.
    Christopher Palmer, arr.
                                       Americana/Films
T&V (rental)

Waltzes from Films: Suite   *14'*
    3[1.pic.pic] 3[1.2.Eh] 3[1.2.Ebcl/bcl] 3[1.2.cbn] – 4 3 3 1 – tmp+4 – hp, pf[cel] – str
      perc: sd, bd, cym, sus cym, tri, bells, vib.
    Includes: *The Age of Innocence* (1993); *The Incredible Sarah* (1976); *Summer & Smoke* (1961); *From the Terrace* (1960); *Thoroughly Modern Millie* (1967).
    Patrick Russ, arr.
                                              Dance/Films
T&V (rental)

Bernstein, Leonard   1918-1990

Candide Overture   *5'*
    3[1.2.pic] 2 4[1.2.Ebcl. bcl] 3[1.2.cbn] – 4 2 3 1 – tmp+5 – hp – str
      perc: bd, cym, sd, td, tri, glock, xyl.
                                           Popular Classics
Boosey (rental)

Candide Suite (1998)   *19'*
    3[1.2.pic] 3[1.2.Eh] 3[1.2.bcl] 3[1.2.cbn] – 4 3 3 1 – tmp+4 – hp – str
      perc: sd, bd, cym, sus cym, finger cym, tri, tamb, cast, woodblk, temple blks, glock.
    Includes: You Were Dead, You Know; Paris Waltz; Bon Voyage; Drowning Music and Kings' Barcarolle; The Ballad of Eldorado; I Am Easily Assimilated; The Best of All Possible Worlds; Make Our Garden Grow.
                                             Broadway Musicals
Boosey

Candide: Glitter and Be Gay   *6'*
    3[1.2/pic] 1[1/Eh] 2[1.2/bcl] 1 – 2 2 2 0 – tmp+2 – hp – str
      perc: tri, sd, bd, cym, glock.
    Solo Soprano.
    Lyrics by Richard Wilbur.
                                             Broadway Musicals
Boosey

Divertimento for Orchestra   *15'*
                  (1' 2' 2' 1' 2' 1' 2' 4')
    4[1.2.3/pic2.pic1] 3[1.2.Eh] 4[1.2.Ebcl.bcl] 3[1.2.cbn] – 4 3 3 1 – tmp+5 – hp, pf – str
      perc: bd, cym, sus cym, 4 sd, td, drumset, tri, tambn, tamtam, glock, xyl, marim, vib, chimes, woodblk, templeblk, marac, congas, 2 Cuban cowbells, rasp, 3 bongos, sandblks.
    Includes: Sennets and Tuckets; Waltz; Mazurka; Samba; Turkey Trot; Sphinxes; Blues; In Memoriam; March: The BSO Forever.
                                             Popular Classics
Boosey (rental)

On the Town: Three Dance Episodes   *11'*
                            (2' 4' 5')
    1[1/pic] 1[1/Eh] 3[1/Ebcl.2/asx.3/bcl] 0 – 2 3 3 1 – tmp+2 – pf – str
      perc: sd, bd, drumset, sus cym, tri, woodblk, xyl.
    Includes: The Great Lover: Allegro pesante; Lonely Town (Pas de deux): Andante; Times Square, 1944: Allegro.
                                      Broadway Musicals/Dance
Boosey (rental)

On the Waterfront: Symphonic Suite   *23'*
    3[1.2.pic] 2 4[1.2.Ebcl.bcl] 3[1.2.cbn] – asx – 4 3 3 1 – 2tmp+3 – hp, pf – str
      perc: xyl, vib, glock, sd, bd, sus cym, cym, tri, woodblk, chimes, 3 tuned dr, 2 tamtams.
                                                  Films
Boosey (rental)

West Side Story Highlights   *4'*
    2 2 3[incl bcl] 1 – sx – 4 3 3 1 – tmp+2 – str
    Includes: I Feel Pretty, Maria, One Hand One Heart, Tonight.
    Frederick Muller, arr.
                                             Broadway Musicals
Schirmer(POP); Luck's (rental)

West Side Story: Overture   *5'*
    2[1.2/pic] 2[1.2/Eh] 2[1/2/Ebcl/bcl] 2 – 4 3 3 1 – tmp+2 – hp, pf, [(elec gtr)] – str
    Maurice Peress, arr.
                                             Broadway Musicals
Boosey (rental); Luck's (rental)

West Side Story: Selections *11'*
   2[1.2/pic] 2[1.2/Eh] 2 2 – 2asx, tsx, bsx –
   4 3 3 1 – tmp+4 – hp – str
   perc: small bd, cast, chimes, glock, claves, cym, hi-hat,
   sd, tambn, tri, vib, xyl.
   Includes: I Feel Pretty; Maria; Something's
   Coming; Tonight; One Hand One Heart; Cool;
   America.
   Jack Mason, arr.
                                        Broadway Musicals
Boosey

West Side Story: Symphonic Dances *23'*
   (Revised Edition)
   3[1.2.3/pic] 3[1.2.Eh] 4[1.2.bcl.Ebcl] 3[1.2.cbn] –
   asx – 4 3 3 1 – tmp+4 – hp, cel/pf – str
   perc: vib, timbales, congas, bd, tomtom, drumset, cym,
   tambn, woodblk, tri, tamtam, xyl, glock, chimes, td, 4
   pitched dr, 2 sd, finger cym, 2 pair marac, 3 cowbells,
   police whistle, 3 bongos, 2 sus cym, guiro.
                                  Broadway Musicals/Dance
Boosey (rental)

Beveridge, Thomas   1938-

Once: Tribute to Martin Luther King
   0 0 0 0 – 4 3 1[basstbn] 1 – 2perc – org – db
   Solo Soprano and Narrator; SATB Chorus.
                                     Martin Luther King
Schirmer (rental)

Binder, Abraham W.   1895-1966

Poem of Freedom *6'*
   3 2 2 2 – 4 4 3 1 – tmp+perc – str
                                             Patriotic
EMI (rental)

Binge, Ronald   1910-1979

Cornet Carillon *3'*
   2 1 0 0 – 0 4 0 0 – 2asx, 2tsx, bsx – str
                                             Fanfare
Novello (rental)

Bishop, Jeffrey S.   1951-

White Nights: Separate Lives
   1 1 2 1 – 1 2 1 1 – perc – pf – str
   John C. Whitney, arr.
                                               Films
Warner

Bizet, Georges   1838-1875

L'Arlésienne: Suite No. 1 *17'*
                                    (6' 3' 3' 5')
   2 2[1/Eh.2] 2 2 – (asx) – 4 4 3 0 – tmp+1 – hp or pf
   – str
   perc: sd.
   Includes: Prélude; Minuet; Adagietto; Carillon
                                         Popular Classics
Breitkopf; Choudens; Kalmus

L'Arlésienne: Suite No. 2 *18'*
                                    (5' 4' 4' 5')
   2[1.2/pic] 2 2 2 – (asx) – 4 4[2tp, 2crt] 3 0 – tmp+3
   – hp or pf – str
                                         Popular Classics
Breitkopf; Choudens; Kalmus

Carmen: "La Fleur que tu m'avais" *4'*
   (Flower Song)
   2 2[incl Eh] 2 2 – 4 0 3 0 – tmp – hp – str
   Solo Tenor.
                                     Ecology/Popular Classics
Kalmus; Luck's

Carmen: Scene & Habanera *2'*
   2 2 2 2 – 4 2 0 0 – tmp+perc – str
                                     Dance/Popular Classics
Kalmus

Carmen: Seguidilla and Duet *5'*
   2 2 2 2 – 4 2 3 0 – tmp – hp – str
   Solo Mezzo Soprano and Tenor.
                                     Dance/Popular Classics
Luck's

Carmen: Suite no. 1   12'
                           (2' 4' 2' 2' 2')
     2[1.2/pic] 2[1.2/Eh] 2 2 – 4 2 3 0 – tmp+4 – hp
     – str
     perc: tri, sd, cast, tambn, cym, bd.
     Optional solo voices. Includes: Prélude &
     Aragonaise; Intermezzo; Seguedille; Les Dragons
     d'Alcala; Les Toréadors.
                                    Popular Classics
     Breitkopf; Choudens; Kalmus

Carmen: Suite no. 2   19'
                           (4' 2' 4' 2' 3' 4')
     2[1/pic.2/pic] 2[1.2/Eh] 2 2 – 4 2 3 1 – tmp+4 –
     hp – str
     perc: tri, tambn, cym, bd.
     Includes: Marche de contrabandiers; Habaner;
     Nocturne; Chanson du toréador; La Garde.
     montante; Danse bohème.
                                    Popular Classics
     Breitkopf; Choudens; Kalmus

Carmen: Toréador Song   2'
     2[incl pic] 2 2 2 – 4 2 3 0 – tmp+perc – str
     Solo Vocals and Men's Chorus.
                              Popular Classics/Sports
     Kalmus; Luck's

Carmen Fantasia   26'
     2[1/pic.2/pic] 3[1.2.Ch] 2 2 – 4 2 3 1 – tmp+4 –
     hp – str
     Includes: Fanfare (Act I): Entracte to Act IV;
     Duet "La Fleur que te m'avais jetée" (Act II);
     Sextet and Chorus (Entry of the Gypsies) (Act III)
     & Chorus of the Street Boys (Act I); Habanera
     (Act I); Toreador Song (Act I).
     Donald Hunsberger, arr.
                                    Popular Classics
     EAM (rental)

Carmen Fantasia
     2[1/pic.2/pic] 2[1.2/Eh] 2 3[1.2.cbn] – 4 2 3 1 –
     tmp+3 – hp – str
     perc: tambn, 4" sd, sd, sm tri, congas, castanets, deep sd
     or field dr, lg tri, maracas, timbales, vib, bongos, xyl,
     cym, sm tri, sus cym bd, med tri, guiro, shaker.
     2 Solo Trumpet. Conductor score is for sale.
                                   Instrumental Pops
     Alfred (rental)

Carmen Fantasie on Themes of Bizet, Op. 25   12'
     2[1.2/pic] 2 2 2 – 4 2[crt] 3 0 – tmp+1 – hp – str
     perc: tambn.
     Solo Violin.
     Pablo de Sarasate, arr.
                                    Popular Classics
     Kalmus

Carmen Fantasie   11'
   (on Themes from George Bizet's Opera)
     2 2 2 2 – 2 2 2 0 – tmp+ perc – hp – str
     Solo Flute.
     The rental orchestral parts are catalogued under the
     arranger's name (Wilson).
     Ransom Wilson, arr.
                                    Popular Classics
     Merion (rental)

A Carmen Fantasy   14'
     2[incl pic] 2 2 2 – 2 2 2 0 – tmp+2 – str
     Alternate: 0 2 0 0 – 2 0 0 0 – str
     Solo Cello.
     Buxton Orr, arr.
                                    Popular Classics
     Novello (rental)

Fantaisie brillante sur Carmen   8'
     3[incl pic] 3[incl Eh] 3[incl bcl] 2 – 4 3 3 1 –
     tmp+perc – hp – str
     Solo Flute transcription.
     Giancarlo Chiaramello, arr.
                                    Popular Classics
     Kalmus

Fantaisie brillante on Themes   11'
   from Bizet's "Carmen"
     2 2 2 2 – 2 2 3 0 – tmp+2 – hp – str
     Solo Flute. Compiled by François Borne.
     James Galway, editor.
                                    Popular Classics
     Schirmer (rental)

Fantaisie brillante sur des airs de Carmen   15'
     2[1.2/pic] 2 2 – 2 2 1[bass tbn] 0 – tmp+3 – str
     Solo flute. Orchestration by Raymond Meylan.
     François Borne, arr.
                                    Popular Classics
     Kunzelmann

Jeux d'enfants: Petite Suite   12'
   (Children's Games), Op. 22   (2' 3' 1' 4' 2')
   2[1.2/pic] 2 2 2 – 4 2 3 1 – tmp+3 – str
   perc: sd, tri, cym.
   Includes: Marche (Trompette et Tambour);
   Berceuse (La Poupée); Impromptu (La Toupie);
   Duo (Petit mari, petite femme); Galop (Le Bal).
                                Popular Classics

Durand (rental); Kalmus

Black, Charlie;
Bourke, Rory;
Fogelberg, Daniel &
Goodrum, Charles Randolph

An Evening at Pops   8'
   2 1 2[incl bcl] 1 – (3sx) – 4 3 2 1 – tmp+perc –
   pf, elec bass – str
   Includes: Longer; Shadows in the Moonlight; You
   Needed Me.
   Bill Holcombe, arr.
                                Instrumental Pops

Leonard (POP); EMS or Luck's (rental)

Blake, Howard   1938-

Agatha: Suite   12'
   2[incl pic] 2[incl Eh] 2 2 – 4 2 3 1 – tmp+3 –
   hp, cel – str
                                Films

Schirmer (rental)

Christmas Lullaby   5'
   1 0 1 0 – 0 0 0 0 – str
   Duet for SA or TB or Chorus.
                                Christmas

Schirmer (rental)

Heartbeat   12'
   0 0 0 0 – 2asx, 2tsx, bsx – 0 4 4 0 – drumset –
   pf – str
   Solo Tenor Saxophone, Big Band and String
   Orchestra.
                                Valentine

Schirmer (rental)

Let Music Live   3'
   3[incl pic] 2[incl Eh] 2[incl bcl] 2[incl cbn] –
   4 3 3 1 – tmp+2 – org or hp – str
   Chorus.
                              Instrumental Pops

Schirmer (rental)

Nursery Rhyme Overture   8'
   2[1/pic.2/pic] 1 2[incl bcl] 1 – 2 1 1 0 – tmp+1 –
   hp – str
                              Popular Song

Schirmer (rental)

The Up and Down Man: Suite   12'
   2[incl pic] 1 2[incl bcl] 1 – 2 1[(crt)] 1 0 – 2perc
   – pf[incl cel], hp – str
   A burlesque for orchestra in 8 short movements.
                              Instrumental Pops

Schirmer (rental)

Blane, Ralph   1914-1995
Martin, Hugh E.   1914-

Have Yourself a Merry Little Christmas   3'
   2 1 2 1 – 2 2 2 1 – tmp+1[incl drumset] – pf – str
   Marty Gold, arr.
                                Christmas

Warner (POP); Luck's (rental)

Have Yourself a Merry Little Christmas   4'
   2 2 2 2 – 4 3 3 1 – tmp+4 – str
   perc: glock, wind chimes, sus cym, slgh-bells.
   John C. Whitney, arr.
                                Christmas

Warner

Bliss, Arthur   1891-1975

Baraza   8'
   2[incl pic] 1 2 2 – 2 2 3 0 – tmp+perc – str
   Solo Piano; Optional Men's Chorus.
                              Black History Month

Schirmer (rental)

Checkmate: Five Dances Suite   20'
   2[incl pic] 2[incl Eh] 2 2 – 4 2 3 0 – tmp+2 – hp
   – str
                                Dance

Schirmer (rental)

Christopher Columbus 5'
   2 2 2 2[incl cbn] – 4 3 3 0 – tmp+2 – hp – str
   Marcus Dodds, arr.
                                       Films

Schirmer (rental)

Things to Come: Overture (1936) 5'
   3[1.2.pic] 3[1.2.Eh] 3[1.2.bcl] 3[1.2.cbn] – 4 4 4 1 – tmp+3 – hp, pf, org[pedals] – str
   perc: chimes, sd, td, bd, cym, sus cym, tamtam.
   Based on a novel by H.G. Wells.
                                         Films

T&V (rental)

Things to Come: Suite 15'
                   (4' 2' 2' 2' 1' 4')
   2[incl 2 pic] 2[incl Eh] 2 2 – 4 3 3 1 – tmp+3 – hp – str
                                         Films

Novello (rental)

Things to Come 11'
   2[incl pic] 1 2 1 – 2 2 3 0 – tmp+2 – hp – str
   Denis Wright, arr.
                                       New Year

Schirmer (rental)

Bloch, Ernest   1880-1959

Suite hébraïque 12'
   2 2 2 2 – 4 3 0 0 – tmp+2 – hp – str   (6' 2' 4')
   Solo Viola or Violin.
                                      Hanukkah

Schirmer (rental)

Trois poèmes juifs 25'
   (Three Jewish Poems)
   3[1.2.3/pic] 3[1.2.Eh] 2 3[1.2/cbn] – 4 3 3 1 – tmp+4 – hp, cel – str
   Solo Piano. Includes: Danse; Rite; Cortège funèbre.
                                      Hanukkah

Kalmus; Schirmer (rental)

Blomdahl, Karl-Birger   1916-1968

The Walpurgis Night:
   Stage Music No. 1 15'
      2 2 2 2 – 2 2 1 0 – str
                                       Halloween

Schirmer (rental)

Blyton, Carey   1932-2002

Cinque Port, Op. 28 15'
   2[incl pic] 2[incl Eh] 2 2 – 4 2 3 1 – tmp+2 – hp – str
   Based on 5 coastal ports on the English Channel in Kent, birthplace of the composer.
                                    International

Novello (rental)

Bock, Jerry   1928-

Fiddler on the Roof, Symphonic Dances from 7'
   2[1.2/pic] 1 3[1.2.bcl] 1 – 4 3 3 1 – tmp+3 – pf – str
   Includes: Tradition; Wedding Dance #1 (The Bottle Dance); Perchik and Hodel Dance; Chava Sequence; To Life.
                               Broadway Musicals

Leonard

Fiddler on the Roof: Medley 4'
   2 1 2 1 – 2 3 2 1 – tmp+perc – pf – str
   Includes: Fiddler on the Roof; If I Were a Rich Man; Sunrise, Sunset; To Life.
   Marty Gold, arr.
                               Broadway Musicals

Warner (POP); Luck's (rental)

Bocook, Jay, Arr.   1953-
(Also See: Elfman, Danny)

Movie Spectacular 6'
   3[1.2.pic]2 3[1.2.bcl] 2 – 4 3 3 1 – tmp+2 – str
   perc: gong, sus cym, sd, tamtam, mark tree, cym, glock, cel or vib, xyl, brake dr, chimes.
   Includes: Theme from Batman; Looks Like Suicide & John Dunbar from Dances with Wolves; Theme from Robin Hood: Prince of Thieves.
                                     Films

Leonard (POP); EMS or Luck's (rental)

Boieldieu, François 1775-1834

The Caliph of Bagdad Overture 8'
2 2 2 2 – 2 2 0 0 – tmp+2 – str
Breitkopf; Heugel; Kalmus
                          Popular Classics

Bolcom, William 1938-

Inventing Flight 17'
3[incl 2 pic] 3[incl Eh] 3[incl bcl] 3[incl cbn] –
4 3[incl pic tp] 3 1 – tmp+3 – pf/cel – hp – str
Includes: I. Daedalus and Icarus; II. Leonardo; III. Wilbur and Orville.
                          Travel
Marks (rental)

Ragomania! 10'
3[incl pic] 3[incl Eh] 3[incl bcl] 3[incl cbn] –
4 3 3 1 – tmp+3 – (hp), pf/(elec pf), elec gtr – str
                          Jazz
Marks (rental)

Seattle Slew Suite 24'
3[incl pic] 3[incl Eh] 3[incl bcl] 3 –
4 3[1.2.flug] 3 1 – tmp+3 – pf, hp – str
Three Dances in Forequarter Time: Derby Dressage, Preakness Promenade, Belmont Bourrée.
                        Animals/Sports
Marks (rental)

Bond, Victoria 1945-

Urban Bird 22'
2[incl pic] 2[incl Eh] 2[incl bcl] 2 – asx – 4 4 3 1 – tmp+2 – str
Solo Alto Saxophone.
                        Animals
Presser (rental)

Borodin, Alexander 1833-1887

In the Steppes of Central Asia 9'
2 2[1.Eh] 2 2 – 4 2 3 0 – tmp – str
                International/Popular Classics
Kalmus; Russian (rental)

In the Steppes of Central Asia 9'
2 2 2 2 – 4 2 3 0 – tmp+perc – str
Transcribed for use by youth and community orchestras.
Steven Rosenhaus, arr.
                International/Popular Classics
Kalmus

Nocturne 9'
Strings
From string quartet no. 2.
Malcolm Sargent, arr.
                        Popular Classics
Boosey

Nocturne 9'
3 2 3 2 – 4 3 3 1 – tmp – hp – str
From string quartet no. 2.
N. Tcherepnin, arr.
                        Popular Classics
Universal

Nocturne 8'
2 2 2 2 – 2 2 0 0 – tmp – str
Solo Violin. From string quartet no. 2.
Nikolai Rimsky-Korsakov, arr.
                        Popular Classics
Kalmus

Nocturne 7'
2 2 2 2 – 2 2 0 0 – tmp – str
From string quartet no. 2. Ideal for youth or community orchestra (part of the *Kalmus Concertmasters* series).
Nikolai Rimsky-Korsakov, orchestrator.
Douglas Stroud, transcriber.
                        Popular Classics
Kalmus

Prince Igor: Overture 10'
3[1.2.pic] 2 2 2 – 4 2 3 1 – tmp – str
Glazunov, arr.
                        Popular Classics
Kalmus

Prince Igor: Polovtsian Dances 14'
                        (2' 12')
3[1.2.pic] 2[1.2/Eh] 2 2 – 4 2 3 1 – tmp+5 – hp – str
perc: bd, chimes, sd, tri, tambn, glock.
Optional Chorus. Nos. 8 & 17 from the opera.
Kalmus edition edited by Bradburd/Wolf.
                 Dance/Popular Classics
Fischer (rental); Kalmus; Schirmer (rental)

Symphony No. 2   26'
                             (8' 5' 6' 7')
    3[1.2.3/pic] 2[1.2/Eh] 2 2 – 4 2 3 1 – tmp+4 – hp – str
    perc: tri, tambn, cym, bd.
    Revised by Rimsky-Korsakov & Glazunov.
    Kalmus edition by Clinton F. Nieweg & Nancy M. Bradburd.
                                 Popular Classics
Breitkopf (rental); Kalmus

Boskerck, Captain Francis Saltus Van

Semper Paratus (1927)   4'
    U.S. Coast Guard March Song
    1 2 2 – 2asx, tsx – 2 3 2 0 – perc – pf – str
    Solo Obligato Violin. Key of A Flat.
    Piano/conductor score.
    William C. Schoenfield, arr.
                                     Patriotic
Fox (POP); Luck's (rental)

Botkin, Perry Jr. &   1933-
DeVorzon, Barry   1934-

Nadia's Theme   3'
    2 1 2 1 – (sxs) – 2 2 1 0 – glock – pf – str
    From the 1971 film *Bless the Beasts and Children*;
    Theme music for "The Young and the Restless."
    Philip Fink, arr.
                                     Films/TV
Luck's (rental)

Boublil, Alain
(See: Schoenberg, Claude-Michel)

Bourke, Rory (See: Black, Charlie)

Bowden, Robert C.

A Christmas Treat   9'
    3[incl pic] 3[incl Eh] 3[incl bcl] 2 – 4 3 3 1 – tmp+4 – hp – str
    Available as a print on demand basis.
                                     Christmas
Shawnee

Brahms, Johannes   1833-1897

Academic Festival Overture, Op. 80   10'
    3[1.2.pic] 2 2 3[1.2.cbn] – 4 3 3 1 – tmp+3 – str
                                     Popular Classics
Breitkopf; Kalmus

Hungarian Dance No. 1   3.5'
    2[incl 2pic] 4 4 4 – 6 3 3 0 – tmp+perc[incl tambn] – hp – str
    Leopold Stokowski, arr.
                 Dance/International/Popular Classics
Stokowski (rental)

Hungarian Dances Nos. 1 and 3   9'
    2[1.pic] 1 2 2 – 4 1(crt) 3 0 – tmp+perc – str
    Riesenfeld, arr.
                 Dance/International/Popular Classics
Broude Bros.; Schirmer (rental)

Hungarian Dances Nos. 1, 3, 10   7'
    3[1.2.pic] 2 2 2 – 4 2 0 0 – tmp+2 – str   *(3' 2' 2')*
    Orchestrated by Brahms.
                                Dance/International/Popular Classics
Breitkopf; Broude Bros.; Kalmus; Luck's

Hungarian Dance No. 4   3'
    2[1/pic.2/pic] 2 2 2 – 4 2 3 0 – tmp – hp – str
    Paul Juon, arr.
                 Dance/Interhational/Popular Classics
Kalmus; Luck's

Hungarian Dance No. 5 & 6   7'
    2[incl pic] 2 2 2 – 4 2 3 0 – tmp+2 – str
    Albert Parlow, arr.
                 Dance/International/Popular Classics
Kalmus; Luck's; Simrock

Hungarian Dance No. 6   3.5'
    2[incl 2pic] 4 4 4 – 6 3 3 0 – tmp+perc[incl tambn]
    – hp – str
    Leopold Stokowski, arr.
                        Dance/International/Popular Classics
    Stokowski (rental)

Liebeslieder Waltzes, Op. 52   15'
    Strings
    Friedrich Hermann, arr.
                        Dance/Popular Classics
    Kalmus; Luck's; Simrock

Tragische Ouverture   13'
    (Tragic Overture), Op. 81
    3[1.2.pic] 2 2 2 – 4 2 3 1 – tmp – str
                        Popular Classics
    Breitkopf; Kalmus

Variations on a Theme by Haydn, Op. 56a   17'
    3[1.2.pic] 2 2 3[1.2.cbn] – 4 2 0 0 – tmp+1 – str
    perc: tri.
                        Popular Classics
    Breitkopf; Kalmus

Brel, McKoel   1929-1978

If You Go Away (Ne me quittez pas)   4'
    2 2 2 2 – 4sx – 4 3 3 1 – tmp+perc – hp, gtr – str
    SoloViolin in orchestra part.
    Richard Hayman, arr.
                        Popular Song
    Kalmus

Britten, Benjamin   1913-1976

Gloriana: The Courtly Dances   9'
                    (1' 1' 2' 1' 2' 2')
    2 2 2 2 – 4 2 3 1 – tmp+2 – str
                        Dance
    Boosey (rental)

Matinees musicales, Op. 24   13'
    2[1.2/pic] 2 2 2 – 2 2 3 0 – tmp+2 – hp or pf,
    cel or pf – str
    perc: sd, tambn, by/cym, sus cym, td, tri, woodblk.
    2nd Suite of 5 mvts from Rossini. Includes: March;
    Nocturne Waltz; Pantomime; Moto Perpetuo.
                        Popular Classics
    Boosey (rental); Luck's (rental)

Soirées musicales, Op. 9   10'
                    (1' 3' 2' 2' 2')
    2[1/pic.2/pic] 2 2 2 – 4 2 3 0 – tmp+3 – hp or pf
    – str
    Alternate: 1 1 1 0 – 0 1 1 0 – 2perc – hp or pf – str
                        Popular Classics
    Boosey (rental)

Young Person's Guide   18'
    to the Orchestra, Op. 34
    3[1.2.pic] 2 2 2 – 4 2 3 1 – tmp+5 – hp – str
    perc: xyl, tri, sd, cym, bd, tambn, gong, whip, cast,
    Chinese blk.
    Optional Narrator.
                        Popular Classics
    Boosey (rental)

Brooks, Mel   1926-

The Producers   7.5'
    2 1 3[1.2.bcl] 1 – 4 3 3 1 – tmp+2 – hp, pf – str
    perc: drumset, cym, xyl, tambn, tri, glock, slapstick, mark
    tree, sus cym, vib.
    Includes: I Wanna Be a Producer; Prisoners of
    Love; The King of Broadway; Der Guten Tag Hop-
    Chop; That Face; Along Came Bialy; Keep it Gay;
    Springtime for Hitler.
    Ted Ricketts, arr.
                        Broadway Musicals/Films
    Leonard

Broughton, Bruce   1945-

The Boy Who Could Fly: Theme (1986)   4'
    2[rec.pic] 2 2 2 – 4 2 3 0 – 2perc –
    hp, pf[tack pf], synth – str
    perc: song bells, vib, glock, tri, sus cym, crotales.
                        Films
    T&V (rental)

Jag: Theme (1994)   4.5'
    3[1.2.pic] 3]1.2.Eh] 3[1.2.bcl] 3[1.2.cbn] – 4 3 3 1 –
    tmp+4 – hp – str
    perc: sd, Field dr, bd, cyms, glock, marim, xyl, tambn, tri.
                        Films
    T&V (rental)

Miracle on 34th Street (1994): Main Title   4'
    3[1.2.3/pic] 3[1.2.Eh] 3[1.2.3/bcl] 3[1.2.cbn] –
    4 3 3 1 – tmp+perc – hp, pf/cel – str
    perc: chimes, crotales, xyl, glock, tri, pic sd, tambn,
    cyms, sus cym, mark tree, slghbells.
    Optional SATB Chorus.
                                                 Christmas/Films
Kane (rental)

Overture to Miracle on 34th Street   4'
    3[1/pic.2.3.] 2 4[1.2.3.bcl] 2 – 2asx, tsx, bsx –
    4 3 4[1.2.3.baritone] 1 – tmp+3 – str
    perc: chimes, crotales, tri, glock, tambn, cym sus cym.
    Johnnie Vinson, arr.
                                                 Christmas/Films
Leonard

Themes from Silverado   5'
    2[incl pic] 2 2[incl Eb] 2[incl cbn] – 4 3 3 1 – perc –
    hp, cel, pf, 2gtr – str
                                                 Films
Schirmer (rental)

Young Sherlock Holmes (1985): Suite   5'
    2[1.pic] 2[1.Eh] 2 2[1.cbn] – 4 2 3 1 – tmp+2 –
    hp, pf – str
    perc: ratchet, sus cym, tamtam, sd, Field dr, bd, anvil,
    chimes, guiro, tri.
    Includes: Prelude, Solving the Crime, The Riddle's
    Solved.
                                                 Films/Halloween
T&V (rental)

Brower, Russell
Duke, Derek &
Hayes, Jason

World of Warcraft (Video Game)   6'
    2 1 3[2+1] 1 – 4 3 3 1 – tmp+4 – pf/synth, hp – str
    perc: vib, tambn, anvil, tri, sus cym, finger cym, bd,
    tam tam, cym, med tom tom, low tom tom.
    Includes: Wrath of the Lich King; Lament of the
    Highborne; Lion's Pride.
    Jerry Brubaker, arr.
                                                 Video Games
Luck's

Brown, Robert Bennett   1917-

Early American Quadrille: 2.5'
   Square Dance
    2 1 2 1 – 2sx – 2 2 1 1 – perc – str
                                                 Dance
Kalmus

Masquerade
    1 1 2 1 – 2sx – 1 2 2 1 – perc – str
                                                 Halloween
Kalmus

Brubaker, Jerry, arr.   1946-

Touch of Jazz!   6'
    2 1 3[1.2.bcl] 1 – 4 3 3 1 – perc (drumset) – str
    Includes: It Don't Mean a Thing; The Swingin'
    Shepherd Blues; 'Round Midnight; Take Five; Li'l
    Darlin'; C Jam Blues; Cute.
                                                 Jazz
Warner

Brubeck, Dave   1920-2012
[David Warren Brubeck]

Brandenburg Gate: Revisited   12'
    Jazz combo; hn – str
    Howard Brubeck, arr.
                                                 Jazz
Schirmer (rental)

Cathy's Waltz   4'
    2 3[1.2.Eh] 2 2 – 4 3 3 1 – tmp+2 – str
    Solo Jazz Combo.
                                                 Dance/Jazz
Schirmer (rental)

La Fiesta de la Posada   45'
    3[1.2.pic] 3[1.2.Eh] 3[1.2.bcl] 3[1.2.cbn] – 4 3 3 1
    – tmp+2 – hp, hpsd, gtr – str
    Alternate instrumentation: 2 0 0 0 – 0 2 0 0 –
    tmp+2 – hp
    Unison Children's Chorus and SATB Chorus.
                                                 International
Schirmer (rental)

Fugal Fanfare: Happy Anniversary   10'
    3[1.2.pic] 3[1.2.Eh] 3[1.2.bcl] 3[1.2.cbn] – 4 3 3 1
    – tmp+3 – str
                                              Celebration/Fanfare
    Schirmer (rental)

The Gates of Justice   60'
    0 0 0 0 – 4 3 3 1 – tmp+2 – db
    Solo Tenor and Baritone; SSAATTBB Chorus.
                                                         Jazz
    Schirmer (rental)

The Gates of Justice: 5'
    Out of the Way of the People
    1[pic] 3[1.2.Eh] 3[1.2.bcl] 2[1.cbn] – 4 3 3 1 –
    2perc – str
    Solo Jazz Combo.
                                                         Jazz
    Schirmer (rental)

In Your Own Sweet Way   5'
    Strings
    Solo Jazz Combo.
                                                   Jazz/Valentine
    Schirmer (rental)

It's About Time
    3[incl pic] 2 2 2 – 4 3 3 1 – tmp+2, drumset –
    elec bass – str
    Includes: Take Five; Unsquare Dance; Blue Rondo
    A La Turk.
    Chuck Sayre, arr.
                                                 Jazz/New Year
    Warner (POP), EMS or Luck's (rental)

The Light in the Wilderness   75'
    3[incl pic] 3[1.2.Eh] 3[1.2.bcl] 3[1.2.cbn] – 4 3 3 1
    – perc – hpsd, org – jazz combo – str
    Solo Baritone; SSAATTBB Chorus.
                                                Ecology/Jazz
    Schirmer (rental)

Summersong   5'
    2 3[1.2.Eh] 3[1.2.bcl] 1 – 4 3 3 1 – 2perc – str
    Jazz Combo.
                                                     Jazz/Seasons
    Schirmer (rental)

They All Sang Yankee Doodle   20'
    3[1.2.pic] 3[1.2.Eh] 3[1.2.bcl] 3[1.2.cbn] – 4 3 3 1
    – tmp+perc – hp, org – str.
    Chorus. Dedicated to the memory of Charles Ives.
                                                Jazz/Patriotic
    Schirmer (rental)

Truth Is Fallen   52'
    3[1.2.pic] 3[1.2.Eh] 3[1.2.bcl] 3[1.2.cbn] – 4 3 3 1
    – 2perc – hpsd, org – str
    Jazz Combo: tbn, elec bass, 2elec gtr, hmn, elec pf.
    Solo Soprano.
                                                         Jazz
    Schirmer (rental)

Brubeck, Howard   1916-1993

Dialogues   25'
    for Jazz Combo and Orchestra
    2[incl pic] 2[incl Eh] 2 2 – 4 3 3 1 – tmp+2 – str
    Jazz combo may be varied in size.
                                                         Jazz
    Shawnee (rental)

Dialogues: Theme for June   5'
    2 3[1.2.Eh] 1[1.Ebcl] 2 – 4 3 3 1 – tmp+2 – str
                                                         Jazz
    Shawnee (rental)

G Flat Theme   7'
    2 3[1.2.Eh] 2 2 – 4 3 3 1 – tmp+2 – str
                                                         Jazz
    Shawnee (rental)

Buck, Dudley   1839-1909

Festival Overture on the American   7'
    National Air: The Star-Spangled Banner
    3[1.2.pic] 2 2 2 – 4 3 3 1 – tmp+3 – str
    perc: sd, cym, bd.
    Optional Chorus.
                                                     Patriotic
    Fleisher

Bullock, Jack, arr.

NYC: Here's to the Big Apple   4.5'
    2 1 3[1.2.bcl] 1 – 4 3 3 1 – tmp+2 – str
    perc: bells, drumset.
    Includes: New York, New York; Give My Regards
    to Broadway; Forty Second St., The Sidewalks of
    New York; Theme from New York, New York.
                                                Popular Songs
    Warner

Patriotic Melodies That Stirred Our Nation   *6'*
    2[1/pic.2] 1 2 1 – 4 3 3 1 – tmp+2 – str
    perc: sd, bd, (Colonial sd [rope tension]), sus cym, cym.
    Includes: Yankee Doodle; Battle Hymn of the Republic; When Johnny Comes Marching Home; Battle Hymn of the Republic; Over There; The Caisson Song (Army); The Halls of Montezuma (Marines); America, The Beautiful.

                                                Patriotic

   Belwin (rental)

Burgon, Geoffrey   1941-

Brideshead Variations   *18'*
    1[incl pic] 1[incl Eh] 0 1 – 1 1 0 0 – hp – str
    6 movements from British TV serial *Brideshead Revisited*, based on a novel by Evelyn Waugh.

                                                TV

   Novello (rental)

Chronicles of Narnia Suite   *12'*
    1[incl pic] 1 0 1 – 1 1 0 0 – perc – str
    For the British TV production of C. S. Lewis work.

                                                TV

   Schirmer (rental)

Fanfare on One Note   *3'*
    0 0 0 0 – 4 3 3 1

                                                Fanfare

   Schirmer (rental)

Nunc Dimittis   *3'*
    0 0 0 0 – 0 1 0 0 – org – str
    Solo Soprano or Tenor.

                                                Christmas

   Schirmer (rental)

Suite from Bleak House   *12'*
    1 0 1 1 – 1 1[crt/(tpt)] 0 0 – (hp) – str
    British TV series.

                                                TV

   Schirmer (rental)

Suite from Martin Chuzzlewit   *24'*
    1[incl pic] 1[incl Eh] 1[incl bcl] 1 – 1 0 0 0 – tmp+perc – str
    British TV series.

                                               TV

   Schirmer (rental)

Suite from Testament of Youth   *10'*
    (tmp) – strings
    British TV series.

                                               TV

   Schirmer (rental)

Bush, Geoffrey   1920-1998

Concerto for Light Orchestra   *15'*
    2[incl pic] 2 2 2 – 4 2 3 0 – tmp+perc – str

                                  Instrumental Pops

   Schirmer (rental)

A Little Concerto (on themes by Arne)   *8'*
    Strings
    Solo Piano.

                                  Instrumental Pops

   Schirmer (rental)

Three Little Pieces for Strings   *10'*
    Strings

                                  Instrumental Pops

   Schirmer (rental)

Yorick Overture   *8'*
    2[incl pic] 2 2 2 – 4 2 3 0 – tmp+perc – str

                                             Films

   Schirmer (rental)

C

Cable, Howard Reid — 1920-

Jingles All the Way: Fantasy — 7'
3[1.2.3/pic] 2 2 2 – 4 3 3 1 – tmp+2 – hp – str
perc: sd, bd, xyl, glock.
Piano/Conductor score.

Mills (rental) — Christmas

Cailliet, Lucien — 1891-1985

Fantasie on "Auld Lang Syne" — 3'
3 3 3 3 – 4 3 3 1 – tmp+perc – hp – str

Fox (rental) — New Year

Variations on Pop Goes the Weasel — 7'
3 3 2 2 – (asx, bsx) – 4 3 3 1 – tmp+perc – str
Animals/Popular Song
Elkan Vogel (rental)

Calandrelli, Jorge — 1939-

Concerto for Jazz Clarinet and Orchestra — 23'
3 2[incl Eh] 3[incl bcl] 2 – (tsx, bsx) –
4 4[opt flug] 4 1 – tmp+3 – hp, cel/pf – str

Presser (rental) — Jazz

Caliendo, Christopher — 1959-

The Iron Horse — 135'
1[1/IndianFl] 1 2[1.bcl] 1 – 2 2 0 0 – tmp+perc –
pf, accordion, gtr – str

Kane (rental) — Films

Camilleri, Charles — 1931-2009

Maltese Dances — 17'
2 2 2 2 – 4 2 3 1 – tmp+perc – hp – str
Dance/International
Schirmer (rental)

Campos, José Carlos — 1957-

Danza Rústica — 3.5'
3[incl pic] 2 2 2 – 2 2 0 0 – tmp+3 – str
Dance/International (Peru)
Filarmonika (rental)

Capua, Eduardo di — 1865-1917

O sole mio — 3'
3[1.2.pic] 2 2 2 – 4 3 3 1 – tmp+perc – hp – str
Solo Tenor in G Major.
Giancarlo Chiaramello, arr.
International/Popular Song
Kalmus

Carey, Julia Scott — 1986-

Legend of Old Befana — 17'
3[incl pic] 2 2 2 – 2 2 0 0 – tmp+3 – hp – str
Narrator. An Italian Christmas story about an old woman who delivers gifts at the Feast of the Epiphany (January 6th). Text by Tomie DePaola.
Christmas/International
Presser (rental)

Carmichael, Hoagy — 1899-1981

Georgia on My Mind — 4'
tbn – rhythm – str
SoloTrombone.
Calvin Custer, arr.
Americana/Popular Song
Warner (POP); Luck's (rental)

Georgia on My Mind   3'
    2 1 2 1 – 2 3 2 1 – tmp+perc – pf – str
    Marty Gold, arr.
                           Americana/Popular Song
Belwin (POP); EMS or Luck's (rental)

Hoagy Carmichael: 15'
   An American Treasure
    3[incl pic] 2 3[incl bcl] 2 – 4 3 3 1 – tmp+perc – hp – cel/pf – str
    Includes: Georgia on My Mind; Heart & Soul; Lazy River; Skylark, Stardust.
    Sammy Nestico, arr.
                           Americana/Popular Song
Leonard

Nearness of You   3'
    2 1 2 1 – 2 3 2 1 – tmp+2 – pf – str
    perc: drumset, vib.
    Marty Gold, arr.
                           Popular Song
Famous (rental)

Romance in the Dark,   3.5'
   Nearness of You
    2 1 2 1 – 2 3 2 1 – tmp+perc – pf – str
    Marty Gold, arr.
                           Valentine
Belwin (POP); EMS or Luck's (rental)

Stardust   4'
    hp, cel – str
    Morton Gould, arr.
                         Popular Song/Space
Kalmus

Carpenter, John Alden   1876-1951

Krazy Kat (original version)   13'
    1[incl pic] 1 1 1 – (asx) – 2 2 1 0 – tmp+perc – hp, pf – str
                           Animals
Schirmer (rental)

Krazy Kat (revised version)   13'
    1[incl pic] 1 2 1 – (ssx) – 2 2 1 0 – tmp+perc – hp, pf – str
                           Animals
Schirmer (rental)

Carr, Benjamin   1768-1831

Federal Overture   8'
    2[incl pic] 2 2 2 – 2 2 2 0 – tmp+perc – str
    Franceschini, arr.
                           Patriotic
Kalmus

Carter, Elliott   1908-

Holiday Overture   10'
    3[1.2.pic] 3[1.2.Eh] 3[1.2.bcl] 3[1.2.cbn] – 4 3 3 1 – tmp+4 – pf – str
    perc: sd, tri, whip, cym, bd, tamtam.
                           Holidays
AMP (rental)

Casey, Warren   1935-
Jacobs, Jim   1942-

Grease!   6'
    3[1.2.pic] 1 3[1.2.bcl] 1 – 4 3 3 1 – tmp+2 – pf – str
    perc: drumset, cym, congas, shakers, tambn, bells.
    Includes: Born to Hand Jive; Summer Nights; Greased Lightnin'; Beauty School Dropout; We Go Together.
    Calvin Custer, arr.
                         Broadway Musicals
Leonard

Cassler, Glenn Winston, arr.   1906-1990

Turtle Dove
    3 3[1.2.Eh] 3[1.2.bcl] 2 – 4 2 3 1 – tmp – hp – str
                           Animals
Kalmus

Castelnuovo-Tedesco, Mario — 1895-1968

Naomi and Ruth: Ruth's Aria — 2'
2 2 2 2 – 3 0 0 0 – tmp – hp – str
Solo Soprano.

Popular Song

Schirmer (rental)

Cervantes, Ignacio — 1847-1905

Three Cuban Dances — 7'
1 1 2 1 – 2 2 1 0 – str
Otto Langey, arr.

Dance/International

Kalmus; Luck's

Chabrier, Emmanuel — 1841-1894

España — 7'
3[1.2.pic] 2 2 2 – 4 3 3 1 – tmp+perc – str
Simpson, arr.

International

Masters

España Rhapsody — 8'
3[1.2.pic] 2 2 4 – 4 4[2tp, 2crt] 3 1 – tmp+4 – 2hp – str
perc: tambn, tri, cym, bd.
Clinton F. Nieweg & Nancy M. Bradburd, editors

International

Kalmus

Chadwick, George — 1851-1931

Symphonic Sketches: Hobgoblin — 5'
3[1.2.pic] 2 3[1.2.bcl] 2 – 4 2 0 0 – tmp+perc – hp – str

Halloween

Kalmus; Schirmer (rental)

Chaplin, Charlie — 1889-1977

City Lights — 87'
1[pic] 1 3 1 – 2 3 2 0 – 3perc – hp, cel/pf, gtr, bnjo – str

Films

Bourne (rental)

The Reel Chaplin: — 20'
A Symphonic Adventure
3 3 3 3 – 4 4 3 1 – tmp+3 – hp, pf – str
Eric Knight, arr.

Films

Bourne (rental)

Chappell, Herbert — 1934-

Caribbean Concerto — 22'
Solo Guitar.

International

Schirmer (rental)

Paddington Bear's First Concert — 18'
2[incl pic] 2[incl 2 Eh] 2[incl asx] 2 – 2 2 0 0 – 2perc – hp – str
Narrator.

Animals

Schirmer (rental)

Chase, Bruce, arr. — 1912-2001

Around the World at Christmas Time — 7'
2 2 3[1.2.bcl] 1 – 4 3 3 1 – tmp+2 – pf – str
perc: sd, bd, cym, chimes, glock, tambn.
Includes: O Tannebaum; Infant Holy, Infant Lowly; What Child is This?; O Sanctissma, The Hanukkah Song; Whence Comes the Rush of Wings; Go Tell It on the Mountain.

Christmas

Leonard

Broadway Tonight — 7'
2 1 3[incl bcl] 1 – (sx) – 4 3 2 1 – perc – pf – str
Includes: Everything's Coming Up Roses; It's Gonna Rain; My Favorite Things; Try to Remember; That's Entertainment; People.
Intended for community and youth orchestras.

Broadway Musicals

Leonard

Christmas Favorites 6'
  2 1 3[1.2.(bcl)] 1 – (asx, tsx) – 4 3 2 1 (tmp)+2 –
  pf – str
  perc: chimes, glock, drumset.
  Includes: It's Beginning to Look Like Christmas;
  Silver Bells; The Christmas Song.
                                                Christmas
  Leonard (POP): Luck's (rental)

Muppet Medley 6'
  2 1 3[1.2.(bcl)] 1 – (asx, tsx) – 4 3 2 1 – 2perc –
  (elec bs), pf – str
  perc: drumset, xyl, glock, tambn.
  Includes: Muppet Theme; Rainbow Connection;
  Moving Right Along.
                                                Films
  Leonard

Chattaway, Jay   1946-

Star Trek: The Next Generation 6.5'
  2[penny whistle.2] 2 3 1 – 4 3 3 1 – tmp+perc –
  2 hp (#2) – str
  perc: sus cym.
  Music from "The Inner Light", the 25th episode of
  the 5th season of Star Trek: The Next Generation.
  Written for the 30th anniversary of Star Trek.
                                                Space/TV
  T&V (rental)

Chávez, Carlos   1899-1978

Cantos de Mexico 4'
  1 1 1 0 – 0 1 0 0 – 7perc – gtr, hp – violins
                                                International
  Schirmer (rental)

Chapultepec: 7'
  Three Famous Mexican Pieces
  6[incl 2pic] 3 4[incl bcl,Ebcl] 3 – ssx, 2asx, tsx –
  4 3 3 1 – tmp+3 – str
  Includes: Marcha Provinciana; Vals Nostalgico;
  Cancion de Adelita.
                                                International
  Schirmer (rental)

Himno nacional Mexicano 2'
  (Mexican National Anthem)
  4 3 4 3 – 6 3 3 1 – tmp+6 – hp, cel – str
                                                International
  Schirmer (rental)

Sinfonia de antigona 11'
  (Symphony No. 1)
  3[1.afl.pic] 3[1.Eh.heckl] 4[1.2.Ebcl.bcl] 3 – 8 3 0 1
  – tmp+3 – 2hp – str
  perc: cym, glock, td, 2sus cym, 2sd, Indian drum.
                                                Popular Classics
  Schirmer (rental)

Sinfonia India (Symphony No. 2) 11'
  4[1.2.3/pic2.pic1] 3 4[1.2.bcl.Ebcl] 3 – 4 2 2 0 –
  tmp+4 – hp – str
  Alternate: 2 1 3 1 – 2 2 1 0 – 4perc – hp – str
  perc: marac, sus cym, td, claves, xyl, sd, guiro, bd, Indian
  drum, metal rattle, soft rattle, rattling string, rasping stick.
  Indian percussion instruments preferred.
                                                Popular Classics
  Schirmer (rental)

El Sol (The Sun) - A Mexican Ballad 36'
  4[incl pic] 3 4[incl bcl, Ebcl] 3 – 4 4 3 1 – tmp+3
  – str
  SATB Chorus.
                                                International/Space
  Schirmer (rental)

Chiarappa, Richard   1948 -

Boom! for Bass Drum & Symphony Orchestra 3'
  3[1.2.pic] 2 2 2 – 4 3 3 1 – tmp+1 – str
  A novelty piece with solo bass drum intended for
  featuring a local celebrity. The work is adapted
  from the historical musical *Lincoln & Booth*.
                                                Instrumental Pops/Novelty
  Clear Mud

Happy, Happy Birthday 5'
  3[1.2.pic] 2 2 2 – 4 3 3 1 – tmp+2 – str
  The melody is set in the following styles, each
  playable individually or as one continuous piece:
  Baroque, Classical, Romantic, and Broadway.
  Richard Chiarappa, orchestrator
                                                Celebration
  Clear Mud

Lincoln & Booth: Good-bye 3'
3[1.2.pic] 2 2 2 – 4 3 3 1 – tmp+1– str
Solo Soprano, Alto, and Tenor.
A ballad of parting sung by a man (Booth) and the two women in his life.
         Instrumental Pops
Clear Mud

Lincoln & Booth: Just Ourselves 4'
3[1.2.pic] 2 2 2 – 4 3 3 1 – tmp+1 – str
Solo Soprano and Tenor.
The waltz sung by President and Mrs. Lincoln in a private moment just before departing for Ford's Theatre.
       Instrumental Pops/Patriotic
Clear Mud

Lincoln & Booth: The President's Waltz 4'
3[1.2.pic] 2 2 2 – 4 3 3 1– tmp+1 – str
       Dance/Instrumental Pops
Clear Mud

Paean to the Scholar, the Athlete, 5'
 and the Artist
3[1.2.pic] 2 2 2 – 4 3 3 1 – tmp+2 – str
SATB Chorus (suitable for high school or adult choruses). Composed for the Scholar-Athlete Games of Rhode Island.
            Sports
Clear Mud

Romp for Symphony Orchestra & 2.5'
 (Celebrity) Triangulist
3[1.2.pic] 2 2 2 – 4 3 3 1 – tmp+2 – str
perc: tri, cym.
A novelty piece with solo triangle intended for featuring a local celebrity.
       Instrumental Pops/Novelty
Clear Mud

Side Effects 3'
3[1.2.pic] 2 2 2 – 4 3 3 1 – drumset+1 – str
Comic song covering a list of warnings printed on a bottle of pills. From the new musical *The Silver Whistle*.
Solo Baritone.
       Instrumental Pops/Novelty
Clear Mud

To Be Young Again 2.5'
3[1.2.pic] 2 2 2 – 4 3 3 1 – drumset+1 – str
A wistful moment of senior romance. From the new musical *The Silver Whistle*.
Solo Alto, Baritone.
         Instrumental Pops
Clear Mud

Chopin, Frédéric   1810-1849

Fantaisie sur des airs nationaux 16'
 polonais (Fantasy on Polish airs), Op. 13
 2 2 2 2 – 2 2 0 0 – tmp – str   (5' 4' 4' 3')
Solo Piano.
      Popular Classics/International
Breitkopf; Fischer; Kalmus; PWM

Variations on "La ci darem la mano", Op. 2 18'
       (5' 2' 1' 1' 1' 1' 7')
2 2 2 2 – 2 0 0 0 – tmp – str
Solo Piano.
          Popular Classics
Kalmus; PWM

Christensen, James   1935-

Snow Chase 2'
2[1/pic.2] 1 3[1.2.bcl] 1 – 2 3 3 0 – 2perc – hp – str
perc: sd, bd, glock, xyl, slgh-bells.
         Holiday/Seasons
Leonard

Christensen, Knud Torben (See: Sebastian)

Churchill, Frank   1901-1942

Snow White: Symphonic Selections 12'
2[incl afl] 2[incl Eh] 2[incl bcl] 2[incl cbn] – 4 4 2[incl bass tbn] 1 – tmp+perc – hp, cel, pf – str
Eric Knight, arr.
            Films
Bourne (rental)

Cifuentes, Santos 1870-1932

Scherzo sobre Aires Tropicales 7'
   1 1 1 1 – 2 1 1 0 – tmp+3 – str
                                           International (Columbia)
Filarmonika (rental)

Cimarosa, Domenico 1749-1801

I Traci Amanti: Overture 7'
   0 2 0 2 – 2 0 0 0 – str
   Napolitano, editor.
                                           Popular Classics
Kalmus

Clark, Larry 1963-

Hooked on Classics 4'
   3[1.2.pic] 2 2 2 – 4 3 3 1 – tmp+2 – str
   perc: drumset, cym, sus cym, tambn.
   Includes: The Flight of the Bumblebee; Mozart Symphony #40; Karelia Suite, The Marriage of Figaro; Tchaikovsky Romeo and Juliet Overture; Trumpet Voluntary; Hallelujah Chorus from *Messiah*; Grieg Piano Concerto; Toreador March from *Carmen*; The 1812 Overture.
   James H. Burden, arr.
                                           Instrumental Pops
Eaton (rental from Luck's)

Coates, Eric 1886-1957

London Suite: 3'
  The Knightsbridge March
   2 3[1.2.Eh] 3[1.2.bcl] 2 – 4 2 3 0 – tmp+2 – pf – str
   Clifford Demarest, arr.
                                           International
Chappell (rental)

London (Every Day) Suite 13'
   2[1.2/pic] 3[1.2.Eh] 3[1.2.bcl] 2 – 4 3 3 0 – 2asx, tsx, bsx – tmp+4 – hp – str
   perc: sd, bd, tri, sus cym.
                                           International
Chappell (rental)

Cohan, George M. 1878-1942

Cohan Medley 9'
   2 2 2 2 – 4 3 3 1 – tmp+2 – hp – str
   Barbershop quartet.
   Pena, arr.
                                           Popular Songs
Marks (rental)

George M.: Choral Overture 14'
   3 2 2 2 – 4 3 3 1 – perc – str
   Chuck Cassey, arr.
   Joseph Erskine, orchestrator
                                       Broadway Musicals
Marks (rental)

George M. Cohan Medley: 6'
  Symphonic Suite
   3[incl pic] 3[incl Eh] 3[incl bcl] 3[incl cbn] – 4 3 3 1 – tmp+3 – hp – str
   Eric Knight, arr.
                                         Popular Songs
Bourne (rental)

George M. Cohan Salute 5'
   3[incl pic] 3[incl Eh] 3[incl bcl] 2 – 4 3 3 1 – tmp+perc[xyl] – hp – str
   Includes: Yankee Doodle Boy; Harrigan; Mary's a Grand Old Name; You're a Grand Old Flag.
   Ralph Hermann, arr.
                                         Popular Songs
Luck's (rental)

Give My Regards to Broadway 2'
   3[1.2.pic] 2 2 2 – (2asx, tsx) – 4 3 3 1 – tmp+perc – str
   William Ryden, arr.
                                         Broadway Musicals
Kalmus

Over There 2'
   3[1.2.pic] 2 2 2 – 3sx – 4 3 3 1 – tmp+perc – str
   William Ryden, arr.
                                             Patriotic
Kalmus

Over There 2'
   3[incl pic] 2 4[all opt; incl Ebcl] 2 – 4 3[crt] 3 1 – tmp+perc – bnjo – str
   SATB Chorus. Key of Ab.
   Carmen Dragon, arr.
                                           Patriotic
Dragon

Royal Vagabond: Selections   6'
1[incl pic] 2 2 1 – 2 2 1 0 – tmp+perc – str
George J. Trinkhaus, arr.

      Travel

Kalmus

Star-Spangled Spectacular   4'
2[incl pic] 1 2 1 – (2sx) – 2 2 1 1 – tmp+perc – str
Philip Gordon, arr.

      Patriotic

Kalmus

Star-Spangled Spectacular   5'
2 2 2 2 – 4 3 3 1 – tmp+2 – pf, (gtr) – str
John Cacavas, arr.

      Patriotic

Marks (rental)

You're a Grand Old Flag   1'
2[incl pic] 2 2 2 – 2 3 3 0 – perc – hp, pf, bnjo – str
Solo Voice. Key of F.
Carmen Dragon, arr.

      Patriotic

Dragon (rental)

You're a Grand Old Flag   2'
3[1.2.pic] 2 2 2 – (2asx, tsx) – 4 3 3 1 – tmp+perc – str
Steven Rosenhaus, arr.

      Patriotic

Kalmus

Cole, Hugo   1917-1995

Black Lion Dances   12'
2[incl pic] 1 2 1 – 2 2 1 0 – tmp+2 – str

      Animals/Dance

Schirmer (rental)

Coleman, Cy   1929-2004

Sweet Charity Medley   7'
3[1.2.pic] 1 4[1.2.3.bcl] 1 – 2asx, tsx, bsx – 4 3 3 1 – perc – (pf, elec bass, gtr) – str
Includes: If My Friends Could See Me Now; Big Spender; It's a Nice Face; I'm a Brass Band.
Bill Holcombe, arr.

      Broadway Musicals

Warner (POP); EMS or Luck's (rental)

Witchcraft   3'
2 1 2 1 – 2 3 2 1 – tmp+perc – pf – str
Marty Gold, arr.

      Halloween

Warner (POP); EMS or Luck's (rental)

Coleridge-Taylor, Samuel   1875-1912

Scenes from The Song of Hiawatha,   32'
    Op. 30: No. 1. Hiawatha's Wedding Feast
3[1.2.pic] 2 2 2 – 4 2 3 1 – tmp+perc – hp, (org) – str

      Americana

Kalmus

Hiawatha's Wedding Feast: 6'
    Onaway! Awake Beloved
2 2 2 2 – 4 0 0 0 – hp – str
Solo Tenor. Text from Henry Wadsworth Longfellow.

      Americana/Valentine

Schirmer (rental)

Conrad, Con   1891-1938

The Gay Divorcee: The Continental (1934)
3[1.2.pic] 3[1.2.Eh] 3[1.2.bcl] 2 – 4 3 3 1 – tmp+2 – hp, pf, gtr – str
perc: drumset, glock.
First Oscar winner for Best Song of the Year.

      Films

T&V (rental)

Constantinescu, Paul   1909-1963

Braul: The Sash Dance
3[1.2.pic] 2 2 2 – 4 3 3 1 – tmp+perc – pf – str
Refers to the cloth belt worn by Rumanian men or women from Egres in the district of Torontál.

      Dance/International

Schirmer (rental)

Ciobănașul: The Shepherd Boy
   3[1.2.pic] 2 2 2 – 4 2[crt] 0 0 – tmp+perc – dulcimer – str
   An energetic Rumanian shepherd line dance.
   Dance/International
   Schirmer (rental)

Olteneasca
   3[1.2.pic] 2 2 2 – 4 2 3 0 – tmp+perc – dulcimer, hp – str
   Rumanian dance from the region of Oltenea.
   Dance/International
   Schirmer (rental)

Tanze aus Rumanien   *10'*
   3 3 3 3 – 4 2 3 1 – tmp+perc – hp, cel, pf – str
   Dance/International
   Universal (rental)

Conti, Bill   1943-

Rocky Highlights   *7'*
   2 2 3[1.2.bcl] 2 – 2asx, tsx, bsx – 4 3 3 1 – tmp+4 – elec gtr, elec bass – str
   perc: chimes, glock, bongos, tambn, sd, bd, cym, hi-hat, toms.
   Includes: Gonna Fly Now; Going the Distance; Philadelphia Morning; You Take My Heart Away; Fanfare for Rocky.
   Bob Lowden, arr.
   Films/Sports
   Warner (POP); Luck's (rental)

Rookie of the Year (1993): End Credits
   2 3[1.2.3/Eh] 2 2 – 4 3 5[(#5)] 1 – tmp+perc – hp, elec pf, synth – str
   Films/Sports
   Kane (rental)

Cook, R. (See: Back, B.)

Coolidge, Peggy Stuart   1913-1982

Pioneer Dances   *11.5'*
   3 2 2 2 – 4 3 3 1 – tmp+4 – hp – str
   Chamber Orch: 1 1 2 1 – 1 2 1 0 – tmp+perc – str
   perc: sd, bd, tambn, xyl, chimes, vib, cym.
   Also available for string orchestra.
   Americana/Dance
   Peer (rental)

Spirituals in Sunshine and Shadow   *14'*
   2[incl pic] 2 2 2 – 4 3 3 1 – tmp+perc – hp – str
   Black History Month
   Peer (rental)

Cooper, Rose Marie   1929-2005

Morning Star: A Christmas Cantata   *16'*
   (3tpt) – Strings
   Solo Tenor; 2-part Children's Chorus.
   Christmas
   Fischer (rental)

Cooper, Paul   1926-1996

A Shenandoah for Charles Ives' Birthday   *8'*
   2 3[1.2.Eh] 3[1.2.bcl] 2 – 4 2 3 1 – tmp+3 – hp, pf[(cel)] – str
   Solo Flute, Trumpet, Viola.
   Americana
   Schirmer (rental)

Coots, J. Fred   1897-1985

For All We Know   *3.5'*
   solo tpt (flug) – drumset – pf, gtr – str
   Calvin Custer, arr.
   Popular Song
   Warner (POP); EMS or Luck's (rental)

Copland, Aaron   1900-1990

Appalachian Spring: Suite   23'
2[1.2/pic] 2 2 2 – 2 2 2 0 – tmp+2 – hp, pf – str
perc: bd, sus cym, sd, tabor, tri, glock, xyl, woodblk, claves.
Full orchestra version.
                           Americana/Dance/
                        Popular Classics/Seasons
Boosey (rental)

Appalachian Spring: Suite   23'
1 0 1 1 – pf – str
Original instrumentation.
                           Americana/Dance/
                        Popular Classics/Seasons
Boosey (rental)

Billy the Kid: 9'
   Prairie Night and Celebration   (5' 4')
3 2 2 2 – 4 3 3 1 – tmp+2 – pf – str
Reduced version:
1 1 2 1 – 1 2 2 0 – tmp+2 – pf – str
perc: bd, sd, xyl.
                     Americana/Celebration/
                      Dance/Popular Classics
Boosey

Billy the Kid: Waltz   4'
1 1 2 1 – 1 2 1 0 – hp or pf – str
                            Americana/Dance
                            /Popular Classics
Boosey (rental)

Down a Country Lane   3'
2 1 2 1 – 2 1 1 0 – str
                     Americana/Popular Classics
Boosey

Fanfare for the Common Man   3'
0 0 0 0 – 4 3 3 1 – tmp+2
perc: bd, tamtam
                                   Fanfare
Boosey

Happy Anniversary (1969)   1'
3(#2) 2 3(#2) 2 – 4 3 3 1 – perc [glock] – str.
Based on Happy Birthday.
                                 Celebration
Boosey (rental)

John Henry   4'
2[1.2/pic] 2 2 2 – 2 2 1 0 – tmp+2 – (pf) – str
perc: sd, tri, bd, anvil, sandpaper blks.
                                  Americana
Boosey

Lincoln Portrait   14'
2[1/pic.2/pic] 3[1.2.(Eh)] 3[1.2.(bcl)] 3[1.2.(cbn)]
– 4 3[(#3)] 3 1 – tmp+3 – hp, (cel or pf) – str
perc: glock, xyl, slgh-bells, sd, tamtam, bd, cym.
Narrator.
                            Americana/Patriotic
Boosey (rental)

Music for the Theatre   21'
                         (6' 3' 5' 3' 4')
1[1/pic] 1[1/Eh] 1[1/Eb] 1 – 0 2 1 0 – 1perc – pf
– str
perc: xyl, glock, td, woodblk, sus cym, bd w/pedal.
                              Popular Classics
Boosey (rental)

Old American Songs   13'/12'
1[1/pic] 1 2 1 – 2 1 1 0 – hp – str
   First Set: (4' 1.5' 3' 1.5' 3')
The Boatmen's Dance (Minstrel Song-1843); The Dodger (Campaign Song); Long Time Ago (Ballad); Simple Gifts (Shaker Song); I Bought Me A Cat (Children's Song).
First Set requires only one horn.

   Second Set: (3' 2' 3.5' 1.5' 2')
The Little Horses (Lullaby); Zion's Walls (Revivalist song); The Golden Willow Tree (Anglo-American Ballad); At the River (Hymn Tune); Ching-A-Ring Chaw (Minstrel Song).
                                 Americana
Boosey (rental)

An Outdoor Overture   9.5'
3[1.2.pic] 2 2 2 – 4 2 3 0 – tmp+4 – pf, (cel) – str
perc: cym, xyl, tri, bd, sd.
                     Popular Classics/Ecology
Boosey

Quiet City   10'
Solo Eh [or Ob], Solo Trumpet – strings
                            Popular Classics
Boosey

The Red Pony 25'
                               (5' 5' 5' 3' 4' 3')
2[1/pic.2/pic] 2[1.2/Eh] 4[1.2.3/bcl.(Ebcl)] 2 – 4[(#4)] 3 3 1 – tmp+4 – hp, cel/pf – str
perc: glock, xyl, vib, marim, sd, td, cym, tri, slgh-bells, bd.
                                             Animals
Boosey (rental)

Rodeo: 1. Buckaroo Holiday 7'
3[1.2/pic1.3/pic2] 3[1.2.(Eh)] 3[1.2.(bcl)] 2 – 4 3 3 1 – tmp+3 – hp, pf/cel – str
perc: xyl, glock, sd, woodblk, tri, cym, whip, bd
                        Americana/Dance/Popular Classics
Boosey

Rodeo: 2. Corral Nocturne 4'
1 1 2 1 – 2 2 1 0 – hp, cel – str
                              Americana/Dance/
                                 Popular Classics
Boosey

Rodeo: 3. Saturday Night Waltz 4'
1 1 3[1.2.(bcl)] 1 – 2 2 1 0 – hp – str
                                Americana/Dance/
                                Popular Classics
Boosey

Rodeo: 4. Hoedown 3'
3[1.2.pic] 3[1.2.(Eh)] 3[1.2.(bcl)] 2 – 4 3 3 1 – tmp+3 – pf – str
perc: xyl, bd, sd, woodblk, tri, cym.
Cued to play without Eh or bcl.
                                Americana/Dance/
                                Popular Classics
Boosey

Rodeo: Hoedown 3'
Strings
                                Americana/Dance/
                                Popular Classics
Boosey

El salón México 11'
3[1.2.pic] 3[1.2.(Eh)] 4[1.2.(Ebcl).(bcl)] 3[1.2.(cbn)] – 4 3[(#3)] 3 1 – tmp+4 – pf – str
perc: sd, woodblk, guiro, cym, bd, xyl, sus cym, templeblks, tambourin provençal.
                  International/Popular Classics
Boosey (rental)

The Tender Land: Suite 19'
3[1.2.pic] 2[1.Eh] 2[1.2/bcl] 2 – 4 3 3 1 – tmp+2 – hp, (cel) – str   (9' 5' 5')
perc: glock, tri, sd, woodblk, xyl, cym, ratch, bd, whip.
Optional Chorus. Includes: Introduction and Love Music; Party Scene; Finale: The Promise of Living.
                        Ecology/Popular Classics
Boosey (rental)

Variations on a Shaker Melody 4'
2[1.2/pic] 2 2 2 – 2 2 2 0 – (tmp+1) – pf, (hp) – str
                      Americana/Popular Classics
Boosey

Corelli, Arcangelo   1653-1713

Concerto grosso in g minor, Op. 6, No. 8: 13'
   Christmas Concerto   (3' 3' 1' 2' 4')
   Strings
   Solo Violin and Cello.
                     Christmas/Popular Classics
Kalmus; Peters; Ricordi

Corigliano, John   1938-

Campane di Ravello: 4'
   A Celebration Piece for Sir Georg Solti
4[1.2.3.pic] 4[1.2.3.Eh] 4[1.2.3.bcl] 4[1.2.3.cbn] – 4 4 3 1 – tmp+5 – hp, pf – str
perc: chimes, glock, crot, marim, xyl, sus cym, bd, 3 tamtams.
Based on Happy Birthday.
                                     Celebrations
Schirmer (rental)

The Cloisters 13'
2 2 2 2 – 2 2 0 0 – tmp+perc – str
Solo Voice. Text by William M. Hoffman; Includes: Fort Tryon Park: September; Song to the Witch of the Cloisters; Christmas at the Cloisters; the Unicorn.
                           Halloween/Christmas
Schirmer (rental)

Gazebo Dances for Orchestra 16'
2[1.2/pic] 2 2 2 – 4 3 3 1 – tmp+3 – pf – str
perc: bd, cym, sus cym, sd, td, tri, tambn, xyl, handbell.
                                           Dance
Schirmer (rental)

Gazebo Dances: 4'
   Overture to the Imaginary Invalid
   2[1.2/pic] 2 2 2 – 4 3 3 1 – tmp+3 – pf – str
                                            Dance
Schirmer (rental)

Midsummer Fanfare (2004) 5'
   3[1.2.pic] 3 3 3 – 4 3 3 1 – tmp+3 – hp, pf – str
                                       Fanfare/Seasons
Schirmer (rental)

Promenade Overture 8'
   3[1.2.pic] 2 2 2 – 4 4 3 1 – tmp+4 – hp – str
   perc: bd, sus cym, finger cym, sd, td, tri, tambn, tamtam, glock, xyl, belltree, templeblk, ratch.
   Based on Haydn's *Farewell* Symphony in reverse.
                         Novelty/Popular Classics
Schirmer (rental)

The Red Violin: Chaconne for Violin 15'
   and Orchestra (1997)
   3[incl 2pic] 2 2 2 – 4 2[C or D tp] 3 1 – tmp+3 – hp, pf(cel) – str
   Solo Violin.
                                               Films
Schirmer (rental)

The Red Violin: Suite for Violin 24'
   and Orchestra (1999)
   0 0 0 0 – 0 0 0 0 – tmp+3 – hp – str
   Solo Violin.
                                               Films
Schirmer (rental)

Three Hallucinations 13'
   3[incl pic] 3 3[incl Ebcl.bcl] 3[incl cbn] – 4 3 3 1 – 2tmp+5 – hp, 2pf, elec org – str
   Based on the film score to *Altered States*.
                                  Halloween/Films
Schirmer (rental)

Tournaments 12'
   3[1.2.3/pic] 3[1.2.Eh] 3[1.2.bcl] 3[1.2.cbn] – 4 4 3 1 – tmp+3 – hp, pf – str
                                             Sports
Schirmer (rental)

Cory, George   1920-1978

I Left My Heart in San Francisco 6'
   3[1.2.3/pic] 2 3[1.2.bcl] 2 – 2asx, tsx, bsx – 4 3 3 1 – tmp+3 – hp – str
   Lyrics by Douglass Cross.
   Robert Russell Bennett, arr.
                                     Popular Song
Leonard (rental)

Costa, Paul Mario   1858-1933

Era di maggio 4'
   3[1.2.pic] 3[1.2.Eh] 2 2 – 4 3 3 1 – tmp+perc – hp – str
   Solo Tenor. Key of D.
   Giancarlo Chiaramello, arr.
                                     Popular Song
Kalmus

A Frangesa March 3'
   2 2 2 2 – 2 2 1 0 – 3perc – pf – str
   Theodore Moses Tobani, arr.
                                   Instrumental Pops
Kalmus

Courage, Alexander   1919-2008

Star Trek: The Television Series, 7.5'
   "The Menagerie" (1964)
   3[1.afl.afl/pic] 2[1.Eh] 3[1.2.bcl] 3]1.2.cbn] – 4 3 3 1 – tmp+4 – hp, pf]cel] – str
   perc: tri, sus cym, bongo, 2 toms, sd, bd, bell tree, tamtam, slgh bells, med gong, glock, marim, vib, tambn, cyms.
                                         Space/TV
T&V (rental)

Courtney, Craig   1965-

A Musicological Journey Through   8'
  Twelve Days of Christmas
  3[1.2.pic] 3[1.2.3/Eh] 3[1.2.bcl] 2 – 4 3 3 1 – tmp+2
  – hp – str
  perc: hand dr, tri, glock, cym, sd, bd.
  SATB Chorus. Arrangement is in various musical
  styles by century including references to familiar
  pieces. Score is in manuscript form.
                                                Christmas/Novelty
  Hinshaw (rental)

Cowell, Henry   1897-1965

Flirtatious Jig (Fiddler's Jig)   2'
  Strings
  Solo Violin.
                                                Dance
  Schirmer (rental)

Four Irish Tales: 13'
  Tales of Our Countryside
  3[incl pic] 3 3 3 – 4 3 3 1 – tmp+perc – str
  Solo Piano.
                                                St. Patrick/International
  Schirmer (rental)

Old American Country Set   12'
  2 2 2 2 – 2 2 1 1 – perc – bnjo – str
                                                Americana
  Schirmer (rental)

Saturday Night at the Firehouse   4'
  1 1 2 1 – 2 2 0 0 – perc – str
                                                Americana
  Schirmer (rental)

Crawford, Robert MacArthur   1899-1961

Air Force March   4'
  Official Song of the United States Army Air Corps
  2 2 2 2 – 2 2 2 0 – perc – str
  Key of B Flat. Piano/Conductor score. Can be
  played with orchestra alone or with voices.
  J. S. Seredy, arr.
                                                Patriotic
  Fischer(POP); Luck's (rental)

Creston, Paul   1906-1985

Concertino for Marimba, Op. 21   15'
  2 1 1 0 – 2 0 0 0 – tmp – str   (5' 5' 5')
  Solo Marimba.
  Includes movements: Vigorous; Calm; Lively.
                                                Popular Classics
  Schirmer (rental)

Concerto for Saxophone and   16'
Orchestra, Op. 26
  3 2 2 2 – asx – 4 2 3 1 – tmp – str
  Solo Saxophone.
                                                Popular Classics
  Schirmer (rental)

Dance Overture   12'
  4[1.2.3.pic] 3[1.2.Eh] 3[1.2.bcl] 3[1.2.cbn] –
  4 3 3 1 – tmp+3 – str
  perc: cast, bd, cym, sd, tamtam, tambn, xyl, tri.
                                                Dance
  Shawnee (rental)

Evening in Texas   3'
  3[incl pic] 3[incl Eh] 3[incl bcl] 3[1.2.cbn] –
  4 3 3 1 – tmp+2 – str
                                                Americana
  Schirmer (rental)

Fantasy for Trombone, Op. 42   10'
  2 2 2 2 – 4 2 3 1 – tmp – str
  Solo Trombone.
                                                Popular Classics
  Schirmer (rental)

Kangaroo Kaper   4'
  2 1 1 1 – 2asx, tsx – 2 2 3 1 – tmp+perc – pf – str
                                                Animals
  Schirmer (rental)

Rumba - Tarantella   4'
  3 2 2 2 – 4 3 3 1 – tmp+3 – str
                                                Dance
  Schirmer (rental)

A Rumor, Op. 27   5'
  1 1 2 1 – 2 2 1 0 – str
                                                Instrumental Pops
  Schirmer (rental)

Sunrise in Puerto Rico   4'
    3[incl pic] 3[incl Eh] 3[incl bcl] 3[1.2.cbn] –
    4 3 3 1 – tmp+2 – str

                                                                  Space/Travel

Schirmer (rental)

Two Choric Dances, Op. 17a   12'
    1 1 1 1 – 1 0 0 0 – tmp+perc – pf – str
    Ballet.

                                                                     Dance

Schirmer (rental)

Two Choric Dances, Op. 17b   12'
    3 2 2 2 – 4 2 3 1 – tmp+perc – pf – str

                                                                     Dance

Schirmer (rental)

Croce, Jim   1943-1973

Jim Croce in Concert   6.5'
    2[1.2/pic] 2 2 2 – 2 3 3 1– tmp+3 – str
    perc: glock, sus cym, hi hat, sd, bd.
    Includes: You Don't Mess Around with Jim;
    Photographs and Memories; Time in a Bottle; I'll
    Have to Say I Love You In a Song; Bad, Bad Leroy
    Brown.
    Ian Polster, arr.

                                                           Popular Songs

Big Three (POP); Luck's (rental)

Cunningham, Arthur   1928-1997

Lullabye for a Jazz Baby   6.5'
    2[incl pic] 2 3[incl bcl] 1 – 2 2 2 0 – perc – hp – str

                                                                    Jazz

Presser (rental)

Rooster Rhapsody   15'
    1 1 2 0 – 3 3 3 0 – 2perc - str
    Narrator; Rock Quartet [drum set, elec gtr,
    elec bass, elec pf, sound effects].

                                                                     Animals

Presser (rental)

Curnow, James, arr.   1943-

TV Spectacular   6'
    2 1 3[1.2.(bcl)] 1 – 2 3 2 1 – tmp+3 – str
    perc: cym, sd, bd, sus cym, glock, xyl, vibraslap,
    congas[or bongos], claves, hi hat, tri, tambn, ride cym.
    Includes themes from NBC News; Growing Pains;
    L.A. Law; Night Court; M*A*S*H; Dynasty.

                                                                     TV

Leonard (POP); EMS or Luck's (rental)

Curtis-Smith, Curtis   1941-

Great American Symphony (GAS!)   22'
    3 3 4 3 – sx –4 4 2 1 – tmp+perc – pf,bnjo – str
    Includes: Kazoo Blues; March; Northern Harmony;
    Dido's Dance. The composer discusses his work at
    website: www.americancomposers.org.

                                                           Americana/Novelty

Marks (rental)

Custer, Calvin, arr.   1939-

The American Frontier   7'
    3[incl pic] 1 3[1.2.bcl] 1 – 4 3 3 1 – tmp+perc – pf
    – str
    Includes: The Girl I Left Behind; Chester;
    Shenandoah; O Susanna; America the Beautiful.

                                                               Americana

Leonard

Beach Boys Medley   6'
    3[1.2.pic] 2 2 1 – 4 3 3 1 – tmp+2 – pf – str
    perc: drumset, 2 tambn, bells.
    Includes: Good Vibrations; I Get Around; California
    Girls.

                                                 Americana/Popular Song

Warner

Birth of the Blues   3.5'
    Clarinet solo – rhythm – strings
    Music by Ray Henderson and lyrics by B. G.
    DeSylva and Lew Brown, but listed under the
    arranger Calvin Custer.

                                                                   Jazz

Warner (POP); EMS or Luck's (rental)

Christmas - That Special Time of the Year   6'
    3[1.2.pic] 2 2 1 – 4 3 3 1 – tmp+2 – pf – str
    perc: tri, drumset, glock, xyl, bd, cym.
    Includes: Rudolph The Red-Nosed Reindeer by Johnny Marks; Sleigh Ride, by Leroy Anderson; The Little Drummer Boy, by Katherine Davis.
                                                             Christmas

Leonard (POP); Luck's (rental)

It's Christmastime (Medley for Orchestra)   6'
    3[1.2.pic] 1 3[1.2.(bcl)] 1 – 4 3 3 1 – tmp+3 – pf – str
    perc: mallets, drumset, accessories.
    Includes: Have Yourself a Merry Little Christmas, I'll be Home for Christmas, Santa Claus is Coming to Town, Silver Bells.
                                                             Christmas

Warner (POP); EMS or Luck's

A Salute to the Big Apple   7'
    2 1 3[1.2.bcl] 1 – 4 3 3 1 – tmp+perc – pf – str
    Includes: Lullaby of Broadway; 42nd Street.
                                                           Americana

Warner

Salute to the Big Bands   8.5'
    2 1 3[1.2.bcl] 1 – 4 3 3 1 – tmp+3 – pf – str
    perc: bells, vib, xylo, drumset, cym, congas, elec phone bell, and cym.
    Includes: April in Paris; I'm Getting Sentimental Over You; PA 6-5000; Serenade in Blue; Sing, Sing, Sing.
                               Jazz/Popular Song

Warner

Star Trek Through the Years   9'
    2[1.2/pic] 2 3[1.2.bcl] 2 – 4 3 3 1 – tmp+4 – pf – str
    perc: drumset, sus cym, sd, bd, cym, vib, bongos, tamtam, glock, (chimes).
    Includes: TV Theme; Deep Space 9; The Inner Light; Star Trek Generations; Star Trek Voyager; Star Trek: The Motion Picture.
                                                              Space

Leonard

Themes from 007: A Medley for Orchestra   7.5'
    3[1.2.pic] 1 3[1.2.bcl] 1 – 4 3 3 1 – tmp+2 – pf – str
    perc: drumset[sd, bd, cym], glock, vib, xyl.
    Includes: The James Bond Theme, music by Monty Norman; for Your Eyes Only, music by Bill Conti; Live and Let Die, music by Paul McCartney; Goldfinger, music by John Barry.
                                                               Films

Warner

D

Damase, Jean-Michel   1928-

Piége de lumiére   22'
    2 2 2 2 – 2 2 2 0 – tmp+1 – hp, pf – str
    Suite from the ballet.
                                                               Dance

Lemoine (rental)

Daniel, Eliot &   1908-1997
Adamson, Harold

I Love Lucy: Theme (1953)   2'
    3[1.2.pic] 2 3[1.2.bcl] 2 – 4 3 3 0 – 4perc – hp, pf – str
    perc: xyl, glock, cowbell, sus cym, bd, bongos, conga, shaker.
                                                               TV

T&V (rental)

Danielpour, Richard   1956-

Toward the Splendid City   9'
    3[1.2.3/pic] 3[1.2.Eh] 3[1.2.3/bcl] 3[1.2.3/bcn] – 4 3 3 1 – tmp+4 – hp, cel/pf – str
    perc: vib, xyl, marim, glock, chimes, sus cym, guiro, tomtom, sd, rototom, cast, brake dr, timbales, tri, bd, cowbell, whip.
    Inspired by New York City.
                                                      Americana

Schirmer (rental)

Dankworth, John   1927-

The Diamond and the Goose   33'
    2[incl pic] 2 2 2 – 4 3 3 1 – tmp+perc – hp – str
    Solo SATB.
                                                            Animals

Schirmer (rental)

Darke, Harold — 1888-1976

In the Bleak Midwinter — 3.5'
  Strings
  Solo Soprano and Tenor; Mixed Chorus. Text by Christina Rossetti.
                    Christmas/Seasons
  Thorpe (rental)

Darzins, Volfgangs — 1906-1962

Latvian Folksongs — Folio
  2 1 2 1 – asx – 2 2 2 0 – perc – (pf) – str
  Includes: White Slippers; I Planted a Mulberry Tree; The Sun Goes Down; Cradle Song; Bride Stealing Song; Sheep Herder's Song; Summer Song; Orphan Song; War Song.
  John David Lamb, orchestrator
                    International
  Kalmus

Daugherty, Michael — 1954-

Metropolis Symphony: 1.Lex — 12'
  3[1.2.pic] 3[1.2.Eh] 3 3 – 4 3 3 1 – tmp+4 – synth or pf – str
  perc: xyl, vib, marim, 3 cowbells, hi-hat, 3woodblk, glock, police whistle, gong, crot, bongo, ratch, cym, whip, finger cym, tambn.
  SoloViolin [concertmaster].
                    Films/TV
  Peer (rental)

Metropolis Symphony: 2.Krypton — 7'
  3[1.2.pic] 3 3[1.Ebcl.bcl] 3 – 4 4 3 1 – 4perc – pf or synth – str
                    Films/TV

Metropolis Symphony: 3.Mxyzptlk — 7'
  2[1.2/pic] 2 2 2 – 2 1 1 0 – 2perc – synth – str
  perc: 2gong, 3tri, 3woodblk, sus cym.
  2 Solo Flutes [II doubles on piccolo].
                    Films/TV
  Peer (rental)

Metropolis Symphony: 4.Oh, Lois! — 6'
  2[1/pic.2] 2 2 2 –4 3 3 0 – tmp+2 – synth –str
  perc: 2 tri (high and low), 2 gongs (large and small), 2 flex, 2 whips or slapsticks.
                    Films/TV
  Peer (rental)

Metropolis Symphony: — 13'
  5. Red Cape Tango
  3[1.2.pic] 3[1.2.Eh] 3[1.2.bcl] 3[1.2.cbn] – 4 4 3 1 – tmp+4 – pf – str
  perc: 2 finger cym, 2 cym (large and small), chimes, sd, cast, large brake dr, cast, marim, large tamtam, tambn.
                    Films/TV
  Peer (rental)

Motown Metal — 7'
  0 0 0 0 – 4 4 3 1 – 2perc
                    Popular Song
  Peer (rental)

Davis, Albert O., arr.

Buffalo Gals: In Blue Grass Style — 4'
  2 2 2 1 – 2 2 2 1 – tmp+perc – gtr – str
  perc: woodblk, tambn, sd, bd, slide whistle.
                    Americana/Popular Song
  Ludwig

Davis, Anthony — 1951-

Esu Variations — 11'
  4[incl pic] 4 4 4[incl cbn] – 4 4 3 1 – tmp+3 – str
                    Black History Month
  Schirmer (rental)

X: The Life and Times of Malcolm X — 8'
  (Malcolm's Prison Aria)
  2[incl pic] 1 2 2[incl cbn] – 2sx – 2 1 2 0 – tmp+3 – pf – str
  Solo Baritone.
                    Black History Month
  Schirmer (rental)

Davis, Chip [Louis Davis, Jr.]   1947-

Christmas Sweet   7.5'
    4[2fl/soprano rec.2pic/sopranino rec]
    2[1/tenor rec.Eh/alto crumhn] 1[incl bass rec] 0 –
    perc – hpsd, 2lutes/gtr – str[vn,vc]
    Mannheim Steamroller arrangement.
                                         Christmas
    Luck's

Davis, B. (See: Back, B.)

Davis, Jimmie   1899-2000

Blue Tail Fly   2.5'
    Strings
    Blue grass version.
                            Americana/Animals
    Ludwig

Buffalo Gals   3'
    2 2 2 1 – 2 2 2 1 – tmp+perc – gtr – str
    Blue grass version.
                                      Americana
    Ludwig

Down In the Valley   3.5'
    1 1 2 1 – 2 2 2 1 – tmp+perc – gtr – str
    Blue grass version.
                                      Americana
    Ludwig

Davis, Katherine K.   1892-1980

Little Drummer Boy   3.5'
    Strings
    Samuel Applebaum, arr.
                                        Christmas
    Warner (POP); Luck's (rental)

Dawson, William   1899-1990

Negro Folk Symphony   35'
    3[1.2.pic] 3[1.2.Eh] 3[1.2.Ebcl.bcl] 3[1.2.cbn]
    – 4 2 3 1 – tmp+3 – hp – str
    perc: gong, chimes, tri, td, sd, xyl, cym, bd, steel plate.
    Includes: The Bond of Africa; Hope in the Night; O
    Le' Me Shine, Shine Like a Morning Star.
                               Black History Month
    Schirmer (rental)

De Rose, Peter   1900-1953

Deep Purple   2'
    2 1 2 1 – 2 3 2 1 – 2perc – pf – str
    perc: drumset, glock.
    Originally a 1933 piano composition, Paul
    Whiteman arranged it for his big band. It has been
    revived by numerous popular artists over the
    decades.
                             Instrumental Pops/Popular Song
    Robbins (POP); EMS or Luck's (rental)

Deep Purple   4'
    2 2 2 2 – sx – 4 2 3 1 – tmp+perc – str
    Originally a 1933 piano composition, Paul
    Whiteman arranged it for his big band. It has been
    revived by numerous popular artists over the
    decades.
    Merle J. Isaac, arr.
                             Instrumental Pops/Popular Song
    Robbins (POP); Luck's (rental)

Deak, John   1943-

The Passion of Scrooge (A Christmas Carol)   49'
    1[incl pic] 0 1[incl bcl] 0 – 1 0 0 0 – perc – hp
    – str[single parts]
    Solo Baritone [Narrator].
                                        Christmas
    Fischer (rental)

Debney, John   1956-

The Passion of the Christ Symphony   70'
 3[1.2.pic] 3[1.2.Eh] 2 2[1.cbn] – 2ethnic
 woodwinds[duduk, tin whistle, pennywhistle, ob, fl]
 – 4 3 3 1 – tmp+perc – hp, pf, (org) – str
 Solo Soprano, Mezzo-soprano, Tenor; SATB
 Chorus.
 Kevin Kaska, arr.
                                          Films
 Kane (rental)

Debussy, Claude   1862-1918

La Cathédrale engloutie   7.5'
 (The Engulfed Cathedral)
 4[incl 2pic] 4[incl Eh] 4[incl bcl] 4[incl cbn]
 – 6 4 3 1 – tmp+4perc – cel, 2hp, org – str
 perc: sus cym, tam-tam, bd, bells, glock, chimes.
 Leopold Stokowski, arr.
                                 Popular Classics
 Presser (rental)

Clair de lune   5'
 2 2 2 2 – 4 0 0 0 – hp, cel – str
 Arthur Luck, arr.
                                     Space/Valentine
 Luck's

Clair de lune   5'
 2 2[incl Eh] 2 2 – 0 1 0 0 – perc[incl vib] – hp – str
 Leopold Stokowski, arr.
                                     Space/Valentine
 Presser (rental)

Clair de lune   5'
 3 3 3 3 – 4 3 3 1 – tmp+perc – hp – str
 Lucien Cailliet, arr.
                                     Space/Valentine
 Presser (rental)

Clair de lune   5'
 2 2 2 2 – 2 0 0 0 – hp – str
 André Caplet, arr.
                                     Space/Valentine
 Presser (rental)

Clair de lune   5'
 2 3 2 2 – 4 3 3 0 – hp – str
 William Gleichmann, arr.
                                     Space/Valentine
 Presser (rental)

Clair de lune   5'
 Strings
 Donald Miller, arr.
                                     Space/Valentine
 Presser (rental)

La Fille aux cheveux de lin   3'
 (Girl with the Flaxen Hair)
 2 2 2 2 – (alto hn or asx) – 2 2 0 0 – tmp – hp – str
 J. C. Cheucle, arr.
                                            Valentine
 Presser (rental)

La Fille aux cheveux de lin   3'
 (Girl with the Flaxen Hair)
 2 2 2 2 – 4 3 3 0 – tmp – hp – str
 William Gleichmann, arr.
                                            Valentine
 Presser (rental)

La Fille aux cheveux de lin   3'
 (Girl with the Flaxen Hair)
 2 1 2 2 – 2 0 0 0 – hp – str
 Leopold Stokowski, arr.
                                            Valentine
 Presser (rental)

Prélude à L'après-midi d'un faune   10'
 (Afternoon of a faun)
 3 3[1.2.Eh] 2 2 – 4 0 0 0 – 1perc – 2hp – str
 perc: crot.
 Kalmus edition by Clinton F. Nieweg.
                                            Valentine
 Breitkopf; Kalmus

La Soirée dans Grenade   7'
 (Night in Grenada)
 3[incl 2pic, afl] 3[incl Eh] 3[incl Ebcl, bcl] 3[incl
 cbn] – 4 3 4 1 – 2perc – cel, pf – str
 perc: sd, bd, cym, tam-tam.
 Leopold Stokowski, arr.
                                           International
 Presser (rental)

DeLarmarter, Eric   1880-1953

Christmastide   12'
2 2 2 2 – 4 3 3 1 – tmp+perc – hp – str
A medley of the following classic Christmas carols:
I Saw Three Ships; The Holly and the Ivy; Jesus,
Gentle Babe.

                                       Christmas

Elkan-Vogel (rental)

Delibes, Leo   1836-1891

Coppelia: Entr'acte & Waltz   4'
2[1.2/pic] 2 2 2 – 2 2 3 1 – tmp – hp – str
                      Dance/Popular Classics

Heugel (rental); Kalmus

Sylvia: Suite   6'
    4. Cortege de Bacchus
2[1.2/pic] 2 2 2 – 4 4 3 1 – tmp+3 – hp – str
                              Popular Classics

Heugel (rental); Kalmus

Delius, Frederick   1862-1934

Two Pieces: 11'
    1. On Hearing the First Cuckoo in Spring;   (6' 5')
    2. Summer-Night on the River
2 1 2 2 – 2 0 0 0 – str
                    Seasons/Popular Classics

Kalmus; Oxford (rental)

Dello Joio, Norman   1913-2008

Christmas Music   17'
1 1 2 1 – 2 2 2 0 – tmp+perc – str
Includes Bright Star [no tmp]; Christmas Carol;
God Rest Ye Merry, Gentlemen; Hark, the Herald
Angels Sing; The Holy Infant's Lullaby; O Come,
All Ye Faithful; Silent Night [only glock needed for
perc].
Can be performed separately.
                                       Christmas

Marks (rental)

Colonial Variants: 26'
    Thirteen Profiles of the Original Colonies
3 3 3 3 – 4 3 3 1 – tmp+perc – hp – str
                                       Patriotic

Schirmer (rental)

Nativity: Canticle for the Child   35'
3[incl pic] 3[incl Eh] 3[incl bcl] 2 – 4 3 3 1 –
tmp+4 – str
Solo Soprano, 2 Tenors, Baritone; SSATTB
Chorus with soli SATB.
                                       Christmas

Schirmer (rental)

Southern Echoes   16'
2 3[1.2.Eh] 3[1.2.bcl] 0 – 4 3 3 1 – 2perc – str
                              Americana/Travel

Schirmer (rental)

Demerest, Clifford   1874–1946

Let Freedom Ring: Overture   6'
2 2 2 2 – 2 2 2 1 – tmp+2 – str
perc: sd, glock, cym.
                                       Patriotic

Remick (rental)

Dennison, Sam   1926-2005

And If Elected...   15'
2[incl pic] 2 2 2 – 4 3 3 1 – tmp+perc – str
Solo Soprano; Narrator; Men's Chorus. Cantata on
Nineteenth-Century election songs.
                                       Patriotic

Kalmus

Denver, John   1943-1997

Annie's Song   3'
3 3 3[1.2.bcl] 3 – 4 0 3 1 – drumset –
pf, Fender bass, gtr – str
Henry Mancini, arr.
                                   Popular Song

Janen (rental)

John Denver Celebration (1987)   10'
    3[1.2.pic] 3[1.2.Eh] 3[1.2.bcl] 3[1.2.cbn] – 4 3 3 1
    – tmp+perc – hp, pf – str
    perc: mark tree, tamtam, sd, bd, cym, sus cym, tri, glock, xyl, tambn.
    Includes: Eagle & Hawk, Rocky Mountain High, Annie's Song, and Take Me Home Country Road. Lee Holdridge, arr.

                                    Popular Song

T&V (rental)

Denza, Luigi   1846-1922

Funiculi - Funicula   3'
    2 2 2 2 – (2asx, tsx) – 4 3 2 0 – tmp+2 – hp, pf – str
    Philip J. Lang, arr.
                                    International

Kalmus

DePonte, Niel   1953-

Bell of Freedom (2002)   4.5'
    2[1.2/pic] 2 2 2 – 4 2 3 1 – tmp+3 –
    hp[(synth or pf)] – str
    perc: 2 low field dr, bd, cym, lg & med sus cym, sd, chimes, orchestra bells.
    Optional Alto and Baritone duet or solos or SATB Chorus. Written in honor of the first responders to the World Trade Center tragedy of 2001. It is available in different versions: chorus, simplified chorus, solos, or a duet version. Includes a timpani/percussion score and Alto-Baritone duet with piano reduction.
                                    Patriotic

Bell

Desplat, Alexandre   1961-

The Curious Case of Benjamin Button: 9.5'
  Suite (2008)
    2[afl/bsfl.afl/bsfl] 1[Eh] 1[bcl] 0 – asx or ssax, 2tsx – 4 1 3 1 – tmp+4 – str
    perc: vib, orch bells, marim, sus cym, sizzle cym, ride cym, small tri, bd, Verdi bd.
    Includes: Postcards; Little Man – Oti; Daisy's Ballet Career; Mr. Button; Love in Murmansk.
                                    Films

T&V (rental)

Harry Potter Symphonic Suite   24.5'
    3[1.2.3/afl/pic] 3[1.2.3/Eh] 3[1.2.3/bcl/Ebcl]
    3[1.2.3/cbn] – 4 3 3 1 – tmp+3perc – hp, pf/cel
    – str
    perc: orch-bells, tubular-bells, xyl, vib, tambn, sm tri, slgh-bells, mark tree, bell tree, sus cyms (sm, med, lg), piatti, sizzle cym, tam-tam, sd, dumbeks(3), tom-toms(3), lg, & sm taiko dms [or tom-toms], bd, verdi bd.
    Optional Solo Female Vocalist in *Lily's Theme*.
    Includes: Prologue/Hedwig's Theme [#1]   (5')
    Buckbeak's Flight [#3]   (2')
    Hogwarts' Hymn [#4]   (1')
    Hogwarts' March [#4]   (1.5')
    Fireworks [#5]   (1')
    The Flight of the Order of the Phoenix [#5]   (1.5')
    Harry & Hermione [#6]   (1.5')
    Obliviate [#7]   (2')
    Lily's Theme [#8]   (2')
    Courtyard Apocalypse [#8]   (2')
    Mischief Managed [#3] & Harry's Wondrous
        World [#2]   (5')
    The number in brackets is the film from which the theme was derived. #1-3 are composed by J.Williams; #4 is composed by P. Doyle; #5& 6 by N. Hooper; and #7 & 8 by A. Desplat. Gary Fry, arr.
                                    Films

Alfred (rental)

The Queen: Suite (2006)   7'
    2[pic.2]1[Eh] 2[bcl.bcl] 0 – 2 1 0 0 – tmp+2 –
    hp, pf[synth/mandolin] cel[hpsd] – str
    perc: marim, glock, bd, shaker.
    Includes: Opening Title; Walk in the Garden; The Queen Drives; Calm Down; The Stag Score; Diana's Life; Difficult Position
                                    Films

T&V (rental)

Dessau, Paul   1894-1979

Alice Helps the Romance   7'
    1[incl pic] 1 1 0 – asx – 0 1 1 0 – tmp+2 – pf – str
    perc: sd, bd with cym, ratch, tri.
    Music to a 1926 Disney silent film from his *Alice in Cartoonland* series produced just before *Steamboat Willie* and the introduction of Mickey Mouse.
                                    Films

Schott (rental)

Alice in the Wooly West   7'
    1 1 1 0 – 0 1 1 0 – tmp+1 – str
    perc: sd, bd with cym, slapstick, tri.
    Music to a 1926 Disney silent film from his *Alice in Cartoonland* series produced just before *Steamboat Willie* and the introduction of Mickey Mouse.

                                                              Films
Schott (rental)

Alice the Firefighter   7'
    1 1 1 0 – 0 1 1 0 – tmp+1 – pf – str
    perc: sd, bd with cym, glock, small bells, xyl, slgh-bells, ratch.
    Music to a 1926 Disney silent film from his *Alice in Cartoonland* series produced just before *Steamboat Willie* and the introduction of Mickey Mouse.

                                                              Films
Schott (rental)

Alice's Monkey Business   7'
    1 1 1 0 – 0 1 1 0 – tmp+perc – pf – str
    perc: sd, bd with cym, ratch, tri.
    Music to a 1926 Disney silent film from his *Alice in Cartoonland* series produced just before *Steamboat Willie* and the introduction of Mickey Mouse.

                                                              Films
Schott (rental)

Deussen, Nancy Bloomer   1931-

American Hymn   4.5'
    3[1.2.pic] 2 2 2 – 4 3 3 1 – tmp+3 – hp – str

                                                              Patriotic
Wendel (rental)

Ascent to Victory   8'
    1 1 2 1 – 2 1 0 0 – tmp+perc – str

                                                              Sports
Wendel (rental)

A Field in Pennsylvania   7'
    3[1.2.pic] 3[1.2.Eh] 3[1.2.bcl] 2 – 4 3 2 1 – tmp+3 – str
    Written in tribute to the passengers and crew of United Airlines Flight 93.

                                                              Patriotic
Wendel (rental)

Regalos   5'
    2[incl pic] 2[incl Eh] 2 2 – 4 3 3 1 – tmp+3 – (hp) – str

                                                          International
Wendel (rental)

DeVorzon, Barry (See: Botkin, Perry Jr.)

Dewitt, Louis O.   1853-19??

Twelve English Songs   Folio
    2[1.pic] 1 2 1 – 2 2 1 0 – perc – str
    Solo Trombone. Includes: The British Grenadiers (Trad.); Sally in our Alley (Trad.); The Anchor's Weigh'd (Braham); My Pretty Jane, or When the Bloom is on the Rye (Bishop); Twickenham Ferry (Marzials); The Midshipmate (Adams); Black Eyed Susan (Trad.); The Bay of Biscay, O! (Davy); The Vicar of Bray (Trad.); Goodbye, Sweetheart Goodbye (Hatton); Ever of Thee (Hall); The Roast Beef of Old England (Trad.)

                                                        International
Kalmus

Diamond, Neil   1941-

Jazz Singer Medley   12'
    2 1 3[1.2.bcl] 1 – 2 2 2 1 – tmp+2 – gtr – str
    perc: drumset, cym, tambn.
    Includes: America, Love on the Rocks, Jerusalem, On the Robert E. Lee, Hello Again.
    Marty Gold, arr.

                                                                Jazz
Leonard (POP); EMS or Luck's (rental)

Dickerson, Roger   1934-

Orpheus an' His Slide Trombone   22'
    3 3 3 3 – 4 3 4 1 – tmp+perc – hp, pf – str
    Narrator.

                                            Instrumental Pops
Presser (rental)

Dickinson, Peter   1934-

Merseyside Echoes   12'
3[incl 2 pic] 3[incl Eh] 3 3[incl cbn] – 4 4 3 1 –
4perc – str
    Instrumental Pops
Schirmer (rental)

Dix, William   1837-1898

Christmas with Renata Scotto: 2'
   8. What Child Is This?
hp – strings
Solo Soprano; SATB Chorus.
John Grady, arr.
    Christmas
Schirmer (rental)

Dodgson, Stephen   1924-

Villanelle   6'
2 1 2 1 – 2 2 1 0 – tmp+perc – str

Schirmer (rental)

Donizetti, Gaetano   1797-1848

La Fille du regiment   7'
   (Daughter of the Regiment): Overture
2[1.2/pic] 2 2 2 – 4 2 3 0 – tmp+2 – str
    Popular Classics
Breitkopf; Kalmus

Lucia di Lammermoor, Act II: Sestetto:
   Chi mi frena
2[1.pic] 2 2 2 – 4 2 3 0 – tmp – str
    Popular Classics
Kalmus

Dorati, Antal   1906-1988

Night Music   22'
0 0 0 0 – 2 0 0 0 – hp – str
Solo Flute.
Includes: Recitativo (Evening Antiphon) *Con moto tranquillo, liberamente*; Arioso (Lullaby) *Andante, affetuoso*; Capriccio (Midnight) *Moderato*; Scherzo (Insects Round the Flame) *Presto*; Postludio (Deep Night - Dawn) *Lento*.
    Halloween
Schirmer (rental)

Dorff, Daniel   1956-

It Takes Four to Tango   2.5'
Strings
This is a Custom Print item and must be
ordered by telephone or email.
    Dance
Presser

The Kiss   14'
2[incl pic, afl] 2[incl Eh] 2 2 – tsx – 4 3 3 1 –
tmp+3 – hp, cel – str
Based on the painting by Klimt.
    Valentine
Presser (rental)

Pachelbel's Christmas   4.5'
2 2 2 2 – 2 2 2 1 – 1perc[incl tmp] – str
    Christmas
Presser (rental)

Philly Rhapsody   11.5'
3[incl pic] 2[opt ob2] 3[incl bcl] 2 –
4[(3-4)] 3[1/(flugelhorn)] 3 1 – 4perc[incl drumset]
– hp, pf – str
Jazzy influence with some improvisation. Options
available for school orchestras.
    Americana
Presser (rental)

Sunburst   4'
Strings
Solo Violin.
    Weather
Presser (rental)

The Tortoise and the Hare   5'
     1 1 1 1[(cbn)] – 1 1 1 0 – 2perc[(#2)] – hp – str
     Features Clarinet and Contrabassoon solos. From *Three Fun Fables*.

                                                       Animals/Sports

MMB (rental)

Dorsey, Jimmy   1904-1957

Oodles of Noodles   5'
     1/pic 1 2 1 – 2asx, tsx, bsx – 2 3 3 0 – tmp+1 – hp – str
     perc: sd, bd.
     Percy Faith, arr.

                                                  Instrumental Pops

Robbins (rental)

Douglas, Bill   1944-

African Drum Ensemble Concerto   10'
     3[incl pic] 3 3 3 – 4 3 3 1 – tmp+drum ensemble – str
     Bill Douglas, arr.

                                                     International

Douglas

Douglas, Samuel Osler   1943-

Millennium Fanfare   3'
     2 2 2 3[incl cbn] – 4 3 3 1 – tmp – str

                                                             Fanfare

SOD

The Night Before Christmas   5'
     3[1.2.(pic)] 2 2 2 – 4 3 3 1 – tmp+3 – str
     perc: sd, cym, tri, chimes, glock, slgh-bells, tambn, vib, xyl, temple blks, ratch, cowbell, siren, bell tree, bd.
     Narrator; Clement Moore poem: *'Twas The Night Before Christmas*.

                                                              Christmas

SMC (rental)

Downey, John W.   1927-2004

Jingalodeon   6.5'
     2 2 2 2 – 4 2 3 1 – tmp+perc – str

                                                                       Jazz

Presser (rental)

Ode to Freedom   8'
     3[incl pic] 3[incl Eh] 3[incl bcl] 3[incl cbn] – 4 3 3 1 – tmp+perc – str

                                                              Patriotic

Presser (rental)

Doyle, Patrick   1953-

Great Expectations Suite   15'
     3[1.2.pic] 3[1.2.3/Eh] 3[1.2.bcl] 3[1.2.3/cbn] – 4 3 0 0 – tmp+perc – hp, synth, 2gtr – str
     Solo Medium Voice.
     Lawrence Ashmore and James Sherman, arr.

                                                            Films

Kane (rental)

Harry Potter Symphonic Suite   24.5'
     3[1.2.3/afl/pic] 3[1.2.3/Eh] 3[1.2.3/bcl/Ebcl] 3[1.2.3/cbn] – 4 3 3 1 – tmp+3perc – hp, pf/cel – str
     perc: orch-bells, tubular-bells, xyl, vib, tambn, sm tri, slgh-bells, mark tree, bell tree, sus cyms (sm, med, lg), piatti, sizzle cym, tam-tam, sd, dumbeks(3), tom-toms(3), lg, & sm taiko dms [or tom-toms], bd, verdi bd.
     Optional Solo Female Vocalist in *Lily's Theme*.
     Includes: Prologue/Hedwig's Theme [#1]   (5')
     Buckbeak's Flight [#3]   (2')
     Hogwarts' Hymn [#4]   (1')
     Hogwarts' March [#4]   (1.5')
     Fireworks [#5]   (1')
     The Flight of the Order of the Phoenix [#5]   (1.5')
     Harry & Hermione [#6]   (1.5')
     Obliviate [#7]   (2')
     Lily's Theme [#8]   (2')
     Courtyard Apocalypse [#8]   (2')
     Mischief Managed [#3] & Harry's Wondrous World [#2]   (5')
     The number in brackets is the film from which the theme was derived. #1-3 are composed by J. Williams; #4 is composed by P. Doyle; #5& 6 by N. Hooper; and #7 & 8 by A. Desplat.
     Gary Fry, arr.

                                                            Films

Alfred (rental)

Henry V: Non Nobis Domine (1989)   3.5'
   3[1.2.pic] 3[1.2.Eh] 3[1.2.bcl] 3[1.2.cbn] –
   4 3 3 1 – tmp+3 – (org) – str
   perc: tri, bd, cym, chimes.
   SATB Chorus. Includes: Opening and Closing
   Titles.
                                       Films
T&V (rental)

Much Ado About Nothing: Suite (1993)   6'
   3 3 2 3[1.2.cbn] – 4 3 3 1 – tmp+3 – hp, synth – str
   perc: sd, sus cym, cym, grand bells, ching ring.
   Chorus. Includes: Overture, Goddess of the Night
   and Take Up Pipers.
                                       Films
T&V (rental)

Sense and Sensibility:Suite (1995)   14'
   2 1 2 0 – 3 0 0 0 – hp, pf – str   *(3' 5.5' 3' 2.5')*
   Solo Voice. Includes: Weep You No More Sad
   Fountains; Norland: (aka My Father's Favorites);
   The Wedding (aka Throw the Coins); The Dreame:
   End Title.
                                       Films
T&V (rental)

Dragon, Carmen, arr.   1914-1984

The Yellow Rose of Texas   3'
   3[incl pic] 3[incl Eh] 3[incl bcl] 2 – 4 4 3 1 –
   tmp+perc – cel – str
                                   Americana
Dragon (rental)

Drdla, Frantisek (Franz) Alois   1868-1944

Souvenir   4'
   1 1 2 1 – 2 2 1 0 – tmp – str
   Adolphe Dumont, arr.
                                   Valentine
Kalmus

Duff, Arthur   1899-1956

Irish Suite   10'
   Strings
                         St. Patrick/International
Schirmer (rental)

Duffy, John   1926-

Heritage Symphonic Dances   16'
   2[incl pic] 2[incl Eh] 2 2 – 4 2 3 1 – tmp+2 –
   pf(cel), hp – str   *(3' 2' 2' 2' 4' 3')*
   Includes: David's Dance; The Rabbi's Dance;
   Renaissance Dance; Spanish Dance; America;
   Waltz. Composed as theme music for the PBS
   Special *Heritage: Civilization and the Jews* for
   which Duffy won an Emmy. Lively dances
   commemorate freedom and cultural heritage.
                          Dance/International
Schott (rental)

Indian Spirits   5'
   3[incl pic] 3[1.2.Eh] 3[1.2.bcl] 3[1.2.cbn] – 4 3 3 1
   – tmp+4 – hp – str
   Composed in celebration of the 400th anniversary
   of the founding of Jamestown, Virginia, and
   inspired by drawings by British artist and explorer
   John White of Virginia of Native Americans.
                                 Americana
Schott (rental)

Dukas, Paul   1865-1935

L'Apprenti Sorcier   12'
(The Sorcerer's Apprentice)
   3[1.2.pic] 2 3[1.2.bcl] 4[1.2.3.cbn] – 4 4 3 0 –
   tmp+4 – hp – str
   perc: glock, sus cym, tri, cym, bd.
   Kalmus edition by Clinton F. Nieweg.
                    Halloween/Popular Classics
Durand (rental); Kalmus

La Peri: Fanfare   3'
   0 0 0 0 – 4 3 3 1
                                    Fanfare
Durand

Duke, Derek   (See: Brower, Russell)

Duke, Vernon [Vladimir Dukelsky] 1903-1969

April in Paris 3'
   2 2 2 1 – 4 3 3 1 – tmp+3 – pf – str
   Chuck Sayre, arr.
                           Travel/Seasons
   Warner (POP); Luck's (rental)

Dun, Tan 1957-

Crouching Tiger, Hidden Dragon (2000) 5'
   4[1.2.afl.afl] 0 0 0 – 4 0 3 0 – tmp+3 –
   hp, cimbalon – str
   perc: woodblk, toms, sd, bd, sus cym
   Includes: Crouching Tiger, Hidden Dragon; The Eternal Vow. Oscar winning film score.
                                     Films
   T&V (rental)

Dunhill, Thomas 1877-1946

The Novello Book of Carols: 3'
   How Soft, Upon the Ev'ning Air
   2 2 0 0 – 0 0 0 0 – str
   Solo Voice.
   William Llewellyn, arr.
                                  Christmas
   Novello (rental)

Dvořák, Antonin 1841-1904

Carnival Overture, Op. 92 10'
   3[1.2.pic] 3[1.2.Eh] 2 2 – 4 2 3 1 – tmp+3 – hp – str
   perc: tambn, tri, cym.
   Kalmus critical edition by Sourek.
                               Popular Classics
   Bärenreiter; Kalmus

Holoubek: 19'
   The Wood (or Forest) Dove, Op. 110
   2[1/pic.2] 3[1.2.Eh] 3[1.2.bcl] 2 – 4 2 3 1 – tmp+3 – hp – str
   perc: tri, cym, bd, tambn.
   Kalmus critical edition by Sourek.
                      Animals/Popular Classics
   Bärenreiter; Kalmus; Simrock

The Midday Witch 14'
   (The Noon Witch), Op. 108
   3[1.2.pic] 2 3[1.2.bcl] 2 – 4 2 3 1 – tmp+3 – str
   perc: tri, chime (a'), cym, bd.
   Kalmus critical edition by Burghauser
                     Halloween/Popular Classics
   Bärenreiter; Kalmus; Simrock

Slavonic Dances Op. 46, Nos. 1-4 19'
   3[1.2/pic.3] 2 2 2 – 4 2 3 0 – tmp+3 – str
   perc: bd, cym, tri.   (4' 5' 4' 6')
   3rd flute only plays in Dance #3.
   Kalmus critical edition by Sourek.
                          Dance/Popular Classics
   Bärenreiter, Breitkopf, Kalmus, Simrock

Slavonic Dances Op. 46, Nos. 5-8 16'
   3[1.2/pic] 2 2 2 – 4 2 3 0 – tmp+3 – str
   perc: bd, cym, tri.   (3' 6' 4' 3')
   Kalmus critical edition by Sourek.
                          Dance/Popular Classics
   Bärenreiter; Breitkopf; Kalmus; Simrock

Slavonic Dances Op. 72, Nos. 1-4 18'
   2 2 2 2 – 4 2 3 0 – tmp+3 – str (4' 6' 3' 5')
   perc: tri, cym, bd.
   Kalmus critical edition by Sourek.
                          Dance/Popular Classics
   Bärenreiter; Kalmus; Simrock

Slavonic Dances Op. 72, Nos. 5-8 17'
   2 2 2 2 – 4 2 3 0 – tmp+3 – str (3' 4' 3' 7')
   perc: bd, cym, tri, handbell (g#).
   Kalmus critical edition by Sourek.
                          Dance/Popular Classics
   Bärenreiter; Kalmus; Simrock

Dworsky, Richard (See: Keillor, Garrison)

Dyson, George — 1883-1964

Concerto da Camera — 20'
   Strings
         Popular Classics
  Novello (rental)

Concerto Leggiero — 20'
   Strings
   Solo piano.
         Popular Classics
  Novello (rental)

Symphony in G — 45'
   2 2 2 2 – 4 2 3 0 – tmp – str
         Popular Classics
  Schirmer (rental)

E

Ebb, Fred (See: Kander, John)

Edwards, Gus — 1879-1945

By the Light of the Silvery Moon — 3'
   2 2 2 2 – 4 3 3 0 – perc – str
   William Ryden, arr.
         Space/Valentine/Popular Song
  Kalmus

By the Light of the Silvery Moon — 3'
   1 1 2 1 – 2 2 1 0 – perc – str
   Anonymous, arr.
         Space/Valentine/Popular Song
  Kalmus

Effinger, Cecil — 1914-

An American Hymn — 5'
   (A Setting of "America the Beautiful")
   0 0 0 0 – 4 3 0 1[euph]
   SATB Chorus [suitable for children's chorus].
         Patriotic
  Schirmer (rental)

Let Your Mind Wander Over America — 8'
   3[1.2.pic] 0 4[1.2.3.bcl] 2 – 2asx, tsx, bsx –
   4 3 3 1+bar – tmp+perc – str
   Chorus.
         Patriotic
  Schirmer (rental)

The St. Luke Christmas Story — 35'
   0 2 0 0 – 0 2 0 0 – tmp – str
   Solo Soprano, Tenor, Baritone; Chorus.
         Christmas
  Schirmer (rental)

Eidelman, Cliff   1964-

Star Trek 6: The Undiscovered Country (1991)   6'
     4]1.sop recorder.pic.4] 2[1.Eh] 1[bcl or bflcbcl]
     2[1.cbn] – 4 3 4 1 – tmp+4 – hp, pf, 2 synth – str
     perc: chimes, bells, song bells, sd, sus cym, cym, xylorimba, orch bells, pic, sd, tri, bd, lg tamtam, small sus cym, key tree.
                                   Films/Space

T&V (rental)

Eiger, Walter   1917-

Concerto Grosso for   28'
    Symphony Orchestra and Jazz Ensemble
     2 2 2 2 – 4 2 1 1 – tmp+perc – str
     Jazz Ensemble: 2asx, 2tsx, bsx – 0 4 4 0 – perc – (gtr) – str bass
     Includes: Adagio; Blue & Scherzo; Fugue on a Latin American Rhythm.
                                     Instrumental Pops

Bourne (rental)

Elfman, Danny   1953-

Beetlejuice: Main Title (1988)   2'
     3[1.2.pic] 3[1.2.Eh] 3[1.2.bcl] 3[1.2.cbn] –
     4 4 4 1 – 4perc – 2 amp kybds[synth.#2=tuba part] – str
     perc: gong, sus cym, shaker, snake shaker, 4 toms, bd, lg bd, sd, xyl, tambn, glock, cym, vibraslap.
                                     Films/Halloween

T&V (rental)

Charlotte's Web: Themes for Flute   7.5'
    and Orchestra (2006)
     1[pic] 1 1 1 – 1 0 0 0 – tmp+perc – hp, pf, gtr – str
     perc: orch bells, popgun, tambn, ethnic tambn, spoons, sd, td, tri.
                                     Animals/Films

T&V (rental)

Edward Scissorhands (1990): Ice Dance   2'
     2 2[1.Eh] 3 3 – 4 3[crt] 4 1 – tmp+perc –
     2Celtic hp, 2cel, synth – str
     Optional SA Chorus and Boys Choir.
                                     Films

Kane (rental)

Edward Scissorhands (1990): Main Title   2.5'
     2[1.2/afl] 2[1/Eh. (Eh)] 3[1.2.bcl.(bcl)] 2[1.cbn] –
     4 3[crt] 4 1 – tmp+perc – hp, cel, synth – str
     (Solo Soprano).
                                     Films

Kane (rental)

Movie Spectacular   6'
     3[1.2.pic] 2 3[1.2.bcl] 2 – 4 3 3 1 – tmp+2 – str
     Includes: Theme from *Batman*; Looks Like Suicide & John Dunbar from *Dances with Wolves*; Theme from *Robin Hood: Prince of Thieves*.
     Jay Bocook, arr.
                                     Films

Leonard (POP); EMS or Luck's (rental)

Serenada Schizophrana (2005)   42'
     3[incl 2pic, afl] 3[incl 2Eh] 3[incl Ebcl, 2bcl, asx] 3[incl 2cbn] – 6 3 3[incl 2 btbn] 1 – tmp+5 –
     hp, 2pf[synth] – str
     Featured music in the IMAX film *Deep Sea 3D*.
                                     Ecology/Films

Schirmer (rental)

Simpsons Main Title   1'
     2[1.2/asx(or 2/cl)] 1 2[1.2/tsx/bsx(or2/bcl)] 0 –
     4 3 3 1 – tmp+perc – hp, pf, synth – str
     Alf Clausen, arr.
                                     TV

20th Century

Simpsons: Main Title   1.5'
     2 [1.2/asx(or 2/cl)] 1 2[1.2/tsx/bsx(or 2/bcl)] 0
     – 4 3 3 1 – tmp+perc – hp, pf/synth, synth – str
     Won an ASCAP for the TV series score.
                                     TV

Kane (rental)

The Simpsons Theme (1991)   2'
     2[incl pic] 2 2 2 – 4 3 3 1 – tmp+2 – hp – str
     Christopher Bankey, arr.
                                     TV

Warner (rental)

Music from Spider-Man   5'
     2 1 3[1.2.bcl] 1 – 4 3 3 1 – tmp+4 – pf – str
     perc: sus cym, bongos, brake dr, gong, bells, sd, mark tree, hi-hat.
     Includes: Main Title and Farewell
     John Wasson, arr.
                                     Films/Halloween

Leonard

Spider-Man: Suite (2004)   6.5'
    3[1.afl.pic] 3[1.2.Eh] 3[1.2.bcl] 3[1.2.cbn] –
    4 4[(#4)] 4[(#4)] 1 – tmp+4 – 2 hp[(#2)], pf[cel]
    – str
    perc: glock, chimes, bongos, hihat, tamtam, sus cym, cym, sd, field drum, bd, toms, 2 hand drums, brake drum.
    SATB Chorus. Includes: Main Title; Declared Love; Finale.

                              Animals/Films
T&V (rental)

Elgar, Edward   1857-1934

Chanson de matin, Op. 15, No. 2   3'
    2 2 2 2 – 2 0 0 0 – hp – str
                      Popular Classics
Kalmus; Novello (rental)

Chanson de nuit, Op. 15, No. 1   4'
    2 2 2 2 – 2 0 0 0 – hp – str
                      Popular Classics
Kalmus; Novello (rental)

Cockaigne Concert Overture Op. 40   13'
(In London Town)
    3[1.2/pic] 2 2 3[1.2.cbn] – 4 4 3 1 – tmp+5 – (org) – str
    perc: sd, tri, slgh-bells, tambn, cym, bd.
                      Popular Classics
Boosey (rental); Kalmus

Enigma Variations, Op. 36: Nimrod   3'
    2 2 2 3 – 4 3 3 1 – tmp – str
                      Popular Classics
Kalmus; Novello (rental)

Froissart Overture, Op. 19   12'
    2 2 2 3 – 4 2 3 0 – tmp+(1) – hp – str
    perc: (cym).
                      Popular Classics
Kalmus; Novello (rental)

In the South: Concert Overture, Op. 50   20'
    3[1.2.3/pic] 3[1.2.Eh] 3 3 – 4 3 3 1 – tmp+2 – 2hp – str
    perc: tri, sd, glock, cym, bd.
                      Popular Classics
Kalmus; Novello (rental)

Nursery Suite   24'
    2[incl pic] 2 2 2 – 4 2 3 1 – tmp+perc – hp – str
                      Popular Classics
Kalmus; Novello (rental)

Pomp and Circumstance March No.1   6'
in D Major, Op. 39
    4[1.2.pic.opt pic2] 2 3[1.2.bcl] 3[1.2.cbn] – 4 4 3 1 – tmp+5 – 2hp, org – str
    perc: sd, tri, tambn, slgh-bells, cym, bd, (glock).
                 Popular Classics/Celebration
Boosey (rental); Kalmus

Pomp and Circumstance March No.1   6'
in D Major, Op. 39
    2 2 2 2 – 4 2 3 1 – tmp+2 – str
    perc: tri, tambn, sd, cym, bd.
    Edition for youth or community orchestras.
    William Ryden, arr.
                 Popular Classics/Celebration
Kalmus

Sea Pictures, Op. 37   23'
                    (4' 5' 4' 6')
    2 2 2 3[1.2.cbn] – 4 2 3 1 – tmp+2 – hp, (org) – str
    perc: bongo, sus cym, bd.
    Solo Alto. Includes: Sea Slumber Song; In Haven; Sabbath Morning at Sea; Where Corals Lie; The Swimmer.
                      Ecology
Boosey (rental); Kalmus

The Snow, Op. 26, No. 1   8'
    2 2 2 2 – 2 0 0 0 – tmp – hp/pf, (org) – str
    SATB Chorus.
                      Christmas/Seasons
Novello (rental)

The Spanish Lady Suite   15'
    Strings   (5' 2' 3' 3' 2')
    Includes: Country Dance; Burlesco; Adagio; Sarabande; Bourree.
    Percy Young, arr.
                 Dance/Popular Classics
Novello (rental)

The Spanish Lady (concert version)   44'
    2 1 2 1 – 2 1 0 0 – 1perc – hp/pf – str
    Percy Young, arr.
                      Popular Classics
Novello (rental)

Wand of Youth Suite No. 1, Op. 1a   18'
    2[incl pic] 2 2 2 – 4 2 3 1 – tmp+2 – hp – str
                              Popular Classics
    Kalmus; Novello (rental)

Wand of Youth Suite No. 2, Op. 1b   15'
    2[incl pic] 2 2 2 – 4 2 3 1 – tmp+2 – hp – str
                              Popular Classics
    Kalmus; Novello (rental)

Ellington, Edward Kennedy (Duke)   1899-1974

Black, Brown and Beige   35'
    2[incl pic] 2[1.Eh] 3[1.2.bcl] 2 – asx – 4 3 3 1 –
    tmp+perc,drumset – hp, pf, jazz bass – str
    Jeff Tyzik, arr.
                              Jazz
    Schirmer (rental)

Black, Brown and Beige: Suite   18'
    3[1.2.pic/afl] 2 3[1.2.bcl/bsx] 3[1.2.cbn] – asx, bsx
    – 4 4 3 1 – tmp+3 [drumset] – hp – str
    Includes: Black (A Work Song); Brown (Come
    Sunday); Beige (Light).
    Maurice Peress, arr.
                              Jazz
    Schirmer (rental)

Caravan   3.5'
    1 1 1 1 + reed1(fl, cl) + reed2(cl, bcl) +
    reed3(fl, cl) + reed4(Eh) – 2 3 3 0 –
    tmp, vib, marim, 2conga – hp, pf, gtr – str
    Morton Gould, arr.
                          Jazz/Travel
    Schirmer (rental)

Duke Ellington! Medley for Orchestra   8'
    3[1.2.3/pic] 2 2 2 – 4 3 3 1 – tmp+3 – pf – str
    perc: drumset, bells, vib, xyl.
    Includes: Don't Get Around Much; Do Nothin' Til
    You Hear From Me; Sophisticated Lady; It Don't
    Mean A Thing, If It Ain't Got That Swing.
    Calvin Custer, arr.
                              Jazz
    Belwin

Ellington Portrait   16'
    3[1.2.pic] 2[1.Eh] 3[1.2.bcl] 2 – (asx) – 4 3 3 1
    – tmp+2, drumset – hp, pf, jazz bass – str
    Includes: Caravan; Sophisticated Lady; Rockin' in
    Rhythm; Mood Indigo; the "C" Jam Blues; Prelude
    to a Kiss; It Don't Mean a Thing, If It Ain't Got
    That Swing.
    Jeff Tyzik, arr.
                              Jazz
    Schirmer (rental)

The Golden Broom   15'
    and the Green Apple
    3[incl pic] 3[incl Eh] 3[incl bcl] 3[incl cbn] –
    4 4 4 1 – tmp+perc, drumset – hp – str
    Includes: Intoduction; Stanza I; Stanza II;
    Stanza III; Coda.
                              Jazz
    Schirmer (rental)

Grand Slam Jam   8'
    2 2[incl Eh] 2[incl bcl] 2 – 2asx, 2tsx, bsx –
    4 4 3 1 – tmp+2 [incl drumset] – hp – str
    Solo Piano, Clarinet, Trumpet.
    Edited by Maurice Peress.
    Luther Henderson, arr.
                          Jazz/Sports
    Schirmer (rental)

Harlem   18'
    3[incl pic] 2[incl Eh] 2[incl bcl] 2 –
    2asx, 2tsx, bsx – 4 3 3 1 – tmp+3 – hp – str
    Luther Henderson & Maurice Peress, arr.
                              Jazz
    Schirmer (rental)

I Got It Bad (and That Ain't Good)   3'
    2 1 2 1 – 2 3 2 1 – tmp+2 – (pf) – str
    Marty Gold, arr.
                              Valentine
    Warner (POP); EMS or Luck's (rental)

Liberian Suite   22'
    0 0 0 0 – 2asx, 2tsx, bsx – 0 5 3 0 –
    tmp+perc, drumset – gtr, pf – vn, db
    David Berger, arr.
                              Jazz
    Schirmer (rental)

Mood Indigo (5 brass setting)   5'
    1 1[Eh] 1 1 – 2asx(fl), 2tsx(2fl) – 0 3 2 0 –
    drumset – hp, pf, gtr – str
    Morton Gould, arr.
                              Jazz
    Schirmer (rental)

Mood Indigo (6 brass setting) — 5'
  1 1[Eh] 1 1 – asx(cl), asx(bcl), tsx(cl), bsx(ob, cl) – 0 3 3 0 – drumset – hp, pf, gtr – str
  Morton Gould, arr.
                              Jazz
  Schirmer (rental)

New World A-Comin' — 10'
  2 3[1.2.Eh] 4[1.2.3.bcl] 2 – 4 4 3 1 – tmp+2 – pf, jazz bass – str
  Luther Henderson, arr.
  Jeff Tyzik, editor
                              Jazz/New Year
  Schirmer

New World A-Comin' — 10'
  2[incl pic] 2 3[1.2.bcl] 2 – 4 4 3 1 – tmp+3 – hp – str
  Solo Piano and Optional Dance Band.
  Maurice Peress, arr.
                              Jazz/New Year
  Schirmer (rental)

Night Creature — 17'
  2 2 2[incl bcl] 2 – 2asx, 2tsx, (bsx) – 4 4 3 1 – tmp+2 – hp – str
  Portrays history of African-Americans through their music.
  David Berger, arr.
                              Black History Month/Jazz
  Schirmer (rental)

Night Creature for Jazz Band and Orchestra — 17'
  3 2 4[1.2.3.bcl] 2 – 4 4 3 1 – tmp+2 – hp – str
  Solo Piano.
  Gunther Schuller, arr.
                              Black History Month/Jazz
  Schirmer (rental)

Non-Violent Integration for Jazz Band and Orchestra — 6'
  Jazz band: 2asx, tsx(cl), bsx – 4tpt, 3tbn – pf
  Orch: 4[1.2.3.pic] 3[1.2.Eh] 4[1.2.3.bcl] 4[1.2.3.cbn] – 6 4 4 1 – str
  Available outside USA only.
  Calvin Jackson, arr.
                              Jazz
  Schirmer

The River — 30'
  2[incl pic] 2[incl Eh] 2[incl bcl] 2 – 4 3 3 1 – tmp+2 – hp, pf – str
  Ron Collier, arr.
  Ballet.
                              Dance/Jazz
  Schirmer (rental)

Satin Doll (instrumental version) — 3'
  2 2 2 2 – 4 4 3 0 – 1perc – pf – str
  Calvin Jackson, arr.
                              Jazz
  Schirmer (rental)

Satin Doll (vocal version) — 3'
  2 2 2 2 – 4 3 3 1 – tmp+2 – hp – str
  Chuck Israels, arr.
                              Jazz
  Schirmer (rental)

Solitude — 3'
  hp, cel – str
  Morton Gould, arr.
                              Jazz
  Schirmer (rental)

Sophisticated Lady — 4'
  hp, cel – 7str
  Morton Gould, arr.
                              Jazz
  Kalmus

Highlights from Sophisticated Ladies — 7.5'
  2 2 3[incl bcl] 2 – 2asx, tsx, bsx – 2 3 3 1 – tmp+2 – gtr, elec bass – str
  Bob Lowden, arr.
                              Jazz
  Belwin (POP); EMS or Luck's (rental)

Three Black Kings:
  Concerto Grosso version — 15'
  3[1.2.pic] 3[1.2.Eh] 3[1.2.bcl] 3[1.2.cbn] – 4 4[all/flug; (#4)] 4[(#4)] 1 – tmp+2 – hp, pf, gtr – str
  A musical depiction of Balthazaar. Includes: King of the Magi, King Solomon, and Martin Luther King.
  Luther Henderson, arr.
                              Black History Month/Christmas/Jazz
  Schirmer (rental)

Three Black Kings: *19'*
   Soloist with Orchestra version
   3[1.2.pic] 3[1.2.Eh] 3[1.2.bcl] 3[1.2.cbn] – 4
   4[all/flug; (#4)] 4[(#4)] 1 – tmp+2 – hp, pf, gtr – str
   Solo Eb, Bb, or C Instrument and Jazz Bass. A
   musical depiction of Balthazaar. Includes: King of
   the Magi, King Solomon, and Martin Luther King.
   Luther Henderson, arr.
                                      Black History Month/
                                            Christmas/Jazz

   Schirmer (rental)

Three Black Kings: *19'*
   Ballet for Orchestra
   3[1.2.pic] 3[1.2.Eh] 3[1.2.bcl] 3[1.2.cbn] –
   4 4[all/flug; (tp4)] 4[(tbn4)] 1 – tmp+2 –
   hp, pf, gtr – str
   A musical depiction of Balthazaar. Includes: King
   of the Magi; King Solomon; Martin Luther King.
   Maurice Peress, arr.
                                      Black History Month/
                                    Christmas/Dance/Jazz

   Schirmer (rental)

Tribute to the Duke   *5.5'*
   2 1 2 1 – 2 3 2 1 – tmp+perc – pf – str
   Includes: Caravan; In a Sentimental Mood;
   Sophisticated Lady.
   Marty Gold, arr.
                                                      Jazz

   Warner (POP); Luck's (rental)

Ellington, Edward K. (Duke)   1899-1974
Mills, Irving   1894-1985

It Don't Mean a Thing (If it Ain't Got That Swing)   *3'*
   2 2 2 1 – 4 3 3 1 – 2perc – elec bs, pf – str
   perc: drumset, xyl.
   Chuck Sayre, arr.
                                             Jazz/Popular Song

   Warner (POP); Luck's (rental)

Ellington, Edward K. (Duke)   1899-1974
Strayhorn, Billy   1915-1967

Deep South Suite: *5'*
   Happy Go Lucky Local
   2 2 2 2 – 4 3 3 1 – tmp+2 – str
   Chuck Israels, arr.
                                                  Jazz

   Schirmer (rental)

The Essential Ellington: *12'*
   Music of Ellington and Strayhorn
   2 2 2 2 – 4 3 3 1 – tmp+3 – hp, pf, elec bass – str
   Includes: Come Sunday (Introduction), Take the A
   Train, Lush Life, Satin Doll, Perdido, Come
   Sunday, Things Ain't What They Used to Be.
   Jeff Tyzik, arr.
                                                  Jazz

   Schirmer (rental)

Ellington, Mercer   1919-1996

Things Ain't What They Used to Be   *10'*
   2[1.pic] 2 4[1.2.3.bcl] 3[1.2.cbn] – 5 4 3 1 –
   vib, drumset – (pf) – str
   Calvin Jackson, arr.
                                                  Jazz

   Schirmer (rental)

Elliot, Jack &   1927-2001
Ferguson, Allyn   1924-2010

Theme from Charlie's Angels   *3'*
   2[1/pic.2/pic.3/pic] 3 3[1/tsx.2.3] 3 –
   3 4[all dbl flug] 3 1 – perc[incl drumset] –
   pf, gtr, elec bs – str
   Henry Mancini, arr.
                                                      TV

   Kane (rental)

Ellis, David   1933-

Carols for an Island Christmas, Op. 34   *6'*
   1 1 1 1 – 0 2 0 0 – tmp+1 – pf – str
   SATB Chorus, Boys' Choir. Chorus parts for sale.
                                                 Christmas

   Novello (rental)

Ellstein, Abraham   1907-1963

Haftorah
Strings
                                   Hanukkah
Schirmer (rental)

Ode to the King of Kings
2 2 2 2 – 4 2 3 1 – tmp+perc – str
Solo Soprano, Baritone; SATB Chorus.
                                   Hanukkah
Schirmer (rental)

Retsei
1 1 1 1 – 2 0 0 0 – tmp – hp – str
Solo Tenor; SATB Chorus.
                                   Hanukkah
Schirmer (rental)

Sh'Ma Yisroel   5'
1 1 1 1 – 2 0 0 0 – tmp – hp – str
Solo Tenor.
                                   Hanukkah
Schirmer (rental)

Vli jeru sholayim ircho
1 1 1 1 – 2 0 0 0 – tmp – hp – str
Solo Voice.
                                   Hanukkah
Schirmer (rental)

Yismechu
1 1 1 1 – 2 0 0 0 – perc – hp – str
                                   Hanukkah
Schirmer (rental)

Enesco, Georges   1881-1955

Roumanian Rhapsody No. 1   11'
in A Major, Op. 11
3[1.2.3/pic] 3[1.2.Eh] 2 2 – 4 4 3 1 – tmp+3 –
2hp – str
perc: cym, sd, tri
                                Popular Classics
Kalmus; Peer (rental)

Erb, Donald   1927-2008

Christmas Music   7'
3 2 2 2 – 2 2 1 0 – 2perc – hp, hpsd, pf, cel – str
                                   Christmas
Presser (rental)

Klangfarbenfunk   16'
2 2 3 3 – 2 2 2 1 – tmp+perc – hp(ampd) – str
Rock group: (gtr), (afl), Fender bass, (tsx), hn, tbn,
elec org or elec pf, perc, and electronic tape.
                              Instrumental Pops
Presser (rental)

Music for a Festive Occasion   7'
3 2 3 3 – 4 3 3 1 – tmp+3 – cel/pf – str – elec tape,
and 20-40 audience volunteers with water goblets
imitating glass harmonicas.
                              Celebration/Novelty
Presser (rental)

Errázuriz, Sebastián   1975-

La Caravana   8'
2[incl pic] 2 2 2 – 4 2 3 1 – tmp+3 – str
                              International (Chile)
Filarmonika (rental)

Eskola, Jari 1973-

Commodore 64 Medley: A Medley of 9.5'
Classic 1980's Computer Game Themes Arranged
for Symphony Orchestra
          (1' 1' 1.5' 1.5' .5' 1.5' 1' .5' 1')
3[1.2.3/pic] 3[1.2.Eh] 3[1.2.bcl] 3[1.2.cbn]
– 4 3 3 1 – tmp+3 – hp, pf/synth/cel – str
perc: sd, tam-tam, tri, cym, tubular bells, glock, elec toms, xyl, sus cym, tambn, tom-tom (med/low), tri.
Includes: Defender of the Crown (Jim Cuomo, 1985); Commando (Rob Hubbard, 1985); Delta (Rob Hubbard, 1987); The Way of the Explodiing Fist (Neil Brennan, 1985); The Last Ninja (Ben Daglish, 1987); M.U.L.E. (Michael Land, 1983); Monty on the Run (Rob Hubbard, 1985); Defender of the Crown Reprise). Includes Commodore 64 cues and fillers (Jari Eskola, 2006).
Available on youtube: original version (live, audience recording): www.youtube.com/watch?v=ji2D83sLJmc and concert performance (steadycam): www.youtube.com/watch?v=MvIozhK9Kgk.
                                Video Games

Eskola (rental)

Esplá, Oscar 1886-1976

Fiesta: Suite de danzas
   4[1.2.3.pic] 3[incl Eh] 3[incl bcl] 3[incl cbn] –
   4 3 3 1 – tmp+perc – hp – str
                           Dance/International

Schirmer (rental)

Esposito, Michele 1855-1929

Irish Suite 21'
   2 2 2 2 – 4 2 3 1 – tmp+perc – str
                        St. Patrick/International

Schirmer (rental)

Estefan, Gloria 1957-

Gloria Estefan: Her Greatest Hits 7'
   3[1.2.pic] 2 2 1 – 4 3 3 1 – tmp+perc – elec bass
   – pf – str
   Chuck Sayre, arr.
                                  Popular Song

Warner (POP); EMS or Luck's (rental)

Reach 4.5'
   2 1 3[1.2.bcl] 1 – 4 3 3 1 – tmp+perc – pf – str
   Commissioned for 1996 Olympics.
   Calvin Custer, arr.
                                        Sports

Warner (POP); EMS or Luck's (rental)

Evans, Dale 1912-2001

Happy Trails to You (1952) 4'
   2 2 3[1.2.bcl] 2 – 4 4 3 1 – tmp+3 – hp, pf, gtr – str
   perc: drumset, temple blk, sus cym, glock, marim.
   Optional Voice. The Roy Rogers Show theme.
                            Americana/Travel/TV

T&V (rental)

F

Fahrbach, Jr., Philipp   1843-1894

Midnight Elopement Galop   5'
1 2 2 2 – 2 2 1 0 – perc – str
                                       New Year/Valentine
Kalmus

Fain, Sammy & Lawrence, Jack

Once Upon a Dream   2'
(1 1 3[1.2.(bcl)] 1) – (2 2 2 1) – tmp+2 – pf – str
perc: sd, bd, sus cym, tri, glock.
From the Walt Disney film *Sleeping Beauty*.
Steven L. Rosenhaus, arr.
                                                 Films
Leonard (rental)

Faith, Percy   1908-1976

Quia, Quia (Kee-a, Kee-a)   2'
2 2 3[1.2.(bcl)] 1 – (asx, tsx) – 2 2 2 1 – 2perc – pf – str
perc: drumset, maracas or bongos.
                                             Popular Song
Leonard (rental)

Falla, Manuel de   1876-1946

El amor brujo (second version 1925)   24'
2[1.2/pic] 1[1/(Eh)] 2 1 – 2 2 0 0 – tmp+1 – pf – str
perc: chimes (a, d', e')
Optional Solo Medium Voice. A ballet; critical edition (1999).
                                       Halloween/Dance/Popular Classics
Chester (rental)

El amor brujo (first version 1915)   34'
1[incl pic] 1 0 0 – 1 1 0 0 – 1perc – pf – str
Optional Solo Medium Voice. A ballet.
                                       Halloween/Dance/Popular Classics
Chester (rental)

El amor brujo: Ritual Fire Dance   5'
2[1.2/pic] 1 2 1 – 2 2 0 0 – tmp – pf – str
                                       Halloween/Dance/Popular Classics
Chester (rental)

El amor brujo: Ritual Fire Dance   4'
3[1.2.pic] 2 2 2 – 4 2 3 0 – tmp+perc – str
William Ryden, arr.
                                       Halloween/Dance/Popular Classics
Kalmus

El amor brujo: Chanson du feu follet   3'
1 0 2 0 – 2 0 0 0 – pf – str
Solo Medium Voice. Text by Martinez Sierra.
                                       Halloween/Dance/Popular Classics
Chester (rental)

El amor brujo: 11'
Pantomime and Ritual Fire Dance(1915)
pf – str
                                       Halloween/Dance/Popular Classics
Chester (rental)

El Corregidor y la Molinera   43'
1[incl pic] 1 1 1 – 1 1 0 0 – pf – str
Solo Mezzo-Soprano. This is the original version of *El sombrero de tres picos*.
                                       International/Popular Classics
Chester (rental)

Danse rituelle du feu (Dance of Fire)   4'
2[incl pic] 1 2 1 – 2 2 0 0 – tmp – pf – str
Leopold Stokowski, arr.
                                       Dance
Stokowski (rental)

Fuego fatuo   45'
2[incl pic] 1[incl Eh] 2 2 – 2 2 3 0 – tmp+perc – hp, pf[4hand] – str
Antoni Ros Marba, arr.
                                       International
Chester (rental)

Homenajes 18'
    3[incl pic] 3[incl Eh] 3[incl bcl] 3[1.2.cbn] –
    4 3 3 0 – tmp+perc – cel, hp – str
                                                          International
Chester (rental)

Noches en los jardines de España 23'
    (Nights in the Gardens of Spain) (10' 5' 8')
    3[1.2.3/pic] 3[1.2.Eh] 2 2 – 4 2 3 1 – tmp+2 –
    hp, cel – str
    Alternate: 2[incl pic] 2[incl Eh] 2 2 – 2 2 0 0 –
    tmp+perc – hp – str
    Solo Piano. Includes: Enel Generalife (In the
    gardens of the Generalife); Danza lejana (A Dance
    Is Heard in the Distance); En los jardines de la
    Sierra de Córdoba (In the Gardens of the Sierra de
    Córdoba).
                                                          International
Chester (rental)

Récit du pêcheur and Pantomime 8'
    2[1.pic] 1 2 1 – 2 2 0 0 – tmp – pf – str
    Solo Mezzo-Soprano.
                                                          International
Chester (rental)

Sept Chansons populaires espagnoles 12'
    (Seven Popular Spanish Songs)
    2 2[1.Eh] 3[1.2.bcl] 2 – 2 0 0 0 – tmp+1 – hp – str
    Solo Medium Voice (Sop or Mezzo-Sop).
    Halffter, arr.
                                                          International
Chester (rental)

El Sombrero de tres picos 35'
    (The Three Cornered Hat)
    3[1/pic2.2.3/pic1] 3[1.2.Eh] 2 2 – 4 3 3 1 – tmp+5
    – hp, cel, pf – str
        perc: bd, cym, sus cym, sd, tri, tamtam, glock, xyl, cast.
    Solo Mezzo Soprano. A ballet in two parts.
                                                Popular Classics/
                                               International/Dance
Chester (rental); Kalmus

El Sombrero de tres picos (Three-Cornered Hat): 14'
    Suite I *(Scenes and Dances from Part I)*
    1[1/pic] 2[1.2/Eh] 2 2 – 2 2 0 0 – tmp+1 –
    hp, pf – str
        perc: xyl, sus cym, glock.
    Includes: Introduction-Afternoon; Dance of the
    Miller's Wife (Fandango); The Corregidor; The
    Grapes.
                                                Popular Classics/
                                             International/Dance
Chester (rental); Kalmus

El Sombrero de tres picos (Three-Cornered Hat): 13'
    Suite 2 *(three dances from Part II)*
    2[incl pic] 3[1.2.Eh] 2 2 – 4 3 3 1 – tmp+5 –
    hp, cel or pf – str
    Includes: The Neighbors; Miller's Dance; Final
    Dance.
    Kalmus edition by Nancy M. Bradburd.
                                               Popular Classics/
                                             International/Dance
Chester (rental); Kalmus

The Three-Cornered Hat: Three Dances 11'
    3[1.2.pic] 2 2 2 – 4 2 0 0 – tmp+perc – str
    Includes: Introduction; Afternoon; The Neighbor's
    Dance (Sequidillas); The Miller's Dance (Farruca).
    Steven L. Rosenhaus, arr.
                                             Popular Classics/
                                        International/Dance
Masters

La vida breve: Interlude and Spanish Dance 8'
3[1.2.pic] 3[1.2.Eh] 3[1.2.bcl] 2 – 4 2 3 1 – tmp+5 –
2hp, cel – str
    perc: glock, tri, cast, cym, bd.
                                                International/Dance
Eschig (rental)

La vida breve: Spanish Dance No. 1 4'
    2[1.pic] 1 2 1 – 2 2 2 0 – tmp+2 – str
    S. Chapelier, arr.
                                               International/Dance
Chester (rental)

Farnan, Robert   1917-2005

The Peanut Polka 5'
    2[1.pic] 1 2 1 – 2 2 3 0 – tmp+ 2 – str
    perc: sd, bd, xyl, glock, cym.
                                       Dance/Instrumental Pops
Chappell (rental)

Portrait of a Flirt 2'
    2[1.2/pic] 2[(#2)] 2 2[(#2)] – (2asx, tsx, bsx) – 2
    3[(#3)] 3 0 – tmp+2 – hp – str
    perc: glock, woodblk, tri, tambn, vib, sd.
                                             Insrumental Pops
Chappell (rental)

Farrar, John   1946-

Grease: You're the One That I Want   2'
    2 1 3[1.2.bcl] 1 – 4 3 3 1 – tmp+1 – pf, elec bass – str
    perc: drumset, bells.
    Douglas E. Wagner, arr.
                             Broadway Musicals/Valentine
  Luck's

Fauré, Gabriel   1845-1924

Pavane, Op. 50   7'
    2 2 2 2 – 2 0 0 0 – str
    Optional SATB Chorus.
                              Popular Classics
  Broude Bros; Kalmus

Pelléas et Mélisande, Op. 80   18'
                          (7' 2' 4' 5')
    2 2 2 2 – 4 2 0 0 – tmp – hp – str
    Includes: Prélude; Entr'acte: Fileuse (The Spinner);
    Sicilienne; La Mort de Mélisande (The Death of
    Melisande).
                              Popular Classics
  Kalmus

Felder, David   1953-
Feller, Sherm   1918-1994

Linebacker Music   7'
    3 3 3 3 – 4 3 3 1 – tmp+2 – pf – str
    Simeone, arr.
                                   Sports
  Presser (rental)

Snow, Snow, Beautiful Snow
    3[1.2.pic] 2 2 2 – 4 3 3 1 – tmp+perc – hp – str
    SATB Chorus.
    Simeone, arr.
                              Christmas/Seasons
  Shawnee (rental)

Feller, Sherm (See: Jameson, Tom)

Ferguson, Allyn (See: Elliot, Jack)

Fernandez, Agustín   1958-

Una Música Escondida   15'
    Strings
    Solo Piano.
                            International (Bolivia)
  Filarmonika (rental)

Fernandez, Caballero   1835-1906

Cielito Lindo   3'
    2 2 2 2 – 3sx – 4 3 3 0 – tmp+perc – hp – str
    Quirino Mencoza Y Cortes is the actual
    composer of this popular Mexican song.
    Some attribute it to Jose Padilla (1889-1960).
    Lang, arr.
                                   International
  Kalmus

Fiedel, Brad   1951-

The Teminator: Theme (1984)   4'
    2[1.pic] 1[Eh] 2[1.bcl] 2[1.cbn] – 4 2 3 1 – tmp+5
    – hp, prepared pf – str
    perc: lg tamtam, xyl, sus cym, sd, lg bd, anvil, 2 roto
    toms, taiko drum or lg tom.
                                     Films
  T&V (rental)

True Lies: Theme (1994)   5'
    3[1.2.pic] 3[1.2.Eh] 3[1.2.bcl] 3[1.2.cbn] – 4 3 3 1
    – tmp+3 – pf[cel] – str
    perc: cast, sd, field drum,Tumbeg[hi bongo], tambn,
    sus cym, floor toms, bd, cym.
                                     Films
  T&V (rental)

Field, John   1782-1837

Irish Concerto for Piano and Orchestra   18'
   2 2 2 2 – 2 2 0 0 – tmp – str
   Solo Piano.
                          St. Patrick/International
Schirmer (rental)

Fillmore, Henry   1881-1956

His Excellency March   3'
   1 1 2 1 – 2 2 1 0 – drumset – str
                                          Patriotic
Kalmus

Fielding, Jerry   1922-1980

The Outlaw Josey Wales: Suite (1976)   5'
   3[1.pic.pic] 2 3[1.2.bcl] 2 – 4 3 3 0 – tmp+3 –
   (hp) pf – str
   perc: sm tris us cym. 2 bd, glock, pic sd, vib, sus cym, sd,
   field drum.
                                            Films
T&V (rental)

The Wild Bunch: Suite in   12.5'
*   Two Movements (1969)*   (6.5' 6')
   3[1.2.pic] 3[1.2.Eh] 3[1.2.bcl] 3[1.2.cbn] – 4 3 3 0
   – tmp+4 – 2 hp, pf, gtr – str
   perc: glock, 2 marim, pic sd, sus cym, sd, field drum, bd,
   choke cym, 3 tuned drums, tri, fishing rod.
   Includes: Train Montage; All Fall Down.
                                           Films
T&V (rental)

Finn, William   1952-

Selections from 25th Annual Putnam   3.5'
*   County Spelling Bee*
   2 1 3[1.2.bcl] 1 – 4 3 3 1 – tmp+3 – (pf) – str
   Includes: The 25th Annual Putnam County Spelling
   Bee; My Friend, The Dictionary; Magic Foot; and
   The I Love You Song.
   Doug Wagner, arr.
                                 Broadway Musicals
Belwin

Fisher, Fred   1875-1942

Peg O' My Heart   3'
   3[incl pic] 2 2 2 – (2asx, tsx) – 4 3 3 1 – tmp+perc
   – str
   William Ryden, arr.
                                        Valentine
Kalmus

Flaherty, Stephen   1960-

Anastasia Medley   7.5'
   2 2 3[1.2.bcl] 1 – 4 3 3 1 – tmp+perc – pf – str
   Calvin Custer, arr.
   Includes: A Rumor in St. Petersburg, Journey To the
   Past, Once Upon a December, Learn To Do It and
   Paris Holds the Key (To Your Heart).
                                          Films
Warner (POP); EMS or Luck's (rental)

Anastasia: In the Dark of the Night   3.5'
   3[1.2.pic] 2 2 2 – 4 3 2 1 – perc – str
   SATB Chorus.
   Douglas Besterman, arr.
                                          Films
Kane (rental)

Anastasia: Journey to the Past   3'
   3[1.2.3/pic] 2[1.2/Eh] 3[1.2.3/bcl] 2 –
   4 3[1/flug.2/flug.3] 3 1 – tmp+perc [incl drumset]
   – hp, pf, synth – str
   Solo Soprano.
   William Brohn, arr.
                                          Films
Kane (rental)

Anastasia: Learn to Do It Waltz   2.5'
   3[1.2.pic] 2 3[1.2.bcl] 2 – 4 3 3 1 – tmp+perc –
   hp, cel – str
   Solo Soprano, Tenor, Bass.
   Douglas Besterman, arr.
                                          Films
Kane (rental)

Anastasia: Once Upon a December   3.5'
   3[1.2.pic] 3[1.2.Eh] 3[1.2.bcl] 3[1.2.cbn] – 4 3 3 1
   – tmp+perc – hp, pf/cel, synth – str
   Solo Soprano and Bass; SATB Chorus.
   Douglas Besterman, arr.
                                          Films
Kane (rental)

Anastasia: Paris Holds the Key   3'
    2[1.2/pic] 1 2 1 – 2asx, tsx, tsx/bcl, bsx – 4 3 3 0 – tmp+perc[incl drumset] – hp, pf/cel, accordion, gtr – str
    Optional Solo Voices; SATB Chorus.
    Douglas Besterman, arr.
                                                 Films
    Kane (rental)

Anastasia: A Rumor in St. Petersburg   3.5'
    3[1.2.3/pic] 3[1.2.3/Eh] 3[1.2.3/bcl] 1[1.cbn] – 4 3 3 1 – tmp+perc – hp, pf, accordion, balalaika, mandolin – str
    Includes a part for choir.
    William Brohn, arr.
                                                 Films
    Kane (rental)

Anastasia Suite
    3[1.2.3/pic] 3[1.2.Eh] 3[1.2.bcl] 3[1.2.cbn] – 4 3 3 1 – tmp+perc – hp, pf, (synth), accordion, mandolin – str
    SATB Chorus.
    Douglas Besterman, arr.
                                                 Films
    Kane (rental)

Ragtime "The Musical" Selections   6'
    3[incl pic] 1 3[incl bcl] 1 – 4 3 3 1 – tmp+perc, drumset – (pf) – str
    Includes: Ragtime; Your Daddy's Son; Wheels of a Dream.
    Kessler, arr.
                                           Films/Jazz
    Warner (POP); Luck's (rental)

Fletcher, H. Grant   1913-

An American Overture   6'
    3 2 2 2 – 4 2 3 1 – tmp+str
                                                 Patriotic
    EMI (rental)

Fogelberg, Daniel (See: Black, Charlie)

Ford, Ralph, arr.

Suite from Video Games Live   11'
    2 1 3[1.2.bcl] 1 – 4 3 3 1 – tmp+8 – synth (hp) – str
    8 percussion parts included (this may not mean the number of players needed). Includes Super Mario Brothers; Halo; Civilization IV; Bounty Hunter; and Kingdom Hearts.
                                                 Video Games
    Belwin

Foss, Lukas   1922-

Elegy for Anne Frank   7'
    0 0 (2) (2) – 1 1 1 1 – 1perc – str
    Alternate brass: 1 upper and 1 lower instrument.
    Solo Piano; Optional Narrator.
                                                 Popular Classics
    Pembroke (rental)

Foster, David W.   1949-

Quest for Camelot Selections   8'
    3[1.2.pic] 2 2 2 – 4 3 3 1 – tmp+perc – str
    Includes: Looking Thru Your Eyes; If I Didn't Love You; I Stand Alone.
    John C. Whitney, arr.
                                                 Films
    Warner

Foster, Stephen Collins   1826-1864

Beautiful Dreamer: Stephen   13.5'
Foster's America
    3 2 2 2 – 4 3 3 1 – tmp+3 – hp – str
    Includes: Beautiful Dreamer, I Dream of Jeannie, Camptown Races, and more.
    Lucas Richman, arr.
                                                 Americana/Popular Song
    LeDor (rental)

Jeannie with the Light Brown Hair   5'
    3[1.2.pic] 2 3[1.2.bcl] 3 – sx – 4 3 3 1 – tmp+perc
    – hp –str
    Lucien Cailliet, arr.
                          Americana/Popular Song
Kalmus

Old Folks At Home;   3'
    Love's Old Sweet Song; Palms
    1 1 2 1 – 2 2 1 0 – tmp+perc – str
    Solo Trombone.
                          Americana/Popular Song
Kalmus

A Stephen Foster Overture   6'
    3[incl pic] 2 2 2 – 4 3 3 1 – tmp+perc – str
    Robert Wendel, arr.
                                Americana
Wendel (rental)

Frackenpohl, Arthur   1924-

Largo and Allegro   8'
    Solo Horn – Strings
                              Popular Classics
Schirmer (rental)

Rondo Marziale   5'
    3[1.2.pic] 2 3[1.2.bcl] 3[1.2.cbn] – 4 3 3 1 –
    tmp+perc – str
                              Popular Classics
Schirmer (rental)

Suite Concertino   9'
    Solo Trumpet – Strings
                              Popular Classics
Schirmer (rental)

Franck, César   1822-1890

Le chasseur maudit   14'
    (The Accursed Huntsman)
    3[1.2.pic] 2 2 4 – 4[2tp, 2crt] 4 3 1 – tmp+3 – str
    perc: chimes, cym, bd, tri.
                              Popular Classics
Kalmus; Lemoine (rental)

Francois, C. (See: Revaux, J.)

Frank, Gabriela Lena   1972-

Three Latin-American Dances   16'
    for Orchestra
    3[incl pic] 3[1.2.Eh] 3[1.2.bcl] 3 – 4 3 3 0 – tmp+4
    – hp, pf – str
                              Dance/International
Schirmer (rental)

Frazelle, Kenneth   1955-

The Swans at Pongo Lake   8'
    3 3 3 3 – 4 3 3 1 – tmp+1 – hp – str
    From the suite *Postcards from North Carolina* by
    6 North Carolina composers. Uses sounds of swans
    and geese in a wildlife refuge.
                              Animals/Ecology
Subito (rental)

Freyhan, Michael   1940-

Toy Symphony   7'
    2 0 2 0 – 0 2 0 0 – perc, toys – str
                              Christmas
Novello (rental)

Fried, Gerald   1928-

Roots: Suite (1977)   35'
    2[sop rec,afl/pic] 2[1.Eh] 2 2 – 4 3 3 1 – tmp+5 –
    gtr[or banjo] harmonica[bs harmonica] – str
    perc: drumset, spoons, washboard, cym, sus cym, conga,
    African gogo bells, African rattles, Dahka Da Bello,
    maracas, woodblk, sandpaper block, sm hand drum, sd,
    bd, rattles, tambn, glock, marim, xyl, chimes.
    Includes: Main Title; New Home; Gathering Mob;
    Walk to Manhood; Kizzy & Chicken George;
    Surrendor/Freedom; Memories; Knoxville Riots &
    Generations.
                              Black History Month
T&V (rental)

Friedhofer, Hugo   1901-1981

An Affair to Remember: The Proposal (1957)   2.5'
3[1.2.afl] 2[1.Eh] 4[1.2.3.bcl] 2 – 3 0 0 0 – 1perc[vib] – hp, pf – str
                               Films/Valentines
T&V (rental)

The Best Years of Our Lives: Suite (1946)   12'
2[1.pic] 2[1.Eh] 2 2[1.cbn] – 4 3 3 1 – tmp+4 – hp, pf[cel] – str
perc: cym, sus cym, marim, xyl, glock, vib, tamtam, bd, 2 temple block.
Includes: Main Title; Homecoming; Homer Goes Upstairs; Wilma's Theme; Citation; Bomber Graveyard; Nightmare; End Title.
Won the Oscar for Best Score of the Year.
                               Films/Valentines
T&V (rental)

The Bishop's Wife: Ice Skater's Waltz (1947)   2.5'
3[1.2.pic] 2 2 – 3 2 3 1 – tmp+3 – hp – str
perc: glock, xyl, chimes, tri, sd, woodblk, sus cym.
                       Christmas/Dance/Films
T&V (rental)

The Mark of Zorro: Suite (1940)   4.5'
3[1.2.pic] 3[1.2.Eh] 3[1.2.bcl] 2 – 4 3 3 1 – tmp+4 – hp, Spanish gtr – str
perc: glock, tri, sd, bd, tambn, castanets, sus cym, cym.
Composed the film score with Alfred Newman, but often uncredited. Nominated for the 1941 Oscar for Best Music.
                                         Films
T&V (rental)

Friml, Rudolf   1879-1972

Melodie   3'
1 1 2 1 – 2 2 1 0 – tmp – str
Schmid, arr.
                                   Popular Classics
Kalmus

Medley from The Firefly   7'
2[incl pic] 2[incl Eh] 2 2 – 2asx, 2tsx – 4 3 3 1 – perc – hp – str
Includes: Allah's Holiday; The Bubble; Giannina Mia; In Sapphire Seas; Rackety Coo; Something Seems; Tingle-ingling; Sympathy; When a Maid Comes; Knocking at Your Heart. This operetta produced by Oscar Hammerstein in 1912 was made into a film in 1937 featuring Jeannette MacDonald.
                         Broadway Musicals/Films
Schirmer (rental)

Frizzell, John

Alien Resurrection (1997): Main Titles
3 3[1.2.Eh] 3[1/Eb.2.bcl] 3[1.2.cbn] – 8[2+6tubens] 3 4[2+2] 1 – tmp+perc – 2 hp – str
SA Choir.
                                               Films
Kane (rental)

Fučik, Julius   1872-1916

Entrance of the Gladiators, Op. 68   4'
2[1.pic] (2) 2 (2) – 4 2 3[opt#2] 0 – 2perc – str
perc: sd, bd.
Clark McAlister, arr.
                                            Sports
Kalmus

Florentiner Marsch, Op. 214   4'
2[1.pic] 1 2 1 – 2 2 3 0 – perc – pf –str
Hartmann, arr.
                                 Instrumental Pops
Kalmus

Unter der Admiralsflagge   5'
(Under the Admiral's Flag), Op. 82
3[incl pic] 2 3[incl bcl] 2 – 4 3 3 1 – tmp+3 – str
Jerome Cohen, arr.
                                 Instrumental Pops
Schirmer (rental)

G

Gabrieli, Giovanni — 1558-1613

Canzon XVI — 3.5'
  2 2[1.Eh] 2 2 – 4 3 3 1 – tmp – str
  Jeff Tyzik, arr.
  Popular Classics
Schirmer (rental)

The Novello Book of Carols: — 3'
  O Magnum Misterium
  0 0 0 0 – 2 2 3 1
  Solo Voice.
  William Llewellyn, arr.
  Christmas
Novello (rental)

Gade, Jacob — 1879-1963

Jalousie (Jealousy) — 6.5'
  2[incl pic] 3[incl Eh] 3[incl bcl] 2 – 4 3 3 0 – tmp+Latin perc – hp, cel, pf – str
  Key of Eb.
  Carmon Dragon, arr.
  Dance
Dragon (rental)

Jalousie (Jealousy) — 4'
  2 2 2 2 – 2asx, tsx – 4 3 3 1 – tmp+3 – pf – str
  F. Campbell-Watson, arr.
  Dance
Warner (rental); Luck's (rental)

Jalousie (Jealousy) — 4'
  1 1 2 1 – 2 3 2 0 – 2perc – pf – str
  perc: sd, bd.
  Solo Voice. Key of C minor. Piano/Conductor score.
  Ken Macomber, arr.
  Dance
Harms (rental)

Tango jalousie (Tango tzigane) — 4'
  3[incl pic] 2 2 2 – 4 2 3 1 – tmp+perc – str
  Peter Ettrup Larsen, arr.
  Dance/International
Schirmer (rental)

Galindo, Blas — 1910-1993

Sones de mariachi — 8'
  3[1.2.pic] 3[1.2.Eh] 4[1.2.Ebcl.bcl] 3 – 4 3 3 1 – tmp+3 – hp – str
  perc: cym, sd, td, bd, marac, xyl, guiro.
  International
EMM (rental)

Galvin, Bob (See: Roylance, Dave)

Gardel, Carlos — 1887-1935

Tango: Por una Cabeza — 4'
  3 3[1.2.3/Eh] 3[1.2.3/bcl] 3[1.2.3/cbn] – 4 0 0 0 – tmp+2 hp, pf/cel, (accordion) str
  perc: sm tambn, sm tri.
  Solo Violin. Written for violinist Itzhak Perlman.
  Signature Edition.
  John T. Williams, arr.
  Dance
Leonard; Luck's

Scent of a Woman: Por una Cabeza — 4'
  2[1.2/pic] 2 2 2 – 4 4 3 1 – tmp+perc – hp, pf/cel – str
  John Neufeld, arr.
  Dance/Films
Kane (rental)

Gardner, John — 1917-

Overture Half-Holiday, Op. 52 — 4'
  2 1 3 1 – 2 2 1 0 – tmp+perc – str
  Holidays
Novello (rental)

Garner, Erroll   1921-1977

Misty   3.5'
 cl – drum set – pf, gtr – str
 Solo Clarinet.
 Calvin Custer, arr.
      Popular Song/Valentine
 Warner (POP); EMS or Luck's (rental)

Misty   3.5'
 2 1 2 1 – 2 3 2 1 – tmp+perc – pf – str
 Marty Gold, arr.
      Popular Song/Valentine
 Warner

Misty   3'
 2 2 2 1 – 4 3 3 1 – tmp+perc – elec bass – str
 Chuck Sayre, arr.
      Popular Song/Valentine
 Warner

Garrido-Lecca, Celso   1926-

Retablos Sinfónicos   20'
 3[incl pic] 3[incl Eh] 3[incl bcl] 3[incl cbn] –
 4 3 3 1 – tmp+4 – hp, pf – str
 Score is available for purchase.
      International (Peru)
 Filarmonika (rental)

Secuencias (Sequences)   13'
 2[incl pic] 2[incl Eh] 2[incl bcl] 2 – 2 2 0 0 –
 tmp+perc – hp, pf – str
 Solo Violin.
      International (Peru)
 Filarmonika (rental)

Garrido-Lecca, Gonzalo   1975-

Arcano (Arcane)   10'
 Strings
      International (Peru)
 Filarmonika (rental)

Toccata Op.1   7'
 3 3[incl Eh] 3[incl bcl] 3[incl cbn] – 4 3 3 1 –
 tmp+2 – pf – str
 Score is available for purchase.
      International (Peru)
 Filarmonika (rental)

Garrop, Stacy   1969-

Thunderwalker   12.5'
 2 2 2 2 – 2 1 2 0 – tmp+2 – pf – str
      Weather
 Presser (rental)

Gauntlett, Henry John   1805-1876
Mann, Arthur Henry   1850-1929

The Novello Book of Carols: 3'
 Once in Royal David's City (Carol #59)
 2 2 2 2 – 2 2 3 1 – tmp+3 – str
 Solo Voice.
 Wells, arr.
      Christmas
 Novello (rental)

Geehl, Henry   1881-1961

A Comedy Overture
 2[incl pic] 2 2 2 – 4 3 1 0 – tmp+perc – hp – str
      Instrumental Pops
 ASH (rental)

Folk Dance Suite   7'
 2 1 2 2 – 2 2 3 0 – tmp+perc – str
      Dance
 ASH (rental)

Overture française
 2 2 2 2 – 4 2 3 0 – tmp+perc – hp, cel – str
      International
 ASH (rental)

Suite Espagnole   18'
 2[incl 2 pic] 2 2 2 – 2 2 3 0 – tmp+perc – str
      International
 ASH (rental)

German, Edward   1862-1936
[born German Edward Jones]

Coronation March and Hymn   5'
2 2 2 2 – 4 4 3 1 – tmp+perc – hp, org – str
                                     International Pops
Kalmus; Novello (rental)

Gypsy Suite: Four Characteristic Dances   12'
2[1.2/pic] 2 2 2 – 4 2 3 0 – tmp+perc – hp – str
Includes: Valse-Lonely Life; Allegro di Bravura;
Menuetto-Love Duet; Tarantella.
                                      International
Novello (rental)

Richard III: Overture   9'
2 2 2 2 – 2 2 3 0 – tmp+perc – str
                                         Films
Kalmus, Novello (rental)

Three Dances: Henry VIII   8'
2[incl pic] 2 2 2 – 2 2 3 0 – tmp+3 – str
Includes: Morris Dance; Shepherd's Dance; Torch Dance.
                                         Dance
Kalmus; Novello (rental)

Valse gracieuse   9'
3 2 2 2 – 4 2 3 1 – tmp+perc – hp – str
                                         Dance
Novello (rental)

Gershwin, George   1898-1937

An American in Paris   16'
3[1.2.3/pic] 3[1.2.Eh] 3[1.2.bcl] 2 – asx, tsx, bsx –
4 3 3 1 – tmp+4 – str
perc: sd, woodblk, cym, bd, tri, 2 tomtoms, xyl, glock
F. Campbell-Watson, editor
                                 Instrumental Pops/Travel
Warner (rental); Luck's (rental)

An American in Paris Suite   10'
3[incl pic] 2 3[incl bcl] 2 – 4 3 3 1 – tmp+3 – str
John Whitney, arr.
                                 Instrumental Pops/Travel
Warner

Concerto in F Major for Piano   31'
   and Orchestra   (13' 1' 7')
3[1.2.pic] 3[1.2.Eh] 3[1.2.bcl] 2 – 4 3 3 1 – tmp+3
– str
F.Campbell-Watson, arr.
                                    Popular Classics
Warner (rental); Luck's (rental)

Crazy for You: Overture   5'
3[1.2.pic] 2 3[1.2.bcl] 1 – 4 3 3 1 – tmp+perc – str
Includes: Embraceable You; I Got Rhythm; Someone
to Watch Over Me, Shall We Dance; Stiff Upper Lip;
I'll Build a Stairway to Heaven.
Jerry Brubaker, arr.
                                       Valentine
Warner (POP); EMS or Luck's (rental)

Cuban Overture   10'
3[1.2.3/pic] 3[1.2.Eh] 3[1.2.bcl] 3[1.2.cbn] – 4 3 3 1
– tmp+6 – str
perc: xyl, glock, sd, bongos, guiro, marac, cym, woodblk, bd, claves.
                                   Instrumental Pops/
                                       Popular Classics
Warner (rental); EMS or Luck's (rental)

Embraceable You   4.5'
Solo flug[tpt] – drumset – pf, gtr – str
Calvin Custer, arr.
                                       Valentine
Warner

Fascinatin' Rhythm   7.5'
3[1.2.pic] 2 2 1 – 4 3 3 1 – perc – pf, elec bass – str
Chuck Sayre, arr.
                                       Jazz
Warner (POP); EMS or Luck's (rental)

Foggy Day   6'
2 2 2 1 – 4 3 3 1 – tmp+perc – pf, elec bass – str
Chuck Sayre, arr.
                                       Weather
Warner (POP); EMS or Luck's (rental)

Gershwin in Concert   5.5'
1 1 3[1.2.bcl] 1 – 2 2 2 1 – tmp+4 – pf – str
perc: sd, bd, cym, sus cym, hi-hat, woodblk, tri, xyl, glock.
Includes: I Got Rhythm; Someone to Watch;
'S Wonderful.
Chuck Sayre, arr.
                                   Instrumental Pops/
                                         Popular Song
Warner (POP); Luck's (rental)

I Got Rhythm   2'
    Strings
    Calvin Custer, arr.
                                        Jazz
    Warner

I Got Rhythm   2'
    3[1.2.pic] 2 2 1 – 4 3 3 1 – tmp+3 – elec bass – str
    perc: bells, drumset, cym, bd, tri.
    Chuck Sayre, arr.
                                        Jazz
    Warner

I Got Rhythm Variations for Piano   9'
    and Orchestra
    2[1.2/pic] 2[1.2/Eh] 4[1.2.3.bcl] 2 – (2asx, tsx, bsx)
    – 4 3 3 1 – tmp+3 – str
    William C. Schoenfeld, arr.
                                        Jazz
    Warner (rental); Luck's (rental)

Love Walked In   3'
    3[incl pic] 2[incl Eh] 3[incl bcl] 2 – 5sx – 4 3 3 1 –
    tmp+perc – str
    Carmen Dragon, arr.
                                        Valentine
    Dragon (rental)

Lullaby for Strings   9'
    Strings
    String quartet version is for sale
                                   Popular Classics
    Warner (rental)

Man I Love   3'
    2 1 2 1 – 2 3 2 1 – tmp+perc – pf – str
    Marty Gold, arr.
                                        Valentine
    Warner (POP); EMS or Luck's (rental)

Prelude No. 2   3'
    Strings
    Carrie Lane Gruselle, arr.
                                   Popular Classics
    Warner

Porgy and Bess Medley
    3[1.2.pic] 3[1.2.(Eh)] 3[1.2.(bcl)) 2 – 4 3 3 1 –
    tmp+perc, drumset – str
    Includes: It Ain't Necessarily So; Summertime; I Got
    Plenty O' Nuttin'; Bess, You Is My Woman; There's
    a Boat Dat's Leavin' Soon for New York.
    John C. Whitney, arr.
                                   Broadway Musicals
    Warner (POP); Luck's (rental)

Porgy and Bess: 4'
    I Got Plenty of Nuttin'
    2 2 2 2 – sx – 2 3 3 0 – perc – gtr – str
    Solo Male Voice.
    Warrington, arr.
                                   Broadway Musicals
    Warner (rental); Luck's (rental)

Porgy and Bess: 3'
    I Got Plenty of Nuttin'
    2 2 2 2 – 4 sx – 4 3 3 1 – tmp+perc – hp, gtr – str
    Key of Bb; From rehearsal 11 on it can be used as a
    vocal solo.
    Spialek, arr.
                                   Broadway Musicals
    Warner (rental); Luck's (rental)

Porgy and Bess: Summertime   2'
    2 2 2 1 – 4 3 3 1 – perc – pf – str
    Chuck Sayre, arr.
                                   Broadway Musicals/
                                         Seasons
    Warner (POP); EMS or Luck's (rental)

Porgy and Bess: Summertime   3'
    2 2 2 1 – 4 3 3 1 – perc – pf – str
    Bob Cerulli, arr.
                                   Broadway Musicals/
                                         Seasons
    Warner (POP); Luck's (rental)

Porgy and Bess: Summertime   3'
    2 2[incl Eh] 4[incl Eb, bcl] 1 – 1 0 0 0 – 1perc – pf
    – str
    Solo Soprano [in A minor or B minor]; Optional
    Choir.
                                   Broadway Musicals/
                                         Seasons
    Warner

Porgy and Bess: Summertime   3'
    drumset – pf – str
    Bert Ligon, arr.
                                   Broadway Musicals/
                                         Seasons
    Alfred

Porgy and Bess: Selections
    2 1 3[1.2.bcl] 2 – 4 3 2 1 – tmp+perc – pf – str
    Chuck Sayre, arr.
                                   Broadway Musicals
    Warner (POP); EMS or Luck's (rental)

Porgy and Bess Selections for Orchestra (1961)   11'
2[1.2/pic] 2[1.2/Eh] 3[1.2.bcl] 2 – (2asx, tsx, bsx) – 4 3 3 1 – tmp+3 – hp – str
Includes: Clara; A Woman Is a Sometime Thing; Summertime; I Got Plenty O' Nuttin'; Bess, You Is My Woman; Oh, I Can't Sit Down; There's A Boat Dat's Leavin'; It Ain't Necessarily So; Oh Lawd, I'm on My Way.
Robert Russell Bennett, arr.
                                            Broadway Musicals
Warner (rental); Luck's (rental)

Porgy and Bess: Selections for Orchestra   13'
2[incl pic] 2 4[incl bcl] 1 – 3 2 2 1 – tmp+perc – pf – str
Solo Scat Singers; SATB Chorus.
Robert Russell Bennett, arr.
                                            Broadway Musicals
Warner (rental)

Porgy and Bess: Symphonic Picture (1943)   24'
3[1.2.pic] 3[1.2.Eh] 3[1.2.bcl] 2 – 2asx, tsx – 4 3 3 1 – tmp+3 – 2hp, bnjo – str
perc: glock, xyl, woodblk, cym, tri, sd, sus cym, bells.
Robert Russell Bennett, arr.
                                            Broadway Musicals
Warner (rental)

Promenade   3'
(aka Walkin' the Dog from The Real McCoy)
2[1.2/pic] 2 3[1.2.bcl] 2 – 4 3 2 1 – tmp+2 – hp, (cel) – str
perc: sus cym, tri, glock, xyl, vib, woodblk.
Sol Berkowitz, arr.
                                                      Animals
Warner (rental)

Rhapsody in Blue (1042 version)   16'
2 2 3[1.2.bcl] 2 – (2asx, tsx) – 3 3 3 1 – tmp+3 – (bnjo) – str
perc: sd, sus cym, cym, glock, tri, bd, tamtam.
Solo Piano.
Ferde Grofé, orchestrator
                                         Jazz/Popular Classics
Warner (rental); Luck's (rental)

Rhapsody in Blue for Trumpet and Orchestra   12.5'
2[1 2/pic] 2[1.Eh] 3[1.2.bcl] 2 – 4 0 3 1 – tmp+3 – pf, hp – str
perc: tambn, tri, bells, bd, gong, cym, xyl.
Solo Trumpet in Bb and C.
Timofei Dokshitzer, arr.
                                         Jazz/Popular Classics
EMR

Strike Up the Band   4.5'
2 2 3[1.2.bcl] 2 – 4 3 3 1 – tmp+3 – str
perc: cow bell, sd, bongos, cym/cabasa or maracas/sus cym, whistle, glock, xyl.
John Whitney, arr.
                                            Broadway Musicals
Belwin

Strike Up the Band   6'
2 2 2 2 – 4 3 3 1 – tmp+2 – hp – str
                                            Broadway Musicals
Viola World

Swanee   4'
3[1.2.pic] 2 2 2 – (2asx, tsx) – 4 3 3 1 – tmp+perc – str
William Ryden, arr.
                                                           Americana
Kalmus

'S Wonderful   3'
2 2 2 1 – 4 3 3 1 – perc – pf – str
Chuck Sayre, arr.
                                       Popular Song/Valentine
Warner (POP); EMS or Luck's (rental)

Two Gershwin Portraits   10'
3[1.2.pic] 2 3[1.2.bcl] 2 – 4 3 3 1 – tmp+4 – hp – str
perc: sus cym, bd, tubular bells, xyl, cym, sd, glock.
2 Solo Trumpets. Includes: Someone To Watch Over Me; Fascinating Rhythm. Written for trumpeters Wynton Marsalis, Philip Smith and commissioned by the New York Philharmonic for the New York 100 Celebration Concert in Central Park.
Joseph Turrin, arr.
                                                  Popular Songs
EAM (rental)

Gestor, Don

First Love   2.5'
2[1.2/pic] 2[1.Eh] 2 2 – 2asx, 2tsx – 4 3 3 1 – perc – hp – str
Jack Mason, arr.
                                       Dance/Instrumental Pops
Schirmer (rental)

Giacchino, Michael — 1967-

Star Trek: End Credits (2009) — 4'
3]1.2.3/pic] 2[1.Eh] 3[1.bcl.(Ebcbcl) 2[1.cbn] – 4[double if possible] 4 4[(#4)] 2[(#2)] – tmp+5 – hp, cel/pf str
perc: vib, tamtam, sus cym, puelli sticks, sticks on hard surface, sd, xyl, piatti, chimes, bd, bells, tomtoms, super tight pic sd.
Optional Chorus.

T&V (rental) — Films/Space

Music from "Up" — 7.5'
3[1/pic.2/pic(asx).3/afl/pic] 2[1/(tsx).2/Eh] 3[1.2/bcl.3/(bsx)/bcl] 2[1.2/cbn] – 4 3[all double on flugelhorn] 4 1 – tmp+4 – (gtr), hp, pf/cel – str
perc: vib, glock, guiro, sand shaker, woodblk, marim, bongos, ride cym, sd, sus cym, cym, tamtam, toms, bd, chimes.
From the Academy award winning Best Animated Picture of 2009.
Andrea Datzman, arr.

Leonard — Films

Gilbertson, Michael — 1990-

Reflections on Rushmore — 9.5'
2[1.2/pic] 2 2 2 – 4 3 3 1 – tmp+perc – str
perc: sd, bd, cym, sus cym, tam-tam, chimes, glock, slapstick.
Includes: Fanfare for the Founding Father; Monticello; Riders in the Rough; Hymn to Lincoln. A short suite representing the 4 presidents at Mount Rushmore monument.

Wendel (rental) — Patriotic

Gilliam, Michell (See: Phillips, John)

Gillis, Don — 1912-1978

Atlanta Suite: — 3.5'
5. Peachtree Promenade (Atlanta: Five Choreographic Impressions of a Southern City)
2[1.2/pic] 2 2 2 – 2asx, tsx – 4 3 3 0 – tmp+perc – pf – str

Kalmus — Americana

The Coming of the King — 26'
2 2 3 1 – 3 0 0 0 – perc – cel, pj – hp – str
Narrator; Mixed Chorus. Text by Norman Vincent Peale.

Presser (rental) — Christmas

The Man Who Invented Music — 14'
3 3 3 2 – 3 3 3 1 – tmp+3 – cel, pf – str
Narrator.

Presser (rental) — Instrumental Pops

The Night Before Christmas — 14'
3 3 3 2 – 3 3 3 1 – tmp+3[incl xyl] – cel, pf – str
Narrator.

Presser (rental) — Christmas

This Is Our America — 16'
1[incl pic] 1[incl Eh] 2[incl bcl] 1 – 3 3 2 1 – 3perc – cel, pf, org – str
Solo Baritone or Alto; Chorus.

Presser (rental) — Patriotic

Twinkletoes Ballet: Tango Lullaby — 3.5'
2 2 3[1.2.bcl] 2 – (2asx, tsx) – 4 3 3 1 – perc – pf or cel – str

Kalmus — Dance

Gilpin, Greg, arr. 1964-

The Music of MGM (A Choral Medley) 8'
1 1 1 0 – 2asx, tsx, bsx – 2 3 3 0 – tmp+3 –
hp, pf, elec bs – str
perc: drumset, sus cym, cym, xyl, glock, sd, tubular bells, sandpaper blk.
SAB Chorus. Includes: That's Entertainment; San Francisco; Trolley Song; Good Morning; Make 'em Laugh; Off to See the Wizard; Over the Rainbow; Singing in the Rain. Must perform with chorus.
Films/Popular Songs
Warner

Gimenez, Jeronimo 1859-1927

La Boda de Luis Alonso: Intermedio 5'
2 2 2 2 – 4 2 3 1 – tmp+perc – str
International
Kalmus

Glass, Philip 1937-

Façades 8'
2ssx(2fl) – strings
Popular Classics
Dvg (rental)

Glassworks 40'
(6' 7' 8' 6' 7' 6')
2 0 0 0 – 2ssx(cl), 2tsx(bcl) – 2 0 0 0 –
pf, (synth), (org) – va, vc
Includes:
Opening: pf
Floe: 2fl, 2ssx, 2tsx, 2hn, synth
Islands: 2fl, ssx, tsx, bcl, 2hn, va, vc
Rubric: fl, ssx, tsx, 2hn, org
Façades: 2ssx, synth, va, vc
Closing: fl, cl, bcl, hn, pf, va, vc
Popular Classics
Dvg (rental)

The Hours: Suite (2002) 25'
(1' 10.5' 2' 7.5' 3' 7')
0 0 0 0 – 0 0 0 0 – hp, pf, cel – str
Includes: Mvt I - The Poet Acts; Morning Passages; Why Does Someone Have to Die?; Dead Things. Mvt II - An Unwelcome Friend; Something She Has to Do; I Going to Make a Cake; The Kiss. Mvt III - The Hours.
2002 Oscar Nomination for Best Score.
Films
T&V (rental)

Modern Love Waltz 12'
1 0 1 0 – 0 0 0 0 – (1perc) – (hp), 2kybd
Robert Moran, arr.
Dance/Valentine
Dvg (rental)

Glazunov, Alexander 1865-1936

The Seasons: Autumn 11'
(4' 4' 3')
3[1.2.pic] 2[1.2/Eh] 2 2 – 4 2 3 1 – tmp+5 –
hp, cel – str
perc: bd, cym, sd, tri, tambn, glock.
Includes: Bacchanal; Petit Adagio; Variation: Le Satyre.
Seasons
Belaieff (rental); Kalmus

The Seasons: Spring 5'
3[1.2.pic] 2 2 2 – 4 2 3 0 – tmp+1 – hp – str
perc: tri.
Seasons
Belaieff (rental); Kalmus

The Seasons: Summer 9'
3[1.2.pic] 2 2 2 – 4 2 3 1 – tmp+4 – hp, cel, pf – str
perc: bd, cym, sus cym, tri, glock.
Seasons
Belaieff (rental); Kalmus

The Seasons: Winter 9'
3[1.2.pic] 2 2 2 – 4 2 3 1 – tmp+1 – hp, cel – str
perc: sus cym, sd, tri, glock.
Includes: Introduction; 4 variations (Frost, Ice, Hail, Show).
Seasons
Belaieff (rental); Kalmus

Glière, Reinhold   1875-1956

The Red Poppy: 7'
Russian Sailor's Dance from Act I
3[1.2.pic] 3[1.2.Eh] 3[1.2.bcl] 3[1.2.cbn] – 4 3 3 1
– tmp+5 – str
perc: tri, tambn, sd, cym, bd.
    Dance
Russian (rental)

The Red Poppy: Suite No. 1   30'
from the ballet, Op. 70a   (4' 9' 3' 7' 2' 4')
3[1.2/pic.3/pic] 3[1.2.Eh] 3[1.2.3/Ebcl/bcl]
3[1.2.3/cbn] – 4 3 3 1 – tmp+7 – 2hp, cel – str
perc: xyl, glock, tamtam, tri, tambn, sd, cym, bd, 2small pitched gongs.
Includes: Victorious Dance of the Coolies; Scene and Dance with the Golden Fingers; Coolie Dance; The Phoenix; Waltz; Russian Sailor's Dance.
    Dance
Russian (rental)

Glinka, Mikhail   1804-1857

Ruslan and Ludmila: Overture   4'
2 2 2 2 – 4 2 3 0 – tmp – str
Corrected edition.
Clark McAlister, editor
    Popular Classics
Masters

Ruslan & Ludmila: Overture   4'
2 2 2 3[1.2.cbn] – 4 2 3 0 – tmp – str
Original edition.
    Popular Classics
Kalmus

Valse Fantaisie in B Minor   6'
2 2 2 2 – 2 2 1 0 – tmp+1 – str
perc: tri.
Revised by Rimsky-Korsakov and Glazunov
    Dance/Popular Classics
Kalmus; Russian (rental)

Gluck, Christoph Willibald   1714-1787

Orfeo ed Euridice: 6'
Dance of the Blessed Spirits
2 1[Eh] 0 0 – 2 0 0 0 – str
Felix Mottl, arr.
    Dance/Popular Classics
Kalmus; Luck's

Gold, Ernest   1921-1999

Boston Pops March   4'
3[1.2.pic] 3[1.2.(Eh)] 2 3[1.2.(cbn)] –
4 4[(#3&4)] 3 1 – tmp+3 – hp – str
perc: bells, tri, tambn, cym, sd, bd.
    Instrumental Pops
Kalmus

Exodus: An Orchestral Tone-Picture   8.5'
2 2 2 2 – (2asx, tsx, bsx) – 4 3 3 1 – tmp+2 –
hp, (pf) – str
Optional Solo Piano.
Robert Russell Bennett, arr.
    Films
Chappell (rental)

Exodus: Rhapsody for Cello   6.5'
and Orchestra (1960)
2[1.pic] 2[1.Eh] 3[1.2.bcl] 2 – 4 2 3 1 – tmp+3 –
hp, cel – str
perc: sus cym, sd, bd, glock, tri.
Solo Cello. Music from the Oscar winning film score.
    Films
T&V (rental)

Exodus: This Land is Mine (1960)   2.5'
2 2 2 2 – 6 3 3 1 – tmp+1 – hp, str
perc: cym, sus cym, tamtam, vib, tubular bells.
SATB Chorus. Lyrics by Pat Boone.
    Films
T&V (rental)

It's a Mad, Mad, Mad, Mad World: 2'
Exit Music (1963)
2[1.pic] 2 4[1.2.3.bcl] 2 – 4 3 3 1 – tmp+3 –
2 hp, pf, cel – str
    Films
T&V (rental)

Ship of Fools: Candlelight & Silver Waltz (1965)   5'
    3[1.2.pic] 2 3[1.2.Ebcl] 2 – 4 2 3 0 – tmp+2 hp
    – str
    perc: sd, bd with attached cym, tambn, tri, glock.
                                           Dance/Films
T&V (rental)

Gold, Julie   1956-

From a Distance
    strings – rhythm
    Larry Moore, arr.
                                           Popular Song
Warner (POP); Luck's (rental)

Gold, Marty, arr.   1915-

Brazil   3'
    2 1 3[incl bcl] 1 – 4 3 3 1 – tmp+3 – pf – str
                                             International
Belwin (POP); Luck's (rental)

Ecstasy   3'
    2 1 2 1 – 2 3 2 1 – tmp+perc – pf – str
                                             Valentine
Warner

Jeopardy Theme
    2 2 2 2 – 2 2 2 1 – 3perc – pf – str
                                             TV
EMI (rental)

Mancini Memories   5'
    2 1 2 1 – 2 3 2 1 – tmp+perc – pf – str
    Theme music from *Breakfast at Tiffany's*
    & Baby Elephant Walk.
                                             Films
Warner (POP); EMS or Luck's (rental)

Rainy Day Medley   6'
    2 1 2 1 – 2 3 2 1 – tmp+perc – pf – str
    Includes: Here's that Rainy Day; Singin' In the Rain;
    Stormy Weather.
                                   Popular Song/Weather
Belwin (POP); EMS or Luck's (rental)

Goldenthal, Elliot   1954-

Alien 3: Adagio
    3[1.2/pic.pic] 2 3[1.2/bcl.Bbcbcl] 3[1.2.cbn] –
    8 3[in C] 6[4+2bass] 1 – tmp+perc – hp – str
                                             Films
Kane (rental)

Goldman, Edwin Franko   1878-1956

Children's March   3'
    1 1 2 1 – 3sx – 2 3 1 0 – tmp+perc – str
    Tom Clark, arr.
                                       Instrumental Pops
Schirmer

Goldsmith, Jerry   1929-2004

The Agony and the Ecstasy (1965): Suite   12.5'
    The Artist Who Did Not Want To Paint
                             (2'   3'   2.5'   3'   2')
    2[1/afl.2/afl] 2 2[1/asx.2] 2 – 8 0 0 0 – tmp+perc
    – hp – str
    This music was composed for a documentary to be
    shown before the actual film. Called *Prologue - The
    Artist Who Did Not Want To Paint*, the Suite
    includes: Rome; Florence; The Crucifix; The Stone
    Giants; The Agony of Creation.
                                             Films
Kane (rental)

Air Force One (1997): Theme   2'
    3 3[1.2.eh] 3 3[1.2.cbn] – 6[all dbl tuben, (#5-6)] 3
    4 1 – tmp+perc – hp, pf – str
                                             Films
Kane (rental)

Alien (1979): End Title   3'
    3[1.2.3/pic] 3[1.2.Eh] 3[1.2.3/bcl] 3[1.2.3/cbn]
    – 6 3 3 1 – tmp+perc – hp, pf/synth – str
                                             Films
Kane (rental)

Basic Instinct (1992): Main Title Theme   2'
    3 2 3 2 – 4 0 0 0 – perc – hp, pf – str
    Won the 1993 Oscar for Best Music/Original Score.
                                             Films
Kane (rental)

Basic Instinct (1992): Suite   13.5'
    3 2 3 2 – 4 0 0 0 – perc – hp, pf – str
    Won the 1993 Oscar for Best Music/Original Score.
                                    Films
    Kane (rental)

The Blue Max (1996): Suite   8'
    3[1/pic/afl.2/pic/afl.3/pic/afl] 3[1.2.3/Eh]
    3[1/Eb/D.2.3/bcl] 3[1.2.3/cbn] – 6 3 3 1 – tmp+perc
    – hp, pf – str
                                    Films
    Kane (rental)

The Boys from Brazil (1978): Waltz & The Boys   7'
    3[1.2/afl.3/pic] 3[1.2.Eh] 3[1.2.bcl] 3[1.2.cbn]
    – 4 3 3 1 – tmp+perc – hp, pf – str
    Nominated for 1979 Oscar Best Original Score.
                                    Films
    Kane (rental)

Capricorn One: Overture & Main Title   3'
    3 3 3 3[1.2.cbn] – 4 3 3 1 – tmp+perc – hp – str
                                 Films/Space
    Kane (rental)

Chinatown (1974): Suite   12'
    0 0 0 0 – 0 1 0 0 – perc – 4hp, 4pf – str
    Won 1975 Oscar for Best Music and Original Score.
    David Newman, arr.
                                    Films
    Kane (rental)

Chinatown: Theme (1974)   2'
    2[1.pic] 1 1 1 – 1 1 2 1 – tmp+perc – gtr, elec bs
    – str
    perc: drumset, bells, vib, marim, tri.
                                    Films
    T&V (rental)

Dennis the Menace (1993): End Credits
    3[1.2.3/pic] 3[1.2.3/Eh] 3[1.2/Eb.3/bcl] 3[1.2.3/cbn]
    – 4 3 3 1 – tmp+perc – hp, pf, synth – str
                                    Films
    Kane (rental)

The Edge (1997): Main Title & Finale   9'
    2 2[1.2/Eh] 2 2[1.cbn] – 4 3 3 1 – tmp+perc –
    hp, pf – str
                                    Films
    Kane (rental)

The Final Conflict (1983)   4'
    3 3 3[1.2.3/bcl] 3 – 6 3 3 1 – tmp+perc –
    hp, pf, elec pf, elec bass – str
    Choir. This is the original title to *Omen III: The
    Final Conflict.*
                                    Films
    Kane (rental)

Fireworks: A Celebration for Los Angeles (1999)   8.5'
    3[1.2.3/pic] 3 3[1.2.3/bcl] 3[1.2.3/cbn] – 4 3 3 1
    – tmp+perc – hp, pf – str
                            Americana/Celebration
    Kane (rental)

The First Knight (1995): Suite   4'
    3[1.2.3/pic] 3[1.2.3/Eh] 3[1.2.3/bcl] 3[1.2.cbn] –
    8 4 4 2 (or 4 3 3 1) – tmp+perc – hp, pf – str
                                    Films
    Kane (rental)

Forever Young (1992): Love Theme   4'
    2 3[1.2.Eh] 3[1.2.bcl] 2 – 4 3 3 1 – tmp+perc
    – hp, pf – str
                                    Films
    Kane (rental)

Four Women: Medley
    3[1.2.pic] 3[1.2.Eh] 3[1.2.bcl] 2 – 4 3 3 1 –
    tmp+perc – hp, pf/cel – str
                                    Films
    Kane (rental)

The Generals: Patton/MacArthur Marches   5'
    3[1.2.3/pic] 3[1.2.3/Eh] 3[1.2.3/Eb] 3[1.2.cbn]
    – 4 3 3 1 – tmp+perc – hp, pf – str
    This is also scored for concert band. The work is
    based on the music from the films *Patton* (1970),
    which was nominated for an Oscar for best original
    score, and from *MacArthur* (1977).
                                  Films/Patriotic
    Kane (rental)

The Great Train Robbery (1979): Suite   7.5'
    3[1.2.pic] 3[1.2.Eh] 3[1.2.bcl] 3[1.2.cbn] –
    4 3 3 1 – tmp+perc – hp, pf – str
                                    Films
    Kane (rental)

Gremlins: Suite   8'
    2[1.2/pic] 2 2 2 – 4 3 3 1 – tmp+perc –
    hp, pf, elec bass – str
                                    Films
    Kane (rental)

Gremlins 2 (1990): The New Batch: Main Title 5'
2 2 2 2 – 4 3 3 1 – tmp+perc – hp, pf, synth, cel – str
                                                  Films
Kane (rental)

Hoosiers (1986): Suite 6'
3[1.2.pic] 3[1.2.Eh] 3[1.2.bcl] 3[1.2.cbn] – 6 3 3 1 – tmp+perc – hp, pf, cel – str
Nominated for the 1987 Oscar for Best Music/Original Score.
                                    Films/Sports
Kane (rental)

The Illustrated Man: Main Title 4'
2[1.2/afl] 2[1.Eh] 2[1.bcl] 1 – 0 0 0 0 – perc – hp, cel – str
                                                  Films
Kane (rental)

King Solomon's Mines (1985): Suite 4'
2[1/pic.2] 3[1.2/Eh.3] 2 3[1.2.cbn] – 3 4 4 1 – tmp+perc – hp, pf – str
                                                  Films
Kane (rental)

L.A. Confidential (1997) 4'
3 2 3[1.2.bcl] 2 – 4 3 3 1 – tmp+perc – hp, pf – str
Nominated for an Oscar for Best Music in 1998.
                                                 Films
Kane (rental)

Lionheart: The Children's Crusade (1987) 4'
3[1.2.3/pic] 3[1.2.Eh] 3[1.2.bcl] 3[1.2.cbn] – 6 3 3 1 – tmp+perc – synth – str
                                                 Films
Kane (rental)

Logan's Run (1976): Monument/End of the City 11'
3[1/pic.2/afl.3/pic] 2[1.2/Eh] 3[1/Eb.2.3/bcl] 2[1.2/cbn] – 4 3 3 1 – tmp+perc – hp, pf, cel – str [no bass]
                                                 Films
Kane (rental)

MacArthur (1977): March 5'
3[1.2.3/pic] 3[1.2.3/Eh] 3[1.2.3/Eb] 3[1.2.cbn] – 4 3 3 1 – tmp+perc – hp, pf – str
                                    Films/Patriotic
Kane (rental)

Masada: Suite 5'
3[1.2.3/pic] 3[1.2.Eh] 3[1.2.3/bcl] 3[1.2.cbn] – 4 3 3 1 – tmp+perc – hp, pf – str
Music for the 1981 TV mini-series. Won the 1982 Emmy for "Outstanding Achievement in Music Composition for a Limited Series or a Special."
                                    International/TV
Kane (rental)

Motion Picture Medley 20'
3[1.2.3/pic] 3[1.2.3/Eh] 3[1.2.3/bcl] 3[1.2.3/cbn] – 4 3 3 1 – tmp+perc – hp, pf/cel – str
                                                 Films
Kane (rental)

Music for Orchestra 8'
3[1.2.pic] 3[1.2.3/Eh] 3[1.2/Eb.3/bcl] 3[1.2.3/cbn] – 4 4 4 1 – tmp+perc – hp, pf/cel – str
Written for Leonard Slatkin and the St. Louis Orchestra, it is a 3 part, dodecophonic work.
                                    Instrumental Pops
Kane (rental)

The Omen (1976): Suite 11'
3 2 2 2 – 4 3 3 1 – tmp+perc – hp, pf, org – str
Chorus. Won the 1977 Oscar for Best Music, Original Score.
                                               Films
Kane (rental)

Papillon: Theme 1.5'
3[1.2.pic] 3[1.2/Eh] 3 3 – 4 3 3 1 – tmp+perc – hp, pf – str
                                               Films
Kane (rental)

A Patch of Blue (1966): Suite 4'
2[1.2/pic] 2[1.2/Eh] 2 2 – 0 0 0 0 – perc – hp, pf, cel, harmonica, elec gtr – str
Won the 1967 Oscar for Best Music Score.
                                               Films
Kane (rental)

Patton (1970): Attack 3'
3[1/afl.2/pic.3/bfl] 2[1/Eh.2/Eh] 3[1.2.bcl] 3[1.2/cbn.cbn] – 4 3 3 1 – tmp+perc – hp, harm, org – str
                                               Films
Kane (rental)

Patton (1970): Main Title 2.5'
3[1/pic.2/pic.3] 2 3[1.2/afl.3] 3[1.2.cbn] – 4 5 3 1 – tmp+perc – hp, org, harm – str
                                               Films
Kane (rental)

Patton (1970): Suite   13.5'
4[1/pic/afl.2/pic/afl.bsfl.3/pic/bsfl.4] 2[1.2/Eh] 3[1.2.bcl/Eb] 3[1.2/cbn] – 4 5 3 1 – tmp+perc – hp, pf/cel/harm, org – str

                                           Films

Kane (rental)

Patton (1970): The Battle Ground   2.5'
2[afl.afl] 0 1 1[cbn] – 2 2 1 0 – perc – hp, pf/cel/harm, harm/org – str

                                           Films

Kane (rental)

Patton (1970): The Hospital   3.5'
2[1/afl.2/afl] 1 3 1 – 2 0 3 0 – tmp+perc – hp, harm – str

                                           Films

Kane (rental)

Patton (1970): The Payoff   2.5'
3 2 3[1.2.Eb] 3[1.2.cbn] – 4 3 3 1 – tmp+perc – hp, pf/harm, org – str

                                           Films

Kane (rental)

Planet of the Apes (1968): Suite   12.5'
3[1/pic/afl.2/pic/afl.3/pic/bsfl] 3[1/bob.2/Eh.3/Eh] 3[1/Eb.2/bcl.3/bcl] 3[1.2.3/cbn] – 4 3 3 0 – tmp+perc – hp, pf – str
Won the 1969 Oscar for Best Music.

                                           Films

Kane (rental)

Poltergeist (1982): Night of the   3'
   Beast (Clown Attack)
2[1.2/pic] 2 3[1.Eb/bscl, 3/bscl] 2[1/cbn,2/cbn] – 6 3 3 2 – tmp+perc – hp, pf/rhodes/cel, saw – str
Won the 1983 Oscar for Best Music.

                                   Films/Halloween

Kane (rental)

Poltergeist (1982): The Calling   2'
2[1.afl] 2[1.Eh] 3[1.2.bscl] 2 – 0 0 0 0 – tmp+perc – hp, pf/rhodes/cel, saw – str
Won the 1983 Oscar for Best Music.

                                   Films/Halloween

Kane (rental)

Poltergeist (1982): The Light   2'
0 1 3[1.2.bcl] 1 – 0 0 0 0 – perc – hp, cel – str
Won the 1983 Oscar for Best Music.

                                   Films/Halloween

Kane (rental)

Poltergeist (1982): Theme (Carol Anne's)   4.5'
3 3[1.2.Eh] 3 3 – 4 3 3 1 – tmp+perc – hp, pf/cel – str
Won the 1983 Oscar for Best Music.

                                   Films/Halloween

Kane (rental)

QB VII: Suite   12'
2 2 2 2 – 4 3 3 1 – tmp+perc – hp, pf/synth, gtr/mand, accordion – str
SATB Chorus. Written for a 1974 TV mini-series and won the 1975 Emmy for Outstanding Achievement in Music Composition for a Special.

                                                 TV

Kane (rental)

Rambo: First Blood, Part 2 (1985): Theme   6'
2[1.2/pic] 2 3[1.2/Eb.3/bcl] 2 – 4 3 3 1 – tmp+perc – hp, 2synth – str

                                           Films

Kane (rental)

Rudy: Suite   23'
2 3[1.2.Eh] 3[1.2.bcl] 2 – 4 3 3 1 – tmp+perc – hp, pf, synth – str
Solo Voice.

                                       Films/Sports

Kane (rental)

Rudy: Theme for Flute and Chamber Orchestra   4'
1 0 1 0 – 0 0 0 0 – tmp+perc – hp, pf – str

                                       Films/Sports

Kane (rental)

The Russia House (1990): Love Theme   5'
3 3[1.2.Eh] 3[1.2.3/bcl] 2 – 4 3 3 1 – tmp+perc – hp, pf – str

                                           Films

Kane (rental)

The Shadow (1994): Main Title   2.5'
2 3[1.2.Eh] 3 3[1.2.cbn] – 4 3 3 1 – tmp+perc – hp, pf – str

                                           Films

Kane (rental)

Six Degrees of Separation (1993): Tango   2'
1 0 1 1 – 0 0 0 0 – perc – hp, pf – str

                                      Dance/Films

Kane (rental)

Sleeping with the Enemy (1991): Theme   4'
    2 2 3[1.2.bcl] 2 – 4 3 3 1 – tmp+perc –
    hp, pf – str
    Won the BMI film music award for 1992.
                                                   Films

Kane (rental)

Soarin' Over California   4.5'
    3[1.2.3/pic] 3[1.2.3/Eh] 3[1.2.3/bcl] 3[1.2.3/cbn] – 6 3 3 1 – tmp+perc – str
    Soundtrack for the popular Disney ride in California and Epcot Center in Florida celebrating flying.
                Americana/Instrumental Pops/Travel

Kane (rental)

Star Trek: Main Theme   2.5'
    2 1 3[1.2.bcl] 1 – 2 2 2 0 – tmp+3 – str
    perc: bells, sd, bd, cym.
    Harry Simeone, arr.
                                               Films/Space

Shawnee (POP); Luck's (rental)

Star Trek: Voyager (1995)   2'
    3[1.2.pic] 3[1.2.Eh] 3[1.Ebcl,bcl] 3[1.2.cbn] – 4 3 3 1 – tmp+2 – hp, cel – str
    perc: vib, sus cym, glock, bd.
                                               Films/Space

T&V (rental)

Star Trek I: The Motion Picture   20'
    "The Director's Cut"
    3[1.2.fl/picc/el. bsfl) 3[1.2.Eh] 3[1.2/Ebcl/cbcl. 3/bcl] 3[1.2.cbn] – 6 4 4 2 – tmp+5 – 2hp, 4kybd[pf. pf/c.s.80/serge synth. elec pf. cel/arp 2600] – str
    perc: vib, bs vib, chimes, big bd, sd, rub rod, tri, tamtam, glock, xyl, piatti, sizzle cym, water crotales, water phone, lg water phone, lg. Angklung, rumble board, slit drum, devil chasers, synth perc, mixing bowls[soft mallets], sus cym, side drum, beam.
    Includes: Floating; Enterprise; Spock Walk; Inner Workings; Vejur Speaks; The Meld; A Good Start.
                                               Films/Space

T&V (rental)

Star Trek I: The Motion Picture   13'
    "The Klingon Battle"
    3[1.pic.3] 3[1.2.Eh] 2 2 – 4 3 3 1 – tmp+perc – 2 hp, pf[cel, synth] – str
    perc: waterphone or bowed tamtam, rumble board or bd, Angklung, boobams, td, bd, timbales, slit drums, sizzle cym, tamtam, vib.
                                               Films/Space

T&V (rental)

Star Trek I: The Motion Picture   6'
    "The New Enterprise"
    3[1.2.pic] 3[1.2.Eh] 3[1.Ebcl.bcl] 3[1.2.cbn] – 6 4 4 2 – tmp+3 – 2 hp, 2 kybd[fender rhodes, midi, kurzweil. ARP 2600, C.S. 80],pf, org, cel – str
    perc: vib, bass vib, glock, bd, big bd, sd, chimes, rub rod, tri, tamtam, cym, sizzle cym.
    John Mauceri, arr.
                                               Films/Space

T&V (rental)

Star Trek I: The Motion Picture Theme (1979)   3.5'
    3[1.2.pic] 3[1.2.Eh] 3[1.2.bcl] 3[1.2.cbn] – 6 4 4 2 – tmp+4 – hp, 2 pf[cel.elec pf] – str
    perc: xyl, glock, vib, sus cym, chimes, bells, bd, cyms, sd.
                                               Films/Space

T&V (rental)

Star Trek 5: The Final Frontier: Suite (1989)   4'
    3 3[1.2.3/Eh] 3[1.2.bcl] 3[1.2.cbn] – 6 3 3 1 – tmp+perc – hp, pf[synth, 2 synth – str
    perc: cym, vib, chimes, glock, lg split drum, sd, bd, cast.
    Includes: End Cast (aka "Life is a Dream" and "Busy Man"); The Barrier.
                                               Films/Space

T&V (rental)

Star Trek 8: First Contact (1996)   5.5'
    3 3[1.Eh.3] 3 3[1.2.cbn] – 4 3 3 1 – tmp+perc – hp, pf, org – str
    perc: chimes, vib, glock, cym, sd, bd.
                                               Films/Space

T&V (rental)

Star Trek 9: Insurrection (1998)   5'
    3[1.2.pic] 3[1.2.Eh] 3 3[1.2.cbn] – 6 3 3 1 – tmp+perc – hp, 2kybd[pf/synth. synth] – str
    perc: vib, glock, chimes, sd, bd, cym.
                                               Films/Space

T&V (rental)

Star Trek 10: Nemesis (2002)   6'
    3[1.2.pic] 3[1.2.Eh] 3 3[1.2.cbn] – 6 3 3 1– tmp+perc – hp, pf – str
    perc: vib, glock, marim, chimes, cym, sd, bd.
                                               Films/Space

T&V (rental)

The Strong Men: Total Recall & Rambo Themes   5'
    3[1.2.3/pic] 3[1.2.3/Eh] 3[1.2/Eb.3/bcl] 3 – 4 3 3 1 – tmp+perc – hp, pf/synth, gtr, elec bass – str
                                               Films

Kane (rental)

The Sum of All Fears (2002) 6'
3[1.2.pic] 3[1.2.Eh] 3 3[1.2.cbn] – 4 3 3 1 – tmp+perc – hp, pf – str
Optional Chorus.
Films/Space
T&V (rental)

Supergirl: Suite
3[1.2.3/pic] 3[1.2.3/Eh] 3 3[1.2.3/cbn] – 6 3[1/pic.2.3] 3 1 – tmp+perc – hp, 3synth – str
Films
Kane (rental)

The Swarm (1978): Bees Arrive/End Title 8'
3[1.2/afl.3/pic] 2[1/Eh.2/Eh] 4[1.2.3/bcl.bcl] 3[1.2.3/cbn] – 6 3 3 1 – tmp+perc – hp, pf/synth – str
Animals/Films
Kane (rental)

Television Themes Medley 10.5'
3[1.2.3/pic] 3[1.2.3/Eh] 3 3 – 4 3 3 1 – tmp+perc – hp, pf /cel – str
TV
Kane (rental)

The Twilight Zone (1961): The Invaders 10.5'
0 0 0 0 – 0 0 0 0 – perc – hp, pf/cel, synth – str
TV
Kane (rental)

Twilight Zone: The Movie (1983): End Title 6'
3[1.2.3/pic] 3[1.2.3/Eh] 3[1.2.3/bcl] 3[1.2.cbn] – 4 3 3 1 – tmp+perc – hp, pf/cel, synth – str
Films
Kane (rental)

Under Fire (1983): Suite 15'
3[1.2.3/pic] 3[1.2.3/Eh] 3[1.2.3/bcl] 3[1.2.cbn] – 6 3 3 1 – hp, pf, 3synth, 2gtr – str
Nominated for 1984 Oscar for Best Music, Original Score.
Films
Kane (rental)

The Wild Rovers (1971): Bronco Busting 2'
2 2 2 2 – 4 3 3 0 – tmp+perc – hp, pf/cel, accordion, gtr, banjo, elec bs – str
Americana/Films
Kane (rental)

The Wind and the Lion (1975) 2'
3[1.2.pic] 3[1.2.3/Eh] 3[1.2.3/bcl] 3[1.2.cbn] – 4 3 3 1 – tmp+perc – hp, pf, mand, bouzouki – str
Nominated for 1976 Oscar for Best Music.
Films
Kane (rental)

Goldsmith, Owen 1932-

Romanza for String Orchestra 2'
Strings
Valentine
Belwin

Goldstein, William 1942-

A.M. America Overture 3'
3[(pic)] 1 2 3 – 2 2 3 0 – tmp+3 – hp, pf, gtr, elec bass – str
Optional SATB chorus.
Patriotic
Merion (rental)

Celebration Overture 1776-1976 11.5'
2[incl pic] 1 1 1 – 2 2 2 0 – perc – hp, pf, gtr – str
Commissioned for the U.S. Bicentennial by ABC TV.
Patriotic
Merion (rental)

'Twas the Night Before Christmas 6'
2[incl pic] 1 1 1 – 2 0 0 0 – 2perc – hp, pf[cel] – str
Narrator, Solo Violin; Girls' and Boys' Choruses.
Christmas
Merion (rental)

Gomez, Alice 1960-

Festive Huapango 2.5'
3[1.2.pic] 2 2 2 – 4 2 0 1 – 4 perc – str
Dance/International(Mexico)
Gomez

Goodrum, Charles Randolph
(See: Black, Charlie)

Goodwin, Ron   1925-2003

Those Magnificent Men in   *6.5'*
Their Flying Machines (1965)
3[1.pic.3] 2 3[1.2.bcl] 3[1.2.cbn] – 4 3 3 1
tmp+4 – hp, gtr – str
perc: drumset, sd, bd, cym, sus cym, glock, tambn.
                                                   Films/Travel
T&V (rental)

Goossens, Eugene   1893-1962

Don Juan de Manara: Intermezzo   *5'*
3[incl pic] 3[incl Eh] 3[incl bcl] 3[incl cbn] –
4 3 3 1 – tmp+perc – 2hp, cel – str
                                                   International
Schirmer (rental)

East of Suez: Incidental Music   *17'*
2[incl pic] 1 1 1 – 2 1 0 0 – tmp+perc –
cel or pf, hp – str
                                                   International
Schirmer (rental)

Fanfare for the Artists   *4'*
0 0 0 0 – 0 4 4 0 – tmp+perc
                                                   Fanfare
Chester (rental)

Flamenco: Ballet   *8'*
3[incl pic] 3[incl Eh] 3[incl bcl] 3[1.2.cbn] – 4 3 3 1
– tmp+perc – 2hp – str
                                   Dance/International
Chester (rental)

The Hurdy-Gurdy Man   *3'*
2 1 2 1 – 1 2[crt] 1 0 – perc – (hp) – str
                                                    Circus
Chester; Schirmer (rental)

Kaleidoscope   *14'*
2[incl pic] 2[incl Eh] 2 2 – 2 2 1 0 – tmp+perc –
hp, cel – str
                                         Instrumental Pops
Chester (rental)

Prelude to "Philip II"   *9'*
1 1 1 1 – 2 1 0 0 – tmp+perc – hp – str
                                         Instrumental Pops
Chester (rental)

Scherzo and Folk Tune   *5'*
3[incl pic] 3[1.2.Eh] 3[1.2.bcl] 3[1.2.cbn] – 4 3 3 1
– tmp+perc – hp – str
                                         Instrumental Pops
Chester (rental)

Tam O'Shanter: Scherzo   *4'*
3[1.2.3/pic] 3[1.2.Eh] 3 3[1.2.cbn] – 4 3 3 1 –
tmp+perc – hp, pf – str
perc: chimes, cym, gong, drum.
                                                   International
Chester (rental)

Two Sketches   *7'*
(cl) – strings
Includes: By the Tarn [(cl)]; Jack O'Lantern [strings only]
                                                    Halloween
Chester (rental)

Gordon, Phillip   1894-1983

Fitzwilliam Suite   *3'*
(1 1 2 1 – asx, tsx – 2 2 1 1 – tmp+1 – pf) – str
perc: sd, bd.
Optional winds and percussion. Includes Fortune, My Foe by William Byrd; Pavana by John Bull; and A Toye by Giles Farnaby. May be performed by strings alone.
                                         Instrumental Pops
Kalmus

Gordon, Michael 1956-

Love Bead 10'
1[incl pic] 1[incl Eh] 1[incl bcl] 1[incl cbn] –
1 1 1 0 – elec bass gtr,elec gtr – vn,va,vc
All instruments are amplified.
                                             Valentine
Schirmer (rental)

Sunshine of Your Love 10'
4 4 4 4 – 4asx – 6 6 4 2 – 2tmp+4 – 4kybd –
2elec gtr, 2elec bass – str
                                Valentine/Weather
Schirmer (rental)

Gottschalk, Louis Moreau 1829-1869

Pasquinade Caprice 3'
1 1 2 1 – 2 2 1 0 – perc – str
Rollinson, arr.
                                    Instrumental Pops
Kalmus

Symphonie romantique: 19'
  Night in the Tropics (13' 6')
2 2 3[Eb] 2 – 3 4[incl Ebtp, pic tp,4crt] 4[4bar]
1[ophicleide] – tmp+4 – str
Includes: La Nuit des tropiques; Une Fête sous les tropiques.
Gunther Schuller, ed.
                          Popular Classics/Valentine
Margun (rental)

L'Union: 8'
  Paraphrase de concert sur les airs nationaux
2 2 2 2 – 2 2 2 1 – tmp+perc – str
Solo Piano.
                                               Patriotic
Schirmer (rental)

L'Union: 8'
  Paraphrase de concert sur les airs nationaux
  (orchestra version)
2 2 2 2 – 2 2 2 1 – tmp+perc – str
Solo Piano.
Samuel Adler, arr.
                                               Patriotic
Schirmer (rental)

Gould, Morton 1913-1996

Adeste fidelis 4'
2 2 2 2 – 2 2 2 1 – tmp+perc – str
                                               Christmas
Schirmer (rental)

American Ballads: 33'
  Settings of American Tunes for Orchestra
3[1.2.pic] 2[1.2/Eh] 3[1.2.3/Ebcl/bcl]) 2[1.cbn] –
4 3 3 1 – tmp+4 – hp – str
perc: bd, cym, sus cym, sd, tri, tambn, chimes, ratch
field dr, glock, gong.
A Bicentennial Commission including National
Anthem; America the Beautiful; We Shall
Overcome; and Taps.
                               Americana/Patriotic
Schirmer (rental)

American Ballads: 7'
  Amber Waves on "America the Beautiful"
3[1.2.pic] 2[1.Eh] 3[1.2.bcl] 2[1.2/cbn] – 4 3 3 1 –
tmp+2 – hp – str
perc: sus cym, gong.
                                               Patriotic
Schirmer (rental)

American Ballads: 7'
  Hymnal on "We Shall Overcome"
3[1.2.pic] 2[1.2/Eh] 3[1.2.bcl] 2[1.2/cbn] – 4 3 3 1 –
tmp+3 – hp – str
perc: sd, sus cym, bd, cym, tambn, gong, bd/cym.
                                               Patriotic
Schirmer (rental)

American Ballads: Jubilo 3'
3[1.2.pic] 2[1.2/Eh] 3[1.2.bcl] 2[1.2/cbn] – 4 3 3 1 –
tmp+3 – hp – str
perc: bd, sus cym, td, tri, tambn, glock.
                                               Patriotic
Schirmer (rental)

American Ballads: 6'
  Memorials - on "Taps"
3[1.2.pic] 2[1.2/Eh] 3[1.2.3/bcl] 2[1.cbn] –
4 3[tp 1 offstage] 3 1 – tmp+3 – hp – str
perc: bd, sd, td, field dr.
                                               Patriotic
Schirmer (rental)

American Ballads: 3'
    Saratoga Quickstep on "The Girl I Left Behind"
    3[1.2.pic] 2[1.2/Eh] 3[1.2.bcl] 2[1.2/cbn] – 4 3 3 1 – tmp+3 – hp – str
    perc: sd, td, field dr, tri, glock.
                                                 Dance/Patriotic
Schirmer (rental)

American Ballads: 5'
    Star-Spangled Overture on "The Star-Spangled Banner"
    3[1.2.pic] 2 3[1.2.Ebcl) 2[1.2/cbn] – 4 3 3 1 – tmp+4 – hp – str
    perc: bd, cym, sus cym, sd, tri, tambn, chimes, ratch.
                                                        Patriotic
Schirmer (rental)

American Caprice   5'
    2 2 2 2 – 4sx – 2 3 2 0 – tmp+3 – hp, cel, pf, gtr – str
                                                        Patriotic
EMI (rental)

American Salute (New Edition, 2000)   4'
    3[incl pic] 2[incl Eh] 3[1.2.bcl] 2 – 4 3 3 1 – tmp+2 – hp, pf, gtr – str
    Based on *When Johnny Comes Marching Home.*
                                                        Patriotic
Belwin

American Sing: Settings of Folk Songs   16'
    3[incl pic] 3 3 3[incl cbn] – 4 3 3 1 – tmp+perc – hp – str
    Solo soprano, mezzo soprano, tenor, bass
                                              Americana/Patriotic
Schirmer (rental)

Audubon: Night Music   5'
    3[incl 2 pic] 2[incl Eh,opt harm] 3[incl bcl] 3 – 0 0 0 0 – perc – gtr or hp – str – tape
                                                    Halloween
Schirmer (rental)

Battle Hymn of the Republic   5'
    2 2 2 2 – 4 2 3 1 – tmp+3 – hp – str
                                                       Patriotic
Schirmer (rental)

Big City Blues   5'
    1[incl pic] 1[incl Eh] 2 1 – 4 3 2 1 – tmp+perc – hp – str
                                                              Jazz
G&C (rental)

Boogie Woogie Etude   2'
    3 1 4[incl bcl] 2 – 4 3 3 1 – tmp+perc – str
    Solo Piano.
                                                               Jazz
EMI (rental)

Café Rio   5'
    1[incl pic] 0 1[asx] 0 – asx, tsx, bsx – 0 2 1 0 – 2perc – hp, pf, gtr – str[44021]
                                                  Instrumental Pops
G&C (rental)

Calypso Souvenir   3'
    3[incl 3 pic] 0 3[1.2.bcl] 1 – 0 3 0 0 – 2 perc – hp – str
                                                            Dance
G&C (rental)

Celebration Strut for Orchestra   3'
    3[incl pic] 2 3 2 – 4 3 3 1 – tmp+3 – hp – str
                                               Dance/Americana
Schirmer (rental)

Cheers! - A Celebration March   5'
    3[incl pic] 3[incl Eh] 3 3[incl cbn] – 4 4 3 1 – tmp+3 – (org) – str
                                                     Celebration
Schirmer (rental)

Christmas Time, Book I   21'
    2 2 2 2 – 4 2 3 1 – perc – hp or pf – str
    SATB Chorus. Chorus parts arr. by Gregg Smith.
                                                    Christmas
G&C (rental)

Christmas Time, Book I: Adeste Fidelis   4'
    2 2 2 2 – 4 2 3 1 – perc – str
    SATB Chorus.
                                                    Christmas
G&C (rental)

Christmas Time, Book I: First Noel   4'
    2 2 2 2 – 4 2 3 1 – perc – hp – str
    SATB Chorus.
                                                  Christmas
G&C (rental)

Christmas Time, Book I: 3'
    It Came Upon a Midnight Clear
    Strings
    SATB Chorus.
                                                 Christmas
G&C (rental)

Christmas Time, Book I: 5'
O Little Town; Away in a Manger
2 2 2 2 – 4 2 3 1 – perc – hp – str
SATB Chorus.

            Christmas

G&C (rental)

Christmas Time, Book I: Silent Night 5'
2 2 2 2 – 4 2 3 1 – 1perc – hp, pf – str
SATB Chorus.

            Christmas

G&C (rental)

Christmas Time, Book II 13'
2[incl 2pic] 2[incl Eh] 2[incl bcl] 2 – 4 3 3 1 – 3perc – hp, cel – str
SATB chorus; chorus parts arr. by Gregg Smith.

            Christmas

G&C (rental)

Christmas Time, Book II: 3'
Home for Christmas
2 2[incl Eh] 2 2 – 2 3 2 1 – 2perc – hp, cel – str
SATB Chorus.

            Christmas

G&C (rental)

Christmas Time, Book II: Jingle Bells 4'
2 2 2 2 – 4 3 3 1 – 3perc – hp – str
SATB Chorus.

            Christmas

G&C (rental)

Cinerama Holiday: Skier's Waltz 3'
2[incl pic] 1 2 1 – 2 2 2 (1) – 2perc – hp, cel – str
SATB Chorus.

          Christmas/Films

G&C (rental)

Cinerama Holiday: Suite 15'
2[incl pic] 1[incl Eh] 2 1 – 2 2 2 (1) – tmp+2 – hp, cel or pf – str

              Films

Schirmer (rental)

Classical Variations on 14'
Colonial Themes
2[1/pic.2/pic] 2 2 2 – 4 2 3 0 – tmp+3 – hp or pf – str

            Patriotic

Schirmer (rental)

Columbia: 13'
Broadsides for Orchestra
3[incl pic] 3[1.2.Eh] 4[incl Ebcl, bcl] 3 – 4 3 3 1 – tmp+3 – hp – str

            Patriotic

G&C (rental)

Cowboy Rhapsody 17'
3[incl pic] 3[incl Eh] 3[incl bcl] 3[incl cbn] – 6 3 3 1 – tmp+4 – hp, (gtr) – str

            Americana

Warner (rental)

Cresta Blanca Waltz 3'
hp, cel – str

         Dance/International

Kalmus

Crinoline and Lace 2.5'
2[incl pic] 2 2 3[1.2.cbn] – 3sx – 4 3 2 0 – perc – hp – str

         Instrumental Pops

Kalmus

Dance Gallery: 4'
Soft Shoe Gavotte
2[incl pic] 2[incl Eh] 3[incl bcl] 2 – 4 2 2 0 – perc – hp – str

              Dance

Schirmer (rental)

Declaration 30'
3[incl pic] 2[incl Eh] 2 2[incl cbn] – 4 3 3 1 – tmp+3 – hp, pf – str
1-2 Narrators; Speaking Male Chorus.

            Patriotic

G&C (rental)

Declaration: Suite 19'
3[incl pic] 2[incl Eh] 2 2[incl cbn] – 4 3 3 1 – tmp+2 – hp – str

            Patriotic

G&C (rental)

Derivations for Solo Clarinet 17'
and Dance Band
0 0 0 0 – 2ssx, tsx – 0 3 3 0 – 2perc – pf – db

              Jazz

G&C (rental)

Deserted Ballroom 3'
1 1 3[1.2.bcl] 1 – 2 3 3 0 – perc – str

              Dance

Kalmus

Dramatic Fanfares from CBS-TV   3'
  Documentary "World War I"
  2[incl pic] 1 2 1 – 2 2 2 1 – tmp+perc – hp, pf or cel
  – str
                                        Fanfare/Patriotic
G&C (rental)

Family Album: Suite   15'
  2[incl pic] 2[incl Eh] 2 2 – 4 3 3 1 – tmp+2 – pf
  – str
  Features percussion.
                                        Instrumental Pops
G&C (rental)

Festive Fanfare   2'
  0 0 0 0 – 0 2 3 0 – tmp+perc
                                                Fanfare
Schirmer (rental)

Festive Music   11'
  3[incl pic] 2 3 2 – 4 3 3 1 – tmp+3 – hp – str
  Solo Trumpet [offstage].
                                              Celebrations
G&C (rental)

First Noel   4'
  2 2 3[1.2.bcl] 2[1.2/cbn] – 4 2 3 1 – chimes – (hp)
  – str
                                                 Christmas
Schirmer (rental)

Five Spirituals   20'
  hp, cel – str   (4' 4' 4' 4' 4')
  Spirituals only available separately: Go Down
  Moses; Deep River; Sometimes I Feel Like a
  Motherless Child; Nobody Knows the Trouble I've
  Seen; Swing Low, Sweet Chariot.
                                            Popular Song
Kalmus

Flares and Declamations   3'
  2[incl 2 pic] 2 2 2 – 4 3[(#3)] 3[(#3)] 1 – tmp+3
  – str
                                               Patriotic
Schirmer (rental)

Flourishes and Galop   4'
  3[1.2.pic] 3 3 3 – 4 3 3 1 – tmp+2 – hp – str
                                               Patriotic
Schirmer (rental)

Folk Suite   11'
  2 2 2 2 – asx, tsx – 4 2 2 0 – tmp+perc – (hp), (pf)
  – str   (3' 5' 3')
  Alternate: 1 1 2 1 – 2 2 1 0 –tmp+perc – str
  Includes: Overture; Blues; Jig.
                                             Americana
G&C (rental)

Foster Gallery   30'
  3[incl pic] 3[incl Eh] 3[incl bcl] 3[1.2.cbn] –
  4 3 3 1 – tmp+3 – hp – bnjo – str
                                             Americana
Schirmer (rental)

Foster Gallery: Suite   18'
  3[incl pic] 3[incl Eh] 3[incl bcl] 3[1.2.cbn] –
  4 3 3 1 – tmp+perc – hp, (bnjo) – str
                                             Americana
Schirmer (rental)

Good King Wenceslas   3'
  2[1/pic.2/pic] 2[1.Eh] 2 1 – 2 2 2 0 – 3 perc – str
  perc: sd, tambn, bells.
                                             Christmas
Schirmer

Hail to a First Lady   2'
  0 0 0 0 – 0 2 3 1 – tmp+perc
                                             Patriotic
Schirmer (rental)

Harvest   12'
  vib – hp – str
                                             Seasons
Schirmer (rental)

Holiday Music   16'
                          (3.5' 3.5' 3' 3' 3' 3')
  Christmas: 2[incl pic] 2[incl Eh] 2 2 – 4 3 3 1
  – tmp+3 – hp, pf, (cel) – str
  Halloween: 2[incl pic] 2[1.Eh] 2 2 – 4 3 3 1
  – tmp+perc – hp, pf – str
  First Thanksgiving: 2[incl pic] 2[incl Eh] 2 2
  – 4 3 3 1 – tmp+3 – hp, cel – str
  Home for Christmas: 2 2[incl Eh] 2 2 – 2 3 2 1
  – 2perc – hp, cel – str
  Easter Morning: 2[incl pic] 2[incl Eh] 2 2 – 4 3 3 1
  – tmp+3 – hp, cel – str
  Fourth of July: 2[incl pic] 2[incl Eh] 2 2 – 4 3 3 1
  – tmp+3 – hp, cel – str
  Each is available separately.
                                               Holidays
G&C (rental)

A Homespun Overture 6'
3[incl pic] 2 3[incl bcl] 2 – 4 3 3 1 – tmp+2 –
bnjo, hp – str

                                              Instrumental Pops

G&C (rental)

Hoofer Suite 13'
1[incl pic] 1 2 1 – 2 2 2 (1) – perc – str
Solo Tap Dancer.

                                                          Dance

G&C (rental)

Hosedown: A Firefighter Fable 18'
3[incl pic] 2 3 2 – 4 3 3 1 – tmp+3 – str
Narrator. Optional hoses, fire tools, cutouts,
projections. Includes 7 movements.

                                              Labor Day/Novelty

Schirmer (rental)

I'm Old Fashioned, Astaire Variations 35'
3[incl pic] 3 3[incl bcl] 3 – 4 3 3 1 – tmp+2 –
hp, pf – str
Ballet choreographed by Jerome Robbins.

                                                          Dance

Schirmer (rental)

It Came Upon a Midnight Clear 3'
Strings

                                                     Christmas

Luck's (rental); Schirmer (rental)

Jekyll and Hyde Variations 22'
3[incl pic] 3[incl Eh] 4[incl Ebcl, bcl] 3[incl cbn] –
6 3 3 1 – tmp+3 – hp, cel or hp – str

                                                    Halloween

G&C (rental)

Jingle Bells 4'
2 2[1.2/Eh] 2 2 – 4 3 3 1 – 3perc – hp or pf – str
perc: slgh-bells, opt bells, whip, sandpaper blocks, tri.

                                                    Christmas

Schirmer (rental)

The Jogger and the Dinosaur 22'
2[1.2/pic] 1 2 1 – 2 2 2 1 – tmp+2 – str
Narrator. The work can be performed in a staged or
concert format. Contact Schirmer to determine
proper licensing for intended performance version.

                                              Animals/Sports

Schirmer (rental)

Latin American Symphonette 17'
(Symphonette No. 4)   (5' 4' 3' 5')
3[1/pic.2.3] 2 4[1.2.3.bcl] 2 – (2asx, tsx, bsx) –
4 3 3 1 – tmp+4 – pf, (gtr) – str
perc: bd, claves, cowbell, cym, guiro, marim, sd, tambn,
templeblks, tomtom, xyl, shakers.
Includes: Rhumba; Tango; Guaracha; Conga.

                                             Dance/International

Kalmus; Schirmer (rental)

Lincoln Legend 18'
2[incl pic] 2[incl Eh] 3 2 – 4 3 3 1 – tmp+2 – hp
– str

                                                    Patriotic

Schirmer (rental)

Minstrel Show 8'
2[incl pic] 2 2 2[1.2.cbn] – 4 3 3 1 – tmp+3 – hp
– str

                                                    Americana

G&C (rental)

Minute Plus Waltz Rag 1.5'
3[1.2.pic] 2 3[incl bcl] 2 – 4 3 3 1 – tmp+perc – hp –
str

                                                   Dance/Jazz

Schirmer (rental)

New China March 9'
3 2 2 2 – 4 3 3 1 – tmp+perc – hp, pf – str

                                              Instrumental Pops

Luck's (rental); Schirmer (rental)

Philharmonic Waltzes 9'
2[incl pic] 2 2[incl bcl] 2[incl cbn] – 4 3 3 1 –
tmp+3 – hp, pf – str

                                                    Dance

G&C (rental)

Pirouette
3[1.2.pic] 2 2 2 – 3sx – 4 3 2 0 – perc – str

                                                   Dance

Kalmus

Pop's Serenade 5'
1 1 1 1 – 4sx – 2 3 3 1 – tmp+3 – hp, pf, gtr – str

                                              Instrumental Pops

EMI (rental)

Red Cavalry March 4'
2 2[incl Eh] 2 2 – 4 3 3 1 – 2perc - hp, pf, gtr – str

                                                   Patriotic

Kalmus

Revival: A Fantasy on Six Spirituals   6'
    2[incl pic] 2 2[incl pic] 2 – 2sx – 2 3 3 1 – tmp+perc
    – hp, pf, gtr or bnjo – str

                                          Americana

Kalmus

Serenade of Carols   15'
    2[incl pic] 2 3[incl bcl] 2 – 2 2 0 0 – hp –
    str[no bass]
    SATB Chorus. Includes: Kings of the Orient; The
    Babe of Bethlehem; Boar's Head Carol; Patapan;
    Carol of Service; Come, Love We God; Coventry
    Carol; The Holly; Irish Carol; God Rest Ye Merry
    Gentlemen; Wassail. Can be performed without
    chorus. Chorus parts arr. by Gregg Smith.

                                          Christmas

G&C (rental)

Something to Do - Labor Cantata   60'
    1[incl pic] 1[incl bcl] 4[incl cbn] 1 – 2 2 2 1 –
    2perc – 2kybd, elec gtr – elec db
    Solo Voice; Narrator; Chorus.

                                          Labor Day

G&C (rental)

A Song of Freedom   10'
    3 2 3 2 – 4 3 3 1 – tmp+5 – hp, gtr – str
    Narrator.

                                          Patriotic

EMI (rental)

Swanee River in the Style of Bach   4'
    1 1 2 1 – 2 2 1 0 – perc – str

                                          Americana

Schirmer (rental)

Swanee River in the Style of Beethoven   4'
    1 1 2 1 – 2 2 0 0 – perc – pf – str

                                          Americana

Schirmer (rental)

Swanee River in the Style of Brahms   4'
    1 1 3 1 – 2 2 1 0 – perc – pf – str

                                          Americana

Schirmer (rental)

Swanee River in the Style of Debussy   4'
    1 1 3 0 – 2 2 1 0 – perc – pf – str

                                          Americana

Schirmer (rental)

Swanee River in the Style of Ellington   4'
    0 0 1 1 – asx – 2 2 1 0 – perc – hp, pf – db

                                          Americana

Schirmer (rental)

Swanee River in the Style of Gershwin   4'
    1 1 1 0 – 3asx – 2 2 1 0 – perc – gtr, pf – str

                                          Americana

Schirmer (rental)

Swanee River in the Style of Liszt   4'
    2 1 2 1 – 2 3 3 1 – perc – pf – str

                                          Americana

Schirmer (rental)

Swanee River in the Style of Mozart   4'
    1 1 2 1 – 2 2 0 0 – str

                                          Americana

Schirmer (rental)

Swanee River in the Style of
Rimsky-Korsakov   4'
    2 1 2 1 – 2 3 3 1 – perc – pf – str

                                          Americana

Schirmer (rental)

Swanee River in the Style of Strauss   4'
(Johann)
    2 2 2 1 – 2 2 1 1 – perc – pf – str

                                          Americana

Schirmer (rental)

Swanee River in the Style of Tchaikovsky   4'
    1 1 1 1 – 3asx – 2 3 2 1 – perc – pf – str

                                          Americana

Schirmer (rental)

Swanee River in the Style of Wagner   4'
    1 1 4[1.2.3.bcl] 1 – asx – 2 3 2 1 – perc – pf – str

                                          Americana

Schirmer (rental)

Symphonette No. 2: Pavanne   3'
    2 2 2 2 – 4 3 3 0 – drumset – hp – str
    2nd mvt features 1st trumpet.

                                         Popular Classics

Belwin; Kalmus

Symphonette No. 2   9'
    (Second American Symphonette)   (3' 3' 3')
    2 2 2 2 – 4 3 3 0 – tmp+1[drumset] – hp or pf – str

                                    Americana/Popular Classics

EMI (rental); Kalmus

Symphonette No. 3
  (Third American Symphonette)
  2 2 2 2 – 2asx, tsx, bsx – 2 3 3 0 – perc – hp, pf, gtr – str
                              Americana/Popular Classics
  EMI (rental)

Tap Dance Concerto   16'
  2[1/pic.2] 2 2 2 – 4 2 2 0 – tmp – str
  Solo Tap Dancer.
                                              Dance/Novelty
  G&C (rental)

Troubadour Music   24'
  2[incl pic] 2[incl Eh] 2 2 – 2 2 2 0 – 2perc – str
  Solo 4 Guitars.
                                           Instrumental Pops
  G&C (rental)

Windjammer: Main Theme, The Ship   3'
  2 2 2 2 – 4 3 3 1 – tmp+2 – hp, cel – str
                                                Films/Travel
  G&C (rental)

Windjammer: Night Watch   3'
  2 1[incl Eh] 2 1 – 2 0 0 0 – perc – hp – str
                                                Films/Travel
  G&C (rental)

Yankee Doodle   3'
  3[1.2.3/pic] 2 2 2 – 2asx, tsx, bsx – 4 3 2 1 – tmp+4 – hp, pf, gtr – str
  perc: sd, bd, temple blks, xylo, vib [tmp only has 3 notes and can be played by 1 of the 2 perc].
                                          Patriotic/Americana
  EMI (rental); Kalmus

Gounod, Charles   1818-1893

Faust: Ballet Music   15'
                              (2' 4' 2' 1' 2' 2' 2')
  2[1.2/pic] 2 3[1.2/bcl] 2 – 4 4[2tp, 2crt] 3 1 – tmp+3 – hp – str
  perc: bd, tri, tambn, cym.
                                                        Dance
  Kalmus

Marche funèbre d'une marionette   6'
  (Funeral March of a Marionette)
  2[1.pic] 2 2 2 – 2 2 3 1 – tmp+3 – str
  perc: tri, cym, bd.
                                             Popular Classics
  Bote & Bock; Kalmus; Luck's

Grady, John arr.   1935-1991?

Christmas with Renata Scotto: 2'
  2. Angels We Have Heard on High
  0 0 0 0 – 3 2 2 0
  Solo Soprano; SATB Chorus.
                                                   Christmas
  AMP (rental)

Christmas with Renata Scotto: 2'
  3. Adeste Fidelis
  0 0 0 0 – 3 2 2 0
  Solo Soprano; SATB Chorus.
                                                   Christmas
  AMP (rental)

Grainger, Percy   1882-1961

Country Gardens   3'
  2 2 2 2 – (asx, tsx) – 4 2 3 1 – tmp+4 – hp – str
  Obbligato Violin.
                                       Ecology/International
  Schirmer (rental)

County Derry Air for 6 or More   4'
  Single Instruments
  6+ instruments
  Available in USA and Canada only.
                                                Popular Song
  Schirmer (rental)

County Derry Air for Pipe Organ   4'
  and Symphony Orchestra
  (2) (1) 4[(1-3).bcl] 1 – ssx, asx, bsx – 2 1 1 1 – org – str
  Solo Organ, 4 Violins. Available in USA and Canada only.
                                                Popular Song
  Schirmer (rental)

Green Bushes   9'
  1[1/pic] 1 2 2 – ssx, 2asx, bsx – 2 1 0 0 – tmp+perc – pf, harm or org – str
  Available in USA and Canada only.
                                                     Ecology
  Schirmer (rental)

In a Nutshell: Suite   15'
                       (2' 2' 8' 3')
    3[incl pic] 3[incl Eh] 3[incl (bcl)] 3[incl (cbn)] –
    4 3 3 1 – tmp+8 to 12 – hp, cel, pf – str
    perc: bd, cym, sus cym, sd, woodblk, glock, tamtam, marim[2 players], vib[2 players], xyl, kybd glock.
    Includes: Arrival Platform Humlet; Gay But Wistful; Pastoral; The Gum-suckers March.
                                   Popular Classics
Kalmus

Irish Tune from County Derry   5'
    1 2 2 1 – asx, tsx – 2 2 1 0 – tmp – str
    Available in USA and Canada only
                                 St. Patrick/International
Schirmer (rental)

Irish Tune from County Derry   5'
    (2hn) – strings
                                 St. Patrick/International
Kalmus; Schirmer (rental)

Irish Tune from County Derry   5'
    1 1 2 1 – asx – 2 2 (1) 0 – tmp – str
    Solo Violin.
    Adolph Schmid, arr.
    Available in USA and Canada only.
                                 St. Patrick/International
Schirmer (rental)

Irish Tune from County Derry   5'
    (Londonderry Air)
    2 1 2 1 – 2 1 0 1[euph] – cym – str
    This version was prepared for Leopold Stokowski who recorded it in 1950.
    Dana P. Perna, arr.
                                 St. Patrick/International
Luck's; Ludwig

Marching Song of Democracy   12'
    for Chorus and Orchestra
    2 2 3[1.2.bcl] 3[1.2.cbn] – 4 3 3 1[euph] – tmp+perc – 2hp, org – str
    Chorus. Available in USA and Canada only.
                                            Patriotic
Schirmer (rental)

Mock Morris for Orchestra   4'
    2[incl pic] 2 2 2 – 2 2 3 0 – perc – str
    Otto Langey, arr.
                                          International
Kalmus

Mock Morris   3'
    2 1 2 1 – 2 2[crt] 1 0 – perc – harm/pf – str
    Solo Violin.
    Available in USA and Canada only.
                                            International
Schirmer (rental)

Molly on the Shore   3'
    Strings
                                            International
Kalmus

Molly on the Shore   3'
    3[1.(2).pic] 2 2 2 – 4 2 3 1 – tmp+5 – cel – str
    perc: bells, xyl, sd, cym, bd.
    Any or all winds can be used.
                                            International
Kalmus

The Power of Love
    3[incl pic] 2 2 3[incl bcl] 2 – ssx, tsx, bsx –
    4 3 3 1 – hp, harm, org – str
    Available in USA and Canada only.
                                              Valentine
Schirmer (rental)

Shepherd's Hey   3'
    2[1.2/pic] 2 2 2 – 4 3 3 1 – tmp+5 – 2hp, pf – str
    perc: sd, bd, cym, sus cym, tri, bells, xyl.
    Alternate for chamber ensemble: 2[1.2/pic] 2 2 – 4 2 3 1 – tmp+3 – hp – str; or 1 0 1 0 – (1) 0 0 0 – str [with 3vn, 2va, 2vc, cb concertina]
                                            International
Kalmus

Tribute to Foster   10'
    3 2 2 2 – 4 2 3 1 – tmp+perc – harm – str – musical glasses
    Solo 5 Voices, Piano; SATB Chorus. Grainger suggests that members of the chorus play the musical glasses. Available in USA and Canada only.
                                            Americana
Schirmer (rental)

Granados, Enrique   1867-1916

Goyescas: Intermezzo   6'
    2 2[incl Eh] 2 2 – 4 1 3 0 – tmp+perc – hp – str
                                         International (Spain)
Filarmonika (rental)

Tres danzas españolas   14'
    3[1.2.3/pic] 2[1.2.Eh] 3[1.2.bcl] 2 – 4 2 3 1 –
    tmp+3 – hp – str
    Includes: Oriental; Andaluza; Rondalla.
    J. Lamote de Grignon, arr.
                                Dance/International
Kalmus

Tonadillas   20'
    1 2[1.Eh] 2[1.bcl] 2[1.cbn] – 0 0 0 0 – tmp – hp – str
    Solo Soprano. Text: Spanish.
    Rafael Ferrer, arr.
                                      International
UME (rental)

Granda, Isabel   1920-1983

La Flor de la Canela   3'
    2 2 2 2 – 3 2 2 0 – tmp+1 – str
    A popular song in the city of Lima, Peru.
    Álvarez, arr.
                                 International (Peru)
Filarmonika

Grant, James   1954-

Lament   10.5'
    Strings
    Often programmed for 9/11 memorial concerts.
                                                Patriotic
Grantwood Music

Waltz for Betz   4.5'
    Solo Viola, Alto Sax, or Clarinet – Strings
    Composed as a musical Valentine's Day card.
                                Dance/Valentine
Grantwood Music

Gray, Allan   1902-1973

African Queen: Portrait (1951)   5'
    2[1.pic] 1 2 1 – 2 2 3 0 – tmp+3 – hp – str
    perc: xyl, tambn, cym, tri, sd, bd.
                                                   Films
T&V (rental)

Green Day (See: Armstrong)

Green, John   1908-1989

Body and Soul   3'
    2 2 2 1 – 4 3 3 1 – tmp+drumset – pf, elec bass – str
    Chuck Sayre, arr.
                                    Jazz/Popular Song
Warner (POP); Luck's (rental)

Body and Soul   5'
    1perc[drumset] – pf, gtr – str
    Solo Tenor or Alto Saxophone.
    Calvin Custer, arr.
                                    Jazz/Popular Song
Warner (POP); Luck's (rental)

Greenway, R. (See: Back, B.)

Greenwood, Lee   1942-

God Bless the U.S.A.   3'
    2 1 3[1.2.bcl] 1 – 2sx – 2 3 3 1 – tmp+perc – pf – str
    Bob Lowden, arr.
                                                Patriotic
Warner (POP); EAM or Luck's (rental)

Gregson-Williams, Harry   1961-

Chronicles of Narnia: 7.5'
*   The Lion, The Witch and The Wardrobe*
    2 1 3[1.2.vcl] 1 – 4 3 3 1 – tmp+4 – (hp), pf/(cel)
    – str
    Includes: Sword; Picnic Talk; The Meeting; Edward
    and the White Witch; Turned in for Sweets; The
    Knighting of Peter; Crossing the River.
    Stephan Bulla, arr.
                                                   Films
Leonard

Grgin, Ante   1945-

Laura: Fantasy for Trumpet in Bb and Orchestra
2 2 2 2 – 0 2 2 0 – tmp+perc – str
perc: sus cym, sd, tom-toms.
Solo Trumpet.

                             Instrumental Pops

EMR

Grieg, Edvard   1843-1907

Erotik   3'
(hp) – strings
Max Spicker, arr.
                 Popular Classics/Valentine

Kalmus; Luck's

Holberg Suite Op. 40   21'
Strings   (4' 4' 4' 5' 4')
                                Popular Classics

Kalmus; Luck's; Peters

ch Liebe Dich   *1*   3'
2 2 2 2 – 4 3 3 1 – tmp – hp – str
Morton Gould, arr.
                 Popular Classics/Valentine

Schirmer (rental)

Lyric Pieces, Suite No. 5,   6'
Op. 68, Nos. 4 and 5
0 1 0 0 – 1 0 0 0 – str
Includes: Evening in the Mountains; At the Cradle.
Spicker, arr.
                                Popular Classics

Kalmus; Peters

Lyric Suite, Op. 54   17'
3[incl pic] 2 2 2 – 4 2 3 1 – tmp+2 – hp – str
                          (5' 4' 4' 4')
Includes: Shepherd's Boy, Norwegian Rustic March, Notturno, March of the Dwarfs.
                     Halloween/Popular Classics

Kalmus; Luck's

Norwegian Dances, Op. 35   17'
                          (6' 2' 4' 5')
3[1.2.pic] 2 2 2 – 4 2 3 1 – tmp+2 – hp – str
Hans Sitt, arr.
                           Popular Classics/Dance/
                                       International

Kalmus; Peters (rental)

Peer Gynt: Suite No. 1, Op. 46   15'
                          (4' 4' 4' 3')
3[1.2.pic] 2 2 2 – 4 2 3 1 – tmp+2 – hp – str
Includes: Morning Mood; Ase's Death; Anitra's Dance; In the Hall of the Mountain King.
                                Popular Classics

Kalmus; Peters (rental)

Sigurd Jorsalfar (Sigurd the Crusader):   17'
  Suite, Op. 56   (4' 5' 8')
2[1/pic.2/pic] 2 2 2 – 4 3 3 1 – tmp+3 – hp – str
perc: sd, cym, bd, tri.
Includes: Introduction-In the King's Hall; Intermezzo; Huldigungsmarsch (Sons of Knute).
Sigurd Jorsalfar was king of Norway from 1103 to 1130.
                                Popular Classics

Kalmus; Luck's

To Spring   4'
2 2 2 2 – 4 3 3 1 – tmp+perc – hp, cel – str
Morton Gould, arr.
                                      Seasons

Schirmer (rental)

Two Norwegian Airs, Op. 63   11'
Strings   (6' 5')
Includes: Popular song; Cow Keeper's Tune and Country Dance
                                    International

Kalmus; Luck's

Wedding Day at Troldhaugen, Op. 65, no. 6   5'
2 2 2 2 – 4 3 3 0 – tmp+1 – hp, cel – str
Breuer, arr.
                                      Valentine

Peters (rental)

Wedding Day at Troldhaugen, Op. 65, no. 6   5'
2 2 2 2 – 4 3 3 1 – tmp+1 – hp, cel – str
Morton Gould, arr.
                                      Valentine

Schirmer (rental)

Wedding Day at Troldhaugen, Op. 65, no. 6   5'
2 2 2 2 – 4 3 3 1 – 2perc – str
Theo. M. Tobani, arr.
                                      Valentine

Luck's

Griffes, Charles Tomlinson   1884-1920

Clouds   5'
3[1.2.3/pic] 3[1.2.3/Eh] 3[1.2.bcl] 3 – 4 0 0 0 – 1perc – 2hp, cel – str
perc: tamtam.
    Popular Classics/Weather
Schirmer (rental)

Five Poems of the Ancient Far East   12'
3 3 2 2 – 2 1 0 0 – perc – hp, cel – str
Solo Medium Voice.
    International
Schirmer (rental)

The Pleasure Dome of Kubla Khan, Op. 8   14'
3[1.2.3/pic] 3[1.2.Eh] 3[1.2.bcl] 3 – 4 3 3 1 – tmp+2 – 2hp, cel, pf – str
perc: bd, cym, gong, tambn.
    Popular Classics
Kalmus; Schirmer (rental)

Poem for Flute and Orchestra   9'
0 0 0 0 – 2 0 0 0 – perc – hp – str
Alternate: 0 0 3[incl acl/bcl] 0 – 2 3[crt] 0 0 – 2perc – hp – db
perc: sd, bd, gong, tambn.
Solo Flute.
    Popular Classics
Schirmer (rental)

Three Tone Pictures   5'
1 1 1 1 – 1 0 0 0 – pf – str
    Popular Classics
Schirmer (rental)

The White Peacock, Op. 7/1   6'
2[1.2/pic] 2 2 2 – 2 3 2 0 – tmp+1 – 2hp, cel – str
perc: cym, tamtam.
    Animals
Kalmus; Schirmer (rental)

Griffin, Merv   1925-2007

An Hour with the Game Shows   4'
1 1 2 1 – 1 2 1 1 – perc – (pf) – str
Can be performed by strings alone. Includes: Jeopardy & Wheel of Fortune.
Bob Cerulli, arr.
    TV
Warner (POP); EMS or Luck's (rental)

Jeopardy Theme   2'
2 1 2 1 – 2 2 2 1 – tmp+perc – pf – str
Marty Gold, arr.
    TV
Warner (POP); EMS (rental)

Grofé, Ferde   1892-1972

Death Valley Suite   18'
3[incl pic] 3[incl Eh] 3[incl bcl] 3[incl cbn] – 4 3 3 1 – tmp+3 – hp, cel – str
Includes: Funeral Mountains, 1849 Emigrant Train; Desert Water Hole; Sand Storm.
    Americana
EMI (rental)

Grand Canyon Suite   35'
    (6' 6' 8' 6' 9')
3[1.2.3/pic] 3[1.2.Eh] 3[1.2.bcl] 3[1.2.cbn] – 4 3 3 1 – tmp+3 – hp,cel/pf – str
perc: glock, tri, chimes, bd, sd, wnd machine, vib, horse hooves, 2sus cym, "lightning machine".
Includes: Sunrise; Painted Desert; On the Trail; Sunset; Cloudburst.
    Americana
EMI (rental)

Hollywood Suite   25'
    3[incl 2pic] 3[incl Eh] 3[1.2.bcl] 3[1.2.cbn] –
    2asx(cl), 2tsx – 4 3 3 1 – tmp+2 – 2hp, cel – str
    On the Set-Sweepers: 3[1.2.pic] 3 3[1.2.bcl]
    3[1.2.cbn] – 4 3 3 1 – tmp+2 – 2hp, cel – str   (4')
    The Stand-In: 3[incl pic] 3[incl Eh] 3[1.2.bcl]
    3[1.2.cbn] – 4 3 3 1 – tmp+perc – hp, cel – str   (4')
    The Stand-In: 3[incl pic] 3[incl Eh] 3[1.2.bcl]
    3[1.2.cbn] – 4 3 3 1 – tmp+perc – hp, cel – str   (4')
    Preview: 3[1.2.pic] 3[incl eh] 3[incl bcl]
    3[1.2.cbn] – 0 0 0 0 – tmp+2 – 2hp, cel – str   (4')
    Production Number: 3[1.2.pic] 3[1.2.Eh] 3[incl Eh]
    3[1.2.bcl] – 2asx(cl), 2tsx – 4 3 3 1 – tmp+2 – cel
    – str   (4')
    Director -Star-Ensemble: 3[1.2.pic]3[1.2.Eh]
    3[1.2.bcl] 3[1.2.cbn] – 2asx, 2tsx – 4 3 3 1 – tmp+2 –
    hp, cel – str   (5')
                                                                      Films
    EMI (rental)

Hudson River Suite   19'
    3[incl pic] 3[incl Eh] 3[incl bcl] 3[incl cbn] –
    4 3 3 1 – tmp+3 – hp, cel, pf – str
    Includes: The River; Hendrik Hudson; Rip Van
    Winkle; Albany Night Boat; New York! With jazz
    trio [opt cl,tp,tbn] cued into orchestra parts.
                                             Americana
    EMI (rental)

Mississippi: A Tone Journey   13'
    (Mississippi Suite)
    3[1.2.pic] 3[1.2.3/Eh] 3[1.2.bcl] 3[1.2.cbn] –
    2asx, tsx, bsx – 4 3 3 1 – tmp+3 – hp, cel – str
    Original 1926 edition by publisher Leo Feist, Inc.,
    NY, NY.
                                               Americana
    EMI (rental)

Mississippi: A Tone Journey   13'
    (Mississippi Suite)
    3[1.2.pic] 3[1.2.Eh] 3[1.2.bcl] 3[1.2.cbn] – 4 3 3 1
    – tmp+3 – hp, cel – str
    perc: small & large Indian tomtom, sd, bd, cym,
    windwhistle, woodblks, tri, sandblks.
    Includes: Father of Waters, Huckleberry Finn,
    Old Creole Days, Mardi Gras.
                                             Americana
    Fleisher; Luck's (rental)

Niagara Falls Suite   22'
                          (3.5' 4.5' 4.5' 10')
    3[incl pic] 3[1.2.Eh] 3[1.2.bcl] 3[1.2.cbn] – 4 3 3 1
    – tmp+3 – hp, pf or cel – str
    Thunder of the Waters; Devil's Hole Massacre;
    Honeymooners; Power of the Niagara.
                                               Americana
    EMI (rental)

Symphony in Steel   15'
    3[incl pic] 2[incl Eh] 3[1.2.bcl] 2 – 2asx, tsx, bsx
    – 4 3 3 1 – tmp+perc – hp, 2pf – str
                         Labor Day/Popular Classics
    EMI (rental); Fleisher

Tabloid   20'
    3[incl 2 pic] 2[incl Eh] 3[incl bcl] 2 –
    asx[(bcl, bsx)], asx[(bcl, bsx)], tsx[(fl/pic, cl)] –
    4 3 3 1 – tmp+2 – 2pf or cel, bnjo – str
    Run of the News:
    3[incl 2 pic] 2[incl Eh] 3[incl bcl] 2 –
    tsx, 2bsx[(2asx)] – 4 3 3 1 – tmp+2 –
    2pf, bnjo – str
    Sob Sister: 2[incl pic] 2[incl Eh] 2 2 –
    tsx, 2bsx[(2asx)] – 4 3 3 1 – tmp+2 –
    2pf or cel, bnjo – str
    Comic Strips: 2 2 2 2 – tsx, 2bsx – 4 3 3 1 –
    cel, pf, bnjo – str;
    Going to Press: 2[incl 2 pic] 2[incl Eh] 2 2 –
    asx[(bcl)], asx[(cl, bsx)], tsx[(fl/pic, cl)] –
    4 3 3 1 – tmp
                                               Americana
    EMI (rental); Fleisher

World's Fair Suite   34'
    3[1.2.pic] 3[1.2.Eh] 3[1.2.bcl] 3[1.2.cbn] – 4 3 3 1
    – tmp+3 – hp, pf – str
    Includes: Unisphere; International; Fun at the Fair;
    Pavilion of Industry; National.
    Albert Glasser, orchestrator.
                                               Americana
    EMI (rental)

Gruber, Franz Xavier   1787-1863

Christmas with Renata Scotto: 2'
    1. Silent Night
    bells – strings
    Solo Soprano; SATB Chorus.
    John Grady, arr.
                                               Christmas
    AMP (rental)

Silent Night   4'
  2 2[1.Eh] 2 2 – 4 3 3 1 – tmp+2,drumset – hp, pf
  – str+jazz bass
  Solo Horn.
  Jeff Tyzik, arr.
      Christmas

  AMP (rental)

Silent Night; O Little Town of Bethlehem   3.5'
  2 2 2 2 – 2 2 0 0 – str
  Silent Night is in the Key of C. Little Town of Bethlehem is in the Key of G and was composed by Lewis Redner.
  Arthur Luck, arr.
      Christmas

  Luck's

Gruenberg, Louis   1884-1964

Jazz Suite, Op. 28   18'
  3[1.2.pic] 3[1.2.Eh] 3[1.2.bcl] 3[1.2.cbn] – 4 3 3 1
  – tmp+4 – hp, cel – str
  Includes: Foxtrot tempo (allegretto ben ritmico); Boston waltz tempo (valse lente e languido); Blues tempo, slow drag (moderato ma non troppo); One-step tempo (allegro assai).
      Jazz

  GunMar (rental)

Grundman, Clare [Mr.]   1913-1996

American Folk Rhapsody No. 1:   6.5'
Four American Folk Songs
  3[1.2.pic] 2 3[1.2.pic] 2 – (3sx) –
  4 3[(#3)] 3[(#3)] 0 – tmp+2 – str
  Includes: My Little Mohee; Shantyman's Life; Sourwood Mountain; Sweet Betsy from Pike.
      Americana

  Boosey

American Folk Rhapsody No. 2   5.5'
  3[incl pic] 2 3[incl bcl] 2 – 3sx – 4 3 3 1 – tmp+3
  – str
  Includes: Billy Boy; Skip to My Lou; Shenandoah.
      Americana

  Boosey

Three Noels   4'
  2[1.2/pic] 2 3[1.2.bcl] 2 – asx, tsx – 2 2 2 0 –
  tmp+2 – (pf) – str
  perc: sd, bd, tri, glock.
  SA, SSA, SAB, or SATB Chorus. Includes: Christmas Hymn; Christmas Eve is Here; Now We Sing of Christmas.
      Chistmas

  Boosey

Grusin, Dave   1907-1993

Theme from On Golden Pond   4'
  2 1 3[1.2.(bcl)] 1 – (asx, tsx) – 2 3 3 1 – 3perc –
  pf – str
  perc: drumset, tri, glock.
  From the film *On Golden Pond*. Nominated for the 1982 Academy Award for Best Music and Original Score.
  Bob Lowden, arr.
      Films

  Leonard (POP); EMS or Luck's (rental)

Guaraldi, Vince & Mendelson, Lee

A Charlie Brown Christmas   6'
  2 2 2 2 – 4 2 2 1 – tmp+2 – pf – str
  perc: drumset [ride cym, hi hat, sd, bd] glock, vib, xyl.
  Includes: Christmas is Coming; Christmas Time is Here; Skating; Linus and Lucy.
  David Pugh, arr.
      Christmas

  Warner

Guarnieri, Camargo   1907-1993

Dansa Brasileira   3'
  3 2 2 2 – 4 2 3 1 – tmp+perc – str
      Dance/International

  Schirmer

Guettel, Adam   1965-

Light in the Piazza: *10'*
   Symphonic Suite   *(5' 1.5' 2.5' 1')*
   3[1.2.pic] 3[1.2.Eh] 3[1.2.bcl] 3[1.2.cbn] – 4 3 3 1
   – tmp+perc – hp, cel – str
   perc: vib, chimes, tri, glock, sus cym, tambn.
   Includes Part 1: The Light in the Pianna; Part 2: Passeggiata; Part 3: Statues and Stories; Coda. All sections of the Suite are available separately.
   Johathan Tunick, orchestrator

                                     Broadway Musicals

R&H (rental)

Guion, David   1892-1981

Arkansas Traveler   *7'*
   2[incl pic] 2 2 2 – asx, tsx – 4 2 3 1 – tmp+3 – hp – str
   Adolf Schmid, arr.

                                     Americana/Travel

Schirmer (rental)

Cowboy's Meditation for Voice and Orchestra
   1 1 1 1 – 1 1 1 0 – tmp – pf – str
   Solo Voice.

                                     Americana

Schirmer (rental)

Home on the Range   *4'*
   1 1 2 1 – 2 2 1 0 – tmp+perc – hp, pf – str
   Optional Solo Voice.
   Adolf Schmid, arr.

                                     Americana

Schirmer (rental)

Home on the Range   *10'*
   for Voice and Orchestra
   1 1 2 1 – 2 2 1 0 – tmp+perc – hp, pf – str
   Solo Voice.

                                     Americana

Schirmer (rental)

De Laud's Baptizin'
   3[1.2.pic] 2[incl Eh] 2 2 – 4 2 3 1 – tmp+perc – hp – str
   Crawford, arr.

                                     Popular Song

Schirmer (rental)

Mam'selle Marie   *9'*
   2 1 2 1 – asx, tsx – 0 0 0 0 – str
   Solo Voice.

                                     Popular Song

Schirmer (rental)

Minuet   *9'*
   1 1 2 1 – 1 1 1 0 – str

                                     Dance

Schirmer (rental)

My Cowboy Love Song
   1 1 2 1 – 4asx – 2 3 2 0 – perc – gtr or bnjo – str
   Agnolucci, arr.

                                     Americana

Schirmer (rental)

Pastorale: Three Little Brown Bulls   *7'*
   1 1 2 1 – 2 1 1 0 – perc – hp, pf – str

                                     Animals

Schirmer (rental)

Pickaninny Dance
   1 1 2 1 – asx, tsx – 2 2 1 0 – tmp+perc – hp, harm – str
   Adolf Schmid, arr.

                                     Dance

Schirmer (rental)

Prairie Suite   *14'*
   2[incl pic] 2 2 2 – 2 2 3 0 – tmp+perc – hp, pf – str

                                     Americana

Schirmer (rental)

Sail Away for the Rio Grande
   1 1 4[incl Ebcl & bcl] 1 – ssx, asx, tsx, bsx – 4 3 3 1+ bar – tmp+3
   Solo Cornet.

                                     Travel/Americana

Schirmer (rental)

Sheep and Goat   *3'*
   1 1 2 1 – asx, tsx – 2 2 1 0 – tmp+perc – hp, harm – str

                                     Animals

Schirmer (rental)

Turkey in the Straw   *4'*
   2[1.pic] 1 2 1 – 2 2 1 0 – tmp+4 – str
   perc: sandblks, tri, sd,bd, cym, bells, xyl, gong, tambn.
   M. Baron, arr.

                                     Americana

Luck's (rental); Schirmer (rental)

Gutierrez, Pedro Elias — 1892-1981

Alma Llanera — 3.5'
2 2 2 2 – 4 2 3 1 – tmp+2 – str
Score available for purchase.
International (Venezuela)

Filarmonika (rental)

H

Hageman, Richard — 1882-1966

At the Well
2 2 2 1 – 2 0 0 0 – tmp+perc – hp – str
Popular Song

Schirmer (rental)

Stagecoach: Suite (1939) — 6.5'
3[1.2.pic] 3[1.2.Eh] 3[1.2.Ebcl/bcl] 3[1.2.cbn] – 4 3 3 1 – tmp+4 – hp, pf/cel– str
perc: cym, sus cym, whip, tri, temple blocks, sd, td, bd, toms, tubophone.
Music from the Oscar winning film score.
Americana/Films

T&V (rental)

Hagen, Earl — 1919-2008

Television Medley — 7'
3[1.2.pic] 3[1.2.Eh] 3[1.2.bcl] 2 – 2asx, tsx, bsx – 4 3[1.flug.flug] 3 1 – tmp+perc[drumset] – hp, pf[cel], elec gtr, elec bs – str
Includes: Mary Tyler Moore; Dick Van Dyke; Gomer Pyle; Make Room for Daddy; I Spy; Will Penny; and Andy Griffith Show.
TV

T&V (rental)

Haggart, Bob — 1914-1998

What's New? — 3'
2 1 2 1 – 2 3 2 1 – drumset+1perc – pf – str
Dixieland-based sound made famous by Linda Ronstadt.
Marty Gold, arr.
New Year/Popular Song

EMS (rental); Warner

Hailstork, Adolphus　　　　1941-

An American Fanfare　　　　4.5'
0 0 0 0 – 4 3 3 1 – tmp+3
　　　　　　　　　　　　Americana
Presser

Four Spirituals　　　　12'
1 1 1 1 – 1 1 1 0 – tmp+perc – str
Includes: Great Day; In Dat Great Gittin Up Morning; Certny Lord; He's Got the Whole World in His Hands.
2 Solo Sopranos; mixed chorus.
　　　　　　　　　　Black History Month
Presser (rental)

I Will Lift Up Mine Eyes　　　　12'
1 1 1 1 – 1 1 1 0 – tmp+perc – str
Solo Tenor; SATB chorus.
　　　　　　　　　　Black History Month
Presser (rental)

Halvorsen, Johan　　　　1864-1935

Entry of the Boyars　　　　5'
1 2 2 2 – 2 2 3 1 – 3perc – str
perc: bd, cym, sd, tri.
Theodore Moses Tobani, transcriber
　　　　　　　　　　　Popular Classics
Kalmus

Entry of the Boyars　　　　5'
2[1.pic] 2 2 2 – 4 2 3 1 – 3perc – str
perc: bd, cym, sd, tri.
　　　　　　　　　　　Popular Classics
Kalmus; Luck's

Norwegian Air　　　　5'
2[incl pic] 2 2 2 – 2 0 0 0 – tmp+perc – str
Solo Violin.
　　　　　　　　　　　　International
Hansen (rental)

Norwegian Fairy Pictures　　　　11'
2[incl pic] 2 2 2 – 4 2 1 0 – tmp+perc – hp – str
　　　　　　　　　　　　International
Hansen (rental)

Norwegian Festival Overture, Op. 16　　　　9'
2 2 2 2 – 4 2 3 0 – tmp+perc – str
　　　　　　　　　　　　International
Hansen (rental)

Norwegian Rhapsody No. 1 in A　　　　10'
2[incl 2 pic] 2 2 2 – 4 2 3 1 – tmp+perc – str
　　　　　　　　　　　　International
Hansen (rental)

Norwegian Rhapsody No. 2 in G　　　　11'
3[1.2.pic] 2 2 2 – 4 2 3 1 – tmp+perc – str
　　　　　　　　　　　　International
Hansen (rental)

Norwegian Song, Op. 31　　　　3'
Strings
Solo Violin.
　　　　　　　　　　　　International
Hansen (rental)

Hamlisch, Marvin　　　　1944-2012

Selections from a Chorus Line　　　　3'
2 1 3[1.2.opt bcl] 1 – (2asx) – 3 3 2 1 – tmp+3 – pf, (elec bass) – str
perc: bells, xylo, drumset [or sus cym, sd, bd, toms].
Includes: I Hope I Get It; At the Ballet; One; What I Did for Love.
Bob Lowden, arr.
　　　　　　　　　　Broadway Musicals/Dance
Leonard

Ice Castles: Through the Eyes of Love　　　　3'
2 1 2 1 – (asx, tsx) – 2 2 2 0 – 1perc – gtr – str
perc: drumset.
Philip H. Fink, arr.
　　　　　　　　　　　Films/Valentine
Gold Horizon/Golden Torch (rental)

Marvin Hamlisch in Concert　　　　3'
2 1 3[1.2.(bcl)] 1 – (asx, tsx) – 4 3 2 1 – tmp+3 – pf – str
perc: drumset, tri, tambn, glock, vib, chimes, xyl.
Includes They're Playing My song; Nobody Does It Better; One; If You Remember Me; The Entertainer; What I Did for Love.
Bob Lowden, arr.
　　　　　　　　　　　Broadway Musicals
Leonard (rental)

Handel, George Frideric 1685-1759

Alexander's Feast: Overture 5'
0 2 0 0 – cnt – str
Novello edition arr. by Granville Bantock.
Kalmus; Novello (rental) Popular Classics

Angels We Have Heard on High; 2'
Joy to the World
2 3[incl Eh] 3 3[incl bcl] – 4 3 3 1 – str
Angels in key of G; Joy in key of D.
Luck's Christmas

Berenice Overture 5'
Strings
Granville Bantock, arr.
Novello (rental) Popular Classics

Hercules Overture 5'
Strings
Granville Bantock, arr.
Novello (rental) Popular Classics

Joy to the World 2'
2 2[incl Eh] 2 2 – 4 3 3 1 – tmp+perc – hp – str
Jeff Tyzik & Tommy Newsom, arr.
Schirmer (rental) Christmas

The Novello Book of Carols: 3'
Joy to the World
2 2 2 2 – 0 2 0 0 – str
Solo Voice.
Novello (rental) Christmas

Christmas with Renata Scotto: 2'
4. Joy to the World
0 0 0 0 – 3 2 2 0
Solo Soprano; mixed chorus.
John Grady, arr.
AMP (rental) Christmas

Julius Caesar Overture 9'
Strings
Granville Bantock, arr.
Novello (rental) Popular Classics

The King Shall Rejoice 13'
0 2 0 1 – 0 3 0 0 – tmp – cnt – str
SAATBB Chorus.
Granville Bantock, arr.
Novello (rental) Popular Classics

Overture in D Minor 6'
3[incl pic] 3[incl EH] 3[incl bcl] 3[incl cbn] –
4 3 3 1 – tmp+perc – (hpsd or org) – str
From *Chandos Anthem No. 2 in D minor*, "In the Lord Put I My Trust", HWV 247.
Edward Elgar, arr.
Fleisher; Novello (rental) Popular Classics

Messiah: Sinfonia Pastoral 5'
0 2 0 2 – 2 0 0 0 – str
Leopold Stokowski, arr.
Presser (rental) Holidays/Ecology

Music for the Royal Fireworks 18'
0 3 0 3[1.2.cbn] – 3 3 0 0 – tmp – hpsd – str
Critical edition.
Hans Redlich, editor
Celebrations/Popular Classics
Breitkopf; Kalmus

Music for the Royal Fireworks 18'
(8' 2' 3' 2' 3')
0 3 0 2 – 3 3 0 0 – tmp – str
Overture; Bourrée; La Paix; La Réjouissance;
Menuet I & II.
Max Seiffert, arr.
Celebrations/Popular Classics
Breitkopf; Kalmus

Music for the Royal Fireworks 19'
2[1/pic.2/pic] 3 3 3[1.2.cbn] – 3 5 3 0 – tmp+3 – str
perc: bd, cym, sd.
Anthony Baines & Charles Mackerras, arr.
Celebrations/Popular Classics
Novello (rental)

Suite from the Royal Fireworks 11'
0 2 0 2 – 4 3 0 0 – tmp+1 – str
perc: sd.
Includes: Overture; Alls Siciliana; Bourrée; Menuetto.
Hamilton Harty, arr.
Celebrations/Popular Classics
Warner (rental)

Variations on a Theme by Handel   4'
   2 2 2 2 – 4 2 3 1 – tmp – str
   Maurice C. Whitney, arr.
   John Whitney, reviser
                                Popular Classics
Alfred

Water Music   20'
   4[incl 2pic, afl] 4 4[incl Ebcl, bcl] 4[incl cbn] –
   6 4 0 0 – tmp+perc[sd] – str
   Leopold Stokowski, arr.
                            Ecology/Popular Classics
Presser (rental)

Water Music Suite   16'
                       (2' 5' 1' 1' 4' 3')
   2[1.2/pic] 2 2 2 – 4 2 0 0 – tmp – str
   Hamilton Harty, arr.
                            Ecology/Popular Classics
Kalmus; Warner (rental)

Handy, W. C.   1873-1958

Saint Louis Blues   3'
   2 1 3[incl bcl] 1 – 3sx – 2 3 3 1 – tmp+perc – pf
   – str
   Bill Holcombe, arr.
                                    Americana/Jazz
Musicians Pub.

Saint Louis Blues   3'
   2[1.pic] 2 2 2 – 4sx – 4 3 3 0 – perc – str
   Vinci, arr.
                                    Americana/Jazz
Kalmus

Harbison, John   1938-

Fanfare for Foley's   2'
   0 0 0 0 – 4 4 3 1 – tmp+perc
                                             Fanfare
AMP (rental)

The Flight into Egypt: Sacred Ricercar   14'
   0 3[incl Eh] 0 1 – 0 0 3 0 – org – str
   Solo Soprano & Baritone; chorus.
   Text: Bible-Matthew 3:13-23; Winner of the 1987
   Pulitzer Prize in Music.
                                          Holidays
Schirmer (rental)

Remembering Gatsby: 7'
Foxtrot for Orchestra
   3[1.2.3/pic] 3[1.2.3/Eh] 3[1.2.3/bcl/ssx] 3[1.2.cbn]
   – 4 3 3 1 – tmp+3[incl drumset] – pf – str
   Alternate: 2[1.2/pic] 2[1.2/Eh] 2[1.2/ssx] 2 – 2 2 2 1
   – tmp+3 – pf – str
   Reduced orchestration by John Moody.
                                        Dance/Jazz
AMP (rental)

Hardiman, Ronan   1961-

The Lord of the Dance   6.5'
   2 1 3[1.2.bcl] 1 – 4 3 3 1 – tmp+3 – elec bass –
   hp or pf – str
   perc: drumset, chimes, tri, low conga, 2 bongos, woodblk,
   tom toms, shaker, sus cym.
   Includes: Cry of The Celts, The Lord of the Dance.
   Larry Moore, arr.
                                                 Dance
Leonard

Music from Lord of the Dance   3'
   drumset – pf – str
   Calvin Custer, arr.
                                               Dance
Leonard

Harris, Arthur E.   1927-1992

Americana   15'
   3[1.2.pic] 2 2 2 – 2 3 3 1– tmp+perc – hp – str
   Includes: When Johnny Comes Marching Home,
   Shenandoah, Camptown Races, Deep River, Yankee
   Doodle.
                                             Americana
Kalmus

Harris, Roy   1898-1979

Acceleration   9'
   3 3 3 3 – 4 3 3 1 – tmp+4 – str
                                          Popular Classics
EMI (rental)

American Creed   18'
    4 3 4 3 – 6 4 4 2 – tmp+4 – str
                                 Patriotic
   AMP (rental)

Concert Overture – March in Time of War   4'
    3 3 4[incl Ebcl,bcl] 3 – 4 3 3 1 – tmp+perc – str
                                 Patriotic
   AMP (rental)

Concerto in One Movement: 14'
   Jamboree
    2 1 5 1 – (sx) – 1 3 3 1 – tmp+3 – str
    Solo Piano.
                           Popular Classics
   AMP (rental)

Epilogue to Profiles in Courage: JFK   10'
    3[1.2.pic] 3[1.2.Eh] 3[1.2.bcl] 3 – 4[+2] 3 3 1 –
    tmp+3 – str
                        Patriotic/Americana
   AMP (rental)

Folksong Symphony: 38'
   Two Interludes
    3 3 4 3 – 4 3 3 1 – tmp+perc – pf – str
                               Americana
   AMP (rental)

Freedom's Land   3'
    1 2 2 1 – 2 2 1 0 – tmp+perc – hp, pf – str
    SATB chorus.
                                 Patriotic
   AMP (rental)

Horn of Plenty   10'
    3[1.2.3/pic] 3[1.2.Eh] 3[1.2.bcl] 3 – 4 4 3 1 –
    baritone horn – tmp+3 – str
    Solo Trumpet.
                                 Seasons
   AMP (rental)

When Johnny Comes Marching Home: 8'
   Overture
    3[1.2.pic] 3[1.2.Eh] 3[1.2.Ebcl.bcl] 3 – 4 3 3 1 –
    euphonium – 2tmp+2 – str
                                 Patriotic
   AMP (rental)

Work   10'
    3 3 3 3 – 4 3 3 1 – tmp+perc[chimes] – pf – str
                                 Labor Day
   EMI (rental)

Haslam, Herbert   1732-1809

Special Starlight   20'
    3 3 0 0 – 1 2 2 1 – perc – pf – str
    Narrator; Mixed Chorus; Treble voices. Text by
    Carl Sandberg.
                                 Christmas
   Presser (rental)

Hawley, C.B.

The Christ Child
    2 2 2 2 – 2 2 2 0 – hp – str
    Solo Tenor or Soprano; 2 Sopranos; Alto; Baritone;
    Bass. SATB Chorus.
    E. B. Immel & J. M. Sayre, arrs.
                                 Christmas
   Presser (rental)

Haydn, Franz Joseph   1732-1809

Kindersymphonie, Hob. II; 47,   10'
   C Major (Toy Symphony)   (5' 3' 2')
    strings[no va] + 7 toy players
    Toys: tpt, drum, cuckoo, nightingale, rattle, triangle,
    quail.
    Leopold Mozart is the likely composer.
                     Christmas/Popular Classics
   Breitkopf; Kalmus; Luck's

Symphony No. 8 in G Major   23'
   (Le soir)   (5' 8' 5' 5')
    1 2 0 1 – 2 0 0 0 – cnt – str
    Critical edition by H.C. Robbins Landon.
                           Popular Classics
   Doblinger

Symphony No. 82   27'
   (The Bear)   (8' 8' 5' 6')
    1 2 0 2 – 2 (2) 0 0 – tmp – str
    Critical edition by H. C. Robbins Landon.
                     Animals/Popular Classics
   Universal

Symphony No. 94 in G Major   23'
   (*Surprise*)   (7' 7' 5' 4')
   2 2 0 2 – 2 2 0 0 – tmp – str
   Critical edition by H. C. Robbins Landon.
                             Popular Classics
Universal

Symphony No. 94 in G Major   6'
   (*Surprise*) (*Mvt. II*)
   2[incl pic] 2 2 2[incl cbn] – 2 2 0 0 – tmp+2 – str
   Catalog calls this a "Mismanagement" for chamber orchestra.
   Sydney Hodkinson, arr.
                             Popular Classics
Presser (rental)

Symphony No. 100 in G Major   24'
   (*Military*)   (7' 5' 6' 6')
   1 2 2 2 – 2 2 0 0 – tmp+3 – str
   perc: bd, cym, tri.
   Critical edition by H. C. Robbins Landon.
                             Popular Classics
Universal

Symphony No. 101 in D Major   29'
   (*The Clock*)   (9' 8' 7' 5')
   2 2 2 2 – 2 2 0 0 – tmp – str
   Critical edition by H. C. Robbins Landon.
                      New Year/Popular Classics
Universal

Hayes, Isaac   1942-2008

Selections from Shaft   20'
   3[1.2.pic] 2 2 2 – 2asx, tsx, bsx – 2 3 3 1 – tmp+3 – gtr, elec bs – str
   perc: tri, drumset, vib, glock, sus cym, cowbell, tambn, bongos.
   Robert W. Lowden, arr.
                                      Films
Big Bells Incorporated (rental)

Hayes, Jack, arr.

Fox Medley No. 1   10'
   3[1.2.3/pic] 3[1.2.Eh] 3[1.2.bcl] 3 – 6 4 3 1 – tmp+perc[incl drumset] – hp, pf, gtr, elec bass – str
                                        Films
Kane (rental)

Fox Medley No. 2   10'
   3[1.2.3/pic/afl] 3[1.2.3/Eh] 3[1.2.3/bcl] 3[1.2.3/cbn] – 6 4 3 1 – tmp+perc[incl drumset] – hp, pf/cel, gtr – str
                                        Films
Kane (rental)

Hayes, Jason (See: Brower, Russell)

Hayman, Richard   1920-

Freddie the Football   12.5'
   3[incl pic] 3 3 3 – 4 3 3 1 – tmp+3 – hp, pf – str
   Narrator.
                                        Sports
Presser

Her Name is Suzanne   2'
   2 2 2 2 – (2asx, tsx) – 4 3 3 1 – tmp+2 – str
   perc: sd, bd, wooblk, glock, (xyl).
                             Instrumental Pops
Mills (rental)

Hullabaloo   4.5'
   2 2 2 2 – 2asx, 2tsx[1.(2)], bsx – 4 3 3 1 – tmp+2 – (gtr) – str
   perc: glock, tambn, sd, bd, cym.
   Includes: Bonaparte's Retreat; Tennessee Waltz; Cold Cold Heart; and Jambalaya.
                                   Americana
Chappell (rental)

Pops Hoe-Down   6'
   3[1.2.pic] 3[1.2.opt Eh] 3[1.2.(bcl)] 3[1.2.(cbn)] – 4 4 3 1 – tmp+4 – hp, pf – str
   perc: wooblk, cym, sd, bd, sus cym, small siren (played by mouth), duck quack, coo coo, slide whistle, bell plate, ratchet, cowbell, chime, large Klaxonhorn, gun, fight gong, metal tray.
                                   Americana
EMI (rental); Kalmus

Heath, Dave   1956-

Alone at the Frontier: Concerto for   30'
Improvised Instrument and Orchestra
2[incl pic & 2afl] 2 2[incl bcl] 2 – 4 3[flug] 3 1 –
tmp+2 – (elec gtr) – str
Solo Violin.

                                         Americana

Chester (rental)

The Frontier   15'
Strings

                                         Americana

Chester (rental)

Out of the Cool   6'
2[1.2/pic] 2 2[1.2/bcl] 2 – 4 0 0 0 – str
Solo Saxophone.

                                           Jazz

Chester (rental)

Hefti, Neil   1922-2008

Batman Theme   2'
(*from the original TV series*)
1 1 2 1 – 1 2 1 1 – 2perc – (pf) – str
perc: drumset, bells, chimes.
Bob Cerulli, arr.

                                    Halloween/TV

Warner

Batman Theme
Strings
From the original TV series.
Calvin Custer, arr.

                                    Halloween/TV

Warner

Heidrich, Peter   1935-

Variations on "Happy Birthday" (1994)   7'
3 2 2 2 – 4 2 3 0 – tmp+perc – gtr, hp - str
Available in the USA and Canada only.

                                       Celebration

Sikorski (rental)

Hely-Hutchinson, Victor   1901-1947

Carol Symphony (1927)   24'
3[incl pic] 2[incl Eh] 3[incl bcl] 3[incl cbn] – 4 3 3 1
– tmp+perc – hp – str
Alternate: 2[incl pic] 1[incl Eh] 2 1 – 2 2 0 0 –
tmp+perc – pf – str

                                         Christmas

Novello (rental)

Henderson, Luther, arr.   1919-2003

A Canadian Brass Christmas   6.5'
3[incl pic] 2 3[incl bcl] 2 – 2 3 3 1 – tmp+3 – pf – str
Includes: Ding Dong, Merrily on High; I Saw Three
Ships; Huron Carol; Here We Come a-Wassailing.
Calvin Custer, arr.

                                         Christmas

Leonard

Henley, Larry   1937-

Wind Beneath My Wings   4'
solo fl – drumset – gtr, pf – str
Calvin Custer, arr.

                             Popular Song/Valentine

Warner (POP); EMS or Luck's (rental)

Wind Beneath My Wings   4'
2 1 2 1[or bcl] – 2 2 2 1 – tmp+2[incl drumset] –
pf – str
Steve Rosenhaus, arr.

                             Popular Song/Valentine

Warner (POP); EMS or Luck's (rental)

Herbert, Victor   1859-1924

Ah Sweet Mystery of Life   4'
2[incl pic] 2 2 – (2asx, tsx) – 4 3 3 1 – tmp+perc
– str
From *Thoroughly Modern Millie*.
Timothy Broege, arr.

                       Broadway Musical/Popular Song

Kalmus

Air de Ballet   2'
1 0 2 0 – 2 1 0 0 – 1perc – str
Violin obbligato.
Otto Langey, arr.
                                           Dance
Schirmer

American Fantasie   4'
3[1.2.3/pic] 3[1.2.EH] 2 2 – 4 0 2 1 – tmp+4 – hp – str
perc: bd, cym, 2 tri, sd.
Seredy, arr.
                                           Americana
Kalmus

Babes in Toyland (March of the Toys)   4'
3[1.2.pic] 2 2 2 – 4 2 3 1 – tmp+perc – str
Clark McAlister, arr.
                                           Christmas
Kalmus

The Enchantress: Art Is Calling for Me   3'
(I Want to Be a Prima Donna)
2[1.pic] 2 2 2 – 4 2 2 0 – perc – hp – str
Solo Voice.
Cohen, arr.
                                           Jazz/Popular Song
Schirmer (rental)

Irish Rhapsody   14'
3[1.2.pic] 2 2 2 – 4 2 3 1 – tmp+perc – hp – str
                                           St. Patrick/International
Kalmus; Schirmer (rental)

Kiss Me Again   4'
1 1 2 1 – 2 2 1 0 – tmp – str
                                           Valentine
Luck's

Natoma: Grand Fantasia
3[incl 2pic] 3[1.2.Eh] 3[1.2.bcl]
3[1.2.cbn] – 4 3 3 1 – tmp+perc – hp – str
Herbert's 1911 opera based on Spanish and American Indian themes from the 1830s.
                                           Popular Classics
Schirmer (rental)

Natoma: Prelude to Act III
3[1.2.pic] 3[1.2.Eh] 3[1.2.bcl] 3[1.2.cbn] – 4 3 3 1 – tmp+perc – hp – str
Herbert's 1911 opera based on Spanish and American Indian themes from the 1830s.
                                           Popular Classics
Schirmer (rental)

Panamericana   4'
1 1 2 1 – 2 2 1 0 – tmp+perc – str
Otto Langey, arr.
                                           Americana
Kalmus

President's March   3'
1 1 2 1 – 3sx – 1 2 1 0 – perc – str
Seredy, arr.
                                           Patriotic
Kalmus

Victorious Herbert   14.5'
  (Music of Victor Herbert)
3[incl pic] 3[incl Eh] 3[incl bcl] 3[incl cbn] –
4 4 3 1 – tmp+3 – hp, pf – str
Eric Knight, arr.
                                           Instrumental Pops
Bourne (rental)

Herman, Jerry   1931-

The Best Christmas of All   3'
3[1.2.pic] 2[1.Eh] 2 2 – 4 3 3 1 – tmp+3[drumset] – hp, cel – str
Solo Alto & Baritone or Chorus.
From his Emmy nominated CBS television special "Mrs. Santa Claus."
Larry Blank, orchestrator
                                           Christmas
Wendel (rental)

La Cage aux Folles: Overture   4.5'
3[1.2.pic] 2 2 2 – 4 3 3 1 – tmp+3[drumset] – hp – str
Includes: Motif Fanfares; La Cage aux Folles; With Anne on My Arm; Song on the Sand; I Am What I Am; The Best of Times Is Now. This edition includes a concert ending approved by Jerry Herman.
Robert Wendel, editor
                                           Broadway Musicals
Wendel (rental)

Selections from La Cage aux Folles   4.5'
2 1 2 1 – 4 3 3 0 – tmp+1 – pf – str
perc: sd, xyl, bd, glock, vib.
Includes: We are What We Are; With You On My Arm; Song on the Sand; The Best of Times.
Philip J. Lang, arr.
                                           Broadway Musicals
Morris (POP); Luck's (rental)

Hello Dolly! (1996 version): Overture 4.5'
 3[1.2.pic] 2 2 2 – 4 3 3 1 – tmp+3[drumset] – hp – str
 Includes: Put On Your Sunday Clothes; It Only Takes a Moment; Before the Parade Passes By; Hello Dolly.
 Don Pippin, arr
 Larry Blank, orch.
  Broadway Musicals
 Wendel (rental)

Hello Dolly Highlights 5'
 2[1/pic.2] 2 3[1.2.(bcl)] 2 – (asx, tsx) – 4 3 3 1 – tmp+3 – hp – str
 perc: sd, bd, cym.
 Includes: Hello Dolly!; Before the Parade Passes By; Dancing; Ribbons Down My Back.
 J. Frederick Muller, arr.
  Broadway Musicals
 Leonard (POP); EMS or Luck's (rental)

Mack & Mabel: Overture 5'
 3[1.2.pic] 2 2 2 – 4 3 3 1 – tmp+3[drumset] – hp, pf/cel, (banjo) – str
 Includes: Movies Were Movies; Look What Happened to Mabel; I Won't Send Roses; Where Ever He Ain't!; When Mabel Comes in the Room.
 Robert Wendel, editor
  Broadway Musicals
 Wendel (rental)

Mame: Overture 4.5'
 3[1.2.pic] 2 2 2 – 4 3 3 1 – tmp+3[drumset] – hp, (banjo) – str
 Includes: Fanfare; Open a New Window; My Best Girl; If He Walked Into My Life; That's How Young I Feel; and Mame.
 Robert Wendel, editor
  Broadway Musicals
 Wendel (rental)

Milk and Honey: Overture 4.5'
 3[1.2.pic] 2 2 2 – 4 3 3 1 – tmp+3[drumset] – hp – str
 Includes: Milk and Honey Fanfares; Shalom; Independence Day Hora; Let's Not Waste a Moment; That Was Yesterday; Milk and Honey.
 Hershey Kay, arr. & orch.
  Broadway Musicals
 Wendel (rental)

Hermann, Ralph 1914-1994

Christmas Fantasy 10'
 3[1.2.3/pic] 3[1.2.Eh] 3[1.2.bcl] 2 – 4 3 3 1 – tmp+1 – hp – str
 perc: tambn, sd, tri, finger cym, glock, cym, chimes, slgh-bells.
 Optional SATB Chorus.
  Christmas
 Luck's (rental)

Farmyard Frolic 4'
 3[1.2.3/pic] 3[1.2.Eh] 3[1.2.bcl] 2 – 4 3 3 1 – tmp+2 – hp – str
 perc: xyl, drumset.
 Includes: Chicken Reel, Home on the Range, Camptown Races, Oh Susannah, Pop! Goes the Weasel, She'll Be Comin' 'Round the Mountain.
  Americana/Instrumental Pops/Popular Songs
 Capital (rental)

Irish Medley 4'
 3[1.2.pic] 3[1.2.Eh] 3[1.2.bcl] 2 – 4 3 3 1 – tmp+2 – hp – str
 perc: sd, bd, cym, xyl, glock.
 Includes: McNamara's Band; My Wild Irish Rose; Sweet Rosie O'Grady; Harrigan; When Irish Eyes are Smiling; Irish Washer Woman.
  International: Ireland/Popular Songs
 Capital (rental)

Italian Fiesta 8'
 3[1.2.pic] 3[1.2.Eh] 3[1.2.bcl] 2 – 4 3 3 1 – tmp+2 – hp – str
 perc: drumset, sd, bd, tambn, cast, tri.
 Includes: Santa Lucia; Tarentella; O Sole Mio; Oh Marie Torna Sorrento; Funiculi Funicula.
  International: Italy/Popular Songs
 Capital (rental)

Jewish Melodies 6.5'
 3[1.2.pic] 3[1.2.Eh] 3[1.2.bcl] 2 – 4 3 3 1 – tmp+2 – hp – str
 perc: xyl, sd, bd, sus cym, glock, tambn.
 Includes: Kolomeike Wollach; Traditional; Russian Sherele; Sha Sha Der Rebbe Gaft; Aufen Pripichok; Mazeltov; Hava Nagiela.
  Holidays/International: Israel/Popular Songs
 Capital (rental)

Old Song Medley 4.5'
3[1.2.pic] 3[1.2.Eh] 3[1.2.bcl] 2 – 4 3 3 1 – tmp+2 – hp – str
perc: sd, bd, xyl, cym.
Includes: A Hot Time in Old Town Tonight; I've Been Working on the Railroad; America; Down by the Old Mill Stream; In the Good Old Summertime; Give My Regards to Broadway.
Score is in manuscript format.
          Popular Songs
Capital (rental)

Old Song Medley No. 2 6'
3[1.2.pic] 3[1.2.Eh] 3[1.2.bcl] 2 – 4 3 3 1 – tmp+2 – hp – str
perc: sd, bd, glock, chimes.
Includes: Reuben and Rachel; Frankie and Johnny; I Love You Truly; Cuddle Up a Little Closer; My Gal Sal; Shine on Harvest Moon.
Score is in manuscript format.
          Popular Songs
Capital (rental)

Old Song Medley No. 3 7'
3[1.2.pic] 3[1.2.Eh] 3[1.2.bcl] 2 – 4 3 3 1 – tmp+2 – hp – str
perc: sd, bd, xyl, glock, woodblk, sus cym.
Includes: My Pony Boy; My Hero; By Light of Silvery Moon, I Wonder Who's Kissing Her Now; Put on Your Old Grey Bonney.
Score is in manuscript format.
          Popular Songs
Capital (rental)

Old Timers Waltz Medley No. 1 4.5'
3[1.2.pic] 3[1.2.Eh] 3[1.2.bcl] 2 – 4 3 3 1 – tmp+3 – hp – str
perc: cym, sd, bd, tri, xyl, glock.
Includes: After the Ball; I Wonder Who's Kissing Her Now; School Days; In My Merry Oldsmobile; Let Me Call You Sweetheart; You Tell Me Your Dreams.
Score is in manuscript format.
        Dance/Popular Songs
Capital (rental)

Old Timers Waltz Medley No. 2 4.5'
3[1.2.pic] 3[1.2.Eh] 3[1.2.bcl] 2 – 4 3 3 1 – tmp+3 – hp – str
perc: cym, sd, bd, xyl.
Includes: Take Me to the Ballgame; And the Band Played On; Meet Me Tonight in Dreamland; In the Shade of the Old Apple Tree; Meet Me in St. Louis; The Sidewalks of New York.
Score is in manuscript format.
        Dance/Popular Songs
Capital (rental)

Polish Polka Party 7.5'
3[1.2.pic] 3[1.2.Eh] 3[1.2.bcl] 2 – 4 3 3 1 – tmp+2 – hp – str
perc: sd, bd, woodblk, xyl, cym.
Includes: Helena Polka; Rain Rain Polka; Clarinet Polka; Barbara Polka. Polkas may be performed individually.
       Dance/International (Poland)
Capital (rental)

Silent Movie 7.5'
3 3[1.2.Eh] 3[1.2.bcl] 2 – 4 3 3 1 – 2perc – 2hp[1.(pf)] – str
perc: bird whistle, woodblk, sd, glock, cowbell, cym, tri, bd, sus cym, train whistle.
Optional Narrator. Includes incidental music for a silent film: Morning on the Farm; Innocent Peg; Rudolph the Villain; Peg Milks the Cow; Rudolph Kidnaps Peg and Rides off with her on his Horse; Enter Jack Dalton of the U.S. Military Service; The Chase via Horse and Train.
         Animals/Films/Novelty
Capital (rental)

Hernández, Rafael   1892-1965

El Cumbanchero 2.5'
2 1 2 1 – 2 3 2 1 – tmp+perc – pf – str
Marty Gold, arr.
        International (Puerto Rico)
Warner (POP); Luck's (rental)

El Cumbanchero 3'
2 2 2 2 – 4 2 2 1 – tmp+3 – str
Gonzalez, arr.
        International (Puerto Rico)
Filarmonika

Hérold, Louis Joseph F.   1791-1833

Zampa Overture   8'
2[1.pic] 2 2 2 – 4 2 3 1 – tmp+3 – str
perc: tri, cym, bd.

Kalmus; Luck's   Popular Classics

Herrmann, Bernard   1911-1975

Anna and the King of Siam Suite (1946)   10.5'
4[1.afl.pic.pic] 6[1.2.3.Eh.Eh.Eh] 4[1.2.bcl.bcl] 3
– 4 3 3 1 – 2 tmp+perc – 2 hp, pf, cel – str
perc: tamtam, Indian dr, bd, cym, chimes, 2 gongs[hi, lo],
2 xyl[hi,lo], glock.
Includes: Prelude; Montage; Elegy; Coronation.

T&V (rental)   Films

The Bride Wore Black: A Musical Scenario (1968)   11.5'
3[1.2.pic] 2[1.Eh] 3[1.2.bcl] 2 – 4 2 3 1 – tmp+3
– hp – str
perc: chimes, tamtam, vib, glock, tri, cyms, bd.
Includes: Prelude, Femme Fatale, The Accident,
Love and Death, Funeral and Finale.
Christopher Palmer, arr.

T&V (rental)   Films

The Bride Wore Black: A Suite in Four Movements   9'
2 3[1.2.Eh] 4[1.2.bcl.bcl] 2 – 4 0 4 0 – 2 perc –
2 hp – str [no vlns,14 va,12 vcl,10 bs]
perc: sus cym, cyms, sd, bd, low tamtam.
Includes: Valse; The Boy; The Shooting.
Edited by Christopher Husted

T&V (rental)   Films

Citizen Kane Overture   2.5'
2 2 3[incl bcl] 2 – 4 3 3 1 – tmp+2 – hp, cel – str

Bourne (rental)   Films

The Day the Earth Stood Still: Arrival (1951)   5'
0 0 0 0 – 0 3 3 4[1.2.cb.cb] – tmp[2 players] –
2 pf, 1 pipe org, 2 Hammond org, 2 theremin –
str[1 elec vln,1 elec cello, 1 elec bs]
perc: 2 vib,2 bd, tamtam.

T&V (rental)   Films/Space

The Day the Earth Stood Still: Suite (1951)   15'   (2' 2.5' 1' 1' 2' 2' 1' 2' 1.5')
0 0 0 0 – 1 3 3 4[1.2.cb.cb] – tmp[3 sets]+perc
– 2 hp, pf, cel, 2 Hammond org, studio org,
2 theremin elec gtr – str [elec vln, elec cello,
elec bs]
perc: 3 vib, lg marim, 2 glock, tamtam, 2bd.
Includes: Outer Space; Radar; Gort; Escape; Lincoln
Memorial; The Robot; Space Control; Terror;
Farewell; Finale 1. Instrumentation includes this
option: combined parts for Theremin, I & II;
Hammond Organs, I & II; piano, I & II.

T&V (rental)   Films/Space

The Devil and Daniel Webster: Suite   21'
2 2 3[incl bcl] 3[incl cbn] – 4 3 3 1 – tmp+4 –
hp, pf, org – str
Includes: Mister Scratch; The Ballad of Springfield
Mountain; The Sleigh Ride; The Miser's Waltz;
Finale "Swing Your Partners."

Bourne (rental)   Films

The Ghost of Mrs. Muir (1947)   3.5'
0 0 0 0 – 0 0 0 0 – hp – str

T&V (rental)   Films/Halloween

It's Alive (1973)   3'
0 0 3 3[bcl.bcl.cbcl] 0 – 8 6 6 2
tmp+perc – 2 hp, org, theremin – elec bass, viola
d'amore [no orchestral strings]
perc: cyms, tambn, chimes, vib.

T&V (rental)   Films/Halloween

Jane Eyre: Suite (1943)   13.5'
3[1.2.pic] 2[Eh] 4[1.2.bcl.cbcl] 3[1.2.cbn] –
4 3 3 1 – tmp+4 – hp, pf(cel) – str
perc: sd, td, sm bd, lg bd, bd, sm tri, woodblk, whip,
2 vib, chimes, cym, sus cym, tamtam.
Includes: Lowood; Thornfield & Rochester; The
Tower; Departure & Retreat.

T&V (rental)   Films

Jason and Argonauts: Suite (1963)   11'
     4[1.2.3.pic] 6[1.2.3.Eh.Eh.Eh]   (2.5'   2.5'   3'   3')
     6[1.2.bcl.bcl.bcl.cbc.] 6[1.2.3.4.cbn.cbn] –
     8 6 6 4 – tmp[2 players]+8 – 4 hp – [no strings]
     perc: 2 sd, 2 bd, td, tamtam, cym, 4 sus cym, 2 tambn, woodblk, castanet.
     Includes: Prelude; Talos; Talos' Death; Triton.
                                       Films
T&V (rental)

Jason and Argonauts: Scherzo macabre (1963)
     4[1.2.pic.pic] 6[1.2.3.4.Eh.Eh.] 6[1.2.3.4.bcl.bcl]
     6[1.2.3.4.cb.cbn] – 8 6 6 4 – tmp+perc – 4 hp –
     [no strings]
     perc: 2sd, 2bd, 2cym[a2 and sus], tri, tambn, glock, xyl.
                                       Films
T&V (rental)

Journey to the Center of the Earth (1959)   15'
     0 0 6[1.2.3.4.bcl.bcl] 6[1.2.3.4.cbn.cbn] – 4 4 3 4 –
     8 perc – 1 pipe org, 4 elec org – [no str]
     perc: 2 bd, 2 tamtam, 2 sus cym, 2 cym, 2 tmp[incl 2sus cym]
     Includes: Mountain Top & Sunrise; Salt Slides; Atlantis; The Shaft & Finale.
                                       Films
T&V (rental)

The Man Who Knew Too Much: 9.5'
     The Storm Clouds Cantata (1956)
     3[1.2.pic] 2 2 2 – 4 3 3 1 – tmp+4 – 2 hp, org – str
     perc: sd, bd, tri, gong, 2 pair cym.
     Solo Mezzo Soprano; SATB Chorus.
     Sir Arthur Benjamin, arr.
                                       Films
T&V (rental)

Mysterious Island: Suite (1961)   2'
                   (2'   3'   2'   5.5'   3.5'   3'   3')
     3[1.2.pic] 4[1.2.3.Eh] 5[1.2.3.bcl.bcl]
     5[1.2.3.cbn.cbn] – 8 3 3 4 – 2 tmp+7 –
     4 hp[2 parts a2] – str
     perc: chimes, 2 cym, 2 bd, 2 tamtam, 2 tri, 2 glock, 2 xyl, woodblk, tambn, whip.
     Includes: Prelude; The Balloon (The Exploration); Marooned (incl. The Rocks, The Stream, The Island, Exploration, The Cliff); The Giant Crab; The Giant Bee; The Giant Bird. Based on the novel by Jules Verne, this film was a sequel to *20,000 Leagues Under the Sea*.
                                       Films
T&V (rental)

North by Northwest
     3[1.2.pic] 3[1.2.Eh] 5[bcl.bcl] 3[1.2.cbn] –
     4 3 3 1 – tmp+5 – 2 hp – str
     perc: castanets, tambn, sd, bd, sus cym, cym, xyl.
                                       Films
T&V (rental)

A Portrait of Hitch   8'
     3 2 3 2 – 4 0 0 0 – tmp – 2hp – str
     From *The Trouble with Harry*.
                                       Films
Novello (rental)

A Portrait of Hitch: The Trouble   8.5'
     with Harry Suite (1954)
     3[1.2.pic] 2 3[1.2.bcl] 2 – 4 0 0 0 –1 perc – 2 hp – str
     perc: sm tri.
                                       Films
T&V (rental)

Psycho (1960)   14.5'
     Strings
     Includes: Prelude; The City; The Rainstorm; The Madhouse; The Murder; The Water; The Swamp; The Stairs; The Knife; The Cellar; Finale.
     The original playthrough edition was restored by John Mauceri in 1990. The complete score is available for performances (109 minutes).
                                Films/Halloween
T&V (rental)

Psycho (1960)   7.5'
     Strings
     Includes: Prelude; Murder; Finale.
                                Films/Halloween
T&V (rental)

Psycho (1960)   5'
     Strings
     Edited by John Mauceri
                                Films/Halloween
T&V (rental)

The Seventh Voyage of Sinbad   8.5'
                                 (2.5'   2'   4')
     3[1.2.pic] 2 4[1.2.bcl.bcl] 3[1.2.cbn] – 4 3 3 2 –
     2 tmp+7 – 2 hps (1 part a2), cel – str
     perc: glock, 2 xyl, tri, sm cyms, 2 castanets, whip, tambn, 2 woodblk.
     Includes: Overture; The Duel With The Skeleton; Baghdad & Finale.
                                Films/Halloween
T&V (rental)

The Snows of Kilimijaro (1952)   14'
                                         (4' 6' 4')
    3[1.2.pic] 2[1.2/Eh] 5[1.2.3.4.bcl] 2 – 4 3 3 0 –
    perc – 2hp – str
    perc: sm, med, & lg sus cym.
    Includes: Overture; Romance; The Memory Waltz.
                                                   Films
T&V (rental)

Taxi Driver: A Night Piece   8.5'
  for Orchestra (1976)
    3 0 2[1.bcl] 3[1.2.cbn] – 4 4 4 2 – tmp+5 –
    2 hp – pf, acoustic gtr, Fender bass – str
    perc: drumset, tamtam, sd, td, bd, lg sus cym, 2 vib.
    Solo Alto Saxophone.
    Includes: Prelude; Blues; Night Prowl; Bloodbath;
    Finale. The alto saxophone solo can be replaced by a
    tenor saxophone.
    Christopher Palmer, arr.
                                                   Films
T&V (rental)

The Three Worlds of Gulliver: Suite (1960)   29'
                                (2.5' 2' 1.5' 3.5' 3.5' 1'
                                2' 2.5' 3' 3' 1.5' 2' 1')
    3[1.2.pic] 3[1.2.Eh] 3[1.2.bcl] 3[1.2.cbn] –
    4 3 3 1– tmp+4 – 2 hp, cel – str
    perc: glock, chimes, sd, bd, cym, tri.
    Includes: Overture; Minuetto-Wapping; Hornpipe;
    Lilliputians; Victory; Escape; The King's March;
    Trees; The Tightrope; Lovers; The Chess Game;
    Pursuit; Finale.
                                                   Films
T&V (rental)

Vertigo: Suite (1958)   10'
                                       (3' 2' 5')
    3 3[1.2.Eh] 5[1.2.3.bcl.bcl] 3[1.2.cbn] –
    4 3 3 1 – tmp+3 – 2 hp, cel, Hammond org – str
    perc: 2 vib, tamtam.
    Includes: Prelude; The Nightmare; Scene d'amour.
                                                   Films
T&V (rental)

The Wrong Man: Prelude (1956)   2'
    3[1.2.pic] 0 4 2 – 4 4 0 1 – tmp+4 – 2 hp, pf,
    Fender bass – str
    perc: maracas, cowbell, guiro, claves, glock, deep pitched
    rattle, conga, timbales.
                                                   Films
T&V (rental)

Herschel, Lee

How the Camel Got His Hump   9'
    2 1 2 1 – 2 2 1 0 – perc – hp – str
    Narrator; 4 Solo Voices.
                                                  Animals
Fox (rental)

How the Whale Got His Tiny Throat   9'
    2 1 2 1 – 2 2 1 0 – perc – hp – str
    Narrator; 4 voices.
                                                  Animals
Fox (rental)

Heuberger, Richard   1850-1914

Melodies of Richard Heuberger   15'
    2 2 2 2 – 4 3 3 0 – tmp+perc – hp, cel – str
    Austrian composer of operas and operettas.
    Fritz Schlenkermann, arr.
                                                  Films
Sikorski (rental)

Hewitt, James   1770-1827

The Battle of Trenton   14'
    2[incl pic] 2 2 2 – 2 2 2 0 – perc – hpsd – str
    Optional Narrator.
    Gunther Schuller, arr.
                                                Patriotic
MarGun (rental)

Higdon, Jennifer   1962-

City Scape   26'
    3[1.2.pic] 3[1.2.Eh] 3[1.2.bcl] 3[1.2.cbn] – 4 3 3 1 –
    tmp+3 – str   (6' 14' 6')
    perc: bd, cym, 2sus cym, szl cym, Chinese cym, sd, floor
    tom, 2tri, brakedrum, tambn, tamtam, glock, wyl, marim,
    vib, crot, woodblk, templeblk, bongo, guiro, watergong.
    Includes: Skyline; River sings a song to trees;
    Peachtree Street. Movements may be ordered and
    performed individually.
                                                Americana
Lawdon (rental)

Higgins, John

Christmas on Broadway 7'
    Strings
    Optional SATB Chorus. Includes: It's Beginning to Look Like Christmas; Pine Cones and Holly Berries; Toyland; March of the toys; My Favorite Things; We Need a Little Christmas; God Bless Us Everyone. Available in Concert Band version as well which can be combined with strings and chorus.
                                                Christmas
Leonard

Hill, Mildred J.   1859-1916
Hill, Patty Smith   1868-1946

Birthday Variations 11'
    2[1.2/pic] 2 2[1.2/asx] 2 – 2 2 1 1 – tmp+1 – hp – str
    Includes nine variations on the familiar tune, including ragtime, blues, latin, and rock and roll.
    Matthew Naughtin, arr.
                                                  Celebration
Naughtin (sale or rental)

Campane di Ravello: 4'
A Celebration Piece for Sir Georg Solti
    4[1.2.3.pic] 4[1.2.3.Eh] 4[1.2.3.bcl] 4[1.2.3.cbn] – 4 4 3 1 – tmp+5 – hp,pf – str
    perc: chimes, glock, crot, marim, xyl, sus cym, bd, 3 tamtams.
    Based on Happy Birthday.
    John Corigliano, arr.
                                                  Celebration
Schirmer (rental)

Happy Anniversary (1969) 1'
    3(#2) 2 3(#2) 2 – 4 3 3 1 – perc [glock] – str
    Aaron Copland, arr.
                                                  Celebration
Boosey (rental)

Happy Birthday Variations 4.5'
    3[1.2.pic] 3[1.2.Eh] 3[1.2.bcl] 3[1.2.cbn] – 4 4 3 1 – tmp+perc – hp, pf – str
    Composed for a concert celebrating birthdays of Seiji Ozawa, Yo-Yo Ma, Itzhak Perlman, and Leon Fleischer. Signature Edition
    John T. Williams, arr.
                                  Celebrations/Fanfare
Leonard

Happy, Happy Birthday 5'
    3[1.2.pic] 2 2 2 – 4 3 3 1 – tmp+2 – str
    The melody is set in the following styles, each playable individually or as one continuous piece: Baroque, Classical, Romantic, and Broadway.
    Richard Chiarappa, orchestrator
                                              Celebration
Clear Mud

Hinds, Thomas

Music for Hannukah: Two Folk Songs 6'
and a Hymn
    3[1.2.pic] 2 3[1.2.bcl] 2 – 4 2 3 1 – tmp+2 – pf – str
    perc: glock, sus cym, tri, cym.
    Conductors score is in manuscript form.
                                                    Holidays
Kalmus (rental)

Hodkinson, Sydney   1934-

Concerto for Clarinet and Orchestra 26'
    2[incl pic] 2[incl Eh] 2[incl bcl] 2 – 2 2 1 0 – tmp+2 – hp, cel/pf – str
    Solo clarinet; string quartet obbligato
                                          Instrumental Pops
Presser (rental)

Overture: A Little Travelin' Music 9'
    2[incl pic] 2 3[incl Ebcl] 2 – 4 3 3 1 – 4tmp+4 – hp – str
                                                        Travel
Presser (rental)

Høffding, Finn — 1899-1997

Celebrations of May-Day — 11'
3[1.2.pic] 2 2 2 – 4 2 3 1 – tmp – pf or cel – str
Celebration

Hansen (rental)

Hoffman, Joel — 1953-

Music from Chartres
0 0 0 0 – 4 2 3 1
International

Shawnee (rental)

Holcombe, Bill — 1924-

Fantasy on Auld Lang Syne — 9'
3[1.2.pic] 3[1.2.Eh] 3[1.2.bcl] 2 – 4 3 3 1 – tmp+3 – hp, (pf) – str
perc: vib, chimes, glock.
New Year's

Musicians Pub.

Casey at the Bat — 6'
3[1.2.3/pic] 3[1.2.Eh] 3[1.2.bcl] 2 – 4 3 3 1 – tmp+2 – hp – str
perc: drumset, glcok, xyl, vib, cym, chimes, ratchet.
Narrator. Words by Ernest L. Thayer.
Sports

Musicians Pub.

Christmas Wishes — 4.5'
(Optional winds and brass) – (2perc) – pf – str
perc: sd, bd, cym, sus cym, tri, sm tri, crotale, slgh-bells, chimes, glock.
Includes: O Christmas Tree; Joy to the World; Deck the Halls; Silent Night; Jingle Bells.
Christmas

Musicians Pub.

Cowboy Fantasy — 9'
3[1.2.pic] 3[1.2.Eh] 3[1.2.cbn] 2 – 4sx – 4 3 3 1 – tmp+2 – hp – str
perc: bells, vib, xyl, marim, chimes.
Based on well-known cowboy airs.
Americana

Musicians Pub.

Evening at Pops — 8'
2 1 2 1 – (3sx) – 4 3 2 1 – tmp+perc – pf, elec bass – str
Includes: "Shadow in the Moonlight" by Charlie Black and Rory Bourke; "Longer" by Daniel Fogelberg; "You Needed Me" by Charles Randolph Goodrum.
Popular Song

Leonard (POP); EMS or Luck's (rental)

Saxanova — 3'
3[incl pic] 2 4[incl Ebcl & bcl] 2 – asx – 4 3 3 1 – tmp+drumset, perc – hp, elec bass – str
Solo Alto Saxophone.
Instrumental Pops

Musicians Pub.

Holdridge, Lee — 1944-

Beauty and the Beast: Theme (1987) — 4'
2 2 2 2 – 4 3 3 1 – tmp+perc – str
perc: sus cym, orch bells.
Introduction music to Ron Koslow's CBS TV series which ran for 3 seasons: 1987-1991.
TV

T&V (rental

Holmboe, Vagn — 1909-1996

Fanfare — 5'
3[1.2.pic] 3 3[1.2.bcl] 0 – 4 4 3 1 – tmp+perc – str
Fanfare

Hansen (rental)

Holst, Gustav — 1874-1934

The Novello Book of Carols:
  In the Bleak Midwinter — 3'
2 2 2 2 – 0 0 0 0 – str
Solo Voice.
Christmas

Novello (rental)

Christmas Day: 8'
   Choral Fantasy on Old Carols
   2[1.2/(pic)] 2 2 2 - 2 2 (2) 0 – tmp+(1) – pf or org
   – str
   perc: glock.
   Chorus. Includes: Good Christian Men Rejoice;
   God Rest You Merry Gentlemen; Come Ye Lofty,
   Come Ye Lowly; The First Nowell.
                                          Christmas
   Kalmus; Schirmer (rental)

Fantasia on Hampshire Folk Songs   6'
   Strings
   Revision by Imogen Holst.
                                         International
   Novello (rental)

A Fugal Overture, Op. 40 No. 1   6'
   3 3 3 3 – 4 3 3 1 – tmp+perc – str
                                  Popular Classics
   Novello (rental)

Let All Mortal Flesh Keep Silence   5'
   Strings – chorus
   Solo Soprano and Bass; SATB Chorus.
   From "Three Festival Choruses."
                                              Holidays
   Stainer

The Perfect Fool: 11'
   Ballet Music Op. 39
   3[1.2.pic] 3[1.2.Eh] 3[1.2.bcl] 3[1.2.cbn] – 4 4 3 1
   – tmp+3 – hp, cel – str
   perc: xyl, slgh-bells, cym, sus cym, tamtam, bd, tambn.
                                  Dance/Popular Classics
   Novello (rental)

The Planets   53'
                                 (7' 10' 5' 7' 11' 6' 7')
   4[1.2.3/pic1.4/afl/pic2] 4[1.2.3/bass ob.Eh]
   4[1.2.3.bcl] 4[1.2.3.cbn] – 6 4 3 2 [1 tenor tuba] –
   2tmp+4 – 2hp, cel, org – str
   perc: glock, xyl, tamtam, chimes, sd, tambn, bd, tri, cym.
   6-part female chorus in last movement.
   Critical edition by Clinton F. Nieweg and Gregory
   Vaught.
                                   Popular Classics/Space
   Kalmus

St. Paul's Suite   12'
   Strings   *(3' 2' 4' 3')*
   Includes: Jig; Ostinato; Intermezzo; Finale: The
   Dargason.
                                        Popular Classics
   Curwen; Kalmus'

St. Paul's Suite, Op. 29   13'
   2 1 2 0 – 2 0 0 0 – tmp – str
   Includes: Jig; Ostinato; Intermezzo; Finale: The
   Dargason.
   Clark McAlister, editor
                                        Popular Classics
   Kalmus

Three Christmas Songs
   2 2 2 2 – 2 0 0 0 – tmp+perc – org – str
   Chorus
                                             Christmas
   Schirmer (rental)

Hooper, Nicolas

Concert Suite from Harry Potter and   6.5'
   the Half-Blood Prince
   3[1.2.pic] 1 3[1.2.bcl] 1 – 4 3 3 1 – tmp+3 –
   pf/cel, hp – str
   perc: glock, cowbell, tri, taiko dr, sd, conga, toms,
   sus cym, cym, drumset.
   Includes: Opening; The Story Begins; In Noctem;
   Wizard Wheezes; Ron's Victory; The Slug Party;
   Journey to the Cave; Dumbledore's Farewell; The
   Friends; The Weasley Stomp.
   Jerry Brubaker, arr.
                                                   Films
   Warner

Harry Potter Symphonic Suite   24.5'
    3[1.2.3/afl/pic] 3[1.2.3/Eh] 3[1.2.3/bcl/Ebcl]
    3[1.2.3/cbn] – 4 3 3 1 – tmp+3perc – hp, pf/cel
    – str
    perc: orch-bells, tubular-bells, xyl, vib, tambn, sm tri, slgh-bells, mark tree, bell tree, sus cyms (sm, med, lg), piatti, sizzle cym, tam-tam, sd, dumbeks(3), tom-toms(3), lg, & sm taiko dms [or tom-toms], bd, verdi bd.
    Optional Solo Female Vocalist in *Lily's Theme*.
    Includes: Prologue/Hedwig's Theme [#1]   *(5')*
    Buckbeak's Flight [#3]   *(2')*
    Hogwarts' Hymn [#4]   *(1')*
    Hogwarts' March [#4]   *(1.5')*
    Fireworks [#5]   *(1')*
    The Flight of the Order of the Phoenix [#5]   *(1.5')*
    Harry & Hermione [#6]   *(1.5')*
    Obliviate [#7]   *(2')*
    Lily's Theme [#8]   *(2')*
    Courtyard Apocalypse [#8]   *(2')*
    Mischief Managed [#3] & Harry's Wondrous
       World [#2]   *(5')*
    The number in brackets is the film from which the theme was derived. #1-3 are composed by J. Williams; #4 is composed by P. Doyle; #5& 6 by N. Hooper; and #7 & 8 by A. Desplat.
    Gary Fry, arr. J.

                                                 Films

Alfred (rental)

Hooper, Nicolas & Williams, John T.

Harry Potter and the Order of the Phoenix: 5'
Concert Suite
    2 1 3[1.2bcl] 2 – 4 3 3 1 – tmp+3 – pf – str
    perc: glock, wyl, sd, bd, sus cym, hi-hat cym, crash cym, tom-tom, wind chimes, taiko dr, tri.
    Includes: Another Story, Flight of the Order of the Phoenix, Professor Umbridge, Dumbledore's Army, The Room of Requirements.
    Victor Lopez, arr.

                                                 Films

Warner

Horner, James   1953-

Aliens Suite No. 1: Main Title & Ripley's   8'
    3[1/pic.2/pic.3/pic] 3[1.2.Eh] 3[1/Ebcl.2.3/bcl]
    3[1.2.3/cbn] – 4 3 3 1 – tmp+perc – hp, pf/cel – str
    Conrad Pope, arr.

                                                 Films

Kane (rental)

Aliens Suite No. 2: Newt & Face Huggers   5.5'
    3[1/pic.2/pic.3/pic/afl] 2 3[1.2.bcl] 3[1.2.cbn] –
    4 2[1/echoplex.2] 3 1 – tmp+perc – hp, pf – str
    Conrad Pope, arr.

                                                 Films

Kane (rental)

An American Tail: 2.5'
Somewhere Out There
    1 1 3[1.2.(bcl)] 1 – (2sx) – 2 3 3 1 – 3perc – (pf)
    – str
    Bob Lowden, arr.

                                                 Films

Leonard (POP); Luck's (rental)

Music from Apollo 13:   5'
Main Title, End Credits, Re-Entry, and Splashdown
    2 2 3[1.2.bcl] 2 – 4 3 3 1 – tmp+2 – pf – str
    perc: field dr, bd, med & lg sus cym, glock, tri, cym, sd, bd, chimes.
    John Moss, arr.

                                              Films/Space

Leonard

Avatar (2009): Suite   9.5'
    3[1.2/pic.(ethnic)] 2 3[1.2.bcl] 2 –
    8 (#5-8) 4 (#4) 3 1 – tmp+perc – hp, pf – str
    Nominated for an Oscar in 2010 for Best Original Score.

                                                 Films

Kane

Braveheart: Main Title & End Credits (1995)   9.5'
    2[afl.2.] 2[1.Eh] 0 2 – 4 2 3 1 – tmp+perc –
    hp, celtic hp, pipes, synth – str
    perc: bd, taiko drum, sus cym, cym, hi crotale, sm gong.
    Chorus.

                                                 Films

T&V

Cocoon (1985): Cocoon Theme   6.5'
    3[1.2.3/pic] 2[1.2/Eh] 2[1.2/bcl] 2 – 6 4 4 1 –
    tmp+perc – 2hp, pf/synth, cel/synth, org – str
    perc: tri, 2 sizzle cym, 2 sus cym, bell tree, 2 tamtam, bd,
    bells, vib.
                                         Films/Space
Kane (rental)

An Irish Party in Third Class   4'
    Strings (winds/perc can be added)
    From the film *Titanic* and made famous by the
    Gaelic Storm band.
    Larry Moore, arr.
                             Films/St. Patrick's
Leonard

James Horner-Hollywood Blockbusters   8'
    2 1 3[1.2.bcl] 1 – 4 3 3 1 – tmp+perc – str
    Includes: Main Title from Apollo 13, Somewhere
    Out There from An American Tale; Bannockburn
    from Braveheart; My Heart Will Go On and
    Southampton from *Titanic*.
    John Moss, arr.
                                              Films
Leonard

Legends of the Fall: The Ludlows (1994)   5'
    3[afl.2.3.] 3[1.2.Eh] 2[1.bcl] 2 – 6 2 4 1 – 1perc
    – hp, pf – str
    perc: sus cym.
    Solo Violin.
                                              Films
T&V (rental)

The Mask of Zorro: Suite (1998)   6.5'
    2[afl.pic] 2[1.Eh] 2[1.bcl] 2[1.cbn] – 6 2 4 1 –
    tmp+6 – 2 hp[1.(2)], synth 2 gtr, guitaron [playable
    on bs gtr] – str
    perc: sd, bd, castanet, tambn, sus cym, cym, chimes,
    palmas.
    John Mauceri, arr.
                                  Films/Halloween
T&V (rental)

Star Trek 2: The Wrath of Khan (1982)   12'
    3[1.pic.pic] 3[Eh.2.Eh] 3[1.2.bcl/bflcbcl]   (3' 9')
    3[1.2.cbn] – 6 4 4 1 – tmp+4 – 2 hp, pf,
    3 synth[serge.jupiter 8.arp 2600] – str
    perc: bd, sus cym, orch bells, sd, mark tree, vib, cym, tri,
    song bells, plastic pipe, sizzle cym, tubophone, bells,
    tamtam.
    Includes: Main Title, Epilogue & End Cast.
                                         Films/Space
T&V (rental)

Star Trek 3: The Search for Spock   8.5'
    "Stealing the Enterprise" (1984)
    4[Ebfl/pic.pic.pic.pic] 2 3[1.2.Bbcbcl] 2[1.cbn]
    – 6[#5&6=tuben] 4 4 1 – tmp+perc –
    2 hp, 3 kybd[pf/CS80/org/DX7,pf.pf/cel], beam,
    cimbalon, EVI – str
    perc: sd, pic sd, field drum, parade drum, 2 bd, sm
    Chinese drum, cym, sizzle cym, sus cym, thunder sheet,
    vib, xyl, marim, bs marim, orch bells, tubophone, trans
    celeste, timbales, tamtam, sm tri, mark tree, plastic tube.
                                     Films/Space
T&V (rental)

Titanic Suite   19'
    3[1/afl/pennywhistle.2/afl.3/(afl)] 3[1.2.Eh.3/(Eh)]
    3[1.2.3(bcl)] 3[1.2.3/cbn] – 4 3 3 1 – tmp+perc –
    hp, pf, synth, elec bass – str
    Don Davis, arr.
                                              Films
Kane (rental)

Titanic Suite   18'
    2[1.2/pic/afl] 2[1.2/Eh] 2[1.2/bcl] 2 – 4 2 4(#4) 1 –
    tmp+perc – hp, pf, synth – str
    Solo Soprano; SATB Chorus.
                                              Films
Leonard

Hovhaness, Alan   1911-2000

Triptych: As on the Night   5'
    (Christmas Ode), Op. 100, No. 1b
    0 2[cl, tp] 0 0 – 2[tbn] 0 0 0 – hp, cel, (pf) – str
    Solo Soprano.
                                        Christmas
AMP (rental)

Howard, James Newton   1951-
(Also See: Zimmer, Hans)

Defiance (2008): Nothing is Impossible   4'
    2[1/afl.2/afl] 0 2[1.bcl] 2[1.2/cbn] – 4 0 4 0
    – tmp+perc – hp – str
    Solo Violin. Nominated for an Oscar for Best
    Original Score.
                                              Films
Kane (rental)

Grand Canyon: Fanfare　　　　　　　　　　　　4'
　　0 0 0 0 – 4 6 4 1 – tmp+perc – str
　　　　　　　　　　　　Americana/Fanfare/Films
Kane (rental)

King Kong　　　　　　　　　　　　　　　　6'
　　tmp+1 to 5 – str
　　Includes: It's Deserted; Tooth and Claw; Beauty
　　Killed the Beast II; Beautiful; Kong Chases Jack;
　　Captured.
　　Ted Ricketts, arr.
　　　　　　　　　　　　　　　　Animals/Films
Leonard

King Kong Soundtrack Highlights　　　　　　8'
　　2 1 3[1.2.bcl] 1 – 4 3 3 1 – tmp+3 – pf – str
　　Includes: Main Title; Wall; Breach; It's Deserted;
　　Beautiful; T Rex and Kong Fight; Jawbreaker;
　　Beauty Killed the Beast V.
　　Ted Ricketts, arr.
　　　　　　　　　　　　　　　　Animals/Films
Leonard

Lady in the Water (2006): The Healing　　　　6'
　　2 2 2 2 – 6 0 4 1 – perc – hp, pf, cel
　　　　　　　　　　　　　　　　　　　　Films
Kane (rental)

Peter Pan (2003): Flying
　　3[1/pic.2.3/pic] 3[1.2.3/Eh] 3[1.2.bcl] 3[1.2.cbn] –6
　　4[all dbl D tpt] 4 1 – tmp+perc – pf, cel – str
　　　SATB Chorus.
　　　　　　　　　　　　　　　　　Films/Travel
Leonard

Peter Pan (2003): Suite for　　　　　　　　23'
　Orchestra with Narrator
　　3[1.2.3/pic] 3[1.2.Eh] 3[1.2.3/bcl] 3[1.2.(cbn)] –
　　4 3 3 1 – tmp+3 – hp, cel, pf – str
　　perc: glock, vib, wind chimes, bd, sus cym, tri, mark tree,
　　bell tree, toms, field dr, cym, sizzle cym, xyl, brake dr,
　　tamtam.
　　Narrator; Optional Child Soprano. Optional SATB
　　Chorus. Narration by Virginia Russell.
　　Includes The Beginning; Dreams in a Drawer,
　　Tinkerbell; Learning to Fly Part I; Learning to Fly
　　Part II; Captain Hook, Fairy Dance; Kidnap and
　　Swordfight; The Flying Ship; Homecoming; Peter
　　Returns.
　　Patrick Russ, arr.
　　　　　　　　　　　　　　　　　　　　Films
Kane (rental)

The Prince of Tides Suite　　　　　　　　　6'
　　3[1.2.3/pic] 2[1.2/Eh] 3[1.2.3/bcl] 2 – 6 3 3 1 –
　　tmp+perc – hp, pf – str
　　　　　　　　　　　　　　　　　　　　Films
Kane (rental)

Signs(2002): Suite　　　　　　　　　　　5.5'
　　3[1/pic.2/pic.pic] 2 3[1.2.bcl] 2 – 4 3 3 1 –
　　tmp+perc – hp, pf – str
　　2 Solo Violins.
　　　　　　　　　　　　　　　　　　　　Films
Kane (rental)

The Sixth Sense Suite　　　　　　　　　　7'
　　3[1/pic/afl.2/pic/afl.3/pic/afl] 3[1.2.Eh] 3 3 – 4 3 3 1
　　– tmp+perc – hp, pf – str
　　SATB Chorus.
　　　　　　　　　　　　　　　　　　　　Films
Kane (rental)

Snow Falling on Cedars Suite　　　　　　　5'
　　3[1.2.3/pic] 3[1.2.Eh] 3 3[1.2.3/cbn] – 4 3 3 1 –
　　tmp+perc – hp, pf – str
　　SATB Chorus.
　　　　　　　　　　　　　　　Films/Weather
Kane (rental)

The Village: The Gravel Road　　　　　　4.5'
　　2[1/recorder.2/recorder] 2 2 2 – 4 0 4 1 – tmp+perc –
　　hp, pf – str
　　Brad Dechter, arr.
　　　　　　　　　　　　　　　　　　　　Films
Kane (rental)

The Village: Suite-Village Romance
　　2[1/rec.2/rec] 1 2 2 – 4 0 3 0 – tmp+perc –
　　hp, pf – str
　　Solo Cello.
　　　　　　　　　　　　　　　　　　　　Films
Kane (rental)

Wyatt Earp (1994)　　　　　　　　　　　5'
　　3[1.afl.pic] 3[1.2.Eh] 3[1.2.bcl] 3 – 4 3 3 1 –
　　tmp+perc – hp, pf – str
　　perc: cym, sus cym, tambn, sd, bd, vib, 2 glock, tri.
　　　　　　　　　　　　　　　Americana/Films
Kane (rental)

Wyatt Earp: End Credits　　　　　　　　　5'
　　2 2[1.Eh] 2 2 – 6[2 are opt] 4 4 1 – tmp+perc –
　　hp, pf – str
　　Brad Dechter, arr.
　　　　　　　　　　　　　　　Americana/Films
Kane (rental)

Hubbell, Raymond 1879-1954

Poor Butterfly 3'
3[1.2.pic] 2 2 2 – 3sx – 4 3 3 1 – tmp+perc – str
William Ryden, arr.
                                                Animals
Kalmus

Hudson, Will & Mills, Irving

Moonglow 4'
drumset – gtr – strings
Solo Clarinet. A jazz standard composed in 1933. It was also used in the soundtrack for the film *The Aviator*.
Calvin Custer, arr.
                        Film/Jazz/Travel/Valentine
Warner (rental)

Humperdinck, Engelbert 1854-1921

Hänsel and Gretel: Overture 8'
3[1.2.pic] 2 2 2 – 4 2 3 1 – tmp+2 – str
perc: tri, tambn, cym.
                                    Popular Classics
Kalmus; Luck's

Hänsel und Gretel: 4'
Hexenritt (Witch's Ride)
3[1.2.pic] 2 2 2 – 4 2 3 1 – tmp+4 – str
perc: bd, cym, sus cym, tri, tambn, cast.
                      Halloween/Popular Classics
Kalmus

Hänsel und Gretel: [Three excerpts] 13'
                    (3' 3' 7')
3[1.2.pic] 2[1.2/Eh] 2 2 – 4 2 3 1 – tmp+1 – hp – str
perc: tri, cym.
Includes: Lied des Sandmännchens (Sandman's Song); Abendsegen (Evening Prayer); Traumpantomime (Dream Pantomime).
                                    Popular Classics
Kalmus; Schott

Hunsberger, Donald

Under Gypsy Skies
2 2 2 2 – 4 2 3 1 – tmp+2 – hp, pf – str
perc: timbales, tambn, marimba, glock, tri, cyms, sus cym, tam tam, bd, castanets, xyl, sd, pic sd, maracas, bongos.
2 Solo Trumpets. Conductor score is for sale.
                                     Instrumental Pops
Alfred (rental)

Hunter, Frank 1920-2005

Fling Went the Strings 4'
3[1.2.pic] 2[1.Eh] 3[1.2.bcl] 2 – 4 3 3 1 – tmp+2 – cel – str
Featuring horns and pizzicato strings.
                      Instrumental Pops/Novelty
Clear Mud

Twinkle Fantasia 4.5'
3 2[1.Eh] 3[1.2.bcl] 2 – 4 3 3 1 – tmp+2 – cel/harp – str
Variations on the familiar melody featuring different sections of the orchestra.
                        Instrumental Pops/Space
Clear Mud

Hupfeld, Herman 1894-1951

As Time Goes By 4'
0 0 0 0 – 0 0 0 0 – drumset – gtr, pf – str
Solo Alto or Tenor Saxophone.
Calvin Custer, arr.
                                Films/Popular Song
Warner (rental)

I

Iannaccone, Anthony   1943-

From Time to Time   13'
3[incl pic] 2 2 2 – 4 2 2 0 – pf/cel – str
Celebrates the history and folk music of Virginia. Written for the Richmond Symphony as part of the Continental Harmony Project.

                                 Americana

Tritone (rental)

Ibert, Jacques   1890-1962

Divertissement   15'
                           (1' 5' 2' 3' 2' 2')
1[1/pic] 0 1 1[1/cbn] – 1 1 1 0 – 1perc – pf/cel – str
perc: timbales, tri, woodblk, sd, tambn, sus cym, bd, cast, tam tam, police whistle.

                               Popular Classics

Durand (rental)

Ippolitov-Ivanov, M.   1859-1935

Caucasian Sketches, Op 10   5'
                           (8' 4' 4' 5')
3[1.2.pic] 3[1.2.Eh] 2 2 – 4 4[2tp,(2crt)] 3 0 – tmp+5 – hp – str
perc: tri, tambn, cym, bd, field dr, 2tmp piccolo orientali.
Includes: In the Mountain Pass; In the Village; In the Mosque; Procession of the Sardar.

                                     Dance

Kalmus; Russian (rental)

Isaac, Merle J., arr.   1898-1996

Salute to the United Nations   8'
1 1 2 1 – 2 2 1 1 – 2perc – pf –str

                                   Patriotic

Fischer (POP); Luck's (rental)

Iturriaga, Enrique   1918-

Canción y Muerte de Rolando   21'
(Song and Death of Rolando)
1 1 2 1 – 2 2 1 1 – str
Solo Soprano.

                                International (Peru)

Filarmonika (rental)

Obertura para una Comedia   3.5'
(Overture for a Comedy)
3[incl pic] 3[incl Eh] 3[incl bcl] 3 – 4 2 3 1 – tmp+perc – hp, pf – str

                                International (Peru)

Filarmonika (rental)

Sinfonía Junín y Ayacucho: 1824   25'
3[incl pic] 3[incl Eh] 3 3 – 4 3 3 1 – tmp+perc – str
Commemorating the battle that secured the independence of Peru and ensured independence for the rest of South America. It is considered the end of the Spanish American wars of independence. Score is available for purchase.

                                International (Peru)

Filarmonika (rental)

Ivanovici, Josef   1845-1902

Waves of the Danube: 7'
The Anniversary Song
1 2 2 2 – 2 2 3 1[euph] – 2perc – str
S.V. Balfour, arr.

                                Celebrations/Dance

Kalmus

Waves of the Danube: 7'
The Anniversary Song
2 2 2 2 – 3sx – 4 3 3 1 – tmp+perc – hp – str
Henry Sopkin, arr.

                                Celebrations/Dance

Kalmus

Ives, Charles   1874-1954

Central Park in the Dark, S.34   7.5'
   2[1.pic] 1 1[1/Ebcl] 1 – 0 1 1 0 – 2perc –2pf
   [3players ideal] – str
   perc: sd, bd/cym.
   No. 1 of *Three Outdoor Scenes*.
                                 Americana
   Boelke (rental)

Christmas Music   8'
   2 2 2 2 – 2 3 3 1 – marimba – pf, hp, (cel) – str
   Optional unison chorus
   Includes: Adeste Fideles; December; A Christmas
   Carol.
   Lou Harrison, arr.
                                   Christmas
   Merion (rental)

Country Band March, S.36   4'
   1[1/pic] 0 1 0 – asx – 0 1[crt] 2 0 – 3perc – pf –
   str(no va)
   perc: drumset[or bd/cym, sd].
   Edited by James Sinclair.
                            Instrumental Pops
   Merion (rental)

Lincoln, the Great Commoner   4'
   for voices and orchestra
   2[incl opt pic] 2 2 2 – 0 2 2 1 – tmp+1[low bell]
   – pf – str
   SATB Chorus.
                                   Patriotic
   Kalmus; Merion (rental)

Symphony Holidays: 8'
   1. Washington's Birthday
   1[1/pic] 0 0 1[opt bn or tbn] – 1 0 1[opt cl or bn] 0
   – glock or pf – 3Jew's hp[1 player] – str
   Critcal edition by James Sinclair.
                                   Patriotic
   AMP (rental)

Symphony Holidays: 10'
   2. Decoration Day
   3[1.2.(pic)] 3[1.2.Eh] 3[1.2.(Ebcl)] 2 –
   4 2 3[opt #3] 1 – tmp+5 – str
   perc: sd, bd, cym, chimes, glock[or cel]
   Critical edition by James Sinclair.
                                   Patriotic
   Peer (rental)

Symphony Holidays: 7'
   3. Fourth of July
   3[1.2.pic] 2 2 3[1.2.cbn] – 4 4[1.2.3.crt] 3 1 – tmp+6
   – pf – str
   perc: xyl, sd, cym, bd, glock.
   Critical edition by Wayne Shirley.
                                   Patriotic
   AMP (rental)

Symphony Holidays: 15'
   4. Thanksgiving and Forefathers' Day
   3[1.2.(pic)] 2 2 3[1.2.(cbn)] – 4 3 3 1 – tmp+1 to 5
   – cel, pf – str
   perc: chimes, glock, churchbells.
   Critical edition by Jonathan Elkus.
                                   Holidays
   Peer (rental)

Symphony No. 3:   19'
   The Camp Meeting   (7' 8' 4')
   1 1 1 1 – 2 0 1 0 – (bells) – str
   Critical edition by Kenneth Singleton.
                                  Americana
   AMP (rental)

Three Places in New England   18'
                                    (8' 6' 4')
   2[1.opt pic] 2[1.Eh] 1 1 – 2[(#2)] 2[(#2)] 1 0 –
   tmp+2 – pf 4-hands[(player2)] – str
   perc: sd, bd/cym.
   Includes: The Saint-Gaudens in Boston Common;
   Putnam's Camp; From the Housatonic at
   Stockbridge.
   1929 small orchestra version edition by James
   Sinclair.
                                  Americana
   Mercury (rental)

Three Places in New England   18'
                                    (8' 6' 4')
   3[1.2.3/pic] 2[1.2/Eh] 2 3[1.2.cbn] – 4 2 3 1 –
   tmp+3 – 2hp[opt #2] cel/pf, org – str
   perc: bd/cym, sd, gong.
   Restored and edited by James Sinclair.
                                  Americana
   Mercury (rental)

Variations on America   8'
   0 0 0 0 – 1 4 4 1
   Arrangement for 10-piece brass ensemble.
   Eric Crees, arr.
                                   Patriotic
   Merion (rental)

Variations on America 8'
   3[1.2/pic.3/pic] 2 2 2 – 4 3 3 1 – tmp+3 – str
   perc: xyl, glock, cast, bd, sd, tri, cym, tambn.
   William Schuman, orchestrator.
                                        Patriotic
   Merion (rental)

Yale-Princeton Football Game 5'
   4[incl pic] 4[incl Eh] 3[(bsx)] 4 – bsx – 4 4 3 1 –
   tmp+perc – pf – str
   Gunther Schuller, editor
                                          Sports
   AMP (rental)

Yale-Princeton Football Game 4'
   3[1.2.pic] 2 2 3[1.2.cbn] 4 3 3 1 – tmp+2 – pf – str
   Optional Kazoo Chorus.
   James Sinclair, editor
                                Novelty/Sports
   AMP (rental)

J

Jackson, Jill (See: Miller, Sy)

Jackson, Michael   1958-2009

A Michael Jackson Spectacular 8.5'
   2 1 2 1 – 4 3 3 1 – tmp+3 – pf – str
   Includes songs from *Thriller*: Billie Jean; The Girl Is
   Mine; Beat It.
   Steven Rosenhaus, arr.
                             Popular Song
   Leonard (POP); EMS or Luck's (rental)

Jackson, Stephen, arr.

The Novello Book of Carols: 3'
   Noel Nouvelet
   2 2 2 2 – 2 2 3 0 – tmp+1 – str
   Solo voice
                               Christmas
   Novello (rental)

Jacob, Gordon   1895-1984

Five Pieces in the Form of a Suite 12'
   Strings – Solo Harmonica
                           Instrumental Pops
   Stainer (rental)

Jacobs, Jim (See: Casey, Warren)

Jager, Robert   1939-

Concerto Grosso   *17'*
(for Dance Band and Orchestra)
3 2 2 2 – 4 3 3 1 – tmp+perc – str
Dance Band: 2asx, tsx, bsx; 4 tp; 4tbn; pf; db; drumset.

Dance

Elkan-Vogel (rental)

Jalbert, Pierre   1971?-

In Aeternam   *13'*
3[incl pic] 3[incl Eh] 3[incl bcl] 3[incl cbn] –
4 3 3 1 – tmp+3 – hp, cel, pf – str
First Prize - Masterprize Competition (2001).

Popular Classics

Merion (rental)

James, Arthur (See: Wilson, Robb)

Jameson, Tom & Feller, Sherm

Summertime, Summertime   *3'*
2 2 2 2 – 4 3 3 1 – tmp+3 – pf – str
Richard Hayman, arr.

Seasons

Music Sales

Jarre, Maurice   1924-1997

Lara's Theme from Doctor Zhivago   *3'*
Strings
Merle J. Isaac, arr.

Films

Robbins(POP); Luck's (rental)

Lara's Theme from Doctor Zhivago   *3'*
1 1 2 1 – 4 3 3 0 tmp+perc – pf, bandoneon, balalaika, 3mandolins, hp – str
Bill Holcomb, arr.

Films

EMI (rental)

Lawrence of Arabia Suite   *12.5'*
3[1.2.pic] 2[1.Eh] 4[1.2.3.Ebcl] 3[1.2.cbn] – 4 3 3 2
– tmp+6 – hp, pf, synth – str
perc: 2 sd, bd, xyl, timb, bongo, cym, 4tambn, 4 toms.
The Overture (5') is available alone.

Films

T&V (rental)

A Passage to India: A Symphonic Journey (1984)   *10'*
3[1.2.afl/pic] 3[1.2.Eh] 3[1.2.bcl] 3[1.2.cbn] –
4 3 3 1 – tmp+4 – 2 hp, pf, cel, ondes – str
perc: drumset, vib, xyl, glock, marim, chimes, cym, sus cym, sd, bd, sm gong, tamtam, bell tree, toms, ruthe, 2 conga, woodblk, tri.
Includes: Prelude; Bombay; Statues; Kashmir & End Titles; Adelia's Theme; Bombay March.
Christopher Palmer, arr.

Films/Travel

T&V (rental)

Ryan's Daughter: Rosy's Theme (1970)   *9'*
2 2 2 2 – 4 2 2 1 – tmp+2 – hp, pf, gtr, ondes – str
perc: drumset, vib, glock.

Films

T&V (rental)

Witness: Building the Barn   *5'*
2[1.pic] 2 2 2 – 4 2 3 1 – tmp – str
Also available for chamber orhestra.
Patrick Russ, arr.

Films

T&V (rental)

Jendras, Louis F.

The Russian Rag   *4'*
3[1,2,pic[2 3[1.2.bcl] 2 – 4 3 3 1 – tmp+2 – str
perc: bd, tri, cym, tambn, sd.
Playable with strings alone.

Instrumental Pops

Luck's (rental)

Appalachian Fling 7'
2 2 3[1.2.bcl] 3[1.2.cbn] – 2asx, 3tsx, bsx – 4 3 3 1 – 2perc – str

        Americana

Luck's (rental)

Jenkins, Karl   1944-

Palladio-Concerto Grosso 18'
  for String Orchestra
Strings
Used in a DeBeers diamond company commercial.

        TV

Boosey

Passacaglia 4.5'
Strings

        Instrumental Pops

Boosey

Jessel, Leon   1871-1942

Parade of the Wooden Soldiers 5'
2 2 3[1.2.bcl] 2 – 4sx – 2 3 3 1 – tmp+perc – str
Morton Gould, arr.

        Christmas

Kalmus

Parade of the Wooden Soldiers 5'
1 1 2 1 – 2 1 1 0 – ssx, 2asx, tsx – 3perc – bnjo – str
M. Lake, arr.

        Christmas

Marks (rental)

Joel, Billy   1949-

The Best of Billy Joel 7'
2 1 2 1 – (asx, tsx, bsx) – 4 3 2 1 – tmp+1– (elec bs), pf – str
perc: drumset, cabasa, tambn.
Includes: Just the Way You Are; My Life; Honesty; Uptown Girl.
Chuck Sayre, arr.

        Popular Song/Rock

Leonard (rental)

Just the Way You Are 2'
2 1 2 1 – 2 2 2 1 – 2perc – pf – str
perc: drumset, vib, maracas, glock, finger cym.
Anita Kerr, arr.

        Popular Song/Rock

Leonard POP (rental)

Movin' Out: Medley 7'
3[1.2.pic] 2 3[1.2.bcl] – 4 3 3 1 – tmp+perc – (pf, gtr, bass gtr) – str
perc: drumset, glock, chimes, xyl, vib, tri, bd, cym, tambn, cabasa, mark tree.
Optional SATB Chorus and/or 1-3 soloists.
Includes: Movin' Out; Just the Way You Are; Uptown Girl; and Big Shot. From the Broadway production "Movin' Out" conceived by Twila Tharp. This medley was commissioned by the Cincinnati Pops for Erich Kunzel.
Robert Wendel, arr.

        Broadway Musicals/Dance

Wendel (rental)

John, Elton   1947-

Suite from the Lion King 15'
3[incl pic] 3[incl Eh] 3[incl bcl] 3[incl cbn] – 4 3 3 1 – tmp+5, drumset – hp, 2kybds[synth/acoustic.org], (accordion), (musette), 2gtr[acoustic.elec gtr] - str
Optional Chorus.
Crafton Beck, arr.

        Broadway Musicals

Wonderland (rental)

Johnson, Francis   1792-1844

Buffalo City Guard Parade March 3'
3[1.2.pic] 2 2 2 – 4 2 3 1 – tmp+perc – str
African-American composer of band music in Philadelphia.
Nightingale, arr.

        Americana

Kalmus

General Cadwalader's Grand March 3'
3[1.2.pic] 2 2 2 – 4 2 3 1 – tmp+perc – str
Nightingale, arr.

        Americana

Kalmus

Philadelphia Grays Quickstep   4'
    3[1.2.pic] 2 2 2 – 4 2 3 1 – tmp+perc – str
    Nightingale, arr.

                                                Americana/Dance
Kalmus

Johnson, Laurence (Laurie)   1927-

The Avengers: Theme (1961)   2.5'
    2[1.pic] 2 3[1.2.bcl] 2 – 4 4 4 0 – tmp+2 –
    hp, upright pf[jangle pf], gtr, bs gtr – str
    perc: drumset, vib.

                                                 TV
T&V (rental

Jones, Ron   1954-

Star Trek, The Next Generation: Suite (1989)   15'
    3 3[1.2.Eh] 3[1.2.bcl] 2 – 4 3 3 1 – tmp+3 –
    hp, 2 kybd[pf/D50/DX7II.D50/DX7II] – str
    perc: vib, marim, xyl, glock, sus cym, sd, bd, gong,
    waterphone, Anklongs, mark tree.
    Includes: Docking at Starbase 74/Beyond Velocity,
    Tasha's Goodbye, The Nursery & Finale.

                                                 Space/TV
T&V (rental)

Jones, Samuel   1935-

Elegy for String Orchestra   6'
    Strings
    Written in response to the assassination of J.F.K.

                                                 Patriotic
Fischer

Jones, Trevor   1949-

Last of the Mohicans: Kiss
    0 1[Eh] 0 0 – 6[(3-5)] 0 0 0 – perc – hp, (gtr),
    EVI(synth) – str
    Solo Violin.
    Brad Dechter, arr.

                                                 Films
Kane (rental)

Last of the Mohicans: Main Title
    3[1.2.pic] 2[1.2.Eh] 2[1.2.bcl] 3[1.2.cbn] – 6 3 3 1
    – tmp+perc – hp – str
    Geoff Alexander, arr.

                                                 Films
Kane (rental)

Last of the Mohicans Suite
    3[1.2.pic] 2[1.2.Eh] 2[1.2.bcl] 3[1.2.cbn] – 6 3 3 1
    – tmp+perc – hp, pf/cel, org – str
    Geoff Alexander, arr.

                                                 Films
Kane (rental)

Joplin, Scott   1868-1917

The Entertainer   5'
    Strings
    Alan Arnold, arr.

                                                 Instrumental Pops/Jazz
Presser (rental)

The Entertainer   3.5'
    3[1.2.pic] 1 4[1.2.3.bcl] 1 – 4sx – 2 3 2 1 – perc –
    (pf) – str
    Optional Solo Piano. Used in the movie *The Sting*.
    Bill Holcombe, arr.

                                                 Jazz
Musicians Pub.

The Entertainer   3.5'
    2[1.pic] 1 3[1.2.bcl] 1 – 2asx, tsx – 3 3 3 (1) –
    3perc – (banjo) – str
    perc: drumset, woodblk, bells, tambn, slide whistle,
    cowbell, ratchet, tri.
    John Cacavas, arr.

                                                 Jazz
Belwin (POP); Luck's (rental)

The Entertainer   3.5'
    1[pic] 0 1 0 – 0 1 1 1 – drumset – pf – str[no bass]
    Gunther Schuller, ed.

                                                 Jazz
Belwin (POP); EMS or Luck's (rental)

The Entertainer   4'
    2 2 2 2 – 4 3 3 1 – tmp+2 – str
    Arthur Frankenpohl, arr.

                                                 Jazz
Shawnee

Maple Leaf Rag   3'
   1[incl pic] 0 1 0 – 0 1 1 1 – drumset – pf – str
   See "Red Back Book."
   Gunther Schuller, arr.

                                                           Jazz

Warner (POP); EMS or Luck's (rental)

Ragtimes for Strings   Collection/Folio
   strings [(bass)]
   Includes: The Ragtime Dance; Original Rags, The
   Favourite, A Ragtime Two-Step.
   Beyer, arr.

                                                           Jazz

Kunzelmann

Ragtime Favorites for Strings   Collection/Folio
   Strings
   Includes: Country Club; Euphonic Sounds;
   Heliotrope Bouquet; Maple Leaf Rag; Paragon Rag;
   Pineapple Rag; Scott Joplin's New Rag.
   William Zinn, arr.

                                                           Jazz

Warner

Red Back Book   Collection/Folio
   1 [pic] 0 1 0 – 0 1[crt] 1 1 – 2perc – pf – str
   perc: sd, bd, drumset.
   The authentic instrumentation is five winds, four
   strings, and rhythm section consisting of piano, string
   bass and drumset.
   Includes: Sun Flower Slow Drag; The
   Chrysanthemum (An Afro-American Intermezzo);
   The Cascades; Maple Leaf Rag; The Easy Winners;
   Ragtime Dance; The Entertainer (A Ragtime Two-
   Step).
   Gunther Schuller, arr.

                                                           Jazz

Belwin (POP); EMS or Luck's (rental)

Joubert, John   1927-

The Novello Book of Carols: 3'
  Torches 1
   2 2 2 2 – 4 2 3 1 – tmp+perc – str
   Solo Voice.

                                                    Christmas

Novello (rental)

The Novello Book of Carols: 3'
  Torches II
   2 2 2 2 – 4 2 3 1 – tmp+perc – str
   Solo Voice.

                                                   Christmas

Novello (rental)

K

Kabalevsky, Dmitri   1904-1987

The Comedians Op. 26: Suite   13'
               (1' 1' 1' 1' 2' 1' 1' 1' 2' 2')
   1[1/pic] 1[1/Eh] 2 1 – 2 2 1 1 – tmp+4 – pf – str
   Includes: Prologue; Galop; March; Waltz;
   Pantomime; Intermezzo; Little Lyrical Scene:
   Gavotte; Scherzo; Epilogue.
                                Popular Classics
Russian (rental)

Romeo and Juliet: Musical Sketches, Op. 56   34'
   3 3 3 3 – 4 3 3 1 – tmp+perc – hp, pf – str
                         Popular Classics/Valentine
Russian (rental)

Kaczmarek, Jan A.P.   1953-

Finding Neverland: Suite (2004)   5'
   2 2[1.Eh] 2 0 – 4 0 0 0 – 2perc – hp, pf, cel,
   accordion, mand – str
   perc: crotales, tri, marim, wind chimes, sus cym, glock.
   Includes: Where is Mr. Barrie?; This is Neverland;
   and Why Does She Have to Die?
   Winner of the Oscar for Best Score of the Year
                                            Films
T&V (rental)

Kalmer, Bert

A Kiss to Build a Dream On   2'
   2 1 2 1 – 2 3 2 1 – tmp+2 – pf – str
   perc: drumset, vib.
   Words & music by Bert Kalmar, Harry Ruby, &
   Oscar Hammerstein II in1935.
   It was recorded by Louis Armstrong in1951 and first
   used in the film *The Strip*, also in *Sleepless In
   Seattle*.
   Marty Gold, arr.
                      Films/Popular Songs/Valentine
Belwin (rental)

Kamen, Michael   1948-2003

Band of Brothers   5.5'
   2 2 3[1.2.bcl] 2 – 4 3 3 1 – tmp+perc – pf – str
   Roy Phillippe, arr.
                                        Patriotic/TV
Belwin

Band of Brothers: Suite (2001)   6'
   3[afl.2.pic] 3[1.2.Eh] 3[1.2.bcl] 3[1.2.cbn] – 6 3 4 1 –
   tmp+3 – hp, pf – str
   perc: sus cym, bd, chimes, sd, tamtam, field drum.
   From the 10 part TV mini-series in 2001.
                                        Patriotic/TV
T&V (rental)

Mr. Holland's Opus: 17'
   American Symphony
   2 2[incl Eh] 3[incl bcl] 3[incl cbn] – 6 3 4 1 –
   tmp+perc – hp, pf, elec gtr[bass] – str
                                              Films
MCA (rental)

Robin Hood: Prince of Thieves (Main Title)   4'
   2 1 3[1.2.(bcl)] 2 – 4[(#3&4)] 3 3 1 – tmp+2 –
   pf or hp – str
   perc: bd, sus cym, glock, tamtam, bell tree, cym, chimes.
   Steven Rosenhaus, arr.
                                             Films
Leonard (rental)

Kander, John   1927-

Chicago   6'
   2 2 3[1.2.bcl] 2 – 2 3 3 1 – tmp+3 – pf – str
   perc: glock, xyl, sd, bd, cym, hi hat, tambn, slapstick,
   woodblk.
   Includes: My Own Best Friend; Razzle Dazzle; And
   All that Jazz.
   Victor Lopez, arr.
                                    Broadway Musicals
Belwin

Chicago: Medley   6'
   2 1 3[1.2.bcl] 1 – 4 3 3 1 – tmp+2 – pf – str
   perc: drumset, xyl, claves, sus cym, glock, woodblk.
   Includes: and All That Jazz; Cell Block Tango;
   Roxie; We Both Reached for the Gun.
                                    Broadway Musicals
Leonard

Kander, John   1927-
Ebb, Fred   1935-2004

Cabaret   3'
    perc – pf, gtr – str
    Calvin Custer, arr.
               Broadway Musicals
Warner (POP); Luck's (rental)

New York, New York Theme   3'
    2 2 2 1 – 4 3 3 1 – tmp+2 – pf,elec bass – str
    perc: drumset, xyl, bells, cym.
    Chuck Sayre, arr.
               Americana
Warner (POP); EMS or Luck's (rental)

Theme from New York, New York   3'
    3[incl pic] 3[1.2.Eh] 3[1.2.bcl] 3[1.2.cbn] – 4 2 3 1
    – tmp+2 – hp – str
    Solo Voice; Key of F.
    Paul McKibbins, arr.
               Americana
EMI (rental)

Theme from New York, New York   3'
    2 2 2 2 – 4 2 3 1 – tmp+5[3] – pf – str
    perc: bells, vib, drumset [sd, bd, ride cym]
    Playable with just strings and piano.
    Bob Cerulli, arr.
               Americana
Warner

Kaper, Bronislau   1902-1983

Auntie Mame: Overture (1958)   3'
    2[1.pic] 2.3[1.Ebcl.bcl] 2 – 4 3 3 1 – tmp+3 –
    hp, pf, cel – str
    perc: sd, bd, cym, sus cym, chimes, tri, sleigh bells, bells, vib, xyl.
               Films
T&V (rental)

Lili: Ballet (1953)   5.5'
    3[1.2.pic] 3[1.2.Eh] 3[1.Ebcl.bcl] 3[1.2.cbn] –
    4 3 3 1 – tmp+3 – hp, pf[cel], accordion[synth] – str
    perc: sd, bd, cym, sus cym, glock, xyl, marim, vib,
    woodblk, tambn, temple blocks, tri, gong.
    Oscar winning film score.
               Dance/Films
T&V (rental)

Mutiny on the Bounty: Suite (1962)   11'
    3[1.2.pic] 3[1.2.Eh] 3[1.2.bcl] 3[1.2.cbn] –
    8 [horns 4-8 are opt] 4 3 1 – tmp+4 –
    2 hp, pf[cel] – str
    perc: sd, field dr, bd, 2 cym, sus cym, glock, xyl, vib, chimes, tambn, tri, tamtam.
    Includes: Overture, Love Theme (Intermezzo), Chase & Idyll (Scherzo), & The Magic Island.
    Christopher Palmer, arr.
               Films
T&V (rental)

Them!: Ant Fugue (1954)
    2 2[1.Eh] 3[1.2.bcl] 2 – 2 1 0 0 – hp – str
               Animals/Films/
               Halloween
T&V (rental)

Kapilow, Robert   1952-

Chris van Allsburg's Polar Express   22'
    2[incl pic] 2 2 2 – 2 2 3 0 – 2perc – hp, cel or pf
    – str
    Alternate: 2[incl pic] 0 2 1 – 2 1 0 0 – perc – pf – str
    Solo Baritone; Children's Chorus.
               Christmas/Films
Schirmer (rental)

City Piece: DC Monuments   29'
    3[incl pic] 3[incl Eh] 3[incl bcl] 3[incl cbn] –
    4 3 3 1 – tmp+3 [incl 8' ocean drums] – hp, cel or pf
    – str
    Solo Rapper. Includes: Beginning; The Truly Great; Rest in Peace; War; Washington Monument; Finale.
               Patriotic
Schirmer (rental)

Dr. Seuss's Gertrude McFuzz   16'
    2[incl pic] 2 2 2 – 2 2 2 0 – 2perc – pf – str;
    Alternate: 1[incl pic] 0 2 1 – 1 1 0 0 – perc – pf – db
    Solo Soprano, Girl Narrator.
               Americana
Schirmer (rental)

Dr. Seuss's Green Eggs and Ham   18'
    2[incl pic] 2 2 2 – 2 2 2 0 – 2perc – pf – str;
    Alternate: 1[incl pic] 0 2 1 – 1 1 0 0 – perc – pf – db
    Solo Soprano, Boy Narrator.
    Performed as fully staged or in concert form. Contact Schirmer about the version desired.
               Americana
Schirmer (rental)

Elijah's Angel 23'
1[incl pic] 1 2 1 – 2 1 0 0 – perc – cel or pf – db
Alternate: 2[incl pic] 2 2 2 – 2 2 0 0 – 2perc – str
Solo Baritone, Bass-Baritone, Boy Soprano;
Children's Chorus. Libretto by Jim Friedland, based on the children's book "Elijah's Angel" by Michael Rosen.

Christmas

Schirmer (rental)

Play Ball!: Casey at the Bat 20'
1 1 2 1 – 2 1 0 0 – perc – pf – db
SATB Chorus. Text English by Ernest L. Thayer.

Sports

Schirmer (rental)

Union Station 30'
3[incl pic] 3[incl Eh] 3[incl bcl] 3[incl cbn] – 4 3 3 1 – tmp+3 – hp,cel or pf – str
Narrator; SATB Chorus. Highlights Kansas City's train station.

Travel

Schirmer (rental)

Union Station: New Year's Eve 2.5'
3[incl pic] 3[incl Eh] 3[incl bcl] 3[incl cbn] – 4 3 3 1 – 3perc – pf – str
Orchestra doubles on noisemakers.

New Year

Schirmer (rental)

You and Hugh 22'
1[incl pic] 1 2 1 – 0 1 1 0 – perc – pf – str
Solo Soprano, Baritone, Boy Soprano. Performed fully staged or in concert form.

Instrumental Pops

Schirmer (rental)

Karlin, Fred (See: Wilson, Robb)

Karmon, Michael 1969-

...And the Rhythm Is Just a Little Bit Off... 10'
3[incl pic] 2 3[incl bcl] 3[incl cbn] – 4 3 3 1 – tmp+3 – hp, cel/pf – str
According to the composer, this work is an energetic concert opener based on a short non-rhyming poem.

Instrumental Pops

Presser (rental)

Kasschau, Howard 1913-1994

Country Concerto
1 1 2 1 – 2 2 1 0 – tmp – str
Solo Piano.

Instrumental Pops

Schirmer (rental)

The Legend of Sleepy Hollow 10'
3 3 3 3 – 4 3 3 0 – tmp+perc – str
Solo Piano. A concerto based on the Washington Irving story.

Halloween

Schirmer (rental)

Katz, S. 1917-1995

Polskie Kwiaty 4'
(Selection of Polish Songs & Dances)
1 1 2 1 – 2 2 1 0 – 2perc – str
perc: sd, bd, tri.
Includes marches and mazurkas.

Dance/Instrumental Pops/
International: Poland

Luck's

Kay, Ulysses 1917-1995

Suite 17'
3[incl pic] 3[incl Eh] 3[incl bcl] 3[incl cbn] – 4 3 3 1 – tmp+3 – pf – str

Black History Month

Schirmer (rental)

Keillor, Garrison & Dworsky, Richard   1942-

Wild Mountain Thyme: *4'*
   Will You Go, Darling, Go?
   2 2 2 2 – 2 0 0 0 – tmp+perc – str
   Traditional Scottish folksong.

                                         International

Williamson (rental)

Kelly, Bryan   1934-

Improvisations on Christmas Carols   *12'*
   2 2 2 2 – 4 2 3 1 – tmp+perc – hp – str

                                         Christmas

Novello (rental)

Kent, Rolfe   1963-

Up In the Air (2009)
   1 0 0 1 – 0 0 0 0 – perc – hp, ukulele – str
   perc: shekere, cabasa, tambn.
   Includes: Milwaukee Wedding; Sitting & Sipping; Who Am I?

                                         Films

T&V (rental)

Kent, Walter   1911-1994

I'll Be Home for Christmas   *2'*
   2 1 2 1 – 2 2 2 1 – tmp+1[incl drumset] – pf – str
   Marty Gold, arr.

                                         Christmas

Warner (POP); Luck's (rental)

Kerchner, Larry

Happy Birthday Medley   *4'*
   2[1.pic] 2 0 0 – 1 3 3 1 – tmp+3 – gtr, pf, hp – str
   perc: glock, sd, cym, bd, (4 toms).
   Solo SATB Vocals. Includes: Happy Birthday to You by Mildred & Patty Hill; For He's a Jolly Good Fellow by traditional; and Happy Days are Here Again by Milton Ager. Choral parts are permanently out of print.

                                         Celebrations

Warner (POP); Luck's (rental)

Kerker, Gustave

The Belle of New York   *3'*
   2[1.pic] 1 2 1 – 2 2 1 0 – 2perc – pf – str
   Only available as a piano score for the conductor.
   F. Beyer, arr.

                          Americana/Instrumental Pops

Luck's

Kern, Jerome   1885-1945

Fluffy Ruffles: Selection   *6'*
   1 1 2 1 – 2 2 1 0 – perc – str
   Franz Mahl, arr.

                                Instrumental Pops

Kalmus

Little Miss Fix-It: Turkey Trot   *2'*
   1 1 2 1 – 2 2 1 0 – perc – str
   Hennenberg, arr.

                               Broadway Musicals

Kalmus

Night Boat Selections   *6'*
   1 1 2 1 – 2 2 1 0 – perc – str
   Includes: Some Fine Day, Left All Alone, Again Blues, Whose Baby Are You, A Heart for Sale, I'd Like a Lighthouse, Good Night Boat.
   Robert Russell Bennett, arr.

                               Broadway Musicals

Kalmus

Night Boat: Whose Baby Are You? 2'
  1 1 2 1 – 2 2 1 0 – perc – str
  Hilding Anderson, arr.
                                     Broadway Musicals
  Kalmus

Ol' Man River 2.5'
  1 1 2[[incl bcl] 1 – 1 3 2 0 – tmp+perc – hp, pf – str
  Solo Voice; Key of Eb.
  Carmen Dragon, arr.
                              Broadway Musicals/Ecology
  Dragon (rental)

Sally Selections for Orchestra 10'
  1 1 2 1 – 2 2 1 0 – perc – str
  Includes: You Can't Keep a Good Girl Down; Look for the Silver Lining; On with the Dance; Sally; Wild Rose; The Church Around the Corner; Look for the Silver Lining Reprise.
  Hilding Anderson, arr.
                                     Broadway Musicals
  Kalmus

She's a Good Fellow Selections 6'
  1[1/pic] 2 1 1 – 2 2 1 0 – tmp+perc – str
  Includes: Some Party; The First Rose of Summer; Happy Wedding Day; Teacher Teacher; Oh You Beautiful; I've Been Waiting for You All the Time.
  Hilding Anderson, arr.
                                     Instrumental Pops
  Kalmus

Show Boat Overture 4'
  2 2 2 2 – 4 3 3 1 – tmp+2 – hp – str
  Includes: Can't Help Lovin' Dat Man; Make Believe; Misery Theme; Ol' Man River; Why Do I Love You?
  Robert Russell Bennett, orchestrator
                                     Broadway Musicals
  R&H

Show Boat Selections 15'
  1 1 2 1 – 2asx, tsx, bsx – 2 3 2 0 – tmp+2 – str
  Includes: Cotton Blossom; Make Believe; Valon's Theme; Ol' Man River; Misery; Can't Help Lovin' Dat Man; You Are Love; Why Do I Love You?; Captain Andy, Hey Fella!
  Walter Paul, arr.
                                     Broadway Musicals
  Harms (POP); Luck's (rental)

Smoke Gets in Your Eyes 2.5'
  2 1 2 2 – 3 3 2 0 – perc – hp, cel, pf – str
  Solo Soprano. Key of Db.
                                Valentine/Popular Song
  Dragon (rental)

They Didn't Believe Me 3'
  2 2 2 1 – 3 3 4 0 – tmp+perc – hp, cel, (pf), gtr – str
  Robert Mandell, arr.
                                             Popular Song
  Kalmus

They Didn't Believe Me 3'
  hp, gtr[or pf] – strings
  Robert Mandell, arr.
                                             Popular Song
  Kalmus

Way You Look Tonight 3'
  3 3[incl Eh] 3[incl bcl] 2 – 4 4[(#4)] 3 1 – tmp+perc – hp, pf, (gtr) – str
  Solo Voice. Key of Eb.
  Carmen Dragon, arr.
                                Valentine/Popular Song
  Dragon (rental)

Way You Look Tonight 3'
  1 1 3[incl bcl] 1 – 2 2 2 1 – perc – pf – str
  Vosbein, arr.
                                                  Valentine
  Leonard (POP); EMS (rental)

Kernis, Aaron Jay   1960-

Goblin Market 45'
  1[afl/pic] 1[Eh] 2[incl bcl Ebcl] 1 – 1 1 0 0 – 1perc – pf – str
  Narrator. Theater-piece; text is based on a poem by Christina Rosetti.
                                                  Halloween
  Schirmer

Valentines 25'
  4[incl 2pic] 3[incl Eh] 3[incl Ebcl & bcl] 3[incl cbn] – 4 3 3 1 – tmp+4 – hp, cel, pf – str
  Solo Soprano.
                                                  Valentine
  Schirmer (rental)

Khachaturian, Aram 1903-1978

Gayaneh: Sabre Dance 3'
3 3 3 2 – asx – 4 3 3 1 – tmp+perc – pf – str
There is also a 1981 arrangement by Günter Noris and Förster Wolfgang.
Dance
Russian (rental)

Gayaneh: Suite No. 1 from the ballet 36'
3[1.2.pic] 3[1.2.Eh] 3[1.2.bcl/asx] 2 – 4 3 3 1 – tmp+4 – hp, pf – str
perc: bd, cym, glock, gong, sd, tambn, tri, xyl, tubaphone.
Includes: Introduction; Dance of the Maidens; Awakening and Dance of Aisha; Mountain Dance "Lullaby" Scene of Gayaneh and Giko; Gayaneh's Adagio; Lezginka.
Dance/Popular Classics
Russian (rental)

Gayaneh: Suite No. 2 from the ballet 30'
3[1.2.pic] 3[1.2.Eh] 3[1.2.bcl] 2 – 4 3 3 1 – tmp+4 – hp, pf – str
perc: bd, cym, glock, sd, tamtam, tambn, tri, vib, woodblk, xyl, frame drum.
Includes: Dance of Welcome; Lyrical Dance; Russian Dance; Nun's Variation; Dance of the Old Man and Carpet Weavers; Armen's Variation; Fire Dance.
Dance/Popular Classics
Russian (rental)

Gayaneh: Suite No. 3 from the ballet 28'
3[1.2.pic] 3[1.2.Eh] 3[1.2.bcl] 2 – asx – 4 3 3 1 – tmp+4 – hp, pf – str
perc: bd, cym, glock, sd, tambn, tri, xyl, frame drum.
Includes: Gathering of the Cotton; Dance of the Young Kurds; Introduction and Dance of the Old Men; Embroidery of the Carpets; Sabre Dance; Hopak.
Dance/Popular Classics
Russian (rental)

Masquerade Suite 18'
(4' 5' 3' 3' 3')
2[1.2/pic] 2 2 2 – 4 2 3 1 – tmp+3 – str
perc: bd, cym, glock, sd, xyl.
Includes: Waltz; Nocturne; Mazurka; Romance; Galop.
Halloween/Popular Classics
Russian (rental)

Spartacus: Suite No. 1 from the ballet 26'
(5' 7' 4' 4' 6')
3[1.2.3/pic] 3[1.2.Eh] 3[1.2.3/bcl] 2 – 4 4 3 1 – tmp+5 – hp, cel, pf – str
perc: tri, tambn, sd, cym, bd, tamtam, glock, xyl, tubaphone.
Includes: Introduction and Dance of the Nymphs; Introduction, Adagio of Aegina and Harmodius; Aegina's Variation and Bacchanale; Scene and Dance with Crotales; Dance of the Gaditanian Maidens and Victory of Spartacus.
Dance/Popular Classics
Russian (rental)

Spartacus: Suite No. 2 from the ballet 21'
(9' 6' 5' 1')
3[1.2.3/pic] 3[1.2.Eh] 3[1.2.3/bcl] 2 – 4 3 3 1 – tmp+4 – hp, pf – str
perc: bd, cym, sus cym, sd, tri, tambn.
Includes: Adagio of Spartacus and Phrygia; Entrance of Merchants, Dance of a Roman Courtesan, General Dance; Entrance of Spartacus, Quarrel, Treachery of Harmodius; The Dance of the Pirates.
Dance/Popular Classics
Russian (rental)

Spartacus: Suite No. 3 from the ballet 16'
(3' 2' 3' 5' 3')
3[1.2.pic] 3[1.2.Eh] 3[1.2.bcl] 2 – 4 3 3 1 – tmp+5 – hp, cel, pf – str
Includes: The Slave Market; Dance of the Greek Slaves; Dance of the Egyptian Girl; Phrgia's Dance and Parting; Dance of the Young; Thracians with Swords.
Dance/Popular Classics
Russian (rental)

Kilar, Wojciech 1932-

Dracula (1992) 5'
1 0 0 0 – 0 0 0 0 – 2 hp, pf – str
Nominated for Best Music by the Academy of Science Fiction, Fantasy, and Horror Films. Based on the original novel by Bram Stoker.
Films/Halloween
T&V (rental)

Theme from the Film The Pianist 2'
Strings
Solo Clarinet. Theme from the 2002 Academy Award winning film, *The Pianist*.
Films
Presser

King, Victor

Gregoriana Christmas Suite — 18'
3[incl pic] 2 3[incl bcl] 2 – 4 3 3 1 – tmp+perc – str
Christmas

EMI (rental)

Kingman, Daniel   1924-2003

A Revolutionary Garland — 8'
2[incl pic] 2 2 2 – 2 2 0 0 – tmp+perc – str
York Fusilliers; Soldier's Joy; St. Patrick's Day in the Morning; Gen'l Washington's March.
Patriotic

Kalmus

Kirk, Theron   1919-1999

An Orchestra Primer — 13'
2[incl pic] 2 2 2 – 4 3 3 1 – tmp+2 – str
Narrator.
Instrumental Pops

Oxford

Kirkpatrick, William J.   1838-1921

The Novello Book of Carols: — 3'
  Away in a Manger
  Strings
  Solo Voice.
  William Llewellyn, arr.
Christmas

Novello (rental)

Kleinsinger, George   1914-1982

Brooklyn Baseball Cantata — 12'
1 0 2 1 – 0 2 2 0 – tmp+perc – (hp), (cel), pf – str
Solo Voices; SATB or Male Chorus.
Sports

EMI (rental)

Tubby the Tuba — 13'
2[1.2/pic] 2 2[1.2/(bcl)] 1 – 2 2 1 0 - tmp+1 – pf/cel – str
perc: sus cym, sd, woodblk, templeblks, xyl.
Solo Tuba; Narrator.
Instrumental Pops

MTI (rental)

Knight, Eric   1932-

Americana Overture — 8'
3[1.2.pic] 3[1.2.Eh] 3[1.2.bcl] 3[1.2.cbn] – 4 4 3 1 – tmp+3, drumset – hp, pf – str
Patriotic

Schirmer (rental)

Canadian Tribute — 8'
2[incl pic] 2 2 2 – 4 4 3 1 – tmp+6, drumset, triangle – hp, pf – str
Written to thank the Canadian people for their assistance during the Iran hostage crisis.
Patriotic/International

Schirmer (rental)

The Great American Bicycle Race — 6'
3[1.2.pic] 3[1.2.Eh] 3[1.2.bcl] 3[1.2.cbn] – 4 4 3 1 – tmp+2, drumset – hp – str
Sports

Schirmer (rental)

Kidnapped: Overture — 7'
2 2 2 2 – 4 3 3 0 – tmp+2 – hp – str
Instrumental Pops

Schirmer (rental)

A Symphony in Four American Idioms — 24'
3[1.2.pic] 3[1.2.Eh] 3[1.2.bcl] 3[1.2.cbn] – 4 4 3 1 – tmp+3, drumset – hp, pf – str
Americana

Schirmer (rental)

Three Musical Elements: — 12'
  Earth, Water, Space
3[incl pic] 2 3[incl bcl] 2 – 4 3 3 1 – tmp+3 – hp, pf – str
Originally composed for slide projections and symphony orchestra in conjunction with photographer Donald Sultner-Wells.
Ecology

Schirmer (rental)

Knight, Vick (See: Russell, Henry)

Koch, Anton — 1972-

The Adventures of Sinbad: Overture — 5'
3[incl pic] 2[1.Eh] 2 2[1.cbn] – 4 3 3 1 – tmp+perc – hp – str
perc: tri, sd, tamb, sus cym, bongos, szl cym, cym, anvil, low conga, bd, bell tree, wind chimes, tam-tam, whip, chimes, glock.
Performed with the staged presentation of Sheherazade's *Tales from the 1001 Nights* during closing ceremonies of the 2006 Asia Games.
International
Wendel (rental)

Kodály, Zoltán — 1882-1967

Dances of Marosszek — 13'
(2' 1' 2' 3' 1' 1' 1' 2')
2[1.2/pic] 2 2 2[1.cbn] – 4 2 0 0 – tmp+3 – str
perc: sd, cym, bd.
Dance/International
Universal (rental)

Variations on a Hungarian Folksong: The Peacock — 25'
3[1.2.3/pic] 2[1.2/Eh] 2 2 – 4 3 3 0 – tmp+1 – hp – str
perc: glock, tri, cym.
Animals/International
Boosey (rental)

Koenig, Hermann Louis — 1800s

Post Horn Galop — 3'
1 0 2 0 – 0 2 1 0 – tmp+perc – str
Published in 1898. Koenig was solo cornetist with Jullien's orchestra from early 1840-1860.
Instrumental Pops
Kalmus

Korngold, Erich Wolfgang — 1897-1957

Korngold: The Adventures of Robin Hood, Symphonic Portrait — 28'
2[1.2/pic] 2[1.2/Eh] 3[1.2.bcl] 2[1.2/cbn] – asx, tsx – 4 3 3 1 – tmp+perc – pf, cel, hp, gtr – str
perc: tambn, sd, cym, tri, gong, vib, marim, xyl, bells.
This arrangement expands the original 16' suite creating a tone poem. The work was dedicated to the Korngold family and premiered November 29, 2007, at the 50th anniversary of the composer's death.
John Mauceri, arr.
Films
Warner (rental)

Kosma, Joseph — 1905-1969

Autumn Leaves — 4'
2[1.2/pic] 2 3[1.2.bcl] 2 – 4 3 3 1 – tmp+2 – (hp), (pf) – str
perc: chimes, vib, glock, cym, sd.
Optional Solo Piano.
Alfred Reed, arr.
Ecology/Popular Songs/Seasons
Kalmus

Kraft, William — 1923-

Contextures: Riots – Decade '60 — 16.5'
4 4[incl Eh] 4[incl Ebcl, bcl] 4[incl cbn] – asx – 4 4 4 1 – tmp+perc – pf or cel, hp – str
Solo Violin & Drum with jazz quartet [ssx, tp, bass gtr, drumset]. Refers to the Watts riots in Los Angeles.
Black History Month
Presser (rental)

A Kennedy Portrait (Contextures III) — 18'
3[incl pic] 3[incl Eh] 3[bcl] 3 – 4 3 3 1 – tmp+3 – pf or cel, hp – str
Narrator.
Includes commentary on race, art, and world peace.
Black History Month/Patriotic
Presser (rental)

Seven Spirituals 20'
  2[incl pic] 1 1 1 – 2 2 1 1 – 2perc – pf – str
  Solo Baritone.
  Tania León, arr.
  Black History Month
Peer (rental)

Simple Introduction to the Orchestra 4'
  4[1.2.opt3.pic] 4[1.2.3.Eh] 4[1.2.3.bcl] 2 – 4 3 3 1 –
  tmp+3 – (hp), (pf) – str
  perc: bells, cym, tri, chimes, sd, field dr.
  Based on *Frère Jacques*.
  Instrumental Pops
Kalmus

Vintage Renaissance 12'
  3[incl pic] 3[incl Eh] 3[incl Ebcl] 3[incl cbn] –
  4 3 3 1 – tmp+3 – hp, cel/pf – str
  Instrumental Pops
Presser (rental)

Kreisler, Fritz 1875-1962

Liebesfreud 3.5'
  2 2 2 2 – 2 3 3 0 – tmp+perc – str
  From *Old Viennese Dances*; no solo violin.
  Clark McAlister, arr.
  Popular Classics/Valentine
Kalmus

Liebesleid 4'
  2 2 2 2 – 2 0 0 0 – str
  Solo Violin.
  Clark McAlister, arr.
  Popular Classics/Valentine
Kalmus

Liebesleid 4'
  2 2 2 2 – 2 0 0 0 – tmp+perc – str
  Orchestral version.
  Clark McAlister, arr.
  Popular Classics/Valentine
Kalmus

Three Old Viennese Dances: 2'
  Schön Rosmarin
  2 2 2 2 – 2 2 0 0 – tmp+perc – str
  Popular Classics/Valentine
Kalmus

Krogstad, Bob, arr.

The Bells of Christmas 7'
  2[1.2/pic] 1 3[1.2.bcl] 1 – 4 3 3 1 – tmp+4 –
  hp, pf/cel, elec bs – str
  perc: mark tree, drumset, cym, woodblk, bd, sus cym,
  slgh-bells, cowbell, chimes, block, xyl, crotales.
  Includes: Ding Dong! Merrily on High!; The Bell
  Carol; Silver Bells; I Heard the Bells on Christmas
  Day; Jingle Bells.
  Christmas
Leonard

Christmas at the Movies 5.5'
  2[1.2/pic] 1 3[1.2.bcl]1 – 4 3 3 1 – tmp+4 –
  elec bs, hp, pf – str
  perc: pic sd, drumset, whip, cym, bd, xyl, chimes,
  crotales, tri, glock, bell tree.
  Includes: Miracle on 34th Street; The Polar Express;
  Somewhere in My Memory; Making Christmas;
  Where Are You Christmas?.
  Christmas/Films
Leonard

Curtain Up! 6.5'
  2[1.2/pic] 1 3[1.2.bcl] 1 – asx, tsx – 4 3 3 1 –
  tmp+4 – elec bs, hp, pf – str
  perc: drum set, cym, sus cym, bd, bongos, chimes, glock.
  Includes: There's No Business Like Show Business;
  The Phantom of the Opera; One; Don't Rain On My
  Parade; If He Walked Into My Life; Everything's
  Coming Up Roses.
  Broadway Musicals
Leonard

Kurtz, Eugene 1923-2006

Chamber Symphony for the 4th of July 15'
  2perc – pf – str
  Patriotic
Jobert (rental)

Kuster, Kristin P. 1973-

Iron Diamond 6'
  3 2 2 2 – 4 3 2 1 – tmp+3 – str
  Celebratory concert opener using a railroad theme.
  Travel
Kuster

L

Lai, Francis 1932-

Love Story: Where Do I Begin 4'
2 1 2 1 – 2 3 2 1 – tmp+2 – pf – str
perc: drumset, vib.
1971 Oscar winning film score for Best Music and Original Score.
Marty Gold, arr.
                                         Films/Valentine
Famous (rental)

Love Story: Theme (1970) 2.5'
3 3 3 0 – 4 0 3 1 – 2perc – pf, 2 gtr, elec bs – str
perc: drumset, song bells, sus cym.
6 Boys' Voices. 1971 Oscar winning film score for Best Music and Original Score.
Henry Mancini, arr.
                                           Films/Valentine
T&V (rental)

A Man and a Woman 2.5'
2 1 2 1 – asx, tsx – 2 3 3 1 – tmp+2 – gtr, elec bs – strings
perc: drumset, tambn.
John Cacavas, arr.
                                         Films/Valentine
Saravah (rental)

Lake, M. L.

Old Timers Waltz 4'
1 1 2 1 – asx, tsx, sx in C – 2 2 1 0 – 2perc – tenor banjo – str
perc: sd, bd, glock.
Includes the Bowery; Sidewalks of New York; Sweet Rosie O'Grady; Daisy Bell; Comrades; Little Annie Rooney; the Band Played On; After the Ball; She May Have Seen Better Days.
Piano/Conductor score.
                                    Dance/Popular Song
Luck's

Lalo, Edouard 1823-1892

Symphonie espagnole, Op. 21 33'
(8' 4' 6' 7' 8')
3[1.2.pic] 2 2 2 – 4 2 3 0 – tmp+2 – hp – str
perc: sd, tri.
Solo Violin.
                         International/Popular Classics
Breitkopf; Kalmus; Luck's

Lamb, Joseph 1887-1960

Ragtime Nightingale 5'
Strings
Clark McAlister, arr.
                                                          Jazz
Breitkopf; Kalmus; Luck's

Lambert, Constant 1905-1951

Eight Poems of Li-Po 14'
1 1 1 0 – 0 0 0 0 – str
Solo Medium Voice.
                                               International
Chester (rental)

Elegiac Blues 3'
2 1 2 1 – 2 2 1 0 – pf – str
                                                          Jazz
Chester (rental)

The Rio Grande 15'
0 0 0 0 – 0 4 3 1 – tmp+4 – str
perc: bd, cym, sus cym, sd, td, tamtam, cast, tri, tambn, woodblk, cowbell, xyl.
Solo Piano; Solo Alto; Chorus.
                                                 Ecology
Oxford (rental)

Lampe, James 1869-1929

Creole Belles 3'
3[1.2.pic] 2 2 2 – 4 3 3 1 – tmp+perc – str
William Ryden, arr.
                                                 International
Kalmus

Lane, Burton

Excerpts from Finian's Rainbow 9.5'
2[1.2/pic] 3[1.2.Eh] 3[1.2.bcl] 2– 4 3 2 1– perc – hp – str
Includes: Look to the Rainbow; How are Things in Glocca Morra?; If This Isn't Love; Something Sort of Grandish; Old Devil Moon; This Time of the Year; That Great Come and Get It Day.
Robert Russell Bennett, arr.
Broadway Musical
Crawford Music (rental from Luck's)

Lane, Philip

Wassail Dances for Orchestra 8'
2[1/pic.2/pic] 2 2 2 – 3 2 2 0 – tmp+2 – cel, hp – str
perc: sd, bd, xyl, glock, sus cym, cym, tri, tambn, tamtam.
The three dances are based on traditional wassail songs of Somerset, Yorkshire, and Gloucestershire.
Christmas/Dance/International (Great Britain)
Goodmusic

Lang, David 1957-

Hunk of Burnin' Love 5'
1 1 1 1 – 1 1 1 0 – 2perc – pf – str
Valentine
Schirmer (rental)

Loud Love Songs 15'
1 2 2 2 – 2 1 1 1 – tmp+3 – pf – str
Solo Percussion.
Valentine
Schirmer (rental)

Lang, Philip J., arr. 1911-1986

Dark Eyes 3'
2 2 2 2 – 3sx – 4 3 3 1 – tmp+perc – pf – str
Popular Song
Kalmus

Langey, Otto

From the Highlands: A Selection of Scotch Melodies 12'
1 1 2 1 – 2 2 1 0 – tmp+2 – str
A medley of 20 popular Scottish melodies including Speed; Bonnie Boat; Duncan Gray; Comin' Thro' the Rye; Annie Laurie; The Campbells are Comin'; and Auld lang Syne.
International: Scotland
Luck's

Lanner, Joseph 1801-1843

Hofball-Tanze Waltz, Op. 161 9.5'
1 1 2 1 – 2 3 0 0 – tmp+2 – str
Dance
Kalmus

Lara, Agustín 1897 or 1900-1970

Granada 3.5'
3[incl (pic)] 2 2 2 – 4 2 3 1 – tmp+2 – str
The composer is Mexican and Granada is in Spain.
International (Mexico/Spain)
Filarmonika

Lawrence, David

High School Musical 6'
2 1 3[1.2.bcl] 1 – 4 3 3 1 – tmp+3 – str
perc: drumset, sd, field dr, bd, mallets.
Includes: Breaking Free; Start of Something New; We're All in This Together. The last 2 are composed by Matthew Gerrard & Robbie Nevil. From the Disney after school TV special. 2006 Emmy for Outstanding Original Music and Lyrics was won by composer Jamie Houston for the song "Breaking Free." David Lawrence scored the musical.
Robert Longfield, arr.
Films/TV
Leonard

High School Musical 2   5'
    2 1 3[1.2.bcl] 1 – 4 3 3 1 – tmp+3 – str
    perc: drumset, mallets, cym.
    Includes: All for One; I Don't Dance; What Time Is It; You Are the Music in Me. David Lawrence scored the musical. Additional composers are Robbie Nevil, Matthew Gerrard, Tim James.
    Robert Longfield, arr.
                                                                     Films/TV
Leonard

Lawrence, Jack (See: Fain, Sammy)

Layton, Billy Jim   1924-2004

An American Portrait   12'
    3[1.2.pic] 3[1.2.Eh] 4[1.2.3.bcl] 2 – 4 3 3 1 – tmp+perc – str
                                                                    Americana
Schirmer (rental)

Dance Fantasy, Op. 7   26'
    3 3 2 3 – 4 3 3 1 – tmp+perc – hp, cel, pf – str
                                                                       Dance
Schirmer (rental)

Three Dylan Thomas Poems, Op. 3   12'
    0 0 0 0 – 2 2 2 0
    SATB Chorus.
                                              Popular Classics
Schirmer (rental)

Lecuona, Ernesto   1896-1963

Andalucia Suite   20'
    2 2 2 2 – 2sx – 4 2 3 0 – perc – gtr – str
    Includes: Malagueña, Andalucia, Gitanerias, Cordoba, Guadalquivir, Alhambra.
    Gordon Jenkins, arr.
                                                             International
Kalmus

Andalucia Suite: Andalucia   3'
    2 2 2 2 – 2asx(2fl), 2tsx(2cl) – 2 3 2 1 – tmp+3 – gtr – str
    Kalmus sells different instrumentation: 2[incl pic] 2 2 1 – 2 3 2 1 – tmp+perc – hp – str
    Morton Gould, arr.
                                                             International
Kalmus; Schirmer (rental)

Andalucia Suite: Gitanerias   3'
    2 2 3[1.2.bcl] 2 – 2 3 3 1 – (4sx) – perc – hp, cel, gtr – str
    Morton Gould, arr.
                                                             International
Kalmus

Andalucia Suite: Malagueña   3.5'
    2[incl pic] 2 2 2 – 4 3 3 1 – tmp+3 – 2hp, cel – str
    Kalmus sells a different instrumentation:
    1 1 2 1 – 3sx – 2 3 2 0 – tmp+perc – str
    Morton Gould, arr.
                                                             International
Kalmus; Schirmer (rental)

Andalucia Suite: Malagueña   3.5'
    1[1/pic] 1 2 1 – 3sx – 2 3 2 0 – tmp+3 – hp – str
    perc: cast, tambn, tri, vib, sd, bd, cym.
    Ferde Grofé, arr.
                                                             International
Kalmus; Marks (rental)

La Comparsa: 3'
    Carnival Procession
    2 2 4[1.2.3.bcl] 2 – 2sx – 2 3 3 1 – perc – hp, cel – str
    Morton Gould, arr.
                                                             International
Kalmus

Danza Afro-Cubanas: 3'
    Danza lucumi
    2[1.2/pic] 2 2 2 – (2sx) – 4 3 3 1 – perc – hp – str
    Solo Violin.
    Guenther, arr.
                                           Dance/International
Kalmus

Jungle Drums   4'
    3[incl 3pic] 1[incl Eh] 3[incl bcl] 2 – asx(fl,pic), asx(cl,bcl), tsx(fl,pic), tsx(cl) – 4 3 3 1 – 3perc – 2hp, cel, pf, gtr – str
    Morton Gould, arr.
                                               Instrumental Pops
Schirmer (rental)

Legrand, Michel 1932-

I Will Wait for You 4'
2 1 2 1 – 4 2 3 1 – tmp+1 – str
perc: drumset.
Optional parts are included for alto sax, tenor sax, and bass clarinet but are not in the score. The arranger suggests they are effective in sections at the option of the conductor.
Frederick Muller, arr.
Popular Song/Valentine

Vogue (rental)

The Windmills of Your Mind 4'
pf – strings
Jaroslav Holesovsky, arr.
Popular Song

Warner (POP); Luck's (rental)

Lehár, Franz 1870-1948

The Count of Luxembourg: Waltz 7'
2[1.2/pic] 2 2 – 2 2 3 0 – tmp+3 – hp – str
Higgs, arr.
Dance

Kalmus

Gold and Silver Waltz, Op. 79 6.5'
2[1/pic.2/pic] 2 2 2 – asx, tsx – 4 2[crt] 3 1 – tmp+3 – hp – str
perc: bd, cym, sd, tri, gong, glock.
Dance

Kalmus

Merry Widow Overture 9'
3[1.2/pic.3/pic] 3[1.2.Eh] 3[1.2.bcl] 3[1.2.cbn] – 4 2 3 1 – tmp+4 – hp,cel – str
perc: bd, cym, glock, sd, tamtam, tri.
Gamley is the arranger of the Glocken edition.
Popular Classics

Glocken (rental); Luck's

The Merry Widow: Selections 8'
2[1.2/pic] 2 2 – 2asx, tsx – 2 2 3 0 – tmp+2 – hp, pf – str
Dan Godfrey, arr.
Popular Classics

Kalmus

The Merry Widow: 10'
Symphonic Paraphrase
2[incl pic] 2[incl Eh] 2 2 – 4 3 3 1 – tmp+perc – hp, cel – str
Morton Gould, arr.
Popular Classics

Schirmer (rental)

Merry Widow Waltz 6'
(Concert Version)
2 1 2 1 – 2 2 3 0 – tmp+perc – hp – str
Harry Dexter, arr.
Popular Classics

Glocken (rental)

Zigeunerliebe (Gypsy Love) Waltzes 4.5'
2[incl pic] 2 2 2 – 2 1 1 0 – tmp+2 – hp – str
perc: bd, glock, sd, tri.
H. M. Higgs, arr.
Dance

Kalmus

Leigh, Mitch 1928-

Man of La Mancha: Selections 8'
2 2 2 2 – 4 3 3 0 – tmp+perc – hp – str
Includes: Man of La Mancha; Dulcinea; Little Bird; A Little Gossip; The Impossible Dream.
Paul Lang, arr.
Broadway Musicals

Scott/Helena (POP); EMS or Luck's (rental)

Man of La Mancha: Orchestra Selection 8'
2[1.2/pic] 2 2 2 – 4 3 3 0 – tmp+4 – str
perc: tambn, cast, sd, bd, cym, tri, glock, maracas, xyl, claves.
Includes: Man of La Mancha; Dulcinea; Little Bird; A Little Gossip; The Impossible Dream.
Broadway Musicals

Sam Fox (rental)

Man of La Mancha: Orchestral Synthesis 7'
3 3 3 3 – 4 4 3 1 – tmp+perc – str
Includes: Dulcinea; I'm Only Thinking of You; Little Bird; To Each His Dulcinea.
Richard Hayman, arr.
Broadway Musicals

Presser (rental)

Leighton, Kenneth   1929-1988

Dance Suite No. 1   26'
3 2 2 2 – 4 3 3 1 – tmp+2 – str
        Dance
Novello (rental)

Dance Suite No. 2   17'
2 2 2 2 – 3 3 2 1 – tmp+3 – pf – str
        Dance
Novello (rental)

Dance suite No. 3:   15'
Scottish Dances, Op. 89
3 2 2 3 – 4 3 3 1 – tmp+perc – hp, pf – str
        Dance
Novello (rental)

Lennon, John   1940-1980
McCartney, Paul   1942-

The Best of the Beatles   7.5'
2 1 3[1.2.bcl] 1 – 1 2 1 1 – 1perc+drumset – pf – str
Includes: Got To Get You Into My Life; When I'm Sixty-Four; Michelle; Get Back.
Calvin Custer, arr.
        Popular Song/Rock
Leonard

Beatles Medley   5.5'
2[incl pic] (1) 3[1.2.bcl] 1 – (3sx) – 2 3 3 1 – tmp+perc – (hp), pf, elec bass – str
Includes: Eleanor Rigby; Yesterday; Sgt. Pepper's; When I'm 64.
Manny Mendelson, arr.
        Popular Song/Rock
Kendor

I Want To Hold Your Hand   4'
2 1 2 1 – asx, tsx – 2 3 3 1 – tmp+drumset – elec gtr, elec bass – str
John Cacavas, arr.
        Popular Song/Rock
Belwin (POP); EMS or Luck's (rental)

Liebermann, Lowell   1961-

Concerto for Piccolo   20'
2 2 2 2 – 2 2 1 0 – tmp+perc – hp, cel – str
The last mvt includes reference to Stars and Stripes Forever.
        Patriotic
Presser (rental)

Revelry   8'
3 2 2 2 – 4 3 3 1 – tmp+3 – str
        New Year/Celebration
Presser (rental)

Lincke, Paul   1886-1946

Kwang Hsu (Chinese March)   3'
1 1 2 1 – 2 2 1 0 – perc – str
        International
Kalmus

Liszt, Franz   1811-1886

Hungarian Rhapsody No. 1, F Minor   11'
3[1.2.pic] 2 2 3 – 4 3 3 1 – tmp+2 – 2hp – str
perc: cym, tri.
Used in the cartoon: *Rhapsody Rabbit* (1946).
Franz Doppler, arr.
        Popular Classics
Kalmus

Hungarian Rhapsody No. 2, in D minor   12'
3[1.2.pic] 2 3[1.2.Ebcl] 2 – 4 2 3 1 – tmp+2 – str
perc: cym, tri.
Franz Doppler, arr.
        Popular Classics
Kalmus; Luck's

Hungarian Rhapsody No. 2 in C minor   12'
2[1/pic.2/pic] 2 2 2 – 4 2 3 0 – tmp+4 – hp – str
perc: sd, tri, bd, cym.
K. Mueller-Berghaus, arr.
        Dance/Popular Classics
Kalmus; Luck's

Mephisto Waltz No. 1 10'
3[1.2.3/pic] 2 2 2 – 4 2 3 1– tmp+2 – hp – str
perc: tri, cym, sus cym.
Episode #2 from Lenau's *Faust (Dance in Village)*.
        Dance/Popular Classics
Kalmus; Luck's

Mephisto Waltz No. 2 10'
3[1.2.pic] 2 2 2 – 4 2 3 1– tmp+2 – hp – str
perc: cym, tri.
        Dance/Popular Classics
Kalmus

Totentanz 16'
3[1.2.pic] 2 2 2 – 2 2 3 1– tmp+3 – str
perc: tri, cym, tamtam.
Piano solo
        Halloween/Popular Classics
Kalmus

Llewellyn, William, arr.

The Novello Book of Carols: 3'
 The Angel Gabriel (Gabriel's Message)
 1 2 0 0 – 0 0 0 0 – str
 Solo Voice(s).
        Christmas
Novello (rental)

The Novello Book of Carols: Come All You 3'
 Worthy People Here (A Somerset Carol)
 2 2 2 2 – 2 2 3 1 – tmp+2 – str
 Solo Voice.
        Christmas
Novello (rental)

The Novello Book of Carols: 3'
 God Rest You Merry Gentlemen
 2 2 2 2 – 2 2 3 1 – tmp+2 – str
 Solo Voice.
        Christmas
Novello (rental)

The Novello Book of Carols: 3'
 The Holly and the Ivy
 2 2 2 2 –2 2 3 1 –tmp+2 –str
 Solo Voice.
        Christmas
Novello (rental)

The Novello Book of Carols: 3'
 Il est né, le divin enfant (See Him Born)
 1 2 0 0 – 0 0 0 0 – str
 Solo Voice.
        Christmas
Novello (rental)

The Novello Book of Carols: 3'
 King Jesus Hath a Garden
 2 2 2 2 – 2 2 0 0 – tmp+2 – str
 Solo Voice.
        Christmas
Novello (rental)

The Novello Book of Carols: 3'
 O Come All Ye Faithful
 2 2 2 2 – 2 2 3 1 – tmp+3 – str
 Solo Voice.
        Christmas
Novello (rental)

The Novello Book of Carols: 3'
 Puer Nobis (*Unto Us Is Born a Son*)
 2 2 2 2 – 2 2 3 1 – tmp+2 – str
 Solo Voice.
        Christmas
Novello (rental)

The Novello Book of Carols: 3'
 De Virgin Mary Had a Baby Boy
 2 2 2 2 – 2 2 3 1 – tmp+2 – str
 Solo Voice.
        Christmas
Novello (rental)

Lloyd Webber, Andrew   1948-

Andrew Lloyd Webber: 8.5'
 A Concert Celebration (Medley)
 3[1.2.pic] 1 3[1.2.pic] 1 – (2asx, tsx, bsx) – 4 3 3 1
 – tmp+5 – elec bass – str
 perc: includes drum set.
 Can be performed with strings alone, concert band,
 or with optional chorus. Includes: Phantom Theme;
 Music of the Night; Don't Cry for Me Argentina;
 Jesus Christ, Superstar; King Herod's Song;
 Memory; Go Go Go Joseph.
 Calvin Custer, arr. of string and orchestra versions.
 Mark Brymer, arr. of band and choral versions.
        Broadway Musicals
Leonard

Cats: Memory   3.5'
    2 1 3[1.2.(bcl)] 0 – (2sx) – 2 3 3 1 – tmp+perc – pf – str
    Key of C to G to Ab.
    Bob Lowden, arr.
                         2004 Animals/Broadway Musicals
Leonard

Cats Selections   7'
    2 1 3[1.2.opt bcl] 1 – (2sx) – 2 3 3 1 – tmp+3 – pf, (elec bass) – str
    perc: drumset, tri, bells, xyl, vib.
    Includes: Overture; Jellicle Songs for Jellicle Cats; The Old Gumbie Cat; Macavity the Mystery Cat; Skimbleshank: The Railway Cat; Memory.
    Bob Lowden, arr.
                               Animals/Broadway Musicals
Leonard (POP); EMS or Luck's (rental)

Evita Highlights   9'
    2 2 3[1.2.bcl] 2 – 2asx, tsx, bsx – 2 3 3 1 – tmp+3 – elec gtr, elec bass – str
    perc: chimes, cowbell, bells, vib, timbales, drumset.
    Includes: Buenos Aires; High Flying Adored; Don't Cry for Me Argentina; She Is a Diamond; Another Suitcase in Another Hall; Finale.
    Bob Lowden, arr.
                                        Broadway Musicals
Leonard

Music from Evita   10'
    2 2 3[1.2.bcl] 2 – 4 3 3 1 – tmp+2 – pf/cel – str
    perc: sd, cym, bd, sus cym, hihat, cowbell, bongos, 2 sizes toms, claves, conga, glock, marim.
    Includes: Buenos Aires; I'd Be Surprisingly Good for You; You Must Love Me; Don't Cry for Me Argentina.
    Calvin Custer, arr.
                                        Broadway Musicals
Leonard

Medley from Jesus Christ Superstar   7'
    2[1/pic.2/pic] 2 3[1.2.(bcl)] 1 – 4[(#4)] 3 3 1 – tmp+3 – (hp) – str
    perc: chimes, drumset, cym, bells, xyl, sus cym.
    Includes: Superstar; Everything's Alright; King Herod's Song; I Don't Know How to Love Him. Optional rhythm parts for gtr/ukelele and bass gtr are included but do not appear in the score.
    Henry Mancini, arr.
                                        Broadway Musicals
Leonard

The Phantom of the Opera Concert Version   4.5'
    2[1/pic.2/pic] 2[1.2/Eh] 2C[1.2/bcl] 2 – 4 3 3 1 – tmp+perc – 3kybds – bass gtr – str
    perc: cym, wind chime, tambn, sd, sus cym.
    Solo Soprano and Tenor for characters Christine and The Phantom. A CD with an organ track is included and necessary for performance.
    David Cullen, orch.
                                        Broadway Musicals
R&H (rental)

The Phantom of the Opera Entr'Acte   3'
    2 2[incl Eh] 2 2 [incl cbn] – 4 2 3 0 – tmp+perc – hp, kybd – str
    perc: sus cym, tri, glock, piatti, bd.
    David Cullen, orch.
                                        Broadway Musicals
R&H (rental)

Phantom of the Opera: Music of the Night   3.5'
    pf – strings
    Bob Lowden, arr.
                                        Broadway Musicals
Leonard

The Phantom of the Opera Overture   2'
    2[pic.2] 1 1 1 – 3 2 1 0 – tmp+perc – hp, pf, synth – str (also CD with organ track)
    perc: cym, sus cym.
    A CD with an organ track is included and necessary for performance.
    David Cullen, orch.
                                        Broadway Musicals
R&H (rental)

The Phantom of the Opera Selections   12'
    2[1/pic.2] 1 3[1.2.bcl] 1 – (asx, tsx) – 4 3 3 1 – tmp+3 – synth – str
    perc: sus cym, cym, hi-hat, sd, bd (or opt drumset), cym, Chinese cym, gong, tri, tambn, xylo, glock, bd, vib.
    Includes: Phantom of the Opera; Think of Me; Angel of Music; All I Ask of You; Masquerade; Music of the Night.
    Calvin Custer, arr.
                                        Broadway Musicals
Leonard

Loeffler, Charles Martin　　1861-1935

Five Irish Fantasies　　30'
4[incl 2pic] 3[incl Eh] 3[incl bcl] 3[incl cbn] – 4 4 3 1 – tmp+4 – 2hp, cel – str
　　　　　　　　　St. Patrick/International
Schirmer (rental)

Loesser, Frank　　1910-1969

Music from Guys and Dolls　　7'
2 2 3[1.2.bcl] 2 – 3 4 3 1 – tmp+3 – pf – str
perc: drumset, cym, woodblk, tri, glock, xyl, vib.
Includes: Guys and Dolls; Luck be a Lady; I've Never Been in Love Before; A Bushel and a Peck; Follow the Fold; If I Were a Bell; Sit Down You're Rockin' the Boat.
Calvin Custer, arr.
　　　　　　　　　Broadway Musicals
Leonard

Selections from Guys and Dolls　　7'
2 2 3 2 – 4 3 3 1 – tmp+perc – pf – str
Includes: If I Were a Bell; Luck Be a Lady Tonight; Sit Down, You're Rockin' the Boat; Bushel & a Peck; I've Never Been in Love Before; Guys and Dolls.
Calvin Custer, arr.
　　　　　　　　　Broadway Musicals
Leonard

The Most Happy Fella: Symphonic Impressions　　10'
2[1.2/pic] 2 2 2 – (2asx, tsx, bsx) – 4 3 3 1 – tmp+3 – hp, cel – str
perc: cym, sus cym, tambn, xyl, sd, bd, glock, woodblk.
Don Walker, arr.
　　　　　　　　　Instrumental Pops
Frank (rental)

Loewe, Frederick　　1901-1988

Brigadoon Suite　　12'
(from the stage production)
3[incl 3pic] 2[incl 2Eh] 3[incl bcl] 0 – 4 3 3 1 – tmp+3 – hp, cel, pf – str
Robert Russell Bennett, arr.
　　　　　　　　　Broadway Musicals
EMI (rental)

Camelot: Selections　　11'
2[1.2/pic] 2[1.Eh] 2 2 – (2asx, tsx, bsx) – 4 3 3 1 – tmp+4 – hp – str
perc: sd, td, bd, tri, cym, xyl, glock.
Robert Russell Bennett, arr.
　　　　　　　　　Broadway Musicals
Chappell (rental); Luck's (rental)

Gigi: Selections　　8.5'
2 2 3[1.2.bcl] 2 – (2asx, tsx, bsx) – 4 3 3 1 – tmp+4 – hp – str
perc: bells, sd, td, bd, cym, small cym.
Includes: The Night They Invented Champagne; Gigi; Waltz at Maxim's; I'm Glad I'm Not Young Anymore; The Parisians, Say a Prayer for Me Tonight; Thank Heaven for Little Girls.
Robert Russell Bennett, arr.
　　　　　　　　　Broadway Musicals
Chappell (rental); Luck's (rental)

My Fair Lady, Highlights　　6.5'
1 1 2 1 – 2asx, tsx – 4 2 2 0 – tmp+perc – str
Includes: Get Me to the Church on Time; On the Street Where You Live; I've Grown Accustomed to Her Face; I Could've Danced all Night.
C. Paul Herfurth, arr.
　　　　　　　　　Broadway Musicals
Chappell (rental); Luck's (rental)

My Fair Lady Medley　　6'
3[1.2.pic] 2 2 2 – 4 3 3 1 – tmp+3 – str
perc: glock, police whistle, sd, bongos, temple or wood blks, sus cym, bd, tri, sand blks.
Includes: I Could Have Danced All Night; On The Street Where You Live; I've Grown Accustomed to Her Face; Get Me to the Church on Time.
John C. Whitney, arr.
　　　　　　　　　Broadway Musicals
Warner

My Fair Lady: Selections　　11'
2 2[1.2/Eh] 3[1.2.bcl] 2 – 2asx, tsx, bsx – 4 3 3 1 – tmp+3 – hp, pf – str
perc: tri, sus cym, sd, bd, cym, glock, xyl.
Robert Russell Bennett, arr.
　　　　　　　　　Broadway Musicals
Chappell (rental); Luck's (rental)

My Fair Lady - Symphonic Picture (1956)
3[1.2/pic.3/pic] 3[1.2.Eh] 3[1.2.bcl] 3[1.2.cbn] –
4 3 3 1 – tmp+perc – hp, pf/cel – str
Includes: Wouldn't It Be Loverly?; With a Little Bit of Luck; The Rain in Spain; I Could Have Danced All Night; Ascot Gavotte; On the Street Where You Live; Embassy Waltz ; Show Me; Get Me to the Church on Time; I've Grown Accustomed to Her Face; I Could Have Danced All Night.
Robert Russell Bennett arr.
                          Broadway Musicals

Chappell (rental)

López, Jimmy   1978-

América Salvaje (Wild America)   14'
2 2 2 2 – 3 3 3 1 – 4perc – pf – str
Score is available for purchase.
                          International (Peru)

Filarmonika (rental)

Fiesta! for chamber orchestra   10'
1 1 1 1 – 1 1 0 0 – 3perc – str
Score is available for purchase.
                Celebration/International (Peru)

Filarmonika (rental)

Fiesta! for orchestra   10'
2[incl pic] 2 2 2 – 4 2 3 1 – tmp+2 – str
Score is available for purchase.
                Celebration/International (Peru)

Filarmonika (rental)

Lago de Lágrimas (Lake of Tears)   20'
2[incl pic] 2 2 2 – 4 2 3 1 – 2perc – hp – str
Solo Flute. Score available for purchase.
                          International (Peru)

Filarmonika (rental)

Perú Negro   14'
3[incl pic] 3[incl Eh] 3[incl bcl] 3[incl cbn] –
4 3 3 1 – tmp+3 – str
                          International (Peru)

Filarmonika (rental)

Love, Mike (See: Wilson, Brian)

Lowden, Robert (Bob), arr.   1920-1999

Armed Forces Salute   4.5'
2[incl pic] 1 3[1.2.bcl] 1 – 4 3 3 1 – tmp+4 – pf – str
Optional SATB Chorus. Official songs of the U.S Army, Coast Guard, Marines, Air Force, and Navy.
                          Patriotic

Leonard (POP); EMS or Luck's (rental)

Disney Magic   8.5'
2 1 3[1.2.bcl] 1 – (2sx) – 2 3 3 1 – tmp+3 – elec bass – str
Includes: Zip-A-Dee-Doo-Dah/Candle on the Water; Chim Chim Cher-ee; A Dream Is a Wish Your Heart Makes; It's a Small World.
                          Films

Leonard (POP); EMS or Luck's (rental)

A Disney Supertime   5'
2 1 3[incl bcl] 1 – 4 3 3 1 – tmp+3 – pf – str
Tunes from *Mary Poppins*.
                          Films

Leonard

Remembering the Beatles   7.5'
1 1 3[1.2.bcl] 1 – 2sx – 2 3 3 1 – tmp+perc – pf – str
Includes: Eleanor Rigby, Yesterday, A Hard Day's Night, The Fool on the Hill, Something, Please Please Me.
                          Popular Song/Rock

Leonard (POP); EMS or Luck's (rental)

Luck, Arthur, arr.   1892-1976

Battle Hymn of the Republic   3'
2 2 2 2 – 2 2 3 1– perc – str
In Key of B flat. Piano/conductor score included. Composer is William Steffe.
                          Patriotic

Luck's

Deck the Hall & We Wish You   2'
a Merry Christmas
2 2 2 2 – 2 2 0 0 – str
Deck the Halls is a Welsh Carol in the Key of F. We Wish You a Merry Christmas is an English Carol in the Key of G.
                          Christmas

Luck's

Luigini, Alexandre — 1850-1906

Ballet Egyptien, Op. 12   20'
(Suite No. 1)
3[1.2/pic.3/pic] 2 2 2 – 4 2 3 1 – tmp+4 – 2hp – str
                                                   Dance
Kalmus

Lumbye, H.C. — 1810-1874

Copenhagen Steam Railway Gallop   4'
2 1 2 1 – 2 2 1 1 – tmp+perc – str
                                          Travel/International
Hansen (rental)

Lundquist, Torbjön — 1920-2000

Round the Orchestra in Ten Minutes   10'
2[1.pic] 1 1 1 – asx, tsx, bsx – 2 2 2 1 – tmp+perc – hp, pf – str
                                          Instrumental Pops
Nordiska (rental)

Lutosławski, Witold — 1913-1994

Fanfare for Louisville   1'
3 3 3 3 – 4 4 3 1 – tmp+perc
                                          Fanfare/Americana
Chester (rental)

Fanfare for the University of Lancaster   1'
0 0 0 0 – 4 4 5 1 – 1perc
                                          Fanfare
Chester (rental)

Twenty Polish Christmas Carols   38'
1 1[incl Eh] 2[incl bcl] 1 – 2 1 1 0 – perc – hp, pf – str
Solo Soprano and Female Chorus.
                      Christmas/International (Poland)
Schirmer (rental)

M

MacColl, Ewan — 1915-1989

The First Time Ever I Saw Your Face   3'
2 2 2 2 – 2 2 2 1 – 1perc[drumset] – str
perc: drumset.
Recorded by Roberta Flack. Piano/Conductor Score.
James D. Ployhar, arr.
                                         Popular Song
Leonard (rental)

MacCunn, Hamish — 1868-1916

Land of the Mountain and Flood,   8'
Op. 3: Overture
2 2 2 2 – 2 2 3 1 – tmp+perc – str
                                          Ecology
Novello (rental)

MacDermot, Galt — 1928-

Aquarius & Let the Sunshine In   3'
drumset – pf, elec gtr, bass gtr – str
From the musical *Hair*.
Rickey, arr.
                                     Broadway Musicals/Weather
Warner.(POP); Luck's (rental)

Hair: Selections   7'
3[1.2.pic] 2 3[1.2.bcl] 2 – 4 2 3 1– tmp+3 – elec gtr, elec bs – str
perc: drumset, bd, tambn, cym, sus cym, gong.
Includes Aguarius; Easy to be Har; Good Morning Starshine; Hair; Aquariue/Let the Sunsine In.
R. Gerry Long, arr.
                                       Broadway Musicals/Rock
United Artists (rental)

Hair: Where Do I Go?/Good Morning Starshine   4.5'
0 0 0 0 – 0 0 0 0 – drumset – elec gtr, bs gtr – pf – str
Alfred Rickey, arr.
                                       Broadway Musicals/Rock
United Artists (rental)

MacLellan, Gene   1939-1995

Put Your Hand in the Hand   2'
2 1 3[1.2.(bcl)] 1 – (asx, tsx) – 2 2 2 1 – tmp+3 – pf – str
Willis Schaefer, arr.
     Popular Song
Leonard (rental)

Snowbird   3'
3 1 3[1.2.bcl] 1 – (asx, tsx) – 2 2 2 1 – 3perc – str
perc: sd, bd, cym, glock, xyl, chimes, tambn, claves.
     Holidays/Seasons
Leonard (rental)

Maggio, Robert   1964-

Big Top   12'
2[incl pic] 2 2 2 – 4 3 3 1 – tmp+3 – str
     Circus
Presser (rental)

Boardwalk   6'
2 2 2 2 – 4 3 3 1 – tmp+2 – str
     Americana
Presser (rental)

The Hand-Prints of Sorcerers   11'
2 2 2 2 – 4 3 3 1 – tmp+3 – pf – str
     Halloween
Presser (rental)

Skylines   7'
3[incl pic] 3[incl Eh] 3[incl bcl] 3[incl cbn] – 4 3 3 1 – hp, pf – str
     Americana
Presser (rental)

Magidson, Herb   1906-1986

The Continental (1934)   4'
3[1.2.pic] 3[1.2.Eh] 3[1.2.bcl] 2 – 4 3 3 1 – tmp+2perc – hp, pf, gtr – str
perc: drumset, glock.
From the motion picture *The Gay Divorcee*. The first Oscar Winner for Best Song of the Year.
     Films
T&V (rental)

Malotte, Albert Hay   1895-1964

The Lord's Prayer (in C)   4'
2 2 2 2 – 2 2 3 0 – tmp+perc – str
SoloVoice or Chorus. SATB, SAB, SSA, and 2-part are published.
     Popular Song
Schirmer

The Lord's Prayer (in E flat, D flat, B flat)   4'
2 2 2 2 – 4 2 3 1 – tmp – str
Solo Voice.
Adolph Schmid, arr.
     Popular Song
Schirmer (rental)

The Lord's Prayer (in E flat)   4'
1 0 2 1 – asx, tsx – 0 2 1 0 – tmp+perc – str
Solo Voice.
Sopkin, arr.
     Popular Song
Schirmer (rental)

Mancina, Mark   1957-

Twister Main Theme   2.5'
3[1.2.pic] 1 3[1.2.bcl] 1 – 4 3 3 1 – tmp+perc – pf – str
Calvin Custer, arr.
     Weather/Films
Warner (POP); Luck's (rental)

Mancini, Henry   1924-1994

10: It's Easy to Say   3.5'
0 0 0 0 – 4 2 2 0 – drumset – 2gtr, elec bs – str
Solo Piano.
     Films
Kane (rental)

Academy Award Medley   11'
2[1.2/pic] 2 3[1.2.bcl] 2 – 4 3 3 1 – tmp+perc – hp, pf, gtr, elec bs – str
perc: includes drumset.
Solo Alto Saxophone.
     Films
Kane (rental)

Astaire! 12'
2 2 2 2 – (2asx, 2tsx) – 4 4[all dbl flug] 3 1 –
tmp+perc[incl drumset] – hp, 2 pf[1/cel.2], gtr – str
Dance/Films
Kane (rental)

Beaver Valley '37 16'
(5.5' 6' 4.5')
4[1.2.3/pic.4/pic] 4[1.2.3.4/Eh] 4[1.2/Eb.3.4/bcl]
4[1.2.3.4/cbn] – 4 3 3 1 – tmp+3 – hp, pf – str
perc: marim, vib, glock, tri, sm & lg sus cym, gong, sd, tambn, bd, cym.
Includes: The River; Black Snow; The Songs of Italy. This is a concert suite for orchestra depicting Mancini's impressions of his home in Pennsylvania. It is separated into 3 different conductor scores.
Americana/Instrumental Pops
Northridge (rental from Kane)

Breakfast at Tiffanys: Moon River 3'
2 1 2 1 – 2 3 2 1 – tmp+2 – pf – str
perc: sus cym, drumset, glock.
Marty Gold, arr.
Films/PopularSongs/Valentine
Famous (rental)

Breakfast at Tiffanys: Moon River (1961) 3'
3 3 3 2 – 4 4 3 1 – tmp+2 – hp, pf[cel] – str
perc: drumset, sd, bells, vib.
Solo Voice or Chorus. The choral version is in D Major.
Films/Popular Songs/Valentine
T&V (rental)

Charade 4'
3[1/pic.2/pic.3/pic] 3[1.2.Eh] 4[1.2.3.bscl] 3 –
4 4 3 1 – tmp+perc[incl drumset] – hp, pf, gtr, elec bs – str
Nominated for the 1964 Oscar for Best Music and Original Song. Lyrics by Johnny Mercer.
Films
Kane (rental)

Days of Wine and Roses 2'
1[alto fl] 0 0 0 – 2 0 0 0 – drumset – hp, pf, gtr, elec bs – str
Choir. Won the 1963 Oscar for Best Music and Original Song.
Films
Kane (rental)

Days of Wine and Roses 2'
0 0 3[1.2.bcl]2 – 3 0 3 1 – drumset – hp, pf, gtr, elec bs – str
Solo Tenor Saxophone. Won the 1963 Oscar for Best Music and Original Song.
Films
Kane (rental)

Dear Heart 2.5'
2 2 3[1.2.bcl] 2 – 4 3 3 1 – perc[incl drumset] – hp, pf, gtr – str
Nominated for the 1965 Oscar for Best Music and Original Song.
Films
Kane (rental)

Dear Heart 2.5'
0 0 0 0 – 4 0 3 1 – perc[incl drumset] – hp, pf, gtr, elec bs[copies orch bs] – str
Choir. Nominated for the 1965 Oscar for Best Music and Original Song.
Films
Kane (rental)

Dream of a Lifetime 3'
2 3[1.2.Eh] 3[1.2.bcl] 2 – 4 0 3 1 – perc –
hp, pf[solo], (hpsd) – str
As Recorded by The Philadelphia Orchestra Pops on the RCA album "Debut," conducted by Henry Mancini.
Instrumental Pops
Northridge (Rental from Kane)

The Glass Menagerie 6'
1 2[1.Eh] 2 2 – 0 0 0 0 – perc – hp, pf – str
Nominated for the 1988 Golden Globe award for Best Original Score - Motion Picture.
Films
Kane (rental)

The Great Mouse Detective 4'
3 3[1.2.Eh] 3[1/Eb.2.bcl] 3 – 4 4 3 1 – tmp+perc –
hp, (elec bs) – str
Films
Kane (rental)

The Great Race: Pie in the Face Polka 2.5'
1 0 0 0 – 3 0 3 1 – perc[incl drumset] – pf, gtr – str
Solo Flute.
Films
Kane (rental)

The Great Race: They're Off   *1.5'*
     1 0 0 0 – 3 0 3 1 – perc[incl drumset] – pf, gtr – str
                                         Films/Sports

Kane (rental)

The Great Waldo Pepper   *2.5'*
     3[1/pic.2/pic.pic] 2 3[1.2.bcl] 2 – 3 3 3 1 – perc –
     pf, (elec bs) – str
                                              Films

Kane (rental)

Hatari!: Baby Elephant Walk (1962)   *2.5'*
     3[all pic] 3[1.2.Eh] 4[1.2.Ebcl.bcl] 2 – 4 4 3 1 –
     tmp+2 drumset, xyl, glock – pf, gtr, Fender bs,
     calliope[4 hands] – str
                                      Animals/Films

T&V (rental)

Henry Mancini for Strings, Vol.1   *Folio*
     Strings
     Includes: Crazy World; Dear Heart; Hong Kong
     Fireworks; Peter Gunn; Pink Panther and more.
     William Zinn, arr.
                                              Films

Warner

Henry Mancini for Strings, Vol. 2   *Folio*
     Strings
     Includes: Baby Elephant Walk; Charade; Moon
     River; Days of Wine and Roses; Thorn Birds Theme;
     and more.
     William Zinn, arr.
                                              Films

Warner

Jingle Bells/Sleigh Ride   *3.5'*
     3[1.2/pic.3/pic] 1 3 2 – 4 4 3 0 – perc – hp, pf, gtr, bs
     – str
     Optional Choir.
                                           Christmas

Kane (rental)

The Lifeforce   *3.5'*
     2 2 3[1.2.bcl] 2 – 3 3 3 1 – tmp+perc – hp, pf – str
                                           Films/Space

Kane (rental)

Mancini Magic   *5'*
     3[incl pic] 1 3[incl bcl] 1 – 2 3 3 1 – tmp+3 – str
     Jerry Brubaker, arr.
                                              Films

Warner (POP); Luck's (rental)

March with Mancini   *14'*
     2 2 3[1.2.bcl] 3 – 4 3 3 1 – tmp+3 – hp, pf – str
     Includes: Timothy; March of the Cue Balls; The
     Swing March; The Great Race March.
                                   Instrumental Pops

Leonard

The Molly Maguires: Pennywhistle Jig (1970)   *4'*
     2 2 3 2 – 4 0 3 1 – 1perc – Irish hp, pf, 12 str gtr,
     Spanish gtr, bs gtr, Fender bs – str
     perc: drumset.
                       Films/ Dance/International (Ireland)

T&V (rental

Monster Movie Music Suite   *15'*
     3[1/pic/afl.2.3/pic] 3[1.2.Eh] 3[1.2.bcl] 3[1.2.3/cbn]
     – 4 4 3 1 – tmp+perc – hp, pf, theremin – str
                                     Films/Halloween

Kane (rental)

Moon River [see *Breakfast at Tiffanys*]

Mystery Movie Theme   *2'*
     2 2 2 2 – 3 3[all tpt/flug] 3 1 – perc [incl drumset]
     – hp, pf, elec bs – str
     Solo Piano.
                                                    TV

Kane (rental)

Oklahoma Crude   *2.5'*
     3 0 3 0 – 4 4 3 1 – (2 asx, 2 tsx, bsx) – tmp+perc –
     gtr[banjo, 12 str, reg], elec bs, harmonica –
     str[(bs)]
     Solo Violin [Fiddle].
                                                 Films

Kane (rental)

Overture to a Pops Concert   *4'*
     3[1.2.3/pic] 3[1.2.Eh] 3[1.2.bcl] 3 – 4 4 (1/pic) 3 1
     – tmp+perc – hp – str
                                   Instrumental Pops

Kane (rental)

Pennywhistle Jig   *2'*
     1 1 3[incl bcl] 1 – 4 3 3 1 – tmp+3 – pf – str
     Solo Piccolo. From the film *The Molly Maguires*.
     Moss, arr.
                       Films/International (Ireland)/Dance

Leonard

Peter Gunn   2'
    3 3 3[1.2.bcl] 3 – (2asx; 2tsx; bsx) – 4 4 3 1
    tmp+perc[incl drumset] – pf, gtr, elec bs – str
    Theme song from the television series. The music
    won an Emmy and 2 Grammys.
        TV

Kane (rental)

Peter Gunn Meets Mr. Lucky   11'
    2 2 3[1.2.bcl] 2 – 4 3 3 1 – tmp+perc –
    hp, pf, gtr – str
    A suite of tunes from the TV shows *Peter Gunn* and
    Mr. Lucky.
        TV

Kane (rental)

Peter Gunn Theme   2.5'
    2 1 3[1.2.(bcl)] 1 – (2asx, tsx, bsx) – 2 3 3 1 – 2perc
    – (gtr, elec bs), pf – str
    perc: xyl, vib, drumset [hi hat, sd, bd].
    Theme song from the television series. The music
    won an Emmy and 2 Grammys.
    Calvin Custer, arr.
        TV

Northridge (rental from Luck's)

The Pink Panther   3'
    3 0 0 0 – 0 4 4 0 – perc [incl drumset] –
    pf, gtr, elec bs – str[no bs]
    Solo Tenor Saxophone.
        Animals/Films

Kane (rental)

The Pink Panther   14'
    2 0 0 0 – 0 4 4 0 – 2perc – elec bs, pf, bs – str
    Solo Tenor Saxophone.
        Animals/Films

Leonard

The Pink Panther   2.5'
    2 1 2 2 – 4 3 3 0 – perc – pf – str
    Cacavas, arr.
        Animals/Films

Warner (POP); Luck's (rental)

The Pink Panther   3'
    2 1 3[1.2.bcl] 1 – (3sx) – 2 3 3 1 – tmp+2 –
    pf, gtr, elec bass – str
    perc: xyl, vib, glock, drumset.
    Calvin Custer, arr.
        Animals/Films

Warner

The Pink Panther: It Had Better Be Tonight   2'
(Meglio Stasera)
    2 2 3[1.2.bcl] 2 – 4 3 3 1 – perc[incl drumset] –
    hp, pf, gtr – str
        Films

Kane (rental)

The Pink Panther: It Had Better Be Tonight   2'
(Meglio Stasera)
    3[1/pic.2/pic.3/pic] 0 0 0 – 0 4 4 0 –
    perc[incl drumset] – pf, gtr, elec bs – str
    Choir.
        Films

Kane (rental)

Revenge of The Pink Panther (1978): Hong   2.5'
Kong Fireworks
    3[1.2.3/pic] 3 3 3 – 4 4 3 1 – tmp+perc[incl
    drumset] – hp, pf, gtr, elec bs – str
        Films

Kane (rental)

Songs for Audrey: Breakfast at Tiffanys,   6'
Charade, Two for the Road
    3 3[1.2.3/Eh] 4[1.2.(3).bscl] 0 – sax[(fl)] –
    4 4 [all with flug] 3 1 – tmp+perc [incl 2 drumsets]
    – hp, pf, bs gtr, gtr – str
        Films

Kane (rental)

The Thorn Birds Theme   3'
    3 3[1.2.Eh] 3[1.2.bscl] 3 – 4 1 3 1 – perc[drumset] –
    hp, pf, gtr, elec bs – st
        TV

Kane (rental)

The Thorn Birds: Meggie's Theme   3.5'
    1 0 0 0 – 4 3 0 1 – perc [drum set] – gtr, elec bs
    – str
    Solo Flute.
        TV

Kane (rental)

Victor, Victoria (1982): Crazy World   2.5'
    1 1 0 0 – 0 0 0 0 – str
    Solo Flute. Won the 1983 Oscar for Best Music.
        Films

Kane (rental)

The White Dawn: Suite (1974)   11.5'
    4[1.2.pic.pic] 3[1.2.Eh] 3[1.2.bcl] 3 – 4 3 3 1 –
    tmp+perc – hp, pf, accordion – str
    perc: orchestra bells, vib, sus cym, cym, lg gong, toms[lo & med hi], 2 sd.
    Includes: Seal Hunt; The Lovers; Horn Pipe; The White Dawn Theme; and Artic Whale Hunt.
                             Animals/Ecology/Films
T&V (rental)

Mandel, Johnny   1925-

The Sandpiper: Shadow of Your Smile   4'
    drumset – gtr – str
    Calvin Custer, arr.
                             Films/Popular Song/Valentine
Warner

The Sandpiper: Shadow of Your Smile   5'
    Piano – Strings
    Jaroslav Holesovsky, arr.
                             Films/Popular Song/Valentine
Warner (POP); Luck's (rental)

The Sandpiper: Shadow of Your Smile   4'
    1 1 2 1 – 2 3 3 1 – perc – pf – str
    Chuck Sayre, arr.
                             Films/Popular Song/Valentine
Warner (POP); Luck's (rental)

Mandell, Robert, arr.

Red River Valley   3.5'
    2 1 2 1 – 2 3 3 1 – tmp+perc – str
                             Americana
Kalmus

Mann, Arthur (See: Gauntlett, Henry John)

Mantovani, Annunzio Paolo   1905-1980

Gypsy Legend   3'
    2 2 2 2 – 2asx, tsx – 4 3 3 0 – tmp+1 – hp – str
    perc: tambn, tamtam.
    Solo Violin.
    Cecil Milner, arr.
                             Instrumental Pops
Kalmus

Poem to the Moon   3'
    2 2 2 2 – 2asx, tsx – 4 3 3 0 – tmp+1 – str
    Piano/Conductor score.
    Ronald Binge, arr.
                             Instrumental Pops
Kalmus

Manzanero, Armando   1935-

It's Impossible (Somos novios)   4'
    2 1 3[1.2.bcl] 1 – asx, tsx – 2 2 2 1 – tmp+1 – pf – str
    perc: chimes, drumset.
    Frederick Muller, arr.
                             Instrumental Pops
Sunbury (rental from Luck's)

Markowitz, Richard   1926-1994

Wild, Wild West   3'
    2[incl pic] 1 3[1.2.bcl] 1 – 4 3 3 1 – tmp+3 – pf – str
    Roy Phillippe, arr.
                             Americana/TV
Warner

Wild, Wild West (1965)   6'
    3[1.2.pic] 2[1.Eh] 5[1.2.3.Ebcl.bcl] 3[1.2.cbn] – 4 4 4[#3/4=bstrb] 1 – tmp+6 – hp or pf – str
    perc: xyl, glock, harmonica or train whistle, 2 sd, bd, sus cym, cym, tambn, Indian bells.
                             Americana/TV
T&V (rental)

Marks, Johnny　　　　　　　　1909-1985

Rudolph the Red-Nosed Reindeer　　　　　　　　*2'*
　　1 1 3[1.2.(bcl)] 1 – (asx, tsx) – 2 2 2 1 – tmp+2 –
　　pf – str
　　perc: sd, bd.
　　Key of C Major.
　　James D. Ployhar, arr.
　　　　　　　　　　　　　　　　　　　Christmas
Leonard (rental)

Marquez, Arturo　　　　　　　　1950-

Danzon No. 2　　　　　　　　　　　　　　*10.5'*
　　2 2 2 2 – 4 2 3 1 – 4perc – pf – str
　　　　　　　　　　　　　Dance/International
Peer (rental)

Marquina, Pascual　　　　　　　　1873-1948

España cani (Spanish Gypsy Dance)　　　　*2'*
　　2[incl pic] 2 3[incl bcl] 2 – 4 2 3 1 – tmp+3 – pf
　　– str
　　Merle J. Isaac, arr.
　　　　　　　　　　　　　Dance/International
Highland/Etling

España cani　　　　　　　　　　　　　*2'*
　　1 1 2 1 – 4sx – 2 3 3 1 – perc – str
　　Graham Prince, arr.
　　　　　　　　　　　　　Dance/International
Kalmus

Marsh, Gerry Jon　　　　　　　　1914-

Hamburger Suite　　　　　　　　　　*4'*
　　1 1 1 1 – 1 2 1 (1) – 5(2)perc – pf – str
　　perc: sd, bd, sus cym, (tri, tambn, vibraslap, bongos).
　　Includes: 1. We're Together by Sid Woloshin &
　　Kevin Gavin; 2. Have It Your Way; 3. Jack in the
　　Box by Steve Karmen.
　　　　　　　　　　　Americana/Popular Songs
Leonard (rental)

Martin, Hugh E.　　　　　　　　1914-

Have Yourself a Merry Little Christmas　　*4'*
　　2 2 2 2 – 4 3 3 1 – tmp+4 – str
　　See additional titles under Blane, Ralph.
　　John Whitney, arr.
　　　　　　　　　　　　　　　　　　Christmas
Warner

Martynov, Vladimir　　　　　　　　1946-

Christmas Music　　　　　　　　　　*40'*
　　1 1 0 2 – 0 0 0 0 – 1perc – str
　　Solo Violin; Solo Cello; Boy Soprano; Boy's Choir.
　　　　　　　　　　　　　　　　　　Christmas
Schirmer (rental)

Mascagni, Pietro　　　　　　　　1863-1945

Cavalleria rusticana:　　　　　　　　*3'*
　　Intermezzo Sinfonica
　　2[incl pic] 2 2 (2) – (2) 0 0 0 – 2hp, org – str
　　Organ may be replaced by 2cl, 2bn.
　　Used in the film *Raging Bull*.
　　　　　　　　　　　　Films/Popular Classics
Kalmus

Cavalleria rusticana:　　　　　　　　*3'*
　　Intermezzo Sinfonica
　　2 2 2 2 – 4 2 2 1 – str
　　Used in the film *Raging Bull*.
　　Carl Simpson, arr.
　　　　　　　　　　　　Films/Popular Classics
Kalmus

Mason, Jack　　　　　　　　1842-1912

O Bury Me Not On the Lone Prairie　　*3'*
　　2 2 3[1.2.bcl] 2 – 2asx, tsx, bsx – 4 3 3 1 – tmp+1
　　– (hp) – str
　　perc: sd, sus cym, temple blks, hi hat, bd.
　　　　　　　　　　　Americana/Popular Song
Remick (rental)

Massenet, Jules 1842-1912

Thaïs: Méditation 5'
2 2[1.Eh] 3[1.2.bcl] 3[1.2.cbn] – 4 0 0 0 –tmp –
hp – str
Solo Violin.

         Popular Classics

Kalmus; Luck's

Masser, Michael 1941-

Greatest Love of All 2.5'
2 1 2 1 – 2 3 3 1 – tmp+2 – pf – str
Playable by string quartet.
John C. Whitney, arr.

        Popular Song/Valentine

Warner (POP); EMS (rental)

Matos Rodríguez, Gerardo (See: Villaldo, Angel G.)

Matthews, H. Alexander 1879-1973

The Story of Christmas: Cantata
1 0 2 0 – 2 2 1 0 – tmp – hp – str
Chorus.

            Christmas

Schirmer (rental)

Maxwell, Robert

Ebb Tide 3'
2 1 2 1 – 2 3 2 1 – tmp+2 – pf – str
perc: drumset, vib.
From the 1962 MGM film "Sweet Bird of Youth" based on the play by Tennessee Williams.
Marty Gold, arr.

             Films

Robbins (POP); EMS or Luck's (rental)

Maxwell Davies, Peter 1934-

The Boyfriend: Concert Suite 25'
1[incl pic] 0 2 0 – ssx, asx, tsx – 0 2 1 1 – perc – hp, cel/pf(4hand), uke/mand, tenor bnjo – str
From soundtrack of Ken Russell's film based on Sandy Wilson's musical.

        Broadway Musicals/Films

Chester (rental)

Caroline Mathilde: 25'
 Concert Suite from Act I
2[1.2/pic/afl] 2[1.2/Eh] 2[1.2/bcl] 2[1.2/cbn] –
2 2 2 0 – tmp+2 – hp – str
perc: cym glock, flexatone, bd, tamtam, crot, 2sus cym, anvil.
Based on the story of princess Caroline Mathilde (1751-1775), sister of George III, forced to marry young to a sadistic Danish prince.

             Dance

Chester (rental)

Caroline Mathilde: 25'
 Concert Suite from Act II
2[1.2/pic/afl] 2[1.2/Eh] 2[1.2/bcl] 21.2/cbn] –
2 2 2 0 – tmp+2 – hp – str
perc: cym, glock, flexatone, bd, tamtam, crot, 2sus cym, anvil.

             Dance

Chester (rental)

The Devils: Suite 20'
1[incl pic/afl] 0 1[incl bcl] 0 – 0 1 1 0 – perc – org (out of tune pf,cel) untuned zither – str
Solo Soprano.

          Films/Halloween

Schirmer (rental)

Maxwell's Reel, 12'
 with Northern Lights
3[incl 2pic.afl] 3[1.2.Eh] 3[1.2.bcl] 3[1.2.cbn] –
4 3 3 1 – tmp+3 – hp – str
Solo Horn.

             Dance

Chester (rental)

Romamor 40'
 (Roma, Amor, Labyrinthos)
4[1.2.pic.afl] 3[1.2.Eh] 4[1.2.Ebcl.bcl] 4[1.2.2cbn] –
4 4 4[cb tbn] 2 – tmp+3 – hp, cel, org – str
Includes: Flamma fumo proxima; PLOUTOS AFANHS; Manet in Aevum.

            Valentine

Chester (rental)

A Spell for Green Corn: *19'*
    The Macdonald Dances
    2[1.2/pic] 2 2[1.bcl] 2[1.2/cbn] – 2 2 (2) 0 –
    (tmp+1) – str
    perc: tambn, glock, crot, bd, belltree.
    Solo Violin.
                                         Americana/Dance

Chester (rental)

Spinning Jenny: A Portrait of   *18'*
    Leigh, Lancashire, circa 1948
    3[1.2.pic] 3[1.2.Eh] 3[1.2.bcl] 3[1.2.cbn] –
    4 3[crt] 3 0 – tmp+4 – str
                                               International

Chester (rental)

Swinton Jig   *15'*
    2[1.pic] 2[1.Eh] 2[1.bcl] 2[1.cbn] – 2 2[crt] 2 1 –
    tmp+2 – pf, concertina, bnjo[out-of-tune] – str
    Solo Horn.
    Based on a nineteenth-century Lancashire fiddle
    tune.
                                  Dance/International

Chester (rental)

Temenos, with Mermaids and Angels   *20'*
    0 0 3[incl bcl] 3[incl cbn] – 2 2 0 0 – tmp+2 – str
    Solo Flute. Christmas theme according to Schirmer
    catalog.
                                                     Christmas

Schirmer (rental)

The Three Kings   *50'*
    3[incl pic] 3[incl Eh] 3[incl bcl] 3[incl cbn] –
    4 3 3 0 – tmp+2 – str
    Solo Soprano, Mezzo-Soprano, Tenor, Baritone;
    SMsTBar Chorus. Text: Christmas poems by
    George Mackay Brown interspersed with related
    Latin fragments from fifteenth-century carols.
                                                     Christmas

Schirmer (rental)

Mayer, William   1925-

Good King Wenceslas   *17'*
    2[incl pic] 2 2 2 – 2 2 1 1 – tmp+perc – pf – str
    Narrator; (SATB Chorus). Text by A.A. Milne.
    Also available for chamber ensemble: 1 1 1 1 –
    1 1 1 0 – pf
                                                     Christmas

Presser (rental)

Good King Wenceslas (chamber version)   *17'*
    1 1 1 1 – 1 1 1 0 – pf
    Narrator; (SATB Chorus). Text by A.A. Milne.
                                                     Christmas

Presser (rental)

Of Rivers and Trains   *15'*
    3[incl pic or ocarina, 2afl] 3[Eh] 2[incl Ebcl, bcl] 2
    – 4 3 3 1 – tmp+2 – pf/cel – hp – str
    Chamber version: 1 1 1 1 – 2 2 1 1 – tmp+perc –
    hp, kbd – str
                                                           Travel

Presser (rental)

Scenes from "The Snow Queen"   *15'*
    3[incl pic] 2[incl Eh] 2[incl Ebcl, bcl] 2[(cbn)] –
    4 3 3 1 – tmp+2 – pf, hp – str
    Chamber orchestra version:
    3[incl pic] 2[incl Eh] 2[incl Ebcl, bcl] 2[(cbn)] –
    2 2 1 1 – 2perc – pf, hp – str
    Based on the Hans Christian Andersen fairy tale.
                                                        Weather

Presser (rental)

McBride, Robert   1911-2007

Pumpkin Eater's Little Fugue   *4'*
    2[1.pic] 2[(#2)] 2 2 – 4 2 3[(#2)] 1 – tmp+2
    – str
                                                         Halloween

AMP (rental); Luck's (rental)

Pumpkin-Eater's Little Fugue for Strings   *4'*
    Strings
                                                         Halloween

AMP (rental); Luck's (rental)

Workout   *5'*
    1 1 1 1 – 1 0 0 0 – perc – pf – str
                                                             Sports

AMP (rental)

McBroom, Amanda   1946-

The Rose   *4.5'*
    2 2 3[1.2.bcl] 1 – 4 3 3 1 – tmp+perc –
    pf, (elec bass) – str
    Calvin Custer, arr.
                                                               Films

Warner (POP); Luck's (rental)

McCabe, John   1939-

The Lion, the Witch, and the   15'
Wardrobe: Suite
     1 1 2 1 – 1 2 1 0 – tmp+2 – pf – str
                                       Halloween
Novello (rental)

Mini Concerto for Organ,   8'
Percussion, Audience
     Percussion – 485 penny whistles
     Solo organ
                              Instrumental Pops
Novello (rental)

Sam (ITV Music)   3'
     1 0 1 0 – 0 1 0 0 – perc
                              Instrumental Pops
Novello (rental)

Sam: Theme Music (orchestra version)   5'
     2[incl pic] 0 2 0 – 0 1 0 0 – perc – str
                              Instrumental Pops
Novello (rental)

McCarthy, Dennis   1945-

Star Trek: Deep Space Nine Suite (1993)   4'
     3[1.2.3/pic] 3[1.2.Eh] 3[1.Ebcl.bcl] 3[1.2.cbn] –
     6 4 3 1 – tmp+4 – hp, pf[cel] – str
     perc: glock, vib, chimes, brass wind chimes, gong, lg bd, tri, sus cym, cym.
     Includes: Theme; Kyra; Through Time & Space.
                                     Films/Space
T&V (rental)

Star Trek 7: Generations "Overture" (1995)   4'
     3[all afl] 3[1.2.Eh] 3[1.2.bcl] 3[1.2.cbn] –
     8 4 5[1.2.3.4.cbstrb] 1 – tmp+3 –
     hp, pf, synth, gtr – str
     perc: cym, lg tamtam, glock, sus cym, tri, mark tree, vib, bd.
     Solo Soprano, Alto, Tenor.
                                     Films/Space
T&V (rental)

McCartney, Paul (See: Lennon, John)

McDonald, Harl   1899-1955

Dirge for Two Veterans   12'
     2 2 3 2 – 2 3 2 1 – tmp+perc – str
     Women's Chorus.
                                            Patriotic
Presser (rental)

Festival of the Workers   15'
     3 3 3 3 – 3 3 3 1 – tmp+perc – hp – str
                                          Labor Day
Elkan-Vogel (rental)

Legend of the Arkansas Traveler   4.5'
     3 3 3 3 – 4 4 3 0 – tmp+3 – str
                                          Americana
Elkan-Vogel (rental)

Saga of the Mississippi   15'
     3 3 3 3 – 4 3 3 1 – tmp+perc – str
                                          Americana
Presser (rental)

Song of Free Nations   3'
     3 3 3 3 – 3 3 3 1 – tmp+perc – str
     Solo Soprano.
                                            Patriotic
Elkan-Vogel (rental)

Suite for Strings on American Negro Themes   9'
     Strings
                                   Black History Month
Presser (rental)

McPartland, Marian   1946-

Melancholy Mood   5'
     2 2 2 2 – 4 0 0 0 – tmp – hp, pf – str
     Brian Torff, arr.
                                                Jazz
Piedmont (rental)

Meacham, Frank W.   1856-1909

American Patrol   4'
     2[1.pic] 2 2 2 – 4 2 2 1 – perc – str
     perc: sd, tambn, bd, (cym).
                                            Patriotic
Luck's

American Patrol 4'
   1 1 2 1 – 3sx – 2 3 2 1 – perc – str
   Henry Sopkin, arr.

                                      Patriotic

Kalmus

Mechem, Kirke   1925-

The Jayhawk, Op. 43:   8'
   Overture to a Mythical Comedy
   3[incl pic] 2 3[incl bcl] 2 – 4 3 3 1 – tmp+2 – pf – str
   Also known as *Magic Bird Overture*.

                                        Animals

Schirmer (rental)

The King's Contest   26'
   3 3 3 3 – 4 3 3 1 – tmp+4 – hp – str
   Alternate: 1 1 1 1 – 1 0 0 0 – (perc) – pf – str
   Solo Mezzo-Soprano[narrator], Tenor, Baritone,
   Bass; Chorus. Text is from the Old Testament
   Apocrypha. A dramatic cantata. More description is
   in the catalog.

                                        Holidays

Schirmer (rental)

Songs of the Slave   34'
   3[incl pic] 3[incl Eh] 3[incl bcl] 3[incl cbn] –
   4 3 3 1 – tmp+4 – hp – str
   Solo Bass-Baritone, Soprano; SATB Chorus.

                            Black History Month

Schirmer (rental)

Meij, Johan de   1953-

The Lord of the Rings: Excerpts from   9.5'
   Symphony No. 1
   3[1.2.pic] 1 3[1.2.bcl] 1 – 4 3 3 1 – tmp+3 –
   synth[pf, hp, cel] – str
   perc: cym, vib, sus cym, bd, whip, td, temple blks, xyl, sd,
   anvil, chimes, deep tom, glock, woodblk, tambn.
   This work is not from the film, but rather an original
   work inspired by Tolkien's books. It includes 5
   movements each depicting a different character or
   episode in the book. This edition offers several
   performance options for cuts varying from 4' to 9.5'
   1st prize winner of the Sudler International
   Composition Competition in 1989.
   Paul Lavender, arr.

                               Instrumental Pops

Leonard

Mejía, Adolfo   1905-1973

Acuarela (Watercolor)   4'
   2 2 3[incl] 2 – 4 3 3 1 – tmp+3 – pf – str

                          International (Columbia)

Filarmonika

Mendelssohn, Felix   1809-1847

Hark! The Herald Angels Sing   3'
   2 2 2 2 – 4 3 2 1 – tmp+perc – str
   8 brass section members form two brass choirs:
   Choir A = hn, 2tp, btbn
   Choir B = hn, tp, tbn, tuba.
   Jeff Tyzik, arr.

                                     Christmas

Schirmer (rental)

Hark! The Herald Angels Sing & Adeste Fidelis   6'
   2 3[1.2.Eh] 3 2[incl cbn] – 4 3 3 1 – tmp+1 – str
   Adeste Fideles (O Come All Ye Faithful) is
   attributed to English hymnist John Francis Wade.
   Hark the Herald is in Key of G and Adeste Fidelis is
   in Key of A.
   Arthur Luck, arr.

                                     Christmas

Luck's

The Novello Book of Carols: 3'
   Hark the Herald Angels Sing
   2 2 2 2 – 2 2 3 1 – tmp+2 – str
   Solo Voice.
   William Llewellyn, arr.

                                     Christmas

Novello (rental)

Hebrides Overture, Op. 26 (Fingal's Cave)   10'
   2 2 2 2 – 2 2 0 0 – tmp – str
   Breitkopf edition by Christian Martin Schmidt.

                              Popular Classics

Breitkopf; Kalmus

Heimkehr aus der Fremde   7'
   (Son and Stranger): Overture, Op. 89
   2 2 2 2 – 2 2 0 0 – str

                            Popular Classics

Breitkopf (rental); Kalmus

Märchen von der schönen Melusine,   *12'*
   (Fair Melusina), Op. 32
   2 2 2 2 – 2 2 0 0 – tmp – str
   Breitkopf edition by Christian Martin Schmidt.
                               Popular Classics

Breitkopf; Kalmus; Luck's

Midsummernight's Dream, Op. 21: Overture   *12'*
   2 2 2 2 – 2 2 0 1 – tmp – str
   Breitkopf edition by Christian Martin Schmidt.
                        Popular Classics/Seasons

Breitkopf; Kalmus

A Midsummernight's Dream: Scherzo   *5'*
   2 2 2 2 – 2 2 0 0 – tmp – str
   Breitkopf edition by Christian Martin Schmidt.
                        Popular Classics/Seasons

Breitkopf; Kalmus

A Midsummer Night's Dream: Wedding March   *5'*
   2 2 2 2 – 2 3 3 1 – tmp+1 – str
   perc: cym
   Breitkopf edition by Christian Martin Schmidt.
                      Popular Classics/Valentine

Breitkopf; Kalmus

Symphony No. 4 in A Major (Italian)   *27'*
   2 2 2 2 – 2 2 0 0 – tmp – str   *(8' 7' 6' 6')*
                                 Popular Classics

Breitkopf; Kalmus

Mendez, Raphael, arr.   1906-1981

La Virgen de la Macarena   *2.5'*
   2 2 3[incl bcl] 3[incl cbn] – 4 3 3 1 – tmp+perc –
   pf – str
   Solo Trumpet.
   The bull fighter's song.
   Charles Koff, arr.
                           International/Sports

Koff

Mendoza Y Cortes, Quirino   1859?-1957
(See: Fernandez, Caballero)

Menken, Alan   1949-

Beauty and the Beast   *4.5'*
   0 0 0 0 – 0 0 0 0 – 2perc – elec bs, pf, gtr – str
   perc: tri, sus cym, sd, claves, toms, tambn, glock.
   This is an arrangement of the main theme.
   Calvin Custer, arr.
                            Broadway Musicals

Leonard

Highlights from Beauty and the Beast   *5'*
   0 0 0 0 – 0 0 0 0 – tmp+2 – str
   perc: drumset, tambn, woodblk.
   Includes: Belle; Beauty and the Beast; Be Our
   Guest.
                            Broadway Musicals

Leonard

Menken, Alan   1949-
Ashman, Howard   1951-1991

Go the Distance   *3'*
   3[incl pic] 3 3[incl bcl] 2 – 4 3 3 1 – tmp+3 –
   pf, hp, synth – str
   Solo Voice; Chorus.
   Greg Prechel, orchestrator
                                      Sports

Wonderland

Menotti, Gian Carlo   1911-2007

Amahl and the Night Visitors: *7'*
   Introduction, March and Shepherd's Dance
   1 2 1 1 – 1 1 0 0 – perc – hp, pf – str
                                   Christmas

Schirmer (rental)

Amahl and the Night Visitors: *5'*
   Shepherd's Chorus
   1 2 1 1 – 1 1 0 0 – perc – hp, pf – str
   Chorus.
                                   Christmas

Schirmer (rental)

Landscapes and Remembrances 45'
   3[1.2.pic] 3[1.2.Eh] 3[1.2.bcl] 2 – 4 3 3 1 –
   tmp+perc – hp, pf – str
   Solo SATB; SATB Chorus.
                                                    Patriotic
   Schirmer (rental)

My Christmas 15'
   1 1 1 1 – 0 0 0 0 – hp – db
   Male Chorus.
                                                    Christmas
   Schirmer (rental)

Mercer, Johnny   1909-1976

Skylark 3'
   2 1 2 1 – 2 3 2 1 – tmp+perc – pf – str
   Marty Gold, arr.
                                                    Animals
   Warner (POP); EMS or *Luck's (rental)*

Mercury, Freddie   1946-1991

Bohemian Rhapsody 6'
   Strings
   From *Wayne's World* and Queen, the rock anthem.
   John Berry, arr.
                                                    International
   Leonard

Merrill, Bob   1921-1998

Take Me Along!: Overture 5'
   3[1.2.pic] 2 2 2 – 4 3 3 1 – tmp+3 – hp, pf – str
   Includes: Did You Do That Sid?; If You Promise
   Me a Rose; I Would Die; Volunteer Fireman's
   Picnic; Nine O'Clock; I'm Staying Young; But
   Yours; and Take Me Along. From the 1959 musical
   that generated the United Airlines theme song.
   Robert Wendel, editor
                                   Broadway Musicals/Travel
   Wendel (rental)

Meyer, George W.   1884-1959

If You Were the Only Girl in the World 3'
   2[incl pic] 2 2 2 – (2asx, tsx) – 4 3 3 1 – tmp+perc
   – str
   Introduced in the film *The Vagabond Lover* by Rudy
   Vallee. Some sources show Nat D. Ayer (1887-1952)
   as the composer.
   Timothy Broege, arr.
                                   Films/Popular Song/
                                                    Valentine
   Kalmus

Meyer, Ranaan   1978-

American Suite 12'
   1 2 2 2 – 2 2 1 0 – tmp – str
   2 Solo Violins, Solo Double Bass.
   Includes Orange Blossom. Ranaan Meyer is the
   bassist with Time for Three (Tf3).
   Hedges, orchestrator
                                                    Americana
   Fleisher

Fox Down 4'
   2 2 2 2 – 2 2 2 0 – tmp+1 – str
   2 Solo Violins, Solo Double Bass.
   Includes Shenandoah.
   Hedges, orchestrator
                                                    Americana
   Fleisher

Meza, Vinicio   1968-

Suite Latinoamericana 17'
   (Tango,Vals,Choro,Son)
   Strings
   Score is available for purchase.
                            Dance/International (Costa Rica)
   Filarmonika (rental)

Milhaud, Darius 1892-1974

Globetrotter Suite 17'
(for Small Orchestra)
2 1 1 1 – asx – 0 2 2 0 –perc – hp – str
                                        Travel
EMI (rental)

Two Marches 6'
2 2 2 2 – 4 3 3 1 – tmp+perc – str
                      Popular Classics
Schirmer (rental)

Miller, Glenn 1904-1944

Moonlight Serenade 4.5'
1 1 2 1 – 1 2 1 1 – tmp+drumset – (pf) – str
Bob Cerulli, arr.
                         Space/Valentine
Warner

Miller, Sy & Jackson, Jill 1913-

Let There Be Peace on Earth 2.5'
3[1.2.pic] 1 2 2 – 4 3[crt] 3 1 – tmp+1 – str
perc: cym.
Hawley Ades, arr.
                                Christmas
Shawnee

Mills, Gordon & Reed, Les

It's Not Unusual 4'
2 1 2 1 – sxs – 2 3 3 1 – tmp+perc – gtr, bs gtr – str
Piano/conductor score.
John Cacavas, arr.
                         Popular Songs
Leeds (POP); Luck's (rental)

Mills, Irving (See: Ellington, Edward K. & Hudson, Will)

Mindreau, Ernesto López

Marinera y Tondero 3'
3[incl (pic)] 2 2 2 – 3 2 3 0 – tmp+3 – (hp) – str
Popular coastal dances in Peru.
                   Dance/International (Peru)
Filarmonika

Mitchell, Darren 1964-

Turok 2 13'
3[pic.2.3] 3[incl Eh] 5[1.2.3.4.bcl] 2 – 4 4 2 1 – tmp+7 – pf, hp – str
                         Video Games
Mitchell

Mitchell, Lyndol 1923-1964

Railroad Suite
3[1.2.pic] 2[incl Eh] 2 2 – 4 3 3 1 – tmp+2 – str
                                 Travel
Shawnee (rental)

Mizzy, Vic 1916-2009

Addams Family Values: Tango for Violin 3'
and Orchestra (1993)
3[1.2.pic] 3[1.2.Eh] 3[1.2.Ebcl] 2[1.cbn] – (tsx) –
4 3 4 1 – tmp+6 – 2 hp[(#2)], pf, (cel[hpsd]), (gtr), (accordion) – str
perc: drumset, xyl, vib, orch bells, cyms, sus cym, bd, maracas, woodblock, shaker, vibraslap, cowbell, tambn, ratchet, conga, cast[2 players], tri.
Solo Violin.
                        Dance/Halloween/TV
T&V (rental)

The Addams Family: Theme & 4'
Waltz Finale (1991)
3[pic.2.3.] 3[1.2.Eh] 3[1.2.Ebcl] 2[1.cbn] – 4 2 4 1 – tmp+4 – 2 hp, pf, cel[hpsd], gtr, accordion – str
perc: drumset, xyl, vib, glock, cyms, sus cym, bd, maracas, woodblk, shaker, vibraslap, cowbell, tambn, ratchet, conga, castanet.
                             Halloween/TV
T&V (rental)

Moeran, E. J.   1894-1950

Lonely Waters   9'
    1 2[incl Eh] 1 1 – 1 0 0 0 – cym – str
    Solo Voice.
                                                   Popular Song
Novello (rental)

Serenade in G   15'
    (6-movement version)
    2[incl pic] 1 2 2 – 2 2 3 0 – tmp+perc – str
                                           Popular Classics
Novello (rental)

Serenade in G   22'
    (original 8-movement version)
    2[incl pic] 1 2 2 – 2 2 3 0 – tmp+perc – str
                                           Popular Classics
Novello (rental)

Whythorne's Shadow   7'
    1 1 1 0 – 1 0 0 0 – str
                                           Instrumental Pops
Novello (rental)

Monaco, James V.   1885-1945

You Made Me Love You   3'
    3[1.2.pic] 2 2 2 – (2asx, tsx) – 4 3 3 1 – tmp+perc
    – str
    Monaco was a Tin Pan Alley composer nicknamed
    "Ragtime Jimmie."
    Steven Rosenhaus, arr.
                                   Popular Song/Valentine
Kalmus

Moncayo, José Pablo   1912-1958

Huapango   7'
    3 2 3 2 - 4 3 3 1 – tmp+perc – hp – str
    Also playable by 1 1 2 1 – 2 2 1 0 – perc – hp or pf
    – str
    perc: guiro, marac, sd, indian dr, bd, claves, sonajas.
                                       Dance/International
Peer (rental)

Monestal, Alexander

The Birth of our Lord: A Christmas Cantata   16.5'
    1 1 2 1 – 2 2 3 0 – str
    Solo Tenor; Baritone; Bass. SATB Chorus.
                                                    Christmas
Fischer (rental)

Monk, Thelonius (See: Williams, Cootie)

Monteverdi, Claudio   1567-1643

Christmas Vespers   43'
    0 0 0 0 – 0 0 4 0 – org – str
    Solos: 2 Sopranos, Alto, 2 Tenors, Baritone, Bass.
    Double SATB Chorus.
    Stevens, editor
                                                    Christmas
Novello (rental)

Montgomery, Bruce   1921-

Concertino for Strings   16'
    Strings
                                           Popular Classics
Novello (rental)

Monti, Vittorio   1868-1922

Czardas   5'
    1[incl pic] 1 2 1 – 2asx, tsx – 2 2 1 0 – tmp+3 – str
    Maurice Baron, arr.
                                           Dance/International
Schirmer (rental)

Czardas   3.5'
    2[incl pic] 2 2 2 – 4 2 3 0 – tmp – hp – str
    Solo Violin.
                                           Dance/International
Kalmus

Czardas 3.5'
 3[1.2.pic] 3[1.2.Eh] 3[1.2.bcl] 2 – 4 3 3 1 –
 tmp+perc – hp – str
 Solo Flute.
 Giancarlo Chiaramello, arr.
                                    Dance/International
 Kalmus

Moore, Donald I.   1910-1998

America   6'
 3 2 2 2 – 2asx, tsx, bsx – 4 3 3 0 – tmp+2 – str
 SATB Chorus.
                                              Patriotic
 EMI (rental)

Moore, Douglas   1893-1969

The Greenfield Christmas Tree   40'
 2 2 2 2 – 2 2 2 0 – perc – hp – str
 Solos: principal players.
                                             Christmas
 Schirmer (rental)

Pageant of P.T. Barnum   16'
 3[1.2.pic] 3[1.2.Eh] 3[1.2.bcl] 3[1.2.cbn] – 4 3 3 1 –
 tmp+6 – hp, cel – str
 Includes: Boyhood at Bethel; Joice Heth, 161 Year
 Old Negress; General and Mrs. Tom Thumb; Jenny
 Lind; Circus Parade.
                                                Circus
 Fischer (rental)

Moroder, Georgio   1940-

Flashdance: What a Feeling (1983)   5'
 3 3[1.2.Eh] 3[1.2.bcl] 3[1.2.cbn] – 4 4 4 1 – tmp+3
 – hp, pf[cel], synth, gtr, Fender bs – str
 perc: drumset, sus cym, cym, finger cym, vib, glock,
 chimes, mark tree, gong, crotales, bd, sm tri.
                                          Dance/Films
 T&V (rental)

Moross, Jerome   1913-1983

The Big Country: Main Title Theme   3'
 3[1.2.3/pic] 2 3 2 – 4 3 3 1 – tmp+2 – hp, cel/pf
 – str
 perc: sd, piatti, glock.
 Won the 1959 Oscar for Best Music.
                                                Films
 Chappell (rental)

The Big Country: Suite   15'
                              (3' 2.5' 4.5' 1.5' 3.5')
 3[1.2.3/pic] 2[1.2/Eh] 3[1/Ebcl.2.3/bcl] 2[1.2/cbn] –
 4 3 3 1 – tmp+perc – hp, cel/pf – str
 perc: sd, piatti, clock, vib, cym, bd, tri.
 Includes: Main Title; Waltz; Ballad; Scherzo;
 Finale.
 Won the 1959 Oscar for Best Music.
                                                Films
 Chappell (rental)

Biguine   5'
 3[incl pic] 2 2[incl bcl] 2 – 4 4 3 1 – tmp+perc –
 pf – str
                                                 Jazz
 Sorom (rental)

Frankie and Johnny   19'
 2 2 3[incl bcl] 2 – 2 2 2 0 – tmp+5 – pf – str
 Vocals: 2 Soprano, 1 Alto.
 Ballet suite for orchestra.
                                                Dance
 Sorom (rental)

Music from the Flicks   20'
 3[incl pic] 3[incl Eh] 3[incl bcl] 2[incl cbn] –
 4 3 3 1 – 2tmp+perc – hp, cel/pf – str
 Includes: Episode from *Vienna* from *The Cardinal*;
 Pastorale from *Proud Rebel*; Romanza from *Five
 Finger Exercise*; Habanera and Danzone from *The
 Shark Fighters*; Nocturnal Procession from *The
 War Lord*.
                                                Films
 Chappell (rental)

A Tall Story for Orchestra   9'
 3[incl pic] 2 3[incl bcl] 2 – 4 3 3 1 – tmp+3 – str
                                    Instrumental Pops
 Sorom (rental)

Variations on a Waltz 14.5'
3[incl pic] 3[incl Eh] 3[incl bcl] 3[incl cbn] –
4 3 3 1 – tmp+4 – hp,cel – str
perc: sd, td, bd, sus cym, cym, glock, xyl, vib.

Dance

Sorom

Wagon Train 3'
2[1.pic] 2[1.Eh] 2 2 – 4 2 2 1 – tmp+1 –
hp, pf(cel), gtr – str

Americana/TV

T&V (rental)

Morricone, Ennio 1928-

Casualties of War: Elegy for Brown (1989) 4'
0 0 0 0 – 1 0 0 0 – str
Solo Cello.
Film by Brian De Palma.

Films

T&V (rental)

Cinema Paradiso Theme 4.5'
1 1[Eh] 3[1.2.bcl] 3 – 0 0 0 0 – pf – str
Henry Mancini, arr.

Films

Janen (rental)

Cinema Paradiso: First Youth 4.5'
3 1 3 1 – 4 0 0 0 – perc – hp, pf – str
perc: bells, glock.
Henry Mancini, arr.

Films

Janen (rental)

Cinema Paradiso: Love Theme 4.5'
3 1 3 1 – 4 0 0 0 – perc – hp, pf – str
perc: bells, glock.
Henry Mancini, arr.

Films

Janen (rental)

Legend of 1900: Romanza (1997) 4'
2 2[1.Eh] 2 2 – 4 1[pic tp] 2 1 – tmp – pf – str
Film by Giuseppe Tornatore originally titled *La leggenda del pianista sull-oceano*.

Films

T&V (rental)

I Knew I Loved You 3'
2 2 3[1.2.bcl] 2 – 4 2 3 1 – tmp+1 – (pf) – str
Also can be performed with strings alone.
Based on "Deborah's Theme" from the film *Once Upon a Time in America*; premiered by Celine Dion on the 2007 Academy Awards telecast.
Roy Phillippe, arr.

Films/Valentine

Belwin

Marco Polo: Main Title (1982) 3'
3 2 3[1.2.bcl] 2 – 4 0 3 1 – tmp+1 – str
perc: sus cym
Solo Cello.

Films

T&V (rental)

The Mission: Gabriel's Oboe 6'
4[pic.3afl] 1 2 2 – tmp+2 – 4 0 0 0 – pf, hp – str
perc: vib, bd.
Film by Roland Joffé.
Henry Mancini, arr.

Films

Janen (rental)

Once Upon a Time in the West: 4.5'
Theme; Man with a Harmonia (1969)
2[afl.2] 1[Eh if no chorus] 2 0 – 4 0 0 0 –
pf, hp, gtr – str
Optional SAA Chorus.
Henry Mancini, arr.

Films

T&V (rental)

The Untouchables: Overture (1987) 2.5'
3[1.2.pic] 3[1.2.Eh] 3[1.2.bcl] 3 – 4 4 3 1 – tmp+3
– hp – str
perc: large bd, large gong, large sus cym, sym.

Films

T&V (rental)

Morris, John 1926-

Blazing Saddles (1973)
3[1.2.pic] 2 2 0 – 4 4 3 0 – tmp+2 – hp, hpsd – str
perc: xyl, orchestra bells, crotales, tri.

Films

T&V (rental)

High Anxiety: Main Title (1973)
　3[1.2.pic] 3[1.2.Eh] 3[1.2.bcl] 3[1.2.cbn] – 4 3 3 1
　– tmp+3 – hp, pf, Theremin – str
　perc: bd, tamtam, sus cym, marim, sd, glock, congas,
　tambn, tri.
　Theme by Mel Brooks.
　　　　　　　　　　　　　　　　　　　　　　　Films
T&V (rental)

The Producers: Main Title (1968)　　　　　　　2'
　3[1.2.pic] 2 2 2 – 4 4 3 1 – tmp+3 – hp, (hpsd) – str
　perc: drumset, crotales, glock, cym, sus cym, tambn, tri,
　xyl, cast.
　Theme by Mel Brooks.
　　　　　　　　　　　　　　　　　　　　　　　Films
T&V (rental)

Young Frankenstein: The Transylvanian Lullaby (1974)
　2[1.pic] 2[1.Eh] 2 2 – 4 2 3 1 – tmp+1 – hp, pf – str
　perc: tamtam, chimes
　　　　　　　　　　　　　　　　　　Films/Halloween
T&V (rental)

Mosolov, Alexander　　　　　　　1900-1973

The Iron Foundry　　　　　　　　　　　　　　3'
　(Machine-Music) Op. 19
　3[1.2.pic] 3[1.2.Eh] 3[1.2.bcl] 3[1.2.cbn] – 4 3 3 1 –
　tmp+5 – str
　Depiction of a Russian factory.
　　　　　　　　　　　　　　　International/Labor Day
Kalmus; Russian (rental)

Moss, John

Salute to Ol' Blue Eyes　　　　　　　　　　　6'
　(Frank Sinatra Medley)
　2 2 3[1.2.bcl] 1 – 4 3 3 1 – perc – pf – str
　Includes: Strangers in the Night; That's Life; Lady
　Is a Tramp; I've Got You Under My Skin.
　　　　　　　　　　　　　　　　　Jazz/Popular Song
Leonard

Mozart, Wolfgang Amadeus　　　1756-1791

Adagio in E, K. 261　　　　　　　　　　　　5'
　2 0 0 0 – 2 0 0 0 – str
　Written for the Violin Concerto, No.5, K.219
　　　　　　　　　　　　　　　　　Popular Classics
Breitkopf; Kalmus

Don Giovanni, K.527: Overture　　　　　　　7'
　2 2 2 2 – 2 2 0 0 – tmp – str
　　　　　　　　　　　　　　　　　Popular Classics
Bärenreiter; Breitkopf; Kalmus

Eine Kleine Nachtmusik, K. 525　　　　　　15'
　(Serenade in G)　　　　　　　　　(5' 5' 2' 3')
　Strings
　　　　　　　　　　　　　　　　　Popular Classics
Kalmus; Luck's

Exsultate Jubilate, K. 165: Alleluja　　　　　3'
　2 2 0 (1) – 2 0 0 0 – org or harm – str
　Solo Soprano.
　　　　　　　　　　　　　　　　　　　　Christmas
Kalmus

German Dance #3, K. 605　　　　　　　　　6'
　2[1.2/flautino] 2 0 2 – 2[2posthorns] 2 0 0 –
　tmp+slghbells – str[no va]
　Including Schlittenfahrt (Sleigh Ride)
　　　　　　　　　　　　　　　　　　　　Christmas
Breitkopf; Kalmus

Il Re Pastore:　　　　　　　　　　　　　　　4'
　Overture, K. 208
　0 2 0 0 – 2 2 0 0 – str
　　　　　　　　　　　　　　　　　Popular Classics
Breitkopf; Kalmus; Luck's

Lucio Silla: Overture, K. 135　　　　　　　　9'
　0 2 0 0 – 2 2 0 0 – tmp – str
　　　　　　　　　　　　　　　　　Popular Classics
Bärenreiter; Breitkopf; Kalmus

Marriage of Figaro: Overture, K. 492　　　　4'
　2 2 2 2 – 2 2 0 0 – tmp – str
　　　　　　　　　　　　　　　Popular Classics/
　　　　　　　　　　　　　　　　　　　　Valentine
Bärenreiter; Breitkopf; Kalmus; Luck's

Marriage of Figaro: 4'
"*Aprite un po'quegl'occhi*"
0 0 2 2 – 2 0 0 0 – str
Solo Bass.

                                      Popular Classics

Kalmus; Luck's

Marriage of Figaro: 5'
"*Deh Vieni non Tardar*"
1 1 0 1 – 0 0 0 0 – strings
Solo Soprano.

                                      Popular Classics

Kalmus; Luck's

Marriage of Figaro: 5'
"*Dove sono i bei momenti*"
0 2 0 2 – 2 0 0 0 – str
Solo Soprano.

                                      Popular Classics

Kalmus; Luck's

Marriage of Figaro: 3'
"*Porgi amor (Cavatina)*"
0 0 2 2 – 2 0 0 0 – str
Solo Soprano.

                                      Popular Classics

Kalmus; Luck's

Der Schauspieldirektor 5'
(The Impresario), K. 486: Overture
2 2 2 2 – 2 2 0 0 – tmp – str

                                      Popular Classics

Breitkopf; Kalmus; Luck's

The Sleigh Ride 3'
1 1 2 1 – 2sx – 2 2 1 0 – tmp+perc – (pf) – str
P. Gordon, arr.

                                    Christmas/Seasons

Presser

Symphony No. 41, C Major 29'
(Jupiter), K.551 (9' 9' 4' 7')
1 2 0 2 – 2 2 0 0 – tmp – str

                                      Popular Classics

Bärenreiter; Breitkopf; Kalmus

Turkish March 3'
(from Piano Sonata No. 11, K. 331, 3rd movement)
2[incl 2pic] 2 0 2[incl cbn] – 2 1 1 1 – 2perc – str
perc: tri, bd, cym.
Leopold Stokowski, arr.

                                      Popular Classics

Stokowski (rental)

Muczynski, Robert   1929-

A Serenade for Summer 7.5'
0 1 0 1 – 1 0 0 0 – tmp – hp, cel – str

                                      Seasons

Presser (rental)

Muller, Frederick

Arkansas Traveler: In Bluegrass Style 3.5'
2 2 3[1.2.bcl] 2 – 2 2 2 1– tmp+2 – str
perc: sd, bd, glock.
Solo Violin.

                                  Americana/Popular Songs

Ludwig

The Rakes of Mallow 1.5'
(with Blue Grass Variation)
2 1 3[1.2.bcl] 1 – 2 2 2 1– tmp+2 – pf, (gtr) – str
perc: sd, bd, glock.

                               Americana/Instrumental Pops

Ludwig

Murray, Lyn   1909-1989

To Catch a Thief: Suite (1955) 6'
4 2 4[1.2.bcl.4] 1 – asx, 2 tsx, bsx – 4 3 3 1 – tmp+3 – hp, 2 pf, gtr, rhythm bs – str
perc: drumset, xyl, bells, sd, bd, woodblk, cyms.

                                          Films

T&V (rental)

Musgrave, Thea   1928-

Night Music 18'
1[1/pic] 2 0 1 – 2 0 0 0 – str

                                      Halloween

Schirmer (rental)

Two Christmas Carols 5'
in traditional style
vn, (va), vc
Solo Soprano, Oboe [or clar or violin]. SA Chorus [(TB chorus)].

                                      Christmas

Schirmer (rental)

Wild Winter II 19'
   Strings
   SATB Chorus.

                              Christmas

Schirmer (rental)

Mussorgsky, Modest Petrovich   1839-1881

The Dream of the Peasant Gritzko 9'
   3[incl pic] 2 2 2 – 4 2 3 1 – tmp+2 – hp – str
   Chorus. From *Soróchinskaya yarmarka*.
   Schebalin, arr.
                        Halloween/Popular Classics

Schirmer (rental)

A Night on Bald Mountain 12'
   3[1.2.pic] 2 2 2 – 4 2 3 1 – tmp+3 –hp – str
   perc: cym, bd, tamtam, chimes (d')
   Nikolai Rimsky-Korsakov, arr.
   Kalmus edition by Clinton F. Nieweg.
                        Halloween/Popular Classics

Kalmus; Russian (rental)

Night on Bare Mountain 10'
   4[incl 2pic] 3[incl Eh] 4[Ebcl, bcl] 3[incl cbn] –
   8 4 4 1 – tmp+3 – 2hp – str
   perc: sd, bd, xyl, tam-tam, chimes.
   Leopold Stokowski, arr.
                        Halloween/Popular Classics

Presser (rental)

Pictures at an Exhibition 35'
   3[1.2/pic.3/pic] 3[1.2.3/Eh] 3[1.2.bcl] 3[1.2.cbn]
   – asx – 4 3 3 1 – tmp+5 – 2hp, cel – str
   perc: xyl., sd, tamtam, tri, whip, ratch, cym, bd, glock,
   sus cym, chimes (d #').
   Includes: Promenade; Gnomus; Promenade; The
   Old Castle; Promenade; Tuileries; Bydlo;
   Promenade; Ballet of the Chicks in Their Shells;
   Samuel Goldenberg and Schmuyle; Limoges;
   Catacombs; Cum mortuis in lingua mortua; The Hut
   on Fowl's Legs; The Great Gate of Kiev.
   Maurice Ravel, arr.
                              Popular Classics

Durand (rental)

The Song of the Flea 3.5'
   2 2 2 2 – 4 2 0 0 – tmp – hp – str
   Solo Voice in key of B Minor.
   Hilding Anderson, arr.
                                  Animals

Kalmus

The Song of the Flea 3.5'
   3[1.2.pic] 2[1.Eh] 2 2 – 4 2 3 1 – tmp – hp – str
   Solo Baritone or Bass.
   Igor Stravinsky, arr.
                                  Animals

Kalmus

Songs and Dances of Death 20'
                        (5' 5' 5' 5')
   2[1.2/pic] 2 2[1.2/bcl] 2[1.2/cbn] – 4 2 3 1 – tmp+2
   – hp – str
   perc: sd, tamtam, cym.
   Solo Soprano. Russian text by Golenishchev-
   Kutuzov. Includes: Kolabelhaya (Lullaby);
   Serenada (Serenade); Trepak; Polkavodets
   (commander in Chief).
   Dmitri Shostakovich, arr.
                        Halloween/Popular Classics

Kalmus; Russian (rental)

Songs and Dances of Death 16'
   2 2 3[incl bcl] 0 – asx – 4 3 3 1 – 2perc – hp, cel
   – str
   Solo Bass. Russian text by Golenishchev-Kutuzov.
   Edison Denisov, arr.
                        Halloween/Popular Classics

Russian (rental)

N

Namenwirth, Micha

Divertimento for Toys and Orchestra   *14.5'*
    1 1 1 1 – 2 0 0 0 – perc – pf[4 hands] – str
    perc: glock, rattles; cast, tri, tambn, sm drums, woodblk, cym, gong, nightingale, quail.
    3 recorders in movement 2. Includes 3 movements.
                              Instrumental Pops
    Schirmer; Luck's (rental)

Naughtin, Matthew, arr.   1947-

Birthday Variations   *11'*
    2[1.2/pic] 2 2[1.2/asx] 2 – 2 2 1 1 – tmp+1 – hp – str
    Includes nine variations on the familiar tune, including ragtime, blues, latin, and rock and roll.
                              Celebration
    Naughtin (sale or rental)

Cinco de Mayo   *3.5'*
    2 2 2 2 – 2 2 1 1 – tmp+2 – hp, pf – str
    Demonstrates the instrumental families of the orchestra for young audiences in Mariachi style.
                              International
    Naughtin (sale or rental)

The Loony Tunes Fugue   *4'*
    2[1.pic] 2[1.2/Eh] 2[1.2/bcl] 2 – 2 2 1 1 – tmp+2 – hp – str
                              Instrumental Pops
    Naughtin (sale or rental)

Mario! Jump!   *4.5'*
    3[1.2.3/pic] 3[1.2.3/Eh] 3[1.2.3/bcl] 3[1.2.3/cbn] – 4 3 3 1 – tmp+2 – hp, cel, pf – str
    Tunes from the popular children's video game.
                              Films
    Naughtin (sale or rental)

This Old Man Sing-Along   *8'*
    2[1.2/pic] 2 2 2 – 2 2 1 1 – tmp+2 – hp, pf – str
    Includes: This Old Man; John Jacob Jingleheimer Schmidt; Day-O; and If You're Happy and You Know It.
                              Instrumental Pops
    Naughtin (sale or rental)

The Wheels on the Bus Sing-Along   *5'*
    2[1.2/pic] 2 2 2 – 2 2 1 1 – tmp+1 – pf – str
    The Wheels on the Bus; B-I-N-G-O; The Itsy-Bitsy Spider; and Old MacDonald.
                              Instrumental Pops
    Naughtin (sale or rental)

Nelson, Ronald J.   1929-

Rocky Point Holiday   *5'*
    2[1.(pic)] 2 2 2 – 4 3 3 1 – tmp+3 – hp – str
    perc: xyl, cym, bd.
    An orchestral arrangement of his popular wind ensemble work. The title refers to a seaside resort on the coast of Rhode Island.
                              Holidays/Instrumental Pops
    Boosey (rental)

Savannah River Holiday   *9'*
    3[incl pic] 2 2 2 – 4 3 3 1 – tmp+perc – cel/pf – str
                              Americana
    Fischer (rental)

Nelson, Steve   1907-?
Rollins, Jack   1906-1973

Frosty the Snowman   *2.5'*
    2 1 3[incl bcl] 1 – 4 3 3 1 – tmp+1,drumset – (pf) – str
    John Moss, arr.
                              Christmas
    Leonard

Newborn, Ira   1949-

The Naked Gun: Theme (1988)   4'
0 0 0 0 – 2asx, 2tsx, 1bsx – 0 4 4 0 – 1perc[drumset]
– pf, gtr, rhythm bs – [no str]
Also known as *Naked Gun 1 1/2* and *Police Story*.
    Films

T&V (rental)

Newman, Alfred   1901-1970

All About Eve: Overture
3[1.2.pic] 2[1.2/Eh] 5[1.2.3.bcl.bcl] 2[1.cbn] –
4 3 3 1 – tmp+perc – hp – str
    Films

Kane (rental)

The Best of Everything: London Calling
1 1 0 1 – 1 0 0 0 – hp, cel – str
    Films

Kane (rental)

Bishop's Wife: Lost April
3 3[1.2.Eh] 3 3 – 4 0 0 0 – tmp+perc – hp, pf/cel,
synth – str
    Films

Kane (rental)

Brigham Young March (1940)   5'
3[1.2.pic] 2[1.2.Eh]3[1.2.bcl] 2 – 4 3 3 1 – 3perc
– hp, cel – str
perc: sd, pic sd, td, bd, cym, tri, glock, xyl.
    Films

T&V (rental)

Captain from Castile: Conquest
3[1.2.pic] 3 4[1.2.3.Ebcl/bcl] 3[1.2.cbn] – 4 4 4 1
– tmp+perc – hp, pf – str
Mel Powell, arr.
    Films

Kane (rental)

Captain from Castile: Pedro and Catania
2[1.afl] 3[1.Eh.3] 4[1.2.3.Ebcbcl] 3[1.2.cbn] –
4 4 3 1 – tmp+4 – hp, cel – str
perc: 2 sd, 2 field dr, bd, cym.
    Films

T&V (rental)

David & Bathsheba   4'
3[1.afl.pic] 2 5[1.2.3.bcl.bcl] 0 – 4 0 0 0 – 3perc
– hp, pf[cel] – str
perc: tambn, finger cym, tri, vib.
    Films

T&V (rental)

Desiree: We Meet Again
1 1 2 1 – 1 0 0 0 – 1perc – hp – str
perc: glock, vib
Elmer Bernstein, arr.
    Films

T&V (rental)

The Diary of Anne Franck: Suite
3 2[1.Eh] 4[1.2.3.bcl] 3[1.2.cbn] – 4 3 3 1 – tmp+4
– hp, pf[cel] – str
perc: sd, field dr, bd, tri, glock, xyl, chimes, sus cym,
cym.
Includes: Overture: Portrait of Anne; Live in Hope;
The First Kiss; Percussion; Anne & Peter.
    Films

T&V (rental)

Fox Fanfare   0.5'
3 2 5[1.2.(3).bcl.(Ebcl)] 2 – 4 4 4 1 – tmp+perc
– str
    Fanfare

20th Century Fox

Gentleman's Agreement Suite
2 2 3[1.2.3/bcl] 2 – (2asx, 2tsx) – 4 2 3 1 –
tmp+perc – hp, pf – str
perc: drumset, cym.
Jon Kull and Patrick Russ, arr.
    Films

Kane; T&V (rental)

How to Marry a Millionaire: Street Scene   5.5'
3[1.2.pic] 2 2[1.2/bcl] 3[1.2.cbn] – ssx, 2asx, tsx
– 4 4 4 1 – tmp+perc – str
    Films

Kane (rental)

How the West Was Won   6'
3[1.2.pic] 2 3[1.2.bcl] 2 – 6 3 3 1 – tmp+perc – pf
– str
    Films

Kane (rental)

How the West Was Won: Suite   19'
    3[1.2.pic] 3[1.2 .Eh] 3[1.2.bcl] 3[1.2.cbn] –
    6 4 3 1 – tmp+4 – 2 hp [1 part a2] – pf[cel] – str
    perc: choked cym, tri, tambn, tamtam, sm tom, lg tom, glock, xyl, wdblk, chimes, pic tmp.
    Includes: Overture; Scherzo: Cleve & the Mule; Chetyenne Attack & Aftermath; Intermezzo; Finale.
    Christopher Palmer, arr.
                                          Americana/Films
T&V (rental)

Keys of the Kingdom Suite
    3 2[1.Eh] 2[bcl.bcl/Ebcbcl] 2[1.cbn] – 4 4 4 1 – tmp+3 – hp, cel – str
    perc: cym, sus cym, chimes, glock, sd, bd, lg gong.
                                                  Films
T&V (rental)

Nevada Smith: Overture
    3[1.2.pic] 2[1.Eh] 4[1.2.bcl.bcl] 3[1.2.cbn] –
    4 3 3 1 – tmp+4 – hp, pf, gtr, accordion – str
    perc: tambn, sd, bd, cym, xyl.
                                                  Films
T&V (rental)

Prisoner of Zenda: A Ruritanian Rhapsody   7'
    for Orchestra
    3[1.2.pic] 2[1.Eh] 3 2 – 4 3 3 1 – tmp+4
    – 2 hp[(#2)] – (cel) – str
    perc: cym, sus cym, sd, field dr, bd, tri, tambn, tamtam, glock.
    This 1937 black-and-white adventure film was based on the Anthony Hope 1894 novel. Alfred Newman received his first Oscar nomination for Best Original Score for this film.
    Christopher Palmer, arr.
                                                 Films
T&V (rental)

The Razors Edge
    3[afl.2.pic] 2[1.Eh] 4[1.2.3.bcl] 3[1.2.cbn] –
    4 4 4 1 – tmp+4 – 2 hp, pf[cel] – str
    perc: sd, bd, tri, cym, chimes, glock, gong.
    Includes: Main Title; Seduction; India.
                                                 Films
T&V (rental)

The Robe: Farewell to Diana
    3[1.2/afl.3/afl] 2[1.2/Eh] 5[1.2.3.Bbcbcl.Ebcbcl]
    2[1.cbn] – 4 3 3 1 – tmp+perc – 2hp, cel – str
    William Ross, arr.
                                                 Films
Kane (rental)

Song of Bernadette (1943): Main Title
    3 2[1.Eh] 5[1.2.bcl.Bbcbcl.Ebcbcl] 3[1.2.cbn] –
    4 3 4 1 – tmp+perc – 2hp, 2cel, org – str
    Won 1944 Oscar for Best Music.
                                               Films
Kane (rental)

Song of Bernadette (1943): Scherzo
    2[1/afl.2/pic] 2 5[1.2.bcl.Bbcbcl.Ebcbcl] 3[1.2.cbn]
    – 4 0 0 0 – perc – hp – str
    Won 1944 Oscar for Best Music.
                                             Films
Kane (rental)

Wuthering Heights: Cathie's Theme (1939)   2.5'
    0 0 0 0 – 0 0 0 0 – hp – str
    Christopher Palmer, arr.
                                           Films/Valentine
T&V (rental)

Wuthering Heights: Concert Suite (1939)   13'
    3[afl.2.pic] 3[1.2.Eh] 3[1.2.bcl] 2 – 4 3 3 0 –
    tmp+2 – hp, pf[cel] – str
    perc: tamtam, cym, sus cym, glock, xyl, tri, tambn, pic sd, bd.
    Fred Steiner, arr.
                                           Films/Valentine
T&V (rental)

Newman, David   1954-

Hoffa Theme   8'
    2[1/afl.2/afl] 2[1.2/Eh] 2[1/bcl.2/EbContra] 2 –
    6 3 3 1 – tmp+perc – hp, pf, synth – str
                                             Films
Kane (rental)

Newman, Lionel   1916-1989

Doctor Dolittle: Talk to the Animals
    3[1.2/pic.3/pic] 3[1.2.3/Eh] 3[1.2.3/bcl] 3[1.2.3/cbn]
    – 4 3 3 1 – tmp+perc[including drumset] – hp, pf
    – str
    Nan Schwartz-Mishkin, arr.
                                           Animals/Films
Kane (rental)

Nicolai, Otto — 1810-1849

Merry Wives of Windsor: Overture — 8'
2[1.2/pic] 2 2 2 – 4 2[crt] 3 0 – tmp+2 – str
perc: bd, cym.
A. Winter, arr.
Popular Classics

Breitkopf; Kalmus; Luck's

Nielsen, Carl August — 1865-1931

Helios Overture, Op. 17 — 12'
3[1.2.3/pic] 2 2 2 – 4 3 3 1 – tmp – str
Popular Classics

Hansen (rental); Kalmus

Little Suite, Op. 1 — 15'
Strings — (4' 5' 6')
Popular Classics

Broude Bros.; Hansen (rental); Kalmus; Luck's

Masquerade: Hanedons (Cock's Dance) — 5'
3[1.2.pic] 2 2 2 – 4 3 3 1 – tmp – str
Animals/Dance

Hansen (rental); Kalmus

Masquerade: Overture — 4'
3[1.2.3/pic] 2 2 2 – 4 3 3 1 – tmp+2 – str
perc: cym, bd.
Halloween

Hansen (rental); Kalmus

Masquerade: Prelude to Act II — 4'
2 2 2 2 – 4 0 0 0 – str
Halloween

Hansen (rental); Kalmus

Rhapsodic Overture — 10'
3[1.2.pic] 2 2 2 – 4 2 3 0 – tmp+perc – str
Popular Classics

Hansen (rental); Kalmus

Niles, John Jacob — 1892-1980

I Wonder as I Wander — 4'
2[incl pic] 1 2 2 – 1 0 0 0 – 1perc – hp – str
perc: bells.
Solo Soprano.
Robert Sadin, arr.
Christmas

Schirmer (rental)

Nitzsche, Jack (See: Sainte-Marie, Buffy)

North, Alex — 1910-1991

2001 Space Odyssey: Fanfare
4[1.2.3.pic] 4[1.2.3.Eh] 4[1.2.3.bcl] 4[1.2.3.cbn] – 6 6 4 2 – tmp+5 – hp, pf, org – str
perc: sd, bd, cym, sus cym, bells, gong, chimes.
Fanfare/Films/Space

Kane (rental)

2001: A Symphonic Suite in Four Movements (1968) — 12'
4[1.2.pic.pic] 3[1.2.Eh] 3[1.2.bcl] 3[1.2.cbn] – 4 4 3 1 – tmp+3 – 2 hp, pf[cel], (org) – str
perc: bd, cym, sus cym, ruthe, 3 toms, xyl, vib, marim, glock, chimes, tamtam.
Includes: Prelude (The Dawn of Man) & The Bluff; Intermezzo: Moon Rocket Bus, The Kill; Epilogue: Space Station Docking (The Waltz).
Alex North created this music for Stanley Kubrick's *2001: A Space Odyssey*, but Kubrick chose not to use it. Erich Kunzel of the Cincinnati Pops introduced North's work in a 1993 recording.
Christopher Palmer, arr.
Films/Space

Kane (rental)

Cheyenne Autumn Suite
  5[pic.2.afl.afl/pic/bsfl.Yugoslav fl]
  4[ob d'amore.bar ob(bs ob).Eh.Eh]
  4[bcl/Ebcl/asx.bcl/asx/barsx.bcl/tsx/barsx/Ebcbcl.
  bssx/barsx/Bbcbcl] 4[1.2.cbn.cbn] – 4 4 4 0 –
  2 tmp+5 – hp, pf[cel] – str[no violins, 6 violas,14
  cellos, 6 basses]
  perc: tambn, sm cym, sd, field dr, bd, sus cym, 2 toms, 2 xyl, marim, bs mar, 2 glock, crotales,ratchet, temple blk, chimes, gong.
  Includes: Overture; Friend Deborah; Dodge City; Cattle Drive; Spring; End Cast.
                                    Americana/Films
Kane (rental)

Cleopatra: Symphonic Portrait (1962)   25'
  4[afl/pic.afl/pic.afl/pic,afl/pic]
  4[1.ob d'amore.Eh.Eh] 4[Ebcl.Ebcl.bcl.bcl]
  4[1.2.cbn.cbn] – 6 4 4 1 – tmp+5 –
  2 hp, pf[cel, clavitimbre, chain pf, org],
  hpsd[chain pf], gtr – str
  perc: crotales, sd, bd, toms, timbales, sus cym, cyms, mar, bs marim, vib, glock, xyl, bell tree, gongs, tri, tambn, giant chimes.
  Symphony in 2 parts: Part 1 is Caesar and Cleopatra; Part 2 is Antony and Cleopatra.
  John Mauceri, arr.
                                    Films/Valentine
Kane (rental)

Spartacus: Camp at Night   2.5'
  6[1.2.3.afl.afl,pic] 4[ob d'amore,2.Eh.Eh]
  3[1.Ebcl/bcl.bcl/Ebcbcl(bflcbcl)] 4[1.2.3.cbn] –
  6 6 6[incl cbtrb] 2 – tmp+9 – 2 hp, 2
  pf[#2=cel,synth], 2 mandolins, 2 gtr, guitarron
  – str
  perc: Napoleon sd, pic sd, 2 sd, 2 Field dr,sm bd, bd, bongo, tuned bongo, anvil, sm tubular bells, xyl, glock, bells, song bells,tambn, cyms, finger cyms, tom tom, tri, woodblk, vib, chimes, gong, lg gong.
                                    Films
Kane(rental)

Spartacus: Draba Fight   4'
  6[1.2.3.afl.afl,pic] 4[ob d'amore, 2.Eh.Eh]
  3[1.Ebcl/bcl.bcl/Ebcbcl(bflcbcl)] 4[1.2.3.cbn] –
  6 6 6[incl cbtrb] 2 – tmp+9 – 2 hp, 2
  pf[#2=cel,synth], 2 mandolins, 2 gtr, guitarron
  – str
  perc: Napoleon sd, pic sd, 2 sd, 2 Field dr,sm bd, bd, bongo, tuned bongo, anvil, sm tubular bells, xyl, glock, bells, song bells,tambn, cyms, finger cyms, tom tom, tri, woodblk, vib, chimes, gong, lg gong.
                                    Films
Kane(rental)

Spartacus: Final Farewell   3'
  6[1.2.3.afl.afl,pic] 4[ob d'amore,2.Eh.Eh]
  3[1.Ebcl/bcl.bcl/Ebcbcl(bflcbcl)] 4[1.2.3.cbn] –
  6 6 6[incl cbtrb] 2 – tmp+9 – 2 hp, 2
  pf[#2=cel,synth], 2 mandolins, 2 gtr, guitarron
  – str
  perc: Napoleon sd, pic sd, 2 sd, 2 Field dr,sm bd, bd, bongo, tuned bongo, anvil, sm tubular bells, xyl, glock, bells, song bells,tambn, cyms, finger cyms, tom tom, tri, woodblk, vib, chimes, gong, lg gong.
                                    Films
Kane(rental)

Spartacus: Forest Meeting   5'
  6[1.2.3.afl.afl,pic] 4[ob d'amore.2.Eh.Eh]
  3[1.Ebcl/bcl.bcl/Ebcbcl(bflcbcl)] 4[1.2.3.cbn] –
  6 6 6[incl cbtrb] 2 – tmp+9 – 2 hp, 2 pf[#2=cel, synth], 2 mandolins, 2 gtr, guitarron
  – str
  perc: Napoleon sd, pic sd, 2 sd, 2 Field dr,sm bd, bd, bongo, tuned bongo, anvil, sm tubular bells, xyl, glock, bells, song bells,tambn, cyms, finger cyms, tom tom, tri, woodblk, vib, chimes, gong, lg gong.
                                    Films
Kane(rental)

Spartacus: Love Theme   3'
  3 3 3[Ebcl.2.bcl] 3[1.2.cbn] – 4 3 3 1 – tmp+4 –
  hp, pf – str
  perc: sd, Field dr, pic sd, med bongo, sm bd, sus cym, cym, xyl, tambn, gong.
                                    Films/Valentine
Kane(rental)

Spartacus: Main Title   3.5'
  6[1.2.3.afl.afl,pic] 4[ob d'amore,2.Eh.Eh]
  3[1.Ebcl/bcl.bcl/Ebcbcl(bflcbcl)] 4[1.2.3.cbn] –
  6 6 6[incl cbtrb] 2 – tmp+9 – 2 hp –
  2 pf[#2=cel,synth], 2 mandolins, 2 gtr, guitarron
  – str
  perc: Napoleon sd, pic sd, 2 sd, 2 Field dr,sm bd, bd, bongo, tuned bongo, anvil, sm tubular bells, xyl, glock, bells, song bells,tambn, cyms, finger cyms, tom tom, tri, woodblk, vib, chimes, gong, lg gong.
                                    Films
Kane(rental)

Spartacus: Vesuvius   2'
     6[1.2.3.afl.afl,pic] 4[ob d'amore,2.Eh.Eh]
     3[1.Ebcl/bcl.bcl/Ebcbcl(bflcbcl)] 4[1.2.3.cbn] –
     6 6 6[incl cbtrb] 2 – tmp+9 – 2 hp –
     2 pf[#2=cel,synth], 2 mandolins, 2 gtr, guitarron
     – str
     perc: Napoleon sd, pic sd, 2 sd, 2 Field dr,sm bd, bd,
     bongo, tuned bongo, anvil, sm tubular bells, xyl, glock.
     bells, song bells, tambn, cyms, finger cyms, tom tom, tri,
     woodblk, vib, chimes, gong, lg gong.
                                                 Films

Kane(rental)

A Streetcar Named Desire: Suite (1951)   10'
     3[1.afl/pic.pic] 2[1.Eh] 3[1.2.Ebcl/bcl] 2[1.cbn]
     – asx – 4 3 3 1 – tmp+3 – hp, pf[cel] – str
     perc: drumset, tamtam, vib, bd, cym, sus cym, tri.
     Mark McGurty, arr.
                                                 Films

Kane (rental)

Unchained Melody (1955)   4'
     2 1 1 0 – 2 0 0 0 – 1 perc[vib] – hp – str
     One of the most recorded songs in the 20th Century.
     From the film *Ghost*.
     Patrick Russ, arr.
                                   Films/Popular Songs

T&V (rental)

Viva Zapata (1952): Gathering Forces
     2 2[1.2/Eh] 3[1.2.bcl] 2[1.2/cbn] – 4 3 3 1 –
     tmp+perc – hp, pf – str
     Nominated for 1953 Oscar for Best Music.
                                                 Films

Kane (rental)

Nørgård, Per   1932-

Three Love Songs   10'
     3[incl 2pic] 2[incl Eh] 2[incl Ebcl] 2[incl cbn] –
     4 4 2 0 – tmp+perc – str
     Solo Alto.
                                                Valentine

Schirmer (rental)

Norton, George A.   1880-1923

Round Her Neck She Wore   3'
a Yellow Ribbon
     3[incl pic] 2 2 2 – (asx, 2tsx) – 4 3 3 1 – tmp+perc
     – str
     Steven Rosenhaus, arr.
                                             Popular Song

Kalmus

Nyman, Michael   1944-

The Piano: 30'
     Concerto (Two-piano version)
     2 2 2 2 – 2 2 1 1 – hp – str
     2 Solo Pianos.
                                                   Films

Chester (rental)

The Piano: 30'
     Concerto (Solo piano version)
     2[incl pic,afl] 2[incl Eh] 2[incl bcl] 2 – 2 2 2 0 –
     hp – str
     Solo Piano.
                                                   Films

Chester (rental)

The Piano: Lost and Found   3'
     Strings
     Solo Soprano Saxophone.
                                                   Films

Chester (rental)

The Piano for String Orchestra   15'
     Strings
                                                   Films

Chester (rental)

Nystroem, Gösta   1890-1966

3 Kärleksvisor (Three Love Songs)   10'
     1 1 2 1 – 2 1 0 0 – tmp – hp,cel – str
     Solo Medium Voice. Text: Swedish;
     Includes: Song of Songs; Österling; Lagerkvist.
                                                 Valentine

Schirmer (rental)

O

O'Boyle, Sean

Country Kazoo Overture   2'
   2[1.pic] 2 2 2 – 4 2 3 1 – tmp+2 – hp – str
   Kazoos.
                                        Novelty
Wendel (rental)

Olympia Australis   2'
   3[1.2.pic] 2 3[1.2.bcl] 2 – 4 3 3 1 – 3perc – hp – str
   Australian Broadcasting Corporation's theme for the 2000 Sydney Olympics.
                                        Sports
Wendel (rental)

Ragtime   1.5'
   3[1.2.pic] 3[1.2.Eh] 3[1.2.bcl] 3[1.2.cbn] – 4 3 3 1 – 1 perc – hp – str
   perc: xyl.
                                          Jazz
Wendel (rental)

River Symphony   11.5'
   3[1.2.3/pic] 3[1.2.Eh] 3[1.2.bcl] 3[1.2.cbn] – 4 3 3 1 – tmp+3 – hp – str
   A shorter version *(4.5')* is available for the same instrumentation. Ask for River Symphony Fanfare.
                                          Ecology
Wendel (rental)

Silent Movie Music   2.5'
   2[1.pic] 2 2[1.bcl] 2 – 4 3 3 1 – 1 perc – hp – str
   perc: xyl.
                                          Films
Wendel (rental)

Waltz of Madness   3'
   (tmp) – strings
                                          Halloween
Wendel (rental)

O'Brien, Richard   1942-

The Rocky Horror Picture Show: Medley   6'
   3[1.2.pic] 2 2 2 – 4 3 3 1 – tmp+perc – (pf) – str
   perc: drumset, mark tree, xyl, glock, chimes, tam-tam, bd.
   Includes: Science Fiction Double Feature; Damn It Janet; Over at the Frankenstein Place; Hot Patootie Bless My Soul; The Time Warp.
   Robert Wendel, arr.
                                   Broadway Musicals/Films
Wendel (rental)

O'Donnell, Martin & Salvatori, Michael   1955-

Halo Suite: Halo Theme   4.5'
   1perc – str
   As performed by VideoGames Live.
   Bob Phillips, arr.
                                     Video Games
Alfred

Offenbach, Jacques   1819-1880

Les contes d'Hoffmann (Tales of Hoffmann):   6'
  Intermezzo & Barcarolle   (2' 4')
   2[1/pic.2/pic] 2 2 2 – 4 2 3 0 – tmp+3 – hp – str
   perc: bd, cym, tri.
                                   Popular Classics
Kalmus; Luck's

Orpheus in the Underworld: Overture   9'
   2[1.pic] 2 2 2 – 4 2 3 1 – tmp+3 – hp – str
   perc: bd, cym, sd, tri.
   Carl Binder, arr.
   Kalmus edition by Clark McAlister.
                                 Halloween/Popular Classics
Kalmus; Luck's

Orpheus in the Underworld: 3.5'
  Galop (Can-Can)
   2 2 2 2 – 4 2 3 0 – tmp – str
   Clark McAlister, editor
                                   Dance/Popular Classics
Masters

La vie parisienne: Overture   5'
    2[1.2/pic] 2 2 2 – 2asx, tsx – 4 2 2 0 – tmp+3 – str
    perc: bd, cym, tri.
    Antal Dorati, arr.
                                      International
    Kalmus

Olcott, Chauncey   1858-1932

My Wild Irish Rose   3.5'
    1 1 2 1 – 3sx – 2 2 1 0 – perc – str
                             Valentine/St. Patrick/
                                        International
    Kalmus

Oliviero, Nino (See: Ortolani, Riz)

Orr, Buxton   1924-1997

A Carmen Fantasy   14'
    2[incl pic] 2 2 2 – 2 2 2 0 – tmp+2 – str;
    Alternate: 0 2 0 0 – 2 0 0 0 – str
    Solo Cello.
                               Popular Classics
    Novello (rental)

Orr, Charles Wilfred   1893-1976

Cotswold Hill Tune   5'
    Strings
    The Cotswolds are a range of hills in
    Gloucestershire.
                             Ecology/International
    Chester (rental)

Ortolani, Riz   1931-
Oliviero, Nino   1918-1980

Mondo Cane: More   4'
    Strings
    Richard Hayman, arr.
                                 Films
    Kalmus

Mondo Cane: More   4'
    3[incl pic] 3[1.2.(Eh)]] 3[1.2.(bcl)] 3[1.2.cbn] –
    4 4[(3&4)] 3 1 – tmp+3 – hp/pf – str
    Boston Pops version.
    Richard Hayman, arr.
                                 Films
    Kalmus

Ottman, John   1964-

Astro Boy (2009): End Titles
    3[1.2.3/pic] 1 3 2 – 8 4 3[2+1] 1 – tmp+perc –
    hp, cel – str
                               Films/Space
    Kane (rental)

Astro Boy (2009): Theme
    3[1.2.3/pic] 1[1/Eh] 3[1.2.3/bcl] 2 – 8 4 3 1 –
    tmp+perc – hp, pf, cel – str
    Choir.
                               Films/Space
    Kane (rental)

Fantastic Four: Main Titles   2.5'
    3 1 3[1.2.bcl] 2 – 8 3 5 1 – tmp+perc – hp, pf – str
    SATB Chorus.
    Rick Giovinazzo, arr.
                                 Films
    Kane (rental)

Fantastic Four 2: Silver Surfer Suite   4.5'
    3[1.2/afl.3/afl] 1/Eh 3[1.2.3/bcl] 2 – 8 3 3 1 –
    tmp+perc – hp, pf/cel – str
    Damon Intrabartolo, arr.
                                 Films
    Kane (rental)

Hide and Seek: Main Titles 2'
    2[1.2/pic] 1[Eh] 2[1.2/bcl] 2[1.cbn] – 3 1 3 1 –
    perc – hp, pf, cel – str
    Optional Solo Voice.
                                          Films

Kane (rental)

Superman Returns Suite (2006) 7'
    3[1/afl.2/afl.3/pic/afl] 2[1.Eh] 3[1.2.3/bcl]
    3[1.2.cbn] – 4 3 3 1 – tmp+perc – hp, pf, cel – str
    John T. Williams also listed as the composer.
    Damon Intrabartolo, arr.
                                          Films

Kane (rental)

The Usual Suspects (1995) 3.5'
    1 2[1.Eh] 1[bcl] 0 – 3 1 0 0 – perc – hp, pf – str
    perc: sus cym, bd, chimes.
    Won Best Music from the Academy of Science
    Fiction, Fantasy, and Horror Films.
                                          Films

T&V (rental)

X2: X-Men United 7'
    3[1.2.3/bfl] 3[1.2.Eh] 3[1.2.bcl] 3[1.2.cbn] –
    6 3[crt] 3 1 – tmp+perc – hp, pf – str
    Optional SATB Chorus.
    Intrabartolo; Tin; Beard, arrs.
                                          Films

Kane (rental)

Owens, Robert   1925-

American Carnival: Ballet Suite 16'
    3 3 3 3 – 4 3 3 1 – tmp+perc[incl xyl] – hp, cel
    – str
    Friedrich Buck, arr.
                                       Americana/Dance

Sikorski (rental)

P

Pachelbel, Johann   1653-1706

Canon in D 5'
    strings – (cnt)
    Extra violin & viola parts fill in for the original
    cembalo.
    Helmut May, arr.
                                       Popular Classics

Schott

Chaconne for String Orchestra 8'
    pf – strings
    Muller-Hartmann, arr.
                                       Popular Classics

Kalmus; Novello (rental)

Kanon in D Major 5.5'
    2 2 2 2 – 4 2 3 1 – tmp+perc – str
    Rock Group: elec gtr, bass gtr, drumset.
    Stephen Simon, arr.
                                  Popular Classics/Rock

Merion (rental)

Ordinary People Theme: Canon in D 5'
    2 1 2 1 – (3sx) – 4 3 2 1 – tmp+perc – pf – str
    Bob Lowden, arr.
                                          Films

Leonard (POP); EMS (rental)

Padilla, José   1889-1960

El Relicario: Paso Doble 3'
    2 2 2 2 – 2sx – 4 2 3 1 – tmp+perc – str
    Merle J. Isaac, arr.
                                       International

Kalmus

Paich, David & 1954-
Porcaro, Jeff 1957-1992

Africa 4'
2 1 2 1 – 4 3 3 1 – tmp+4 – str
Song recorded by Toto in the 1980s.
Steven L. Rosenhaus, arr.
International/Popular Song/Rock

Leonard (POP); EMS or Luck's (rental)

Pankow, James

Colour My World
2 1 3[1.2.bcl] 1 – (sx) – 2 2 2 1 – perc – pf – str
1970 composition by James Pankow, founding member of rock band Chicago.
Willis Schaefer, arr.
Rock/Valentine

Leonard (rental)

Pann, Carter 1972-

Slalom 10'
3[1.2/pic.3/pic] 3 3[1.2.3/bcl] 3[1.2.3/cbn] –
4 3 3 1 – tmp+3 – hp,cel/pf – str
perc: bd, cym, 2sus cym, 2hi-hat, 4toms, 2tri, tambn, tamtam, glock, xyl, marim, crot, woodblk, templeblk, 3whip, 3sandblks, rute, thunderdheet, siren whistle.
Sports

Presser (rental)

Two Portraits of Barcelona 13.5'
3[incl pic] 3[incl Eh] 4[incl Ebcl & bcl] 2 – 4 3 3 1 – tmp+5 – hp, cel/pf – str
Includes: Antoni Gaudi's Cathedral; The Bullfight.
International

Presser (rental)

Parker, Alice 1925-

Seven Carols for Christmas 17.5'
(2.5' 2.5' 2' 2.5' 2' 3' 3')
2 2 2 2 – 4 2 2 1 – tmp+perc – (hp, pf) – str
SATB Chorus. Carols can be played separately or as a suite: O Come Emanuel; Away in a Manger; Fum, Fum, Fum; Good Christian Men, Rejoice; So Blest a Sight; God Rest You Merry; Masters in this Hall.
The composer recommends this order as a suite or to split the above list into two parts: the first three as a suite from varied sources, and the final four celebrating their British heritage.
Christmas

Fischer (rental)

Payne, Anthony 1936-

Fanfares and Processional 12'
0 0 0 0 – 1 4 4 1
Fanfare

Chester (rental)

Pearson, Leslie, arr.

Early One Morning 3'
1 1 1 1 – 2 0 0 0 – str
Instrumental Pops

Kalmus

Peaslee, Richard 1930-

Arrows of Time 14'
2[incl pic] 2 2[incl bcl] 2 – 4 3 2 1 – tmp+3 – hp – str
Solo Trombone.
New Year

Margun (rental)

Chicago Concerto 17'
0 0 0 0 – 2asx(cl, fl, acl), 2tsx(cl, bcl) – 0 4 5 0 – (2perc), drumset – gtr – (4vc)db
Solo Baritone Saxophone.
Americana

Margun (rental)

Peck, Russell   1945-2009

Playing With Style   10'
2 2 2 2 – 4 2 3 1 – tmp+2 - str; Alternate: 2 2 2 2 – 2 2 1 1 – tmp+1 – str
perc: xyl, glock, sd, bd, hi-hat, sus cym, cym, tri, woodblk, tambn, vibrslp, belltree, ratch, 3tomtoms, sandblks, siren whistle, police whistle, klaxon.
Narrator/Conductor.
                                            Instrumental Pops
Pecktackular (rental)

The Thrill of the Orchestra   13'
3[1,2,3/pic] 3[1.2.Eh] 3[1.2.bcl] 3[1.2.cbn] – 4 3 3 1 – tmp+3 – str; Alternate: 2 2 2 2 – 2 2 (1) (1) – tmp+1[or 1 player] – str
perc: tambn, glock, bd, szl cym, tamtam, sd, templeblks, belltree, xyl, chimes, cym, marac, metal wrench, 3sus cym, 3tomtoms, 2tri, (vib).
Narrator.
                                            Instrumental Pops
Pecktackular (rental)

Penderecki, Krysztof   1933-

Threnody: 9'
   To the Victims of Hiroshima
Strings
[24 vln, 10 vla, 10 vc, 8 bass]
                                            Popular Classics
EMI (rental)

Penella, Manuel   1880-1939

El Gato Montés (The Bobcat)   3'
2 2 2 2 – 4 2 3 1 – tmp+2 – str
Score is available for purchase.
                               Animals/International (Spain)
Filarmonika (rental)

Perillo, Steve

Hangoverture   12'
2 2 2 2 – 4 2 2 1 – tmp+perc – str
                                                New Year
Presser (rental)

Perry, Sam   1884-1936

The Phantom of the Opera (1930)   5"
2[1.pic] 2 3]1.2.bcl] 2 – 4 3 3 1 – perc – hp, cel – str
perc: sus cym, tri, bd, tamtam.
Includes: Through the Looking Glass. The publisher confirms that this is just 5 seconds long!
Mark McGurty, arr.
                                            Films/Halloween
T&V (rental)

Perry, William   1930-

The Gasoline Can-Can   3'
3[1.2.3/pic] 3[1.2.Eh] 3[1.2.bcl] 2 – 4 3 3 1 – tmp+4 – hp, pf – str
A novelty piece describing the Grand Prix with optional pots and pans for the crash scene.
                                            Novelty/Sports
Wendel (rental)

Graduation March   3'
3[1.2.pic] 3[1.2.Eh] 3[1.2.bcl] 2 – 4 4 3 1 – tmp+3 – hp, (org) – str
                                            Celebrations
Wendel (rental)

Joy Shall Be Yours in the Morning   2.5'
3[1.2.pic] 2 2 2 – 4 3 3 1 – tmp+3 – (hp, cel) – str
Solo SSATB soloists or SATB Chorus.
A Christmas carol from the musical "Wind in the Willows."
                           Broadway Musicals/Christmas
Wendel (rental)

Persichetti, Vincent   1915-1987

A Lincoln Address   11'
4 3 4 3 – 4 3 3 1 – tmp+perc – str
Narrator
                                               Patriotic
Presser (rental)

Sinfonia Janiculum, Op. 113   23'
4 3 4 3 – 4 3 3 1 – tmp+2 – hp – str
Symphony No. 9, based on the Roman god Janus.
                                            Popular Classics
Presser (rental)

Phillips, John

Monday, Monday   *3'*
   2 1 3[1.2.(bcl)] 1 – (asx, tsx) – 2 2 2 1 – tmp+2
   – pf – str
   perc: drumset, tri, maracas, tambn.
   A hit by the Mamas and the Papas.
   Willis Schaefer, arr.
                               Films/Popular Songs
Leonard (rental)

Phillips, John & Gilliam, Michelle   1935-2001 / 1944-

California Dreamin'   *3'*
   2 1 3[1.2.bcl] 1 – (2sxs) – 2 2 2 1 – perc – pf – str
   perc: drumset, tambn, cowbell.
   A hit by the Mamas and the Papas.
   Willis Schaefer, arr.
                               Popular Songs
Leonard(POP); Luck's (rental)

California Dreamin'   *3'*
   Strings
                               Popular Songs
Leonard

Phillips, Peter   1930-

Interplays: Concerto for Jazz Drums,
Percussion Ensemble and Orchestra
   3[1.2.pic] 2[1.Eh] 2[1.bcl] 2 – 4 3 2 1 – 4perc –
   hp, pf – str
   Solo Jazz Drums.
                               Jazz
AMP (rental)

Piazzolla, Astor   1921-1992

Cuatro Estaciones Porteñas (The Four   *25.5'*
  Seasons in Buenas Aires)   *(5.5' 8.5' 5' 6.5')*
   2 2 2 2 – 4 4 4 1 – perc – str
   perc: orch. bells, xyl.
   Includes: Primavera porteña; Verano porteño; Otoño
   porteño; Invierno porteño.
   Carlos Franzetti, arr.
                               Popular Classics/Seasons
Lagos (rental)

Cuatro Estaciones Porteñas
  (The Four Seasons in Buenas Aires)
   Strings
   Solo Violin.
   Jose Bragato, arr.
                               Popular Classics/Seasons
Lagos (rental)

Cuatro Estaciones Porteñas
  (The Four Seasons in Buenas Aires)
   Strings
   Solo Violin.
   Leonid Desyatnikov, arr.
                               Popular Classics/Seasons
Lagos (rental)

Libertango   *3'*
   Strings
   From *Astor Piazzolla for String Quartet,* Volume 1
                               Dance/International
Curci-Pagani

Michelangelo   *3.5'*
   pf, bandoleon – str
                               Dance/International
Tonos

Milonga del Angel   *6.5'*
   Strings
                               Dance/International
Tonos

Tango No. 1: Coral   *3'*
   Strings
                               Dance/International
Tonos

Tango No. 2: Canyengue   *3'*
   Strings
                               Dance/International
Tonos

Tanguedia 3'
  Strings
                              Dance/International
  Tonos

Tres minutos con la realidad: Tango 3'
  (Three Minutes of Reality)
  Strings
                              Dance/International
  Tonos

Piket, Frederick   1903-1974

Curtain Raiser to an American Play: 6'
  Overture
  3 2 3 2 – 4 3 3 1 – perc – str
                                      Americana
  AMP (rental)

Piston, Walter   1894-1976

Bicentennial Fanfare 2'
  3[1.2.pic] 3[1.2.Eh] 3[1.2.bcl] 3[1.2.cbn] – 4 3 3 1
  – tmp+4 – str
  perc: bd, cym, sd, tamtam, tambn, tri, woodblk.
                              Americana/Fanfare
  AMP (rental)

The Incredible Flutist: 17'
  Ballet Suite for Orchestra
  3[1.2.pic] 31.2.Eh] 3[1.2.bcl] 3[1.2.cbn] – 4 3 3 1
  – tmp+4 – pf – str
  perc: cast, cym bd, glock, sd, tambn, tri.
                              Dance/Popular Classics
  AMP (rental)

Lincoln Center Festival Overture 12'
  3[1.2.pic] 31.2.Eh] 3[1.2.bcl] 3[1.2.cbn] – 4 3 3 1
  – tmp+4 – 2hp, pf – str
  perc: bd, cym, gong, sd, tambn, tri.
  Chorus.
                                      Americana
  AMP (rental)

Plowman, Michael Richard
(See: Tallarico, Tommy)

Pola, Eddie   1907-1995
Wyle, George   1916-2003

It's the Most Wonderful Time of the Year 3'
  1 1 2 1 – 1 2 1 1 – tmp+2 – pf – str
  bells, tri, drumset.
  SATB or SAB chorus.
  Mark Hayes, arr.
                                      Holidays
  Shawnee

Poledouris, Basil   1945-2006

Free Willy Suite (1993) 6'
  3[1.2.3/pic] 3[1.2.Eh] 3[1.2.bcl] 3[1.2.cbn] –
  4 3 3 1 – tmp+5 – hp, pf, 2 synths – str
  perc: drumset, glock, guiro, jingle stix, shaker, tamtam,
  maracas, sus cym, sizzle cym, bd, tri.
                                      Animals/Films
  T&V (rental)

Polster, Ian, arr.   1938 -

Salute to MGM: That's Entertainment 7'
  2[1.2/pic] 2 2 2 – 2 3 3 1 – tmp+5 – str
  perc: temple blks, sus cym, hi hat, sd,bd, bells, chimes,
  xyl, small cowbell.
  Includes: You are My Lucky Star; The Trolley
  Song; Be My Love; Honeysuckle Rose; It's a Most
  Unusual Day; On the Atchison; Topeka and the
  Santa Fe; Singin' in the Rain; San Francisco; Over
  the Rainbow; You Made Me Love You; The Boy
  Next Door; Broadway Melody.
                                      Films
  Leonard (POP); Luck's (rental)

Ponce, Manuel   1882-1948

Estrellita (Star of Love)   3'
     1 1 2 1 – 2 1 1 0 – perc – cel – str
     Adolph Lotter, arr.
                                                         Space
Kalmus

Estrellita   4'
     2hp – strings
     Morton Gould, arr.
                                                         Space
Schirmer (rental)

Ponchielli, Amilcare   1834-1886

La Gioconda: Dance of the Hours   9.5'
     3[1.2.pic] 2 2 2 – 4 4[2crt] 3 1 –tmp+3 – 2hp – str
     perc: glock, tri, bd/(cym).
                                      Dance/New Year
Kalmus

La Gioconda: Dance of the Hours   6'
     3[1.2.pic] 2 2 2 – 4 2 3 0 – tmp+perc – str
     Steven L. Rosenhaus, arr.
                                      Dance/New Year
Masters

Popp, André

Love is Blue (L'Amour est bleu)   4'
     2 2 3[1.2.bcl] 2 – 4 3 3 1 – 1perc – pf – str
     perc: drumset.
     Optional Chorus. In 1967, Paul Mauriat conducted an orchestral "easy listening" version that was a number-one hit in the USA for five weeks on the Billboard Hot 100.
     Fred Barovick, arr.
                                                Popular Songs
Warner Brothers/The Big 3 Music Corporation/ Criterion Music Corp (rental from Luck's)

Popper, David   1843-1913

Hungarian Rhapsodie, Op. 68   8'
     2 2 2 2 – 4 2 3 0 – tmp+1 – str
     perc: glock, tri.
     Solo Cello.
     Schlegel, arr.
                              International/Popular Classics
Kalmus; Luck's

Porcaro, Jeff (See: Paich, David)

Porter, Cole   1891-1964

Cole Porter Classics   2.5'
     1 1 2 1 – 1 2 1 1 – tmp+3 – str
     Includes: Begin the Beguine; Love for Sale; Anything Goes.
     Douglas E. Wagner, arr.
                      Broadway Musicals/Films/Popular Song
Warner

Cole Porter Salute   5.5'
     3[1.2.pic] 2 3[incl bcl] 2 – 4 3 3 1 – tmp+3 – str
     perc: xyl, bells, sd, wind chimes, sus cym, ride cym, shaker.
     Includes: Another Op'nin', Another Show; In the Still of the Night; Anything Goes; Night and Day.
     John Whitney, arr.
                                             Popular Songs
Chappell

Gay Divorcée: Night and Day   4'
     drumset – pf, gtr – strings
     Calvin Custer, arr.
                                        Broadway Musicals/
                                        Films/Popular Song
Warner

Gay Divorcée: Night and Day   4'
     2 1 2 1 – 2 3 2 1 – tmp+4 – (pf) – str
     Steven L. Rosenhaus, arr.
                                        Broadway Musicals/
                                        Films/Popular Song
Warner (POP); EMS or Luck's (rental)

I Get a Kick Out of You 4'
   1 1 1 1 – 4asx – 2 3 3 1 – perc – hp, pf – str
   Morton Gould, arr.
                    Broadway Musicals/Popular Song
Schirmer (rental)

You Do Something to Me 3'
   2 2 2 1 – 4 3 3 1 – drumset – pf, elec bass – str
   From "50 Million Frenchmen"
   Chuck Sayre, arr.
                          Popular Song/Valentine
Warner (POP); EMS

Portman, Rachel 1960-

Chocolat: Suite (2000) 9'
   1[(ethnic fl)] 1 1 1 – 3 0 0 0 – 2perc – hp, pf, (gtr), accordion – str
   perc: vib, tubaphone, tri.
   Includes: Opening; Guillaume's Confession; Greater Problem; The Story of Grandmere and Grandpere; Ashes to the Wind; Roux Returns.
   Music was nominated for an Oscar.
                                     Films
T&V (rental)

The Cider House Rules (1999) 4.5'
   2 1 1 2 – 4 0 3 1 – 2 hp, pf – str
   Nominated for Best Original Score.
                                     Films
T&V (rental)

Emma (1996) 4.5'
   1 0 1 2 – 3 1 2 1 – 2 hp – str
   Won the Oscar for Best Music and Best Original Score.
                                     Films
T&V (rental)

Oliver Twist: Suite (2005) 5.5'
   1 1 1 1 – 4 0 3 0 – 2 hp, pf – str
                                     Films
T&V (rental)

Poulenc, Francis 1899-1963

Fanfare 3'
   0 0 2 3[1.2.cbn] – 2 2 2 0 – tmp+perc
                                     Fanfare
Chester (rental)

Gloria 28'
                            (3' 3' 5' 1' 8' 8')
   3[1.2/pic.pic] 3[1.2.Eh] 3[1.2.bcl] 3[1.2.cbn] – 4 3 3 1 – tmp – hp – str
   Solo Soprano; Chorus.
                                   Christmas
Salabert (rental)

L'histoire de Babar: 22'
The Story of Babar, the Little Elephant
   2[1/pic.2/pic] 2[1.2/Eh] 2[1.2/bcl] 2[1.2/cbn] – 2 1 0 1 – tmp – hp – str
   Solo Narrator.
   Bastiaan Blomhert, arr.
                                   Animals
Chester (rental)

L'histoire de Babar: 22'
The Story of Babar, the Little Elephant
   1[1/pic] 1[1/Eh] 1[1/Ebcl/bcl]] 1 – 1 0 0 0 – perc – pf – str
   Solo Narrator.
   David Matthews, arr.
                                   Animals
Chester (rental)

L'histoire de Babar: 22'
The Story of Babar, the Little Elephant
   2[1/pic.2/pic] 2[1.2/Eh] 2[1.2/bcl] 2[1.2/cbn] – 2 2[1/crt,2] 1 1 – tmp – hp – str
   Solo Narrator.
   Jean Françaix, arr.
                                   Animals
Chester (rental)

Sinfonietta 24'
   2 2 2 2 – 2 2 0 0 – tmp – hp – str
                              Popular Classics
Chester (rental)

Powell, John H. 1882-1963

At the Fair
   2 2 2 2 – 2 2 3 1 – tmp+perc – hp – str
                                   Americana
Schirmer (rental)

The Bourne Identity 6'
   0 0 0 1 – 0 0 0 0 – tmp+perc – synth – str
                                     Films
Kane (rental)

Chicken Run: Final Escape   5'
    3[1.2.3/pic] 3[1.2.3/Eh] 3 3[1.2.3/cbn] – 6 3 4 1 – tmp+perc – hp, balalaika
    SATB Chorus with kazoos.
                                                 Animals/Films
Kane (rental)

Chicken Run: Make a Crate   3.3'
    2[1/pic.2/pic] 2[1.2Eh] 2 2[1.2/cbn] – 6 3 4 1 – tmp+perc – hp, pf, gtr, balalaika
    SATB Chorus with kazoos.
                                                 Animals/Films
Kane (rental)

Happy Feet: The Story of Mumble   4'
    2 1 3[1.2.bcl] 1 – 4 3 3 1 – tmp+5 – str
    perc: xyl, chimes, sd, bd, Mambo bell (or opt. drumset), td, claves, police whistle, congas, bongos.
    Jack Bullock, arr.
                                                 Animals/Films
Warner

Endurance: The Great Tree
    3[1.2.pic] 2 2 1 – 4 0 0 0 – cel – str
                                                            Films
Kane (rental)

Suite from Ice Age: The Meltdown   4.5'
    3[1.2.3/pic] 3[1.2.3/Eh] 3[1.2.3/bcl] 3[1.2.3/cbn] – 4 3 4 1 – tmp+perc – hp, pf/cel, gtr (ukelele) – str
                                                             Films
Kane (rental)

In Old Virginia: Overture, Op. 28   11'
    4 3 3 2 – 4 2 3 1 – tmp+perc – hp – str
                                                           Americana
Schirmer (rental)

Mr. and Mrs. Smith: Tango de los Asesinos   4.5'
    1 0 0 0 – 4 3 3 1 – tmp+perc – hp, pf, accordion, gtr – str
                                                         Dance/Films
Kane (rental)

Natchez on the Hill: 4'
   Three Virginia Country Dances
    3[1.2.pic] 2 2 2 – 4 2 2 1 – tmp+2 – hp – str
    perc: tri, sd, bells
    Composed for the Bicentennial Musical Celebration (gift from J. C. Penney).
                                                 Americana/Dance
Schirmer (rental)

A Set of Three   16'
    3 3 3 3 – 4 3 3 1 – tmp+perc – hp – str
                                                 Instrumental Pops
Schirmer (rental)

X-Men: The Last Stand
    3[1.2.3/pic] 3[1.2.3/Eh] 3 3[1.2.cbn] – 4 3 3 1 – tmp+perc – hp, pf, org – str
                                                             Films
Kane (rental)

Prima, Louis   1910-1978

Jump, Jive an' Wail   3.5'
    drumset – pf – strings
    Lloyd Edgar Conley, arr.
                                                              Jazz
Leonard

Prizeman, Robert   1952-

Songs of Praise: Toccata   6'
    0 0 0 0 – 4 3 3 0 – tmp+perc – org
                                                Holidays (Easter)
Chester (rental)

Prokofiev, Sergei   1891-1953

Cinderella: Suite No. 1, Op. 107   26'
                                (3' 3' 3' 5' 5' 3' 3' 2')
    3[1.2.pic] 3[1.2.Eh] 3[1.2.bcl] 3[1.2.cbn] – 4 3 3 1 – tmp+6 – hp – str
    perc: glock, xyl, tri, tambn, field dr, cym, bd, chimes (c'), tamtam, woodblk, cast.
    Includes: Introduction; Pas de Chat; Quarrel; Fairy Godmother & Fairy Winter; Mazurka; Cinderella Goes to the Ball; Cinderella's Waltz; Midnight.
                                 Dance/New Year (final mvt)/ Popular Classics
Russian (rental)

Cinderella: Suite No.2, Op. 108 17'
    3[1.2.pic] 3[1.2.Eh] 3[1.2.bcl] 3[1.2.cbn] – 4 3 3 1
    – tmp+4 – hp, cel/pf – str
    perc: xyl, tri, tambn, field dr, cym, marac, glock, bd, woodblk, cast.
    Includes: Cinderella's Dream; Dancing Lesson and Gavotte; Fairy of Spring & Fairy of Summer; Bourrée; Cinderella in the Castle; Galop.
                                      Dance/Popular Classics
Russian (rental)

Lieutenant Kijé: Suite, Op. 60 20'
                          (4' 5' 3' 2' 6')
    3[1.2.pic] 2 2 2 – tsx – 4 3[1.2.(crt)] 3 1 – 3perc
    – hp, cel/pf – str
    perc: sd, slgh-bells, cym, tambn, bd, tri.
    Includes: The Birth of Kijé; Romance; Kijé's Wedding; Troika; The Burial of Kijé.
    Optional Baritone Voice.
                                                  Popular Classics
Boosey (rental)

Love for Three Oranges: 4'
March & Scherzo
    3[1.2.pic] 3[1.2.Eh] 3[1.2.bcl] 3[1.2.cbn] – 4 3 3 1
    – tmp+6 – 2hp – str
    perc: glock, xyl, tri, field dr., cym, bd.
                                                  Popular Classics
Boosey (rental)

Peter and the Wolf: 25'
Symphonic Tale for Narrator and Orchestra, Op. 67
    1 1 1 1 – 3 1 1 0 – tmp+2 – str
    perc: bd, sd(field dr), cast, cym, sus cym, tri, tambn.
    Narrator.
                                          Animals/Popular Classics
Russian (rental)

Romeo and Juliet: Scenes from the Ballet 45'
    3 3 3 3 – tsx – 6 3[crt] 3 1 – tmp+perc – hp, cel, pf
    – str
    Rudolf Barshai, arr.
                                      Popular Classics/Valentine
Russian (rental)

Romeo and Juliet: Suite No. 1, Op. 64a 28'
    3[1.2.pic] 3[1.2.Eh] 3[1.2.bcl] 3[1.2.cbn] – tsx
    – 4 3[1.2.crt] 3 1 – tmp+5 – hp, pf – str
    perc: glock, xyl, tambn, field dr, tri, cym, bd, sd.
    Includes: Folk Dance; Scene; Madrigal; Minuet; Masks; Romeo and Juliet; The Death of Tybalt.
                                      Popular Classics/Valentine
Russian (rental)

Romeo and Juliet: Suite No. 2, Op. 64b 30'
    3[1.2.pic] 3[1.2.Eh] 3[1.2.bcl] 3[1.2.cbn] – tsx
    – 4 3[1.2.crt] 3 1 – tmp+2 – hp, pf/cel
    – str[(va d'amore)]
    perc: glock, tambn, cym, sd, bd, marac, tri.
    Includes: The Montagues and the Capulets; Juliet - The Young Girl; Friar Laurence; Dance; Romeo and Juliet before Parting; Dance of the Maids from the Antilles; Romeo at Juliet's Grave.
                                      Popular Classics/Valentine
Russian (rental)

Romeo and Juliet: Suite No. 3, Op. 101 20'
    3[1.2.pic] 3[1.2.Eh] 3[1.2.bcl] 3[1.2.cbn] – 4 3 3 1
    – tmp+2 – hp, pf, cel – str
    perc: woodblk, glock, bd, cym, tambn, tri, sd.
    Includes: Romeo at the Fountain; Morning Dance; Juliet; Nurse; Morning Serenade; Juliet's Death.
                                    Dance/Popular Classics
Russian (rental)

Winter Bonfire: Suite, Op. 122 20'
    2 1 2 1 – 4 2 1 1 – tmp+perc – cel, pf – str
    Narrator; Boys' Chorus.
                                                        Christmas
Schirmer (rental)

Proto, Frank 1941-

Casey at the Bat 13'
    3[incl pic] 3[incl Eh] 3[incl bcl] 3 – 4 3 3 1 – tmp+4
    – hp, pf, elec bass – electronic tape (crowd noises)
    – str
    Narrator.
                                                            Sports
Liben (rental)

Fantasy on the Saints 8-12'
    3[incl pic] 3[incl Eh] 3[incl bcl] 3 – 4 3 3 1 – tmp+4
    – hp, cel/pf, (elec bass) – str
    Optional jazz section.
                                                               Jazz
Liben (rental)

Pryor, Arthur 1870-1942

The Whistler and His Dog 3.5'
    1 1 2 1 – 2 2[crt] 1 0 – perc – str
                                                            Animals
Kalmus

Puccini, Giacomo 1858-1924

I crisantemi 6'
(The Chrysanthemums)
   Strings
                                    Popular Classics
   Kalmus; Luck's; Ricordi

Gianni Schicchi: 5'
   O mio babbino caro
   2 3[1.2.Eh] 2 2 – 4 0 0 0 – hp – str
   Solo Soprano.
                                    Popular Classics
   Kalmus

Madam Butterfly for Orchestra 8'
   3 3 3 3 – 4 3 3 1 – tmp+perc – hp – str
   Alfredo Antonini, arr.
                                    Popular Classics
   Bourne (rental)

Le Villi: Intermezzo – La Tregenda 4'
"The Witches' Sabbath"
   3[incl pic] 2 2 2 – 4 0 3 1 – tmp+perc – str
                                      Halloween
   Boccaccini (rental)

Putman, Curly

Green Green Grass of Home 2'
   2 1 3[1.2.bcl] 1 – 2 2 2 1 – tmp+ 2 – pf – str
   perc: temple blks, sd, bd, vib, glock.
   Piano/Conductor Score.
   Willis Schaefer, arr.
                                    Instrumental Pops
   Leonard (rental)

Q

Quilter, Roger 1877-1953

Where the Rainbow Ends Suite 11'
   2 2 2 2 – 4 2 3 0 – tmp+perc – hp – str
                                    Weather
   Novello (rental)

R

Rachmaninoff, Sergei   1873-1943

The Isle of the Dead, Op. 29   20'
3[1.2.3/pic] 3[1.2.Eh] 3[1.2.bcl] 3[1.2.cbn] –
6 3 3 1 – tmp+2 – hp – str
perc: bd, cym.
                        Halloween/Popular Classics
Boosey; Kalmus; Luck's

Raksin, David   1912-2004

The Bad and the Beautiful:
   I. Love Is for the Very Young
2[1.2.3/pic] 3[1.2.Eh] 3[1.2.3/cbn] – asx – 4 3 4 1 –
tmp+perc – hp, pf/cel – str
                        Films
Kane (rental)

The Bad and the Beautiful:
   II. The Acting Lesson
Strings
                        Films
Kane (rental)

The Bad and the Beautiful:
   III. The Quickies and Sneak Preview
3[1.2/afl. 3/pic] 3[1.2.Eh] 3[1.2.3/bcl] 3[1.2.3/cbn]
– asx – 4 3[c.Bb.Bb] 4 1 – tmp+perc – hp, pf/cel
– str
                        Films
Kane (rental)

Forever Amber: I. Main Title "Amber"
3[1.2/afl.3/afl/pic] 2 3 3[1.2.cbn] – 4 4 3 1 –
tmp+perc – hp, cel – str
1974 record version
                        Films
Kane (rental)

Forever Amber: II. The King's Mistress
2 3[1.2.Eh] 3 3 – 4 3 3 1 – tmp+perc – hp, cel – str
1974 record version
                        Films
Kane (rental)

Forever Amber: III. Whitefriars;
   IV. The Great Fire
4[1.2/pic.3/afl/pic.4/afl/pic] 3[1/Eh.2/Eh.Eh]
4[1.2.(3).bcl/contrabcl] 4[1.2.3.4/cbn] – 4 4 4 1 –
tmp+perc hp, pf/cel – str
1974 record version.
                        Films
Kane (rental)

Forever Amber: V. End Title "Finale"
3[1.2.3/pic] 3[1.2.Eh] 3 3[1.2.3/cbn] – 4 3 3 1 –
tmp+perc – hp – str
1974 record version.
                        Films
Kane (rental)

Forever Amber: Suite (1947)
4[I.afl/pic.afl/pic.afl/pic] 3[1.(Eh).Eh]
4[1.2.3.bcl/(Ebcl)] 0 – 4 4 4 1 – tmp+3 –
hp, pf[cel] – str
perc: cym, sus cym, chimes, bd[w. attached cym], tri,
sm tri, lg gong, sd, td, xyl, glock.
Nominated for an Oscar.
                        Films
T&V (rental)

Laura   3'
2 2 3[1.2.bcl] 2 – asx, tsx – 4 2 3 1 – tmp+2 – str
perc: glock, sd, bd, sus cym.
Theme melody from the 20th Century-Fox film
"Laura."
Alfred Rickey, arr.
                        Films
Robbins (POP); Luck's (rental)

Laura: Laura's Theme
3[1.2.pic] 3[1.2.Eh] 3[1.2.3/bcl] 3[1.2.3/cbn] –
4 3 3 1 – tmp+perc – hp, pf/cel – str
Optional Baritone Voice.
From the 1944 film directed by Otto Preminger.
                        Films
Kane (rental)

Toy Concertino   6'
2[1.2/pic] 1 2 1 – 2 2 0 0 – tmp+1 – str
perc: bd/cym.
concertino = 8 players: tin fife, pic tpt, ocarina in G
and C, toy glock, bird warble, toy sd, cuckoo call.
                        Instrumental Pops
Broude Bros. (rental)

Ramsey, Elmer

Rhapsody for Trumpet   6'
    2[1.pic] 2 3[1.2.bcl] 2 – 4 3 3 1 – tmp+1 – str
    perc: sus cym, sd, bd, cym.
    Solo Trumpet. Optional SATB Chorus.
                                    Instrumental Pops
Sherwood (rental)

Ran, Shulamit   1949-

Chicago Skyline   5.5'
    0 0 0 0 – 6 4 3 2 – tmp+3 – [no str]
                                      Americana
Presser (rental)

Ranjbaran, Behzad   1955-

Seven Passages   14'
    3 3 3 3 – 4 3 3 1 – tmp+3 – hp, cel – str
    From his "Persian Trilogy." Based on the Persian legend about the seven labors of Rostam – a Persian Hercules.
                                      International
Presser (rental)

Thomas Jefferson   16'
    2[incl pic] 2 2 2 – 4 3 3 1 – tmp+2 – hp – str
    Narrator; Solo Cello.
                                      Patriotic
Presser (rental)

Rasmussen, Karl Aage   1947-

Symphony for Young Lovers   18'
    3 3[incl Eh] 3[incl bcl] 2 – tsx – 4 3 3 1 – tmp+perc – hp, pf – str
                                      Valentine
Schirmer (rental)

Ravel, Maurice   1875-1937

Bolero   13'
    3[1.2.pic] 3[1.2/ob d'amour.Eh] 3[1.2/Ebcl.bcl] 3[1.2.cbn] – ssx, tsx – 4 4 3 1 – tmp+4 – hp, cel – str
    perc: bd, cym, 2sd, tamtam, cel.
                                     Dance/Popular Classics
Durand (rental)

Bolero   5'
    3 3[1.2.Eh] 3[incl Ebcl] 3 – 4 4 3 1 – tmp+3 – pf, hp, (Fender bass) – str
    From the Blake Edwards movie "10."
    Henry Mancini, arr.
                                      Films
Janen (rental)

Daphnis et Chloé: Suite No. 1   12'
                                      (5' 3' 4')
    4[1.2/pic2.pic1.afl] 3[1.2.Eh] 4[1.2.Ebcl.bcl] 4[1.2.3.sarr] – 4 4 3 1 – tmp+6 – 2hp, cel – str
    perc: bd, cym, sd, tri, tambn, tamtam, glock, crot, wind machine.
    Optional Chorus.
    Includes: Nocturne; Interlude; Danse guerrière.
    Kalmus edition by Clark McAlister.
                                     Dance/Popular Classics
Durand (rental); Kalmus

Daphnis et Chloé: Suite No. 2   18'
                                      (6' 7' 5')
    4[1.2/pic2.pic1.afl] 3[1.2.Eh] 4[1.2.Ebcl.bcl] 4[1.2.3.sarr] – 4 4 3 1 – tmp+7 – 2hp, cel – str
    perc: bd, cym, sd, military drum, tri, tambn, cast, jeu de timbres à clavier.
    Optional Chorus. Percussion can be covered by 5 players. Includes: Lever Du Jour; Pantomime; Danse générale.
    Kalmus edition by Clinton F. Nieweg.
                                     Dance/Popular Classics
Durand (rental); Kalmus

Ma Mère l'Oye (Mother Goose: Suite) 16'
                                             (2' 3' 3' 4' 4')
    2[1.2/pic] 2[1.2/Eh] 2 2[1.2/cbn] – 2 0 0 0 – tmp+3
    – hp, cel – str
    perc: bd, cym, tri, tamtam, xyl, jeu de timbres à clavier.
    Includes: Pavane de la Belle au bois dormant (Pavane of the Sleeping Beauty); Petit Poucet (Tom Thumb); Laideronnette, impératrice des pagodes (Laideronnette, empress of the pagodas); Les Entretiens de la Belle et de la Bête (Conversations of Beauty and the Beast); Le Jardin féerique (The enchanted garden).
    Kalmus edition by Bradburd and Nieweg.
                                                         Popular Classics
    Durand (rental); Kalmus

Ma Mère l'Oye: Prélude et Danse du rouet 7'
                                                  (3' 4')
    2[1.2/pic] 2[1.2/Eh] 2 2 – 2 0 0 0 – tmp+3 – hp, cel – str
    perc: cym, sus cym, sd, tri, tamtam, jeu de timbres à clavier, xyl.
    Kalmus edition by Clinton F. Nieweg.
                                           Dance/Popular Classics
    Durand (rental); Kalmus

Pavane pour une infante défunte 6'
(Pavane for a dead princess)
    2 1 2 2 – 2 0 0 0 – hp – str
    Kalmus edition by Carl Simpson
                                                Popular Classics
    Eschig; Kalmus

Rapsodie espagnole 17'
                                            (5' 3' 3' 6')
    4[1.2.pic1.pic2] 3[1.2.Eh] 3[1.2.bcl] 4[1.2.3.sarr]
    – 4 3 3 1 – tmp+7 – 2hp, cel – str
    perc: bd, cym, sd, tri, tambn, tamtam, xyl, cast.
    Includes: Prélude à la nuit; Malagueña; Habanera; Feria.
    Kalmus edition by Nieweg & Bradburd.
                                     International/Popular Classics
    Durand (rental); Kalmus

Rebagliati, Claudio   1843-1909

Rapsodia Peruana 12'
    2 2 2 2 – 4 2 2 1 – tmp+3 – str
    Score available for purchase.
                                                 International (Peru)
    Filarmonika (rental)

Reed, Alfred   1921-2005

A Festival Prelude 5'
    3[1.2.pic] 3[1.2.(Eh)] 4[1.2.bcl.(cbcl)] 3]1.2.cbn]
    – (2asx, tsx, bsx) – 4 3 3 1 – tmp+2 – str
    perc: cym, tri, sd, bd.
                                              Instrumental Pops
    Leonard

Greensleeves 5'
    2[1.2/pic] 3[1.2.Eh] 3[1.2.bcl] 3[1.2.cbn] – 4 3 3 1
    – tmp+perc – hp – str
                                                    Christmas
    Kalmus

Pledge of Allegiance 2.5'
    2 3[1.2.Eh] 3[1.2.bcl] 2 – 4 3 3 1 – tmp+perc – str
    Mixed Chorus.
                                                      Patriotic
    Kalmus

Reed, Les (See: Mills, Gordon)

Reger, Max   1873-1916

Christmas with Renata Scotto: 2'
    7. *Virgin's Slumber Song*
    Strings
    Solo Soprano. Original title is *Weihnachten* and is one of a set of 7 organ works.
    John Grady, arr.
                                                    Christmas
    AMP (rental)

Weihnachten (Christmas), Op. 145/3 5'
    1 1 2 1 – 2 2 1 0 –perc – str
    Also available in a version for strings. Originally from a set of 7 organ works.
    O. Meyer, arr.
                                                    Christmas
    Breitkopf (rental); Kalmus (strings only)

Regney, Noel & Shayne, Gloria

Do You Hear What I Hear   3'
2 2 3[1.2.bcl] 2 – 2asx, tsx, bsx – 2 3 3 1 – tmp+2 – str
perc: chimes, glock, drumset.
Key of C Major, changing to D, then F Major.
Robert W. Lowden, arr.

                               Christmas

Regent (rental)

Do You Hear What I Hear   4'
2 1 4[1.2.3.4/acl/bcl] 1 – 2asx, tsx, bsx – 4 3 3 1 – tmp+2 – str
perc: includes mallets.
SATB Chorus. 25 chorus copies available on rental. Must perform with chorus. Key of Eb Major modulating to F.
Warren Barker, arr.

                               Christmas

Regent (rental)

Reinagle, Alexander   1756-1809

Federal March   3'
1[incl pic] 2 2 1 – 2 0 0 0 – tmp – str
Sam Dennison, arr.

                               Patriotic

Kalmus

Madison's March   3'
1 2 2 1 – 2 0 0 0 – tmp – str
Sam Dennison, arr.

                          Instrumental Pops

Kalmus

Mrs. Madison's Minuet   4'
1 2 2 1 – 2 0 0 0 – tmp – str
Sam Dennison, arr.

                                    Dance

Kalmus

Reisfeld, Bert   1906-

California Concerto   10'
2 1 2 1 – 4 3 3 0 – tmp+perc – str
Solo Piano.

                               Americana

Sikorski (rental)

Reitz, Ric

To the Flag   5'
3[incl pic] 3[1.2.Eh] 3[1.2.bcl] 2 – 4 3 3 1 – tmp+2 – hp – str
perc: drumset, mallets.
Based on Francis Bellamy's 1892 "Pledge of Allegiance."
Bill Holcombe, arr.

                               Patriotic

Luck's (rental)

Respighi, Ottorini   1879-1936

Antiche danze ed arie (Ancient Airs and Dances):
   Suite I   16'
                   (3' 4' 5' 4')
     2 3[1.2.Eh] 0 2 – 2 1 0 0 – hp, hpsd – str

                Dance/Popular Classics

Kalmus; Ricordi (rental)

   Suite II   19'
                   (4' 4' 5' 6')
     3[1.2.3/pic] 3[1.2.Eh] 2 2 – 3 2 3 0 – tmp – hp, hpsd [4hands] – str

                Dance/Popular Classics

Ricordi (rental)

   Suite III   19'
                   (4' 8' 3' 4')
   Strings

                Dance/Popular Classics

Ricordi (rental)

La boutique fantasque: Suite (after Rossini)   18'
[The Fantastic Toy Shop]
               (2' 2' 2' 2' 2' 4' 4' 2')
3[1.2.pic] 3[1.2.Eh] 2 2 – 4 3 3 1 – tmp+5 – hp, cel – str
perc: glock, tambn, tri, xyl, sd, cym, bd, cast.
Includes: Overture; Tarantella; Mazurka; Danse cosaque; Can-can; Valse lente; Nocturne; Galop.
Kalmus edition by Nancy M. Bradburd.

               Halloween/Popular Classics

Chester (rental); Kalmus

Gli uccelli (The Birds)   19'
                                   (3' 5' 3' 4' 4')
   2[incl pic] 1 2 2 – 2 2 0 0 – hp, cel – str
   Preludio (Prelude); La colomba (The Dove); La gallina (The Hen); L'usignolo (The Nightingale); Il cuccù (The Cuckoo).

                                                 Animals

Ricordi (rental)

The Pines of Rome: 20'
  Pines of the Appian Way   (3' 6' 6' 5')
   3[1.2.3/pic] 3[1.2.Eh] 3[1.2.bcl] 3[1.2.bcl] – 6 4 3 1 – tmp+5 – hp, cel, pf, org – 6 buccine – str
   perc: glock, tamtam, tri, cym, tambn, bd, 2small cym, nightingale recording[supplied with parts], ratch.
   Includes: I pini di Villa Borghese (The pines of the Villa Borghese); Pini presso una catacomba (Pines near a catacomb); I pini del Gianicolo (The Pines of the Janiculum); I pini della Fia Appia (The pines of the Appian Way).
                                      Ecology/PopularClassics

Ricordi (rental)

Trittico Botticelliano: 2. Adoration of the Magi   7'
   1 1 1 1 – 1 1 0 0 – 1perc – hp, cel, pf – str
   perc: glock, tri.
                                              Christmas

Ricordi (rental)

Revaux, J. & Francois, C.

My Way   4'
   2 1 2 1 – asx, tsx – 2 3 3 1 – tmp+1 – gtr, elec bs – str
   perc: drumset.
   Arrangement of the popular song performed by Paul Anka.
   John Cacavas, arr.
                                            Popular Song

Spanka (rental)

Revueltas, Silvestre   1899-1940

Paisajes (Landscapes)   20'
   1 0 1 1 – 1 2 1 1 – tmp+perc – pf – str
                                                    Ecology

Peer (rental)

Sensemaya   7'
   4[1.2.pic1.pic2] 3[1.2.Eh] 3[1.2.Ebcl.bcl] 4[incl cbn] – 4 4 3 1 – tmp+3 – pf – str
   Alternate: 1[incl pic] 0 2[incl Ebcl,bcl] 1 – 0 2 1 0 – 5perc – pf – vn, db
   perc: xyl, claves, cym, glock, bd, 2gongs, 2tomtoms, small Indian drum, raspador, gourd.
   Mexican folk and street music.
                                             International

Schirmer (rental)

Reznicek, Emil Nikolaus von   1860-1945

Donna Diana: Overture   5'
   3[1.2.3/pic] 2 2 2 – 4 2 0 0 – tmp+1 – (hp) – str
   perc: tri.
                                       Popular Classics

Kalmus

Rhodes, Phillip   1940-

Bluegrass Festival: Suite for Bluegrass   18'
  Quartet and Orchestra
   2 2 2 2 – 4 2 3 1 – tmp+2 – str
   Solo Bluegrass Quartet: bnjo, mand, gtr, db.
   Includes: Breakdown; Ballad [incl singer]; Variations. Also known as *Concerto for Bluegrass Band and Orchestra*.
                                            Americana

EMI (rental)

Richards, Johnny   1911-1968

Cuban Fire Suite: La Suerte de los Tontos   4.5'
(Fortune of Fools)
   3[1.2.pic] 2 1[1.2.bcl] 2 – 4 3 3 1 – tmp+4 – pf – str
   perc: bongos, maracas, conga, claves, cowbell, timbales, drumset.
   John Whitney, arr.
                                   Instrumental Pops/
                                   International (Cuba)

Warner

La Suerte de los Tantos   5'
(Fortune of Fools)
    3[1.2.pic] 2 3[1.2.bcl] 2 – 4 3 3 1 – tmp+5/6 – pf – str
    perc: bongos, maracas, conga, claves, timbales/cowbell, drumset.
    Richards was the chief arranger for Stan Kenton. John Whitney, arr.

                                    Jazz
Warner

Richardson, Clive, arr.   1910-1999

British Grenadiers   1.5'
    2[1.pic] 1 2 1 – 2sx – 2 2 2 0 – tmp+perc – pf – str
                                   International
Kalmus

Polly-Wolly-Doodle   1.5'
    2 1 2 1 – 2sx – 2 2 2 0 – tmp+drumset – str
                       Americana/Popular Song
Kalmus

Richman, Lucas   1964-

Beautiful Dreamer: Stephen Foster's America   13.5'
    3 2 2 2 – 4 3 3 1 – tmp+3 – hp – str
    Includes: Beautiful Dreamer, I Dream of Jeannie, Camptown Races, and more.
                     Americana/Popular Song
LeDor (rental)

The Brentwood Rag   3'
    2 2 2 2 – 2 2 1 0 – perc – str
                                     Jazz
LeDor (rental)

Christmas Is Coming   3'
    2 2 2 2 – 2 2 2 1 – tmp+2 – hp – str
    Children's Choir.
    An original melody is sung in counterpoint to the carol: *Sing We Now of Christmas.*
                                 Holidays
LeDor (rental)

Christmas Singalong   10'
    3 2 2 2 – 4 3 3 1 – tmp+2 – str
                                 Holidays
LeDor (rental)

A Christmas Wish   55'
    2 2 2 2 – 2 2 2 1 – tmp+2 – hp – str
    A one-act musical suitable for full theatrical presentations or in concert version.
                                 Holidays
LeDor (rental)

Colonial Liberty Overture   6'
    3 2 2 2 – 4 3 3 1 – tmp+2 – hp – str
                                 Patriotic
LeDor (rental)

Coventry Carol   3'
    hp – str
    Chorus.
                                   Holidays
LeDor (rental)

Hanukkah Festival Overture   6.5'
    3 2 2 2 – 4 3 3 1 – tmp+2 – hp – str
                                 Holidays
LeDor (rental)

Hanukkah Medley   4.5'
    2 2 2 2 – 2 2 0 0 – tmp+2 – hp – str
    Includes: Mi Yimalel, S'vi-von.
    Solo Soprano.
                                 Holidays
LeDor (rental)

Ho! Ho! Ho!   2.5'
    2 2 2 2 – 2 2 2 1 – tmp+2 – hp – str
    Solo Baritone; Chorus.
                                 Holidays
LeDor (rental)

In the Day When I Cried Out (Cantata)   15'
    2 2 2 2 – 4 2 3 1 – tmp+2 – hp, pf – str
    Solo Vocal Quartet; Gospel Choir.
                     Black History Month/
                         Martin Luther King
LeDor (rental)

An Overture to Blanche   9'
    2 2 2 2 – tsx – 2 2 2 1 – tmp+2 – pf – str
    Inspired by Tennessee Williams play *A Streetcar Named Desire.*
                                      Films
LeDor (rental)

Presents from Santa   3'
    2 2 2 2 – 2 2 2 1 – tmp+2 – hp – str
    Solo Baritone.
                                 Holidays
LeDor (rental)

Reindeer Variations   7.5'
    2 2 2 2 – 2 2 2 1 – tmp+2 – hp – str
    From the one-act musical *A Christmas Wish*.
                                           Holidays
    LeDor (rental)

Shena B'rachot   7'
    cl – hp – str
    Solo Tenor or Soprano.
    Traditionally sung at Jewish weddings.
                                           Celebration
    LeDor (rental)

Take a Ride With Santa   3'
    2 2 2 2 – 2 2 2 1 – tmp+2 – hp – str
    Solo Child Alto.
                                             Holidays
    LeDor (rental)

Thanksgiving Hymn   2.5'
    2 2 2 2 – 2 2 2 1 – tmp+2 – hp – str
    Solo Soprano and Baritone; Chorus
                                           Holidays
    LeDor (rental)

A Western Fanfare   3'
    2 2 2 2 – 2 2 1 0 – tmp+1 – hp –str
                                       Americana/Fanfare
    LeDor (rental)

Ricketts, Ted, arr.

Satchmo!: A Tribute to Louis Armstrong   4.5'
    2 1 3[incl bcl] 1 – 4 3 3 1 – tmp+3 – pf – str
    Includes Hello, Dolly!; St. Louis Blues; What A
    Wonderful World; When the Saints Go Marching
    In.
                                           Jazz
    Leonard

Riege, Ernst   1885-1976

Bezaubernde Gloriette, Konzertwalzer   8'
    2 1 2 1 – 4 2 3 0 – tmp+perc – hp – str
                                      Dance/International
    Sikorski (rental)

Ewiges Wien   11'
    2 2 2 2 – 4 2 3 1 – tmp+perc – hp – str
                                        International
    Sikorski (rental)

Katharinen-Waltz   9'
    2 2 2 2 – 4 2 3 0 – tmp+perc – hp – str
                                           Dance
    Sikorski (rental)

Riegger, Wallingford   1885-1961

Dance Rhythms, Op. 58   8'
    2[1.2/pic] 2 2 2 – 2 2 2 0 – tmp+4 – hp – str
                                           Dance
    AMP (rental)

New Dance, Op. 18b: Finale from the Ballet   5'
    3[1.2.pic] 3[incl Eh] 3[incl bcl] 3 – asx – 4 3 3 1
    – tmp+2 – hp – str
    Choreographed by Martha Graham under the title
    Steps in the Street.
                                         Dance
    AMP (rental)

Quintuple Jazz, Op. 72   7'
    3 3 2 2 – asx – 4 3 3 1 – tmp+perc – str
                                           Jazz
    AMP (rental)

Rimelis, David   1954-

Please Turn Your Cell Phones On! (2003)   8.5'
    2 2 2 2 – 4 3 3 1 – tmp+2[incl drumset] – str
    A duet between cell phones ringing and the
    orchestra playing with a section where the audience
    rings their phones on cue to the music.
                                           Novelty
    LKMP (rental)

Rimsky-Korsakov, Nicolai   1844-1908

Capriccio Espagnol, Op. 34   15'
(1' 5' 1' 5' 3')
3[1.2.pic] 2[1/Eh.2] 2 2 – 4 2 3 1 – tmp+5 – hp – str
perc: bd, cym, sd, tri, tambn, cast.
Includes: Alborada; Variazioni; Alborada; Scena e canto gitano; Fandango asturiano.
Kalmus edition by Clinton F. Nieweg and Stuart S. Serio.
                         International/Popular Classics
Belaieff; Kalmus

Christmas Eve: Polonaise   5'
3[1.2.pic] 2 3 2 – 4 3 3 1 – tmp+4 – hp – str
                         Christmas
Belaieff; Kalmus; Luck's

Le coq d'or (The Golden Cockerel):   9'
Introduction & Wedding March
3[1.2.pic] 3[1.2.Eh] 3[1.2.bcl] 3[1.2.cbn] – 4 3[1.2.alto tp] 3 1 – tmp+4 – 2hp, cel – str
perc: bd, cym, sd, tri, chimes.
                         Popular Classics/Valentine
Kalmus; Luck's

May Night: Overture   8'
2 2 2 2 – 4 2 3 0 – tmp – str
                         Popular Classics/Seasons
Belaieff (rental); Kalmus

Scheherazade: 4. The Sea-Shipwreck   11'
3[1.2.pic] 2[1.2/Eh] 2 2 – 4 2 3 1 – tmp+5 – hp – str
Included in the complete work. Kalmus edition by Clinton F. Nieweg and Andrew S. Holmes.
                         Popular Classics
Belaieff (rental); Kalmus

The Tale of Tsar Saltan: 3'
Flight of the Bumble Bee
2 2 2 2 – 4 2 3 1 – tmp+1 – str
Can be played with 2 2 2 2 – 2 0 0 0 – str
perc: cym.
The 3rd & 4th hrns, trumpets, tbns, tuba, timpani & percussion only play the 1st chord.
                         Animals
Kalmus; Russian (rental)

The Tale of Tsar Saltan: 3'
Flight of the Bumble Bee (Hummelflüg)
1 1 1 1 – 3 1 0 0 – tmp+1 – str
perc: sd.
Solo Trumpet.
Dokshitser, arr.
                         Animals
EMR

Ringwald, Roy   1910-1995

O Brother Man
3[1.2.pic] 2 3 2 – 2asx, tsx, bsx – 4 3 3 1 – perc – str
SATB or TTBB or SAB or two-part Chorus.
Hawley Ades, arr.
                         Popular Song
Shawnee (rental)

The Song of America   12'
2 2 3[1.2.bcl] 2 – 3 4 3 1 – tmp+perc – hp, pf – str
Narrator; SATB Chorus.
                         Patriotic
Shawnee (rental)

The Song of Easter
2 0 2 1 – 3 3 3 0 – tmp+perc – str
SATB Chorus.
                         Holidays
Shawnee (rental)

The Song of Christmas   7'
2[1.2.pic] 2 4[1.2.bcl] 1 – 2asx, tsx, bsx – 3 3[crt] 3 1 – tmp+perc – str
SATB or SSA or SAB Chorus.
Includes: O Come Emanuel; While Shepherds Watched Over Their Flocks; Angels We Have Heard On High; What Child Is This?; We Three Kings.
William Schoenfeld, orchestrator
                         Christmas
Shawnee

Rio, Chuck (Daniel Flores)   1929-2006

Tequila   1.5'
3[1.2.pic] 2 2 1 – 4 3 2 1 – 3perc – str
Chuck Sayre, arr.
                         International
Warner (POP); EMS or Luck's (rental)

Robinson, Earl   1910-1991

A Country They Call Puget Sound   16'
2[incl pic] 2 2[1.2.bcl] 2 – 4 3 3 1 – perc – str
Solo Tenor.

                                        Americana
Shawnee (rental)

In the Folded and Quiet Yesterdays   8'
2[incl pic] 3[1.2.Eh] 3[1.2.bcl] 3[1.2.cbn] – 2 2 2 1
– perc – hp, pf – str
Solo Voice; SATB Chorus. Text by Carl Sandburg.
                                          New Year
Shawnee (rental)

The Lonesome Train   35'
2[incl pic] 2[1.Eh] 2 2 – 2 3 2 1 – tmp+perc –
hp, pf, gtr, bnjo – str;
Alternate: afl(cl) 0 1(bcl) 0 – 0 0 1 0 – tmp+perc –
4gtr(3bnjo), harmonica (melodica), accordion –
vn, db
Solo High Baritone; 2 Narrators; Double SATB
Chorus.

                                             Travel
Shawnee (rental)

Robinson, Walter H.   1952-

Harriet Tubman   5'
3[incl pic] 2 3[incl bcl] 3[incl cbn] – 4 3 3 1 – perc
– pf, org, elec bass, gtr – str
Chorus.
Michael Runyan, arr.

                               Black History Month
Schirmer (rental)

Robinson, Wayne & Giovannini, Caesar

Brazilian Polka   2'
2[1.2/pic] 2 2 – 4 3 3 1– tmp+2 – str
perc: tambn, marim, xyl, glock, sd, bd, cym, tri.
Although the title says "Polka," it is actually a
Samba.
                                               Dance
Dorabet

Robles, Daniel Alomia   1871-1942

El Condor Pasa   7.5'
(The Condor Flies Past)
2 2 2 2 – 4 2 3 1 – tmp+2 – str
Written in 1913 and based on traditional Andean
folk tunes. It is possibly the best-known Peruvian
song due to a cover version by Simon & Garfunkel
in 1970 on their Bridge Over Troubled Water
album.
Gonzalez, arr.

                         Animals/International (Peru)/
                                   Popular Song
Filarmonika

Rodgers, Richard   1902-1979

Carousel: Selections   9.5'
2 2 2 2 – 2asx, 2tsx – 4 3 3 1 – tmp+2 – hp – str
Includes: Carousel Waltz, June is Bustin' Out All
Over, You'll Never Walk Alone, Mr. Snow, If I
Loved You, A Real Nice Clambake, What's the Use
of Wonderin'.
Walter Paul, arr.

                                 Broadway Musicals
Williamson (POP); Luck's (rental)

Carousel Waltz   8'
3 3 3 3 – 4 3 3 1 – perc – hp – str
Don Walker, arr.

                           Broadway Musicals/Dance
R&H (rental)

Carousel Waltz   4.5'
3[incl pic] 1 3[incl bcl] 1 – 4 3 3 1 – tmp+3 – pf
– str
Calvin Custer, arr.

                           Broadway Musicals/Dance
Leonard

Carousel: You'll Never Walk Alone   5'
1 1 3[incl bcl] 1 – 2 2 2 1 – tmp+perc – pf – str
Optional Chorus.
J. Frederick Muller, arr.

                       Broadway Musicals/Valentine
Leonard (POP); EMS or Luck's (rental)

King and I Selections   *10'*
     2[1.2/pic] 2[1.2/Eh] 2 2 – 4 3 3 1 – tmp+2 – hp – str
     perc: gong, sd, bd, slgh bells, sus cym.
     Robert Russell Bennett, arr.
                               Broadway Musicals
Williamson Music (rental)

King and I Selections   *5'*
     2 1 3[incl bcl] 1 – 4 3 3 1 – tmp+perc – pf – str
     Includes: Getting To Know You; I Whistle a Happy Tune; Shall We Dance?; The March of the Siamese Children.
     Bob Lowden, arr.
                               Broadway Musicals
Leonard

Love Me Tonight: Lover   *2.5'*
     2 2 2 2 – 4 3 3 1 – tmp+perc – hp, pf – str
     Solo Voice. Key of D.
     Carmen Dragon, arr.
                      Broadway Musicals/Valentine
Dragon (rental)

Oklahoma: Selections   *11'*
     2[1.2/pic] 2[1.2/Eh] 3[1.2.bcl] 2 – 2asx, 2tsx – 4 3 3 1 – tmp+2 – hp – str
     perc: tri, sd, bd, bells, cym, vib, temple blks(tic toc).
     Includes: I Can't Say No, Kansas City; Many a New Day; Oh, What a Beautiful Mornin'; Oklahoma, Out of My Dreams; People Will Say We're in Love, Pore Jud, The Farmer and the Cowman; The Surrey with the Fringe on Top.
     Robert Russell Bennett, arr.
                               Broadway Musicals
Leonard

Richard Rodgers in Concert   *9'*
     2[1.pic] 1 3[1.2.bcl] 1 – 2 3 3[(#3)] 1 – (asx, tsx, bsx) – tmp+3 – (str)
     Chorus.
     Includes: Do-Re-Mi; I Whistle a Happy Tune; June Is Bustin' Out All Over; The March of the Siamese Children; My Funny Valentine; Oklahoma; Slaughter on Tenth Avenue; The Sound of Music; The Surrey with the Fringe on Top; There Is Nothin' Like A Dame.
     Mac Huff and Paul Murtha, arr.
                               Broadway Musicals
Leonard

Sound of Music: Selections   *10.5'*
     2[1.2/pic] 2 3[1.2.bcl] 2 – 2asx, tsx, bsx – 4 3 3 1 – tmp+4 – hp – str
     perc: xyl, glock, sd, bd, cym.
     Robert Russell Bennett, arr.
                               Broadway Musicals
Leonard

State Fair: *2'*
     It's a Grand Night for Singing
     3[incl pic] 2 2 2 – 4 3 3 1 – hp, cel, pf, (gtr) – tmp+perc – str
     SATB Chorus. Key of F.
                               Broadway Musicals
Dragon (rental)

Victory at Sea: Symphonic Scenario   *7'*
     2[1.2/pic] 2[1.2./Eh] 3[1.2.bcl] 2 – 4 3 3 1 – tmp+3 – hp – str
     perc: sd, sus cym, glock, bd, cym, sand pan, field drum, wood blk, gong.
     Robert Russell Bennett, arr.
                               Popular Classics
Leonard

Rodrigo, Joaquin   1901-1999

Concierto andaluz   *24'*
     2[1.2/pic] 2 2 2 – 4 2 0 0 – str   *(8' 10' 6')*
     4 Solo Guitars.
                               International
Schott (rental)

Cuatro madrigales amatorios   *9'*
                             (3' 3' 1' 2')
     2[1.2/pic] 2 1 0 – 1 1 0 0 – 1perc – str
     Solo High or Medium Voice.
                          International/Valentine
Chester (rental)

Rodríguez, Robert Xavier   1946-

Adoracion ambulante   *60'*
(A Mexican Folk Celebration)
     3[1.2.pic] 2 2 2 – 4 4 3 1 – tmp+4 – hp – str
     Solo Tenor and Bass. Mariachi band; percussion ensemble; church bells; conch shells; and singing audience.
                               International
Schirmer (rental)

Adoracion ambulante: Con flor y canto   15'
3[1.2. pic] 2 2 2 – 4 4 3 1 – tmp+4 – hp – str
Solo Tenor and Bass. SSAA Children's Chorus;
SATB Chorus.
                               Celebration/International
Schirmer (rental)

A Colorful Symphony   20'
3[1.2.3/pic] 2 2 2 – 4 2 3 1 – tmp+3 – hp, pf – str
Solo Narrator. Text: Norton Juster from *The Phantom Toll Booth*. An introduction to the instruments of the orchestra.
                               Instrumental Pops
Schirmer (rental)

Fanfare for Trumpets and Caracolas   5'
4 conch shells[or 4hn]. 4tpt
                               Fanfare
Schirmer (rental)

Flight: The Story of Wilbur and Orville Wright   23'
3[incl pic] 2[incl Eh] 2 2[incl cbn] – 4 3[C tp] 3 1 – tmp+3 – str
Female narrator and recorded sounds of airplane engines.
                               Travel
Schirmer (rental)

A Gathering of Angels: Bolero for Orchestra   8'
3[incl 3pic] 3[incl Eh] 3[incl Ebcl] 2 – 4 3 3 1 – tmp+3 – hp, pf – str
Optional Handbell Choir: 12 players
                               Christmas
Schirmer (rental)

Hot Buttered Rumba   5'
3[1.2.pic] 2 2 2 – asx – 4 3 3 1 – tmp+3 – pf – str
                               Dance
Schirmer (rental)

Jargon: 15'
  The Story of the American Constitution
2[incl pic] 2 2 2 – 4 2 3 1 – tmp+3 –pf – str
Narrator. Optional Chorus. Text: in English by Mary (Duren) Medrick.
                               Patriotic
Schirmer (rental)

Mascaras   18'
2[incl pic] 2[incl Eh] 2[incl Ebcl, bcl] 2 – 2 2 1 0 – tmp+2 – hp, pf – str
Solo Cello.
                               Halloween
Schirmer (rental)

Oktoechos: Fanfare   1.5'
13tp, 13tbn
For four spatially separated choirs of trumpets and trombones.
                               Fanfare
Schirmer (rental)

Piñata   5'
3[1.2.pic] 2 2 2 – asx – 4 3 3 1 –tmp+3 – hp, pf – str
Solo Violin and Percussion. Catalog suggests programming this for Christmas.
                               Celebration/International
Schirmer (rental)

The Salutation Rag   5'
3[1.2.3/pic] 2 2 2 – 4 3 3 1 – tmp+3 – str
Ragtime variations alluding to Happy Birthday at the end.
                               Celebration/Jazz
Schirmer (rental)

Scrooge: 8'
  Concert Scenes from "A Christmas Carol"
2[incl pic] 2[incl Eh] 2[incl Ebcl, bcl] 2[incl cbn] – 2 2 2 0 – tmp+3 – hp, pf or hpsd – str
Solo Bass-Baritone; Chorus. Libretto by the composer; cantata in one act.
                               Christmas
Schirmer (rental)

Sinfonia a la mariachi   24'
3[1.2.pic] 3[incl Eh] 2[incl Ebcl] 2 – 4 2 3 0 – tmp+2 – hpsd – str
Orch II [Mariachi]: 0 0 0 0 – 0 2 0 0 – 1perc – accordion,hp,gtr – str
Opt Orch III: 2 tpt or Mariachi band in finale.
                               International
Schirmer (rental)

The Tempest   34'
3[incl 3pic] 3[1.2.Eh] 3[1.2.bcl] 3[1.2.cbn] – 4(conch shells) 3 3 1 – tmp+3 –hp, pf or hpsd – str
Solo Puppeteers or Actors [2-4 male voices; 1 female voice]. Includes bird songs on tape. Based on Shakespeare.
                               Instrumental Pops
Schirmer (rental)

Tequila Sunrise   3'
0 0 0 0 – 4 3 3 1 – tmp+4 – hp
                               International/Space
Schirmer (rental)

Trunks: 18'
  A Circus Story for Narrator and Orchestra
  2[1.pic] 2 2 2[1.cbn] – 4 2 3 1 – tmp+3 – hp, pf
  – str
  Solo Narrator. The text is based on a story by H. C.
  Bunner about the friendship of a trumpet-playing
  boy and an elephant.
  Animals/Circus

  ALH (rental)

Rollins, Jack (See: Nelson, Steve)

Romberg, Sigmund 1887-1951

A Tribute to Romberg 10.5'
  2 2 2 2 – 2asx, tsx – 4 3 3 1 – tmp+1 – str
  Includes: French Military Marching Song; The
  Desert Song; Deep in My Heart; Your Land and
  My Land; One Alone; Softly as a Morning Sunrise;
  Golden Days; One Kiss; Stout Hearted Men.
  Douglas Maclean & F. Campbell-Watson, arr.
  Popular Song

  Warner (POP); EMS or Luck's (rental)

Rome, Harold

Fanny: Selection for Orchestra 9'
  2[1/pic.2] 2[1.2/Eh] 2 2 – 2asx, tsx, bsx – 4 3 3 1
  – tmp+2 – hp – str
  Includes: Fanny; Never too Late for Love; Why Be
  afraid to Dance; Restless Heart; Love is a Very
  Light thing; Welcome Home.
  Philip F. Lang, arr.
  Broadway Musical

  Chappell (rental)

Ronell, Ann 1908-1993

Willow Weep for Me 5.5
  Solo fl – drumset – pf, gtr – str
  Made famous by Billie Holiday.
  Calvin Custer, arr.
  Jazz

  Warner (POP); EMS or Luck's (rental)

Rose, David 1910-1990

Holiday for Strings 3.5'
  drumset – (gtr) – pf – str
  Calvin Custer, arr.
  Christmas

  Warner (POP); EMS or Luck's (rental)

Holiday for Strings 2.5'
  2 2 2 1 – 2 3 2 1 – tmp+perc – pf – str
  Marty Gold, arr.
  Christmas

  Warner (POP); EMS or Luck's (rental)

Little House on the Prairie: Meet Me at 7'
  the Fair (1974)
  3 2 2 2 – 3 3 3 1 – tmp+2 – hp, org, gtr, Fender bs
  – str
  perc: drumset, vib, chimes.
  Americana/TV

  T&V (rental)

Rosenberg, Hilding Constantin 1892-1985

Die Heligea Natten (The Holy Night): 32'
  A Christmas Oratorio
  1 1 2 0 – 2 2 0 0 – tmp+perc – cel, org – str
  Solo Soprano, Alto, Tenor, Bass. SATB Chorus.
  Text: Swedish and English by Hjalmar Gullberg.
  Christmas

  Schirmer (rental)

Rosenhaus, Steven L., arr. 1952-

American Spiritual Festival 5.5'
  1 1 3[1.2.bcl] 1 – 2 2 2 1 – tmp+2 – banjo, pf – str
  perc: sd, bd, sus cym, tambn.
  The winds and brass are optional. Includes: Steal
  Away; Give Me that Old Time religion; sometimes I
  Fell Like a Motherless Child; Ev'ry Time I Fell the
  Spirit.
  Popular Song

  Leonard (POP); Luck's (rental)

Kitchen Percussion March for   3'
  Special Guests and Orchestra
  2 2 2 2 – 2 3 2 1 – tmp+2 – str
  perc: sd, bd, sus cym.
  3 percussion soloists (amateurs). Solo I=2 pot lids, wood spoon; Solo II=veg grater, wood spoon; Solo III=plastic bucket, box of rice.
                                                           Novelty
  Warner (rental from Luck's)

Lionel Richie in Concert   3'
  2 1 2 1 – 4 3 3 1 – tmp+3 – (pf) – str
  perc: drumset, tambn, claves, bells, maracas.
  Includes: All Night Long; Hello: Stuck on You.
                                         Popular Song
  Leonard (POP); EMS or Luck's (rental)

Rosenman, Leonard   1924-2008

Star Trek 4: The Voyage Home (1986)   8'
  3[pic.2.pic] 3[1.2.Eh] 3[Ebcl.bcl.Ebcbcl] 3[1.2.cbn] – 4 4 3 1 – tmp+4 – hp, cel, synth – str
  perc: cym, sus cym, bd, vib, bells, chimes, tamtam, tri.
  Won the 1987 ASCAP award and nominated for an Oscar for Best Music, Original Score.
                                        Films/Space
  T&V (rental)

Rossini, Gioacchino   1792-1868

Il barbiere di Siviglia   8'
  (Barber of Seville): Overture (Elizabetta, Regina d'Inghiterra)
  2[1.pic] 2 2 2 – 2 2 3 0 – tmp+1 – str
  perc: bd/cym
  Ricordi edition by Alberto Zedda uses one trombone.
                                     Popular Classics
  Kalmus; Luck's; Ricordi (rental)

Il barbiere di Siviglia   8'
  (Barber of Seville): Sinfonia (Aureliano in Palmira)
  2 2 2 2 – 2 2 0 0 – (tmp+1) – str
  (perc: bd/cym)
  Kalmus edition by Clark McAlister
                                     Popular Classics
  Kalmus

La Cenerentola (Cinderella):   8'
  Overture or Sinfonia
  2[1/pic.2] 2 2 2 – 2 2 1 0 – tmp+1 – str
  perc: bd.
                                     Popular Classics
  Kalmus; Luck's; Ricordi (rental)

Duetto buffo di due gatti (Cat Duet)   5'
  1 1 1 1 – 0 0 0 0 – str
  2 Solo Female Voices.
  John Grande, orchestrator (Attributed to Rossini)
                                           Animals
  Kalmus

La gazza ladra (The Thieving Magpie):   10'
  Overture or Sinfonia
  2[1.pic] 2 2 2 – 4 2 1 0 – tmp+4 – str
  perc: bd, tri, 2sd.
  Kalmus edtion by Clark McAlister; Ricordi edition by Alberto Zedda.
                                     Popular Classics
  Kalmus; Luck's; Ricordi (rental)

Guillaume Tell (William Tell):   12'
  Overture or Sinfonia
  2[1.pic] 2[1.2/Eh] 2 2 – 4 2 3 0 – tmp+3 – str
  perc: tri, cym, bd.
                                     Popular Classics
  Breitkopf; Kalmus; Luck's; Ricordi (rental)

L'Italiana in Algeri: Overture or Sinfonia   9'
  1[pic] 2 2 1 – 2 2 0 0 – 2perc – str
  perc: bd, Turkish crescent.
  Kalmus edition by Clark McAlister; Ricordi edition by Azio Corghi.
                                     Popular Classics
  Kalmus; Luck's; Ricordi (rental)

Semiramide: Overture   12'
  2[1.pic] 2 2 2 – 4 2 3 0 – tmp+1 – str
  perc: cym, bd.
                                     Popular Classics
  Breitkopf; Kalmus; Luck's; Ricordi (rental)

Rota, Nino   1911-1979

Amarcord   3.5'
  3 2 3[1.2.bcl] 3 – 4 0 0 1 – perc – gtr, accordion, hp – str
  Henry Mancini, arr.
                                             Films
  Janen (rental)

Romeo and Juliet (1968)   6.5'
    2[1.afl] 2[1.Eh] 0 1 – 2 0 0 0 – hp – str
    Won the Golden Globe for Best Original Score.
    Patrick Russ, arr.
                                           Films/Valentine
T&V (rental)

Romeo and Juliet: A Time for Us (1968)   3'
    0 0 0 0 – 4 3[flugelhorns] 3 1 – 1perc –
    2 gtr[1 part a2], pf, bs gtr – str
    perc: drumset.
    Female Chorus [16 girls].
    Henry Mancini, arr.
                                           Films/Valentine
T&V (rental)

Romeo and Juliet: Suite (1968)   11.5'
    2[1.pic] 2 2[1.bcl] 2 – 4 3 3 1– tmp+1 –
    hp, Spanish gtr, harmonium, org – str
    perc: bd.
    Includes: Prologue & Fanfare for a Prince; Romeo;
    But this I Pray...Consent to Marry Us Today; The
    Ride to Mantua; Love Theme.
                                           Films/Valentine
T&V (rental)

The Godfather (1972)   13'
    3[1.2.pic] 3[1.2.Eh] 3[1.2.bcl] 2 – 3 3 3 1 – tmp+1
    – hp, pf[tack pf], cel, org, gtr, elec gtr, 12 str gtr,
    elec bs, accordion – str
    perc: drumset, vib.
    Includes: Sicilian Pastorale; A New Carpet:
    Tarantella;Waltz; Michael & Kay; Love Theme.
    Oscar winning film score.
                                                   Films
T&V (rental)

The Godfather II (1974)   4'
    2 2[1.Eh] 2 2 – 3 1 3 1 – tmp+1 – hp, pf[tack pf],
    gtr, 2 mandolins – str
    perc: tri.
    Includes: Main Title; The Immigrant.
                                                   Films
T&V (rental)

The Godfather III: Suite   32'
    3[1.2.pic] 3[1.2.Eh] 3[1.2.bcl] 2 – asx, 2tsx, bsx
    – 3 3 3 1 – tmp+2 – hp, pf, cel, org, gtr, elec bs,
    elec gtr, 2 mandolins, 12 str gtr[no more than
    3 plectrists are needed at one time], accordion – str
    perc: drumset tri, vib, xyl.
    Includes: Marcia Religioso; Marcia Festa; Marcia
    Stilo Italiano (from *The Godfather Part II*);
    The Immigrant/Love Theme; Intermezzo;
    Preludio from Cavalleria Rusticana
    (Mascagni/Coppola); Finale (Coda).
    Carmine Coppola, arr.
                                                   Films
T&V (rental)

The Godfather: Reminicences for   5'
Orchestra (1972)
    2[1.pic] 2[1.Eh] 3[1.2.bcl] 2 – 2 asx – 3 2 3 1 –
    tmp+5 – hp, 2 kybd[pf/tack pf.elec org/cel/hpsd/ toy
    pf/tack pf] 2gtr[12str/acoustic/elec/ mandolin.(#2)],
    bs gtr, accordion – str
    perc: drumset, vib, xyl, marim, claves, tgl, reco-reco, cym.
    John Mauceri, arr.
                                                   Films
T&V (rental)

War and Peace: Suite (1956)   7.5'
    3[1.2.pic] 2 2 2 – 4 3 3 1 – tmp+perc –
    hp, pf, cel, org – str
    perc: tamtam, cym, sd, bd, chimes.
    Includes: Introduction; Waltz; La Rosa Di
    Novgorod; N 73[Finale]. Additional movements
    available for a longer suite: Musical Moment;
    Polonaise; Exodus From Moscow; N 54; Andrea &
    Natasha; Retreat of the Grand Army; N 66; N 67;
    Return to Moscow.
                                                   Films
T&V (rental)

Rouse, Christopher   1949-

Karolju   23'
    2[1.2/pic] 2 2 2 – 4 3 3 1 – tmp+4 – hp – str
    perc: glock, sd, tri, bd, chimes, slgh-bells, marac, guiro,
    2tambn, 2pr cym, rute, sm cym.
    Chorus. Carols in Latin, Swedish, French, Spanish,
    Russian, Czech, German, and Italian.
                                                   Christmas
Boosey (rental)

Rouse, Ervin T.   ?-1980

Orange Blossom Special   2.5'
perc – pf – str
Calvin Custer, arr.
    Americana
MCA

Orange Blossom Special   3'
2[incl pic] 2 2 2 – 4 3 3 1 – timp+ 3[incl drumset] – str
    Americana
Wendel (rental)

Roxburgh, Edwin   1937-

How Pleasant to Know Mr. Lear   24'
1[incl pic] 1 1 1 – 1 0 0 0 – tmp+perc – str
Narrator. Text from *The Complete Nonsense Book*; limericks by Edward Lear; popular in the 1850s.
    Instrumental Pops
UMP (rental)

Roylance, Dave & Galvin, Bob

Ocean Fantasia   19'
3 3 3 3 – 4 3 3 1 – tmp+3 – hp – str
    Ecology
Novello (rental)

Tall Ships Suite   29'
3 3 3 3 – 4 3 3 1 – tmp+3 – hp – pf – str
In three movements.
    Films/Travel
Novello (rental)

Voyager   9'
3 3 3 3 – 4 3 3 1 – tmp+3 – hp – str
    Travel
Novello (rental)

Rózsa, Miklós   1907-1995

Ben-Hur: Choral Suite   20'
2[1.2/opt pic.pic] 2[incl (Eh)] 3[incl bcl + (Ebcl)] 2[incl (cbn)] – 4 3 3 1 – tmp+perc – (cel), pf, (org) – str
SATB Chorus.
Daniel Robbins, editor
    Films
EMI (rental)

Ben-Hur: Love Theme   3'
2 2 3 2 – 4 3 3 0 – tmp – 2hp – str
Solo violin
    Films/Valentine
EMI (rental)

Ben Hur: Parade of the Charioteers   4'
3[1.2.pic] 2 3 2 – 4 3 3 2 – tmp+perc – pf – str
    Films/Sports
EMI (rental)

Ben-Hur: Prelude   2'
3[incl pic] 2 3 2 – 4 3 3 2 – tmp+2 – 2hp, pf, org – str
    Films
EMI (rental)

Ben Hur: Rowing of the Galley Slaves   3'
3[incl pic]2 3 2 – 2 2 2[incl cbn] – 4 2 2 1 – tmp+2 – hp, pf – str
    Films
EMI (rental)

El Cid: Love Scene   5'
3 2 3 2 – 4 3 3 1 – tmp+2 – pf, hp – str
    Films/Valentine
EMI (rental)

El Cid: Main Title   4'
3[1.2.3/pic] 3 3[1.2.bcl] 3[1.2.cbn] – 4 4 3 1 – tmp+perc – (org) – str
Joel Rosenbaum, arr.
    Films
Kane (rental)

El Cid: Overture   4'
3[incl pic] 2 3 2 – 4 3 3 1 – tmp+2 – hp, pf – str
    Films
EMI (rental)

El Cid: Overture and March   6'
   3[1.2.pic] 2 3[(bcl)] 2[(cbn)] – 4 3 3 1 – tmp+3 –
   pf, (cel), hp – str

                                                Films

EMI (rental)

Dead Men Don't Wear Plaid: 4.5'
   End Cast (1982)
   3[1.2.3/pic] 2 3 2 – 6 4 3 1 – tmp+4 – 2hp, pf – str

                                                Films

T&V (rental)

Double Indemnity: Suite (1944)   6.5'
   2[1.pic] 2[1.Eh] 2[1.bcl] 2 – 4 3 3 1 – tmp+3
   – hp, pf – str
   Includes: Prelude; Narration; The Meeting; The
   Lovers; The Murder; Finale.
   perc: vib, xyl, tam tam, sd, field dr, bd, cym, sus
   cym, tambn.
   Christopher Palmer, arr.

                                                Films

T&V (rental)

Ivanhoe   8'
   3[1.2.pic] 3[1.2.Eh] 3[1.2.bcl] 3[1.2.cbn] – 4 3 3 1
   – tmp+4 – hp, pf – str
   Includes: Prelude, Lady Rowena, Finale, Epilogue.
   Patrick Russ, arr.

                                                Films

EMI (rental)

The Killers: Concert Suite (1946)   12'
   3 2[incl (Eh)] 3[incl (bcl)] 2[incl (cbn)] –
   4 3 3 1 – tmp+3 – pf or cel, hp – str

                                                Films

EMI (rental)

The Lost Weekend: Suite (1945)   6'
   3[1.2.pic] 2 3[1.2.bcl] 2 – 4 3 3 1 – tmp+2 –
   2hp,cel/pf, ondes or synth – str
   perc: sd, military dr, bd, cym, sus cym, vib, glock, tam
   tam.
   Includes: Prelude; New York Skyline; Alcohol;
   Love Theme; The Walk; and Finale.
   Christopher Palmer, arr.

                                                Films

T&V (rental)

Quo Vadis Suite   20'
   3 3 3 3 – 4 3 3 1 – tmp+3 – hp, cel, pf – str
   Includes: Ave Caesar, Romanza, Arabesque, Quo
   Vadis.

                                               Films

EMI (rental)

The Red House Suite   12.5'
   3[1.2.pic] 3[1.2.Eh] 3[1.2.bcl] 3[1.2.cbn] – 4 3 3 1
   – tmp+3 – 2hp, cel or pf – str
   perc: cym, sus cym, sd, bd, glock, vib, xyl, chimes,
   tri, gong, opt flexatone, theremin or synth, tam tam.
   Female Chorus. Includes: Pastorale, Storm, and
   Sunrise.

                                               Films

T&V (rental)

Ruders, Poul   1949-

Saaledes saae Johannes   11'
   (Thus Saw St. John...)
   3[incl 3pic] 3[incl Eh] 3[incl Ebcl, bcl] 3[incl cbn]
   – 4 3 2 1 – 3perc – hp, cel, pf[4hand] – str

                                            Halloween

Schirmer (rental)

Ruggles, Carl   1876-1968

Sun-Treader   14'
   5[1.2.3.4/pic.5/pic] 5[3ob, 2Eh] 5[1.2.3.bcl.Ebcl]
   4[1.2.3.cbn] – 6 5 5 2 – tmp+1 – 2hp – str
   perc: cym, 2sus cym.

                                              Space

AME (rental)

Russell, Henry & Knight, Vick

The Halls of Ivy   3'
   1 1 2 1 – asx – 2 2 1 1 – 2perc – str
   perc: glock, sd, bd.
   Ralph Matesky, arr.

                                      Instrumental Pops

Chappell (rental)

Rutter, John   1945-

Jesus Child!   3'
    2 2 2 1 – 2 0 0 0 – 2perc – hp – str
    perc: includes claves and glock.
    SATB Chorus. Additional version for brass:
    0 4 3 1 – 2perc.
                                          Christmas
Oxford

The Very Best Time of the Year   6'
    1 1 0 0 – 0 0 0 0 – hp – str
    SATB Chorus. Key of D, modulates to F.
                                            Christmas
Hinshaw

Ryden, William

Amazing Grace   3'
    2 2 2 2 – 4 3 3 1 – tmp+1 – str
    perc: chimes, sus cym.
                            Holidays/Popular Song
Kalmus

S

Sainte-Marie, Buffy   1941-
Nitzsche, Jack   1937-

An Officer & A Gentleman: 3.5'
    Up Where We Belong
    1 1 2 1 – 1 3 3 1 – tmp+perc – hp, pf – str
    SATB Chorus.
    Charles Sayre, arr.
                                              Films
    Warner (POP); EMS or Luck's (rental)

Saint-Saëns, Camille   1835-1921

Le Carnaval des animaux   21'
    (Carnival of the Animals)
    1[1/pic] 0 1 0 – 2perc – str
    perc: xyl, glock.
    2 Solo Pianos. Optional Narrator. Includes: Intro
    and Royal March of the Lion; Hens and Roosters;
    Fast Animals; Tortoises; Elephant; Kangaroos; The
    Aquarium; Personages with Long Ears; The Cuckoo
    in the Heart of the Woods; Aviary;Pianists; Fossils;
    The Swan; Finale.
    Kalmus edition by Clinton Nieweg & Nancy
    Bradburd.
                                              Animals
    Durand; Kalmus

Le Carnaval des animaux   5'
    (Carnival of the Animals): The Swan
    pf, cel – str
    Solo Cello.
    Arthur Luck, arr.
                                              Animals
    Luck's

Carnival of the Animals   18.5'
    2[1.2/pic] 2 2 1 – 3 2 1 1 – tmp+2 – hp – str
    Narrator. Rescored for orchestra with no pianos and
    a new narration which is child friendly and features
    the instruments in each movement. Words by
    Barbara Goehrig.
    Bill Holcombe, arr.
                                              Animals
    Musicians Pub.

Christmas Oratorio, Op. 12   38'
   hp, org – str
   Solo SSATBar; Chorus.
                                       Christmas

   Kalmus; Schirmer (rental)

Christmas Oratorio, Op. 12:   6'
   Praise Ye the Lord of Hosts
   1 1 2 1 – asx, tsx – 2 3 2 0 – perc – pf – str
   Optional SA Chorus.
   E. Jurey, arr.
                                         Christmas

   EMI (rental)

Danse macabre, Op. 40   8'
   3[1.2.pic] 2 2 2 – 4 2 3 1 – tmp+4 – (hp) – str
   perc: xyl, bd, tri, cym.
   Kalmus edition by Clinton F. Nieweg.
                     Halloween/Popular Classics

   Durand; Kalmus

Havanaise, Op. 83   11'
   2 2 2 2 – 2 2 0 0 – tmp – str
   Solo Violin.
   Kalmus edited by Nieweg & Bradburd.
                               Popular Classics

   Fischer (rental); Kalmus; Luck's

Introduction and Rondo Capriccioso:
   Trumpet in Bb and Orchestra
   2 2 2 2 – 2 2 0 0 – tmp – str
   Solo Trumpet.
   Mikhail Nakariakov, arr.
                               Popular Classics

   EMR

La nuit, Op. 114   10'
   2 2 2 2 – 0 0 3 0 – tmp – str
   Solo Soprano; Female Chorus.
                               Popular Classics

   Durand (rental)

Romance in F, Op. 36   5'
   2 1 2 1 – 0 0 0 0 – str
   Solo Horn or Cello.
                       Popular Classics/Valentine

   Durand; Kalmus; Luck's

Samson et Delilah: Danse Bacchanale   8'
   3[1.2.pic] 3[1.2.Eh] 3[1.2.bcl] 3[1.2.cbn] – 4 4 3 1
   – tmp+4 – hp – str
   perc: tri, cym, bd, finger cym, cast.
   Kalmus edition by Nieweg & Bradburd.
                               Popular Classics

   Durand; Kalmus; Luck's

Sakamoto, Ryuichi   1952-

The Last Emperor: Theme (1987)   6'
   2 2[1.Eh] 2 2 – 4 2 3 1 – tmp+2 – 2 hp,
   Chinese koto, Chinese ErHu, Chinese Stone Flute,
   cimbalom – str
   perc: glock, tubular bells, tamtam, sus cym, bd.
   Oscar winning film score.
                                            Films

   T&V (rental)

Sallinen, Aulis   1935-

At the Palace Gates: Overture, Op. 68a   4'
   2[incl pic] 2 2[incl bcl] 2[incl cbn] – 4 2 2 1 –
   tmp+2 – hp, pf – str
   Overture to the opera: Palace (Palaton Porteilla)
                                  Popular Classics

   Novello (rental)

Salvatori, Michael (See: O'Donnell, Martin)

Salzedo, Leonard   1921-

The Witch Boy: Suite from the Ballet   19'
   2[incl pic] 2 2 – 4 3 3 1 – tmp+perc – hp, pf – str
                                  Dance/Halloween

   Schirmer (rental)

The Witch Boy: 12'
   Three Dances from the Ballet
   2[incl pic] 2 2 – 4 3 3 1 – tmp+perc – hp, pf – str
                                  Dance/Halloween

   Chester (rental)

The Witch Boy: 4'
   Square Dance from the Ballet
   2 1 2 1 – 2 2 3 0 – perc – hp – str
   Harry Dexter, arr.
                                  Dance/Halloween

   Schirmer (rental)

Sarasate, Pablo de   1844-1908

Carmen Fantasie   12'
on Themes of Bizet, Op. 25
    2[1.2/pic] 2 2 2 – 4 2[crt] 3 0 – tmp+1 – hp – str
    perc: tambn.
    Solo Violin.
    Pablo de Sarasate, arr.
                               Popular Classics
Kalmus

Zigeunerweisen (Gypsy Airs), Op. 2   10'
    2 2 2 2 – 2 2 0 0 – tmp+(tri) – str
    Solo Violin.
                               Popular Classics
Fischer (rental); Kalmus

Satie, Erik   1866-1925

Gymnopedie No. 1 & 3   7'
    2 1 0 0 – 4 0 0 0 – 1perc – 2hp – str   (4' 3')
    perc: sus cym.
    Claude Debussy, arr.
    Kalmus edition by Carl Simpson.
                               Popular Classics
Kalmus; Luck's; Salabert (rental)

Sayre, Charles [Chuck], arr.   1939-

Broadway on Parade   4'
    (1 1 3[1.2.bcl] 1 – 2 2 2 1) – 2perc – pf – str
    perc: sd, bd, cym, sus cym, temple blk or woodblk, (gong), tambn.
    Wind and brass parts are optional. Includes: I Have Confidence; The March of the Siamese Children; Seventy Six Trombones; Before the Parade Passes By.
                               Broadway Musicals
Leonard (POP); Luck's (rental)

Broadway Showstoppers   6'
    3[1.2.pic] 2 2 1 – 4 3 3 1 – tmp+3 – pf, elec bs – str
    perc: drumset, cym, xyl, glock, temple blks.
    Includes: That's Entertainment; Cabaret; Mame; There's No business Like Show Business.
                               Broadway Musicals
Leonard

A Christmas Tradition   6'
    2 2 2 1 – 4 3 3 1 – tmp+3 – str
    perc: glock, sd, sus cym, cym, chimes, (tri).
    Includes: Joy to the World; Good King Wenceslas; Hark the Herald Angels Sing.
                               Christmas
Warner

Christmas Vision   4'
    2 2 3[1.2.bcl] 1 – 4 3 2 1 – tmp+2 – pf – str
    perc: chimes, glock, sd, bd, cym, sus cym, tri, tambn.
    Includes: Angels We Have Heard On High; Away in a Manger; I Am So Glad Each Christmas Eve; Joy to the World.
                               Christmas
Leonard (rental)

Disney Adventure   4'
    2 1 3[1.2.bcl] 1 – 2 2 2 1 – perc – pf – str
    Includes: Zip-A-Dee-Doo-Dah; Once Upon a Dream; Micky Mouse March; A Dream Is a Wish Your Heart Makes; It's a Small World.
                               Films
Leonard (POP); EMS or Luck's (rental)

Jerome Robbins Broadway   6.5'
    2[incl pic] 1 3[1.2.bcl] 1 – 4 3 3 1 – tmp+perc – pf – str
    Includes: Sunrise, Sunset; America; Somewhere; Comedy Tonight.
                               Broadway Musicals/Dance
Leonard (POP); EMS or Luck's (rental)

A Rockin' Christmas   4'
    2 1 2 1 – (asx, tsx, bsx) – 4 3 2 1 – 2perc – pf – str
    perc: drumset, chimes, glock, tubular bells, slgh-bells.
    Includes: Have a Holly Jolly Christmas; Rudolph the Red-Nosed Reindeer; Rockin' Around the Christmas Tree; Jingle Bell Rock.
                               Christmas
Leonard (rental)

Schickele, Peter   1935-

1712 Overture   11'
    3 3 3 3 – 4 4 3 1 – tmp+4 – org – str
    Enter in program as composed by PDQ Bach.
                               Instrumental Pops
Presser (rental)

American Birthday Card   8'
    3 2 3 2 – 4 3 3 1 – tmp+3 – str
    Narrator.
                                          Patriotic
    Presser (rental)

A Bach Portrait   15'
    2 2 2 2 – 2 2 3 1 – tmp+2 – pf – str
    Narrator.
    Enter in program as composed by PDQ Bach.
                                  Instrumental Pops
    Presser (rental)

Birthday Ode to "Big Daddy" Bach   8'
    0 0 0 0 – 0 3[all pic] 0 0 – tmp – hpsd – str
    Solo Soprano, Mezzo, Tenor, Baritone; Narrator;
    Mixed Chorus. Enter in program as composed
    by PDQ Bach.
                                       Celebrations
    Presser (rental)

Broadway Boogie   5'
    1 1 0 0 – 0 0 0 0 – hp,pf – str
    Solo Dog. Enter in program as composed by PDQ
    Bach.
                                            Animals
    Presser (rental)

Canine Cantata "Wachet Arf!"   9'
    0 0 0 2 – 2 2 0 0 – tmp – str
    Solo dog
    Enter in program as composed by PDQ Bach.
                                   Animals/Novelty
    Presser (rental)

The Chenoo Who Stayed to Dinner   22'
    2 2 2 2 – 3 2 2 1 – 2perc – str
    Narrator. Based on a Native American Micmac
    legend.
                                       Americana
    Presser (rental)

Classical Rap   9'
    0 0 0 0 – 0 2 0 0 – hpsd – str
    Narrator [rapper]. Enter in program as composed
    by PDQ Bach.
                                 Instrumental Pops
    Presser (rental)

Prelude to Einstein on the Fritz, S.E=mc2   7'
    2 2 2 2 – 2 2 3 1 – 2perc – str
    Solo Piano, Foghorn, Bell, Kazoo, Balloon with
    pitchpipes.
    Enter in program as composed by PDQ Bach.
                         Instrumental Pops/Novelty
    Presser (rental)

Fanfare for the Common Cold   2'
    0 0 0 0 – 2 2 1 0 – [no str]
                                          Fanfare
    Presser (rental)

The Fantastic Garden   25'
    3 3 3 2 – 4 4 4 1 – tmp+4 – hp, cel – str
    Rock group: elec pf, pf, elec org, elec hpsd
    [3players]; singers.
                                          Ecology
    Presser (rental)

Legend   22'
    2 2 2 2 – 3 2 2 1 – 2perc – str
    Instrumental version of *The Chenoo Who Stayed to
    Dinner*.
                                     Americana
    Presser (rental)

Overture to "The Civilian Barber"   3'
    0 2 0 2 – 2 0 0 0 – str
                               Instrumental Pops
    Presser

Requiem Mantras   15'
    3 2 2 2 – 4 3 3 1 – 3perc – cel, pf – str
    Rock group.
                             Instrumental Pops
    Presser (rental)

Royal Firewater Musick   15'
    0 2 0 1 – 2 0 0 0 – 10 bottle players – str
                             Instrumental Pops
    Presser (rental)

Three Strange Cases   6'
    1 1 1 1 – 0 0 0 0 – 2perc – str
    Narrator; poems of Ogden Nash.
                             Instrumental Pops
    Presser (rental)

Thurber's Dogs   20'
    2 2 2 2 – 2 2 0 0 – tmp+perc – hp – str
                                          Animals
    Presser (rental)

Unbegun Symphony 10'
    1 1 1 1 – 1 1 0 0 – str
                                      Instrumental Pops
Presser (rental)

Uptown Hoedown 4.5'
    1[incl pic] 1 1 1 – (3) 1 1 0 – tmp+perc – str
                                        Dance
Presser (rental)

A Zoo Called Earth 15'
    2[incl pic] 2 2 2 – 4 3 3 1 – tmp+3 – str
    Taped narration.
                                        Ecology
Presser (rental)

Schiff, David   1945-

Infernal 6'
    3[1.2.pic] 3[1.2.Eh] 3 2 – 4 3 3 1 –
    tmp+1perc[incl   drumset] – pf – str
    Jazzy version of Stravinsky *Firebird* (1919).
                                        Instrumental Pops
MMB

Schifrin, Lalo   1932-

Dialogues
    2 2 1 2 – 2 3 2 0 – tmp+perc – str
    Solo Jazz Quintet: asx, tp[crt], drumset, pf, db;
    optional bass trombone with jazz ensemble.
                                        Jazz
AMP (rental)

Mission Impossible (1966): *Theme* 2'
    2[1.pic] 2 3 2 – 6 3 3 1 – tmp+perc –
    hp, pf, gtr, Fender bass – str
    perc: drumset, tri, bongo, claves, 4 Latin hand perc,
    sus cym, xyl.
                                        TV
T&V (rental)

Mission: Impossible Theme 3'
    2 1 2 1 – 4 3 3 1 – tmp+2 – pf – str
    perc: drumset, sus cym, bongos.
    Calvin Custer, arr.
                                        TV
Leonard

Schnittke, Alfred   1934-1998

Concerto grosso No. 1 25'
    0 0 0 0 – 0 0 0 0 – hpsd, player pf – str
    2 Solo Violins.
                                        Halloween
Schirmer (rental)

Schocker, Gary   1959-

Green Places 15'
    0 2[incl Eh] 1 1 – 3 0 0 0 – hp – str
    Solo Flute.
                                        Ecology
Presser (rental)

Schoenberg, Claude-Michel   1944-

Les Misérables: The ABC Café 5'
    1 1 1 0 – 2 3 1 0 – perc, drumset – 2kybd, gtr – str
    Solo Voice; Key of C minor.
                                        Broadway Musicals
BOU (rental)

Les Misérables: At the End of the Day 5'
    1 1 1 0 – 2 3 1 0 – perc, drumset – 2kybd, gtr – str
    Solo Voice; Key of A flat major.
                                        Broadway Musicals
BOU (rental)

Les Misérables: Bring Him Home 3'
    3[incl pic] 2 3[1.2.bcl] 1 – 4 0 3 1 – tmp+perc –
    hp, cel/pf – str
    Solo Male Voice.
    Bob Krogstad, arr.
                                        Broadway Musicals
Leonard

Les Misérables: Bring Him Home 5'
    1 1 1 0 – 2 3 1 0 – perc,drumset – 2kybd, gtr – str
    Solo Voice; Key of F Major.
                                        Broadway Musicals
BOU (rental)

Les Misérables: Do You Hear the People Sing? 5'
    1 1 1 0 – 2 3 1 0 – perc, drumset – 2kybd, gtr – str
    Solo Voice; Key of F Major.
                                        Broadway Musicals
BOU (rental)

Les Misérables: 5'
   Empty Chairs at Empty Tables
    1 1 1 0 – 2 3 1 0 – perc, drumset – 2kybd, gtr – str
    Solo Voice.
                                            Broadway Musicals
  BOU (rental)

Les Misérables: I Dreamed a Dream   3'
    3[incl pic] 2 3[1.2.bcl] 1 – 4 3 3 1 – tmp+perc –
    hp, cel/pf – str
    Solo Female Voice.
    Bob Krogstad, arr.
                                            Broadway Musicals
  Leonard

Les Misérables: I Dreamed a Dream   5'
    1 1 1 0 – 2 3 1 0 – perc,drumset – 2kybd, gtr – str
    Solo Voice; Key of E flat major.
                                            Broadway Musicals
  BOU (rental)

Les Misérables: 5'
   Little Cosette-Castle on a Cloud
    1 1 1 0 – 2 3 1 0 – 2perc – 2kybd, gtr – str
    Solo Voice; Key of in A minor.
                                            Broadway Musicals
  BOU (rental)

Les Misérables: Master of the House   5'
    1 1[incl Eh] 1 0 – 2 3 1 0 – perc, drumset –
    2kybd, gtr – str
    Solo Voice; Key of C major.
                                            Broadway Musicals
  BOU (rental)

Les Misérables: On My Own   5'
    1 1[incl Eh] 1 0 – 2 3 1 0 – perc[drumset]
    2kybd, gtr – str
    Solo Voice; Key of D major.
                                            Broadway Musicals
  BOU (rental)

Les Misérables: One Day More   5'
    1 1 1 0 – 2 3 1 0 – perc, drumset – 2kybd, gtr – str
    Solo Voice; Key of A major.
                                            Broadway Musicals
  BOU (rental)

Les Misérables: Stars   5'
    1 1 1 0 – 2 3 1 0 – perc, drumset – 2kybd, gtr – str
    Solo Voice; Key of C major.
                                            Broadway Musicals
  BOU (rental)

Selections from Les Miserables   7'
    2 2 3[1.2.(bcl)] 1 – (asx, tsx) – 4 3 3 1 tmp+4 –
    pf – str
    perc: sd, bd, cym, (drumset), tri, tambn, chimes, glock,
    marim, xyl.
    Includes: At the End of the Day; I Dreamed a
    Dream; Master of the House; On My Own; Do You
    Hear the People Sing?
    Bob Lowden, arr.
                                            Broadway Musicals
  Leonard

Les Misérables: Symphonic Suite   30'
    2[incl pic] 2[incl Eh] 2[incl bcl] 2[incl cbn] –
    4 4 2 1 – tmp+perc – 2hp, pf – str
                                            Broadway Musicals
  BOU (rental)

Miss Saigon: Finale   6'
    2 1 2 1 – 2 2 3 0 – tmp+3 – hp, cel/pf, gtr – str
    Solo Voices; Chorus.
                                            Broadway Musicals
  BOU (rental)

Miss Saigon: I Still Believe This   5'
    2[incl Asian fl] 1[Eh] 2 1 – 2 2 3 0 – 3perc –
    2kbd, gtr – str
    Solo Voice.
                                            Broadway Musicals
  BOU (rental)

Miss Saigon: Last Night of the World   5'
    2 1 1 1 – asx – 2 2[flug] 3 0 – 3perc –
    hp, cel, kybd, gtr – str
    Solo Voice.
                                            Broadway Musicals
  BOU (rental)

Miss Saigon Medley   10'
    2[incl pic] 1 3[1.2.bcl] 2 – 4 3 3 1 – tmp+perc
    – pf – str
    Includes: Overture; Sun and Moon; The Heat Is on
    in Saigon; Last Night of the World; The American
    Dream.
    Calvin Custer, arr.
                                            Broadway Musicals
  Leonard

Miss Saigon Rhapsody   15'
    3[1.2.pic] 3[1.2.Eh] 3[1.2.bcl] 2 – asx – 4 2 3 1
    – tmp – hp, cel/kybd, (gtr), bass gtr – str
    W. D. Broan, arr.
    Solo Piano.
                                            Broadway Musicals
  BOU (rental)

Miss Saigon: Sun and Moon 5'
2 1 2[incl bcl] 1 – 2 2 3 0 – 3perc – hp, cel/pf, gtr – str
Solo Voice.
                                                                Broadway Musicals
BOU (rental)

Miss Saigon: This Is the Hour 5'
2[incl Eh] 1 2 1 – 2 2 3 0 – tmp+perc – 2kybd[(pf)], gtr, bass gtr – str
Solo Voice.
                                                  Broadway Musicals
BOU (rental)

Miss Saigon: Why God Why 5'
2 1 2 1 – 2 2[flug] 3 0 – tmp+3 – hp, cel/pf, gtr – str
Solo Voice.
                                                  Broadway Musicals
BOU (rental)

Schreiner, Adolph   1841-1894

The Worried Drummer(der Pauker im Aengsten) 8'
2[1.2/pic] 2 2 2 – 2 2 3 0 – Solo or tmp+3 – str
perc: bells, tambn, tri, cym, bd, sd, xyl, slgh bells, whip, cast.
Saul Goodman, arr.
The composer is often confused with Alexander Schreiner, organist with the Morman Tabernacle, who lived from 1901-1987.
                                   Instrumental Pops/Novelty
EMI (rental); Kalmus

Schubert, Franz   1797-1828

Ave Maria 5'
2 2 2 2 – 4 0 3 1 – tmp – hp – str
Solo Soprano or Tenor or SATB Chorus.
Jeff Tyzik, arr.
                                                                           Christmas
Schirmer (rental)

Ave Maria (choral version) 5'
2 2 2 2 – 4 0 3 1 – tmp – hp – str
SATB Chorus.
Jeff Tyzik, arr.
                                                                             Christmas
Schirmer (rental)

Christmas with Renata Scotto: 6. Ave Maria 3'
1 1 2 2 – 2 0 0 0 – str
Solo Soprano; SATB Chorus.
John Grady, arr.
                                                                          Christmas
Schirmer (rental)

Marche militaire Nos. 1&2 6'
1 2 2 1 – 2 2 2 0 – tmp+1 – str
Moses Tobani, arr.; revised by J.S. Seredy.
                                                           Popular Classics
Kalmus

Der Teufel als Hydraulicus, D. 4: Overture 5'
2 0 2 2 – 2 0 0 0 – str
                                                           Popular Classics
Breitkopf; Carisch; Kalmus

Die Zauberharfe(Rosamunde), D. 644: Overture 10'
2 2 2 2 – 4 2 3 0 – tmp – str
                                                           Popular Classics
Breitkopf; Kalmus; Luck's

Schuller, Gunther   1925-

And They All Played Ragtime 20'
3[1.2.pic] 3[1.2.Eh] 4[incl 2bcl, cbcl] 3[incl cbn] – 4 3 3 1 – tmp+4 – pf[cel+synth] – str
                                                                                      Jazz
AMP (rental)

Concertino for Jazz Quartet & Orchestra (1959) 19'
2 1 2 1 – 2 3 2 0 – tmp+perc – str
Solo Vibraphone, Piano, String Bass, Drumset.
                                                                                    Jazz
MJQ (rental)

Journey into Jazz 15'
1 1 1 1 – 1 1 0 0 – 1perc – hp – str
perc: hi-hat, szl cym, sd, sus cym.
Solo Narrator and Jazz Quintet: asx, tsx – tpt – drumset – db
Text compares learning to play jazz with getting along with people.
                                                                                    Jazz
AMP (rental)

Music for a Celebration: 6'
 A Fantasy on National Themes
  3[incl 3pic] 3[1.2.Eh] 3[1.2.bcl] 3[1.2.cbn] –
  4 3 3 1 – tmp+6 – hp, cel, pf – str
  SATB Chorus & Audience.
                                                    Patriotic
AMP (rental)

Schuman, William   1910-1992

American Festival Overture 9'
  3[1.2.3/pic] 3[1.2.Eh] 3[1.2.bcl] 3[1.2.(cbn)] –
  4 3 3 1 – tmp+3 – str
                                                    Patriotic
AMP (rental)

American Hymn 27'
  3 3 3 3 – 4 3 3 1 – tmp+perc – cel – str
                                                    Patriotic
Merion (rental)

Casey at the Bat: A Baseball Cantata 40'
  3[incl pic] 3[incl Eh] 3[incl bcl] 2 – 4 3 3 1 –
  tmp+3 – pf – str
  Solo Soprano, Baritone [reciter]; SATB Chorus.
  Libretto and vocal scores for sale.
                                                    Sports
Schirmer (rental)

Circus Overture: Sideshow 7'
  3[incl 2pic] 3[1.2.Eh] 4[1.2.Ebcl.bcl] 3[1.2.cbn] -
  4 3 3 1 – tmp+perc – pf – str
  Alternate: 2 2 3 0 – 2 3 3 1 – tmp+perc – pf – str
  Can be used as an introduction to the instruments of
  the orchestra.
                                                    Circus
AMP (rental)

New England Triptych 15'
                                                 (6' 6' 3')
  3[1.2.3/pic] 3[1.2.Eh] 4[1.2.bcl.Ebcl] 2 – 4 3 3 1
  – tmp+3 – str
  perc: bd, cym, sd, td; (2 or 3 sd or field dr at end).
  Three Pieces for Orchestra after William Billings:
  Be Glad Then America; When Jesus Wept;
  Chester.
                                                    Americana
Merion (rental)

Newsreel in 5 Shots 8'
  3[1.2.3/pic] 3[1.2.Eh] 5[1.2.3.Ebcl.bcl] 4[1.2.3.cbn]
  – 2asx, tsx – 4 3 3 1 – tmp+4 – str
  Alternate: 2[incl pic] 1 2 1 – 2 3 3 1 – tmp+4 – str
  Includes: Horse-Race; Fashion Show; Tribal Dance;
  Monkeys at the Zoo; Parade.
                                                    Instrumental Pops
Schirmer (rental)

On Freedom's Ground: 40'
 An American Cantata for Baritone, Chorus &
 Orchestra
  3[incl 3pic] 3[incl Eh] 3[incl bcl] 2 – 4 3 3 1 –
  tmp+4 – pf/cel – str
  Solo Baritone and SATB Chorus. Text by Richard
  Wilbur.
                                                    Black History Month
Merion (rental)

Schumann, Robert   1810-1856

New Year Song, Op. 144 20'
  "Mit eherner Zunge, da ruft es: Gebt acht"
  2 2 2 2 – 2 2 4 0 – tmp – str
  Solo SATB with SATB Chorus.
                                                    New Year/Popular Classics
Schirmer (rental)

Overture, Scherzo and Finale, Op. 52 17'
  2 2 2 2 – 2 2 (2) 0 – tmp – str   (7' 4' 6')
                                                    Popular Classics
Breitkopf (rental); Kalmus

Schurmann, Gerard   1928-

Attack and Celebration 8'
  2[incl pic] 2[incl Eh] 2 2 – 4 2 3 1 – tmp+2 –
  hp – str
                                                    Celebration
Novello (rental)

Schütz, Heinrich   1585-1672

Christmas Story, SWV 435a   40'
    2 0 0 1 – 0 2 2 0 – cnt – str
    Solo Soprano, Tenor, Bass; SSAAATTTBBBB Chorus.
    A. Schering, arr.

                                    Christmas

Schirmer (rental)

Schwantner, Joseph   1943-

A New Morning for the World   27'
    4[1.2.3/pic.4/pic] 3[1.2.Eh] 3[1.2.3/bcl] 3 – 4 3 4 1 – tmp+4 – hp, cel, pf – str
    perc: vib, glock, marim, crot, xyl, chimes, 3tomtoms, buttongong, 2pr timbales, 2sus cym, 2tri, 2tamtams, 2bd.
    Narrator. Words of Martin Luther King, Jr.

                     Black History Month/
                         Martin Luther King

Helicon (rental)

Schwartz, Stephen   1948-

Dancing in the Dark   4'
    2 2 2 1 – 4 3 3 1 – tmp+perc – pf, elec bass – str
    Chuck Sayre, arr.

                                       Dance

Warner (POP); EMS or Luck's (rental)

The Prince of Egypt Medley   8.5'
    3[1.2.pic] 2 3[1.2.bcl] 2 – 4 3 3 1 – tmp+perc – pf – str
    Includes: Deliver Us; Through Heaven's Eyes; When You Believe.
    Chuck Sayre, arr.

                                       Films

Leonard

Rock-a-Bye Your Baby with a Dixie Melody   3'
    3[1.2.pic] 2 2 2 – (2asx, tsx) – 4 3 3 1 – tmp+perc – str
    Steven Rosenhaus, arr.

                                   Americana

Kalmus

Scott, Cyril   1879-1970

Irish Serenade
    Strings

                         St. Patrick/International

Schirmer (rental)

Scott, Raymond   1908-1994

Dinner Music for a Pack of Hungry Cannibals   3'
    3[1.2.pic] 2[1.2.Eh] 2 2 – 4 3 3 1 – tmp+drumset+perc – str
    Robert Wendel, arr.

                                 Animals/Novelty

Music Sales (rental)

Huckleberry Duck   3'
    3[1.2.pic] 2 2 2 – 4 3 3 1 – tmp+perc – pf – str
    perc: drumset, xyl, glock.
    Robert Wendel, arr.

                                      Animals

Schirmer (rental)

Minuet in Jazz   3'
    2gtr, cel – str[vn divisi, no va or vc]
    Szathmary, arr.

                                 Dance/Jazz

Music Sales (rental)

The Penguin   4'
    3[1.2.pic] 2 2 2 – 4 3 3 1 – tmp+perc – str
    perc: drumset, xyl, glock, mark tree, temple blks.
    Robert Wendel, arr.

                                      Animals

Schirmer (rental)

Powerhouse   4'
    2[incl pic] 2 2 2 – 4 3 3 1 – tmp+3 – pf – str
    Orchestration of late '30s jazz piece used in more than 40 Warner Brothers Cartoons.
    Robert Wendel, arr.

                                         Jazz

Music Sales (rental)

A Raymond Scott Fantasia   7'
    3[1.2.pic] 2 2 2 – 4 3 3 1 – tmp+3 – hp, pf[or cel] – str
    Includes: Dinner Music for a Pack of Hungry Cannibals, Powerhouse, A Boy Scout in Switzerland, The Toy Trumpet, The Penguin, Huckleberry Duck, Twilight in Turkey.
    Robert Wendel, arr.

                                                       TV

Music Sales (rental)

The Toy Trumpet   3'
    3[1.2.pic] 2 2 2 – 4 3 3 1 – tmp+2 – hp, cel – str
    perc: incl drumset, glock, xyl.
    Robert Wendel, arr.

                                        Christmas

Music Sales (rental)

Twilight in Turkey   3'
    3[1.2.pic] 2 4[1.2.Ebcl.bcl] 2 – 4 3 3 1 – tmp+perc – (pf) – str

                                   International

Music Sales (rental)

"Sebastian"   1949-

A Fairytale: 15'
    Suite from the Ballet
    2 2 2 2 – 4 2 3 1 – tmp+3 – hp – str
    Single pieces available. Born as Knud Torben Christensen, the composer is better known by the stage name Sebastian. A Danish singer, guitarist and composer who is one of the most prominent pop/rock musicians in Denmark and has scored numerous films and plays.
    Wolfgang Käfer, arr.

                                        Dance

Hansen (rental)

Secunda, Sholom   1926-1971

Tango de la luna
    2[1.2/pic] 2 2 2 – (3sx) – 4 3 3 0 – tmp+perc – str

                                   Dance/Space

Kalmus

Serly, Tibor   1901-1978

A Little Christmas Cantata   7'
    1 1 2 2 – 2 2 3 1 – tmp+perc – str
    Chorus & audience

                                      Christmas

Schirmer (rental)

Shaiman, Marc   1901-1978

Addams Family Values (1993): Tango   2.5'
    3[1.2.pic] 3[1.2.Eh] 3[1.2.Ebcl] 3[1.2.cbn] – (tsx) – 4 3 4 1 – tmp+6 – 2 hp[(#2)], pf, (cel[hpsd]), (gtr), (accordion) – str
    perc: drumset, xyl, vib, orch bells, cym, sus cym, bd, maracas, woodblk, shaker, vibraslap, cowbell, tambn, ratchet, conga, castanets[2 players], tri.
    Solo Violin. Includes the original theme by Vic Mizzy.

                                   Dance/Films

T&V (rental)

The Addams Family (1991): Theme   4'
and Waltz Finale
    3[pic.2.3] 3[1.2Eh] 3[1.2.Ebcl] 2[1.cbn] – 4 2 4 1 – tmp+4 – 2 hp, pf, cel[hpsd], gtr, accordion – str
    perc: drumset, xyl, vib, glock, cyms, sus cym, bd, maracas, woodblk, shaker, vibraslap, cowbell, tambn, ratchet, conga, castanets.
    Won a 1992 ASCAP award.

                                   Dance/Films

T&V (rental)

The American President (1995):   7.5'
Big Speech, Big Finish
    2 2[1.2/Eh] 2 2 – 4 2 3 1 – tmp+5 – hp, pf/cel – str
    perc: vib, glock, song bells, sus cym, sm finger cyms, tri, sd, pic sd.
    Nominated for 1996 Oscar for Best Music.

                                 Films/Patriotic

Kane (rental)

Shapiro, Michael — 1951-

Frankenstein — 70'
1 1 1 1 – 1 1 1 0 – tmp+1 – elec kybd – str
Music for the film Frankenstein directed by James Whale starring Boris Karloff and Colin Clive. Premiered 2002 at Film Society of Lincoln Center's Jacob Burns Film Center.
                        Films/Halloween
Paumanok

Sharp, Cecil — 1859-1924

Country Gardens, in F
1 1 2 1 – 2 2 3 0 – tmp+perc – hp – str
Solo Voice.
Henry Geehl, arr.
                    Ecology/International
ASH (rental)

Shaw, Artie — 1927-1978

Concerto for Clarinet and Jazz Band — 10'
2 2 4 1 – 2asx, 2bsx – 4 3 3 0 – drumset – gtr – str
                          Jazz
Music Sales (rental)

Shaw, Robert — 1927-1978

The Many Moods of Christmas: Suite 1 — 6'
3[incl 2pic] 3[1.2.Eh] 3[1.2.bcl] 3[1.2.cbn] – 4 3 3 1 – tmp+perc – hp, cel, org – str
SATB Chorus. Includes: Good Christian Men, Rejoice; Silent Night; Patapan; O Come, All Ye Faithful.
Robert Russell Bennett, arr.
                         Christmas
Lawson Gould (rental)

The Many Moods of Christmas: Suite 2 — 13'
3[incl pic] 3[1.2.Eh] 3[1.2.bcl] 3[1.2.cbn] – 4 3 3 1 – tmp+perc – hp – str
SATB Chorus. Includes: O Sanctissima; Joy to the World; Away in a Manger; Fum Fum Fum; March of the Kings.
Robert Russell Bennett, arr.
                         Christmas
Lawson Gould (rental)

The Many Moods of Christmas: Suite 3 — 13'
3[incl pic] 3[1.2.Eh] 3[1.2.bcl] 3[1.2.cbn] – 4 3 3 1 – tmp+perc – hp, lute, viola d'amore – str
SATB Chorus. Includes: What Child Is This?; Hark! The Herald Angels Sing; Bring a Torch, Jeanette, Isabella; Angels We Have Heard on High.
Robert Russell Bennett, arr.
                         Christmas
Lawson Gould (rental)

The Many Moods of Christmas: Suite 4 — 9'
3[incl pic] 3[1.2.Eh] 3[1.2.bcl] 3[1.2.cbn] – 4 3 3 1 – tmp+perc – hp, org – str
Includes: Break Forth, O Beauteous Heavenly Light; The First Nowell; O Little Town of Bethlehem; I Saw Three Ships; Deck the Halls with Boughs of Holly.
Robert Russell Bennett, arr.
                         Christmas
Lawson Gould (rental)

Shchedrin, Rodion — 1932-

Carmen Suite (after Georges Bizet) — 46'
5perc – str
Ballet in 1 act.
                         Dance
Sikorski (rental)

Concerto No. 1 for Orchestra, — 8'
  "Naughty Limericks" (or "Mischievous Melodies")
3 3 3 3 – 4 4 4 0 – tmp+perc – hp, pf – str
                        Halloween
Sikorski (rental)

Sheldon, Robert, arr.

A Most Wonderful Christmas 8.5'
2 1 3[1.2.bcl] 1 – 4 3 3 1 – tmp+3 – str
perc: chimes, glock, sd, hi hat, bd, sus cym, slgh-bells.
Includes: Winter Wonderland; I'll Be Home for Christmas; Santa Claus is Comin' to Town; Have Yourself a Merry Little Christmas; It's the Most Wonderful Time of the Year.

Christmas

Warner

Sheriff, Noam   1935-

Israel Suite 20'
2 2[incl Eh] 3[incl bcl] 1 – 3 3 3 1 – tmp+perc – hp – str

International

Presser (rental)

Shire, David   1937-

The Conversation (1974) 2.5'
0 0 2 0 – 0 0 0 0 – str
Solo Piano.

Films

T&V (rental)

Farewell My Lovely (1975): Suite 2.5'
3[1.2.pic] 3[1.2.Eh] 3[1.2.bcl] 3[1.2.cbn] – 4 3 3 1 – tmp+perc – hp, pf[cel], gtr, elec bs – str
perc: drumset, vib.

Films

T&V (rental)

Norma Rae: It Goes Like It Goes 3'
0 0 0 0 – 0 0 0 0 – pf – str
Solo Vocal.

Films/Labor Day

T&V (rental)

Raid on Entebbe (1977): Theme 3'
2 2 2[1.Ebcl] 2 – 4 3 3 1 – tmp+perc – hp, pf – str
perc: marim, tabla or dumbec, tambn.

TV

T&V (rental)

Return to Oz (1985): Theme 4.5'
3[1.2.pic] 3[1.2.Eh] 3[1.2.bcl] 3[1.2.cbn] – 4 3 3 1 – tmp+perc – hp, pf, cel – str
perc: glock, chimes, crotales, sus cym.
Solo Violin and Cello.

Films

T&V (rental)

Taking of Pelham One Two Three (1974): Theme 3'
3[1.2.pic] 2 2[1.Ebcl] 3[1.2.cbn] – ssx or asx, tsx – 4 3 3 1 – tmp+perc – elec pf, gtr, elec bs – str
perc: drumset, ahatsi or lg cabasa, mellow dr or squeeze dr, bd.

Films

T&V (rental)

With You I'm Born Again 4'
2 2 2 0 – ssx – 4 0 0 0 – tmp+perc – hp, gtr, elec bs – str
perc: drumset.
Solo Piano. Credited to and made popular by Billy Preston and Syreeta Wright.

Popular Song

T&V (rental)

Shore, Howard   1946-

The Lord of the Rings: Highlights from the Fellowship of the Ring 7'
1 1 2 1 – 1 2[1/(flug).2] 1 1 - tmp+perc – hp/pf – str
perc: chimes, mark tree, Bodhran, opt large tom-tom, tam-tam, bd, sus cym, cym.
Includes: Many Meetings, The Ring Goes South, Shadow of the Past.
Bob Cerulli, arr.

Films

Warner

The Lord of the Rings: 10'
Fellowship of the Ring (Symphonic Suite)
3[incl pic] 2 3[incl bcl] 2 – 4 3 3 1 – tmp+perc – str
Solo Boy Soprano. Includes: The Fellowship Theme, Prophecy, Concerning Hobbits, Three Is Company, In Dreams, Shortcut, Knife in the Dark, Argonath, Breaking of the Fellowship.
John C. Whitney, arr.

Films

Warner

The Lord of the Rings: *8.5'*
   Suite from The Return of the King
     2[1/pic/(pan fl). 2] 2 3[1.2.bcl] 1 – 4 3 3 1 –
     tmp+5 – pf/synth[harp patch] – str
     perc: bells, xyl, sd, bd, sus cym, tri, tenor dr, wind
     chimes, Bodhran, vibraslap, tam-tam.
     Includes: The Steward of Gondor, Minas Tinth,
     The End of All Things, The Return of the King.
     Victor Lopez, arr.
                                                       Films
Warner

The Lord of the Rings: The Two Towers   *7'*
   3[1.2.pic] 2 3[1.2.bcl] 2 – 4 3 3 1 – tmp+3 – str
   perc: tam-tam, brake dr, woodblk, sd, large tom-tom, cym,
   bd, sus cym.
   John Whitney, arr.
                                                         Films
Warner

Symphonic Suite from The Lord of the Rings: *7'*
   The Two Towers
     2 3[1.2.Eh] 3[1.2.bcl] 2 – 4 3 3 1 – tmp+3 –
     pf, synth [harp and vocal patch] – str
     perc: chimes, vib, bd, Bodhran, (med. tom-tom), sd,
     sus cym, tam-tam, cym, bell tree.
     Includes: Forth Eorlingas; Evenstar; Rohan; The
     March of the Ents; Isengard Unleashed; Breath of
     Life; Gollum's Song.
     Jerry Brubaker, arr.
                                                        Films
Warner

Shostakovich, Dmitri   1906-1975

Ballet Suite No. 1 (1949)   *13'*
   3[incl pic] 3[incl Eh] 3[1.2.Ebcl] 3[1.2.cbn] –
   4 3 3 1 – tmp+perc – cel, pf – str
   perc: glock, vib, xyl.
   Levon Atovmian, arr.
                                     Dance/Popular Classics
Russian (rental)

Ballet Suite No. 2 (1951)   *20'*
   3[incl pic] 3[incl Eh] 3[1.2.Ebcl] 3[1.2.cbn] –
   4 3 3 1 – tmp+perc – cel, pf – str
   Levon Atovmian, arr.
                                     Dance/Popular Classics
Russian (rental)

Ballet Suite No. 3 (1921)   *20'*
   3[incl pic] 3[incl Eh] 3[1.2.Ebcl] 3[1.2.cbn] –
   4 3 3 1– tmp+perc – cel, pf – str
   Levon Atovmian, arr.
                                     Dance/Popular Classics
Russian (rental)

Ballet Suite No. 4 (1953)   *13'*
   3[incl pic] 3[incl Eh] 3[1.2.Ebcl] 3[1.2.cbn] -
   4 3 3 1 – tmp+perc – cel, pf – str
   Levon Atovmian, arr.
                                     Dance/Popular Classics
Russian (rental)

Bolt: Suite from the Ballet, Op. 27a   *27'*
   (Ballet Suite No. 5)
     3[incl pic] 3[1.2.Eh] 4[1.2.Ebcl.(bcl)] 3[1.2.cbn]
     – 6 3 3 1 – tmp+perc – str
     banda: crt[Eb], 2crt[Bb], 2tp, 2alto hn[Eb], 2tenor
     hn[Bb], 2bar.hn[Bb], 2bass hn
                                     Dance/Popular Classics
Russian (rental)

Eight English and American Folk Songs: *6'*
   When Johnny Comes Marching Home
     2 2 2 2 – 4 0 0 0 – tmp+2 – str
     Solo Voice.
                                                     Patriotic
Schirmer (rental)

Festive Overture, Op. 96   *6'*
   3[1.2.pic] 3 3 3[1.2.cbn] – 4 3 3 1 – tmp+4 – str
   Optional additional brass: 4 3 3 0
   perc: tri, sd, cym, bd.
                                               Popular Classics
Russian (rental)

The Gadfly: Suite from the Film, Op. 97a   *42'*
   3[1.2.pic] 3 3[1/asx.2/asx.3/asx] 3[1.2.cbn] –
   4 3 3 1 – tmp+4 – hp, cel/pf – str
   perc: glock, xyl, tri, sd, tambn, tamtam, cym, bd.
                                                        Films
Russian (rental)

Hamlet: Incidental Music   *20'*
   to the Stage Production, Op. 32a
     2[incl pic] 1 1 1 – 2 2 1 1 – tmp+3 – str
     perc: sd, tri, cym, tamtam, bd, tambn.
                                           Popular Classics
Russian (rental)

Hamlet: Music from the Film, Op. 116   35'
    3[1.2.pic] 2 2 2 – 4 3 3 1 – tmp+5 –
    hp, cel, hpsd/pf – str
    Includes: Introduction; Ball at the Palace; The
    Ghost; In the Garden; Scene of the Poisoning; The
    Arrival and Scene of the Players; Ophelia; The Duel
    and Death of Hamlet.
                                                                                  Films
Russian (rental)

Hamlet: Music from the Film, Op. 116a   42'
    3[1.2.pic] 2 2 2 – 4 3 3 1 – tmp+5[incl xyl] –
    hp, cel, hpsd, pf – str
    Levon Atovmian, arr.
                                                                                 Films
Russian (rental)

Hypothetically Murdered, Op. 31a   42'
    2[1.pic] 1 2[1.bcl] 2 – ssx, tsx – 1 2 2 1 – tmp+4
    – Upright pf[out-of-tune], (accordion) – str
    Gerard McBurney, arr.
                                       Popular Classics
Russian (rental)

The Limpid Stream: Suite from the Ballet, Op. 39a
    3[1.2.pic] 3[1.2.Eh] 3[1.2.Ebcl] 3[incl cbn] –
    4 3 3 1 – tmp+perc – hp – str
                                     Dance/ Popular Classics
Russian (rental)

Overture on Russian and   8'
   Kirghiz Folk Themes, Op. 115
    3[1.2.pic] 2 2 3[1.2.cbn] – 4 2 3 1 – tmp+perc – str
                                                     International
Russian (rental)

Suite for Jazz Orchestra No. 1   7'
    0 0 0 0 – ssx, asx, tsx – 0 2 1 0 – 3perc –
    bnjo, Hawaiian gtr, pf – str
    Includes: Waltz; Polka; Foxtrot (Blues).
                             Dance/Jazz/Popular Classics
Russian (rental)

Suite for Jazz Orchestra No. 2   8'
    0 0 0 0 – 2asx, 2tsx, bsx – 0 4 2 1 – 2perc –
    pf, 4gtr, bnjo – vn, db
    Formerly known as The "Lost" Jazz Suite.
    Includes: Scherzo; Lullaby; Serenade.
    Gerard McBurney, arr.
                                                                       Jazz
Russian (rental)

Suite for Variety Orchestra No. 1   25'
    2[incl pic] 1 4 1 – 2asx, 2tsx – 3 3 3 1 – tmp+3 –
    hp, cel, pf – str
    This Suite has been recorded under many titles
    including *Second Suite for Variety Orchestra, Jazz*
    Suite No. 2, Second Jazz Suite.
                           Dance/Jazz/Popular Classics
Russian (rental)

Suite for Variety Orchestra No. 2   12'
    2[incl pic] 1 2 1 – 2asx, 2tsx – 3 3 3 1 – tmp+3
    – hp, cel, pf, accordion, gtr – str
    Includes: Introduction; Waltz; Intermezzo; Finale.
                                 Dance/Popular Classics
Russian (rental)

Tahiti-Trot, Op. 16   3.5'
    2[1.pic] 2[1.Eh] 3[1.Ebcl.bcl] 2[1.cbn] – 2sx –
    4 3 3 1 – tmp+3 – hp, cel – str
    perc: includes glock, xyl.
    This smaller wind section is available:
    2[1.pic] 2 1 1 – 4 2 1 0.
    This is an arrangement of *Tea for Two* by Victor
    Youmans.
                                 Dance/Popular Classics
Russian (rental)

United Nations March   2.5'
    2[incl pic] 2[incl Eh] 3[incl bcl] 2 – 2 2 2 1 –
    3perc – str
    Premiered at United Nations Day Concert on
    October 24, 1954 for the newly built New York
    headquarters. Arranged from Shostakovich's song
    The Counterplan from the film *The Song of the*
    Counterplan. Text refers to peace and united
    nations.
    Leopold Stokowski, arr.
                                                        Patriotic
Presser (rental)

Shulman, Alan   1915-2002

The Bop Gavotte   3'
    Strings
                                         Instrumental Pops
EAM (rental)

Hup Two Three Four   2.5'
    2 2 2 2 – 4 3 3 1 – tmp+3 – hp – str
    Jazz march.
                               Jazz/Instrumental Pops
Shawnee (rental)

J. S. On The Rocks: Nightcap   2.5'
    0 0 1 0 – 0 0 0 0 – hp, gtr – str
                          Instrumental Pops/Novelty
    Shawnee (rental)

Popocatepeti   6'
    3[incl pic] 2 2 2 – 4 3 3 1 – tmp+3 – hp – str
                          Instrumental Pops
    Shawnee (rental)

Ricky-Tick Serenade   3'
    0 0 0 0 – 0 0 0 0 – 1perc – hp, pf, gtr – str
                          Instrumental Pops
    Shawnee (rental)

Shur, Itaal & Thomas, Rob   1972-

Smooth: Santana   3.5'
    1 1 2 1 – 1 2 1 1 – 4 perc – (elec bass) – str
    perc: drumset, vib, congas, tambn, guiro.
    Jerry Brubaker, arr.
                          Popular Song
    Warner

Sibelius, Jean   1865-1957

Academic March   4'
    2 2 2 2 – 4 2 0 0 – tmp – hp – str
                          Popular Classics
    Hansen (rental)

Finlandia, Op. 26, No. 7   8'
    2 2 2 2 – 4 3 3 1 – tmp+1 – str
    perc: cym, bd, tri.
                        International/Popular Classics
    Breitkopf; Kalmus

Hymn to the Earth   8'
    2 2 2 2 – 4 2 3 0 – tmp – str
                          Ecology
    Peer (rental)

Karelia Suite, Op. 11   14'
    3[1.2.pic] 3[1.2.(Eh)] 2 2 – 4 3 3 1 – tmp+3 – str
    perc: tambn, bd, cym.   (4' 6' 4')
    Includes: Intermezzo; Ballade; March.
                          Popular Classics
    Breitkopf (rental); Kalmus

Kuolema (Death), Op. 44, No. 1: Valse Triste   6'
    1 0 1 0 – 2 0 0 0 – tmp – str
                          Dance
    Breitkopf; Kalmus; Luck's

Legends, Op. 22: 2. The Swan of Tuonela   10'
    0 2[1.Eh] 1[bcl] 2 – 4 0 3 0 – tmp+1 – hp – str
    perc: bd.
    Solo English Horn.
                          Animals/Popular Classics
    Breitkopf (rental); Kalmus; Luck's

Rakastave the Lover   12.5'
    Strings & percussion
                          Valentine
    Peer (rental)

Romance in C Major, Op. 42   5'
    Strings
                          Popular Classics/Valentine
    Breitkopf; Kalmus; Luck's

Suite Champêtre, Op. 98b   9'
    Strings
                          Popular Classics
    Hansen (rental)

Valse chevaleresque, Op. 96c   4'
    2 2 2 2 – 4 2 3 0 – tmp+perc – str
                          Dance/Popular Classics
    Hansen (rental)

Valse lyrique, Op. 96a   5'
    2 2 2 2 – 4 2 3 0 – tmp+perc – str
                          Dance/Popular Classics
    Breitkopf (rental); Kalmus

Sieczynsky, Rudolf   1879-1952

Vienna-City of My Dreams   3'
    (Wien, Wien, Nur Du Allein)
    2 2 2 2 – 4 2 3 1 – tmp+perc – hp – str
    Solo Voice in key of G. Also available for solo
    voice in the key of A flat (score is in G).
                          International
    Mapleson (rental)

Vienna-City of My Dreams   3'
    (Wien, Wien, Nur Du Allein)
    2[1.pic] 2 2 2 – 4 2 3 0 – tmp+perc – hp – str
    Arthur Luck, arr.
                          International
    Luck's

Vienna-City of My Dreams   3'
(Wien, Wien, Nur Du Allein)
    2 2 2 2 – 4 0 0 0 – tmp+perc – hp, cel, pf – str
    Key of G.

                                             International

Dragon (rental)

Vienna-City of My Dreams   3'
(Wien, Wien, Nur Du Allein)
    Strings
    Solo Voice.
    Kennedy, arr.

                                             International

Kalmus

Sierra, Roberto   1953-

A Joyous Overture   5'
    3[1.2.pic] 2 2 2 – 4 3 2 1 – tmp+2 – str

                             Instrumental Pops

Schirmer (rental)

Tropicalia: Celebration   7'
    3[1.2.pic] 3[1.2.Eh] 3[1.2.bcl] 3[1.2.cbn] – 4 3 3 1 – tmp+4 – hp, pf[or cel] – str

                                     Celebration

Schirmer (rental)

Silvers, Louis   1889-1954

April Showers   3'
    3[incl pic] 2 2 2 – (2asx, tsx) – 4 3 3 1 – perc – str
    Timothy Broege, arr.

                                                Weather

Kalmus (rental)

Silvestri, Alan   1950-

The Abyss: Finale   7'
    3[1.2.3/pic] 3 3 3[1.2.cbn] – 4 4 4 1 – tmp+perc – hp, pf – str
    SATB Chorus.

                                                    Films

Kane (rental)

Back to the Future (Madrid Version)   8'
    3 3 3[1.2.bcl]3[1.2.cbn] – 4 4 4 2 – tmp+4 – 2hp, 2pf – str
    Chorus. This version was created for a Silvestri festival in Madrid, 2007.

                                                    Films

Kane (rental)

Back to the Future Suite   4'
    3[1/pic.2/pic.3/pic] 3[1.2.3/Eh] 3[1.2.bcl] 3 – 4 4 4 1 – tmp+perc – hp, pf, mandolin – str
    Also listed by the publisher as *Back to the Future III (1990): End Credits.*

                                                    Films

Kane (rental)

Beowulf (2007): I Shouldn't Have Told You
    3[1/afl.2.3] 3[1.2.3/Eh] 3[1.2.3/bcl] 3[1.2.3/cbn] – 8 4 4 1 – tmp+perc – 2hp, pf – str
    SATB Chorus.

                                                    Films

Kane (rental)

Cast Away: Crossroads   3.5'
    0 2[1.Eh] 0 0 – 0 0 0 0 – pf – str

                                                    Films

Kane (rental)

Fools Rush In
    3 3[1.2.Eh] 3[1/tsx.2.bcl] 2 – 6 3 2 1 – tmp+perc – hp, pf, cel – str

                                                    Films

Kane (rental)

Forrest Gump: Suite   7'
    2[1.2/pic] 2 3[1.2.bcl] 2 – 4 3 3 1 – tmp+5 – pf – str
    perc: sd, bd, sus cym, mark tree, cym, bells, vib.
    Calvin Custer, arr.

                                                    Films

Leonard

Forrest Gump (1994): Suite   6.5'
    2[1.afl] 2[1.Eh] 3[1.bcl.3] 2 – 4 0 3 1 – 3perc – hp, pf, acoustic gtr – str
    perc: vib glock, sus cym, sm tri.
    Won 1995 Oscar for Best Music.

                                                    Films

T&V (rental)

Forrest Gump (1994): The Feather   2.5'
    2[1.afl] 2[1.Eh] 3 2 – 4 0 3 1 – 3perc –
    hp, 2 pf, gtr – str
    perc: vib, glock, sus cym, sm tri.
    Won 1995 Oscar for Best Music.

                                Films
T&V (rental)

Forrest Gump: 3'
   Main Title for Piano & Orchestra (Feather Theme)
    2[incl afl] 2[incl Eh] 3 2 – 4 0 3 1 – 3perc –
    hp, pf, gtr – str
    Winds and brass are optional.
    Solo Piano.
    Paul Lavender, arr.

                                Films
Leonard

Judge Dredd (1995): Suite   5.5'
    3[1.2.3/pic] 2 2 2 – 8 3 3 1 – tmp+perc –
    hp, 2 pf – str

                                Films
Kane (rental)

Mouse Hunt (1997): Suite   5.5'
    3[1.2/afl.3/pic] 3[1.2.Eh] 3[1.2.bcl] 3[1.2.3/cbn] –
    asx, asx/tsx – 8 4 4 2 – tmp+perc –
    2hp, pf, pf/cel/accordion – str

                            Animals/Films
Kane (rental)

The Mummy Returns (2001)
    3[1.2/afl.3/afl] 3[1.2.3/Eh] 3[1.2.3/bcl] 3[1.2.3/cbn]
    – 8 3 3 1 – tmp+perc – 2 hp, pf, saz or oud [Turkish
    stringed instruments] – str
    SATB Chorus. Won an ASCAP award in 2002.
                                Films
Kane (rental)

Night at the Museum (2006): Suite
    3[1.2.3/pic] 3[1.2.Eh] 3[1.2.3/bcl] 3[1.2.3/cbn] –
    6 3 3 1– tmp+perc – hp, pf – str
                                Films
Kane (rental)

Polar Express: Believe
    3[1.2.afl] 2[1.Eh] 3[1.2.bcl] 2 – 4 0 3 1 – tmp+perc
    – hp – str
    SA Chorus.
    William Ross, arr.
                            Christmas/Films
Kane (rental)

Polar Express: O Tannenbaum
    3[1.2.3/pic/rec] 3[1.2.Eh/rec] 3[1.2.3/bcl]
    3[1.2.3/cbn] – 8 3 4 1 – tmp+perc –
    2hp, pf/cel, pf – str
    Conrad Pope, arr.
                            Christmas/Films
Kane (rental)

Polar Express: Spirit of the Seasons   2.5'
    3[1.2.3/pic] 3[1.2.3/Eh] 3[1.2.3/Ebcl/bcl]
    3[1.2.3/cbn] – 8 3 4 1 – tmp+perc –
    2hp, pf/cel, pf – str
    SATB Chorus and Boys' Choir.
    Conrad Pope, arr.
                            Christmas/Films
Kane (rental)

Polar Express Suite   6'
    3[1.2.3/pic] 3[1.2.3/Eh/alto recorder]
    3[1.2.3/Eb/bcl] 3[1.2.3/cbn] – 4 3 3 1 – tmp+perc
    – hp, pf, pf/cel/synth – str
    Conrad Pope, arr.
                            Christmas/Films
Kane (rental)

Polar Express: When Christmas Comes to Town
    3[1.2.afl] 2[1.Eh] 3[1.2.bcl] 2 – 4 0 0 0 – perc –
    hp, pf/synth, synth – str
    SA Chorus.
    William Ross, arr.
                            Christmas/Films
Kane (rental)

Silvestri, Alan & Ballard, Glen   1950-/?

God Gless Us Everyone   3'
    3[1.2.3/afl/pic] 3[1.2.Eh] 3[1.2.bcl] 2 – 4 3 3 1
    – tmp+4 – hp, pf, cel – str
    perc: bd, cym, sus cym, chimes, glock.
    Solo Tenor; SATB Chorus. May be performed with
    tenor solo with chorus or chorus alone. From the
    Disney *A Christmas Carol*.
    William Ross, arr.
                                  Christmas
Leonard

Simeone, Harry

Flute Cocktail: 3'
    Scherzo and Blues for 3 or 2 Solo Flutes and Orchestra
       3[solos] 2 3[1.2.bcl] 2 – (asx, tsx) – 3 3 3 1 – tmp+2 – hp, pf – str
       perc: drumset, chimes.
       2 or 3 Solo Flutes.
       Arthur Fiedler, editor

                                   Instrumental Pops
    Shawnee (rental)

Simons, Moises   1888-1945

Peanut Vendor (El manisaro)   3'
       2 1 2 2 – 2asx, tsx – 2 2 1 0 – tmp+2 – str
       perc: maracas, claves, bells.
       Philip J. Lang, arr.

                                                Circus
    Kalmus

Simons, Netty   1913-

Big Sur   30'
       3[incl pic] 2[incl Eh] 2[incl bcl] 2[cbn] – 4 3 3 1 – tmp+perc – 2hp – str

                                           Ecology
    Merion (rental)

Pied Piper of Hamelin   18'
       Solo flute – pf – 3 part violins
       Narrator.

                                           Animals
    Merion (rental)

Slatkin, Leonard   1944-

The Raven   18'
       3 3 3 3 – 4 4 3 1 – tmp+perc – 2hp, pf – str
       Narrator. Text by Edgar Allan Poe.

                                   Animals/Halloween
    Schirmer (rental)

Slonimsky, Nicolas   1894-1995

My Toy Balloon   6'
    (Variations on a Brazilian Tune)
       3[1.2.pic] 2 2[Ebcl] 2 – 2 2 3 1 – tmp+6 – (hp), pf/(cel) – str

                                       International
    Shawnee (rental)

Smetana, Bedrich   1824-1884

The Bartered Bride: Three Dances   11'
       3[1.2.pic] 2 2 2 - 4 2 3 0 – tmp+3 – str
       perc: bd, cym, td, tri.
       Includes: Polka; Furiant; Dance of the Comedians.
       Clark McAlister, arr.

                                 Dance/Popular Classics
    Kalmus

Má vlast (My Fatherland):   11.5'
    2. Vltava (Moldau)
       3[1.2.pic] 2 2 2 – 4 2 3 1 – tmp+3 – hp – str
       perc: tri, bd, cym.

                             Popular Classics/Ecology
    Breitkopf; Kalmus

Má vlast: 3.Sárka   9'
       3[1.2.pic] 2 2 2 – 2 4 3 1 – tmp+2 – str
       perc: tri, cym.

                                      Popular Classics
    Kalmus; Luck's

Smith, Claude T.

A Rhapsody on Christmas Carols   7'
       3[1.2.pic] 2[1.2/Eh] 3[1.2.(bcl)] 2 – 4 3 4 2 – tmp+4 – str
       perc: sd, bd, tambn, cym, sus cym, chime tree, tri, finger cym, tamtam, glock, vib, marim, chimes, xyl.
       Includes: In Dulci Jubilo; O Come, O Come, Emmanuel; We three Kings; Greensleeves/What Child Is This?; Joy to the World; Away in a Manger; Deck the Halls; Angels We Have Heard on High.

                                           Christmas
    Leonard

Smith, Hale   1925-

Abide With Me   2.5'
2 2 1 1 – 0 0 0 0 – str
No. 1 from *A Set of Protestant Hymns*.

        Popular Song

Presser (rental)

Amazing Grace   2.5'
2 2 2 2 – 2 2 2 1 – str
No. 2 from *A Set of Protestant Hymns*.

        Popular Song

Presser (rental)

America the Beautiful   4.5'
2 0 1 0 – 2 0 0 0 – str
No. 3 from *A Set of Protestant Hymns*.

        Patriotic

Presser (rental)

Meditations in Passage   27'
2 2 2[incl bcl] 2[incl cbn] – 4 2 3 0 – tmp+2 –
hp, pf – str
Solo Soprano & Baritone. Based on the story of The Amistad.

        Black History Month

Presser (rental)

A Mighty Fortress Is Our God   4.5'
2 2 2 2 – 2 2 2 1 – tmp+perc – str
No. 4 from *A Set of Protestant Hymns*.

        Popular Song

Presser (rental)

Smith, Harry C.

Admiral Dewey's March   3'
1 1 2 1 – 2 2 1 0 – perc – str

        Patriotic

Kalmus

Smith, John Stafford   1750-1836

Star-Spangled Banner   2'
3[1.2.pic] 3[1.2.Eh] 3[1.2.bcl] 3[1.2.cbn] –
4 3 3 1 – tmp+perc – str
Key of A flat.

        Patriotic

Kalmus

Star-Spangled Banner   5'
2 3[1.2.Eh] 3[1.2.bcl] 3[1.2.cbn] – 4 3 3 1 –
tmp+perc – str
Key of B flat.
Alfred Luck, arr.

        Patriotic

Luck's

Star-Spangled Banner   5'
2 3[1.2.Eh] 3[1.2.bcl] 3[1.2.cbn] – 4 3 3 1 –
tmp+perc – str
Key of B flat.
Ward, arr.

        Patriotic

Luck's

Star-Spangled Banner   5'
3[1.2.pic] 2 2 2 – 4 2 3 1 – tmp+3 – hp – str
Key of B flat.
Walter Damrosch, arr.

        Patriotic

Kalmus; *Schirmer (rental)*

Star-Spangled Banner   1.5'
3[1.2.pic] 2 3[1.2.bcl] 2 – 4 2 3 1 – tmp+5 – hp – str
perc: sd, bd, cym, tri, chimes. 2004 Summer Olympics version. Key of E flat.
Peter Breiner, arr.

        Patriotic

Belwin

Star-Spangled Banner   3'
3[1.2.pic] 3[1.2.Eh] 3[1.2.bcl] 3[1.2.cbn] – 4 3 3 1
– tmp+perc – hp, pf – str
perc: includes a cannon.
Signature Edition: 2004 Rose Bowl version.
John T. Williams, arr.

        Patriotic

Leonard

Star-Spangled Banner   3'
    4[1.2.pic] 4[1.2.3.Eh] 4[1.2.3.bcl] 4[1.2.3.cbn]
    – 8 4 4 1 – tmp+2 – str
    perc: 2sd.
    Can be done with three in each woodwind section and 4331 brass. A note on the score says if only 4 horns, #3 should play the #5 part and #4 should play #6. Key of G.
    Leopold Stokowski, arr.
                                                    Patriotic

Tetra

Smith, Julia   1911-

American Dance Suite   20'
    2 2 2 1 – 2 2 1 0 – tmp+perc – str
                                           Americana/Dance

Presser (rental)

Smith, Robert W.   1958-

Great Steamboat Race   4.5'
    1[opt pic] 3[1.2.bcl] 1 – 2 2 2 1 – tmp+5 – str
    perc: xyl, chimes, bells, sd, bd, mark tree or wind chimes, ship's bell, hi-hat, congas, cym, sus cym, ocean drum, water jugs, cabasa, train whistle, brake dr.
                                               Sports/Travel

Belwin

Jingle Bells Forever   4'
    2[1/pic.2] 1 4[1.2.3.bcl] 1 – 3 3 3 1 – tmp+5 – str
    perc: glock, sd, bd, cym, slgh-bells.
    Based on melodies by Pierpont and Sousa. String parts edited by Robert McCashin.
                                                   Christmas

Boosey

Snow, Mark   1946-

X-Files: Main Title Theme
    2[1.2.pic] 3[1.2.Eh] 3[1.2.3/Eh] 3 3[1.2.cbn] – 4 3 3 1 – tmp+perc – hp, pf, org – str
    Jonathan Sacks, arr.
                                                           Films

Kane (rental)

Sondheim, Stephen   1930-

A Little Night Music: Send In the Clowns   3'
    2 1 3[1.2.bcl] 1 – (3sx) – 4 3 2 1 – tmp+2 – pf – str
    perc: tri, drumset, bells.
    Bob Lowden, arr.
                             Circus/Films/Popular Songs
Leonard (POP); EMS or Luck's (rental)

Soro, Enrique   1884-1954

Danza Fantástica   4'
    3[incl pic] 2 2 2 – 4 2 3 1 – tmp+2 – hp – str
    Score available for purchase.
                             Dance/International (Chile)
Filarmonika (rental)

Tres Aires Chilenos   14'
    (Three Chilean Aires)
    3[incl pic] 2 3[incl bcl] 2 – 4 3 4 0 – tmp+3 – 2hp – str
    Score available for purchase.
                                   International (Chile)
Filarmonika (rental)

Sousa, John Philip   1854-1932

El Capitan March   3'
    3[1.2.pic] 2 3[1.2.(bcl)] 2 – 4 2 3 1 – (tmp)+3 – str
    perc: sd, bd, cym, bells.
    Clark McAlister, editor
                                                   Patriotic
Kalmus

Fairest of the Fair March   3'
    3[1.2.pic] 2 3[1.2.(bcl)] 2 – 4 2 3 1 – 3perc – str
    Clark McAlister, editor
                                                   Patriotic
Kalmus

Hands Across the Sea   3'
    3[1.2.pic] 2 3[1.2.(bcl)] 2 – 4 2 3 1 – 3perc – str
    Clark McAlister, editor
                                                   Patriotic
Kalmus

High School Cadets March   3'
    1[1/pic] 2 2 1 – 2 2 0 0 – 3perc – str
    perc: sd, bd, cym.
                                                Patriotic
Kalmus

King Cotton March   3'
    3[1.2.pic] 2 3[1.2.(bcl)] 2 – 4 2 3 1 – 3perc – str
    Clark McAlister, editor
                                                Patriotic
Kalmus

King Cotton March   3'
    1/pic 2 2 2 – 2 2 3 1 – perc – str
                                                Patriotic
Church

The Liberty Bell March   3'
    3[1.2.pic] 2 3[1.2.(bcl)] 2 – 4 2 3 1 – perc – str
    Clark McAlister, editor
                                                Patriotic
Kalmus

The Liberty Bell March   3'
    2 2 2 2 – asx, tsx – 2 2[crt] 3 0 – 2perc – str
    perc: sd, bd.
    Aubrey Winter, arr.
                                                Patriotic
Novello (rental)

Semper Fidelis March   3'
    3[1.2.pic] 2 3[1.2.(bcl)] 2 – 4 2 3 1 – 2perc – str
    perc: sd, bd, cym.
    Clark McAlister, editor
                                              Patriotic
Kalmus

The Stars and Stripes Forever   3.5'
    Strings
    Samuel Adler, arr.
                                              Patriotic
Presser (rental)

The Stars and Stripes Forever   3.5'
    3[1.2.pic] 2 3[1.2.bcl] 2 – 4 4 3 1 – perc – (hp) – str
    Key of D.
    Keith Brion & Schissel, arr.
                                              Patriotic
Leonard

The Stars and Stripes Forever   3.5'
    Strings
    Bruce Dukov, arr.
                                            Patriotic
Kane (rental)

The Stars and Stripes Forever   5'
    3[incl 2pic] 3[1.2.Eh] 3 3[incl cbn] – 4 3 3 1 –
    tmp+perc – str
    Solo 3+ pianos
    Morton Gould, arr.
                                            Patriotic
Schirmer (rental)

The Stars and Stripes Forever   3.5'
    2 2 2 2 – 2 2 1 0 – perc – str
    Jansen, arr.
                                            Patriotic
Schirmer (rental)

The Stars and Stripes Forever   3.5'
    3[1/pic2.2/pic3.pic1] 2 2 2 – asx, tsx, bsx –
    4 4[(4)] 3[(2&3)] 1 – tmp+5 - (pf), (hp) – str
    perc: bells, slgh-bells, xyl, sd, cym, bd.
    Key of G.
    Leopold Stokowski, arr.
                                            Patriotic
Tetra

The Stars and Stripes Forever   3'
    3[1.2.pic] 2 3[1.2.(bcl)] 2 – 4 2 3 1 – 3perc – str
    Corrected edition. Key of D.
    Clark McAlister, editor
                                            Patriotic
Kalmus

Thunderer March   3'
    3[1.2.pic] 2 3[1.2.(bcl)] 2 – 4 2 3 1 – 3perc – str
    Clark McAlister, editor
                                      Weather/Patriotic
Kalmus

Washington Post March   3'
    2 2 2 2 – 2 2 3 1 – 3perc – str
    perc: sd, bd, cym, tri.
                                            Patriotic
Novello (rental)

Washington Post March   3'
    3[1.2.pic] 2 3[1.2.(bcl)] 2 – 4 2 3 1 –(tmp) + perc
    – str
    Clark McAlister, arr.
                                            Patriotic
Kalmus

Sowerby, Leo — 1895-1968

Monotony: A Symphony for Metronome & Jazz Orchestra — 24'
Stage band and strings
                                                                Jazz
Presser (rental)

Song for America — 9'
3[incl pic] 3[incl Eh] 3[incl bcl] 2 – 4 3 3 1 – tmp+perc – str
Chorus
                                                     Patriotic
Presser (rental)

Synconata — 10'
Stage band and strings
                                        Instrumental Pops
Presser (rental)

Two Romantic Pieces — 15'
3 3 2 2 – 4 2 3 1 – perc – str
                                               Valentine
Presser (rental)

Stanford, Charles Villiers — 1852-1924

Irish Rhapsody No. 1, Op. 78 — 12'
2[1.2/pic] 2[1.2/Eh] 3[1.2.(bcl)] 3[1.2.cbn] – 4 3 3 1 – tmp+3 – hp – str
Based on *Leitherbags Donnell* (an Irish battle song) and *Emer's Farewell to Cuchullin* (also known as *Londonderry Air* or *O Danny Boy*).
                  St. Patrick/International
Kalmus

Steffe, William — 1830-1890

Battle Hymn of the Republic — 5'
3[incl pic] 2 3[1.2.bcl] 2 – 4 3 3 1 – tmp+perc – hp – str
Solo Baritone. SATB Chorus.
Robert Russell Bennett, arr.
                                                 Patriotic
Alfred (rental)

Battle Hymn of the Republic — 5'
2[incl pic] 2 2 2 – 2asx, tsx – 4 3 3 1 – tmp+3 – hp – str
Optional Mixed Chorus.
Peter J. Wilhousky, arr.
                                                 Patriotic
Fischer

Battle Hymn of the Republic — 3'
2 2 2 2 – 2 2 3 1 – perc – str
Optional Chorus. In the of Key of B flat.
Piano/conductor score included.
Arthur Luck, arr.
                                                 Patriotic
Luck's

Battle Hymn of the Republic — 5'
2 2 2 2 – 4 3 3 1 – tmp+3 – str;
Alternate: 2 2 2 2 – 2asx, 2tsx – 4 3 3 1 – tmp+3 – db
perc: sd, bd, bells, chimes.
Roy Ringwald, arr.
William Schoenfeld, orchestrator.
                                                 Patriotic
Shawnee (rental)

Battle Hymn of the Republic — 5'
2[1.2/pic] 1 2 1 – 2 3 3 1 – tmp+2 – hp – str
perc: sd, tri, sus cym, cym.
Optional SATB or SSA or TTBB or SAB or two-part Chorus.
Roy Ringwald, arr.
Brant Adams, orchestrator
                                                 Patriotic
Shawnee (rental)

Battle Hymn of the Republic — 4.5'
2 1 2 1 – 4[(3&4)] 4[(3&4)] 3 0 – tmp+2 – hp, (org) – str
SATB Chorus.
John Rutter, arr.
                                                 Patriotic
Hinshaw

Steiner, Fred

Perry Mason (1956): Theme — 1.5'
3[1.2.pic] 2[1.Eh] 2 2 – 4 3 3 1 – tmp+2 sus – pf – str
perc: cym, 2 sd, bd [all perc playable on drumset].
                                                   TV
T&V (rental)

Steiner, Max   1888-1971

The Caine Mutiny (1954): The March   2.5'
     3[1.2.pic] 3[1.2.Eh] 3[Ebcl/(Bbcl).2.bcl] 3[1.2.cbn]
     – 4 4 4 1 – tmp+4 – hp – str
     perc: sd, cym, bd, tamtam, chimes, xyl, glock.
     Won the 1955 Oscar for Best Music.
                                                             Films/Patriotic/TV

T&V (rental)

Gone With the Wind (1939): Dance Montage   4'
     3[1.2.pic] 2 3[1.2.bcl] 2 – 4 4 3 1 – tmp+4 –
     2 hp, pf – str
     perc: sd, bd, cym, tri, glock, xyl.
     Nominated for the 1940 Oscar for Best Music.
                                                             Dance/Films

T&V (rental)

Gone With the Wind: 4'
     Tara - Short Poem for Orchestra (1941)
     2 2 3[1.2.bcl] 2 – 4 3 3 1 – tmp+2 – hp, pf – str
     perc: sd, bd, cym, sus cym, gong, glock, tri.
     F. Campbell-Watson, arr.
                                                                          Films

Luck's; Warner (rental)

Jezebel (1938): Waltz   2.5'
     2 2 2 2 – 3 2 2 0 – tmp+2 – hp – str
     perc: tri, glock.
     Nominated for 1939 Oscar for Best Music.
                                                             Dance/Films

T&V (rental)

King Kong (1933): Overture   5'
     3[afl.2.pic] 2[1.Eh] 4[1.Ebcl.3.bcl/barisx] 2[1.cbn]
     – 4 4 4 2 – 3 tmp+8 – 2 hp, 2 pf – str
     perc: cym[2players], sd, bd, native dr[2 players], toms,
     xyl, Turkish cym, chimes, sus cym, lg tamtam, hi tamtam.
                                                             Animals/Films

T&V (rental)

King Kong: Jungle Dance   8.5'
     2 2 2 2 – 2 3 3 1 – tmp+perc – hp, pf – str
                                                          Animals/Dance/Films

Bourne (rental)

King Kong: Theme   4'
     3 2 3 2 – 2 3 3 2 – tmp+perc – hp, pf
                                                                    Animals/Films

Bourne (rental)

Now, Voyager (1942): Main Title   5'
     and Final Scene
     2 2([1.Eh] 3[1.2.bcl] 2 – 4 3 3 1 – tmp+3 –
     2 hp, pf, cel – str
     perc: 2 vib, (chimes).
     Won 1943 Oscar for Best Music.
                                                                Films

T&V (rental)

The Treasure of Sierra Madre (1948): Suite   7'
     3[1.pic.pic] 2[1.Eh] 5[Ebcl.Ebcl.tsx.4.bcl] 2
     – asx[#1&2=cl], tsx[ssx] – 4 4 4 1 – tmp+5 –
     2 hp, 2 pf[#2=cel], 2 gtr – str
     perc: tom tom, cym, 2 vib, glock, marim, tambn, tri,
     2 sm Mexican dr, 2 carracas, gong.
                                                                Films

T&V (rental)

Stephenson, James M. III, arr.   1969-

BaSOON It Will Be Christmas   4'
     3[1.2.pic] 3[1.2.Eh] 3[1.2.bcl] 3[soloists] –
     4 3 3 1 – tmp+2 – hp – str
     perc: glock, tri, ratchet, crotales, sd, sus cym, xyl, cym.
     3 Solo Bassoons.
                                                                Christmas

Stephenson (rental)

Bells of Christmas Suite   7.5'
     3[1.2.pic] 3[1.2.Eh] 3[1.2.bcl] 2 – 3 2 2 0 –
     tmp+3 – hp – str
     perc: glock, chimes, tri, sus cym, cym, finger cym, bd,
     slgh bells, sd, tambn, xyl, td.
     Solo Brass Quintet. Includes: Carol of the Bells;
     Jingle Bells; Ding Dong Merrily on High; I Heard
     the Bells on Christmas Day.
                                                                Christmas

Stephenson (rental)

Concerto for Cell Phone (2006)   5.5'
     3[1.2.pic] 3[1.2.Eh] 3[1.2.bcl] 2 – 4 3 3 1 –
     tmp+4 – str
     Solo Cell Phone.
                                                                 Novelty

Stephenson (rental)

God Rest Ye Merry Gentlemen　　　　　　　　　4'
　2 3[1.2.Eh] 3[1.2.bcl] 2 – 3 2 2 0 – tmp+3 – hp
　– str
　perc: drum set; finger cym, bd, sus cym, tri, cym, td, sd,
　tambn.
　Solo Brass Quintet.
　　　　　　　　　　　　　　　　　　　　　Christmas

Stephenson (rental)

Go Tell It On the Mountain　　　　　　　　　　4'
　3[1.2.pic] 2 3[1.2.bcl] 2 – 4 3 3 1 – tmp+3 –
　elec bs, pf – str
　perc: drumset, tambn, bongos, shaker, sus cym, tri,
　vibraslap.
　S. Moore, arr.
　J. Stephenson, trans.
　　　　　　　　　　　　　　　　　　　　　Christmas

Stephenson (rental)

Holiday Fanfare Medley No. 2　　　　　　　　　4'
　3[incl pic] 3[incl Eh] 3 2 – 4 3 3 1 – tmp+3 –
　hp, pf, cel – str
　perc: drumset, slgh bells, mark tree, sus cym, glock, tri,
　ratchet, sd, bd, tambn, crotales, temple blks.
　Includes: A Snowy Christmas; Let It Snow;
　Snow Flake Waltz; Winter Wonderland;
　Jingle Bells.
　　　　　　　　　　　　　　　　　　　　　Christmas

Stephenson (rental)

Holiday Overture　　　　　　　　　　　　　　　8'
　3[incl pic] 3[incl Eh] 3[1.2.bcl] 2 – 4 3 3 1 –
　tmp+3 – hp, pf, cel – str
　perc: drumset, cym, chimes, slgh bells, sus cym, glock,
　tri, sd, bd, tambn.
　Includes: Deck to the Hall; Oy Chanukah; I Have a
　Little Dreydl; O Christmas Tree; Away in a
　Manger; Jingle Bells; Up on the Housetop; Good
　King Wenceslas.
　　　　　　　　　　　　　　　　　　　　　Christmas

Stephenson (rental)

A Holly and Jolly Sing-Along!　　　　　　　　9.5'
　3[incl pic] 3[incl Eh] 3 2 – 4 3 3 1 – tmp+3 –
　hp, (kybds) – str
　Optional SATB and/or Children's Chorus.
　Includes: Introduction; Deck the Hall; Jingle Bells;
　The Holly and the Ivy; Jolly Old St. Nicholas;
　Frosty the Snowman; Up on the Housetop;
　Rudolph the Red-Nosed Reindeer; Joy to the
　World; We Wish You a Merry Christmas. This
　work has many optional cuts and can be used as an
　audience sing-along.
　　　　　　　　　　　　　　　　　　　　　Christmas

Stephenson (rental)

I Saw Three Ships/Jeanette, Isabella Medley　　3'
　3[1.2.pic] 3[1.2.Eh] 3[1.2.bcl] 2 – 4 3 3 1 –
　tmp+2 – hp, cel – str
　perc: sus cym, chimes, tambn, tri, sd, td, glock, cym.
　Solo Female Vocal.
　　　　　　　　　　　　　　　　　　　　　Christmas

Stephenson (rental)

Joy to the World　　　　　　　　　　　　　　　2'
　3[incl pic] 2 3[1.2.bcl] 0 – 3 2 3 1 – tmp+3 – hp
　– str
　perc: glock, chimes, cym, tri, sd, bd, tambn.
　　　　　　　　　　　　　　　　　　　　　Christmas

Stephenson (rental)

Lo, How a Rose E'er Blooming　　　　　　　　　3'
　Es ist ein Ros 'entsprungen
　2 0 2 2 – 4 0 3 1 – tmp – str
　Solo Mezzo-Soprano. The solo can be played by an
　instrument instead. The composer suggests using
　trumpet.
　　　　　　　　　　　　　　　　　　　　　Christmas

Stephenson (rental)

The Magic of Christmas　　　　　　　　　　　　8'
　3[1.2.pic] 3[1.2.Eh] 3[1.2.bcl] 2 – 4 3 3 1 –
　tmp+2 – hp, kybd – str
　perc: glock, wind chimes, tri, sus cym, chimes, tambn,
　slgh bells, cym, (hand bells).
　Solo Soprano (child). SATB Choir and Children's
　Choir.
　　　　　　　　　　　　　　　　　　　　　Christmas

Stephenson (rental)

O Christmas Tree　　　　　　　　　　　　　　　3'
　3[1.2.pic] 2 3[1.2.bcl] 2 – 3 2 2 0 – tmp+3 – hp
　– str
　perc: glock, chimes, cym, tri, sd, bd, tambn.
　　　　　　　　　　　　　　　　　　　　　Christmas

Stephenson (rental)

Swing Carol Fantasy　　　　　　　　　　　　　　8'
　3[1.2.pic] 3[1.2.Eh] 3[1.2.bcl] 2 – 4 3 3 1 –
　tmp+4 – hp, kybd – str
　perc: drumset, glock, cym, tri, sus cym, xyl, slgh bells,
　claves, vibraslap, slapstick, tambn, sd, ratchet, (chimes).
　Includes: Rudolf the Red-Nosed Reindeer; Jingle
　Bells; Up on the Housetop; Winter Wonderland;
　We Wish You a Merry Christmas.
　　　　　　　　　　　　　　　　　　　　　Christmas

Stephenson (rental)

Wassail, Wassail All Over the Tuba   5'
    2[incl pic] 3[1.2.Eh] 2 2 – 3 2 2 0 – tmp+3 – str
    perc: tambn, sd, bd, glock, drum set, vib.
    Solo Tuba.
                                        Christmas

Stephenson (rental)

We Three Basses!   4'
    from *We Three Kings*
    1 1 1 1 – 1 0 0 0 – 2perc – str
    perc: bell tree, tri, td, sus cym, sd, bd.
    3 Solo String Basses.
                                        Christmas

Stephenson (rental)

We Three Kings of Orient Are   5'
    3[1.2.pic] 3[1.2.Eh] 2 2 – 4 3 3 1 – tmp+3 –
    hp, kybd – str
    perc: glock, cym, tri, sd, sus cym, td, wind chimes, tambn, bd.
    SATB Chorus and optional audience sing-along.
                                        Christmas

Stephenson (rental)

We Three Strings!   4'
    from *We Three Kings*
    1 1 1 1 – 1 0 0 0 – 2perc – str
    perc: bell tree, tri, td, sus cym, woodblk, tambn, sd, bd.
    3 Solo Violins.
                                        Christmas

Stephenson (rental)

Stevens, Leith   1909-1970

The Wild One (1953)
    3[1.2.pic] 2 0 3 – 2asx, tsx – 4 3 3 1 – tmp+perc
    – hp – str
    perc: sd, bd, sus cym, cym, tamtam.
                                        Films

T&V (rental)

Stevens, Morton   1929-1991

Hawaii Five O (1968)   1'
    3[1.2.pic] 3[1.2.Eh] 3[1.2.bcl] 2 – 4 3 3 1 –
    tmp+perc – hp, pf, gtr, elec bs – str
    perc: drumset, tambn, congas.
    Won for 1974 Emmy for Best Music Composition.
                                        TV

T&V (rental)

Stevens, Ray

Everything is Beautiful   3'
    2 1 3[1.2.bcl] 1 – (sxs) – 2 2 2 1 – tmp+perc – (pf) – str
    Piano/conductor score.
    Jerry Lehmeier, arr.
                                       Popular Song

Leonard (rental)

Still, William Grant   1895-1978

Symphony No. 1   24'
    (Afro-American Symphony)   (7' 5' 5' 7')
    3[incl pic] 3[incl Eh] 4[incl bcl] 2 – 4 3 3 1 –
    tmp+2 – hp, cel – str
                                 Black History Month

Novello (rental)

Wood Notes   20'
    2[(#2)] 2[(#2)] 2[(#2)] 2 – 2 3 2 0 – tmp+2 –
    hp, cel, (pf) – str
    perc: sus cym, drumset, sd, tri, glock, vib.
    Includes: Singing River; Autumn Night; Moon Dusk; Wippoorwill's Shoes.
    Inspired by poems of J. Mitchell Pilcher.
                       Ecology/Black History Month

Peer

Stillman, Al & Allen, Robert

Home for the Holidays   5'
    2[1.2/pic] 1 1 1 – 2 2 2 0 – 2perc – hp – str
    perc: sus cym, slgh-bells, xyl, glock, mark tree, vib.
    Solo Soprano and Baritone. SATB Chorus.
    Mark Hayes, arr.
                                        Christmas

Shawnee

Stokowski, Leopold, arr.   1882-1977

3 Christmas Carols   5.5'
    4 2[incl Eh] 4[incl bcl, cbcl] 4[incl cbn] – 4 2 3 1 – str
                                        Christmas

Stokowski (rental)

Traditional Slavic Christmas Music   4'
    0 0 0 0 – 4 3 3 1 – str
                               Christmas/International
Stokowski (rental)

What Child Is This?   1'
    0 0 0 0 – 0 4 4 0 – tmp+perc[sd] – str
                               Christmas
Stokowski (rental)

Strauss, Johann, Jr.   1825-1899

An der schönen blauen Donau Walzer   11'
    (On the Beautiful Blue Danube), Op. 314
    2[1.2/pic] 2 2 2 – 4 2 1 1 – tmp+2 – hp – str
    perc: tri, sd, bd.
    Optional Male Chorus.
                               Dance/New Year
Breitkopf; Doblinger; Kalmus

An der schönen blauen Donau Walzer   3'
    (On the Beautiful Blue Danube), Op. 314
    1 1 2 1 – 2 2 1 0 – hp – str
    Solo Voice.
    Henry Geehl, arr.
                               Dance/New Year
ASH (rental)

Annen Polka, Op. 117   4'
    2[incl pic] 2 2 2 – 4 2 1 0 – tmp+1 – str
    Rudolf H. Führer, arr.
                               Dance/New Year
Doblinger

Annen Polka, Op. 117   4'
    2[incl pic] 2 2 2 – 4 2 3 0 – tmp+perc – hp – str
    G. Walter, arr.
                               Dance/New Year
Boosey (rental)

Banditen Galopp   2.5'
    (Bandit's Galop), Op. 378
    2[1.pic] 2 2 2 – 4 2 3 0 – tmp/tri+2 – str
    Doblinger edition by Isabella Sommer.
                       New Year/Popular Classics
Doblinger; Kalmus

Champagne Polka, Op. 211   3'
    2[1.pic] 2 2[1.Ebcl] 2 – 4 2 1 1 – tmp+1 – str
                               Dance/New Year
Kalmus, Luck's

Eine nacht in Venedig: Frühlingsstimmen Walzer   6'
    (Voices of Spring), Op. 410
    2[1.pic] 2 2 2 – 4 2 3 0 – tmp+1 – hp – str
    perc: bd, sd.
                               Dance/New Year/
                      Popular Classics/Seasons
Breitkopf; Kalmus; Luck's

Eljen A Magyar! Polka   3'
    (Long Live the Magyar), Op. 332
    2[1.pic] 2 2 2 – 4 3 3 0 – tmp+1 – str
    Doblinger edition by Norbert Nischkauer.
                             Popular Classics
Doblinger; Kalmus

Egyptian March, Op. 335   4'
    2[1.pic] 2 2 2 – 4 2 3 1 – 5perc – str
    perc: chimes, cym, bd, sd, tambn, tri.
    Doblinger edition by Fritz Racek uses no tuba.
                             Popular Classics
Doblinger; Kalmus; Luck's

Eine Nacht in Venedig: 11'
    Lagunenwalzer, Op. 411
    3[incl pic] 2 2 2 – 4 2 3 0 – tmp+perc – pf – str
    Kalmus also lists a smaller arrangement by Wright
    as 1 1 2 1 – 2 2 1 0 – perc – pf – str.
                               Dance/New Year/
                               Popular Classics
Breitkopf (rental); Kalmus

Die Fledermaus: Du und du   5'
    (You and You Waltz), Op. 367
    2[1.2/pic] 2 2 2 – 4 2 3 0 – tmp+2 – str
    Doblinger edition by Isabella Sommers.
                     New Year/Popular Classics
Breitkopf; Doblinger; Kalmus; Luck's

Die Fledermaus: Mein Herr Marquis   5'
    (Laughing Song)
    2 2 2 2 – 4 2 3 0 – tmp – str
    Solo Soprano.
                             Popular Classics
Kalmus

Die Fledermaus: Overture   8'
    2[1.2/pic] 2 2 2 – 4 2 3 0 – tmp+2 – str
    perc: sd, cym, bd, tri, chime [E]
                     New Year/Popular Classics
Kalmus

Die Fledermaus Waltz   6'
    3[incl pic] 3[incl Eh] 3[incl bcl] 3[incl cbn] –
    4 3 3 1 – tmp +5 – hp – str
    perc: bd, tri, sd, cym, marim.
    Leopold Stokowski, arr.
                      Dance/New Year/Popular Classics
Stokowski (rental)

Geschichten aus dem Wienerwald
(Tales from the Vienna Woods), Op. 325
    2[1.2/pic] 2 2[1/Ebcl.2] 2 – 4 3 3 1 – tmp+2 –
    hp, (zither) – str
    perc: bd, sd, tri.
                  Popular Classics/Seasons
                         Ecology/New Year/
Breitkopf; Kalmus

Graduation Ball: Ballet in One Act   40'
    2[incl pic] 2 2 2 – 4 2 3 0 – tmp+4 – hp – str
    Antal Dorati, arr.
                           Dance/Popular Classics
EMI (rental)

Im Krapfenwaldl,   3'
Polka Française, Op. 336
    2[1.pic] 2 2 2 – 4 2 3 0 – tmp+2 – str
    Includes cuckoo calls.
    Schoenherr, arr.
                           Animals/Ecology/
                           Popular Classics
Kalmus

Kaiser Walzer   11'
(Emperor Waltzes), Op. 437
    2 2 2 2 – 4 2 3 0 – tmp+1 – hp – str
    perc: sd, bd.
                        New Year/Popular Classics
Breitkopf; Doblinger; Kalmus; Luck's

Künstler (Artist's) Quadrille, Op. 201   6'
    2[1.pic] 2 2 2 – 4 2 1[bass tbn] 1 – tmp+1 – str
                           Dance/New Year/
                           Popular Classics
Kalmus; Luck's

Künstlerleben (Artist's Life) Waltz, Op. 316   10'
    2[1.pic] 1 2 2 – 4 2 3 1 – tmp+perc – str
    Doblinger edition by Fritz Racek with brass listed
    as 4210.
                           Dance/New Year/
                           Popular Classics
Doblinger; Kalmus

Lucifer Polka, Op. 266   3'
    2[1.pic] 2 2 2 – 4 2 0 0 – tmp+2 – str
                           Dance/Halloween
                           Popular Classics
Kalmus

Morgenblätter (Morning Papers), Op. 279   10'
    2[1.2/pic] 2 2 2 – 4 2 3 1 – tmp+2 – str
    Doblinger edition by Thomas Aigner uses 1 tbn.
                           Dance/New Year/
                           Popular Classics
Doblinger; Kalmus; Luck's

Moulinet Polka, Op. 57   3'
    2[incl pic] 2 2 2 – 4 2 3 1 – 2perc – hp, (accordion)
    – str
    Max Schoenherr, arr.
                           Dance/New Year/
                           Popular Classics
Doblinger; Kalmus

Perpetuum mobile, Op. 257   3'
(Musical Joke)
    2[1.2/pic] 2 2[1.Ebcl] 2 – 4 2 1 0 – tmp+1 – hp
    – str
    perc: glock, tamtam.
    Doblinger edition by Norbert Rubey; Kalmus
    edition by Clark McAlister.
                           Popular Classics
Doblinger; Kalmus; Luck's

Persian March, Op. 289   3'
    2[1.pic] 2 2 2 – 4 2 3 0 – perc – str
                           International/
                           Popular Classics
Doblinger; Kalmus; Novello (rental)

Rosen aus dem Süden   10'
(Roses from the South Waltzes), Op. 388
    2[1.pic] 2 2 2 – 4 2 3 0 – tmp+3 – hp – str
    perc: bd, cym, sd, tri.
    Edition by Howard K. Wolf.
                           Dance/New Year/
                           Popular Classics
Kalmus

Telegramme Walzer, Op. 318   10'
    2[1.pic] 2 2 2 – 4 2 1 0 – tmp – str
                           Dance/New Year/
                           Popular Classics
Kalmus

Thousand and One Nights Waltzes, Op. 346   7'
    2[incl pic] 2 2 2 – 4 2 3 0 – tmp+perc – str
                               Dance/New Year/
                               Popular Classics
    Kalmus; Luck's

Tick-Tack Polka, Op. 365   2.5'
    2[incl pic] 2 2 2 – 4 2 3 0 – tmp+2 – str
    Based on motifs from *Die Fledermaus*.
    Kalmus edition by Clark McAlister.
                               Dance/New Year/
                               Popular Classics
    Kalmus; Luck's

Tritsch-Tratsch Polka (Chit-Chat), Op. 214   3'
    2[1.pic] 2 2 2 – 4 2 3 0 – perc – str
    Kalmus edition by Clark McAlister.
                               Dance/New Year/
                               Popular Cassics
    Kalmus; Luck's

Tritsch-Tratsch Polka (Chit-Chat), Op. 214   3'
    3[incl pic] 2 2 2 – 4 2 3 0 – tmp+3 – str
    Aubrey Winter, arr.
                               Dance/New Year/
                               Popular Classics
    Boosey (rental)

Tritsch-Tratsch Polka (Chit-Chat), Op. 214   3'
    1 1 2 1 – 2 2 2 0 – perc – str
    A. Wood, arr.
                               Dance/New Year/
                               Popular Classics
    Novello (rental)

Unter Donner und Blitz   3'
    (Thunder and Lightning Polka), Op. 324
    2[1.pic] 2 2 2 – 4 3 3 1 – tmp+3 – str
    perc: bd, cym, sd.
    Doblinger edition by Fritz Racek; Kalmus edition
    by Clark McAlister.
                               Dance/Weather/
                            New Year/Popular Classics
    Doblinger; Kalmus; Luck's

Unter Donner und Blitz   3'
    (Thunder and Lightning Polka), Op. 324
    2[incl pic] 2 2 2 – 4 2 3 0 – tmp+perc – str
    H. Perry, arr.
                            Dance/Weather/New Year/
                               Popular Classics
    Novello (rental)

Vergnügungszug Polka   2.5'
    (Excursion or Pleasure Train), Op. 281
    2[1.pic] 1 2[incl Ebcl] 2 – 4 2 1 0 - tmp+3 – str
    perc includes Signalhorn.
    Doblinger edition by Norbert Rubey.
                             Dance/Popular Classics/Travel
    Doblinger; Kalmus; Luck's

Von der Borse,   3'
    Polka française, Op. 337
    2[incl pic] 2 2 2 – 4 2 3 0 – tmp+2 – hp – str
    Fritz Racek, ed.
                                       Dance
    Doblinger

Waldmeister Overture   5'
    2 2 2 2 – 4 2 3 0 – tmp+1 – hp – str
    Boosey edition by Benatzky.
                                 Popular Classics
    Boosey; Novello (rental)

Wein, Weib und Gesang Waltzer   9'
    (Wine, Women, and Song), Op. 333
    2[1,2/pic] 2 2[1/Ebcl.2] 2 – 4 2 3 0 – tmp+2 – hp
    – str
    perc: bd, sd, tri.
    Doblinger edition by Fritz Racek; Kalmus edition
    by Howard K. Wolf.
                             Popular Classics/Valentine
    Breitkopf; Doblinger; Kalmus

Wiener Blut (Vienna Blood), Op. 354   7'
    2[1.2/pic] 2 2 2 – 4 2 3 0 – tmp+2 – str
    perc: bd, sd, tri.
                               Dance/New Year/
                               Popular Classics
    Breitkopf; Kalmus; Luck's; Novello (rental)

Zigeunerbaron (Gypsy Baron): Overture   8'
    2[1.2/pic] 2 2 2 – 4 2 3 0 – tmp+3 – hp –str
                             New Year/Popular Classics
    Doblinger; Kalmus; Luck's; Novello (rental)

Strauss, Johann Jr. and Josef

Pizzicato Polka   3'
    2[1.pic] 2 2 2 – 4 2 3 1 – tmp+2 – str
    Also available for strings and optional
    glockenspiel.
                               Dance/New Year/
                               Instrumental Pops
    Kalmus

Pizzicato Polka   3'
    3[1.2.pic] 2 2 2 – 4 2 2 0 – glock – str
    Norbert Rubey, editor

                               Dance/New Year/
                               Instrumental Pops
Doblinger

Pizzicato Polka   3'
    2[1.pic] 2 2 2 – 2 2 0 0 – tmp+perc – str
    Clark McAlister, editor

                               Dance/New Year/
                               Instrumental Pops
Masters

Pizzicato Polka   3'
    (glock) – strings

                               Dance/New Year/
                               Instrumental Pops
Breitkopf; Kalmus

Strauss, Johann, Sr.   1804-1849

Carnival Nights (Emperor Waltz) in F   3'
    1 1 2 1 – 2 2 3 0 – perc – str
    Henry Geehl, arr.

                               Dance/New Year
ASH (rental)

Radetzky March, Op. 228   3'
    3[1.2.pic] 2 2 2 – 4 2 3 0 – 2perc – str
    perc: bd, cym.
    Kalmus edition by Clark McAlister.
                               New Year/Popular Classics
Kalmus; Luck's

Radetzky March, Op. 228   3'
    1 1 2 1 – 2 2 3 0 – 3 perc – str
    perc: sd, bd, cym.
    Aubrey Winter, arr.
                               New Year/Popular Classics
Boosey (rental)

Tritsch-Tratsch (The Circus)   3'
    1 1 2 1 – 2 2 1 0 – 2perc – str
    Solo Voice.
    Henry Geehl, arr.

                               Circus/Dance/
                               New Year/Popular Classics
ASH (rental)

Strauss, Josef   1827-1870

Aus Ferienreisen, Polka Schnell, Op. 133   3'
    2[1.pic] 2 2 1 – 4 2 1 0 – tmp+perc – str
                               Popular Classics/Travel
Kalmus; Luck's

Dorfschwalben aus Österreich   8'
(Austrian Village Swallows Waltz), Op. 164
    2[1.2/pic] 2 2[incl Ebcl] 2 – 4 2 1 0 – tmp+3 – hp
    – str
    perc: tri, sd, bd, birdcall.
                               Animals/Dance
Kalmus; Luck's

Elfen Polka, Op. 74   3'
    3[incl pic] 2 2 2 – 4 2 1 1 – perc – hp – str
    Kalmus lists the instrumentation as
    2[1.pic] 2 2[1.Ebcl] 2 – 4 2 1 0 – tmp+perc – str.
                               Dance
Kalmus; Luck's

Ohne Sorgen (Carefree) Polka, Op. 271   3'
    2[1.pic] 2 2 2 – 4 3 3 1 – tmp+2 – str
                               Dance/New Year/Popular Classics
Kalmus

Plappermaulchen Polka (Chatterbox), Op. 245   3'
    2[1.pic] 2 2 2 – 4 3 3 1 – tmp+2 – str
                               Dance
Kalmus

Sphärenklänge   9'
(Music of the Spheres Waltz), Op. 235
    2[1.2/pic] 2 2[incl Ebcl] 2 – 4 4 3 1 – tmp+2 – hp
    – str
                               Dance/Popular Classics/Space
Kalmus

Strauss, Richard   1864-1949

Also sprach Zarathustra, Op. 30   33'
    4[1.2.3/pic2.pic1] 4[1.2.3.Eh] 4[1.2.bcl.Ebcl]
    4[1.2.3.cbn] – 6 4 3 2 – tmp+3 – 2hp, org – str
    perc: glock, tri, cym, bd, sus cym, chimes [E]
                               Popular Classics
Kalmus; Peters

Burleske   17'
   3[1.2.pic] 2 2 2 – 4 2 0 0 – tmp – str
   Solo Piano.
                                      Dance
Kalmus

Introduction: (Sunrise)   2'
   4[1.2.3.pic] 3 3[1.2.Ebcl] 4[1.2.3.cbn] – 6 4 2 1
   – tmp+perc – org – str
   From *Also sprach Zarathustra* as used in the film
   2001: A Space Odyssey.
                       Films/Space/Weather
Kalmus

Romanze   12'
   2 2 2 2 – 2 0 0 0 – str
   Solo Cello.
                     Popular Classics/Valentine
Schott

Till Eulenspiegels lustige Streiche, Op. 28   15'
   (Till Eulenspiegel's Merry Pranks)
   4[1.2.3.pic] 4[1.2.3.Eh] 4[1.2.bcl.Ebcl] 4[1.2.3.cbn]
   – 4 3 3 1 – tmp+2 – str
   perc: bd, cym, ratch, sd, tri.
   Kalmus critical edition by Clinton F. Nieweg.
                             Popular Classics
Kalmus; Peters

Stravinsky, Igor   1882-1971

Circus Polka: 4'
   Composed for a Young Elephant
   2[1.pic] 2 2 2 – 4 2 3 1 – tmp+3 – str
   perc: sd, cym, bd.
                          Circus/Dance/Novelty/
                                Popular Classics
Schott

L'Oiseau de feu (Firebird): Suite (1919)   22'
                     (3' 2' 6' 5' 6')
   2[1.2/pic] 2[1.2/Eh] 2 2 – 4 2 3 1 – tmp+3 –
   hp, pf/(cel) – str
   perc: xyl, tambn, tri, cym, bd.
   Includes: Introduction; L'Oiseau de feu et sa danse
   & Variation de l'oiseau de feu; Ronde des
   princesses; Danse infernale du roi Kastcheï;
   Berceuse et Final.
   Kalmus edition by Clark McAlister.
                                Animals/Dance/
                                Popular Classics
Kalmus; Schott

L'Oiseau de feu (Firebird):   6'
   Berceuse & Finale (1919)
   2[1.2/pic] 2 2 2 – 4 2 3 1 – tmp+3 – hp, cel – str
   perc: tri, bd, cym.
   Clark McAlister, editor
                                Animals/Dance/
                                Popular Classics
Kalmus

Ragtime   6'
   1 0 1 0 – 1 1[crt] 1 0 – 1perc – cimbalom –
   str[no cello]
   perc: bd, sus cym, 2sd, 3tomtoms.
   Original version.
                                         Jazz
Chester (rental); Kalmus

Song of the Volga Boatmen   4'
   2[1.pic] 2 2 3 – 4 3 3 1 – tmp+2 – [no str]
   perc: tamtam, bd.
                                    International
Chester (rental); Kalmus

Strayhorn, Billy   1915-1967
(Also See: Ellington/Strayhorn)

Chelsea Bridge   5'
   2 2[1.Eh] 2 2 – 4 3 3 1 – tmp+2 – hp – str
   Chuck Israels, arr.
                                         Jazz
TPO (rental)

Pinturas de tamayo   18'
   3[1.2/pic1.3/pic2] 3[1.2.3/Eh] 3[1.2/Ebcl.2/bcl]
   3[1.2.3/cbn] – 4 3[1/pic tp.2.3] 3 1 – 3perc – hp, pf
   – str
   perc: bd, Chinese cym, tamtam, glock, xyl, marim,
   chimes, vib, marac, claves, tambn, 2tri, 2sus cym,
   2woodblks.
   Inspired by Mexican artist Rufino Tamayo.
                                    International
Presser (rental)

Strommen, Carl

A Salute to Broadway 7.5'
2[1/pic.2[1 3[1.2.bcl] 1 – 4 3 3 1 – tmp+2 – str
perc: drumset, xyl, glock.
Includes: Give My Regards to Broadway; Ain't Misbehavin'; My Funny Valentine; I've Grown Accustomed to Her Face Thou Swell.
                                    Broadway Musicals
Warner

A Salute to the Cinema 8'
2 1 3[1.2.bcl] 1 – 4 3 3 1 – tmp+3 – str
perc: xyl, glock, drumset, sd, woodblk, sus cym, bd, cym.
Includes: Hooray for Hollywood; Singin' In the Rain; Over the Rainbow; As Time Goes By; A Day in the Life of a Fool.
                                                 Films
Warner

Salute to TV 7'
2 1 3[1.2.bcl] 2 – 4 3 3 1– tmp+3 – str
perc: xyl, tri, 2woodblks[or temple blks], cowbell, slide whistle, drumset.
Includes: Masterpiece Theater; M A S H; The Alfred Hitchcock Hour; The Late and the Late, Late show; the Flintstones; Bonanza.
                                                    TV
Belwin

Strouse, Charles

Musical Highlights from Annie 6'
2[1.2/pic] 2 3[1.2.bcl] 2 – 4 3 3 1 – tmp+3 – gtr, elec bs – str
perc: chimes, woodblk, sd, bd, cym, xyl, glock.
Includes: It's the Hard Knock Life; N.Y.C.; You're Never Fully Dressed Without a Smile; Maybe; Easy Street; I Don't Need Anything But You; Tomorrow.
Philip J. Lang, arr.
                                    Broadway Musicals/Films
Morris (rental)

Selections from Annie 7.5'
2 2 3[1.2.bcl] 2 – 2asx, tsx, bsx – 4 3 3 1 – tmp+2 – (elec bs) – str
perc: chimes, glock, marim, vib, drumset [sd, bd, cym, hi-hat, toms]
Includes: Tomorrow; It's the Hard Knock Life; Maybe; Let's Go to the Movies; Easy Street; I Don't Need Anything But You; We Got Annie!; Finale-Tomorrow.
Robert W. Lowden, arr.
                                    Broadway Musicals/Films
Morris (rental)

Stucky, Steven 1949-

Fanfare for Cincinnati 2'
3[incl pic] 3[incl Eh] 3[incl bcl] 3[incl cbn] – 4 3 3 1 – tmp+perc – hp, pf – str
                                    Americana/Fanfare
Presser (rental)

Fanfare for Los Angeles 2'
2 2 2[incl Ebcl & bcl] 2[incl cbn] – 4 3 3 1 – 2perc – hp – str
                                    Americana/Fanfare
Presser (rental)

Styne, Jule 1905-1994

Gypsy: Overture 5'
3[1.2.pic]2 3[1.2.(bcl)] 2 – (3sx) – 4 3 3 1 – tmp+3[drumset] – hp – str
Includes: Fanfare; Everything's Coming Up Roses; You'll Never Get Away from Me; Small World Isn't It; The Strippers' Music; and Mister Goldstone.
Robert Wendel, editor
                                        Broadway Musicals
Wendel (rental)

Let It Snow! Let It Snow! Let It Snow 2.5'
2 2 2 2 – 4 3 3 1 – 4 perc – elec bass – str
perc: drumset, bells, tri, conga dr.
Chuck Sayre, arr.
                                        Seasons/Christmas
Warner

Let It Snow! Let It Snow! Let It Snow!   3'
    1 1 3[1.2.(bcl)] 1 – (asx, tsx) – 2 2 2 1 – tmp+2
    – pf – str
    perc: sd, bd, sus cym.
    James D. Ployhar, arr.
                                                      Christmas/Seasons
Leonard (rental)

Sullivan, Arthur   1842-1900

The Mikado: Overture   8'
    2[1.2/pic] 1 2 1 – 2 2 2 0 – tmp+1 – str
    perc: bd, cym, tri.
                                   Popular Classics
Kalmus

The Mikado: Overture   7'
    2[incl pic] 1 2 1 – 2 2 0 0 –tmp+perc – str
    Cruikshank, arr.
                                   Popular Classics
Novello (rental)

Mikado Selections   8'
    2[incl pic] 2 2 2 – 4 2 3 1 – perc – str
    Cruikshank, arr.
                                   Popular Classics
Novello (rental)

Onward Christian Soldiers
    2 2 2 2 – 4 3 3 1 – tmp+perc – str;
    Alternate: 2 2 2 2 – 2asx, 2tsx – 4 3 3 1 – tmp+perc
    – db
    Optional SATB or TTBB Chorus.
    Harry Simeone & William Schoenfeld, arr.
                                   Popular Song
Shawnee

Patience Selections   8'
    2[incl pic] 1 2 1 – 2 2 3 0 – tmp+perc – str
    Cruikshank, arr.
                                   Popular Classics
Novello (rental)

Pineapple Poll: Suite   21'
    3[1/pic.2/pic.pic] 3[1.2.Eh] 3[1.2.bcl]
    3[1.2.cbn] – 4 3 3 1 – tmp+4 – hp, cel – str
    perc: bd, cast, cym, glock, sd, tamtam, tambn, tri, xyl.
    Suite from the ballet.
    Charles Mackerras, arr.
                                Dance/Popular Classics
Chappell (rental)

Pirates of Penzance Selections   8'
    1[incl pic] 1 2 1 – 2 2 1 0 – tmp+perc – str
    Hellier, arr.
                                   Popular Classics
Novello (rental)

Ruddigore: Overture   8'
    2[incl pic] 1 2 1 – 2 2 2 0 – tmp+1 – str
    Cruikshank, arr.
                                   Popular Classics
Novello (rental)

Ruddigore Selections   8'
    2[incl pic] 2 2 2 – 4 2 3 1 – tmp+perc – str
    Cruikshank, arr.
                                   Popular Classics
Novello (rental)

Yeoman of the Guard: Overture   4'
    2[incl pic] 1 2 1 – 2 2 3 0 – tmp – str
    Rapley, arr.
                                   Popular Classics
Novello (rental)

Yeoman of the Guard: Selections   8'
    2[incl pic] 2 2 2 – 2 2 3 1 – tmp+perc – str
    C. Godfrey, arr.
                                   Popular Classics
Novello (rental)

Suppé, Franz von   1819-1895

Dichter und Bauer (Poet and Peasant):   10'
  Overture
    2[1.2/pic] 2 2 2 – 4 2 3 1 – tmp+2 – hp – str
    perc: sd, tri, cym, bd.
    Clark McAlister, editor
                                   Popular Classics
Kalmus

Die leichte Kavallerie (Light Cavalry):   7'
  Overture
    2[1.pic] 2 2 2 – 4 2 3 1[(euph)] – 3perc – str
    perc: sd, bd cym.
    Kalmus edition by Clark McAlister.
                                   Popular Classics
Kalmus; Luck's; Novello (rental)

Ein Morgen, Mittag und   7'
  Abend in Wien: Overture (Morning,
  Noon, and Night in Vienna)
  2[1.2/pic] 2 2 2 – 4 2 3 0 – tmp+2 – str
  perc: bd, sd, cym.
  Kalmus edition by Clark McAlister.
                               New Year/Popular Classics
  Kalmus; Luck's

Die schöne Galathea: Overture   8'
  (The Beautiful Galatea)
  2[1.pic] 2 2 2 – 4 2 3 0 – tmp+2 – str
  perc: bd, sd, tri, cym.
  Clark McAlister, editor
                                    Popular Classics
  Kalmus

Surinach, Carlos   1915-1997

Feria Mágica (Magic Fair): Overture   6'
  2[1/pic.2/pic] 2 2 2 – 4 2 3 1 – tmp+2 – hp – str
  Highlights the piccolo, oboe, horn, and percussion.
                                             Halloween
  AMP (rental)

Ritmo jondo: 20'
  Flamenco for Orchestra
  1[1/pic] 1[1/Eh] 1 1 – 1 1 1 0 – tmp+4 – str
  Also uses 3 hand clappers.
  Includes: Of Men; Of Women; Of Meeting and
    Parting.
                                      Dance/International
  AMP (rental)

Sinfonietta flamenca   12'
  2[incl 2pic] 2[incl Eh] 2 2 – 4 2 3 1 – tmp+perc –
    hp – str
                                      Dance/International
  AMP (rental)

Svoboda, Tomáš   1939-

Overture of the Season, Op. 89   8'
  3[1.2.pic] 2 2 2 – 4 3 3 1 – tmp+2 – str
  perc: chimes, 2sus cym.
                                                 Seasons
  Stangland (rental)

Swanson, Howard   1907-1978

Night Music   9'
  1 1 1 1 – 1 0 0 0 – str
                                                 Halloween
  Weintraub (rental)

Short Symphony   11'
  2[incl pic] 2 2 2 – 2 2 1 0 – tmp – str
                                  Black History Month
  Weintraub (rental)

Swayne, Giles   1946-

Naaotwa Lala, Op. 39   13'
  2 0 2 0 – 2 2 0 0 – hp – str
                                     Instrumental Pops
  Novello (rental)

T

Talbot, Joby   1971-

Lover's Ink   20'
    Strings
                                Valentine
Schirmer (rental)

Tallarico, Tommy &   1968-
Plowman, Michael Richard   1965-

Advent Rising Suite: 5.5'
    Bounty Hunter Theme
    2 1 3[1.2.bcl] 1 – 4 3 3 1 – tmp+6 – pf – str
    From "Video Games Live."
    Victor Lopez, arr.
                             Video Games
Belwin

Tan Dun   1957-

Crouching Tiger Concerto   45'
    2[incl afl/(bawu).pic/(dizi)] 0 0 0 – 0 0 0 0 – 5perc – hp – str
    Solo Cello. Optional bawu and dizi are Asian flutes.
                       Animals/Films
PAR (rental)

Tanara, Fernando

Two Venetian Dialect Songs   4'
    1 0 1 0 – 0 1 1 0 – perc – str
    Includes: Nina; A Night in Venice.
    Andor Pinter, arr.
                             International
Kalmus

Tchaikovsky, Piotr Ilyich   1840-1893

Eugen[e] Onegin: Polonaise   4'
    2 2 2 2 – 4 2 3 0 – tmp – str
                          Popular Classics
Kalmus; Simrock (rental)

Festival Coronation March   5'
    for Alexander III
    3[1.2.pic] 3[1.2.Eh] 2 2 – 4 4 3 1 – tmp+3 – str
                       Popular Classics
Kalmus

Humoresque   2.5'
    2[incl pic] 2 2 2 – 3 1 1 0 – tmp – str
    Leopold Stokowski, arr.
                       Popular Classics
Stokowski (rental)

Marche Slave, Op. 31   10'
    4[1.2.pic1.pic2] 2 2 2 – 4 4 3 1 – tmp+4 – str
    perc: bd, cym, sd, tamtam.
                       Popular Classics
Kalmus; Luck's; Simrock (rental)

The Nutcracker, Op. 71a: Suite No. 1   24'
           (4' 3' 2' 1' 2' 1' 4' 7')
    3[1.2.3/pic] 3[1.2.Eh] 3[1.2.bcl] 2 – 4 2 3 1 – tmp+1 – hp, cel – str
    perc: glock, tambn, tri, cym.
    Includes: Overture miniature; Marche; Danse de la fée-dragée; Danse russe trepak; Danse arabe; Danse chinoise; Danse des mirlitons; Valse des fleurs.
                     Christmas/Dance/
                     Popular Classics
Breitkopf; Kalmus

The Nutcracker, Op. 71b: Suite No. 2   33'
           (4' 5' 1' 8' 7' 2' 6')
    3[1.2.3/pic] 3[1.2.Eh] 3[1.2.bcl] 2 – 4 2 3 1 – tmp+1 – 2hp, cel – str
    perc: bd, cast, cym, glock, ratch, tambn, tri.
    Divertissement Chocolate; Pas de deux; Decorating and Lighting of the Christmas Tree; Little Galop of the Children and Entrance of the Parents; Tempo di Grossvater.
                     Christmas/Dance/
                     Popular Classics
Kalmus

Nutcracker Dances, Set I   7'
    2 2 2 2 – 4 2 3 0 – tmp+1 – str
    perc: sus cym
    Includes: March; Little Flutes (Mirlitons); Trepak.
    Clark McAlister, editor
                            Christmas/Dance/
                             Popular Classics
LudwigMasters

Nutcracker Dances, Set II   10'
    3[1.2.3/pic] 2 2 2 – 4 2 3 1 – tmp+1 – str
    perc: glock, tri.
    Includes: Dance of the Sugar-Plum Fairy; Chinese Dance; Waltz of the Flowers. Celesta part is written for glock.
    Clark McAlister, editor
                             Christmas/Dance/
                             Popular Classics
LudwigMasters

The Nutcracker Suite   17.5'
    2 2[1.Eh] 3[1.2.bcl] 2 – asx [(tsx)] – 4 3 3 1 – drumset – jazz bass – str
    Movements available separately:
    1. Overture   (3.5')
    2. Toot Toot Tootie Toot (Dance of the Reed Pipes)   (2.5')
    3. Dance of the Foreadores (Waltz of the Flowers)   (4')
    4. Sugar Rum Cherry (Dance of the Sugar-Plum Fairy)   (3')
    5. Peanut Brittle Brigade (March)   (4.5')
    Duke Ellington and Billy Strayhorn, arr.
    Jeff Tyzik, adapted
                             Christmas/Dance/
                             Popular Classics
Schirmer (rental)

The Nutcracker Suite   9'
    3 0 3 2 – 0 4 3 1 – perc – hp, cel – str
    SATB Chorus.
    Harry Simeone, arr.
                             Christmas/Dance/
                             Popular Classics
Schirmer (rental)

The Nutcracker Suite
    1 1 0 0 – ssx, asx, tsx – 4 2[crt] 1 0 – tmp+1 – str
    Rebmann-Clark, arr.
                             Christmas/Dance/
                             Popular Classics
Schirmer (rental)

Ouverture solennelle: 16'
1812 Overture, Op. 49
    3[1.2.pic] 3[1.2.Eh] 2 2 – 4 4[2crt, 2tp] 3 1 – tmp+5 – str
    perc: bd, cym, sd, tri, tambn, chimes, cannon.
    Optional extra brass: 4 2 2 2 – perc
                             Celebration/Popular Classics
Breitkopf; Kalmus

Pique Dame: Prince Yeletsky's   5'
Aria (I Love You, Dear)
    3[1.2.pic] 2[incl Eh] 2 2 – 4 0 0 0 – tmp+perc – hp, pf – str
    Solo Baritone.
                             Popular Classics/Valentine
Kalmus

Romeo and Juliet: Duet   12'
    2 3[1.2.Eh] 2 2 – 4 2 0 0 – tmp – hp – str
    Solo Soprano and Tenor.
    Sergei Taneyev, arr.
                             Popular Classics/Valentine
Billaudot

Romeo and Juliet: Fantasy Overture   19'
(Third Version, 1880)
    3[1.2.pic] 3[1.2.Eh] 2 2 – 4 2 3 1 – tmp+2 – hp – str
    perc: cym, bd.
    Third version: 1880.
                             Popular Classics/Valentine
Bote & Bock (rental); Kalmus; Luck's

Symphony No. 1 in G Minor, Op. 13   44'
(Winter Dreams)   (11' 12' 8' 13')
    3[1.2.pic] 2 2 2 – 4 2 3 1 – tmp+2 – str
    perc: bd, cym.
                             Popular Classics/Seasons
Kalmus

Templeton, Alec   1909-1963

Ballad de ballet
    asx – drumset – hp, pf, gtr – str
                             Dance
Schirmer (rental)

Give Me Your Heart   3'
    drumset – hp, cel, pf, gtr – str
                             Valentine
Schirmer (rental)

Merry Christmas
   2 2 2 2 – 2 0 0 0
   Paul Jouard, arr.

   Christmas

   Schirmer (rental)

Night Pieces
   Strings

   Halloween

   Schirmer (rental)

Operation Mambo   3'
   2[incl pic] 2 2 2 – 4 3 3 1 – perc – str

   Dance

   Schirmer (rental)

Tesori, Jeanine   1961-

Thoroughly Modern Millie   3.5'
   3 2 3[1.2.bcl] 2 – 4 4 3 1 – tmp+2 – hp, pf – str
   2 Solo Voices.
   Bill Holcombe, arr.

   Broadway Musicals

   Musicians Pub. (rental)

Thomas, Augusta Read   1964-

Sunlight Echoes   5'
   3 3[incl Eh] 3 3 – 4 3 3 1 – 3perc – hp – str
   Chorus. Text by Emily Dickinson.

   Valentine/Weather

   Schirmer (rental)

Theodorakis, Mikis

Zorba the Greek (1964): Theme   4.5'
   3[1.2.pic] 2 2 2 – 4 2 2 1 – tmp+4 –
   hp, 2 gtr[1 part a2], accordion, 2 bouzoukis – str
   perc: sd, bd, cym, gong, tambn, sm tri, lg tri, cowbell, guiro, bells, xyl, washboard.
   Nominated for a Golden Globe and Grammy for Best Original Score.

   Films

   T&V (rental)

Thomas, Augusta Read   1964-

Sunlight Echoes   5'
   3 3[incl Eh] 3 3 – 4 3 3 1 – 3perc – hp – str
   Chorus. Text by Emily Dickinson.

   Valentine/Weather

   Schirmer (rental)

Thomas, Rob (See: Shur, Itaal)

Thomson, Virgil   1896-1989

Fugue and Chorale on   5'
Yankee Doodle
   2 1 3[incl bcl] 1 – 2 3 2 0 – tmp+1 – str
   Used in the film *Tuesday in November*.

   Films/Patriotic

   Schirmer (rental)

Louisiana Story: 15'
Acadian Songs and Dances
   2[1.2/pic] 2[1.2/Eh] 2 2 – 2 2 2 0 – 2perc –
   hp, accordion or pf – str
   perc: sd, field dr, bd, cym, xyl, sus cym.

   Films/Americana

   Schirmer (rental)

Louisiana Story: 18'
Orchestral Suite
   2[1.2/pic] 2[1.2/Eh] 2[1.2/bcl] 2[1.2/cbn] – 4 2 3 1 –
   tmp+3 – hp – str
   perc: glock, xyl, cym, sd, field dr, sus cym, bd, tamtam.
   Won the 1949 Pulitzer Prize in Music.

   Films/Americana

   Schirmer (rental)

The Nativity   7'
   2 2 2 2 – 2 2 0 0 – perc – org – str
   Solo: Alto, Tenor, Bass; SATB Chorus.

   Christmas

   Schirmer (rental)

The Plow that Broke the Plains: Suite   15'
                          (1' 2' 3' 3' 1' 5')
     1 1[1/(Eh_] 2[1.2/(bcl)] 2[(bn2)] – (asx, tsx) –
     2 2 2 0 – tmp+2 – gtr/bnjo – str
     perc: bd, sd, tri, cym, sus cym, tambn, tomtom, woodblk, cowbell, horse hooves.
     Optional Narrator. Includes: Prelude; Pastoral (Grass); Cattle; Blues (Speculation); Drought; Devastation.
                                         Americana
Schirmer (rental)

The River: Suite   25'
     1[1/pic] 2[1.2/Eh] 2[1.2/bcl] 1 – 2 2 2 0 – tmp+2 – bnjo – str
     perc: sd, bd, cym, tri, tamtam, glock, iron ratchet, 2iron bars.
                                  Ecology/Films
Peer (rental)

Sea Piece with Birds   5'
     3[1.2.3/pic] 3 3 3 – 4 3 3 0 – 2perc – (hp) – str
     perc: cym, sus cym, tamtam.
                                  Animals/Ecology
Schirmer (rental)

The Seine at Night   8'
     3[1.2.3/pic] 3[1.2.3/Eh] 3[1.2.3/bcl] 3[1.2.3/cbn] – 4 3 3 1 – 1perc – 2hp, cel – str
     perc: cym, sus cym, tamtam, 2tri.
                         Ecology/Popular Classics/Travel
Schirmer (rental)

Wheat Field at Noon   6'
     3[1.2.3/pic] 3[1.2.3/Eh] 3[1.2.3/bcl] 3[1.2.3/cbn] – 4 3 3 0 – 3perc – hp – str
                      Ecology/Popular Classics
Schirmer (rental)

Thurlow, Jeremy, arr.   1967-

The Novello Book of Carols: 3'
    All and Some (Nowell We Sing)
     1 1 1 1 – 1 1 1 1 – 3perc – str
     Solo Voice.
                                            Christmas
Novello (rental)

Ticheli, Frank   1958-

Angels in Architecture   14.5'
     3 3 3 2 – 4 3 3 1 – tmp+4 – cel, (org) – str
     Solo Soprano.
                                Instrumental Pops
MBM (rental)

Blue Shades   11'
     3 2 3 2 – asx – 4 3 3 1 – tmp+3 – str
                                Instrumental Pops
MBM (rental)

Postcard for Symphony Orchestra   5'
     3 2 2 2 – 4 3 3 1 – tmp+3 – str
                                Instrumental Pops
MBM (rental)

Shooting Stars   5'
     3 2 3 2 – 4 3 3 1 – tmp+3 – pf – str
                                               Space
MBM (rental)

Tilzer, Albert von   1878-1956

Take Me Out to the Ball Game   3'
     3[1.2.pic] 2 2 2 – 4 3 3 1 – tmp+3 – str
     perc: bells, sd, bd, cym.
     Optional Narrator as broadcaster.
                                                Sports
Kalmus

Time for Three (Also See: Meyer, Ranaan)

Sweet Georgia Brown   2'
     1 1 0 1 – 2asx, 2tsx – 4 4 4 0 – vib – pf – str
     2 Solo Violins, Double Bass.
                                           Americana
Fleisher

Tiomkin, Dimitri 1894-1979

55 Days at Peking (1963): Suite 27.5'
(4' 4' 4' 3' 3' 3' 5' 1.5')
3[pic.pic/afl.pic/afl] 2[1.Eh] 3 2[1.cbn] – ssx –
4 4 4 1 – tmp+5 – 2 hp, pf, cel, elec gtr, accordion – str
perc: drumset, 2 xyl, vib, marim, glock, 2 bells, cym, sus cym, broken cym, Chinese cym, finger cym, gong, Chinese gong, 2 sd, 2 field dr, bd, tri, lg tri, chimes, 2 toms, temple blk, tambn, 2 woodblk, timbales.
SATB Chorus. Includes: Overture; Main Title; Welcome Marines/Tuan's Procession; The Ball; Attack and Explosion; Children's Corner/Peking Theme ("So Little Time"; Chinese Victory Celebration/Hauling the Gun; Finale.
Nominated for 1964 Oscar for Best Music.
Christmas Palmer, arr.

Films

T&V (rental)

The Alamo (1960): Short Suite
3[1.pic.afl/pic] 2[1.Eh] 3[1.2.bcl] 2 – 4 4[(#4)] 3 1 – tmp+perc – 2 hp, pf – str
perc: sd, pic sd, td, field dr, bd, glock, xyl, vib, chimes, cym, sus cym, tambn, tamtam, gong.
Includes: Overture and Prologue; Davy Crockett; The Battle of the Alamo/Epilogue.
Patrick Russ, arr.

Americana/Films

T&V (rental)

The Alamo (1960): Suite 25.5'
(7' 2.5' 3.5' 8.5' 2.5' 1.5')
3[1.pic.afl/pic] 2[1.Eh] 3[1.2.bcl] 2 – 4 4 3 1 – tmp+4 – 2 hp, pf[cel] – str
perc: drumset, sd, pic sd, field dr, td, bd, sm bd, cym, sus cym, tambn, tom tom, tamtam, glock, xyl, vib, chimes.
Vocal Solo. SATB Chorus. Includes: Overture and Prologue; Davy Crockett; The Green Leaves of Summer; The Battle of the Alamo; Tennessee Babe; Finale: The Ballad of the Alamo. Nominated for 1961 Oscar for Best Music.
Christopher Palmer, arr.

Americana/Films

T&V (rental)

The Big Sky (1952): Suite 8'
3[1.2. afl] 2[1.Eh] 5[1.2.(3).bcl.(bcl)] 2 – 4 4 3 1 – tmp+4 – 2 hps, pf, cel – str
perc: sus cym, cyms, glock, marim, vib, tub bells, Indian drum, bd, tamtam, 2 toms.
Includes: Prelude; Forrest at Night(Nocturne); The Wide Missouri (Epilogue).
Patrick Russ, arr.

Films

T&V (rental)

Circus World (1964): John Wayne March 2.5'
2[1.pic] 2[1.Eh] 2 2[1.cbn] – 2 3 4[1.2.3.baritone hn]1 – 4perc – pf, gtr, accordion – str
perc: sd, bd, cym, vib, glock.
Patrick Russ, arr.

Circus/Films

T&V (rental)

Cyrano De Bergerac (1950): Suite 18'
(3' 3' 5.5' 6.5')
3[1.2.pic] 3[1.2.Eh] 2 2 – 4 3 3 1 – tmp+4 – 2 hp, pf[cel], (hpsd), org – str
perc: drumset, sd, field dr, bd, tri, tamtam, cym, whip, xyl, vib, low chime.
SA Chorus. Includes: Overture; Roxanne: 16th Century Blues; Street Fight; Requiem: Cyrano's Death.
Christopher Palmer, arr.

Films

T&V (rental)

Dial M for Murder (1954): Suite 7'
3[1.afl/pic.3] 2[1.Eh] 5[1.2.asx.bcl.bcl] 2[1.cbn] – 4 4 4 1 – tmp+4 – 2 hp, pf, synth[novachord] – str
perc: xyl, vib, bells, marim, chimes, sus cym, tri, bd, gong, temple blk.
Includes: Main Title;The Telephone; The Trap; Finale.
Christopher Palmer, arr.

Films

T&V (rental)

DOA (1950) 3.5'
3 2 3 2 – 4 3 3 0 – tmp+perc – pf, rhythm bs – str
perc: drumset, sd, sus cym, great cym, xyl, gong, tri.
Solo Trumpet; Tenor Saxophone (optional Alto Saxophone).
Patrick Russ, arr.

Films

T&V (rental)

Duel in the Sun (1946): Suite   13'
     3[1.2.pic] 2[1.Eh] 2[1.bcl] 2 – 4 3 3 1 – tmp+3
     – 2 hp[(#2)], pf[cel), 2 Spanish gtr [1 part a2],
     harmonica, accordion – str
     perc: sd, bd, cym, sus cym, tamtam, tri, 3 temple blk,
     glock.
     Includes: Prelude (Theme); The Buggy Ride; Love
     Theme.
     Christopher Palmer, arr.
                                                                  Films

T&V (rental)

The Fall of the Roman Empire(1964): Themes   12'
     3[incl pic] 3[1.2.Eh] 3[1.2.bcl] 2 – 6 6 6 1 –
     tmp+4 – 2hp, 2pf, org, 4 mandolins – str
     Includes: Overture; Main Title; The Fall of Love.
     Won the Golden Globe for Best Original Score and
     nominated for 1969 Oscar for Best Music.
     Patrick Russ, arr.
                                                                  Films

T&V (rental)

The Four Poster (1952)
     3[1.2.pic] 2 3 2 – 4 3 3 0 – tmp+4 – 2 hp, pf – str
     perc: sd, field dr, bd, cym, glock, xyl, tri, chimes,
     lg gong.
                                                                   Films

T&V (rental)

Friendly Persuasion (1956)   8'
     3[1.2.pic] 2[1.Eh] 3 2 – 4 3 3 1 – tmp+2 – hp, pf
     – str
     perc: bd, cym.
     SATB Chorus. Includes: Thee I Love; Marry Me;
     Lead Her Like A Pigeon; Mocking Bird and Willow
     Tree; Coax Me A Little; Indiana Holiday; Finale.
     Nominated for 1957 Oscar for Best Music and
     Original Song: "Friendly Persuasion (Thee I
     Love)."
     Christopher Palmer, arr.
                                                                  Films

T&V (rental)

Friendly Persuasion (1956)
     3[1.2.pic] 2[1.2/Eh] 3[1.2.3/bcl] 2 – 4 3 3 1 – tmp+3
     – 2hp, 2pf, (banjo), mandolin, accordion – str
     perc: sd, bd, sus cym, cym, glock, marim, vib, chimes,
     2xyl, tri, 4temple blocks, woodblk, tambn, slgh-bells,
     drumset, field dr.
     Includes: Prelude; Thee I Love; Little Jess;
     Samantha;Carriage Chase; The Fair; Love Scene;
     The War; Finale. Nominated for 1957 Oscar for
     Best Music and Original Song: *Friendly Persuasion*
     (Thee I Love).
     Carroll Huxley, arr.
                                                                 Films

T&V (rental)

Friendly Persuasion (1956): Thee I Love   4'
     3[1.2.pic] 2[1.Eh] 3 2 – 4 3 3 1 – tmp+2 – hp – str
     perc: sd, bd, sus cym, cym, glock.
     Nominated for a 1957 Oscar for Original Song.
     Christopher Palmer and Patrick Russ, arr.
                                                                  Films

T&V (rental)

Giant (1956): Suite   4'
     3[1.2.pic] 2[1.Eh] 3[1.2.bcl] 2 –   (2' 3' 3')
     4 3 3 1 – tmp+3 – hp, pf[cel], gtr, (accordion) – str
     perc: drumset, sd, field dr, bd, sus cym, cym, tri, glock,
     chimes, temple blk, claves.
     TB Chorus. Includes: Prelude *This Then is Texas*
     (vocal optional); Love Theme *There's Never Been*
     Anyone Else But You; The Ballad of Jett Rink (aka
     The James Dean Ballad); Finale. Nominated for
     1957 Oscar for Best Music.
     Christopher Palmer and Patrick Russ, arr.
                                                                  Films

T&V (rental)

The Great Waltz (1938)   6'
     3[1.pic.pic] 2[1.Eh] 3[1.2.bcl] 3[1.2.cbn] 4 4 3 1
     – tmp+4 – 2 hp[(#2)], 2 pf, cel – str
     perc: sd, bd, tamtam, tri, woodblk, cym, vib, glock, xyl,
     chimes.
     Based on *The Blue Danube* by Johann Strauss II.
     Recorded by John Mauceri with the Hollywood
     Bowl Orchestra on *The Great Waltz* CD (Phillips
     Classics).
                                                               Dance/Films

T&V (rental)

Gunfight at the OK Corral (1957):   12'
   Ballad and Theme   (9' 3')
   3[1.2.afl/pic] 2[1.Eh] 3[1.2.bcl] 2 – 4 3 3 1 –
   tmp+4 – hp, pf, gtr – str
   perc: drumset, sd, field dr, bd, cym, sus cym, vib, xyl, tri, 3 woodblk, tambn, tamtam, anvil, chimes, bass chime, temple blk.
   Solo Baritone (Ballad only). Optional TTBB Chorus.
   Christopher Palmer, arr.
                                            Americana/Films
T&V (rental)

The Guns of Navarone (1961): Suite   9.5'
   3[1.pic.pic/afl] 2[1.Eh] 3[1.2.bcl] 2 – 4 4 3 1 –
   tmp+4 – hp, pf – str
   perc: chimes, tambn, bd, cym, finger cym, sus cym, tri, sd, military dr, tamtam, marim, vib, glock, xyl.
   Includes: Prologue; Legend of Navarone; Epilogue.
   Nominated for 1962 Oscar for Best Music.
   Christopher Palmer, arr.
                                            Americana/Films
T&V (rental)

The High and the Mighty (1954): Suite   7'
   3[1.pic.pic] 2 3 2 – 4 3 3 1– tmp+5 –
   2 hp[1 part a2], pf – str
   perc: sd, field dr, bd, cym, sus cym, glock, chimes, tamtam, tri.
   STB Chorus. Includes: Prelude; Safe Landing & Jubilo. Won the 1955 Oscar for Best Music.
   Christopher Palmer and Patrick Russ, arr.
                                            Films/Travel
T&V (rental)

High Noon (1952): Do Not Forsake   2.5'
  Me Oh My Darling
   2 2[1.Eh] 2 2 – 2 1 0 0 – 1perc –
   hp [omit if gtr], gtr – str
   perc: 2 toms.
   Optional Solo Vocal. Won the 1953 Oscar for Original Song.
                                            Americana/Films
T&V (rental)

High Noon (1952): Suite   9'
   2[1.pic] 2[1.Eh] 2 2[1.cbn] – 4 3 3 1 – tmp+4 –
   hp or gtr, pf – str
   perc: 2 toms, tamtam, marim, xyl, chimes, sus cym, cym, sd, td, bd, thunder dr, tmp 2.
   Includes: Prelude; The Clock & The Showdown; Postlude. Won 1953 Oscar for Best Music.
   Christopher Palmer, arr.
                                            Americana/Films
T&V (rental)

It's a Wonderful Life (1947): Suite   12'
   3[1.2.pic] 2[1.Eh] 3[1.2.bcl] 2 – 4 3 3 1 –
   tmp+3 – 2 hp[(#2)], pf[cel], gtr – str
   perc: glock, xyl, vib, sd, bd, chimes, tri, drumset, sus cym, tamtam, slgh-bells.
   Optional SATB Chorus in the Finale. Includes: Prelude and It's A Wonderful Life Theme; Nightmare: George Unborn; and Chistmas Eve Finale.
   Christopher Palmer, arr.
                                            Christmas/Films
T&V (rental)

It's a Wonderful Life (1947): Theme   2.5'
   2 2[1.Eh] 2 2 – 4 0 1 1 – 1perc – hp, pf, (gtr) – str
   perc: drumset.
   Optional Solo Vocal.
   Christopher Palmer, arr.
                                            Christmas/Films
T&V (rental)

Suite from It's a Wonderful Life   8'
   3[1.2.pic] 2 2 2 – 4 3 3 1 – tmp+3 – (gtr), hp, pf/cel – str
   Includes: Prologue, Theme, Christmas Eve Finale. Theme may be performed as a single movement year round. 40 chorus parts in the set.
   Paul Marquart and Christopher Palmer are the original arrangers. This Suite was revised by Patrick Russ and Paul Henning.
                                            Christmas/Films
Leonard

The Men (1950): Suite   7'
   3[1.2.pic] 3[1.2.Eh] 3[1.2.bcl] 3[1.2.cbn] – asx –
   4 3 2 1 – tmp+4 – hp, pf – str
   Patrick Russ, arr.
                                                       Films
T&V (rental)

Night Passage (1957): Follow the River   2'
   2 2[1.Eh] 2 2 – 4 3 3 1 – tmp+2 – pf – str
   perc: cyms, bd, glock, temple blk.
   Optional Solo Vocal. TTBB Chorus. Won 1959 Oscar for Best Music.
   Christopher Palmer, arr.
                                            Americana/Films
T&V (rental)

A President's Country (1966): Medley   10.5'
    2[1.afl/pic] 2[1.Eh] 2 2 – 4 2 2 1 – tmp+3 –
    hp, pf, Spanish gtr – str
    perc: drumset, 3 temple blk, glock, vib, bd, wdbl, 2 toms.
    A medley assembled by the composer of music from his great epic Westerns: Red River; Duel in the Sun; Giant; Rawhide; High Noon; and The Alamo: *The Green Leaves of Summer*.
    Christopher Palmer, arr.
        Americana/Films

T&V (rental)

Rawhide (1959): Theme   2.5'
    Instrumental edition: 3[1.2.pic] 2[1.Eh] 3 2 – 4 3 3 1 – tmp+4 – hp, pf, (gtr) – str
    perc: drumset, xyl, glock, whip, sus cym, cyms, tambn.
    Vocal: 2[1.pic] 2 2 2 – 4 3 3 1 – tmp+3 – pf, gtr – str
    perc: drumset, wdblk, tambn, xyl, whip, cyms, bd.
    Optional Solo Vocal.
    Christopher Palmer and Patrick Russ, arr.
        Americana/TV

T&V (rental)

Red River (1948): Suite   3.5'
    3[1.2.afl/pic] 2[1.Eh] 2[1.bcl] 2[1.cbn] – 6 4 3 1 – tmp+3 – 2 hp, pf, banjo – str
    perc: sd, td, bd, cyms, sus cym, glock, tamtam.
    TTBB Chorus. Includes: Prelude; The Red River Crossing; The Challenge; The Finale.
    Christopher Palmer, arr.
        Americana/Films

T&V (rental)

Rhapsody of Steel (1959)   22'
    3[1.2.pic] 3[1.2.Eh] 3[1.2.bcl] 3[1.2.cbn] – 4 4 3 1 – tmp+perc – hp, pf(cel) – str
    perc: drumset, tri, vib, glock, xyl, marim, chimes, tamtam, anvil, gong, pic sd, sd, bd, wdblk.
    A Tone Poem in Three Parts: The Past; The Present; The Future. Commissioned by the United States Steel Company to create music for an animated industrial film.
        Films/Labor Day

T&V (rental)

Rio Bravo (1959): Suite   6.5'
    2[1.afl,pic] 2[1.Eh] 2[asx.bcl] 2 –   (1.5' 2' 3')
    4 3 3 1 – 3 perc – hp, pf, 2 gtr[Spanish gtr.(2)], accordion, harmonica – str
    perc: vib, 2 marim, bongo, conga.
    Includes: Main Theme; Love Theme; De Guella.
    Patrick Russ, arr.
        Films

T&V (rental)

Strangers on a Train (1951): Suite   8'
    3[1.2.pic/afl] 2[1.Eh] 4[Ebcl.2.bcl/ssx.bcl] 2[1.cbn] – 4 3 3 0 – tmp+3 – hp, 2 pf[#2=cel, novachord] – str
    perc: sd, Field drum, vib, glock, xyl, marim, chimes, sm gong, lg gong, tri, temple blk, cyms, sus cym.
    Includes: Main Title and Approaching the Train; The Tennis Game; The Cigarette Lighter; Finale.
    Christopher Palmer, arr.
        Films

T&V (rental)

The Sundowners (1960): Suite
    3[1.2.pic] 3[1.2.Eh] 3[1.2.bcl] 3[1.2.cbn] – 4 3 3 1 – tmp+4 – hp, pf(cel), (gtr), (accordion), harmonica – str
    perc: glock, mariim, xyl, vib, chimes, sd, bd, sus cym, cyms, sizzle cym, tri, sm bongo, temple blk.
    Includes: Main Title; Mad Dog; The Fire; Dingo; End Credits.
    Patrick Russ, arr.
        Films

T&V (rental)

Tarzan and the Mermaids (1948): Suite   6'
    3[1.2.pic] 3[1.2.Eh] 3[1.2.bcl] 3[1.2.cbn] – 4 4 3 1 – tmp+3 – 2 hp, pf[cel] – str
    perc: cym, hand cym, sus cym, lg gong, low gong, field dr, vib, xyl, marim, 2 bells, chimes, toms.
    This was the last of the Tarzan movies to star Johnny Weissmuller in the title role.
    Patrick Russ and Jeff Atmajian, arr.
        Films

T&V (rental)

Tension at Table Rock (1956): Suite   5'
        (2.5' 2.5' 2')
    3[1.2.pic] 3[1.2.Eh] 3[1.2.bcl] 3[1.2.cbn] – 4 3 3 1 – tmp+3 – hp, pf[cel] –str
    perc: xyl, glock, vib, sus cym, sd, field dr, gong, tri, chimes, tamtam.
    Patrick Russ, arr.
        Films

T&V (rental)

The Thing from Another World (1951): Suite   6'
                                                           (2' 1.5' 2.5')
    3[1.pic.(3)] 3[1.Eh] 3[1.Ebcl.bcl] 2[1.cbn] – 2 ssx – 4 4 4 1 – tmp+5 – hp, 2 pf[I=cel], org, theremin, novachord – string basses [no other strings]
        perc: 2 vib, low chimes, bells, xyl, marim, toms, deep tom, tamtam, sus cym, soft cym, sd, bd, gong, short deep gong, anvil, hollow pipe.
    4 High Voices. Includes: Main Title; The Melting Sequence; The Thing Electrocuted.
    Patrick Russ, arr.

                                                                          Films

    T&V (rental)

Town Without Pity (1961): Theme   4'
    2 2[1.Eh] 2[1.bcl] 2 – asx – 4 2 2 1 – tmp+1 – pf – str
        perc: drumset.
    Won the Golden Globe and was nominated for an Oscar for this song: Town Without Pity.
    Christopher Palmer, arr.

                                                                           Films

    T&V (rental)

The Unforgiven   8'
                                                         (2.5' 3' 2.5')
    2[1.pic] 2[1.Eh] 3[1.2.bcl] 2 – 4 3 3 1 – tmp+3 – hp, pf, gtr[or banjo], accordion – str
        perc: vib, glock, xyl, marim, chimes, cyms, sus cym, choke cym, gong, tambn, tri, woodblk, slapstick, tambn.
    Across the Texas Panhandle; The Need for Love; Horse Ballet.

                                                                            Films

    T&V (rental)

The War Wagon (1967): Suite   5'
    2 2[1.Eh] 3[1.2.bcl] 2[1.cbn] – 4 3 4 1 – tmp+3 – hp, pf, gtr, harmonica – str
        perc: vib, glock, marim, chimes, choked cym, sus cym, cym, claves, tri, sandpaper blk, woodblk, shaker, tambn.
    Includes: Ballad of The War Wagon; Senorita.
    Patrick Russ, arr.

                                                                            Films

    T&V (rental)

The Well (1951): Suite   4.5'
    3[1.2.pic] 3[1.2.Eh] 3[1.2.bcl] 3[1.2.cbn] – 4 3 3 1 – tmp+3 – hp, pf – str
        perc: xyl, 3 chimes, sus cym, stopped cym, gong, lg gong, broken gong, field dr, bd, 2 anvils.
    Nominated for a Golden Globe for Best Motion Picture Score.
    Patrick Russ, arr.

                                                                            Films

    T&V (rental)

Wild is the Wind (1958): Theme   2.5'
    2 2[1.Eh] 2 2 – 4 3 3 1 – tmp+1 – hp, pf[cel], gtr – str
        perc: drumset.
    Nominated for an Oscar for Best Music and Original Song (Wild is the Wind).
    Christopher Palmer, arr.

                                                                            Films

    T&V (rental)

The Wild, Wild West (1965): Suite   5'
    2[1.pic] 2[1.Eh] 3[1.2.bcl] 2 – 4 3 3 1 –   (3' 2')
    tmp+3 – hp, pf – str
        perc: cym, sus cym, woodblk, sd, tamtam, tri, xyl, glock, tambn.
    Includes: The Wild Wild West Main Theme; The Ballad of Jim West.
    Patrick Russ, arr.

                                                                      Americana/TV

    T&V (rental)

The Young Land (1959): Strange are   3'
    the Ways of Love
    2[1.pic] 1 2 1 – 2 1 0 0 – 1perc – pf, gtr, rhythm bs – str
        perc: drumset.
    This song was nominated for a 1960 Oscar.
    Christopher Palmer, arr.

                                                                            Films

    T&V (rental)

Toch, Ernst   1887-1964

Big Ben, Variation: Fantasy   20'
    on the Westminster Chimes, Op. 62
    3 3 3 2 – 4 4 3 1 – perc – hp, cel – str

                                                                          International

    AMP (rental)

Circus Overture   6'
    3[1.2.3/pic] 2 2 2 – 3 3 3 1 – 4perc – pf – str
        perc: bd, cym, sd, tri, woodblk, cast, whip, glock, xyl.

                                                                            Circus

    EMI (rental); Kalmus

Pinocchio: A Merry Overture   7'
    3[1.2.pic] 2 2 2 – 2 2 3 0 – tmp+2 – str
        perc: cym, sd, tri, xyl.

                                                           Instrumental Pops

    AMP (rental)

Tomlinson, Ernest   1924-

Suite of English Folk Dances   12'
2[incl pic] 2 2 2 – 4 2 3 0 – tmp+perc – hp – str
                              Dance/International
Novello (rental)

Torelli, Giuseppe   1658-1709

Concerto Grosso for Two Violins and Orchestra   7'
  in G Minor, Op. 8, No. 6: Christmas Concerto
  cnt – strings
  Schroeder, arr.
                              Christmas/Popular Classics
Peters

Torme, Mel & Wells, Robert

Christmas Song (Chestnuts Roasting   4'
  on an Open Fire)
  2 2 3[1.2.(bcl=bassoon 2)] 2 – 4 3 3 1 – tmp+3
  – str
  perc: glock, sd, bd, cym, slgh-bells, tri, tambn.
  Key of Eb Major, changing to G Major, then
  F Major.
  Frederick Muller, arr.
                              Christmas
Warner (rental)

Christmas Song (Chestnuts Roasting   3'
  on an Open Fire)
  2 1 2 1 – (asx, tsx, bsx) – 2 3 3 1 – tmp+2 – pf – str
  perc: chimes, glock, drumset, tri.
  Key of C Major, changing to F Major.
  Bob Lowden, arr.
                              Christmas
Leonard

Tower, Joan   1938-

Fanfare for the Uncommon   3'
  Woman (1986)
  0 0 0 0 – 4 3 3 1 – tmp+4 – [no str]
                              Fanfare/Popular Classics
AMP (rental)

Stepping Stones: 4'
  Celebration Fanfare
  0 0 0 0 – 4 3 3 1 – tmp+2 – [no str]
  Version for brass and percussion
  Daniel Forlano, arr.
                              Fanfare
AMP (rental)

Traditional

Football Song Hits: Eastern   4'
  0 0 0 0 – 2asx, tsx, bsx – 0 2 3 0 – 3perc – gtr – str
  perc: sd, bd, cym.
  Includes: Syracuse, Washington & Jefferson, West
  Point, Yale, Amherst, Colgate, Columbia, Cornell,
  Dartmouth, Harvard, Lehigh, New York
  University, University of Pennsylvania, Penn State,
  Princeton, and Swarthmore.
                              Sports
Allen (POP); Luck's (rental)

Football Song Hits No. 2: Western   4'
  0 0 0 0 – 2asx, tsx, bsx – 0 2 3 0 – 3perc – gtr – str
  perc: sd, bd, cym.
  Includes: University of California, University of
  Chicago, University of Illinois, Indiana, University
  of Michigan, University of Minnesota, Notre
  Dame, Ohio State, Oregon State, Purdue,
  University of Southern California, University of
  Wisconsin.
                              Sports
Allen (POP); Luck's (rental)

Football Song Hits No. 4: East-South   4'
  0 0 0 0 – 2asx, tsx, bsx – 0 2 3 0 – 3perc – gtr – str
  perc: sd, bd, cym.
  Includes: Carnegie, Davidson, Duke, Florida,
  Lafayette, Lehigh, Penn State, Princeton,
  Vanderbilt, Virginia Military Institute.
                              Sports
Allen (POP); Luck's (rental)

Tsontakis, George   1951-

Let the River Be Unbroken   14'
  3 3 2 2 – 4 2 3 1 – perc – hp – str
  Civil War and traditional themes appear.
  Written for the Alexandria Symphony, Virginia.
                              Americana/Ecology
Merion (rental)

Winter Lightning 15'
  3[incl pic] 3[incl Eh] 3[incl bcl] 3[incl cbn] –
  4 3 3 1 – tmp+3 – hp, pf/cel – str
  One of his *Four Symphonic Quartets,* drawn from
  East Coker by T. S. Eliot.
                                        Weather/Seasons
Merion (rental)

Turina, Joaquín   1882-1949

Canto a Sevilla, Op. 37 40'
  3[incl pic] 2 2 2 – 4 3 3 1 – tmp+2 – hp – str
  Solo Soprano; Narrator.
  Includes: Preludio; Semana Santa; Las frentecitas
  des Parque; Noche de feria; El fantasma; La
  Giralda; Ofrenda.
                                        International
UME (rental)

Danzas fantásticas, Op. 22 15'
  3[1.2.3/pic] 3[1.2.Eh] 3[1.2.bcl] 3[1.2.cbn] –
  4 3 3 1 – tmp+3 – hp – str
  perc: block, chimes, tri, tambn, cym, sus cym, bd.
  Includes: Exaltación; Ensueño; Orgía.
                                        Dance/International
Kalmus; UME (rental)

La oración del torero, Op. 34 8'
  Strings
                                        International
UME (rental)

Rapsodia sinfónica, Op. 66 10'
  Strings
  Solo Piano.
                                        International
UME (rental)

Turok, Paul   1929-

Great Scott! 20'
  Orchestral Suite after Joplin
  3[1.2.pic] 3[1.2.Eh] 3[1.2.bcl] 2 – 4 3 3 1 – tmp+3
  – hp – str
  Includes: Overture; Slow Dance; Scherzo; Ragtime;
  Rondo: Finale.
                                        Jazz
Schirmer (rental)

A Joplin Overture 6'
  3[1.2.pic] 3[1.2.Eh] 3[1.2.bcl] 2 – 4 3 3 1 – tmp+3
  – hp – str
                                        Jazz
Schirmer (rental)

Ragtime Caprice, Op. 45 10'
  2[incl pic] 2 2[1.2.bcl] 2 – 2 2 2 1 – tmp+perc
  – hp – str
  Solo Piano.
                                        Jazz
Schirmer (rental)

Reeling in the New Year 5'
  2 2 2 2 – 2 2 0 0 – tmp – str
                                        New Year
Presser (rental)

A Sousa Overture, Op. 43 8'
  3[1.2.pic] 3[1.2.Eh] 4[1.2.Ebcl.bcl] 3[1.2.cbn] –
  4 3 3 1 – tmp+3 – hp – str
                                        Patriotic
Schirmer (rental)

Turrin, Joseph   1947-

Civil War Suite 20'
                        (5' 3' 4.5' 4.5' 3')
  2 2[incl Eh] 2 2 – 4 3 3 1 – tmp+perc – hp,pf – str
  perc: sd, bd, chimes, bells, cym, xyl, brake drum, tri,
  gong.
  Includes: Into Battle; Hymn; The Charge; Far from
  Thee; Honor and Glory. Most of the music is
  original; but these tunes from the Civil War period
  are included: *Marching Along* and *For the Dear Old
  Flag.*
                                        Patriotic
Presser (rental)

Fanfare for George Gershwin 3'
  3[1.2.pic] 2 2 2 – 4 3 3 1 – perc – str
                                        Fanfare
Turrin (rental)

The Fir Tree   20'
1 1 1 1 – 1 1 1 0 – perc – hp – str
Solo Vocalist; Narrator. Based on a story by Hans Christian Andersen. Adapted by Gloria Nissenson. The work is also available for double brass quintet, percussion, narrator and vocalist. Commissioned by the Canadian Brass and the NY Philharmonic Principal Brass.
                                             Christmas
Turrin (rental)

Lullaby of Broadway   15'
3[1.2.pic] 2 2 2 – 4 3 3 1 – perc – str
Chorus
                                   Instrumental Pops
Turrin (rental)

Steadfast Tin Soldier   15'
1 1 1 1 – 1 1 0 0 – perc – pf – str
Solo Piano. Text by Hans Christian Andersen.
                                   Instrumental Pops
Presser (rental)

When Tony Played the Sax   8'
2[incl pic] 1 2 2 – 2 2 1 0 – perc – str
Narrator; Solo Jazz Vocal; Alto Saxophone; String Bass; Drum set; Piano.
Text by Gloria Nissenson.
                                                     Jazz
Turrin (rental)

Tyzik, Jeff, arr.   1952-

Amazing Grace   5'
2[incl pic] 2[incl Eh] 2 2 – 4 3 3 1 – tmp+2 – hp, pf – str
                                           Holidays
Schirmer (rental)

American Celebration   8.5'
3[1.2.pic] 2 3[1.2.bcl] 2 – 4 3 3 1 – tmp+2 – pf, hp – str
Solo Soprano and Baritone or SATB Chorus.
Includes: Yankee Doodle Dandy; America; My Country; America (My Country 'Tis of Thee); You're a Grand Old Flag; America the Beautiful.
                                            Patriotic
Schirmer (rental)

The Big Movie Suite   16.5'
3[incl pic] 2 3[incl bcl] 2 – asx or tsx – 4 3 3 1 – tmp+2[incl drumset] – pf, hp, elec bass – str
Includes: Tara's Theme from *Gone With the Wind*; *Ben Hur*; *Laura*; *Dr. Zhivago*; Main Theme from *Lawrence of Arabia*; Gonna Fly Now from *Rocky*; *The Pink Panther*; *The Way We Were*.
                                               Films
Schirmer (rental)

Chanukah Suite   8'
2[incl pic] 2[incl Eh] 2 2 – 4 3 3 1 – tmp+2, drumset – hp, pf, jazz bass – str
Includes Rock of Ages, My Dredl, Al Hanissim, Who Can Retell, and Hanukkah.
                                             Hanukkah
Schirmer (rental)

A Christmas Overture: 3'
  Variations on Deck the Halls
2[incl pic] 2 2 2 – (2asx, tsx, bsx) – 4 3 3 1 – tmp+perc, drumset – hp, jazz bass – str
                                           Christmas
Schirmer (rental)

Fantasy On American Themes   10'
3[1.2.pic] 2 2[1.2.bcl] 2 – 4 3 3 1 – tmp+2 – hp, pf – str
Includes: Yankee Doodle, America the Beautiful, When Johnny Comes Marching Home.
                                   Americana/Patriotic
Schirmer (rental)

The Great Westerns Suite   11'
3[incl pic] 2 2 2 – 4 3 3 1 – tmp+3 – pf, cel, synth, hp – str
Includes: *The Magnificent Seven*; *How the West Was Won*; *Silverado*; *Dances with Wolves*.
                                      Americana/Films
Schirmer (rental)

Holiday Moods: 12'
  Suite No. 1 for chorus and orchestra
2 2 2 2 – 4 2 3 1 – tmp+2 – hp, kybd – str
SATB Chorus. Includes: Hark! The Herald Angels Sing; Silent Night; Angels We Have Heard on High; What Child Is This?; Joy to the World.
                                           Christmas
Schirmer (rental)

Holiday Moods: 10'
Suite No. 2 for chorus and orchestra
2 2 2 2 – 4 2 3 1 – tmp+2 – hp, kybd – str
SATB Chorus. Includes: Deck the Hall; O Christmas Tree; Here We Come A-Wassailing; Carol of the Bells; Jingle Bells
                                  Christmas
Schirmer (rental)

Holiday Moods: 10'
Suite No. 3 for chorus and orchestra
2 2 2 2 – 4 2 3 1 – tmp+2 – hp, kybd – str
SATB Chorus. Includes: Adeste Fideles; God Rest Ye Merry Gentlemen; The First Noel; Lo! How a Rose E'er Blooming; We Wish You a Merry Christmas.
                                  Christmas
Schirmer (rental)

Hot Soul Medley 11.5'
2[incl pic] 2 2 2 – 4 3 3 1 – tmp+perc, drumset – pf, bass gtr – str
                        Popular Song/Valentine
Schirmer (rental)

Mis zeh Hidlik (Behold the Lights) 3.5'
0 0 0 0 – 0 0 0 0 – bells – cel, pf, hp – str
Solo English Horn.
                                    Hanukah
Schirmer (rental)

A Skater's Overture: 3.5'
Variations on a Theme of Waldteufel
2 2 2 2 – (asx) – 4 3 3 1 – tmp+2, drumset – jazz pf, jazz bass – str
                                  Christmas
Schirmer (rental)

Symphonic Swing 10'
2 2 2 2 – 4 3 3 1 – tmp+drumset,vib – hp, pf, elec bass – str
Arrangements of Big Band tunes from the 1940's: Jersey Bounce; Opus 1; Sunrise Serenade; Tuxedo Junction; Satin Doll; Back Bay Shuffle.
                                        Jazz
Schirmer (rental)

Twelve Gifts of Christmas 10'
2 2 3[1.2.bcl] 2 – 4 3 3 1 – tmp+2 – hp, cel/pf – str
perc: bd, cym, sd, tri, glock, chimes, slgh-bells, sus cym, 3tomtoms.
Solo Soprano or Tenor.
                                  Christmas
Schirmer (rental)

What Child Is This 5'
0 1 0 0 – 0 0 0 0 – tmp+perc – hp, pf – str
Solo Soprano or Tenor or Oboe.
                                  Christmas
Schirmer (rental)

U

V

Ulbrich, Siegfried 1922-

Blue City: 7'
Impression for Piano and Orchestra
  2 2 2 2 – 4 3 3 0 – tmp+3 – hp – str
  Solo Piano.
                              Instrumental Pops
Sikorski (rental)

Valens, Ritchie 1941-1959

La Bamba 3'
  2 2 3[1.2.bcl] 1 – 4 3 3 1– tmp+3 – pf – str
  perc: cowbell, conga, drumset, claves.
  Calvin Custer, arr.
                                    Popular Song
Warner (rental)

Van Vactor, David

The New Light: Prologue and 3 Canticles 20'
for Christmas
  3[incl pic] 3[incl Eh] 2 2 – 4 3 3 1 – tmp+perc
  – org – str
  Narrator. Chorus.
                                         Christmas
Presser (rental)

Vandervalk, Bruce

A Reagan Portrait 6'
  2 2[1.Eh] 3[1.2.bcl] 2 – 4 3 3 1 – tmp+1 – str
  perc: tambn, cym.
                                          Patriotic
Sherwood Press (rental)

Vangelis 1943-

Chariots of Fire 2.5'
  2 2 3[1.2.bcl] 1 – 2asx, bsx – 2 2 2 1 – tmp+4 –
  pf/synth, (gtr) – str
  perc: sd, bd, cym, (bells).
  Jim Riley, arr.
                                       Films/Sports
Warner (POP); EMS or Luck's (rental)

Chariots of Fire
    Strings
    Vangelis' real name is Evanghelos Odyssey Papathanassiou. The original music was entirely electronic and initiated a new style in film scoring.
    Paul Jennings, arr.
                                            Films/Sports
  Leonard

Chariots of Fire: Theme   5'
    3[incl pic] 2 3[incl bcl] 2[incl cbn] – 4 4 4 1 – tmp+5 – hp, pf[cel] – str
    Thomas Pasatieri, arr.
                                              Films/Sports
  EMI (rental)

Chariots of Fire Suite   7'
    3[incl pic, opt afl] 3[incl Eh] 3[incl bcl] 3[incl cbn] – 4 3 3 1 – tmp+3 – hp, cel – str
    Solo Piano.
    Don Rose, arr.
                                              Films/Sports
  EMI (rental)

Hymne   2.5'
    tmp+1 – pf – str
    perc: sus cym, glock, tri.
    Used as music in a Gallo wine commercial.
    Curnow, arr.
                                                      TV
  Warner (POP); EMS or Luck's (rental)

Vardi, Emanuel   1917-

Suite on American Folk Songs   8'
    2 2 2 2 – 2 2 0 0 – tmp+perc – str
    Solo Viola.
                                                   Patriotic
  Schirmer (rental)

Vaughan Williams, Ralph   1872-1958

English Folk Songs Suite   10'
    2[1.2/pic] 1 2 1 – 2 2 2 0 – tmp+2 – str (3' 4' 3')
    perc: cym, bd, sd, tri.
    Gordon Jacob, arr.
                                              International
  Boosey

Fantasia on Christmas Carols   8.5'
    2 2 2 2 – 4 2 3 1 – tmp+perc – org – str
    SATB Chorus. Also available for just organ and strings.
                                                  Christmas
  Thorpe (rental)

Fantasia on Greensleeves   4'
    2[or 1, opt vn] 0 0 0 – 0 0 0 0 – hp or pf – str
    Ralph Greaves, arr.
                                              Popular Classics
  Goodmusic

Fantasia on Greensleeves   4'
    2 1 3 1 – 2 0 0 0 – hp or pf, (gtr) – str
    Stone, arr.
                                              Popular Classics
  Goodmusic

Fantasia on a Theme by Thomas Tallis   14'
    Solo string quartet and 2 string orchestras.
                                              Popular Classics
  Broude Bros.; Kalmus

Greensleeves   5'
    2[1.2/pic] 3[1.2.Eh] 3[1.2.bcl] 3[1.2.cbn] – 4 3 3 1 – tmp+perc – hp – str
    Alfred Reed, arr.
                                                 Christmas
  Kalmus

Hodie, a Christmas Cantata   54'
    3[1.2.3/pic] 3[1.2.Eh] 2 3[1.2.(cbn)] – 4 3 3 1 – tmp+4 – hp, cel, pf, (org) – str;
    Alternate: 2[1.2.3/pic] 2[1.3/Eh] 2 2 – 2 2 3 1 – tmp+4 – cel, pf – str
    perc: sd, td, bd, cym, sus cym, tri, glock, chimes (b, d', e')
    Solo Soprano, Tenor, and Bass; Chorus.
                                                 Christmas
  Oxford (rental)

The Lark Ascending   13'
    2 1 2 2 – 2 0 0 0 – 1perc – str
    perc: tri.
    Solo Violin.
                                     Animals/Popular Classics
  Oxford (rental)

Rhosymedre   4'
    2 1 2 2 – 2 1 0 0 – str
    Arnold Foster, arr.
                                              Popular Classics
  Galaxy

Three Choral Hymns: 12'
  Easter, Christmas, Whitsunday
  2 2 2 2 – 4 2 3 1 – tmp+perc – hp – str
  Solo Tenor or Baritone.

  Holidays
  Curwen (rental)

The Wasps: Overture 9'
  2[1.2/pic] 2 2 2 – 2 1 0 0 – tmp+3 – hp – str
  perc: tri, cym, bd, sus cym.

  Animals
  Curwen (rental); Kalmus; Luck's

Verdi, Giuseppe 1813-1901

Aïda: 11'
  Triumphal March and Ballet (7' 4')
  3[1.2.pic] 2 2 2 – 4 4 3 1 – tmp+3 – str
  perc: bd, cym, tri.

  Popular Classics
  Luck's

Aïda: 7'
  Triumphal March (Concert version)
  2[1.2.pic] 2 2 2 – 4 4 3 1 – tmp+2 – str
  From Act II.
  Clark McAlister, editor

  Popular Classics
  Kalmus

Aïda: 10'
  Triumphal March (original version)
  3[1.2.pic] 2 2 2 – 4 2 3 1 – tmp+2 – str –
  (banda: 0 3[Eb] 3 4[Egyptian trp] 4[bar] 2)
  Mixed Chorus.
  From Act II.

  Popular Classics
  Kalmus

La forza del destino: Overture 8'
  2[1.pic] 2 2 2 – 4 2 3 1 – tmp+1 – 2hp – str
  perc: bd/cym

  Popular Classics
  Kalmus; Luck's; Ricordi (rental)

Nabucco: Overture 8'
  2[1.pic] 2 2 2 – 4 2 3 1 – tmp+3 – str
  perc: sd, cym, bd.

  Popular Classics
  Kalmus; Ricordi (rental)

I vespri siciliani: Overture 9'
  2[1.pic] 2 2 2 – 4 4 3 1 – tmp+3 – str
  perc: sd, bd, cym.

  Popular Classics
  Kalmus; Ricordi (rental)

Vianello, Hugo

Christmas Kaleidoscope 12'
  4[incl pic] 2 2 2 – 4 3 3 1 – tmp+perc – cel, org
  – str

  Christmas
  Fischer (rental)

Villa-Lobos, Heitor 1887-1959

Bachianas Brasileiras No. 1 17'
  8 cellos

  International/Popular Classics
  AMP (rental)

Bachianas Brasileiras No. 5 11'
  8 cellos
  Solo Soprano.

  International/Popular Classics
  AMP (rental)

Bachianas Brasileiras No. 5: Aria 7'
  2[1.2/pic] 2[1.Eh] 2[1.2/bcl] 2 – 2 2 2 0 – tmp+7
  – (hp), cel, (gtr) – str
  Also arranged for strings alone.
  John Krance, arr.

  International/Popular Classics
  AMP (rental)

Concerto for Harmonica 20'
  1 1 1 1 – 2 0 1 0 – tmp+perc – hp – str

  Popular Classics
  AMP (rental)

Villaldo, Angel G. 1864-1921

El Choclo: Tango Argentina 3'
  2 1 2 2 – 3sx – 2 2 3 0 – tmp+perc – str

  Dance/International
  Kalmus

Villaldo, Angel G. & Matos Rodríguez, Gerardo 1864-1921

El Choclo & La Cumparsita 7.5'
2 2 2 2 – 4 2 3 1 – tmp+2 – str
Dance/International (Argentina)
Filarmonika

Vivaldi, Antonio 1678-1741

Concerto, Op. 44, No. 16, R.V. 570 7'
F Major (3' 2' 2')
cnt – strings
Solo Flute, Oboe, Bassoon.
La tempesta di mare (Sea Storm).
Popular Classics/Weather
Eulenburg

Le quattro staggioni 37'
(The Four Seasons) Op. 8, Nos.1-4
cnt – strings
Solo Violin.
La primavera (Spring) R.V. 269 (11')
L'estate (Summer) R.V. 315 (10')
L'autunno (Autumn) R.V. 293 (9')
L'inverno (Winter) R.V. 297 (7')
Popular Classics/Seasons/Weather
Bärenreiter; Eulenburg; Kalmus; Luck's; Ricordi

Vognar, Frank, arr.

Bohemian Folksongs 6'
1 1 2 1 – 2 2 1 0 – tmp+perc – str
Intenational
Kalmus

W

Wagenaar, Bernard 1894-1971

Concert Overture 7'
3 2 2 2 – 2 2 0 0 – tmp+perc – hp – str
Popular Classics
Shawnee (rental)

Wagner, Joseph Franz 1856-1908

Unter dem Doppeladler (Under the 3'
Double Eagle March), Op. 159
2[1.pic] 1 2 1 – 2 2 1 0 – perc – str
Patriotic
Kalmus

Unter dem Doppeladler (Under the 3'
Double Eagle March), Op. 159
1[1/pic] 1 2 1 – 2sx – 2 2 1 0 – 2perc – str
Ellis Brooks, arr.
Patriotic
Kalmus

Wagner, Joseph Frederick 1900-1974

Ballad of Brotherhood 15'
3[incl pic] 2 2 2 – 4 3 3 1 – tmp+perc – str
Chorus. Text by Alfred Kreymborg based on Walt Whitman.
Black History Month
Presser (rental)

Radio City Snapshots 7'
3 2 2 2 – 2asx, tsx – 4 3 3 1 – tmp+perc – hp, cel – str
Americana
EMI (rental)

Wagner, Richard — 1813-1883

Eine Faust Ouvertüre — 12'
(A Faust Overture)
3[1.2.pic] 2 2 3 – 4 2 3 1 – tmp – str
         Popular Classics
Breitkopf; Kalmus

Götterdämmerung: — 9'
 Siegfried's Rhine Journey
3[1.(2).pic] 2 2 2 – 4 3[(#3)] 3 1 – tmp+2 – hp – str
perc: tri, cym, (glock).
Englebert Humperdinck, arr.
        Popular Classics/Travel
Kalmus; Luck's; Schott

Lohengrin: Bridal Chorus — 4'
2 2 2 2 – 2 2[crt] 1 0 – tmp+1 – str
perc: tri, tambn.
From Act III, Scene 1: Treulich geführt.
J. Louis von der Mehden, Jr., arr.
       Popular Classics/Valentine
Kalmus

Tristan und Isolde: — 17'
 Prelude and Liebestod
3[1.2.3/pic] 3[1.2.Eh] 3[1.2.bcl] 3 – 4 3 3 1 – tmp
– hp – str
          Popular Classics
Breitkopf; Kalmus

Die Walküre: — 5'
 Ride of the Valkyries
4[1.2.pic1.pic2] 4[1.2.3.Eh] 4[1.2.3.bcl] 3[(#3)] –
8 3 4 1 – 2tmp+3 – str
perc: sd, tri, cym.
       Halloween/Popular Classics
Kalmus

Die Walküre: Ride of the Valkyries — 5'
3[1.2.pic] 3[1.2.Eh] 4[1.2.3.(bcl)] 3[(#3)] –
6[(#5&6)] 3 3 1 – tmp+3 – str
perc: sd, tri, cym.
Wouter Hutschenruyter, arr.
       Halloween/Popular Classics
Breitkopf; Kalmus

Die Walküre: Wotan's Farewell — 18'
 and Magic Fire Music (concert version)
2[1.2/pic] 2 2[1/Ebcl.2] 2 – 4 2 3 1 – tmp+2
– hp – str
perc: sus cym, tri, glock.
         Popular Classics
Kalmus

Waldteufel, Emile — 1837-1915

Les Patineurs (Skater's Waltz) ,Op.183 — 7'
2[1.pic] 2 2 2 – 4 2 3 1 – tmp+4 – str
perc: sd, bd, cym, tri, slgh-bells.
Kalmus edition by Clark McAlister.
         Christmas/Sports
Kalmus; Luck's

Walker, Robert — 1946-

My Dog Has Fleas: — 8'
 A Capriccio for Scratch Orchestra
2[incl pic] 2 2 2 – 4 3 3 1 – tmp+perc – hp – str
         Animals/Novelty
Novello (rental)

Walton, William — 1902-1983

Crown Imperial: — 7'
 Coronation March
3[1.2.3/pic] 3[1.2.Eh] 3[1.2.bcl] 3[1.2.cbn] – 4 3 3 1
– tmp+3 – hp, (org) – str
Alternate winds: 2 2 2 2 – 4 2 3 0
perc: sd, glock, tri, td, cym, bd, gong,
chimes [pitches: f ", c '"].
         Popular Classics
Oxford (rental)

Ward-Steinman, David

Season's Greetings: Festive Overture — 2'
3 3 3 3 – 4 3 3 1 – 3perc – cel, hp – str
         Christmas
Merion (rental)

Ward, Samuel A.   1848-1903

America the Beautiful   4.5'
2 2[1.Eh] 2 2 – 4 3 3 1 – tmp+2 – str
perc: sd, cym, chimes, cel.
Optional Chorus.
Carmen Dragon, arr.

    Patriotic

Dragon (rental)

America the Beautiful   4'
3[1.2.pic] 2 2 2 – 4 3 3 1 – tmp+perc – hp – str
Alfred Reed, arr.

    Patriotic

Kalmus

America the Beautiful   4.5'
2 0 1 0 – 2 0 0 0 – str
Hale Smith, arr.

    Patriotic

Presser (rental)

Warlock, Peter   1894-1930

Aspects of Love and Contentment   16'
1 0 1 0 – 1 0 0 0 – hp – str
Solo Soprano.
Anthony Payne, arr.

    Valentine

Schirmer (rental)

Warren, Diane   1956-

Music of My Heart   4'
strings – rhythm
Optional Chorus. From *Music of the Heart*;
compatible choral arrangements by Jerry Ray;
recorded by Gloria Estefan & 'NSYNC.
Roy Phillipps, arr.

    Films

Warner (POP); EMS (rental)

Warren, Harry   1893-1981

42nd Street (1981)   5'
3[incl pic] 2[incl Eh] 3[1.2.bcl] 2 –
4 4 3 1 – tmp+perc – hp, gtr, elec bass – str
perc: marching machine, sd, bd, cym, woodblk, hi-hat, vib, sus cym, sandblk, tambn, glock, xyl.
Bill Holcombe, arr.

    Broadway Musicals

Warner/Chappell (rental)

42nd Street: Overture   5'
3[1.2.pic] 2[1.Eh] 3[1.2.bcl] 2 – 4 4 3 1 –
tmp+perc – hp – str
perc: bongos, glock, xyl, vib, cym, large cym, hi-hat, sd, bd.
Marty Gold, arr.

    Broadway Musicals

Warner/Chappell (rental)

Lullaby of Broadway   5'
3[1.2.3/pic] 2 3[1.2.bcl] 2 – 4 4 3 1 – tmp+3 –
hp, elec bass – str
perc: glock, vib, sus cym, xyl, sd, drum set.
Peter Nero, arr.

    Films

Warner/Chappell (rental)

Serenade in Blue   3'
2 1 2 1 – 2 3 2 1 – tmp+1, drumset – pf – str
Glenn Miller sound.
Marty Gold, arr.

    Jazz

Warner/Chappell

Warrington, John

Yuletide Festival   4.5'
2 2 2 2 – 2sx – 4 2 3 0 – tmp+perc – str
Includes: Jingle Bells; Deck the Hall; I Heard the
Bells On Christmas Day; Rudolph, the Red-Nosed
Reindeer. Suitable for school orchestras also.

    Christmas

Presser

Warshauer, Meira   1949-

Symphony No. 1: Living, Breathing, Earth   25'
                                       (6.5'   6'   7'   7.5')
     3 3 2 2 – 4 3 3 1 – tmp+2 – hp, pf – str
     Includes: Call of the Cicadas; Tahuayo Rive at
     Night; Wings in Flight; Living, Breathing, Earth.
     Movement 3 refers to the Monarch butterfly.

                                                     Ecology
MMB (rental)

Washington, Ned & Bassman, George

I'm Getting Sentimental Over You   3'
     2 2 2 2 – 3sx – 4 2 3 0 – tmp+perc – str
     Lyrics by Washington and music by Bassman.
     Henry Sopkin, arr.

                                         Popular Songs
Kalmus

Waxman, Franz   1906-1967

Anne of the Indes (1951): Overture   4.5'
     3[1.pic.pic] 2 5[1.2.3.bcl.Ebcl/bcl] 2[1.cbn] –
     4 3 3 1 – tmp+2 – hp, pf – str
     perc: tri, glock, cyms, sus cym, tambn,vib, gong.
     Includes: Prelude; Sheba Queen; Jamaica; Finale.
     Recorded by Richard Mills with the Queensland
     Symphony Orchestra on "Franz Waxman: Legends
     of Hollywood Vol.2" (Vrese Sarabande).
                                                           Films
T&V (rental)

Beloved Infidel (1959): Theme   2'
     3[1.2.pic] 2[1.Eh] 3 2 – 4 1 3 1 – tmp+2
     – hp, pf(cel) – str
     perc: vib, glock, bd.
                                                           Films
T&V (rental)

Botany Bay (1953): Suite   9'
     2[1.pic] 1 3[1.2.bcl] 1[cbn] – 4 3 3[incl baritone] 1
     – tmp+2 – hp, pf(cel) – str
     perc: sd, bd, cyms, sus cym, vib, chimes, gong.
                                                           Films
T&V (rental)

The Bride of Frankenstein (1935)   75'
     3[1.2.pic] 3[1.2.Eh] 3[1.2.bcl] 3[1.2.cbn] –
     4 3 3 1 – tmp+perc – hp, 2 pf
     [cel/synth.org/synth/church org] – str
     perc: cym, sizzle cym, sus cym, sd, bd, gong, tamtam,
     tambn, woodblk, tri, 2 xyl(can share 1 xyl), vib, chimes.
     This is the music to accompany the entire film.
                                                      Films/Halloween
T&V (rental)

The Bride of Frankenstein (1935)   6'
     3[1.2.pic] 3[1.2.Eh] 3[1.2.bcl] 3[1.2.cbn] –
     4 3 3 1 – tmp+perc – hp, synth – str
     perc: xyl, glock, tri, tamtam, bd, sus cym, cym, chimes.
                                                      Films/Halloween
T&V (rental)

The Bride of Frankenstein (1935)   9'
     3[afl.afl/pic.pic] 3[1.2.Eh] 3[1.2.bcl] 3[1.2.cbn] –
     4 3 3 1 – tmp+5 – hp, pf, cel, Hammond org, synth
     – str
     perc: sizzle cym, sus cym, cyms, crotales, glock, xyl, vib,
     chimes, tri, ratchet, tamtam, sd, bd.
     Includes: Prelude; Minuet; Pastorale & March; The
     Creation of the Female Monster. The first three
     movements (*Suite 5'*) can be ordered separately and
     was recorded by Erich Kunzel and the Cincinnati
     Pops on "Reel Chillers" (Telarc). The final
     movement (*The Creation of the Female Monster 7'*)
     is available to order separately and was recorded on
     SUNSET BOULEVARD: The Classic Film Scores
     by Franz Waxman, Charles Gerhardt, conductor,
     National Philharmonic Orchestra, RCA.
                                                     Films/Halloween
T&V (rental)

The Bride of Frankenstein (1935)   2'
     2[1.pic] 2[1.Eh] 2[1.bcl] 2 – 3 3 0 0 – tmp+2 –
     hp, synth, org – str
     perc: temple blk, tri, tambn, sd, bd, cym, xyl, chimes.
                                                      Films/Halloween
T&V (rental)

Captains Courageous (1937): Suite   7'
     3[1.2.pic] 2[1.Eh] 3[1.2.bcl] 2 – 4 3 3 1 – tmp+4
     – hp, pf[cel] – str
     perc: tri, cym, sd, bd, xyl, marim, glock, vib, tambn,
     woodblk, chimes.
     Christopher Palmer, arr.
                                                           Films
T&V (rental)

A Christmas Carol (1939): Christmas Morning & Finale   3'
    2[1.pic] 2 2 2 – 4 2 1 0 – tmp+2 – hp, pf[cel] – str
    perc: sus cym, cym, bd.
    Christopher Palmer, arr.

                                                  Christmas/Films

T&V (rental)

A Christmas Carol (1939): Five Sketches after Dickens   10'
                       (3' 1.5' 2' 2' 1.5')
    2[1.pic] 2 2 2 – 4 2 1 0 – tmp+2 – hp, pf[cel] – str
    perc: sus cym, cym, bd.
    Includes: Prelude & Threadneedle Street;
    Mr. Scrooge, Ghosts & Spirits; Snowball Fight;
    Christmas Morning; Finale.
    Christopher Palmer, arr.

                                                  Christmas/Films

T&V (rental)

Cimarron (1960): Suite   3'
    2[bsfl.pic] 2[1.Eh] 3[1.2.bcl] 2[1.cbn] – 4 3 3 1
    – tmp+3 – hp, pf[cel] – str
    perc: sus cym, cym, gong, tmp 2, sd, bd, xyl, vib, chimes,
    tambn, tom tom.

                                                  Films

T&V (rental)

Come Back, Little Sheba (1953): Reminiscences for Orchestra   5'
    2 1 3[1.2.bcl] 1 – 3 3 3 0 – tmp+2 – hp, pf – str
    perc: sus cym, cym, tri, glock.

                                                  Films

T&V (rental)

Dark City (1950)   13'
                       (3' 4' 6')
    3[1.afl.pic] 2[1.Eh] 3[1.2.bcl] 3[1.2.cbn] – tsx –
    4 3 3 1 – tmp+2 – hp, pf[cel] – str
    perc: sd, bd, low gong, sm gong, cym, sus cym, xyl, vib.
    Includes: Prelude; Stroll in the Dark; Finale.

                                                  Films

T&V (rental)

The Devil Doll (1936): Waltzes   6.5'
    2[1.pic] 1[Eh] 2 1 – 2 2 0 1 – tmp+3 – hp, pf – str
    perc: glock, sd, bd, cym, sus cym, tri, tambn.

                                                  Dance/Films

T&V (rental)

Dr. Jekyll and Mr. Hyde (1941): Suite   10'
    3[1.2.pic] 2[1.Eh] 2[1.Ebcl/bcl] 2[1.cbn] – 4 3 3 1 –
    tmp+3 – hp, pf, cel, org – str
    perc: drumset, sd, bd, sus cym, cym, glock, vib, chimes,
    tamtam, police whistle.
    SATB Chorus.
    Includes: The Laboratory; The Transformation; The
    Music Hall; Fight & Pursuit; Finale.
    Nominated for 1942 Oscar for Best Music.
    Recorded by John Mauceri and the Hollywood
    Bowl Orchestra on "Hollywood Nightmares"
    (Phillips Classics).
    Christopher Palmer, arr.

                                                  Films/Halloween

T&V (rental)

Elephant Walk (1954): Suite   12.5'
    3[1.2.pic] 2[1.Eh] 3[1.2.bcl] 3[1.2.cbn] –
    (asx, tsx, barsx) – 4 3 3 1 – tmp+2 – 2 hp, pf[cel]
    – str
    perc: cym, finger cym, tambn, (bass marim), glock, xyl,
    sd, bd, tri, tamtam.
    Includes: Prelude; The Plantation; Appeal for Help;
    Cylon Romance; Elephant Stampede & Finale
    Christopher Palmer, arr.

                                                  Animals/Films

T&V (rental)

The Furies (1950): Suite   7'
    2[1.pic] 2[1.Eh] 3[1.2.bcl] 2[1.cbn] – 4 3 3 1
    – tmp+3 – hp, pf[cel], gtr – str
    perc: sd, bd, cym, sus cym, xyl, vib, whip.
    Includes: Prelude; Juan & Vance; The Mark of the
    Furies; The Romance Revived; The King of the
    Furies. Recorded by Richard Mills with the
    Queensland Symphony Orchestra on "Franz
    Waxman: Legends of Hollyuwood Vol. 3" (Varese
    Sarabande) and Erich Kunzel & Cincinnati Pops on
    "Round Up" (Telarc).

                                                  Films

T&V (rental)

Hemingway's Adventures of a Young Man   18'
                       (4' 2.5' 3' 4.5' 4')
    3[1.2.pic] 2[1.Eh] 3[1.2.bcl] 2 – 2 barsx –
    4 3 3 1 – tmp+2 – 2 hp, 2 pf, cel – str
    perc: sd, bd, xyl, vib, bells, marim, slapstick, temple blk,
    cowbells, gong, sus cym, choke cym.
    Includes: The Northern Woods - Moderato;
    A Soldier Home - Allegro; On His Own - Lento;
    War - Allegro; Home Again - Moderato.

                                                  Films

T&V (rental)

Hemingway's Adventures of a Young Man: 7'
Rosanna
   3[1.2.pic] 3[1.2.EH) 3[1.2.bcl] 3[1.2.cbn] – 4 3 3 1
   – tmp+3 – hp, cel – str
   perc: cym, sus cym, sd, bd, bells, xyl, vib, tambn, tri.
   Solo Trumpet.
                                            Films

T&V (rental)

Huckleberry Finn (1939): Overture 6'
   2[1.pic] 2 2 2 – 4 3 3 1 – tmp+4 – hp, pf[cel] – str
   perc: sd, bd, cym, sus cym, woodblk, xyl, vib, tamtam, tri,
   whip, (wind machine), tmp 2.
   Includes: Main Title; The River Queen; At Night;
   Huck's Disapointment; The First Adventure; End
   Title.
   Christopher Palmer, arr.
                                            Films

T&V (rental)

The Ice Follies of 1939 6'
   2[1.pic] 2[1.Eh] 3[1.2.bcl] 3[1.2.cbn] –
   (2asx, 2tsx, barsx) – 4 4 3 0 – tmp+3 –
   hp, pf[cel], gtr – str
   perc: drumset, cym, bd, glock, vib.
   Optional Solo Soprano; Optional SATB Chorus.
   Roger Edens, arr.
                                        Films/Sports

T&V (rental)

The Lost Command (1966): Aicha's Theme 2.5'
   3 2[1.Eh] 3[1.bcl.Ebcl] 2 – 4 1 0 0 – hp, cel – str
                                            Films

T&V (rental)

Man on a Tightrope (1953): March 2'
   3[1.2.pic] 2 3[(#3)] 3[(#3)] – 4 4[(#4)] 4[(#4)] 1
   – tmp+3 – (cel) – str
   perc: sd, bd, cym, sus cym, glock, tri, tambn.
                                      Circus/Films

T&V (rental)

Medley: Classic Film Themes 10'
   3[1/afl.afl.pic].3[1.2.Eh] 3[1.2.bcl] 2 – 2asx[can be
   doubled by flute players].barsx[can be doubled by
   bcl player] – 4 3 3 1 – tmp+3 – 2 hp, pf[cel] – str
   perc: sus cym, cym, lions roar, tri, bells, celeste, bells, vib,
   marim, 2 toms[sm,med], sd, tamtam,
   2 gongs[sm, lg].
   Solo Alto Saxophone. Includes: The Philadelphia
   Story; A Place in the Sun; This is My Love;
   "Katsumi" Love Theme from Sayonara.
                                          Films

T&V (rental)

Medley: Classic Love Themes 8.5'
   3[pic.2.pic] 3[1.2.EH] 3[1/Ebcl.2.bcl/tsx] 3[1.2.cbn]
   – tsx[(bcl)] – 4 3 3 1 – tmp+1 –
   2 hp, pf[cel], 3 mandolins – str
   perc: glock,chimes, vib, xyl, sus cym, cym, bd.
   Includes: Peyton Place: Prelude; *Rosanna* from
   Hemingway's Adventures of a Young Man; *Many
   Dreams Ago* from Elephant Walk; *Aicha's Theme*
   from The Lost Command; *The Wonderful Season of
   Love* from Peyton Place.
                                       Films/Valentine

T&V (rental)

Medley: Nostalgic Film Themes 10'
   3[1.afl.pic] 3[1.2.Eh] 3[1.2.bcl/tsx] 3[1.2.cbn]
   4 3 3 1 tmp+4 – 2 hp, pf[cel] – str
   perc: cym, sus cym, glock, chimes, 2 vib, 2 marim, xyl,
   bd.
   Includes: Suspicion; My Geisha; Beloved Infidel;
   Prince Valiant.
                                         Films

T&V (rental)

My Cousin Rachel (1952): Suite 7.5'
   3[1.2.pic] 2[1.Eh] 4[1.2.3.bcl/tsx.Ebcbcl] 0 – tsx
   – 4 3 3 1 – tmp+4 – hp, pf[cel] str
   perc: sus cym, cym, lg bd, glock, vib, chimes, gong.
   Includes: Prelude; Tisana; Philip's Birthday;
   At Night & Finale.
   The publisher posts a ? for bassoons, but Waxman
   typically uses 3[1.2.cbn].
                                         Films

T&V (rental)

My Geisha (1961): Goodbye Love - Finale 2.5'
   3[1.2.pic] 3[1.2.Eh] 3[1.2.bcl] 2 – 4 3 3 1 –
   tmp+1 – 2 hp, pf – str
   perc: vib.
                                         Films

T&V (rental)

My Geisha (1961): Suite 5.5'
   3(I.afl.pic] 3[1.2.Eh] 3[1.2.bcl] 2 – 4 3 3 1 –
   tmp+5 – 2 hp, pf[cel] – str
   perc: sd, bd, cym, vib, sm marim, bs marim, glock, xyl,
   tri, tambn.
   Includes: Prelude; Work Montage & Wedding;
   Goodbye Love (Finale).
                                         Films

T&V (rental)

My Geisha (1961): You Are Sympathy to Me 3.5'
   2[1.afl]1 3[1.2.bcl] 0 – 3 0 0 0 – perc – hp, pf – str
   perc: drumset, vib, glock.
                                         Films

T&V (rental)

Night and the City (1950): Suite   10'
  Nightride for Orchestra
    3[1.pic.pic] 2[1.Eh] 2[Ebcl.bcl] 2[1.cbn] – asx, tsx, (barsx or bcl) – 4 3 3 1 – tmp+4 – hp, pf[cel] – str
    perc: tamtam, 2 chimes, xyl, vib, glock, cym, sus cym, tri, bd, (tmp 2).
                                            Films
  T&V (rental)

The Nun's Story (1958)   11'
    3[1.2.pic] 3[1.2.Eh] 3[1.2.bcl] 3[1.2.cbn] – 4 3 3 1 – tmp+1 – 2 hp, 2 pf[1.cel], (synth) – str
    perc: glock, chimes, xyl, muffled "Mahler" chime.
    Includes: Prelude; I Accuse Myself; Haircutting; Killing of Aurelie; Finale. Nominated for an Oscar and a Grammy in 1959.
                                            Films
  T&V (rental)

The Nun's Story (1958): Short Suite   4'
    3[1.2.pic] 3[1.2.Eh] 3[1.2.bcl] 3[1.2.cbn] – 4 3 3 1 – tmp+perc – 2 hp[combined part for 1 hp included], 2 pf[cel.(#2)] – str
    perc: glock, xyl, chimes, Mahler chime.
    Includes: Prelude; Finale.
                                            Films
  T&V (rental)

Peyton Place (1957): Suite   9.5'
    3[incl pic] 3[1.2.Eh] 3[1.2.bcl] 3 – 4 3 3 1 – tmp+2 – hp, pf[cel] – str
    perc: glock, vib, chimes, sus cym, tri.
    Includes: Prelude; Entering Peyton Place; Going to School; Swimming; The Hilltop.
                                            Films
  T&V (rental)

Peyton Place (1957): Theme   4'
  "The Wonderful Seasons of Love" or "For Those Who Are Young"
    3[1.2.pic] 2[1.Eh] 3 3 – 4 0 3 1 – tmp+1 – hp, pf[cel] – str
    perc: vib, glock.
                                  Films/Valentine
  T&V (rental)

The Philadelphia Story (1939): Suite   3.5'
    0 – asx – 4 3 3 1 – tmp+2 – hp, pf – str
    perc: vib, glock, sus cym, cyms, tri.
    Includes: Metro-Goldwyn-Mayer Fanfare (featuring "Leo the Lion"); Main Title; The True Love.
                                            Films
  T&V (rental)

The Pioneer (1951): Suite   10.5'
    2[bsfl.pic] 2[1.Eh] 3[1.2.bcl] 2[1.cbn] – 4 3 3 1 – tmp+3 – hp, pf[cel] – str
    perc: sus cym, cym, gong, tmp 2, sd, bd, xyl, vib, chimes, tambn, tom tom.
    Includes music from the films: *Red Mountain*; *Cimarron*; *The Indian Fighter*.
                                  Americana/Films
  T&V (rental)

A Place in the Sun (1951)   8.5'
    3[afl/pic,2.3] 2[Eh.2] 3[1.2.bcl] 2 – 4 4[(#4)] 4 1 – tmp+2 – hp, pf – str
    perc: sus cym, cyms, vib, xyl, sd, bd.
    Solo Alto Saxophone or Guitar. Includes: Prelude; Angela; Loon Lake; Farewell & Frenzy; The Farewell.
    Won the 1952 Oscar for Best Music.
                                            Films
  T&V (rental)

A Place in the Sun (1951): A Symphonic Scenario   12.5'
    3[afl/pic.2.3] 2[Eh.2] 3[1.2.bcl] 2 – asx – 4 4[(#4)] 4 1 – tmp+2 – hp, pf – str
    perc: sus cym, xyl, vib, sd, bd, cym.
    Includes: Prelude & First Scene; The First Mile; Angela Vicker's Theme; The Drowning; Farewell & Frenzy; The Courtroom; The Last Mile.
    Christopher Palmer, arr.
                                            Films
  T&V (rental)

Possessed (1947)   12'
    2[1.pic] 2[1.Eh] 4[1.2.3.Ebcl/bcl] 2[1.cbn] – 6 4 4 1 – tmp+2 – 2 hp, 2 pf, synth – str
    perc: sd, sus cym, cym, vib, glock, bs marim.
                                            Films
  T&V (rental)

Prince Valiant (1954)   12'
    3[1.2.pic] 2 4[1.2.3.bcl] 3 – 4 3 3 1 – tmp+2 – hp, pf[cel, org] – str
    perc: field dr, bd, glock, vib, pic xyl, gong, chimes, cym.
    Includes: Prelude; King Aguar's Escape; The Fens; The First Chase; The Tournament; Sir Brack's Death; Finale.
                                      Films/Sports
  T&V (rental)

Rear Window (1954)   12'
    3[1.pic.3] 2 1[bcl] 2 – asx, (tsx) – 4 3 3 1 –
    tmp+2 – hp, pf[cel], gtr – str
    perc: drumset, sus cym, sd, glock, xyl, vib, claves, (shakers).
    Includes: Prelude; Rhumba; Lisa: Intermezzo; Ballet; Finale.
    Christopher Palmer, arr.
                                                   Films

T&V (rental)

Rebecca (1940): Suite   8'
    3[1.afl/pic.pic] 2[1.Eh] 3[1.2.bcl] 2 – 4 3 3 1 –
    tmp+3 – hp, pf – str
    perc: chimes, gong, vib, xyl, marim, 2 glock, cym, sd, bd, tri.
    Includes: Prelude; After the Ball; Mrs. Danvers; Confession Scene; Manderly in Flames.
    Nominated for 1941 Oscar for Best Music.
                                                   Films

T&V (rental)

The Silver Chalice (1954): Short Suite   7'
    2 2[1.Eh] 5[1.2.3.bcl.bcl] 2[1.cbn] – 4 3 3 1 –
    tmp+perc – 2 hp, pf, novachord – str
    perc: cym, bells, chimes, vib.
    Includes: Prelude; Fight for the Cup; Finale.
    Nominated for the 1955 Oscar for Best Music.
    Richard Kaufman (editor).
                                                   Films

T&V (rental)

The Silver Chalice (1954): Suite   16'
    2[1.pic] 2[1.Eh] 5[Ebcl.2.3.bcl.(bcl)] 2[1.cbn] –
    3 3 3 1 – tmp+perc – 2 hp, 2 pf [1.cel] – str
    perc: 2 glock, vib, chimes, cym, gong, 2 sd, bd[with cym], choke cym, finger cym, tuned toms, tambn.
    Includes: Prelude - Maestoso; The Chase - Allegro; Deborah's Lament - Largo; Simon the Magician - Moderato; Fight for the Cup - Allegro; Finale - Broadly.
    Arnold Freed, arr.
                                                   Films

T&V (rental)

Sorry, Wrong Number (1948): Passacaglia   7'
    2[1.pic] 2[1.Eh] 2[1.bcl] 2[1.cbn] – 4 3 3 1 –
    tmp+3 – hp, pf[cel] – str
    perc: sus cym, vib, sd, bd, ruthe, tri, tamtam.
                                                   Films

T&V (rental)

The Story of Ruth (1960): A Suite in   13.5'
    Three Movements   (5.5' 4' 4')
    4[1.2.pic.pic] 3[1.2.Eh] 1[(EbcbcI] 3[1.2.cbn]
    – ssx, bcl, 2tsx – 6 4 4 2 – tmp+5 –
    2 hp, 2 pf[cel/mandolin, elec org or synth] – str
    perc: 2 vib, 2 xyl, marim, glock, gong, cym, field dr, lg bd, bd.
                                                   Films

T&V (rental)

Sunset Boulevard (1950): Staged Reading   108.5'
    in Two Acts   (55' 53.5')
    2[1/pic.2/pic/afl] 2[1.Eh] 3[1.2/Ebcl/bcl.3/bcl]
    2[1.cbn] – asx, tsx – 3 3 3 1 – tmp+3 –
    set accordion, hp, 2kbd[pf.cel.nova/chord org.wind effect/org.(pf 2)] – str
    perc: drumset, sd, sus cym, xyl, gong, bd, cym, 2vib, tambn, marim, tri, bells.
    Adapted as a reading with Orchestra by David Rambo. World Concert Premiere by John Mauceri, conducting the Hollywood Bowl Orchestra at the Hollywood Bowl on August 6, 2006.
                                                   Films

T&V (rental)

Sunset Boulevard (1950): Suite   8'
    2[afl/pic.pic] 1[Eh] 3[1.Ebcl.bcl] 2[1.cbn] –
    3 3 3 1 – tmp+3 – hp, pf[cel] – str
    perc: sd, cym, sus cym, choke cym, finger cym, gong, xyl, vib, glock, tambn.
    Includes: Prelude; Norma Desmond; The Studio Stroll; The Comeback: Norma as Salome; Paramount on Parade. Won the 1951 Oscar and Golden Globe awards for Best Music.
    Charles Gerhardt and Leonid Raab, arr.
                                                   Films

T&V (rental)

Suspicion (1941): Suite   12'
    2[pic.afl]1 3[1.Ebaltcl.bcl] 1 – 3 3 3 1 – tmp+3 –
    2 hp, 2 pf, novachord – str
    perc: bells, vib, xyl, marim(bs marim), chimes, sd, bd, sus cym, cym.
    Includes: Prelude;Sunday Morning; The Chairs are Back; Melbeck's Office; Looking for Johnny; Too Fast & Finale.
    Nominated for the 1942 Oscar for Best Music.
                                                   Films

T&V (rental)

Taras Bulba (1962): Suite 17.5'
    (3.5' 3.5' 4' 5')
2[1.pic] 3[ob d'amore.2.Eh] 3[1.2.bcl/(eflcl)] 3[1.2.cbn] – 4 4 3 1 – tmp+3 – hp, pf[cel] – str
perc: sus cym, cym, xyl, vib, glock, sd, field dr, bd, tambn, slgh-bells.
Includes: Overture; Torchlight Parade; Pastorale; The Black Plague; Finale: The Ride of the Cossacks. Nominated for the 1963 Oscar and Golden Globe for Best Music.
    Films

T&V (rental)

Taras Bulba (1962): The Ride of the Cossacks 5'
3[1.2.pic] 2 3[1.bcl.Dbcl] 3[1.2.cbn] – (ssax) – 6[4tuben.5.6] 3 3 1 – 2 tmp+4] – (hp), (pf) – str
Nominated for the 1963 Oscar and Golden Globe for Best Music.
    Films

T&V (rental)

Untamed (1955) 7.5'
3[1.2.pic] 2[1.Eh] 5[1.2.3.bcl.bcl/Ebcbcl] 3[1.2.cbn] – 8 3 3 1 – tmp+4 – hp, pf – str
perc: cym, sus cym, tri, 2 sd, marim, bs marim, xyl
Includes: Prelude; Capetown Street; By the River; Vorwarts & Finale.
    Films

T&V (rental)

Young at Heart (1938) 5'
3[1.2.pic] 2 3[1.2.bcl] 2 – 2 asx, 2 tsx – 4 3 3 1 – tmp+3 sus cym, cym – hp, cel[hpsd] – str
perc: drumset, glock, xyl, chimes, vib.
Includes: Main Title; The Rivera; The Yacht Club; Engineering Office; Finale. Won the 1939 Oscars for Best Music and Scoring.
Christopher Palmer, arr.
    Films

T&V (rental)

Weatherly, Fred Edward   1848-1929

Danny Boy 4'
1 1 2 1 – 2 2 1 (1) – tmp – str
Optional Solo Voice in Key of E flat. Tuba plays string bass part.
    Popular Song

Boosey (POP); Luck's

Webb, Jimmy   1946-

The Animals' Christmas 50'
2 1 2 1 – 2 3 2 0 – tmp+perc – pf, org, gtr – str
3 Solo Voices.
    Christmas

Schirmer (rental)

MacArthur Park 4.5'
2 2 3[incl bcl] 1 – 2sx – 4 3 3 1 – tmp+perc – pf, (elec gtr) – str
Muller, arr.
    Popular Song

Belwin (POP); EMS or Luck's (rental)

Webb, Roy   1888-1982

Notorious (1946): Suite 6'
3[1.2.pic] 3[1.2.Eh] 3[1.2.bcl] 3[1.2.cbn] – 4 3 3 1 – tmp+3 – hp, pf[cel] – str
perc: sus cym, cym, sd, bd, vib, tamtam, tmp 2.
Includes: Main Title; Troubled Mind; Alicia Collapses; Finale & End Cast.
Christopher Palmer, arr.
    Films

T&V (rental)

Webber [see Lloyd Webber]

Weber, Carl Maria von   1786-1826

Invitation to the Dance 9'
2[incl pic] 2[Eh] 3[incl bcl] 2 – 3 2 3 0 – 2hp – str
Leopold Stokowski, arr.
    Dance

Presser (rental)

Oberon: Overture 9'
2 2 2 2 – 4 2 3 0 – tmp – str
    Popular Classics

Breitkopf; Kalmus

Turandot: Overture and March   6'
    2[1.pic] 2 2 2 – 2 2 1 0 – tmp+4 – str
    perc: bd, cym, sd, tri.
                                                  Popular Classics
Kalmus

Weill, Kurt   1900-1950

Kleine Dreigroschenmusik   22'
    (*Suite from Little Three Penny Opera*)
    2[incl pic] 0 2 2 – asx, tsx/ssx – 0 2 1 1 – tmp+1
    – hp, pf, bnjo, (gtr), accordion
                                                 Instrumental Pops
EAM (rental)

The Two Worlds of Kurt Weill: Berlin Suite   18'
    2[incl 2pic] 1[Eh] 3[1.2.bcl] 1 – 0 2 3 1 –
    3perc – hp, pf, gtr, bnjo, mand – str
    Includes:
    Mack the Knife: (2')
    2[incl pic] 1 3[1.2.bcl] 1 – 0 2 3 1 – 3perc –
    hp, pf, mand, bnjo – str
    J'attends un navire   (3')
    hp, cel - str
    Surabaya Johnny   (3')
    2[(pic)] 1[Eh] 3[1.2.bcl] 1 – 0 2 3 0 – 3perc –
    hp, bnjo – str
    Theme from "Mahogonny"   (5')
    2 1[Eh] 3[1.2.bcl] 1 – 0 0 0 0 – hp, pf – str
    Polly's Lied   (3')
    2 1[Eh] 3[1.2.bcl] 1 – 0 0 0 0 – gtr, hp, mand –
    str[no db]
    Bilbao Song   (2')
    2[incl 2pic] 1 3[1.2.bcl] 1 – 0 2 3 1 – 3perc –
    hp, pf, gtr, bnjo – str
    Movements are available separately.
    Morton Gould, arr.
                                    Instrumental Pops/
                                           Popular Song
GEA (rental)

The Two Worlds of Kurt Weill: New York Suite   21'
    2[incl pic] 1[incl Eh] 3[1.2.bcl] 1 – 0 2 3 1 –
    3perc – hp, (cel), pf, (player pf), gtr, bnjo – str
    Includes:
    Mack the Knife   (3')
    2[incl pic] 1 3[1.2.bcl] 1 – 0 2 3 1 – 3perc –
    hp, player pf, gtr, bnjo – str
    Speak Low   (2')
    2 1 3[1.2.bcl] 1 – 0 0 0 0 – hp, cel, gtr – str
    Lost in the Stars   (3')
    2 1[incl Eh] 3[1.2.bcl] 1 – 0 2 3 0 – perc –
    hp – str
    Train to Johannesburg   (2')
    2[incl pic] 1 3[1.2.bcl] 1 – 0 2 3 0 – 3perc –
    gtr, hp – str
    My Ship   (4')
    2 1[Eh] 3[1.2.bcl] 1 – 0 0 0 0 – gtr, hp, mand –
    str[no db]
    I Got a Marble and a Star   (2')
    2 1 3[1.2.bcl] 1 – 0 2 3 1 – 2perc –
    gtr, pf, hp, bnjo – str
    September Song   (5')
    1 1[incl Eh] 3[1.2.bcl] 1 – 0 0 0 0 – 2perc –
    hp, gtr – str
    Movements are available separately.
    Morton Gould, arr.
                                    Instrumental Pops/
                                           Popular Song
GEA (rental)

Weinberger, Jaromir   1896-1967

Bohemian Songs and Dances:
    Six Dances
        2 2 2 2 – 4 2 3 0 – tmp+perc – cel, hp –str
        Solo Violin in no.1. Dances available separately.
                                                Dance/International
AMP (rental)

The Devil on the Belfry   4'
    0 0 0 0 – 0 0 0 0 – 2perc – cel – str
    Solo Violin.
                                                          Halloween
Schirmer (rental)

Prelude and Fugue on "Dixie"   5'
    3 2 2 2 – 4 3 3 1 – perc – hp – str
    Optional stage band: 2hn, 2tp, 2tbn – perc – str
                                                     Americana
AMP (rental)

Svandadudák (Shvanda the Bagpiper): 10'
  Polka and Fugue (2' 6')
    3[incl pic] 2 2 2 – 4 3 3 1 – tmp+3 – hp, (org) – str
    4 offstage trumpets in unison.
                              Dance/International
    AMP (rental); EMS (rental); Luck's (rental)

Under the Spreading Chestnut Tree 12'
    3[incl 2pic] 2 2 2 – 4 3 3 1 – tmp+3 – hp, pf – str
                                           Ecology
    AMP (rental)

Welcher, Dan   1948-

Castle Creek: Fanfare 1.5'
    4 3 3 1 – tmp+4
                                  Americana/Fanfare
    Presser (rental)

Castle Creek: Fanfare & Overture 5'
    3 2 2 3 – 4 3 3 1 – tmp+4 – hp, pf – str
                                           Americana
    Presser (rental)

Haleakala: How Maui Snared the Sun 21'
    3[incl 2pic] 3[incl Eh] 3[incl bcl] 3[incl cbn] –
    4[incl 1 conch shell] 3 3 1 – tmp+4 – hp, cel/pf
    – str
    Narrator.
                                    Americana/Space
    Elkan-Vogel (rental)

JFK: The Voice of Peace 46'
    2[1.2/pic] 2 2 2 – 2 2 0 0 – tmp+perc – pf, hp – str
    Solo Cello; SATB chorus; 1 Male & 1 Female
    Speaker; Mezzo-Sop or Boy Soprano.
                                           Patriotic
    Presser (rental)

Prairie Light: Three Texas Watercolors of Georgia
    O'Keeffe
    3 2 2 2 – 4 3 3 1 – tmp+3 – pf/cel – hp – str
    Also available with Solo Piano as 1 2 2 2 –
    2 0 0 0 – perc – str
                                           Americana
    Presser (rental)

Spumante 7'
    3 3 3 3 – 4 4 3 1 – tmp+4 – hp, pf – str
                                   Instrumental Pops
    Presser (rental)

Symphony No. 2 "Night Watchers" 25'
    3 3 3 3 – 4 3 3 1 – tmp+4 – pf/cel, hp – str
    Written for the centenary of the Lowell
    Observatory in Arizona. The Scherzo movement
    may be played separately (4').
                                              Space
    Presser (rental)

The Visions of Merlin 21'
    2 2 2 2 – 3 2 0 0 – tmp+3 – pf, cel – str
                                          Halloween
    Presser (rental)

The Yellowstone Fires 8'
    4[incl 2pic] 3[incl Eh] 7[incl Ebcl & bcl]
    2[incl cbn] – ssx, asx, tsx, bsx – 5 4 4 0 – pf
    Bissell, arr.
                                  Americana/Ecology
    Presser (rental)

Zion 10'
    3 3 3 3 – 4 4 3 1 – tmp+4 – hp, pf – str
                                           Americana
    Presser (rental)

Wells, Robert (See: Torme, Mel)

Wells, Robin, arr.

The Novello Book of Carols: 6'
  A Fanfare for Christmas (Hodie, Hodie); (3' 3')
  A Gallery Carol (Rejoice and Be Merry)
    2 2 2 2 – 2 2 3 1 – tmp+2 – str
    Solo Voice.
                                          Christmas
    Novello (rental)

Wendel, Robert, arr.   1951-

The April Fool Concerto 8'
    3[1.2.pic] 2 2 2 – 4 3 3 1 – tmp+3 – pf – str
    Solo Piano.
    Includes many musical quotes and novelty
    activities creating comic relief.
                            Instrumental Pops/Novelty
    Wendel (rental)

The Armed Forces March   3'
    3[1.2.pic] 2 2 2 – 4 3 3 1 – tmp+3[drumset] – str
    A salute to the Army, Marines, Coast Guard, Navy, and Air Force with a tag from the Star Spangled Banner.
                                           Patriotic

Wendel (rental)

Back to the Fifties!   6'
    3[1.2.pic] 2[1.2/tsx] 2 – 4 3 3 1 – tmp+3[drumset] – hp, (pf) – str
    Includes: Mister Sandman; The Great Pretender; Que Sera Sera; Sh-Boom Sh-Boom; and Tequila!
                                          Popular Songs

Wendel (rental)

Baile Chruiach (Bally Croy)   6'
    3 3 3 3 – 4 5[2 offstage] 3 1 – tmp+2 – hp – str
    From the Celtic legend of Grainne Ni Mhaille.
                                   International/St. Patrick

Wendel (rental)

The Bells of Christmas   3.5'
    3[1.2.pic]2 3[1.2.(bcl)] 2 – 4 3 3 1 – tmp+3 – hp, (cel or pf) – str
    Chorus with optional handbells.
    Vince Trani, co-lyricist
                                            Christmas

Wendel (rental)

Carol of the Bells   3.5'
    3[1.2.pic] 2 2 2 – 4 3 3 1 – tmp+3 – hp, cel – str
    perc: bd, sus cym, sd, tri, tamtam, glock, chimes, belltree, (3 Turandot gongs or low synthesizer bells).
    Optional handbell choir (parts available on request).
                                            Christmas

Wendel (rental)

A Chanukah Overture   5.5'
    3[1.2.pic] 2 2 2 – 4 3 3 1 – tmp+3[drumset] – str
    perc: bd, cym, drumset, tri, tambn, glock.
    Overture based on Maoz T'zur; Rock of My Security (Rock of Ages); Al HaNisim; S'vivon; and I Have a Little Dreidel.
    Dana Friedman and Robert Wendel, composers.
                                            Hanukkah

Wendel (rental)

Christmas a la Valse!   6'
    3[1.2.pic] 2 2 2 – 4 3 3 1 – tmp+3 – hp – str
    perc: bd, cym, tri, tambn, tamtam, glock, chimes.
    Includes: Bring a Torch, Jeanette Isabella; We Three Kings; The Skaters' Waltz; Greensleeves; It Came Upon a Midnight Clear; Wassail, Wassail; We Wish You a Merry Christmas.
                                            Christmas

Wendel (rental)

Christmas Through Children's Eyes   4'
    3[1.2.pic] 2 2 2 – 4 3 3 1 – tmp+3 – (toy pf), hp – str
    Chorus.
    Vince Trani, co-lyricist.
                                            Christmas

Wendel (rental)

A Classical Christmas Suite   14.5'
    3[1.2.pic] 2 2 2 – 4 3 3 1 – tmp+3 – hp – str
    Alternate for Movements I, II, III: 2 2 2 2 – 2 2 0 0 – tmp+1 – str
    I. Overture to a Merry Christmas
        Combines Mozart's Marriage of Figaro with Joy to the World.
    II. We three Kings (So Unfinished Are…)
        Based on Schubert's Unfinished Symphony.
    III. Jingle Fourth
        Uses Mahler's Fourth Symphony and Jingle Bells.
    IV. Little Bolero Boy
        The Little Drummer Boy in the style of Ravel's Bolero.
    All movements available separately.
                                            Christmas

Wendel (rental)

Commemoration   4'
    3[1.2.5/pic] 2[1.Eh] 2 2 – 4[or2] 3[or4] 3 1 – tmp+3 – (org) – str
    perc: sus cym, sd, tamtam, glock, chimes.
                                          Celebration/Fanfare

Wendel (rental)

An Evergreen Christmas   4'
    3[1.2.pic] 2 2 2 – 4 3 3 1 – tmp+3[drumset] – hp – str
    Chorus. Includes: Oh Christmas Tree; The Holly and the Ivy; and Deck the Hall.
                                            Christmas

Wendel (rental)

Fanfare for Freedom 3.5'
3[1.2.pic] 2 2 2 – 4 3 3 1 – tmp+3 – (pf) – str
perc: cym, tri, glock, chimes.
                                            Fanfare/Patriotic
Wendel (rental)

Fantasia on "Yeroushalaim Shel Zahav" 5.5'
1 2[1.Eh] 1 1 – 0 0 0 0 – 1perc – hp – str
perc: non-pitched antique cym (or tri or windchime).
Based on the Israeli folk song "Jerusalem of Gold."
                                     Holidays/International
Wendel (rental)

Fiesta Mexicana 4.5'
3[1.2.pic] 2 2 2 – 4 3 3 0 – tmp+3[drumset] – str
Includes Mexican Hat Dance; La Cucaracha; and Ritchie Valens' version of La Bamba.
                                                        International
Wendel (rental)

The Flintstones Meet the Jetsons 4'
3[1.2.pic] 2 2 2 – 4 3 3 1 – tmp+3[drumset] – str
                                                                           TV
Wendel (rental)

From Sea to Shining Sea 9'
3[1.2.pic] 3[1.2.(bcl)] 2 – 4 3 3 1 – tmp+3[drumset] – str
Includes: America the Beautiful; San Francisco; Deep in the Heart of Texas; Meet Me in Saint Louis; Chicago; The Tennessee Waltz; My Old Kentucky Home; Georgia on My Mind; Carolina in the Morning; and New York, New York.
                                          Americana/Travel
Wendel (rental)

A George M. Cohan Overture 6.5'
3[1.2.pic] 2 2 2 – 4 3 3 1 – tmp+3[drumset] – str
Also available in a vocal version for Mezzo Soprano and/or Baritone soloists or SATB Chorus. Includes: Give My Regards to Broadway; Mary; Harrigan; Over There; Yankee Doodle Dandy; and You're a Grand Old Flag.
                                Americana/Popular Songs
Wendel (rental)

A Halloween Trilogy 13.5'
  I. *The Pit and the Pendulum* (5.5')
     2 2 2 2 – 4 2 3 1 – tmp+perc – str
     perc: xyl, glock, tam-tam, sus cym, guerro, td, cym, bd.
     Based on Edgar Allen Poe's story and includes The Inquisition; The Pit; The Pendulum; The Walls Close In; A Blast of Noise and Liberation by the French Army.
  II. *Trick or Treat* (3')
     2 2 2 2 – 0 0 0 0 – perc – str
     perc: xyl, sd, sus cym.
  III. *Ride of the Headless Horseman* (5')
     3[1.2.pic] 2[1.Eh] 2 2 – 4 3 3 1 – tmp+4 – hp – str
     perc: drumset, mark tree, xyl, glock, chimes, tam-tam, tri, cym, bd.
All movements available separately.
                                                         Halloween
Wendel (rental)

A Hollywood Salute 3'
3[1.2.pic] 2 3[1.2.(bcl)] 2 – 4 3 3 1 – tmp+3[drumset] – hp – str
Includes 20th Century Fox Fanfare and Hooray for Hollywood and 15 other movie themes.
                                                                 Films
Wendel (rental)

Hymn of Thanksgiving: We Gather Together 3'
3[1.2.pic] 2[1.Eh] 2 2 – 4 3 3 1 – tmp+3 – hp, cel, (org) – str
Optional Soloists and/or Chorus.
                                                        Thanksgiving
Wendel (rental)

In the Manger 4'
3[1.2.pic] 2[1.Eh] 2 2 – 4 0 (3) 0 – tmp+3 – hp, cel – str
perc: tri, glock, chimes, belltree.
Optional handbell choir and vocal version available [2 solos or any combination of 2 choirs].
Combines Away in a Manger and Gesu Bambino.
                                                          Christmas
Wendel (rental)

An Irish Trilogy 4.5'
2 2 3[incl bcl] 2 – 4 3 3 1 – tmp+perc – str
                                                  International/St. Patrick
Wendel (rental)

Jonny Quest 2'
3[1.2.pic] 2 2 2 – 4 3 3 1 – tmp+3[drumset] – str
                                                                           TV
Wendel (rental)

An Old Fashioned Summer 4'
3[1.2.pic] 2 2 2 – 4 3 3 1 – tmp+3[drumset] – hp – str
Includes: School Days; In the Good Old Summertime; Sidewalks of New York; Bicycle Built for Two; Take Me Out to the Ball Game; and By the Sea
       Popular Songs/Seasons
Wendel (rental)

Orange Blossom Special 3'
3[1.2.pic] 2 2 2 – 4 3 3 1 – tmp+3[drumset] – str
Includes: Choo-Choo Charlie; Flight of the Bumble Bee; I've Been Working on the Railroad; and Chattanooga Choo-Choo.
       Americana
Wendel (rental)

The Original Ragtime Band 4'
3[1.2.pic] 2 2 2 – 4 3 3 1 – tmp+3[drumset] – pf – str
Includes: Ragtime Dance; The Entertainer; and The Maple Leaf Rag.
       Jazz
Wendel (rental)

Rock Around the Clock 3'
3[1.2.pic] 2 2 2 – 4 3 3 1 – tmp+3[drumset] – str
      New Year/Instrumental Pops/
       Popular Songs
Wendel (rental)

Saint Bailey's Rag 3.5'
3[1.2.pic] 2 3[1.2.bcl] 2 – 4 3 3 1 – tmp+3[drumset] – str
Dixieland-style march from When the Saints Go Marching In; Won't You Come Home Bill Bailey; 12th Street Rag.
       Jazz
Wendel (rental)

The Saint Louis Blues 3.5'
3[1.2.pic] 2 2 2 – 4 3 3 1 – tmp+3[drumset] – str
       Jazz
Wendel (rental)

Santa Dear 3'
2 2 2 2 – 0 0 0 0 – tmp+2 – cel or pf, hp – str
Children's Chorus.
Vince Trani, co-lyricist.
       Christmas
Wendel (rental)

The Smurfs: March 2'
3[1.2.pic] 2 2 2 – 4 3 3 1 – tmp+3[drumset] – str
       TV
Wendel (rental)

Stephen Foster Overture 6'
3[1.2.pic] 2 2 2 – 4 3 3 1 – tmp+3 – str
Includes: Oh! Susanna; My Old Kentucky Home; Jeannie With the Light Brown Hair; Swannee River; Beautiful Dreamer; Camptown Races; references to Dvořák's *Humoresque* and Rossini's *William Tell*.
       Americana
Wendel (rental)

Surf's Up! 3'
3[1.2.pic] 2 2 2 – 4 3 3 1 – tmp+3[drumset] – str
Includes: The Beach Boys' - Surfin'; Surfer Girl; and Surfin' Safari; and Wipe Out.
     Instrumental Pops/Popular Songs
Wendel (rental)

Swing, Ludwig, Swing! 3.5'
3[1.2.pic]2 2 2 – 4 3 3 1 – tmp+3[drumset] – str
       Instrumental Pops
Wendel (rental)

Take Flight 5.5'
3[1.2.pic] 2 3[1.2.(bcl)] 2 – 4 3 3 1 – tmp+3 – hp, cel – str
perc: bd, cym, sus cym, tri, tamtam, glock, marktree.
       Travel
Wendel (rental)

The Tall Ships 6'
3[1.2.pic] 2 2 2 – 4 3 3 1 – tmp+3 – str
       Travel
Wendel (rental)

That's It, That's All...The End! 5.5'
3[1.2.pic] 2 2 2 – 4 3 3 1 – tmp+3 – str
Includes *Auld Lang Syne* and excerpts from Schubert 9th, Brahms 2nd, Dvorak 9th, Beethoven 3rd & 5th, Mahler 1st and Beethoven 9th symphonies.
       New Year
Wendel (rental)

Towers of Light 7'
    2 2[1.2/Eh] 2 2 – 2[or 4] 0 0 0 – tmp+perc – cel, hp – str
    perc: glock, chimes, sus cym, tri, mark trees, tam-tam.
    Refers to light tributes held at "ground zero" in New York.
Patriotic

Wendel (rental)

Under the Big Top 6.5'
    3[1.2.pic] 2 2 2 – 4 2 3 1 – tmp+3[drumset] – str
Circus

Wendel (rental)

We Need a Little Christmas 3'
    3[1.2.pic] 2 2 2 – 4 3 3 1 – tmp+3[drumset] – hp – str
    Includes Jingle Bells; Deck the Halls, and White Christmas.
Christmas

Wendel (rental)

When TV Was Young 4.5'
    3[1.2.pic] 2 2 2 – 4 3 3 1 – tmp+3[drumset] – hp – str
    Includes: Dragnet; Alfred Hitchcock Presents; The Honeymooners; The Lone Ranger; I Love Lucy; and N-B-C theme.
TV

Wendel (rental)

Wenrich, Percy   1887-1952

Put On Your Old Grey Bonnet 3'
    1 1 2 1 – 2 2 1 0 – perc – str
    Ribe Danmark, arr.
Popular Song

Kalmus

When You Wore a Tulip 3'
    2[1.2/pic] 2 2 2 – (2asx, tsx) – 4 3 3 1 – tmp+perc – str
    Timothy Broege, arr.
Popular Song/Valentine

Kalmus

Wernick, Richard   1934-

Chanukah Festival Overture 3'
    2[incl (pic)] 2 0 2 – 2asx, tsx – 4 3 3 1 – tmp+3 – str
    Optional Chorus.
Hanukkah

Schirmer (rental)

Whelan, Bill   1950-

Riverdance Theme 6'
    2[incl pic] 2 2[incl bcl] 2 – 4 3 3 0 – tmp+3, drumset – hp, pf or cel, gtr – str
    Solo Violin.
Dance/International/
St. Patrick

Schirmer (rental)

Whitney, John   1942-

Coming of Age 7'
    3[1.2.pic] 2 3[1.2.bcl] 2 – 4 3 3 1 – tmp+4 – str
    perc: xyl, temple blks, sus cym, vibraslap, tambn, sd, bd, tom tom.
Instrumental Pops

Belwin

Light Rays 4.5'
    2 2 2 2 – 4 3 3 1 – drumset+2 – pf,elec bass – str
    Solo Alto Sax, Flute, or Flugel Horn (trumpet).
Weather

Belwin

Wilby, Philip   1949-

The Highland Express 13'
    Instrumentation varies from opt synth and strings to 2[incl pic] 2 2 2 – 4 2 3 1 – 3perc – str
    Narrator with audience participation.
Travel/International

Schirmer (rental)

Williams, Charles — 1893-1978

The Apartment: — 4'
  Theme (Jealous Lover)
  2 1[1/Eh] 2 1 – (asx, tsx) – 4 3 3 0 – tmp+1 –
  (hp) – str
  Solo Piano. Originally composed as *Jealous Lover* for an obscure 1949 British film, *The Romantic Age*. It became popular with this 1969 Academy Award winning film by Billy Wilder.
  Piano/Conductor score.

  Films
  EMI (rental); Kalmus

The Apartment: — 3.5'
  Theme (Jealous Lover)
  2 1 2 1 – 2sx – 2 3 3 1 – tmp+1 – gtr, elec bs – str
  Originally composed as *Jealous Lover* for an obscure 1949 British film, *The Romantic Age*. It became popular with this 1969 Academy Award winning film by Billy Wilder. Piano/Conductor score.
  John Cacavas, arr.

  Films
  Belwin(POP); Luck's (rental)

The Dream of Olwen — 4'
  2 1 2 1 – (2sx) – 2 2 3 0 – tmp+perc, hp – str
  Solo Piano in the score. From the film *While I Live*: a WWII war drama. Used as the theme song for "The Hallmark Hall of Fame."
  Henry Ernest Geehl, arr.

  Films/TV
  Kalmus

Williams, Cootie — 1910-1985
Monk, Thelonius — 1917-1982

'Round Midnight — 5'
  1tpt/flug – drumset – pf, gtr – str
  Solo Trumpet.
  Calvin Custer, arr.

  Jazz/New Year
  Warner (POP); Luck's (rental)

Williams, Ernest S.

Revolutionary Fantasy — 8'
  3[1.2.3/pic] 2 2 2 – 4 3 3 1 – tmp+2 – str
  perc: sd, bd, tambn, tamtam.
  From the opera "Rip van Winkle." Fantasy on the themes *Rule Britania* and *Yankee Doodle*.

  Instrumental Pops
  Ernest Williams (POP); Luck's (rental)

Williams, John T. — 1932-
(Also See: Hooper, Nicolas)

1941: March of 1941 — 4'
  3[incl 2pic] 2 2[1.2/Ebcl] 2[1.2/cbn] – 4 4 4 1 –
  tmp+13perc – hp, pf – str

  Films
  Leonard

Amistad: Dry Your Tears, Afrika — 3'
  3[incl 2pic] 3[1.2.Eh] 3[incl bcl] 3[incl cbn] –
  4 3 3 1 – tmp+perc – hp, pf – str
  SATB and Children's Chorus. Signature Edition

  Films
  Leonard

Angela's Ashes: — 11'
  Two Concert Pieces
  3[incl pic] 3[incl Eh] 3[incl bcl] 3[incl cbn] –
  4 0 0 0 – perc – hp, cel/pf – str
  Includes: Theme from Angela's Ashes; Angela's Prayer. Signature Edition

  Films
  Leonard

Call of the Champions: — 9'
  2002 Olympic Theme
  3[1.2.pic] 3[incl Eh] 3 3[incl cbn] – 4 3 3 1 –
  tmp+perc – hp, pf(cel) – str
  Optional Chorus. Signature Edition.

  Sports
  Leonard

Catch Me If You Can: 13'
Escapades for Alto Sax
3[1.2.pic] 3[incl Eh] 3 3[incl cbn] – 4 3 3 1 –
tmp+3 – hp, pf(cel) – str
Solo Alto Saxophone. Includes: Catch Me If You
Can; Recollections (Father's Theme); The Float.
Signature Edition.

                                                    Films

Leonard

Close Encounters of the Third Kind 15'
(Excerpts)
3[1.2/pic.pic] 2[1.2/Eh] 2[1.2/bcl] 3[1.2.cbn] –
4 4 4 1 – tmp+3 – hp, pf/cel(org) – str
perc: cym, bd, tamtam, tri,bell tree, chimes, sus cym, vib,
glock.
Optional Chorus. Signature Edition.

                                      Films/Space

Leonard

Theme from Close Encounters of the Third Kind 3'
1 1 2 1 – asx, tsx–1 2 1 0 –tmp+2 – (elec bs) – str
Bob Lowden, arr.

                                    Films/Space

Gold Horizon (rental from Luck's)

The Cowboys Overture 9'
3[1.2.pic] 2 3[1.2.bcl 3[1.2.cbn] – 4 3 3 1 – tmp+perc
– hp, cel/pf – str
Signature Edition.

                                Americana/Films

Leonard

Selections from E.T. 8'
3[incl pic] 2 4[incl bcl] 2 – 2asx, tsx, bsx –
4 3 3 1 – tmp+7 – (pf) – str
John Cacavas, arr.

                                    Films/Space

Warner (POP); Luck's (rental)

Theme from E.T. 3.5'
2 1 2 2 – 4 3 3 1 – tmp+3 – pf – str
James Ployhar, arr.

                                    Films/Space

Leonard

E.T. Suite: Adventures on Earth 10'
3[incl pic] 2[incl Eh] 3[incl bcl] 3[incl cbn] –
4 3 3 1 – tmp+3 – hp, cel/pf – str
Includes: Bicycle Chase; E.T.'s Theme & Farewell;
Closing Fanfare. Signature Edition.

                                Films/Space

Leonard

E.T.: Flying Theme 4'
3[incl pic] 2 2 3 – 4 3 3 1 – tmp+2 – hp, cel/pf – str
Signature Edition.

                                Films/Space

Leonard

The Empire Strikes Back Medley 4.5'
2[1.2.pic] 1 2 1 – 4 3 3 0 – tmp+5 – str
Includes: Star Wars (main theme); May the Force Be
With You; Han Solo and the Princess; Yoda's
Theme; The Imperial March (Darth Vader's Theme).
John Whitney, arr.

                                Films/Space

Warner

Far and Away: Excerpts 7.5'
3[incl 2pic] 3[1.2.Eh] 3[1.2.bcl] 3[1.2.cbn] –
4 3 3 1 – tmp+6 – hp, pf – str
Includes: County Galway 1892; The Fighting
Donelly's; Joseph & Shannon; Blowing off Steam;
Finale. Signature Edition.

                                          Films

Leonard

Happy Birthday Variations 4.5'
3[1.2.pic] 3[1.2.Eh] 3[1.2.bcl] 3[1.2.cbn] – 4 4 3 1 –
tmp+perc – hp, pf – str
Composed for a concert celebrating birthdays of
Seiji Ozawa, Yo-Yo Ma, Itzhak Perlman, and Leon
Fleischer. Signature Edition.

                            Celebrations/Fanfare

Leonard

Harry Potter and the 13'
Chamber of Secrets
3[1.2.pic] 3[incl Eh] 3 3[1.2.cbn] – 4 3 3 1 – tmp+6
– hp, pf – str
Includes: Chamber of Secrets; Dobby the House Elf;
Fawkes the Phoenix; Gilderoy Lockhart. Signature
Edition.

                                                    Films

Leonard

Harry Potter and the Prisoner of 6'
Azkaban Concert Suite
3[1.2(pic/ recorder)] 1 3[1.2.bcl]1– 4 3 3 1 –
tmp+6 – kybd[cel, pf, hpsd] – str
perc: mar, bells, xyl, vib, sd, bd, td, wind chimes,
sus cym, tambn, tri, slgh-bells, finger cym, sm tambn,
sm drum, cym, tamtam, bell tree.
Includes: Hedwig's Theme, Hagrid the Professor,
Double Trouble, A Window to the Past.
Victor Lopez, arr.

                                                    Films

Warner

Harry Potter and the   16'
  Prisoner of Azkaban
    3[1/pic.2/pic.3/pic] 3[1.2.3/Eh] 3[1.2.3/Ebcl/bcl]
    3[1.2.3/cbn] – asx – 4 4 3 1 – tmp+6 – hp, cel/pf
    – str
    perc: cym, xyl, hi & med sus cym, sm tambn, vib, chimes, glock, sizzle cym, sm & lg tri, bd, sm slap tick, sm Japanese block, song bells, slgh bells, sd, 2 slide whistles, woodblks, cowbells, police whistle, Trolley klang, metal plate, drumset, temple blks, toms, train whistle, siren, conga, marim, tamtam, ratchet, bell tree.
    SATB Chorus. Signature Edition. Includes: Aunt Margie's Waltz; Bridge to the Past; Double Trouble; Knight Bus; Witches Wands and Wizards. 40 chorus parts included in set.

                                              Films

Leonard

Harry Potter and the   28'
  Sorcerer's Stone: Children's Suite
    3[incl pic,afl] 3[incl Eh] 3[incl bcl,Ebcl] 3[incl cbn] – 4 3 3 1 – tmp+3 – hp, cel/pf – str
    4 recorders [(fl,ob,cl)]
    Includes: Hedwig's Flight; Hogwarts Forever; Voldemort; Nimbuw 2000; Fluffy and His Harp; Quidditch; Family Portrait; Diagon Alley; Harry's Wondrous World. Signature Edition.

                                              Films

Leonard

Harry Potter and the   17'
  Sorcerer's Stone: Suite for Orchestra
    3[incl pic &afl] 3[incl Eh] 3[incl Ebcl, 2bcl, (cbcl)] 3[incl cbn] – 4 3 3 1 – tmp+4 – hp, cel/pf – str
    perc: vib, sm tri, tambn, med & hi sus cym, glock, slgh bells, cym, mark tree, chimes, bd, tri, tamtam, xyl, sizzle cym, side dr.
    Includes: Hedwig's Theme; The Sorcerer's Stone; Nimbus; Harry's Wondrous World. Signature Edition.

                                  Films/Halloween

Leonard

Harry Potter and the Sorcerer's Stone: 7.5'
  Harry Potter Symphonic Suite
    2[incl pic, alto fl, (recorder)]
    2[incl Eh] 3[1.2.bcl] 1 – 4 3 3 1 – tmp+4 – hp, cel – str
    perc: bells, xyl, antique bells, marim, glock, hand drs, vib, chimes, small tuned drums, tambn, sd, sus cym, tri, tam-tam, bd, cym.
    Jerry Brubaker, arr

                                              Films

Warner

Harry Potter Symphonic Suite   24.5'
    3[1.2.3/afl/pic] 3[1.2.3/Eh] 3[1.2.3/bcl/Ebcl]
    3[1.2.3/cbn] – 4 3 3 1 – tmp+3perc – hp, pf/cel
    – str
    perc: orch-bells, tubular-bells, xyl, vib, tambn, sm tri, slgh-bells, mark tree, bell tree, sus cyms (sm, med, lg), piatti, sizzle cym, tam-tam, sd, dumbeks(3), tom-toms(3), lg, & sm taiko dms [or tom-toms], bd, verdi bd.
    Optional Solo Female Vocalist in *Lily's Theme* only.
    Includes: Prologue/Hedwig's Theme [#1]   *(5')*
    Buckbeak's Flight [#3]   *(2')*
    Hogwarts' Hymn [#4]   *(1')*
    Hogwarts' March [#4]   *(1.5')*
    Fireworks [#5]   *(1')*
    The Flight of the Order of the Phoenix [#5]   *(1.5')*
    Harry & Hermione [#6]   *(1.5')*
    Obliviate [#7]   *(2')*
    Lily's Theme [#8]   *(2')*
    Courtyard Apocalypse [#8]   *(2')*
    Mischief Managed [#3] & Harry's Wondrous
        World [#2]   *(5')*
    The number in brackets is the film from which the theme was derived. #1-3 are composed by John Williams; #4 is composed by Patrick Doyle; #5 & 6 by Nicholas Hooper; and #7 & 8 by Alexandre Desplat.
    Gary Fry, arr.

                                              Films

Alfred (rental)

Home Alone: Three Holiday Songs   15'
    3[incl pic] 3[incl Eh] 3[incl bcl] 3[incl cbn] – 4 3 3 1 – tmp+3 – hp, kybd, org – str
    Includes: Somewhere in My Memory; Star of Bethlehem; Merry, Merry Christmas.
    SATB Chorus and Children's Chorus. Signature Edition.

                                Christmas/Films

Leonard

Hook: Flight to Neverland   4.5'
    3[1.2.pic] 3[incl Eh] 3 3[incl cbn] – 4 3 3 1 – tmp+3 – hp, cel/pf – str
    Signature Edition.

                                              Films

Leonard

Suite from Jaws
    3[1.2.pic] 3[incl Eh] 3 3[incl cbn] – 4 3 3 1 – tmp+6 – hp, cel/pf – str
    Includes: Out to Sea; Shark Cage Fugue; Theme from Jaws.

                                              Films

Leonard

Suite from J.F.K. 16'
3[incl 3pic] 3[incl Eh] 2 2 – 4 3 3 1 – tmp+3 –
hp, cel/pf – str
Includes: Theme from J.F.K.; Motorcade; Arlington.
Signature Edition
             Patriotic

Leonard

Highlights from Jurassic Park 3'
3[1.2.3/pic] 2 3[1.2.bcl] 2 – 4 3 3 1 – tmp+3 –
synth or pf – str
perc: bd, sd, sus cym, cym, slgh-bells, tri, bell tree, glock, chimes.
Calvin Custer, arr.
             Films

Leonard

Liberty Fanfare 4'
3[incl pic] 3[1.2.Eh] 2 3[1.2.cbn] – 4 3 3 1 –
tmp+perc – hp, pf – str
Composed for the re-dedication of the Statue of Liberty in 1986. Signature Edition.
             Patriotic

Leonard

The Lost World: Jurassic Park 6'
(Main Theme)
3[1.2.pic] 3[1.2.Eh] 3[1.2.bcl] 3[1.2.cbn] –
4 4 4 1 – tmp+perc – hp, pf – str
Signature Edition.
             Films

Leonard

The Lost World: Jurassic Park 3.5'
2 1 3[incl bcl] 1 – 4 3 3 1 – 3perc – pf – str
John Moss, arr.
             Films

Warner

Memoirs of a Geisha: Sayuri's Theme 4'
3[incl pic] 3[1.2.pic] 2 3 – 4 3 3 1 – tmp+3 –
hp, cel – str
Signature Edition.
             Films

Leonard

Midway: Midway March 4'
3[1.2.pic] 2 3 2 – 4 3 3 1 – tmp+6 – hp, pf – str
Signature Edition.
             Films

Leonard

The Mission (NBC News Theme) 3.5'
3[incl pic] 3[1.2.Eh] 2 3 – 4 3 3 1 – tmp+3 –
hp, pf – str
Signature Edition.
             TV

Leonard

Munich: A Prayer for Peace 4'
Harp and Strings
Nominated for the 2006 Academy Award in Best Achievement in Music Written for Motion Pictures and Original Score.
             Films

Leonard

Munich: Hatikva (The Hope) 2'
(1 1 1) 0 – (3) 0 0 0 – (hp) – str
Arrangement of the Israel national anthem for the Steven Spielberg film Munich. Nominated for the 2006 Academy Award in Best Achievement in Music Written for Motion Pictures and Original Score.
        Films/International: Israel

Leonard

Olympic Fanfare and Theme 4'
3[1.2.pic] 3 3[1.2.bcl] 3[1.2.cbn] – 4 4 4 1 –
tmp+4 – hp, pf – str
perc: sd, field dr, cym, bd, sus cym, chimes, bells, vib, tri.
Written for the 1984 Olympic Games in Los Angeles.
Signature Edition.
             Sports

Leonard

Olympic Fanfare and Theme 4'
3[1.2.pic] 2 2 2 – 4 3 3 1 – tmp+3 – pf – str
Riggio, arr.
             Sports

Leonard

Olympic Spirit 4'
3[1.2.pic] 3[1.2.Eh] 2 2 – 4 4 3 1 – tmp+perc –
hp, pf – str
Signature Edition.
             Sports

Leonard

The Patriot 6.5'
3[1.2/pic.3/pic] 3[1.2.3/Eh] 3[1.2.bcl/Ebcl]
3[1.2.cbn] – 4 4 3 1 – tmp+perc – hp, cel/pf – str
Signature Edition.
             Films

Leonard

Raiders of the Lost Ark: 6'
  Raiders March
  3[incl pic] 3[incl Eh] 3[incl bcl] 3[incl cbn] –
  4 4 4 1 – tmp+3 – hp, cel/pf – str
  Signature Edition.
                                                    Films/Space
Leonard

Highlights from Return of the Jedi 8'
  2 1 2 1 – 4 3 3 1 – tmp+4 – str
  perc: sd, bd, cym, glock, vib, sus cym, marim.
  Includes: Main Title; Luke & Leia; Ewok
  Celebration.
  Steven Rosenhaus, arr.
                                                    Films/Space
Leonard

Saving Private Ryan: 6'
  Hymn to the Fallen
  2 3[1.2.Eh] 5[1.2.3.(Ebcl).(bcl)] 3[1.2.cbn] –
  4 3 3 1 – tmp+perc – hp – str
  Optional Mixed Chorus. Set includes 40 octavo
  (SSATBB) wordless chorus parts. Signature Edition.
                                                    Films/Patriotic
Leonard

Theme from Schindler's List 3'
  bells – (hp), pf – str
  Calvin Custer, arr.
                                                    Films
Warner

Three Pieces from Schindler's List 14.5'
  3[1.2.3/pic/afl] 2[1.Eh] 3[1.2.3/bcl] 3[1.2.cbn]
  – 3 0 3 0 – tmp+1 – hp, cel – str
  perc: vib, bd.
  Schindler's List: 3[incl 2afl] 1[incl Eh]   (4')
  3[incl bcl] 2 – 1 0 0 0 – 1perc – hp, cel – str
  Jewish Town(Krakow Ghetto-Winter '41)   (4.5')
  3[incl pic,afl] 2[1.Eh] 3[incl bcl] 3[1.2.cbn]
  – 3 0 0 0 – tmp+perc – hp, cel – str
  Remembrances: (6')
  2 2[1.Eh] 3[incl bcl] 1 – 1 0 3 0 – hp – str
  Solo Violin. Signature Edition.
                                                    Films
Leonard

Star-Spangled Banner 3'
  3[1.2.pic] 3[1.2.Eh] 3[1.2.bcl] 3[1.2.cbn] –
  4 3 3 1 – tmp+perc – hp, pf – str
  perc: includes a cannon
  The 2004 Rose Bowl Version. Signature Edition.
                                                    Patriotic
Leonard

Star Wars Suite 25'
  3[1.2.3/pic] 2 3[1.2.bcl] 2 – 4 3 3 1 – tmp+4 –
  hp, cel/pf – str
  perc: tri, bells, cym, sus cym, 2 sd, vib, large tam-tam, bd.
  Optional Chorus.
  Includes: Main Title; Princess Leia's Theme;
  Imperial March; Yoda's Theme; Throne Room; End
  Title.
  Signature Edition.
                                                    Films/Space
Leonard

Star Wars: 16'
  Episode I: Phantom Menace (Suite for Orchestra)
  3[1.2.3/pic/afl] 3[1.2.3/Eh] 3[1.2.3/Eb/bcl]
  3[1.2.3/cbn] – 4 4 4 1 – tmp+6 – hp, cel or pf – str
  perc: sd, field dr, cym, bd, bells, xyl.
  Optional Wordless Chorus. Includes: Flag Parade;
  Anakin's Theme; Adventures of Jar Jar; Duel of the
  Fates. Signature Edition.
                                                    Films/Space
Leonard

Star Wars:
  Episode I: Phantom Menace (Duel of the Fates)
  1 1 2 1 – 1 2 1 1 – tmp+perc – pf – (str)
  Includes: Star Wars Main Theme, Anakin's Theme,
  Jar Jar's Introduction, Augie's Great Municipal
  Band, Duel of Fates, End Credits.
  Jerry Brubaker, arr.
                                                    Films/Space
Warner

Star Wars: 4'
  Episode II: Attack of the Clones (Across the Stars
  Love Theme)
  3[incl pic] 3[incl Eh] 3 3[incl cbn] – 4 3 3 1 –
  tmp+perc – hp, cel, pf – str
  Signature Edition .
                                                    Films/Space
Leonard

Star Wars: 3.5'
  Episode III: Revenge of the Sith (Battle of the
  Heroes)
  3[incl pic] 3[1.2.Eh] 3[incl Ebcl,bcl] 3[incl cbn] –
  4 4 3 1 – tmp+perc – hp, pf – str
  Optional SATB Chorus.
                                                    Films/Space
Leonard

Star Wars Main Theme   2'
   3[1.2.pic] 2 2 1 – 4 3 3 1 – tmp+4 – str
   perc: glock, chimes, sd, bd, cym.
   Charles Sayre, arr.
                                Films/Space
Warner

Star Wars Medley   7.5'
   3[incl pic] 2 4[incl (bcl)] 2 – (asx, tsx, bsx) –
   4 3 3 1 – tmp+3 – hp – str
   perc: bells, vib, xyl, cym, tri, field dr, gong, sd, bd
   James H. Burden, arr.
                                Films/Space
20th Century

Star Wars: Parade of the Ewoks   3.5'
  (Return of the Jedi)
   3[incl pic] 2 2 2 – 4 3 3 1 – tmp+perc – pf – str
   Luck's lists winds as 1[incl pic] 1 1 1.
   Riggio, arr.
                                Films
Leonard (POP); EMS or Luck's (rental)

Star Wars: Selections from   3.5'
  The Phantom Menace
   2 2 3[1.2.bcl] 1 – 4 3 3 1 – tmp+3 – elec bs – str
   perc: chimes, glock, vib, xyl, slide whistle, cym,
   sus cym, temple blks, police whistle, deep-tuned muffled
   drums.
     Includes: Star Wars Main Theme; Anakin's Theme;
     Jar Jar's Introduction; Augie's Great Municipal
     Band; Duel of Fates; End Credits.
   Jerry Brubaker, arr.
                                Films/Space
Warner

Summon the Heroes   8'
   3[1.2.pic] 2 2 3[1.2.bcl] 2 – 4 3 3 1 – tmp+5 –
   (hp), pf – str
   perc: sd, bd, field drum, chimes, cym, tri, sus cym, glock.
   Calvin Custer, arr.
                                  Sports
Leonard

Summon the Heroes   6'
   3[incl pic] 3[incl Eh] 3[incl bcl] 3[1.2.cbn] –
   4 6 4 1 – tmp+perc – hp,pf – str
   1996 Olympic Games theme; Signature Edition.
                                  Sports
Leonard

Superman March: Main Theme   4.5'
   3[1.2.pic] 2 3[1.2.bcl] 2 – 4 4 3 1 – tmp+5 –
   hp, pf – str
   perc: sd, tri, cym, sus cym, bells, vib.
   Signature Edition.
                                  Films
Leonard

Superman Returns: 5'
  Concert Selections
   2 1 3[1 2 bcl] 1 – 4 3 3 1 – tmp+8 – pf – str
   Includes: Superman Theme; Memories; Rough
   Flight; Can You Read My Mind?; Love Theme from
   Superman.
   Lopez, arr.
                                  Films
Warner

Superman Returns Suite   7'
   3[1/afl.2/afl.3/pic/afl] 2[1.Eh] 3[1.2.3/bcl]
   3[1.2.cbn] – 4 3 3 1 – tmp+perc – hp, cel, pf – str
   John Ottman also listed as composer.
   Damon Intrabartolo, arr.
                                  Films
JoAnn Kane

The Terminal: Viktor's Tale   4.5'
   3[incl pic] 3 3[incl bcl] 2 – 4 3 3 1 – tmp+perc
   – hp, pf, (accordion) – str
   Solo Clarinet in clarinet 1 part.
                                  Films
Leonard

Three Themes for Strings   6.5'
   Strings
   Includes: Schindler's List, Angela's Ashes, and
   Hymn to the Fallen (from Saving Private Ryan).
   John Moss, arr.
                                  Films
Leonard

Williams, John T. & Hooper, Nicolas &

Harry Potter and the Order of the Phoenix: 5'
   Concert Suite
   2 1 3[1.2bcl] 2 – 4 3 3 1 – tmp+3 – pf – str
   perc: glock, xyl, sd, bd, sus cym, hi-hat cym, crash cym, tom-tom, wind chimes, taiko dr, tri.
   Includes: Another Story, Flight of the Order of the Phoenix, Professor Umbridge, Dumbledore's Army, The Room of Requirements.
   Victor Lopez, arr.
                                                  Films

Warner

Williams, Paul   1940-

Rainy Days and Mondays   5'
   2 1 3[1.2.bcl] 1 – 2 2 2 1 – 3perc – pf – str
   perc: sd, bd, sus cym, glock, chimes.
   Willis Schaefer, arr.
                               Popular Song/Weather

Leonard (rental)

Willson, Meredith   1902-1984

The Music Man: Overture   3'
   Reed 1: fl/pic.
   Reed 2: cl/Eh/Ob.
   Reed 3: cl, Ebcl/ssx.
   Reed 4: bcl/cl/fl/pic.
   Reed 5: bsx/bn/cl/bass sx.
   Brass: 0 3 3 0
   Strings: 3 vln, vc, bass.
   perc: bd, bells, cym, glock, hi-hat, sd, Temple blks, tom tom, tri, tmp, vib, whistle, wdblk, xyl.
   Alternate instrumentation:
   Reed 1: cl/fl/pic. Reed 2: cl/tsx.
   Reed 3: bcl/cl. Reed 4: bsx/cl.
   perc: glock, Temple blks, tri, tmp, vib, whistle, wdblk, xyl.
   Don Walker, arr.
                                       Broadway Musicals

MTI (rental)

The Music Man: 3'
   Seventy-Six Trombones
   3[1.2/pic.pic] 3[1.2.Eh] 3[1.2.bcl] 3[1.2.cbn] – 4 4 3 1 – tmp+3 – pf – str
   perc: sd, bd, whistle, cym.
   Leroy Anderson, arr.
                                       Broadway Musicals

Leonard

The Music Man: 3'
   Seventy-Six Trombones
   2[incl pic] 1 3[1.2.bcl] 1 – 4 3 3 1 – tmp+perc – pf – str
   Ted Ricketts, arr.
                                       Broadway Musicals

Leonard

Wilson, Don, arr.

Scrambled Opera (An Orchestral Antic)   5'
   1/pic 1 2 1 – 2asx, tsx – 2 3 3 1[Baritone] – tmp+2 – str
   perc: sd, bd, cym, tambn, tri, cym.
   Optional Solo Voice parts. Includes: Carmen, Hillbilly Trio; Maddelena & Duke Duet.
   Principals, chorus & orchestra don't agree on which opera to play as a musical joke.
                                Instrumental Pops/Novelty

Remick (rental)

Wilson, Brian & Love, Mike

Beach Boys: Medley for Orchestra   5'
   3[1.2.pic] 2 2 1 – 4 3 3 1 – tmp+2 – pf – str
   perc: drumset, tambn, glock.
   Includes: Good Vibrations; I Get Around; California Girls.
   Calvin Custer, arr.
                                         Popular Songs

Warner (POP); Luck's (rental)

Wilson, Robb & James, Arthur & Karlin, Fred

For All We Know   6'
    2 1 3[1.2.(bcl)] 1 – asx, tsx – 2 2 2 1 – 2perc
    – pf – str
    perc: drumset, glock, vib, chimes.
    Willis Schaefer, arr.
                                  Popular Song
    Leonard (rental)

Wonder, Stevie   1950-

Stevie Wonder Sounds   6'
    2[incl pic] 2 2 2 – asx, tsx – 4 3 3 1 –
    tmp+2, drumset – pf, elec bass – str
    Includes: You Are the Sunshine of My Life; All in
    Love Is Fair; Isn't She Lovely.
    John Whitney, arr.
                       Popular Song/Valentine
    Warner (POP); Luck's (rental)

Wood, Arthur   1875-1953

Moorland Fiddlers for Orchestra
    2 2 2 2 – 3sx – 2 2 3 0 – tmp – str
                                   International
    Kalmus

Woodgate, Leslie   1902-1961

English Dance Suite   9'
    Strings
                               Dance/International
    Novello (rental)

Wyle, George (See: Pola, Eddie)

Y

Yared, Gabriel   1938-

The English Patient (1996)   4'
    2 2[1.Eh] 2 2 – 3 0 0 0 – tmp+1 – hp, cel, synth,
    mandolin – str
    perc: bd.
    Won the 1997 Oscar for Best Music and Original
    Score.
                                          Films
    T&V (rental)

Yarrow, Peter   1938-

Puff the Magic Dragon
    Strings
    This tune was best known with the '60s folk group:
    Peter, Paul, and Mary
    Douglas E. Wagner, arr.
                           Animals/Popular Song
    Warner

Yeston, Maury   1945-

Beneath all the Stripes and Stars   6'
    Strings
    SATB Chorus. Also available for Concert Band
    which can be combined with the strings.
    John Moss, arr.
                                      Patriotic
    Leonard

Yon, Pietro A.   1886-1943

Gesu Bambino   6'
    1 1 0 0 – 2 0 0 0 – perc – hp, pf – str
    Jeff Tyzik, arr.
                                      Christmas
    Schirmer (rental)

Gesu Bambino   6'
    2 2 2 2 – 2 2 3 0 – tmp+1 – (hp) – str
    perc: glock, chimes.
    Solo High Voice. Available for high voice in
    Key of F or for low voice in Key of D.
    William Ryden, arr.
                                                               Christmas

Kalmus

Young, Christopher

Species (1995): End Credits   8'
    3 2 3[1.2.bcl] 2[1.cbn] – 4 2 3 1 – tmp+5 –
    2 hp, 2 pf, cel – str
    perc: bd, vib, glock, 2 marim, chimes, claves.
    3 Violins and Chorus.
                                         Films/Halloween

T&V (rental)

Young, Victor   1899-1956

Around the World in 80 Days (1956):   9'
   Overture & Epilogue   (3' 6')
    3 3[1.Eh] 3[1.2.bcl] 3[1.2.cbn] – 4 4 3 1 – tmp+2
    – hp, pf – str
    perc: sd, marim, cym.
    Won 1957 Oscars for Best Music and Scoring.
                                              Films/Travel

T&V (rental)

For Whom the Bell Tolls (1943): Suite   9'
    2 2 2 3 – 4 3 4[inc euph] 1 – tmp+2 –
    hp, pf[cel], 2 gtr – str
    perc: church bell, gong, cym, vib, marim.
    Nominated for two 1944 Oscars for Best Music and
    Scoring.
                                                          Films

T&V (rental)

Medley: Victor Young Tribute   10'
    3 3 4[1.2.3.bcl] 3 – 4 3 3 1 – tsx – tmp+3 –
    hp, pf, Fender bs – str
    perc: drumset, toms, woodblk, cowbell, tri, cym,
    sus cym, finger cym, tree bells, conga, glock, xyl, (vib).
    Includes: Golden Earrings; When I Fall In Love;
    Sweet Sue; Stella by Starlight; My Foolish Heart;
    Love Letters; Around the World in Eighty Days.
    Henry Mancini, arr.
                                                          Films

T&V (rental)

The Quiet Man (1952): Suite   8.5'
    3[1.2.pic] 2[1.Eh] 3[1.2.bcl] 3[1.2.cbn] –
    4 3 3 1 – tmp+3 – hp, pf[cel] – str
    perc: cym, sus cym, sd, bd, tri.
    Includes: St. Patrick's Day; Kathleen; Innesfree.
    Nominated for the 1953 Golden Globe award for
    Best Motion Picture Score.
                                                        Films

T&V (rental)

Samson and Delilah (1949)   8'
    2[pic] 2[1.Eh] 3[1.2.bcl] 1[cbn] – 3 3 3 1 –
    tmp+4 – hp, pf[cel] – str
    perc: gong, vib, marim, cym, finger cym, slgh-bells, toms,
    tambn, lg cym.
    Includes: Prelude; Dance to Dagon; Hebrew
    Lament; Feather Dance; Interlude; The Fall of
    Samson; Exit Music.
                                                        Films

T&V (rental)

Scaramouche (1952): Suite   13'
    2[1.pic] 2[1.Eh] 3[1.2.bcl] 1[cbn] – 3 3 3 1 –
    tmp+4 – hp, pf[cel] – str
    perc: gong, vib, marim, cym, finger cym, slgh-bells,
    toms, tambn, lg cym.
    Includes: Main Title; Vanished Merchant;
    The Tomb; Andre & Aline; Pavane; Andre Escapes;
    The Big Apple; The Magic Box
     Roses; Napoleon.
                                                        Films

T&V (rental)

Shane (1953): Suite   11'
    3[1.2.pic] 2[1.Eh] 3[1.2.bcl(tsx)] 2[1.cbn) –
    4 3 3 1 – tmp+3 – hp, pf[cel], accordion – str
    perc: cym, sus cym, sd, bd, xyl, vib, marim, tamtam.
    Includes: Prelude; The Tree Stump; Rodeo Music;
    Wyoming Sketched; Cemetery Hill.
                                                        Films

T&V (rental)

The Uninvited (1944): Stella by Starlight   6'
    2 2 2 1 – asx – 2 3 3 1 – 3perc – pf, rhythm bs – str
    perc: drumset, bells, sus cym.
                                                        Films

T&V (rental)

Young, Victor & Auric, George   1899-1956 / 1899-1983

Roman Holiday (1953): Main Title and Prelude   8.5'
3[1.2.pic] 3 3[1.2.bcl] 2 – 3 2 2 0 – tmp+2 – hp, pf[cel] – str
perc: glock, tri, tambn, cym, sus cym, gong.
Victor Young is the uncredited composer of the film's title music.
                                            Films

T&V (rental)

Yradier, Sebastian   1809-1865

La Paloma (The Dove):   3'
Spanish Serenade
1 1 2 1 – 2 2 1 0 – perc – str
Wright, arr.
                                 Animals/International

Kalmus

Z

Zador, Eugene   1894-1977

A Christmas Overture   8'
3 2 2 2 – 4 3 3 1 – tmp+3[incl glock] – hp, pf – str
                                     Christmas

EMI (rental)

Zaninelli, Luigi   1932-

For Spacious Skies   8'
2[1.pic] 1 5[1.2.3.bcl.(cbcl)] 1 – asx, tsx, bsx – 4 3 4 2[incl (bar)] – tmp+4 – hp or pf – str
Antiphonal brass: 12 tp, 12 tbn
SATB Chorus and audience.
                                         Patriotic

Shawnee (rental)

A Lexicon of Beasties   24'
1 1 1 1 – 1 1 1 1 – 2perc – (str)
perc: tmp, bd, sus cym, tri, tamtam, glock, xyl, vib, finger cym.
Narrator, Solo Piano. English text by Edward Lear (adapted by the composer).
                                         Halloween

Shawnee (rental)

Night Voices   11'
2[1.2/pic] 2 3[1.2.bcl] 2 – 4 3 3 1 – 2perc – cel, pf – str
perc: sus cym, tamtam, vib.
                                         Halloween

Shawnee (rental)

Zawinul, Joseph   1932- 2007

Birdland   5.5'
2 2 2 2 – asx, tsx – 4 3 3 1 – perc – pf, gtr, elec bass – str
Robert Cowart, arr.
                                               Jazz

Presser (rental)

Ziehrer, Carl Michael   1843-1922

Herreinspaziert! Waltz, Op. 518   8'
    2[incl pic] 2 2 2 – 4 2 3 0 – tmp – 2perc – hp – str
    From the operetta *Der Schätzmeister*.
    Max Schonherr, arr.
                                Dance/New Year/
                                  Popular Classics

Doblinger

Zimmer, Hans   1957-

Da Vinci Code (2006): Chevaliers de Sangreal   4'
    2 2 2 2 – 4 0 3 1 – tmp+perc – pf – str
    perc: bd, cym, tubular bells.
    SATB Chorus. Nominated for the 2007 Golden
    Globe Best Original Score.
                                              Films

T&V (rental)

Gladiator: Music from the Movie   6.5'
    2 1 3[1.2.bcl] 1 – 4 3 3 1 – tmp+4 – pf – str
    Includes: Barbarian Horde; The Battle; Earth.
    John Wasson, arr.
                                        Films/Sports

Leonard

The Last Samurai: The Way of the Sword   8'
    2[1/pic.2/pic] 2[1.2/Eh] 3[1.2/bcl.bcl] 2 –
    2 3 3 0 – tmp+perc – pf – str
    Y. S. Moriarty
                                              Films

Kane (rental)

Pirates of the Carribean: 6'
Dead Man's Chest (Soundtrack Highlights)
    2 1 3[1.2.bcl] 1 – 4 3 3 1 – tmp+6 – pf – str
    Includes: I've Got My Eye on You, Jack Sparrow.
    Paul Lavender, arr.
                                              Films

Leonard

Zimmer, Hans &   1957-
Howard, James Newton   1951-

The Dark Knight: Concert Suite   7'
    2 1 3[1.2.bcl] 1 – 4 3 3 1 – tmp+6 – pf – str
    perc: tamtam, wind gong/xyl, marim, glock, sd, bd,
    2 Odaiko dr, Surdo or toms, lg Taiko bd, sus cym,
    3 Djembe, (Roto toms).
    Includes: Harvey Two-Face; Introduce a Little
    Anarchy; Like a Dog Chasing Cars.
    Victor Lopez, arr.
                                              Films

Alfred

Zinn, William

Symphony in Ragtime   31'
    3[incl pic] 3[incl Eh] 2 2 – (ssx) – 4 2 3 1 –
    tmp+perc – hp, upright pf, banjo – str
                                              Jazz

Excelsior

Zwilich, Ellen Taaffe   1939-

American Concerto   16'
    2 2 3 2 – 4 2 3 1 – 2perc – str
    Solo Trumpet.
                                            Americana

Merion (rental)

Celebration   10'
    4[incl pic] 3[incl Eh] 3[incl bcl] 3[incl cbn] –
    4 3 3 1 – tmp+3 – hp, cel/pf – str
                                           Celebrations

Merion (rental)

Jubilation   6.5'
    3[1.2.pic] 3[1.2.Eh] 3[1.2.bcl] 3[1.2.cbn] –
    4 3 3 1 – tmp+4 – str
    perc: glock, vib, cym, szl cym, 3sus cym.
                                           Celebrations

Merion (rental)

One Nation   *5'*
    0 0 0 0 – 2 4 3 1 – tmp – str
    SATB Chorus. Reflections on the Pledge of Allegiance.
                                                  Patriotic
    Merion (rental)

Peanuts ® Gallery (1996)   *14'*
    1 2 2 2 – 2 0 0 0 – perc – str
    Solo Piano. 6 mvts: including Snoopy Does the Samba, Peppermint Patty, and Marcie Leads the Parade.
                                                Americana
    Merion (rental)

Upbeat! (1999)   *4'*
    3[1.2.pic] 3[1.2.Eh] 3[1.2.bcl] 3[1.2.cbn] – 4 3 3 1 – tmp+2 – str
                                               Celebrations
    Merion (rental)

Zyman, Samuel   1956-

Encuentros (1992)   *10.5'*
    2[incl pic] 2 2 2 – 4 2 3 1 – tmp+3 – hp – str
    Written to be played at the Mexican pavilion during the Expo 1992 in Seville, Spain.
                              Dance/International: Mexico
    Merion; Presser (rental)

APPENDIX A

Works Listed by Instrumentation

Refer to the composer listing in the main body of the volume for complete information on a work. Works for full orchestra are listed in order of increasing brass sections and within those sections, they are listed by increasing woodwind size. Repertoire using saxophone are only listed in a separate category. These charts list the instrumental combinations included in this appendix.

STRINGS	WOODWINDS	BRASS	PAGE
no strings	any	any	284
str orch			285
str	(with kybd or harp)		286
	(with guitar, kybd, hp, & perc)		
str	1111	1111	287
str	0303	0330	288
str	0222	2000	
str	0033	2200	
str	1111	2200	
str	1121	2200	
str	1202	2200	
str	1221	2200	
str	2022	2200	289
str	2122	2200	
str	2222	2200	
str	3222	2211	290
str	1141	2220	292
str	2222	2221	
str	2222	2241	293
str	2222	2331	
str	2232	2331	294
str	2222	3321	295
str	2222	4000	
str	2222	4200	
str	2222	4211	

STRINGS	WOODWINDS	BRASS	PAGE
str	2222	4221	295
str	3222	4221	296
str	2222	4230	
str	3222	4230	297
str	2222	4231	
str	3322	4231	298
str	2222	4321	299
str	2322	4330	
str	2222	4331	
str	2232	4331	301
str	2332	4331	302
str	3131	4331	303
str	3222	4331	
str	3232	4331	305
str	3233	4331	306
str	3323	4331	
str	3332	4331	307
str	4343	4331	308
str	2223	4431	310
str	2333	4431	
str	3222	4431	
str	3333	4441	
str	4444	8666	312
Miscellaneous Instrumental Ensembles			318

Turn page for *Orchestra with Saxophones; Orchestra with Voices;* and *Orchestra with Solo Instruments.*

→

Orchestra with Saxophones

STRINGS	WOODWINDS	BRASS	SAX	PAGE
str			1	314
str	1131	2331	1	
str	2252	2231	1	
str	2232	4331	1	
str	4454	6432	1	
str			2	315
str	1131	2331	2	
str	2252	2331	2	
str	2242	4431	2	
str	3342	4431	2	316
str	1231	2331	3	
str	2232	2331	3	
str	2232	4331	3	
str	3222	4331	3	317
str	4344	6431	3	
str	1131	2331	4	
str	2232	2231	4	
str	2242	4431	4	318
str	3222	4331	4	
str	3342	6431	4	
str	6444	6642	4	

Orchestra with Solo Voices/Chorus/Narrator

SECTION	PAGE
Soprano	318
Alto/Ms	319
Tenor	
Bass	
Vocalist	
Vocal Ensembles	320
Solo with Chorus	321
Chorus	322
Narrator	324

Orchestra with Solo Instruments

INSTRUMENT	PAGE
Keyboard	325
Strings	
Woodwinds	326
Brass	327
Percussion	
Jazz Combo	
Miscellaneous	328

WORKS WITHOUT STRINGS

Brass Alone

Berkeley, Lennox
 - Fanfare for the Royal Academy of Music Banquet
Burgon, Geoffrey
 - Fanfare on One Note
Dukas, Paul
 - La Peri
Hoffman, Joel
 - Music from Chartres
Rodríguez, Robert Xavier
 - Fanfare from "Oktoechos"
 - Fanfare for Trumpets and Caracolas

Brass with Chorus

Effinger, Cecil
 - An American Hymn

Brass and Percussion

Arnaud, Leo
 - Fanfare to the Olympic Games: Divertissement for Brass and Percussion
Copland, Aaron
 - Fanfare for the Common Man
Daugherty, Michael
 - Motown Metal
Goossens, Eugene
 - Fanfare for the Artists
Gould, Morton
 - Festive Fanfare
 - Hail to a First Lady
Hailstork, Adolphus
 - An American Fanfare
Handel, George Frideric
 - Music for the Royal Fireworks
 - Water Music
Harbison, John
 - Fanfare for Foley's
Lutosławski, Witold
 - Fanfare for the University of Lancaster
Prizeman, Robert
 - Songs of Praise: Toccata
Ran, Shulamit
 - Chicago Skyline
Rodríguez, Robert Xavier
 - Tequila Sunrise
Rutter, John
 - Jesus Child!
Tower, Joan
 - Celebration Fanfare (from "Stepping Stones")
 - Fanfare for the Uncommon Woman (1986)

Brass and Percussion with Chorus

Beveridge, Thomas
 - Once:Tribute to Martin Luther King
Brubeck, Dave
 - The Gates of Justice

Winds and Brass

Poulenc, Francis
 - L'Histoire de Babar (The Story of Babar, the Little Elephant)
Templeton, Alec
 - Merry Christmas
Welcher, Dan
 - The Yellowstone Fires

Winds, Brass, and Percussion

Gould, Morton
- Something to Do
- Labor Cantata
- Swanee River in the Style of Ellington

Herrmann, Bernard
- It's Alive (1973)
- Jason and Argonauts: Suite (1963
- Jason and Argonauts: Scherzo macabre (1963)
- Journey to the Center of the Earth (1959)

Maxwell Davies, Peter
- The Boyfriend: Concert Suite

Poulenc, Francis
- Fanfare

STRING ORCHESTRA

Adolphe, Bruce
- I'm Inclined to New Music: A Comic Parody of Mozart's Eine Kleine Nachtmusik

Anderson, Leroy
- Arietta
- Fiddle Faddle
- Jazz Legato
- Jazz Pizzicato
- Leroy Anderson for Strings
- Plink Plank Plunk!
- Suite of Carols
- The Syncopated Clock

Antheil, George
- Lithuanian Night
- Water Music for 4th of July Evening

Arban, Jean Baptiste
- The Carnival of Venice: for Trumpet and Strings

Arnold, Alan
- Cartoon Sketches of the Baroque Suite

Bach, J.S.
- Three Choral Preludes

Bagley, E.E.
- National Emblem March

Barber, Samuel
- Adagio for Strings, Op. 11

Bartók, Béla
- Rumanian Folk Dances

Berners, Lord
- The Triumph of Neptune

Borodin, Alexander
- Nocturne

Brahms, Johannes
- Liebeslieder Waltzes, Op. 52

Burgon, Geoffrey
- Suite from Testament of Youth

Bush, Geoffrey
- Three Little Pieces for Strings

Copland, Aaron
- Rodeo: Hoedown

Corigliano, John
- The Red Violin: Suite for Violin and Orchestra

Corelli, Arcangelo
- Concerto grosso, Op. 6, #8 in G minor (Christmas Concerto)

Cowell, Henry
- Flirtatious Jig (Fiddler's Jig)

Darke, Harold
- In the Bleak Midwinter

Davis, Jimmy
- Blue Tail Fly

Davis, Katherine
- Little Drummer Boy

Debussy
- Clair de lune

Dorff, Daniel
- It Takes Four to Tango
- Sunburst

Duff, Arthur
- Irish Suite

Dyson, George
- Concerto da Camera
- Concerto Leggiero

Elgar, Edward
- Spanish Lady Suite

Ellstein, Abraham
- Haftorah

Garrido-Lecca, Gonzalo
- Arcano (Arcane)

Gershwin, George
- I Got Rhythm
- Lullaby for Strings
- Porgy and Bess: Summertime
- Prelude No. 2

Goldsmith, Owen
- Romanza for String Orchestra

Goossens, Eugene
- Two Sketches

Gould, Morton
- It Came Upon a Midnight Clear

Grainger, Percy
- Molly on the Shore

Grant, James
- Lament
- Waltz for Betz

Grieg, Edvard
- Erotik
- Holberg Suite Op. 40
- Two Norwegian Airs, Op. 63

Halvorsen, Johan
- Norwegian Song, Op. 31

Handel, George Frideric
- Berenice Overture
- Hercules Overture
- Julius Caesar Overture

Heath, Dave
- The Frontier

Hefti, Neil
- Batman Theme

Herrmann, Bernard
- Psycho (1960)

Higgins, John
- Christmas on Broadway

Holst, Gustav
- Fantasia on Hampshire Folk Songs
- St. Paul's Suite

Horner, James
- An Irish Party in Third Class

Jarre, Maurice
- Lara's Theme from Doctor Zhivago

Jendras, Louis F.
- The Russian Rag

Jenkins, Karl
- Palladio-Concerto Grosso
- Passacaglia

Jones, Samuel
- Elegy for String Orchestra

Joplin, Scott
- The Entertainer
- Ragtimes for Strings
- Ragtime Favorites for Strings

Kilar, Wojciech
- Theme from the Film The Pianist

Lamb, Joseph
- Ragtime Nightingale

Lloyd Webber, Andrew
- Andrew Lloyd Webber: A Concert Celebration (Medley)

Mancini, Henry
- Henry Mancini for Strings, Vol.1 & Vol.2

Mandel, Johnny
- Sandpiper: Shadow of Your Smile

McBride, Robert
- Pumpkin-Eater's Little Fugue

McDonald, Harl
- Suite for Strings on American Negro Themes

Mercury, Freddie
- Bohemian Rhapsody

Meza, Vinicio
- Suite Latinoamericana

Montgomery, Bruce
- Concertino for Strings

Mozart, Wolfgang Amadeus
- Eine Kleine Nachtmusik, K. 525

Nielsen, Carl August
- Little Suite, Op. 1

Nyman, Michael
- The Piano

O'Boyle, Sean
- Waltz of Madness

Orr, Charles Wilfred
- Cotswold Hill Tune

Ortolani & Oliviero
- Mondo Cane: More

Pachelbel, Johann
- Canon in D
- Chaconne

(String Orchestra cont.)

Penderecki, Krysztof
- Threnody: To the Victims of Hiroshima

Piazzolla, Astor
- Cuatro Estaciones Porteñas (The Four Seasons in Buenas Aires)
- Libertango
- Milonga del Angel
- Tango No. 1 (Coral)
- Tango No. 2 (Canyengue)
- Tanguedia
- Three Minutes of Reality (Tango)

Porter, Cole
- Gay Divorcee: Night and Day

Puccini, Giacomo
- I Crisantemi (The Chrysanthemums)

Raksin, David
- The Bad and the Beautiful: Mvt. II: The Acting Lesson

Reger, Max
- Weihnachten (Christmas), Op.145/3c

Respighi, Ottorini
- Antiche danze ed arie (Ancient Airs and Dances): Set III

Scott, Cyril
- Irish Serenade

Shulman, Alan
- The Bop Gavotte

Sibelius, Jean
- Romance in C Major, Op. 42
- Suite Champêtre, Op. 98b

Sousa, J.P.
- Semper Fidelis
- The Stars and Stripes Forever

Strauss, Johann and Josef
- Pizzicato Polka

Talbot, Joby
- Lover's Ink

Templeton, Alec
- Night Pieces

Turina, Joaquín
- La oración del Torero, Op. 34
- Rapsodia sinfónica, Op. 66

Vangelis
- Chariots of Fire

Vaughan Williams, Ralph
- Fantasia on a Theme by Thomas Tallis
- Rhosymedre

Villa-Lobos, Heitor
- Bachianas Brasileiras No. 1
- Bachianas Brasileiras No. 5

Williams, John T.
- Munich: Hatikva (The Hope)
- Three Themes

Woodgate, Leslie
- English Dance Suite

Yarrow, Peter
- Puff the Magic Dragon

STRING ORCHESTRA WITH KEYBOARD OR HARP

Anderson, Leroy
- Plink Plank Plunk!

Arnold, Malcolm
- Toy Symphony, Op. 62

Bacon, Ernst
- Christmas Fantasia for Strings

Berlin, Irving
- Alexander's Ragtime Band

Falla, Manuel de
- El Amor brujo: Pantomime and Ritual Fire Dance

Holcombe, Bill
- Christmas Wishes

Legrand, Michel
- The Windmills of Your Mind

Mandel, Johnny
- Shadow of Your Smile

Newman, Alfred
- Wuthering Heights: Cathie's Theme

Piazzolla, Astor
- Michelangelo

Richman, Lucas
- Coventry Carol

Saint-Saëns, Camille
- Carnival of the Animals: The Swan

Schnittke, Alfred
- Concerto Grosso No. 1

Torelli, Giuseppe
- Concerto Grosso for Two Violins and Orchestra in G Minor, Op. 8, No. 6 (Christmas Concerto)

Vaughan Williams, Ralph
- Fantasia on Christmas Carols

Williams, John T.
- Munich: A Prayer for Peace
- Munich: Hatikva (The Hope)

Vivaldi, Antonio
- Concerto, Op. 44, No. 16, R.V. 570, F Major
- Le quattro staggioni (The Four Seasons) Op. 8, Nos.1-4

STRING ORCHESTRA WITH GUITAR, HARP, KEYBOARD, AND PERCUSSION

Arlen, Harold
- Stormy Weather

Bach, J.S.
- Toccata and Fugue in D Minor, BWV 565

Carmichael, Hoagy
- Stardust

Ellington, Edward K. (Duke)
- Solitude
- Sophisticated Lady

Glass, Philip
- The Hours: Suite (2002)

Gold, Julie
- From a Distance

Goldsmith, Jerry
- The Twilight Zone (1961): The Invaders

Gould, Morton
- Cresta Blanca Waltz
- Five Spirituals
- Harvest

Hudson, Will & Mills, Irving
- Moonglow

Kander, John
- Cabaret

Kern, Jerome
- Jerome Kern Medley

MacDermot, Gal
- Aquarius: Let the Sunshine In
- Hair: Where Do I Go?/Good Morning Starshine

Menken, Alan
- Beauty and the Beast
- Highlights from Beauty and the Beast

O'Donnell & Salvatori
- Halo Suite: Halo Theme

Rodgers, Richard
- Pal Joey: Bewitched, Bothered, and Bewildered

Rose, David
- Holiday for Strings

Saint-Saëns, Camille
- Christmas Oratorio, Op. 12

Sayre, Charles
- Broadway on Parade

Shulman, Alan
- Ricky-Tick Serenade

Silvestri, Alan
- Forrest Gump Main Title (Feather Theme)

Templeton, Alec
- Give Me Your Heart

Weill, Kurt
- The Two Worlds of Kurt Weill: Berlin Suite (J'Attends un navire)

Strings with Guitar, Harp

Dix, William
- Christmas with Renata Scotto: 8. What Child Is This?

Grieg, Edvard
- Erotik

Herrmann, Bernard
- The Ghost of Mrs. Muir (1947)

Kern, Jerome
- They Didn't Believe Me

Strings and Percussion

Shchedrin, Rodion
- Carmen Suite

Sibelius
- Rakastave the Lover

Warren, Diane
- Music of My Heart

Strings with Keyboard and Percussion

Fain, Sammy
- Once Upon a Dream

Prima, Louis
- Jump, Jive an' Wail

Rose, David
- Holiday for Strings

Rouse, Ervin T.
- Orange Blossom Special

Weinberger, Jaromir
- The Devil on the Belfry

STRINGS, SINGLE WIND & PERCUSSION, HARP, KEYBOARD, GUITAR

Aguila, Miguel del
- Conga

Amram, David
- Three Songs for America

Arlen, Harold
- Wizard of Oz: Over the Rainbow

Bach, J.S.
- Prelude from Partita in E Major

Barber, Samuel
- Capricorn Concerto

Bazelon, Irwin
- Early American Suite

Bennett, Richard Rodney
- Nocturnes

Berlioz, Hector
- The Novello Book of Carols:The Shepherds' Farewell (Thou Must Leave)

Blake, Howard
- Christmas Lullaby

Burgon, Geoffrey
- Brideshead Variations
- Chronicles of Narnia Suite
- Nunc Dimittis
- Suite from Bleak House
- Suite from Martin Chuzzlewit

Carmichael, Hoagy
- Georgia On My Mind

Chávez, Carlos
- Cantos de México

Coots, J. Fred
- For All We Know

Copland, Aaron
- Appalachian Spring: Suite
- Quiet City

Creston, Paul
- Two Choric Dances, Op. 17a

Custer, Calvin
- Birth of the Blues

Dessau, Paul
- Alice the Firefighter
- Alice's Monkey Business
- Alice in the Wooly West
- Alice Helps the Romance

Dorff, Daniel
- Tortoise and the Hare

Elfman, Danny
- Charlotte's Web: Themes for Flute and Orchestra (2006)

Falla, Manuel de
- El Amor brujo
- El Corregidor y la Molinera

Frackenpohl, Arthur
- Largo and Allegro
- Suite Concertino

Garner, Erroll
- Misty

Gershwin, George
- Embraceable You

Glass, Philip
- Modern Love Waltz

Goldsmith, Jerry
- Chinatown (1974): Suite
- Rudy: Theme for Flute and Chamber Orchestra
- Six Degrees of Separation (1993): Tango

Goossens, Eugene
- Two Sketches

Gordon, Michael
- Love Bead

Green, John
- Body and Soul

Griffes, Charles Tomlinson
- Three Tone Pictures

Guion, David
- Cowboy's Meditation for Voice and Orchestra

Haggart, Bob
- What's New?

Handel, George Frideric
- Alexander's Feast Overture

Haydn, Franz Joseph
- Kindersymphonie, Hob. II;47, C Major (Toy Symphony)

Henley, Larry
- Wind Beneath My Wings

Ibert, Jacques
- Divertissement

Ives, Charles
- Symphony Holidays: 1.Washington's Birthday

Joplin, Scott
- The Entertainer
- Red Back Book

Kapilow, Robert
- Dr. Seuss's Gertrude McFuzz
- Dr. Seuss's Green Eggs and Ham

Kent, Rolfe
- Up In the Air (2009)

Kilar, Wojciech
- Dracula (1992)

Lambert, Constant
- Eight Poems of Li-Po

Lang, David
- Hunk of Burnin' Love

Mancini, Henry
- Victor, Victoria (1982): Crazy World

Maxwell Davies, Peter
- The Devils: Suite

Mayer, William
- Good King Wenceslas

McBride, Robert
- Workout

McCabe, John
- Sam (ITV Music)

Mechem, Kirke
- The King's Contest

Menotti, Gian Carlo
- My Christmas

Moeran, E.J.
- Whythorne's Shadow

Monteverdi, Claudio
- Christmas Vespers

Morricone
- Casualties of War: Elegy for Brown

Mozart, Wolfgang Amadeus
- Marriage of Figaro: "Deh Vieni non Tardar"

Newman, Alfred
- The Best of Everything: London Calling

Poulenc, Francis
- L'Histoire de Babar (The Story of Babar, the Little Elephant)

Powell, John
- The Bourne Identity

Respighi, Ottorino
- Trittico Botticelliano: 2.Adoration of the Magi

Richman, Lucas
- Shena B'rachot

Ronell, Ann
- Willow Weep for Me

Roxburgh, Edwin
- How Pleasant to Know Mr. Lear

Rutter, John
- The Very Best Time of the Year

Saint-Saëns, Camille
- Le Carnaval des animaux (Carnival of the Animals)

Schickele, Peter
- Birthday Ode to "Big Daddy" Bach
- Broadway Boogie

(Str, Single Wind & Perc, Hp, Kybd, Gtr – SCHICKELE, cont.)

- Classical Rap
- Three Strange Cases
- Unbegun Symphony
- Uptown Hoedown

Schuller, Gunther
- Journey into Jazz

Shapiro, Michael
- Frankenstein

Shulman, Alan
- J. S. on The Rocks (Nightcap)

Silvestri, Alan
- Cast Away: Crossroads
- Forrest Gump Main Title for Piano & Orchestra (Feather Theme)

Simons, Netty
- Pied Piper of Hamelin

Stravinsky, Igor
- Ragtime

Surinach, Carlos
- Ritmo jondo, Flamenco

Swanson, Howard
- Night Music

Tan Dun
- Crouching Tiger Concerto

Tanara
- Two Venetian Dialect Songs

Thurlow, Jeremy
- The Novello Book of Carols: All and Some (Nowell We Sing)

Tyzik, Jeff
- Mis zeh Hidlik (Behold the Lights)

Vaughan Williams, Ralph
- Fantasia on Greensleeves

Wendel
- Fantasia on "Yeroushalaim Shel Zahav"

Zaninelli, Luigi
- A Lexicon of Beasties

STRINGS
0 3 0 3 – 0 3 3 0 – PERC

Amundson, Steven
- Three's Company

Effinger, Cecil
- The St. Luke Christmas Story

Handel, George Frideric
- The King Shall Rejoice

Harbison, John
- The Flight into Egypt: Sacred Ricercar

Willson, Meredith
- The Music Man: Overture

STRINGS
0 2 2 2 – 2 0 0 0 – PERC

Cimarosa, Domenico
- I Traci Amanti: Overture

Griffes, Charles Tomlinson
- Poem for flute and orchestra

Handel, George Frideric
- Messiah: Sinfonia Pastoral

Jones, Trevor
- Last of the Mohicans: Kiss

Kreisler, Fritz
- Liebesleid

STRINGS
0 0 3 3 – 2 2 0 0 – PERC

Maxwell Davies, Peter
- Temenos, with Mermaids and Angels

Schickele, Peter
- Canine Cantata "Wachet Arf!"

STRINGS
1 1 1 1 – 2 2 0 0 – PERC

Baker, David
- Concerto for Cello

Dorati, Antal
- Night Music

Ellis, David
- Carols for an Island Christmas

Ellstein, Abraham
- Retsei
- Sh'Ma Yisroel
- Vli Jeru Sholayim Ircho
- Yismechu

Goossens, Eugene
- Prelude to "Philip II"

Martynov, Vladimir
- Christmas Music

Pearson, Leslie
- Early One Morning

Revueltas, Silvestre
- Paisajes (Landscapes)

Yon, Pietro
- Gesu Bambino

STRINGS
1 1 2 1 – 2 2 0 0 – PERC

Caliendo, Christopher
- Iron Horse

Cowell, Henry
- Saturday Night at the Firehouse

Deussen, Nancy
- Ascent to Victory

Falla, Manuel de
- El Amor brujo: Chanson du feu follet
- El Amor Brujo: Ritual Fire Dance
- El Sombrero de tres picos (Three-Cornered Hat): Suite I

Gould, Morton
- Swanee River in the Style of Beethoven
- Swanee River in the Style of Mozart

Kapilow, Robert
- Elijah's Angel
- Play Ball! (Casey at the Bat)

Nystroem, Gösta
- Three Love Songs (3 Kärleksvisor)

Rosenberg, Hilding Constantin
- The Holy Night (Die Heligea Natten): A Christmas Oratorio

Schubert, Franz
- Christmas with Renata Scotto: 6. Ave Maria
- March Militaire Nos. 1&2

Sibelius, Jean
- Kuolema, Op. 44 (Valse Triste)

STRINGS
1 2 0 2 – 2 2 0 0 – PERC

Beethoven, Ludwig van
- Romance No. 1 in G Major, Op.40
- Romance No. 2 in F Minor, Op. 50

Handel, George Frideric
- Water Music

Haydn, Franz Joseph
- Symphony No. 8 in G Major (Le soir)
- Symphony No. 82 "The Bear"

Llewellyn, William
- The Novello Book of Carols: Il est né, le divin enfant (See Him Born)
- The Novello Book of Carols: The Angel Gabriel (Gabriel's Message)

Mozart, Wolfgang Amadeus
- Symphony No. 41, K.551, C Major (Jupiter) K. 551

Musgrave, Thea
- Night Music

Zwilich, Ellen Taaffe
- Peanuts Gallery (1996)

STRINGS
1 2 2 1 – 2 2 0 0 – PERC

Bazelon, Irwin
- Fairy Tale

Kern, Jerome
- She's a Good Fellow Selections

Menotti, Gian Carlo
- Amahl and the Night Visitors: Introduction, March and Shepherd's Dance

- Amahl and the Night Visitors: Shepherd's Chorus
Reinagle, Alexander
- Federal March
- Madison's March
- Mrs. Madison's Minuet
Rossini, Gioacchino
- L'Italiana in Algeri: Overture

STRINGS
2 0 2 2 – 2 2 0 0 – PERC

Bartók, Béla
- Rumanian Folk Dances
Freyhan, Michael
- Toy Symphony
McCabe, John
- Sam: Theme music
Mozart, Wolfgang Amadeus
- Adagio in E, K. 261
Schubert, Franz
- Der Teufel als Hydraulicus, D. 4: Overture
Swayne, Giles
- Naaotwa Lala, Op. 39
Ward, Samuel A.
- America the Beautiful

STRINGS
2 1 2 2 – 2 2 0 0 – PERC

Arnold, Malcolm
- The Belles of St.Trinians: Comedy Suite
- Whistle Down the Wind
Copland, Aaron
- Down A Country Lane
Creston, Paul
- Concertino for Marimba, Op. 21
Debussy
- La Fille aux cheveux de lin
Delius, Frederick
- Two Pieces: 1. On Hearing the First Cuckoo in Spring; 2. Summer Night on the River
Desplat, Alexandre
- The Queen: Suite (2006)
Dodgson, Stephen
- Villanelle
Elgar, Edward
- The Spanish Lady (concert version)
Falla, Manuel de
- El Amor brujo
- Danse rituelle du feu
- Seven Popular Spanish Songs
- Récit du pécheur and Pantomime
Gershwin, George
- Porgy and Bess: Summertime

Gluck, Christoph Willibald
- Orfeo ed Euridice (Dance of the Blessed Spirits)
Goldsmith, Jerry
- Poltergeist (1982): The Light
- Star Trek Main Theme
Goossens, Eugene
- East of Suez: Incidental Music
- The Hurdy-Gurdy Man
Gould, Morton
- Windjammer: Night Watch
Grainger, Percy
- Irish Tune from County Derry (LondonderryAir)
Griffin, Merv
- Jeopardy Theme
Hely-Hutchinson, Victor
- Carol Symphony
Herschel, Lee
- How the Camel Got His Hump
- How the Whale Got His Tiny Throat
Kent, Walter
- I'll Be Home for Christmas
Lambert, Constant
- Elegiac Blues
Lumbye, H.C.
- Copenhagen Steam Railway Gallop
Mancini, Henry
- The Glass Menagerie
Namenwirth, Micha
- Divertimento for Toys and Orchestra
Newman, Alfred
- Desiree: We Meet Again
Niles, John Jacob
- I Wonder as I Wander
Raksin, David
- Toy Concertino
Ravel, Maurice
- Pavane pour une infante défunte (Pavane for a Dead Princess)
Respighi, Ottorini
- Gli uccelli (The Birds)
Saint-Saëns, Camille
- Romance, Op. 36
Sullivan, Arthur
- Mikado Overture
Tiomkin, Dimitri
- The Young Land (1959): Strange are the Ways of Love
Vaughan Williams, Ralph
- Fantasia on Greensleeves
- The Lark Ascending
Yon, Pietro A.
- Gesu Bambino

STRINGS
2 2 2 2 – 2 2 0 0 – PERC

Adler, Samuel
- Judah's Song of Praise
- Show an Affirming Flame

Arlen, Harold
- Wizard of Oz: Over the Rainbow
Bennett, Richard Rodney
- Diversions
- Partita
Bernstein, Elmer
- My Left Foot: Suite
Boieldieu, Francois
- The Caliph of Bagdad Overture
Borodin, Alexander
- String Quartet No.2: Nocturne
Chappell, Herbert
- Caribbean Concerto
- Paddington Bear's First Concert
Chopin, Frédéric
- Fantaisie sur des airs nationaux polonais, Op. 13 (Fantasy on Polish Airs)
- Variations on "La ci darem la mano," Op. 2
Corigliano, John
- The Cloisters
Debussy
- Clair de lune
- La fille au cheveux de lin
Dunhill, Thomas
- The Novello Book of Carols: How Soft, Upon the Ev'ning Air
Elgar, Edward
- Chanson de matin, Op. 15
- Chanson de nuit, Op. 15
- The Snow, Op. 26, No. 1
Falla, Manuel de
- Seven Popular Spanish Songs
- El Sombrero de tres picos (Three-Cornered Hat): Suite No. 1
Fauré, Gabriel
- Pavane, Op. 50
Field, John
- Irish Concerto for Piano and Orchestra
Garrop, Stacy
- Thunderwalker
Goldsmith, Jerry
- The Illustrated Man: Main Title
- A Patch of Blue (1966): Suite
- Poltergeist (1982): The Calling
Gould, Morton
- Serenade of Carols
Gruber, Franz & Redner
- Silent Night; O Little Town of Bethlehem
Hageman, Richard
- At the Well
Halvorsen, Johan
- Norwegian Air
Handel, George Frideric
- The Novello Book of Carols (Joy to the World)
Haydn, Franz Joseph
- Symphony No. 100 in G Major (Military)

(Str – 2 2 2 2 – 2 2 0 0 – Perc – HAYDN, cont.)

- Symphony No. 101 in D Major (The Clock)
- Symphony No. 94 in G Major, "Surprise!" (mvt. II)

Holst, Gustav
- The Novello Book of Carols (In the Bleak Midwinter)

Holst, Gustav, cont.
- Three Christmas Songs
- The Novello Book of Carols (In the Bleak Midwinter)

Keillor, Garrison
- Wild Mountain Thyme: Will You Go, Darling, Go?

Kingman, Daniel
- A Revolutionary Garland

Kreisler, Fritz - Liebesleid
- Three Old Viennese Dances; No. 3 (Schön Rosmarin)

Llewellyn, William, arr.
- The Novello Book of Carols (King Jesus Hath a Garden)

Luck, Arthur
- Deck the Hall & We Wish You a Merry Christmas

Mascagni, Pietro
- Cavalleria Rusticana (Intermezzo)

Maxwell Davies, Peter
- A Spell for Green Corn: The MacDonald Dances

Mendelssohn, Felix
- Hebrides Overture, Op. 26 (Fingal's Cave)
- Heimkehr aurs der Fremde, Op. 89 (Son and Stranger): Overture
- Märchen von der Schönen Melusine, Op. 32 DI (Fair Melusina)
- Midsummernight's Dream, Op. 21: Overture
- A Midsummernight's Dream: Scherzo
- Symphony No. 4 in A Major (Italian)

Mozart, Wolfgang Amadeus
- Don Giovanni, K.527: Overture
- Exsultate Jubilate, K. 165
- German Dance #3, K. 605
- Le Nozze di Figaro (Marriage of Figaro) K. 492: Overture
- Der Schauspieldirektor (The Impresario) K. 486: Overture

North, Alex
- Unchained Melody (1955)

Poulenc, Francis
- Sinfonietta

Ravel, Maurice
- Ma Mère l'Oye (Mother Goose)
- Ma Mère l'Oye: Prélude et Danse du rouet

Richman, Lucas
- The Brentwood Rag
- Hanukkah Medley
- A Western Fanfare

Rimsky-Korsakov, Nicolai
- The Tale of Tsar Saltan (Flight of the Bumble Bee)

Rodrigo, Joaquin
- Cuatro madrigales amatorios

Rossini, Gioacchino
- La Cenerentola (Cinderella) Overture
- Il barbiere di Siviglia (Barber of Seville): Sinfonia

Rota, Nino
- Romeo and Juliet (1968)

Rutter, John
- Jesus Child!

Saint-Saëns, Camille
- Havanaise, Op. 83

Sarasate, Pablo de
- Zigeunerweisen, Op. 20

Schickele, Peter
- Thurber's Dogs

Schumann, Robert
- Overture, Scherzo and Finale

Smith, Hale
- Abide with Me

Strauss, Richard
- Romanze

Templeton, Alec
- Merry Christmas

Thomson, Virgil
- The Nativity

Tiomkin, Dimitri
- High Noon (1952): Do Not Forsake Me Oh My Darling

Turok, Paul
- Reeling in the New Year

Vardi, Emanuel
- Suite on American Folk Songs

Vaughan-Williams, Ralph
- The Wasps Overture

Welcher, Dan
- JFK: The Voice of Peace

Wendel
- A Halloween Trilogy: Trick or Treat
- Santa Dear

STRINGS
3 2 2 2 – 2 2 1 1 – PERC

Alwyn, William
- Suite of Scottish Dances

Anderson, Leroy
- First Day of Spring
- Jazz Legato

Antheil, George
- Music to a World's Fair Film

Arditi, Luigi
- Kiss (Il Bacio)

Arlen, Harold
- Wizard of Oz: Munchkinland
- Wizard of Oz: Yellow Brick Road

Armand, Charles (Puerner, Charles)
- Neapolitan Songs for Orchestra

Armstrong, Billie Joe
- Best of Green Day

Bagley, Edwin Eugene
- National Emblem March

Bendix, Victor
- Grand American Fantasia: Tone Pictures of the North and South

Bennett, Richard Rodney
- London Pastoral
- Suite française

Bishop, Stephen
- White Nights: Separate Lives

Blake, Howard
- Nursery Rhyme Overture
- The Up and Down Man: Suite

Blomdahl, Karl-Birger
- The Walpurgis Night (Stage Music No. 1)

Botkin, Perry
- Nadia's Theme

Campos, José Carlos
- Danza Rústica

Carpenter, John Alden
- Krazy Kat

Cervantes
- Three Cuban Dances

Cohan, George M.
- Royal Vagabond: Selections
- Star-Spangled Spectacular

Cole, Hugo
- Black Lion Dances

Copland, Aaron
- Billy the Kid (Waltz)
- Down A Country Lane
- John Henry
- Music for the Theatre
- Old American Songs
- Rodeo: 2.Corral Nocturne

Costa, Paul Mario
- A Frangesa March

Cowell, Henry
- Old American Country Set

Creston, Paul
- A Rumor, Op. 27

Daugherty, Michael
- Metropolis Symphony (3.Mwyzptlk)

Denza, Luigi
- Funiculi, Funicula

Dewitt, Louis O.
- Twelve English Songs

Dodgson, Stephen
- Villanelle

Drdla, Frantisek (Franz) Alois
- Souvenir

Edwards, Gus
- By the Light of the Silvery Moon

Erb, Donald
- Christmas Music

Fahrbach, Philipp, Jr.
- Midnight Elopement Galop

Fernandez, Caballero
- Cielito Lindo

Fillmore, Henry
- His Excellency March

Foss, Lukas
- Elegy for Anne Frank

Foster, Stephen
- Old Folks At Home; Love's Old Sweet Song: Palms

Friml, Rudolf
- Melodie

Glinka, Mikhail
- Valse Fantaisie

Goldsmith, Jerry
- Star Trek Main Theme
- Patton (1970): The Battle Ground

Goossens, Eugene
- Kaleidoscope

Gottschalk, Louis Moreau
- Pasquinade Caprice

Gould, Morton
- Swanee River in the Style of Bach
- Swanee River in the Style of Strauss (Johann)

Grainger, Percy
- Mock Morris

Greenwood
- God Bless the U.S.A.

Griffin, Merv
- An Hour with the Game Shows

Guion, David
- Home on the Range
- Minuet
- Pastorale (Three Little Brown Bulls)
- Turkey in the Straw

Hageman, Richard
- At the Well

Harris, Roy
- Freedom's Land

Haydn, Franz Joseph
- Symphony No. 94 in G Major (Surprise)

Hefti, Neal Paul
- Batman Theme

Herbert, Victor
- Panamericana

Herschel, Lee
- How the Camel Got His Hump
- How the Whale Got His Tiny Throat

Hodkinson, Sydney
- Concerto for Clarinet and Orchestra

Isaac, Merle
- Salute to the United Nations

Ivanovici, Josif
- Waves of the Danube: The Anniversary Song

Ives, Charles
- Central Park in the Dark
- Symphony No. 3: The Camp Meeting
- Three Places in New England

Joplin, Scott
- Maple Leaf Rag

Kabalevsky, Dmitri
- The Comedians, Op. 26: Suite

Kapilow, Rober
- You and Hugh

Kasschau, Howard
- Country Concerto

Kerker, Gustave
- The Belle of New York

Kern, Jerome
- Fluffy Ruffles: Selection
- Night Boat: Whose Baby Are You?
- Night Boat Selections
- Sally Selections for Orchestra

Kleinsinger, George
- Tubby the Tuba

Koenig, Hermann Louis
- Post Horn Galop

Lambert, Constant
- Elegiac Blues

Lang, David
- Loud Love Songs

Langey, Otto
- From the Highlands: A Selection of Scotch Melodies

Lehár, Franz
- Zigeunerliebe (Gypsy Love) Waltzes

Liebermann, Lowell
- Concerto for Piccolo

Lincke, Paul
- Kwang Hsu (Chinese March)

Lumbye, H.C.
- Copenhagen Steam Railway Gallop

Lutosławski, Witold
- Twenty Polish Christmas Carols

Marsh, Gerry Jon
- Hamburger Suite

Matthews, H. Alexander
- The Story of Christmas Cantata

Mayer, William
- Good King Wenceslas
- Scenes from "Snow Queen"

McCabe, John
- The Lion, the Witch, and the Wardrobe: Suite

Mendelssohn, Felix
- Midsummernight's Dream, Op. 21: Overture

Meyer, Ranaan
- American Suite

Mozart
- Turkish March

Naughtin, Matthew
- Birthday Variations
- Cinco de Mayo
- The Loony Tunes Fugue
- This Old Man Sing-Along

- The Wheels on the Bus Sing-Along

Nyman, Michael
- The Piano (Concerto: Two-piano version)

Peck, Russell
- Playing With Style
- The Thrill of the Orchestra

Phillips & Gilliam
- California Dreamin'

Pola, Eddie & George Wyle
- It's the Most Beautiful Time of the Year

Ponce, Manuel
- Estrellita (Star of Love)

Porter, Cole
- Cole Porter Classics

Poulenc, Francis
- L'histoire de Babar (The Story of Babar, The Little Elephant)

Pryor, Arthur
- The Whistler and His Dog

Reger, Max
- Weihnachten (Christmas), Op.145/3

Rimsky-Korsakov, Nicolai
- The Tale of Tsar Saltan: Flight of the Bumble Bee

Rodríguez, Robert Xavier
- Mascaras

Schreiner, Aldolph
- The Worried Drummer

Schubert, Franz
- Der Teufel als Hydraulicus, D. 4: Overture

Shore, Howard
- The Lord of the Rings: Highlights from the Fellowship of the Ring

Shostakovich, Dmitri
- Hamlet: Incidental Music to the Stage Production, Op. 32a

Shur, Thomas
- Smooth (Santana)

Sibelius, Jean
- Kuolema, Op. 44 (Valse Triste)

Smith, Harry C.
- Admiral Dewey's March

Smith, Julia
- American Dance Suite

Sousa, John Philip
- High School Cadets March
- King Cotton March
- The Stars and Stripes Forever

Strauss, Johann, Sr.
- An der schönen Donau Walzer (On the Blue Danube), Op. 314
- Tritsch-Tratsch (The Circus)

Sullivan, Arthur
- Pirates of Penzance Selections

Swanson, Howard
- Short Symphony

Villa-Lobos, Heitor - Concerto for Harmonica

(Str – 3 2 2 2 – 2 2 1 1 – Perc, cont.)

Vognar, Frank
- Bohemian Folksongs

Wagner, Joseph Franz
- Unter dem Doppeladler (Under the Double Eagle March), Op. 159

Wagner, Richard
- Lohengrin: Bridal Chorus

Washington, Ned
- I'm Getting Sentimental Over You

Waxman, Franz
- The Devil Doll (1936): Waltzes

Weatherly, Fred E.
- Danny Boy

Weber, Carl Maria von
- Turandot: Overture and March

Wenrich, Percy
- Put On Your Old Grey Bonnet

Williams, John T.
- Star Wars: Episode I Phantom Menace (Duel of the Fates)

Wood, Arthur
- Moorland Fiddlers for Orchestra

Yradier, Sebastian
- La Paloma (Spanish Serenade)

STRINGS
1 1 4 1 – 2 2 2 0 – PERC

Antheil, George
- A Jazz Symphony (1955 version)

Arlen, Harold
- The Wizard of Oz: Over the Rainbow

Copland, Aaron
- Rodeo: 3.Saturday Night Waltz

Gershwin, George
- Gershwin in Concert

Gould, Morton
- Something to Do: Labor Cantata
- Swanee River in the Style of Brahms
- Swanee River in the Style of Debussy

Kern, Jerome
- Way You Look Tonight

Rodgers, Richard
- Carousel: You'll Never Walk Alone

Sayre, Charles
- Broadway on Parade

Weill, Kurt
- The Two Worlds of Kurt Weill - New York Suite: September Song

STRINGS
2 2 2 2 – 2 2 2 1 – PERC

Adler, Samuel
- The Feast of Lights
- A Song of Hanukkah

Antheil, George
- Cabeza de vaca

Barab, Seymour
- G.A.G.E., A Christmas Story

Bartok, Bela
- Hungarian Sketches

Bennett, Richard Rodney
- Lovesongs

Blane, Ralph
- Have Yourself a Merry Little Christmas

Carr, Benjamin
- Federal Overture

Cifuentes, Santos
- Scherzo sobre Aires Tropicales

Copland, Aaron
- Appalachian Spring: Suite
- Billy the Kid (Prairie Night and Celebration)
- Variations on a Shaker Melody

Crawford, Robert MacArthur
- Air Force March: Official Song of the United States Army Air Corps

Damase, Jean-Michel
- Piege de lumiere

Davis, Albert O.
- Buffalo Gals: In Blue Grass Style

Davis, Jimmy
- Buffalo Gals
- Down In the Valley

Demerest, Clifford
- Let Freedom Ring: Overture

Dorff, Daniel
- Pachelbel's Christmas

Falla, Manuel de
- La vida breve: Spanish Dance No. 1

Garrop, Stacy
- Thunderwalker

Goldstein, William
- Celebration Overture 1776-1976

Gottschalk, Louis Moreau
- L'Union: Paraphrase de concert sur les airs nationaux

Gould, Morton
- Adeste fidelis
- Christmas Time, Book II: Cinerama Holiday (Skier's Waltz)
- Christmas Time, Book II: Good King Wenceslas
- Dramatic Fanfares from CBS-TV Documentary "World War I"
- Cinerama Holiday: Skier's Waltz
- Cinerama Holiday: Suite
- Dramatic Fanfares from CBS-TV documentary "World War I"
- Hoofer Suite
- The Jogger and the Dinosaur
- Troubadour Music

Griffin, Merv
- Jeopardy Theme

Hewitt, James
- The Battle of Trenton

Joel, Billy
- Just the Way You Are

Ives, Charles
- Three Places in New England

Kapilow, Robert
- Dr. Seuss's Gertrude McFuzz
- Dr. Seuss's Green Eggs and Ham

Katz, S
- Polskie Kwiaty (Selection of Polish Songs & Dances)

Kent, Walter
- I'll Be Home for Christmas

Kleinsinger, George
- Brooklyn Baseball Cantata

MacColl, Ewan
- The First Time Ever I Saw Your Face

Marks, Johnny
- Rudolph the Red-Nosed Reindeer

Maxwell Davies, Peter
- Caroline Mathilde: Concert Suite from Act I
- Caroline Mathilde: Concert Suite from Act II
- Swinton Jig, on a Nineteenth Century Lancashire Fiddle Tune

Meyer, Ranaan
- Fox Down

Moore, Douglas
- The Greenfield Christmas Tree

Nyman, Michael
- The Piano (Concerto)

Orr, Buxton
- A Carmen Fantasy

Richman, Lucas
- Christmas Is Coming
- A Christmas Wish
- Ho! Ho! Ho!
- Presents from Santa
- Reindeer Variations
- Take a Ride with Santa
- Thanksgiving Hymn

Riegger, Wallingford
- Dance Rhythms, Op. 58

Rodríguez, Robert Xavier
- Scrooge: Concert Scenes from "A Christmas Carol"

Schumann, Robert
- Overture, Scherzo, Finale, Op. 52

Schutz, Heinrich
- Christmas Story SWV 435a

Smith, Hale
- Amazing Grace
- A Mighty Fortress

Strauss, Johann, Jr.
- Tritsch-Tratsch Polka, Op. 214

Sullivan, Arthur
- Mikado: Overture
- Ruddigore Overture

Thomson, Virgil
- Louisiana Story: Acadian Songs and Dances
- The Plow that Broke the Plains: Suite
- The River: Suite

Turok, Paul
- Ragtime Caprice, Op. 45

Vaughan Williams, Ralph
- English Folk Songs Suite

Villa-Lobos, Heitor
- Bachianas Brasileiras No. 5: Aria

Weill, Kurt
- Kleine Dreigroschenmusik (Suite from Little Three Penny Opera)

Williams, John T.
- Munich: Hatikva (The Hope)

STRINGS
2 2 2 2 – 2 2 4 1 – PERC

Adams, John
- The Chairman Dances: Foxtrot for Orchestra

Adler, Samuel
- Summer Stock: A Short Merry Overture

Alford, Kenneth
- Colonel Bogey March

Álvarez, Teófilo
- Marinera Trujillana

Austin, Frederic
- Twelve Days of Christmas

Balakirev, Mily
- Overture on Russian Folk Themes

Barry, John
- Out of Africa: Main Title

Beethoven
- Die Ruinen von Athen, Op. 113 (Ruins of Athens): Turkish March and Chorus

Bizet, Georges
- Fantaisie Brilliante on Themes from Bizet's "Carmen"

Bliss, Arthur
- Baraza
- Things to Come

Britten, Benjamin
- Matinees musicales, Op. 24

Delibes, Leo
- Coppelia: Entr'acte & Waltz

Falla, Manuel de
- Fuego fatuo

Farnan, Robert
- The Peanut Polka

Fučik, Julius
- Florentiner March, Op. 214

Gauntlett & Mann & Wells
- The Novello Book of Carols: Once in Royal David's City

Geehl, Henry
- Folk Dance Suite
- Suite Espagnole

German, Edward
- Richard III Overture
- Three Dances: Henry VIII

Gounod, Charles
- Marche funèbre d'une marionette (Funeral March of a Marionette)

Grainger, Percy
- Mock Morris for Orchestra

Gray, Allan
- African Queen: Portrait (1951)

Guion, David
- Prairie Suite

Jackson, Stephen
- The Novello Book of Carols: Noel Nouvelet

Kapilow, Robert
- Chris van Allsburg's Polar Express

Lehár, Franz
- Merry Widow Waltz

Llewellyn, William
- The Novello Book of Carols: Come All You Worthy People Here (A Somerset Carol)
- The Novello Book of Carols: De Virgin Mary had a Baby Boy
- The Novello Book of Carols: God Rest You Merry Gentlemen
- The Novello Book of Carols: Puer Nobis (Unto Us Is Born a Son)
- The Novello Book of Carols: O Come All Ye Faithful
- The Novello Book of Carols: The Holly and the Ivy

López, Jimmy
- Fiesta! for chamber orchestra

MacCunn, Hamish
- Land of the Mountain and Flood, Op. 3: Overture

Mendelssohn, Felix
- The Novello Book of Carols: Hark the Herald Angels Sing

Moeran, E.J.
- Serenade in G

Saint-Saëns, Camille
- La nuit, Op. 114

Salzedo, Leonard
- The Witch Boy: Square Dance from the Ballet

Schickele, Peter
- A Bach Portrait
- Prelude to Einstein on the Fritz

Schoenberg, Claude-Michel
- Miss Saigon: Finale
- Miss Saigon: Sun and Moon
- Miss Saigon: Why God Why

Schumann, Robert
- New Year Song, Op. 144 "Mit eherner Zunge, da ruft es: Gebt acht"

Serly, Tibor
- A Little Christmas Cantata

Sharp, Cecil
- Country Gardens

Sousa, John Philip
- Washington Post March

Steffe, William
- Battle Hymn of the Republic

Strauss, Johann, Sr.
- Carnival Nights (Emperor Waltz)
- Radetzky March, Op. 228

Sullivan, Arthur
- Patience Selections
- Yeoman of the Guard Overture
- Yeoman of the Guard Selections

Tiomkin, Dimitri
- Circus World (1964): John Wayne March

Vaughan Williams, Ralph
- Hodie, a Christmas Cantata

Wells, Robin
- The Novello Book of Carols: A Fanfare for Christmas (Hodie, Hodie); A Gallery Carol (Rejoice and Be Merry)

Williams, Charles
- The Dream of Olwen

STRINGS
2 2 2 2 – 2 3 3 1 – PERC

Balada, Leonardo
- Sinfonia en Negro (Homage to Martin Luther King)

Berlin, Irving
- Annie Get Your Gun: Overture
- When I Lost You
- White Christmas

Bock, Jerry
- Fiddler on the Roof: Medley

Carmichael, Hoagy
- Georgia on My Mind
- Nearness of You
- Romance in the Dark, Nearness of You

Chaplin, Charlie
- City Lights

Cohan, George M.
- You're a Grand Old Flag

Coleman, Cy
- Witchcraft

Croce, Jim
- Jim Croce in Concert

Ellington, Edward K. (Duke)
- I Got it Bad and That Ain't Good
- Tribute to the Duke

Gade, Jacob
- Jalousie (Jealousy)

Garner, Erroll
- Misty

(Str – 2 2 2 2 – 2 3 3 1 – Perc, cont.)

Gershwin, George
- Man I Love

Gold, Marty
- Ecstasy
- Mancini Memories
- Rainy Day Medley

Goldsmith, Jerry
- Chinatown: Theme (1974)
- Patton (1970): The Hospital

Gould, Morton
- Swanee River in the Style of Liszt
- Swanee River in the Style of Rimsky-Korsakov

Griffes, Charles Tomlinson
- The White Peacock

Haggart, Bob
- What's New?

Hernandez, Rafael
- El Cumbanchero

Holst, Gustav
- Let All Mortal Flesh Keep Silence

Ives, Charles
- Christmas Music

Kern, Jerome
- Ol' Man River
- Show Boat Selections

Kreisler, Fritz
- Liebesfreud

Lai, Francis
- Love Story: Where Do I Begin

Lanner, Joseph
- Hofball-Tanze Waltz, Op. 161

Lloyd Webber, Andrew
- Cats Selections

Mancini, Henry
- Breakfast at Tiffanys: Moon River

Mandel, Johnny
- The Sandpiper: Shadow of Your Smile

Mandell, Robert
- Red River Valley

Masser, Michael
- Greatest Love of All

Maxwell, Robert
- Ebb Tide

Mendelssohn, Felix
- A Midsummer Night's Dream: Wedding March

Mercer, Johnny
- Skylark

Mills, Gordon & Reed, Les
- It's Not Unusual

Polster, Ian
- Salute to MGM: That's Entertainment

Porter, Cole
- Gay Divorcee: Night and Day

Powell, John H.
- At the Fair

Robinson, Earl
- The Lonesome Train

Rose, David
- Holiday for Strings

Rosenhaus, Steven L.
- Lionel Richie in Concert

Sainte-Marie & Nitzsche
- An Officer & A Gentleman: Up Where We Belong

Saint-Saëns, Camille
- La nuit Op. 114

Schifrin, Lalo
- Dialogues

Schoenberg, Claude-Michel
- Les Miserables: The ABC Café
- Les Miserables: At the End of the Day
- Les Miserables: Bring Him Home
- Les Miserables: Do You Hear the People Sing?
- Les Miserables: Empty Chairs at Empty Tables
- Les Miserables: I Dreamed A Dream
- Les Miserables: Little Cosette
- Les Miserables: Master of the House
- Les Miserables: On My Own
- Les Miserables: One Day More
- Les Miserables: Stars

Schuller, Gunther
- Concertino for Jazz Quartet & Orchestra (1959)

Schuman, William
- Newsreel in 5 Shots

Steffe, William
- Battle Hymn of the Republic

Steiner, Max
- King Kong: Jungle Dance

Still, William Grant
- Wood Notes: Singing River

Torme & Wells
- Christmas Song (Chestnuts Roasting on an Open Fire)

Warren, Harry
- Serenade in Blue

Webb, Jimmy
- The Animals' Christmas

STRINGS
2 2 3 2 – 2 3 3 1 – PERC

Bach, J. S.
- Arioso

Bernstein, Leonard
- On the Town: Three Dance Episodes

Christensen, James
- Snow Chase

Cunningham, Arthur
- Lullabye for a Jazz Baby

Curnow, James, arr.
- TV Spectacular

Diamond, Neil
- Jazz Singer Medley

Faith, Percy
- Quia, Quia (Kee-a, Kee-a)

Fain, Sammy
- Once Upon a Dream

Farnan, Robert
- Portrait of a Flirt

Goldsmith, Jerry
- Poltergeist (1982): The Calling

Gould, Morton
- Deserted Ballroom
- Holiday Music: Home for Christmas
- Holiday Music: Easter Morning
- Serenade of Carols (Choral Setting)

Griffes, Charles Tomlinson
- Poem for flute and orchestra

Grusin, Dave
- Theme from On Golden Pond

Kander, John
- Chicago

Lennon, John & McCartney, Paul
- The Best of the Beatles

Lloyd Webber, Andrew
- Cats: Memory
- Cats Selections

McDonald, Harl
- Dirge for Two Veterans

MacLellan, Gene
- Put Your Hand in the Hand

Phillips, John
- Monday, Monday

Phillips & Gilliam
- California Dreamin'

Polster
- Salute to MGM: That's Entertainment

Putman, Curly
- Green Green Grass of Home

Rodgers, Richard
- Richard Rodgers in Concert

Rosenhaus, Steven L.
- American Spiritual Festival
- Kitchen Percussion March for Special Guests and Orchestra

Sayre, Chuck
- Disney Adventure

Shostakovich, Dmitri
- United Nations March

Smith, Robert W.
- Great Steamboat Race

Stevens, Ray
- Everything is Beautiful

Styne, Jule
- Let It Snow! Let It Snow! Let It Snow!

Thomson, Virgil
- Fugue & Chorale on Yankee Doodle

Weill, Kurt
- The Two Worlds of Kurt Weill: Berlin Suite (Mack the Knife)

- The Two Worlds of Kurt Weill: New York Suite
- The Two Worlds of Kurt Weill: New York Suite (I Got a Marble and a Star)
- The Two Worlds of Kurt Weill: New York Suite (Mack the Knife)
- The Two Worlds of Kurt Weill: New York Suite (Speak Low)
- The Two Worlds of Kurt Weill: New York Suite (Train to Johannesburg)

Williams, Paul
- Rainy Days and Mondays

Zimmer, Hans
- The Last Samurai: The Way of the Sword

STRINGS
2 2 2 2 – 3 3 2 1 – PERC

Aguila, Miguel del
- Conga

Bach, J. S.
- Jesu, Joy of Man's Desiring

Castelnuovo-Tedesco, Mario
- Naomi and Ruth: Ruth's Aria

Gillis, Don
- This s Our America

Granda, Isabel
- La Flor de la Canela

Hamlisch, Marvin
- Selections from a Chorus Line

Handel, George Frideric
- Music for the Royal Fireworks

Kaper, Bronislau
- Them!: Ant Fugue (1954)

Lane, Philip
- Wassail Dances for Orchestra

Leighton, Kenneth
- Dance Suite No. 2

Lloyd Webber, Andrew
- The Phantom of the Opera Overture

Ottman, John
- The Usual Suspects (1995)

Portman, Rachel
- Chocolat: Suite (2000)
- Emma (1996)

Prokofiev, Sergei
- Peter and the Wolf

Schocker, Gary
- Green Places

Steiner, Max
- Jezebel (1938): Waltz

Tchaikovsky, Piotr Ilyich
- Humoresque

Welcher, Dan
- The Visions of Merlin

Yared, Gabriel
- The English Patient (1996)

STRINGS
2 2 2 2 – 4 0 0 0 – PERC

Bax, Arnold
- A Christmas Carol

Beck, Christophe
- Under the Tuscan Sun (2003): Suite

Coleridge-Taylor, Samuel
- Hiawatha's Wedding Feast: Onaway! Awake Beloved

Debussy, Claude
- Clair de lune

Heath, Dave
- Out of the Cool

Kaczmarek, Jan A.P.
- Finding Neverland: Suite (2004)

McPartland, Marian
- Melancholy Mood

Nielsen, Carl August
- Masquerade: Prelude to Act II

Ottman, John
- Superman Returns Suite

Satie, Erik
- Gymnopedie No. 1 & 3

Sieczynsky
- Vienna-City of My Dreams

Shostakovich, Dmitri
- Eight English and American Folk Songs: When Johnny Comes Marching Home

Waxman, Franz
- The Bride of Frankenstein (1935)

Wendel, Robert
- Towers of Light

STRINGS
2 2 2 2 – 4 2 0 0 – PERC

Bantock, Granville
- Old English Suite

Beethoven, Ludwig van
- Egmont: Overture

Fauré, Gabriel
- Pelleas et Melisande, Op. 80

Handel, George Frideric
- Water Music Suite

Kodaly, Zoltán
- Dances of Marosszek

Rodrigo, Joaquin
- Concierto andaluz

Sibelius, Jean
- Academic March

Strauss, Johann, Jr.
- Lucifer Polka, Op. 266

STRINGS
2 2 2 2 – 4 2 1 1 – PERC

Bizet, Georges
- Carmen: Flower Song

Barry, John
- Somewhere in Time

Eiger, Walter
- Concerto Grosso

Halvorsen, Johan
- Norwegian Fairy Pictures

Mussorgsky, Modest
- The Song of the Flea

Prokofiev, Sergei
- Winter Bonfire: Suite, Op. 122

Rossini, Gioacchino
- La gazza ladra (The Thieving Magpie): Overture

Shostakovich, Dmitri
- Tahiti-Trot, Op. 16

Strauss, Johann, Jr.
- An der schönen blauen Donau (On the Beautiful Blue Danube), Op. 314
- Annen Polka, Op. 117
- Champagne Polka, Op. 211
- Eine Nacht in Venedig: Lagunenwalzer, Op. 411
- Künstler (Artist's) Quadrille, Op. 201
- Morgenblätter (Morning papers), Op. 279
- Perpetuum mobile, Op. 257
- Telgramme Walzer, Op. 318
- Vergnugungszug Polka (Excursion Train), Op. 281

Strauss, Josef
- Aus Ferienreisen, Op. 133
- Dorfschwalben aus Osterreich (Austrian Village Swallows), Op. 164

Waxman, Franz
- A Christmas Carol (1939): Christmas Morning & Finale
- A Christmas Carol (1939): Five Sketches after Dickens

STRINGS
2 2 2 2 – 4 2 2 1 – PERC

Abreu, Zequinha de
- Tico Tico

Adam, Adolphe
- Christmas with Renata Scotto: 5. Christmas Song (Cantique deNoel)

Arnold, Malcolm
- Hobson's Choice

Bartók, Béla
- Dance Suite

Gould, Morton
- Classical Variations on Colonial Themes

(Str – 2 2 2 2 – 4 2 2 1 – Perc – GOULD, cont.)

- Flares and Declamations
- Tap Dance Concerto

Guaraldi, Vince
- A Charlie Brown Christmas

Hamlisch, Marvin
- Chorus Line

Herbert, Victor
- The Enchantress: Art Is Calling for Me (I Want to Be a Prima Donna)

Hernández, Rafael
- El Cumbanchero

Jarre, Maurice
- Ryan's Daughter: Rosy's Theme (1970)

Moross, Jerome
- Wagon Train

Perillo, Steve
- Hangoverture

Rebagliati, Claudio
- Rapsodia Peruana

Sallinen, Aulis
- At the Palace Gates: Overture, Op. 68a

Schickele, Peter
- The Chenoo Who Stayed to Dinner
- Legend

Tiomkin, Dimitri
- It's a Wonderful Life (1947): Theme
- A President's Country (1966): Medley

STRINGS
3 2 2 2 – 4 2 2 1 – PERC

Bernstein, Elmer
- Ghostbusters: Theme

Bernstein, Leonard
- Candide: Glitter and Be Gay

Brahms, Johannes
- Hungarian Dances Nos. 1,3,10

Constantinescu, Paul
- Ciobănașul: The Shepherd Boy

Holst, Gustav
- Christmas Day

Iannaccone, Anthony
- From Time to Time

Nórgård, Per
- Three Love Songs

Powell, John
- Endurance: the Great Tree
- A Set of Three

Reznicek, Emil Nikolaus von
- Donna Diana: Overture

Rózsa, Miklos
- Ben Hur: Rowing of the Galley Slaves

Sousa, John Philip
- Semper Fidelis March
- Washington Post March

Strauss, Josef
- Elfen Polka Op. 74

Strauss, Richard
- Burleske

Theodorakis, Mikis
- Zorba the Greek (1964): Theme

Wagenaar, Bernard
- Concert Overture

Wendel, Robert
- In the Manger

STRINGS
2 2 2 2 – 4 2 3 0 – PERC

Arlen, Harold
- Wizard of Oz: Over the Rainbow

Arnold, Malcolm
- Anniversary Overture, Op. 99
- Four Scottish Dances
- Solitaire, Op. 141: Sarabande and Polka

Auber, Daniel-François
- Fra Diavolo: Overture

Bach, J. S.
- Prelude in E flat minor

Bernstein, Elmar
- To Kill a Mockingbird: Suite

Bizet, Georges
- Carmen Fantasia
- Carmen: Seguidilla and Duett
- Carmen: Suite no. 1
- Carmen: Toreador Song

Bliss, Arthur
- Checkmate: Five Dances Suite

Borodin, Alexander
- In the Steppes of Central Asia

Brahms, Johannes
- Hungarian Dance No. 1
- Hungarian Dances Nos. 1 & 3
- Hungarian Dance No. 4
- Hungarian Dance No. 5 & 6

Britten, Benjamin
- Soirees Musicales, Op. 9

Broughton, Bruce
- The Boy Who Could Fly: Theme

Bush, Geoffrey
- Concerto for Light Orchestra
- Yorick Overture

Donizetti, Gaetano
- La fille du régiment (Daughter of the Regiment): Overture
- Lucia di Lammermoor, Act II: Sestetto: Chi mi frena

Dvořák, Antonin
- Slavonic Dances Op. 72

Dyson, George
- Symphony in G

Fučik, Julius
- Entry of the Gladiators, Op. 68

Geehl, Henry
- Overture Française

German, Edward
- Gypsy Suite

Granados, Enrique
- Goyescas: Intermezzo

Halvorsen, Johan
- Norwegian Festival Overture, Op. 16

Liszt, Franz
- Hungarian Rhapsody No. 2

Lloyd Webber, Andrew
- The Phantom of the Opera Entr'Acte

Monti, Vittorio
- Czardas

Nicolai, Otto
- Merry Wives of Windsor Overture

Offenbach, Jacques
- Les Contes d'Hoffmann (Tales of Hoffmann): Intermezzo & Barcarolle

Popper, David
- Hungarian Rhapsodie, Op. 68

Ponchielli, Amilcare
- La Gioconda: Dance of the Hour

Quilter, Roger
- Where the Rainbow Ends Suite

Riege, Ernst
- Bezaubernde Gloriette, Konzertwalzer
- Katharinen-Waltz

Rimsky-Korsakov, Nicolai
- May Night: Overture

Rossini, Gioacchino
- Guillaume Tell (William Tell): Overture
- Semiramide: Overture

Sarasate, Pablo de
- Carmen Fantasie on Themes of Bizet, Op. 25

Schubert, Franz
- Die Zauberharfe (Rosamunde) D. 644: Overture

Sibelius, Jean
- Hymn to the Earth
- Valse chevaleresque, Op. 96c
- Valse lyrique, Op. 96a

Simons, Netty
- Big Sur

Strauss, Johann, Jr.
- Annen Polka, Op. 117
- Banditen Galopp (Bandit's Galop), Op. 378
- Die Fledermaus (Laughing Song)
- Die Fledermaus: Du und du (You and You Waltz), Op.367
- Die Fledermaus: Overture
- Eine nacht in Venedig: Fruhlingsstimmen Waltz (Voices of Spring), Op. 410
- Graduation Ball (Ballet in one act)

- Im Krapfenwald, Polka française, Op. 336
- Kaiser Walzer (Emperor Waltzes), Op. 437
- Perpetuum Mobile, Op. 257
- Persian March, Op. 289
- Rosen aus dem Süden (Roses from the South Waltzes), Op. 388
- Thousand and One Nights Waltz, Op. 346
- Tick-Tack Polka, Op. 365
- Unter Donner und Blitz (Thunder and Lightning Polka), Op. 324
- Von der Borse, Polka française, Op. 337
- Waldmeister Overture
- Wein, Weib und Gesang (Wine, Women, and Song), Op. 333
- Wiener Blut (Vienna Blood), Op. 354
- Zigeunerbaron (Gypsy Baron): Overture

Strauss, Johann and Josef
- Pizzicato Polka

Suppé, Franz von
- Die schöne Galathea (The Beautiful Galatea): Overture
- Ein Morgen, ein Mittag und ein Abend in Wien (Morning, Noon, and Night in Vienna): Overture

Tchaikovsky, Peter Ilyich
- Eugen Onegin: Polonaise
- Nutcracker Dances, Set I

Tomlinson, Ernest
- Suite of English Folk Dances

Walton, William
- Crown Imperial (Coronation March)

Weber, Carl Maria von
- Oberon: Overture

Weinberger, Jaromir
- Bohemian Songs and Dances

Ziehrer, C. M.
- Herreinspaziert! Waltz, Op. 518

STRINGS
3 2 2 2 – 4 2 3 0 – PERC

Constantinescu, Paul
- Olteneasca

Copland, Aaron
- An Outdoor Overture

Dvořák, Antonin
- Slavonic Dances Op. 46, Nos. 1-4
- Slavonic Dances Op. 46, Nos. 5-8

Falla, Manuel de
- El amor brujo: Ritual Fire Dance

Fučik, Julius
- Entrance of the Gladiators, Op. 68

Gomez, Alice
- Festive Huapango

Lalo, Edouard
- Symphonie Espagnole, Op. 21

Mindreau, Ernesto López
- Marinera y Tondero

Portman, Rachel
- Oliver Twist: Suite (2005)

Rodríguez, Robert Xavier
- Sinfonia a la mariachi

Strauss, Johann, Sr.
- Radetzky March

Smetana, Bedrich
- The Bartered Bride: Three Dances

Toch, Ernst
- Pinocchio, A Merry Overture

STRINGS
2 2 2 2 – 4 2 3 1 – PERC

Adam, Adolphe Charles
- O Holy Night (Cantique de Noel)

Antheil, George
- Hot-Time Dance

Barroso, Ary
- Brazil (Aquarela do Brasil)

Barry, John
- Robin and Marian

Bellini, Vincenzo
- Romeo and Juliet: Overture

Bennett, Richard Rodney
- Variations on a Nursery Tune

Berkeley, Lennox
- Palm Court Music, Op. 81, No. 2

Bizet, Georges
- Carmen: Suite no. 2
- Jeux d'enfants, Op. 22: Petite Suite (Children's Games)

Blake, Howard
- Agatha: Suite

Blyton, Carey
- Cinque Port, Op. 28

Britten, Benjamin
- Gloriana: The Courtly Dances

Broughton, Bruce
- Young Sherlock Holmes (1985): Suite

Camilleri, Charles
- Maltese Dances

Creston, Paul
- Fantasy for Trombone, Op. 42

DePonte, Niel
- Bell of Freedom (2002)

Downey, John
- Jingalodeon

Duffy, John
- Heritage Symphonic Dances

Elgar, Edward
- Nursery Suite
- Wand of Youth Suite No. 1, Op. 1a
- Wand of Youth Suite No. 2, Op. 1b

Ellstein, Abraham
- Ode to the King of Kings

Errázuriz, Sebastián
- La Caravana

Esposito, Michele
- Irish Suite

Fiedel, Brad
- The Teminator: Theme (1984)

Gimenez, Jeronimo
- La Boda de Luis Alonso: Intermedio

Glinka, Mikhail
- Ruslan and Ludmilla: Overture

Gould, Morton
- Battle Hymn of the Republic
- Christmas Time, Book I
- Christmas Time, Book I: Adeste Fidelis- Christmas Time, Book I: First Noel
- Christmas Time, Book I: O Little Town/Away in a Manger
- Christmas Time, Book 1: Silent Night

Grainger, Percy
- Country Gardens
- Molly on the Shore

Gutierrez, Pedro Elias
- Alma Llanera

Halvorsen, Johan
- Entry of the Boyars
- Norwegian Rhapsody No.1 in A

Handel, George Frideric
- Variations on a Theme by Handel

Hérold, Louis
- Zampa Overture

Ivanovici, Josif
- Waves of the Danube: The Anniversary Song

Joubert, John
- The Novello Book of Carols: Torches 1
- The Novello Book of Carols: Torches II

Kelly, Bryan
- Improvisations on Christmas Carols

Khachaturian, Aram
- Masquerade Suite

Legrand, Michel
- I Will Wait for You

López, Jimmy
- Fiesta! for orchestra
- Lago de Lágrimas (Lake of Tears)

Malotte, Albert Hay
- The Lord's Prayer

Mancini, Henry
- The Great Race: They're Off

Marquez, Arturo
- Danzon No. 2

McBride, Robert
- Pumpkin Eater's Little Fugue

Morricone, Ennio
- Legend of 1900: Romanza

Morris, John
- Young Frankenstein: The Transylvanian Lullaby (1974)

(Str – 2 2 2 2 – 4 2 3 1 – Perc, cont.)

Mussorgsky, Modest
- Songs and Dances of Death
O'Boyle, Sean
- Country Kazoo Overture
Offenbach, Jacques
- Orpheus in the Underworld Overture
Pachelbel, Johann
- Kanon in D Major
Peck, Russell
- Playing With Style
Penella, Manuel
- El Gato Montés (The Bobcat)
Portman, Rachel
- The Cider House Rules (1999)
Rhodes, Phillip
- Bluegrass Festival: Suite for Bluegrass Quartet and Orchestra
Richman, Lucas
- In the Day When I Cried Out
Riege, Ernst
- Ewiges Wien
Rimsky-Korsakov, Nicolai
- The Tale of Tsar Saltan (Flight of the Bumble Bee)
Robles, Daniel Alomia
- El Condor Pasa (The Condor Flies Past)
Rodriguez, Robert Xavier
- Jargon: The Story of the American Constitution
- Trunks, A Circus Story for Narrator and Orchestra
Rota, Nino
- The Godfather II (1974)
Sakamoto, Ryuichi
- The Last Emperor: Theme (1987)
Schubert, Franz
- Ave Maria
Schurmann, Gerard
- Attack and Celebration
Sebastian
- A Fairytale: Suite from the Ballet
Shaiman, Marc
- American President: Big Speech, Big Finish
Sieczynski, Rudolf
- Vienna-City of My Dreams
Strauss, Johann, Jr.
- Egyptian March, Op. 335
- Künstlerleben (Artist's Life) Waltz, Op. 316
- Morgenblätter (Morning Papers), Op. 279
- Moulinet Polka, Op. 57
Strauss, Josef
- Dorfschwalben aus Osterreich (Austrian Village Swallows), Op. 164

Stravinsky, Igor
- Circus Polka
- L'Oiseau de feu (Firebird): Suite (1919)
Sullivan, Arthur
- Mikado Selections
- Ruddigore Selections
Suppé, Franz von
- Dichter und Bauer (Poet and Peasant): Overture
- Die leichte Kavallerie (Light Cavalry): Overture
Surinach, Carlos
- Feria Mágica (Magic Fair), Overture
- Sinfonietta flamenca
Thomson, Virgil
- Louisiana Story: Orchestral Suite
Tyzik, Jeff
- Holiday Moods: Suite No. 1 for chorus and orchestra
- Holiday Moods: Suite No. 2 for chorus and orchestra
- Holiday Moods: Suite No. 3 for chorus and orchestra
Vaughan Williams, Ralph
- Three Choral Hymns: Easter, Christmas, Whitsunday
Verdi, Giuseppe
- La forza del destino: Overture
- Nabucco: Overture
Villaldo & Matos Rodríguez
- El Choclo & La Cumparsita
Wagner, Richard
- Die Walküre: Wotan's Farewell and Magic Fire Music
Waldteufel, Emile
- Les Patineurs (Skater's Waltz), Op. 183
Wendel
- A Halloween Trilogy: The Pit and the Pendulum
Zyman, Samuel
- Encuentros (1992)

STRINGS
3 3 2 2 – 4 2 3 1 – PERC

Anderson, Leroy
- Penny Whistle Song
Berlioz, Hector
- Damnation de Faust: Hungarian March (Rakoczy)
Borodin, Alexander
- Prince Igor: Overture
- Prince Igor: Polovtsian Dances
- Symphony No. 2
Brahms, Johannes
- Tragische Ouverture (Tragic Overture), Op. 81

Britten, Benjamin
- Young Person's Guide to the Orchestra, Op. 34
Buck, Dudley
- Festival Overture on the American National Air: The Star-Spangled Banner
Coleridge-Taylor, Samuel
- Scenes from The Song of Hiawatha, Op. 30: No. 1. Hiawatha's Wedding Feast
Corigliano, John
- The Red Violin: Chaconne for Violin and Orchestra
Creston, Paul
- Two Choric Dances, Op. 17B
Fletcher, H. Grant
- An American Overture
Friedhofer, Hugo
- The Bishop's Wife: Ice Skater's Waltz (1947)
Gade, Jacob
- Tango Jalousie (Tango Tzigane)
German, Edward
- Valse gracieuse
Grainger, Percy
- Tribute to Foster
Grieg, Edvard
- Peer Gynt: Suite No. 1
- Lyric Suite: March of the Dwarfs
- Norwegian Dances, Op. 35
Guarnieri, Camargo
- Dansa Brasileira
Guion, David
- De Laud's Baptizin'
Halvorsen, Johan
- Norwegian Rhapsody No. 2 in G
Herbert, Victor
- American Fantasie
- Irish Rhapsody
Høffding, Finn
- Celebrations of May-Day
Humperdinck, Engelbert
- Hansel and Gretel: Overture
- Hansel und Gretel: Hexenritt (Witch's Ride)
- Hansel und Gretel: Three Excerpts
Johnson, Francis
- Buffalo City Guard Parade March
- General Cadwalader's Grand March
- Philadelphia Grays Quickstep
Lara, Agustín
- Granada
Lehár, Franz
- The Count of Luxembourg: Waltz
Liszt, Franz
- Mephisto Waltz No. 1 (from Lenau's Faust)
- Mephisto Waltz No. 2 (from Lenau's Faust)
- Totentanz

Luigini, Alexandre
- Ballet Egyptien

Mussorgsky, Modest
- A Night on Bald Mountain
- The Dream of the Peasant Gritzko

Newman, Alfred
- David & Bathsheba

Nielsen, Carl August
- Rhapsodic Overture

Powell, John
- Natchez on the Hill, Three Virginia Country Dances

Puccini, Giocomo
- Le Villi: The Witches' Sabbath

Rimsky-Korsakov, Nicolai
- Capriccio Espagnol, Op. 34
- Scheherazade: 4. The Sea-Shipwreck

Rodríguez, Robert Xavier
- A Colorful Symphony

Saint-Saëns, Camille
- Danse Macabre, Op. 40

Slonimsky, Nicolas
- My Toy Balloon: Variations on a Brazilian Tune

Smetana, Bedrich
- Má Vlast (My Fatherland): 2. Vltava (Moldau)

Smith, John Stafford
- Star-Spangled Banner

Soro, Enrique
- Danza Fantástica

Sowerby, Leo
- Two Romantic Pieces

Strauss, Johann, Sr.
- Radetzky March, Op. 228

Tchaikovsky, Piotr Ilyich
- Nutcracker Dances, Set II
- Symphony No. 1 in G Minor, Op. 13: Winter Dreams

Toch, Ernst
- Circus Overture

Verdi, Giuseppe
- Aïda: Triumphal March

Wendel, Robert
- Under the Big Top

Zinn, William
- Symphony in Ragtime

STRINGS
2 2 2 2 – 4 3 2 1 – PERC

Antheil, George
- Archipelago "Rhumba"

Berlin, Irving
- God Bless America

Barroso, Ary
- Brazil

Bloch, Ernest
- Suite Hébraïque

Chase, Bruce
- Broadway Tonight

Geehl, Henry
- A Comedy Overture

Gillis, Don
- This Is Our America

Gould, Morton
- Big City Blues
- Christmas Time, Book II: Home for Christmas
- Holiday Music: Home for Christmas

Jarre, Maurice
- Lara's Theme from Dr. Zhivago
- Witness: Building the Barn

Joel, Billy
- The Best of Billy Joel

Kern, Jerome
- Smoke Gets in Your Eyes

Knight, Eric
- Kidnapped: Overture

Mendelssohn
- Hark! The Herald Angels Sing

Pachelbel, Johann
- Ordinary People Theme: Canon in D

Peaslee, Richard
- Arrows of Time

Reisfeld, Bert
- California Concerto

Sayre, Charles
- A Rockin' Christmas

Schifrin, Lalo
- Dialogues

Schoenberg, Claude-Michel
- Les Miserables: Master of the House
- Les Miserables: On My Own

Sondheim, Stephen
- Little Night Music: Send in the Clowns

STRINGS
2 3 2 2 – 4 3 3 0 – PERC

Alwyn, William
- Elizabethan Dances

Berlioz, Hector
- Béatrice et Bénédict: Overture

Cunningham, Arthur
- Rooster Rhapsody

Daugherty, Michael
- Metropolis Symphony: 4. Oh, Lois!

Debussy
- Clair de lune
- La fille au cheveux de lin

Edwards, Gus
- By the Light of the Silvery Moon

Gershwin, George
- Porgy and Bess: Summertime

Goldsmith, Jerry
- The Wild Rovers (1971): Bronco Busting

Gould, Morton
- Symphonette No. 2
- Symphonette No. 2: Pavane

Grieg, Edvard
- Wedding Day at Troldhaugen, Op. 65, No. 6

Herman, Jerry
- Selections from La Cage aux Folles

Herrmann, Bernard
- The Snows of Kilimijaro (1952)

Heuberger, Richard
- Melodies of Richard Heuberger

Leigh, Mitch
- Man of La Mancha: Selections

Mancini, Henry
- The Pink Panther

Offenbach, Jacques
- Orpheus in the Underworld: Galop (Can Can)

Strauss, Johann, Jr.
- Eljen A Magyar! (Long Live the Magyar), Op. 332

Ulbrich, Siegfried
- Blue City, Impression for Piano and Orchestra

Weill, Kurt
- The Two Worlds of Kurt Weill: Berlin Suite (Theme from "Mahogonny")
- The Worlds of Kurt Weill: New York Suite (My Ship)
- The Two Worlds of Kurt Weill: New York Suite (Polly's Lied)

Whelan, Bill
- Riverdance Theme

Williams, John T.
- The Empire Strikes Back Medley

STRINGS
2 2 2 2 – 4 3 3 1 – PERC

Anderson, Leroy
- The First Day of Spring
- Forgotten Dreams
- Jazz Legato
- Jazz Pizzicato
- The Phantom Regiment
- Summer Skies
- The Syncopated Clock
- A Trumpeter's Lullaby

Antheil, George
- Accordion Dance
- Tom Sawyer Overture (California Overture)

Arlen, Harold
- Blues in the Night

Arnold, Alan
- Israeli Work Song
- Three Colombian Songs
- Three Crazy Pieces
- Variations for Orchestra

(Str – 2 2 2 2 – 4 3 3 1 – Perc, cont.)

Arnold, Malcolm
 - A Grand, Grand Overture, Op. 57
 - Sarabande and Polka from Solitaire, Op. 141
 - Symphonic Study: Machines, Op. 30
 - Tam O'Shanter: Overture, Op. 51
Ayars, Bo
 - American Fanfare
Bach, J. S.
 - Jesu, Joy of Man's Desiring
 - Sleepers Awake (Wachet Auf)
Baerwald, David
 - Moulin Rouge: Come What May
Balada, Leonardo
 - Homage to Sarasate
Ball, Ernest R.
 - When Irish Eyes Are Smiling
Barry, John
 - The Best of Bond
Beatles
 - Beatles Hits Medley
Bennett, Richard Rodney
 - Murder on the Orient Express Suite
 - Murder on the Orient Express Theme: Foxtrot Theme
 - Murder on the Orient Express Waltz
Berlin, Irving
 - Berlin Patriotic Overture
 - Easter Parade
 - Irving Berlin: A Symphonic Portrait for Chorus & Orchestra
Bernstein, Elmer
 - The Birdman of Alcatraz: Finale
Bernstein, Leonard
 - West Side Story Highlights
 - West Side Story Overture
Bizet, Georges
 - Carmen: Flower Song
Blane, Ralph
 - Have Yourself A Merry Little Christmas
Bliss, Arthur
 - Christopher Columbus
 - Things to Come: Suite
Borodin, Alexander
 - In the Steppes of Central Asia
Broughton, Bruce
 - Themes from Silverado
Brubeck, Dave
 - The Gates of Justice: Out of the Way of the People
Cohan, George M.
 - Cohan Medley
 - Star-Spangled Spectacular
Coolidge, Peggy
 - Spirituals in Sunshine and Shadow
Copland, Aaron
 - Happy Anniversary

Corigliano, John
 - Gazebo Dances: Overture to the Imaginary Invalid
 - Gazebo Dances for Orchestra
DeLarmarter, Eric
 - Christmastide
Dankworth, John
 - The Diamond and the Goose
Dennison, Sam
 - And If Elected…
Deussen, Nancy Bloomer
 - Regalos
Duke, Vernon
 - April in Paris
Elfman, Danny
 - Simpsons Theme
Ellington, Edward K. (Duke) and Strayhorn, Billy
 - Deep South Suite: Happy Go Lucky Local
 - The Essential Ellington: Music of Ellington and Strayhorn
Ellington, Edward K. (Duke)
 - It Don't Mean a Thing (If it Ain't Got That Swing)
 - Satin Doll (vocal version)
 - The River
Fried, Gerald
 - Roots: Suite (1977)
Friedhofer, Hugo
 - The Best Years of Our Lives: Suite
Gabrieli, Giovanni
 - Canzon XVI
Garner, Erroll
 - Misty
Gershwin, George
 - Foggy Day
 - A Gershwin Portrait
 - Porgy and Bess: Summertime
 - Strike Up the Band
 - 'S Wonderful
Gilbertson, Michael
 - Reflections on Rushmore
Goldsmith, Jerry
 -The Edge (1997): Main Title & Finale
 - Gremlins: Suite
 - Gremlins 2 (1990): The New Batch: Main Title
Gould, Morton
 - Christmas Time, Book II
 - Christmas Time, Book II: Jingle Bells
 - Family Album: Suite
 - Holiday Music
 - Holiday Music: Christmas
 - Holiday Music: First Thanksgiving
 - Holiday Music: Fourth of July
 - Holiday Music: Halloween
 - Minstrel Show
 - Philharmonic Waltzes
 - Red Cavalry March

 - Windjammer: Main Theme; The Ship
Green, John
 - Body and Soul
Grieg, Edvard
 - Ich Liebe Dich
 - To Spring
 - Wedding Day at Troldhaugen
Gruber, F.X.
 - Silent Night
Handel
 - Joy to the World
Hayman, Richard
 - Her Name is Suzanne
Heath, Dave
 - Alone at the Frontier: Concerto for Improvised Instrument and Orchestra
Herbert, Victor
 - Ah Sweet Mystery of Life
Holdridge, Lee
 - Beauty and the Beast: Theme
Jackson, Michael
 - A Michael Jackson Spectacular
Jameson, Tom & Feller, Sherm
 - Summertime, Summertime
Kander
 - New York, New York Theme
Kern, Jerome
 - Show Boat Overture
Kirk, Theron
 - An Orchestra Primer
Kern, Jerome
 - They Didn't Believe Me
Lecuona, Ernesto
 - Andalucia Suite: Malagueña
Lehár, Franz
 - The Merry Widow: Symphonic Paraphrase
Lloyd Webber, Andrew
 - The Phantom of the Opera: Concert Version
López, Jimmy
 - América Salvaje (Wild America)
Maggio, Robert
 - Big Top
 - The Hand-Prints of Sorcerers
Mancini, Henry
 - The Pink Panther
Meyer, George W.
 - If You Were the Only Girl in the World
Milhaud, Darius
 - Two Marches
Nelson, Ronald J.
 - Rocky Point Holiday
O'Boyle, Sean
 - Silent Movie Music
Ottman, John
 - Hide and Seek: Main Titles
Paich & Porcaro
 - Africa

Porter, Cole
- You Do Something to Me

Powell, John
- Mr. and Mrs. Smith: Tango de los Asesinos

Ranjbaran, Behzad
- Thomas Jefferson

Rimelis, David
- Please Turn Your Cell Phones On!

Ringwald, Roy
- The Song of Easter

Robinson, Earl
- A Country They Call Puget Sound

Robinson & Giovannini
- Brazilian Polka

Rodgers, Richard
- King and I Selections
- Love Me Tonight: Lover

Rota, Nino
- Romeo and Juliet: Suite (1968)

Rouse, Christopher
- Karolju

Rouse, Ervin
- Orange Blossom Special

Rósza, Miklós
- Double Indemnity: Suite

Ryden, William
- Amazing Grace

Salzedo, Leonard
- The Witch Boy: Suite from the Ballet
- The Witch Boy: Three Dances from the Ballet

Sayre, Charles
- A Christmas Tradition

Schickele, Peter
- A Zoo Called Earth

Schifrin, Lalo
- Mission Impossible: Theme

Schwartz, Stephen
- Dancing in the Dark

Scott, Raymond
- Powerhouse

Shulman, Alan
- Hup Two Three Four

Sibelius, Jean
- Finlandia, Op. 26, No. 7

Shire, David
- Raid on Entebbe (1977): Theme

Steffe, William
- Battle Hymn of the Republic

Stokowski, Leopold
- Traditional Slavic Christmas

Strauss, Johann, Jr.
- Geschichten aus dem Wienerwald (Tales from the Vienna Woods), Op. 325
- Unter Donner und Blitz (Thunder and Lightning Polka), Op.324

Strauss, Josef
- Ohne Sorgen Polka, Op. 271
- Plappermaulchen Polka Schnell (Chatterbox), Op. 245

Strayhorn, Billy
- Chelsea Bridge

Stucky, Steven
- Fanfare for Los Angeles

Styne, Jule
- Let It Snow! Let It Snow! Let It Snow!

Templeton, Alec
- Operation Mambo

Tiomkin, Dmitri
- High Noon (1952): Suite
- Rio Bravo (1959): Suite
- Wild is the Wind (1958): Theme

Towers, Joan
- Stepping Stones: Celebration Fanfare

Turrin, Joseph
- Civil War Suite

Tyzik, Jeff
- Amazing Grace
- Chanukah Suite
- A Christmas Overture (Variations on Deck the Halls)
- Hot Soul Medley
- Symphonic Swing

Walker, Robert
- My Dog Has Fleas: A Capriccio for Scratch Orchestra

Waxman, Franz
- Huckleberry Finn (1939): Overture
- Sorry, Wrong Number (1948): Passacaglia

Wenrich, Percy
- When You Wore a Tulip

Whitney, John
- Light Rays

Williams, Charles
- The Apartment

Williams, John T.
- E.T., Theme from
- Highlights from Return of the Jedi

STRINGS
2 2 3 2 – 4 3 3 1 – PERC

Badelt, Klaus
- Pirates of the Caribbean: The Black Pearl

Bagley, Edwin Eugene
- National Emblem March

Barber, Samuel
- Die Natali (Chorale Preludes for Christmas) Op. 37: Silent Night

Barry, John
- Dances with Wolves: Concert Suite
- Somewhere In Time

Bennett, Robert Russell
- Columbia, the Gem of the Ocean
- Suite of Old American Dances

Bernard, Felix
- Winter Wonderland

Bock, Jerry
- Fiddler on the Roof

Brower, Russell
- World of Warcraft (Video Game)

Brubaker, Jerry
- Touch of Jazz!

Bullock, Jack
- NYC: Here's to the Big Apple

Chase, Bruce
- Christmas Favorites
- Muppet Medley

Custer, Calvin
- A Salute to the Big Apple
- Salute to the Big Bands Medley
- Star Trek Through the Years

Elfman, Danny
- Music from Spider Man

Estefan, Gloria
- Reach

Farrar, John
- Grease: You're the One that I Want

Finn, William
- Selections from 25th Annual Putnam County Spelling Bee

Flaherty, Stephen
- Anastasia Medley

Ford, Ralph
- Suite from Video Games Live

Gershwin, George
- Porgy and Bess: Selections for Orchestra (1961)
- Promenade: Walkin' the Dog or The Real McCoy

Gold, Marty
- Brazil

Goldsmith, Jerry
- Rambo: First Blood, Part 2 (1985): Theme
- Sleeping with the Enemy (1991): Theme

Gould, Morton
- Dance Gallery: Soft Shoe Gavotte
- Lincoln Legend

Gounod, Charles
- Faust: Ballet Music

Gregson-Williams, Harry
- Chronicles of Narnia: The Lion, the Witch and the Wardrobe

Hardiman, Ronan
- Lord of the Dance

Herrmann, Bernard
- Citizen Kane Overture

Hodkinson, Sydney
- Overture: A Little Travelin' Music

Hooper, Nicolas & Williams, John T.
- Harry Potter and the Order of the Phoenix: Concert Suite

Horner, James
- Apollo 13: Main Title, End Credits, Re-Entry and Splashdown

(Str – 2 2 3 2 – 4 3 3 1 – Perc – HORNER, cont.)

- James Horner-Hollywood Blockbusters: Apollo 13; American Tail; Braveheart; Titanic

Jessel, Leon
- Parade of the Wooden Soldiers

Kamen, Michael
- Band of Brothers
- Robin Hood: Prince of Thieves (Main Title)

Kander, John
- Chicago: Medley

Kaper, Bronislau
- Auntie Mame: Overture (1958)

Kosma, Joseph
- Autumn Leaves

Krogstad, Bob
- The Bells of Christmas
- Christmas at the Movies

Lawrence, David
- High School Musical

Lawrence, David
- High School Musical 2

Lloyd Webber, Andrew
- Music from Evita
- Medley from Jesus Christ Superstar
- The Phantom of the Opera Selections

Loesser, Frank
- Selections from Guys and Dolls

Lowden, Bob
- Armed Forces Salute
- A Disney Supertime (from Mary Poppins)

Mancini, Henry
- Dear Heart
- The Lifeforce
- The Molly Maguires: Pennywhistle Jig (1970)
- Pennywhistle Jig
- Peter Gunn Meets Mr. Lucky
- The Pink Panther
- The Pink Panther: It Had Better Be Tonight (Meglio Stasera)

Markowitz, Richard
- Wild, Wild West

Marquina, Pascual
- Espana Cani

McBroom, Amanda
- The Rose

Mejía, Adolfo
- Acuarela (Watercolor)

Moross, Jerome
- Frankie and Johnny

Morricone, Ennio
- I Knew I Loved You

Moss, John
- Salute to Ol' Blue Eyes

Nelson, Steve & Rollins, Jack
- Frosty the Snowman

Newman, Alfred
- Gentleman's Agreement Suite

North, Alex
- Viva Zapata (1952): Gathering Forces

Perry, Sam
- The Phantom of the Opera (1930)

Powell, John
- Happy Feet: The Story of Mumble

Ricketts, Ted
- Satchmo! (A Tribute to Louis Armstrong)

Rodgers, Richard
- King and I Selections
- Victory at Sea

Rózsa, Miklós
- Ben-Hur: Love Theme

Sayre, Chuck
- Christmas Vision
- Jerome Robbins Broadway

Schoenberg, Claude-Michel
- Les Miserables Selections
- Miss Saigon Medley

Schuman, William
- Circus Overture: Sideshow

Sheldon, Robert
- A Most Wonderful Christmas

Shore, Howard
- The Lord of the Rings: Suite from The Return of the King

Silvestri
- Forrest Gump: Suite

Sondheim, Stephen
- A Little Night Music: Send In the Clowns

Steiner, Max
- Gone With the Wind: Tara's Short Poem for Orchestra
- Now, Voyager (1942): Main Title and Final Scene

Strauss, Johann, Jr.
- Perpetuum mobile, Op. 257

Strommen, Carl
- A Salute to Broadway
- A Salute to the Cinema
- Salute to TV

Strouse, Charles
- Muscal Highlights from Annie

Tallarico, Tommy & Plowman, Michael
- Advent Rising Suite: Bounty Hunter Theme

Tiomkin, Dimitri
- The Unforgiven
- The Wild, Wild West (1965): Suite

Torme & Wells
- Christmas Song (Chestnuts Roasting on an Open Fire)

Tyzik, Jeff
- Twelve Gifts of Christmas

Valens, Ritchie
- La Bamba

Vandervalk, Bruce
- A Reagan Portrait

Vangelis
- Chariots of Fire

Waxman, Franz
- Botany Bay (1953): Suite
- Cimarron (1960): Suite
- Come Back, Little Sheba (1953): Reminiscences for Orchestra
- The Furies (1950): Suite
- My Geisha (1961): You Are Sympathy to Me
- The Pioneer (1951): Suite
- The Silver Chalice (1954): Short Suite
- The Silver Chalice (1954): Suite
- Sunset Boulevard (1950): Staged Reading in Two Acts
- Sunset Boulevard (1950): Suite

Weber, Carl Maria von
- Invitation to the Dance

Weill, Kurt
- The Two Worlds of Kurt Weill - Berlin Suite
- The Two Worlds of Kurt Weill - Berlin Suite: Bilbao Song

Wendel, Robert
- An Irish Trilogy

Williams, John T.
- Star Wars: Selections from The Phantom Menace
- Superman Returns, Concert Selections

Williams & Hooper
- Harry Potter and the Order of the Phoenix: Concert Suite

Willson, Meredith
- Music Man: Seventy-Six Trombones

Young, Victor
- Samson and Delilah (1949)
- Scaramouche (1952): Suite
- Shane (1953): Suite

Zaninelli, Luigi
- Night Voices

Zimmer, Hans
- Gladiator: Music from the Movie
- Pirates of the Caribbean: Dead Man's Chest (Soundtrack Highlights)

Zimmer & Howard
- The Dark Knight: Concert Suite

Zwilich, Ellen Taaffe
- American Concerto

STRINGS
2 3 3 2 – 4 3 3 1 – PERC

Barber, Samuel
- Die Natali (Chorale Prelude on Silent Night)

Brubeck, Dave
- Cathy's Waltz

- Summersong
Brubeck, Howard
- Dialogues
- Dialogues: Theme for June
- G Flat Theme
Chase, Bruce
- Around the World at Christmas Time
Chattaway, Jay
- Star Trek: The Next Generation
Coates, Eric
- London Suite: Knightsbridge March
Cooper, Paul
- A Shenandoah for Charles Ives' Birthday
Dello Joio, Norman
- Southern Echoes
Dvořák, Antonin
- Holoubek (The Wood Dove) Op. 110
Falla, Manuel de
- El Sombrero de tres picos (Three-Cornered Hat): Suite 2
Gade, Jacob
- Jalousie
Lane, Burton
- Excerpts from Finian's Rainbow
Mancini, Henry
- Dream of a Lifetime
Mendelssohn, Felix
- Hark! The Herald Angels Sing & Adeste Fidelis
Puccini, Giacomo
- Gianni Schicchi: O mio babbino caro
Reed, Alfred
- Pledge of Allegiance
Respighi, Ottorini
- Antiche danze ed arie (Ancient Airs and Dances): Set I
Shore, Howard
- Symphonic Suite from The Lord of the Rings: The Two Towers
Tchaikovsky, Peter Ilyich
- Romeo and Juliet: Duet

STRINGS
3 1 3 1 – 4 3 3 1 – PERC

Arlen, Harold
- Wizard of Oz Choral Review
Casey, Warren & Jacobs, Jim
- Grease!
Custer, Calvin
- The American Frontier
- It's Christmastime (Medley for Orchestra)
- Themes from 007: A Medley for Orchestra
Elfman, Danny
- Movie Spectacular

Flaherty, Stephen
- Ragtime Selections
Hooper, Nicolas
- Concert Suite from Harry Potter and the Half-Blood Prince
Lloyd Webber, Andrew
- Andrew Lloyd Webber: A Concert Celebration (Medley)
MacLellan, Gene
- Snowbird
Mancina, Mark
- Twister Main Theme
Mancini, Henry
- Mancini Magic
Meij, Johan de
- The Lord of the Rings: Excerpts from Symphony No. 1
Morricone, Ennio
- Cinema Paradiso: First Youth
- Cinema Paradiso: Love Theme
Rodgers, Richard
- Carousel Waltz

STRINGS
3 2 2 2 – 4 3 3 1 – PERC

Ades, Thomas
- Twentiana
Anderson, Leroy
- Arietta
- Balladette
- Belle of the Ball
- Birthday Party
- The Bluebells of Scotland
- Blue Tango
- Bonnie Dundee
- Bugler's Holiday
- The Campbells Are Coming
- The Captains and the Kings
- Chicken Reel
- China Doll
- A Christmas Festival
- Clarinet Candy
- Fiddle Faddle
- The Girl in Satin
- The Golden Years
- Goldilocks: I Never Know When
- Goldilocks: Lady In Waiting
- Goldilocks: Lazy Moon
- Goldilocks: Overture
- Goldilocks: Pirate Dance
- Goldilocks: Pussyfoot
- Goldilocks: Pyramid Dance
- Goldilocks: Save a Kiss
- Goldilocks: Shall I Take My Heart
- Goldilocks: Town House Maxixe
- Goldilocks: Who's Been Sitting in My Chair?
- Governor Bradford's March
- Home Stretch

- Horse and Buggy
- The Irish Suite
- Leroy Anderson Favorites
- Lullaby of the Drums for Orchestra
- March of the Two Left Feet
- Old MacDonald Had a Farm
- The Penny Whistle Song
- Promenade
- Sandpaper Ballet
- Saraband
- Second Regiment Connecticut National Guard March
- Serenata
- Sleigh Ride
- Song of the Bells
- The Typewriter
- The Waltzing Cat
Arlen, Harold
- It's Only a Paper Moon
- The Wizard of Oz Selections
- Wizard of Oz Orchestra Suite: Wizard of Oz Medley
Arnold, Malcolm
- Comedy Overture: Beckus the Dandipratt
- Commonwealth Christmas Overture, Op. 64
- English Dances: Set I
- English Dances: Set.2
- Four Cornish Dances, Op. 91
- Four Irish Dances, Op. 126
- The Holly and the Ivy: Fantasy on Christmas Carols
- The Sound Barrier Rhapsody, Op. 38
Bennett, Richard Rodney
- Celebration
Berlin, Irving
- God Bless America
Bernstein, Elmer
- Great Escape March
Blake, Howard
- Let Music Live
Brubeck, Dave
- It's About Time
Capua, Eduardo di
- O sole mio
Chabrier, Emmanuel
- España
Chiarappa, Richard
- Boom!: A Waltz for Symphony Orchestra and Bass Drum
- Happy, Happy Birthday
- Lincoln & Booth: Good-bye
- Lincoln & Booth: Just Ourselves
- Lincoln & Booth: The President's Waltz
- Romp for Symphony & Triangulist
- Paean to he Scholar, The Athlete and The Artist
Clark, Larry
- Hooked on Classics

(Str – 3 2 2 2 – 4 3 3 1 – Perc, cont.)

Cohan, George M.
- George M.: Choral Overture
- Give My Regards to Broadway
- Over There
- You're a Grand Old Flag

Constantinescu, Paul
- Braul (The Sash Dance)

Coolidge, Peggy Stuart
- Pioneer Dances

Copland, Aaron
- The Tender Land: Suite

Creston, Paul
- Rumba-Tarantella

Custer, Calvin
- Beach Boys Medley
- Christmas - That Special Time of the Year

Deussen, Nancy Bloomer
- American Hymn

Edwards, Gus
- By the Light of the Silvery Moon

Ellington, Edward (Duke)
- Duke Ellington! Medley

Estefan, Gloria
- Gloria Estefan: Her Greatest Hits

Flaherty, Stephen
- Anastasia: In the Dark of the Night

Foster, David W.
- Quest for Camelot Selections

Foster, Stephen
- A Stephen Foster Overture

Gershwin, George
- Fascinatin' Rhythm

Gould, Morton
- New China March
- American Salute
- Calypso Souvenir
- Declaration: Suite
- New China March

Grainger, Percy
- Shepherd's Hey

Harris, Arthur E.
- Americana

Herman, Jerry
- The Best Christmas of All
- La Cage aux Folles
- Hello Dolly!
- Mack & Mabel
- Mame
- Milk and Honey

Ives, Charles
- Variations on America

Jager, Robert
- Concerto Grosso

Koch, Anton
- Adverntures of Sinbad: Overture

Kodály, Zoltán
- Variations on a Hungarian Folksong: The Peacock

Kuster, Kristin
- Iron Diamond

Lampe, James
- Creole Belles

Leighton, Kenneth
- Dance Suite No. 1

Liebermann, Lowell
- Revelry

Loewe, Frederick
- My Fair Lady Medley

Merrill, Bob
- Take Me Along!

Mitchell, Lyndol
- Railroad Suite

Monaco, James V.
- You Made Me Love You

Morris, John
- Blazing Saddles (1973)

Nelson, Ronald J.
- Savannah River Holiday

Nielsen, Carl August
- Helios Overture, Op. 17
- Masquerade: Hanedons (Cock's Dance)
- Masquerade Overture

Norton, George A.
- Round Her Neck She Wore a Yellow Ribbon

O'Brien, Richard
- The Rocky Horror Picture Show

Perry, William
- Joy Shall Be Yours in the Morning

Richards, Johnny
- Cuban Fire Suite: La Suerte de los Tontos (Fortune of Fools)

Richman, Lucas
- Beautiful Dreamer: Stephen Foster's America
- Christmas Singalong
- Colonial Liberty Overture

Rodgers, Richard
- State Fair: It's a Grand Night for Singing

Rodríguez, Robert Xavier
- Flight: The Story of Wilbur and Orville Wright
- The Salutation Rag

Rota, Nino
- War and Peace: Suite (1956)

Rose, David
- Little House on the Prairie: Meet Me at the Fair (1974)

Sayre, Charles
- Broadway Showstoppers

Schickele, Peter
- Requiem Mantras

Scott, Raymond
- Dinner Music for a Pack of Hungry Cannibals
- Huckleberry Duck
- The Penguin
- A Raymond Scott Fantasia
- The Toy Trumpet

Shostakovich, Dmitri
- Hamlet: Music from the Film, Op. 116
- Hamlet: Music from the Film, Op.116a

Shulman, Alan
- Popocatepeti

Sierra, Roberto
- A Joyous Overture

Silvers, Louis
- April Showers

Steiner, Fred
- Perry Mason (1956): Theme

Steiner, Max
- King Kong: Jungle Dance

Styne, Jule
- Gypsy: Overture

Svoboda, Tomáš
- Overture of the Season, Op. 89

Tichili, Frank
- Postcard for Symphony Orchestra

Tiomkin, Dimitri
- Duel in the Sun (1946): Suite

Turina, Joaquin
- Canto a Sevilla, Op. 37

Turrin, Joseph
- Fanfare for George Gershwin
- Lullaby of Broadway

Tyzik, Jeff
- Fantasy On American Themes
- The Great Westerns Suite

Verdi, Giuseppe
- Aida:Triumphal March

Waxman, Franz
- Suspicion (1941): Suite

Weinberger, Jaromir
- Prelude and Fugue on "Dixie"
- Svandadudák (Shvanda the bagpiper): Polka and Fugue
- Under the Spreading Chestnut Tree

Welcher, Dan
- Prairie Light: Three Texas Watercolors of Georgia O'Keeffe

Wendel, Robert
- The April Fool Concerto
- The Armed Forces March
- Back to the Fifties!
- The Bells of Christmas
- Carol of the Bells
- A Chanukah Overture
- Christmas a la Valse!
- Christmas Through Children's Eyes
- A Classical Christmas Suite
- Commemoration
- An Evergreen Christmas
- Fanfare for Freedom
- Fiesta Mexicana
- The Flintstones Meet the Jetsons
- From Sea to Shing Sea
- A George M. Cohan Overture

- A Halloween Trilogy: Ride of the Headless Horseman
- A Hollywood Salute
- Hymn of Thanksgiving: We Gather Together
- Jonny Quest
- An Old Fashioned Summer
- Orange Blossom Special
- The Original Ragtime Band
- Rock around the Clock
- Saint Bailey's Rag
- The Saint Louis Blues
- The Smurfs
- Stephen Foster Overture
- Surf's Up!
- Swing, Ludwig, Swing!
- Take Flight
- The Tall Ships
- That's It, That's All… The End!
- Under the Big Top
- We Need a Little Christmas
- When TV Was Young

Williams, Ernest S.
- Revolutionary Fantasy

Williams, John T.
- Olympic Fanfare and Theme
- Star Wars Main Theme
- Star Wars: Parade of the Ewoks (Return of the Jedi)

Wilson & Love
- Beach Boys: Medley for Orchestra

Zador, Eugene
- A Christmas Overture

STRINGS
3 2 3 2 – 4 3 3 1 – PERC

Ades, Hawley
- Twentiana

Alford, Kenneth
- Colonel Bogey March

Arlen, Harold & Harburg & Stothart
- Wizard of Oz Orchestral Suite

Arnold, Malcolm
- The Inn of the Sixth Happiness

Bagley, Edwin
- National Emblem March

The Beatles
- Beatles!!! A Medley of Lennon and McCartney Favorites

Bennett, Robert Russell
- The Four Freedoms
- Overture to the Mississippi

Berlin, Irvin
- White Christmas

Bernstein, Elmar
- True Grit: Concert Suite

Bernstein, Leonard
- Candide Overture

Bocook, Jay
- Movie Spectacular

Borodin, Alexander
- Nocturne

Carmichael, Hoagy
- Hoagy Carmichael: An American Treasure

Chadwick, George
- Symphonic Sketches: Hobgoblin

Copland, Aaron
- Happy Anniversary

Daniel, Eliot
- I Love Lucy: Theme

Dorff, Daniel
- Philly Rhapsody

Dvořák, Antonin
- The Midday Witch (The Noon Witch), Op. 108

Ellington, Edward K. (Duke)
- Ellington Portrait

Fielding, Jerry
- The Outlaw Josey Wales: Suite (1976)
- The Wild Bunch: Suite in Two Movements (1969)

Flaherty, Stephen
- Anastasia: Journey to the Past
- Anastasia: Learn to Do It Waltz

Foster, Stephen Collins
- Jeanie with the Light Brown Hair

Fučik, Julius
- Under the Admiral's Flag (Unter der Admiralsflagge), Op. 82

Gershwin, George
- An American in Paris Suite
- Crazy for You Overture
- Love Walked In

Goldsmith, Jerry
- L.A. Confidential (1997)
- Logan's Run (1976): Monument/End of the City

Gould, Morton
- American Ballads: Amber Waves on "America the Beautiful"
- American Ballads: Hymnal on "We Shall Overcome"
- American Ballads: Jubilo
- American Ballads: Memorials Setting of "Taps"
- American Ballads: Saratoga Quickstep on "The Girl I Left Behind"
- American Ballads: Settings of American Tunes for Orchestra
- American Ballads: Star-Spangled Overture on "The Star-Spangled Banner"
- Celebration Strut for Orchestra
- Festive Music
- A Homespun Overture
- Hosedown: A Firefighter Fable
- Minute Plus Waltz Rag
- A Song of Freedom

Granados, Enrique
- Tres danzas españolas

Grundman, Clare
- American Folk Rhapsody No.1: Four American Folk Songs

Henderson, Luther
- A Canadian Brass Christmas

Herrmann, Bernard
- The Bride Wore Black: A Musical Scenario (1968)
- A Portrait of Hitch
- A Portrait of Hitch: The Trouble with Harry Suite (1954)

Hinds, Thomas
- Music for Hannukah: Two Folk Songs and a Hymn

Jendras, Louis F.
- The Russian Rag

Joel, Billy
- Movin' Out

King, Victor
- Gregoriana Christmas Suite

Knight, Eric
- Three Musical Elements: Earth, Water, Space

Loewe, Frederick
- Brigadoon: Suite

MacDermot, Gal
- Hair: Selections

Mancini, Henry
- The Great Waldo Pepper

Mechem, Kirke
- The Jayhawk, Op. 43: Overture to a Mythical Comedy

Miller, Sy & Jackson, Jill
- Let There Be Peace on Earth

Moncayo, José Pablo
- Huapango

Moross, Jerome
- The Big Country: Main Title Theme
- A Tall Story for Orchestra

Morricone, Ennio
- Marco Polo Main Title

Mussorgsky, Modest Petrovich
- The Song of the Flea

Newman, Alfred
- All About Eve: Overture
- Brigham Young March (1940)
- Prisoner of Zenda: A Ruritanian Rhapsody for Orchestra

O'Boyle, Sean
- Olympia Australis

Piket, Frederick
- Curtain Raiser to an American Play: Overture

Popp, André
- Love is Blue (L'Amour est bleu)

Porter, Cole
- Cole Porter Salute

Richards, Johnny
- La Suerte de los Tantos (Fortune of Fools)

(Str – 3 2 3 2 – 4 3 3 1 – Perc, cont.)

Rimsky-Korsakov, Nicolai
- Christmas Eve: Polonaise

Rózsa, Miklós
- Ben Hur: Choral Suite
- Ben Hur: Parade of the Charioteers
- Ben-Hur Prelude
- El Cid: Love Scene
- El Cid: Overture
- El Cid: Overture and March
- The Killers: Concert Suite
- The Lost Weekend: Suite

Schickele, Peter
- American Birthday Card

Schoenberg, Claude-Michel
- Les Miserables: Bring Him Home
- Les Miserables: I Dreamed A Dream

Schwartz, Stephen
- Prince of Egypt Medley

Shore, Howard
- The Lord of the Rings: Fellowship of the Ring (Symphonic Suite)
- The Lord of the Rings: The Two Towers

Silvestri, Alan
- Polar Express: Believe
- Polar Express: When Christmas Comes to Town

Sousa, John Philip
- El Capitan March
- Fairest of the Fair March
- Hands Across the Sea
- King Cotton March
- The Liberty Bell March
- Semper Fidelis March
- The Stars and Stripes Forever
- Thunderer March

Steiner, Max
- King Kong: Theme

Stephenson, James M. III
- Go Tell It On the Mountain
- Joy to the World
- O Christmas Tree

Tchaikovsky, Peter Ilyich
- The Nutcracker Suite

Ticheli, Frank
- Shooting Stars

Tiomkin, Dimitri
- The Four Poster (1952)
- Friendly Persuasion (1956)
- Friendly Persuasion (1956): Thee I Love
- It's a Wonderful Life (1947): Suite
- Rawhide (1959): Theme

Verdi, Giuseppe
- Aida:Triumphal March (original version)

Wagner, Richard
- Gotterdämmerung: Siegfried's Rhine Journey

Waxman, Franz
- Beloved Infidel (1959): Theme
- Captains Courageous (1937): Suite -
The Lost Command (1966): Aicha's Theme
- Rebecca (1940): Suite

Williams, John T.
- Midway: Midway March
- Star Wars Suite
- Summon The Heroes
- Superman March: Main Theme

STRINGS
3 2 3 3 – 4 3 3 1 – PERC

The Beatles
- Abbey Road Suite

Brahms, Johannes
- Academic Festival Overture, Op 80
- Variations on a Theme by Haydn, Op. 56a

Bernstein, Elmer
- American Werewolf in London

Courage, Alexander
- Star Trek: The Television Series "The Menagerie" (1964)

Douglas, Samuel
- Millennium Fanfare

Erb, Donald
- Music for a Festive Occasion

Frackenpohl, Arthur
- Rondo Marziale

Gold, Ernest
- Ship of Fools: Candlelight & Silver Waltz (1965)

Goldsmith, Jerry
- Basic Instinct (1992): Main Title Theme
- Basic Instinct (1992): Suite
- Patton (1970): Attack
- Patton (1970): The Payoff

Goodwin, Ron
- Those Magnificent Men in Their Flying Machines (1965)

Gould, Morton
- Audubon: Night Music

Hely-Hutchinson, Victor
- Carol Symphony

Hermann, Bernard
- The Devil and Daniel Webster: Suite

Horner, James
- Aliens Suite No. 2: Newt & Face Huggers

Ives, Charles
- Symphony Holidays:
4. Thanksgiving/Forefathers' Day

Karmon, Michael
- …And The Rhythm Is Just A Little Bit Off…

Liszt, Franz
- Hungarian Rhapsody No. 1, F Minor

Mancini, Henry
- March with Mancini

Moross, Jerome
- The Big Country: Suite

Morricone, Ennio
- Cinema Paradiso Theme

Newman, Alfred
- Song of Bernadette (1943): Scherzo

Ottman, John
- Superman Returns Suite

Robinson, Walter H.
- Harriet Tubman

Roto, Nino
- Amarcord

Schoenberg, Claude-Michel
- Les Miserables: I Dreamed a Dream

Shostakovich, Dmitri
- Overture on Russian and Kirghiz Folk Themes, Op. 115

Wagner, Richard
- Eine Faust Ouvertüre (A Faust Overture)

Waxman, Franz
- Peyton Place (1957): Theme "The Wonderful Seasons of Love" or "For Those Who Are Young"

Whitney, John
- Coming of Age

Williams, John T.
- The Cowboys Overture
- E.T. Suite: Adventures on Earth
- E.T.: Flying Theme
- Schindler's List: Three Pieces
- Superman Returns Suite

Young, Victor
- The Quiet Man (1952): Suite

STRINGS
3 3 2 3 – 4 3 3 1 – PERC

Anderson, Leroy
- Mother's Whistler

Baker, David
- Concertino for Cellular Phones and Symphony Orchestra

Bloch, Ernest
- Trois Poèmes Juifs

Caillet, Lucien
- Variations on Pop Goes the Weasel

Debussy, Claude
- Prélude a L'après-midi d'un faune (Afternoon of a Faun)

Goldsmith, Jerry
- Star Trek I: The Motion Picture "The Klingon Battle"

Goldstein, William
- A.M.America Overture

Howard, James
- Signs Suite

Ives, Charles
- Symphony Holidays: 3. Fourth of July

Mayer, William
- Of Rivers and Trains
- Scenes from "The Snow Queen"

Schiff, David
- Infernal

Shostakovich, Dmitri
- Ballet Suite No. 1 (1949)
- Ballet Suite No. 2 (1951)
- Ballet Suite No. 3 (1951)
- Ballet Suite No. 4 (1953)

Vaughan Williams, Ralph
- Hodie: A Christmas Cantata

Warshauer Meira
- Symphony No. 1 "Living, Breathing, Earth"

Williams, John T.
- Liberty Fanfare

STRINGS
3 3 3 2 – 4 3 3 1 – PERC

Amundson, Steven
- Angels' Dance

Ayars, Bo
- Christmas Medley
- Cowboy Medley: Cielito lindo
- Cowboy Medley: Mexican Hat Dance
- Cowboy Medley: She'll Be Comin' 'Round the Mountain
- Cowboy Medley: Shenandoah
- Cowboy Medley: Sweet Betsy from Pike
- Cowboy Medley: The Yellow Rose of Texas
- Shave and a Haircut March

Barber, Samuel
- Die natali, Op. 37 (Chorale Preludes for Christmas)
- The Lovers, Op. 43
- The School for Scandal: Overture

Bart, Lionel
- Oliver Selections

Beethoven
- Moonlight Sonata

Bennett, Robert Russell
- Hollywood

Berlin, Irving
- White Christmas

Bowden, Robert C.
- A Christmas Treat

Cailliet, Lucien
- Variations on "Pop! Goes the Weasel"

Cohan, George M.
- George M. Cohan Salute

Conrad, Con
- The Gay Divorcee: The Continental

Costa, Francesco Antonio
- Era di maggio

Debney, John
- The Passion of the Christ Symphony

Dello Joio, Norman
- Nativity: Canticle for the Child

Deussen, Nancy Bloomer
- A Field in Pennsylvania

Dvořák, Antonin
- Carnival Overture, Op. 92

Falla, Manuel de
- Noches en los jardines de Espana (Nights in the Gardens of Spain)
- El Sombrero de tres picos (Three-Cornered Hat)
- El Sombrero de tres picos (Three-Cornered Hat): Suite No. 2
- La vida breve: Interlude and Spanish Dance

Flaherty, Stephen
- Anastasia: A Rumor in St. Petersburg

Friedhofer, Hugo
- The Mark of Zorro: Suite (1940)

Gershwin, George
- Concerto in F Major for Piano and Orchestra

Gillis, Don
- The Man Who Invented Music
- The Night Before Christmas

Goldsmith, Jerry
- Forever Young (1992): Love Theme
- Four Women: Medley
- The Russia House (1990): Love Theme

Gould, Morton
- American Salute (New Edition, 2000)

Griffes, Charles Tomlinson
- Five Poems of the Ancient Far East

Guettel, Adam
- Light in the Piazza: Symphonic Suite

Hermann, Ralph
- Christmas Fantasy
- Farmyard Frolic
- Irish Medley
- Italian Fiesta
- Jewish Melodies
- Old Song Medley
- Old Song Medley No. 2
- Old Song Medley No. 3
- Old Timers Waltz Medley No. 1
- Old Timers Waltz Medley No. 2
- Polish Polka Party
- Silent Movie

Holcombe, Bill
- Fantasy on Auld Lang Syne

Jones, Ron
- Star Trek, The Next Generation: Suite (1989)

Ives, Charles
- Symphony Holidays: 2. Decoration Day

Kern, Jerome
- Way You Look Tonight

Khachaturian, Aram
- Gayane, Suite No. 1 from the ballet
- Gayane, Suite No. 2 from the ballet
- Spartacus, Suite No. 2 from the ballet
- Spartacus, Suite No. 3 from the ballet

Lai, Francis
- Love Story: Theme (1970)

Layton, Billy Jim
- An American Portrait
- Dance Fantasy, Op. 7

Magidson, Herb
- The Continental (1934)

Menken, Alan
- Go the Distance

Menotti, Gian Carlo
- Landscapes and Remembrances

Monti, Vittorio
- Czardas

Moross, Jerome
- Music from the Flicks

Newman, Alfred
- Wuthering Heights: Concert Suite

Perry, William
- The Gasoline Can-Can

Reitz, Ric
- To the Flag

Respighi, Ottorino
- Antiche danze ed arie (Ancient Airs and Dances): Set II
- La Boutique fantasque: Suite (after Rossini)

Rodríguez, Robert Xavier
- A Gathering of Angels: Bolero for Orchestra

Rota, Nino
- The Godfather (1972)

Schuman, William
- Casey at the Bat: A Baseball Cantata

Scott, Raymond
- Twilight in Turkey

Sibelius, Jean
- Karelia Suite, Op. 11

Snow, Mark
- X-Files: Main Title Theme

Sowerby, Leo
- Song for America

Stephenson, James M. III
- Bells of Christmas Suite
- Concerto for Cell Phone (2006)
- Holiday Fanfare Medley No. 2
- Holiday Overture
- A Holly and Jolly Sing-Along!

(Str – 3 3 3 2 – 4 3 3 1 – Perc – STEPHENSON, cont.)

- I Saw Three Ships/Jeanette, Isabella Medley
- Swing Carol Fantasy

Stevens, Morton
- Hawaii Five O (1968)

Strauss, Johann
- Die Fledermaus Waltz

Tchaikovsky, Peter Ilyich
- The Nutcracker, Op. 71a Suite No.1
- The Nutcracker, Op. 71b Suite No.2
- Romeo and Juliet: Fantasy Overture

Tsontakis, George
- Let the River Be Unbroken

Turok, Paul
- Great Scott! Orchestral Suite after Joplin
- A Joplin Overture

Waxman, Franz
- My Geisha (1961): Goodbye Love – Finale

Williams, John T.
- Harry Potter Symphonic Suite
- Suite from J.F.K.
- Memoirs of a Geisha: Sayuri's Theme
- The Mission
- The Terminal: Viktor's Tale

Young & Auric
- Roman Holiday (1953): Main Title and Prelude

Zinn, William
- Symphony in Ragtime

STRINGS
4 3 4 3 – 4 3 3 1 – PERC

Addinsell, Richard
- A Christmas Carol (Suite: Scrooge)

Alfvén, Hugo
- Midsommarvaka: Swedish Rhapsody No. 1, Op. 19

Anderson, Leroy
- Classical Jukebox

Bach, J.S.
- Jesu, Joy of Man's Desiring

Bacon, Ernst
- Suite From These States: Gathered Along Unpaved Roads

Baker, David
- Le chat qui pêche
- Kosbro
- Two Improvisations

Barber, Samuel
- Commando March for Orchestra

Bazelon, Irwin
- Spirits of the Night

The Beatles
- Abbey Road Suite Classic Beatles: A Medley
- The Great Beatles Singles Suite I: Strawberry Fields Forever
- The Great Beatles Singles Suite II: All You Need Is Love
- Sergeant Pepper's Lonely Hearts Club Band
- Songs from the White Album

Bennett, Richard Rodney
- Love Spells

Bernstein, Leonard
- Candide Suite

Berlin, Irving
- God Bless America

Bolcom, William
- Inventing Flight
- Ragomania!
- Seattle Slew Suite

Broughton, Bruce
- Miracle on 34th Street

Brubeck, Dave
- La Fiesta de la Posada
- Fugal Fanfare (Happy Anniversary)
- The Light in the Wilderness
- They All Sang Yankee Doodle
- Truth Is Fallen

Caillet, Lucien
- Fantasie on "Auld Lang Syne"

Carter, Elliott
- Holiday Overture

Chávez, Carlos
- Sinfonia India (Symphony No. 2)

Constantinescu, Paul
- Tanze Aus Rumanien

Copland, Aaron
- Rodeo: 1.Buckaroo Holiday
- Rodeo: 4.Hoedown

Corigliano, John
- Midsummer Fanfare
- Three Hallucinations

Cowell, Henry
- Four Irish Tales: Tales of Our Countryside

Creston, Paul
- Evening in Texas
- Sunrise in Puerto Rico

Danielpour, Richard
- Toward the Splendid City

Daugherty, Michael
- Metropolis Symphony: 1.Lex

Dawson, William
- Negro Folk Symphony

Debussy, Claude
- Clair de lune

Dello Joio, Norman
- Colonial Variants: Thirteen Profiles of the Original Colonies

Denver, John
- Annie's Song

Douglas, Bill
- Concerto for African Percussion Ensemble and Orchestra

Downey, John
- Ode to Freedom

Doyle, Patrick
- Great Expectations Suite

Duffy, John
- Indian Spirits

Dun, Tan
- Crouching Tiger, Hidden Dragon (2000)

Elgar, Edward
- In the South: Concert Overture, Op. 50

Falla, Manuel de
- Homenajes

Felder, David
- Linebacker Music

Flaherty, Stephen
- Anastasia: Once Upon a December
- Anastasia Suite

Frank, Gabriela Lena
- Three Latin-American Dances

Frazelle, Kenneth
- The Swans of Pongo Lake

Friedhofer, Hugo
- An Affair to Remember: The Proposal (1957)

Galindo, Blas
- Sones de Mariachi

Garrido-Lecca, Celso
- Retablos Sinfónicos

Gershwin, George
- Cuban Overture
- Porgy and Bess Medley

Glière, Reinhold
- The Red Poppy: Russian Sailor's Dance from Act I
- The Red Poppy: Suite No. 1 from the ballet, Op. 70a

Gold, Ernest
- It's a Mad, Mad, Mad, Mad World: Exit Music (1963)

Goossens, Eugene
- Don Juan de Manara: Intermezzo
- Flamenco: Ballet
- Scherzo and Folk Tune
- Tam O'Shanter: Scherzo

Goldsmith, Jerry
- MacArthur (1977): March
- Masada: Suite
- Motion Picture Medley
- Papillon: Theme
- The Strong Men: Total Recall & Rambo Themes
- The Sum of All Fears (2002)
- Television Themes Medley
- Twilight Zone: The Movie (1983): End Title
- The Wind and the Lion (1975)

Gould, Morton
- American Sing: Settings of Folk Songs
- Cowboy Rhapsody
- Flourishes and Galop
- Foster Gallery
- Foster Gallery: Suite
- I'm Old Fashioned, Astaire Variations

Grainger, Percy
- In a Nutshell: Suite

Griffes, Charles Tomlinson
- Clouds
- The Pleasure Dome of Kubla Khan, Op. 8

Grofé, Ferde
- Death Valley Suite
- Grand Canyon Suite
- Hudson River Suite
- Mississippi: A Tone Journey
- Mississippi Suite
- Niagara Falls Suite
- World's Fair Suite

Gruenberg, Louis
- Jazz Suite, Op. 28

Handel, George Frideric
- Overture in D Minor

Harris, Roy
- Acceleration
- Epilogue to Profiles in Courage: JFK
- Horn of Plenty
- Work

Hayman, Richard
- Freddie the Football

Herbert, Victor
- Natoma: Grand Fantasia
- Natoma: Prelude to Act III

Herrmann, Bernard
- Anna and the King of Siam Suite (1946)
- The Bride Wore Black: A Suite in Four Movements
- Jane Eyre: Suite (1943)

Higdon, Jennifer
- Cityscape

Holst, Gustav
- A Fugal Overture, Op. 40, No. 1

Horner, James
- Aliens Suite No. 1: Main Title & Ripley's Rescue
- Titanic Suite

Howard, James
- The Sixth Sense Suite
- Snow Falling on Cedars Suite

Ives, Charles
- Three Places in New England

Jalbert, Pierre
- In Aeternam

John, Elton
- Suite from The Lion King

Kabalevsky, Dmitri
- Romeo and Juliet: Musical Sketches, Op. 56

Kaper, Bronislau
- Lili: Ballet (1953)

Kapilow, Robert
- City Piece: DC Monuments
- Union Station
- Union Station: New Year's Eve

Kasschau, Howard
- The Legend of Sleepy Hollow

Kay, Ulysses
- Suite

Kraft, William
- A Kennedy Portrait
- Vintage Renaissance

Lehár, Franz
- Merry Widow Overture

Leighton, Kenneth
- Dance Suite No. 3 (Scottish Dances), Op. 89

López, Jimmy
- Perú Negro

Maggio, Robert
- Skylines

Mancini, Henry
- The Thorn Birds Theme
- The White Dawn: Suite (1974)

McDonald, Harl
- Saga of the Mississippi

Morricone, Ennio
- The Mission: Gabriel's Oboe

Newman, Alfred
- The Diary of Anne Franck: Suite
- Nevada Smith: Overture

Newman, Lionel
- Doctor Dolittle: Talk to the Animals

O'Boyle, Sean
- Ragtime
- River Symphony

Poledouris, Basil
- Free Willy Suite (1993)

Powell, John
- In Old Virginia: Overture, Op. 28
- Natchez on the Hill: Three Virginia Country Dances
- Suite from X-Men: The Last Stand

Raksin, David
- Forever Amber: II. The King's Mistress
- Forever Amber: V. End Title "Finale"
- Laura's Theme

Reed, Alfred
- Greensleeves

Ruders, Poul
- Thus Saw St. John...(Saaledes saae Johannes)

Schuller, Gunther
- Music for a Celebration: A Fantasy on National Themes

Schuman, William
- American Festival Overture
- American Hymn
- Circus Overture: Sideshow

Shire, David
- Farewell My Lovely (1975): Suite

Shostakovich, Dmitri
- Ballet Suite No. 1 (1949)
- Festive Overture, Op. 96
- The Gadfly: Suite from the Film, Op. 97a
- The Limpid Stream: Suite from the ballet, Op. 39a

Sierra, Roberto
- Tropicalia: Celebration

Silvestri, Alan
- Polar Express Suite

Smith, John Stafford
- Star-Spangled Banner

Smith, Robert W.
- Jingle Bells Forever

Stokowski, Leopold
- 3 Christmas Carols

Stucky, Steven
- Fanfare for Cincinnati
- Pinturas de Tamayo

Sullivan, Arthur
- Pineapple Poll: Suite

Thomas, Augusta Read
- Sunlight Echoes

Thomson, Virgil
- Sea Piece with Birds
- The Seine at Night
- Wheat Field at Noon

Tiomkin, Dimitri
- Strangers on a Train (1951): Suite
- The Sundowners (1960): Suite
- Tension at Table Rock (1956): Suite
- The Well (1951): Suite

Tsontakis, George
- Winter Lightning

Turina, Joaquín
- Danzas fantásticas, Op. 22

Turok, Paul
- A Sousa Overture, Op. 43

Vangelis
- Chariots of Fire Suite

Vianello, Hugo
- Christmas Kaleidoscope

Wagner, Richard
- Tristan und Isolde: Prelude and Liebestod

Walton, William
- Crown Imperial: Coronation March

Ward-Steinman, David
- Season's Greetings: Festive Overture

Waxman, Franz
- Anne of the Indes (1951): Overture - The Bride of Frankenstein (1935)
- Magnificent Seven, The: Suite
- Medley: Classic Love Themes
- Medley: Nostalgic Film Themes

(Str – 4 3 4 3 – 4 3 3 1 – Perc – WAXMAN, cont.)

- My Geisha (1961): Suite
- The Nun's Story (1958)
- The Nun's Story (1958): Short Suite
- Peyton Place (1957): Suite
- Prince Valiant (1954)

Webb, Roy
- Notorious (1946): Suite

Welcher, Dan
- Castle Creek: Fanfare & Overture
- Haleakala: How Maui Snared the Sun

Williams, John T.
- Amistad: Dry Your Tears, Afrika
- Angela's Ashes: Two Concert Pieces
- Call of the Champions: 2002 Olympic Theme
- Catch Me If You Can: Escapades for Alto Sax
- Far and Away: Excerpts
- Harry Potter and the Chamber of Secrets
- Harry Potter and the Sorcerer's Stone: Children's Suite
- Harry Potter and the Sorcerer's Stone: Suite for Orchestra
- Home Alone: Three Holiday Songs
- Hook: Flight to Neverland
- Suite from Jaws
- Star Spangled Banner
- Star Wars: Episode II: Attack of the Clones (Across the Stars Love Theme)

Zwilich, Ellen Taaffe
- Jubilation
- Upbeat!

STRINGS
2 2 2 3 – 4 4 3 1 – PERC

Beethoven, Ludwig van
- Konig Stephan Overture, Op. 117

Berkeley, Lennox
- Voices of the Night, Op. 86

Bizet, Georges
- L'Arlésienne: Suite No. 1
- L'Arlésienne: Suite No. 2

Cohan, George M.
- George M. Cohan Medley

Elgar, Edward
- Enigma Variations, Op. 36: Nimrod
- Froissart Overture, Op. 19
- Sea Pictures

Glinka, Mikhail
- Russlan & Ludmilla Overture

Verdi, Giuseppe
- Aïda: Triumphal March

STRINGS
2 3 3 3 – 4 4 3 1 – PERC

Alfvén, Hugo
- Dalarapsodi: Swedish Rhapsody No.3, Op. 47

Copland, Aaron
- Lincoln Portrait

Elgar, Edward
- Pomp and Circumstance March No. 1 in D Major, Op. 39

Ellington, Edward K. (Duke)
- New World A-Comin'

Elliot, Jack
- Theme from Charlie's Angels

Erb, Donald
- Klangfarbenfunk

Evans, Dale
- Happy Trails to You (1952)

Goldsmith, Jerry
- The Shadow (1994): Main Title

Gottschalk, Louis Moreau
- Symphonie romantique: Night in the Tropics

Gounod, Charles
- Faust: Ballet Music

Grainger, Percy
- Marching Song of Democracy for Chorus and Orchestra

Handel, G.F.
- Angels We Have Heard on High; Joy to the World

Loesser, Frank
- Music from Guys and Dolls

Mancini, Henry
- Astaire!

Massenet, Jules
- Méditation from Thaïs

Maxwell Davies, Peter
- Maxwell's Reel, with Northern Lights

Mendez, Raphael
- La Virgin de la Macarena

Newman, Alfred
- Captain from Castile: Pedro and Catania

Reed, Alfred
- Greensleeves

Revueltas, Silvestre
- Sensemaya

Robinson, Earl
- In the Folded and Quiet Yesterdays

Stanford, Charles Villiers
- Irish Rhapsody No. 1, Op. 78

Stravinsky, Igor
- Song of the Volga Boatmen

Waxman, Franz
- Taras Bulba (1962): Suite

Williams, John T.
- Saving Private Ryan: Hymn to the Fallen

STRINGS
3 2 2 2 – 4 4 3 1 – PERC

Berlioz, Hector
- Carnaval romain (Roman Carnival)

Binder, Abraham W.
- Poem of Freedom

Copland, Aaron
- The Red Pony

Corigliano, John
- Promenade Overture

Delibes, Leo
- Sylvia: Suite (4. Cortege de Bacchus)

Ellington, Edward K. (Duke)
- New World A-Comin'
- Satin Doll (instrumental version)

Gardel, Carlos
- Scent of a Woman: Por una Cabeza

German, Edward
- Coronation March and Hymn

Herrmann, Bernard
- The Wrong Man: Prelude (1956)

Knight, Eric
- Canadian Tribute

Moross, Jerome
- Biguine

Ponchielli, Amilcare
- La Gioconda: "Dance of the Hours"

Ringwald, Roy
- The Song of America

Rio, Chuck
- Tequila

Rodríguez, Robert Xavier
- Adoracion ambulante (A Mexican Folk Celebration)
- Adoracion Ambulante: Con flor y canto

Schoenberg, Claude-Michel
- Les Miserables: Symphonic Suite

Smetana, Bedrich
- Má Vlast: 3.Sárka

Strauss, Josef
- Spharenklänge (Music of the Spheres Waltz), Op. 235

Verdi, Giuseppe
- I vespri siciliani: Overture

Waxman, Franz
- The Ice Follies of 1939

STRINGS
3 3 3 3 – 4 4 4 1 – PERC

Anderson, Leroy
- Old MacDonald Had A Farm

Arnold, Malcolm
- The Bridge on the River Kwai

Bart, Lionel
- Oliver! for Orchestra

Bavil, Zamir
- David and the Ark of the Covenant
- Hanukkah Light (1998)
- Israeli Rhapsody

Beatles
- A Long and Winding Road

Benzecry, Esteban
- Colores de la Cruz del Sur (Colors of the Southern Cross)

Berezovsky, Nicolai
- Christmas Festival Overture: Ukrainian Noel

Bernstein, Elmer
- The Babe: End Credits
- The Man with the Golden Arm: Suite
- The Ten Commandments: Suite
- Thoroughly Modern Millie: Sky-Hi Waltz
- Waltzes from Films: Suite

Bernstein, Leonard
- Divertimento for Orchestra

Broughton, Bruce
- Jag: Theme
- Miracle on 34th Street (1994): Main Title

Chaplin, Charlie
- The Reel Chaplin

Churchill, Frank
- Snow White

Cohan, George M.
- George M. Cohan Medley: Symphonic Suite

Copland, Aaron
- El Salón México

Corigliano, John
- Tournaments

Daugherty, Michael
- Metropolis Symphony: 2.Krypton
- Metropolis Symphony: 5.Red Cape Tango

Debussy, Claude
- La Soirée dans Grenade

Denver, John
- John Denver Celebration (1987)

Dickinson, Peter
- Merseyside Echoes

Dragon, Carmen
- The Yellow Rose of Texas

Elfman, Danny
- Beetlejuice: Main Title (1988)

Elgar, Edward
- Cockaigne Concert Overture Op. 40

Ellington, Edward K. (Duke)
- Three Black Kings: Ballet for Orchestra
- Three Black Kings for Soloist and Orchestra

Elliot, Jack
- Theme from Charlie's Angels

Enesco, Georges
- Roumanian Rhapsody No. 1 in A Major, Op. 11

Eskula, Jari
- Commodore 64 Medley: A Medley of Classic 1980's Computer Game Themes

Fiedel, Brad
- True Lies: Theme (1994)

Gardel, Carlos
- Tango: Por una Cabeza

Garrido-Lecca, Gonzalo
- Toccata Op.1

Giacchino, Michael
- Music from "Up"

Glière, Reinhold
- The Red Poppy: Russian Sailor's Dance from Act I

Gold, Ernest
- Boston Pops March

Goldsmith, Jerry
- The Boys from Brazil (1978): Waltz & The Boys
- Capricorn One: Overture & Main Title
- Dennis the Menace (1993): End Credits
- Fireworks: A Celebration for Los Angeles (1999)
- The Generals: Patton/MacArthur Marches
- The Great Train Robbery (1979): Suite
- King Solomon's Mines (1985): Suite
- Music for Orchestra
- Planet of the Apes (1968): Suite
- Poltergeist (1982): Theme (Carol Anne's)
- Star Trek: Voyager (1995)
- Star Trek 8: First Contact (1996)
- The Sum of All Fears (2002)

Gould, Morton
- Cheers!-A Celebration March

Hageman, Richard
- Stagecoach: Suite (1939)

Harris, Roy
- Concert Overture-March in Time of War

Hayman, Richard
- Pops Hoe-Down

Herbert, Victor
- Victorious Herbert

Herrmann, Bernard
- The Three Worlds of Gulliver: Suite (1960)
- Vertigo: Suite (1958)

Holmboe, Vagn
- Fanfare

Holst, Gustav
- The Perfect Fool: Ballet Music, Op. 39

Howard, James
- Wyatt Earp (1994)
- Wyatt Earp: End Credits

Ippolitov-Ivanov, M.
- Caucasian Sketches: Procession of the Sardar

Iturriaga, Enrique
- Obertura para una Comedia (Overture for a Comedy)
- Sinfonía Junín y Ayacucho: 1824

Jarre, Maurice
- A Passage to India: A Symphonic Journey (1984)

Johnson, Laurence (Laurie)
- The Avengers: Theme (1961)

Khachaturian, Aram
- Spartacus, Suite No. 1 from the ballet

Knight, Eric
- Americana Overture
- The Great American Bicycle Race
- A Symphony in Four American Idioms

Leigh, Mitch
- Man of La Mancha

Lutosławski, Witold
- Fanfare for Louisville

Mancini, Henry
-Monster Movie Music Suite
- Overture to a Pops Concert
- Peter Gunn

Maxwell Davies, Peter
- Romamor: Roma, Amor, Labyrinthus

McDonald, Harl
- Legend of the Arkansas Traveler

Mancini, Henry
- The Great Mouse Detective
- Jingle Bells/Sleigh Ride
- Revenge of The Pink Panther (1978): Hong Kong Fireworks

Markowitz, Richard
- Wild, Wild West (1965)

Mitchell, Darren
- Turok 2

Mizzy, Vic
- The Addams Family: Theme & Waltz Finale (1991)

Moroder, Georgio
- Flashdance: What a Feeling (1983)

Morricone, Ennio
- The Untouchables: Overture

Morris, John
- High Anxiety: Main Title (1973)
- The Producers: Main Title (1968)

Newman, Alfred
- Keys of the Kingdom Suite

North, Alex
- 2001: A Symphonic Suite in Four Movements
- Cheyenne Autumn Suite
- Spartacus: Love Theme

Ortolani & Oliviero
- Mondo Cane: More

(Str – 3 3 3 3 – 4 4 4 1 – Perc – NORTH, cont.)

Perry, William
 - Graduation March
Piazzolla, Astor
 - Cuatro Estaciones Porteñas (The FourSeasons in Buenas Aires)
Raksin, David
 - Forever Amber: Main Title "Amber"
Rosenman, Leonard
 - Star Trek 4: The Voyage Home (1986)
Rózsa, Miklos
 - El Cid: Main Title
Saint-Saëns, Camille
 - Samson and Delilah: Bacchanale
Schickele, Peter
 - 1712 Overture
Schuller, Gunther
 - And They All Played Ragtime
Schuman, William
 - New England Triptych
Shaiman, Marc
 - The Addams Family (1991): Theme and Waltz Finale
Shchedrin, Rodion
 - Concerto No. 1 for Orchestra, "Naughty Limericks" (or "Mischievous Melodies")
Silvestri, Alan
 - Back to the Future Suite
Slatkin, Leonard
 - The Raven
Smith, Claude T.
 - A Rhapsody on Christmas Carols
Soro, Enrique
 - Tres Aires Chilenos (Three Chilean Aires)
Steiner, Max
 - The Caine Mutiny (1954): The March
 - Gone With the Wind (1939): Dance Montage
Stephenson, James M. III
 - BaSOON It Will Be Christmas
Stokowski, Leopold
 - What Child Is this?
Tchaikovsky, Peter Ilyich
 - Festival Coronation March for Alexander III
 - Ouverture Solennelle (1812 Overture) Op. 49
Tiomkin, Dimitri
 - The Alamo (1960): Short Suite
 - The Great Waltz (1938)
 - The Guns of Navarone (1961): Suite
 - Rhapsody of Steel (1959)
 - Tarzan and the Mermaids (1948): Suite
 - The War Wagon (1967): Suite
Toch, Ernst
 - Big Ben, Variation-Fantasy on the Westminster Chimes, Op. 62
Vangelis
 - Chariots of Fire: Theme
Warren, Harry
 - 42nd Street (1981)
 - 42nd Street: Overture
 - Lullaby of Broadway
Waxman, Franz
 - Magnificent Seven, The: Suite
 - Man on a Tightrope (1953): March
Welcher, Dan
 - Spumante
 - Zion
Williams, John T.
 - Happy Birthday Variations
 - Close Encounters of the Third Kind
 - Harry Potter and the Prisoner of Azkaban
 - Olympic Spirit
 - The Patriot
 - Star Wars Episode III: Revenge of the Sith (Battle of the Heroes)
Willson, Meredith
 - The Music Man: Seventy-Six Trombones
Young, Victor
 - Around the World in 80 Days (1956): Overture & Epilogue
 - For Whom the Bell Tolls (1943): Suite

STRINGS
4 4 4 4 – 8 6 6 6 – PERC

Adomian, Lan
 - Cantata de la Revolucion Mexicana
Arnold, David
 - Independence Day Suite
 - Independende Day Suite: End Tags
Arnold, Malcolm
 - Bridge on the River Kwai: March
Bach, J. S.
 - Chaconne
 - Fugue in C minor
 - Toccata and Fugue, BWV 565, D minor
 - Toccata and Fugue in C for Organ: Adagio
Barry, John
 - Out of Africa: Main Title
Berlin, Irving
 - God Bless America
 - A Pretty Girl Is Like a Melody
 - White Christmas
Brahms, Johannes
 - Hungarian Dance No. 1
 - Hungarian Dance No. 6

Calandrelli, Jorge
 - Concerto for Jazz Clarinet
Chabrier, Emmanuel
 - España Rhapsody
Chávez, Carlos
 - Himno nacional mexicano (Mexican National Anthem)
 - Sinfonia de antigona (Symphony No. 1)
 - Sinfonia India (Symphony No. 2)
 - El Sol (The Sun)-A Mexican Ballad
Conti, Bill
 - Rookie of the Year: End Credits
Corigliano, John
 - Campane di Ravello: A Celebration Piece for Sir Georg Solti
Creston, Paul
 - Dance Overture
Davis, Anthony
 - Esu Variations
Davis, Chip
 - Christmas Sweet
Debussy, Claude
 - La Cathédrale engloutie
Dukas, Paul
 - L'Apprenti Sorcier (The Sorcerer's Apprentice)
Eidelman, Cliff
 - Star Trek 6: The Undiscovered Country (1991)
Elfman, Danny
 - Edward Scissorhands: Ice Dance
 - Edward Scissorhands: Main Title
 - Serenada Schizophrana
Ellington, Edward K. (Duke)
 - The Golden Broom and the Green Apple
Ellington, Mercer
 - Things Ain't What They Used to Be
Esplá, Oscar
 - Fiesta: Suite de danzas
Franck, César
 - Le Chasseur maudit (The Accursed Huntsman)
Giacchino, Michael
 - Star Trek: End Credits (2009)
Goldenthal, Elliot
 - Alien 3: Adagio
Goldsmith, Jerry
 - The Agony and the Ecstasy (1965): Suite
 - Air Force One (1997): Theme
 - Alien (1979): End Title
 - The Blue Max (1996): Suite
 - The First Knight (1995): Suite
 - Hoosiers (1986): Suite
 - Lionheart: The Children's Crusade (1987)
 - Patton (1970): Main Title
 - Patton (1970): Suite
 - Poltergeist (1982): Night of the Beast (Clown Attack)

- Soarin' Over California
- Star Trek I: The Motion Picture "The Director's Cut"
- Star Trek I: The Motion Picture "The New Enterprise"
- Star Trek I: The Motion Picture Theme (1979)
- Star Trek 5: The Final Frontier: Suite (1989)
- Star Trek 9: Insurrection (1998)
- Star Trek 10: Nemesis (2002)
- Supergirl: Suite
- The Swarm (1978): Bees Arrive/End Title
- Under Fire (1983): Suite

Gould, Morton
- Columbia: Broadsides for Orchestra
- Jekyll and Hyde Variations
- Latin American Symphonette

Handel, George Frideric
- Water Music

Harris, Roy
- American Creed
- Folksong Symphony: Two Interludes
- When Johnny Comes Marching Home: Overture

Hayes, Jack
- Fox Medley No. 1; No. 2

Herrmann, Bernard
- Mysterious Island: Suite (1961)
- North by Northwest
- The Seventh Voyage of Sinbad
- The Day the Earth Stood Still: Arrival (1951)

Holst, Gustav
- The Planets

Horner, James
- Avatar (2009): Suite
- Cocoon Theme
- The Mask of Zorro: Suite (1998)
- Star Trek 2: The Wrath of Khan (1982)
- Star Trek 3: The Search for Spock "Stealing the Enterprise" (1984)

Howard, James
- Grand Canyon Fanfare
- Lady in the Water (2006): The Healing
- Prince of Tides Suite
- Wyatt Earp: End Credits

Ives, Charles
- Yale-Princeton Football Game

Jarre, Maurice
- Lawrence of Arabia

Jones, Trevor
- Last of the Mohicans: Main Title
- Last of the Mohicans Suite

Kamen, Michael
- Band of Brothers: Suite (2001)

Kaper, Bronislau
- Mutiny on the Bounty: Suite (1962)

Kernis, Aaron Jay
- Valentines

Kraft, William
- Simple Introduction to the Orchestra

Loeffler, Charles Martin
- Five Irish Fantasies

Mancini, Henry
- Beaver Valley '37
- Charade
- Hatari!: Baby Elephant Walk (1962)

McCarthy, Dennis
- Star Trek 7: Generations "Overture"
- Star Trek: Deep Space Nine Suite

Mussorgsky, Modest
- Night on Bare Mountain

Newman, Alfred
- Captain from Castile: Conquest
- Fox Fanfare
- How the West Was Won
- How the West Was Won: Suite
- The Razors Edge
- The Robe: Farewell to Diana
- Song of Bernadette (1943): Main Title

Newman, David
- Hoffa Theme

North, Alex
- 2001 Space Odyssey: Fanfare
- Cleopatra: Symphonic Portrait
- Spartacus: Camp at Night
- Spartacus: Draba Fight
- Spartacus: Final Farewell
- Spartacus: Forest Meeting
- Spartacus: Main Title
- Spartacus: Vesuvius

Ottman, John
- Astro Boy (2009): End Titles
- Astro Boy (2009): Theme
- Fantastic Four: Main Titles
- Fantastic Four: Silver Surfer Suite
- Suite from X2: X-Men United

Pann, Carter
- Two Portraits of Barcelona

Persichetti, Vincent
- A Lincoln Address
- Sinfonia Janiculum, Op. 113

Powell, John
- Chicken Run: Final Escape; Make a Crate
- Ice Age: The Meltdown

Rachmaninoff, Sergei
- The Isle of the Dead, Op. 29

Raksin, David
- Forever Amber: III. Whitefriars & The Great Fire
- Forever Amber: Suite (1947)

Ravel, Maurice
- Daphnis et Chloé: Suite No. 1
- Daphnis et Chloé: Suite No. 2
- Rapsodie espagnole

Respighi, Ottorino
- The Pines of Rome: Pines of the Appian Way

Ringwald, Roy
- The Song of Christmas

Rósza, Miklós
- Dead Men Don't Wear Plaid: End Cast

Ruggles, Carl
- Sun-Treader

Schickele, Peter
- The Fantastic Garden

Schifrin, Lalo
- Mission Impossible (1966): Theme

Schumann, Robert
- New Year Song, Op. 144 "Mit eherner Zunge, da ruft es: Gebt acht"

Schwantner, Joseph
- A New Morning for the World

Shchedrin, Rodion
- Concerto No. 1 for Orchestra, "Naughty Limericks" (or "Mischievous Melodies")

Silvestri, Alan
- The Abyss: Finale
- Back to the Future Suite
- Fools Rush In
- Judge Dredd (1995): Suite
- Night at the Museum (2006): Suite
- Polar Express: O Tannenbaum
- Polar Express: Spirit of the Seasons

Steiner, Max
- King Kong (1933): Overture

Still, William Grant
- Symphony No. 1 (Afro-American Symphony)

Strauss, Richard
- Also sprach Zarathustra, Op. 30
- Introduction (Sunrise)
- Till Eulenspiegels lustige Streiche (Till Eulenspiegel's Merry Pranks), Op. 28

Tchaikovsky, Peter Ilyich
- Marche Slave, Op. 31

Tiomkin, Dimitri
- The Big Sky (1952): Suite
- Dial M for Murder (1954): Suite
- The Fall of the Roman Empire (1964): Themes

Wagner, Richard
- Die Walkure: Ride of the Valkyries

Waxman, Franz
- Possessed (1947)
- Taras Bulba (1962): The Ride of the Cossacks
- Untamed (1955)

Welcher, Dan
- Castle Creek: Fanfare
- The Yellowstone Fires

Williams, John T.
- 1941: March of 1941

(Str – 4 4 4 4 – 8 6 6 6 – Perc – WILLIAMS, cont.)
- Close Encounters of the Third Kind
- The Lost World: Jurassic Park
- Olympic Fanfare and Theme
- Raiders of the Lost Ark: Raiders March
- Star Wars: Episode I Phantom Menace: Suite for Orchestra
- Summon the Heroes

Zwilich, Ellen Taaffe
- Celebration

ENSEMBLES WITH ONE SAXOPHONE

Strings with percussion
Hupfeld, Herman
- As Time Goes By
Templeton, Alec
- Ballad de ballet

---

1 1 3 1 – 2 3 3 1 – perc – str
Antheil, George
- Jazz Sonata
- A Jazz Symphony (ensemble version)
Benjamin, Arthur
- Two Jamaican Pieces
Bernstein, Leonard
- On the Town: Three Dance Episodes
Carpenter, John Alden
- Krazy Kat
Gould, Morton
- Swanee River in the Style of Ellington
- Swanee River in the Style of Wagner
Ives, Charles
- Country Band March
Russell & Knight
- The Halls of Ivy
Turrin, Joseph
- When Tony Played the Sax

---

2 2 5 2 – 2 2 3 1 – perc – str
Bach, J.S.
- Jesu, Joy of Man's Desiring: from Cantata no. 147
Chappell, Herbert
- Paddington Bear's First Concert
Darzins, Emils
- Latvian Folksongs
De Rose, Peter
- Deep Purple

Harris, Roy
- Concerto in One Movement: Jamboree
Milhaud, Darius
- Globetrotter Suite
Pankow, James
- Colour My World
Richman, Lucas
- An Overture to Blanche
Schoenberg, Claude-Michel
- Miss Saigon: Last Night of the World
Simons, Moises
- Peanut Vendor
Sousa, John Philip
- The Stars and Stripes Forever
Villaldo, Angel
- El Choclo: Tango Argentina
Young, Victor
- The Uninvited (1944): Stella by Starlight

---

2 2 3 2 – 4 3 3 1 – perc – str
Bernstein, Leonard
- West Side Story Highlights
Dorff, Daniel
- The Kiss
Ellington, Edward (Duke)
- Black, Brown and Beige
Mancini, Henry
- Academy Award Medley
- Days of Wine and Roses
Mussorgsky, Modest
- Songs and Dances of Death
Shire, David
- With You I'm Born Again
Tiomkin, Dimitri
- Town Without Pity (1961): Theme
Tyzik, Jeff
- The Skater's Overture: Variations on a Theme of Waldteufel

---

4 4 5 4 – 6 4 3 2 – perc - str
Anderson, Leroy
- China Doll
Bach, J. S.
- Fantasia & Fugue in G minor
Bernstein, Leonard
- West Side Story: Symphonic Dances
- On the Waterfront: Symphonic Suite
Bizet, Georges
- L'Arlesienne Suite No. 1
Bond, Victoria
- Urban Bird
Creston, Paul
- Concerto for Saxophone, Op. 26

Curtis-Smith, Curtis
- Great American Symphony
Ellington, Edward (Duke)
- Ellington Portrait
Harbison, John
- Remembering Gatsby: Foxtrot for Orchestra
Herrmann, Bernard
- Taxi Driver: A Night Piece for Orchestra (1976)
Holcombe, Bill
- Saxanova
Khachaturian, Aram
- Gayaneh: Sabre Dance
- Gayaneh, Suite No. 1
- Gayaneh, Suite No. 3
Mancini, Henry
- The Pink Panther
- Songs for Audrey: Breakfast at Tiffanys, Charade, Two for the Road
Mussorgsky, Modest
- Pictures at an Exhibition
North, Alex
- A Streetcar Named Desire: Suite
Prokofiev, Sergei
- Lieutenant Kije Suite, Op. 60
- Romeo and Juliet: Scenes from the Ballet
- Romeo and Juliet: Suite No. 1, Op. 64a
- Romeo and Juliet: Suite No. 2, Op. 64b
Raksin, David
- The Bad and the Beautiful: Mvt. I: Love Is For the Very Young
- The Bad and the Beautiful: Mvt III: The Quickies and Sneak Preview
Rasmussen, Karl Aage
- Symphony for Young Lovers
Riegger, Wallingford
- New Dance, Op. 18b: Finale from the Ballet
- Quintuple Jazz, Op. 72
Rodríguez, Robert Xavier
- Hot Buttered Rumba
- Piñata
Schoenberg, Claude-Michel
- Miss Saigon Rhapsody
Ticheli, Frank
- Blue Shades
Tiomkin, Dimitri
- The Men (1950): Suite
Tyzik, Jeff
- The Big Movie Suite
Waxman, Franz
- Dark City (1950)
- My Cousin Rachel (1952): Suite
- The Philadelphia Story (1939): Suite
- A Place in the Sun (1951): A Symphonic Scenario
- Rear Window (1954)

- Taras Bulba (1962): The Ride of the Cossacks
Young, Victor
- Medley: Victor Young Tribute

ENSEMBLES WITH TWO SAXOPHONES

Strings
Glass, Philip
- Façades
Gordon, Phillip
- Fitzwilliam Suite

1 1 3 1 – 2 3 3 1 – perc – str
Arlen, Harold
- Wizard of Oz: Munchkin Land
Brown, Robert Bennett
- Masquerade
Gordon, Phillip
- Fitzwilliam Suite
Grainger, Percy
- Irish Tune from County Derry
Guion, David - Pickaninny Dance
- Sheep and Goat
Herbert, Victor
- Babes in Toyland: March of the Toys
Horner, James
- An American Tail: Somewhere Out There
Lowden, Bob
- Remembering the Beatles
Marks, Johnny
- Rudolph the Red-Nosed Reindeer
Mozart, Wolfgang Amadeus
- The Sleigh Ride
Saint-Saëns, Camille
- Christmas Oratorio, Op. 12: Praise Ye the Lord of Hosts
Styne, Jule
- Let It Snow! Let It Snow! Let It Snow!
Thomson, Virgil
- The Plow that Broke the Plains: Suite
Williams, John T.
- Theme from Close Encounters of the Third Kind
Willson, Meredith
- The Music Man Entr'acte
- The Music Man Overture

2 2 5 2 – 2 3 3 1 – perc – str
Brown, Robert Bennett
- Early American Quadrille: Square Dance
Davis, Anthony
- X: The Life and Times of MalcolmX: Malcolm's Prison Aria
Faith, Percy
- Quia, Quia (Kee-a, Kee-a)
Gould, Morton
- Revival: A Fantasy on Six Spirituals
Greenwood, Lee
- God Bless the U.S.A
Guion, David
- Mam'selle Marie
Hamlisch, Marvin
- Ice Castles Through the Eyes of Love
Lai, Francis
- A Man and a Woman
Lecuona, Ernesto
- La Comparsa: Carnival Procession
Lennon, John & McCartney, Paul
- I Want To Hold Your Hand
Lloyd Webber, Andrew
- Cats: Memory
- Cats Selections
Lowden, Bob
- Disney Magic
MacLellan, Gene
- Put Your Hand in the Hand
Manzanero, Armando
- It's Impossible (Somos novios)
Phillips, John
- Monday, Monday
Phillips & Gilliam
- California Dreamin'
Revaux, J. & Francois, C.
- My Way
Richardson, Clive
- British Grenadiers
- Polly-Wolly Doodle
Schoenberg, Claude-Michel
- Les Miserables: I Dreamed A Dream
Shostakovich, Dmitri
- Hypothetically Murdered, Op. 31a
Sousa, John Philip
- The Liberty Bell March
Weill, Kurt
- Kleine Dreigroschenmusik (Three Penny Opera): Mack the Knife
Williams, Charles
- The Apartment: Theme (Jealous Lover)
Williams, Charles
- Dream of Olwen
Wilson & James & Karlin
- For All We Know

2 2 4 2 – 4 4 3 1 – perc – str
Anderson, Leroy
- Forgotten Dreams
Chase, Bruce
- Christmas Favorites
- Muppet Medley
Falla, Manuel de
- Three Cornered Hat: Miller's Dance
Gould, Morton
- Folk Suite
Grainger, Percy
- Country Gardens
Guion, David
- Arkansas Traveler
Hamlisch, Marvin
- Selections from a Chorus Line
- Marvin Hamlisch in Concert
Herbert, Victor
- Ah Sweet Mystery of Life
Herman, Jerry
- Hello Dolly Highlights
Korngold, Erich
- Korngold: The Adventures of Robin Hood, Symphonic Portrait
Krogstad, Bob
- Curtain Up!
Lecuona, Ernesto
- Andalucia Suite
Lehár, Franz
- Gold and Silver Waltz
Lloyd Webber, Andrew
- Phantom of the Opera Selections
Monti, V.
- Czardas   Padilla, José
- El Relicario: Paso Doble
Raksin, David
- Laura
Rota, Nino
- The Godfather: Reminiscences for Orchestra (1972)
Schoenberg, Claude-Michel
- Les Miserables Selections
Shaw, Artie
- Concerto for Clarinet and Jazz Band
Warrington, John
- Yuletide Festival
Webb, Jimmy
- MacArthur Park
Williams, Charles
- The Apartment: Theme (Jealous Lover)
Wonder, Stevie
- Stevie Wonder Sounds
Zawinul, Joseph
- Birdland

(Ensembles with Two Saxs, cont.)

3 3 4 2 – 4 4 3 1 – perc – str

Alzedo, José Bernardo
- Himno Nacional del Perú

Anderson, Leroy
- Arietta for Orchestra
- Bugler's Holiday

Cailliet, Lucien
- Variations on "Pop! Goes the Weasel"

Calandrelli, Jorge
- Concerto for Jazz Clarinet and Orchestra

Ellington, Edward (Duke)
- Black, Brown and Beige: Suite

Lecuona, Ernesto
- Danza Lucumi: Danza Afro-Cubanas

MacLellan, Gene
- Snowbird

Ravel, Maurice
- Bolero

Shire, David
- Taking of Pelham One Two Three (1974): Theme

Silvestri, Alan
- Mouse Hunt (1997): Suite

Steiner, Max
- The Treasure of Sierra Madre (1948): Suite

Tiomkin, Dimitri
- The Thing from Another World (1951): Suite

Waxman, Franz
- Hemingway's Adventures of a Young Man
- Rear Window (1954)

ENSEMBLES WITH THREE SAXOPHONES

1 2 3 1 – 2 3 3 1 – perc – str

Antheil, George
- A Jazz Symphony: 1925 version

Boskerck, Captain Francis Saltus Van
- Semper Paratus (1927): U.S. Coast Guard March Song

Goldman, Edwin Franko
- Children's March

Gould, Morton
- Café Rio
- Derivations for Solo Clarinet and Dance Band
- Swanee River in the Style of Gershwin
- Swanee River in the Style of Tchaikovsky

Herbert, Victor
- President's March

Lake, M. L.
- Old Timers Waltz

Lecuona, Ernesto
- Andalucia Suite: Malagueña

Maxwell Davies, Peter
- The Boyfriend: Concert Suite

Meacham, Frank W.
- American Patrol

Monti, Vittorio
- Czardas

Olcott, Chauncey
- My Wild Irish Rose

Shostakovich, Dmitri
- Suite for Jazz Orchestra No. 1

Wilson, Don
- Scrambled Opera (An Orchestral Antic)

2 2 3 2 – 2 3 3 1 – perc – str

Creston, Paul
- Kangaroo Kaper

Grainger, Percy
- County Derry Air for Pipe Organ and Symphony Orchestra

Handy, W. C.
- Saint Louis Blues

Lehár, Franz
- The Merry Widow

Lennon, John & McCartney, Paul
- Beatles Medley

Lundquist, Torbjön
- Round the Orchestra in Ten Minutes

Mancini, Henry
- The Pink Panther

Mills, Gordon & Reed, Les
- It's Not Unusual

Stevens, Ray
- Everything is Beautiful

Torme & Wells
- Christmas Song (Chestnuts Roasting on an Open Fire)

Vangelis
- Chariots of Fire

Weill, Kurt
- Kleine Dreigroschenmusik (Three Penny Opera): Mack the Knife Wood
- Moorland Fiddlers

2 2 3 2 – 4 3 3 1 – perc – str

Adams, Emmett A.
- Bells of St. Mary's

Anderson, Leroy
- A Christmas Festival
- First Day of Spring
- Jazz Legato
- Jazz Pizzicato
- Summer Skies
- Syncopated Clock
- Trumpeter's Lullaby

Ball, Ernest R.
- When Irish Eyes Are Smiling

Conti, Bill
- Rocky Highlights

Denza, Luigi
- Funiculi, Funicula

Desplat, Alexandre
- The Curious Case of Benjamin Button: Suite

Fernandez, Caballero
- Cielito Lindo

Gade, Jacob
- Jalousie

Gershwin, George
- Rhapsody in Blue

Gillis, Don
- Atlanta Suite: Peachtree Promenade
- Twinkletoes Ballet: Tango Lullaby

Gould, Morton
- Crinoline and Lace

Hayman, Richard
- Her Name is Suzanne

Herbert, Victor
- Ah Sweet Mystery of Life

Holcombe, Bill
- Evening at Pops

Ivanovici, Josif
- Waves of the Danube: The Anniversary Song

Joel, Billy
- The Best of Billy Joel

Lang, Philip J.
- Dark Eyes

Loewe, Frederick
- My Fair Lady

Mantovani, Annunzio Paolo
- Gypsy Legend
- Poem to the Moon

Meyer, George W.
- If You Were the Only Girl in the World

Pachelbel, Johann
- Ordinary People Theme (Canon)

Romberg, Sigmund
- A Tribute to Romberg

Sayre, Charles
- A Rockin' Christmas

Secunda, Sholom
- Tango de la luna

Sondheim, Stephen
- A Little Night Music: Send In the Clowns

Tchaikovsky, Peter Ilyich
- The Nutcracker Suite

Washington, Ned & Bassman, George
- I'm Getting Sentimental Over You

Wenrich, Percy
- When You Wore a Tulip
Wernick, Richard
- Chanukah Festival Overture
Willson, Meredith
- Music Man Selections
Zaninelli, Luigi
- For Spacious Skies

3 2 2 2 – 4 3 3 1 – perc – str

Anderson, Leroy
- Blue Tango
- Captains and the Kings
- Chicken Reel
- Fiddle Faddle
- Girl in Satin
- Golden Years for Orchestra
- Goldilocks: Pyramid Dance
- Goldilocks: Pirate Dance
- Horse and Buggy
- Penny Whistle Song
- The Phantom Regiment
- Promenade for Orchestra
- Sandpaper Ballet
- Saraband
- Serenata
- Sleigh Ride
- Song of the Bells-Waltz
- The Typewriter
- The Waltzing Cat

Cohan, George M.
- Give My Regards to Broadway
- Over There
- You're a Grand Old Flag

Cory, George
- I Left My Heart in San Francisco

Fisher, Fred
- Peg O' My Heart

Gershwin, George
- Swanee

Gould, Morton
- Pirouette

Grundman, Clare
- American Folk Rhapsody, No. 1 & No. 2

Hubbell, Raymond
- Poor Butterfly

Monaco, James V.
- You Made Me Love You

Norton, George A.
- Round Her Neck She Wore a Yellow Ribbon

Offenbach, Jacques
- La Vie Parisienne: Overture

Puccini, Giacomo
- Madam Butterfly

Schwartz, Stephen
- Rock-a-Bye Your Baby with a Dixie Melody

Silvers, Louis
- April Showers

Sousa, John Philip
- The Stars and Stripes Forever

Stevens, Leith
- The Wild One (1953)

Tilzer, Albert von
- Take Me Out to the Ball Game

Wagner, Joseph
- Radio City Snapshots

Waxman, Franz
- Night and the City (1950): Suite
Nightride for Orchestra

4 3 4 4 – 6 4 3 1 – perc – str

Anderson, Leroy
- Clarinet Candy
- Penny Whistle Song

Arnold, David
- Independence Day: Highlights
- Independence Day Suite

Effinger, Cecil
- Let Your Mind Wander Over America

Elfman, Danny
- Simpsons Main Title

Ellington, Edward K. (Duke)
- Non-Violent Integration, for Jazz Band and Orchestra

Foster, Stephen Collins
- Jeanie with the Light Brown Hair

Gershwin, George
- American in Paris
- Porgy and Bess: Symphonic Picture

Grainger, Percy
- The Power of Love

Grofé, Ferde
- Symphony in Steel
- Tabloid

Murray, Lyn
- To Catch a Thief: Suite (1955)

Schuman, William
- Newsreel in 5 Shots

Waxman, Franz
- Elephant Walk (1954): Suite

ENSEMBLES WITH FOUR OR MORE SAXOPHONES

Brass-perc (jazz band)

Blake, Howard
- Heartbeat

Ellington, Edward K. (Duke)
- Liberian Suite

Peaslee, Richard
- Chicago Concerto

Shostakovich, Dmitri
- Suite for Jazz Orchestra No. 2

1 1 3 1 – 2 3 3 1 – perc – str

Blake, Howard
- Heartbeat

Ellington, Edward K. (Duke)
- Liberian Suite
- Mood Indigo: 5 brass setting
- Mood Indigo: 6 brass setting

Gilpin, Greg
- The Music of MGM (A Choral Medley)

Grainger, Percy
- Green Bushes

Gould, Morton
- Pop's Serenade

Guion, David
- My Cowboy Love Song
- Sail Away for the Rio Grande

Marquina
- España cani

Newborn, Ira
- The Naked Gun: Theme (1988)

Peaslee, Richard
- Chicago Concerto

Porter, Cole
- I Get a Kick Out of You

Shostakovich, Dmitri
- Suite for Jazz Orchestra No. 2

Traditional
- Football Song Hits: Eastern
- Football Song Hits No. 2: Western
- Football Song Hits No. 4: East-South

2 2 3 2 – 2 2 3 1 – perc – str

Beatles
- Beatles Medley

Gershwin, George
- I Got Plenty of Nuttin'

Glass, Philip
- Glassworks

Mancini, Henry
- The Pink Panther

Jessel, Leon
- Parade of the Wooden Soldiers

Ellington, Edward (Duke)
- Highlights from Sophisticated Ladies

Lecuona, Ernesto
- Andalucia

Gould, Morton
- Symphonette No. 3 (Third American Symphonette)

Mancini, Henry
- Peter Gunn Theme

(Ensembles with Four or More Saxs, cont.)

2 2 4 2 – 4 4 3 1 – perc – str

Ades, Hawley
- Sholom Aleichem

Bernstein, Leonard
- West Side Story Selections

Binge, Ronald
- Cornet Carillon

Brel, Jacques
- If You Go Away

Eiger, Walter
- Concerto Grosso

Ellington, Edward K. (Duke)
- Harlem
- Grand Slam Jam
- Night Creature

Flaherty, Stephen
- Anastasia: Paris Holds the Key

Farnan, Robert
- Portrait of a Flirt

Friml, Rudolf
- Medley from The Firefly

Gershwin, George
- I Got Rhythm Variations for Piano and Orchestra
- Porgy and Bess: I Got Plenty of Nuttin'
- Porgy and Bess: Selections for Orchestra (1961)

Gould, Morton
- American Caprice

Handy, W. C.
- Saint Louis Blues

Hayman, Richard
- Hullabaloo

Jendras, Louis F.
- Appalachian Fling

Loesser, Frank
- The Most Happy Fella: Symphonic Impressions

Loewe, Frederick
- My Fair Lady: Selections
- Gigi: Selections

Lloyd Webber, Andrew
- Evita Highlights

Mancini, Henry
- Astaire!
- Oklahoma Crude

Mason, Jack
- O Bury Me Not On the Lone Prairie

Newman, Alfred
- Gentleman's Agreement Suite

Regney & Shayne
- Do You Hear What I Hear

Rodgers, Richard
- Carousel: Selections
- Oklahoma Selections
- Sound of Music Selections

Rome, Harold
- Fanny: Selection for Orchestra

Shostakovich, Dmitri
- Suite for Variety Orchestra No. 1
- Suite for Variety Orchestra No. 2

Strouse, Charles
- Selections from Annie

3 2 2 2 – 4 3 3 1 – perc – str

Anderson, Leroy
- Belle of the Ball

Gestor, Don
- First Love

Gold, Ernest
- Exodus: An Orchestral Tone-Picture

Gould, Morton
- Yankee Doodle

Hayes, Isaac
- Selections from Shaft

Leigh, Mitch
- Man of La Mancha: The Impossible Dream

Lloyd Webber, Andrew
- Andrew Lloyd Webber: A Concert Celebration (Medley)

Loewe, Frederick
- Camelot: Selections

Moore, Donald I.
- America

3 3 4 2 – 6 4 3 1 – perc – str

Berlin, Irving
- Irving Berlin in Hollywood Overture

Coleman, Cy
- Sweet Charity Medley

Gershwin, George
- Love Walked In
- Porgy and Bess: Symphonic Picture

Gould, Morton
- Latin American Symphonette

Grofé, Ferde
- Hollywood Suite

Hagen, Earl
- Television Medley

Holcombe, Bill
- Cowboy Fantasy

Joplin, Scott
- The Entertainer

Lecuona, Ernesto
- Jungle Drums

Mancini, Henry
- Peter Gunn

Newman, Alfred
- How to Marry a Millionaire: Street Scene

Reed, Alfred
- A Festival Prelude

Ringwald, Roy
- O Brother Man

Rota, Nino
- The Godfather III: Suite

Styne, Jule
- Gypsy: A Musical Fable

Time for Three
- Sweet Georgia Brown

Waxman, Franz
- The Ice Follies of 1939
- Young at Heart (1938)

Williams, John T.
- Selections from E.T.

6 4 4 4 – 6 6 4 2 – perc – str

Bernstein, Elmer
- The Sweet Smell of Success: Main Title

Broughton, Bruce
- Overture to Miracle on 34th Street

Chávez, Carlos
- Chapultepec: Three Famous Mexican Pieces

Gordon, Michael
- Sunshine of Your Love

MISCELLANEOUS INSTRUMENTAL COMBINATIONS

Andriessen, Louis
- Workers' Union

Arnold, Malcolm
- A Grand, Grand Overture, Op. 57

Brubeck, Dave
- Brandenburg Gate: Revisited

Grainger, Percy
- County Derry Air for 6 or More Single Instruments

Haydn, Franz Joseph
- Kindersymphonie, Hob. II:47, C Major (Toy Symphony)

McCabe, John
- Mini Concerto for Organ, Percussion, Audience

Tan Dun
- Crouching Tiger Concerto

Wilby, Philip
- The Highland Express

ORCHESTRA WITH SOLO VOICES

Solo Soprano

Baker, David
- Le chat qui pêche

Bennett, Richard Rodney
  - Love Spells
Berlin, Irving
  - God Bless America
Brubeck, Dave
  - Truth Is Fallen
Burgon, Geoffrey
  - Nunc Dimittis
Castelnuovo-Tedesco, Mario
  - Naomi and Ruth (Ruth's Aria)
Falla, Manuel de
  - Seven Popular Spanish Songs
Gershwin, George
  - Porgy and Bess: Summertime
Granados, Enrique
  - Tonadillas
Hawley, C.B.
  - The Christ Child
Horner, James
  - Titanic Suite
Hovhaness, Alan
  - Triptych: As on the Night,
    Op. 100, No. 1b (Christmas Ode)
Iturriaga, Enrique
  - Canción y Muerte de Rolando
    (Song and Death of Rolando)
Kapilow, Robert
  - Dr. Seuss's Gertrude McFuzz
  - Dr. Seuss's Green Eggs and Ham
Kern, Jerome
  - Smoke Gets In Your Eyes
Kernis, Aaron Jay
  - Valentines
Maxwell Davies, Peter
  - The Devils: Suite
McDonald, Harl
  - Song of Free Nations
Mozart, Wolfgang Amadeus
  - Exsultate Jubilate, K. 165
  - The Marriage of Figaro: Deh Vieni
    non Tardar
  - The Marriage of Figaro: Porgi amor
    (Cavatina)
Mussorgsky, Modes
  - Songs and Dances of Death
Niles, John Jacob
  - I Wonder as I Wander
Puccini, Giacomo
  - Gianni Schicchi: O mio babbino
    caro
Reger, Max
  - Christmas with Renata Scotto:
    7. Virgin's Slumber Song
Rodrigo, Joaquin
  - Cuatro madrigales amatorios
Schubert, Franz
  - Ave Maria
Strauss, Johann, Jr.
  - Die Fledermaus: Mein Herr
    Marquis (Laughing Song)
Ticheli, Frank
  - Angels in Architecture

Turina, Joaquin
  - Canto a Sevilla, Op. 37
Tyzik, Jeff
  - Twelve Gifts of Christmas
  - What Child Is This
Villa-Lobos, Heitor
  - Bachianas Brasileiras No. 5
Warlock, Peter
  - Aspects of Love and Contentment
Waxman, Franz
  - The Ice Follies of 1939

Solo Alto or Mezzo-Soprano
Bax, Arnold
  - A Christmas Carol
Berlin, Irving
  - God Bless America
Bizet, Georges
  - Carmen: Seguidilla and Duett
DePonte, Niel
  - Bell of Freedom (2002)
Elgar, Edward
  - Sea Pictures
Falla, Manuel de
  - El Amor brujo
  - El Sombrero de tres picos (The Three
    Cornered Hat)
  - Récit du pécheur and Pantomime
  - Sept Chansons populaires espagnoles
    (Seven Popular Spanish Songs)
Herrmann, Bernard
  - The Man Who Knew Too Much: The
    Storm Clouds Cantata (1956)
Hupfeld, Herman
  - As Time Goes By
Nórgård, Per
  - Three Love Songs
Nystroem, Gösta
  - Three Love Songs (3 Kärleksvisor)
Rodrigo, Joaquin
  - Cuatro madrigales amatorios
Stephenson, James M. III
  - Lo, How a Rose E'er Blooming
Wendel, Robert
  - A George M. Cohan Overture

Solo Tenor
Bennett, Richard Rodney
  - London Pastoral
  - Lovesongs
Berlin, Irving
  - White Christmas
Burgon, Geoffrey
  - Nunc Dimittis
Capua, Eduardo di
  - O sole mio
Costa, Francesco Antonio
  - Era di maggio

Ellstein, Abraham
  - Sh'Ma Yisroel
Gershwin, George
  - I Got Plenty of Nuttin'
Hawley, C.B.
  - The Christ Child
Hupfeld, Herman
  - As Time Goes By
Robinson, Earl
  - A Country They Call Puget Sound
Schubert, Franz
  - Ave Maria
Tyzik, Jeff
  - Twelve Gifts of Christmas
  - What Child Is This
Vaughan Williams, Ralph
  - Three Choral Hymns: Easter,
    Christmas, Whitsunday

Solo Baritone or Bass
Davis, Anthony
  - X: The Life and Times of
    Malcolm X: Malcolm's Prison Aria
Deak, John
  - The Passion of Scrooge (A Christmas
    Carol)
DePonte, Niel
  - Bell of Freedom (2002)
Gershwin, George
  - I Got Plenty of Nuttin'
Kern, Jerome
  - Ol' Man River
Kraft, William
  - Seven Spirituals
Mozart, Wolfgang Amadeus
  - The Marriage of Figaro: Aprite un
    po'quegl'occhi
Mussorgsky, Modest
  - Songs and Dances of Death
  - The Song of the Flea
Tiomkin, Dimitri
  - Gunfight at the OK Corral
    (1957): Ballad and Theme
Vaughan Williams, Ralph
  - Three Choral Hymns: Easter,
    Christmas, Whitsunday
Wendel, Robert
  - A George M. Cohan Overture

Solo Vocalist
Arias, Clotilde
  - Huiracocha for voice and orchestra
Arlen, Harold
  - Blues in the Night
  - The Wizard of Oz: Over the
    Rainbow
Berlin, Irving
  - White Christmas

(Orchestra with Solo Voices, cont. Solo Vocalist)

Berlioz, Hector
- The Novello Book of Carols: The Shepherds' Farewell (Thou Must Leave)

Cohan, George M.
- You're a Grand Old Flag

Corigliano, John
- The Cloisters

Doyle, Patrick
- Sense and Sensibility: Suite (1995)

Dunhill, Thomas
- The Novello Book of Carols: How Soft, Upon the Ev'ning Air

Ellstein, Abraham
- Vli jeru sholayim ircho

Gauntlett & Mann & Wells
- The Novello Book of Carols: Once in Royal David's City

Goldsmith, Jerry
- Rudy: Suite

Guion, David
- Home on the Range
- Cowboy's Meditation
- Mam'selle Marie

Handel, George Frideric
- The Novello Book of Carols: Joy to the World

Herbert, Victor
- The Enchantress: Art Is Calling for Me: I Want to Be a Prima Donna
- Naughty Marietta: I'm Falling in Love with Someone

Holst, Gustav
- The Novello Book of Carols: In the Bleak Midwinter

Jackson, Stephen
- The Novello Book of Carols: Noel Nouvelet

Kirkpatrick, W. F.
- The Novello Book of Carols: Away in a Manger

Lambert, Constant
- Eight Poems of Li-Po

Llewellyn, William
- The Novello Book of Carols: The Angel Gabriel (Gabriel's Message)
- The Novello Book of Carols: Come All You Worthy People Here (A Somerset Carol)
- The Novello Book of Carols: De Virgin Mary had a Baby Boy
- The Novello Book of Carols: God Rest You Merry Gentlemen
- The Novello Book of Carols: The Holly and the Ivy
- The Novello Book of Carols: Il est né, Le divin enfant (See Him Born)
- The Novello Book of Carols: King Jesus Hath A Garden
- The Novello Book of Carols: O Come All Ye Faithful
- The Novello Book of Carols: Puer Nobis: Unto Us Is Born a Son

Malotte, Albert Hay
- The Lord's Prayer

Mancini, Henry
- Breakfast at Tiffanys: Moon River

Mendelssohn, Felix
- The Novello Book of Carols: Hark the Herald Angels Sing

Moeran, E.J.
- Lonely Waters

Schoenberg, Claude-Michel
- Les Miserables: At the End of the Day
- Les Miserables: Bring Him Home
- Les Miserables: Do You Hear the People Sing?
- Les Miserables: Empty Chairs at Empty Tables
- Les Miserables: I Dreamed A Dream
- Les Miserables: Little Cosette (Castle on a Cloud)
- Les Miserables: Master of the House
- Les Miserables: On My Own
- Les Miserables: One Day More
- Les Miserables: Stars
- Les Miserables: The ABC Café
- Miss Saigon: Last Night of the World
- Miss Saigon: Why God Why

Sharp, Cecil
- Country Gardens

Shire, David
- Norma Rae: It Goes Like It Goes

Shostakovich, Dmitri
- Eight English and American Folk Songs: When Johnny Comes Marching Home

Stephenson, James M. III
- I Saw Three Ships/Jeanette, Isabella Medley

Strauss, Johann, Sr.
- On the Blue Danube
- Tritsch-Tratsch (The Circus)

Thurlow, Jeremy
- The Novello Book of Carols: All and Some (Nowell We Sing)

Tiomkin, Dimitri
- High Noon (1952): Do Not Forsake Me Oh My Darling
- It's a Wonderful Life (1947): Theme
- Rawhide (1959): Theme

Turrin, Joseph
- The Fir Tree

Wells, Robin
- The Novello Book of Carols: A Fanfare for Christmas (Hodie, Hodie); A Gallery Carol (Rejoice and Be Merry)

Yon, Pietro A.
- Gesu Bambino

ORCHESTRA WITH VOCAL ENSEMBLES

Duo

Anderson, Leroy
- Goldilocks: Save a Kiss [SBar]

Baerwald, David
- Moulin Rouge! (2001): Come What May [Male and Female]

Berlin, Irving
- White Christmas [Male and Female]

Bizet, Georges
- Carmen: Seguidilla and Duet [MsT]

Blake, Howard
- Christmas Lullaby [S, A or T, Bs]

Chiarappa, Richard
- To Be Young Again [ABar]
- Lincoln & Booth: Just Ourselves [ST]

DePonte, Niel
- Bell of Freedom (2002) [ABar]

Rodgers, Richard
- Love Me Tonight: Lover

Rodríguez, Robert Xavier
- Adoracion Ambulante: Con flor y canto [TBs]
- Adoracion ambulante (A Mexican Folk Celebration) [TBs]

Rossini, Gioacchino
- Cat Duet (Duetto buffo di due gatti) [Female]

Smith, Hale
- Meditations in Passage [SBar]

Tchaikovsky, Peter Ilyich
- Romeo and Juliet: Duet [ST]

Tesori, Jeanine
- Thoroughly Modern Millie

Tyzik, Jeff
- American Celebration [ST]

Wendel, Robert
- A George M. Cohan Overture [SBar]

Trio

Chiarappa, Richard
- Lincoln & Booth: Good-bye [SAT]

Flaherty, Stephen
- Anastasia: Learn to Do It Waltz [SABar]

Kapilow, Robert
- You and Hugh [SBar, Boy Soprano]

McCarthy, Dennis
- Star Trek 7: Generations "Overture" [SAT]

Moross, Jerome
- Frankie and Johnny [SSA]

Webb, Jimmy
- The Animals' Christmas

Quartet

Berlin, Irving
- White Christmas [SATB]

Chiarappa, Richard
- Lincoln & Booth: Good-bye [SAT]

Dankworth, John
- The Diamond and the Goose [SATB]

Gould, Morton
- American Sing: Settings of Folk Songs [SATB]

Kerchner, Larry
- Happy Birthday Medley [SATB]

McCarthy, Dennis
- Star Trek 7: Generations "Overture" [SAT]

Perry, William
- Joy Shall Be Yours in the Morning [SSATB]

Tiomkin, Dimitri
- The Thing from Another World (1951): Suite

ORCHESTRA WITH SOLO VOICES AND CHORUS

Strings with Solo Voices

Kirkpatrick, W. F.
- The Novello Book of Carols: Away in a Manger

Reger, Max
- Christmas with Renata Scotto: 7. Virgin's Slumber Song [S]

Solo

Adam, Adolphe
- Christmas with Renata Scotto: 5. Christmas Song (Cantique de Noel) [Soprano]

Arlen, Harold
- Wizard of Oz: Yellow Brick Road

Barber, Samuel
- The Lovers, Op. 43 [Baritone]

Berlin, Irving
- God Bless America [Mezzo Soprano]

Beveridge, Thomas
- Once: Tribute to Martin Luther King [Soprano]

Boccadoro, Carol
- Snowtime! Christmas Fantasy [Soprano]

Brubeck, Dave
- The Light in the Wilderness [Baritone]

Cooper, Rose Marie
- Morning Star: A Christmas Cantata [T]

Dennison, Sam
- And If Elected… [S]

Dix, William
- Christmas with Renata Scotto: 8. What Child Is This? [S]

Ellstein, Abraham
- Retsei [T]

Gershwin, George
- Porgy and Bess: Summertime [S]

Gillis, Don
- This Is Our America [ABar]

Gould, Morton
- Something to Do-Labor Cantata

Grady, John
- Christmas with Renata Scotto: 2. Angels We Have Heard on High [S]
- Christmas with Renata Scotto: 3. Adeste Fidelis [S]

Gruber, F. X.
- Christmas with Renata Scotto: 1. Silent Night [S]

Hailstork, Adolphus
- I Will Lift Up Mine Eyes [T]

Handel, George Frideric
- Christmas with Renata Scotto: 4. Joy to the World [S]

Herrmann, Bernard
- The Man Who Knew Too Much: The Storm Clouds Cantata [Ms]

Horner, James
- Titanic Suite [S]

Howard, James
- Peter Pan (2003): Suite for Orchestra with Narrator [(Child Soprano)]

Kapilow, Robert
- Chris van Allsburg's Polar Express [Bar]

Lambert, Constant
- The Rio Grande [A]

Lutoslawski, Witold
- Twenty Polish Christmas Carols [S]

Martynov, Vladimir
- Christmas Music [Boy Soprano]

Musgrave, Thea
- Two Christmas Carols in traditional style [S]

Poulenc, Francis
- Gloria [S]

Richman, Lucas
- Ho! Ho! Ho! [Bar]

Robinson, Earl
- In the Folded and Quiet Yesterdays
- The Lonesome Train [Bar]

Rodriguez, Robert Xavier
- Scrooge: Concert Scenes from "A Christmas Carol" [Bs-Bar]

Saint-Saëns, Camille
- La Nuit, Op. 114 [S]

Schubert, Franz
- Ave Maria [S or T]
- Christmas with Renata Scotto: 6. Ave Maria [S]

Schuman, William
- On Freedom's Ground [Bar]

Silvestri & Ballard
- God Gless Us Everyone [T]

Steffe, William
- Battle Hymn of the Republic [Bar]

Stephenson, James M. III
- The Magic of Christmas [Child Soprano]

Tiomkin, Dimitri
- The Alamo (1960): Suite
- Gunfight at the OK Corral (1957): Ballad and Theme [Bar]
- Night Passage (1957): Follow the River

Welcher, Dan
- JFK: The Voice of Peace [Ms or Boy Soprano]

Duo

Blake, Howard
- Christmas Lullaby [Male & Female]

Brubeck, Dave
- The Gates of Justice [T Bar]

Chiarappa, Richard
- Lincoln & Booth: Just Ourselves [ST]

Darke, Harold
- In the Bleak Midwinter [ST]

Ellstein, Abraham
- Ode to the King of Kings [SBar]

Flaherty, Stephen
- Anastasia: Once Upon a December [SBs]

Hailstork, Adolphus
- Four Spirituals [SS]

Harbison, John
- The Flight into Egypt; Sacred Ricercar [SBar]

Hawley, C.B.
- The Christ Child [BarBs]

Herman, Jerry
- The Best Christmas of All [ABar]

Holst, Gustav
- Let All Mortal Flesh Keep Silence [SBs]

Mechem, Kirke
- Songs of the Slave [SB-Bar]

Menken, Alan
- Go the Distance

Richman, Lucas- Thanksgiving Hymn [SBar]

Rodríguez, Robert Xavier
- Adoracion Ambulante: Con flor y canto [TBs]

(Orchestra with Solo Voices and Chorus – DUO – RODRIGUEZ, cont)

- Adoracion ambulante: A Mexican Folk Celebration *[TBs]*

Schuman, William
- Casey at the Bat: A Baseball Cantata *[SBar]*

Stillman & Allen
- Home for the Holidays *[SBar]*

Tchaikovsky, Piotr Ilyich
- Romeo and Juliet: Duet *[S T]*

Tyzik, Jeff
- American Celebration *[SBar]*

Trio

Antheil, George
- Cabeza de vaca *[TBar, Boy Soprano]*

Debney, John
- Passion of the Christ, The Symphony *[SMsT]*

Effinger, Cecil
- The St. Luke Christmas Story *[STBs]*

Kapilow, Robert
- Elijah's Angel *[Bar, Bs-Bar, Boy Soprano]*

Monestal, Alexander
- The Birth of our Lord: A Christmas Cantata *[TBarBs]*

Schutz, Heinrich
- Christmas Story SWV 435a *[STBs]*

Thomson, Virgil
- The Nativity *[ATBs]*

Vaughan Williams, Ralph
- Hodie, A Christmas Cantata *[STBs]*

Quartet or more

Arlen, Harold
- Wizard of Oz: Munchkin Land

Bach, P.D.Q.
- Birthday Ode to "Big Daddy" Bach *[SATB]*

Dello Joio, Norman
- Nativity: Canticle for the Child *[STTBar]*

Grainger, Percy
- Tribute to Foster

Hawley, C.B.
- The Christ Child *[T or S,SSABarBs]*

Kleinsinger, George
- Brooklyn Baseball Cantata

Maxwell Davies, Peter
- The Three Kings *[SMsTBs]*

Mechem, Kirke
- The King's Contest *[Ms/Nar,TBarBs]*

Menotti, Gian Carlo
- Landscapes and Remembrances *[SATB]*

Monteverdi, Claudio
- Christmas Vespers *[SSATTBarBs]*

Perry, William
- Joy Shall Be Yours in the Morning *[SSATB]*

Richman, Lucas
- In the Day When I Cried Out

Rosenberg, Hilding Constantin
- Die Heligea Natten (The Holy Night): A Christmas Oratorio *[SATB]*

Saint-Saëns, Camille
- Christmas Oratorio, Op. 12 *[SATB]*

Schickele, Peter
- Birthday Ode to "Big Daddy" Bach *[SATB]*

Schoenberg, Claude-Michel
- Miss Saigon: Finale

Schumann, Robert
- New Year Song, Op. 144 "Mit eherner Zunge, da ruft es: Gebt acht" *[SATB]*

Schütz, Heinrich
- Christmas Story, SWV 435a *[STBs]*

ORCHESTRA WITH CHORUS

Strings with Chorus

Gould, Morton
- Christmas Time, Book I: It Came Upon a Midnight Clear

Lloyd Webber, Andrew
- Andrew Lloyd Webber: A Concert Celebration (Medley)

Musgrave, Thea
- Two Christmas Carols
- Wild Winter II

Warren, Diane
- Music of My Heart

Yeston, Maury
- Beneath all the Stripes and Stars

Children's Chorus

Effinger, Cecil
- An American Hymn: A Setting of "America the Beautiful"

Goldstein, William
- 'Twas the Night Before Christmas

Kapilow, Robert
- Chris van Allsburg's Polar Express

Lai, Francis
- Love Story: Theme (1970)

Stephenson, James M. III
- A Holly and Jolly Sing-Along!

Children's Chorus and SATB Chorus

Brubeck, Dave
- La Fiesta de la Posada

Ellis, David
- Carols for an Island Christmas

Stephenson, James M. III
- A Holly and Jolly Sing-Along!
- The Magic of Christmas

Female Chorus

Berlin, Irving
- God Bless America

Grundman, Clare
- Three Noels

Holst, Gustav
- The Planets

Lutosławski, Witold
- Twenty Polish Christmas Carols

Rota, Nino
- Romeo and Juliet: A Time for Us (1968)

Male Chorus

Berlin, Irving
- God Bless America

Bizet, Georges
- Carmen: Toréador Song

Bliss, Arthur
- Baraza

Gould, Morton
- Declaration

Menotti, Gian Carlo
- My Christmas

Strauss, Johann Jr.
- An der schönen blauen Donau, Op. 314

Tiomkin, Dimitri
- Giant (1956): Suite
- Gunfight at the OK Corral (1957): Ballad and Theme
- Night Passage (1957): Follow the River
- Red River (1948): Suite

Two Part Chorus

Berlin, Irving
- God Bless America

Bernstein, Elmer
- Airplane!: Suite

Blake, Howard
- Christmas Lullaby

Ringwald, Roy
- O Brother Man

Malotte, Albert Hay
- The Lord's Prayer
Saint-Saëns, Camille
- Christmas Oratorio, Op. 12: Praise Ye the Lord of Hosts
Tiomkin, Dimitri
- Cyrano De Bergerac (1950): Suite

SATB Chorus

Adam, Adolphe
- Cantique de noel (O Holy Night)
Addinsell, Richard
- A Christmas Carol (Suite: Scrooge)
Ades, Thomas
- Twentiana
Adler, Samuel
- A Song of Hanukkah
- Judah's Song of Praise
- The Feast of Lights
Adomian, Lan
- Cantata de la revolución Mexicana
Arlen, Harold
- Wizard of Oz Choral Review
Arnold, David
- Independence Day Suite
Bach, J. S.
- Jesu, Joy of Man's Desiring
Bavel, Zamir
- Hanukkah Light (1998)
Beethoven, Ludwig van
- Die Ruinen von Athen, Op. 113 (Ruins of Athens): Turkish March and Chorus
Bennett, Robert Russell
- A Commemoration Symphony: Stephen Collins Foster
- The Many Moods of Christmas: Suite 1
- The Many Moods of Christmas: Suite 2
- The Many Moods of Christmas: Suite 3
- The Many Moods of Christmas: Suite 4
Berlin, Irving
- God Bless America
- White Christmas
Borodin, Alexander
- Prince Igor: Polovtsian Dances
Broughton, Bruce
- Miracle on 34th Street (1994): Main Title
Brubeck, Dave
- They All Sang Yankee Doodle
Chávez, Carlos
- El Sol (The Sun)-A Mexican Ballad
Chiarappa, Richard
- Paean for The Scholar, The Athlete and The Artist

Cohan, George M.
- Over There
Courtney, Craig
- A Musicological Journey Through Twelve Days of Christmas
Dello Joio
- Christmas Music
DePonte, Niel
- Bell of Freedom (2002)
Doyle, Patrick
- Henry V: Non Nobis Domine
- Much Ado About Nothing: Suite
Effinger, Cecil
- Let Your Mind Wander Over America
Elfman, Danny
- Spider-Man: Suite (2004)
Elgar, Edward
- The Snow, Op. 26, No. 1
Feller, Sherm
- Snow, Snow, Beautiful Snow
Gershwin, George
- Love Walked In
- Porgy and Bess: Selections for Orchestra
Gillis, Don
- The Coming of the King
Gilpin, Greg
- The Music of MGM (A Choral Medley)
Goldstein, William
- A.M. America Overture
Giacchino, Michael
- Star Trek: End Credits (2009)
Gold, Ernest
- Exodus: This Land is Mine (1960)
Goldsmith, Jerry
- The Final Conflict (1983)
- The Omen (1976): Suite
- QB VII: Suite
- The Sum of All Fears (2002)
Gould, Morton
- Christmas Time, Book I
- Christmas Time, Book I: Adeste Fidelis
- Christmas Time, Book I: First Noel
- Christmas Time, Book I: It Came Upon a Midnight Clear
- Christmas Time, Book I: O Little Town; Away in a Manger
- Christmas Time, Book I: Silent Night
- Christmas Time, Book II
- Christmas Time, Book II: Cinerama Holiday: Skier's Waltz
- Christmas Time, Book II: Good King Wenceslas
- Christmas Time, Book II: Home for Christmas
- Christmas Time, Book II: Jingle Bells
- Serenade of Carols (Choral Setting)
Grainger, Percy
- Marching Song of Democracy

- Tribute to Foster
Grundman, Clare
- Three Noels
Handel, George Frideric
- The King Shall Rejoice
Harris, Roy
- Freedom's Land
Haslam, Herbert
- Special Starlight
Hermann, Ralph
- Christmas Fantasy
Herrmann, Bernard
- The Man Who Knew Too Much: The Storm Clouds Cantata (1956)
Holst, Gustav
- Christmas Day
- Let All Mortal Flesh Keep Silence
- Three Christmas Songs
Horner, James
- Braveheart: Main Title & End Credits (1995)
Howard, James
- Peter Pan (2003): Flying
- Peter Pan (2003): Suite for Orchestra with Narrator
Joel, Billy
- Movin' Out
Kapilow, Robert
- Play Ball!: Casey at the Bat
Layton, Billy Jim
- Three Dylan Thomas Poems, Op. 3
Leigh, Mitch
- Man of La Mancha: The Impossible Dream
Lehár, Franz
- The Count of Luxembourg: Waltz
Lloyd Webber, Andrew
- Andrew Lloyd Webber: A Concert Celebration
Lowden, Bob
- Armed Forces Salute
Malotte, Albert Hay
- The Lord's Prayer
Mancini, Henry
- Breakfast at Tiffanys: Moon River
- Days of Wine and Roses
- Dear Heart
- Jingle Bells/Sleigh Ride
- The Pink Panther: It Had Better Be Tonight (Meglio Stasera)
Matthews, H. Alexander
- The Story of Christmas Cantata
Mayer, William
- Good King Wenceslas
Menotti, Gian Carlo
- Amahl and the Night Visitors: Shepherd's Chorus
Moore, Donald I.
- America
Musgrave, Thea
- Wild Winter II

(Orchestra with Chorus, cont.)

Ottman, John
- Astro Boy (2009): Theme

Parker, Alice
- Seven Carols for Christmas

Perry, William
- Joy Shall Be Yours in the Morning

Ringwald, Roy
- O Brother Man
- The Song of America
- The Song of Christmas
- The Song of Easter

Robinson, Walter H.
- Harriet Tubman

Rutter, John
- Jesus Child!
- The Very Best Time of the Year

Saint-Saëns, Camille
- Christmas Oratorio, Op. 12

Schubert, Franz
- Ave Maria

Serly, Tibor
- A Little Christmas Cantata

Shaw, Robert
- The Many Moods of Christmas: Suites 1, 2, 3, or 4

Silvestri, Alan
- The Abyss: Finale
- Back to the Future (Madrid Version)
- Beowulf (2007): I Shouldn't Have Told You
- The Mummy Returns (2001)

Silvestri & Ballard
- God Gless Us Everyone

Steffe, William
- Battle Hymn of the Republic

Stephenson, James M. III
- A Holly and Jolly Sing-Along!
- We Three Kings of Orient Are

Tchaikovsky, Peter Ilyich
- The Nutcracker Suite

Thomas, Augusta Read
- Sunlight Echoes

Tiomkin, Dimitri
- 55 Days at Peking (1963): Suite
- Friendly Persuasion (1956)
- The High and the Mighty (1954): Suite
- It's a Wonderful Life (1947): Suite
- Suite from It's a Wonderful Life

Tyzik, Jeff
- American Celebration
- Holiday Moods: Suite Nos. 1, 2, 3

Van Vactor, David
- The New Light: Prologue and 3 Canticles for Christmas

Vaughan Williams, Ralph
- Fantasia on Christmas Carols

Verdi, Giuseppe
- Aïda: Triumphal March

Wagner, Joseph
- Ballad of Brotherhood

Waxman, Franz
- Dr. Jekyll and Mr. Hyde (1941): Suite
- The Ice Follies of 1939

Wendel, Robert
- A George M. Cohan Overture

Wernick, Richard
- Chanukah Festival Overture

Williams, John T.
- Amistad: Dry Your Tears, Afrika
- Call of the Champions: 2002 Olympic Theme
- Close Encounters of the Third Kind
- Saving Private Ryan: Hymn to the Fallen

Young, Christopher
- Species (1995): End Credits

Zwilich, Ellen Taaffe
- One Nation

Chorus and Audience

Kapilow, Robert
- Union Station

Schuller, Gunther
- Music for a Celebration: A Fantasy on National Themes

Serly, Tibor
- A Little Christmas Cantata

Zaninelli, Luigi
- For Spacious Skies

Zaninelli, Luigi
- Americana

Zimmer, Hans
- Da Vinci Code (2006): Chevaliers de Sangreal

ORCHESTRA WITH NARRATOR

Antheil, George
- Music to a World's Fair Film

Arnold, Alan
- Cartoon Sketches of the Baroque Suite

Barab, Seymour
- G.A.G.E., A Christmas Story

Berlin, Irving
- God Bless America

Beveridge, Thomas
- Once: Tribute to Martin Luther King

Britten, Benjamin
- Young Person's Guide to the Orchestra, Op. 34

Carey, Julia Scott
- Legend of Old Befana

Chappell, Herbert
- Paddington Bear's First Concert

Copland, Aaron
- Lincoln Portrait

Cunningham, Arthur
- Rooster Rhapsody

Gillis, Don
- The Coming of the King
- The Man Who Invented Music
- The Night Before Christmas

Goldstein, William
-'Twas the Night Before Christmas

Gould, Morton
- A Song of Freedom
- Declaration
- Hosedown: A Firefighter Fable
- The Jogger and the Dinosaur

Haslam, Herbert
- Special Starlight

Hawley, C.B.
- The Christ Child

Hayman, Richard
- Freddie the Football

Hermann, Ralph
- Silent Movie

Herschel, Lee
- How the Camel Got His Hump
- How the Whale Got His Tiny Throat

Hewitt, James
- The Battle of Trenton

Holcombe, Bill
- Casey at the Bat

Howard, James
- Peter Pan (2003): Suite for Orchestra with Narrator

Kapilow, Robert
- City Piece: DC Monuments
- Dr. Seuss's Gertrude McFuzz
- Dr. Seuss's Green Eggs and Ham
- Union Station

Kirk, Theron
- An Orchestra Primer

Kleinsinger, George
-Tubby the Tuba

Mayer, William
- Good King Wenceslas

Peck, Russell
- The Thrill of the Orchestra

Persichetti, Vincent
- A Lincoln Address

Poulenc, Francis
- L'Histoire de Babar (The Story of Babar, The Little Elephant)

Prokofiev, Sergei
- Peter and the Wolf: Symphonic Tale for Narrator and Orchestra, Op. 67

Proto, Frank
- Casey at the Bat

Ringwald, Roy
- The Song of America

Robinson, Earl
- The Lonesome Train

Rodríguez, Robert Xavier
- A Colorful Symphony

- Flight: The Story of Wilbur and Orville Wright
- Jargon: the Story of the American Constitution
- Trunks, A Circus Story for Narrator and Orchestra

Saint-Saëns, Camille
- Le Carnaval des animaux (Carnival of the Animals)

Schickele, Peter
- A Bach Portrait
- American Birthday Card
- A Zoo Called Earth

Schuller, Gunther
- Journey into Jazz

Schwantner, Joseph
- A New Morning for the World

Simons, Netty
- Pied Piper of Hamelin

Slatkin, Leonard
- The Raven

Thomson, Virgil
- The Plow that Broke the Plains: Suite

Tilzer, Albert von
- Take Me Out to the Ball Game

Turina, Joaquín
- Canto a Sevilla, Op. 37

Turrin, Joseph
- The Fir Tree
- When Tony Played the Sax

Van Vactor, David
- The New Light: Prologue and 3 Canticles for Christmas

Welcher, Dan
- Haleakala: How Maui Snared the Sun
- JFK: The Voice of Peace

Wilby, Philip
- The Highland Express

Zaninelli, Luigi
- A Lexicon of Beasties

ORCHESTRA WITH SOLO INSTRUMENTS

Keyboard

Antheil, George
- A Jazz Symphony: 1955 version
- A Jazz Symphony: 1925 version

Arlen, Harold
- Wizard of Oz: Over the Rainbow

Bliss, Arthur
- Baraza

Bloch, Ernest
- Trois Poèmes Juifs

Bush, Geoffrey
- A Little Concerto

Chopin, Frédéric
- Fantaisie sur des airs nationaux polonais, Op.13 (Fantasy on Polish airs)
- Variations on "La ci darem la mano," Op. 2

Cowell, Henry
- Four Irish Tales: Tales of Our Countryside

Ellington, Edward K. (Duke)
- New World A-Comin'

Falla, Manuel de
- Noches en los jardines de España (Nights in the Gardens of Spain)

Fernandez, Agustín
- Una Música Escondida

Field, John
- Irish Concerto for Piano

Foss, Lukas
- Elegy for Anne Frank

Gold, Ernest
- Exodus: An Orchestral Tone-Picture

Gottschalk, Louis Moreau
- L'Union: Paraphrase de Concert sur les Airs Nationaux

Harris, Roy
- Concerto in One Movement (Jamboree)

Kasschau, Howard
- Country Concerto

Kosma, Joseph
- Autumn Leaves

Lambert, Constant
- The Rio Grande

Liszt, Franz
- Totentanz

McCabe, John
- Mini Concerto for Organ, Percussion, Audience

Mancini, Henry
- 10: It's Easy to Say
- Mystery Movie Theme

Messiaen, Olivier
- Des canyons aux etoiles

Nyman, Michael
- The Piano

Reisfeld, Bert
- California Concerto

Saint-Saëns, Camille
- Le Carnaval des animaux (Carnival of the Animals)

Schickele, Peter
- Prelude to Einstein on the Fritz

Schoenberg, Claude-Michel
- Miss Saigon Rhapsody

Silvestri, Alan
- Forrest Gump Main Title for Piano & Orchestra: Feather Theme
- Forrest Gump Suite for Orchestra

Shire, David
- The Conversation (1974)

Strauss, Richard
- Burleske

Turina, Joaquín
- Rapsodia Sinfonica, Op. 66

Turok, Paul
- Ragtime Caprice, Op. 45

Turrin, Joseph
- Steadfast Tin Soldier

Ulbrich, Siegfried
- Blue City, Impression for Piano and Orchestra

Vangelis
- Chariots of Fire Suite

Zwilich, Ellen Taaffe
- Peanuts Gallery (1996)

Strings

[Violin]

Beethoven, Ludwig van
- Romance No. 1 in G Major, Op. 40
- Romance No. 2 in F Minor, Op. 50

Bizet, Georges
- Carmen Fantasie, Op. 25

Bloch, Ernest
- Suite hébraïque

Borodin, Alexander
- String Quartet No.2: Nocturne

Boskerck, Captain Francis Saltus Van
- Semper Paratus

Corigliano, John
- The Red Violin: Chaconne for Violin and Orchestra
- The Red Violin: Suite for Violin and Orchestra

Cowell, Henry
- Flirtationus Jig (Fiddler's Jig)

Dorff, Daniel
- Sunburst

Gardel, Carlos
- Tango: Por Una Cabeza

Garrido-Lecca, Celso
- Secuencias (Sequences)

Goldstein, William
- 'Twas the Night Before Christmas

Grainger, Percy
- Country Gardens
- Mock Morris

Halvorsen, Johan
- Norwegian Air
- Norwegian Song, Op. 31

Heath, Dave
- Alone at the Frontier: Concerto for Improvised Instrument and Orchestra

Herbert, Victor
- Air de Ballet

Horner, James
- Legends of the Fall: The Ludlows

Howard, James Newton
- Defiance (2008): Nothing is Impossible
- Signs (2002): Suite

(Orchestra with Solo Instruments – Violin, cont.)

Jones, Trevor
- Last of the Mohicans: Kiss

Kreisler, Fritz
- Liebesleid

Lalo, Edouard
- Symphonie Espagnole, Op. 21

Lecuona, Ernesto
- Danza lucumi: Danza Afro-Cubanas

Mancini, Henry
- Oklahoma Crude

Mantovani, Annunzio Paolo
- Gypsy Legend

Massanet, Jules
- Thaïs: Méditation

Maxwell Davies, Peter
- A Spell for Green Corn: The Macdonald Dances

Mizzy, Vic
- Addams Family Values: Tango for Violin and Orchestra (1993)

Monti, Vittorio
- Czardas

Muller, Frederick
- Arkansas Traveler: In Bluegrass Style

Piazzolla, Astor
- Cuatro Estaciones Porteñas (The Four Seasons in Buenas Aires)

Rózsa, Miklós
- Ben-Hur: Love Theme

Saint-Saëns, Camille
- Havanaise, Op. 83

Sarasate, Pablo de
- Carmen Fantasie on Themes of Bizet, Op. 25
- Zigeunerweisen, Op. 20

Schnittke, Alfred
- Concerto Grosso No. 1

Shaiman, Marc
- Addams Family Values (1993): Tango

Stephenson, James M. III
- We Three Strings! from We Three Kings

Vaughan Williams, Ralph
- The Lark Ascending

Vivaldi. Antonio
- Le quattro staggioni (The Four Seasons) Op. 8, Nos.1-4

Weinberger, Jaromir
- Bohemian Songs and Dances: Six Dances
- The Devil on the Belfry

Whelan, Bill
- Riverdance Theme

Williams, John T.
- Three Pieces from Schindler's List

Young, Christopher
- Species (1995): End Credits

[Viola]
Bloch, Ernest
- Suite hébraïque

Grant, James
- Waltz for Betz

Vardi, Emanuel
- Suite on American Folk Songs

[Cello]
Baker, David
- Concerto for Cello

Bizet, Georges
- A Carmen Fantasy

Gold, Ernest
- Exodus: Rhapsody for Cello and Orchestra (1960)

Howard, James Newton
- The Village: Suite-Village Romance

Morricone, Ennio
- Casualties of War: Elegy for Brown
- Marco Polo: Main Title

Orr, Buxton
- A Carmen Fantasy

Popper, David
- Hungarian Rhapsodie, Op. 68

Ranjbaran, Behzad
- Thomas Jefferson

Rodríguez, Robert Xavier
- Mascaras

Saint-Saëns, Camille
- Carnival of the Animals: The Swan
- Romance, Op. 36

Strauss, Josef
- Romanze

Tan Dun
- Crouching Tiger Concerto

[Double Bass]
Stephenson, James M. III
- We Three Basses! from We Three Kings

[Violin & Cello]
Corelli, Arcangelo
- Concerto grosso,Op. 6, #8 in g minor: Christmas Concerto

Shire, David
- Return to Oz (1985): Theme

[Guitar]
Chappell, Herbert
- Caribbean Concerto

Gould, Morton
- Troubadour Music

Rodrigo, Joaquin
- Concierto Andaluz

Waxman, Franz
- A Place in the Sun (1951)

Woodwind
[Flute]
Simeone, Harry
- Flute Cocktail Scherzo and Blues for 3 or 2 Solo Flutes and Orchestra

Bizet, Georges
- Fantaisie Brillante on Themes from Bizet's "Carmen"

Dorati, Antal
- Night Music

Goldsmith, Jerry
- Rudy: Theme for Flute and Chamber Orchestra

Griffes, Charles Tomlinson
- Poem for Flute and Orchestra

López, Jimmy
- Lago de Lágrimas (Lake of Tears)

Mancini, Henry
- The Great Race: Pie in the Face Polka
- Pennywhistle Jig
- The Thorn Birds: Meggie's Theme
- Victor, Victoria (1982): Crazy World

Maxwell Davies, Peter
- Temenos, with Mermaids and Angels

Monti, Vittorio
- Czardas

Schocker, Gary
- Green Places

Whitney, John
- Light Rays

[Oboe]
Livingston, Jay
- Mona Lisa (1950) *[Oboe d'amore]*

Sibelius, Jean
- Legends, Op. 22: 2. The Swan of Tuonela *[English Horn]*

Tyzik, Jeff
- Mis zeh Hidlik (Behold the Lights) *[English Horn]*
- What Child Is This

[Clarinet]
Arnold, Malcolm
- Comedy Overture: Beckus the Dandipratt

Custer, Calvin
- Birth of the Blues

Ellington, Edward K. (Duke)
- Three Black Kings

Garner, Erroll
- Misty

Hodkinson, Sydney
- Concerto for Clarinet and Orchestra

Williams, John T.
- The Terminal: Viktor's Tale

Hudson, Will & Mills, Irving
- Moonglow

Kilar, Wojciech
- Theme from the Film The Pianist

[Bassoon]
Alford, Kenneth J.
- Hexen (Witches)
Stephenson, James M. III
- BaSOON It Will Be Christmas

[Saxophone]
Anderson, Leroy
- Clarinet Candy
Bennett, Richard Rodney
- Concerto for Stan Getz
Blake, Howard
- Heartbeat
Bond, Victoria
- Urban Bird
Creston, Paul
- Concerto for Saxophone and Orchestra, Op. 26
Ellington, Edward K. (Duke)
- Three Black Kings
Grant, James
- Waltz for Betz
Heath, Dave
- Out of the Cool
Herrmann, Bernard
- Taxi Driver: A Night Piece for Orchestra
Holcombe, Bill
- Saxanova
Hupfeld, Herman
- As Time Goes By
Mancini, Henry
- Academy Award Medley
- The Pink Panther
Nyman, Michael
- The Piano: Lost and Found
Peaslee, Richard
- Chicago Concerto
Waxman, Franz
- Medley: Classic Film Themes
- A Place in the Sun (1951)
Whitney, John
- Light Rays
Williams, John T.
- Catch Me If You Can: Escapades for Alto Sax

[Woodwind Ensemble]
Vivaldi, Antonio
- Concerto, Op. 44, No. 16, R.V. 570, F Major *[Flute, Oboe, Bassoon]*

Brass
[Horn]
Gruber, F. X.
- Silent Night
Maxwell Davies, Peter
- Maxwell's Reel, with Northern Lights
- Swinton Jig, on a Nineteenth Century Lancashire Fiddle Tune
Saint-Saëns, Camille
- Romance, Op. 36

[Trumpet]
Arban, Jean Baptiste
- The Carnival of Venice
Bizet, Georges
- Carmen Fantasia
Coots, J. Fred
- For All We Know
Ellington, Edward K. (Duke)
- Three Black Kings
Frackenpohl, Arthur
- Suite Concertino
Gershwin, George
- Embraceable You
- Rhapsody in Blue for Trumpet and Orchestra
- Two Gershwin Portraits
Grgin, Ante
- Laura: Fantasy for Trumpet in Bb and Orchestra
Guion, David
- Sail Away for the Rio Grande
Harris, Roy
- Horn of Plenty
Hunsberger, Donald
- Under Gypsy Skies
Mendez, Raphael
- La Virgen de la Macarena
Ramsey, Elmer
- Rhapsody for Trumpet
Rimsky-Korsakov, Nicolai
- The Tale of Tsar Saltan: Flight of the Bumble Bee (Hummelflüg)
Saint-Saëns, Camille
- Introduction and Rondo Capriccioso: Trumpet in Bb and Orchestra
Stephenson, James M. III
- Lo, How a Rose E'er Blooming
Waxman, Franz
- Hemingway's Adventures of a Young Man: Rosanna
Whitney, John
- Light Rays
Williams, Cootie & Monk, Thelonius
- 'Round Midnight
Zwilich, Ellen Taaffe
- American Concerto

[Trombone]
Carmichael, Hoagy
- Georgia On My Mind
Creston, Paul
- Fantasy, Op. 42
Dewitt, Louis O.
- Twelve English Songs
Ellington, Edward K. (Duke)
- Three Black Kings
Foster, Stephen
- Old Folks At Home; Love's Old Sweet Song: Palms
Peaslee, Richard
- Arrows of Time

[Tuba]
Kleinsinger, George
- Tubby the Tuba
Stephenson, James M. III
- Wassail, Wassail All Over the Tuba

[Brass Quintet]
Stephenson, James M. III
- Bells of Christmas Suite
- God Rest Ye Merry Gentlemen
- Lo, How a Rose E'er Blooming
Turrin, Joseph
- The Fir Tree

Percussion
Aguila, Miguel del
- Conga
Creston, Paul
- Concertino for Marimba, Op. 21
Lang, David
- Loud Love Songs
Phillips, Peter
- Interplays: Concerto for Jazz Drums, Percussion Ensemble and Orchestra
Schreiner, Adolph
- The Worried Drummer

Jazz Combo
Brubeck, Dave
- Brandenburg Gate: Revisited
- Cathy's Waltz
- Gates of Justice, The: Out of the Way of the People
- In Your Own Sweet Way
- Summersong
Ellington, Edward Kennedy (Duke)
- Grand Slam Jam *[Solo Piano, Clarinet, Trumpet]*
Kraft, William
- Contextures: Riots – Decade '60 *[Solo Violin & Drum with Jazz Quartet]*
Schifrin, Lalo
- Dialogues

(Orchestra with Solo Instruments, cont.)

Schuller, Gunther
- Concertino for Jazz Quartet & Orchestra
- Journey into Jazz

Turrin, Joseph
- When Tony Played the Sax

Miscellaneous Solo Instruments

Barber, Samuel
- Capricorn Concerto *[Solo Flute, Oboe, Trumpet]*

Brubeck, Dave
- In Your Own Sweet Way *[Solo Jazz Combo]*

Cooper, Paul
- A Shenandoah for Charles Ives' Birthday *[Solo Flute, Trumpet, Viola]*

Ellington, Edward K. (Duke)
- Grand Slam Jam *[Solo Piano, Clarinet, Trumpet.]*

Gould, Morton
- Hoofer Suite *[Tap Dancer]*
- Tap Dance Concerto

Jacob, Gordon
- Five Pieces in the Form of a Suite *[Harmonica]*

Kraft, William
- Contextures: Riots – Decade '60 *[Solo Violin & Drum with Jazz Quartet]*

McCabe, John
- Mini Concerto for Organ, Percussion, Audience

Meyer, Ranaan
- American Suite *[2 Solo Violins & Double Bass]*
- Fox Down *[2 Solo Violins & Double Bass]*

Time for Three
- Sweet Georgia Brown *[2 Solo Violins & Double Bass]*

Tiomkin, Dimitri
- DOA (1950) *[Solo Trumpet; Tenor Saxophone (Alto Saxophone)]*

Villa-Lobos, Heitor
- Concerto for Harmonica

APPENDIX B

Works Listed by Duration

Orchestral works are grouped by theme categories under each duration heading. Within each group, the works are listed in alphabetical order by composer. Refer to the composer listing in the main body of the document for complete information on a work.

5' or Less

AMERICANA

Anderson, Leroy
- Mother's Whistler
- Old MacDonald Had a Farm

Ayars, Bo
- American Fanfare
- Cowboy Medley: Cielito lindo
- Cowboy Medley: Mexican Hat Dance
- Cowboy Medley: She'll Be Comin' Round the Mountain
- Cowboy Medley: Shenandoah
- Cowboy Medley: Sweet Betsy from Pike
- Cowboy Medley: The Yellow Rose of Texas
- Shave and a Haircut March

Bendix, Victor
- Grand American Fantasia: Tone Pictures of the North and South

Carmichael, Hoagy
- Georgia On My Mind

Copland, Aaron
- Billy the Kid: Prairie Night and Celebration
- Down a Country Lane
- John Henry
- Rodeo: 2. Corral Nocturne
- Rodeo: 4. Hoedown
- Variations on a Shaker Melody

Cowell, Henry
- Saturday Night at the Firehouse

Creston, Paul
- Evening in Texas

Davis, Albert O.
- Buffalo Gals: In Blue Grass Style

Davis, Jimmy
- Blue Tail Fly
- Buffalo Gals

- Down In the Valley

Dragon, Carmen
- The Yellow Rose of Texas

Duffy, John
- Indian Spirits

Evans, Dale
- Happy Trails to You (1952)

Foster, Stephen
- Old Folks At Home; Love's Old Sweet Song: Palms
- Jeanie with the Light Brown Hair

Gershwin, George
- Swanee

Gillis, Don
- Atlanta Suite: Peachtree Promenade

Goldsmith, Jerry
- Soarin' Over California
- The Wild Rovers (1971): Bronco Busting

Gould, Morton
- Swanee River in the Style of Bach
- Swanee River in the Style of Beethoven
- Swanee River in the Style of Brahms
- Swanee River in the Style of Debussy
- Swanee River in the Style of Ellington
- Swanee River in the Style of Gershwin
- Swanee River in the Style of Liszt
- Swanee River in the Style of Mozart
- Swanee River in the Style of Rimsky-Korsakov
- Swanee River in the Style of Strauss (Johann)
- Swanee River in the Style of Tchaikovsky
- Swanee River in the Style of Wagner
- Yankee Doodle

Grundman, Clare
- American Folk Rhapsody No. 2

Guion, David
- Home on the Range
- Turkey in the Straw

Hailstork, Adolphus
- An American Fanfare

Handy, W. C.
- Saint Louis Blues

Hayman, Richard
- Hullabaloo

Herbert, Victor
- American Fantasie
- Panamericana

Hermann, Ralph
- Farmyard Frolic

Howard, James
- Wyatt Earp (1994)
- Wyatt Earp: End Credits

Johnson, Francis
- Buffalo City Guard Parade March
- General Cadwalader's Grand March
- Philadelphia Grays Quickstep

Kander, John
- New York, New York Theme

Kerker, Gustave
- The Belle of New York

Lutosławski, Witold
- Fanfare for Louisville

MacDonald, Harl
- Legend of the Arkansas Traveler

Mandell, Robert
- Red River Valley

Markowitz, Richard
- Wild, Wild West

Marsh, Gerry Jon
- Hamburger Suite

Mason, Jack
- O Bury Me Not On the Lone Prairie

Meyer, Ranaan
- Fox Down

Moross, Jerome
- Wagon Train

Muller, Frederick
- Arkansas Traveler: In Bluegrass Style

[5' or less]

(AMERICANA - Muller, cont.)

- The Rakes of Mallow
 (with Blue Grass Variation)
Piston, Walter
- Bicentennial Fanfare
Powell, John
- Natchez on the Hill, Three Virginia Country Dances
- A Set of Three
Ran, Shulamit
- Chicago Skyline
Richardson, Clive
- Polly-Wolly Doodle
Schwartz, Stephen
- Rock-a-Bye Your Baby with a Dixie Melody
Stucky, Steven
- Fanfare for Cincinnati
- Fanfare for Los Angeles
Time for Three
- Sweet Georgia Brown
Tiomkin, Dimitri
- High Noon (1952): Do Not Forsake Me Oh My Darling
- Night Passage (1957): Follow the River
- Rawhide (1959): Theme
- Red River (1948): Suite
- The Wild, Wild West (1965): Suite
Tyzik, Jeff
- Amazing Grace
Weinberger, Jaromir
- Prelude and Fugue on "Dixie"
Welcher, Dan
- Castle Creek: Fanfare
Wendel, Robert
- Orange Blossom Special

ANIMALS

Anderson, Leroy
- Chicken Reel
- Old MacDonald Had a Farm
- The Waltzing Cat
Barry, John
- Dances with Wolves: Concert Suite
Creston, Paul
- Kangaroo Kaper
Davis, Jimmy
- Blue Tail Fly
Dorff, Daniel
- Tortoise and the Hare
Gershwin, George
- Promenade: Walkin' the Dog or The Real McCoy
Guion, David
- Sheep and Goat
- Turkey in the Straw

Hubbell, Raymond
- Poor Butterfly
Lloyd Webber, Andrew
- Cats: Memory
Mancini, Henry
- Hatari!: Baby Elephant Walk (1962)
- The Pink Panther
Mercer, Johnny
- Skylark
Mussorgsky, Modest Petrovich
- The Song of the Flea
Nielsen, Carl August
- Masquerade: Hanedons (Cock's Dance)
Penella, Manuel
- El Gato Montés (The Bobcat)
Powell, John
- Chicken Run: Final Escape
Pryor, Arthur
- The Whistler and His Dog
Rimsky-Korsakov, Nikolai
- The Tale of Tsar Saltan: Flight of the Bumble Bee
Rossini, Giocchino
- Cat Duet (Duetto buffo di due gatti)
Saint-Saëns, Camille
- Carnival of the Animals: The Swan
Schickele, Peter
- Broadway Boogie
Scott, Raymond
- Dinner Music for a Pack of Hungry Cannibals
- Huckleberry Duck
- The Penguin
Steiner, Max
- King Kong (1933): Overture
- King Kong: Theme
Strauss, Johann, Jr.
- Im Krapfenwaldl, Polka française, Op. 336
Thomson, Virgil
- Sea Piece with Birds
Yarrow, Peter
- Puff the Magic Dragon
Yradier, Sebastian
- La Paloma (The Dove): Spanish Serenade

BLACK HISTORY MONTH/ MARTIN LUTHER KING

Robinson, Walter H.
- Harriet Tubman

BROADWAY MUSICALS

Anderson, Leroy
- Goldilocks: I Never Know When
- Goldilocks: Lady in Waiting
- Goldilocks: Lazy Moon

- Goldilocks: Overture
- Goldilocks: Pirate Dance
- Goldilocks: Pussyfoot
- Goldilocks: Pyramid Dance
- Goldilocks: Save a Kiss
- Goldilocks: Shall I Take My Heart
- Goldilocks: Town House Maxixe
- Goldilocks: Who's Been Sitting In My Chair?
Berlin, Irving
- Annie Get Your Gun: Overture
Bernstein, Leonard
- West Side Story Highlights
- West Side Story Overture
Bock, Jerry
- Fiddler on the Roof Selections
Cohan, George M.
- Give My Regards to Broadway
Farrar, John
- Grease: You're the One that I Want
Finn, William
- Selections from 25th Annual Putnam County Spelling Bee
Gershwin, George
- I Got Plenty of Nuttin'
- Porgy and Bess: Summertime
Hamlisch, Marvin
- Chorus Line, Selections from a
- Marvin Hamlisch in Concert
Herman, Jerry
- La Cage aux Folles
- Hello Dolly!
- Mack & Mabel
- Mame
- Milk and Honey
Kander & Ebb
- Chicago: All That Jazz
Kander, John
- Cabaret
Kern, Jerome
- Little Miss Fix-It: Turkey Trot
- Night Boat: Whose Baby Are You?
- Ol' Man River
- Show Boat Overture
Leigh, Mitch
- Man of La Mancha: The Impossible Dream
Lloyd Webber, Andrew
- Cats: Memory
- The Phantom of the Opera: Concert Version
- The Phantom of the Opera Entr'Acte
- Phantom of the Opera: Music of the Night
- The Phantom of the Opera Overture
MacDermot, Galt
- Aquarius: Let the Sunshine In
- Hair: Where Do I Go?/Good Morning Starshine
Menken, Alan
- Beauty and the Beast

[5' or less]

- Highlights from Beauty and the Beast

Merrill, Bob
- Take Me Along!

O'Brien, Richard
- The Rocky Horror Picture Show

Perry, William
- Joy Shall Be Yours in the Morning

Porter, Cole
- Cole Porter Classics
- Gay Divorcée: Night and Day

Rodgers, Richard
- Carousel Waltz- Carousel: You'll Never Walk Alone
- Love Me Tonight: Lover
- State Fair: It's a Grand Night for Singing

Sayre, Charles
- Broadway on Parade
- Broadway Showstoppers

Schoenberg, Claude-Michel
- Les Miserables: The ABC Café
- Les Miserables: At the End of the Day
- Les Miserables: Bring Him Home
- Les Miserables: Do You Hear the People Sing
- Les Miserables: Empty Chairs at Empty Tables
- Les Miserables: I Dreamed a Dream
- Les Miserables: Little Cosette (Castle on a Cloud)
- Les Miserables: Master of the House
- Les Miserables: On My Own
- Les Miserables: One Day More
- Les Miserables: Stars
- Miss Saigon: I Still Believe This
- Miss Saigon: Last Night of the World
- Miss Saigon: Sun and Moon
- Miss Saigon: This Is the Hour
- Miss Saigon: Why God Why

Styne, Jule
- Gypsy

Tesori, Jeanine
- Thoroughly Modern Millie

Warren, Harry
- 42nd Street (1981)
- 42nd Street: Overture

Willson, Meredith
- The Music Man: Entr'acte
- The Music Man: Overture
- The Music Man: Seventy-Six Trombones

CELEBRATIONS

Anderson, Leroy
- Birthday Party

Arnold, Malcolm
- Anniversary Overture, Op. 99

Bennett, Richard Rodney
- Celebration

Chiarappa, Richard
- Happy, Happy Birthday

Copland, Aaron
- Billy the Kid: Prairie Night and Celebration
- Happy Anniversary

Corigliano, John
- Campane di Ravello: A Celebration Piece for Sir Georg Solti

Gould, Morton
- Celebration Strut for Orchestra
- Cheers!: A Celebration March

Kerchner, Larry
- Happy Birthday Medley

Perry, William
- Graduation March

Rodríguez, Robert Xavier
- Piñata
- The Salutation Rag

Tower, Joan
- Stepping Stones: Celebration Fanfare

Wendel, Robert
- Commemoration

Williams, John T.
- Happy Birthday Variations

Willson, Meredith
- The Music Man: Seventy-Six Trombones

Zwilich, Ellen Taaffe
- Upbeat!

CIRCUS

Goossens, Eugene
- The Hurdy-Gurdy Man

Simons, Moises
- Peanut Vendor

Sondheim, Stephen
- Little Night Music: Send In the Clowns

Strauss, Johann, Sr.
- Tritsch-Tratsch (The Circus)

Stravinsky, Igor
- Circus Polka

Tiomkin, Dimitri
- Circus World (1964): John Wayne March

Waxman, Franz
- Man on a Tightrope (1953): March

DANCE

Anderson, Leroy
- Belle of the Ball
- Blue Tango
- Chicken Reel
- Goldilocks: Lady in Waiting
- Goldilocks: Pirate Dance
- Goldilocks: Pyramid Dance
- Sandpaper Ballet
- Song of the Bells
- The Waltzing Cat

Antheil, George
- Accordion Dance
- Hot-Time Dance

Ayars, Bo
- Cowboy Medley: Mexican Hat Dance

Bennett, Richard Rodney
- Murder on the Orient Express Theme: Foxtrot Theme
- Murder on the Orient Express Waltz

Bernstein, Elmar
- Thoroughly Modern Millie: Sky-Hi Waltz

Bizet, Georges
- Carmen: Habanera
- Carmen: Seguidilla and Duett
- Carmen: Sequidilla

Brahms, Johannes
- Hungarian Dance No. 1
- Hungarian Dance No. 4
- Hungarian Dance No. 8

Brown, Robert Bennett
- Early American Quadrille: Square Dance

Brubeck, Dave
- Cathy's Waltz

Campos, José Carlos
- Danza Rústica

Copland, Aaron
- Billy the Kid: Prairie Night and Celebration
- Billy the Kid: Waltz
- Rodeo: 2. Corral Nocturne
- Rodeo: 3. Saturday Night Waltz
- Rodeo: 4. Hoedown

Corigliano, John
- Gazebo Dances: Overture to the Imaginary Invalid

Cowell, Henry
- Flirtatious Jig: Fiddler's Jig

Creston, Paul
- Rumba – Tarantella

Delibes, Leo
- Coppelia: Entr'acte & Waltz

Dorff, Daniel
- It Takes Four to Tango

Elfman, Danny
- Simpsons Main Title

Ellington, Edward (Duke)
- The Perfume Suite: Dancers in Love

Falla, Manuel de
- Danse rituelle du feu
- La vida breve: Spanish Dance No. 1

Farnan, Robert
- The Peanut Polka

[5' or less]

(DANCE, cont.)

Friedhofer, Hugo
- The Bishop's Wife: Ice Skater's Waltz (1947)

Gade, Jacob
- Jalousie
- Tango Jalousie (Tango Tzigane)

Gardel, Carlos
- Tango: Por una Cabeza

Gestor, Don
- First Love

Gillis, Don
- Twinkletoes Ballet: Tango Lullaby

Gold, Ernest
- Ship of Fools: Candlelight & Silver Waltz (1965)

Goldsmith, Jerry
- Six Degrees of Separation (1993): Tango

Gomez, Alice
- Festive Huapango

Gould, Morton
- American Ballads: Saratoga Quickstep - on "The Girl I Left Behind"
- Calypso Souvenir
- Celebration Strut for Orchestra
- Cinerama Holiday: Skier's Waltz
- Cresta Blanca Waltz
- Dance Gallery: Soft Shoe Gavotte
- Deserted Ballroom
- Minute Plus Waltz Rag

Grant, James
- Waltz for Betz

Guarnieri, Camargo
- Dansa Brasileira

Hamlisch, Marvin
- Chorus Line, Selections from a

Herbert, Victor
- Air de Ballet

Hermann, Ralph
- Old Timers Waltz Medley No. 1
- Old Timers Waltz Medley No. 2

Howard, James
- Snow Falling on Cedars Suite

Johnson, Francis
- Philadelphia Grays Quickstep

Kaper, Bronislau
- Lili: Ballet (1953)

Katz, S.
- Polskie Kwiaty (Selection of Polish Songs & Dances)

Khachaturian, Aram
- Gayane: Sabre Dance

Lake, M. L.
- Old Timers Waltz

Lecuona, Ernesto
- Danza lucumi (Danza Afro-Cubanas)

Lehár, Franz
- Zigeunerliebe (Gypsy Love) Waltzes

Mancini, Henry
- The Molly Maguires: Pennywhistle Jig (1970)
- Pennywhistle Jig

Marquina, Pascual
- España Cani

Mindreau, Ernesto López
- Marinera y Tondero

Mizzy, Vic
- Addams Family Values (1993): Tango

Monti, Vittorio
- Czardas

Moroder, Georgio
- Flashdance: What a Feeling (1983)

Moross, Jerome
- Variations on a Waltz

Nielsen, Carl August
- Masquerade: Hanedons (Cock's Dance)

Offenbach, Jacques
- Orpheus in the Underworld: Galop (Can Can)

Piazzolla, Astor
- Libertango
- Michelangelo
- Milonga del Angel
- Tango No. 1: Coral
- Tango No. 2: Canyengue
- Tanguedia
- Tres minutos con la realidad: Tango (Three Minutes of Reality)

Powell, John
- Mr. and Mrs. Smith: Tango de los Asesinos
- Natchez on the Hill, Three Virginia Country Dances
- A Set of Three

Reinagle, Alexander
- Mrs. Madison's Minuet

Riegger, Wallingford
- New Dance, Op. 18b: Finale from the Ballet

Robinson & Giovannini
- Brazilian Polka

Rodríguez, Robert Xavier
- Hot Buttered Rumba

Salzedo, Leonard
- The Witch Boy: Square Dance from the Ballet

Schickele, Peter
- Uptown Hoedown

Scott, Raymond
- Minuet in Jazz

Shaiman, Marc
- Addams Family Values (1993): Tango
- The Addams Family (1991): Theme and Waltz Finale

Shostakovich, Dmitri
- Tahiti-Trot, Op. 16

Sibelius, Jean
- Valse chevaleresque, Op. 96c
- Valse lyrique, Op. 96a

Silvestri, Alan
- Polar Express: Spirit of the Seasons
- The Quick and the Dead

Soro, Enrique
- Danza Fantástica

Steiner, Max
- Gone With the Wind (1939): Dance Montage
- Jezebel (1938): Waltz

Strauss, Johann and Josef
- Pizzicato Polka

Strauss, Johann Jr.
- Annen Polka, Op. 117
- Champagne Polka, Op. 211
- Eljen A Magyar!, Op. 332: Long Live the Magyar
- Im Krapfenwaldl, Polka française, Op. 336
- Moulinet Polka, Op. 57
- Tick-Tack Polka, Op. 365
- Tritsch Tratsch Polka, Op. 214 (Chit-Chat)
- Unter Donner und Blitz (Thunder and Lightning Polka), Op. 324
- Von der Borse, Polka française, Op. 337

Strauss, Josef
- Elfen Polka Op. 74
- Ohne Sorgen Polka, Op. 271

Stravinsky, Igor
- Circus Polka

Templeton, Alec
- Operation Mambo

Tiomkin, Dimitri
- The Great Waltz (1938)

Villaldo, angel
- El Choclo: Tango Argentina

Youmans, Vincent
- No, No, Nanette: Tea for Two

ECOLOGY

Bizet, Georges
- Carmen: Flower Song

Grainger, Percy
- Country Gardens

Handel, George Frideric
- Messiah: Sinfonia Pastoral

Kern, Jerome
- Ol' Man River

Kosma, Joseph
- Autumn Leaves

Strauss, Johann, Jr.
- Im Krapfenwaldl Polka, Polka française, Op. 336

[5' or less]

FANFARE

Arnaud, Leo
- Fanfare to the Olympic Games (Divertissement for Brass and Percussion)

Berkeley, Lennox
- Fanfare for the Royal Academy of Music Banquet

Binge, Ronald
- Cornet Carillon

Burgon, Geoffrey
- Fanfare on One Note

Copland, Aaron
- Fanfare for the Common Man

Corigliano, John
- Midsummer Fanfare

Douglas, Samuel
- Millenium Fanfare

Dukas, Paul
- La Peri (Fanfare)

Goossens, Eugene
- Fanfare for the Artists

Gould, Morton
- Dramatic Fanfares from CBS-TV documentary "World War I"
- Festive Fanfare

Harbison, John
- Fanfare for Foley's

Holmboe, Vagn
- Fanfare

Lutosławski, Witold
- Fanfare for Louisville
- Fanfare for the University of Lancaster

Newman, Alfred
- Fox Fanfare

Piston, Walter
- Bicentennial Fanfare

Poulenc, Francis
- Fanfare

Rodríguez, Robert Xavier
- Fanfare for Trumpets and Caracolas
- Fanfare from "Oktoechos"

Schickele, Peter
- Fanfare for the Common Cold

Stucky, Steven
- Fanfare for Cincinnati

Tower, Joan
- Stepping Stones: Celebration Fanfare
- Fanfare for the Uncommon Woman

Turrin, Joseph
- Fanfare for George Gershwin

Welcher, Dan
- Castle Creek: Fanfare

Wendel, Robert
- Commemoration
- Fanfare for Freedom

Williams, John T.
- Happy Birthday Variations

FILMS

Adams, Emmett A.
- Bells of St. Mary's

Alford, Kenneth
- Colonel Bogey March

Arlen, Harold
- The Wizard of Oz: Over the Rainbow
- The Wizard of Oz: Yellow Brick Road

Arnold, David
- Independence Day Suite

Arnold, Malcolm
- Bridge on the River Kwai: March

Baerwald, David
- Moulin Rouge: Come What May

Barry, John
- Dances with Wolves: Concert Suite
- Out of Africa: Main Title
- Robin and Marian

Bennett, Richard Rodney
- Murder on the Orient Express Theme: Foxtrot Theme
- Murder on the Orient Express Waltz

Berlin, Irving
- Easter Parade

Bernstein, Elmer
- American Werewolf in London
- The Babe: End Credits
- The Birdman of Alcatraz: Finale
- Ghostbusters: Theme
- The Man with the Golden Arm: Suite
- The Sweet Smell of Success: Main Title
- Thoroughly Modern Millie: Sky-Hi Waltz

Bliss, Arthur
- Christopher Columbus

Botkin, Perry, Jr.
- Nadia's Theme

Broughton, Bruce
- The Boy Who Could Fly: Theme
- Jag: Theme
- Miracle on 34th Street (1994): Main Title
- Miracle on 34th Street, Overture to
- Silverado
- Young Sherlock Holmes (1985): Suite

Doyle, Patrick
- Henry V: Non Nobis Domine

Dun, Tan
- Crouching Tiger, Hidden Dragon (2000)

Elfman, Danny
- Beetlejuice: Main Title (1988)
- Edward Scissorhands: Ice Dance
- Edward Scissorhands: Main Title
- Music from Spider Man

Fain, Sammy
- Once Upon a Dream

Fiedel, Brad
- The Teminator: Theme (1984)
- True Lies: Theme (1994)

Fielding, Jerry
- The Outlaw Josey Wales: Suite

Flaherty, Stephen
- Anastasia: A Rumor in St. Petersburg
- Anastasia: In the Dark of the Night
- Anastasia: Journey to the Past
- Anastasia: Learn to Do It Waltz
- Anastasia: Once Upon a December
- Anastasia: Paris Holds the Key

Friedhofer, Hugo
- An Affair to Remember: The Proposal
- The Bishop's Wife: Ice Skater's Waltz (1947)
- The Mark of Zorro: Suite (1940)

Giacchino, Michael
- Star Trek: End Credits (2009)

Gold, Ernest
- Exodus: This Land is Mine (1960)
- It's a Mad, Mad, Mad, Mad World: Exit Music (1963)
- Ship of Fools: Candlelight & Silver Waltz (1965)

Gold, Marty
- Mancini Memories

Goldsmith, Jerry
- Air Force One (1997): Theme
- Alien (1979): End Title
- Basic Instinct (1992): Main Title Theme
- Capricorn One: Overture & Main Title
- Chinatown: Theme (1974)
- The Final Conflict (1983)
- The First Knight (1995): Suite
- Forever Young (1992): Love Theme
- The Generals: Patton/MacArthur Marches
- Gremlins 2 (1990): The New Batch: Main Title
- The Illustrated Man: Main Title
- King Solomon's Mines (1985): Suite
- L.A. Confidential (1997)
- Lionheart: The Children's Crusade (1987)
- MacArthur (1977): March
- Papillon: Theme
- Patton (1970): Attack
- Patton (1970): The Hospital
- Patton (1970): The Payoff
- Poltergeist (1982): Night of the Beast (Clown Attack)
- Poltergeist (1982): The Calling
- Poltergeist (1982): The Light
- Poltergeist (1982): Theme (Carol Anne's)

[5' or less]

(FILMS – Goldsmith, cont.)

- Rambo: First Blood, Part 2 (1985): Theme
- Rudy: Theme for Flute and Chamber Orchestra
- The Russia House (1990): Love Theme
- The Shadow (1994): Main Title
- Six Degrees of Separation (1993): Tango
- Sleeping with the Enemy (1991): Theme
- Sleeping with the Enemy (1991): Theme
- Star Trek Main Theme
- Star Trek: Voyager (1995)
- Star Trek I: The Motion Picture Theme (1979)
- Star Trek 5: The Final Frontier: Suite (1989)
- Star Trek 8: First Contact (1996)
- Star Trek 9: Insurrection (1998)
- The Strong Men: Total Recall & Rambo Themes
- Twilight Zone: The Movie (1983): End Title
- The Wild Rovers (1971): Bronco Busting
- The Wind and the Lion (1975)

Gray, Allan
- African Queen: Portrait (1951)

Grusin, Dave
- Theme from On Golden Pond

Hamlisch, Marvin
- Ice Castles Through the Eyes of Love

Herrmann, Bernard
- Citizen Kane Overture
- The Ghost of Mrs. Muir (1947)
- It's Alive (1973)
- Psycho (1960)
- The Day the Earth Stood Still: Arrival (1951)
- The Wrong Man: Prelude (1956)

Hooper, Nicolas & Williams, John T.
- Harry Potter and the Order of the Phoenix: Concert Suite

Horner, James
- Apollo 13: Main Title, End Credits, Re-Entry and Splashdown - An Irish Party in Third Class
- Legends of the Fall: The Ludlows (1994)
- The Mask of Zorro: Suite (1998)

Howard, James
- Defiance (2008): Nothing is Impossible
- Grand Canyon Fanfare
- Snow Falling on Cedars Suite
- The Village: The Gravel Road
- Wyatt Earp (1994)
- Wyatt Earp: End Credits

Hudson, Will & Mills, Irving
- Moonglow

Hupfeld, Herman
- As Time Goes By

Jarre, Maurice
- Lara's Theme from Doctor Zhivago
- Lawrence of Arabia: Overture
- Witness: Building the Barn

Kaczmarek, Jan A.P.
- Finding Neverland: Suite (2004)

Kamen, Michael
- Robin Hood: Prince of Thieves (Main Title)

Kaper, Bronislau
- Auntie Mame: Overture (1958)
- Lili: Ballet (1953)

Kilar, Wojciech
- Dracula (1992)
- Theme from the Film The Pianist

Krogstad, Bob
- Christmas at the Movies

Lai, Francis
- Love Story: Where Do I Begin
- Love Story: Theme (1970)
- A Man and a Woman

Lawrence, David
- High School Musical 2

Magidson, Herb
- The Continental (1934)

Mancina, Mark
- Twister Main Theme

Mancini, Henry
- 10: It's Easy to Say
- Breakfast at Tiffanys: Moon River
- Charade
- Days of Wine and Roses
- Dear Heart
- The Great Mouse Detective
- The Great Race: Pie in the Face Polka
- The Great Race: They're Off
- The Great Waldo Pepper
- Hatari!: Baby Elephant Walk (1962)
- The Lifeforce
- Mancini Magic
- The Molly Maguires: Pennywhistle Jig (1970)
- Oklahoma Crude
- Pennywhistle Jig
- The Pink Panther
- The Pink Panther : It Had Better Be Tonight (Meglio Stasera)
- Revenge of The Pink Panther (1978): Hong Kong Fireworks
- Victor, Victoria (1982): Crazy World

Mandel, Johnny
- The Sandpiper: Shadow of Your Smile

Mascagni, Pietro
- Cavalleria Rusticana: Intermezzo

Maxwell, Robert
- Ebb Tide

McCarthy, Dennis
- Star Trek: Deep Space Nine Suite
- Star Trek 7: Generations "Overture"

McBroom, Amanda
- The Rose

Meyer, George W.
- If You Were the Only Girl in the World

Moroder, Georgio
- Flashdance: What a Feeling (1983)

Moross, Jerome
- The Big Country: Main Title Theme
- Wagon Train

Morricone, Ennio
- Casualties of War: Elegy for Brown
- Cinema Paradiso Theme
- Cinema Paradiso: First Youth
- Cinema Paradiso: Love Theme
- I Knew I Loved You
- Legend of 1900: Romanza
- Marco Polo: Main Title
- Once Upon a Time in the West Theme
- The Untouchables: Overture

Morris, John
- The Producers: Main Title (1968)

Newborn, Ira
- The Naked Gun: Theme (1988)

Newman, Alfred
- Brigham Young March (1940)
- David & Bathsheba
- Wuthering Heights: Cathie's Theme

North, Alex
- Unchained Melody (1955)
- Spartacus: Camp at Night
- Spartacus: Draba Fight
- Spartacus: Final Farewell
- Spartacus: Forest Meeting
- Spartacus: Main Title
- Spartacus: Vesuvius

Nyman, Michael
- The Piano: Lost and Found

O'Boyle, Sean
- Silent Movie Music

O'Brien, Richard
- The Rocky Horror Picture Show

Ortolani & Oliviero
- Mondo Cane: More

Ottman, John
- Fantastic Four: Main Title
- Fantastic Four 2: Silver Surfer Suite
- Hide and Seek: Main Titles
- The Usual Suspects (1995)

Pachelbel, Johann
- Ordinary People Theme: Canon

Perry, Sam
- The Phantom of the Opera (1930)

[5' or less]

Phillips, John
- Monday, Monday

Porter, Cole
- Cole Porter Classics
- Gay Divorcée: Night and Day

Portman, Rachel
- The Cider House Rules (1999)
- Emma (1996)
- Oliver Twist: Suite (2005)

Powell, John
- Chicken Run: Final Escape; Make a Crate
- Happy Feet: The Story of Mumble
- Suite from Ice Age: The Meltdown
- Mr. and Mrs. Smith: Tango de los Asesinos

Raksin, David
- Laura

Rota, Nino
- Amarcord
- Romeo and Juliet: A Time for Us
- The Godfather II (1974)
- The Godfather: Reminicences for Orchestra (1972)

Rózsa, Miklós
- Ben Hur: Parade of the Charioteers
- Ben Hur: Rowing of the Galley Slaves
- Ben-Hur Prelude
- Ben-Hur: Love Theme
- Dead Men Don't Wear Plaid: End Cast
- El Cid: Love Scene
- El Cid: Main Title
- El Cid: Overture

Sainte Marie, Nitzsche
- An Officer & A Gentleman: Up Where We Belong

Sayre, Chuck
- Disney Adventure

Shaiman, Marc
- Addams Family Values (1993): Tango
- The Addams Family (1991): Theme and Waltz Finale

Shire, David
- The Conversation (1974)
- Farewell My Lovely (1975): Suite
- Norma Rae: It Goes Like It Goes
- Return to Oz (1985): Theme
- Taking of Pelham One Two Three (1974): Theme

Silvestri, Alan
- Back to the Future Suite
- Cast Away: Crossroads
- Forrest Gump Main Title for Piano & Orchestra: Feather Theme

Sondheim, Stephen
- A Little Night Music: Send In the Clowns

Steiner, Max
- The Caine Mutiny (1954): The March
- Gone With the Wind (1939): Dance Montage
- Gone With the Wind: Tara's Theme
- Jezebel (1938): Waltz
- King Kong (1933): Overture
- King Kong: Theme
- Now, Voyager (1942): Main Title and Final Scene

Strauss, Richard
- Introduction (Sunrise)

Theodorakis, Mikis
- Zorba the Greek (1964): Theme

Thomson, Virgil
- Fugue and Chorale on Yankee Doodle

Tiomkin, Dimitri
- Circus World (1964): John Wayne March
- DOA (1950)
- Friendly Persuasion (1956): Thee I Love
- Giant (1956): Suite
- The Great Waltz (1938)
- High Noon (1952): Do Not Forsake Me Oh My Darling
- It's a Wonderful Life (1947): Theme
- Night Passage (1957): Follow the River
- Red River (1948): Suite
- Tarzan and the Mermaids (1948): Suite
- Tension at Table Rock (1956): Suite
- Town Without Pity (1961): Theme
- The War Wagon (1967): Suite
- The Well (1951): Suite
- Wild is the Wind (1958): Theme
- The Young Land (1959): Strange are the Ways of Love

Vangelis
- Chariots of Fire

Warren, Diane
- Music of My Heart

Warren, Harry
- Lullaby of Broadway

Waxman, Franz
- Anne of the Indes (1951): Overture
- Beloved Infidel (1959): Theme
- A Christmas Carol (1939): Christmas Morning & Finale
- Cimarron (1960): Suite
- Come Back, Little Sheba (1953): Reminiscences for Orchestra
- The Lost Command (1966): Aicha's Theme
- The Magnificent Seven: Suite
- Man on a Tightrope (1953): March
- My Geisha (1961): Goodbye Love–Finale
- My Geisha (1961): Suite
- My Geisha (1961): You Are Sympathy to Me
- The Nun's Story (1958): Short Suite
- Peyton Place (1957): Theme "The Wonderful Seasons of Love" or "For Those Who Are Young"
- The Philadelphia Story (1939): Suite
- Taras Bulba (1962): The Ride of the Cossacks
- Young at Heart (1938)

Wendel, Robert
- A Hollywood Salute

Williams, Charles
- The Dream of Olwen
- The Apartment: Theme (Jealous Lover)

Williams, John T.
- 1941: March of 1941
- Theme from Close Encounters of the Third Kind
- Theme from E.T.
- E.T.: Flying Theme
- The Empire Strikes Back Medley
- Hook: Flight to Neverland
- Suite from Jaws
- The Lost World: Jurassic Park
- Memoirs of a Geisha: Sayuri's Theme
- Midway: Midway March
- Munich: A Prayer for Peace
- Munich: Hatikva (The Hope)
- Star Wars: Episode II: Attack of the Clones (Across the Stars Love Theme)
- Star Wars: Episode III: Revenge of the Sith (Battle of the Heroes)
- Star Wars Main Theme
- Star Wars: Parade of the Ewoks (Return of the Jedi)
- Star Wars: Selections from The Phantom Menace
- Superman March: Main Theme
- Superman Returns, Concert Selections
- The Terminal: Viktor's Tale

Williams & Hooper
- Harry Potter and the Order of the Phoenix: Concert Suite

Yared, Gabriel
- The English Patient (1996)

Zimmer, Hans
- Da Vinci Code (2006): Chevaliers de Sangreal

[5' or less]

HOLIDAYS

Christmas

Adam, Adolphe
- Christmas with Renata Scotto: 5. Christmas Song (Cantique de Noel)
- O Holy Night (Cantique de Noel)

Amundson, Steven
- Angels' Dance

Anderson, Leroy
- A Christmas Festival
- Bugler's Holiday
- Sleigh Ride

Arnold, Malcolm
- Holly and the Ivy: Fantasy on Christmas Carols

Austin, Frederic
- Twelve Days of Christmas

Bach, J. S.
- Jesu, Joy of Man's Desiring
- Sheep May Safely Graze

Bacon, Ernst
- Christmas Fantasia for Strings

Barber, Samuel
- Die Natali (Chorale Preludes for Christmas) Op. 37: Silent Night

Bax, Arnold
- A Christmas Carol

Berlin, Irving
- White Christmas

Berlioz, Hector
- The Novello Book of Carols: The Shepherds' Farewell

Blake, Howard
- Christmas Lullaby

Blane, Ralph
- Have Yourself a Merry Little Christmas

Broughton, Bruce
- Miracle on 34th Street (1994): Main Title
- Miracle on 34th Street, Overture to

Burgon, Geoffrey
- Nunc Dimittis

Christensen, James
- Snow Chase

Darke, Harold
- In the Bleak Midwinter

Davis, Katherine
- Little Drummer Boy

Dix, William
- Christmas with Renata Scotto: 8. What Child Is This?

Dorff, Daniel
- Pachelbel's Christmas

Dunhill, Thomas
- The Novello Book of Carols: How Soft, Upon the Ev'ning Air

Friedhofer, Hugo
- The Bishop's Wife: Ice Skater's Waltz (1947)

Gabrielli, Giovanni
- The Novello Book of Carols: O Magnum Misterium

Gauntlett & Mann & Wells
- The Novello Book of Carols: Once in Royal David's City

Gould, Morton
- Adeste Fidelis
- Christmas Time, Book I: Adeste Fidelis
- Christmas Time, Book I: First Noel
- Christmas Time, Book I: It Came Upon a Midnight Clear
- Christmas Time, Book I: O Little Town/Away in a Manger
- Christmas Time, Book 1: Silent Night
- Christmas Time, Book II: Cinerama Holiday: Skier's Waltz
- Christmas Time, Book II: Good King Wenceslas
- Christmas Time, Book II: Home for Christmas
- Christmas Time, Book II: Jingle Bells
- First Noel
- Good King Wenceslas
- Holiday Music: Christmas
- Holiday Music: Home for Christmas
- It Came Upon a Midnight Clear
- Jingle Bells

Grady, John
- Christmas with Renata Scotto: 2. Angels We Have Heard on High
- Christmas with Renata Scotto: 3. Adeste Fidelis

Grainger, Percy
- Shepherd's Hey

Gruber, F. X.
- Christmas with Renata Scotto: 1. Silent Night
- Silent Night

Gruber, Franz & Redner
- Silent Night; O Little Town of Bethlehem

Grundman, Clare
- Three Noels

Handel, G. F.
- Angels We Have Heard on High; Joy to the World
- Christmas with Renata Scotto: 4. Joy to the World
- Joy to the World
- Messiah: Sinfonia Pastoral
- The Novello Book of Carols: Joy to the World

Herbert, Victor
- Babes in Toyland: March of the Toys

Herman, Jerry
- The Best Christmas of All

Holcombe, Bill
- Christmas Wishes

Holst, Gustav
- The Novello Book of Carols: In the Bleak Midwinter

Hovhaness, Alan
- Triptych: 1b. As on the Night, Op.100 (Christmas Ode)

Jackson, Stephen
- The Novello Book of Carols: Noel nouvelet

Jessel, Leon
- Parade of the Wooden Soldiers

Joubert, John
- The Novello Book of Carols: Torches 1
- The Novello Book of Carols: Torches II

Kent, Walter
- I'll Be Home for Christmas

Kilar, Wojciech
- Dracula (1992)

Kirkpatrick, W. F.
- The Novello Book of Carols: Away in a Manger

Krogstad, Bob
- Christmas at the Movies

Llewellyn, William
- The Novello Book of Carols: Come All You Worthy People
- The Novello Book of Carols: De Virgin Mary Had a Baby Boy
- The Novello Book of Carols: God Rest You Merry Gentlemen
- The Novello Book of Carols: Il est ne, le divin enfant (See Him Born)
- The Novello Book of Carols: King Jesus Hath A Garden
- The Novello Book of Carols: O Come All Ye Faithful
- The Novello Book of Carols: Puer Nobis (Unto Us is Born a Son)
- The Novello Book of Carols: The Angel Gabriel
- The Novello Book of Carols: The Holly and the Ivy

Luck, Arthur
- Deck the Hall & We Wish You a Merry Christmas

MacLellan, Gene
- Snowbird

Mancini, Henry
- Jingle Bells/Sleigh Ride

Marks, Johnny
- Rudolph the Red-Nosed Reindeer

Mendelssohn
- Hark! The Herald Angels Sing
- The Novello Book of Carols: Hark the Herald Angels Sing

Menotti, Gian Carlo
- Amahl and the Night Visitors: Shepherd's Chorus

[5' or less]

Miller, Sy & Jackson, Jill
- Let There Be Peace on Earth
Mozart, Wolfgang Amadeus
- Exsultate Jubilate, K. 165
- The Sleigh Ride
Musgrave, Thea
- Two Christmas Carols
Nelson, Steve & Rollins, Jack
- Frosty the Snowman
Niles, John Jacob
- I Wonder as I Wander
Perry, William
- Joy Shall Be Yours in the Morning
Pola, Eddie & Wyle, George
- It's the Most Wonderful Time of the Year
Reed, Alfred
- Greensleeves
Reger, Max
- Christmas with Renata Scotto: 7. Virgin's Slumber Song
- Weihnachten (Christmas), Op. 145/3
Regney & Shayne
- Do You Hear What I Hear
Rimsky-Korsakov, Nicolai
- Christmas Eve: Polonaise
Rose, David
- Holiday for Strings
Rutter, John
- Jesus Child!
Sayre, Charles
- A Christmas Tradition
- Christmas Vision
- A Rockin' Christmas
Schubert, Franz
- Ave Maria
- Christmas with Renata Scotto: 6. Ave Maria
Scott, Raymond
- The Toy Trumpet
Silvestri & Ballard
- God Gless Us Everyone
Smith, Robert W.
- Jingle Bells Forever
Stephenson, James M. III
 - BaSOON It Will Be Christmas
- God Rest Ye Merry Gentlemen
- Go Tell It On the Mountain
- Holiday Fanfare Medley No. 2
- I Saw Three Ships/Jeanette, Isabella Medley
- Joy to the World
- Lo, How a Rose E'er Blooming
- O Christmas Tree
Stillman & Allen
- Home for the Holidays
Stokowski, Leopold
- Traditional Slavic Christmas Music
- What Child Is This?

Styne, Jule
- Let It Snow! Let It Snow! Let It Snow!
Thurlow, Jeremy
- The Novello Book of Carols: All and Some (Nowell We Sing)
Tiomkin, Dimitri
- It's a Wonderful Life (1947): Theme
Torme & Wells
- Christmas Song (Chestnuts Roasting on an Open Fire)
Tyzik, Jeff
- A Christmas Overture
- The Skater's Overture: Variations on a Theme of Waldteufel
- What Child Is This
Vaughan Williams
- Greensleeves
Ward-Steinman, David
- Season's Greetings: Festive Overture
Warrington, John
- Yuletide Festival
Waxman, Franz
- A Christmas Carol (1939): Christmas Morning & Finale
Wells, Robin
- The Novello Book of Carols: A Fanfare for Christmas
- The Novello Book of Carols: A Gallery Carol (Rejoice and Be Merry)
Wendel
- The Bells of Christmas
- Carol of the Bells
- Christmas Through Children's Eyes
- An Evergreen Christmas
- In the Manger
- Santa Dear
- We Need a Little Christmas
Yon, Pietro
- Gesu Bambino

Halloween

Alford, Kenneth
- Hexen
Anderson, Leroy
- The Phantom Regiment
Bernstein, Elmer
- American Werewolf in London
- Ghostbusters: Theme
Chadwick, George
- Symphonic Sketches: Hobgoblin
Coleman, Cy
- Witchcraft
Elfman, Danny
- Beetlejuice: Main Title (1988)
Falla, Manuel de
- El Amor brujo: Chanson du feu follet
- El Amor Brujo: Ritual Fire Dance

Goldsmith, Jerry
- Poltergeist (1982): Night of the Beast (Clown Attack)
- Poltergeist (1982): The Calling
- Poltergeist (1982): The Light
- Poltergeist (1982): Theme (Carol Anne's)
Gould, Morton
- Audubon: Night Music
- Holiday Music: Halloween
Hefti, Neal Paul
- Batman TV Theme
Herrmann, Bernard
- The Ghost of Mrs. Muir (1947)
- It's Alive (1973)
- Psycho (1960)
- The Mask of Zorro: Suite (1998)
Humperdink, Engelbert
- Hansel und Gretel: Hexenritt (Witch's Ride)
McBride, Robert
- Pumpkin Eater's Little Fugue
Mizzy, Vic
- Addams Family Values: Tango for Violin and Orchestra (1993)
- The Addams Family: Theme & Waltz Finale (1991)
Nielsen, Carl August
- Masquerade (Prelude to Act II)
- Masquerade Overture
O'Boyle, Sean
- Waltz of Madness
O'Brien, Richard
- The Rocky Horror Picture Show: Medley
Perry, Sam
- The Phantom of the Opera (1930)
Salzedo, Leonard
- The Witch Boy: Square Dance from the Ballet
Strauss, Johann, Jr.
- Lucifer Polka, Op. 266
Wagner, Richard
- Die Walküre: Ride of the Valkyries
Weinberger, Jaromir
- The Devil on the Belfry
Wendel, Robert
- A Halloween Trilogy

Hanukkah

Adler, Samuel
- The Feast of Lights
- A Song of Hanukkah
- Judah's Song of Praise
Bavel, Zamir
- Hanukkah Light (1998)
Ellstein, Abraham
- Sh'Ma Yisroel
Wernick, Richard
- Chanukah Festival Overture
Wendel, Robert
- A Chanukah Overture

[5' or less]

(Hanukkah - Wendel, cont.)

- Fantasia on "Yeroushalaim Shel Zahav"

Tyzik, Jeff
- Mis zeh Hidlik (Behold the Lights)

Labor Day

Mosolov, Alexander
- The Iron Foundry, Op. 19

Shire, David
- Norma Rae: It Goes Like It Goes

New Year

Anderson, Leroy
- The Syncopated Clock

Barry, John
- Somewhere In Time

Caillet, Lucien
- Fantasie on "Auld Lang Syne"

Haggart, Bob
- What's New?

Kapilow, Robert
- Union Station: New Year's Eve

Strauss, Johann and Josef
- Pizzicato Polka

Strauss, Johann, Jr.
- Annen Polka, Op. 117
- Banditen Galopp, Op. 378 (Bandit's Galop)
- Champagne Polka, Op. 211
- Die Fledermaus: Du und du (You and You Waltz), Op.367
- Im Krapfenwaldl Polka, Polka française, Op. 336
- Thousand and One Nights Waltz, Op. 346
- Tick-Tack Polka, Op. 365
- Tritsch Tratsch Polka, Op. 214 (Chit-Chat)
- Unter Donner und Blitz (Thunder and Lightning Polka), Op. 324

Strauss, Johann, Sr.
- Radetzky March, Op. 228

Strauss, Josef
- Ohne Sorgen Polka, Op. 271

Turok, Paul
- Reeling in the New Year

Wendel, Robert
- Rock Around the Clock
- That's It, That's All...The End!

Williams, Cootie & Monk, Thelonius
- 'Round Midnight

St. Patrick

Anderson, Leroy
- The Irish Suite

Ball, Ernest R.
- When Irish Eyes Are Smiling

Grainger, Percy
- Irish Tune from County Derry

Horner, James
- An Irish Party in Third Class

Wendel, Robert
- An Irish Trilogy

Valentine

Anderson, Leroy
- Goldilocks: Save a Kiss

Arditi, Luigi
- Kiss (Il Bacio)

Barry, John
- Robin and Marian

Bellini, Vincenzo
- Romeo and Juliet: Overture

Brubeck, Dave
- In Your Own Sweet Way

Carmichael, Hoagy
- Romance in the Dark, Nearness of You

Debussy, Claude
- Clair de lune
- La fille au cheveux de lin

Drdla, Frantisek (Franz) Alois
- Souvenir

Edwards, Gus
- By the Light of the Silvery Moon

Ellington, Edward (Duke)
- I Got It Bad and That Ain't Good

Fahrbach, Philipp, Jr.
- Midnight Elopement Galop

Farrar, John
- Grease: You're the One that I Want

Fisher, Fred
- Peg O' My Heart

Friedhofer, Hugo
- An Affair to Remember: The Proposal (1957)

Garner, Erroll
- Misty

Gershwin, George
- Crazy for You Overture
- Embraceable You
- Love Walked In
- Man I Love
- 'S Wonderful

Gold, Marty
- Ecstasy

Goldsmith, Owen
- Romanza for String Orchestra

Grant, James
- Waltz for Betz

Grieg, Edvard
- Erotik
- Ich Liebe Dich
- Wedding Day at Troldhaugen Op. 65, no. 6

Hamlisch, Marvin
- Ice Castles Through the Eyes of Love

Henley, Larry
- Wind Beneath My Wings

Herbert, Victor
- Ah Sweet Mystery of Life

Herbert, Victor
- Kiss Me Again

Hudson, Will & Mills, Irving
- Moonglow

Kern, Jerome
- Smoke Gets In Your Eyes
- Way You Look Tonight

Kreisler, Fritz
- Liebesfreud
- Liebesleid
- Three Old Viennese Dances; No. 3 (Schön Rosmarin)

Lai, Francis
- Love Story: Where Do I Begin
- Love Story: Theme (1970)
- A Man and a Woman

Lang, David
- Hunk of Burnin' Love

Legrand, Michel
- I Will Wait for You

Lennon, John & McCartney, Paul
- I Want to Hold Your Hand

Mancini, Henry
- Breakfast at Tiffanys: Moon River

Mandel, Johnny
- Sandpiper: Shadow of Your Smile

Masser, Michael
- Greatest Love of All

Mendelssohn, Felix
- A Midsummer Night's Dream: Wedding March

Meyer, George W.
- If You Were the Only Girl in the World

Monaco, James
- You Made Me Love You

Morricone, Ennio
- Cinema Paradiso: Love Theme
- I Knew I Loved You

Mozart, Wolfgang Amadeus
- Le Nozze di Figaro (Marriage of Figaro) K. 492: Overture

Newman, Alfred
- Wuthering Heights: Cathie's Theme

Olcott, Chauncey
- My Wild Irish Rose

Porter, Cole
- I Get a Kick Out of You
- You Do Something to Me

Puccini, Giocomo
- Le Villi: "The Witches' Sabbath"

Rodgers, Richard
- Love Me Tonight: Lover

Rota, Nino
- Romeo and Juliet: A Time for Us

Rózsa, Miklós
- Ben-Hur Love Theme
- El Cid: Love Scene

[5' or less]

Saint-Saëns, Camille
- Romance Op. 36
Sibelius, Jean
- Romance in C Major, Op. 42
Tchaikovsky, Peter Ilyich
- Pique Dame: Prince Yeletsky's Aria: I Love You, Dear
Templeton, Alec
- Give Me Your Heart
Thomas, Augusta Read
- Sunlight Echoes
Wagner, Richard
- Lohengrin: Bridal Chorus
Washington & Bassman, George
- I'm Getting Sentimental Over You
Waxman, Franz
- Peyton Place (1957): Theme "The Wonderful Seasons of Love" or "For Those Who Are Young"
Wenrich, Percy
- When You Wore a Tulip

Other Holidays

Berlin, Irving
- Easter Parade
Gardner, John
- Overture Half-Holiday
Gould, Morton
- Holiday Music: Easter Morning
- Holiday Music: First Thanksgiving
Holst, Gustav
- Let All Mortal Flesh Keep Silence
Nelson, Ronald J.
- Rocky Point Holiday
Ryden, William
- Amazing Grace
Wendel, Robert
- Hymn of Thanksgiving

INSTRUMENTAL POPS

Ades, Hawley
- Sholom aleichem
Armstrong, Billie Joe
- Best of Green Day
Anderson, Leroy
- Arietta
- Balladette
- Bonnie Dundee
- The Campbells Are Coming
- The Captain and the Kings
- China Doll
- Clarinet Candy
- Classical Jukebox
- Golden Years for Orchestra
- Fiddle Faddle
- Forgotten Dreams
- The Girl in Satin
- The Golden Years
- Home Stretch
- Lullaby of the Drums
- March of the Two Left Feet
- The Penny Whistle Song
- Plink Plank Plunk1
- Promenade
- Saraband
- Serenata
- A Trumpeter's Lullaby
- The Typewriter
Bernstein, Elmer
- Great Escape March
Blake, Howard
- Let Music Live
Costa, Paul Mario
- A Frangesa March
Chiarappa, Richard
- Boom! for Bass Drum & Orchestra
- Lincoln & Booth: Good-bye
- Lincoln & Booth: Just Ourselves
- Lincoln & Booth: The President's Waltz
- Romp for Symphony Orchestra and (Celebrity) Triangulist
- Side Effects
- To Be Young Again
Clark, Larry
- Hooked on Classics
Creston, Paul
- A Rumor, Op. 27
De Rose, Peter
- Deep Purple
Farnan, Robert
- The Peanut Polka
- Portrait of a Flirt
Fučik, Julius
- Florentiner Marsch, Op. 214
- Under the Admiral's Flag, Op. 82 (Unter der Admiralsflagge)
German, Edward
- Coronation March and Hymn
Gershwin, George
- Gershwin in Concert
Gestor, Don
- First Love
Gold, Ernest
- Boston Pops March
Goldman, Edwin Franko
- Children's March
Goldsmith, Jerry
- Soarin' Over California
Goossens, Eugene
- Scherzo and Folk Tune
Gordon, Phillip
- Fitzwilliam Suite
Gottschalk, Louis Moreau
- Pasquinade Caprice
Gould, Morton
- Café Rio
- Crinoline and Lace
- Pop's Serenade
Hayman, Richard
- Her Name is Suzanne
Hermann, Ralph
- Farmyard Frolic
Holcombe, Bill
- Saxanova
Hunter, Frank
- Fling Went the Strings
- Twinkle Fantasia
Ives, Charles
- Country Band March
Jendras, Louis F.
- The Russian Rag
Jenkins, Karl
- Passacaglia
Katz, S.
- Polskie Kwiaty (Selection of Polish Songs & Dances)
Kerker, Gustave
- The Belle of New York
Koenig, Hermann Louis
- Post Horn Galop
Kraft, William
- Simple Introduction to the Orchestra
Lecuona, Ernesto
- Jungle Drums
- Overture to a Pops Concert
MacDowell, Edward
- To a Wild Rose
Mantovani, Annunzio Paolo
- Gypsy Legend
- Poem to the Moon
Manzanero, Armando
- It's Impossible (Somos novios)
McCabe, John
- Sam (ITV Music)
- Sam: Theme music (orchestra version)
- Dream of a Lifetime
Meij, Johan de
- The Lord of the Rings: Excerpts from Symphony No. 1
Muller, Frederick
- The Rakes of Mallow (with Blue Grass Variation)
Naughtin, Matthew
- The Loony Tunes Fugue
- Mario! Jump!
- The Wheels on the Bus Sing-Along
Nelson, Ronald J.
- Rocky Point Holiday
Pearson, Leslie
- Early One Morning
Putman, Curly
- Green Green Grass of Home
Reed, Alfred
- A Festival Prelude
Reinagle
- Madison's March

[5' or less]

(INSTRUMENTAL POPS, cont.)

Richards, Johnny
- Cuban Fire Suite: La Suerte de los Tontos (Fortune of Fools)

Russell & Knight
- The Halls of Ivy

Schickele, Peter
- Overture to "The Civilian Barber"

Shulman, Alan
- The Bop Gavotte
- Hup Two Three Four
- J. S. On The Rocks (Nightcap)
- Ricky-Tick Serenade

Sierra, Roberto
- A Joyous Overture

Simeone, Harry
- Flute Cocktail Scherzo and Blues for 3 or 2 Solo Flutes and Orchestra

Strauss, Johann and Josef
- Pizzicato Polka

Tichili, Frank
- Postcard for Symphony Orchestra

Wendel, Robert
- Rock Around the Clock
- Surf's Up!
- Swing, Ludwig, Swing!

Weill, Kurt
- Berlin Suite (Bilbao Song)
- Berlin Suite (J'Attends un navire)
- Berlin Suite (Mack the Knife)
- Berlin Suite (Surabaya Johnny)
- New York Suite (I Got a Marble and a Star)
- New York Suite (Mack the Knife)
- New York Suite (Polly's Lied)
- New York Suite (Speak Low)
- The Two Worlds of Kurt Weill: Berlin Suite (Theme from "Mahogonny")
- The Two Worlds of Kurt Weill: New York Suite

Wilson, Don
- Scrambled Opera (An Orchestral Antic)

INTERNATIONAL

African
Paich & Porcaro
- Africa

Asian
Lincke, Paul
- Kwang Hsu (Chinese March)

British/Scottish
Anderson, Leroy
- The Bluebells of Scotland

Coates, Eric
- London Suite: Knightsbridge March

Orr, Charles Wilfred
- Cotswold Hill Tune

Richardson, Clive
- British Grenadiers

Eastern European
Katz, S.
- Polskie Kwiaty (Selection of Polish Songs & Dances)

Monti, Vittorio
- Czardas

Stokowski, Leopold
- Traditional Slavic Christmas Music

French
Offenbach, Jacques
- La vie parisienne: Overture

Irish
Anderson, Leroy
- The Irish Suite

Ball, Ernest R.
- When Irish Eyes Are Smiling

Goossens, Eugene
- Tam O'Shanter: Scherzo

Grainger, Percy
- Irish Tune from County Derry (Londonderry Air)
- Mock Morris
- Molly on the Shore

Hermann, Ralph
- Irish Medley

Mancini, Henry
- The Molly Maguires: Pennywhistle Jig (1970)

Olcott, Chauncey
- My Wild Irish Rose

Wendel, Robert
- An Irish Trilogy

Italian
Armand, Charles (Puerner, Charles)
- Neapolitan Songs for Orchestra

Capua, Eduardo di
- O sole mio

Denza, Luigi
- Funiculi, Funicula

Latin American
Abreu, Zequinha de
- Tico Tico

Álvarez, Teófilo
- Marinera Trujillana

Alzedo, José Bernardo
- Himno Nacional del Perú

Arias, Clotilde
- Huiracocha for voice and orchestra

Ayars, Bo
- Cowboy Medley: Cielito lindo
- Cowboy Medley: Mexican Hat Dance

Barroso, Ary
- Brazil

Benjamin, Arthur
- Two Jamaican Pieces

Campos, José Carlos
- Danza Rústica

Chávez, Carlos
- Cantos de México
- Himno Nacional Mexicano (Mexican National Anthem)

Deussen, Nancy
- Regalos

Gimenez, Jeronimo
- La de Luis Alonso

Gold, Marty
- Brazil

Gomez, Alice
- Festive Huapango

Goossens, Eugene
- Don Juan de Manara: Intermezzo

Granda, Isabel
- La Flor de la Canela

Guarnieri, Camargo
- Dansa Brasileira

Gutierrez, Pedro Elias
- Alma Llanera

Hernandez, Rafael
- El Cumbanchero

Iturriaga, Enrique
- Obertura para una Comedia (Overture for a Comedy)

Lara, Agustín
- Granada

Marquina, Pascual
- Espana Cani

Mindreau, Ernesto López
- Marinera y Tondero

Naughtin, Matthew
- Cinco de Mayo

Piazzolla, Astor
- Libertango
- Michelangelo
- Milonga del Angel
- Tango No. 1: Coral
- Tango No. 2: Canyengue
- Tanguedia
- Tres minutos con la realidad: Tango (Three Minutes of Reality) Rio
- Tequila

Richards, Johnny
- Cuban Fire Suite: La Suerte de los Tontos (Fortune of Fools)

Rodríguez, Robert Xavier
- Tequila Sunrise

Soro, Enrique
- Danza Fantástica

Villaldo, Angel
- El Choclo (Tango Argentina)

Wendel, Robert
- Fiesta Mexicana

[5' or less]

Middle East
Goldsmith, Jerry
- Masada: Suite
Koch, Anton
- Adventures of Sinbad: Overture
Scott, Raymond
- Twilight in Turkey
Williams, John T.
- Munich: Hatikva (The Hope)

Russian
Antheil, George
- Lithuanian Night
Mosolov, Alexander
- The Iron Foundry, Op. 19
Stravinsky, Igor
- Song of the Volga Boatmen

Scandinavian
Halvorsen, Johan
- Norwegian Air
- Norwegian Song, Op. 31
Keillor, Garrison
- Wild Mountain Thyme: Will You Go, Darling, Go?
Lumbye, H.C.
- Copenhagen Steam Railway Gallop

Spanish
Falla, Manuel de
- La vida breve: Spanish Dance No. 1
Fernandez
- Cielito Lindo
Gade, Jacob
- Tango Jalousie (Tango Tzigane)
Lara, Agustín
- Granada
Lecuona, Ernesto
- Andalucia
- Andalucia Suite (Malagueña)
- Danza Lucumi (Danza Afro-Cubanas)
- La Comparsa (Carnival Procession)
Marquina, Pascual
- España Cani
Mendez, Raphael
- La Virgin de la Macarena
Penella, Manuel
- El Gato Montés (The Bobcat)
Piazzolla, Astor
- Libertango
Yradier, Sebastian
- La Paloma (The Dove): Spanish Serenade

Viennese
Sieczynsky
- Vienna: City of My Dreams

JAZZ

Anderson, Leroy
- Jazz Legato
- Jazz Pizzicato
Arnold, Alan
- The Entertainer
Antheil, George
- Jazz Sonata
Arlen, Harold
- Blues in the Night
Berlin, Irving
- Alexander's Ragtime Band
Bernstein, Elmer
- The Man with the Golden Arm: Suite
- The Sweet Smell of Success: Main Title
Brubeck, Dave
- Summersong
- The Gates of Justice: Out of the Way of the People
Brubeck, Howard
- Dialogues: Theme for June
Custer, Calvin
- Birth of the Blues
Ellington, Edward K. (Duke)
- Tribute to the Duke
- Caravan
- I Got It Bad and That Ain't Good
- It Don't Mean a Thing (If it Ain't Got That Swing)
- Mood Indigo: 5 brass setting
- Mood Indigo: 6 brass setting
- Satin Doll
- Solitude
- The Perfume Suite: Dancers in Love
Ellington, Edward K. (Duke) and Strayhorn, Billy
- Deep South Suite: Happy Go Lucky
Gershwin, George
- Gershwin in Concert
- I Got Fascinating Rhythm
- I Got Rhythm
- Big City Blues
- Boogie Woogie Etude
- Minute Plus Waltz Rag
- Body and Soul
Green, John
- Body and Soul
Handy, W. C.
- Saint Louis Blues
Herbert, Victor
- The Enchantress: Art Is Calling for Me (I Want to Be a Prima Donna)
Hudson, Will & Mills, Irving
- Moonglow
Joplin, Scott
- Maple Leaf Rag
- The Entertainer
- The Entertainer Rag
- Ragtimes for Strings

Lamb, Joseph
- Ragtime Nightingale
Lambert, Constant
- Elegiac Blues Local
McPartland, Marian
- Melancholy Mood
Moross, Jerome
- Biguine
O'Boyle, Sean
- Ragtime
Prima, Louis
- Jump, Jive an' Wail
Richards, Johnny
- La Suerte de los Tantos (Fortune of Fools)
Richman, Lucas
- The Brentwood Rag
- Christmas is Coming
- Coventry Carol
- Hanukkay Medley
- Ho! Ho! Ho!
- Presents from Santa
- Take a Ride with Santa
- Thanksgiving Hymn
- A Western Fanfare
Ricketts, Ted
- Satchmo!: A Tribute to Louis Armstrong
Rodríguez, Robert Xavier
- The Salutation Rag
Ronell, Ann
- Willow Weep for Me
Scott, Raymond
- Powerhouse
Shulman, Alan
- Hup Two Three Four
Strayhorn, Billy
- Chelsea Bridge
Warren, Harry
- Serenade in Blue
Wendel, Robert
- The Original Ragtime Band
- Saint Bailey's Rag
- The Saint Louis Blues
Williams, Cootie & Monk, Thelonius
- 'Round Midnight
Zawinul, Joseph
- Birdland

NOVELTY

Anderson, Leroy
- Sandpaper Ballet
- The Typewriter
Chiarappa, Richard
- Boom!: A Waltz for Symphony Orchestra & Bass Drum
- Romp for Symphony Orchestra & (Celebrity) Triangulist

[5' or less]

(NOVELTY, cont.)

Ives, Charles
- Yale-Princeton Football Game

O'Boyle, Sean
- Country Kazoo Overture

Perry, William
- The Gasoline Can-Can

Scott, Raymond
- Dinner Music for a Pack of Hungry Cannibals

Shulman, Alan
- J. S. on the Rocks: Nightcap

Stephenson, James M. III
- Concerto for Cell Phone (2006)

Stravinsky, Igor
- Circus Polka: Composed for a Young Elephant

Wilson, Don
- Scrambled Opera (An Orchestral Antic)

PATRIOTIC

Alford
- Colonel Bogey March

Anderson, Leroy
- Governor Bradford March
- Second Regiment Connecticut National

Bagley, E. E.
- National Emblem March

Bendix, Victor
- Grand American Fantasia: Tone Pictures of the North and South

Bennett, Robert Russell
- Columbia, the Gem of the Ocean

Berlin, Irving
- God Bless America

Boskerck, Captain Francis Saltus Van
- Semper Paratus (1927): U.S. Coast Guard March Song

Chiarappa, Richard
- Lincoln & Booth: Just Ourselves

Cohan, George M.
- Over There
- Star Spangled Spectacular
- You're a Grand Old Flag

Crawford, Robert MacArthur
- Air Force March: Official Song of the United States Army Air Corps

DePonte, Niel
- Bell of Freedom (2002)

Deussen, Nancy
- American Hymn

Effinger, Cecil
- An American Hymn (A Setting of "America the Beautiful")

Falla, Manuel de
- El Amor brujo: Chanson du feu follet
- El Amor Brujo: Ritual Fire Dance

Fillmore, Henry
- His Excellency March

Goldsmith, Jerry
- The Generals: Patton/MacArthur Marches

Goldstein, William
- A. M. America Overture

Gould, Morton
- American Ballads: Jubilo
- American Ballads: Saratoga Quickstep "The Girl I Left Behind"
- American Ballads: Star-Spangled Overture on "The Star-Spangled Banner"
- American Caprice
- American Salute
- Battle Hymn of the Republic
- Dramatic Fanfares from CBS-TV documentary "World War I"
- Flares and Declamations
- Flourishes and Galop
- Hail to a First Lady
- Holiday Music: Fourth of July
- Red Cavalry March
- Yankee Doodle

Greenwood, Lee
- God Bless the U.S.A.

Grieg, Edvard
- Lyric Suite (March of the Dwarfs)

Harris, Roy
- Concert Overture: March in Time of War
- Freedom's Land

Heaton-Smith, Roy
- Admiral Dewey's March

Herbert, Victor
- President's March

Humperdink, Engelbert
- Hansel und Gretel: Hexenritt (Witch's Ride)

Kamen, Michael
- Band of Brothers: Suite (2001)

Ives, Charles
- Lincoln, the Great Commoner

Johnson, Francis
- General Cadwalader's Grand March

Lowden, Bob
- Armed Forces Salute

McDonald, Harl
- Song of Free Nations

Meacham, Frank W.
- American Patrol

Reed, Alfred
- Pledge of Allegiance

Reinagle, Alexander
- Federal March

Reitz, Ric
- To the Flag

Rosenhaus, Steven L.
- Kitchen Percussion March for Special Guests and Orchestra

Shostakovich
- United Nations March

Smith, Harry C.
- Admiral Dewey's March

Smith, John Stafford
- Star-Spangled Banner

Sousa, John Philip
- El Capitan March
- Fairest of the Fair March
- Hands Across the Sea
- King Cotton March
- Semper Fidelis March
- The Liberty Bell March
- The Stars and Stripes Forever
- Thunderer March
- Washington Post March

Steffe, William
- Battle Hymn of the Republic

Steiner, Max
- The Caine Mutiny (1954): The March

Strauss, Johann, Jr.
- Banditen Galopp, Op. 378
- Die Fledermaus: Du und du (You and You Waltz), Op.367
- Thousand and One Nights Waltz, Op. 346

Strauss, Johann, Sr.
- Tritsch-Tratsch (The Circus)

Thomson, Virgil
- Fugue on Yankee Doodle

Wagner, Joseph Franz
- Unter dem Doppeladler (Under the Double Eagle March), Op. 159

Ward, Samuel A.
- America the Beautiful

Wendel, Robert
- The Armed Forces March
- Fanfare for Freedom

Williams, John T.
- Star Spangled Banner

Zwilich, Ellen Taaffe
- One Nation

POPULAR CLASSICS

Anderson, Leroy
- Arietta
- Captains and the Kings
- Clarinet Candy
- Fiddle-Faddle

Bach, J. S.
- Fugue in C minor
- Jesu, Joy of Man's Desiring
- Prelude in E flat minor
- Prelude from Partita in E Major
- Toccata and Fugue in C for Organ: Adagio

DURATION

[5' or less]

- Toccata and Fugue in D Minor, BWV 565

Barber, Samuel
- Commando March for Orchestra

Berlioz, Hector
- Damnation de Faust: Hungarian March (Rakoczy)

Bernstein, Leonard
- Candide Overture

Bizet, Georges
- Carmen: Flower Song
- Carmen: Habanera
- Carmen: Seguidilla and Duett
- Carmen: Sequidilla
- Carmen: Toreador Song

Brahms, Johannes
- Hungarian Dance No. 4

Copland, Aaron
- Billy the Kid: Prairie Night and Celebration
- Rodeo: 3. Saturday Night Waltz
- Rodeo: Hoedown
- Billy the Kid: Waltz

Delibes, Leo
- Coppelia: Entr'acte & Waltz

Elgar, Edward
- Chanson de Matin, Op. 15
- Chanson de Nuit, Op. 15
- Enigma Variations, Op. 36: Nimrod

Frackenpohl, Arthur
- Rondo Marziale

Friml, Rudolf
- Melodie

Gabrieli, Giovanni
- Canzon XVI

Gershwin, George
- Prelude No. 2

Glinka, Mikhail
- Russlan and Ludmilla: Overture

Goldsmith, Jerry
- MacArthur (1977): March

Gould, Morton
- Symphonette No. 2: Pavane

Grieg, Edvard
- Huldigungsmarsch: Sons of Knute
- Ich Liebe Dich

Griffes, Charles Tomlinson
- Clouds
- Three Tone Pictures

Halvorsen, Johan
- Entry of the Boyards

Handel, George Frideric
- Alexander's Feast Overture
- Berenice Overture
- Hercules Overture
- Julius Caesar Overture
- Variations on a Theme by Handel

Herbert, Victor
- Natoma: Prelude to Act III

Khachaturian, Aram
- Gayane: Sabre Dance

Kreisler, Fritz
- Liebesfreud
- Liebesleid
- Three Old Viennese Dances, No. 3: Schön Rosmarin

Mascagni, Pietro
- Cavalleria Rusticana: Intermezzo

Massenet, Jules
- Méditation from Thaïs

Mendelssohn, Felix
- A Midsummer Night's Dream: Wedding March
- A Midsummernight's Dream: Scherzo

Mozart, Wolfgang Amadeus
- Adagio in E, K. 261
- Der Schauspieldirektor (The Impresario) K. 486: Overtur
- Il Re Pastore, K. 208: Overture
- Marriage of Figaro "Deh Vieni non Tardar"
- The Marriage of Figaro, K. 492: Overture
- The Marriage of Figaro: Aprite un po' quegl' occhi
- The Marriage of Figaro: Dove sono i bei momenti
- The Marriage of Figaro: Porgi amor (Cavatina)
- Turkish March

Offenbach, Jacques
- Orpheus in the Underworld: Galop (Can Can)

Pachelbel, Johann
- Canon in D

Prokofiev, Sergei
- Love for Three Oranges: March & Scherzo

Puccini, Giacomo
- Gianni Schicchi: O mio babbino caro

Reznicek, Emil Nikolaus von
- Donna Diana: Overture

Saint-Saëns, Camille
- Romance Op. 36

Sallinen, Aulis
- At the Palace Gates: Overture, Op. 68a

Schubert, Franz
- Der Teufel als Hydraulicus, D. 4: Overture

Shostakovich, Dmitri
- Tahiti-Trot, Op. 16

Sibelius, Jean
- Academic March
- Romance in C Major, Op. 42
- Valse chevaleresque, Op. 96c
- Valse lyrique, Op. 96a

Strauss, Johann Jr.
- Die Fledermaus: Mein Herr Marquis (Laughing Song)
- Im Krapfenwaldl, Polka française, Op. 336
- Waldmeister Overture
- Lucifer Polka, Op. 266
- Perpetuum mobile, Op. 257
- Persian March, Op. 289
- Unter Donner und Blitz (Thunder and Lightning Polka), Op. 324
- Tick-Tack Polka, Op. 365
- Tritsch Tratsch Polka, Op. 214 (Chit-Chat)
- Annen Polka, Op. 117
- Egyptian March, Op. 335
- Eljen A Magyar!, Op. 332 (Long Live the Magyar)

Strauss, Johann, Sr.
- Radetzky March, Op. 228

Strauss, Josef
- Aus Ferienreisen, Op. 133
- Plappermaulchen Polka Schnell, Op. 245 (Chatterbox)

Stravinsky, Igor
- Circus Polka

Sullivan, Arthur
- Yeoman of the Guard Overture

Tchaikovsky, Peter Ilyich
- Eugen Onegin: Polonaise
- Festival Coronation March for Alexander III
- Humoresque
- Pique Dame: Prince Yeletsky's Aria: I Love You, Dear

Tower, Joan
- Fanfare for the Uncommon Woman

Vaughan Williams, Ralph
- Fantasia on Greensleeves
- Rhosymedre

Wagner, Richard
- Die Walküre: Ride of the Valkyries
- Lohengrin: Bridal Chorus

POPULAR SONGS

Anderson, Leroy
- Old MacDonald Had A Farm

Arlen, Harold
- Stormy Weather

Berlin, Irving
- A Pretty Girl Is Like a Melody
- When I Lost You

Brel, Jacques
- If You Go Away

Bullock, Jack
- NYC: Here's to the Big Apple

Carmichael, Hoagy
- Georgia on My Mind
- Nearness of You

[5' or less]

*(POPULAR SONGS
Carmichael, cont.)*

- Romance in the Dark, Nearness of You
- Stardust

Castelnuovo-Tedesco, Mario
- Naomi and Ruth: Ruth's Aria

Coots, J. Fred
- For All We Know

Costa, Francesco Antonio
- Era di maggio

Davis, Albert O.
- Buffalo Gals: In Blue Grass Style

Denver, John
- Annie's Song

De Rose, Peter
- Deep Purple

Edwards, Gus
- By the Light of the Silvery Moon

Ellington, Edward K. (Duke)
- It Don't Mean a Thing (If it Ain't Got That Swing)

Faith, Percy
- Quia, Quia (Kee-a, Kee-a)

Foster, Stephen
- Old Folks At Home; Love's Old Sweet Song: Palms

Garner, Erroll
- Misty

Gershwin, George
- Embraceable You
- Gershwin in Concert
- Man I Love
- 'S Wonderful

Grainger, Percy
- County Derry Air

Green, John
- Body and Soul

Henley, Larry
- Wind Beneath My Wings

Herbert, Victor
- Ah Sweet Mystery of Life
- Kiss Me Again
- The Enchantress: Art Is Calling for Me

Hermann, Ralph
- Farmyard Frolic
- Irish Medley
- Old Song Medley
- Old Timers Waltz Medley No. 1
- Old Timers Waltz Medley No. 2

Hupfeld, Herman
- As Time Goes By

Joel, Billy
- Just the Way You Are

Kern, Jerome
- Smoke Gets In Your Eyes
- They Didn't Believe Me
- Way You Look Tonight

Kosma, Joseph
- Autumn Leaves

Lake, M. L.
- Old Timers Waltz

Lang, Philip J.
- Dark Eyes

Legrand, Michel
- I Will Wait for You
- The Windmills of Your Mind

Lennon, John & McCartney, Paul
- Beatles Medley
- I Want to Hold Your Hand

MacColl, Ewan
- The First Time Ever I Saw Your Face

MacLellan, Gene
- Put Your Hand in the Hand

Malotte, Albert Hay
- The Lord's Prayer

Mancini, Henry
- Breakfast at Tiffanys: Moon River

Mandel, Johnny
- Shadow of Your Smile

Marsh, Gerry Jon
- Hamburger Suite

Mason, Jack
- O Bury Me Not On the Lone Prairie

Masser, Michael
- Greatest Love of All

Meyer, George W.
- If You Were the Only Girl in the World

Mills, Gordon & Reed, Les
- It's Not Unusual

Monaco, James
- You Made Me Love You

Muller, Frederick
- Arkansas Traveler: In Bluegrass Style

North, Alex
- Unchained Melody (1955)

Norton, George
- Round Her Neck She Wore a Yellow Ribbon

Paich & Porcaro, Jeff
- Africa

Phillips, John
- Monday, Monday

Phillips & Gilliam
- California Dreamin'

Popp, André
- Love is Blue (L'Amour est bleu)

Porter, Cole
- Cole Porter Classics
- Gay Divorcée: Night and Day
- I Get a Kick Out of You
- You Do Something to Me

Revaux, J. & François, C.
- My Way

Richardson, Clive
- Polly-Wolly Doodle

Rosenhaus, Steven L.
- American Spiritual Festival
- Lionel Richie in Concert for Orchestra

Ryden, William
- Amazing Grace

Shire, David
- With You I'm Born Again

Shur, Thomas
- Smooth (Santana)

Smith, Hale
- Abide With Me
- Amazing Grace
- A Mighty Fortress

Sondheim, Stephen
- A Little Night Music: Send In the Clowns

Stevens, Ray
- Everything is Beautiful

Valens, Ritchie
- La Bamba

Webb, Jimmy
- MacArthur Park

Washington & Bassman, George
- I'm Getting Sentimental Over You

Weatherly, Fred E.
- Danny Boy

Weill, Kurt
- The Two Worlds of Kurt Weill: Berlin Suite (Bilbao Song)
- The Two Worlds of Kurt Weill: Berlin Suite (J'Attends un navire)
- The Two Worlds of Kurt Weill: Berlin Suite (Mack the Knife)
- The Two Worlds of Kurt Weill: Berlin Suite (Surabaya Johnny)
- The Two Worlds of Kurt Weill: Berlin Suite (Theme from "Mahogonny")
- The Two Worlds of Kurt Weill: New York Suite (I Got a Marble and a Star)
- The Two Worlds of Kurt Weill: New York Suite (Mack the Knife)
- The Two Worlds of Kurt Weill: New York Suite (Polly's Lied)
- The Two Worlds of Kurt Weill: New York Suite (Speak Low)

Wendel, Robert
- An Old Fashioned Summer
- Back to the Fifties!
- Surf's Up!

Wenrich, Percy
- Put On Your Old Grey Bonnet
- When You Wore a Tulip

Williams, Paul
- Rainy Days and Mondays

Wilson & Love
- Beach Boys: Medley for Orchestra

Yarrow, Peter
- Puff the Magic Dragon

[5' or less]

SEASONS

Adler, Samuel
- Summer Stock: A Short Merry Overture

Anderson, Leroy
- First Day of Spring
- Summer Skies

Brubeck, Dave
- Summersong

Christensen, James
- Snow Chase

Corigliano, John
- Midsummer Fanfare

Darke, Harold
- In the Bleak Midwinter

Duke, Vernon
- April in Paris

Gershwin, George
- Porgy and Bess: Summertime

Gould, Morton
- Cinerama Holiday: Skier's Waltz

Grieg, Edvard
- To Spring

Jameson, Tom & Feller, Sherm
- Summertime, Summertime

Kosma, Joseph
- Autumn Leaves

MacLellan, Gene
- Snowbird

Mendelssohn, Felix
- A Midsummernight's Dream: Scherzo

Mozart, W. A.
- The Sleigh Ride

Strauss, Richard
- Introduction (Sunrise)

Styne, Jule
- Let It Snow! Let It Snow! Let It Snow!

Wendel, Robert
- An Old Fashioned Summer

Weill, Kurt
- The Two Worlds of Kurt Weill: New York Suite (September Song)

SPACE

Anderson, Leroy
- Goldilocks: Lazy Moon

Berners, Lord
- The Triumph of Neptune

Carmichael, Hoagy
- Stardust

Corigliano, John
- Midsummer Fanfare

Creston, Paul
- Sunrise in Puerto Rico

Debussy, Claude
- Clair de lune

Edwards, Gus
- By the Light of the Silvery Moon

Giacchino, Michael
- Star Trek: End Credits (2009)

Goldsmith, Jerry
- Capricorn One: Overture & Main Title
- Star Trek Main Theme
- Star Trek: Voyager (1995)
- Star Trek I: The Motion Picture Theme (1979)
- Star Trek 5: The Final Frontier: Suite (1989)
- Star Trek 8: First Contact (1996)
- Star Trek 9: Insurrection (1998)

Herrmann, Bernard
- The Day the Earth Stood Still: Arrival (1951)

Horner, James
- Apollo 13 (Main Title, End Credits, Re-Entry and Splashdown)

Hunter, Frank
- Twinkle Fantasia

Mancini, Henry
- The Lifeforce

McCarthy, Dennis
- Star Trek: Deep Space Nine Suite
- Star Trek 7: Generations "Overture"

Ponce, Manuel
- Estrellita (Star of Love)

Rodriguez, Robert Xavier
- Tequila Sunrise

Ticheli, Frank
- Shooting Stars

Welcher, Dan
- "Night Watchers" Symphony No. 2: Scherzo

Williams, John T.
- Theme from Close Encounters of the Third Kind
- Theme from E.T.
- Selections from E.T.
- Parade of the Ewoks: Return of the Jedi
- Star Wars: Episode II: Attack of the Clones (Across the Stars Love Theme)
- Star Wars Main Theme
- Star Wars: Selections from The Phantom Menace
- The Empire Strikes Back Medley

SPORTS

Arnaud, Leo
- Fanfare to the Olympic Games (Divertissement for Brass and Percussion)

Bernstein, Elmer
- The Babe: End Credits

Bizet, Georges
- Carmen: Toreador Song

Chiarappa, Richard
- Paean to The Scholar, The Athlete and The Artist

Dorff, Daniel
- Tortoise and the Hare

Estefan, Gloria
- Reach

Fučik, Julius
- Entrance of the Gladiators, Op. 68

Goldsmith, Jerry
- Rudy: Theme for Flute and Chamber Orchestra

Ives, Charles
- Yale-Princeton Football Game

Mancini, Henry
- The Great Race: They're Off

McBride, Robert
- Workout

Mendez, Raphael
- La Virgen de la Macarena

Menken, Alan
- Go the Distance

O'Boyle, Sean
- Olympia Australis

Perry, William
- The Gasoline Can-Can

Rózsa, Miklós
- Ben Hur: Parade of the Charioteers

Smith, Robert W.
- Great Steamboat Race

Traditional
- Football Song Hits: Eastern
- Football Song Hits No. 2: Western
- Football Song Hits No. 4: East-South

Tyzik, Jeff
- The Skater's Overture: Variations on a Theme of Waldteufel Vangelis
- Chariots of Fire

Williams, John T.
- Olympic Fanfare and Theme
- Olympic Spirit
- Call of the Champions: 2002 Olympic Theme

TRAVEL

Anderson, Leroy
- Horse and Buggy

Creston, Paul
- Sunrise in Puerto Rico

Duke, Vernon
- April in Paris

Ellington, Edward K. (Duke)
- Caravan

Evans, Dale
- Happy Trails to You (1952)

Goldsmith, Jerry
- Soarin' Over California

[5' or less]

Gould, Morton
 - Windjammer: Main Theme, The Ship
 - Windjammer: Night Watch
Hudson, Will & Mills, Irving
 - Moonglow
Smith, Robert W.
 - Great Steamboat Race
Strauss, Johann, Jr.
 - Vergnugungszug Polka, Op. 281 (Excursion Train)
 - Perpetuum Mobile. Op. 257
Strauss, Josef
 - Aus Ferienreisen, Op. 133
Weill, Kurt
 - The Two Worlds of Kurt Weill: New York Suite (My Ship)
 - The Two Worlds of Kurt Weill: New York Suite (Train to Johannesburg)

TV

Alford, Kenneth J.
 - Colonel Bogey March
Daniel, Eliot
 - I Love Lucy: Theme
Elfman, Danny
 - Simpsons Theme
Elliot, Jack
 - Theme from Charlie's Angels
Evans, Dale
 - Happy Trails to You (1952)
Goldsmith, Jerry
 - Masada: Suite
Griffin, Merv
 - An Hour with the Game Shows
 - Jeopardy Theme
Hefti, Neal Paul
 - Batman TV Theme
Holdridge, Lee
 - Beauty and the Beast: Theme
Johnson, Laurence (Laurie)
 - The Avengers: Theme (1961)
Kamen, Michael
 - Band of Brothers
 - Band of Brothers: Suite (2001)
Lawrence, David
 - High School Musical 2
Mancini, Henry
 - Mystery Movie Theme
 - Peter Gunn
 - Peter Gunn Theme
 - The Thorn Birds Theme
 - The Thorn Birds: Meggie's Theme
Mizzy, Vic
 - Addams Family Values: Tango for Violin and Orchestra (1993)
 - The Addams Family: Theme & Waltz Finale (1991)

Schifrin, Lalo
 - Mission Impossible: Theme
Shire, David
 - Raid on Entebbe (1977): Theme
Steiner, Fred
 - Perry Mason (1956): Theme
Steiner, Max
 - The Caine Mutiny (1954): The March
Stevens, Morton
 - Hawaii Five O (1968)
Tiomkin, Dimitri
 - Rawhide (1959): Theme
 - The Wild, Wild West (1965): Suite
Vangelis
 - Hymne
Wendel, Robert
 - The Flintstones Meet the Jetsons
 - Jonny Quest
 - The Smurfs
 - When TV Was Young
Williams, Charles
 - The Dream of Olwen
Williams, John T.
 - The Mission (NBC News Theme)

VIDEO GAMES

O'Donnell & Salvatori
 - Halo Suite: Halo Theme
Tallarico, Tommy & Plowman, Michael Richard
 - Advent Rising Suite: Bounty Hunter Theme
Wendel, Robert
 - Take Flight
 - The Tall Ships

WEATHER

Arlen, Harold
 - The Wizard of Oz: Over the Rainbow
 - Stormy Weather
Dorff, Daniel
 - Sunburst
Griffes, Charles Tomlinson
 - Clouds
Howard, James
 - Snow Falling on Cedars Suite
MacDermot, Galt
 - Aquarius: Let the Sunshine In
Mancina, Mark
 - Twister Main Theme
Silvers, Louis
 - April Showers
Sousa, John Philip
 - Thunderer March
Steiner, Max
 - Gone With the Wind: Tara's Theme

Strauss, Johann, Jr.
 - Unter Donner und Blitz (Thunder and Lightning Polka), Op.324
Strauss, Richard
 - Introduction (Sunrise)
Thomas, Augusta Read
 - Sunlight Echoes
Whitney, John
 - Light Rays
Williams, Paul
 - Rainy Days and Mondays

6' to 10'

AMERICANA

Antheil, George
 - Tom Sawyer Overture: California Overture
Bennett, Robert Russell
 - Overture to the Mississippi
Bernstein, Elmar
 - True Grit: Concert Suite
Coleridge-Taylor, Samuel
 - Hiawatha's Wedding Feast: Onaway! Awake Beloved
Cooper, Paul
 - Shenandoah for Charles Ives' Birthday
Copland, Aaron
 - Rodeo: 1. Buckaroo Holiday
Custer, Calvin
 - A Salute to the Big Apple
 - The American Frontier
Danielpour, Richard
 - Toward the Splendid City
Foster, Stephen
 - A Stephen Foster Overture
Goldsmith, Jerry
 - Fireworks: A Celebration for Los Angeles (1999)
Gould, Morton
 - Minstrel Show
 - Revival: A Fantasy on Six Spirituals
Grainger, Percy
 - Tribute to Foster
Grundman, Clare
 - American Rhapsody No. 1: Four Folk Songs
Guion, David
 - Arkansas Traveler
 - Home on the Range for Voice and Orchestra
Hageman, Richard
 - Stagecoach: Suite (1939)
Harris, Roy
 - Epilogue to Profiles in Courage: JFK

[6' to 10']

Hayman, Richard
- Pops Hoe-Down
Holcombe, Bill
- Cowboy Fantasy
Ives, Charles
- Central Park in the Dark
Jendras, Louis F.
- Appalachian Fling
Maggio, Robert
- Boardwalk
- Skylines
Markowitz, Richard
- Wild, Wild West (1965)
Nelson, Ronald J.
- Savannah River Holiday
Piket, Frederick
- Curtain Raiser to an American Play: Overture
Reisfeld, Bert
- California Concerto
Rose, David
- Little House on the Prairie: Meet Me at the Fair (1974)
Tiomkin, Dimitri
- The Guns of Navarone (1961): Suite
- High Noon (1952): Suite
Tyzik, Jeff
- Fantasy On American Themes
Wagner, Joseph
- Radio City Snapshots
Waxman, Franz
- The Pioneer (1951): Suite
Welcher, Dan
- Zion
Wendel, Robert
- From Sea to Shining Sea
- A George M. Cohan Overture
- Stephen Foster Overture

ANIMALS

Cailliet, Lucien
- Variations on "Pop! Goes the Weasel"
Elfman, Danny
- Charlotte's Web: Themes for Flute and Orchestra (2006)
- Spider-Man: Suite (2004)
Frazelle, Kenneth
- Swans at Pongo Lake
Goldsmith, Jerry
- The Swarm (1978): Bees Arrive/End Title
Griffes, Charles Tomlinson
- The White Peacock
Guion, David
- Pastorale: Three Little Brown Bulls
Hermann, Ralph
- Silent Movie

Herschel, Lee
- How the Camel Got His Hump
- How the Whale Got His Tiny Throat
Lloyd Webber, Andrew
- Cats Selections
Mechem, Kirke
- The Jayhawk Op. 43: Overture to a Mythical Comedy
Poledouris, Basil
- Free Willy Suite (1993)
Ravel, Maurice
- Ma Mère l'Oye: Prélude et Danse du rouet
Robles, Daniel Alomia
- El Condor Pasa (The Condor Flies Past)
Schickele, Peter
- Canine Cantata "Wachet Arf!"
Sibelius, Jean
- Legends, Op. 22: 2. The Swan of Tuonela
Silvestri, Alan
- Mouse Hunt (1997): Suite
Steiner, Max
- King Kong: Jungle Dance
Strauss, Josef
- Dorfschwalben aus Osterreich (Austrian Village Swallows), Op.164
Tiomkin, Dimitri
- A President's Country (1966): Medley
Walker, Robert
- My Dog Has Fleas: A Capriccio for Scratch Orchestra
Vaughan-Williams, Ralph
- The Wasps Overture
Zaninelli, Luigi
- Americana

BLACK HISTORY MONTH

Bliss, Arthur
- Baraza
Baker, David
- Two Improvisations
Davis, Anthony
- X: The Life and Times of Malcolm X: Malcolm's Prison Aria
McDonald, Harl
- Suite for Strings on American Negro Themes

BROADWAY MUSICALS

Bart, Lionel
- Oliver Selections
- Oliver! for Orchestra
Bernstein, Leonard
- Candide: Glitter and be Gay
- West Side Story Selections

Bock, Jerry
- Fiddler on the Roof
Brubeck, Dave
- Fugal Fanfare: Happy Anniversary
Chase, Bruce
- Broadway Tonight
Coleman, Cy
- Sweet Charity Medley
Erb, Donald
- Music for a Festive Occasion
Friml, Rudolf
- Medley from The Firefly
Gershwin, George,
- Strike Up the Band
Guettel, Adam
- Light in the Piazza: Symphonic Suite
Joel, Billy
- Movin' Out
Kander, John
- Chicago
- Chicago: Medley
Kern, Jerome
- Jerome Kern Medley
- Sally Selections for Orchestra
Krogstad, Bob
- Curtain Up!
Lane, Burton
- Excerpts from Finian's Rainbow
Leigh, Mitch
- Man of La Mancha: Selections
- Man of La Mancha: Orchestral Synthesis
Lloyd Webber, Andrew
- Andrew Lloyd Webber: A Concert Celebration
- Cats Selections
- Music from Evita
- Medley from Jesus Christ Superstar
Loesser, Frank
- Music from Guys and Dolls
- Selections from Guys and Dolls
- The Most Happy Fella: Symphonic Impressions
Loewe, Frederick
- Highlights My Fair Lady
- Gigi: Selections
- My Fair Lady
MacDermot, Gal
- Hair: Selections
Rodgers, Richard
- Carousel: Selections
- Carousel: The Carousel Waltz
- King and I Selections
- Richard Rodgers in Concert
- Rodgers and Hart Medley
Rome, Harold
- Fanny: Selection for Orchestra
Sayre, Chuck
- Jerome Robbins Broadway
Schoenberg, Claude-Michel
- Les Miserables Selections

[6'-10']

(BROADWAY MUSICALS Schoenberg, cont.)

- Miss Saigon: Finale
- Miss Saigon Medley

Strommen, Carl
- A Salute to Broadway

Strouse, Charles
- Muscal Highlights from Annie
- Selections from Annie

Willson, Meredith
- Music Man Selections

CELEBRATION

Brubeck, Dave
- Fugal Fanfare: Happy Anniversary

Elgar, Edward
- Pomp and Circumstance March No. 1 in D Major, Op. 39

Erb, Donald
- Music for a Festive Occasion

Goldsmith, Jerry
- Fireworks: A Celebration for Los Angeles (1999)

Ivanovici, Josef
- Danube Waves Waltz: The Anniversary Song

Liebermann, Lowell
- Revelry

López, Jimmy
- Fiesta! for chamber orchestra
- Fiesta! for orchestra

Richman, Lucas
- Shena B'rachot

Schickele, Peter
- Birthday Ode to "Big Daddy" Bach

Schurmann, Gerard
- Attack and Celebration

Sierra, Roberto
- Tropicalia (Celebration)

Zwilich, Ellen Taaffe
- Celebration
- Jubilation

CIRCUS

Schuman, William
- Circus Overture: Sideshow

Toch, Ernst
- Circus Overture

Wendel, Robert
- A George M. Cohan Overture

DANCE

Alwyn, William
- Suite of Scottish Dances

Antheil, George
- Archipelago "Rhumba"

Arnold, Malcolm
- English Dances, Suite No.2
- English Dances: Set I
- Four Cornish Dances, Op. 91
- Four Scottish Dances
- Solitaire, Op. 141: Sarabande and Polka

Bartók, Béla
- Rumanian Folk Dances

Brahms, Johannes
- Hungarian Dance No. 5 & 6
- Hungarian Dances Nos. 1, 3, 10

Britten, Benjamin
- Gloriana: The Courtly Dances

Cervantes, Ignacio
- Three Cuban Dances

Constantinescu, Paul
- Tanze Aus Rumanien

Copland, Aaron
- Rodeo: 1. Buckaroo Holiday

Dodgson, Stephen
- Villanelle

Falla, Manuel de
- La Vida Breve: Interlude & Dance

Gade, Jacob
- Jalousie

Geehl, Henry
- Folk Dance Suite

German, Edward
- Three Dances: Henry VIII
- Valse Gracieuse

Gliere, Reinhold
- The Red Poppy: Russian Sailor's Dance from Act I

Glinka, Mikhail
- Valse Fantaisie

Gluck, Christoph Willibald
- Orfeo ed Euridice: Dance of the Blessed Spirits

Goossens, Eugene
- Flamenco: Ballet

Gould, Morton
- Philharmonic Waltzes

Grant, James
- Waltz for Betz

Guion, David
- Minuet

Hardiman, Ronan
- Lord of the Dance

Hermann, Ralph
- Polish Polka Party

Ivanovici, Josef
- Danube Waves Waltz: The Anniversary Song

Joel, Billy
- Movin' Out

Lane, Philip
- Wassail Dances for Orchestra

Lanner, Joseph
- Hofball-Tanze Waltz, Op. 161

Lehár, Franz
- Gold and Silver Waltz

Liszt, Franz
- Mephisto Waltz No. 1 (from Lenau's Faust)
- Mephisto Waltz No. 2 (from Lenau's Faust)

Mancini, Henry
- Astaire!

Marquez, Arturo
- Danzon No. 2

Moncayo, José Pablo
- Huapango

Piazzolla, Astor
- Milonga del Angel

Ponchielli, Amilcare
- La Gioconda: "Dance of the Hours"

Ravel, Maurice
- Ma Mère l'Oye: Prélude et Danse du rouet

Riege, Ernst
- Katharinen-Waltz

Riegger, Wallingford
- Dance Rhythms, Op. 58

Rodgers, Richard
- Carousel: The Carousel Waltz

Sayre, Chuck
- Jerome Robbins Broadway

Sibelius, Jean
- Kuolema, Op. 44: Valse Triste

Steiner, Max
- King Kong: Jungle Dance

Strauss, Johann, Jr.
- Die Fledermaus Waltz
- Eine nacht in Venedig: Fruhlingsstimmen Waltz (Voices of Spring), Op. 410
- Künstler (Artist's) Quadrille, Op. 201
- Künstlerleben (Artist's Life) Waltz, Op. 316
- Morgenblätter (Morning papers), Op. 279
- Rosen aus dem Süden (Roses from the South Waltzes), Op. 388
- Telegramme Walzer, Op. 318
- Wiener Blut (Vienna Blood), Op. 354

Strauss, Josef
- Sphärenklänge (Music of the Spheres Waltz), Op. 235

Stravinsky, Igor
- L'Oiseau de feu (Firebird): Berceuse & Finale

Tchaikovsky, Peter Ilyich
- Nutcracker Dances
- The Nutcracker Suite

[6'-10']

Villaldo &Matos Rodríguez
- El Choclo & La Cumparsita
Waxman, Franz
- The Devil Doll (1936): Waltzes
Weber, Carl Maria von
- Invitation to the Dance
Weinberger, Jaromir
- Svandadudák (Shvanda the Bagpiper): Polka and Fugue
Whelan, Bill
- Riverdance Theme
Woodgate, Leslie
- English Dance Suite
Zyman, Samuel
- Encuentros (1992)

ECOLOGY

Copland, Aaron
- An Outdoor Overture
Frazelle, Kenneth
- Swans at Pongo Lake
Grainger, Percy
- Green Bushes
MacCunn, Hamish
- Land of the Mountain and Flood, Op. 3: Overture
Sibelius, Jean
- Hymn to the Earth
Thomson, Virgil
- The Seine at Night
- Wheat Field at Noon
Welcher, Dan
- The Yellowstone Fires

FANFARE

Brubeck, Dave
- Fugal Fanfare: Happy Anniversary

FILMS

Arlen, Harold
- The Wizard of Oz Selections
- Wizard of Oz Choral Review
- Wizard of Oz: Munchkin Land
Arnold, David
- Independence Day Suite: End Tags
Arnold, Malcolm
- The Belles of St. Trinians: Comedy Suite
- The Sound Barrier Rhapsody, Op. 38
- Whistle Down the Wind
Badelt, Klaus
- Pirates of the Caribbean: Curse of the Black Pearl

Barry, John
- Somewhere in Time
Berlin, Irving
- Irving Berlin in Hollywood Overture
Bernstein, Elmer
- Airplane!: Suite
- My Left Foot: Suite
- The Ten Commandments: Suite
- To Kill a Mockingbird: Suite
- True Grit: Concert Suite
Bock, Jerry
- Fiddler on the Roof: Medley
Bocook, Jay
- Movie Spectacular
Bush, Geoffrey
- Yorick Overture
Chase, Bruce
- Muppet Medley
Conti, Bill
- Rocky Highlights
Custer, Calvin
- Themes from 007: A Medley for Orchestra
Daugherty, Michael
- Metropolis Symphony: 1. Lex
- Metropolis Symphony: 2. Krypton
- Metropolis Symphony: 3. Mxyzptlk
- Metropolis Symphony: 4. Oh, Lois!
Desplat, Alexandre
- The Curious Case of Benjamin Button: Suite
- The Queen: Suite (2006)
Dessau, Paul
- Alice the Firefighter
- Alice's Monkey Business
- Alice in the Wooly West
- Alice Helps the Romance
Doyle, Patrick
- Much Ado About Nothing: Suite
Eidelman, Cliff
- Star Trek 6: The Undiscovered Country (1991)
Elfman, Danny
- Charlotte's Web: Themes for Flute and Orchestra (2006)
- Movie Spectacular
- Spider-Man: Suite (2004)
Flaherty, Stephen
- Ragtime Selections
- Anastasia Medley
Foster, David W.
- Quest for Camelot Selections
Friml, Rudolf
- Medley from The Firefly
German, Edward
- Richard III Overture
Giacchino, Michael
- Music from "Up"
Gilpin, Greg
- The Music of MGM (A Choral Medley)

Gold, Ernest
- Exodus: An Orchestral Tone-Picture
- Exodus: Rhapsody for Cello and Orchestra (1960)
Goldsmith, Jerry
- The Blue Max (1996): Suite
- The Boys from Brazil (1978): Waltz & The Boys
- The Edge (1997): Main Title & Finale
- The Great Train Robbery (1979): Suite
- Gremlins: Suite
- Hoosiers (1986): Suite
- Star Trek I: The Motion Picture *The New Enterprise*
- Star Trek 10: Nemesis (2002)
- The Sum of All Fears (2002)
- The Swarm (1978): Bees Arrive/End Title
Goodwin, Ron
- Those Magnificent Men in Their Flying Machines (1965)
Gregson-Williams, Harry
- Chronicles of Narnia: The Lion, The Witch and The Wardrobe
Hageman, Richard
- Stagecoach: Suite (1939)
Hayes, Jack
- Fox Medley No. 1; No. 2
Hermann, Ralph
- Silent Movie
Herrmann, Bernard
- Anna and the King of Siam Suite
- The Man Who Knew Too Much: The Storm Clouds Cantata (1956)
- A Portrait of Hitch
- A Portrait of Hitch: The Trouble with Harry Suite (1954)
- Psycho (1960)
- The Seventh Voyage of Sinbad
- Taxi Driver: A Night Piece for Orchestra (1976)
- Vertigo: Suite (1958)
Hooper, Nicolas
- Concert Suite from Harry Potter and the Half-Blood Prince
Horner, James
- Aliens Suite No. 1: Main Title & Ripley's Rescue
- Aliens Suite No. 2: Newt & Face Huggers
- Avatar (2009): Suite
Horner, James
- Braveheart: Main Title & End Credits
- Cocoon Theme
- James Horner-Hollywood Blockbusters: Apollo13; American Tail; Braveheart; Titanic

[6'-10']

*(FILMS
Horner, cont.)*

- Star Trek 3: The Search for Spock *Stealing the Enterprise* (1984)

Howard, James
 - Lady in the Water (2006): The Healing
 - The Prince of Tides Suite
 - Signs Suite
 - The Sixth Sense Suite

Jarre, Maurice
 - Lawrence of Arabia: Overture
 - A Passage to India: A Symphonic Journey (1984)
 - Ryan's Daughter: Rosy's Theme

Kamen, Michael
 - Mr. Holland's Opus: American Symphony

Kaper, Bronislau
 - Mutiny on the Bounty: Suite (1962)

Lawrence, David
 - High School Musical

Lowden, Bob
 - A Disney Supertime
 - Disney Magic

Mancini, Henry
 - Academy Award Medley
 - Astaire!
 - The Glass Menagerie
 - Songs for Audrey: Breakfast at Tiffanys, Charade, Two for the Road

Morricone, Ennio
 - The Mission: Gabriel's Oboe

Murray, Lyn
 - To Catch a Thief: Suite (1955)

Newman, Alfred
 - Prisoner of Zenda: A Ruritanian Rhapsody for Orchestra

Newman, David
 - Hoffa Theme
 - How to Marry a Millionaire
 - How the West Was Won

North, Alex
 - A Streetcar Named Desire: Suite

Ottman, John
 - Superman Returns Suite
 - X2: X-Men United

Poledouris, Basil
 - Free Willy Suite (1993)

Polster, Ian
 - Salute to MGM: That's Entertainment

Portman, Rachel
 - Chocolat: Suite (2000)

Powell, John
 - The Bourne Identity

Richman, Lucas
 - An Overture to Blanche

Rosenman, Leonard
 - Star Trek 4: The Voyage Home

Rota, Nino
 - Romeo and Juliet (1968)
 - War and Peace: Suite (1956)

Rózsa, Miklós
 - Double Indemnity: Suite
 - El Cid: Overture and March
 - El Cid: Suite
 - Ivanhoe
 - The Lost Weekend: Suite

Sakamoto, Ryuichi
 - The Last Emperor: Theme (1987)

Schwartz, Stephen
 - Prince of Egypt Medley

Shore, Howard
 - The Lord of the Rings: The Two Towers
 - The Lord of the Rings: Highlights from the Fellowship of the Ring
 - The Lord of the Rings: Suite from The Return of the King
 - Symphonic Suite from The Lord of the Rings: The Two Towers

Shaiman, Marc
 - The American President: Big Speech, Big Finish

Sheldon, Robert
 - A Most Wonderful Christmas

Shore, Howard
 - Symphonic Suite from The Lord of the Rings: The Two Towers

Silvestri Alan
 - The Abyss: Finale
 - Back to the Future (Madrid Version)
 - Back to the Future Suite
 - Forrest Gump: Suite
 - Judge Dredd (1995): Suite
 - Mouse Hunt (1997): Suite
 - Polar Express Suite

Steiner, Max
 - King Kong: Jungle Dance
 - The Treasure of Sierra Madre (1948): Suite

Strommen, Carl
 - A Salute to the Cinema

Strouse, Charles
 - Muscal Highlights from Annie
 - Selections from Annie

Tiomkin, Dimitri
 - The Big Sky (1952): Suite
 - Dial M for Murder (1954): Suite
 - Friendly Persuasion (1956)
 - The Guns of Navarone (1961): Suite
 - The High and the Mighty (1954): Suite
 - High Noon (1952): Suite
 - Suite from It's a Wonderful Life
 - The Men (1950): Suite

 - A President's Country (1966): Medley
 - Rio Bravo (1959): Suite
 - Strangers on a Train (1951): Suite
 - The Thing from Another World (1951): Suite
 - The Unforgiven

Vangelis
 - Chariots of Fire Suite

Waxman, Franz
 - Botany Bay (1953): Suite
 - The Bride of Frankenstein (1935)
 - Captains Courageous (1937): Suite
 - A Christmas Carol (1939): Five Sketches after Dickens
 - The Devil Doll (1936): Waltzes
 - Dr. Jekyll and Mr. Hyde (1941): Suite
 - The Furies (1950): Suite
 - Hemingway's Adventures of a Young Man: Rosanna
 - Huckleberry Finn (1939): Overture
 - The Ice Follies of 1939
 - Medley: Classic Film Themes
 - Medley: Classic Love Themes
 - My Cousin Rachel (1952): Suite
 - Night and the City (1950): Suite Nightride for Orchestra
 - The Nun's Story (1958)
 - Peyton Place (1957): Suite
 - The Pioneer (1951): Suite
 - A Place in the Sun (1951)
 - Rebecca (1940): Suite
 - The Silver Chalice (1954): Short Suite
 - Sorry, Wrong Number (1948): Passacaglia
 - Sunset Boulevard (1950): Suite
 - Untamed (1955)

Webb, Roy
 - Notorious (1946): Suite

Williams, John T.
 - The Cowboys Overture
 - E.T. Suite: Adventures on Earth
 - Far and Away: Excerpts
 - Harry Potter and the Sorcerer's Stone: Harry Potter Symphonic Suite
 - The Lost World: Jurassic Park
 - Raiders of the Lost Ark: Raiders March
 - Highlights from Return of the Jedi
 - Saving Private Ryan: Hymn to the Fallen
 - Selections from E.T.
 - The Patriot
 - Theme from Schindler's List
 - Superman Returns Suite
 - Star Wars Medley
 - Three Themes

Willson, Meredith
 - The Music Man: Overture

[6'-10']

Young, Christopher
 - Species (1995): End Credits
Young, Victor
 - Around the World in 80 Days (1956): Overture & Epilogue
 - For Whom the Bell Tolls (1943): Suite
 - Medley: Victor Young Tribute
 - The Quiet Man (1952): Suite
 - Samson and Delilah (1949)
 - The Uninvited (1944): Stella by Starlight
Young & Auric
 - Roman Holiday (1953): Main Title and Prelude
Zimmer, Hans
 - Gladiator, Music from the Movie
 - The Last Samurai: The Way of the Sword
 - Pirates of the Caribbean: Dead Man's Chest (Soundtrack Highlights)
Zimmer & Howard
 - The Dark Knight: Concert Suite

HOLIDAYS

Christmas

Anderson, Leroy
 - Suite of Carols
Arnold, Malcolm
 - The Holly and the Ivy
 - Toy Symphony, Op. 62
Berezovsky, Nicolai
 - Christmas Festival Overture: Ukrainian Noel
Chase, Bruce
 - Around the World at Christmas Time
 - Christmas Favorites
Courtney, Craig
 - A Musicological Journey Through Twelve Days of Christmas
Custer, Calvin
 - Christmas - That Special Time of the Year
 - It's Christmastime (Medley for Orchestra)
Davis, Chip
 - Christmas Sweet
Elgar, Edward
 - The Snow, Op. 26, No. 1
Erb, Donald
 - Christmas Music
Ellis, David
 - Carols for an Island Christmas
Freyhan, Michael
 - Toy Symphony
Goldstein, William
 - 'Twas the Night Before Christmas

Guaraldi, Vince
 - A Charlie Brown Christmas
Haydn, Franz Joseph
 - Kindersymphonie, Hob. II; 47, C Major (Toy Symphony)
Henderson, Luther
 - A Canadian Brass Christmas
Hermann, Ralph
 - Christmas Fantasy
Higgins, John
 - Christmas on Broadway
Holst, Gustav
 - Christmas Day
Krogstad, Bob
 - The Bells of Christmas
Ives, Charles
 - Christmas Music
Lane, Philip
 - Wassail Dances for Orchestra
Mendelssohn, Felix
 - Hark! The Herald Angels Sing & Adeste Fidelis
Menotti, Gian-Carlo
 - Amahl and the Night Visitors
Mozart, Wolfgang Amadeus
 - German Dance #3, K. 605: Schlittenfahrt (sleigh ride)
Rutter, John
 - The Very Best Time of the Year
Respighi, Ottorino
 - Trittico Botticelliano: 2. Adoration of the Magi
Richman, Lucas
 - Christmas Singalong
 - Reindeer Variations
Ringwald, Roy
 - The Song of Christmas
Rodríguez, Robert Xavier
 - A Gathering of Angels: Bolero for Orchestra
Saint-Saëns, Camille
 - Christmas Oratorio, Op. 12: Praise Ye the Lord of Hosts
Serly, Tibor
 - A Little Christmas Cantata
Shaw, Robert
 - The Many Moods of Christmas: Suites 1 & 4
Smith, Claude T.
 - A Rhapsody on Christmas Carols
Stephenson, James M. III
 - Bells of Christmas Suite
 - Holiday Overture
 - A Holly and Jolly Sing-Along!
 - The Magic of Christmas
 - Swing Carol Fantasy
 - Wassail, Wassail All Over the Tuba
 - We Three Basses! from We Three Kings
 - We Three Kings of Orient Are
 - We Three Strings! from We Three Kings

Tchaikovsky, Peter Ilyich
 - Nutcracker Dances
 - The Nutcracker Suite
Thomson, Virgil
 - The Nativity
Tiomkin, Dimitri
 - Suite from It's a Wonderful Life
Torelli, Giuseppe
 - Concerto Grosso for Two Violins and Orchestra in G Minor, Op. 8, No. 6: Christmas Concerto
Tyzik, Jeff
 - Holiday Moods: Suite No. 2
 - Holiday Moods: Suite No. 3
 - Twelve Gifts of Christmas
Vaughan Williams, Ralph
 - Fantasia on Christmas Carols
Waldteufel, Emile
 - Les Patineurs (Skater's Waltz), Op. 183
Waxman, Franz
 - A Christmas Carol (1939): Five Sketches after Dickens
Wendel, Robert
 - Christmas a la Valse!
Yon, Pietro A.
 - Gesu Bambino
Zador, Eugene
 - A Christmas Overture

Halloween

Arnold, Malcolm
 - Tam O'Shanter: Overture, Op. 51
Auber, Daniel-Francois
 - Fra Diavolo: Overture
Berkeley, Lennox
 - Voices of the Night, Op. 86
Goossens, Eugene
 - Two Sketches
Kasschau, Howard
 - The Legend of Sleepy Hollow
Herrmann, Bernard
 - Psycho (1960)
 - The Seventh Voyage of Sinbad
Mussorgsky, Modest
 - The Dream of the Peasant Gritzko
 - Night on Bare Mountain
Offenbach, Jacques
 - Orpheus in the Underworld Overture
Saint-Saëns, Camille
 - Danse Macabre, Op. 40
Shchedrin, Rodion
 - Concerto No. 1 for Orchestra, "Naughty Limericks" (or "Mischievous Melodies")
Surinach, Carlos
 - Feria Mágica (Magic Fair): Overture
Swanson, Howard
 - Night Music

[6'-10']

(Halloween, cont.)

Waxman, Franz
  - The Bride of Frankenstein (1935)
  - Dr. Jekyll and Mr. Hyde (1941): Suite
Young, Christopher
  - Species (1995): End Credits

Hanukkah

Hermann, Ralph
  - Jewish Melodies
Hinds, Thomas
  - Music for Hannukah: Two Folk Songs and a Hymn
Richman, Lucas
  - Hanukkah Festival Overture
Tyzik, Jeff
  - Chanukah Suite

Labor Day

Arnold, Malcolm
  - Symphonic Study: Machines, Op. 30

New Year

Barry, John
  - Somewhere in Time
Ellington, Edward K. (Duke)
  - New World A-Comin'
Holcombe, Bill
  - Fantasy on Auld Lang Syne
Liebermann, Lowell
  - Revelry
Ponchielli, Amilcare
  - La Gioconda: "Dance of the Hours"
Robinson, Earl
  - In the Folded and Quiet Yesterdays
Strauss, Johann, Jr.
  - An der schönen blauen Donau (On the Beautiful Blue Danube), Op. 314
  - Die Fledermaus: Overture
  - Die Fledermaus Waltz
  - Eine nacht in Venedig: Fruhlingsstimmen Waltz (Voices of Spring), Op. 410
  - Künstler (Artist's) Quadrille, Op. 201
  - Künstlerleben (Artist's Life) Waltz, Op. 316
  - Morgenblätter (Morning Papers), Op. 279
  - Rosen aus dem Süden (Roses from the South Waltzes), Op. 388
  - Telegramme Walzer, Op. 318
  - Wiener Blut (Vienna Blood), Op. 354
  - Zigeunerbaron (Gypsy Baron): Overture
Suppe, Franz von
  - Ein Morgen, ein Mittag und ein Abend in Wien (Morning, Noon, and Night in Vienna): Overture

Valentine

Beethoven, Ludwig van
  - Romance No.1 in G Major, Op.40
  - Romance No. 2 in F Minor, Op. 50
Coleridge-Taylor, Samuel
  - Hiawatha's Wedding Feast: Onaway! Awake Beloved
Gordon, Michael
  - Love Bead
  - Sunshine of Your Love
Horner, James
  - Titanic Medley
Leigh, Mitch
  - Man of La Mancha: Orchestral Synthesis
Nørgård, Per
  - Three Love Songs
Nystroem, Gösta
  - Three Love Songs: 3. Kärleksvisor
Prokofiev, Sergei
  - Lieutenant Kijé Suite, Op. 60
Rimsky-Korsakov, Nicolai
  - Suite from La coq d'or (The Golden Cockerel): Introduction & Wedding March
Rota, Nino
  - Romeo and Juliet (1968)
Strauss, Johann, Jr.
  - Wein, Weib und Gesang (Wine, Women, and Song), Op. 333
Waxman, Franz
  - Medley: Classic Love Themes
  - Medley: Nostalgic Film Themes

Other Holidays

Carter, Elliott
  - Holiday Overture
Prizeman, Robert
  - Songs of Praise: Toccata

INSTRUMENTAL POPS

Adolphe, Bruce
  - I'm Inclined to New Music: A Comic Parody of Mozart's Eine Kleine Nachtmusik
Anderson, Leroy
  - Leroy Anderson Favorites
Arnold, Alan
  - Three Crazy Pieces
Arnold, Malcolm
  - A Grand, Grand Overture, Op. 57
  - Comedy Overture: Beckus the Dandipratt
  - Symphonic Study: Machines, Op. 30
Berkeley, Lennox
  - Palm Court Music, Op. 81, No. 2
Bush, Geoffrey - A Little Concerto
  - Three Little Pieces for Strings

Gershwin, George
  - Strike Up the Band
Goldsmith, Jerry
  - Music for Orchestra
Goosens, Eugene
  - Prelude to "Philip II"
Gould, Morton
  - A Homespun Overture
  - New China March
Karmon, Michael
  - …And The Rhythm Is Just A Little Bit Off…
Kern, Jerome
  - Fluffy Ruffles: Selection
  - She's a Good Fellow Selections
Knight, Eric
  - Kidnapped: Overture
Lundkrist, Torbjön
  - Round the Orchestra in Ten Minutes
McCabe, John
  - Mini Concerto for Organ, Percussion, Audience
Meij, Johan de
  - The Lord of the Rings: Excerpts from Symphony No. 1
Moeran, E. J.
  - Whythorne's Shadow
Moross, Jerome
  - A Tall Story for Orchestra
Naughtin, Matthew
  - This Old Man Sing-along
Peck, Russell
  - Playing With Style
Raksin, David
  - Toy Concertino
Schickele, Peter
  - Classical Rap
  - Prelude to Einstein on the Fritz
  - Three Strange Cases
  - Unbegun Symphony
Schiff, David
  - Infernal
Schreiner, Adolph
  - The Worried Drummer
Schuman, William
  - Newsreel in 5 Shots
Shulman, Alan
  - Popocatepeti
Sowerby, Leo
  - Synconata
Toch, Ernst
  - Pinocchio, A Merry Overture
Ulbrich, Siegfried
  - Blue City, Impression for Piano and Orchestra
Welcher, Dan
  - Spumante
Wendel, Robert
  - The April Fool Concerto

[6'-10']

Williams, Ernest S.
- Revolutionary Fantasy
Whitney, John
- Coming of Age

INTERNATIONAL

African
Douglas, Bill
- Concerto for African Percussion Ensemble and Orchestra

British/Scottish
Alwyn, William
- Suite of Scottish Dances
Arnold, Malcolm
- English Dances, Suite No.2
- Four Scottish Dances
Holst, Gustav
- Fantasia on Hampshire Folk Songs
Lane, Philip
- Wassail Dances for Orchestra
Vaughan Williams, Ralph
- English Folk Songs Suite
Woodgate, Leslie
- English Dance Suite

Eastern European
Bartók, Béla
- Rumanian Folk Dances
Constantinescu, Paul
- Tanze Aus Rumanien
Hermann, Ralph
- Polish Polka Party
Mercury, Freddie
- Bohemian Rhapsody
Popper, David
- Hungarian Rhapsodie, Op. 68
Vognar, Frank
- Bohemian Folksongs
Weinberger, Jaromir
- Svandadudák (Shvanda the bagpiper): Polka and Fugue

French
Bennett, Richard Rodney
- Suite française

Irish
Duff, Arthur
- Irish Suite
Hermann, Ralph
- Italian Fiesta
Whelan, Bill
- Riverdance Theme

Latin American
Cervantes, Ignacio
- Three Cuban Dances
Chávez, Carlos
- Chapultepec: Three Famous Mexican Pieces
Cifuentes, Santos
- Scherzo sobre Aires Tropicales
Debussy, Claude
- La Soirée dans Grenade
Errázuriz, Sebastián
- La Caravana
Galindo, Blas
- Sones de Mariachi
Garrido-Lecca, Gonzalo
- Arcano (Arcane)
- Toccata Op.1
Gershwin, George
- Cuban Overture
López, Jimmy
- Fiesta! for chamber orchestra
- Fiesta! for orchestra
Mejía, Adolfo
- Acuarela (Watercolor)
Moncayo, José Pablo
- Huapango
Robles, Daniel Alomia
- El Condor Pasa (The Condor Flies Past)
Slonimsky, Nicolas
- My Toy Balloon: Variations on a Brazilian Tune
Villaldo & Matos Rodríguez
- El Choclo & La Cumparsita
Zyman, Samuel
- Encuentros (1992)

Middle Eastern
Arnold, Alan
- Israeli Work Song
Hermann, Ralph
- Jewish Melodies

Russian
Balakirev, Mily
- Overture on Russian Folk Themes
Shostakovich, Dmitri
- Overture on Russian and Kirghiz Folk Themes, Op. 115

Scandinavian
Halvorsen, Johan
- Norwegian Festival Overture, Op. 16
- Norwegian Rhapsody No. 1 in A
Sibelius, Jean
- Finlandia, Op. 26, No. 7

Spanish
Chabrier, Emmanuel
- España
- España Rhapsody
Falla, Manuel de
- Récit du pécheur and Pantomime
- La Vida Breve: Interlude and Spanish Dance
Goossens, Eugene
- Flamenco: Ballet
Granados, Enrique
- Goyescas: Intermezzo
Marquez, Arturo
- Danzon No. 2
Piazzolla, Astor
- Milonga del Angel
Rodrigo, Joaquin
- Cuatro madrigales amatorios
Turina, Joaquín
- La oración del torero, Op. 34
- Rapsodia sinfónica, Op. 66
Villa-Lobos, Heitor
- Bachianas Brasileiras No. 5: Aria

JAZZ

Antheil, George
- A Jazz Symphony (1955 version)
Baker, David
- Two Improvisations
Berlin, Irving
- Irving Berlin: A Symphonic Portrait for Chorus & Orchestra
Bolcom, William
- Ragomania!
Brubaker, Jerry
- Touch of Jazz!
Brubeck, Howard
- G Flat Theme
Cunningham, Arthur
- Lullabye for a Jazz Baby
Custer, Calvin
- Salute to the Big Bands Medley
Downey, John
- Jingalodeon
Ellington, Edward K. (Duke)
- Grand Slam Jam
- Highlights from Sophisticated Ladies
- Duke Ellington! Medley
- New World A-Comin'
- Non-Violent Integration
Ellington, Mercer
- Things Ain't What They Used to Be
Flaherty, Stephen
- Ragtime Selections
Gershwin, George
- Fascinatin' Rhythm
- I Got Rhythm Variations for Piano and Orchestra
Harbison, John
- Remembering Gatsby: Foxtrot for Orchestra
Heath, Dave
- Out of the Cool
Moss, John
- Salute to Ol' Blue Eyes

[6'-10']

(JAZZ, cont.)

Proto, Frank
- Fantasy on the Saints

Riegger, Wallingford
- Quintuple Jazz, Op. 72

Shaw, Artie
- Concerto for Clarinet and Jazz Band

Shostakovich, Dmitri
- Suite for Jazz Orchestra No. 1
- Suite for Jazz Orchestra No. 2

Stravinsky, Igor
- Ragtime

Turok, Paul
- A Joplin Overture
- Ragtime Caprice, Op. 45

Turrin, Joseph
- When Tony Played the Sax

Tyzik, Jeff
- Symphonic Swing

Wonder, Stevie
- Stevie Wonder Sounds

NOVELTY

Courtney, Craig
- A Musicological Journey Through Twelve Days of Christmas

Erb, Donald
- Music for a Festive Occasion

Hayman, Richard
- Pops Hoe-Down

Hermann, Ralph
- Silent Movie

Rimelis, David
- Please Turn Your Cell Phones On!

Schickele, Peter
- Canine Cantata: "Wachet Arf"
- Prelude to Einstein on the Fritz S.E=mc2

Schreiner, Adolph
- The Worried Drummer

Walker, Robert
- My Dog Has Fleas: A Capriccio for Scratch Orchestra

Wendel, Robert
- The April Fool Concerto

PATRIOTIC

Adler, Samuel
- Show an Affirming Flame

Amram, David
- Three Songs for America

Berlin, Irving
- Berlin Patriotic Overture

Binder, Abraham W.
- Poem of Freedom

Buck, Dudley
- Festival Overture on the American National Air: The Star-Spangled Banner

Carr, Benjamin
- Federal Overture

Demerest, Clifford
- Let Freedom Ring: Overture

Deussen
- A Field in Pennsylvania

Downey, John
- Ode to Freedom

Effinger, Cecil
- Let Your Mind Wander over America

Fletcher, H. Grant
- An American Overture

Gilbertson, Michael
- Reflections on Rushmore

Gottschalk, Louis Moreau
- L'Union

Gould, Morton
- A Song of Freedom
- American Ballads: Amber Waves on "America the Beautiful"
- American Ballads: Hymnal - on "We Shall Overcome"
- American Ballads: Memorials - on "Taps"

Grant, James
- Lament for Strings

Harris, Roy
- Epilogue to Profiles in Courage: JFK
- When Johnny Comes Marching Home Overture

Isaac, Merle J.
- Salute to the United Nations

Ives, Charles
- Symphony Holidays: 1. Washington's Birthday
- Symphony Holidays: 2. Decoration Day
- Symphony Holidays: 3. Fourth of July
- Variations on America

Jones, Samuel
- Elegy for String Orchestra

Kingman, Daniel
- A Revolutionary Garland

Knight, Eric
- Americana Overture
- Canadian Tribute

Moore, Donald I.
- America

Peterson, O.
- Hymn to Freedom

Richman, Lucas
- Colonial Liberty Overture

Ringwald, Roy
- The Song of America

Schickele, Peter
- American Birthday Card

Schuller, Gunther
- Music for a Celebration: A Fantasy on National Themes

Schuman, William
- American Festival Overture

Shostakovich, Dmitri
- Eight English and American Folk Songs: When Johnny Comes Marching Home

Sowerby, Leo
- Song for America

Turok, Paul
- A Sousa Overture, Op. 43

Tyzik, Jeff
- American Celebratioin
- Fantasy on American Themes

Vandervalk, Bruce
- A Reagan Portrait

Vardi, Emanuel
- Suite on American Folk Songs

Williams, John T.
- Saving Private Ryan: Hymn to the Fallen

Yeston, Maury
- Beneath all the Stripes and Stars

Zaninelli, Luigi
- For Spacious Skies

POPULAR CLASSICS

Arban, Jean Baptiste
- Carnival of Venice, The: for Trumpet and Strings

Bach, J. S.
- Arioso
- Brandenburg Concerto No. 3, BWV 1048, G major
- Toccata & Fugue, BWV 565, D minor

Balada, Leonardo
- Homage to Sarasate

Barber, Samuel
- Adagio for Strings, Op. 11
- The School for Scandal: Overture

Bartók, Béla
- Rumanian Folk Dances
- Rumanian Folk Dances

Beethoven, Ludwig van
- Die Ruinen von Athen, Op. 113 (Ruins of Athens): Turkish March and Chorus
- König Stephan Overture, Op. 117
- Moonlight Sonata
- Overture to Egmont
- Romance No. 1 in G Major, Op. 40
- Romance No. 2 in F Minor, Op. 50

Berlioz, Hector
- Beatrice et Bénédict: Overture
- Carnaval romain (Roman Carnival)

Bizet, Georges
- Carmen Fantasy

[6'-10']

Boieldieu, François
- The Caliph of Bagdad Overture

Borodin, Alexander
- In the Steppes of Central Asia
- Nocturne
- Prince Igor: Overture
- String Quartet No.2: Nocturne

Brahms, Johannes
- Academic Festival Overture, Op. 80
- Hungarian Dances No. 5 & 6
- Hungarian Dances Nos. 1 and 3
- Hungarian Dances Nos. 1, 3, 10

Britten, Benjamin
- Soirées Musicales, Op. 9

Cimarosa, Domenico
- I Traci Amanti: Overture

Copland, Aaron
- An Outdoor Overture
- Quiet City
- Rodeo: 1. Buckaroo Holiday

Corigliano, John
- Promenade Overture

Creston, Paul
- Fantasy for Trombone, Op. 42

Debussy, Claude
- La Cathédrale engloutie
- Prélude à L'après-midi d'un faune (Afternoon of a Faun)

Delibes, Leo
- Sylvia: Suite: 4. Cortege de Bacchus

Donizetti, Gaetano
- La fille du régiment (Daughter of the Regiment): Overture

Dvořák, Antonin
- Carnival Overture, Op. 92

Elgar, Edward
- Pomp and Circumstance March No.1 in D Major, Op. 39

Fauré, Gabriel
- Pavane, Op. 50

Foss, Lukas
- Elegy for Anne Frank

Frackenpohl, Arthur
- Largo and Allegro
- Suite Concertino

Gershwin, George
- Cuban Overture
- Lullaby for Strings

Glass, Philip
- Façades

Glière, Reinhold
- The Red Poppy: Russian Sailor's Dance from Act I

Glinka, Mikhail
- Valse Fantaisie

Gluck, Christoph Willibald
- Orfeo ed Euridice: Dance of the Blessed Spirits

Goossens, Eugene
- Prelude to "Philip II"

Gould, Morton
- Symphonette No. 2

Gounod, Charles
- Marche funèbre d'une marionette (Funeral March of a Marionette)

Grant, James
- Lament

Grieg, Edvard
- Lyric Pieces, Op. 68, Nos. 4 and 5

Griffes, Charles Tomlinson
- Poem for Flute and Orchestra

Handel, George Frideric
- Overture in D Minor

Handel, George Frideric
- Water Music

Harris, Roy
- Acceleration

Haydn, Franz Joseph
- Kindersymphonie, Hob. II; 47, C Major (Toy Symphony)
- Symphony No. 94 in G Major, "Surprise!" (mvt II)

Herold, Louis
- Zampa Overture

Holst, Gustav
- A Fugal Overture, Op. 40 No. 1

Humperdinck, Engelbert
- Hansel and Gretel: Overture

Lehár, Franz
- Merry Widow Overture
- Merry Widow Waltz
- The Merry Widow: Symphonic Paraphrase
- Mephisto Waltz No. 1: from Lenau's Faust
- Mephisto Waltz No. 2: from Lenau's Faust

Mendelssohn, Felix
- Hebrides Overture, Op. 26 (Fingal's Cave)
- Heimkehr aus der Fremde, Op. 89 (Son and Stranger): Overture
- Marchen von der Schönen Melusine, Op. 32 (Fair Melusina)

Milhaud, Darius
- Two Marches

Mozart, Wolfgang Amadeus
- Don Giovanni, K.527: Overture
- Lucio Silla, K. 135: Overture

Mussorgsky, Modest
- The Dream of the Peasant Gritzko
- Night on Bare Mountain

Nicolai, Otto
- Merry Wives of Windsor Overture

Nielsen, Carl August
- Rhapsodic Overture

Offenbach, Jacques
- Les Contes d'Hoffmann (Tales of Hoffmann): Intermezzo & Barcarolle
- Orpheus in the Underworld: Overture, Op. 314

Pachelbel, Johann
- Chaconne for String Orchestra

Penderecki, Krysztof
- Threnody: To the Victims of Hiroshima

Popper, David
- Hungarian Rhapsodie, Op. 68

Puccini, Giacomo
- I Crisantemi (The Chrysanthemums)
- Madam Butterfly

Ravel, Maurice
- Ma Mère l'Oye: Prélude et Danse du rouet
- Pavane pour une Infante Defunte (Pavane for a dead princess)

Revueltas, Silvestre
- Sensemaya

Rimsky-Korsakov, Nicolai
- May Night Overture
- Suite from La coq d'or (The Golden Cockerel): Introduction & Wedding March

Rodgers, Richard
- Victory at Sea

Rossini, Gioacchino
- Il barbiere di Siviglia (Barber of Seville): Overture
- Il barbiere di Siviglia (Barber of Seville): Sinfonia
- L'Italiana in Algeri: Overture
- La Cenerentola (Cinderella) Overture
- La Gazza Ladra (The Thieving Magpie): Overture

Saint-Saëns, Camille
- Danse Macabre, Op. 40
- La Nuit, Op. 114
- Samson and Delilah: Bacchanale

Sarasate, Pablo de
- Zigeunerweisen, Op. 20

Satie, Erik
- Gymnopedie No. 1 & 3

Schubert, Franz
- Die Zauberharfe (Rosamunde) D. 644: Overture
- March Militaire Nos. 1 & 2

Shostakovich, Dmitri
- Festive Overture, Op. 96
- Suite for Jazz Orchestra No. 1

Sibelius, Jean
- Finlandia, Op. 26, No. 7
- Legends, Op. 22: 2. The Swan of Tuonela
- Suite champétre, Op. 98b

Smetana, Bedrich
- Má Vlast (3.Sarka)

Strauss, Johann, Jr.
- An der schönen blauen Donau (On the Beautiful Blue Danube), Op. 314
- Artist's Life Waltz, Op. 316

[6'-10']

*(POPULAR CLASSICS
Strauss, Johann, Jr.,cont.)*

- Die Fledermaus: Overture
- Die Fledermaus Waltz
- Eine nacht in Venedig: Fruhlingsstimmen Waltz (Voices of Spring), Op. 410
- Künstler (Artist's) Quadrille, Op. 201
- Künstlerleben (Artist's Life) Waltz, Op. 316
- Telegramme Walzer, Op 318
- Zigeunerbaron (Gypsy Baron): Overture

Strauss, Josef
- Sphärenklänge (Music of the Spheres Waltz), Op. 235

Stravinsky, Igor
- L'Oiseau de feu (Firebird): Berceuse & Finale

Sullivan, Arthur
- Mikado: Overture
- Patience Selections
- Pirates of Penzance Selections
- Ruddigore Overture
- Ruddigore Selections
- Yeoman of the Guard Selections

Suppé, Franz von
- Dichter und Bauer (Poet and Peasant): Overture
- Die leichte Kavallerie (Light Cavalry): Overture
- Die schöne Galathea (The Beautiful Galatea): Overture
- Ein Morgen, ein Mittag und ein Abend in Wien (Morning, Noon, and Night in Vienna): Overture

Tchaikovsky, Peter Ilyich
- Marche Slave, Op. 31
- Nutcracker Dances

Thomson, Virgil
- The Seine at Night
- Wheat Field at Noon

Verdi, Giuseppe
- Aïda: Triumphal March
- Aïda: Triumphal March
- I vespri siciliani: Overture
- La Forza del Destino: Overture
- Nabucco: Overture

Villa-Lobos, Heitor
- Bachianas Brasileiras No. 5: Aria

Vivaldi, Antonio
- Concerto, Op. 44, No. 16, R.V. 570, F Major

Wagenaar, Bernard
- Concert Overture

Wagner, Richard
- Götterdämmerung: Siegfried's Rhine Journey

Walton, William
- Crown Imperial: Coronation March

Weber, Carl Maria von
- Oberon: Overture
- Turandot: Overture and March

Williams, John T.
- Cowboys Overture

POPULAR SONGS

Ades, Hawley
- Twentiana
Beatles
- Beatles Medley
Berlin, Irving
- Irving Berlin: A Symphonic Portrait for Chorus & Orchestra
Blake, Howard
- Nursery Rhyme Overture
Cailliet, Lucien
- Variations on "Pop! Goes the Weasel"
Cohan, George M.
- Cohan Medley
- George M. Cohan Medley
Cory, George
- I Left My Heart in San Francisco
Croce, Jim
- Jim Croce in Concert
Custer, Calvin
- Beach Boys Medley
- Salute to the Big Bands Medley
Daugherty, Michael
- Motown Metal
Denver, John
- John Denver Celebration (1987)
Estefan, Gloria
- Gloria Estefan-Her Greatest Hits
Gershwin, George
- Two Gershwin Portraits
Gilpin, Greg
- The Music of MGM (A Choral Medley)
Gold, Marty
- Rainy Day Medley
Hermann, Ralph
- Italian Fiesta
- Jewish Melodies
- Old Song Medley No. 2
- Old Song Medley No. 3
Holcombe, Bill
- Evening at Pops (Shadow in the Moonlight; Longer; You Needed Me)
Jackson, Michael
- A Michael Jackson Spectacular
Joel, Billy
- The Best of Billy Joel
Lennon, John & McCartney, Paul
- The Best of the Beatles
Lowden, Bob
- Remembering the Beatles

Moeran, E. J
- Lonely Waters
Moss, John
- Salute to Ol' Blue Eyes
Porter, Cole
- Cole Porter Salute
Robles, Daniel Alomia
- El Condor Pasa (The Condor Flies Past)
Romberg, Sigmund
- A Tribute to Romberg
Wilson & James & Karlin
- For All We Know
Wonder, Stevie
- Stevie Wonder Sounds

SEASONS

Custer, Calvin
- Star Trek Through the Years
Harris, Roy
- Horn of Plenty
Muczynski, Robert
- A Serenade for Summer
Rimsky-Korsakov, Nicolai
- May Night: Overture
Strauss, Johann, Jr.
- Frühlingsstimmen Waltz, Op. 410 (Voices of Spring)
Svoboda, Tomáš
- Overture of the Season, Op. 89
Vivaldi, Antonio
- L'autunno (Autumn)
- L'estate (Summer)
- L'inverno (Winter)

SPACE

Beethoven
- Moonlight Sonata
Chattaway, Jay
- Star Trek: The Next Generation
Courage, Alexander
- Star Trek: The Television Series "The Menagerie" (1964)
Eidelman, Cliff
- Star Trek 6: The Undiscovered Country (1991)
Goldsmith, Jerry
- Star Trek I: The Motion Picture "The New Enterprise"
- Star Trek 10: Nemesis (2002)
- The Sum of All Fears (2002)
Horner, James
- Star Trek 3: The Search for Spock "Stealing the Enterprise" (1984)
Rosenman, Leonard
- Star Trek 4: The Voyage Home (1986)

[6'-10']

Strauss, Josef
- Sphärenklänge (Music of the Spheres Waltz), Op. 235

Williams, John T.
- E.T. Suite: Adventures on Earth
- Raiders of the Lost Ark: Raiders March
- Highlights from Return of the Jedi
- Star Wars Medley

SPORTS

Conti, Bill
- Rocky Highlights

Deussen, Nancy
- Ascent to Victory

Ellington, Edward K. (Duke)
- Grand Slam Jam

Felder, David
- Linebacker Music

Goldsmith, Jerry
- Hoosiers (1986): Suite

Holcombe, Bill
- Casey at the Bat

Knight, Eric
- The Great American Bicycle Race

Pann, Carter
- Slalom

Vangelis
- Chariots of Fire Suite

Waxman, Franz
- The Ice Follies of 1939

Williams, John T.
- Summon the Heroes

TRAVEL

Arnold, Malcolm
- The Sound Barrier Rhapsody, Op. 38

Bennett, Robert Russell
- Overture to the Mississippi

Bernstein, Elmer
- Airplane!: Suite

Cohan, George M.
- Royal Vagabond: Selections

Gershwin, George
- An American in Paris Suite

Goodwin, Ron
- Those Magnificent Men in Their Flying Machines (1965)

Guion, David
- Arkansas Traveler

Hodkinson, Sydney
- Overture: A Little Travelin' Music

Jarre, Maurice
- A Passage to India: A Symphonic Journey (1984)

Kuster, Kristin
- Iron Diamond

Roylance, Dave and Galvin, Bob
- Voyager

Thomson, Virgil
- The Seine at Night

Tiomkin, Dimitri
- The High and the Mighty (1954): Suite

Wagner, Richard
- Götterdämmerung: Siegfried's Rhine Journey

Wendel, Robert
- From Sea to Shinging Sea

Young, Victor
- Around the World in 80 Days (1956): Overture & Epilogue

TV

Amundson, Steven
- Three's Company

Burgon, Geoffrey
- Suite from Testament of Youth

Chattaway, Jay
- Star Trek: The Next Generation

Courage, Alexander
- Star Trek: The Television Series "The Menagerie" (1964)

Curnow, James, arr.
- TV Spectacular

Daugherty, Michael
- Metropolis Symphony: 1. Lex
- Metropolis Symphony: 2. Krypton
- Metropolis Symphony: 3. Mxyzptlk
- Metropolis Symphony: 4. Oh, Lois!

Goldsmith, Jerry
- Television Themes Medley
- The Twilight Zone (1961): The Invaders

Hagen, Earl
- Television Medley

Lawrence, David
- High School Musical

Markowitz, Richard
- Wild, Wild West (1965)

Rose, David
- Little House on the Prairie: Meet Me at the Fair (1974)

Scott, Raymond
- A Raymond Scott Fantasia

Strommen, Carl
- Salute to TV

VIDEO GAMES

Brower, Russell
- World of Warcraft

Eskula, Jari
- Commodore 64 Medley: A Medley of Classic 1980's Computer Game Themes

WEATHER

Arnold, Malcolm
- Whistle Down the Wind

Elgar, Edward
- The Snow, Op. 26, No. 1

Gershwin, George
- Foggy Day

Gold, Marty
- Rainy Day Medley

Vivaldi, Antonio
- Concerto, Op. 44, No. 16, R.V. 570, F Major
- L'autunno (Autumn)
- L'estate (Summer)
- L'inverno (Winter)

11' to 15'

AMERICANA

Bazelon, Irwin
- Early American Suite

Coolidge, Peggy Stuart
- Pioneer Dances

Copland, Aaron
- Lincoln Portrait
- Old American Songs: Set 1
- Old American Songs: Set 2

Cowell, Henry
- Old American Country Set

Dorff, Daniel
- Philly Rhapsody

Gould, Morton
- Folk Suite

Grofé, Ferde
- Mississippi: A Tone Journey

Guion, David
- Prairie Suite

Harris, Arthur E.
- Americana

Heath, Dave
- The Frontier

Iannaccone, Anthony
- From Time to Time

Layton, Billy Jim
- An American Portrait

McDonald, Harl
- Saga of the Mississippi

Meyer, Ranaan
- American Suite

Piston, Walter
- Lincoln Center Festival Overture

Powell, John
- In Old Virginia: Overture, Op. 28

Richman, Lucas
- Beautiful Dreamer: Stephen Foster's America

Rodgers, Richard
- All Points West

[11'-15']

(AMERICANA, cont.)

Schuman, William
- New England Triptych

Welcher, Dan
- Prairie Light: Three Texas Watercolors of Georgia O'Keeffe

Thomson, Virgil
- Louisiana Story: Acadian Songs and Dances
- The Plow that Broke the Plains: Suite

Tiomkin, Dimitri
- Gunfight at the OK Corral (1957): Ballad and Theme

Tsontakis, George
- Let the River Be Unbroken

Tyzik, Jeff
- The Great Westerns Suite

Zwilich, Ellen Taaffe
- Peanuts Gallery

ANIMALS

Barry, John
- Dances with Wolves: Concert Suite

Carpenter, John Alden
- Krazy Kat

Cole, Hugo
- Black Lion Dances

Cunningham, Arthur
- Rooster Rhapsody

Mancini, Henry
- The Pink Panther
- The White Dawn: Suite (1974)

Vaughan Williams, Ralph
- The Lark Ascending

Waxman, Franz
- Elephant Walk (1954): Suite

BLACK HISTORY MONTH

Coolidge, Peggy
- Spirituals in Sunshine and Shadow

Davis, Anthony
- Esu Variations

Hailstork, Adolphus
- Four Spirituals
- I Will Lift Up Mine Eyes

Richman, Lucas
- In the Day When I Cried Out

Swanson, Howard
- Short Symphony

Wagner, Joseph
- Ballad of Brotherhood

BROADWAY MUSICALS

Bernstein, Leonard
- On the Town: Three Dance Episodes
- West Side Story Selections

Cohan, George M.
- George M.: Choral Overture

Gershwin, George
- A Gershwin Portrait
- Porgy and Bess: Selections for Orchestra

John, Elton
- Suite from The Lion King

Kern, Jerome
- Show Boat Selections

Leigh, Mitch
- Man of La Mancha: Orchestra

Lloyd Webber, Andrew
- Phantom of the Opera Selections

Loewe, Frederick
- Brigadoon Suite
- Camelot: Selections
- My Fair Lady: Selections

Rodgers, Richard
- Oklahoma Selections

Schoenberg, Claude-Michel
- Miss Saigon Rhapsody

CELEBRATIONS

Gould, Morton
- Festive Music

Høffding, Finn
- Celebrations of May-Day

Naughtin, Matthew
- Birthday Variations

CIRCUS

Maggio, Robert
- Big Top

DANCE

Adams, John
- The Chairman Dances: Foxtrot for Orchestra

Aguila, Miguel del
- Conga

Arnold, Malcolm
- Four Irish Dances, Op. 126

Bernstein, Elmar
- Waltzes from Films: Suite

Bernstein, Leonard
- On the Town: Three Dance Episodes

Bowden, Alexander
- Prince Igor: Polovtsian Dances

Brahms, Johannes
- Liebeslieder Waltzes, Op. 52

Cole, Hugo
- Black Lion Dances

Coolidge, Peggy Stuart
- Pioneer Dances

Creston, Paul
- Two Choric Dances, Op. 17a
- Two Choric Dances, Op. 17b

Falla, Manuel de
- El Sombrero de tres picos (Three-Cornered Hat): Suite No. 2

Glass, Philip
- Modern Love Waltz

Gould, Morton
- Hoofer Suite

Gounod, Charles
- Faust: Ballet Music

Kodály, Zoltán
- Dances of Marosszek

Leighton, Kenneth
- Dance Suite No. 3 (Scottish Dances), Op. 89

Maxwell Davies, Peter
- Maxwell's Reel, with Northern Lights

Ravel, Maurice
- Daphnis et Chloé: Suite No. 1

Salzedo, Leonard
- The Witch Boy: Three Dances from the Ballet

Sebastian
- A Fairytale; Suite from the Ballet

Shostakovich, Dmitri
- Ballet Suite No. 1 (1949)

Smetana, Bedrich
- The Bartered Bride: Three Dances

Strauss, Johann, Jr.
- Lagunenwalzer, Op. 411

Surinach, Carlos
- Sinfonietta Flamenca

Tchaikovsky, Peter Ilyich
- The Nutcracker, Op. 71b Suite No.2

ECOLOGY

Knight, Eric
- Three Musical Elements: Earth, Water, Space

Lambert, Constant
- The Rio Grande

Mancin, Henry
- The White Dawn: Suite (1974)

O'Boyle, Sean
- River Symphony

Schickele, Peter
- A Zoo Called Earth

Schocker, Gary
- Green Places

[11'-15']

Smetana, Bedrich
- Má Vlast (My Fatherland) 2. Vltava (Moldau)

Strauss, Johann, Jr.
- Geschichten aus dem Wienerwald (Tales from the Vienna Woods), Op. 325

Weinberger, Jaromir
- Under the Spreading Chestnut Tree

FANFARE

Payne, Anthony
- Fanfares and Processional

FILMS

Antheil, George
- Music to a World's Fair Film

Arlen, Harold & Harburg & Stothart
- Wizard of Oz Orchestral Suite

Arnold, David
- Independence Day Suite

Arnold, Malcolm
- The Inn of the Sixth Happiness

Barry, John
- The Best of Bond
- Dances With Wolves: Concert Suite

Bennett, Richard Rodney
- Murder on the Orient Express Suite

Bennett, Robert Russell
- Hollywood

Bernstein, Elmar
- Waltzes from Films: Suite

Blake, Howard
- Agatha: Suite

Bliss, Arthur
- Things to Come: Suite

Churchill, Frank
- Snow White

Corigliano, John
- The Red Violin: Chacoone for Violin and Orchestra
- Three Hallucinations

Daugherty, Michael
- Metropolis Symphony: 5. Red Cape Tango

Doyle, Patrick
- Sense and Sensibility: Suite (1995)

Fielding, Jerry
- The Wild Bunch: Suite in Two Movements (1969)

Friedhofer, Hugo
- The Best Years of Our Lives: Suite

Goldsmith, Jerry
- The Agony and the Ecstasy (1965): Suite
- Basic Instinct (1992): Suite
- Chinatown (1974): Suite
- Logan's Run (1976): Monument/ End of the City
- The Omen (1976): Suite
- Patton (1970): Suite
- Patton (1970): The Battle Ground
- Planet of the Apes (1968): Suite
- Star Trek I: The Motion Picture "The Klingon Battle"
- Under Fire (1983): Suite

Gould, Morton
- Cinerama Holiday: Suite

Herrmann, Bernard
- The Bride Wore Black: A Musical Scenario (1968)
- The Bride Wore Black: A Suite in Four Movements
- Jane Eyre: Suite (1943)
- Journey to the Center of the Earth (1959)
- Psycho (1960)
- The Snows of Kilimijaro (1952)
- The Day the Earth Stood Still: Suite

Heuberger, Richard
- Melodies of Richard Heuberger

Horner, James
- Star Trek 2: The Wrath of Khan (1982)

Jarre, Maurice
- Lawrence of Arabia

Mancini, Henry
- Monster Movie Music Suite
- The Pink Panther
- The White Dawn: Suite (1974)

Moross, Jerome
- The Big Country: Suite

Newman, Alfred
- Wuthering Heights: Concert Suite

North, Alex
- 2001: A Symphonic Suite in Four Movements

Nyman, Michael
- The Piano for String Orchestra

Rózsa, Miklós
- The Killers: Concert Suite
- The Red House Suite

Thomson, Virgil
- Louisiana Story: Acadian Songs and Dances

Tiomkin, Dimitri
- Duel in the Sun (1946): Suite
- The Fall of the Roman Empire (1964): Themes
- Gunfight at the OK Corral (1957): Ballad and Theme
- It's a Wonderful Life (1947): Suite

Waxman, Franz
- Dark City (1950)
- Elephant Walk (1954): Suite
- A Place in the Sun (1951): A Symphonic Scenario
- Possessed (1947)
- Prince Valiant (1954)
- Rear Window (1954)
- Suspicion (1941): Suite

Williams, John T.
- Angela's Ashes: Two Concert Pieces
- Close Encounters of the Third Kind
- Harry Potter and the Chamber of Secrets
- Home Alone: Three Holiday Songs
- Three Pieces from Schindler's List

Young, Victor
- Scaramouche (1952): Suite
- Shane (1953): Suite

HOLIDAYS

Christmas

Addinsell, Richard
- A Christmas Carol (Suite: Scrooge)

Bennett, Robert Russell
- The Many Moods of Christmas: Suite 1
- The Many Moods of Christmas: Suite 2
- The Many Moods of Christmas: Suite 3
- The Many Moods of Christmas: Suite 4

Borodin, Alexander
- Prince Igor: Polovtsian Dances

Corelli, Arcangelo
- Concerto grosso, Op. 6, #8 in g minor: Christmas Concerto

Corigliano, John
- The Cloisters

Creston, Paul
- Dance Overture

DeLarmarter, Eric
- Christmastide

Ellington, Edward (Duke)
- Three Black Kings (Ballet for Orchestra)

Falla, Manuel de
- El Amor brujo: Pantomime and Ritual Fire Dance
- El Sombrero de tres picos (Three-Cornered Hat): Suite 1
- El Sombrero de tres picos (Three-Cornered Hat): Suite 2

Gould, Morton
- Christmas Time, Book II
- Serenade of Carols

Holst, Gustav
- The Perfect Fool: Ballet Music, Op. 39

Kelly, Bryan
- Improvisations on Christmas Carols

Liszt, Franz
- Hungarian Rhapsody No. 2

Maxwell Davies, Peter
- Swinton Jig, on a Nineteenth Century Lancashire Fiddle Tune

[11'-15']

(HOLIDAYS-Christmas, cont.)

Menotti, Gian Carlo
- My Christmas

Ravel, Maurice
- Bolero

Rodriguez, Robert Xavier
- Con Flor y Canto from "Adoracion Ambulante"

Rota, Nino
- Romeo and Juliet: Suite (1968)
- The Godfather (1972)

Shaw, Robert
- The Many Moods of Christmas, Suites 2 & 3

Shostakovich, Dmitri
- Ballet Suite No. 1 (1949)
- Ballet Suite No. 4 (1953)
- Suite for Variety Orchestra No. 2

Tchaikovsky, Peter Ilyich
- The Nutcracker, Op. 71b: Suite No. 2

Tiomkin, Dimitri
- It's a Wonderful Life (1947): Suite

Turina, Joaquín
- Danzas fantásticas, Op. 22

Tyzik, Jeff
- Holiday Moods: Suite No. 1

Vianello, Hugo
- Christmas Kaleidoscope

Wendel, Robert
- A Classical Christmas Suite

Williams, John T.
- Home Alone: Three Holiday Songs

Halloween

Bazelon, Irwin
- Fairy Tale
- Spirits of the Night

Blomdahl, Karl-Birger
- The Walpurgis Night (Stage Music No. 1)

Corigliano, John
- The Cloisters
- Three Hallucinations

Dukas, Paul
- L'Apprenti Sorcier (The Sorcerer's Apprentice)

Dvořák, Antonin
- The Midday Witch, Op. 108 (The Noon Witch)

Herrmann, Bernard
- Psycho (1960)

McCabe, John
- The Lion, the Witch, and the Wardrobe: Suite

Maggio, Robert
- The Hand-Prints of Sorcerers

Mancini, Henry
-Monster Movie Music Suite

Mussorgsky, Modest
- A Night on Bald Mountain

Ruders, Poul
- Saaledes saae Johannes: (Thus Saw St. John)

Salzedo, Leonard
- The Witch Boy: Three Dances from the Ballet

Wendel, Robert
- A Halloween Trilogy

Zaninelli, Luigi
- Night Voices

Hanukkah

Bavil, Zamir
- David and the Ark of the Covenant

Bloch, Ernest
- Suite hébraïque

Labor Day

Grofé, Ferde
- Symphony in Steel

McDonald, Harl
- Festival of the Workers

New Year

Bliss, Arthur; Denis Wright
- Things to Come

Peaslee, Richard
- Arrows of Time

Perillo, Steve
- Hangoverture

Strauss, Johann, Jr.,
- Lagunenwalzer, Op. 411 (from "Eine Nacht in Venedig")
- Kaiser Walzer (Emperor Waltzes), Op. 437
- Geschichten aus dem Wienerwald (Tales from theVienna Woods), Op. 325

St. Patrick

Cowell, Henry
- Four Irish Tales: Tales of Our Countryside

Herbert, Victor
- Irish Rhapsody

Stanford, Charles Villiers
- Irish Rhapsody No. 1, Op. 78

Valentine

Bennett, Richard Rodney
- Love Spells

Blake, Howard
- Heartbeat

Dorff, Daniel
- The Kiss

Friedhofer, Hugo
- The Best Years of Our Lives: Suite

Glass, Philip
- Modern Love Waltz

Lang, David
- Loud Love Songs

Newman, Alfred
- Wuthering Heights: Concert Suite

Rota, Nino
- Romeo and Juliet: Suite (1968)

Sibelius, Jean
- Rakastave the Lover

Sowerby, Leo
- Two Romantic Pieces

Strauss, Richard
- Romanze

Tchaikovsky, Peter Ilyich
- Romeo and Juliet: Duet

Tyzik, Jeff
- Hot Soul Medley

Other Holidays

Harbison, John
- The Flight into Egypt; Sacred Ricercar

Ives, Charles
- Symphony Holidays: 4. Thanksgiving/Forefathers' Day

Vaughan Williams, Ralph
- Three Choral Hymns: Easter, Christmas, Whitsunday

INSTRUMENTAL POPS

Baker, David
- Concerto for Cello

Bennett, Richard Rodney
- London Pastoral
- Nocturnes

Blake, Howard
- The Up and Down Man: Suite

Bush, Geoffrey
- Concerto for Light Orchestra

Dickinson, Peter
- Merseyside Echoes

Gillis, Don
- The Man Who Invented Music

Goossens, Eugene
- Kaleidoscope

Gould, Morton
- Family Album: Suite

Herbert, Victor
- Victorious Herbert

Jacob, Gordon
- Five Pieces in the Form of a Suite

Kirk, Theron
- An Orchestra Primer

Kleinsinger, George
- Tubby the Tuba

Kraft, William
- Vintage Renaissance

Mancini, Henry
- March with Mancini

[11'-15']

Namenwirth, Micha
- Divertimento for Toys and Orchestra

Peck, Russell
- The Thrill of the Orchestra

Schickele, Peter
- 1712 Overture
- A Bach Portrait
- Requiem Mantras
- Royal Firewater Musick

Swayne, Giles
- Naaotwa Lala, Op. 39

Ticheli, Frank
- Angels in Architecture
- Blue Shades

INTERNATIONAL

Asian
Griffes, Charles Tomlinson
- Five Poems of the Ancient Far East

Lambert, Constant
- Eight Poems of Li-Po

British/Scottish
Bennett, Richard Rodney
- London Pastoral

Blyton, Carey
- Cinque Port, Op. 28

Langey, Otto
- From the Highlands: A Selection of Scotch Melodies

Tomlinson, Ernest
- Suite of English Folk Dances

Turrin, Joseph
- Lullaby of Broadway
- Steadfast Tin Soldier

Wilby, Philip
- The Highland Express

Eastern European
Bartók, Béla
- Hungarian Sketches

Enesco, Georges
- Roumanian Rhapsody No. 1, A Major, Op. 11

German, Edward
- Gypsy Suite

Kodály, Zoltán
- Dances of Marosszek

Irish
Arnold, Malcolm
- Four Irish Dances, Op. 126

Cowell, Henry
- Four Irish Tales: Tales of Our Countryside

Herbert, Victor
- Irish Rhapsody

Stanford, Charles Villiers
- Irish Rhapsody No. 1, Op. 78

Latin American
Adomian, Lan
- Cantata de la revolución Mexicana

Arnold, Alan
- Three Columbian Songs

Benzecry, Esteban
- Colores de la Cruz del Sur (Colors of the Southern Cross)

Copland, Aaron
- El salón Mèxico

Fernandez, Agustín
- Una Música Escondida

López, Jimmy
- América Salvaje (Wild America)
- Perú Negro

Pann, Carter
- Two Portraits of Barcelona

Rebagliati, Claudio
- Rapsodia Peruana

Soro, Enrique
- Tres Aires Chilenos (Three Chilean Aires)

Villa-Lobos, Heitor
- Bachianas Brasileiras No. 5

Middle Eastern
Ranjbaran, Behzad
- Seven Passages

Russian
Borodin, Alexander
- In the Steppes of Central Asia

Scandinavian
Alfvèn, Hugo
- Midsommarvaka: Swedish Rhapsody No. 1, Op. 19

Grieg, Edvard
- Two Norwegian Airs, Op. 63

Halvorsen, Johan
- Norwegian Fairy Pictures
- Norwegian Rhapsody No. 2 in G

Spanish
Falla, Manuel de
- El Sombrero de tres picos (Three-Cornered Hat): Suite No. 2
- Sept Chansons populaires espagnoles (Seven Popular Spanish Songs)

Granados, Enrique
- Tres danzas españolas

Lambert, Constant
- Eight Poems of Li-Po

Rimsky-Korsakov, Nicolai
- Capriccio Espagnol, Op. 34

Surinach, Carlos
- Sinfonietta Flamenca

Viennese
Riege, Ernst
- Ewiges Wien (Eternal Vienna)

JAZZ

Antheil, George
- A Jazz Symphony (1925 version)
- A Jazz Symphony (ensemble version)

Baker, David
- Kosbro

Brubeck, Dave
- Brandenburg Gate: Revisited

Carmichael, Hoagy
- Hoagy Carmichael: An American Treasure

Diamond, Neil
- Jazz Singer Medley

Ellington, Edward K. (Duke)
- The Golden Broom and the Green Apple

Ellington, Edward K. (Duke) and Strayhorn, Billy
- The Essential Ellington: Music of Ellington and Strayhorn

Gershwin, George
- Rhapsody in Blue for Trumpet and Orchestra

Schuller, Gunther
- Journey into Jazz

NOVELTY

Baker, David
- Concertino for Cellular Phones and Symphony Orchestra

Gould, Morton
- Hoofer Suite

PATRIOTIC

Copland, Aaron
- Lincoln Portrait

Dennison, Sam
- And If Elected…

Goldstein, William
- Celebration Overture 1776-1976

Gould, Morton
- Classical Variations on Colonial Themes
- Columbia: Broadsides for Orchestra

Grainger, Percy
- Marching Song of Democracy for Chorus and Orchestra

Hewitt, James
- The Battle of Trenton

[11'-15']

(PATRIOTIC, cont.)

Kurtz, Eugene
- Chamber Symphony for the 4th of July

McDonald, Harl
- Dirge for Two Veterans

Persichetti, Vincent
- A Lincoln Address

Rodríguez, Robert Xavier
- Jargon: the Story of the American Constitution

POPULAR CLASSICS

Bach, J. S.
- Fantasia & Fugue in G minor

Barber, Samuel
- Capricorn Concerto

Bartók, Béla
- Hungarian Sketches

Bernstein, Leonard
- Divertimento for Orchestra

Bizet, Georges
- Carmen: Suite no. 1
- Fantaisie Brilliante on Themes from Bizet's "Carmen"
- Jeux d'enfants, Op. 22: Petite Suite (Children's Games)

Borodin, Alexander
- Prince Igor: Polovtsian Dances

Brahms, Johannes
- Tragische Ouverture, Op. 81

Brahms, Johannes
- Liebeslieder Waltzes, Op. 52

Britten, Benjamin
- Matinees musicales, Op. 24

Chávez, Carlos
- Sinfonia de Antigona (Symphony No. 1)
- Sinfonia India (Symphony No. 2)

Copland, Aaron
- El Salón México

Creston, Paul
- Concertino for Marimba, Op. 21
- Dance Overture

Delius, Frederick
- Two Pieces: 1. On Hearing the First Cuckoo in Spring; 2. Summer-Night on the River

Dukas, Paul
- L'Apprenti Sorcier (The Sorcerer's Apprentice)

Dvořák, Antonin
- The Midday Witch, Op. 108 (The Noon Witch)

Elgar, Edward
- Cockaigne Concert Overture, Op. 40
- Froissart Overture, Op. 19
- Wand of Youth Suite No. 2, Op. 1b

Falla, Manuel de
- El Amor brujo: Pantomime and Ritual Fire Dance
- El Sombrero de tres picos (Three-Cornered Hat): Suite No. 1
- El Sombrero de tres picos (Three-Cornered Hat): Suite No. 2
- El Sombrero de tres picos (Three-Cornered Hat): Suite 2 - El Sombrero de tres picos (Three-Cornered Hat): Suite 1

Franck, César
- Le Chasseur maudit (The Accursed Huntsman)

Gershwin, George
- Rhapsody in Blue for Trumpet and Orchestra

Grainger, Percy
- In a Nutshell: Suite

Grieg, Edvard
- Peer Gynt: Suite No. 1

Griffes, Charles Tomlinson
- The Pleasure Dome of Kubla Khan, Op. 8

Grofé, Ferde
- Symphony in Steel

Handel, George Frideric
- The King Shall Rejoice

Harris, Roy
- Concerto in One Movement: Jamboree

Holst, Gustav
- St. Paul's Suite
- The Perfect Fool: Ballet Music, Op. 39

Humperdink, Engelbert
- Hansel und Gretel: Three Excerpts

Ibert, Jacques
- Divertissement

Jalbert, Pierre
- In Aeternam

Kabalevsky, Dmitri
- The Comedians, Op. 26: Suite

Layton, Billy Jim
- Three Dylan Thomas Poems, Op. 3

Liszt, Franz
- Hungarian Rhapsody No. 1, F Minor
- Hungarian Rhapsody No. 2

Mendelssohn, Felix
- Midsummernight's Dream, Op. 21: Overture

Moeran, E. J.
- Serenade in G (6 movement version)

Mussorgsky, Modest
- A Night on Bald Mountain

Nielsen, Carl August
- Helios Overture, Op. 17
- Little Suite, Op. 1

Orr, Buxton
- A Carmen Fantasy

Ravel, Maurice
- Bolero

Rimsky-Korsakov, Nicolai
- Capriccio Espagnol, Op. 34
- Scheherazade: 4. The Sea-Shipwreck

Rossini, Gioacchino
- Guillaume Tell (William Tell): Overture
- Semiramide: Overture

Saint-Saëns, Camille
- Havanaise, Op. 83

Sarasate, Pablo de
- Carmen Fantasie on Themes of Bizet, Op. 25

Shostakovich, Dmitri
- Ballet Suite No. 1 (1949)
- Ballet Suite No. 4 (1953)
- Suite for Variety Orchestra No. 2

Sibelius, Jean
- Karelia Suite, Op. 11

Smetana, Bedrich
- The Bartered Bride Three Dances

Smetana, Bedrich
- Má Vlast (My Fatherland) 2. Vltava (Moldau)

Strauss, Johann, Jr.
- Kaiser Walzer (Emperor Waltzes), Op. 437
- Lagunenwalzer, Op. 411

Strauss, Richard
- Also sprach Zarathustra, Op. 30
- Romanze
- Till Eulenspiegels lustige Streiche (Till Eulenspiegel's Merry Pranks), Op. 28

Tchaikovsky, Peter Ilyich
- Romeo and Juliet: Duet

Vaughan Williams, Ralph
- Fantasia on a Theme by Thomas Tallis
- The Lark Ascending

Verdi, Giuseppe
- Aïda: Triumphal March and Ballet

Villa-Lobos, Heitor
- Bachianas Brasileiras No. 5

Wagner, Richard
- Eine Faust Ouvertüre (A Faust Overture)

POPULAR SONGS

The Beatles
- Classic Beatles: A Medley
- Beatles!!! A Medley of Lennon and McCartney Favorites
- Beatles Hits Medley

Bennett, Richard Rodney
- Variations on a Nursery Tune

Cohan, George M.
- George M. Cohan Salute

[11'-15']

Richman, Lucas
- Beautiful Dreamer: Stephen Foster's America

SEASONS

Alfvén, Hugo
- Midsommarvaka: Swedish Rhapsody No. 1, Op. 19

Delius, Frederick
- Two Pieces: On Hearing the First Cuckoo in Spring; Summer-Night on the River

Gould, Morton
- Harvest

Mendelssohn, Felix
- Midsummernight's Dream, Op. 21: Overture

Vivaldi, Antonio
- La primavera (Spring)

SPACE

Barber, Samuel
- Capricorn Concerto

Goldsmith, Jerry
- Star Trek I: The Motion Picture "The Klingon Battle"

Herrmann, Bernard
- The Day the Earth Stood Still: Suite

Jones, Ron
- Star Trek, The Next Generation: Suite (1989)

North, Alex
- 2001: A Symphonic Suite in Four Movements

Ruggles, Carl
- Sun-Treader

SPORTS

Corigliano, John
- Tournaments

Hayman, Richard
- Freddie the Football

Horner, James
- Star Trek 2: The Wrath of Khan (1982)

Kleinsinger, George
- Brooklyn Baseball Cantata

Proto, Frank
- Casey at the Bat

Waxman, Franz
- Prince Valiant (1954)

TRAVEL

Mayer, William
- Of Rivers and Trains

Wilby, Philip
- The Highland Express

TV

Burgon, Geoffrey
- Chronicles of Narnia Suite
- Suite from Bleak House

Daugherty, Michael
- Metropolis Symphony: 5.Red Cape Tango

Goldsmith, Jerry
- QB VII: Suite

Jones, Ron
- Star Trek, The Next Generation: Suite (1989)

Mancini, Henry
- Peter Gunn Meets Mr. Lucky

VIDEO GAMES

Ford, Ralph
- Video Games Live

Mitchell, Darren
- Turok 2

WEATHER

Mayer, William
- Scenes from "The Snow Queen"

Garrop, Stacy
- Thunderwalker

Quilter, Roger
- Where the Rainbow Ends Suite

Tsontakis, George
- Winter Lightning

Vivaldi, Antonio
- La primavera (Spring)

16' to 20'

AMERICANA

Bacon, Ernst
- From These States, Suite: Gathered Along Unpaved Roads

Dello Joio, Norman
- Southern Echoes

Gould, Morton
- American Sing: Settings of Folk Songs
- Cowboy Rhapsody

Grofé, Ferde
- Death Valley Suite
- Hudson River Suite
- Mississippi Suite
- Tabloid

Ives, Charles
- Symphony No. 3: The Camp Meeting
- Three Places in New England

Kapilow, Robert
- Dr. Seuss's Gertrude McFuzz
- Dr. Seuss's Green Eggs and Ham

Mancini, Henry
- Beaver Valley '37

Maxwell Davies, Peter
- A Spell for Green Corn: The Macdonald Dances

Newman, Alfred
- How the West Was Won: Suite

Owens, Robert
- American Carnival
- Ballet Suite

Peaslee, Richard
- Chicago Concerto

Rhodes, Phillip
- Suite for Bluegrass Quartet and Orchestra

Robinson, Earl
- A Country They Call Puget Sound

Smith, Julia
- American Dance Suite

Thomson, Virgil
- Louisiana Story: Orchestral Suite

Zwilich, Ellen Taaffe
- American Concerto

ANIMALS

Chappell, Herbert
- Paddington Bear's First Concert

Dvořák, Antonin
- Holoubek (The Wood Dove), Op.110

Respighi, Ottorini
- Gli uccelli (The Birds)

Rodríguez, Robert Xavier
- Trunks, A Circus Story for Narrator and Orchestra

Saint-Saëns, Camille
- Carnival of the Animals

Simons, Netty
- Pied Piper of Hamelin

Slatkin, Leonard
- The Raven

BLACK HISTORY MONTH

Balada, Leonardo
- Sinfonia en Negro: Homage to Martin Luther King

[16'-20']

(BLACK HISTORY MONTH, cont.)

Ellington, Edward K. (Duke)
- Night Creature
- Three Black Kings for Soloist and Orchestra
- Three Black Kings: Concerto Grosso version

Kay, Ulysses
- Suite

Kraft, William
- Seven Spirituals

Still, William Grant
- Wood Notes

BROADWAY MUSICALS

Bernstein, Leonard
- Candide Suite

CELEBRATIONS

Handel, George Frideric
- Music for the Royal Fireworks

CIRCUS

Moore, Douglas
- Pageant of P. T. Barnum

Rodríguez, Robert Xavier
- Trunks, A Circus Story for Narrator and Orchestra

DANCE

Alwyn, William
- Elizabethan Dances

Bartók, Béla
- Dance Suite

Bennett, Robert Russell
- Suite of Old American Dances

Bliss, Arthur
- Checkmate: Five Dances Suite

Camilleri, Charles
- Maltese Dances

Corigliano, John
- Gazebo Dances for Orchestra

Duffy, John
- Heritage Symphonic Dances

Dvořák, Antonin
- Slavonic Dances Op. 46

Elgar, Edward
- Spanish Lady Suite

Frank, Gabriela Lena
- Three Latin-American

Gould, Morton
- Latin American Symphonette
- Tap Dance Concerto

Grieg, Edvard
- Norwegian Dances, Op. 35

Jager, Robert
- Concerto Grosso

Khachaturian, Aram
- Spartacus, Suite No. 3 from the ballet

Leighton, Kenneth
- Dance Suite No. 2

Luigini, Alexandre
- Ballet Egyptien

Maxwell Davies, Peter
- A Spell for Green Corn: The Macdonald Dances

Meza, Vinicio
- Suite Latinoamericana (Tango, Vals, Choro, Son)

Moross, Jerome
- Frankie and Johnny

Owens, Robert
- American Carnival: Ballet Suite

Prokofiev, Sergei
- Cinderella, Suite No.2 from the ballet, Op. 108
- Romeo and Juliet, Suite No. 3, Op. 101

Ravel, Maurice
- Daphnis et Chloé, Suite No. 2

Respighi, Ottorini
- Antiche danze ed arie (Ancient Airs and Dances): Set I
- Antiche danze ed arie (Ancient Airs and Dances): Set II
- Antiche danze ed arie (Ancient Airs and Dances): Set III

Salzedo, Leonard
- The Witch Boy: Suite from the Ballet

Shostakovich, Dmitri
- Ballet Suite No. 2 (1951)
- Ballet Suite No. 3 (1951)
- The Limpid Stream: Suite from the ballet, Op. 39a

Smith, Julia
- American Dance Suite

Strauss, Richard
- Burleske

Surinach, Carlos
- Ritmo Jondo, Flamenco for Orchestra

Tchaikovsky, Peter Ilyich
- The Nutcracker Suite

ECOLOGY

Copland, Aaron
- The Tender Land: Suite

Handel, George Frideric
- Water Music

Respighi, Ottorino
- The Pines of Rome (Pines of the Appian Way)

Revueltas, Silvestre
- Paisajes

Roylance, Dave and Galvin, Bob
- Ocean Fantasia

Still, William Grant
- Wood Notes

FILMS

Arnold, Malcolm
- Hobson's Choice

Chaplin, Charlie
- The Reel Chaplin

Goldsmith, Jerry
- Motion Picture Medley
- Star Trek I: The Motion Picture "The Director's Cut"

Horner, James
- Titanic Suite

Maxwell Davies, Peter
- The Devils: Suite

Moross, Jerome
- Music from the Flicks

Newman, Alfred
- How the West Was Won: Suite

Rózsa, Miklós
- Ben Hur: Choral Suite
- Quo Vadis Suite

Thomson, Virgil
- Louisiana Story: Orchestral Suite

Tiomkin, Dimitri
- Cyrano De Bergerac (1950): Suite

Tyzik, Jeff
- The Big Movie Suite

Waxman, Franz
- Hemingway's Adventures of a Young Man
- The Silver Chalice (1954): Suite
- Taras Bulba (1962): Suite

Williams, John T.
- Harry Potter and the Prisoner of Azkaban
- Harry Potter and the Sorcerer's Stone (Suite for Orchestra)
- Star Wars: Episode I Phantom Menace (Suite for Orchestra)

HOLIDAYS

Christmas

Arnold, Malcolm
- Commonwealth Christmas Overture, Op. 64

Barab, Seymour
- G.A.G.E., A Christmas Story

[16'-20']

Barber, Samuel
- Die Natali, Op. 37: Chorale Preludes for Christmas

Bennett, Robert Russell
- The Many Moods of Christmas: Suite 1
- The Many Moods of Christmas: Suite

Carey, Julia Scott
- Legend of Old Befana

Dello Joio, Norman
- Christmas Music

Gould, Morton
- Holiday Music

Haslam, Herbert
- Special Starlight

Hayes, Isaac
- Selections from Shaft

King, Victor
- Gregoriana Christmas Suite

Maxwell Davies, Peter
- Temenos, with Mermaids and Angels

Mayer, William
- Good King Wenceslas

Monestal, Alexander
- The Birth of our Lord: A Christmas Cantata

Musgrave, Thea
- Wild Winter II

Parker, Alice
- Seven Carols for Christmas

Prokofiev, Sergei
- Winter Bonfire: Suite, Op. 122

Rodríguez, Robert Xavier
- Scrooge: Concert Scenes from "A Christmas Carol"

Tchaikovsky, Peter Ilyich
- The Nutcracker Suite

Van Vactor, David
- The New Light: Prologue and 3 Canticles for Christmas

Halloween

Grieg, Edvard
- Lyric Suite, Op. 54

Khachaturian, Aram
- Masquerade Suite

Liszt, Franz
- Totentanz

Maxwell Davies, Peter
- The Devils: Suite

Musgrave, Thea
- Night Music

Mussorgsky, Modest
- Songs and Dances of Death

Rachmaninoff, Sergei
- The Isle of the Dead, Op. 29

Respighi, Ottorino
- La Boutique fantasque: Suite (after Rossini)

Rodríguez, Robert Xavier
- Mascaras

Salzedo, Leonard
- The Witch Boy: Suite from the Ballet

Slatkin, Leonard
- The Raven

Labor Day

Andriessen, Louis
- Workers' Union

Gould, Morton
- Hosedown: A Firefighter Fable

New Year

Schumann, Robert
- New Year Song, Op. 144 "Mit eherner Zunge, da ruft es: Gebt acht"

St. Patrick

Anderson, Leroy
- The Irish Suite

Field, John
- Irish Concerto for Piano and Orchestra

Valentine

Berlioz, Hector
- Roméo and Juliette: Scene d'amour, Op. 17

Gottschalk, Louis Moreau
- Symphonie Romantique: Night in the Tropics

Rasmussen, Karl Aage
- Symphony for Young Lovers

Talbot, Joby
- Lover's Ink

Tchaikovsky, Peter Ilyich
- Romeo and Juliet: Fantasy Overture

Warlock, Peter
- Aspects of Love and Contentment

Other Holidays

Gould, Morton
- Holiday Music

INSTRUMENTAL POPS

Arnold, Alan
- Variations for Orchestra

Bennett, Richard Rodney
- Diversions
- Partita

Erb, Donald
- Klangfarbenfunk

Gershwin, George
- American in Paris

Gould, Morton
- Family Album: Suite

Mancini, Henry
- Beaver Valley '37

Powell, John
- Natchez on the Hill: Three Virginia Country Dances
- A Set of Three

Rodríguez, Robert Xavier
- A Colorful Symphony

Weill, Kurt
- The Two Worlds of Kurt Weill: Berlin Suite

INTERNATIONAL

British/Scottish

Maxwell Davies, Peter
- Spinning Jenny: A Portrait of Leigh, Lancashire, circa 1948

Toch, Ernst
- Big Ben, Variation-Fantasy on the Westminster Chimes, Op. 62

Eastern European

Chopin, Frédéric
- Fantaisie sur des airs nationaux polonais, Op. 13 (Fantasy on Polish Airs)

Irish

Anderson, Leroy
- The Irish Suite

Field, John
- Irish Concerto for Piano and Orchestra

Italian

Camilleri, Charles
- Maltese Dances

Carey, Julia Scott
- Legend of Old Befana

Latin American

Frank, Gabriela Lena
- Three Latin-American Dances

Garrido-Lecca, Celso
- Retablos Sinfónicos

Goossens, Eugene
- East of Suez: Incidental Music

Gould, Morton
- Latin American Symphonette

López, Jimmy
- Lago de Lágrimas (Lake of Tears)

Meza, Vinicio
- Suite Latinoamericana (Tango, Vals, Choro, Son)

Stucky, Steven
- Pinturas de Tamayo

Villa-Lobos, Heitor
- Bachianas Brasileiras No. 1

Middle Eastern

Bavil, Zamir
- Israeli Rhapsody

Duffy, John
- Heritage Symphonic Dances

Sheriff, Noam
- Israel Suite

[16'-20']

(INTERNATIONAL, cont.)

Scandinavian

Alfvén, Hugo
- Dalarapsodi – Swedish Rhapsody No. 3, Op. 47

Grieg, Edvard
- Norwegian Dances, Op. 35

Spanish

Falla, Manuel de
- Homenajes

Geehl, Henry
- Suite Espagnole

Granados, Enrique
- Tonadillas

Lecuona, Ernesto
- Andalucia Suite

Ravel, Maurice
- Rapsodie Espagnole

Surinach, Carlos
- Ritmo Jondo, Flamenco for Orchestra

JAZZ

Ellington, Edward K. (Duke)
- Ellington Portrait
- Black, Brown and Beige: Suite
- Harlem
- Night Creature
- Three Black Kings

Gershwin, George
- Rhapsody in Blue

Gould, Morton
- Derivations for Solo Clarinet and Dance Band

Gruenberg, Louis
- Jazz Suite, Op. 28

Schuller, Gunther
- And They All Played Ragtime
- Concertino for Jazz Quartet & Orchestra (1959)

Turok, Paul
- Great Scott! Orchestral Suite after Joplin

NOVELTY

Gould, Morton
- Hosedown: A Firefighter Fable
- Tap Dance Concerto

PATRIOTIC

Bennett, Robert Russell
- The Four Freedoms

Brubeck, Dave
- They All Sang Yankee Doodle

Gillis, Don
- This Is Our America

Gould, Morton
- American Sing: Settings of Folk Songs
- Declaration: Suite
- Foster Gallery: Suite
- Lincoln Legend

Harris, Roy
- American Creed

Kraft, William
- A Kennedy Portrait

Liebermann, Lowell
- Concerto for Piccolo

Ranjbaran, Behzad
- Thomas Jefferson

Turrin, Joseph
- Civil War Suite

Williams, John T.
- Suite from J.F.K.

POPULAR CLASSICS

Bach, J.S.
- Chaconne

Bantock, Granville
- Old English Suite

Berlioz, Hector
- Roméo and Juliette: Scene d'amour, Op. 17

Bizet, Georges
- Carmen: Suite no. 2
- L'Arlésienne Suite No. 1
- L'Arlésienne Suite No. 2

Brahms, Johannes
- Variations on a Theme by Haydn, Op. 56a

Britten, Benjamin
- Young Person's Guide to the Orchestra, Op. 34

Chopin, Frédéric
- Fantaisie sur des airs nationaux polonais, Op.13 (Fantasy on Polish airs)
- Variations on "La ci darem la mano," Op. 2

Creston, Paul
- Concerto for Saxophone and Orchestra, Op. 26

Dvořák, Antonin
- Slavonic Dances Op. 46
- Slavonic Dances Op. 72, Nos. 1-4
- Slavonic Dances Op. 72, Nos. 5-8

Dyson, George
- Concerto da Camera
- Concerto Leggiero

Elgar, Edward
- In the South: Concert Overture, Op. 50
- Wand of Youth Suite No. 1, Op. 1a

Faure, Gabriel
- Pelleas et Melisande, Op. 80

Gershwin, George
- Rhapsody in Blue

Gottschalk, Louis Moreau
- Symphonie Romantique: Night in the Tropics

Gould, Morton
- Latin American Symphonette

Grieg, Edvard
- Lyric Suite, Op. 54
- Norwegian Dances, Op. 35

Handel, George Frideric
- Music for the Royal Fireworks
- Water Music

Khachaturian, Aram
- Masquerade Suite
- Spartacus, Suite No. 3 from the ballet

Liszt, Franz
- Totentanz

Montgomery, Bruce
- Concertino for Strings

Mussorgsky, Modest
- Songs and Dances of Death

Piston, Walter
- The Incredible Flutist: Ballet Suite for Orchestra

Prokofiev, Sergei
- Cinderella, Suite No.2 from the ballet, Op. 108
- Lieutenant Kijé Suite, Op. 60
- Romeo and Juliet, Suite No. 3, Op. 101

Ravel, Maurice
- Daphnis et Chloé, Suite No. 2
- Ma Mère l'Oye (Mother Goose)
- Rapsodie Espagnole

Respighi, Ottorini
- Antiche danze ed arie (Ancient Airs and Dances): Set I
- Antiche danze ed arie (Ancient Airs and Dances): Set II
- Antiche danze ed arie (Ancient Airs and Dances): Set III
- La Boutique fantasque: Suite (after Rossini)
- The Pines of Rome (Pines of the Appian Way)

Schumann, Robert
- New Year Song, Op. 144 "Mit eherner Zunge, da ruft es: Gebt acht"
- Overture, Scherzo and Finale

Shostakovich, Dmitri
- Ballet Suite No. 2 (1951)
- Ballet Suite No. 3 (1951)
- The Limpid Stream: Suite from the Ballet, Op. 39a
- Hamlet, Incidental Music to the Stage Production, Op. 32a

[16'-20']

Tchaikovsky, Peter Ilyich
  - Ouverture Solennelle (1812 Overture) Op. 49
  - Romeo and Juliet: Fantasy Overture
Villa-Lobos, Heitor
  - Concerto for Harmonica
Wagner, Richard
  - Die Walküre: Wotan's Farewell and Magic Fire Music
  - Tristan und Isolde: Prelude and Liebestod

POPULAR SONGS

Anderson, Leroy
  - Old MacDonald Had a Farm
Gould, Morton
  - Five Spirituals
The Beatles
  - Abbey Road Suite
  - Sergeant Pepper's Lonely Hearts Club Band
  - Songs from the White Album
  - The Great Beatles Singles Suite I
  - The Great Beatles Singles Suite I: All You Need Is Love
  - The Great Beatles Singles Suite I: Strawberry Fields Forever
  - The Great Beatles Singles Suite II
Villa-Lobos, Heitor
  - Bachianas Brasileiras No. 1
Weill, Kurt
  - The Two Worlds of Kurt Weill: Berlin Suite

SEASONS

Tsontakis, George
  - Winter Lightning

SPACE

Goldsmith, Jerry
  - Star Trek I: The Motion Picture "The Director's Cut"
Williams, John T.
  - Close Encounters of the Third Kind

SPORTS

Kapilow, Robert
  - Play Ball!: Casey at the Bat

TRAVEL

Bolcom, William
  - Inventing Flight
Gershwin, George
  - An American in Paris
Milhaud, Darius
  - Globetrotter Suite

TV

Burgon, Geoffrey
  - Brideshead Variations
Jenkins, Karl
  - Palladio: Concerto Grosso for String Orchestra

21' to 25'

AMERICANA

Copland, Aaron
  - Appalachian Spring: Suite
Curtis-Smith, Curtis
  - Great American Symphony
Grofé, Ferde
  - Niagara Falls Suite
Knight, Eric
  - A Symphony in Four American Idioms
Schickele, Peter
  - The Chenoo Who Stayed to Dinner
  - Legend

ANIMALS

Bond, Victoria
  - Urban Bird
Copland, Aaron
  - The Red Pony
Gould, Morton
  - The Jogger and the Dinosaur
Kodály, Zoltán
  - Variations on a Hungarian Folksong: The Peacock
Poulenc, Francis
  - L'Histoire de Babar (The Story of Babar, the Little Elephant)
Saint-Saëns, Camille
  - Le Carnaval des animaux (Carnival of the Animals)
Stravinsky, Igor
  - L'Oiseau de feu (Firebird): Suite (1919)

BLACK HISTORY MONTH

Ellington, Edward K. (Duke)
  - Liberian Suite
Still, William Grant
  - Afro-American Symphony

BROADWAY MUSICALS

Bernstein, Leonard
  - West Side Story: Symphonic Dances
Gershwin, George
  - Porgy and Bess: Symphonic Pictures
Maxwell Davies, Peter
  - The Boyfriend: Concert Suite

DANCE

Bernstein, Leonard
  - West Side Story: Symphonic Dances
Copland, Aaron
  - Appalachian Spring: Suite
Damase, Jean-Michel
  - Piége de lumiére
Ippolitov-Ivanov, M.
  - Caucasian Sketches (Procession of the Sardar)
Kapilow, Robert
  - Chris van Allsburg's Polar Express
Khachaturian, Aram
  - Spartacus, Suite No. 2 from the ballet
Maxwell Davies, Peter
  - Caroline Mathilde: Concert Suite from Act I
  - Caroline Mathilde: Concert Suite from Act II
Piston, Walter
  - The Incredible Flutist: Ballet Suite for Orchestra
Stravinsky, Igor
  - L'Oiseau de feu (Firebird): Suite (1919)
Sullivan, Arthur
  - Pineapple Polka: Suite
Tchaikovsky, Peter Ilyich
  - The Nutcracker, Op. 71a, Suite No. 1

ECOLOGY

Elgar, Edward
  - Sea Pictures
Schickele, Peter
  - The Fantastic Garden

[21'-25']

(ECOLOGY, cont.)

Thomson, Virgil
- The River: Suite

Warshauer, Meira
- Symphony No. 1 "Living, Breathing, Earth"

FILMS

Arnold, Malcolm
- The Bridge on the River Kwai

Bernstein, Leonard
- On the Waterfront: Symphonic Suite

Corigliano, John
- The Red Violin: Suite for Violin and Orchestra

Glass, Philip
- The Hours: Suite (2002)

Goldsmith, Jerry
- Rudy: Suite

Grofé, Ferde
- Hollywood Suite

Hermann, Bernard
- The Devil and Daniel Webster: Suite
- Mysterious Island: Suite (1961)

Howard, James
- Peter Pan (2003): Suite for Orchestra with Narrator

Maxwell Davies, Peter
- The Boyfriend: Concert Suite

North, Alex
- Cleopatra: Symphonic Portrait

Thomson, Virgil
- The River: Suite

Tiomkin, Dimitri
- Rhapsody of Steel (1959)

Williams, John T.
- Harry Potter Symphonic Suite

HOLIDAYS

Christmas

Ayars, Bo
- Christmas Medley

Gould, Morton
- Christmas Time, Book I

Hely-Hutchinson, Victor
- Carol Symphony

Kapilow, Robert
- Chris van Allsburg's Polar Express
- Elijah's Angel

Rouse, Christopher
- Karolju

Tchaikovsky, Piotr Ilyich
- The Nutcracker, Op. 71a, Suite No. 1

Turrin, Joseph
- The Fir Tree

Halloween

Dorati, Antal
- Night Music

Falla, Manuel de
- El Amor brujo

Gould, Morton
- Jekyll and Hyde Variations

Schnittke, Alfred
- Concerto Grosso No. 1

Welcher, Dan
- The Visions of Merlin

Zaninelli, Luigi
- A Lexicon of Beasties

Hanukkah

Bloch, Ernest
- Trois Poèmes Juifs

Labor Day

Bernstein, Leonard
- On the Waterfront: Symphonic Suite

Grofé, Ferde
- Hollywood Suite

Tiomkin, Dimitri
- Rhapsody of Steel (1959)

St. Patrick

Esposito, Michele
- Irish Suite

Valentine

Bennett, Richard Rodney
- Lovesongs

Brahms, Johannes
- Liebeslieder Waltzes, Op. 52

Kernis, Aaron Jay
- Valentines

North, Alex
- Cleopatra: Symphonic Portrait

INSTRUMENTAL POPS

Dickerson, Roger
- Orpheus an' his Slide Trombone

Eiger, Walter
- Concerto Grosso

Gould, Morton
- Troubadour Music

Kapilow, Robert
- You and Hugh

Roxburgh, Edwin
- How Pleasant to Know Mr. Lear

Weill, Kurt
- Kleine Dreigroschenmusik (Suite from Little Three Penny Opera)
- The Two Worlds of Kurt Weill: New York Suite

INTERNATIONAL

Eastern European

Kodály, Zoltán
- Variations on a Hungarian Folksong: The Peacock

Irish

Esposito, Michele
- Irish Suite

Latin American

Chappell, Herbert
- Caribbean Concerto

Iturriaga, Enrique
- Canción y Muerte de Rolando (Song and Death of Rolando)
- Sinfonía Junín y Ayacucho: 1824

Rodríguez, Robert Xavier
- Sinfonia a la Mariachi

Spanish

Falla, Manuel de
- Noches en los jardines de España (Nights in the Gardens of Spain)

Rodrigo, Joaquin
- Concierto Andaluz

JAZZ

Bennett, Richard Rodney
- Concerto for Stan Getz

Brubeck, Howard
- Dialogues

Calandrelli, Jorge
- Concerto for Jazz Clarinet and Orchestra

Shostakovich, Dmitri
- Suite for Variety Orchestra No. 1

Sowerby, Leo
- Monotony: A Symphony for Metronome & Jazz Orchestra

PATRIOTIC

Bennett, Robert Russell
- A Commemoration Symphony: Stephen Collins Foster

POPULAR CLASSICS

Copland, Aaron
- Appalachian Spring: Suite
- Music for the Theatre

[21'-25']

Elgar, Edward
- Nursery Suite

Falla, Manuel de
- El Amor brujo
- Noches en los jardines de España (Nights in the Garden of Spain)

Haydn, Franz Joseph
- Symphony No. 100 in G Major: Military
- Symphony No. 8 in G Major (Le soir)
- Symphony No. 94 in G Major: (Surprise)

Ippolitov-Ivanov, M.
- Caucasian Sketches: Procession of the Sardar

Moeran, E. J.
- Serenade in G

Persichetti, Vincent
- Sinfonia Janiculum, Op. 113

Piazzolla, Astor
- Cuatro Estaciones Porteñas (The Four Seasons in Buenas Aires)

Poulenc, Francis
- Sinfonietta

Prokofiev, Sergei
- Peter and the Wolf

Rachmaninoff, Sergei
- The Isle of the Dead, Op. 29

Shostakovich, Dmitri
- Suite for Variety Orchestra No. 1

Stravinsky, Igor
- L'Oiseau de feu (Firebird): Suite (1919)

Sullivan, Arthur
- Pineapple Poll Suite

POPULAR SONGS

The Beatles
- A Long and Winding Road

SEASONS

Piazzolla, Astor
- Cuatro Estaciones Porteñas (The Four Seasons in Buenas Aires)

SPACE

Welcher, Dan
- "Night Watchers" Symphony No. 2

SPORTS

Bolcom, William
- Seattle Slew Suite

Goldsmith, Jerry
- Rudy: Suite

Gould, Morton
- The Jogger and the Dinosaur

Welcher, Dan
- Haleakala: How Maui Snared the Sun

TRAVEL

Rodríguez, Robert Xavier
- Flight: The Story of Wilbur and Orville Wright

TV

Burgon, Geoffrey
- Suite from Martin Chuzzlewit

26' to 30'

AMERICANA

Gould, Morton
- Foster Gallery

Heath, Dave
- Alone at the Frontier: Concerto for Improvised Instrument and Orchestra

Higdon, Jennifer
- Cityscape

Schuman, William
- American Hymn

Tiomkin, Dimitri
- The Alamo (1960): Suite

ANIMALS

Haydn, Franz Joseph
- Symphony No. 82 "The Bear"

Prokofiev, Sergei
- Peter and the Wolf, Symphonic Tale for Narrator and Orchestra, Op. 67

BLACK HISTORY MONTH

Schwantner, Joseph
- A New Morning for the World

Smith, Hale
- Meditations in Passage

DANCE

Glière, Reinhold
- The Red Poppy, Suite No. 1 from the ballet, Op. 70a

Khachaturian, Aram
- Gayaneh, Suite No. 2 from the ballet
- Gayaneh, Suite No. 3 from the ballet
- Spartacus, Suite No. 1 from the ballet

Layton, Billy Jim
- Dance Fantasy, Op. 7

Leighton, Kenneth
- Dance Suite No. 1

Maxwell Davies, Peter
- Caroline Mathilde: Concert Suite from Act I

Maxwell Davies, Peter
- Caroline Mathilde: Concert Suite from Act II

Piston, Walter
- The Incredible Flutist, Ballet

Prokofiev, Sergei
- Cinderella Suite No. 1, Op. 107

Shostakovich, Dmitri
- Bolt, Suite from the ballet, Op. 27a (Ballet Suite No. 5)

ECOLOGY

Ellington, Edward K. (Duke)
- The River

Schickele, Peter
- The Fantastic Garden

Simons, Netty
- Big Sur

Thomson, Virgil
- The River: Suite

FILMS

Grofé, Ferde
- Hollywood Suite

Herrmann, Bernard
- The Three Worlds of Gulliver: Suite (1960)

Korngold, Erich
- Korngold: The Adventures of Robin Hood, Symphonic Portrait

Maxwell Davies, Peter
- The Boyfriend: Concert Suite

Nyman, Michael
- The Piano

Tiomkin, Dimitri
- 55 Days at Peking (1963): Suite
- The Alamo (1960): Suite

[26'-30']

(FILMS, cont.)

Williams, John T.
- Harry Potter and the Sorcerer's Stone: Children's Suite

Roylance, Dave & Bob Galvin
- Tall Ships Suite

HOLIDAYS

Christmas

Gillis, Don
- The Coming of the King

Poulenc, Francis
- Gloria

Halloween

Schnittke, Alfred
- Concerto Grosso No. 1

Thomas, Richard
- Ghosts of Alder Gulch

New Year

Haydn, Franz Joseph
- Symphony No. 101 in D Major: The Clock

Prokofiev, Sergei
- Cinderella Suite No. 1, Op. 107

Valentine

Kernis, Aaron Jay
- Valentines

Prokofiev, Sergei
- Romeo and Juliet, Suite No. 1, Op. 64a
- Romeo and Juliet, Suite No. 2, Op. 64b

Other Holidays

Mechem, Kirke
- The King's Contest

INSTRUMENTAL POPS

Hodkinson, Sydney
- Concerto for Clarinet and Orchestra

INTERNATIONAL

Eastern European

Kodály, Zoltán
- Variations on a Hungarian Folksong: The Peacock

Irish

Loeffler, Charles Martin
- Five Irish Fantasies

JAZZ

Brubeck, Howard
- Dialogues

PATRIOTIC

Dello Joio, Norman
- Colonial Variants: Thirteen Profiles of the Original Colonies

Gould, Morton
- Declaration

Kapilow, Robert
- City Piece: DC Monuments

POPULAR CLASSICS

Bizet, Georges
- Carmen Fantasia

Borodin, Alexander
- Symphony No. 2

Falla, Manuel de
- El Sombrero de tres picos (Three-Cornered Hat)

Haydn, Franz Joseph
- Symphony No. 101 in D Major: The Clock

Khachaturian, Aram
- Gayaneh, Suite No. 2 from the ballet
- Gayaneh, Suite No. 3 from the ballet
- Spartacus, Suite No. 1 from the ballet

Mendelssohn, Felix
- Symphony No. 4 in A Major: Italian

Mozart, Wolfgang Amadeus
- Symphony No. 41, K.551, C Major K. 551: Jupiter

Prokofiev, Sergei
- Cinderella Suite No. 1, Op. 107
- Peter and the Wolf, Symphonic Tale for Narrator and Orchestra, Op. 67
- Romeo and Juliet, Suite No. 1, Op. 64a
- Romeo and Juliet, Suite No. 2, Op. 64b

Shostakovich, Dmitri
- Bolt, Suite from the ballet, Op. 27a: Ballet Suite No. 5

POPULAR SONGS

The Beatles
- A Long and Winding Road

TRAVEL

Kapilow, Robert
- Union Station

Roylance, Dave and Galvin, Bob
- Tall Ships Suite

31' to 35'

AMERICANA

Coleridge-Taylor, Samuel
- Scenes from The Song of Hiawatha, Op. 30, No. 1: Hiawatha's Wedding Feast

Gould, Morton
- American Ballads, Settings of American Tunes for Orchestra

ANIMALS

Baker, David
- Le Chat qui pêche

BLACK HISTORY MONTH

Dawson, William
- Negro Folk Symphony

Fried, Gerald
- Roots: Suite (1977)

Mechem, Kirke
- Songs of the Slave

DANCE

Gould, Morton
- I'm Old Fashioned: Astaire Variations

FILMS

Rota, Nino
- The Godfather III: Suite

Shostakovich, Dmitri
- Hamlet: Music from the Film, Op.116

HOLIDAYS

Christmas

Dello Joio, Norman
- Nativity: Canticle for the Child

Effinger, Cecil
- The St. Luke Christmas Story

Rosenberg, Hilding Constantin
- The Holy Night (Die Heligea Natten): A Christmas Oratorio

Halloween

Falla, Manuel de
- El Amor brujo: first version

[31'-35']

INSTRUMENTAL POPS

Rodríguez, Robert Xavier
- The Tempest

INTERNATIONAL

Spanish

Falla, Manuel de
- El Sombrero de tres picos (The Three Cornered Hat)

Lalo, Edouard
- Symphonie espagnole, Op. 21

Valentine

Barber, Samuel
- The Lovers, Op. 43

Kabalevsky, Dmitri
- Romeo and Juliet: Musical Sketches, Op. 56

JAZZ

Baker, David
- Le Chat qui pêche

Ellington, Edward K. (Duke)
- Black, Brown and Beige

Zinn, William
- Symphony in Ragtime

POPULAR CLASSICS

Barber, Samuel
- The Lovers, Op. 43

Falla, Manuel de
- El Amor brujo: first version

Gershwin, George
- Concerto in F Major for Piano

Grofé, Ferde
- Grand Canyon Suite
- World's Fair Suite

Kabalevsky, Dmitri
- Romeo and Juliet: Musical Sketches, Op. 56

Lalo, Edouard
- Symphonie espagnole, Op. 21

Mussorgsky, Modest
- Pictures at an Exhibition

Strauss, Richard
- Also Sprach Zarathustra, Op. 30

TRAVEL

Robinson, Earl
- The Lonesome Train

36' to 40'

AMERICANA

Harris, Roy
- Folksong Symphony: Two Interludes

BLACK HISTORY MONTH

Dawson, William
- Negro Folk Symphony

Schuman, William
- On Freedom's Ground

DANCE

Khachaturian, Aram
- Gayaneh, Suite No. 1 from the ballet

Strauss, Johann, Jr.
- Graduation Ball: Ballet in One Act

HOLIDAYS

Christmas

Lutosławski, Witold
- Twenty Polish Christmas Carols

Martynov, Vladimir
- Christmas Music

Moore, Douglas
- The Greenfield Christmas Tree

Saint-Saëns, Camille
- Christmas Oratorio, Op. 12

Schutz, Heinrich
- Christmas Story SWV 435a

Valentine

Maxwell Davies, Peter
- Romamor

INTERNATIONAL

Eastern European

Lutosławski, Witold
- Twenty Polish Christmas Carols

Spanish

Turina, Joaquín
- Canto a Sevilla, Op. 37

JAZZ

Baker, David
- Le Chat qui pêche

POPULAR CLASSICS

Glass, Philip
- Glassworks

Khachaturian, Aram
- Gayaneh, Suite No. 1 from the ballet

SEASONS

Vivaldi, Antonio
- Le quattro staggioni (The Four Seasons)

SPACE

Chávez, Carlos
- El Sol (The Sun): A Mexican Ballad

SPORTS

Schuman, William
- Casey at the Bat: A Baseball Cantata

WEATHER

Vivaldi, Antonio
- Le quattro staggioni (The Four Seasons)

41' and Longer

AMERICANA

Antheil, George
- Cabeza de vaca

ANIMALS

Tan Dun
- Crouching Tiger Concerto

CELEBRATION

Rodríguez, Robert Xavier
- Adoracion ambulante - A Mexican Folk Celebration

[41' or longer]

DANCE

Shchedrin, Rodion
- Carmen Suite (after Georges Bizet)

ECOLOGY

Brubeck, Dave
- The Light in the Wilderness
Elfman, Danny
- Serenada Schizophrana

FILMS

Caliendo, Christopher
- The Iron Horse
Chaplin, Charlie
- City Lights
Debney, John
- The Passion of the Christ Symphony
Elfman, Danny
- Serenada Schizophrana
Shapiro, Michael
- Frankenstein
Shostakovich, Dmitri
- The Gadfly: Suite from the Film, Op. 97a
- Hamlet: Music from the Film, Op. 116a
Tan Dun
- Crouching Tiger Concerto
Waxman, Franz
- The Bride of Frankenstein (1935)
- Sunset Boulevard (1950): Staged Reading in Two Acts

HOLIDAYS

Christmas
Deak, John
- The Passion of Scrooge (A Christmas Carol)
Maxwell Davies, Peter
- The Three Kings
Monteverdi, Claudio
- Christmas Vespers
Richman, Lucas
- A Christmas Wish
Vaughan Williams, Ralph
- Hodie, A Christmas Cantata
Webb, Jimmy
- The Animals' Christmas

Halloween
Shapiro, Michael
- Frankenstein

Waxman, Franz
- The Bride of Frankenstein (1935)

Labor Day
Gould, Morton
- Something to Do-Labor Cantata

Valentine
Prokofiev, Sergei
- Romeo and Juliet, Scenes from the Ballet

INTERNATIONAL

Spanish
Brubeck, Dave
- La Fiesta de la Posada
Falla, Manuel de
- El Corregidor y la Molinera
Falla, Manuel de
- Fuego fatuo
Rodríguez, Robert Xavier
- Adoracion ambulante: A Mexican Folk Celebration

JAZZ

Brubeck, Dave
- Truth Is Fallen
- The Gates of Justice
- The Light in the Wilderness

PATRIOTIC

Menotti, Gian Carlo
- Landscapes and Remembrances
Welcher, Dan
- JFK: The Voice of Peace

POPULAR CLASSICS

Dyson, George
- Symphony in G
Elgar, Edward
- The Spanish Lady
Handel, George Frideric
- Water Music
Holst, Gustav
- The Planets
Prokofiev, Sergei
- Romeo and Juliet, Scenes from the Ballet
Shostakovich, Dmitri
- Hypothetically Murdered, Op. 31a
Tchaikovsky, Peter Ilyich
- Symphony No. 1 in G Minor, Op. 13 (Winter Dreams)

Vivaldi, Antonio/ Malipiero, G.F.
- Le Quattro staggioni (The Four Seasons) Op. 8, Nos.1-4

SEASONS

Tchaikovsky, Peter Ilyich
- Symphony No. 1 in G Minor, Op.13 (Winter Dreams)

SPACE

Holst, Gustav
- The Planets

Collection/Folio

Anderson, Leroy
- Leroy Anderson for Strings
Mancini, Henry
- Henry Mancini for Strings, Vol. 1
- Henry Mancini for Strings, Vol. 2

APPENDIX C

Works Listed by Themes

Orchestral "pops" concerts are often programmed by themes. To help locate possible selections for a program, entries are divided among the following groups alphabetically by composer. Often titles will share themes. For example you will find *Ben Hur: Parade of the Chariots* by Miklós Rózsa under both Films and Sports. Refer to the main body of the document for complete information on a work.

Americana	p. 374	Jazz	p. 398
Animals	p. 375	Novelty	p. 399
Black History Month	p. 376	Patriotic	p. 399
Broadway Musicals	p. 377	Popular Classics	p. 401
Celebrations	p. 378	Popular Songs	p. 404
Circus	p. 378	Seasons	p. 406
Dance	p. 378	Space	p. 406
Ecology	p. 381	Sports	p. 407
Fanfare	p. 381	Travel	p. 407
Films	p. 382	TV	p. 408
Holidays	p. 387	Video Games	p. 409
Instrumental Pops	p. 393	Weather	p. 409
International	p. 395		

AMERICANA

Anderson, Leroy
- Fiddle-Faddle
- Mother's Whistler
- Old MacDonald Had a Farm

Antheil, George
- Cabeza de vaca
- Tom Sawyer Overture: California Overture

Ayars, Bo
- American Fanfare
- Cowboy Medley: Mexican Hat Dance
- Cowboy Medley: She'll Be Comin' Round the Mountain
- Cowboy Medley: Shenandoah
- Cowboy Medley: Sweet Betsy from Pike
- Cowboy Medley: The Yellow Rose of Texas
- Shave and a Haircut March

Bacon, Ernst
- Gathered Along Unpaved Roads
- From These States: Suite

Bendix, Victor
- Grand American Fantasia: Tone Pictures of the North and South

Bernstein, Elmar
- True Grit: Concert Suite

Bazelon, Irwin
- Early American Suite

Bennett, Robert Russell
- Overture to the Mississippi

Bishop, Henry
- Home Sweet Home

Carmichael, Hoagy
- Georgia On My Mind
- Hoagy Carmichael: An American Treasure

Chambers, William Paris
- Chicago Tribune March

Coleridge-Taylor, Samuel
- Scenes from The Song of Hiawatha Op. 30: No. 1.
- Hiawatha's Wedding Feast: Onaway! Awake Beloved

Coolidge, Peggy Stuart
- Pioneer Dances

Cooper, Paul
- Shenandoah for Charles Ives' Birthday

Copland, Aaron
- Appalachian Spring
- Billy the Kid
- Down a Country Lane
- John Henry
- Lincoln Portrait
- Old American Songs
- Rodeo
- Variations on a Shaker Melody

Cowell, Henry
- Old American Country Set
- Saturday Night at the Firehouse

Creston, Paul
- Evening in Texas

Curtis-Smith, Curtis
- Great American Symphony

Custer, Calvin
- The American Frontier
- Beach Boys Medley
- A Salute to the Big Apple

Danielpour, Richard
- Toward the Splendid City

Davis, Albert O.
- Buffalo Gals: In Blue Grass Style

Davis, Jimmie
- Blue Tail Fly
- Buffalo Gals
- Down in the Valley

Dello Joio, Norman
- Southern Echoes

Dorff, Daniel
- Philly Rhapsody

Dragon, Carmen
- The Yellow Rose of Texas

Duffy, John
- Indian Spirits

Evans, Dale
- Happy Trails to You (1952)

Foster, Stephen
- Beautiful Dreamer: Stephen Foster's America
- Jeanie with the Light Brown Hair
- Old Folks at Home; Love's Old Sweet Song: Palms
- A Stephen Foster Overture

Gershwin, George
- Swanee

Gillis, Don
- Atlanta Suite: Peachtree Promenade

Goldsmith, Jerry
- Fireworks: A Celebration for Los Angeles (1999)

Gould, Morton
- American Ballads: Settings of American Tunes for Orchestra
- America Sing: Settings of Folk Songs
- Cowboy Rhapsody
- Folk Suite: Overture; Blues; Jig
- Foster Gallery
- Minstrel Show
- Revival: A Fantasy on Six Spirituals
- Swanee River in the Style of Bach
- Swanee River in the Style of Beethoven
- Swanee River in the Style of Brahms
- Swanee River in the Style of Debussy
- Swanee River in the Style of Ellington
- Swanee River in the Style of Gershwin
- Swanee River in the Style of Liszt
- Swanee River in the Style of Mozart
- Swanee River in the Style of Rimsky-Korsakov
- Swanee River in the Style of Strauss (Joh., Jr.)
- Swanee River in the Style of Tchaikovsky
- Swanee River in the Style of Wagner
- Symphonette No. 3 (Third American Symphonette)
- Yankee Doodle

Grainger, Percy
- Tribute to Foster

Grofé, Ferde
- Death Valley Suite
- Grand Canyon Suite
- Hudson River Suite
- Mississippi: A Tone Journey
- Niagara Falls Suite
- Tabloid
- World's Fair Suite

Grundman, Clare
- American Folk Rhapsody No. 1: Four American Folk Songs
- American Folk Rhapsody No. 2

Guion, David
- Arkansas Traveler
- Cowboy's Meditation
- Home on the Range
- My Cowboy Love Song
- Prairie Suite
- Turkey in the Straw

Hageman, Richard
- Stagecoach: Suite (1939)

Hailstork, Adolphus
- An American Fanfare

Handy, W. C.
- Saint Louis Blues

Harris, Arthur
- Americana

Harris, Roy
- Epilogue to Profiles in Courage: JFK
- Folksong Symphony: Two Interludes

Hayman, Richard
- Hullabaloo
- Pops Hoe-Down

Heath, Dave
- Alone at the Frontier: Concerto for Improvised Instrument
- The Frontier

Herbert, Victor
- American Fantasie
- Panamericana

Hermann, Ralph
- Farmyard Frolic

Higdon, Jennifer
- Cityscape: Peachtree Street

Holcombe, Bill
- Cowboy Fantasy
Howard, John
- Grand Canyon Fanfare
- Wyatt Earp (1994)
- Wyatt Earp: End Credits
Iannaccone, Anthony
- From Time to Time
Ives, Charles
- Central Park in the Dark
- Symphony No. 3: The Camp Meeting
- Three Places in New England
Kerker, Gustave
- The Belle of New York
Jendras, Louis F.
- Appalachian Fling
Johnson, Francis
- Buffalo City Guard Parade March
- General Cadwalader's Grand March
- Philadelphia Grays Quickstep
Kander, John
- New York, New York
Kapilow, Robert
- Dr. Seuss's Gertrude McFuzz
- Dr. Seuss's Green Eggs and Ham
Knight, Eric
- A Symphony in Four American Idioms
Layton, Billy Jim
- An American Portrait
Lutosławski, Witold
- Fanfare for Louisville
Maggio, Robert
- Boardwalk
- Skylines
Mandell, Robert
- Red River Valley
Markowitz, Richard
- Wild, Wild West
Maxwell Davies, Peter
- A Spell for Green Corn: The MacDonald Dances
Mancini, Henry
- Beaver Valley '37
Marsh, Gerry Jon
- Hamburger Suite
Mason, Jack
- O Bury Me Not On the Lone Prairie
McDonald, Harl
- Legend of the Arkansas Traveler
- Saga of the Mississippi
Meyer, Ranaan
- American Suite
- Fox Down
Moross, Jerome
- Wagon Train
Muller, Frederick
- Arkansas Traveler: In Bluegrass Style
- The Rakes of Mallow (with Blue Grass Variation)

Nelson, Ronald J.
- Savannah River Holiday
Newman, Alfred
- How the West Was Won: Suite
North, Alex
- Cheyenne Autumn Suite
Owens, Robert
- American Carnival: Ballet Suite
Peaslee, Richard
- Chicago Concerto
Piket, Frederick
- Curtain Raiser to an American Play: Overture
Piston, Walter
- Bicentennial Fanfare
- Lincoln Center Festival Overture
Powell, John H.
- At the Fair
- In Old Virginia: Overture, Op. 28
- Natchez on the Hill: Three Virginia Country Dances
- A Set of Three
Ran, Shulamit
- Chicago Skyline
Reisfeld, Bert
- California Concerto
Rhodes, Phillip
- Bluegrass Festival: Suite for Bluegrass Quartet
Richman, Lucas
- Beautiful Dreamer: Stephen Foster's America
- A Western Fanfare
Richardson, Neil
- Polly-Wolly Doodle
Robinson, Earl
- A Country They Call Puget Sound
Rose, David
- Little House on the Prairie: Meet Me at the Fair (1974)
Rouse, Ervin T.
- Orange Blossom Special
Schuman, William
- New England Triptych
Schwartz, Stephen
- Rock-a-Bye Your Baby with a Dixie Melody
Smith, Julia
- American Dance Suite
Stucky, Steven
- Fanfare for Cincinnati
- Fanfare for Los Angeles
Thomson, Virgil
- Louisiana Story: Acadian Songs and Dances
- Louisiana Story: Orchestral Suite
- The Plow that Broke the Plains: Suite
Time for Three
- Sweet Georgia Brown
Tiomkin, Dimitri
- The Alamo (1960): Short Suite
- The Alamo (1960): Suite

- Gunfight at the OK Corral (1957): Ballad and Theme
- The Guns of Navarone (1961): Suite
- High Noon (1952): Do Not Forsake Me Oh My Darling
- High Noon (1952): Suite
- Night Passage (1957): Follow the River
- A President's Country (1966): Medley
- Rawhide (1959): Theme
- Red River (1948): Suite
- The Wild, Wild West (1965): Suite
Tsontakis, George
- Let the River Be Unbroken
Tyzik, Jeff
- Amazing Grace
- Fantasy on American Themes
Wagner, Joseph
- Radio City Snapshots
Waxman, Franz
- The Pioneer (1951): Suite
Weinberger, Jaromir
- Prelude and Fugue on "Dixie"
Welcher, Dan
- Castle Creek: Fanfare & Overture
- Haleakala: How Maui Snared the Sun
- Prairie Light: Three Texas Watercolors of Georgia O'Keeffe
- The Yellowstone Fires
- Zion
Wendel, Robert
- From Sea to Shining Sea
- George M. Cohan Overture
- Orange Blossom Special
- Stephen Foster Overture
Williams, John T.
- Cowboys Overture
Zwilich, Ellen Taaffe
- American Concerto
- Peanuts Gallery (1996)

ANIMALS

Anderson, Leroy
- Old MacDonald Had a Farm
- The Waltzing Cat
Bach, P.D.Q.
- Broadway Boogie
- Canine Cantata "Wachet Arf!"
Baker, David
- Le chat qui pêche
Barry, John
- Dances with Wolves: Concert Suite
Bolcom, William
- Seattle Slew Suite
Bond, Victoria
- Urban Bird

(ANIMALS, cont.)

Caillet, Lucien
- Pop! Goes the Weasel

Carpenter, John Alden
- Krazy Kat

Cassler, Glenn
- Turtle Dove

Chappell, Herbert
- Paddington Bear's First Concert

Cole, Hugo
- Black Lion Dances

Copland, Aaron
- The Red Pony

Creston, Paul
- Kangaroo Kaper

Cunningham, Arthur
- Rooster Rhapsody

Dankworth, John
- The Diamond and the Goose

Davis, Jimmie
- Blue Tail Fly

Dvořák, Antonin
- Holoubek (The Wood Dove), Op. 110

Elfman, Danny
- Charlotte's Web: Themes for Flute and Orchestra (2006)
- Spider-Man: Suite (2004)

Frazelle, Kenneth
- The Swans at Pongo Lake

Friml, Rudolf
- Medley from The Firefly

Gershwin, George
- Promenade: Walkin' the Dog or The Real McCoy

Goldsmith, Jerry
- The Swarm (1978): Bees Arrive/End Title

Gould, Morton
- The Jogger and the Dinosaur

Griffes, Charles Tomlinson
- The White Peacock

Guion, David
- Pastorale: Three Little Brown Bulls
- Sheep and Goat

Haydn, Franz Joseph
- Symphony No. 82 "The Bear"

Hermann, Ralph
- Silent Movie

Herschel, Lee
- How the Camel Got His Hump
- How the Whale Got His Tiny Throat

Howard, James
- King Kong

Hubbell, Raymond
- Poor Butterfly

John, Elton
- Crocodile Rock

Kaper, Bronislau
- Them!: Ant Fugue (1954)

Kodály, Zoltán
- Variations on a Hungarian Folksong: The Peacock

Lloyd Webber, Andrew
- Cats Selections
- Cats: Memory

Mancini, Henry
- Hatari!: Baby Elephant Walk (1962)
- Pink Panther
- The White Dawn: Suite (1974)

Mechem, Kirke
- The Jayhawk Op. 43: Overture to a Mythical Comedy (Magic Bird Overture)

Mercer, Johnny
- Skylark

Mussorgsky, Modest Petrovich
- The Song of the Flea

Newman, Lionel
- Doctor Dolittle: Talk to the Animals

Nielsen, Carl
- Masquerade: Hanedons (Cock's Dance)

Penella, Manuel
- El Gato Montés (The Bobcat)

Poledouris, Basil
- Free Willy Suite (1993)

Poulenc, Francis
- L'Histoire de Babar

Powell, John
- Chicken Run: Final Escape
- Chicken Run: Make a Crate

Prokofiev, Sergei
- Peter and the Wolf, Op. 67

Pryor, Arthur
- The Whistler and His Dog

Respighi, Ottorini
- Gli uccelli (The Birds)

Rimsky-Korsakov, Nicolai
- The Tale of Tsar Saltan: Flight of the Bumble Bee

Robles, Daniel Alomia
- El Condor Pasa (The Condor Flies Past)

Rodríguez, Robert Xavier
- Trunks: A Circus Story

Rossini, Giocchino
- Cat Duet

Saint-Saëns, Camille
- Le Carnaval des animaux

Schickele, Peter
- Broadway Boogie
- Canine Cantata "Wachet Arf!"
- Thurber's Dogs

Scott, Raymond
- Dinner Music for a Pack of Hungry Cannibals
- Huckleberry Duck
- The Penguin

Sibelius, Jean
- Legends, Op. 22: 2. The Swan of Tuonela

Silvestri, Alan
- Mouse Hunt (1997): Suite

Simons, Netty
- Pied Piper of Hamelin

Slatkin, Leonard
- The Raven

Steiner, Max
- King Kong (1933): Overture

Strauss, Johann, Jr.
- Im Krapfenwaldl, Polka française, Op. 336

Strauss, Josef
- Dorfschwalben aus Österreich (Austrian Village Swallows), Op. 164

Stravinsky, Igor
- L'Oiseau de feu (Firebird): Suite

Tan Dun
- Crouching Tiger Concerto

Thomson, Virgil
- Sea Piece with Birds

Vaughan Williams, Ralph
- The Lark Ascending
- The Wasps: Overture

Walker, Robert
- My Dog Has Fleas: A Capriccio for Scratch Orchestra

Waxman, Franz
- Elephant Walk (1954): Suite

Yarrow, Peter
- Puff the Magic Dragon

Yradier, Sebastian
- La Paloma (The Dove): Spanish Serenade

BLACK HISTORY MONTH

Baker, David
- Two Improvisations

Balada, Leonardo
- Sinfonia en negro: Homage to Martin Luther King

Beveridge, Thomas
- Once: Tribute to Martin Luther King

Bland, James A.
- O dem Golden Slippers

Bliss, Arthur
- Baraza

Davis, Anthony
- Esu Variations
- X: The Life and Times of Malcolm X: Malcolm's Prison Aria

Dawson, William
- Negro Folk Symphony: The Bond of Africa; Hope in the Night; O Le' Me Shine, Shine Like a Morning Star

Ellington, Edward K. (Duke)
- Night Creature
- Three Black Kings

Fried, Gerald
- Roots: Suite (1977)

Hailstork, Adolphus
 - Four Spirituals
 - I Will Lift Up Mine Eyes
Kay, Ulysses
 - Suite
Kraft, William
 - Contextures: Riots – Decade '60
 - Kennedy Portrait (Contextures III)
 - Seven Spirituals
McDonald, Harl
 - Suite for Strings on American Negro Themes
Mechem, Kirke
 - Songs of the Slave
Richman, Lucas
 - In the Day When I Cried Out
Robinson, Walter H.
 - Harriet Tubman
Schuman, William
 - On Freedom's Ground: An American Cantata
Schwantner, Joseph
 - A New Morning for the World
Still, William Grant
 - Symphony No. 1 (Afro-American Symphony)
 - Wood Notes: Singing River
Swanson, Howard
 - Short Symphony
Wagner, Joseph
 - Ballad of Brotherhood

BROADWAY MUSICALS

Anderson, Leroy
 - Goldilocks: I Never Know When
 - Goldilocks: Lady in Waiting
 - Goldilocks: Lazy Moon
 - Goldilocks: Overture
 - Goldilocks: Pirate Dance
 - Goldilocks: Pussyfoot
 - Goldilocks: Pyramid Dance
 - Goldilocks: Save a Kiss
 - Goldilocks: Shall I Take My Heart
 - Goldilocks: Town House Maxixe
 - Goldilocks: Who's Been Sitting In My Chair?
Arnold, Alan
 - Gershwin Portrait
Bart, Lionel
 - Oliver Selections
 - Oliver! for Orchestra
Bernstein, Leonard
 - Candide: Glitter and Be Gay
 - Candide Suite
 - On the Town: Three Dance Episodes
 - West Side Story Highlights
 - West Side Story: Selections
 - West Side Story: Symphonic Dances
Bock, Jerry
 - Fiddler on the Roof: Medley
 - Fiddler on the Roof: Symphonic Dances from
Berlin, Irving
 - Annie Get Your Gun: Overture
Casey, Warren & Jacobs, Jim
 - Grease!
Chase, Bruce
 - Broadway Tonight
Cohan, George M.
 - George M.: Choral Overture
 - Give My Regards to Broadway
Coleman, Cy
 - Sweet Charity Medley
Farrar, John
 - Grease: You're the One that I Want
Finn, William
 - Selections from 25th Annual Putnam County Spelling Bee
Friml, Rudolf
 - Medley from The Firefly
Gershwin, George
 - A Gershwin Portrait
 - Porgy and Bess
Guettel, Adam
 - Light in the Piazza: Symphonic Suite
Hamlisch, Marvin
 - Chorus Line, Selections from a
 - Marvin Hamlisch in Concert
Herbert, Victor
 - Ah Sweet Mystery of Life
Herman, Jerry
 - La Cage aux Folles: Overture
 - Selections from La Cage aux Folles
 - Hello Dolly Highlights
Joel, Billy
 - Movin' Out: Medley
John, Elton
 - Suite from The Lion King
Kander, John
 - Chicago
 - Chicago: Medley
Kander & Ebb
 - Cabaret
Kern, Jerome
 - Little Miss Fix-It: Turkey Trot
 - Night Boat: Whose Baby Are You
 - Night Boat Selections Ol' Man River
 - Sally Selections for Orchestra
 - Show Boat Overture
 - Show Boat Selections
Krogstad, Bob
 - Curtain Up!
Lane, Burton
 - Excerpts from Finian's Rainbow
Leigh, Mitch
 - Man of La Mancha: Selections
Lloyd Webber, Andrew
 - Andrew Lloyd Webber: A Concert Celebration
 - Cats Selections
 - Cats: Memory
 - Evita Highlights
 - Music from Evita
 - Medley from Jesus Christ Superstar
 - The Phantom of the Opera: Concert Version
 - The Phantom of the Opera Entr'Acte
 - Phantom of the Opera: Music of the Night
 - The Phantom of the Opera Overture
 - Phantom of the Opera Selections
Loesser, Frank
 - Music from Guys and Dolls
 - Selections from Guys and Dolls
 - The Most Happy Fella: Symphonic Impressions
Loewe, Ferdinand
 - Brigadoon Suite
 - Camelot: Selections
 - Gigi: Selections
 - My Fair Lady Medley
 - My Fair Lady: Selections
 - My Fair Lady: Highlights
MacDermot, Galt
 - Aquarius: Let the Sunshine In
 - Hair: Selections
 - Hair: Where Do I Go?/Good Morning Starshine
Mascagni, Pietro
 - Cavalleria Rusticana: Intermezzo
Maxwell Davies, Peter
 - The Boyfriend: Concert Suite
Menken, Alan
 - Beauty and the Beast
 - Highlights from Beauty and the Beast
Merrill, Bob
 - Take Me Along!: Overture
O'Brien, Richard
 - Rocky Horror Picture Show: Medley
Perry, William
 - Joy Shall Be Yours in the Morning
Porter, Cole
 - Cole Porter Classics
 - Gay Divorcée: Night and Day; I Get a Kick Out of You
Rodgers, Richard
 - Carousel: Selections
 - Carousel Waltz
 - Carousel: You'll Never Walk Alone
 - King and I Selections
 - Love Me Tonight: Lover
 - Oklahoma Selections
 - Richard Rodgers in Concert
 - Sound of Music Selections
 - State Fair: It's a Grand Night for Singing
Rome, Harold
 - Fanny: Selection for Orchestra
Sayre, Charles
 - Broadway on Parade
 - Broadway Showstoppers
 - Jerome Robbins Broadway

(BROADWAY MUSICALS, cont.)

Schoenberg, Claude-Michel
- Les Miserables: At the End of the Day
- Les Miserables: Bring Him Home
- Les Miserables: Do You Hear the People Sing?
- Les Miserables: Empty Chairs at Empty Tables
- Les Miserables: I Dreamed a Dream
- Les Miserables: Little Cosette-Castle on a Cloud
- Les Miserables: Master of the House
- Les Miserables: On My Own
- Les Miserables: One Day More
- Les Miserables: Stars
- Les Miserables: The ABC Café
- Les Miserables: Symphonic Suite
- Miss Saigon: Finale
- Miss Saigon: I Still Believe This
- Miss Saigon: Last Night of the World
- Miss Saigon: Sun and Moon
- Miss Saigon: This Is the Hour
- Miss Saigon: Why God Why
- Miss Saigon Rhapsody
- Miss Saigon Medley

Strommen, Carl
- A Salute to Broadway

Strouse, Charles
- Muscal Highlights from Annie
- Selections from Annie

Styne, Jule
- Gypsy: Overture

Tesori, Jeanine
- Thoroughly Modern Millie

Warren, Harry
- 42nd Street (1981)
- 42nd Street: Overture

Willson, Meredith
- The Music Man: Overture
- The Music Man: Seventy-Six Trombones

CELEBRATION

Anderson, Leroy
- Birthday Party

Arnold, Malcolm
- Anniversary Overture, Op. 99

Bach, P.D.Q.
- Birthday Ode to "Big Daddy" Bach

Bennett, Richard Rodney
- Celebration

Brubeck, Dave
- Fugal Fanfare: Happy Anniversary

Chiarappa, Richard
- Happy, Happy Birthday

Corigliano, John
- Campane di Ravello: A Celebration Piece for Sir Georg Solti

Erb, Donald
- Music for a Festive Occasion

Goldsmith, Jerry
- Fireworks: A Celebration for Los Angeles (1999)

Gould, Morton
- Cheers! -A Celebration March
- Festive Music

Handel, George Frideric
- Music for the Royal Fireworks

Hill & Hill
- Birthday Variations
- Campane di Ravello: A Celebration Piece for Sir Georg Solti
- Happy Anniversary
- Happy Birthday Variations
- Happy, Happy Birthday

Høffding, Finn
- Celebrations of May-Day

Ivanovici, Josif
- Waves of the Danube: The Anniversary Song

Liebermann, Lowell
- Revelry

López, Jimmy
- Fiesta! for chamber orchestra
- Fiesta! for orchestra
- Lago de Lágrimas (Lake of Tears)
- Perú Negro

Kerchner, Larry
- Happy Birthday Medley

Naughtin, Matthew
- Birthday Variations

Perry, William
- Graduation March

Richman, Lucas
- Shena B'rachot

Rodríguez, Robert Xavier
- The Salutation Rag

Schickele, Peter
- Birthday Ode to "Big Daddy" Bach

Schurmann, Gerard
- Attack and Celebration

Sierra, Roberto
- Tropicalia: Celebration

Tower, Joan
- Stepping Stones: Celebration Fanfare

Wendel, Robert
- Commemoration

Williams, John T.
- Happy Birthday Variations

Zwilich, Ellen Taaffe
- Celebration
- Jubilation
- Upbeat!

CIRCUS

Alford, Harry L.
- Clownette Novelty

Goossens, Eugene
- The Hurdy-Gurdy Man

Maggio, Robert
- Big Top

Moore, Douglas
- Pageant of P.T. Barnum

Rodríguez, Robert Xavier
- Trunks: A Circus Story

Schuman, William
- Circus Overture: Sideshow

Simons, Moises
- Peanut Vendor (also known as El manisero)

Sondheim, Stephen
- A Little Night Music: Send In the Clowns

Strauss, Johann, Sr.
- Tritsch-Tratsch: The Circus

Stravinsky, Igor
- Circus Polka

Tiomkin, Dimitri
- Circus World (1964): John Wayne March

Toch, Ernst
- Circus Overture

Waxman, Franz
- Man on a Tightrope (1953): March

Wendel, Robert
- Under the Big Top

DANCE

Adams, John
- The Chairman Dances: Foxtrot for Orchestra

Aguila, Miguel del
- Conga

Alwyn, William
- Elizabethan Dances
- Suite of Scottish Dances

Anderson, Leroy
- Belle of the Ball
- Blue Tango
- Chicken Reel
- Goldilocks: Lady in Waiting
- Goldilocks: Pirate Dance
- Goldilocks: Pyramid Dance
- Sandpaper Ballet
- Song of the Bells
- The Waltzing Cat

Antheil, George
- Accordion Dance
- Archipelago "Rhumba"
- Hot-Time Dance

Arnold, Malcolm
- English Dances: Suite No. 1
- English Dances, Suite No. 2

- Four Cornish Dances, Op. 91
- Four Irish Dances, Op. 126
- Four Scottish Dances, Op. 59
- Solitaire, Op. 141: Sarabande and Polka
- Sweeney Todd Concert Suite, Op. 68a

Ayars, Bo
- Cowboy Medley: Mexican Hat Dance

Bartók, Béla
- Dance Suite
- Rumanian Folk Dances

Bennett, Richard Rodney
- Murder on the Orient Express Theme: Foxtrot Theme
- Murder on the Orient Express Waltz

Bennett, Robert Russell
- Suite of Old American Dances

Bernstein, Elmar
- Thoroughly Modern Millie: Sky-Hi Walt
- Waltzes from Films: Suite

Bernstein, Leonard
- On the Town: Three Dance Episodes
- West Side Story: Symphonic Dances

Bizet, Georges
- Carmen: Scene & Habanara
- Carmen: Seguidilla and Duett

Bliss, Arthur
- Checkmate: Five Dances Suite

Borodin, Alexander
- Prince Igor: Polovtsian Dances

Brahms, Johannes
- Hungarian Dances
- Liebeslieder Waltzes, Op. 52

Britten, Benjamin
- Gloriana: The Courtly Dances

Brown, Robert Bennett
- Early American Quadrille: Square Dance

Brubeck, Dave
- Cathy's Waltz

Camilleri, Charles
- Maltese Dances

Campos, José Carlos
- Danza Rústica

Cervantes, Ignacio
- Three Cuban Dances

Cole, Hugo
- Black Lion Dances

Constantinescu, Paul
- Braul: The Sash Dance
- Ciobănaşul: The Shepherd Boy
- Olteneasca
- Tanze Aus Rumanien

Coolidge, Peggy Stuart
- Pioneer Dances

Copland, Aaron
- Appalachian Spring
- Billy the Kid
- Rodeo

Corigliano, John
- Gazebo Dances: Overture to the Imaginary Invalid
- Gazebo Dances for Orchestra

Cowell, Henry
- Flirtatious Jig: Fiddler's Jig

Creston, Paul
- Dance Overture
- Rumba-Tarantella
- Two Choric Dances, Op. 17a
- Two Choric Dances, Op. 17b

Damase, Jean-Michel
- Piége de lumiére

Delibes, Leo
- Coppelia: Entr'acte & Waltz

Dodgson, Stephen
- Villanelle

Dorff, Daniel
- It Takes Four to Tango

Duffy, John
- Heritage Symphonic Dances

Dvořák, Antonin
- Slavonic Dances

Elgar, Edward
- Spanish Lady Suite

Ellington, Edward (Duke)
- The River
- Three Black Kings

Esplá, Oscar
- Fiesta: Suite de danzas

Falla, Manuel de
- El Amor brujo: Pantomime and Ritual Fire Dance
- El Sombrero de tres picos (Three-Cornered Hat)
- La vida breve: Interlude & Spanish Dance

Frank, Gabriela Lena
- Three Latin-American Dances

Friedhofer, Hugo
- The Bishop's Wife: Ice Skater's Waltz (1947)

Gade, Jacob
- Jalousie
- Tango Jalousie (Tango Tzigane)

Gardel, Carlos
- Scent of a Woman: Por una Cabeza

Geehl, Henry
- Folk Dance Suite

German, Edward
- Three Dances: Henry VIII
- Valse Gracieuse

Gestor, Don
- First Love

Gillis, Don
- Twinkletoes Ballet: Tango Lullaby

Glass, Philip
- Modern Love Waltz

Glière, Reinhold
- The Red Poppy: Russian Sailor's Dance from Act I
- The Red Poppy, Suite No. 1 from the ballet, Op. 70a

Glinka, Mikhail
- Valse Fantaisie

Gluck, Christopher Willibald
- Orfeo ed Euridice: Dance of the Blessed Spirits

Goossens, Eugene
- Flamenco: Ballet

Gold, Ernest
- Ship of Fools: Candlelight & Silver Waltz (1965)

Goldsmith, Jerry
- Six Degrees of Separation (1993): Tango

Gomez, Alice
- Festive Huapango

Gould, Morton
- American Ballads: Saratoga Quickstep on "The Girl I Left Behind"
- Calypso Souvenir
- Celebration Strut
- Cinerama Holiday: Skier's Waltz
- Cresta Blanca Waltz
- Dance Gallery: Soft Shoe Gavotte
- Deserted Ballroom
- Hoofer Suite
- I'm Old Fashioned, Astaire Variations
- Latin American Symphonette
- Minute Plus Waltz Rag
- Philharmonic Waltzes
- Pirouette
- Tap Dance Concerto

Gounod, Charles
- Faust: Ballet Music

Granados, Enrique
- Tres danzas españolas: Oriental; Andaluza; Rondalla

Grant, James
- Waltz for Betz

Grieg, Edvard
- Norwegian Dances, Op. 35

Guarnieri, Camargo
- Dansa Brasileira

Guion, David
- Minuet
- Pickaninny Dance

Hamlisch, Marvin
- Chorus Line, Selections from a

Harbison, John
- Remembering Gatsby: Foxtrot for Orchestra

Hardiman, Ronan
- Lord of the Dance

Herbert, Victor
- Air de Ballet

Hermann, Ralph
- Old Timers Waltz Medley No. 1
- Old Timers Waltz Medley No. 2
- Polish Polka Party

THEMES 380 THEMES

(DANCE, cont.)

Holst, Gustav
- The Perfect Fool: Ballet Music, Op. 39

Ippolitov-Ivanov, M.
- Caucasian Sketches

Ivanovici, Josef
- Danube Waves (Anniversary) Waltz

Jager, Robert
- Concerto Grosso

Joel, Billy
- Movin' Out: Medley

Johnson, Francis
- Philadelphia Grays Quickstep

Kaper, Bronislau
- Lili: Ballet (1953)

Katz, S.
- Polskie Kwiaty (Selection of Polish Songs & Dances)

Khachaturian, Aram
- Gayane: Sabre Dance
- Gayane: Suite No. 1
- Gayane: Suite No. 2
- Gayane: Suite No. 3
- Spartacus: Suite No. 1
- Spartacus: Suite No. 2
- Spartacus: Suite No. 3

Kodály, Zoltán
- Dances of Marosszek

Lake, M. L.
- Old Timers Waltz

Lanner, Joseph
- Hofball-Tanze Waltz, Op. 161

Layton, Billy Jim
- Dance Fantasy, Op. 7

Lecuona, Ernesto
- Danza lucumi: Danza Afro-Cubanas

Lehár, Franz
- The Count of Luxembourg: Waltz
- Gold and Silver Waltz
- Gypsy Love Waltzes
- Waltz on Melodies from Zigeunerliebe (Gypsy Love)

Lane, Philip
- Wassail Dances for Orchestra

Leighton, Kenneth
- Dance Suite No. 1
- Dance Suite No. 2
- Dance suite No. 3: Scottish Dances, Op. 89

Liszt, Franz
- Hungarian Rhapsody No. 2
- Lenau's Faust: Mephisto Waltz No. 1
- Lenau's Faust: Mephisto Waltz No. 2

Luigini, Alexandre
- Ballet Egyptien

Mancini, Henry
- Astaire!
- The Molly Maguires: Pennywhistle Jig (1970)
- Pennywhistle Jig

Marquez, Arturo
- Danzon No. 2

Marquina, Pascual
- España cani

Maxwell Davies, Peter
- Caroline Mathilde: Concert Suite from Act I
- Caroline Mathilde: Concert Suite from Act II
- Maxwell's Reel, with Northern Lights
- Swinton Jig, on a Nineteenth Century Lancashire Fiddle Tune
- A Spell for Green Corn: The Macdonald Dances
- Swinton Jig on a Nineteenth Century Lancashire Fiddle Tune

Meza, Vinicio
- Suite Latinoamericana (Tango, Vals, Choro, Son)

Mindreau, Ernesto López
- Marinera y Tondero

Mizzy, Vic
- Addams Family Values (1993): Tango

Moncayo, José
- Huapango

Monti, Vittorio
- Czardas

Moroder, Georgio
- Flashdance: What a Feeling (1983)

Moross, Jerome
- Frankie and Johnny
- Variations on a Waltz

Nielsen, Carl August
- Masquerade: Hanedons (Cock's Dance)

Offenbach, Jacques
- Orpheus in the Underworld: Galop (Can Can)

Owens, Robert
- American Carnival: Ballet Suite

Piazzolla, Astor
- Libertango
- Michelangelo
- Milonga del Angel
- Tango No. 1: Coral
- Tango No. 2: Canyengue
- Tanguedia
- Three Minutes of Reality: Tango

Piston, Walter
- The Incredible Flutist: Ballet

Ponchielli, Amilcare
- La Gioconda: Dance of the Hours

Powell, John
- Mr. and Mrs. Smith: Tango de los Asesinos
- Natchez on the Hill: Three Virginia Country Dances
- A Set of Three

Prokofiev, Sergei
- Cinderella: Suite No. 1, Op. 107
- Cinderella: Suite No.2, Op. 108
- Romeo and Juliet: Suite No. 3, Op. 101

Ravel, Maurice
- Bolero
- Daphnis et Chloé: Suite No. 2
- Ma Mère l'Oye (Mother Goose)

Reinagle, Alexander
- Mrs. Madison's Minuet

Respighi, Ottorini
- Antiche danze ed arie (Ancient Airs and Dances)
- La Boutique fantasque: Suite (after Rossini)
- The Pines of Rome: Pines of the Appian Way

Riege, Ernst
- Bezaubernde

Gloriette, Konzertwalzer
- Katharinen-Waltz

Riegger, Wallingford
- Dance Rhythms, Op. 58
- New Dance, Op. 18b: Finale from the Ballet

Robinson & Giovannini
- Brazilian Polka

Rodríguez, Robert Xavier
- Hot Buttered Rumba

Salzedo, Leonard
- The Witch Boy: Three Dances from the Ballet

Sayre, Chuck
- Jerome Robbins Broadway: Sunrise, Sunset; America; Somewhere; Comedy Tonight

Schickele, Peter
- Uptown Hoedown

Schwartz, Stephen
- Dancing in the Dark

Scott, Raymond
- Minuet in Jazz

Sebastian
- A Fairytale: Suite from the Ballet

Secunda, Sholom
- Tango de la luna

Shaiman, Marc
- Addams Family Values (1993): Tango
- The Addams Family (1991): Theme and Waltz Finale

Shchedrin, Rodion
- Carmen Suite (after Georges Bizet)

Shostakovich, Dmitri
- Ballet Suite No. 1 (1949)
- Ballet Suite No. 2 (1951)
- Ballet Suite No. 3 (1951)
- Ballet Suite No. 4 (1953)
- Bolt: Suite from the ballet, Op. 27a (Ballet Suite No. 5)
- The Limpid Stream: Suite from the ballet, Op. 39a
- Suite for Jazz Orchestra No. 1

- Suite for Variety Orchestra No. 1
- Suite for Variety Orchestra No. 2
- Tahiti-Trot, Op. 16

Sibelius, Jean
- Kuolema, Op. 44: Valse Triste
- Valse chevaleresque, Op. 96c
- Valse lyrique, Op. 96a

Smetana, Bedrich
- The Bartered Bride: Dance of the Comedians

Smith, Julia
- American Dance Suite

Soro, Enrique
- Danza Fantástica

Steiner, Max
- Gone With the Wind (1939): Dance Montage
- Jezebel (1938): Waltz

Strauss, Johann Jr.
- Annen Polka, Op. 117
- Champagne Polka, Op. 211
- Eine nacht in Venedig: Frühlingsstimmen Waltz, Op. 410 (Voices of Spring)
- Graduation Ball: Ballet in one act
- Künstler (Artist's) Quadrille, Op. 201
- Künstlerleben (Artist's Life) Waltz, Op. 316
- Eine nacht in Venedig: Lagunenwalzer, Op. 411
- Lucifer Polka, Op. 266
- Morgenblätter (Morning Papers), Op. 279
- Moulinet Polka, Op. 57
- Rosen aus dem Süden (Roses from the South), Op. 388
- Telegramme Walzer, Op. 318
- Thousand and One Nights Waltz, Op. 346
- Tick-Tack Polka, Op. 365
- Tritsch-Tratsch Polka, Op.214
- Unter Donner und Blitz (Thunder and Lightning Polka)
- Vergnügungszug Polka, Op. 281
- Von der Borse, Polka française, Op. 337
- Wiener Blut (Vienna Blood), Op. 354

Strauss, Johann, Sr.
- Carnival Nights (Emperor Waltz)
- Tritsch-Tratsch (The Circus)

Strauss, Johann and Josef
- Pizzicato Polka

Strauss, Josef
- Elfen Polka
- Ohne Sorgen Polka, Op. 271
- Plappermaulchen Polka, Op. 245
- Sphärenklänge (Music of the Spheres Waltz), Op. 235

Strauss, Richard
- Burleske

Stravinsky, Igor
- Circus Polka
- L'Oiseau de feu (Firebird)

Sullivan, Arthur
- Pineapple Polka: Suite

Surinach, Carlos
- Ritmo Jondo: Flamenco
- Sinfonietta Flamenca

Tchaikovsky, Peter Ilyich
- The Nutcracker Suite

Templeton, Alec
- Ballad de ballet
- Operation Mambo

Tiomkin, Dimitri
- The Great Waltz (1938)

Tomlinson, Ernest
- Suite of English Folk Dances

Turina, Joaquin
- Danzas Fantásticas, Op. 22

Villaldo
- El Choclo: Tango Argentina

Waxman, Franz
- The Devil Doll (1936): Waltzes

Weinberger, Jaromir
- Bohemian Songs and Dances: Six Dances
- Svandadudák (Shvanda the Bagpiper): Polka and Fugue

Whelan, Bill
- Riverdance Theme

Woodgate, Leslie
- English Dance Suite

Ziehrer, Carl
- Herreinspaziert! Waltz, Op. 518

Zyman, Samuel
- Encuentros (1992)

ECOLOGY

Bizet, Georges
- Carmen: Flower Song

Brubeck, Dave
- The Light in the Wilderness

Copland, Aaron
- The Tender Land: Suite

Elfman, Danny
- Serenada Schizophrana

Elgar, Edward
- Sea Pictures

Frazelle, Kenneth
- The Swans at Pongo Lake

Grainger, Percy
- Country Gardens
- Green Bushes

Knight, Eric
- Three Musical Elements: Earth, Water, Space

Kosma, Joseph
- Autumn Leaves

Lambert, Constant
- The Rio Grande

MacCunn, Hamish
- Land of the Mountain and Flood, Op. 3: Overture

Mancini, Henry
- The White Dawn: Suite (1974)

O'Boyle, Sean
- River Symphony

Orr, Charles Wilfred
- Cotswald Hill Tune

Respighi, Ottorino
- The Pines of Rome: Pines of the Appian Way

Revueltas, Silvestre
- Paisajes (Landscapes)

Roylance, Dave and Galvin, Bob
- Ocean Fantasia

Schickele, Peter
- The Fantastic Garden
- A Zoo Called Earth

Schocker, Gary
- Green Places

Sharp, Cecil
- Country Gardens

Smetana, Bedrich
- Má Vlast (My Fatherland): 2. Vltava (Moldau)

Still, William Grant
- Wood Notes: Singing River

Strauss, Johann, Jr
- Im Krapfenwaldl, Polka française, Op. 336

Thomson, Virgil
- The River: Suite
- Sea Piece with Birds
- The Seine at Night
- Wheat Field at Noon

Tsontakis, George
- Let the River Be Unbroken

Warshauer, Meira
- Symphony No. 1: Living, Breathing Earth

Weinberger, Jaromir
- Under the Spreading Chestnut Tree

Welcher, Dan
- The Yellowstone Fires

FANFARE

Arnaud, Leo
- Bugler's Dream, Fanfare to the Olympic Games

Berkeley, Lennox
- Fanfare for the Royal Academy of Music Banquet

Binge, Ronald
- Cornet Carillon

Brubeck, Dave
- Fugal Fanfare: Happy Anniversary

Burgon, Geoffrey
- Fanfare on One Note

THEMES

(FANFARE, cont.)

Copland, Aaron
- Fanfare for the Common Man

Corigliano, John
- Midsummer Fanfare

Douglas, Samuel
- Millennium Fanfare

Dukas, Paul
- La Peri

Gardel, Carlos
- Tango: Por una Cabeza

Goossens, Eugene
- Fanfare for the Artists

Gould, Morton
- Dramatic Fanfares "World War I"
- Festive Fanfare

Harbison, John
- Fanfare for Foley's

Holmboe, Vagn
- Fanfare

Howard, John
- Grand Canyon Fanfare

Lutosławski, Witold
- Fanfare for Louisville

Newman, Alfred
- Fox Fanfare

North, Alex
- 2001 Space Odyssey: Fanfare

Payne, Anthony
- Fanfares and Processional

Piston, Walter
- Bicentennial Fanfare

Poulenc, Francis
- Fanfare

Richman, Lucas
- A Western Fanfare

Rodríguez, Robert Xavier
- Fanfare from "Oktoechos"

Schickele, Peter
- Fanfare for the Common Cold

Stucky, Steven
- Fanfare for Cincinnati
- Fanfare for Los Angeles

Tower, Joan
- Stepping Stones: Celebration Fanfare
- Fanfare for the Uncommon Woman

Turrin, Joseph
- Fanfare for George Gershwin

Welcher, Dan
- Castle Creek: Fanfare

Wendel, Robert
- Commemoration
- Fanfare for Freedom

Williams, John T.
- Happy Birthday Variations

FILMS

Adams, Emmett A.
- Bells of St. Mary's

Alford, Harry L.
- Colonel Bogey March

Antheil, George
- Music to a World's Fair Film

Arlen, Harold
- Wizard of Oz Choral Review
- Wizard of Oz: Munchkin Land
- Wizard of Oz: Over the Rainbow
- Wizard of Oz: Orchestral Suite
- Wizard of Oz Selections
- Wizard of Oz: Yellow Brick Road

Arnold, David
- Independence Day: Highlights
- Independence Day Suite
- Independence Day Suite: End Tags

Arnold, Malcolm
- The Belles of St. Trinians: Comedy Suite
- The Bridge on the River Kwai
- Hobson's Choice
- The Inn of the Sixth Happiness
- The Sound Barrier Rhapsody, Op. 38
- Whistle Down the Wind

Badelt, Klaus
- Pirates of the Caribbean: Curse of the Black Pearl

Baerwald, David
- Moulin Rouge: Come What May

Barry, John
- Best of Bond
- Dances with Wolves: Concert Suite
- Out of Africa: Main Title
- Robin and Marian
- Somewhere in Time

Beck, Christophe
- Under the Tuscan Sun (2003): Suite

Bennett, Richard Rodney
- Murder on the Orient Express Theme: Foxtrot Theme
- Murder on the Orient Express Suite
- Murder on the Orient Express Waltz

Bennett, Robert Russell
- Hollywood

Berlin, Irving
- Easter Parade
- Irving Berlin in Hollywood Overture

Bernstein, Elmer
- Airplane!: Suite
- American Werewolf in London
- The Babe: End Credits
- The Birdman of Alcatraz: Finale
- The Man with the Golden Arm: Suite
- My Left Foot: Suite
- The Sweet Smell of Success: Main Title
- The Ten Commandments: Suite
- Thoroughly Modern Millie: Sky-Hi Waltz
- To Kill a Mockingbird: Suite
- True Grit: Concert Suite
- Waltzes from Films: Suite

Bernstein, Leonard
- On the Waterfront: Symphonic Suite

Bishop, Jeffrey
- White Nights: Separate Lives

Blake, Howard
- Agatha: Suite

Bliss, Arthur
- Christopher Columbus
- Things to Come: Suite

Bocook, Jay
- Movie Spectacular

Botkin, Perry
- Nadia's Theme

Broughton, Bruce
- The Boy Who Could Fly: Theme
- Miracle on 34th Street: Main Title
- Themes from Silverado
- Jag: Theme
- Miracle on 34th Street (1994): Main Title
- Miracle on 34th Street, Overture to
- Young Sherlock Holmes(1985): Suite

Bush, Geoffrey
- Yorick Overture

Caliendo, Christopher
- The Iron Horse

Chaplin, Charlie
- City Lights
- The Reel Chaplin

Chase, Bruce
- Muppet Medley

Churchill, Frank
- Snow White: Symphonic Selections

Conrad, Con
- The Gay Divorcee: The Continental

Conti, Bill
- Rocky Highlights
- Rookie of the Year

Corigliano, John
- The Red Violin: Chaconne for Violin and Orchestra
- The Red Violin: Suite for Violin and Orchestra
- Three Hallucinations

Custer, Calvin
- Themes from 007: A Medley for Orchestra

Daugherty, Michael
- Metropolis Symphony

Debney, John
- The Passion of the Christ Symphony

Desplat, Alexandre
- The Curious Case of Benjamin Button: Suite
- The Queen: Suite (2006)

Dessau, Paul
- Alice the Firefighter
- Alice's Monkey Business
- Alice in the Wooly West
- Alice Helps the Romance

Doyle, Patrick
- Great Expectations Suite
- Henry V: Non Nobis Domine
- Much Ado About Nothing: Suite (1993)
- Sense and Sensibility: Suite (1995)

Dun, Tan
- Crouching Tiger, Hidden Dragon (2000)

Eidelman, Cliff
- Star Trek 6: The Undiscovered Country (1991)

Elfman, Danny
- Beetlejuice: Main Title (1988)
- Charlotte's Web: Themes for Flute and Orchestra (2006)
- Edward Scissorhands: Ice Dance
- Edward Scissorhands: Main Title
- Movie Spectacular: Batman; Dances with Wolves; Robin Hood
- Serenada Schizophrana
- Simpsons Main Title
- Spider Man, Music from
- Spider-Man: Suite (2004)

Fain, Sammy
- Once Upon a Dream

Fiedel, Brad
- The Teminator: Theme (1984)
- True Lies: Theme (1994)

Fielding, Jerry
- The Outlaw Josey Wales: Suite (1976)
- The Wild Bunch: Suite in Two Movements (1969)

Flaherty, Stephen
- Anastasia: A Rumor in St. Petersburg
- Anastasia Medley
- Anastasia Suite
- Anastasia: In the Dark of the Night
- Anastasia: Journey to the Past
- Anastasia: Learn to Do It Waltz
- Anastasia: Once Upon a December
- Anastasia: Paris Holds the Key
- Ragtime "The Musical" Selections

Foster, David W.
- Quest for Camelot Selections

Friedhofer, Hugo
- An Affair to Remember: The Proposal (1957)
- The Best Years of Our Lives: Suite
- The Bishop's Wife: Ice Skater's Waltz (1947)
- The Mark of Zorro: Suite (1940)

Friml, Rudolf
- Medley from The Firefly

Gardel, Carlos
- Scent of a Woman: Por una Cabeza

German, Edward
- Richard III: Overture

Giacchino, Michael
- Star Trek: End Credits (2009)
- Music from "Up"

Gilpin, Greg
- The Music of MGM (A Choral Medley)

Glass, Philip
- The Hours: Suite (2002)

Gold, Marty
- Mancini Memories: Breakfast at Tiffany's & Baby Elephant Walk

Gold, Ernest
- Exodus: An Orchestral Tone-Picture
- Exodus: Rhapsody for Cello and Orchestra (1960)
- Exodus: This Land is Mine (1960)
- It's a Mad, Mad, Mad, Mad World: Exit Music (1963)
- Ship of Fools: Candlelight & Silver Waltz (1965)

Goldenthal, Elliot
- Alien 3: Adagio

Goldsmith, Jerry
- The Agony and the Ecstasy (1965): Suite
- Alien (1979): End Title
- Air Force One (1997): Theme
- Basic Instinct (1992): Main Title Theme
- Basic Instinct (1992): Suite
- The Blue Max (1996): Suite
- The Boys from Brazil (1978): Waltz & The Boys
- Capricorn One: Overture & Main Title
- Chinatown (1974): Suite
- Chinatown: Theme (1974)
- Dennis the Menace (1993): End Credits
- The Edge (1997): Main Title & Finale
- The Final Conflict (1983)
- The First Knight (1995): Suite
- Forever Young (1992): Love Theme
- Four Women: Medley
- The Generals: Patton/MacArthur Marches
- The Great Train Robbery (1979): Suite
- Gremlins: Suite
- Gremlins 2 (1990): The New Batch: Main Title
- Hoosiers (1986): Suite
- The Illustrated Man: Main Title
- King Solomon's Mines (1985): Suite
- L.A. Confidential (1997)
- Lionheart: The Children's Crusade (1987)
- Logan's Run (1976): Monument/End of the City
- MacArthur (1977): March
- Motion Picture Medley
- The Omen (1976): Suite
- Papillon: Theme

- A Patch of Blue (1966): Suite
- Patton (1970): Attack
- Patton (1970): Suite
- Patton (1970): The Battle Ground
- Patton (1970): The Hospital
- Patton (1970): The Payoff
- Planet of the Apes (1968): Suite
- Poltergeist (1982): Night of the Beast (Clown Attack)
- Poltergeist (1982): The Calling
- Poltergeist (1982): The Light
- Poltergeist (1982): Theme (Carol Anne's)
- Rambo: First Blood, Part 2 (1985): Theme
- Rudy: Theme for Flute and Chamber Orchestra
- The Russia House (1990): Love Theme
- The Shadow (1994): Main Title
- Six Degrees of Separation (1993): Tango
- Sleeping with the Enemy (1991): Theme
- Star Trek: Main Theme
- Star Trek: Voyager (1995)
- Star Trek I: The Motion Picture "The Director's Cut"
- Star Trek I: The Motion Picture "The Klingon Battle"
- Star Trek I: The Motion Picture "The New Enterprise"
- Star Trek I: The Motion Picture Theme (1979)
- Star Trek 5: The Final Frontier: Suite (1989)
- Star Trek 8: First Contact (1996)
- Star Trek 9: Insurrection (1998)
- Star Trek 10: Nemesis (2002)
- The Sum of All Fears (2002)
- Supergirl: Suite
- The Swarm (1978): Bees Arrive/End Title
- Twilight Zone: The Movie (1983): End Title
- Under Fire (1983): Suite
- The Wild Rovers (1971): Bronco Busting
- The Wind and the Lion (1975)

Goodwin, Ron
- Those Magnificent Men in Their Flying Machines (1965)

Gould, Morton
- Cinerama Holiday: Suite

Gray, Allan
- African Queen: Portrait (1951)

Gregson-Williams, Harry
- Chronicles of Narnia: The Lion, The Witch and The Wardrobe

(FILMS, cont.)

Grofé, Ferde
 - Hollywood Suite: On the Set-Sweepers; The Stand-in; Carpenters and Electricians; Preview; Production Number

Grusin, Dave
 - Theme from On Golden Pond

Hageman, Richard
 - Stagecoach: Suite (1939)

Hamlisch, Marvin
 - Ice Castles Through the Eyes of Love

Hayes, Isaac
 - Selections from Shaft

Hayes, Jack
 - Fox Medley No. 1 & No. 2

Hermann, Ralph
 - Silent Movie

Herrmann, Bernard
 - Anna and the King of Siam Suite (1946)
 - The Bride Wore Black: A Musical Scenario (1968)
 - The Bride Wore Black: A Suite in Four Movements
 - Citizen Kane Overture
 - The Day the Earth Stood Still: Arrival (1951)
 - The Devil and Daniel Webster: Suite
 - The Ghost of Mrs. Muir (1947)
 - It's Alive (1973)
 - Jane Eyre: Suite (1943)
 - Jason and Argonauts: Suite (1963)
 - Jason and Argonauts: Scherzo macabre (1963)
 - Journey to the Center of the Earth (1959)
 - The Man Who Knew Too Much: The Storm Clouds Cantata (1956)
 - Mysterious Island: Suite (1961)
 - North by Northwest
 - A Portrait of Hitch
 - A Portrait of Hitch: The Trouble with Harry Suite (1954)
 - Psycho (1960)
 - The Seventh Voyage of Sinbad
 - The Snows of Kilimijaro (1952)
 - Taxi Driver: A Night Piece for Orchestra (1976)
 - The Three Worlds of Gulliver: Suite (1960)
 - Vertigo: Suite (1958)
 - The Wrong Man: Prelude (1956)

Heuberger, Richard
 - Melodies of Richard Heuberger

Hooper, Nicolas
 - Concert Suite from Harry Potter and the Half-Blood Prince

Hooper, Nicolas & Williams, John T.
 - Harry Potter and the Order of the Phoenix: Concert Suite

Horner, James
 - Aliens Suite No. 1: Main Title & Ripley's
 - Aliens Suite No. 2: Newt & Face Huggers
 - Apollo 13: Main Title; End Credits; Re-Entry; and Splashdown
 - An American Tail: Somewhere Out There
 - Avatar (2009): Suite
 - Braveheart: Main Title & End Credits (1995)
 - Cocoon Theme
 - An Irish Party in Third Class
 - James Horner-Hollywood Blockbusters: Apollo 13; American Tail; Braveheart; Titanic
 - Legends of the Fall: The Ludlows (1994)
 - The Mask of Zorro: Suite (1998)
 - Star Trek 2: The Wrath of Khan (1982)
 - Star Trek 3: The Search for Spock "Stealing the Enterprise" (1984)
 - Titanic Suite

Howard, James
 - Defiance (2008): Nothing is Impossible
 - Grand Canyon Fanfare
 - King Kong
 - Lady in the Water (2006): The Healing
 - Peter Pan (2003): Flying
 - Peter Pan (2003): Suite for Orchestra with Narrator
 - Prince of Tides Suite
 - Signs Suite
 - The Sixth Sense Suite
 - Snow Falling on Cedars Suite
 - The Village
 - The Village: Suite-Village Romance
 - Wyatt Earp (1994)
 - Wyatt Earp: End Credits

Hudson, Will & Mills, Irving
 - Moonglow

Hupfeld, Herman
 - As Time Goes By

Ivanovici, Josef
 - Danube Waves Waltz: The Anniversary Song

Jarre, Maurice
 - Lara's Theme from Doctor Zhivago
 - Lawrence of Arabia
 - A Passage to India: A Symphonic Journey (1984)

Jarre, Maurice
 - Ryan's Daughter: Rosy's Theme (1970)
 - Witness: Building the Barn

Jones, Trevor
 - Last of the Mohicans: Kiss
 - Last of the Mohicans: Last of the Mohicans Suite
 - Last of the Mohicans: Main Title

Kaczmarek, Jan A.P.
 - Finding Neverland: Suite (2004)

Kamen, Michael
 - Mr. Holland's Opus: American Symphony
 - Robin Hood: Prince of Thieves (Main Title)

Kaper, Bronislau
 - Auntie Mame: Overture (1958)
 - Lili: Ballet (1953)
 - Mutiny on the Bounty: Suite (1962)
 - Them!: Ant Fugue (1954)

Kapilow, Robert
 - Chris van Allsburg's Polar Express

Kent, Rolfe
 - Up In the Air (2009)

Kilar, Wojciech
 - Dracula (1992)
 - Theme from the Film The Pianist

Korngold, Erich
 - Korngold: The Adventures of Robin Hood, Symphonic Portrait

Krogstad, Bob
 - Christmas at the Movies

Lai, Francis
 - Love Story: Where Do I Begin
 - Love Story: Theme (1970)
 - A Man and a Woman

Lawrence, David
 - High School Musical
 - High School Musical 2

Lowden, Bob
 - Disney Magic
 - A Disney Supertime: From Mary Poppins

Magidson, Herb
 - The Continental (1934)

Mancina, Mark
 - Twister: Main Theme

Mancini, Henry
 - 10: It's Easy to Say
 - Academy Award Medley
 - Astaire!
 - Breakfast at Tiffanys: Moon River
 - Charade
 - Days of Wine and Roses
 - Dear Heart
 - The Great Mouse Detective
 - The Great Race: Pie in the Face Polka
 - The Great Race: They're Off
 - The Great Waldo Pepper
 - Hatari!: Baby Elephant Walk (1962)
 - Henry Mancini for Strings
 - The Lifeforce
 - Mancini Magic

- The Molly Maguires: Pennywhistle Jig (1970)
- Monster Movie Music Suite
- Oklahoma Crude
- The Pink Panther
- The Pink Panther: It Had Better Be Tonight (Meglio Stasera)
- Revenge of The Pink Panther (1978): Hong Kong Fireworks
- Songs for Audrey: Breakfast at Tiffanys, Charade, Two for the Road
- Victor, Victoria (1982): Crazy World
- The White Dawn: Suite (1974)

Mandel, Johnny
- The Sandpiper: Shadow of Your Smile

Mascagni, Pietro
- Cavalleria rusticana: Intermezzo Sinfonica

Maxwell, Robert
- Ebb Tide

Maxwell Davies, Peter
- The Boyfriend: Concert Suite
- The Devils: Suite

McBroom, Amanda
- The Rose

McCarthy, Dennis
- Star Trek: Deep Space Nine Suite
- Star Trek 7: Generations "Overture"

Meyer, George W.
- If You Were the Only Girl in the World

Moroder, Georgio
- Flashdance: What a Feeling (1983)

Moross, Jerome
- The Big Country: Main Title Theme
- The Big Country: Suite
- Music from the Flicks
- Wagon Train

Morricone, Ennio
- Casualties of War: Elegy for Brown
- Cinema Paradiso: First Youth
- Cinema Paradiso: Love Theme
- Cinema Paradiso Theme
- I Knew I Loved You
- Legend of 1900: Romanza
- Marco Polo: Main Title
- The Mission: Gabriel's Oboe
- Once Upon a Time in the West: Theme; Man With a Harmonia
- The Untouchables: Overture

Morris, John
- Blazing Saddles (1973)
- High Anxiety: Main Title (1973)
- The Producers: Main Title (1968)
- Young Frankenstein: The Transylvanian Lullaby (1974)

Murray, Lyn
- To Catch a Thief: Suite (1955)

Newborn, Ira
- The Naked Gun: Theme (1988)

Newman, Alfred
- All About Eve: Overture
- The Best of Everything: London Calling
- Bishop's Wife: Lost April
- Brigham Young March (1940)
- Captain from Castile: Conquest
- Captain from Castile: Pedro and Catania
- David & Bathsheba
- Desiree: We Meet Again
- The Diary of Anne Franck: Suite
- Gentleman's Agreement Suite
- How to Marry a Millionaire: Street Scene
- How the West Was Won
- How the West Was Won: Suite
- Keys of the Kingdom Suite
- Nevada Smith: Overture
- Prisoner of Zenda: A Ruritanian Rhapsody for Orchestra
- The Razors Edge
- The Robe: Farewell to Diana
- Song of Bernadette (1943): Main Title
- Song of Bernadette (1943): Scherzo
- Wuthering Heights: Cathie's Theme
- Wuthering Heights: Concert Suite

Newman, David
- Hoffa Theme

Newman, Lionel
- Doctor Dolittle: Talk to the Animals

North, Alex
- 2001 Space Odyssey: Fanfare
- 2001: A Symphonic Suite in Four Movements
- Cheyenne Autumn Suite
- Cleopatra: Symphonic Portrait
- Spartacus: Camp at Night
- Spartacus: Draba Fight
- Spartacus: Final Farewell
- Spartacus: Forest Meeting
- Spartacus: Love Theme
- Spartacus: Main Title
- Spartacus: Vesuvius
- A Streetcar Named Desire: Suite
- Unchained Melody (1955)
- Viva Zapata (1952): Gathering Forces

Nyman, Michael
- The Piano: Concerto
- The Piano: Lost and Found
- The Piano for String Orchestra

O'Boyle, Sean
- Silent Movie Music

Ortolani & Oliviero
- Mondo Cane: More

Ottman, John
- Astro Boy (2009): End Titles
- Astro Boy (2009): Theme
- Fantastic Four: Main Titles
- Fantastic Four 2: Silver Surfer Suite
- Superman Returns Piano Suite
- Superman Returns Suite
- The Usual Suspects (1995)
- X2: X-Men United

Pachelbel, Johann
- Ordinary People Theme: Canon

Perry, Sam
- The Phantom of the Opera (1930)

Phillips, John
- Monday, Monday

Poledouris, Basil
- Free Willy Suite (1993)

Polster, Ian
- Salute to MGM: That's Entertainment

Porter, Cole
- Gay Divorcée: Night and Day

Portman, Rachel
- Chocolat: Suite (2000)
- The Cider House Rules (1999)
- Emma (1996)
- Oliver Twist: Suite (2005)

Powell, John
- The Bourne Identity
- Chicken Run: Final Escape
- Chicken Run: Make a Crate
- Endurance: The Great Tree
- Happy Feet: the Story of Mumble
- Suite from Ice Age: The Meltdown
- Mr. and Mrs. Smith: Tango de los Asesinos
- X-Men: The Last Stand

Raksin, David
- The Bad and the Beautiful: Mvt. I: Love Is for the Very Young; Mvt. II: Acting Lesson; Mvt. III: The Quickies and Sneak Preview
- Forever Amber: I. Main Title "Amber"; II. The King's Mistress; III. Whitefriars; IV. The Great Fire; V. End Title "Finale"
- Forever Amber: Suite (1947)
- Laura
- Laura's Theme

Richman, Lucas
- An Overture to Blanche

Rosenman, Leonard
- Star Trek 4: The Voyage Home

Rota, Nino
- Amarcord
- Romeo and Juliet (1968)
- Romeo and Juliet: A Time for Us
- The Godfather (1972)
- The Godfather II (1974)
- The Godfather III: Suite
- The Godfather: Reminicences for Orchestra (1972)
- War and Peace: Suite (1956)

Roylance, Dave & Galvin, Bob
- Tall Ships Suite

Rózsa, Miklós
- Ben Hur: Choral Suite

*(FILMS –
Rózsa, Miklós, cont.)*

- Ben Hur: Parade of the Charioteers
- Ben-Hur: Prelude
- Ben Hur: Rowing of the Galley Slaves
- El Cid: Main Title
- El Cid: Overture
- El Cid: Overture and March
- Dead Men Don't Wear Plaid: End Cast
- Double Indemnity: Suite
- Ivanhoe: Prelude, Lady Rowena; Finale; Epilogue
- The Killers: Concert Suite
- The Lost Weekend: Suite
- Quo Vadis Suite: Ave Caesar; Romanza; Arabesque; Quo Vadis
- The Red House Suite

Sakamoto, Ryuichi
- The Last Emperor: Theme (1987)

Sainte-Marie, Buffy
- An Officer & A Gentleman: Up Where We Belong

Sayre, Chuck
- Disney Adventure

Schwartz, Stephen
- Prince of Egypt Medley

Shaiman, Marc
- Addams Family Values (1993): Tango
- The Addams Family (1991): Theme and Waltz Finale
- American President: Big Speech, Big Finish

Shapiro, Michael
- Frankenstein

Shire, David
- The Conversation (1974)
- Farewell My Lovely (1975): Suite
- Norma Rae: It Goes Like It Goes
- Return to Oz (1985): Theme
- Taking of Pelham One Two Three (1974): Theme

Shore, Howard
- The Lord of the Rings: The Two Towers
- The Lord of the Rings: Fellowship of the Ring
- Suite from The Return of the King
- Symphonic Suite from The Lord of the Rings: The Two Towers

Shostakovich, Dmitri
- The Gadfly: Suite from the Film, Op. 97a
- Hamlet: Music from the Film, Op. 116

Silvestri, Alan
- The Abyss: Finale
- Back to the Future (Madrid Version)
- Back to the Future Suite
- Beowulf (2007): I Shouldn't Have Told You
- Cast Away: Crossroads
- Fools Rush In
- Forrest Gump: Suite
- Forrest Gump Main Title: Feather Theme
- Judge Dredd (1995): Suite
- Mouse Hunt (1997): Suite
- The Mummy Returns (2001)
- Night at the Museum (2006): Suite
- Polar Express: Believe
- Polar Express: O Tannenbaum
- Polar Express: Spirit of the Seasons
- Polar Express Suite
- Polar Express: When Christmas Comes to Town

Sondheim, Stephen
- A Little Night Music: Send In the Clowns

Snow, Mark
- X-Files: Main Title Theme

Steiner, Max
- The Caine Mutiny (1954): The March
- Gone With the Wind (1939): Dance Montage
- Gone With the Wind: Tara's Theme
- Jezebel (1938): Waltz
- King Kong: Jungle Dance
- King Kong (1933): Overture
- King Kong: Theme
- Now, Voyager (1942): Main Title and Final Scene
- The Treasure of Sierra Madre (1948): Suite

Stevens, Leith
- The Wild One (1953)

Strauss, Richard
- Introduction (Sunrise)

Strommen, Carl
- A Salute to the Cinema

Strouse, Charles
- Muscal Highlights from Annie
- Selections from Annie

Tan Dun
- Crouching Tiger Concerto

Theodorakis, Mikis
- Zorba the Greek (1964): Theme

Thomson, Virgil
- Fugue and Chorale on Yankee Doodle
- Louisiana Story: Acadian Songs and Dances
- Louisiana Story: Orchestral Suite
- The River: Suite

Tiomkin, Dimitri
- 55 Days at Peking (1963): Suite
- The Alamo (1960): Short Suite
- The Alamo (1960): Suite
- The Big Sky (1952): Suite
- Circus World (1964): John Wayne March
- Cyrano De Bergerac (1950): Suite
- Dial M for Murder (1954): Suite
- DOA (1950)
- Duel in the Sun (1946): Suite
- The Fall of the Roman Empire (1964): Themes
- The Four Poster (1952)
- Friendly Persuasion (1956)
- Friendly Persuasion (1956): Thee I Love
- Giant (1956): Suite
- The Great Waltz (1938)
- Gunfight at the OK Corral (1957):Ballad and Theme
- The Guns of Navarone (1961): Suite
- The High and the Mighty (1954): Suite
- High Noon (1952): Do Not Forsake Me Oh My Darling
- High Noon (1952): Suite
- It's a Wonderful Life (1947): Suite
- Suite from It's a Wonderful Life
- It's a Wonderful Life (1947): Theme
- The Men (1950): Suite
- Night Passage (1957): Follow the River
- A President's Country (1966): Medley
- Red River (1948): Suite
- Rhapsody of Steel (1959)
- Rio Bravo (1959): Suite
- Strangers on a Train (1951): Suite
- The Sundowners (1960): Suite
- Tarzan and the Mermaids (1948): Suite
- Tension at Table Rock (1956): Suite
- The Thing from Another World (1951): Suite
- Town Without Pity (1961): Theme
- The Unforgiven
- The War Wagon (1967): Suite
- The Well (1951): Suite
- Wild is the Wind (1958): Theme
- The Young Land (1959): Strange are the Ways of Love

Tyzik, Jeff
- The Big Movie Suite

Vangelis
- Chariots of Fire

Warren, Diane
- Music of My Heart

Warren, Harry
- Lullaby of Broadway

Waxman, Franz
- Anne of the Indes (1951): Overture
- Beloved Infidel (1959): Theme
- Botany Bay (1953): Suite
- The Bride of Frankenstein (1935)
- Captains Courageous (1937): Suite

- A Christmas Carol (1939): Christmas Morning & Finale
- A Christmas Carol (1939): Five Sketches after Dickens
- Cimarron (1960): Suite
- Come Back, Little Sheba (1953): Reminiscences for Orchestra
- Dark City (1950)
- The Devil Doll (1936): Waltzes
- Dr. Jekyll and Mr. Hyde (1941): Suite
- Elephant Walk (1954): Suite
- The Furies (1950): Suite
- Hemingway's Adventures of a Young Man
- Hemingway's Adventures of a Young Man: Rosanna
- Huckleberry Finn (1939): Overture
- The Lost Command (1966): Aicha's Theme
- Magnificent Seven, The: Suite
- Man on a Tightrope (1953): March
- Medley: Classic Film Themes
- Medley: Classic Love Themes
- Medley: Nostalgic Film Themes
- My Cousin Rachel (1952): Suite
- My Geisha (1961): Goodbye Love – Finale
- My Geisha (1961): Suite
- My Geisha (1961): You Are Sympathy to Me
- Night and the City (1950): Suite Nightride for Orchestra
- The Nun's Story (1958)
- The Nun's Story (1958): Short Suite
- Peyton Place (1957): Suite
- Peyton Place (1957): Theme "The Wonderful Seasons of Love" or "For Those Who Are Young"
- The Philadelphia Story (1939): Suite
- The Pioneer (1951): Suite
- A Place in the Sun (1951)
- A Place in the Sun (1951): A Symphonic Scenario
- Possessed (1947)
- Prince Valiant (1954)
- Rear Window (1954)
- Rebecca (1940): Suite
- The Silver Chalice (1954): Short Suite
- The Silver Chalice (1954): Suite
- Sorry, Wrong Number (1948): Passacaglia
- Sunset Boulevard (1950): Staged Reading in Two Acts
- Sunset Boulevard (1950): Suite
- Suspicion (1941): Suite
- Taras Bulba (1962): Suite
- Taras Bulba (1962): The Ride of the Cossacks
- Untamed (1955)
- Young at Heart (1938)

Webb, Roy
- Notorious (1946): Suite
Wendel, Robert
- Hollywood Salute
Williams, Charles
- The Apartment: Theme (Jealous Lover)
- The Dream of Olwen
Williams, John T.
- 1941: March of 1941
- Amistad: Dry Your Tears, Afrika
- Angela's Ashes: Two Concert Pieces
- Catch Me If You Can
- Close Encounters of the Third Kind
- Close Encounters of the Third Kind, Theme from
- The Cowboys Overture
- The Empire Strikes Back Medley
- Episode I Phantom Menace: Duel of the Fates
- E.T.: Flying Theme
- Selections from E.T.
- E.T. Suite: Adventures on Earth
- Theme from E.T.
- Empire Strikes Back Medley
- Far and Away: Excerpts
- Harry Potter and the Chamber of Secrets
- Harry Potter and the Prisoner of Azkaban
- Harry Potter and the Sorcerer's Stone: Children's Suite
- Harry Potter and the Sorcerer's Stone: Suite for Orchestra
- Harry Potter and the Sorcerer's Stone: Harry Potter Symphonic Suite
- Harry Potter Symphonic Suite
- Home Alone: Three Holiday Songs
- Hook: Flight to Neverland
- Suite from Jaws
- Jurassic Park: Highlights
- The Lost World: Jurassic Park
- Memoirs of a Geisha: Sayuri's Theme
- Midway: Midway March
- Munich: A Prayer for Peace
- Munich: Hatikva (The Hope)
- The Patriot
- Raiders of the Lost Ark: Raiders March
- Highlights from Return of the Jedi
- Saving Private Ryan: Hymn to the Fallen
- Theme from Schindler's List
- Three Pieces from Schindler's List
- Star Spangled Banner
- Star Wars Suite
- Star Wars: Episode I Phantom Menace
- Star Wars: Selections from The Phantom Menace
- Star Wars: Episode II: Attack of the Clones (Across the Stars Love Theme)
- Star Wars: Episode III: Revenge of the Sith (Battle of the Heroes)
- Star Wars: Main Theme
- Star Wars: Medley
- Star Wars: Parade of the Ewoks (Return of the Jedi)
- Superman March: Main Theme
- Superman Returns: Concert Selections
- Superman Returns Suite
- The Terminal: Viktor's Tale
- Three Themes: Schindler's List Theme; Angela's Ashes; Hymn to the Fallen
Williams & Hooper
- Harry Potter and the Order of the Phoenix: Concert Suite
Yared, Gabriel
- The English Patient (1996)
Young, Christopher
- Species (1995): End Credits
Young, Victor
- Around the World in 80 Days (1956): Overture & Epilogue
- For Whom the Bell Tolls (1943): Suite
- Medley: Victor Young Tribute
- The Quiet Man (1952): Suite
- Samson and Delilah (1949)
- Scaramouche (1952): Suite
- Shane (1953): Suite
- The Uninvited (1944): Stella by Starlight
Young & Auric
- Roman Holiday (1953): Main Title and Prelude
Zimmer, Hans
- Da Vinci Code (2006): Chevaliers de Sangreal
- Gladiator: Music from the Movie
- The Last Samurai: The Way of the Sword
- Pirates of the Caribbean: Dead Man's Chest (Soundtrack Highlights)
Zimmer & Howard
- The Dark Knight: Concert Suite

HOLIDAYS

Christmas
Adam, Adolphe Charles
- Cantique de Noel (O Holy Night)
- Christmas with Renata Scotto: 5. Christmas Song (Cantique de Noel)
Addinsell, Richard
- A Christmas Carol (Suite: Scrooge)
Amundson, Steven
- Angels' Dance

(Christmas, cont.)

Anderson, Leroy
- Bugler's Holiday
- A Christmas Festival
- Sleigh Ride
- Suite of Carols

Arnold, Malcolm
- Commonwealth Christmas Overture, Op. 64
- The Holly and the Ivy Fantasy on Christmas Carols
- Toy Symphony, Op. 62

Austin, Frederic
- Twelve Days of Christmas

Ayars, Bo
- Christmas Medley

Bach, J. S.
- Jesu, Joy of Man's Desiring
- Sheep May Safely Graze

Bacon, Ernst
- Christmas Fantasia for Strings

Barab, Seymour
- G.A.G.E., A Christmas Story

Barber, Samuel
- Die natali (Chorale Preludes for Christmas), Op. 37:
- Die natali (Chorale Preludes for Christmas) Op. 37: Silent Night

Bax, Arnold
- A Christmas Carol

Bennett, Robert Russell
- The Many Moods of Christmas: Suite 1
- The Many Moods of Christmas: Suite 2
- The Many Moods of Christmas: Suite 3
- The Many Moods of Christmas: Suite 4

Berezovsky, Nicolai
- Christmas Festival Overture: Ukrainian Noel

Berlin, Irving
- White Christmas

Berlioz, Hector
- The Novello Book of Carols: The Shepherds' Farewell (Thou Must Leave)

Bernard, Felix
- Winter Wonderland

Blake, Howard
- Christmas Lullaby

Blane, Ralph
- Have Yourself a Merry Little Christmas

Bowden, Robert C.
- A Christmas Treat

Broughton, Bruce
- Miracle on 34th Street (1994): Main Title
- Miracle on 34th Street, Overture to

Burgon, Geoffrey
- Nunc Dimittis

Carey, Julia Scott
- Legend of Old Befana

Chase, Bruce
- Around the World at Christmas Time
- Christmas Favorites

Christensen, James
- Snow Chase

Corelli, Arcangelo
- Concerto grosso, Op. 6, #8 in g minor: Christmas Concerto

Corigliano, John
- The Cloisters

Courtney, Craig
- A Musicological Journey Through Twelve Days of Christmas

Custer, Calvin
- Christmas - That Special Time of the Year
- It's Christmastime (Medley for Orchestra)

Darke, Harold
- In the Bleak Midwinter

Davis, Chip
- Christmas Sweet

Davis, Katherine
- The Little Drummer Boy

Deak, John
- The Passion of Scrooge (A Christmas Carol)

DeLarmarter, Eric
- Christmastide

Dello Joio, Norman
- Christmas Music
- Nativity: Canticle for the Child

Dix, William
- Christmas with Renata Scotto: 8. What Child Is This?

Dunhill, Thomas
- The Novello Book of Carols: How Soft, Upon the Ev'ning Air

Effinger, Cecil
- The St. Luke Christmas Story

Elgar, Edward
- The Snow Op. 26, No. 1

Ellington, Edward (Duke)
- Three Black Kings

Ellis, David
- Carols for an Island Christmas

Feller, Sherm
- Snow, Snow, Beautiful Snow

Freyhan, Michael
- Toy Symphony

Friedhofer, Hugo
- The Bishop's Wife: Ice Skater's Waltz (1947)

Gabrielli, Giovanni
- The Novello Book of Carols: O Magnum Misterium

Gauntlett & Mann & Wells
- The Novello Book of Carols: Once in Royal David's City

Goldstein, William
- 'Twas the Night Before Christmas

Gould, Morton
- Adeste fidelis
- Christmas Time, Book I
- Christmas Time, Book II
- First Noel
- Good King Wenceslas
- Holiday Music: Christmas
- Holiday Music: Easter Morning
- Holiday Music: Home for Christmas
- It Came Upon a Midnight Clear
- Jingle Bells
- Serenade of Carols
- Serenade of Carols: Choral Setting

Grady, John
- Christmas with Renata Scotto: 2. Angels We Have Heard on High
- Christmas with Renata Scotto: 3. Adeste Fidelis

Grainger, Percy
- Shepherd's Hey

Gruber, F. X
- O Little Town of Bethlehem
- Silent Night

Grundman, Clare
- Three Noels

Guaraldi, Vince
- A Charlie Brown Christmas

Handel, George Frideric
- Joy to the World

Haslam, Herbert
- Special Starlight

Hawley, C.B.
- The Christ Child

Haydn, Franz Joseph
- Kindersymphonie, Hob. II; 47, C Major

Hely-Hutchinson, Victor
- Carol Symphony

Henderson, Luther
- A Canadian Brass Christmas

Herbert, Victor
- Babes in Toyland: March of the Toys

Herman, Jerry
- Best Chrsitmas of All

Hermann, Ralph
- Christmas Fantasy

Higgins, John
- Christmas on Broadway

Holcombe, Bill
- Christmas Wishes

Holdridge, Lee
- Beauty and the Beast: Theme (1987)

Holst, Gustav
- The Novello Book of Carols: In the Bleak Midwinter
- Christmas Day
- Three Christmas Songs

Hovhaness, Alan
- Triptych: 1b. As on the Night, Op. 100, No. 1b (Christmas Ode)

Jackson, Stephen, arr.
- The Novello Book of Carols: Noel Nouvelet

Jessel, Leon
- Parade of the Wooden Soldiers

Joubert, John
- The Novello Book of Carols: Torches 1
- The Novello Book of Carols: Torches II

Kapilow, Robert
- Elijah's Angel
- Chris van Allsburg's Polar Express

Kelly, Bryan
- Improvisations on Christmas Carols

Kent, Walter
- I'll Be Home for Christmas

King, Victor
- Gregoriana Christmas Suite

Kirkpatrick, W. F.
- The Novello Book of Carols: Away in a Manger

Krogstad, Bob
- The Bells of Christmas
- Christmas at the Movies

Lane, Philip
- Wassail Dances for Orchestra

Llewellyn, William
- The Novello Book of Carols: Come All You Worthy People Here; De Virgin Mary Had a Baby Boy; God Rest You Merry Gentlemen; Il est né, le divin enfant (See Him Born); King Jesus Hath A Garden;O Come All Ye Faithful; Puer Nobis (Unto Us is Born a Son); The Angel Gabriel: Gabriel's Message; The Holly and the Ivy

Luck, Arthur
- Deck the Hall & We Wish You a Merry Christmas

Lutosławski, Witold
- Twenty Polish Christmas Carols

MacLellan, Gene
- Snowbird

Mancini, Henry
- Jingle Bells/Sleigh Ride

Marks, Johnny
- Rudolph the Red-Nosed Reindeer

Martin, Hugh E.
- Have Yourself A Merry Little Christmas

Martynov, Vladimir
- Christmas Music

Matthews, H. Alexander
- The Story of Christmas: Cantata

Maxwell Davies, Peter
- Temenos, with Mermaids and Angels
- The Three Kings

Mayer, William
- Good King Wenceslas

Mendelssohn, Felix
- Hark! The Herald Angels Sing & Adeste Fidelis
- The Novello Book of Carols: Hark the Herald Angels Sing

Menotti, Gian Carlo
- Amahl and the Night Visitors:
- My Christmas

Miller, Sy & Jackson, Jill
- Let There Be Peace on Earth

Monestal, Alexander
- The Birth of our Lord: A Christmas Cantata

Monteverdi, Claudio
- Christmas Vespers

Moore, Douglas
- The Greenfield Christmas Tree

Mozart, Wolfgang Amadeus
- Exsultate Jubilate, K. 165
- German Dance #3, K. 605: Schlittenfahrt (sleigh ride)

Musgrave, Thea
- Two Christmas Carols in traditional style
- Wild Winter II

Nelson, Steve & Rollins, Jack
- Frosty the Snowman

Niles, John Jacob
- I Wonder as I Wander

Parker, Alice
- Seven Carols for Christmas

Perry, William
- Joy Shall Be Yours in the Morning

Pola & Wyle
- It's the Most Wonderful Time of the Year

Poulenc, Francis
- Gloria

Prokofiev, Sergei
- Winter Bonfire: Suite, Op. 122

Rachmaninoff, Sergei
- The Isle of the Dead, Op. 29

Reed, Alfred
- Greensleeves

Reger, Max
- Christmas with Renata Scotto: 7. Virgin's Slumber Song
- Weihnachten (Christmas), Op. 145/3

Regney & Shayne
- Do You Hear What I Hear

Respighi, Ottorino
- Trittico Botticelliano: 2. Adoration of the Magi

Richman, Lucas
- Christmas Is Coming
- Christmas Singalong
- A Christmas Wish
- Coventry Carol
- Ho! Ho! Ho!
- Presents from Santa

- Reindeer Variations
- Take a Ride with Santa

Rimsky-Korsakov, Nicolai
- Christmas Eve: Polonaise

Ringwald, Roy
- The Song of Christmas

Rodríguez, Robert Xavier
- Con Flor y Canto: from "Adoracion ambulante"
- A Gathering of Angels: Bolero for Orchestra
- Scrooge: Concert Scenes from "A Christmas Carol"

Rose, David
- Holiday for Strings

Rosenberg, Hilding Constantin
- The Holy Night (Die Heligea Natten): A Christmas Oratorio

Rouse, Christopher
- Karolju

Rutter, John
- Jesus Child!
- The Very Best Time of the Year

Saint-Saëns, Camille
- Christmas Oratorio, Op. 12

Sayre, Charles
- A Christmas Tradition
- Christmas Vision
- A Rockin' Christmas

Schubert, Franz
- Ave Maria
- Christmas with Renata Scotto: 6 Ave Maria

Schutz, Heinrich
- Christmas Story SWV 435a

Scott, Raymond
- The Toy Trumpet

Serly, Tibor
- A Little Christmas Cantata

Shaw, Robert
- The Many Moods of Christmas: Suites 1, 2, 3, 4

Sheldon, Robert
- A Most Wonderful Christmas

Silvestri & Ballard
- God Gless Us Everyone

Smith, Claude T.
- A Rhapsody on Christmas Carols

Smith, Robert W.
- Jingle Bells Forever

Stephenson, James M. III
- BaSOON It Will Be Christmas
- Bells of Christmas Suite
- God Rest Ye Merry Gentlemen
- Go Tell It On the Mountain
- Holiday Fanfare Medley No. 2
- Holiday Overture
- A Holly and Jolly Sing-Along!
- I Saw Three Ships/Jeanette, Isabella Medley
- Joy to the World
- Lo, How a Rose E'er Blooming

*(Christmas –
Stephenson, cont.)*

- The Magic of Christmas
- O Christmas Tree
- Swing Carol Fantasy
- Wassail, Wassail All Over the Tuba
- We Three Basses! from We Three Kings
- We Three Kings of Orient Are
- We Three Strings! from We Three Kings

Stillman & Allen
- Home for the Holidays

Stokowski, Leopold
- 3 Christmas Carols
- Traditional Slavic Christmas Music
- What Child Is This?

Styne, Jule
- Let It Snow! Let It Snow! Let It Snow!

Tchaikovsky, Peter Ilyich
- The Nutcracker Suite

Templeton, Alec
- Merry Christmas

Thomson, Virgil
- The Nativity

Thurlow, Jeremy, arr.
- The Novello Book of Carols: All and Some (Nowell We Sing)

Tiomkin, Dimitri
- It's a Wonderful Life (1947): Suite
- Suite from It's a Wonderful Life
- It's a Wonderful Life (1947): Theme

Torelli, Giuseppe
- Concerto Grosso for Two Violins and Orch. In G Minor, Op. 8, No. 6: Christmas Concerto

Torme & Wells
- Christmas Song (Chestnuts Roasting on an Open Fire)

Turrin, Joseph
- The Fir Tree

Tyzik, Jeff
- A Christmas Overture: Variations on Deck the Halls
- Holiday Moods: Suites No. 1, 2, 3
- The Skater's Overture: Variations on a Theme of Waldteufel
- Twelve Gifts of Christmas
- What Child is This?

Van Vactor, David
- The New Light: Prologue and 3 Canticles for Christmas

Vaughan Williams, Ralph
- Fantasia on Christmas Carols
- Fantasia on Greensleeves
- Greensleeves
- Hodie, a Christmas Cantata
- Three Chorale Hyms

Vianello, Hugo
- Christmas Kaleidoscope

Waldteufel, Emile
- Les Patineurs (Skater's Waltz), Op. 183

Ward-Steinman, David
- Season's Greetings: Festive Overture

Warrington, John
- Yuletide Festival

Waxman, Franz
- A Christmas Carol (1939): Christmas Morning & Finale
- A Christmas Carol (1939): Five Sketches after Dickens

Webb, Jimmy
- The Animals' Christmas

Wells, Robin, arr.
- The Novello Book of Carols: A Fanfare for Christmas: Hodie, Hodie; A Gallery Carol: Rejoice and Be Merry

Wendel, Robert
- Bells of Christmas
- Carol of the Bells
- Christmas a la Valse!
- Christmas Through Children's Eyes
- Classical Christmas Suite
- Evergreen Christmas
- In the Manger
- Santa Dear
- We Need a Little Christmas

Williams, John T.
- Home Alone: Three Holiday Songs

Yon, Pietro
- Gesu Bambino

Zador, Eugene
- A Christmas Overture

Halloween

Alford, Kenneth
- Hexen (Witches)

Anderson, Leroy
- The Phantom Regiment

Arnold, Malcolm
- Tam O'Shanter: Overture, Op. 51

Auber, Daniel-François
- Fra Diavolo: Overture

Bazelon, Irwin
- Fairy Tale
- Spirits of the Night

Berkeley, Lennox
- Voices of the Night, Op. 86

Bernstein, Elmer
- American Werewolf in London

Blomdahl, Karl-Birger
- The Walpurgis Night: Stage Music No. 1

Brown, Robert Bennett
- Masquerade

Chadwick, George
- Symphonic Sketches: Hobgoblin

Coleman, Cy
- Witchcraft

Corigliano, John
- The Cloisters
- Three Hallucinations

Dorati, Antal
- Night Music

Dukas, Paul
- L'Apprenti sorcier (The Sorcerer's Apprentice)

Dvořák, Antonin
- The Midday Witch, Op. 108

Elfman, Danny
- Beetlejuice: Main Title (1988)
- Music from Spider Man

Falla, Manuel de
- El amor brujo

Goldsmith, Jerry
- Poltergeist (1982): Night of the Beast (Clown Attack)
- Poltergeist (1982): The Calling
- Poltergeist (1982): The Light
- Poltergeist (1982): Theme (Carol Anne's)

Gould, Morton
- Audubon: Night Music
- Holiday Music: Halloween
- Jekyll and Hyde Variations

Grieg, Edvard
- Lyric Suite: March of the Dwarfs

Hefti, Neil
- Batman TV Theme

Herrmann, Bernard
- The Ghost of Mrs. Muir (1947)
- It's Alive (1973)
- Psycho (1960)
- The Seventh Voyage of Sinbad

Horner, James
- The Mask of Zorro: Suite (1998)

Humperdinck, Engelbert
- Hänsel und Gretel: Hexenritt (Witch's Ride)

Kaper, Bronislau
- Them!: Ant Fugue (1954)

Kasschau, Howard
- The Legend of Sleepy Hollow

Kernis, Aaron Jay
- Goblin Market

Kilar, Wojciech
- Dracula (1992)

Liszt, Franz
- Totentanz

Maggio, Robert
- Hand-Prints of Sorcerers

Mancini, Henry
- Monster Movie Music Suite

McBride, Robert
- Pumpkin Eater's Little Fugue

McCabe, John
- The Lion, the Witch, and the Wardrobe: Suite

Maxwell Davies, Peter
- The Devils: Suite

Mizzy, Vic
- Addams Family Values: Tango for Violin and Orchestra (1993)
- The Addams Family: Theme & Waltz Finale (1991)

Morris, John
- Young Frankenstein: The Transylvanian Lullaby (1974)

Musgrave, Thea
- Night Music

Mussorgsky, Modest
- Songs and Dances of Death
- A Night on Bald Mountain
- The Dream of the Peasant Gritzko

Nielsen, Carl August
- Masquerade: Overture
- Masquerade: Prelude to Act II

O'Boyle, Sean
- Waltz of Madness

Offenbach, Jacques
- Orpheus in the Underworld: Overture

Perry, Sam
- The Phantom of the Opera (1930)

Puccini, Giacomo
- Le Villi: Intermezzo – La Tregenda

Respighi, Ottorino
- La Boutique fantasque: Suite

Revueltas, Silvestre
- Sensemaya

Rodríguez, Robert Xavier
- Mascaras

Ruders, Poul
- Thus Saw St. John

Saint-Saëns, Camille
- Danse macabre, Op. 40

Salzedo, Leonard
- The Witch Boy: Suite from the Ballet
- The Witch Boy: Three Dances from the Ballet

Schnittke, Alfred
- Concerto Grosso No. 1

Shapiro, Michael
- Frankenstein

Shchedrin, Rodion
- Concerto No. 1 for Orchestra, "Naughy Limericks" (or "Mischievous Melodies")

Slatkin, Leonard
- The Raven

Strauss, Johann, Jr
- Lucifer Polka, Op. 266

Surinach, Carlos
- Feria Mágica (Magic Fair): Overture

Swanson, Howard
- Night Music

Templeton, Alec
- Night Pieces

Wagner, Richard
- Die Walkure: Ride of the Valkyries

Waxman, Franz
- The Bride of Frankenstein (1935)
- Dr. Jekyll and Mr. Hyde (1941): Suite

Weinberger, Jaromir
- The Devil on the Belfry

Welcher, Dan
- Visions of Merlin

Wendel, Robert
- Halloween Trilogy

Williams, John T.
- Harry Potter and the Sorcerer's Stone: Suite

Young, Christopher
- Species (1995): End Credits

Zaninelli, Luigi
- A Lexicon of Beasties
- Night Voices

Hanukkah

Adler, Samuel
- The Feast of Lights
- Judah's Song of Praise
- A Song of Hanukkah

Bavil, Zamir
- David and the Ark of the Covenant
- Hanukkah Light (1998)

Bloch, Ernest
- Suite hébraïque
- Trois poèmes juifs

Ellstein, Abraham
- Haftorah
- Ode to the King of Kings
- Retsei
- Sh'Ma Yisroel
- Vli Jeru Sholayim Ircho
- Yismechu

Hermann, Ralph
- Jewish Melodies

Hinds, Thomas
- Music for Hannukah: Two Folk Songs and a Hymn

Richman, Lucas
- Hanukkah Festival Overture
- Hanukkah Medley

Tyzik, Jeff
- Chanukah Suite

Wendel, Robert
- Chanukah Overture

Wernick, Richard
- Chanukah Festival Overture

Labor Day

Andriesson, Louis
- Worker's Union

Arnold, Malcolm
- Symphonic Study: Machines, Op. 30

Gould, Morton
- Something to Do - Labor Cantata

Grofé, Ferde
- Symphony in Steel

Harris, Roy
- Work

McDonald, Harl
- Festival of the Workers

Mesolov, Alexander
- The Iron Foundry, Op. 19

Shire, David
- Norma Rae: It Goes Like It Goes

Tiomkin, Dimitri
- Rhapsody of Steel (1959)

New Year

Anderson, Leroy
- Syncopated Clock

Barry, John
- Somewhere in Time

Bliss, Arthur
- Things to Come

Brubeck, Dave
- It's About Time

Cailliet, Lucien
- Fantasie on "Auld Lang Syne"

Ellington, Edward K. (Duke)
- New World A-Comin'

Haggart, Bob
- What's New?

Haydn, Franz Joseph
- Symphony No. 101 in D Major "The Clock"

Holcombe, Bill
- Fantasy on Auld Lang Syne

Kapilow, Robert
- Union Station: New Year's Eve

Liebermann, Lowell
- Revelry

Peaslee, Richard
- Arrows of Time

Perillo, Steve
- Hangoverture

Ponchielli, Amilcare
- La Gioconda: Dance of the Hours

Prokofiev, Sergei
- Cinderella: Suite No. 1, Op. 107 (Midnight)

Robinson, Earl
- In the Folded and QuietYesterdays

Schumann, Robert
- New Year Song, Op. 144 "Mit eherner Zunge, da ruft es: Gebt acht"

Strauss, Johann, Jr.
- An der schönen blauen Donau (On the Beautiful Blue Danube), Op. 314
- Annen Polka, Op. 117
- Banditen Galopp, Op. 378
- Champagne Polka, Op. 211
- Die Fledermaus: Overture
- Die Fledermaus: Du und du (You and You Waltz), Op.367
- Eine nacht in Venedig: Frühlingsstimmen Waltz, Op. 410 (Voices of Spring)

*(New Year –
STRAUSS, Johann, Jr., cont.)*
- Geschichten aus dem Wienerwald (Tales from theVienna Woods), Op. 325
- Kaiser Walzer (Emperor Waltzes), Op. 437
- Künstler (Artist's) Quadrille, Op. 201
- Künstlerleben (Artist's Life) Waltz, Op. 316
- Lagunenwalzer, Op. 411
- Morgenblätter Walzer, Op. 279
- Moulinet Polka, Op. 57
- Rosen aus dem Süden, Op. 388
- Telegramme Walzer, Op. 318
- Thousand and One Nights Waltz, Op. 346
- Tick-Tack Polka, Op. 365
- Tritsch-Tratsch Polka, Op. 214
- Unter Donner und Blitz (Thunder and Lightning Polka), Op. 324
- Wiener Blut (Vienna Blood), Op. 354
- Zigeunerbaron (Gypsy Baron): Overture

Strauss, Johann, Sr.
- Carnival Nights (Emperor Waltz) in F
- On the Beautiful Blue Danube
- Radetzky March, Op. 228

Strauss, Johann and Josef
- Pizzicato Polka

Strauss, Josef
- Ohne Sorgen Polka, Op. 245 (Chatterbox)

Suppé, Franz von
- Ein Morgen, ein Mittag und ein Abend in Wien (Morning, Noon, and Night in Vienna): Overture

Wendel, Robert
- Fantasia on "Yeroushalaim Shel Zahav"
- Rock Around the Clock
- That's It, That's All . . . The End!

Williams, Cootie & Monk, Thelonius
- 'Round Midnight

Ziehrer, Carl
- Herreinspaziert! Waltz, Op. 518

St. Patrick's

Anderson, Leroy
- Irish Suite

Ball, Ernest
- When Irish Eyes Are Smiling

Cowell, Henry
- Four Irish Tales: Tales of Our Countryside

Duff, Arthur
- Irish Suite

Esposito, Michele
- Irish Suite

Field, John
- Irish Concerto for Piano and Orchestra

Grainger, Percy
- Irish Tune from County Derry

Herbert, Victor
- Irish Rhapsody

Horner, James
- An Irish Party in Third Class

Loeffler, Charles Martin
- Five Irish Fantasies

Olcott, Chauncey
- My Wild Irish Rose

Scott, Cyril
- Irish Serenade

Stanford, Charles Villiers
- Irish Rhapsody No. 1, Op. 78

Wendel, Robert
- Baile Chruiach (Bally Croy)
- An Irish Trilogy

Whelan, Bill
- Riverdance Theme

Valentine

Arditi, Luigi
- Kiss: Il Bacio

Barber, Samuel
- The Lovers, Op. 43

Barry, John
- Robin and Marian

The Beatles
- The Great Beatles Singles Suite II: All You Need Is Love

Beethoven, Ludwig van
- Romance No. 1 in G Major, Op. 40
- Romance No. 2 in F Minor, Op. 50

Bellini, Vincenzo
- Romeo and Juliet: Overture

Bennett, Richard Rodney
- Lovesongs
- Love Spells

Berlioz, Hector
- Roméo and Juliette: Scene d'amour, Op. 17

Blake, Howard
- Heartbeat

Brubeck, Dave
- In Your Own Sweet Way

Carmichael, Hoagy
- Romance in the Dark, Nearness of You

Coleridge-Taylor, Samuel
- Hiawatha's Wedding Feast: Onaway! Awake Beloved

Drdla, Frantisek
- Souvenir

Edwards, Gus
- By the Light of the Silvery Moon

Ellington, Edward (Duke)
- I Got It Bad and That Ain't Good

Fahrbach, Jr., Philipp
- Midnight Elopement Galop

Farrar, John
- Grease: You're the One that I Want

Fisher, Fred
- Peg O' My Heart

Friedhofer, Hugo
- An Affair to Remember: The Proposal (1957)
- The Best Years of Our Lives: Suite

Garner, Erroll
- Misty

Gershwin, George
- Girl Crazy: Overture
- Crazy for You: Overture
- Embraceable You
- Love Walked In
- Man I Love
- 'S Wonderful

Glass, Philip
- Modern Love Waltz

Gold, Marty
- Ecstasy

Goldsmith, Owen
- Romanza for String Orchestra

Gordon, Michael
- Love Bead
- Sunshine of Your Love

Gottschalk, Louis Moreau
- Symphonie romantique: Night in the Tropics

Grainger, Percy
- The Power of Love

Green, John
- Body and Soul

Grieg, Edvard
- Erotik
- Ich Liebe Dich
- Wedding Day at Troldhaugen, Op. 65, no. 6

Hamlisch, Marvin
- Ice Castles Through the Eyes of Love

Henley, Larry
- Wind Beneath My Wings

Herbert, Victor
- Kiss Me Again

Hudson, Will & Mills, Irving
- Moonglow

Kabalevsky, Dmitri
- Romeo and Juliet: Musical Sketches, Op. 56

Kern, Jerome
- Smoke Gets In Your Eyes
- Way You Look Tonight

Kernis, Aaron Jay
- Valentines

Kreisler, Fritz
- Liebesfreud
- Liebesleid

- Schön Rosmarin
Lai, Francis
- Love Story: Where Do I Begin
- Love Story: Theme (1970)
- A Man and a Woman
Lang, David
- Hunk of Burnin' Love
- Loud Love Songs
Legrand, Michel
- I Will Wait for You
Lennon, John & McCartney, Paul
- I Want To Hold Your Hand
Lloyd Webber, Andrew
- Aspects of Love: Love Changes Everything
Loesser, Frank
- Heart and Soul
Lyman, Levy
- Why Do Fools Fall in Love
Mancini, Henry
- Breakfast at Tiffanys: Moon River
Mandel, Johnny
- The Sandpiper: Shadow of Your Smile
Masser, Michael
- Greatest Love of All
Maxwell Davies, Peter
- Romamor: Roma, Amor, Labyrinthus
Mendelssohn, Felix
- Midsummernight's Dream: Wedding March
Meyer, George W.
- If You Were the Only Girl in the World
Miller, Glenn
- Moonlight Serenade
Monaco, James V.
- You Made Me Love You
Mozart, Wolfgang Amadeus
- Le Nozze di Figaro (Marriage of Figaro) K. 492: Overture
Newman, Alfred
- Wuthering Heights: Cathie's Theme
- Wuthering Heights: Concert Suite
Nørgård, Per
- Three Love Songs
North, Alex
- Cleopatra: Symphonic Portrait
- Spartacus: Love Theme
Nystroem, Gösta
- Three Love Songs: 3 Kärleksvisor
Olcott, Chauncey
- My Wild Irish Rose
Pankow, James
- Colour My World
Porter, Cole
- Gay Divorcée: Night and Day
- I Get a Kick Out of You
- You Do Something to Me

Prokofiev, Sergei
- Romeo and Juliet: Suite No. 1, Op. 64a
- Romeo and Juliet: Suite No. 2, Op. 64b
- Romeo and Juliet: Scenes from the Ballet
Rasmussen, Karl Aage
- Symphony for Young Lovers
Rimsky-Korsakov, Nicolai
- Suite from La coq d'or (The Golden Cockerel): Introduction & Wedding March
Rodgers, Richard
- Carousel Waltz
- Love Me Tonight: Lover
Rodrigo, Joaquin
- Cuatro madrigals amatorios
Rota, Nino
- Romeo and Juliet (1968)
- Romeo and Juliet: A Time for Us (1968)
Rózsa, Miklós
- Ben-Hur: Love Theme
- El Cid: Love Scene
Saint-Saëns, Camille
- Romance Op. 36
Sibelius, Jean
- Romance in C Major, Op. 42
Sowerby, Leo
- Two Romantic Pieces
Strauss, Johann, Jr.
- Wein, Weib und Gesang (Wine, Women, and Song), Op. 333
Strauss, Richard
- Romanze
Talbot, Joby
- Lover's Ink
Tchaikovsky, Piotr Ilyich
- Pique Dame: Prince Yeletsky's Aria: I Love You, Dear
- Romeo and Juliet: Duet
- Romeo and Juliet: Fantasy Overture
Templeton, Alec
- Give Me Your Heart
Thomas, Augusta Read
- Sunlight Echoes
Tyzik, Jeff
- Hot Soul Medley
Washington, Ned & Bassman, George
- I'm Getting Sentimental Over You
Wagner, Richard
- Lohengrin: Bridal Chorus
Warlock, Peter
- Aspects of Love and Contentment
Waxman, Franz
- Medley: Classic Love Themes
- Peyton Place (1957): Theme "The Wonderful Seasons of Love" or "For Those Who Are Young"
Wenrich, Percy
- When You Wore a Tulip

Wonder, Stevie
- Stevie Wonder Sounds

Other Holidays

Berlin, Irving
- Easter Parade
Carter, Elliott
- Holiday Overture
Gardner, John
- Overture Half-Holiday
Gould, Morton
- Holiday Music: Easter Morning
- Holiday Music: First Thanksgiving;
Harbison, John
- The Flight into Egypt
- Sacred Ricercar
Holst, Gustav
- Let All Mortal Flesh Keep Silence
Ives, Charles
- Symphony Holidays: 4. Thanksgiving/Forefathers' Day
Mechem, Kirke
- The King's Contest
Nelson, Ronald J.
- Rocky Point Holiday
Prizeman, Robert
- Songs of Praise: Toccata (Easter)
Richman, Lucas
- Thanksgiving Hymn
Ringwald, Roy
- The Song of Easter
Ryden, William
- Amazing Grace
Vaughan Williams, Ralph
- Three Choral Hymns: Easter, Christmas, Whitsunday
Wendel, Robert
- Hymn of Thanksgiving: We Gather Together

INSTRUMENTAL POPS

Adolphe, Bruce
- I'm Inclined to New Music: A Comic Parody of Mozart's Eine Kleine Nachtmusik
Alford, Harry L.
- Clownette Novelty
Armstrong, Billie Joe
- Best of Green Day
Anderson, Leroy
- Arietta
- Balladette
- Bonnie Dundee
- Campbells Are Coming
- The Captains and The Kings
- China Doll
- Clarinet Candy
- Classical Jukebox
- Fiddle Faddle

(INSTRUMENTAL POPS – ANDERSON, cont.)

- Forgotten Dreams
- The Girl in Satin
- The Golden Years
- Home Stretch
- Leroy Anderson Favorites
- Leroy Anderson for Strings
- Lullaby of the Drums
- March of the Two Left Feet
- The Penny Whistle Song
- Plink Plank Plunk!
- Promenade
- Saraband
- Serenata
- A Trumpeter's Lullaby
- The Typewriter

Arnold, Alan
- Cartoon Sketches of the Baroque Suite
- Three Crazy Pieces
- Strike Up the Band
- Variations for Orchestra

Arnold, Malcolm
- Belles of St. Trinians: Comedy Suite
- Comedy Overture: Beckus the Dandipratt
- A Grand, Grand Overture, Op. 57
- Symphonic Study: Machines, Op. 30
- Toy Symphony, Op. 62

Bach, P.D.Q.
- 1712 Overture
- Bach Portrait
- Classical Rap
- Prelude to Einstein on the Fritz, S.E=mc2
- Requiem Mantras

Baker, David
- Concerto for Cello

Bennett, Richard Rodney
- Diversions
- Nocturnes
- Partita

Berkeley, Lennox
- Palm Court Music, Op. 81, No. 2

Bernstein, Elmer
- Great Escape March

Black, Charlie
- An Evening at Pops

Blake, Howard
- Let Music Live
- The Up and Down Man: Suite

Bush, Geoffrey
- Concerto for Light Orchestra
- A Little Concerto
- Three Little Pieces for Strings

Chiarappa, Richard
- Boom!: A Waltz for Symphony Orchestra & Bass Drum
- Lincoln & Booth: Good-bye
- Lincoln & Booth: Just Ourselves
- Lincoln & Booth: The President's Waltz
- Romp for Symphony Orchestra and (Celebrity) Triangulist
- Side Effects
- To Be Young Again

Clark, Larry
- Hooked on Classics

Costa, Paul Mario
- A Frangesa March

Creston, Paul
- A Rumor, Op. 27

De Rose, Peter
- Deep Purple

Dickerson, Roger
- Orpheus an' His Slide Trombone

Dickinson, Peter
- Merseyside Echoes

Eiger, Walter
- Concerto Grosso

Erb, Donald
- Klangfarbenfunk

Farnan, Robert
- The Peanut Polka
- Portrait of a Flirt

Fernandez, Agustín
- Una Música Escondida

Fučik, Julius
- Florentiner Marsch, Op. 214
- Under the Admiral's Flag, Op. 82

Geehl, Henry
- A Comedy Overture

Geiger, Loren
- Harpist's Heritage

German, Edward
- Coronation March and Hymn

Gershwin, George
- An American in Paris
- Gershwin in Concert

Gestor, Don
- First Love

Gillis, Don
- The Man Who Invented Music

Gold, Ernest
- Boston Pops March

Goldman, Edwin Franko
- Children's March

Goldsmith, Jerry
- Music for Orchestra

Goossens, Eugene
- Kaleidoscope
- Scherzo and Folk Tune

Gordon, Phillip
- Fitzwilliam Suite

Gottschalk, Louis Moreau
- Pasquinade Caprice

Gould, Morton
- Crinoline and Lace
- Family Album: Suite
- A Homespun Overture
- New China March
- Pop's Serenade
- Troubadour Music
- Café Rio

Hayman, Richard
- Her Name is Suzanne

Herbert, Victor
- Victorious Herbert

Hermann, Ralph
- Farmyard Frolic

Hodkinson, Sydney
- Concerto for Clarinet and Orchestra

Holcombe, Bill
- Saxanova

Hunsberger, Donald
- Under Gypsy Skies

Hunter, Frank
- Fling Went the Strings
- Twinkle Fantasia

Ives, Charles
- Country Band March

Jacob, Gordon
- Five Pieces in the Form of a Suite

Jendras, Louis F.
- The Russian Rag

Jenkins, Karl
- Passacaglia

Joplin, Scott
- The Entertainer

Kapilow, Robert
- You and Hugh

Karmon, Michael
- And the Rhythm Is Just a Little Bit Off…

Kasschau, Howard
- Country Concerto

Katz, S.
- Polskie Kwiaty (Selection of Polish Songs & Dances)

Kerker, Gustave
- The Belle of New York

Kern, Jerome
- Fluffy Ruffles: Selection
- She's a Good Fellow Selections

Kirk, Theron
- An Orchestra Primer

Kleinsinger, George
- Tubby the Tuba

Knight, Eric
- Kidnapped: Overture

Koenig, Hermann Louis
- Post Horn Galop

Kraft, William
- Simple Introduction to the Orchestra
- Vintage Renaissance

Lecuona, Ernesto
- Jungle Drums

Lundkrist, Torbjön
- Round the Orchestra in Ten Minute

MacDowell, Edward
- To a Wild Rose

Mancini, Henry
- Beaver Valley '37
- Dream of a Lifetime

- March with Mancini
- Overture to a Pops Concert
- Pennywhistle Jig

Mantovani, Annunzio Paolo
- Gypsy Legend
- Poem to the Moon

Manzanero, Armando
- It's Impossible (Somos novios)

McCabe, John
- Mini Concerto for Organ, Percussion, Audience
- Sam: ITV Music
- Sam: Theme music

Meij, Johan de
- The Lord of the Rings: Excerpts from Symphony No. 1

Moeran, E. J.
- Whythorne's Shadow

Moross, Jerome
- A Tall Story for Orchestra

Muller, Frederick
- The Rakes of Mallow (with Blue Grass Variation)

Namenwirth, Micha
- Divertimento for Toys and Orchestra

Naughtin, Matthew
- The Loony Tunes Fugue
- This Old Man Sing-Along
- The Wheels on the Bus Sing-Along

Nelson, Ronald J.
- Rocky Point Holiday

Pearson, Leslie
- Early One Morning

Peck, Russell
- Playing with Style
- The Thrill of the Orchestra

Powell, John
- Natchez on the Hill: Three Virginia Country Dances
- A Set of Three

Putman, Curly
- Green Green Grass of Home

Raksin, David
- Toy Concertino

Reed, Alfred
- A Festival Prelude

Reinagle
- Madison's March

Richards, Johnny
- Cuban Fire Suite: La Suerte de los Tontos (Fortune of Fools)

Rodríguez, Robert Xavier
- A Colorful Symphony
- The Tempest

Russell & Knight
- The Halls of Ivy

Roxburgh, Edwin
- How Pleasant to Know Mr. Lear

Russell & Knight
- The Halls of Ivy

Schickele, Peter
- 1712 Overture
- A Bach Portrait
- Classical Rap
- Prelude to Einstein on the Fritz
- Overture to "The Civilian Barber"
- Requiem Mantras
- Royal Firewater Musick
- Three Strange Cases
- Unbegun Symphony

Schreiner, Adolph
- The Worried Drummer

Schuman, William
- Newsreel in 5 Shots: Horse-Race; Fashion Show; Tribal Dance; Mondays at the Zoo; Parade

Shulman, Alan
- The Bop Gavotte
- Hup Two Three Four
- J.S. on the Rocks: Nightcap
- Popocatepeti
- Ricky-Tick Serenade

Sierra, Roberto
- A Joyous Overture

Simeone, Harry
- Flute Cocktail Scherzo and Blues for 3 or 2 Solo Flutes and Orchestra

Sowerby, Leo
- Synconata

Strauss, Johann and Josef
- Pizzicato Polka

Swayne, Giles
- Naaotwa Lala, Op. 39

Ticheli, Frank
- Angels in Architecture
- Blue Shades
- Postcard for Symphony Orchestra

Toch, Ernst
- Pinocchio, A Merry Overture

Turrin, Joseph
- Lullaby of Broadway
- Steadfast Tin Soldier

Ulbrich, Siegfried
- Blue City: Impression for Piano and Orchestra

Welcher, Dan
- Spumante

Weill, Kurt
- Kleine Dreigroschenmusik
- The Two Worlds of Kurt Weill: Berlin Suite
- The Two Worlds of Kurt Weill: New York Suite

Wendel, Robert
- April Fool Concerto
- Rock Around the Clock
- Surf's Up!
- Swing, Ludwig, Swing!

Whitney, John
- Coming of Age

Williams, Ernest S.
- Revolutionary Fantasy

Wilson, Don
- Scrambled Opera (An Orchestral Antic)

INTERNATIONAL

African

Douglas, Bill
- Concerto for African Percussion Ensemble and Orchestra

Paich & Porcaro
- Africa

Asian

Griffes, Charles Tomlinson
- Five Poems of the Ancient Far East

Lambert, Constant
- Eight Poems of Li-Po

Lincke, Paul
- Kwang Hsu (Chinese March)

British/Scottish

Anderson, Leroy
- The Bluebells of Scotland
- The Irish Suite

Arnold, Malcolm
- English Dances: Suite No. 1
- English Dances: Suite No. 2
- Four Scottish Dances

Bennett, Richard Rodney
- London Pastoral

Blyton, Carey
- Cinque Port, Op. 28

Coates, Eric
- London Suite: Knightsbridge March

Coombes, Douglas
- Sailors' Hornpipe

Dewitt, Louis O.
- Twelve English Songs

Geiger, Loren
- Rhapsody on Welsh Airs

Holst, Gustav
- Fantasia on Hampshire Folk Songs

Keillor, Garrison
- Wild Mountain Thyme: Will You Go, Darling, Go?

Lane, Philip
- Wassail Dances for Orchestra

Langey, Otto
- From the Highlands: A Selection of Scotch Melodies

Maxwell Davies, Peter
- Spinning Jenny
- A Portrait of Leigh, Lancashire, circa 1948
- Swinton Jig, on a Nineteenth Century Lancashire Fiddle Tune

Orr, Charles Wilfred
- Cotswold Hill Tune

(British/Scottish, cont.)

Richardson, Clive
- British Grenadiers

Sharp, Cecil
- Country Gardens, in F

Toch, Ernst
- Big Ben, Variation: Fantasy on the Westminster Chimes, Op. 62

Tomlinson, Ernest
- Suite of English Folk Dances

Vaughan Williams, Ralph
- English Folk Songs Suite

Wilby, Philip
- The Highland Express

Eastern European

Bartók, Béla
- Hungarian Sketches
- Rumanian Folk Dances

Brahms, Johannes
- Hungarian Dances

Constantinescu, Paul
- Ciobanasul: The Shepherd Boy

Darzins, Emils
- Latvian Folksongs

German, Edward
- Gypsy Suite

Hermann, Ralph
- Polish Polka Party

Katz, S.
- Polskie Kwiaty (Selection of Polish Songs & Dances)

Kodály, Zoltán
- Dances of Marosszek
- Variations on a Hungarian Folksong: The Peacock

Lutosławski, Witold
- Twenty Polish Christmas Carols

Mercury, Freddie
- Bohemian Rhapsody

Popper, David
- Hungarian Rhapsodie, Op. 68

Vognar, Frank, arr.
- Bohemian Folksongs

Weinberger, Jaromir
- Bohemian Songs and Dances: Six Dances
- Svandadudák (Shvanda the Bagpiper): Polka and Fugue

French

Bennett, Richard Rodney
- Suite française

Geehl, Henry
- Overture française

Offenbach, Jacques
- La vie parisienne: Overture

Irish

Anderson, Leroy
- Irish Suite

Arnold, Malcolm
- Four Irish Dances, Op. 126

Ball, Ernest R.
- When Irish Eyes Are Smiling

Cowell, Henry
- Four Irish Tales: Tales of Our Countryside

Esposito, Michele
- Irish Suite

Field, John
- Irish Concerto for Piano and Orchestra

Goossens, Eugene
- Tam O'Shanter: Scherzo

Grainger, Percy
- Country Gardens
- Irish Tune from County Derry (Londonderry Air)
- Mock Morris
- Molly on the Shore

Herbert, Victor
- Irish Rhapsody

Hermann, Ralph
- Irish Medley

Loeffler, Charles Martin
- Five Irish Fantasies

Mancini, Henry
- The Molly Maguires: Pennywhistle Jig (1970)

Olcott, Chauncey
- My Wild Irish Rose

Stanford, Charles Villiers
- Irish Rhapsody No. 1, Op. 78

Wendel, Robert, arr.
- An Irish Trilogy

Wood, Arthur
- Moorland Fiddlers for Orchestra

Italian

Armand, Charles (Puerner, Charles)
- Neapolitan Songs for Orchestra

Camilleri, Charles
- Maltese Dances

Capua, Eduardo di
- O sole mio

Carey, Julia Scott
- Legend of Old Befana

Denza, Luigi
- Funiculi-Funicula,

Hermann, Ralph
- Italian Fiesta

Tanara, Fernando
- Two Venetian Dialect Songs

Latin American

Abreu, Zequinha de
- Tico Tico

Adomian, Lan
- Cantata de la revolución Mexicana

Álvarez, Teófilo
- Marinera Trujillana

Alzedo, José Bernardo
- Himno Nacional del Perú

Arias, Clotilde
- Huiracocha for voice and orchestra

Arnold, Alan
- Three Colombian Songs

Ayars, Bo
- Cowboy Medley: Cielito lindo

Barroso, Ary
- Brazil

Benjamin, Arthur
- Two Jamaican Pieces

Benzecry, Esteban
- Colores de la Cruz del Sur (Colors of the Southern Cross)

Brubeck, Dave
- La Fiesta de la Posada

Campos, José Carlos
- Danza Rústica

Cervantes, Ignacio
- Three Cuban Dances

Chappell, Herbert
- Caribbean Concerto

Chávez, Carlos
- Cantos de México
- Chapultepec: Three Famous Mexican Pieces
- Himno nacional Mexicano (Mexican National Anthem)
- El Sol (The Sun): A Mexican Ballad

Cifuentes, Santos
- Scherzo sobre Aires Tropicales

Copland, Aaron
- El salón México

Deussen, Nancy
- Regalos

Errázuriz, Sebastián
- La Caravana

Fernandez, Carlos
- Cielito Lindo

Frank, Gabriela Len
- Three Latin-American Dances

Gade, Jacob
- Tango jalousie (Tango tzigane)

Gershwin, George
- Cuban Overture

Galindo, Blas
- Sones de mariachi

Garrido-Lecca, Celso
- Retablos Sinfónicos
- Secuencias (Sequences)

Garrido-Lecca, Gonzalo
- Arcano (Arcane)

- Toccata Op.1
Gimenez, Jeronimo
- La Boda de Luis Alonso
Gold, Marty
- Brazil
Gomez, Alice
- Festive Huapango
Goossens, Eugene
- Don Juan de Manara
- East of Suez: Incidental Music
Gould, Morton
- Latin American Symphonette
Granda, Isabel
- La Flor de la Canela
Guarnieri, Camargo
- Dansa Brasileira
Gutierrez, Pedro Elias
- Alma Llanera
Hernandez, Rafael
- El Cumbanchero
Iturriaga, Enrique
- Canción y Muerte de Rolando (Song and Death of Rolando)
- Obertura para una Comedia (Overture for a Comedy)
- Sinfonía Junín y Ayacucho: 1824
Lampe, James
- Creole Belles
Lara, Agustín
- Granada
Lecuona, Ernesto
- Danza lucumi: Danza Afro-Cubanas
López, Jimmy
- América Salvaje (Wild America)
- Fiesta! for chamber orchestra
- Fiesta! for orchestra
Marquez, Arturo
- Danzon No. 2
Marquina
- España Cani
Mejía, Adolfo
- Acuarela (Watercolor)
Mendez, Raphael
- La Virgin de la Macarena
Meza, Vinicio
- Suite Latinoamericana (Tango, Vals, Choro, Son)
Mindreau, Ernesto López
- Marinera y Tondero
Moncayo, José Pablo
- Huapango
Naughtin, Matthew
- Cinco de Mayo
Padilla, José
- El Relicario: Paso doble
Pann, Carter
- Two Portraits of Barcelona
Piazzolla, Astor
- Libertango
- Michelangelo
- Milonga del Angel
- Tango No. 1: Coral

- Tango No. 2: Canyengue
- Tangredia
- Three Minutes of Reality:
- Tango
Rebagliati, Claudio
- Rapsodia Peruana
Revueltas, Silvestre
- Sensemaya
Richards, Johnny
- Cuban Fire Suite: La Suerte de los Tontos (Fortune of Fools)
Rio, Chuck
- Tequila
Robles, Daniel Alomia
- El Condor Pasa (The Condor Flies Past)
Rodríguez, Robert Xavier
- Adoracion ambulante (A Mexican Folk Celebration)
- Piñata
- Sinfonia a la Mariachi
- Tequila Sunrise
Slonimsky, Nicolas
- My Toy Balloon: Variations on a Brazilian Tune
Soro, Enrique
- Danza Fantástica
- Tres Aires Chilenos (Three Chilean Aires)
Stucky, Steven
- Pinturas de tamayo
Villardo, Angel
- El Choclo: Tango Argentina
Villa-Lobos, Heitor
- Bachianas Brasileiras No. 1
- Bachianas Brasileiras No. 5
Zyman, Samuel
- Encuentros (1992)

Middle Eastern

Arnold, Alan
- Israeli Work Song
- Three Columbian Songs
Bavil, Zamir
- Israeli Rhapsody
Duffy, John
- Heritage Symphonic Dances
Goldsmith, Jerry
- Masada: Suite
Hermann, Ralph
- Jewish Melodies
Koch, Anton
- Adventures of Sinbad: Overture
Ranjbaran, Behzad
- Seven Passages
Scott, Raymond
- Twilight in Turkey
Sheriff, Noam
- Israel Suite

Wendel, Robert
- Fantasia on "Yeroushalaim Shel Zahav"
- Fiesta Mexicana
Williams, John T.
- Munich: Hatikva (The Hope)

Russian

Antheil, George
- Lithuanian Night
Balakirev, Mily
- Overture on Russian Folk Themes
Borodin, Alexander
- In the Steppes of Central Asia
Darzins, Volfgangs
- Latvian Folksongs
Mosolov, Alexander
- The Iron Foundry, Op. 19
Shostakovich, Dmitri
- Overture on Russian and Kirghiz Folk Themes, Op. 115

Scandinavian

Alfvén, Hugo
- Dalarapsodi - Swedish Rhapsody No. 3, Op. 47
- Midsommarvaka - Swedish Rhapsody No. 1, Op. 19
Grieg, Edvard
- Norwegian Dances, Op. 35
- Two Norwegian Airs, Op. 63
Halvorsen, Johan
- Norwegian Air
- Norwegian Fairy Pictures
- Norwegian Festival Overture, Op. 16
- Norwegian Rhapsody No. 1 in A
- Norwegian Rhapsody No. 2 in G
- Norwegian Song, Op. 31
Sibelius, Jean
- Finlandia, Op. 26, No. 7

Spanish

Chabrier, Emmanuel
- España
- España Rhapsody
Esplá, Oscar
- Fiesta: Suite de danzas
Falla, Manuel de
- El Corregidor y la Molinera
- Fuego fatuo
- Homenajes
- Noches en los jardines de España (Nights in the Gardens of Spain)
- Récit du pécheur and Pantomime
- Sept Chansons populaires espagnoles (Seven Popular Spanish Songs)
- El Sombrero de Tres Picos (The Three Cornered Hat)
- Three Cornered Hat: Three Dances

*(Spanish –
FALLA, cont.)*

- La vida breve: Interlude and Spanish Dance
- La vida breve: Spanish Dance No. 1

Fernandez, Carlos
- Cielito Lindo

Geehl, Henry
- Suite Espagnole

Granados, Enrique
- Goyescas: Intermezzo
- Tres danzas españolas
- Tonadillas

Lalo, Edouard
- Symphonie Espagnole, Op. 21

Lara, Agustín
- Granada

Lecuona, Ernesto
- Andalucia Suite
- Andalucia Suite: Malagueña
- La Comparsa (Carnival Procession)
- Malagueña

Pann, Carter
- Two Portraits of Barcelona

Penella, Manuel
- El Gato Montés (The Bobcat)

Ravel, Maurice
- Rapsodie Espagnole

Rimsky-Korsakov, Nicolai
- Capriccio Espagnol, Op. 34

Rodrigo, Joaquin
- Concierto Andaluz
- Cuatro Madrigales Amatorios

Surinach, Carlos
- Ritmo Jondo, Flamenco for Orchestra
- Sinfonietta Flamenca

Turina, Joaquin
- Canto a Sevilla, Op. 37
- Danzas fantásticas, Op. 22
- La oración del torero
- Rapsodia sinfónica, Op. 66

Yradier, Sebastian
- La Paloma (The Dove): Spanish Serenade

Viennese

Riege, Ernst
- Bezaubernde Gloriette, Konzertwalzer
- Ewiges Wien

Sieczynsky, Rudolf
- Vienna: City of My Dreams

JAZZ

Anderson, Leroy
- Jazz Legato
- Jazz Pizzicato

Antheil, George
- Jazz Sonata
- A Jazz Symphony

Arlen, Harold
- Blues in the Night

Baker, David
- Le Chat qui pêche
- Kosbro
- Two Improvisations

Bennett, Richard Rodney
- Concerto for Stan Getz

Berlin, Irving
- Alexander's Ragtime Band
- Irving Berlin-A Symphonic Portrait for Chorus & Orchestra

Bernstein, Elmer
- The Man with the Golden Arm: Suite
- The Sweet Smell of Success: Main Title

Bolcom, William
- Ragomania!

Brubaker, Jerry
- Touch of Jazz

Brubeck, Dave
- Brandenburg Gate: Revisited
- Cathy's Waltz
- The Gates of Justice
- The Gates of Justice: Out of the Way of the People
- In Your Own Sweet Way
- It's About Time
- The Light in the Wilderness
- Summer Song
- They All Sang Yankee Doodle
- Truth Is Fallen

Brubeck, Howard
- Dialogues
- Dialogues: Theme for June
- G Flat Theme

Calandrelli, Jorge
- Concerto for Jazz Clarinetand Orchestra

Carmichael, Hoagy
- Hoagy Carmichael: An American Treasure: Georgia on My Mind; Heart & Soul; Lazy River; Skylark, Stardust

Cunningham, Arthur
- Lullabye for a Jazz Baby

Custer, Calvin
- Birth of the Blues
- Duke Ellington Medley
- Salute to the Big Bands Medley for Orchestra: April in Paris; I'm Getting Sentimental Over You; PA 6-5000; Serenade in Blue; Sing, Sing, Sing

Diamond, Neil
- Jazz Singer Medley

Downey, John
- Jingalodeon

Ellington, Edward K. (Duke)
- Black, Brown and Beige
- Caravan
- Duke Ellington! Medley
- Ellington Portrait
- The Golden Broom and the Green Apple
- Grand Slam Jam
- Harlem
- It Don't Mean a Thing (If it Ain't Got That Swing)
- Liberian Suite
- Mood Indigo
- New World A-Comin'
- Night Creature
- Non-Violent Integration
- The River
- Satin Doll
- Solitude
- Sophisticated Lady
- Three Black Kings
- Tribute to the Duke

Ellington, Edward K. (Duke) and Strayhorn, Billy
- Deep South Suite: Happy Go Lucky Local
- The Essential Ellington: Music of Ellington and Strayhorn

Ellington, Mercer
- Things Ain't What They Used to Be

Flaherty, Stephen
- Ragtime "The Musical" Selections

Gershwin, George
- Fascinatin' Rhythm
- Gershwin in Concert
- I Got Rhythm
- I Got Rhythm Variations for Piano and Orchestra
- Rhapsody in Blue
- Rhapsody in Blue for Trumpet and Orchestra

Gould, Morton
- Big City Blues
- Boogie Woogie Etude
- Derivations for Solo Clarinet and Dance Band
- Minute Plus Waltz Rag

Green, John
- Body and Soul

Gruenberg, Louis
- Jazz Suite, Op. 28

Handy, W. C.
- Saint Louis Blues

Harbison, John
- Remembering Gatsby: Foxtrot for Orchestra

Heath, Dave
- Out of the Cool

Herbert, Victor
- The Enchantress: Art Is Calling for Me

Hudson, Will & Mills, Irving
- Moonglow

Joplin, Scott
- The Entertainer

- The Entertainer Rag
- Maple Leaf Rag
- Ragtime for Strings
- Ragtime Favorites for Strings
- Red Back Book

Lamb, Joseph
- Ragtime Nightingale

Lambert, Constant
- Elegiac Blues

McPartland, Marian
- Melancholy Mood

Moross, Jerome
- Biguine

Moss, John
- Salute to Ol' Blue Eyes

O'Boyle, Sean
- Ragtime

Phillips, Peter
- Interplays: Concerto for Jazz Drums, Percussion Ensemble and Orchestra

Prima, Louis
- Jump, Jive an' Wail

Proto, Frank
- Fantasy on the Saints

Richards, Johnny
- La Suerte de los Tantos (Fortune of Fools)

Richman, Lucas
- A Brentwood Rag

Ricketts, Ted
- Satchmo!: A Tribute to Louis Armstrong

Riegger, Wallingford
- Quintuple Jazz, Op. 72

Rodríguez, Robert Xavier
- Salutation Rag

Ronell, Ann
- Willow Weep for Me

Schifrin, Lalo
- Dialogues

Schuller, Gunther
- And They All Played Ragtime
- Concertino for Jazz Quartet & Orchestra (1959)
- Journey into Jazz

Scott, Raymond
- Powerhouse

Shaw, Artie
- Concerto for Clarinet and Jazz Band

Shostakovich, Dmitri
- Suite for Jazz Orchestra No. 1
- Suite for Jazz Orchestra No. 2 (formerly The "Lost" Jazz Suite)
- Suite for Variety Orchestra 1

Shulman, Alan
- Hup Two Three Four

Sowerby, Leo
- Monotony: A Symphony for Metronome & Jazz Orchestra

Stravinsky, Igor
- Ragtime

Strayhorn, Billy
- Chelsea Bridge

Turok, Paul
- Great Scott! Orchestral Suite after Joplin
- A Joplin Overture
- Ragtime Caprice, Op. 45

Turrin, Joseph
- When Tony Played the Sax

Tyzik, Jeff
- Symphonic Swing

Warren, Harry
- Serenade in Blue

Wendel, Robert
- Original Ragtime Band
- Saint Bailey's Rag
- Saint Louis Blues

Williams, Cootie
- 'Round Midnight

Wonder, Stevie
- Stevie Wonder Sounds

Zawinul, Joseph
- Birdland

Zinn, William
- Symphony in Ragtime

NOVELTY

Anderson, Leroy
- Sandpaper Ballet
- The Typewriter

Arnold, Malcolm
- A Grand, Grand Overture, Op. 57
- Toy Symphony, Op. 62

Bach, P.D.Q.
- Broadway Boogie
- Canine Cantata "Wachet Arf!"
- Prelude to Einstein on the Fritz, S.E=mc2

Baker, David
- Concertino for Cellular Phones and Symphony Orchestra

Chiarappa, Richard
- Boom!: A Waltz for Symphony Orchestra & Bass Drum
- Romp for Symphony Orchestra & (Celebrity) Triangulist
- Side Effects

Courtney, Craig
- A Musicological Journey Through Twelve Days of Christmas

Curtis-Smith, Curtis
- Great American Symphony (GAS!)

Erb, Donald
- Music for a Festive Occasion

Gould, Morton
- Hoofer Suite
- Hosedown: A Firefighter Fable
- Tap Dance Concerto

Hayman, Richard
- Pops Hoe-Down

Hermann, Ralph
- Silent Movie

Hunter, Frank
- Fling Went the Strings

Ive, Charles
- Yale-Princeton Football Game

O'Boyle, Sean
- Country Kazoo Overture

Perry, William
- Gasoline Can-Can

Rimelis, David
- Please Turn Your Cell Phones On!

Rosenhaus, Steven L.
- Kitchen Percussion March for Special Guests and Orchestra

Schickele, Peter
- Canine Cantata: "Wachet Arf"
- Prelude to Einstein on the Fritz, S.E=mc2

Schreiner, Adolph
- The Worried Drummer

Scott, Raymond
- Dinner Music for a Pack of Hungry Cannibals

Shulman, Alan
- J.S. on the Rocks: Nightcap

Stephenson, James M. III
- Concerto for Cell Phone (2006)

Stravinsky, Igor
- Circus Polka: Composed for a Young Elephant

Walker, Robert
- My Dog Has Fleas: A Capriccio for Scratch Orchestra

Wendel, Robert
- April Fool Concerto

Wilson, Don
- Scrambled Opera (An Orchestral Antic)

Wilson & Love
- Beach Boys: Medley for Orchestra

Wilson & James & Karlin
- For All We Know

PATRIOTIC

Adler, Samuel
- Show an Affirming Flame (2001)

Alford, Harry
- Colonel Bogey March

Amram, David
- Three Songs for America

Anderson, Leroy
- Governor Bradford's March
- Second Regiment Connecticut National Guard march

Antheil, George
- Water Music for 4th of July Evening

Bagley, Edwin Eugene
- National Emblem March

(PATRIOTIC, cont.)

Bendix, Victor
- Grand American Fantasia: Tone Pictures of the North and South

Bennett, Robert Russell
- Columbia, the Gem of the Ocean
- A Commemoration Symphony: Stephen Collins Foster
- The Four Freedoms

Berlin, Irving
- Berlin Patriotic Overture
- God Bless America

Binder, Abraham W.
- Poem of Freedom

Boskerck, Captain Francis Saltus Van
- Semper Paratus (1927): U.S. Coast Guard March Song

Brubeck, Dave
- They All Sang Yankee Doodle

Buck, Dudley
- Festival Overture on the American National Air: The Star-Spangled Banner

Carr, Benjamin
- Federal Overture

Cohan, George M.
- Over There
- Star-Spangled Spectacular
- You're a Grand Old Flag

Copland, Aaron
- Lincoln Portrait

Crawford, Robert MacArthur
- Air Force March: Official Song of the United States Army Air Corps

Dello Joio, Norman
- Colonial Variants: Thirteen Profiles of the Original Colonies

Demerest, Clifford
- Let Freedom Ring: Overture

Dennison, Sam
- And If Elected…

DePonte, Niel
- Bell of Freedom (2002)

Deussen, Nancy
- American Hymn
- A Field in Pennsylvania

Downey, John
- Ode to Freedom

Effinger, Cecil
- An American Hymn: A Setting of "America the Beautiful"
- Let Your Mind Wander Over America

Fillmore, Henry
- His Excellency March

Fletcher, H. Grant
- An American Overture

Gilbertson, Michael
- Reflections on Rushmore

Gillis, Don
- This Is Our America

Goldsmith, Jerry
- The Generals: Patton/MacArthur Marches

Goldstein, William
- A.M. America Overture
- Celebration Overture 1776-1976

Gottschalk, Louis Moreau
- L' Union: Paraphrase de Concert sur les Airs Nationaux

Goldsmith, Jerry
- MacArthur (1977): March

Gould, Morton
- American Ballads: Amber Waves - on "America the Beautiful"
- American Ballads: Memorials (Setting of "Taps")
- American Ballads: Saratoga Quickstep - on "The Girl I Left Behind"
- American Ballads: Star-Spangled Overture on "The Star-Spangled Banner"
- American Ballads: Settings of American Tunes for Orchestra
- American Caprice
- American Salute
- American Salute: New Edition, 2000
- America Sing: Settings of Folk Songs
- Battle Hymn of the Republic
- Classical Variations on Colonial Themes
- Columbia: Broadsides for Orchestra
- Declaration: Suite
- Dramatic Fanfares from CBS-TV documentary "World War I"
- Flares and Declamations
- Flourishes and Galop
- Foster Gallery: Suite
- Hail to a First Lady
- Holiday Music: Fourth of July
- Lincoln Legend
- Red Cavalry March
- A Song of Freedom
- Yankee Doodle

Grainger, Percy
- Marching Song of Democracy for Chorus and Orchestra

Grant, James
- Lament

Greenwood, Lee
- God Bless the U.S.A

Harris, Roy
- American Creed
- Concert Overture - March in Time of War
- Epilogue to Profiles in Courage: JFK
- Freedom's Land
- When Johnny Comes Marching Home Overture

Herbert, Victor
- President's March

Hewitt, James
- The Battle of Trenton

Isaac, Merle
- Salute to the United Nations

Ives, Charles
- Symphony Holidays: 1.Washington's Birthday
- Symphony Holidays: 3. Fourth of July
- Symphony No. 3: The Camp Meeting
- Variations on America

Johnson, Francis
- General Cadwalader's Grand March

Jones, Samuel
- Elegy for String Orchestra

Kapilow, Robert
- City Piece: DC Monuments
- Play Ball!: Casey at the Bat

Kingman, Daniel
- A Revolutionary Garland

Knight, Eric
- Americana Overture
- Canadian Tribute

Kraft, William
- Kennedy Portrait (Contextures III)

Kurtz, Eugene
- Chamber Symphony for the 4th of July

Liebermann, Lowell
- Concerto for Piccolo

Lowden, Bob
- Armed Forces Salute

McDonald, Harl
- Song of Free Nations

Meacham, Frank W.
- American Patrol

Menotti, Gian Carlo
- Landscapes and Remembrances

Moore, Donald I.
- America

Persichetti, Vincent
- A Lincoln Address

Ranjbaran, Behzad
- Thomas Jefferson

Reed, Alfred
- Pledge of Allegiance

Reinagle, Alexander
- Federal March

Reitz, Ric
- To the Flag

Richman, Lucas
- Colonial Liberty Overture

Ringwald, Roy
- The Song of America

Rodríguez, Robert Xavier
- Jargon: The Story of the American Constitution

Schickele, Peter
- American Birthday Card

Schuller, Gunther

- Music for a Celebration: A Fantasy on National Themes
Schuman, William
- American Festival Overture
- American Hymn
Shaiman, March
- American President: Big Speech, Big Finish
Shostakovich, Dmitri
- Eight English and American Folk Songs: When Johnny Comes Marching Home
Smith, Hale
- America the Beautiful
Smith, Harry C.
- Admiral Dewey's March
Smith, John Stafford
- Star-Spangled Banner
Sousa, J. P.
- El Capitan March
- Fairest of the Fair March
- Hands Across the Sea
- High School Cadets March
- King Cotton March
- The Liberty Bell March
- Semper Fidelis March
- The Stars and Stripes Forever
- Thunderer March
- Washington Post March
Sowerby, Leo
- Song for America
Steffe, William
- Battle Hymn of the Republic
Steiner, Max
- The Caine Mutiny (1954): The March
Thomson, Virgil
- Fugue on Yankee Doodle
Turok, Paul
- A Sousa Overture, Op. 43
Turrin, Joseph
- Civil War Suite
Tyzik, Jeff, arr.
- American Celebration
- Fantasy on American Themes
Vandervalk, Bruce
- A Reagan Portrait
Vardi, Emanuel
- Suite on American Folk Songs
Wagner, Joseph Franz
- Unter dem Doppeladler (Under the Double Eagle March), Op. 159
Ward, Samuel A.
- America the Beautiful
Welcher, Dan
- JFK: The Voice of Peace
Wendel, Robert
- Armed Forces March
- Fanfare for Freedom
- Towers of Light
Williams, John T.
- Suite from J.F.K.

- Liberty Fanfare
- Saving Private Ryan: Hymn to the Fallen
Yeston, Maury
- Beneath all the Stripes and Stars
Zaninelli, Luigi
- For Spacious Skies
Zwilich, Ellen Taaffe
- One Nation

POPULAR CLASSICS

Anderson, Leroy
- Arietta
- Captains and the Kings
- Clarinet Candy
- Fiddle-Faddle
Arban, Jean Baptiste
- Carnival of Venice, The: for Trumpet and Strings
Bach, J. S.
- Arioso
- Chaconne
- Fantasia & Fugue in G Minor
- Fugue in C Minor
- Prelude in E flat Minor
- Prelude from Partita in E Major
- Sheep May Safely Graze
- Sleepers Awake (Wachet Auf)
- Three Choral Preludes
- Toccata and Fugue in C for Organ: Adagio
- Toccata & Fugue in D minor, BWV 565
Balada, Leonardo
- Homage to Sarasate
Bantock, Granville
- Old English Suite
Barber, Samuel
- Adagio for Strings, Op. 11
- Commando March for Orchestra,
- The School for Scandal: Overture
Bartók, Béla
- Hungarian Sketches
- Rumanian Folk Dances
Beethoven, Ludwig van
- Konig Stephan Overture, Op. 117
- Egmont: Overture
- König Stephan: Overture, Op. 117
- Moonlight Sonata
- Romance No. 1 in G Major, Op. 40
- Romance No. 2 in F Minor, Op. 50
- Die Ruinen von Athen (Ruins of Athens), Op. 113: Turkish March and Chorus
Berkeley, Lennox
- Divertimento in B flat, Op. 18
Berlioz, Hector
- Béatrice et Bénédict: Overture
- Carnaval romain (Roman Carnival)

- Damnation de Faust: Hungarian March (Rakoczy)
- Romeo and Juliette: Scene d'amour, Op. 17
Bernstein, Leonard
- Candide Overture
- Divertimento for orchestra
Bizet, Georges
- L'Arlésienne Suite No. 1
- L'Arlésienne Suite No. 2
- Carmen: Flower Song
- Carmen: Scene & Habanera
- Carmen: Seguidilla and Duett
- Carmen: Suite no. 1
- Carmen: Suite no. 2
- Carmen: Toreador Song
- Carmen Fantasia
- Carmen Fantasie on Themes of Bizet, Op. 25
- Carmen Fantasy
- Fantaisie Brillante sur Carmen
- Fantaisie Brilliante on Themes from Bizet's "Carmen"
- Jeux d'enfants, Op. 22: Petite Suite (Children's Games)
- Symphony No. 1 in C Major
Boieldieu, François
- The Caliph of Bagdad Overture
Borodin, Alexander
- In the Steppes of Central Asia
- Nocturne
- Prince Igor: Overture
- Prince Igor: Polovtsian Dances
- String Quartet No.2: Nocturne
- Symphony No. 2
Brahms, Johannes
- Academic Festival Overture, Op 80
- Hungarian Dances
- Tragische Ouverture, Op. 81 (Tragic Overture)
- Variations on a Theme by Haydn, Op. 56a
Britten, Benjamin
- Matinees musicales, Op. 24
- Soirées musicales, Op. 9
- Young Person's Guide to the Orchestra, Op. 34
Chávez, Carlos
- Sinfonia de antigona (Symphony No. 1)
- Sinfonia India (Symphony No. 2)
Cherubini, Luigi
- Sinfonia in D Major
Chopin, Frédéric
- Fantaisie sur des airs nationaux polonais, Op. 13 (Fantasy on Polish airs)
- Polonaise Militaire, Op. 40
Cimarosa, Domenico
- I Traci Amanti: Overture

(POPULAR CLASSICS, cont.)

Copland, Aaron
- Appalachian Spring
- Billy the Kid
- Down a Country Lane
- El salón México
- Music for the Theatre
- An Outdoor Overture
- Quiet City
- Rodeo
- The Tender Land: Suite
- Variations on a Shaker Melody

Corigliano, John
- Promenade Overture

Creston, Paul
- Concertino for Marimba, Op. 21
- Concerto for Saxophone and Orchestra, Op. 26
- Fantasy for Trombone, Op. 42

Debussy, Claude
- Clair de lune

Delibes, Leo
- Sylvia: Suite: 4. Cortege de Bacchus

Delius, Frederick
- Two Pieces: 1. On Hearing the First Cuckoo in Spring; 2. Summer-Night on the River

Donizetti, Gaetano
- La fille du regiment (Daughter of the Regiment): Overture
- Lucia di Lammermoor, Act II: Sestetto: Chi mi frena

Dukas, Paul
- L'Apprenti Sorcier (The Sorcerer's Apprentice)

Dvořák, Antonin
- Carnival Overture, Op. 92
- Holoubek: The Wood Dove, Op. 110
- The Midday Witch, Op. 108 (The Noon Witch)
- Slavonic Dances
- Symphony No. 8 in G Major, Op. 88

Dyson, George
- Concerto da Camera
- Concerto Leggiero

Effinger, Cecil
- Capriccio, Op. 91

Elgar, Edward
- Chanson de matin, Op. 15
- Chanson de nuit, Op. 15
- Cockaigne Concert Overture Op. 40
- Enigma Variations, Op. 36: Nimrod
- Froissart Overture, Op. 19
- In the South: Concert Overture, Op. 50
- Introduction and Allegro, Op. 47
- Nursery Suite
- Pomp and Circumstance March No. 1 in D Major, Op. 39
- The Spanish Lady
- Wand of Youth Suite No. 1, Op. 1a
- Wand of Youth Suite No. 2, Op. 1b

Enesco, Georges
- Roumanian Rhapsody No. 1 in A Major, Op. 11

Falla, Manuel de
- Noches en los jardines de España (Nights in the Garden of Spain)
- El Sombrero de tres picos (Three-Cornered Hat)
- El Sombrero de tres picos (Three-Cornered Hat): Suite No. 2

Faure, Gabriel
- Pelleas et Melisande, Op. 80
- Pavane, Op. 50

Foss, Lukas
- Elegy for Anne Frank

Frackenpohl, Arthur
- Largo and Allegro
- Rondo Marziale
- Suite Concertino

Franck, César
- Le chasseur maudit (The Accursed Huntsman)

Friml, Rudolf
- Melodie

Gabrieli, Giovanni
- Canzon XVI

Gershwin, George
- Concerto in F Major for Piano and Orchestra
- Cuban Overture
- Lullaby for Strings
- Prelude No. 2
- Rhapsody in Blue for Trumpet and Orchestra
- Two Gershwin Portraits

Glass, Philip
- Façades
- Glassworks

Glinka, Mikhail
- Russlan and Ludmilla: Overture
- Valse Fantaisie

Gluck, Christoph Willibald
- Orfeo ed Euridice: Dance of the Blessed Spirits

Goossens, Eugene
- Prelude to "Philip II"

Gottschalk, Louis Moreau
- Symphonie romantique: Night in the Tropics

Gould, Morton
- Latin American Symphonette
- Symphonette No. 2: Pavanne
- Symphonette No. 2 (Second American Symphonette)
- Symphonette No. 3 (Third American Symphonette)

Gounod, Charles
- Marche funèbre d'une marionette (Funeral March of a Marionette)

Grainger, Percy
- In a Nutshell: Suite

Grant, James
- Lament

Grieg, Edvard
- Erotik
- Holberg Suite Op. 40
- Ich Liebe Dich
- Lyric Pieces, Op. 68, Nos. 4 and 5
- Lyric Suite: March of the Dwarfs
- Norwegian Dances, Op. 35
- Peer Gynt: Suite No. 1

Griffes, Charles Tomlinson
- Clouds
- The Pleasure Dome of Kubla Khan, Op. 8
- Poem for flute and orchestra
- Three Tone Pictures

Grofé, Ferde
- Symphony in Steel
- World's Fair Suite

Halvorsen, Johan
- Entry of the Boyards

Handel, G. F.
- Alexander's Feast Overture
- Berenice Overture
- Hercules Overture
- Julius Caesar Overture
- The King Shall Rejoice
- Music for the Royal Fireworks
- Overture in D Minor
- Water Music

Harris, Roy
- Acceleration
- Concerto in One Movement: Jamboree

Haydn, Franz Joseph
- Kindersymphonie, Hob. II; 47, C Major "Toy Symphony"
- Symphony No. 8 in G Major "Le soir"
- Symphony No. 82 "The Bear"
- Symphony No. 94 in G Major "Surprise"
- Symphony No. 100 in G Major "Military"
- Symphony No. 101 in D Major "The Clock"

Herbert, Victor
- Natoma: Grand Fantasia
- Natoma: Prelude to Act III

Herold, Louis
- Zampa Overture

Holst, Gustav
- A Fugal Overture, Op. 40, No. 1
- The Perfect Fool: Ballet Music Op. 39
- St. Paul's Suite
- The Planets

Humperdinck, Engelbert
- Hansel and Gretel

Ibert, Jacques
- Divertissement

Jalbert, Pierre
- In Aeternam

Kabalevsky, Dmitri
- The Comedians, Op. 26: Suite

Khachaturian, Aram
- Gayeneh: Suite No. 1
- Gayeneh: Suite No. 2
- Gayeneh: Suite No. 3
- Masquerade Suite
- Spartacus: Suite No. 1
- Spartacus: Suite No. 2
- Spartacus: Suite No. 3

Kreisler, Fritz
- Liebesfreud
- Liebesleid
- Three Old Viennese Dances: Schön Rosmarin

Lalo, Edouard
- Symphonic Espagnole, Op. 21

Layton, Billy Jim
- Three Dylan Thomas Poems, Op. 3

Lehár, Franz
- Merry Widow Overture
- Merry Widow Waltz
- The Merry Widow: Symphonic Paraphrase

Lemare, Edwin
- Andantino in D Flat

Liszt, Franz
- Hungarian Rhapsody No. 1, F Minor
- Hungarian Rhapsody No. 2
- Mephisto Waltz No. 1: from Lenau's Faust
- Mephisto Waltz No. 2: from Lenau's Faust
- Totentanz

Mascagni, Pietro
- Cavalleria Rusticana: Intermezzo

Massenet, Jules
- Thaïs: Méditation

Mendelssohn, Felix
- Hebrides Overture, Op. 26: Fingal's Cave
- Heimkehr aus der Fremde, Op. 89 (Son and Stranger)
- Märchen von der Schönen Melusine, Op. 32 (Fair Melusina)
- Midsummernight's Dream, Op. 21

Milhaud, Darius
- Two Marches

Moeran, E. J.
- Serenade in G

Montgomery, Bruce
- Concertino for Strings

Mozart, Wolfgang Amadeus
- Adagio in E, K. 261
- Der Schauspieldirektor (The Impresario) K. 486: Overture
- Don Giovanni, K.527: Overture
- Eine Kleine Nachtmusik, K. 525
- Il Re Pastore, K. 208: Overture
- Le Nozze di Figaro (Marriage of Figaro) K. 492: Overture
- Lucio Silla, K. 135: Overture
- The Marriage of Figaro: Aprite un po'quegl'occhi
- The Marriage of Figaro: Deh vieni non tardar
- The Marriage of Figaro: Dove sono i bei momenti
- The Marriage of Figaro: Porgi amor (Cavatina)
- Symphony No. 41, K.551, C Major (Jupiter) K. 551

Mussorgsky, Modest
- Pictures at an Exhibition

Nicolai, Otto
- Merry Wives of Windsor: Overture

Nielsen, Carl August
- Helios Overture, Op. 17
- Little Suite, Op. 1
- Rhapsodic Overture

Offenbach, Jacques
- Les Contes d'Hoffmann (Tales of Hoffmann): Intermezzo & Barcarolle
- Grande Cancan
- Orpheus in the Underworld: Galop (Can Can)
- Orpheus in the Underworld: Overture

Orr, Buxton
- A Carmen Fantasy

Pachelbel, Johann
- Canon in D
- Chaconne for String Orchestra
- Kanon in D Major

Penderecki, Krysztof,
- Threnody: To the Victims of Hiroshima

Persichetti, Vincent
- Sinfonia Janiculum, Op. 113

Piazzolla, Astor
- Cuatro Estaciones Porteñas (The Four Seasons in Buenas Aires)

Piston, Walter
- The Incredible Flutist: Ballet Suite for Orchestra

Popper, David
- Hungarian Rhapsodie, Op. 68

Poulenc, Francis
- Sinfonietta

Prokofiev, Sergei
- Cinderella: Suite No. 1, Op. 107
- Cinderella: Suite No. 2, Op. 108
- Lieutenant Kijé Suite, Op. 60
- Love for Three Oranges: March & Scherzo
- Peter and the Wolf: Symphonic Tale for Narrator and Orchestra, Op. 67
- Romeo and Juliet: Scenes from the Ballet
- Romeo and Juliet: Suite No.1, Op. 64a
- Romeo and Juliet: Suite No.2, Op. 64b
- Romeo and Juliet: Suite No. 3, Op. 101

Puccini, Giacomo
- I Crisantemi (The Chrysanthemums)
- Madam Butterfly

Rachmaninoff, Sergei
- The Isle of the Dead, Op. 29

Ravel, Maurice
- Bolero
- Daphnis et Chloé, Suite No. 1 and 2
- Ma Mère l'Oye (Mother Goose)
- Ma Mère l'Oye: Prelude et Danse du rouet
- Pavane pour une infante défunte (Pavane for a dead princess)
- Rapsodie Espagnole

Respighi, Ottorini
- Antiche danze ed arie (Ancient Airs and Dances): Set II
- Antiche danze ed arie (Ancient Airs and Dances): Set III

Revueltas, Silvestre
- Sensemaya

Reznicek, Emil Nikolaus von
- Donna Diana: Overture

Rimsky-Korsakov, Nicolai
- Capriccio Espagnol, Op. 34
- May Night: Overture
- Scheherazade: 4.The Sea-Shipwreck
- Suite from La Coq d'or (The Golden Cockerel): Introduction & Wedding March

Rodgers, Richard
- Victory at Sea

Rossini, Gioacchino
- La cenerentola (Cinderella): Overture
- La gazza ladra (The Thieving Magpie): Overture
- Guillaume Tell (WilliamTell): Overture
- Il barbiere di Siviglia (Barber of Seville): Overture
- L'Italiana in Algeri: Overture
- Semiramide: Overture

Saint-Saëns, Camille
- Introduction and Rondo Capriccioso: Trumpet in Bb and Orchestra
- Havanaise, Op. 83
- La nuit Op. 114
- Romance in F, Op. 36
- Samson and Delilah: Bacchanale

Sallinen, Aulis
- At the Palace Gates, Op. 68a: Overture

Sarasate, Pablo de
- Carmen Fantasie on Themes of Bizet, Op. 25
- Zigeunerweisen, Op. 20

(POPULAR CLASSICS, cont.)

Satie, Erik
- Gymnopedie No. 1 & 3

Schubert, Franz
- Der Teufel als Hydraulicus, D. 4: Overture
- Die Zauberharfe (Rosamunde), D. 644: Overture
- Symphony No.5 in B flat Major, D. 485
- March Militaire Nos. 1&2

Schumann, Robert
- Overture, Scherzo and Finale

Shostakovich, Dmitri
- Festive Overture, Op. 96
- Hamlet: Incidental Music to the Stage Production, Op. 32a
- Hypothetically Murdered, Op. 31a

Sibelius, Jean
- Academic March
- Karelia Suite, Op. 11
- Suite Champêtre, Op. 98b

Smetana, Bedrich
- Má Vlast (My Fatherland): 2.Vltava (Moldau)
- Má Vlast: 3.Sarka

Steffe, William
- Battle Hymn of the Republic

Strauss, Johann Jr.
- Die Fledermaus (Laughing Song)
- Egyptian March, Op. 335
- Eine nacht in Venedig: Fruhlingsstimmen Waltz (Voices of Spring), Op. 410
- Eljen A Magyar! Polka, Op.332 (Long Live the Magyar)
- Geschichten aus dem Wienerwald (Tales from the Vienna Woods), Op. 325
- Im Krapfenwaldl, Polka française, Op. 336
- Künstler Quadrille, Op. 201
- Künstlerleben (Artist's Life) Waltz, Op. 316
- Morgenblätter (Morning Papers) Walzer, Op. 279
- Moulinet Polka, Op. 57
- Perpetuum mobile, Op. 257
- Persian March, Op. 289
- Rosen aus dem Süden (Roses of the South), Op. 388
- Telegramme Walzer, Op. 318
- Tick-Tack Polka, Op. 365
- Tritsch-Tratsch Polka, Op.214
- Waldmeister Overture

Strauss, Josef
- Aus Ferienreisen, Op. 133
- Plappermaulchen Polka Schnell, Op. 245 (Chatterbox)

Strauss, Richard
- Also Sprach Zarathustra, Op. 30
- Till Eulenspiegels lustige Streiche (Till Eulenspiegel's Merry Pranks), Op. 28

Stravinsky, Igor
- L'Oiseau de feu (Firebird): Suite (1919)

Sullivan, Arthur
- Mikado: Overture
- Mikado Selections
- Patience Selections
- Pineapple Poll Suite
- Pirates of Penzance Selections
- Ruddigore Overture
- Ruddigore Selections
- Yeoman of the Guard: Overture
- Yeoman of the Guard Selections

Suppé, Franz von
- Dichter und Bauer (Poet and Peasant): Overture
- Die leichte Kavallerie (Light Cavalry): Overture
- Ein Morgen, ein Mittag und ein Abend in Wien (Morning, Noon, and Night in Vienna): Overture
- Die schöne Galathea (The Beautiful Galatea): Overture

Tchaikovsky, Piotr Ilyich
- Eugen Onegin: Polonaise
- Festival Coronation March for Alexander III
- Marche slave, Op. 31
- Ouverture solennelle (1812 Overture) Op. 49
- Pique Dame: Prince Yeletsky's Aria: I Love You, Dear

Thomson, Virgil
- The Seine at Night
- Wheat Field at Noon

Tower, Joan
- Fanfare for the Uncommon Woman (1986)

Vaughan Williams, Ralph
- Fantasia on Greensleeves
- Fantasia on a Theme by Thomas Tallis
- Rhosymedre

Verdi, Giuseppe
- Aïda: Triumphal March
- Aïda: Triumphal March and Ballet
- La Forza del Destino: Overture
- Nabucco: Overture
- I vespri siciliani: Overture

Villa-Lobos, Heitor
- Bachianas Brasileiras no. 1
- Bachianas Brasileiras no. 5
- Concerto for Harmonica

Vivaldi, Antonio
- Concerto, Op. 44, No. 16, R.V. 570, F Major
- Le Quattro staggioni (The Four Seasons) Op. 8, Nos. 1-4

Wagenaar, Bernard
- Concert Overture

Wagner, Richard
- Eine Faust Ouvertüre (A Faust Overture)
- Götterdämmerung: Siegfried's Rhine Journey
- Lohengrin: Bridal Chorus
- Tristan und Isolde: Prelude and Liebestod
- Die Walküre: Ride of the Valkyries
- Die Walküre: Wotan's Farewell and Magic Fire Music

Walton, William
- Crown Imperial: Coronation March

Weber, Carl Maria von
- Oberon: Overture
- Turandot: Overture and March

Ziehrer, C. M.
- Herreinspaziert! Waltz, Op. 518

POPULAR SONGS

Ades, Hawley
- Twentiana

Anderson, Leroy
- Old MacDonald Had a Farm

Arlen, Harold
- Stormy Weather

The Beatles
- Abbey Road Suite
- Beatles!!! A Medley of Lennon and McCartney Favorites
- Beatles Medley
- Beatles Hits Medley
- Classic Beatles: A Medley
- The Great Beatles Singles Suite I: Strawberry Fields Forever
- A Long and Winding Road
- Sergeant Pepper's Lonely Hearts Club Band
- Songs from the White Album

Bennett, Richard Rodney
- Variations on a Nursery Tune

Berlin, Irving
- A Pretty Girl Is Like a Melody
- When I Lost You

Blake, Howard
- Nursery Rhyme Overture

Brahms, Johannes
- Hungarian Dances

Brel, Jacques
- If You Go Away

Bullock, Jack
- NYC: Here's to the Big Apple

Cailliet, Lucien
- Variations on "Pop! Goes the Weasel"

Capua, Eduardo di
- O sole mio

Carmichael, Hoagy
- Georgia on My Mind
- Hoagy Carmichael: An American Treasure
- Nearness of You
- Stardust

Castelnuovo-Tedesco
- Naomi and Ruth: Ruth's Aria

Cohan, George M.
- Cohan Medley
- George M. Cohan Medley: Symphonic Suite
- George M. Cohan Salute

Coots, J. Fred
- For All We Know

Cory, George
- I Left My Heart in San Francisco

Costa, Francesco Antonio
- Era di maggio

Croce, Jim
- Jim Croce in Concert

Custer, Calvin
- Beach Boys Medley
- Salute to the Big Bands Medley for Orchestra

Davis, Albert O.
- Buffalo Gals: In Blue Grass Style

Daugherty, Michael
- Motown Metal

Denver, John
- Annie's Song
- John Denver Celebration (1987)

De Rose, Peter
- Deep Purple

Edwards, Gus
- By the Light of the Silvery Moon

Ellington, Edward K. (Duke)
- It Don't Mean a Thing (If it Ain't Got That Swing)

Estefan, Gloria
- Gloria Estefan: Her Greatest Hits

Faith, Percy
- Quia, Quia (Kee-a, Kee-a)

Foster, Stephen
- Jeanie with the Light Brown Hair

Garner, Erroll
- Misty

Gershwin, George
- Gershwin in Concert
- 'S Wonderful

Gilpin, Greg
- The Music of MGM (A Choral Medley)

Gold, Julie
- From a Distance

Gold, Mary
- Rainy Day Medley

Gould, Morton
- Five Spirituals

Grainger, Percy
- County Derry Air

Green, John
- Body and Soul

Guion, David
- Mam'selle Marie
- De Laud's Baptizin'

Hageman, Richard
- At the Well

Haggart, Bob
- What's New?

Herbert, Victor
- Ah Sweet Mystery of Life
- The Enchantress: Art Is Calling for Me

Hermann, Ralph
- Farmyard Frolic
- Irish Medley
- Italian Fiesta
- Jewish Melodies
- Old Song Medley
- Old Song Medley No. 2
- Old Song Medley No. 3
- Old Timers Waltz Medley No. 1
- Old Timers Waltz Medley No. 2

Holcombe, Bill
- Evening at Pops

Hupfeld, Herman
- As Time Goes By

Jackson, Michael
- A Michael Jackson Spectacular

Joel, Billy
- The Best of Billy Joel
- Just the Way You Are

Kern, Jerome
- Smoke Gets in Your Eyes
- They Didn't Believe Me
- Way You Look Tonight

Kosma, Joseph
- Autumn Leaves

Lake, M. L.
- Old Timers Waltz

Lang, Philip J.
- Dark Eyes

Legrand, Michel
- I Will Wait for You
- The Windmills of Your Mind

Lennon, John & McCartney, Paul
- The Best of the Beatles
- Beatles Medley
- I Want to Hold Your Hand

Lowden, Bob
- Remembering the Beatles

MacColl, Ewan
- The First Time Ever I Saw Your Face

MacLellan, Gene
- Put Your Hand in the Hand

Malotte, Albert Hay
- The Lord's Prayer

Mancini, Henry
- Breakfast at Tiffanys: Moon River

Mandel, Johnny
- The Sandpiper: The Shadow of Your Smile

Marsh, Gerry Jon
- Hamburger Suite

Mason, Jack
- O Bury Me Not On the Lone Prairie

Masser, Michael
- Greatest Love of All

Meyer, George W.
- If You Were the Only Girl in the World

Mills, Gordon & Reed, Les
- It's Not Unusual

Moeran, E. J.
- Lonely Waters

Monaco, James V.
- You Made Me Love You

Moss, John
- Salute to Ol' Blue Eyes

Muller, Frederick
- Arkansas Traveler: In Bluegrass Style

North, Alex
- Unchained Melody (1955)

Norton, George A.
- Round Her Neck She Wore a Yellow Ribbon

Phillips, John
- Monday, Monday

Phillips & Gilliam
- California Dreamin'

Popp, André
- Love is Blue (L'Amour est bleu)

Porter, Cole
- Cole Porter Suite
- Gay Divorcée: Night and Day

Revaux, J. & Francois, C.
- My Way

Richardson, Neil
- Polly-Wolly Doodle

Richman, Lucas
- Beautiful Dreamer: Stephen Foster's America

Ringwald, Roy
- O Brother Man

Robles, Daniel Alomia
- El Condor Pasa (The Condor Flies Past)

Romberg, Sigmund
- A Tribute to Romberg

Rosenhaus, Steven L.
- American Spiritual Festival
- Lionel Richie in Concert

Ryden, William
- Amazing Grace

Shire, David
- With You I'm Born Again

Shur, Thomas
- Smooth: Santana

Smith, Hale
- Abide With Me

(POPULAR SONGS – SMITH, cont.)
- Amazing Grace

Sondheim, Stephen
- A Little Night Music: Send In the Clowns

Stevens, Ray
- Everything is Beautiful

Tyzik, Jeff
- Amazing Grace
- Hot Soul Medley

Valens, Ritchie
- La Bamba

Washington, Ned & Bassman, George
- I'm Getting Sentimental Over You

Weatherly, Fred E.
- Danny Boy

Webb, Jimmy
- MacArthur Park

Weill, Kurt
- The Two Worlds of Kurt Weill - Berlin Suite
- The Two Worlds of Kurt Weill - Berlin Suite: Bilbao Song)
- The Two Worlds of Kurt Weill - Berlin Suite: J'Attends un navire
- The Two Worlds of Kurt Weill - Berlin Suite: Mack the Knife
- The Two Worlds of Kurt Weill - Berlin Suite: Surabaya Johnny
- The Two Worlds of Kurt Weill - Berlin Suite: Theme from "Mahogonny"
- The Two Worlds of Kurt Weill - New York Suite
- The Two Worlds of Kurt Weill - New York Suite: I Got a Marble and a Star
- The Two Worlds of Kurt Weill - New York Suite: Mack the Knife
- The Two Worlds of Kurt Weill - New York Suite: Polly's Lied
- The Two Worlds of Kurt Weill - New York Suite: Speak Low

Wendel, Robert
- Back to the Fifties!
- George M. Cohan Overture
- An Old Fashioned Summer
- Rock Around the Clock
- Surf's Up!

Wenrich, Percy
- Put On Your Old Grey Bonnet
- When You Wore a Tulip

Williams, Paul
- Rainy Days and Mondays

Wonder, Stevie
- Stevie Wonder Sounds

Yarrow, Peter
- Puff the Magic Dragon

SEASONS

Adler, Samuel
- Summer Stock: A Short Merry Overture

Anderson, Leroy
- The First Day of Spring
- Summer Skies

Brubeck, Dave
- Summersong

Christensen, James
- Snow Chase

Corigliano, John
- Midsummer Fanfare

Darke, Harold
- In the Bleak Midwinter

Delius, Frederick
- Two Pieces

Duke, Vernon
- April in Paris

Felder & Feller
- Snow, Snow, Beautiful Snow

Gershwin, George
- Porgy and Bess: Summertime

Glazunov, Alexander
- The Seasons: Autumn
- The Seasons: Spring
- The Seasons: Summer
- The Season: Winter

Gould, Morton
- Cinerama Holiday: Skier's Waltz
- Harvest

Grieg, Edvard
- To Spring

Harris, Roy
- Horn of Plenty

Jameson & Feller
- Summertime, Summertime

Kosma, Joseph
- Autumn Leaves

MacLellan, Gene
- Snowbird

Mayer, William
- Scenes from "The Snow Queen"

Mendelssohn, Felix
- Midsummernight's Dream, Op. 21: Overture
- Midsummernight's Dream, Op. 21: Scherzo

Muczynski, Robert
- A Serenade for Summer

Piazzolla, Astor
- Cuatro Estaciones Porteñas (The Four Seasons in Buenas Aires)

Strauss, Johann, Jr.
- Frühlingsstimmen Waltz, Op. 410 (Voices of Spring)

Styne, Jule
- Let It Snow! Let It Snow! Let It Snow!

Svoboda, Tomáš
- Overture of the Season, Op. 89

Tchaikovsky, Peter Ilyich
- Symphony No. 1 in G Minor, Op. 13 (Winter Dreams)

Tsontakis, George
- Winter Lightning

Vivaldi, Antonio
- Le quattro staggioni (The Four Seasons), Op. 8, Nos. 1-4

Wendel, Robert
- An Old Fashioned Summer

SPACE

Arlen, Harold
- It's Only a Paper Moon

Barber, Samuel
- Capricorn Concerto

Beethoven, Ludwig van
- Moonlight Sonata

Berners, Lord
- Triumph of Neptune: Adagio, Variations and Hornpipe

Carmichael, Hoagy
- Stardust

Chattaway, Jay
- Star Trek: The Next Generation

Chávez, Carlos
- El Sol (The Sun)-A Mexican Ballad

Creston, Paul
- Sunrise in Puerto Rico

Courage, Alexander
- Star Trek: The Television Series "The Menagerie" (1964)

Custer, Calvin
- Star Trek Through the Years

Debussy, Claude
- Clair de lune

Edwards, Gus
- By the Light of the Silvery Moon

Eidelman, Cliff
- Star Trek 6: The Undiscovered Country (1991)

Giacchino, Michael
- Star Trek: End Credits (2009)

Goldsmith, Jerry
- Capricorn One: Overture & Main Title
- Star Trek: Main Theme
- Star Trek: Voyager (1995)
- Star Trek I: The Motion Picture "The Director's Cut"
- Star Trek I: The Motion Picture "The Klingon Battle"
- Star Trek I: The Motion Picture "The New Enterprise"
- Star Trek I: The Motion Picture Theme (1979)
- Star Trek 5: The Final Frontier: Suite (1989)
- Star Trek 8: First Contact (1996)
- Star Trek 9: Insurrection (1998)

- Star Trek 10: Nemesis (2002)
- The Sum of All Fears (2002)

Herrmann, Bernard
- The Day the Earth Stood Still: Arrival (1951)

Holst, Gustav
- The Planets

Horner, James
- Apollo 13: Main Title, End Credits, Re-Entry, and Splashdown
- Cocoon: Cocoon Theme
- Star Trek 2: The Wrath of Khan (1982)
- Star Trek 3: The Search for Spock "Stealing the Enterprise" (1984)

Hunter, Frank
- Twinkle Fantasia

Jones, Ron
- Star Trek, The Next Generation: Suite (1989)

Mancini, Henry
- The Lifeforce

McCarthy, Dennis
- Star Trek: Deep Space Nine Suite
- Star Trek 7: Generations "Overture"

Miller, Glenn
- Moonlight Serenade

North, Alex
- 2001 Space Odyssey: Fanfare
- 2001: A Symphonic Suite in Four Movements

Ottman, John
- Astro Boy (2009): End Titles
- Astro Boy (2009): Theme

Ponce, Manuel
- Estrellita (Star of Love)

Rosenman, Leonard
- Star Trek 4: The Voyage Home

Ruggles, Carl
- Sun-Treader

Secunda, Sholom
- Tango de la luna

Strauss, Josef
- Sphärenklänge (Music of the Spheres Waltz), Op. 235

Strauss, Richard
- Introduction (Sunrise)

Ticheli, Frank
- Shooting Stars

Welcher, Dan
- Haleakala: How Maui Snared the Sun
- Symphony No. 2 "Night Watchers"

Williams, John T.
- Close Encounters of the Third Kind
- Close Encounters of the Third Kind, Theme from
- E.T. Suite: Adventures on Earth
- Selections from E.T.
- Theme from E.T.
- Empire Strikes Back Medley
- Raiders of the Lost Ark: Raiders March
- Highlights from Return of the Jedi
- Star Wars Suite
- Star Wars: Episode I Phantom Menace
- Star Wars: Selections from The Phantom Menace
- Star Wars: Episode II: Attack of the Clones (Across the Stars Love Theme)
- Star Wars: Main Theme

SPORTS

Anderson, Leroy
- Home Stretch

Arnaud, Leo
- Bugler's Dream, Fanfare to the Olympic Games

Bernstein, Elmer
- The Babe: End Credits

Bizet, Georges
- Carmen: Toreador Song

Bolcom, William
- Seattle Slew Suite

Chiarappa, Richard
- Paean to the Scholar, the Athlete and the Artist

Conti, Bill
- Rocky Highlights
- Rookie of the Year

Corigliano, John
- Tournaments

Deussen, Nancy
- Ascent to Victory

Ellington, Edward K. (Duke)
- Grand Slam Jam

Estefan, Gloria
- Reach

Felder & Feller
- Linebacker Music

Fučik, Julius
- Entrrance of the Gladiators, Op. 68

Goldsmith, Jerry
- Hoosiers (1986): Suite
- Rudy: Theme for Flute and Chamber Orchestra

Gould, Morton
- The Jogger and the Dinosaur

Hayman, Richard
- Freddie the Football

Holcombe, Bill
- Casey at the Bat

Ives, Charles
- Yale-Princeton Football Game

Kapilow, Robert
- Play Ball!: Casey at the Bat

Kleinsinger, George
- Brooklyn Baseball Cantata

Knight, Eric
- The Great American Bicycle Race

Mancini, Henry
- The Great Race: They're Off

Mendez, Raphael
- La Virgin de la Macarena

Menken & Ashman
- Go the Distance

O'Boyle, Sean
- Olympia Australis

Pann, Carter
- Slalom

Perry, William
- Gasoline Can-Can

Proto, Frank
- Casey at the Bat

Rózsa, Miklós
- Ben Hur: Parade of the Charioteers

Schuman, William
- Casey at the Bat: A Baseball Cantata

Smith, Robert W.
- Great Steamboat Race

Tilzer, Albert von
- Take Me Out to the Ball Game

Traditional
- Football Song Hits: Eastern
- Football Song Hits No. 2: Western
- Football Song Hits No. 4: East-South

Vangelis
- Chariots of Fire Suite

Waldteufel, Emile
- Le Patineurs (Skater's Waltz), Op. 183

Waxman, Franz
- Prince Valiant (1954)

Williams, John T.
- Call of the Champions: 2002 Olympic Theme
- Olympic Fanfare and Theme
- Olympic Spirit
- Summon the Heroes

Zimmer, Hans
- Gladiator: Music from the Movie

TRAVEL

Adams, John
- Short Ride in a Fast Machine

Anderson, Leroy
- Horse and Buggy

Arnold, Malcolm
- Sound Barrier Rhapsody, Op. 38

Bennett, Robert Russell
- Overture to the Mississippi

Bernstein, Elmer
- Airplane!: Suite

Bolcom, William
- Inventing Flight

Cohan, George M.
- Royal Vagabond Selections for Orchestra

Creston, Paul
- Sunrise in Puerto Rico

(TRAVEL, cont.)

Danielpour, Richard
- Toward the Splendid City

Dello Joio, Norman
- Southern Echoes

Duke, Vernon
- April in Paris

Ellington, Duke
- Caravan

Evans, Dale
- Happy Trails to You (1952)

Gershwin, George
- An American in Paris

Gillis, Don
- Atlanta Suite: 5. Peachtree Promenade

Goodwin, Ron
- Those Magnificent Men in Their Flying Machines (1965)

Gould, Morton
- Windjammer: Main Theme, The Ship

Guion, David
- Arkansas Traveler

Hodkinson, Sydney
- Overture: A Little Travelin' Music

Howard, James
- Peter Pan (2003): Flying

Hudson, Will & Mills, Irving
- Moonglow

Jarre, Maurice
- A Passage to India: A Symphonic Journey (1984)

Kapilow, Robert
- Union Station

Kuster, Kristin
- Iron Diamond

Lambert, Constant
- The Rio Grande

Lumbye, H. C.
- Copenhagen Steam Railway Gallop

Maggio, Robert
- Boardwalk

Mayer, William
- Of Rivers and Trains

Merrill, Bob
- Take Me Along!: Overture

Milhaud, Darius
- Globetrotter Suite

Mitchell, Lyndol
- Railroad Suite

Robinson, Earl
- The Lonesome Train

Rodríguez, Robert Xavier
- Flight: The Story of Wilbur and Orville Wright

Roylance, Dave & Galvin, Bob
- Tall Ships Suite
- Voyager

Smith, Robert W.
- Great Steamboat Race

Strauss, Johann, Jr.
- Vergnugungszug Polka, Op. 281 (Excursion Train)

Thomson, Virgil
- The Seine at Night

Toch, Ernst
- Big Ben, Variation – Fantasy on the Westminster Chimes, Op. 62

Tiomkin, Dimitri
- The High and the Mighty (1954): Suite

Turina, Joaquin
- Canto a Sevilla, Op. 37

Wagner, Richard
- Götterdämmerung: Siegfried's Rhine Journey

Wendel, Robert
- From Sea to Shining Sea
- The Tall Ships
- That's It, That's All. . . The End!

Wilby, Philip
- The Highland Express

Young, Victor
- Around the World in 80 Days (1956): Overture & Epilogue

TV

Alford, Harry L.
- Colonel Bogey March

Amundson, Steven
- Three's Company

Burgon, Geoffrey
- Brideshead Variations
- Chronicles of Narnia Suite
- Suite from Bleak House
- Suite from Martin Chuzzlewit
- Suite from Testament of Youth

Chattaway, Jay
- Star Trek: The Next Generation

Courage, Alexander
- Star Trek: The Television Series "The Menagerie" (1964)

Curnow, James arr.
- TV Spectacular

Daniel, Eliot
- I Love Lucy: Theme

Daugherty, Michael
- Metropolis Symphony

DeVorzon & Botkin
- Nadia's Theme: Young and the Restless

Elfman, Danny
- Simpsons Theme

Elliot, Jack
- Theme from Charlie's Angels

Evans, Dale
- Happy Trails to You (1952)

Gold, Marty
- Jeopardy theme

Goldsmith, Jerry
- Masada: Suite
- QB VII: Suite
- Television Themes Medley
- The Twilight Zone (1961): The Invaders

Griffin, Merv
- An Hour with the Game Shows
- Jeopardy Theme

Hagen, Earl
- Television Medley

Hefti, Neil
- Batman Theme

Holdridge, Lee
- Beauty and the Beast: Theme (1987)

Jenkins, Karl
- Palladio: Concerto Grosso for String Orchestra

Johnson, Laurence (Laurie)
- The Avengers: Theme (1961)

Jones, Ron
- Star Trek, The Next Generation: Suite (1989)

Kamen, Michael
- Band of Brothers

Lawrence, David
- High School Musical
- High School Musical 2

Mancini, Henry
- Mystery Movie Theme
- Peter Gunn
- Peter Gunn Meets Mr. Lucky
- Peter Gunn Theme
- The Thorn Birds Theme
- The Thorn Birds: Meggie's Theme

Markowitz, Richard
- Wild, Wild West (1965)

Mizzy, Vic
- Addams Family Values: Tango for Violin and Orchestra (1993)
- The Addams Family: Theme & Waltz Finale (1991)

Rose, David
- Little House on the Prairie: Meet Me at the Fair (1974)

Schifrin, Lalo
- Mission Impossible: Theme

Shire, David
- Raid on Entebbe (1977): Theme

Steiner, Fred
- Perry Mason (1956): Theme

Steiner, Max
- The Caine Mutiny (1954): The March

Stevens, Morton
- Hawaii Five O (1968)

Strommen, Carl
- Salute to TV

Tiomkin, Dimitri
- Rawhide (1959): Theme
- The Wild, Wild West (1965): Suite

Vangelis
- Hymne
Wendel, Robert
- Flintstones Meet the Jetsons
- Jonny Quest
- Smurfs: March
- When TV Was Young
Williams, Charles
- The Dream of Olwen
Williams, John T.
- The Mission (NBC News Theme)

VIDEO GAMES

Brower, Russell
- World of Warcraft
O'Donnell & Salvatori
- Halo Suite: Halo Theme
Eskula, Jari
- Commodore 64 Medley: A Medley of Classic 1980's Computer Game Themes
Ford, Ralph
- Suite from Video Games Live
Mitchell, Darren
- Turok 2
Naughtin, Matthew
- Mario! Jump!
Tallarico, Tommy & Plowman, Michael Richard
- Advent Rising Suite: Bounty Hunter Theme

WEATHER

Anderson, Leroy
- First Day of Spring
Arnold, Malcolm
- Whistle Down the Wind
Arlen, Harold
- Stormy Weather
- Wizard of Oz: Over the Rainbow
Berners, Lord
- Triumph of Neptune: Adagio, Variations and Hornpipe
Copland, Aaron
- Appalachian Spring: Suite
Dorff, Daniel
- Sunburst
Garrop, Stacy
- Thunderwalker
Gershwin, George
- Foggy Day
Gold, Marty
- Rainy Day Medley
Gordon, Michael
- Sunshine of Your Love
Griffes, Charles Tomlinson
- Clouds
Howard, James
- Snow Falling on Cedars Suite
MacDermot, Galt
- Aquarius: Let the Sunshine In
Mancina, Mark
- Twister: Main Theme

Mendelssohn, Felix
- A Midsummernight's Dream: Scherzo
Quilter, Roger
- Where the Rainbow Ends Suite
Rimsky-Korsakov, Nicolai
- Scheherazade: 4. The Sea-Shipwreck
Silvers, Louis
- April Showers
Sousa, John Philip
- Thunderer March
Strauss, Johann, Jr.
- Unter Donner und Blitz (Thunder and Lightning Polka), Op. 324
Strauss, Richard
- Introduction (Sunrise)
Thomas, Augusta Read
- Sunlight Echoes
Tsontakis, George
- Winter Lightning
Vivaldi, Antonio
- Concerto, Op. 44, No. 16, R.V. 570, F Major
- Le quattro staggioni (The Four Seasons), Op. 8, Nos. 1-4
Whitney, John
- Light Rays
Williams, Paul
- Rainy Days and Mondays

APPENDIX D

Works Listed by Title

Refer to the composer listing in the main body of the volume for complete information on a work.

3 Christmas Carols – Stokowski
007, Themes from: A Medley for Orchestra – Custer, Calvin
10: It's Easy to Say – Mancini, Henry
25th Annual Putnam County Spelling Bee – Finn
42nd Street (1981) – Warren, H.
42nd Street: Overture – Warren, H.
55 Days at Peking (1963): Suite – Tiomkin, Dimitri
1712 Overture – Schickele
1941: March of 1941 – Williams, J.
2001 Space Odyssey: Fanfare – North, Alex
2001: A Symphonic Suite in Four Movements – North, Alex

A

A.M. America Overture – Goldstein
Abbey Road Suite – The Beatles
Abduction of Figaro: Overture – Schickele
Abide With Me – Smith, H.
Abyss, The: Finale – Silvestri, Alan
Academic Festival Overture, Op 80 – Brahms
Academic March – Sibelius
Academy Award Medley – Mancini, Henry
Acceleration – Harris, R.
Accordion Dance – Antheil
Acuarela (Watercolor) – Mejía, Adolfo
Adagio for Strings, Op. 11 – Barber
Adagio in E, K. 261 – Mozart
Addams Family: Theme & Waltz Finale (1991) – Mizzy, Vic
Addams Family, The (1991): Theme and Waltz Finale – Shaiman, Marc
Addams Family Values: Tango for Violin and Orchestra (1993) – Mizzy, Vic
Addams Family Values (1993): Tango – Shaiman, Marc

Adeste fidelis – Gould
Admiral Dewey's March – Smith, H.
Adoracion Ambulante: A Mexican Folk Celebration – Rodriguez
Advent Rising Suite: Bounty Hunter Theme – Tallarico, Plowman, & Richard
Adventures of Sinbad: Overture – Koch
Affair to Remember, An: The Proposal (1957) – Friedhofer, Hugo
Africa – Paich & Porcaro
African Queen: Portrait (1951) – Gray, Allan
African Trilogy – Diamond
Afro-American Symphony – Still
Agatha: Suite – Blake
Agony and the Ecstasy, The (1965): Suite – Goldsmith, Jerry
Ah Sweet Mystery of Life – Herbert
Aïda: Triumphal March and Ballet – Verdi
Air de Ballet – Herbert, Victor
Air Force March: Official Song of the United States Army Air Corps – Crawford, Robert MacArthur
Air Force One (1997): Theme – Goldsmith, Jerry
Airplane!: Suite – Bernstein, Elmer
Alamo, The (1960): Short Suite – Tiomkin, Dimitri
Alexander's Feast Overture – Handel
Alexander's Ragtime Band – Berlin
Alfie – Bacharach
Alice the Firefighter – Dessau
Alice's Monkey Business – Dessau
Alice in the Wooly West – Dessau
Alice Helps the Romance – Dessau
Alien (1979): End Title – Goldsmith, Jerry
Alien 3: Adagio – Goldenthal, Elliot
Aliens Suite No. 1 – Horner
Aliens Suite No. 2 – Horner
Alma Llanera – Gutierrez, Pedro Elias
Alone at the Frontier: Concerto for Improvised Instrument – Heath

Also Sprach Zarathustra, Op. 30 – Strauss, R.
Amahl and the Night Visitors – Menotti
Amarcord – Rota, Nino
Amazing Grace – Smith, H.
Amazing Grace – Ryden, William
Amber Waves – on "America the Beautiful" from American Ballads – Gould
America – Moore, D.
America the Beautiful – Ward
América Salvaje (Wild America) – López, Jimmy
American Variations on – Ives
American Ballads [Jubilo] – Gould
American Birthday Card – Schickele
American Caprice – Gould
American Carnival: Ballet Suite – Owens, R.
American Celebration – Tyzik
American Concerto – Zwilich
American Creed – Harris, R.
American Dance Suite – Smith, J.
American Fanfare – Ayars, Bo
American Fanfare – Hailstork
American Fantasie – Herbert
American Festival Overture – Schuman
American Folk Rhapsody, No. 1: Four American Folk Songs – Grundman
American Folk Rhapsody, No. 2 – Grundman
American Folk Songs – Vardi
American Frontier – Custer
American Hymn – Deussen
American Hymn – Schuman
American Hymn: A Setting of "America the Beautiful" – Effinger
American in Paris – Gershwin
American in Paris Suite – Gershwin
American Overture – Fletcher
American Patrol – Meacham
American Portrait – Layton
American Salute – Gould

American Sing: Settings of Folk Songs – Gould
American Spiritual Festival – Rosenhaus, Steven L.
American Suite – Meyer, R.
American Tail: Somewhere Out There – Horner
American Werewolf in London – Bernstein, Elmer
Americana – Harris, A.
Americana Overture – Knight
Amistad: Dry Your Tears, Afrika – Williams, J.
Amor brujo – Falla
An der schönen blauen Donau (On the Beautiful Blue Danube), Op. 314 – Strauss, Joh., Jr.
Anastasia: In the Dark of the Night; Journey to the Past; Learn to Do It Waltz; Once Upon a December; Paris Holds the Key; Rumor in St. Petersburg – Flaherty
Anastasia Medley – Flaherty
Anastasia Suite – Flaherty
And If Elected… – Dennison
And the Rhythm Is Just a Little Bit Off… – Karmon
And They All Played Ragtime – Schuller
Andalucia – Lecuona
Andrew Lloyd Webber: A Concert Celebration – Lloyd Webber
Angela's Ashes: Two Concert Pieces – Williams, J.
Angels' Dance – Amundson
Angels in Architecture – Ticheli, Frank
Angels We Have Heard on High; Joy to the World – Handel
Animals' Christmas – Webb, Jimmy
Anna and the King of Siam Suite (1946) – Herrmann, Bernard
Anne of the Indes (1951): Overture – Waxman, Franz
Annen Polka, Op. 117 – Strauss, Joh., Jr.
Annie, Muscal Highlights from – Strouse, Charles
Annie, Selections from – Strouse, Charles
Annie Get Your Gun: Overture – Berlin
Annie's Song – Denver
Anniversary Overture, Op. 99 – Arnold, M.
Antiche danze ed arie (Ancient Airs and Dances) – Respighi
Apartment – Theme [Jealous Lover] – Williams, C.
Apollo 13: Main Title, End Credits, Re-Entry and Splashdown – Horner, James
Appalachian Fling – Jendras, Louis F.
Appalachian Spring: Suite – Copland

Apprenti Sorcier (Sorcerer's Apprentice) – Dukas
April Fool Concerto – Wendel
April in Paris – Duke
April Showers – Silvers
Aquarius: Let the Sunshine In – MacDermot
Arcano (Arcane) – Garrido-Lecca, Gonzalo
Archipelago "Rhumba" – Antheil
Arietta – Anderson
Arioso – Bach, J. S.
Arkansas Traveler – Guion
Arkansas Traveler: In Bluegrass Style – Muller, Frederick
Arlesienne Suites – Bizet
Armed Forces March – Wendel
Armed Forces Salute – Lowden
Around the World at Christmas Time – Chase, Bruce
Around the World in 80 Days (1956): Overture & Epilogue – Young, Victor
Arrows of Time – Peaslee
As Time Goes By – Custer
Ascent to Victory – Deussen
Aspects of Love and Contentment – Warlock
Astaire! – Mancini, Henry
As Time Goes By – Hupfeld, Herman
Astro Boy (2009): End Titles – Ottman, John
Astro Boy (2009): Theme – Ottman, John
At the Fair – Powell, John H.
At the Palace Gates: Overture, Op. 68a – Sallinen
At the Well – Hageman
Atlanta Suite: Peachtree Promenade – Gillis
Attack and Celebration – Schurmann
Audubon: Night Music – Gould
Auntie Mame: Overture (1958) – Kaper, Bronislau
Aus Ferienreisen, Op. 133 – Strauss, Jos.
Autumn Leaves – Kosma, Joseph
Avatar (2009): Suite – Horner, James
Ave Maria – Schubert
Avengers: Theme, The (1961) – Johnson, Laurence (Laurie)

B

Babe, The: End Credits – Bernstein, Elmer
Babes in Toyland (March of the Toys) – Herbert
Bach Portrait – Schickele

Bachianas Brasileiras No. 1 – Villa-Lobos
Bachianas Brasileiras No. 5 – Villa-Lobos
Back to the Fifties! – Wendel
Back to the Future (Madrid Version) – Silvestri, Alan
Back to the Future Suite – Silvestri, Alan
Bad and the Beautiful: Mvt. I: Love Is for the Very Young – Raksin
Bad and the Beautiful: Mvt. II: The Acting Lesson – Raksin
Bad and the Beautiful: Mvt. III: The Quickies and Sneak Preview – Raksin
Ballad de Ballet – Templeton
Ballad of Brotherhood – Wagner, Joseph
Balladette – Anderson
Ballet Egyptien – Luigini
Ballet Suite No. 1 (1949) – Shostakovich
Ballet Suite No. 2 (1951) – Shostakovich
Ballet Suite No. 3 (1951) – Shostakovich
Ballet Suite No. 4 (1953) – Shostakovich
Band of Brothers – Kamen
Band of Brothers: Suite (2001) – Kamen
Banditen Galopp, Op. 378 (Bandit's Galop) – Strauss, Joh., Jr.
Baraza – Bliss
Bartered Bride: Three Dances – Smetana
Basic Instinct (1992): Main Title Theme – Goldsmith, Jerry
Basic Instinct (1992): Suite – Goldsmith, Jerry
BaSOON It Will Be Christmas – Stephenson, James M. III
Batman TV Theme – Hefti
Battle Hymn of the Republic – Gould
Battle Hymn of the Republic – Steffe
Battle of Trenton – Hewitt
Beach Boys Medley – Custer
Beach Boys: Medley for Orchestra – Wilson & Love
Beatles Medley – The Beatles
Beatles Hits Medley – The Beatles
Beatles Medley – Lennon & McCartney
Beatles!!! A Medley of Lennon and McCartney Favorites – The Beatles
Beatrice et Bénédict: Overture – Berlioz
Beautiful Dreamer: Stephen Foster's America – Richman
Beauty and the Beast – Menken, Alan

Beauty and the Beast, Highlights from – Menken, Alan
Beauty and the Beast: Theme (1987) – Holdridge, Lee
Beaver Valley '37 – Mancini, Henry
Beetlejuice: Main Title (1988) – Elfman, Danny
Bell of Freedom (2002) – DePonte, Niel
Belle of New York, The – Kerker, Gustave
Belle of the Ball – Anderson
Belles of St. Trinians: Comedy Suite – Arnold, M.
Bells of Christmas, The – Krogstad, Bob
Bells of Christmas – Wendel
Bells of Christmas Suite – Stephenson, James M. III
Bells of St. Mary's – Adams, Emmett
Beloved Infidel (1959): Theme – Waxman, Franz
Beneath all the Stripes and Stars – Yeston, Maury
Ben Hur: Choral Suite – Rózsa
Ben Hur: Parade of the Charioteers – Rózsa
Beowulf (2007): I Shouldn't Have Told You – Silvestri, Alan
Berenice Overture – Handel
Berlin Patriotic Overture – Berlin
Best Christmas of All – Herman, Jerry
Best of the Beatles – Lennon & McCartney
Best of Bond – Barry
Best of Everything: London Calling – Newman, Alfred
Best of Green Day – Armstrong, Billie Joe
Best Years of Our Lives, The: Suite – Friedhofer, Hugo
Bezauberndre Gloriette, Konzertwalzer – Riege
Bicentennial Fanfare – Piston
Big Ben, Variation – Fantasy on the Westminster Chimes, Op. 62 – Toch
Big City Blues – Gould
Big Country: Main Title Theme – Moross
Big Country: Suite – Moross
Big Movie Suite – Tyzik
Big Sky, The (1952): Suite – Tiomkin, Dimitri
Big Sur – Simons, Netty
Big Top – Maggio
Biguine – Moross
Billy Joel, The Best of – Joel, Billy
Billy the Kid: Prairie Night and Celebration – Copland
Birdland – Zawinul
Birdman of Alcatraz: Finale – Bernstein, Elmer

Birth of the Blues – Custer
Birth of our Lord, The: A Christmas Cantata – Monestal, Alexander
Birthday Ode to "Big Daddy" Bach – Schickele
Birthday Variations – Naughtin
Bishop's Wife, The: Ice Skater's Waltz (1947) – Friedhofer, Hugo
Black Lion Dances – Cole, Hugo
Black, Brown and Beige – Ellington
Blanche, Overture to – Richman
Blazing Saddles (1973) – Morris, John
Bleak House – Burgon
Bluebells of Scotland – Anderson
Blue City, Impression for Piano – Ulbrich
Blue Max, The (1996): Suite – Goldsmith, Jerry
Blue Shades – Ticheli, Frank
Blue Tail Fly – Davis, Jimmy
Blue Tango – Anderson
Bluegrass Festival: Suite for Bluegrass Quartet – Rhodes, P.
Blues in the Night – Arlen
Boardwalk – Maggio
Boda de Luis Alonso: Intermedio – Gimenez
Body and Soul – Green, John
Bohemian Folksongs – Vognar
Bohemian Rhapsody – Mercury
Bohemian Songs and Dances: Six Dances – Weinberger
Bolero – Ravel
Bolt, Suite from the ballet, Op. 27a (Ballet Suite No. 5) – Shostakovich
Bonnie Dundee – Anderson, Leroy
Boogie Woogie Etude – Gould
Boom! for Bass Drum & Orchestra – Chiarappa
Bop Gavotte – Shulman
Boston Pops March – Gold, E.
Botany Bay (1953): Suite – Waxman, Franz
Bourne Identity – Powell, John
Boutique fantasque: Suite (after Rossini) [The Fantastic Toy Shop] – Respighi
Boy Who Could Fly, The: Theme – Broughton, Bruce
Boyfriend: Concert Suite – Maxwell Davies
Boys from Brazil, The (1978): Waltz & The Boys – Goldsmith, Jerry
Brandenburg Gate: Revisited – Brubeck, Dave
Braul: The Sash Dance – Constantinescu
Braveheart: Main Title & End Credits (1995) – Horner, James
Brazil – Barroso
Brazil – Gold, M.

Brazilian Polka – Robinson & Giovannini
Breakfast at Tiffanys: Moon River (1961) – Mancini, Henry
Brentwood Rag – Richman, Lucas
Bride of Frankenstein, The (1935) – Waxman, Franz
Bride Wore Black, The: A Musical Scenario – Herrmann, Bernard
Bride Wore Black: A Suite in Four Movements – Herrmann, Bernard
Brideshead Variations – Burgon, G.
Bridge on the River Kwai – Arnold, M.
Brigadoon Suite – Loewe, F.
Brigham Young March (1940) – Newman, Alfred
British Grenadiers – Richardson
Broadway Boogie – Schickele
Broadway on Parade – Sayre, Charles
Broadway Showstoppers – Sayre, Charles
Broadway Tonight – Chase, Bruce
Brooklyn Baseball Cantata – Kleinsinger
Buffalo Gals: In Blue Grass Style – Davis, Albert O.
Buffalo Gals – Davis, Jimmy
Bugler's Holiday – Anderson
Burleske – Strauss, R.
By the Light of the Silvery Moon – Edwards, Gus

C

Cabaret – Kander, John
Cabeza de vaca – Antheil
Café Rio – Gould
Caine Mutiny, The (1954): The March – Steiner, Max
California Concerto – Reisfeld
California Dreamin' – Phillips & Gilliam
Caliph of Bagdad Overture – Boieldieu
Call of the Champions: 2002 Olympic Theme – Williams, J.
Calypso Souvenir – Gould
Camelot: Selections – Loewe, F
Campane di Ravello: A Celebration Piece for Sir Georg Solti – Corigliano
Campbells Are Coming – Anderson, L.
Canadian Brass Christmas – Henderson
Canadian Tribute – Knight, E.
Canción y Muerte de Rolando (Song and Death of Rolando) – Iturriaga, Enrique
Candide: Glitter and Be Gay – Bernstein, L.
Candide Overture – Bernstein, L.
Candide Suite – Bernstein, L.

Canine Cantata "Wachet Arf!" – Schickele
Canon in D – Pachelbel
Cantata de la revolución Mexicana – Adomian
Canto a Sevilla, Op. 37 – Turina
Cantos de Mexico – Chavez
Canzon XVI – Gabrieli
Capitan March – Sousa
Capriccio Espagnol, Op. 34 – Rimsky-Korsakov
Capricorn Concerto – Barber
Captain from Castile – Newman, Alfred
Captain from Castile: Pedro and Catania – Newman, Alfred
Captains and the Kings – Anderson, L.
Captains Courageous (1937): Suite – Waxman, Franz
Capricorn One: Overture & Main Title – Goldsmith, Jerry
Caravan – Ellington, E.
Caravana, La – Errázuriz, Sebastián
Caribbean Concerto – Chappell
Carmen – Bizet, Georges
Carmen Fantasie – Bizet
Carmen Fantasie on Themes of Bizet, Op. 25 – Sarasate
Carmen Fantasy – Bizet
Carmen Fantasy – Orr, Buxton
Carmen Suite (after Georges Bizet) – Shchedrin
Carmen: Suites no. 1 and no. 2 – Bizet
Carnaval des animaux (Carnival of the Animals) – Saint-Saëns, Camille
Carnaval romain (Roman Carnival) – Berlioz
Carnival Nights (Emperor Waltz) in F – Strauss, Joh., Sr.
Carnival of Venice, The: for Trumpet and Strings – Arban, Jean Baptiste
Carnival Overture, Op. 92 – Dvořák
Carol of the Bells – Wendel
Carol Symphony – Hely-Hutchinson
Caroline Mathilde: Concert Suites from Act I and Act II – Maxwell Davies
Carols for an Island Christmas – Ellis, D.
Carols, The Novello Book of:
　All and Some [Nowell We Sing] – Thurlow
　Angel Gabriel [Gabriel's Message] – Joubert
　Away in a Manger – Kirkpatrick, W.
　Come All You Worthy People Here [A Somerset Carol] – Llewellyn
　Divin enfant, Le [See Him Born]; King Jesus Hath a Garden – Llewellyn
　Gallery Carol [Rejoice and Be Merry] – Wells, Robin

(Carols, The Novello Book of, cont.)
　God Rest You Merry Gentlemen – Llewellyn
　Hark the Herald Angels Sing – Mendelssohn
　Holly and the Ivy – Llewellyn
　How Soft, Upon the Ev'ning Air – Dunhill
　Il est né – Llewellyn
　In the Bleak Midwinter – Holst
　Joy to the World – Handel
　Noel nouvelet – Jackson, Stephen
　O Come All Ye Faithful – Llewellyn
　O Magnum Misterium – Gabrielli
　Once in Royal David's City – Gauntlett & Mann & Wells
　Puer Nobis [Unto Us Is Born a Son] – Llewellyn
　Torches 1 and II – Joubert
　Virgin Mary Had a Baby Boy – Llewellyn
Carousel – Rodgers, R.
Cartoon Sketches of the Baroque Suite – Arnold, A.
Casey at the Bat – Holcombe, Bill
Casey at the Bat – Proto
Casey at the Bat: A Baseball Cantata – Schuman
Cast Away: Crossroads – Silvestri
Castle Creek: Fanfare & Overture – Welcher
Casualties of War: Elegy for Brown – Morricone
Cat Duet: Duetto buffo di due gatti – Rossini
Catch Me If You Can (Escapades for Alto Sax) – Williams, J.
Cathédrale engloutie – Debussy
Cathy's Waltz – Brubeck, Dave
Cats – Lloyd Webber
Caucasian Sketches: Procession of the Sardar – Ippolitov-Ivanov
Cavalleria Rusticana: Intermezzo – Mascagni
Celebration – Bennett, Richard
Celebration – Zwilich
Celebration Overture 1776-1976 – Goldstein
Celebration Strut for Orchestra – Gould
Celebrations of May-Day – Høffding
Cenerentola (Cinderella) Overture – Rossini
Central Park in the Dark – Ives
Chaconne – Bach, J. S.
Chaconne for String Orchestra – Pachelbel
Chairman Dances: Foxtrot for Orchestra – Adams, John

Chamber Symphony for the 4th of July – Kurtz
Champagne Polka, Op. 211 – Strauss, Joh., Jr.
Chanson de Matin, Op. 15 – Elgar
Chanson de Nuit, Op. 15 – Elgar
Chanukah Festival Overture – Wernick
Chanukah Overture – Wendel
Chanukah Suite – Tyzik
Chapultepec (Three Famous Mexican Pieces) – Chávez
Charade – Mancini, Henry
Chariots of Fire – Vangelis
Charlie's Angels, Theme from – Elliot, Jack
Charlie Brown Christmas, A – Guaraldi, Vince
Charlotte's Web: Themes for Flute and Orchestra – Elfman, Danny
Chasseur maudit, Le (The Accursed Huntsman) – Franck
Chat qui pèche – Baker, David
Checkmate: Five Dances Suite – Bliss
Cheers!-A Celebration March – Gould
Chelsea Bridge – Strayhorn
Chenoo Who Stayed to Dinner – Schickele
Chestnuts Roasting on an Open Fire – Torme & Wells
Cheyenne Autumn Suite – North, Alex
Chicago – Kander, John
Chicago: Medley – Kander, John
Chicago Concerto – Peaslee
Chicago Skyline – Ran
Chicken Reel – Anderson
Chicken Run: Final Escape; Make a Crate – Powell
Children's March – Goldman.
China Doll – Anderson
Chinatown (1974): Suite – Goldsmith, Jerry
Chinatown: Theme (1974) – Goldsmith, Jerry
Choclo, El (Tango Argentina) – Villaldo
Chocolat: Suite (2000) – Portman, Rachel
Chorus Line, Selections from a – Hamlisch, Marvin
Chris van Allsburg's Polar Express – Kapilow
Christ Child, The – Hawley, C.B.
Christmas a la Valse – Wendel
Christmas at the Movies – Krogstad, Bob
Christmas is Coming – Richman.
Christmas Carol – Bax
Christmas Carol (Suite: Scrooge) – Addinsell
Christmas Carol, A (1939): Christmas Morning & Finale – Waxman, Franz

Christmas Carol, A (1939): Five Sketches after Dickens – Waxman, Franz
Christmas Day – Holst
Christmas Eve: Polonaise – Rimsky-Korsakov
Christmas Fantasia for Strings – Bacon
Christmas Fantasy – Hermann, Ralph
Christmas Favorites – Chase, Bruce
Christmas Festival Overture: Ukrainian Noel – Berezovsky
Christmas Festival – Anderson
Christmas Kaleidoscope – Vianello, Hugo
Christmas Lullaby – Blake
Christmas Medley – Ayars
Christmas Music – Dello Joio
Christmas Music – Erb
Christmas Music – Ives
Christmas Music – Martynov
Christmas on Broadway – Higgins, John
Christmas Oratorio, Op. 12 – Saint-Saëns
Christmas Overture – Zador
Christmas Overture: Variations on Deck the Halls – Tyzik
Christmas Singalong – Richman
Christmas Song (Chestnuts Roasting on an Open Fire) – Torme & Wells
Christmas Story, SWV 435a – Schutz
Christmas Sweet – Davis, C.
Christmas - That Special Time of the Year – Custer, Calvin
Christmas Through Children's Eyes – Wendel
Christmastide – DeLarmarter, Eric
Christmas Time, Book I – Gould
Christmas Time, Book II – Gould
Christmas Tradition, A – Sayre, Charles
Christmas Treat – Bowden
Christmas Vespers – Monteverdi
Christmas Vision – Sayre, Charles
Christmas Wish – Richman
Christmas Wishes – Holcombe, Bill
Christmas with Renata Scotto:
  1. Silent Night – Gruber
  2. Angels We Have Heard on High – Grady
  3. Adeste Fidelis – Grady
  4. Joy to the World – Handel
  5. Christmas Song (Cantique de Noel) – Adam, Adolphe
  6 Ave Maria – Schubert
  7. Virgin's Slumber Song – Reger
  8. What Child Is This? – Dix
Christmas (See Weihnachten), Op. 145/3 – Reger, Max
Christopher Columbus – Bliss
Chronicles of Narnia Suite – Burgon

Chronicles of Narnia: The Lion, The Witch and The Wardrobe – Gregson-Williams
Cid, El – Rózsa
Cider House Rules, The (1999) – Portman, Rachel
Cinco de Mayo–Naughtin
Cielito lindo – Fernandez
Cielito lindo [See Cowboy Medley] – Ayars, Bo
Cimarron (1960): Suite – Waxman, Franz
Cinderella Suite No. 1, Op. 107 – Prokofiev
Cinderella, Suite No.2, Op. 108 – Prokofiev
Cinema Paradiso: First Youth; Love Theme; Theme – Morricone
Cinerama Holiday: Skier's Waltz; Suite – Gould
Cinque Port, Op. 28 – Blyton
Ciobanasul (The Shepherd Boy) – Constantinescu
Circus Overture – Toch
Circus Overture: Sideshow – Schuman
Circus Polka – Stravinsky
Circus World (1964): John Wayne March – Tiomkin, Dimitri
Citizen Kane Overture – Herrmann, B.
City Lights – Chaplin, Charlie
City Piece: DC Monuments – Kapilow
Cityscape – Higdon
Civil War Suite – Turrin
Civilian Barber, Overture to The – Schickele
Clair de lune – Debussy
Clarinet Candy – Anderson
Classic Beatles: A Medley – The Beatles
Classical Christmas Suite – Wendel
Classical Jukebox – Anderson
Classical Rap – Schickele
Classical Variations on Colonial Themes – Gould
Cleopatra: Symphonic Portrait – North, Alex
Cloisters – Corigliano
Close Encounters of the Third Kind – Williams, J.
Close Encounters of the Third Kind, Theme from – Williams, J.
Clouds – Griffes
Cockaigne Concert Overture Op. 40 – Elgar
Cocoon Theme – Horner
Cohan Medley – Cohan
Cole Porter Classics – Porter
Cole Porter Salute – Porter
Columbia, the Gem of the Ocean – Bennett, R. R.
Colonel Bogey March – Alford
Colonial Liberty Overture – Richman

Colonial Variants: Thirteen Profiles of the Original Colonies – Dello Joio
Colores de la Cruz del Sur (Colors of the Southern Cross) – Benzecry, Esteban
Colorful Symphony – Rodriguez
Colour My World – Pankow, James
Columbia: Broadsides – Gould
Come Back, Little Sheba (1953): Reminiscences for Orchestra – Waxman, Franz
Comedians, The, Op. 26: Suite – Kabalevsky
Comedy Overture – Geehl
Comedy Overture: Beckus the Dandipratt – Arnold, Malcolm
Commemoration Symphony: Stephen Collins Foster – Bennett, Robert Russell
Coming of Age – Whitney
Coming of the King – Gillis
Commando March – Barber
Commemoration – Wendel
Commodore 64 Medley: A Medley of Classic 1980's Computer Game Themes – Eskula, Jari
Commonwealth Christmas Overture, Op. 64 – Arnold, Malcolm
Comparsa, La (Carnival Procession) – Lecuona
Con flor y canto from "Adoracion ambulante" – Rodríguez
Concert Overture – Wagenaar
Concert Overture: March in Time of War – Harris, Roy
Concertino for Cellular Phones and Symphony Orchestra – Baker, David
Concertino for Jazz Quartet & Orchestra (1959) – Schuller, Gunther
Concertino for Marimba, Op. 21 – Creston
Concertino for Strings – Montgomery
Concerto da Camera – Dyson
Concerto for African Percussion Ensemble – Douglas, Bill
Concerto for Cello – Baker, David
Concerto for Cell Phone (2006) – Stephenson, James M. III
Concerto for Clarinet – Hodkinson
Concerto for Clarinet and Jazz Band – Shaw, Artie
Concerto for Flute, Oboe, Bassoon, Op. 44, No. 16, F Major – Vivaldi
Concerto for Harmonica – Villa-Lobos
Concerto for Jazz Clarinet and Orchestra – Calandrelli
Concerto for Light Orchestra – Bush
Concerto for Piccolo – Liebermann
Concerto for Saxophone, Op. 26 – Creston
Concerto for Stan Getz – Bennett, Rob.

Concerto Grosso for Two Violins and Orch. In G Minor, Op. 8, No. 6 (Christmas Concerto) – Torelli
Concerto Grosso No. 1 – Schnittke
Concerto Grosso, Op. 6, #8 in g minor (Christmas Concerto) – Corelli
Concerto in F Major for Piano – Gershwin
Concerto in One Movement (Jamboree) – Harris, Roy
Concerto Grosso – Eiger
Concerto Grosso – Jager
Concerto Leggiero – Dyson
Concerto No. 1 for Orchestra, "Naughty Limericks" (or "Mischievous Melodies") – Shchedrin
Concierto Andaluz – Rodrigo
Condor Flies Past, The (El Condor Pasa) – Robles, Daniel Alomia
Conga – Aguila
Contes d'Hoffmann (Tales of Hoffmann): Intermezzo & Barcarolle – Offenbach
Contextures: Riots – Decade '60 – Kraft, William
Continental, The (1934) – Magidson, Herb
Conversation, The (1974) – Shire, David
Copenhagen Steam Railway Gallop – Lumbye, H. C.
Coppelia: Entr'acte & Waltz – Delibes
Coq d'or (The Golden Cockerel): Introduction & Wedding March – Rimsky-Korsakov
Cornet Carillon – Binge
Coronation March and Hymn – German
Corregidor y la Molinera – Falla
Cotswold Hill Tune – Orr, Charles
Count of Luxembourg (Waltz) – Lehar
Country Band March – Ives
Country Concerto – Kasschau
Country Gardens – Grainger
Country Gardens in F – Sharp, C.
Country Kazoo Overture – O'Boyle, Sean
Country They Call Puget Sound – Robinson, E.
County Derry Air – Grainger
Coventry Carol – Richman
Cowboy Fantasy – Holcombe
Cowboy Medley – Ayars, Bo
Cowboy Rhapsody – Gould
Cowboy's Meditation – Guion
Cowboys Overture – Williams, J.
Crazy for You Overture – Gershwin
Creole Belles – Lampe
Cresta Blanca Waltz – Gould
Crinoline and Lace – Gould
Crouching Tiger Concerto – Tan Dun
Crouching Tiger, Hidden Dragon (2000) – Dun, Tan
Crown Imperial: Coronation March – Walton
Cuatro Estaciones Porteñas (The Four Seasons in Buenas Aires) – Piazzolla, Astor
Cuatro Madrigales Amatorios – Rodrigo
Cuban Fire Suite: La Suerte de los Tontos (Fortune of Fools) – Richards, Johnny
Cuban Overture – Gershwin
Cumbanchero – Hernandez
Curious Case of Benjamin Button, The: Suite – Desplat, Alexandre
Curtain Raiser to an American Play: Overture – Piket
Curtain Up! – Krogstad, Bob
Cyrano De Bergerac (1950): Suite – Tiomkin, Dimitri
Czardas – Monti

D

Dalarapsodi: Swedish Rhapsody No. 3, Op. 47 – Alfvén
Damnation de Faust: Hungarian March (Rakoczy) – Berlioz
Dance Fantasy, Op. 7 – Layton
Dance Gallery: Soft Shoe Gavotte – Gould
Dance Overture – Creston
Dance Rhythms, Op. 58 – Riegger
Dance Suite – Bartók
Dance Suites No. 1, 2, and 3 – Leighton
Dances of Marosszek – Kodály
Dances with Wolves – Barry
Dancing in the Dark – Schwartz
Danny Boy – Weatherly
Dansa Brasileira – Guarnieri
Danse Macabre, Op. 40 – Saint-Saëns
Danse rituelle du feu – Falla, Manuel de
Danza Afro-Cubanas: Danza lucumi – Lecuona
Danza Fantástica – Soro, Enrique
Danza Rústica – Campos, José Carlos
Danzas fantásticas, Op. 22 – Turina
Danzon No. 2 – Marquez
Daphnis et Chloe, Suite No. 1 and 2 – Ravel
Dark City (1950) – Waxman, Franz
Dark Eyes – Lang, Philip J.
Dark Knight, The: Concert Suite – Zimmer & Howard
David and the Ark of the Covenant – Bavil, Zamir

David & Bathsheba – Newman, Alfred
Da Vinci Code (2006): Chevaliers de Sangreal – Zimmer, Hans
Day the Earth Stood Still, The: Arrival – Herrmann, Bernard
Day the Earth Stood Still, The: Suite – Herrmann, Bernard
Days of Wine and Roses – Mancini, Henry
Dead Men Don't Wear Plaid: End Cast – Rózsa
Dear Heart – Mancini, Henry
Death Valley Suite – Grofé
Deck the Hall & We Wish You a Merry Christmas – Luck, Arthur
Declaration – Gould
Deep Purple – De Rose, Peter
Deep South Suite: Happy Go Lucky Local – Ellington & Strayhorn
Defiance (2008): Nothing is Impossible – Howard, James
Dennis the Menace (1993): End Credits – Goldsmith, Jerry
Derivations for Solo Clarinet and Dance Band – Gould
Desiree: We Meet Again – Newman, Alfred
Deserted Ballroom – Gould
Devil on the Belfry – Weinberger
Devil and Daniel Webster: Suite – Herrmann, B.
Devil Doll, The (1936): Waltzes – Waxman, Franz
Devils: Suite – Maxwell Davies
Dial M for Murder (1954): Suite – Tiomkin, Dimitri
Dialogues – Brubeck, Howard
Dialogues – Schifrin
Dialogues: Theme for June – Brubeck, H.
Diamond and the Goose – Dankworth
Diary of Anne Franck, The: Suite – Newman, Alfred
Dichter und Bauer (Poet and Peasant): Overture – Suppé
Dinner Music for a Pack of Hungry Cannibals – Scott, R.
Dirge for Two Veterans – McDonald, Harl
Disney Adventure – Sayre
Disney Magic – Lowden
Disney Supertime (from Mary Poppins) – Lowden, Bob
Diversions – Bennett, Richard
Divertimento for Toys and Orchestra – Namenwirth, Micha
Divertimento for Orchestra – Bernstein
Divertissement – Ibert
DOA (1950) – Tiomkin, Dimitri
Doctor Dolittle: Talk to the Animals – Newman, Lionel

Don Giovanni, K.527: Overture – Mozart
Don Juan de Manara: Intermezzo – Goossens
Donna Diana: Overture – Reznicek
Dorfschwalben aus Osterreich (Austrian Village Swallows), Op. 164 – Strauss, Josef
Double Indemnity: Suite – Rósza
Double O Seven, Themes from: A Medley for Orchestra – Custer, Calvin
Down a Country Lane – Copland
Down in the Valley – Davis, Jimmy
Do You Hear What I Hear – Regney & Shayne
Dr. Jekyll and Mr. Hyde (1941): Suite – Waxman, Franz
Dr. Seuss's Gertrude McFuzz – Kapilow
Dr. Seuss's Green Eggs and Ham – Kapilow
Dracula (1992) – Kilar, Wojciech
Dramatic Fanfares from CBS-TV Documentary "World War I" – Gould
Dream of a Lifetime – Mancini, Henry
Dream of Olwen – Williams, C.
Dream of the Peasant Gritzko – Mussorgsky
Duel in the Sun (1946): Suite – Tiomkin, Dimitri
Duke Ellington! Medley – Ellington

E

E.T. Suite: Adventures on Earth – Williams, J.
E.T.: Flying Theme – Williams, J.
Early American Quadrille (Square Dance) – Brown, R. B.
Early American Suite – Bazelon
Early One Morning – Pearson
East of Suez: Incidental Music – Goossens
Easter Parade – Berlin
Ebb Tide – Maxwell, Robert
Ecstasy – Gold, Marty
Edge, The (1997): Main Title & Finale – Goldsmith, Jerry
Edward Scissorhands: Ice Dance; Main Title – Elfman
Egmont Overture – Beethoven
Egyptian March, Op. 335 – Strauss, Joh., Jr.
Eight English and American Folk Songs: When Johnny Comes Marching Home – Shostakovich
Eight Poems of Li-Po – Lambert
Eine Kleine Nachtmusik, K. 525 – Mozart
Einstein on the Fritz – Schickele

El Choclo & La Cumparsita – Villaldo & Matos Rodríguez
El Cid: Main Title – Rózsa
El Condor Pasa (The Condor Flies Past) – Robles, Daniel Alomia
El Gato Montés (The Bobcat) – Penella, Manuel
Elegiac Blues – Lambert
Elegy for Anne Frank – Foss
Elegy for String Orchestra – Jones, Samuel
Elephant Walk (1954): Suite – Waxman, Franz
Elfen Polka Op. 74 – Strauss, Jos.
Elijah's Angel – Kapilow, Robert
Elizabethan Dances – Alwyn, William
Eljen A Magyar! (Long Live the Magyar), Op. 332 – Strauss, Joh., Jr.
Ellington Portrait – Ellington
Embraceable You – Gershwin
Emma (1996) – Portman, Rachel
Empire Strikes Back Medley – Williams, J.
Enchantress: Art Is Calling for Me – Herbert
Encuentros (1992) – Zyman, Samuel
Endurance: The Great Tree – Rózsa
English Dance Suite – Woodgate
English Dances – Arnold, M.
English Folk Songs Suite – Vaughan Williams
English Patient, The (1996) – Yared, Gabriel
Enigma Variations, Op. 36: Nimrod – Elgar
Entertainer Rag – Joplin
Entertainer – Joplin
Entry of the Boyards – Halvorsen
Entrance of the Gladiators, Op. 68 – Fučik
Epilogue to Profiles in Courage: JFK – Harris, Roy
Era di maggio – Costa
Erotik – Grieg
España Cani – Marquina
España – Chabrier
España Rhapsody – Chabrier
Essential Ellington – Ellington & Strayhorn
Estrellita (Star of Love) – Ponce
Esu Variations – Davis, Anthony
Eugen Onegin: Polonaise – Tchaikovsky
Evening at Pops – Holcombe
Evening in Texas – Creston
Evergreen Christmas – Wendel
Everything is Beautiful – Stevens, Ray
Evita Highlights – Lloyd Webber
Evita, Music from – Lloyd Webber, Andrew
Ewiges Wien – Riege
Exodus: An Orchestral Tone-Picture

– Gold, Ernest
Exodus: Rhapsody for Cello and Orchestra (1960) – Gold, Ernest
Exodus: This Land is Mine (1960) – Gold, Ernest
Exsultate Jubilate, K. 165 – Mozart

F

Façades – Glass
Fairest of the Fair March – Sousa
Fairy Tale – Bazelon, Irwin
Fairytale: Suite from the Ballet – Sebastian
Fall of the Roman Empire (1964): Themes – Tiomkin, Dimitri
Family Album: Suite – Gould
Fanfare – Holmboe, Vagn
Fanfare – Poulenc
Fanfare for the Artists – Goossens
Fanfare for Christmas [Hodie, Hodie] – Wells, Robin
Fanfare for Cincinnati – Stucky
Fanfare for the Common Man – Copland
Fanfare for the Common Cold – Schickele
Fanfare for Foley's – Harbison
Fanfare for Freedom – Wendel
Fanfare for George Gershwin – Turrin, Joseph
Fanfare for Los Angeles – Stucky
Fanfare for Louisville – Lutosławski
Fanfare for the Royal Academy of Music Banquet – Berkeley
Fanfare for the Uncommon Woman (1986) – Tower, Joan
Fanfare for the University of Lancaster – Lutosławski
Fanfare for Trumpets and Caracolas – Rodríguez
Fanfare from "Oktoechos" – Rodriguez
Fanfare on One Note – Burgon
Fanfare to the Olympic Games: Divertissement for Brass and Percussion – Arnaud
Fanfares and Processional – Payne
Fanny: Selection for Orchestra – Rome, Harold
Fantaisie Brilliante on Themes from Bizet's "Carmen" – Bizet
Fantaisie sur des airs nationaux polonais (Fantasy on Polish Airs), Op. 13 – Chopin
Fantasia & Fugue – Bach, J. S.
Fantasia on Christmas Carols – Vaughan Williams
Fantasia on Greensleeves – Vaughan Williams
Fantasia on Hampshire Folk Songs

– Holst
Fantasia on a Theme by Thomas Tallis – Vaughan Williams
Fantasia on "Yeroushalaim Shel Zahav" – Wendel
Fantasie on "Auld Lang Syne" – Caillet
Fantastic Four: Main Titles – Ottman
Fantastic Four 2: Silver Surfer Suite – Ottman
Fantastic Garden – Schickele
Fantasy on Auld Lang Syne – Holcombe, Bill
Fantasy for Trombone, Op. 42 – Creston
Fantasy on American Themes – Tyzik
Fantasy on the Saints – Proto
Far and Away: Excerpts – Williams, J.
Farewell [Thou Must Leave] – Berlioz
Farewell My Lovely (1975): Suite – Shire, David
Farmyard Frolic – Hermann, Ralph
Fascinatin' Rhythm – Gershwin
Faust: Ballet Music – Gounod
Faust Ouvertüre – Wagner, R.
Feast of Lights – Adler
Federal March – Reinagle
Federal Overture – Carr, Benjamin
Feria Mágica (Magic Fair): Overture – Surinach
Festival Coronation March for Alexander III – Tchaikovsky
Festival of the Workers – McDonald, H.
Festival Prelude, A – Reed, Alfred
Festival Overture on the American National Air (Star-Spangled Banner) – Buck
Festive Fanfare – Gould
Festive Huapango – Gomez, Alice
Festive Music – Gould
Festive Overture, Op. 96 – Shostakovich
Fiddle Faddle – Anderson
Fiddler on the Roof – Bock
Field in Pennsylvania – Deussen
Fiesta! for chamber orchestra – López, Jimmy
Fiesta! for orchestra – López, Jimmy
Fiesta Mexicana – Wendel
Fiesta de la Posada – Brubeck, Dave
Fiesta: Suite de danzas – Esplá
Fifty-Five Days at Peking (1963): Suite – Tiomkin, Dimitri
Fille aux cheveux de lin – Debussy
Fille du régiment (Daughter of the Regiment): Overture – Donizetti
Final Conflict, The (1983) – Goldsmith, Jerry
Finding Neverland: Suite (2004) – Kaczmarek, Jan A.P.
Finian's Rainbow, Excerpts from – Lane, Burton
Finlandia, Op. 26, No. 7 – Sibelius
Firefly, Medley – Friml
Fireworks: A Celebration for Los Angeles (1999) – Goldsmith, Jerry
First Day of Spring – Anderson
First Knight, The (1995): Suite – Goldsmith, Jerry
First Love – Gestor, Don
First Time Ever I Saw Your Face, The – MacColl, Ewan
First Noel – Gould
Fir Tree, The – Turrin, Joseph
Fitzwilliam Suite – Gordon, Phillip
Five Irish Fantasies – Loeffler
Five Poems of the Ancient Far East – Griffes
Five Spirituals – Gould
Flamenco: Ballet – Goossens
Flares and Declamations – Gould
Flashdance: What a Feeling (1983) – Moroder, Georgio
Fledermaus – Strauss, Joh., Jr.
Flight into Egypt; Sacred Ricercar – Harbison
Flight: The Story of Wilbur and Orville Wright – Rodriguez
Fling Went the Strings – Hunter
Flintstones Meet the Jetsons – Wendel
Flirtatious Jig (Fiddler's Jig) – Cowell
Florentiner Marsch, Op. 214 – Fučik
Flourishes and Galop – Gould
Fluffy Ruffles: Selection – Gould
Flute Cocktail: Scherzo and Blues for 3 or 2 Solo Flutes and Orchestra – Simeone, Harry
Foggy Day – Gershwin, George
Folk Dance Suite – Geehl
Folk Suite – Gould
Folksong Symphony: Two Interludes – Harris, Roy
Fools Rush In – Silvestri, Alan
For All We Know – Coots
For Spacious Skies – Zaninelli
Forever Amber: Main Title "Amber"; The King's Mistress; Whitefriars; The Great Fire; End Title "Finale" – Raksin
Forever Amber: Suite (1947) – Raksin
Forever Young (1992): Love Theme – Goldsmith, Jerry
Forgotten Dreams – Anderson
For Whom the Bell Tolls (1943): Suite – Young, Victor
Football Song Hits: Eastern – Traditional
Football Song Hits No. 2: Western – Traditional
Football Song Hits No. 4: East-South – Traditional
For All We Know – Wilson & James & Karlin
Forrest Gump Main Title: Feather Theme – Silvestri
Forrest Gump: Suite – Silvestri
Forty-Second Street (1981) – Warren, H.
Forty-Second Street: Overture – Warren, H.
Forza del Destino: Overture – Verdi
Foster Gallery – Gould
Four Cornish Dances, Op. 91 – Arnold, M.
Four Freedoms – Bennett, Robert
Four Irish Dances – Arnold, M.
Four Irish Tales (Tales of Our Countryside) – Cowell
Four Poster, The (1952) – Tiomkin, Dimitri
Four Scottish Dances – Arnold, M.
Four Seasons in Buenas Aires, The (Cuatro Estaciones Porteñas) – Piazzolla, Astor
Four Spirituals – Hailstork
Four Women: Medley –Goldsmith, Jerry
Fox Down – Meyer, Ranaan
Fox Fanfare – Newman, Alfred
Fox Medley No. 1; No. 2 – Hayes
Française, Overture – Geehl
Fra Diavolo: Overture – Auber
Frangesa March – Costa
Frankenstein – Shapiro, Michael
Frankie and Johnny – Moross
Freddie the Football – Hayman
Freedom's Land – Harris, Roy
Free Willy Suite (1993) – Poledouris, Basil
Friendly Persuasion (1956) – Tiomkin, Dimitri
Friendly Persuasion (1956): Thee I Love – Tiomkin, Dimitri
Froissart Overture, Op. 19 – Elgar
From a Distance – Gold, Julie
From Sea to Shining Sea – Wendel
From These States, Suite: Gathered Along Unpaved Roads – Bacon
From Time to Time – Iannaccone
Frontier – Heath
Frosty the Snowman – Nelson & Rolli
Fruhlingsstimmen Waltz (Voices of Spring), Op. 410 – Strauss, Joh., Jr.
Fuego fatuo – Falla
Fugue in C minor – Bach, J. S.
Fugal Fanfare: Happy Anniversary – Brubeck, Dave
Fugal Overture, Op. 40 No. 1 – Holst
Fugue on Yankee Doodle – Thomson, V.
Funiculi, Funicula – Denza
Furies, The (1950): Suite – Waxman, Franz

G

G Flat Theme – Brubeck, H.
G.A.G.E., A Christmas Story – Barab
Gadfly: Suite from the Film, Op. 97a – Shostakovich
Gasoline Can-Can – Perry, William
Gates of Justice – Brubeck, D.
Gathering of Angels: Bolero – Rodríguez
Gay Divorcee: Night and Day – Porter
Gay Divorcee: The Continental – Conrad, Con
Gayaneh, Suites – Khachaturian
Gazebo Dances: Overture to the Imaginary Invalid – Corigliano
Gazza Ladra (The Thieving Magpie) Overture – Rossini
General Cadwalader's Grand March – Johnson, Francis
Generals, The: Patton/MacArthur Marches – Goldsmith, Jerry
Gentleman's Agreement Suite: Newman, Alfred
George M.: Choral Overture – Cohan
George M. Cohan Medley – Cohan
George M. Cohan Overture – Wendel
George M. Cohan Salute – Cohan
Georgia on My Mind – Carmichael
German Dance #3, K. 605 – Mozart
Gershwin in Concert – Gershwin
Gershwin Portrait – Arnold, A.
Geschichten aus dem Wienerwald (Tales from the Vienna Woods), Op. 325 – Strauss, Joh., Jr.
Gesu Bambino – Yon, Pietro
Ghost of Mrs. Muir, The (1947) – Herrmann, Bernard
Ghostbusters: Theme – Bernstein, Elmer
Gianni Schicchi (O mio babbino caro) – Puccini
Giant (1956): Suite – Tiomkin, Dimitri
Gigi: Selections – Loewe
Gioconda: "Dance of the Hours" – Ponchielli
Girl in Satin – Anderson
Give Me Your Heart – Templeton
Give My Regards to Broadway – Cohan
Gladiator, Music from the Movie – Zimmer
Glass Menagerie, The – Mancini, Henry
Glassworks – Glass
Gli uccelli (The Birds) – Respighi
Globetrotter Suite – Milhaud
Gloria – Poulenc
Gloria Estefan: Her Greatest Hits – Estefan
Gloriana: The Courtly Dances – Britten
Go the Distance – Menken
God Bless America – Berlin
God Bless the U.S.A – Greenwood
God Gless Us Everyone – Silvestri & Ballard
Godfather, The (1972) – Rota, Nino
Godfather II, The (1974) – Rota, Nino
Godfather III, The: Suite – Rota, Nino
Godfather: Reminicences for Orchestra (1972) – Rota, Nino
God Rest Ye Merry Gentlemen – Stephenson, James M. III
Gold and Silver Waltz – Lehár
Golden Broom and the Green Apple – Ellington
Golden Years – Anderson
Goldilocks – Anderson
Gone With the Wind (1939): Dance Montage – Steiner, Max
Gone With the Wind: Tara's Theme – Steiner, Max
Good King Wenceslas – Gould
Good King Wenceslas – Mayer
Go Tell It On the Mountain – Stephenson, James M. III
Götterdämmerung (Siegfried's Rhine Journey) – Wagner, R.
Governor Bradford's March – Anderson
Goyescas: Intermezzo – Granados, Enrique
Graduation Ball: Ballet in One Act – Strauss, Joh., Jr.
Graduation March – Perry, William
Granada – Lara, Agustín
Grand American Fantasia: Tone Picture of the North and South – Bendix
Grand Canyon Fanfare – Howard, J.
Grand Canyon Suite – Grofé
Grand, Grand Overture, A, Op. 57 – Arnold, M.
Grand Slam Jam – Ellington
Grease! – Casey & Jacobs
Grease: You're the One that I Want – Farrar
Great American Bicycle Race – Knight
Great American Symphony – Smith, C.
Great Beatles Singles Suite I – The Beatles
Great Beatles Singles Suite II – The Beatles
Great Escape March – Bernstein, E.
Great Expectations Suite – Doyle, Patrick
Great Mouse Detective, The – Mancini, Henry
Great Race, The: Pie in the Face Polka – Mancini, Henry
Great Race, The: They're Off – Mancini, Henry
Great Scott! Orchestral Suite after Joplin – Turok
Great Steamboat Race – Smith, R.W.
Great Train Robbery, The (1979): Suite – Goldsmith, Jerry
Great Waldo Pepper, The – Mancini, Henry
Great Waltz, The (1938) – Tiomkin, Dimitri
Greatest Love of All – Masser
Green Green Grass of Home – Putman, Curly
Green Places – Schocker
Greenfield Christmas Tree – Moore, D.
Greensleeves – Reed
Greensleeves – Vaughan Williams
Gregoriana Christmas Suite – King, V.
Gremlins: Suite – Goldsmith, Jerry
Gremlins 2 (1990): The New Batch: Main Title – Goldsmith, Jerry
Guillaume Tell (William Tell): Overture – Rossini
Gunfight at the OK Corral (1957): Ballad and Theme – Tiomkin, Dimitri
Guns of Navarone, The (1961): Suite – Tiomkin, Dimitri
Guys and Dolls – Loesser
Gymnopedie No. 1 & 3 – Satie
Gypsy – Styne
Gypsy Legend – Mantovani, Annunzio Paolo
Gypsy Suite – German, E.

H

Haftorah – Ellstein
Hail to a First Lady – Gould
Hair: Selections – MacDermot, Gal
Hair: Where Do I Go?; Good Morning Starshine – MacDermot, Gal
Haleakala: How Maui Snared the Sun – Welcher
Half-Holiday, Overture – Gardner
Halloween Trilogy – Wendel
Halls of Ivy, The – Russell & Knight
Halo Suite: Halo Theme – O'Donnell & Salvatori
Hamburger Suite – Marsh, Gerry Jon
Hamlet, Incidental Music to the Stage Production, Op. 32a – Shostakovich
Hamlet: Music from the Film, Op. 116 – Shostakovich
Hamlet: Music from the Film, Op. 116a – Shostakovich
Hands across the Sea – Sousa
Hand-Prints of Sorcerers – Maggio
Hangoverture – Perillo, Steve
Hansel and Gretel – Humperdinck
Hanukkah Festival Overture – Richman
Hanukkah Light (1998) – Bavel, Zamir
Happy Anniversary – Copland

Happy Feet: The Story of Mumble – Powell, John
Happy Birthday Medley – Kerchner, Larry
Happy Birthday Variations – Williams, J.
Happy, Happy Birthday – Chiarappa
Hark! The Herald Angels Sing & Adeste Fidelis – Mendelssohn, Felix
Harlem – Ellington, Edward (Duke)
Harriet Tubman – Robinson, Walter H.
Harry Potter and the Chamber of Secrets – Williams, J.
Harry Potter and the Half-Blood Prince, Concert Suite from – Hooper, Nicolas
Harry Potter and the Order of the Phoenix: Concert Suite – Williams & Hooper
Harry Potter and the Prisoner of Azkaban – Williams, J.
Harry Potter and the Sorcerer's Stone: Children's Suite – Williams, J.
Harry Potter Symphonic Suite – Williams, J.
Harry Potter and the Sorcerer's Stone: Suite for Orchestra – Williams, J.
Harvest – Gould
Hatari!: Baby Elephant Walk (1962) – Mancini, Henry
Havanaise, Op. 83 – Saint-Saëns
Have Yourself a Merry Little Christmas – Blane
Hawaii Five O (1968) – Stevens, Morton
Heartbeat – Blake
Hebrides Overture, Op. 26 (Fingal's Cave) – Mendelssohn
Heimkehr aus der Fremde (Son and Stranger), Op. 89: Overture – Mendelssohn
Helios Overture, Op. 17 – Nielsen
Hello Dolly! – Herman
Hello Dolly Highlights – Herman, J.
Hemingway's Adventures of a Young Man – Waxman, Franz
Hemingway's Adventures of a Young Man: Rosanna – Waxman, Franz
Henry Mancini for Strings, Vol.1 and 2 – Mancini, H.
Henry V: Non Nobis Domine – Doyle, Patrick
Hercules Overture – Handel
Her Name is Suzanne – Hayman, Richard
Herreinspaziert! Waltz, Op. 518 – Ziehrer
Heritage Symphonic Dances – Duffy
Hexen – Alford, Kenneth
Hiawatha's Wedding Feast: Onaway! Awake Beloved – Coleridge-Taylor
Hide and Seek: Main Titles – Ottman

High and the Mighty, The (1954): Suite – Tiomkin, Dimitri
High Anxiety: Main Title (1973) – Morris, John
High Noon (1952): Do Not Forsake Me Oh My Darling – Tiomkin, Dimitri
High Noon (1952): Suite – Tiomkin, Dimitri
High School Cadets March – Sousa
High School Musical – Lawrence, David
High School Musical 2 – Lawrence, David
Highland Express – Wilby
Highlands, From the: A Selection of Scotch Melodies – Langey, Otto
Himno Nacional Mexicano (Mexican National Anthem) – Chavez
Himno Nacional del Perú – Alzedo
His Excellency March – Fillmore
Histoire de Babar (The Story of Babar, the Little Elephant) – Poulenc
Hoagy Carmichael: An American Treasure – Carmichael
Hobson's Choice – Arnold, M.
Hodie, a Christmas Cantata – Vaughan Williams
Hofball-Tanze Waltz, Op. 161 – Lanner
Hoffa Theme – Newman, David
Ho! Ho! Ho! – Richman
Holberg Suite Op. 40 – Grieg
Holiday Fanfare Medley No. 2 – Stephenson, James M. III
Holiday for Strings – Rose, D.
Holiday Moods: Suites – Tyzik
Holiday Music – Gould
Holiday Music: Christmas – Gould
Holiday Music: Easter Morning – Gould
Holiday Music: First Thanksgiving – Gould
Holiday Music: Fourth of July – Gould
Holiday Music: Halloween – Gould
Holiday Music: Home for Christmas – Gould
Holiday Overture – Carter
Holiday Overture – Stephenson, James
Holly and the Ivy: Fantasy on Christmas Carols – Arnold, M.
Holly and Jolly Sing-Along, A! – Stephenson, James M. III
Hollywood Salute – Wendel
Hollywood Suite – Grofé
Holoubek (The Wood Dove) Op. 110 – Dvořák
Holy Night (Die Heligea Natten): A Christmas Oratorio – Rosenberg
Homage to Sarasate – Balada

Home Alone: Three Holiday Songs – Williams, J.
Home for the Holidays – Stillman & Allen
Home On the Range – Guion
Home Stretch – Anderson
Homenajes – Falla
Homespun Overture – Gould
Hoofer Suite – Gould
Hook: Flight to Neverland – Williams, J.
Hooked on Classics – Clark, Larry
Horn of Plenty – Harris, Roy
Horse and Buggy – Anderson
Hosedown: A Firefighter Fable – Gould
Hot Buttered Rumba – Rodríguez
Hot Soul Medley – Tyzik
Hot-Time Dance – Antheil
Hour with the Game Shows – Griffin
Hours, The: Suite (2002) – Glass, Philip
How Pleasant to Know Mr. Lear – Roxburgh
How the Camel Got His Hump – Herschel
How to Marry a Millionaire – Newman, Alfred
How the West Was Won – Newman, Alfred
How the West Was Won: Suite – Newman, Alfred
How the Whale Got His Tiny Throat – Herschel
Huapango – Moncayo
Huckleberry Duck – Scott, R.
Huckleberry Finn (1939): Overture – Waxman, Franz
Hudson River Suite – Grofé, Ferde
Huiracocha for voice and orchestra – Arias, Clotilde
Huldigungsmarsch (Sons of Knute) – Grieg
Hullabaloo – Hayman, Richard
Humoresque – Tchaikovsky
Hungarian Dances – Brahms
Hungarian March – Berlioz
Hungarian Rhapsodie, Op. 68 – Popper
Hungarian Rhapsody No. 1, F Minor – Liszt
Hungarian Rhapsody No. 2 – Liszt
Hungarian Sketches – Bartók
Hunk of Burnin' Love – Lang, D.
Hup Two Three Four – Shulman
Hurdy-Gurdy Man – Goossens
Hymn to the Earth – Sibelius
Hymn of Thanksgiving – Wendel
Hymnal on "We Shall Overcome": from American Ballads – Gould
Hymne – Vangelis
Hypothetically Murdered, Op. 31a – Shostakovich

I

Ice Castles Through the Eyes of Love – Hamlisch, Marvin
Ice Follies of 1939 – Waxman, Franz
I Crisantemi (The Chrysanthemums) – Puccini
I Get a Kick Out of You – Porter
I Got Fascinating Rhythm – Gershwin
I Got It Bad and That Ain't Good – Ellington
I Got Plenty of Nuttin' – Gershwin
I Got Rhythm – Gershwin
I Got Rhythm Variations for Piano – Gershwin
I Knew I Loved You – Morricone
I Left My Heart in San Francisco – Cory, George
I Love Lucy: Theme – Daniel, Eliot
I Traci amanti: Overture – Cimarosa
I vespri siciliani: Overture – Verdi
I Want to Hold Your Hand – Lennon & McCartney
I Will Lift Up Mine Eyes – Hailstork
I Will Wait for You – Legrand, Michel
I Wonder as I Wander – Niles, J.
Ice Age: the Meltdown – Powell, John
Ich Liebe Dich – Grieg
If You Go Away – Brel
If You Were the Only Girl in the World – Meyer, G.
Il barbiere di Siviglia (Barber of Seville): Overture – Rossini
Il barbiere di Siviglia (Barber of Seville): Sinfonia – Rossini
Illustrated Man, The: Main Title – Goldsmith, Jerry
Il re pastore, K. 208: Overture – Mozart
I'll Be Home for Christmas – Kent, W.
I'm Getting Sentimental Over You – Washington & Bassman
I'm Inclined to New Music: A Comic Parody of Mozart's Eine Kleine Nachtmusik – Adolphe
Im Krapfenwaldl, Polka Française, Op. 336 – Strauss, Joh., Jr
I'm Old Fashioned, Astaire Variations – Gould
Improvisations on Christmas Carols – Kelly, Bryan
In Aeternam – Jalbert
In a Nutshell: Suite – Grainger
In Old Virginia: Overture, Op. 28 – Powell, John
In the Bleak Midwinter – Darke, Harold
In the Day When I Cried Out – Richman
In the Folded and Quiet Yesterdays – Robinson, Earl
In the Manger – Wendel
In the South: Concert Overture, Op. 50 – Elgar
In the Steppes of Central Asia – Borodin
In Your Own Sweet Way – Brubeck, D.
Incredible Flutist – Piston
Independence Day: Highlights; End Tags – Arnold, David
Independence Day Suite – Arnold, David
Indian Spirits – Duffy
Infernal – Schiff
Inn of the Sixth Happiness – Arnold, M.
Interplays: Concerto for Jazz Drums, Percussion Ensemble – Phillips, P.
Introduction (Sunrise) – Strauss, R.
Introduction and Rondo Capriccioso: Trumpet in Bb and Orchestra – Saint-Saëns, Camille
Inventing Flight – Bolcom
Invitation to the Dance – Weber
Irish Concerto for Piano – Field, J.
Irish Party in Third Class – Horner
Irish Rhapsody – Herbert, V.
Irish Rhapsody No. 1, Op. 78 – Stanford
Irish Serenade – Scott, C.
Irish Suite – Anderson
Irish Suite – Duff, A.
Irish Suite – Esposito
Irish Trilogy – Wendel
Irish Tune from County Derry – Grainger
Iron Diamond – Kuster
Iron Foundry, Op. 19 – Mosolov
Iron Horse – Caliendo
Irving Berlin: A Symphonic Portrait – Berlin
Irving Berlin in Hollywood Overture – Berlin
I Saw Three Ships/Jeanette, Isabella Medley – Stephenson, James M. III
Isle of the Dead, The, Op. 29 – Rachmaninoff, Sergei
Israel Suite – Sheriff
Israeli Rhapsody – Bavil, Zamir
Israeli Work Song – Arnold, A.
Italian Fiesta – Hermann, Ralph
Italiana in Algeri: Overture – Rossini
I Traci Amanti: Overture – Cimarosa
It Came Upon a Midnight Clear – Gould
It Don't Mean a Thing (If it Ain't Got That Swing) – Ellington, Edward K. (Duke)
It Takes Four to Tango – Dorff
It's About Time – Brubeck, D.
It's a Wonderful Life (1947): Suite – Tiomkin, Dimitri
It's a Wonderful Life, Suite from – Tiomkin, Dimitri
It's a Wonderful Life (1947): Theme – Tiomkin, Dimitri
It's Christmastime (Medley for Orchestra) – Custer, Calvin
It's a Mad, Mad, Mad, Mad World: Exit Music (1963) – Gold, Ernest
It's Impossible (Somos novios) – Manzanero, Armando
It's Not Unusual – Mills, Gordon & Reed, Les
It's Only a Paper Moon – Arlen
It's the Most Wonderful Time of the Year – Pola & Wyle
Ivanhoe – Rózsa

J

J.F.K. – Williams, J.
JFK: The Voice of Peace – Welcher, Dan
J. S. on The Rocks: Nightcap – Shulman
Jag: Theme – Broughton, Bruce
Jalousie – Gade, J.
Jane Eyre: Suite (1943) – Herrmann, Bernard
James Horner – Hollywood Blockbusters: Apollo 13; American Tail; Braveheart; Titanic – Horner
Jargon: The Story of the American Constitution – Rodriguez
Jason and Argonauts: Suite (1963) – Herrmann, Bernard
Jason and Argonauts: Scherzo macabre (1963) – Herrmann, Bernard
Jaws – Williams, J.
Jayhawk, Op. 43, Overture to a Mythical Comedy – Mechem
Jazz Legato – Anderson
Jazz Pizzicato – Anderson
Jazz Singer Medley – Diamond
Jazz Sonata – Antheil
Jazz Suite, Op. 28 – Gruenberg
Jazz Symphony – Antheil
Jeanie with the Light Brown Hair – Foster, S.
Jekyll and Hyde Variations – Gould
Jeopardy Theme – Griffin
Jerome Kern Medley – Kern
Jerome Robbins Broadway – Sayre, C.
Jesu, Joy of Man's Desiring – Bach
Jesus Child! – Rutter
Jesus Christ Superstar – Lloyd-Webber
Jeux d'enfants, Op. 22: Petite Suite (Children's Games) – Bizet
Jewish Melodies – Hermann, Ralph
Jezebel (1938): Waltz – Steiner, Max

Jim Croce in Concert – Croce, Jim
Jingalodeon – Downey
Jingle Bells – Gould
Jingle Bells Forever – Smith, Robert W.
Jingle Bells/Sleigh Ride – Mancini, Henry
Jogger and the Dinosaur – Gould
John Denver Celebration (1987) – Denver, John
John Henry – Copland
Jonny Quest – Wendel
Joplin Overture – Turok, Paul
Journey into Jazz – Schuller
Journey to the Center of the Earth (1959) – Herrmann, Bernard
Joy Shall Be Yours in the Morning – Perry, William
Joy to the World – Handel
Joy to the World – Stephenson, James M. III
Joyous Overture – Sierra
Jubilation – Zwilich
Judah's Song of Praise – Adler, S.
Judge Dredd (1995): Suite – Silvestri, Alan
Julius Caesar Overture – Handel
Jump, Jive an' Wail – Prima
Jungle Drums – Lecuona
Just the Way You Are – Joel, Billy

K

Kaiser Walzer (Emperor Waltzes), Op. 437 – Strauss, Joh., Jr.
Kaleidoscope – Goossens
Kangaroo Kaper – Creston
Kanon in D Major – Pachelbel
Karelia Suite, Op. 11 – Sibelius
Karolju – Rouse
Katharinen: Waltz – Riege
Kennedy Portrait – Kraft, William
Keys of the Kingdom Suite – Newman, Alfred
Kidnapped: Overture – Knight
Killers: Concert Suite – Rósza
Kindersymphonie, Hob. II; 47, C Major (Toy Symphony) – Haydn
King and I Selections – Rodgers, R.
King Cotton March – Sousa
King Kong: Jungle Dance – Steiner, Max
King Kong (1933): Overture – Steiner, Max
King Kong: Theme – Steiner, Max
King Shall Rejoice – Handel
King Solomon's Mines (1985): Suite – Goldsmith, Jerry
King's Contest – Mechem
Kiss, The – Dorff, Daniel

Kiss (Il Bacio) – Arditi
Kiss Me Again – Herbert
Kitchen Percussion March for Special Guests and Orchestra – Rosenhaus, Steven L.
Klangfarbenfunk – Erb
Kleine Dreigroschenmusik (Suite from Little Three Penny Opera) – Weill
König Stephan Overture, Op. 117 – Beethoven
Korngold: The Adventures of Robin Hood, Symphonic Portrait – Korngold
Kosbro – Baker, D.
Krazy Kat – Carpenter, J.
Künstler (Artist's) Quadrille, Op. 201 – Strauss, Joh., Jr.
Künstlerleben (Artist's Life) Waltz, Op. 316 – Strauss, Joh., Jr.
Kuolema, Op. 44 (Valse Triste) – Sibelius
Kwang Hsu (Chinese March) – Lincke

L

La Bamba – Valens, Ritchie
L.A. Confidential (1997) – Goldsmith, Jerry
La Cage aux Folles: Overture – Herman, Jerry
La Cage aux Folles, Selections from – Herman, Jerry
Lady in the Water (2006): The Healing – Howard, James
La Flor de la Canela – Granda, Isabel
Lago de Lágrimas (Lake of Tears) – López, Jimmy
Lagunenwalzer, Op. 411: from "Eine Nacht in Venedig" – Strauss, Joh., Jr.
Lament – Grant, J.
Land of the Mountain and Flood, Op. 3: Overture – MacCunn
Landscapes and Remembrances – Menotti
Lara's Theme from Doctor Zhivago – Jarre
Largo and Allegro – Frackenpohl
Lark Ascending – Vaughan Williams
Last Emperor, The: Theme (1987) – Sakamoto, Ryuichi
Last of the Mohicans: Kiss; Main Title – Jones, Trevor
Last of the Mohicans: Main Title – Jones, Trevor
Last of the Mohicans Suite – Jones, Trevor
Last Samurai: The Way of the Sword – Zimmer, Hans
Latin American Symphonette – Gould
Latvian Folksong – Darzins

Laud's Baptizin' – Guion
Laura – Raksin
Laura's Theme – Raksin
Lawrence of Arabia – Jarre
Legend – Schickele
Legend of 1900: Romanza – Morricone
Legend of the Arkansas Traveler – McDonald, H.
Legend of Sleepy Hollow – Kasschau
Legends, Op. 22 (2. The Swan of Tuonela) – Sibelius
Legends of the Fall: The Ludlows (1994) – Horner, James
Leichte Kavallerie (Light Cavalry): Overture – Suppé
Leroy Anderson Favorites – Anderson
Leroy Anderson for Strings – Anderson
Let All Mortal Flesh Keep Silence – Holst
Let Freedom Ring: Overture – Demerest, Clifford
Let It Snow! Let It Snow! Let It Snow – Styne
Let Music Live – Blake
Let the River Be Unbroken – Tsontakis
Let There Be Peace on Earth – Miller & Jackson
Let Your Mind Wander Over America – Effinger
Lexicon of Beasties – Zaninelli
Liberian Suite – Ellington
Libertango – Piazzolla
Liberty Bell March – Sousa
Liberty Fanfare – Williams, J.
Liebesfreud – Kreisler
Liebesleid – Kreisler
Liebeslieder Waltzes, Op. 52 – Brahms
Lieutenant Kijé, Op. 60 – Prokofiev
Lifeforce, The – Mancini, Henry
Light in the Piazza – Guettel
Light in the Wilderness – Brubeck, D.
Light Rays – Whitney
Lili: Ballet (1953) – Kaper, Bronislau
Limpid Stream, Op. 39a – Shostakovich
Lincoln Address – Persichetti
Lincoln & Booth: Good-bye – Chiarappa
Lincoln & Booth: Just Ourselves – Chiarappa
Lincoln & Booth: The President's Waltz – Chiarappa
Lincoln Center Festival Overture – Piston
Lincoln Legend – Gould
Lincoln Portrait – Copland
Linebacker Music – Felder, D.
Lionheart: The Children's Crusade (1987) – Goldsmith, Jerry
Lion King – John, Elton
Lion, the Witch, and the Wardrobe: Suite – McCabe

Lionel Richie in Concert – Rosenhaus
Lithuanian Night – Antheil
Little Christmas Cantata, A – Serly
Little Concerto (on themes by Arne) – Bush
Little Drummer Boy – Davis, Katherine
Little House on the Prairie: Meet Me at the Fair (1974) – Rose, David
Little Miss Fix-It: Turkey Trot – Kern
Little Night Music: Send In the Clowns – Sondheim
Little Suite, Op. 1 – Nielsen
Little Travelin' Music, Overture: A – Hodkinson
Logan's Run (1976): Monument/End of the City – Goldsmith, Jerry
Lohengrin: Bridal Chorus – Wagner, R.
Lo, How a Rose E'er Blooming – Stephenson, James M. III
London Pastoral – Bennett, Richard
London Suite: Knightsbridge March – Coates
Lonely Waters – Moeran, E. J.
Lonesome Train – Robinson, Earl
Long and Winding Road – The Beatles
Loony Tunes Fugue – Naughtin
Lord of the Dance – Hardiman
Lord of the Rings, The: Excerpts from Symphony No. 1 – Meij, Johan de
Lord of the Rings: Fellowship of the Ring – Shore
Lord of the Rings: The Return of the King – Shore
Lord of the Rings: The Two Towers – Shore
Lord of the Rings, Symphonic Suite from The: The Two Towers – Shore
Lord's Prayer – Malotte
Lost Command (1966): Aicha's Theme – Waxman, Franz
Lost Weekend: Suite – Rósza
Lost World: Jurassic Park – Williams, J.
Loud Love Songs – Lang, David
Louisiana Story: Acadian Songs and Dances – Thomson
Louisiana Story: Orchestral Suite – Thomson
Love Bead – Gordon
Love for Three Oranges: March & Scherzo – Prokofiev
Love is Blue (L'Amour est bleu) – Popp, André
Love Me Tonight: Lover – Rodgers, Richard
Love Spells – Bennett, Richard
Love Story: Where Do I Begin – Lai, Francis
Love Story: Theme (1970) – Lai, Francis
Love Walked In – Gershwin
Lover's Ink – Talbot
Lovers, Op. 43 – Barber
Lovesongs – Bennett, Richard
Lucia di Lammermoor, Act II: Sestetto: Chi mi frena – Donizetti
Lucifer Polka, Op. 266 – Strauss, Joh, Jr.
Lucio Silla, K. 135: Overture – Mozart
Lullabye for a Jazz Baby – Cunningham
Lullaby for Strings – Gershwin
Lullaby of Broadway – Turrin, Joseph
Lullaby of Broadway – Warren, H.
Lullaby of the Drums – Anderson
Lyric Pieces, Op. 68 – Grieg
Lyric Suite: March of the Dwarfs – Grieg

M

Má vlast (My Fatherland) – Smetana
Ma Mère l'Oye: Prélude et Danse du rouet – Ravel
Ma Mère l'Oye (Mother Goose) – Ravel
MacArthur (1977): March – Goldsmith, Jerry
MacArthur Park – Webb
Mack & Mabel – Herman, Jerry
Madam Butterfly for Orchestra – Puccini
Madison's March – Reinagle
Magic of Christmas, The – Stephenson, James M. III
Magnificent Seven, The: Suite – Bernstein, E.
Malagueña – Lecuona
Maltese Dances – Camilleri
Mame – Herman, Jerry
Mam'selle Marie – Guion
Man and a Woman, A – Lai, Francis
Man I Love – Gershwin
Man of La Mancha: Selections – Leigh
Man of La Mancha: Orchestral Synthesis – Leigh
Man on a Tightrope (1953): March – Waxman, Franz
Man Who Invented Music – Gillis
Man Who Knew Too Much, The: The Storm Clouds Cantata (1956) – Herrmann, Bernard
Man with the Golden Arm: Suite – Bernstein, Elmer
Mancini Magic – Mancini
Mancini Memories – Gold, Marty
Many Moods of Christmas: Suite 1 – Bennett, Robert Russell

Many Moods of Christmas: Suite 2 – Bennett, Robert Russell
Many Moods of Christmas: Suite 3 – Bennett, Robert Russell
Many Moods of Christmas: Suite 4 – Bennett, Robert Russell
Many Moods of Christmas – Shaw
Maple Leaf Rag – Joplin
March Militaire Nos. 1&2 – Schubert
March of the Two Left Feet – Anderson
March with Mancini – Mancini, Henry
Marche funèbre d'une marionette (Funeral March of a Marionette) – Gounod
Marche Slave, Op. 31 – Tchaikovsky
Marchen von der Schönen Melusine, Op. 32 (Fair Melusina) – Mendelssohn
Marching Song of Democracy – Grainger
Marco Polo: Main Title – Morricone
Marinera y Tondero – Mindreau, Ernesto López
Marinera Trujillana – Álvarez, Teófilo
Mario! Jump! – Naughtin, Matthew
Mark of Zorro, The: Suite (1940) – Friedhofer, Hugo
Marriage of Figaro (Aprite un po'quegl'occh, Deh Vieni non Tardar, Dove sono i bei momenti; Porgi amor) – Mozart
Marvin Hamlisch in Concert – Hamlisch, Marvin
Masada: Suite – Goldsmith, Jerry
Mascaras – Rodriguez
Mask of Zorro: Suite (1998) – Horner, James
Masquerade – Brown, Robert Bennett
Masquerade: Hanedons (Cock's Dance) – Nielsen
Masquerade: Prelude to Act II – Nielsen
Masquerade: Overture – Nielsen
Masquerade Suite – Khachaturian
Matinees musicales, Op. 24 – Britten
Maxwell's Reel, with Northern Lights – Maxwell Davies
May Night: Overture – Rimsky-Korsakov
Méditation from Thaïs – Massenet
Meditations in Passage – Smith, Hale
Medley: Classic Film Themes – Waxman, Franz
Medley: Classic Love Themes – Waxman, Franz
Medley: Nostalgic Film Themes – Waxman, Franz
Medley: Victor Young Tribute – Young, Victor
Melancholy Mood – McPartland
Melodie – Friml

Melodies of Richard Heuberger – Heuberger
Memoirs of a Geisha: Sayuri's Theme – Williams, J.
Men, The (1950): Suite – Tiomkin, Dimitri
Mephisto Waltz (from Lenau's Faust) – Liszt
Merry Christmas – Templeton
Merry Widow: Overture – Lehár
Merry Widow Waltz – Lehár
Merry Widow: Selection – Lehár
Merry Widow: Symphonic Paraphrase – Lehár
Merry Wives of Windsor: Overture – Nicolai
Merseyside Echoes – Dickinson
Messiah: Sinfonia Pastoral – Handel
Metropolis Symphony – Daugherty
Mexican Hat Dance [See Cowboy Medley] – Ayars, Bo
MGM, The Music of (A Choral Medley) – Gilpin, Greg
Michael Jackson Spectacular – Jackson
Michelangelo – Piazzolla
Midday Witch, Op. 108 (The Noon Witch) – Dvořák
Midnight Elopement Galop – Fahrbach
Midsommarvaka: Swedish Rhapsody No. 1, Op. 19 – Alfvén
Midsummer Fanfare – Corigliano
Midsummer Night's Dream – Mendelssohn
Midway: Midway March – Williams, J.
Mighty Fortress Is Our God – Smith, Hale
Mikado: Overture – Sullivan
Mikado: Selections – Sullivan
Milk and Honey – Herman, Jerry
Millennium Fanfare – Douglas, S.
Milonga del Angel – Piazzolla
Mini Concerto for Organ, Percussion, Audience – McCabe
Minstrel Show – Gould
Minuet – Guion
Minuet in Jazz – Scott, R.
Minute Plus Waltz Rag – Gould
Miracle on 34th Street (1994): Main Title – Broughton, Bruce
Miracle on 34th Street, Overture to – Broughton, Bruce
Miserables, Les – Schoenberg, C-M
Miss Saigon – Schoenberg, C-M
Miss Saigon Medley – Schoenberg, C-M
Miss Saigon Rhapsody – Schoenberg, C-M
Mission – Williams, J.
Misson: Gabriel's Oboe – Morricone
Mission Impossible: Theme – Schifrin
Mississippi, Overture to the – Bennett, Robert Russell
Mississippi Suite – Grofé
Misty – Garner
Mock Morris – Grainger
Mock Morris for Orchestra – Grainger
Modern Love Waltz – Glass
Molly on the Shore – Grainger
Molly Maguires, The: Pennywhistle Jig (1970) – Mancini, Henry
Monday, Monday – Phillips, John
Mondo Cane (More) – Ortolani
Monotony: A Symphony for Metronome & Jazz Orchestra – Sowerby
Monster Movie Music Suite – Mancini, Henry
Mood Indigo – Ellington
Moonglow – Hudson, Will & Mills, Irving
Moonlight Sonata – Beethoven
Moon River [see Breakfast at Tiffanys]
Moorland Fiddlers for Orchestra – Wood
Morgen, ein Mittag und ein Abend in Wien (Morning, Noon, and Night in Vienna): Overture – Suppé
Morgenblätter (Morning Papers), Op. 279 – Strauss, Joh., Jr.
Most Happy Fella, The: Symphonic Impressions – Loesser, Frank
Most Wonderful Christmas, A – Sheldon, Robert
Mother's Whistler – Anderson
Motion Picture Medley – Goldsmith, Jerry
Motown Metal – Daugherty
Moulin Rouge: Come What May – Baerwald
Moulinet Polka, Op. 57 – Strauss, Joh., Jr.
Mouse Hunt (1997): Suite – Silvestri, Alan
Movie Spectacular – Bocook, Jay
Movie Spectacular – Elfman, D.
Movin' Out – Joel, Billy
Mr. Holland's Opus: American Symphony – Kamen
Mr. and Mrs. Smith: Tango de los Asesinos – Powell, John
Mrs. Madison's Minuet – Reinagle
Much Ado About Nothing: Suite (1993) – Doyle, Patrick
Munich: A Prayer for Peace – Williams, John T.
Munich: Hatikva (The Hope) – Williams, John T.
Muppet Medley – Chase, Bruce
Murder on the Orient Express – Bennett, Richard
Music for a Celebration: A Fantasy on National Themes – Schuller
Music for a Festive Occasion – Erb
Music for Hannukah: Two Folk Songs and a Hymn – Hinds, Thomas
Music of My Heart – Warren, D.
Music for Orchestra – Goldsmith, Jerry
Music for the Royal Fireworks – Handel
Music for the Theatre – Copland
Music from Chartres – Hoffman
Music from the Flicks – Moross
Music Man: Overture – Willson
Music Man: Seventy-Six Trombones – Willson
Music to a World's Fair Film – Antheil
Musicological Journey Through Twelve Days of Christmas – Courtney, Craig
Mummy Returns (2001) – Silvestri, Alan
Mutiny on the Bounty: Suite (1962) – Kaper, Bronislau
My Christmas – Menotti
My Cousin Rachel (1952): Suite – Waxman, Franz
My Cowboy Love Song – Guion
My Dog has Fleas: A Capriccio for Scratch orchestra – Walker, R.
My Fair Lady – Loewe, F.
My Geisha (1961): Goodbye Love – Finale – Waxman, Franz
My Geisha (1961): Suite – Waxman, Franz
My Geisha (1961): You Are Sympathy to Me – Waxman, Franz
My Left Foot: Suite – Bernstein, Elmer
Mysterious Island: Suite (1961) – Herrmann, Bernard
Mystery Movie Theme – Mancini, Henry
My Toy Balloon: Variations on a Brazilian Tune – Slonimsky
My Way – Revaux, J. & Francois, C.
My Wild Irish Rose – Olcott

N

Naaotwa Lala, Op. 39 – Swayne
Nabucco: Overture – Verdi
Nadia's Theme – Botkin
Naked Gun, The: Theme (1988) – Newborn, Ira
Naomi and Ruth: Ruth's Aria – Castelnuovo-Tedesco
Natali (Chorale Preludes for Christmas), Op. 37 – Barber
Natchez on the Hill, ThreeVirginia Country Dances – Powell, John
National Emblem March – Bagley
Nativity – Thomson
Nativity: Canticle for the Child – Dello Joio

Natoma: Grand Fantasia – Herbert
Natoma: Prelude to Act III – Herbert
Naughty Marietta: I'm Falling in Love with Someone – Herbert
Neapolitan Songs for Orchestra – Armand, Charles
Nearness of You – Carmichael, Hoagy
Negro Folk Symphony – Dawson
Nevada Smith: Overture – Newman, Alfred
New China March – Gould
New Dance, Op. 18b: Finale from the Ballet – Riegger
New England Triptych – Schuman
New Light, The: Prologue and 3 Canticles for Christmas – Van Vactor, David
New Morning for the World – Schwantner
New World A-Comin' – Ellington
New Year Song, Op. 144 "Mit eherner Zunge, da ruft es: Gebt acht" – Schumann
New York, New York Theme – Kander
Newsreel in 5 Shots – Schuman
Niagara Falls Suite – Grofé
Night and the City (1950): Suite Nightride for Orchestra – Waxman, Franz
Night at the Museum (2006): Suite – Silvestri, Alan
Night Boat: Whose Baby Are You? – Kern
Night Boat Selections – Kern
Night Creature – Ellington
Night Music – Dorati
Night Music – Musgrave
Night Music – Swanson, Howard
Night on Bald Mountain – Mussorgsky
Night Passage (1957): Follow the River – Tiomkin, Dimitri
Night Pieces – Templeton
Night Voices – Zaninelli
"Night Watchers" Symphony No. 2 – Welcher, Dan
Nineteen Forty-One: March of 1941 – Williams, J.
Noches en los jardines de Espana (Nights in the Gardens of Spain) – Falla
Nocturne – Borodin
Nocturnes – Bennett, Richard
Non-Violent Integration – Ellington
Norma Rae: It Goes Like It Goes – Shire, David
North by Northwest – Herrmann, Bernard
Norwegian Air – Halvorsen
Norwegian Dances, Op. 35 – Grieg
Norwegian Fairy Pictures – Halvorsen,
Norwegian Festival Overture, Op. 16 – Halvorsen

Norwegian Rhapsody No. 1 in A – Halvorsen
Norwegian Rhapsody No. 2 in G – Halvorsen
Norwegian Song, Op. 31 – Halvorsen
Notorious (1946): Suite – Webb, Roy
Now, Voyager (1942): Main Title and Final Scene – Steiner, Max
Nozze di Figaro (Marriage of Figaro) K. 492: Overture – Mozart
Nuit, Op. 114 – Saint-Saëns
Nunc Dimittis – Burgon
Nun's Story, The (1958) – Waxman, Franz
Nun's Story (1958): Short Suite – Waxman, Franz
Nursery Rhyme Overture – Blake
Nursery Suite – Elgar
Nutcracker Dances – Tchaikovsky
Nutcracker Suites – Tchaikovsky
NYC: Here's to the Big Apple – Bullock

O

Obertura para una Comedia (Overture for a Comedy) – Iturriaga, Enrique
O Brother Man – Ringwald
O Bury Me Not On the Lone Prairie – Mason, Jack
O Christmas Tree – Stephenson, James
O Holy Night (Cantique de Noel) – Adam, Adolphe Charles
O sole mio – Capua, Eduardo di
Oberon: Overture – Weber
Ocean Fantasia – Roylance & Galvin
Ode to Freedom – Downey, John
Ode to the King of Kings – Ellstein
Of Rivers and Trains – Mayer, William
Officer & A Gentleman: Up Where We Belong – Sainte-Marie & Nitzsche
Ohne Sorgen Polka, Op. 271 – Strauss, Josef
Oiseau de feu (Firebird): Suite (1919) – Stravinsky
Oiseau de feu (Firebird): Berceuse & Finale – Stravinsky
Oklahoma Crude – Mancini, Henry
Oklahoma Selections – Rodgers, R.
Ol' Man River – Kern
Old American Country Set – Cowell
Old American Dances – Bennett, Robert
Old American Songs – Copland
Old English Suite – Bantock
Old Fashioned Summer – Wendel
Old Folks At Home; Love's Old Sweet Song: Palms – Foster

Old MacDonald Had a Farm – Anderson
Old Song Medley – Hermann, Ralph
Old Song Medley No. 2 – Hermann, Ralph
Old Song Medley No. 3 – Hermann, Ralph
Old Timers Waltz – Lake, M. L.
Old Timers Waltz Medley No. 1 – Hermann, Ralph
Old Timers Waltz Medley No. 2 – Hermann, Ralph
Oliver Selections – Bart
Oliver! for Orchestra – Bart
Oliver Twist: Suite (2005) – Portman, Rachel
Olteneasca – Constantinescu
Olympia Australis – O'Boyle, Sean
Olympic Fanfare and Theme – Williams, J.
Olympic Spirit – Williams, J.
Omen, The (1976): Suite – Goldsmith, Jerry
On the Blue Danube – Strauss, Joh., Sr.
On Freedom's Ground – Schuman, William
On Golden Pond, Theme from – Grusin, Dave
On the Town: Three Dance Episodes – Bernstein, L.
On the Waterfront: Symphonic Suite – Bernstein, L
Once: Tribute to Martin Luther King – Beveridge
Once Upon a Dream – Fain, Sammy
One Nation – Zwilich
Operation Mambo – Templeton
Oración del Torero, Op. 34 – Turina
Orange Blossom Special – Rouse, Ervin
Orchestra Primer – Kirk
Ordinary People Theme (Canon) – Pachelbel
Orfeo ed Euridice: Dance of the Blessed Spirits – Gluck
Original Ragtime Band – Wendel
Orpheus an' His Slide Trombone – Dickerson
Orpheus in the Underworld: Galop (Can Can) – Offenbach
Orpheus in the Underworld: Overture – Offenbach
Out of the Cool – Heath
Out of Africa: Main Title – Barry
Outdoor Overture – Copland
Outlaw Josey Wales, The: Suite (1976) – Fielding, Jerry
Ouverture Solennelle (1812 Overture), Op. 49 – Tchaikovsky
Over There – Cohan
Overture to Blanche – Richman
Overture française – Geehl

Overture Half-Holiday – Gardner
Overture to the Mississippi – Bennett, Robert Russell
Overture in D Minor – Handel
Overture of the Season, Op. 89 – Svoboda
Overture on Russian and Kirghiz Folk Themes, Op. 115 – Shostakovich
Overture on Russian Folk Themes – Balakirev
Overture to a Pops Concert – Mancini, Henry
Overture to "The Civilian Barber" – Schickele
Overture, Scherzo and Finale – Schumann
Overture: A Little Travelin' Music – Hodkinson

P

Pachelbel's Christmas – Dorff
Paddington Bear's First Concert – Chappell
Paean to the Scholar, the Athlete and the Artist – Chiarappa
Pageant of P.T. Barnum – Moore, Douglas
Paisajes – Revueltas, Silvestre
Pal Joey: Bewitched, Bothered, and Bewildered – Rodgers, R.
Palladio: Concerto Grosso – Jenkins
Palm Court Music, Op. 81, No. 2 – Berkeley
Paloma (Spanish Serenade) – Yradier
Panamericana – Herbert
Papillon: Theme – Goldsmith, Jerry
Parade of the Wooden Soldiers – Jessel
Partita – Bennett, Richard
Pasquinade Caprice – Gottschalk
Passacaglia – Jenkins, Karl
Passage to India, A: A Symphonic Journey (1984) – Jarre, Maurice
Passion of the Christ Symphony – Debney
Passion of Scrooge, The (A Christmas Carol) – Deak, John
Pastorale: Three Little Brown Bulls – Guion
Patch of Blue, A (1966): Suite – Goldsmith, Jerry
Patience Selections – Sullivan
Patineurs (Skater's Waltz), Op. 183 – Waldteufel
Patriot – Williams, J.
Patton (1970): Attack – Goldsmith, Jerry
Patton (1970): Main Title – Goldsmith, Jerry
Patton (1970): Suite – Goldsmith, Jerry
Patton (1970): The Battle Ground – Goldsmith, Jerry
Patton (1970): The Hospital – Goldsmith, Jerry
Patton (1970): The Payoff – Goldsmith, Jerry
Pavane pour une Infante Defunte (Pavane for a dead princess) – Ravel
Pavane, Op. 50 – Fauré, Gabriel
Peanut Vendor – Simons
Peanut Polka, The – Farnan, Robert
Peanuts Gallery (1996) – Zwilich
Peer Gynt: Suite No. 1 – Grieg
Peg O' My Heart – Fisher
Pelleas et Melisande, Op. 80 – Faure
Penguin – Scott, R.
Penny Whistle Song – Anderson
Pennywhistle Jig – Mancini
Perfect Fool: Ballet Music Op. 39 – Holst
Perfume Suite (Dancers in Love) – Ellington
Peri: Fanfare – Dukas, Paul
Perpetuum mobile, Op. 257 – Strauss, Joh., Jr.
Perry Mason (1956): Theme – Steiner, Fred
Persian March, Op. 289 – Strauss, Joh., Jr.
Perú Negro – López, Jimmy
Peter and the Wolf, Op. 67 – Prokofiev
Peter Gunn – Mancini, Henry
Peter Gunn Meets Mr. Lucky – Mancini, Henry
Peter Gunn Theme – Mancini, Henry
Peter Pan (2003): Flying – Howard, James
Peter Pan (2003): Suite for Orchestra with Narrator – Howard, James
Peyton Place (1957): Suite – Waxman, Franz
Peyton Place (1957): Theme "The Wonderful Seasons of Love" or "For Those Who Are Young" – Waxman, Franz
Phantom of the Opera, The (1930) – Perry, Sam
Phantom of the Opera, The: Concert Version – Lloyd Webber
Phantom of the Opera, The: Entr'Acte – Lloyd Webber
Phantom of the Opera: Music of the Night – Lloyd Webber
Phantom of the Opera, The: Overture – Lloyd Webber
Phantom of the Opera Selections – Lloyd Webber
Phantom Regiment – Anderson
Philadelphia Grays Quickstep – Johnson
Philadelphia Story, The (1939): Suite – Waxman, Franz
Philharmonic Waltzes – Gould
Philly Rhapsody – Dorff
Pianist, Theme from the Film The – Kilar, Wojciech
Piano – Nyman
Pickaninny Dance – Guion
Pictures at an Exhibition – Mussorgsky
Pied Piper of Hamelin – Simons, Netty
Piége de lumiére – Damase
Piñata – Rodríguez
Pineapple Poll Suite – Sullivan
Pines of Rome: Pines of the Appian Way – Respighi
Pink Panther – Mancini
Pink Panther: It Had Better Be Tonight (Meglio Stasera) – Mancini
Pinocchio, A Merry Overture – Toch
Pinturas de Tamayo – Stucky
Pioneer, The (1951): Suite – Waxman, Franz
Pioneer Dances – Coolidge
Pique Dame: Prince Yeletsky's Aria: I Love You, Dear – Tchaikovsky
Pirates of the Caribbean: Curse of the Black Pearl – Badelt
Pirates of the Carribean: Dead Man's Chest (Soundtrack Highlights) – Zimmer
Pirates of Penzance Selections – Sullivan
Pirouette – Gould
Pizzicato Polka – Strauss, Joh. & Jos.
Place in the Sun, A (1951) – Waxman, Franz
Place in the Sun, A (1951): A Symphonic Scenario – Waxman, Franz
Planet of the Apes (1968): Suite – Goldsmith, Jerry
Planets – Holst
Plappermaulchen Polka Schnell, Op. 245 (Chatterbox) – Strauss, Jos.
Play Ball!: Casey at the Bat – Kapilow
Playing with Style – Peck
Please Turn Your Cell Phones On! – Rimelis, David
Pleasure Dome of Kubla Khan, Op. 8 – Griffes
Pledge of Allegiance – Reed
Plink Plank Plunk! – Anderson
Plow that Broke the Plains: Suite – Thomson, Virgil
Poem for Flute and Orchestra – Griffes
Poem of Freedom – Binder
Poem to the Moon – Mantovani, Annunzio Paolo
Polar Express: Believe; O Tannenbaum; Spirit of the Seasons; When Christmas Comes to Town – Silvestri

Polar Express Suite – Silvestri
Polish Polka Party – Hermann, Ralph
Polly-Wolly Doodle – Richardson
Polskie Kwiaty (Selection of Polish Songs & Dances) – Katz, S.
Poltergeist (1982): Night of the Beast (Clown Attack) – Goldsmith, Jerry
Poltergeist (1982): The Calling – Goldsmith, Jerry
Poltergeist (1982): The Light – Goldsmith, Jerry
Poltergeist (1982): Theme (Carol Anne's) – Goldsmith, Jerry
Pomp and Circumstance March No.1, Op. 39 – Elgar
Poor Butterfly – Hubbell
Popocatepeti – Shulman
Pops Concert, Overture to a – Mancini, Henry
Pops Hoe-Down – Hayman
Pop's Serenade – Gould
Porgy and Bess: Summertime – Gershwin
Porgy and Bess Medley – Gershwin
Porgy and Bess: Selections – Gershwin
Porgy and Bess: Symphonic Picture – Gershwin
Portrait of a Flirt – Farnan, Robert
Portrait of Hitch – Herrmann, Bernard
Portrait of Hitch: The Trouble with Harry Suite (1954) – Herrmann, Bernard
Possessed (1947) – Waxman, Franz
Postcard for Symphony Orchestra – Tichili, Frank
Post Horn Galop – Koenig
Power of Love – Grainger
Powerhouse – Scott, R.
Prairie Light: Three Texas Watercolors of Georgia O'Keeffe – Welcher, Dan
Prairie Suite – Guion
President's Country, A (1966): Medley – Tiomkin, Dimitri
Pretty Girl is Like Melody – Berlin
Prelude in E flat minor – Bach, J. S.
Prélude à L'après-midi d'un faune (Afternoon of a faun) – Debussy
Prelude and Fugue on "Dixie" – Weinberger
Prelude No. 2 – Gershwin
Prelude from Partita in E Maor – Bach, J. S.
Prelude to "Philip II" – Goossens
Presents from Santa – Richman
President's March – Herbert
Prince Igor – Borodin
Prince of Egypt Medley – Schwartz
Prince of Tides Suite – Howard, James
Prince Valiant – Waxman, Franz

Prisoner of Zenda: A Ruritanian Rhapsody for Orchestra – Newman, Alfred
Producers, The: Main Title (1968) – Morris, John
Promenade: Walkin' the Dog or The Real McCoy – Gershwin
Promenade – Anderson
Promenade Overture – Corigliano
Psycho (1960) – Herrmann, Bernard
Puff the Magic Dragon – Yarrow
Pumpkin-Eater's Little Fugue – McBride
Put On Your Old Grey Bonnet – Wenrich
Put Your Hand in the Hand – MacLellan, Gene

Q

QB VII: Suite – Goldsmith, Jerry
Quattro Staggioni, Le (The Four Seasons) Op. 8, Nos.1-4 – Vivaldi
Queen: Suite (2006) – Desplat, Alexandre
Quest for Camelot Selections – Foster
Quia, Quia (Kee-a, Kee-a) – Faith, Percy
Quiet City – Copland
Quiet Man, The (1952): Suite – Young, Victor
Quintuple Jazz, Op. 72 – Riegger
Quo Vadis Suite – Rózsa

R

Radetzky March, Op. 228 – Strauss, Joh., Sr.
Radio City Snapshots – Wagner, Joseph
Ragomania! – Bolcom
Ragtime – O'Boyle, Sean
Ragtime – Stravinsky
Ragtime Caprice, Op. 45 – Turok
Ragtime for Strings – Joplin
Ragtime Favorites for Strings – Joplin
Ragtime Nightingale – Lamb, Joseph
Ragtime Selections – Flaherty
Raid on Entebbe (1977): Theme – Shire, David
Raiders of the Lost Ark: Raiders March – Williams, J.
Railroad Suite – Mitchell
Rainy Day Medley – Gold, Marty
Rainy Days and Mondays – Williams, Paul
Rakastave the Lover – Sibelius

Rakes of Mallow, The (with Blue Grass Variation) – Muller, Frederick
Rambo: First Blood, Part 2 (1985): Theme – Goldsmith, Jerry
Rapsodia Peruana – Rebagliati, Claudio
Rapsodia sinfónica, Op. 66 – Turina
Rapsodie Espagnole – Ravel
Raven – Slatkin
Rawhide (1959): Theme – Tiomkin, Dimitri
Raymond Scott Fantasia – Scott, R.
Razors Edge, The – Newman, Alfred
Reach – Estefan, Gloria
Reagan Portrait, A – Vandervalk, Bruce
Rear Window (1954) – Waxman, Franz
Rebecca (1940): Suite – Waxman, Franz
Récit du pécheur and Pantomime – Falla, Manuel de
Red Back Book – Joplin
Red Cavalry March – Gould
Red House Suite – Rózsa
Red Pony – Copland
Red Poppy: Russian Sailor's Dance from Act I – Glière
Red Poppy, Suite No. 1 from the Ballet, Op. 70a – Glière
Red River (1948): Suite – Tiomkin, Dimitri
Red River Valley – Mandell
Red Violin: Chaconne – Corigliano
Red Violin: Suite – Corigliano
Reel Chaplin – Chaplin
Reeling in the New Year – Turok
Reflections on Rushmore – Gilbertson
Regalos – Deussen
Reindeer Variations – Richman, Lucas
Relicarlo – Padilla
Remembering Gatsby: Foxtrot for Orchestra – Harbison
Remembering the Beatles – Lowden
Requiem Mantras – Schickele
Retablos Sinfónicos – Garrido-Lecca, Celso
Retsei – Ellstein
Return of the Jedi, Highlights from – Williams, John T.
Return to Oz (1985): Theme – Shire, David
Revelry – Liebermann
Revenge of The Pink Panther (1978): Hong Kong Fireworks – Mancini
Revival: A Fantasy on Six Spirituals – Gould
Revolutionary Fantasy – Williams, Ernest S.
Revolutionary Garland – Kingman
Rhapsodic Overture – Nielsen
Rhapsody in Blue – Gershwin
Rhapsody in Blue for Trumpet and Orchestra – Gershwin, George

Rhapsody of Steel (1959) – Tiomkin, Dimitri
Rhapsody on Christmas Carols, A – Smith, Claude T.
Rhosymedre – Vaughan Williams
Richard III Overture – German
Richard Rodgers in Concert – Rodgers
Ricky-Tick Serenade – Shulman
Rio Bravo (1959): Suite – Tiomkin, Dimitri
Rio Grande – Lambert
Ritmo Jondo, Flamenco for Orchestra – Surinach
River – Ellington
River: Suite – Thomson
River Symphony – O'Boyle, Sean
Riverdance Theme – Whelan
Robe: Farewell to Diana – Newman, Alfred
Robin Hood: Prince of Thieves (Main Title) – Kamen, Michael
Robin and Marian – Barry, John
Rock Around the Clock – Wendel
Rock-a-Bye Your Baby with a Dixie Melody – Schwartz
Rockin' Christmas, A – Sayre, Charles
Rocky Highlights – Conti
Rocky Horror Picture Show – O'Brien
Rocky Point Holiday – Nelson, Ronald
Rodeo – Copland
Romamor (Roma, Amor, Labyrinthus) – Maxwell Davies
Romance in C Major, Op. 42 – Sibelius
Romance in the Dark, Nearness of You – Carmichael
Romance No. 1 in G Major, Op.40 – Beethoven
Romance No. 2 in F Minor, Op. 50 – Beethoven
Romance Op. 36 – Saint-Saëns
Romanza for String Orchestra – Goldsmith, O.
Romanze – Strauss, R.
Roman Holiday (1953): Main Title and Prelude – Young & Auric
Romeo and Juliet (1968) – Rota, Nino
Romeo and Juliet: A Time for Us – Rota, Nino
Romeo and Juliet: Duet – Tchaikovsky
Romeo and Juliet: Fantasy Overture – Tchaikovsky
Romeo and Juliet: Musical Sketches, Op. 56 – Kabalevsky
Romeo and Juliet: Overture – Bellini
Romeo and Juliet, Scenes from the Ballet – Prokofiev
Romeo and Juliet: Suite (1968) – Rota, Nino
Romeo and Juliet, Suite No. 1, Op. 64a – Prokofiev
Romeo and Juliet, Suite No. 2, Op. 64b – Prokofiev

Romeo and Juliet, Suite No. 3, Op. 101 – Prokofiev
Roméo and Juliette (Scene d'amour), Op.17 – Berlioz
Romp for Symphonic Orchestra and (Celebrity) Triangulist – Chiarappa
Rondo Marziale – Frackenpohl
Rookie of the Year: End Credits – Conti, Bill
Rooster Rhapsody – Cunningham
Roots: Suite (1977) – Fried, Gerald
Rose – McBroom
Rosen aus dem Süden (Roses from the South Waltzes), Op. 388 – Strauss, Joh., Jr.
Roumanian Rhapsody No. 1 A Major, Op. 11 – Enesco
Round Her Neck She Wore a Yellow Ribbon – Norton
'Round Midnight – Williams, Cootie & Monk
Round the Orchestra in Ten Minutes – Lundquist
Royal Firewater Musick – Schickele
Royal Fireworks Music – Handel
Royal Vagabond: Selections – Cohan
Rudolph the Red-Nosed Reindeer – Marks, Johnny
Rudy: Suite – Goldsmith, Jerry
Rudy: Theme for Flute and Chamber Orchestra – Goldsmith, Jerry
Ruddigore: Overture – Sullivan
Ruddigore Selections – Sullivan
Ruinen von Athen, Op. 113 Ruins of Athens: Turkish March and Chorus – Beethoven
Rumanian Folk Dances – Bartók
Rumba-Tarantella – Creston
Rumor, Op. 27 – Creston
Russia House, The (1990): Love Theme – Goldsmith, Jerry
Russian Folk Themes, Overture on – Balakirev
Russian and Kirghiz Folk Themes, Overture on, Op. 115 – Shostakovich
Russian Rag, The – Jendras, Louis F.
Russlan & Ludmilla: Overture – Glinka
Ryan's Daughter: Rosy's Theme – Jarre, Maurice

S

'S Wonderful – Gershwin
Saaledes saae Johannes (Thus Saw St. John…) – Ruders
Saga of the Mississippi – McDonald, Harl
Sail Away for the Rio Grande – Guion
Saint Bailey's Rag – Wendel
Saint Louis Blues – Handy

Saint Louis Blues – Wendel
Sally Selections for Orchestra – Kern
Salón México – Copland
Salutation Rag – Rodríguez
Salute to Ol' Blue Eyes – Moss
Salute to the Big Apple – Custer
Salute to the Big Bands Medley – Custer
Salute to Broadway, A – Strommen, Carl
Salute to the Cinema, A – Strommen, Carl
Salute to MGM: That's Entertainment – Polster
Salute to TV – Strommen, Carl
Salute to the United Nations – Isaac, Merle
Sam: ITV Music – McCabe
Sam: Theme Music – McCabe
Samson and Delilah (1949) – Young, Victor
Samson and Delilah (Bacchanale) – Saint-Saens
Sandpaper Ballet – Anderson
Sandpiper: Shadow of Your Smile – Mandel
Santa Dear – Wendel
Sarabande – Anderson
Satchmo!: A Tribute to Louis Armstrong – Ricketts
Satin Doll – Ellington
Saturday Night at the Firehouse – Cowell
Savannah River Holiday – Nelson, R.
Saving Private Ryan (Hymn to the Fallen) – Williams, J.
Saxanova – Holcombe
Scenes from "The Snow Queen" – Mayer, William
Scaramouche (1952): Suite – Young, Victor
Scent of a Woman: Por una Cabeza – Gardel
Schauspieldirektor (The Impresario) K. 486: Overtur – Mozart
Scheherazade: 4.The Sea-Shipwreck – Rimsky-Korsakov
Scherzo and Folk Tune – Goossens
Scherzo sobre Aires Tropicales – Cifuentes, Santos
Schindler's List – Williams, J.
Schöne Galathea (The Beautiful Galatea): Overture – Suppé
School for Scandal – Barber
Scrambled Opera (An Orchestral Antic) – Wilson, Don
Scrooge: Concert Scenes from A Christmas Carol – Rodríguez
Sea Pictures – Elgar
Sea Piece with Birds – Thomson
Season's Greetings: Festive Overture – Ward-Steinman, David

Seattle Slew Suite – Bolcom
Second Regiment Connecticut National Guard March – Anderson, Leroy
Secuencias (Sequences) – Garrido-Lecca, Celso
Seine at Night – Thomson
Semiramide: Overture – Rossini
Semper Fidelis – Sousa
Semper Paratus (1927): U.S. Coast Guard March Song – Boskerck, Captain Francis Saltus Van
Send In the Clowns – Sondheim
Sense and Sensibility: Suite (1995) – Doyle, Patrick
Sensemaya – Revueltas
Serenada Schizophraha – Elfman
Serenade for Summer – Muczynski
Serenade in Blue – Warren, H.
Serenade in G – Moeran
Serenade of Carols – Gould
Serenata – Anderson
Sergeant Pepper's Lonely Hearts Club Band – The Beatles
Set of Three, A – Powell
Seven Carols for Christmas – Parker, Alice
Seven Passages – Ranjbaran
Seven Popular Spanish Songs – Falla
Seven Spirituals – Kraft, William
Seventeen-Twelve Overture – Schickele
Seventh Voyage of Sinbad – Herrmann, Bernard
Shadow, The (1994): Main Title – Goldsmith, Jerry
Shaft, Selections from – Hayes, Isaac
Shane (1953): Suite – Young, Victor
Shave and a Haircut March – Ayars
Sheep and Goat – Guion
She'll be Comin' Round the Mountain [See Cowboy Medley] – Ayars, Bo
Shena B'rachot – Richman
Shenandoah [See Cowboy Medley] – Ayars, Bo
Shenandoah for Charles Ives' Birthday – Cooper
Shepherd's Hey – Grainger
She's a Good Fellow Selections – Kern
Ship of Fools: Candlelight & Silver Waltz (1965) – Gold, Ernest
Sh'Ma Yisroel – Ellstein
Shooting Stars – Ticheli, Frank
Short Symphony – Swanson
Show an Affirming Flame – Adler
Show Boat Overture – Kern
Show Boat Selections – Kern
Side Effects – Chiarappa
Signs Suite – Howard, James
Silent Movie – Hermann, Ralph
Silent Movie Music – O'Boyle, Sean
Silent Night – Gruber
Silent Night; O Little Town of Bethlehem – Gruber

Silverado – Broughton
Silver Chalice, The (1954): Short Suite – Waxman, Franz
Silver Chalice (1954): Suite – Waxman, Franz
Simple Introduction to the Orchestra – Kraft
Simpsons Theme – Elfman/Barry
Sinfonia a la Mariachi – Rodríguez
Sinfonia de Antigona (Symphony No. 1) – Chávez
Sinfonia en Negro: Homage to Martin Luther King – Balada
Sinfonia India (Symphony No. 2) – Chávez
Sinfonia Janiculum, Op. 113 – Persichetti
Sinfonía Junín y Ayacucho: 1824 – Iturriaga, Enrique
Sinfonietta – Poulenc
Sinfonietta Flamenca – Surinach
Six Degrees of Separation (1993): Tango – Goldsmith, Jerry
Sixth Sense Suite – Howard, James
Skater's Overture: Variations on a Theme of Waldteufel – Tyzik
Skylark – Mercer
Skylines – Maggio
Slalom – Pann
Slavonic Dances Op. 46 – Dvořák
Slavonic Dances Op. 72 – Dvořák
Sleepers Awake (Wachet Auf) – Bach
Sleeping with the Enemy (1991): Theme – Goldsmith, Jerry
Sleigh Ride – Anderson
Sleigh Ride – Mozart
Smoke Gets In Your Eyes – Kern
Smooth: Santana – Shur
Smurfs: March – Wendel
Snow, Op. 26, No. 1 – Elgar
Snow Falling on Cedars Suite – Howard, James
Snow, Snow, Beautiful Snow – Feller
Snow White – Churchill, Frank
Soirée dans Grenade – Debussy
Soiress Musicales, Op. 9 – Britten
Sol (The Sun): A Mexican Ballad – Chávez
Solitaire, Op. 141: Sarabande and Polka – Arnold, M.
Solitude – Ellington
Sombrero de tres picos (The Three Cornered Hat) – Falla
Something to Do: Labor Cantata – Gould
Somewhere In Time – Barry
Sones de Mariachi – Galindo
Song of Hiawatha, Op. 30: No. 1: Hiawatha's Wedding Feast – Coleridge-Taylor
Song for America – Sowerby
Song of America – Ringwald

Song of Bernadette (1943): Main Title – Newman, Alfred
Song of Bernadette (1943): Scherzo – Newman, Alfred
Song of Christmas – Ringwald
Song of Easter – Ringwald
Song of Free Nations – McDonald
Song of Freedom – Gould
Song of Hanukkah – Adler
Song of the Bells – Anderson
Song of the Flea – Mussorgsky
Song of the Volga Boatmen – Stravinsky
Songs and Dances of Death – Mussorgsky
Songs for Audrey: Breakfast at Tiffanys, Charade, Two for the Road – Mancini, Henry
Songs from the White Album – The Beatles
Songs of Praise: Toccata – Prizeman
Songs of the Slave – Mechem
Sophisticated Ladies – Ellington
Sorry, Wrong Number (1948): Passacaglia – Waxman, Franz
Sound Barrier Rhapsody, Op. 38 – Arnold, M.
Sound of Music Selections – Rodgers
Soarin' Over California – Goldsmith, Jerry
Sousa Overture, Op. 43 – Turok, Paul
Southern Echoes – Dello Joio, Norman
Souvenir – Drdla
Snow Chase – Christensen, James
Snows of Kilimijaro (1952) – Herrmann, Bernard
Spanish Lady Suite – Elgar
Spartacus: Camp at Night – North, Alex
Spartacus: Draba Fight – North, Alex
Spartacus: Final Farewell – North, Alex
Spartacus: Forest Meeting – North, Alex
Spartacus: Love Theme – North, Alex
Spartacus: Main Title – North, Alex
Spartacus: Vesuvius – North, Alex
Spartacus, Suites Nos. 1, 2, & 3 – Khachaturian
Special Starlight – Haslam, Herbert
Species (1995): End Credits – Young, Christopher
Spell for Green Corn: The Macdonald Dances – Maxwell Davies
Sphärenklänge (Music of the Spheres Waltz), Op. 235 – Strauss, Jos.
Spider Man – Elfman
Spinning Jenny: A Portrait of Leigh, Lancashire, circa 1948 – Maxwell Davies
Spirits of the Night – Bazelon
Spirituals in Sunshine and Shadow – Coolidge, Peggy

Spumante – Welcher
St. Luke Christmas Story – Effinger
St. Paul's Suite – Holst
Stagecoach: Suite (1939) – Hageman, Richard
Star-Spangled Banner – Smith, J. S.
Star-Spangled Spectacular – Cohan
Star Trek: Deep Space Nine Suite – McCarthy, Dennis
Star Trek: End Credits (2009) – Giacchino, Michael
Star Trek Main Theme – Goldsmith, J.
Star Trek, The Next Generation: Suite (1989) – Jones, Ron
Star Trek Through the Years – Custer
Star Trek: Voyager (1995) – Goldsmith, Jerry
Star Trek I: The Motion Picture "The Director's Cut" – Goldsmith, Jerry
Star Trek I: The Motion Picture "The Klingon Battle" – Goldsmith, Jerry
Star Trek I: The Motion Picture "The New Enterprise" – Goldsmith, Jerry
Star Trek I: The Motion Picture Theme (1979) – Goldsmith, Jerry
Star Trek 2: The Wrath of Khan (1982) – Horner, James
Star Trek 3: The Search for Spock "Stealing the Enterprise" (1984) – Horner, James
Star Trek 4: The Voyage Home – Rosenman, Leonard
Star Trek 5: The Final Frontier: Suite (1989) – Goldsmith, Jerry
Star Trek 6: The Undiscovered Country (1991) – Eidelman, Cliff
Star Trek 7: Generations "Overture" – McCarthy, Dennis
Star Trek 8: First Contact (1996) – Goldsmith, Jerry
Star Trek 9: Insurrection (1998) – Goldsmith, Jerry
Star Trek 10: Nemesis (2002) – Goldsmith, Jerry
Star Wars: Parade of the Ewoks (Return of the Jedi) – Williams, J.
Star Wars Main Theme – Williams, J.
Star Wars Suite – Williams, J.
Star Wars Episode I: Phantom Menace – Williams, J.
Star Wars: Selections from The Phantom Menace – Williams, J.
Star Wars: Episode II: Attack of the Clones (Across the Stars Love Theme) – Williams, J.
Star Wars: Episode III: Revenge of the Sith – Williams, J.
Stardust – Carmichael
Star Spangled Banner – Williams, J.

Star Wars Medley – Williams, J.
Stars and Stripes Forever – Sousa
State Fair (It's a Grand Night for Singing) – Rodgers
Steadfast Tin Soldier – Turrin, Joseph
Stephen Foster Overture – Foster, S.
Stephen Foster Overture – Wendel
Stepping Stones: Celebration Fanfare – Tower, Joan
Stevie Wonder Sounds – Wonder
Stormy Weather – Arlen
Story of Christmas Cantata – Matthews
Strangers on a Train (1951): Suite – Tiomkin, Dimitri
Streetcar Named Desire, A: Suite – North, Alex
Strike Up the Band – Gershwin
String Quartet No.2: Nocturne – Borodin, Alexander
Strong Men, The: Total Recall & Rambo Themes – Goldsmith, Jerry
Suerte de los Tantos (Fortune of Fools) – Richards
Suite – Kay
Suite on American Folk Songs – Vardi
Suite of Carols – Anderson
Suite Champêtre, Op. 98b – Sibelius
Suite Concertino – Frackenpohl
Suite Espagnole – Geehl
Suite for Jazz Orchestra No. 1 and No. 2 – Shostakovich
Suite for Strings on American Negro Themes – McDonald, Harl
Suite for Variety Orchestra No. 1 and No. 2 – Shostakovich
Suite française – Bennett, Richard
Suite from Martin Chuzzlewit – Burgon
Suite from Testament of Youth – Burgon
Suite hébraïque – Bloch
Suite of English Folk Dances – Tomlinson
Suite of Scottish Dances – Alwyn
Suite Latinoamericana (Tango, Vals, Choro, Son) – Meza, Vinicio
Sum of All Fears, The (2002) – Goldsmith, Jerry
Summer Skies – Anderson
Summer Stock: A Short Merry Overture – Adler
Summersong – Brubeck, Dave
Summertime – Gershwin
Summertime, Summertime – Jameson & Feller
Summon the Heroes – Williams, J.
Sunburst – Dorff, Daniel
Sundowners, The (1960): Suite – Tiomkin, Dimitri
Sunlight Echoes – Thomas, A.
Sunrise in Puerto Rico – Creston

Sunset Boulevard (1950): Staged Reading in Two Acts – Waxman, Franz
Sunset Boulevard (1950): Suite – Waxman, Franz
Sunshine of Your Love – Gordon
Sun-Treader – Ruggles
Supergirl: Suite – Goldsmith, Jerry
Superman March (Main Theme) – Williams, J.
Superman Returns: Concert Selections – Williams, J.
Superman Returns Suite – Williams, J.
Surf's Up! – Wendel
Suspicion (1941): Suite – Waxman, Franz
Svandadudák (Shvanda the Bagpiper): Polka and Fugue – Weinberger
Swanee – Gershwin, George
Swanee River in the Style of . . . (Bach, Beethoven, Brahms, Debussy, Ellington, Gershwin, Liszt, Mozart, Rimsky-Korsakov, Strauss (Johann), Tchaikovsky, Wagner) – Gould
Swans of Pongo Lake – Frazelle
Swarm, The (1978): Bees Arrive/End Title – Goldsmith, Jerry
Sweet Betsy from Pike [See Cowboy Medley] – Ayars, Bo
Sweet Charity Medley – Coleman
Sweet Smell of Success: Main Title – Bernstein, Elmer
Swing Carol Fantasy – Stephenson, James M. III
Swing, Ludwig, Swing! – Wendel
Swinton Jig, on a Nineteenth Century Lancashire Fiddle Tune – Maxwell Davies
Sylvia: Suite (4.Cortege de Bacchus) – Delibes
Symphonette No. 2 – Gould
Symphonette No. 2: Pavanne – Gould
Symphonette No. 3 (Third American Symphonette) – Gould
Symphonic Sketches: Hobgoblin – Chadwick
Symphonic Study: Machines, Op. 30 – Arnold, M.
Symphonic Swing – Tyzik
Symphonie Espagnole, Op. 21 – Lalo, Edouard
Symphonie Romantique: Night in the Tropics – Gottschalk, Louis Moreau
Symphony for Young Lovers – Rasmussen
Symphony Holidays – Ives
Symphony in Four American Idioms – Knight
Symphony in G – Dyson
Symphony in Ragtime – Zinn
Symphony in Steel – Grofé

Symphony No. 1 in G Minor, Op. 13: (Winter Dreams) – Tchaikovsky
Symphony No. 1: Living, Breathing, Earth – Warshauer
Symphony No. 100 in G Major (Military) – Haydn
Symphony No. 101 in D Major (The Clock) – Haydn
Symphony No. 2 – Borodin
Symphony No. 2 "Night Watchers" – Welcher
Symphony No. 3 The Camp Meeting – Ives
Symphony No. 4 in A Major (Italian) – Mendelssohn
Symphony No. 8 in G Major (Le soir) – Haydn
Symphony No. 41, K.551, C Major (Jupiter) K. 551 – Mozart
Symphony No. 82 "The Bear" – Haydn
Symphony No. 94 in G Major (Surprise) – Haydn
Synconata – Sowerby
Syncopated Clock – Anderson

T

Tabloid – Grofé
Tahiti-Trot, Op. 16 – Shostakovich
Take Flight – Wendel
Take Me Along! – Merrill, Bob
Take a Ride with Santa – Richman
Take Me Out to the Ball Game – Tilzer
Taking of Pelham One Two Three (1974): Theme – Shire, David
Tale of Tsar Saltan: Flight of the Bumble Bee – Rimsky-Korsakov
Tall Ships – Wendel
Tall Ships Suite – Roylance & Galvin
Tall Story for Orchestra – Moross
Tam O'Shanter: Overture, Op. 51 – Arnold, M.
Tam O'Shanter: Scherzo – Goossens
Tango de la Luna – Secunda, Sholom
Tango Jalousie (Tango Tzigane) – Gade
Tango No. 1 (Coral) – Piazzolla
Tango No. 2 (Canyengue) – Piazzolla
Tango: Por una Cabeza – Gardel, Carlos
Tanguedia – Piazzolla
Tanze aus Rumanien – Constantinescu
Tap Dance Concerto – Gould
Taras Bulba (1962): Suite – Waxman, Franz
Taras Bulba (1962): The Ride of the Cossacks – Waxman, Franz
Tarzan and the Mermaids (1948): Suite – Tiomkin, Dimitri

Taxi Driver: A Night Piece for Orchestra – Herrmann, Bernard
Telegramme Walzer – Strauss, Joh., Jr.
Television Themes Medley – Goldsmith, Jerry
Television Medley – Hagen, Earl
Temenos, with Mermaids and Angels – Maxwell Davies
Tempest – Rodriguez
Tender Land: Suite – Copland
Ten Commandments: Suite – Bernstein, Elmer
Ten: It's Easy to Say – Mancini, Henry
Tension at Table Rock (1956): Suite – Tiomkin, Dimitri
Tequila – Rio
Tequila Sunrise – Rodríguez
Terminal: Viktor's Tale – Williams, J.
Teminator, The: Theme (1984) – Fiedel, Brad
Teufel als Hydraulicus, D. 4: Overture – Schubert
Thanksgiving Hymn – Richman
That's It, That's All...The End! – Wendel
Them!: Ant Fugue (1954) – Kaper, Bronislau
They All Sang Yankee Doodle – Brubeck, Dave
They Didn't Believe Me – Kern
Thing from Another World, The (1951): Suite – Tiomkin, Dimitri
Things Ain't What They Used to Be – Ellington, M.
Things to Come – Bliss
This Old Man Sing-Along – Naughtin
This Is Our America – Gillis
Thomas Jefferson – Ranjbaran
Thorn Birds Theme, The – Mancini
Thorn Birds: Meggie's Theme, The – Mancini
Thoroughly Modern Millie – Tesori, Jeanine
Thoroughly Modern Millie: Sky-Hi Waltz – Bernstein, Elmar
Those Magnificent Men in Their Flying Machines (1965) – Goodwin, Ron
Thousand and One Nights Waltz, Op.346 – Strauss, Joh., Jr.
Three Black Kings – Ellington, E.
Three Choral Hymns – Vaughan Williams
Three Choral Preludes – Bach
Three Christmas Carols – Stokowski
Three Christmas Songs – Holst
Three Columbian Songs – Arnold, A.
Three Cornered Hat: Miller's Dance – Falla, Manuel de
Three Crazy Pieces – Arnold, A.
Three Cuban Dances – Cervantes
Three Dances: Henry VIII – German

Three Dylan Thomas Poems, Op. 3 – Layton
Three Hallucinations – Corigliano
Three Kings – Maxwell Davies
Three Latin-American Dances – Frank
Three Little Pieces for Strings – Bush
Three Love Songs – Nørgård
Three Minutes of Reality (Tango) – Piazzolla
Three Musical Elements: Earth, Water, Space – Knight
Three Noels – Grundman, Clare
Three Old Viennese Dances; No. 3 (Schoen Rosmarin) – Kreisler
Three Places in New England – Ives
Three Songs for America – Amram
Three Strange Cases – Schickele, Peter
Three Themes – Williams, John
Three Tone Pictures – Griffes
Three Worlds of Gulliver: Suite – Herrmann, Bernard
Three's Company – Amundson
Threnody: To the Victims of Hiroshima – Penderecki
Thrill of the Orchestra – Peck
Thunderer March – Sousa
Thunderwalker – Garrop
Thurber's Dogs – Schickele, Peter
Thus Saw St. John... (Saaledes saae Johannes) – Ruders
Tick-Tack Polka – Strauss, Joh., Jr.
Tico Tico – Abreu, Zequinha de
Till Eulenspiegels lustige Streiche (Till Eulenspiegel's Merry Pranks), Op. 28 – Strauss, R.
Titanic Suite – Horner
To Be Young Again – Chiarappa
To Catch a Thief: Suite (1955) – Murray, Lyn
To Kill a Mockingbird: Suite – Bernstein, Elmer
To Spring – Grieg
To the Flag – Reitz
Toccata Op.1 – Garrido-Lecca, Gonzalo
Toccata & Fugue, BWV 565, D minor – Bach
Toccata and Fugue in C for Organ: Adagio – Bach
Tom Sawyer Overture (California Overture) – Antheil
Tonadillas – Granados
Tortoise and the Hare – Dorff
Totentanz – Liszt
Touch of Jazz! – Brubaker
Tournaments – Corigliano
Toward the Splendid City – Danielpour
Towers of Light – Wendel
Town Without Pity (1961): Theme – Tiomkin, Dimitri
Toy Concertino – Raksin

Toy Symphony – Freyhan
Toy Symphony, Op. 62 – Arnold, M.
Toy Trumpet – Scott, R.
Traditional Slavic Christmas Music – Stokowski
Tragische Ouverture, Op. 81 (Tragic Overture) – Brahms
Treasure of Sierra Madre, The (1948): Suite – Steiner, Max
Tres Aires Chilenos (Three Chilean Aires) – Soro, Enrique
Tres Danzas españolas – Granados
Tribute to Foster – Grainger
Tribute to Romberg – Romberg
Tribute to the Duke – Ellington
Triptych: As on the Night, Op. 100, No. 1b (Christmas Ode) – Hovhaness
Tristan und Isolde: Prelude and Liebestod – Wagner, R.
Tritsch Tratsch Polka, Op. 214 (Chit-Chat) – Strauss, Joh., Jr.
Tritsch-Tratsch (The Circus) – Strauss, Joh., Jr.
Trittico Botticelliano: 2.Adoration of the Magi – Respighi
Triumph of Neptune: Adagio, Variations and Hornpipe – Berners
Trois Poèmes Juifs – Bloch
Tropicalia: Celebration – Sierra
Troubadour Music – Gould
True Lies: Theme (1994) – Fiedel, Brad
Trumpeter's Lullaby – Anderson
Trunks: A Circus Story – Rodríguez
Truth Is Fallen – Brubeck, Dave
Tubby the Tuba – Kleinsinger
Turandot: Overture and March – Weber
Turkey in the Straw – Guion
Turkish March – Mozart
TV Spectacular – Curnow
'Twas the Night Before Christmas – Goldstein, William
Twelve Days of Christmas – Austin
Twelve English Songs – Dewitt
Twelve Gifts of Christmas – Tyzik
Twentiana – Ades
Twenty Fifth Annual Putnam County Spelling Bee – Finn
Twenty Polish Christmas Carols – Lutosławski
Twilight in Turkey – Scott, R.
Twilight Zone, The (1961): The Invaders – Goldsmith, Jerry
Twilight Zone: The Movie (1983): End Title – Goldsmith, Jerry
Twinkle Fantasia – Hunter
Twinkletoes Ballet: Tango Lullaby – Gillis
Twister Main Theme – Mancina
Two Choric Dances, Op. 17a and Op. 17b – Creston

Two Christmas Carols in Traditional Style – Musgrave
Two Gershwin Portraits – Gershwin, George
Two Improvisations – Baker
Two Jamaican Pieces – Benjamin
Two Marches – Milhaud
Two Norwegian Airs, Op. 63 – Grieg
Two Pieces: 1. On Hearing the First Cuckoo in Spring; 2. Summer-Night on the River – Delius
Two Portraits of Barcelona – Pann
Two Romantic Pieces – Sowerby, Leo
Two Sketches – Goossens, Eugene
Two Thousand One Space Odyssey: Fanfare – North, Alex
Two Thousand One: A Symphonic Suite in Four Movements – North, Alex
Two Venetian Dialect Songs – Tanara
Two Worlds of Kurt Weill: Berlin Suite – Weill
Two Worlds of Kurt Weill: New York Suite – Weill
Typewriter – Anderson, Leroy

U

Una Música Escondida – Fernandez, Agustín
Unbegun Symphony – Schickele
Unchained Melody (1955) – North, Alex
Under Fire (1983): Suite – Goldsmith, Jerry
Under Gypsy Skies – Hunsberger, Donald
Under the Admiral's Flag, Op. 82 (Unter der Admiralsflagge) – Fučik
Under the Big Top – Wendel
Under the Spreading Chestnut Tree – Weinberger
Under the Tuscan Sun (2003): Suite – Beck, Christophe
Unforgiven, The – Tiomkini, Dimitri
Uninvited, The (1944): Stella by Starlight – Young, Victor
Union Station – Kapilow
Union: Paraphrase de concert sur les airs nationaux – Gottschalk
United Nations March – Shostakovich
Untamed (1955) – Waxman, Franz
Unter dem Doppeladler (Under the Double Eagle March), Op. 159 – Wagner, J. F.
Unter Donner und Blitz (Thunder and Lightning Polka), Op. 324 – Strauss, Joh., Jr.
Up In the Air (2009) – Kent, Rolfe
Up, Music from – Giacchino, Michael

Up and Down Man: Suite – Blake
Upbeat! – Zwilich
Uptown Hoedown – Schickele
Urban Bird – Bond
Usual Suspects, The (1995) – Ottman, John

V

Valentines – Kernis
Valse chevaleresque, Op. 96c – Sibelius
Valse Fantaisie – Glinka
Valse Gracieuse – German
Valse lyrique, Op. 96a – Sibelius
Variations for Orchestra – Arnold, A.
Variations on America – Ives
Variations on "La ci darem la mano," Op. 2 – Chopin
Variations on a Hungarian Folksong: The Peacock – Kodály
Variations on a Nursery Tune – Bennett, Richard
Variations on "Pop! Goes the Weasel" – Cailliet
Variations on a Shaker Melody – Copland
Variations on a Theme by Handel – Handel
Variations on a Theme by Haydn, Op.56a – Brahms
Variations on a Waltz – Moross
Vergnugungszug Polka, Op. 281 (Excursion Train) – Strauss, Joh. Jr.
Vertigo: Suite (1958) – Herrmann, Bernard
Very Best Time of the Year – Rutter
Victor, Victoria (1982): Crazy World – Mancini, Henry
Victorious Herbert – Herbert, Victor
Victory at Sea – Rodgers
Vida breve: Interlude & Dance – Falla
Vida breve: Spanish Dance No. 1 – Falla, Manuel de
Video Games Live, Suite from – Ford, Ralph
Vie parisienne: Overture – Offenbach
Vienna: City of My Dreams – Sieczynsky
Villi: "The Witches' Sabbath" – Puccini
Village, The: The Gravel Road – Howard, James
Village, The: Suite-Village Romance – Howard, James
Villanelle – Dodgson
Vintage Renaissance – Kraft
Virgin de la Macarena – Mendez
Visions of Merlin – Welcher, Dan

Viva Zapata (1952): Gathering Forces – North, Alex
Vli Jeru Sholayim Ircho – Ellstein
Voices of the Night, Op. 86 – Berkeley
Von der Borse, Polka française, Op. 337 – Strauss, Joh. Jr.
Voyager – Roylance & Galvin

W

Wagon Train – Moross
Waldmeister Overture – Strauss, Joh. Jr.
Walkure – Wagner, Richard
Walpurgis Night: Stage Music No. 1 – Blomdahl
Waltz for Betz – Grant
Waltz of Madness – O'Boyle, Sean
Waltzes from Films: Suite – Bernstein, Elmar
Waltzing Cat – Anderson
Wand of Youth Suite No. 1, Op. 1a & No. 2, Op. 1b – Elgar
War and Peace: Suite (1956) – Rota, Nino
War Wagon, The (1967): Suite – Tiomkin, Dimitri
Washington Post March – Sousa
Wasps Overture – Vaughan Williams
Wassail Dances for Orchestra – Lane, Philip
Wassail, Wassail All Over the Tuba – Stephenson, James M. III
Water Music – Handel
Water Music for 4th of July Evening – Antheil, George
Waves of the Danube: The Anniversary Song – Ivanovici, Josif
Way You Look Tonight – Kern
We Need a Little Christmas – Wendel
Wedding Day at Troldhaugen, Op. 65, No. 6 – Grieg
Weihnachten (Christmas), Op. 145/3 – Reger
Wein, Weib und Gesang (Wine, Women, and Song), Op. 333 – Strauss, Joh., Jr.
Well, The (1951): Suite – Tiomkin, Dimitri
Western Fanfare – Richman
West Side Story Highlights – Bernstein, L.
West Side Story Overture – Bernstein, L.
West Side Story Selections – Bernstein, L.
West Side Story: Symphonic Dances – Bernstein, L.
We Three Basses! from We Three Kings – Stephenson, James M. III

We Three Kings of Orient Are – Stephenson, James M. III
We Three Strings! from We Three Kings – Stephenson, James M. III
What Child Is This? – Stokowski
What Child Is This – Tyzik
What's New? – Haggart
Wheat Field at Noon – Thomson
Wheels on the Bus Sing-Along – Naughtin
When Irish Eyes Are Smiling – Ball
When Johnny Comes Marching Home: Overture – Harris
When Tony Played the Sax – Turrin, Joseph
When TV Was Young – Wendel
When You Wore a Tulip – Wenrich
Where the Rainbow Ends Suite – Quilter
Whistle Down the Wind – Arnold, M.
Whistler and His Dog – Pryor
White Christmas – Berlin
White Dawn, The: Suite (1974) – Mancini, Henry
White Nights: Separate Lives – Bishop
White Peacock – Griffes
Whythorne's Shadow – Moeran
Wiener Blut (Vienna Blood), Op.354 – Strauss, Joh., Jr.
Wild Bunch, The: Suite in Two Movements (1969) – Fielding, Jerry
Wild is the Wind (1958): Theme – Tiomkin, Dimitri
Wild One, The (1953) – Stevens, Leith
Wild Mountain Thyme: Will You Go, Darling, Go? – Keillor
Wild Rovers, The (1971): Bronco Busting – Goldsmith, Jerry
Wild Winter II – Musgrave
Wild, Wild West – Markowitz
Willow Weep for Me – Ronell
Wind and the Lion (1975) – Goldsmith, Jerry
Wind Beneath My Wings – Henley
Windjammer – Gould
Windmills of Your Mind – Legrand
Winter Bonfire: Suite, Op. 122 – Prokofiev
Winter Lightning – Tsontakis
Winter Wonderland – Bernard
Witch Boy: Square Dance from the Ballet – Salzedo
Witch Boy: Suite from the Ballet – Salzedo
Witch Boy: Three Dances from the Ballet – Salzedo
Witchcraft – Coleman
With You I'm Born Again – Shire, David
Witness: Building the Barn – Jarre
Wizard of Oz – Arlen

Wizard of Oz Choral Review – Arlen
Wizard of Oz Orchestral Suite: "Wizard of Oz Medley" – Arlen
Wizard of Oz Selections – Arlen
Wood Notes – Still
Work – Harris
Workers' Union – Andriessen
Workout – McBride
World's Fair Suite – Grofé
World of Warcraft – Brower, Russell
Worried Drummer – Schreiner
Wrong Man, The: Prelude (1956) – Herrmann, Bernard
Wuthering Heights: Cathie's Theme – Newman, Alfred
Wuthering Heights: Concert Suite – Newman, Alfred
Wyatt Earp: End Credits – Howard, James

X

X: The Life and Times of Malcolm X (Malcolm's Prison Aria) – Davis, A.
X-Files: Main Title Theme – Snow, Mark
X-Men: The Last Stand – Powell, John
X2: X-Men United – Ottman, John

Y

Yale-Princeton Football Game – Ives
Yankee Doodle – Gould
Yellow Rose of Texas – Dragon
Yellow Rose of Texas [See Cowboy Medley] – Ayars, Bo
Yellowstone Fires – Welcher
Yeoman of the Guard Overture – Sullivan
Yeoman of the Guard Selections – Sullivan
Yismechu – Ellstein
Yorick Overture – Bush
You and Hugh – Kapilow
You Do Something to Me – Porter, Cole
You Made Me Love You – Monaco
Young at Heart (1938) – Waxman, Franz
Young Frankenstein: The Transylvanian Lullaby (1974) – Morris, John
Young and the Restless (Nadia's Theme) – Botkin
Young Land, The (1959): Strange are the Ways of Love – Tiomkin, Dimitri

Young Person's Guide to the Orchestra, Op. 34 – Britten
Young Sherlock Holmes (1985): Suite – Broughton, Bruce
You're a Grand Old Flag – Cohan
Yuletide Festival – Warrington, John

Z

Zampa Overture – Herold
Zauberharfe (Rosamunde) D. 644: Overture – Schubert
Zigeunerbaron (Gypsy Baron): Overture – Strauss, Joh., Jr.
Zigeunerliebe (Gypsy Love) Waltzes – Lehár
Zigeunerweisen, Op. 20 – Sarasate
Zion – Welcher
Zoo Called Earth – Schickele
Zorba the Greek (1964): Theme – Theodorakis, Mikis

APPENDIX E

Publishers and Sources

On the left of each entry is the abbreviated version of the publisher as used in the main body of this book. Current contact information, at the time of this handbook's completion, is listed on the right. International telephone numbers are intended for calls from the United States. Publishers without a U.S. rental agent must be contacted directly. Frequent changes occur in the publishing industry, so the reader is encouraged to contact the following sources or a music dealer for updates as needed:

American Society of Composers, Authors, and Publishers (ASCAP):
    Tel: 212.621.6000
    Tel: 212.621.6160 (ACSAP clearance representative)
    Fax: 212.724.9064
    Direct link: www.ascap.com/index.html

Broadcast Music, Inc. (BMI):
    Tel: 212.586.2000
    Tel: 212.830.8362 (Publisher contact information)
    Direct link: www.bmi.com

Major Orchestra Librarians' Association (MOLA):
    Direct link: www.mola-inc.org
    Direct link to MOLA PAD (list of orchestral publishers):
        www.mola-inc.org/cgi-bin/fudpaddb/fudpadndx.cgi

Music Publishers' Association (MPA):
    Direct link: www.mpa.org

20th Century	20th Century Fox U.S. Agent: Kane
A. Spelling	U.S. Agent: Famous Music Corporation
Alfred	Alfred Publishing P.O. Box 10003 Van Nuys, CA 91410-0003 USA Tel: 818.891.5999; (818) 891-5999 Fax: 818.895.1846 E-mail: rental@alfred.com; customerservice@alfred.com Web site: www.alfred.com/rental Web site: www.alfred.com *Agent for EAM rentals; Belwin; High Touch Music (Christmas selections arranged by Gary Fry); Lawson-Gould; Sam Fox Music; Warner Brothers Music; Warner/Chappell. Alfred Music is the sales agent for Warner/Chappell/Belwin.*
Allen	Thornton W. Allen Co New York See Luck's for rental

Almo/BadAzz	Almo Music Corp and BadAzz Music U.S Agent: Rondor Music International 2440 Sepulveda Blvd. #119 Los Angeles CA 90064 Tel: 310.235.4800 310.235.4800 Toll Free Fax: 310.235.4801 E-mail: rondorla@umusic.com Website: www.universalmusicpublishing.com
ALH	Alhambra RXR U.S. Agent: Schirmer (rental)
AME	American Music Edition U.S. Agent: Presser
AMP	Associated Music Publishers U.S. Agent: Schirmer (rental); Leonard (sales)
ASH	Ashdown U.S. Agent: Schirmer (rental)
ATV	Sony/ATV Songs LLC U.S. Agent: Schirmer (rental)
Bärenreiter	Bärenreiter-Verlag Heinrich-Schütz-Allee 35-37 D - 34131 Kassel Germany Tel: +49.561.3105.0 Fax: +49.561.3105.240 E-mail: info@baerenreiter.com; ny@baerenreiter.com (perusal scores) Web site: www.baerenreiter.com U.S. Agent: Alfred (rental); No exclusive U.S. sales agent.
Belaieff	M. P. Belaieff U.S. Agent: EAM (rental)
Bell	Bell of Freedom Niel DePonte 0240 SW Canby Street Portland, OR 97219 E-mail: info@BellOfFreedom.com Web site: www.belloffreedom.com
Belwin	CCP/Belwin Inc. U.S. Agent: Alfred
Berlin Music	U.S. Agent: Williamson Music (rental); Leonard (sales)
Big Three	Big Three Music Corporation U.S. Agent: Schirmer (rental); Leonard (sales)

Billaudot	Gérard Billaudot Editeur 14 Rue de L'Echiquier 75010 Paris France Tel: +33.147.70.1446 Fax: +33.145.23.2254 E-mail: info@billaudot.com Web site: www.billaudot.com U.S. Agent: Presser
Boccaccini	Boccaccini & Spada Edizioni Musicali U.S. Agent: Presser
Boelke	Boelke-Bomart/Mobart Music Publishers U.S. Agent: EAM
Boosey	Boosey & Hawkes, Inc. 35 East 21st Street, 4th Floor New York, NY 10010-6212 Tel: 212.358.5300 212.358.5300 (ext. 2 for rental department) Fax: 212.358.5301 (5307 for rentals) (5306 for perusal materials) E-mail: usrental@boosey.com Web site: www.boosey.com U.S. Agent: Boosey (rental); Leonard (sales) *Agent for Ricordi, Durand-Eschig-Salabert, Amphion, Rideau Rouge, EMB-Editio Musica Budapest, Weinberger, Carisch, Sugarmusic, Gehrmans, and Fennica Gehrmans.*
Bosworth	Bosworth & Co. Limited U.S. Agent: Schirmer (rental); Music Sales (sales)
Bote & Bock	Bote & Bock U.S. Agent: Boosey (rental); Leonard (sales)
BOU	Alain Boublil Music, Ltd 1775 Broadway, Suite 708 New York, NY 10019 Tel: 212.246.7203 Fax: 212.246.7217 U.S. Agent: Schirmer (rental)
Bourne	Bourne Company 5 West 37th Street New York, NY 10018 Tel: 212.391.4300 Fax: 212.391.4306 E-mail: bourne@bournemusic.com Web site: www.bournemusic.com
Breitkopf	Breitkopf & Härtel Walkmühlstrasse 52 D-65195 Wiesbaden Germany E-mail: sales@breitkopf.com Web site: www.breitkopf.com U.S. Agent: Schirmer (rental); No exclusive U.S. sales agent

Broude Bros.	Broude Brothers Ltd. 141 White Oaks Rd. or PO Box 547 Williamstown, MA 01267-0547 Tel. 800.225.3197 Fax: 413.458.5242 E-mail: broude@sover.net Web site: Process orders by E-mail.
Capital	Capital Press ASCAP U.S. Agent: Luck's (rental)
Chappell	Chappell & Co., Inc.; Warner/Chappell U.S. Agent: Alfred
Chester	J. & W. Chester, Ltd. and Novello & Co. (Chester/Novello) Head Office: 14-15 Berners Street London W1T 3LJ England Tel: +44. (0)20.7612.7400 Fax: +44. (0)20.7612.7545 E-mail: promotion@musicsales.co.uk 　　　or Hire and Distribution: Newmarket Road Bury St. Edmonds Suffolk IP33 3YB England Tel: +01.284.70.5705 Fax: +01.284.70.3401 E-mail: hire@musicsales.co.uk Web site: www.chesternovello.com U.S. Agent: Schirmer (rental); Music Sales (sales) Web site: www.newmusicals.com
Choudens	Choudens Editions, Paris 38 rue Jean Mermoz 75008 Paris France Tel: 011.42.66.6297 Fax: 011.42.66.6279 E-mail: editions.choudens@wanadoo.fr U.S. Agent: Schirmer
Church	The John Church Co. U.S. Agent: Presser
Clear Mud	Clear Mud Publications Richard Chiarappa 22 Grenhart Street West Hartford, CT 06117-2105 E-mail: info@cmpub.com 　　　chiarappa@comcast.net
CPP/Belwin	CPP/Belwin Music U.S. Agent: Alfred
Crawford Music	Crawford Music Corporation See Luck's for rental

Curci-Pagano	Edizioni Curci S.r.l Galleria del Corso, 4 I-20122 Milano Italia Web site: www.edizionicurci.it U.S. Agent: Curci USA Corp.
Curwen	J. Curwen & Sons U.S. Agent: Schirmer (rental); Leonard (sales)
Disney	Disney Concert Library 500 South Buena Vista Street Burbank, CA 91521-6431 Tel: 818.567.5015 Fax: 818.567.5178 E-mail: Concert.library@library@disney.com Web site: www.disneyconcertlibrary.com
Doblinger	Doblinger Music Publishers Dorotheergasse Postfach 882 10 A-1010 Vienna Austria Tel: +43.1515.03.0 Fax: +43.1515.03.51 E-mails: music@doblinger; rent@doblinger.at Web site: www.doblinger-musikverlag.at No U.S. Agent
Dorabet	Dorabet Music U.S. Agent: RBC Publications
Douglas	Douglas Music 1527 North St. Boulder, CO 80304 E-mail: billdouglas@comcast.net Web site: www.billdouglas.cc
Dragon	Carmen Dragon Music Company 28908 Grayfox Street Malibu, CA 90265 USA Tel: 310.457.9902 Fax: 310.457.8470 E-mail: dragon.music@verizon.net Web site: www.carmendragon.com
Durand	Durand-Salabert-Eschig (BMG) 16 rue des Fossés Saint-Jacques 75005 Paris, France Tel: +33. (0)1.44.41.5090 Fax: +33. (0)1.44.41.5091 E-mail: durand-salabert-eschig@bmg.com location.rental.durant-salabert-eschig@bmg.com (rentals) Web site: www.durand-salabert-eschig.com U.S. Agent: Boosey (rental); Leonard (sales)

Dvg	Dunvagen Music Publishers, Inc. 40 Exchange Place, Suite 1906 New York, NY 10005 Tel: 212.979.2080 Fax: 212.473.2842 E-mail: info@dunvagen.com Web site: www.dunvagen.com U.S. Agent: Schirmer Outside the US: Chester	
E. H. Morris	U.S. Agent: MPL Communications	
EAM	European American Music Distributors LLC (Schott Music International/European American Music) 254 West 31st Street Floor 15 New York, NY 10001-2813 USA Tel: 212.461.6940 Fax: 212.810.4565 E-mail: info@eamdllc.com Web site: www.eamdllc.com U.S. Agent: Alfred (rental) *For sales works in these catalogs contact Hal Leonard Corporation: Schott Music, Eulenburg, European American Music Corporation, Schott Helicon Music Corporation, Glocken Verlag, Moeck Verlag, Hug Musikverlag, Schott Frères, Zen-On Music Company Ltd. Also: works by Kurt Weill.* *For sales works in the Universal Edition Catalog contact the Theodore Presser Company.* *For sales and rental works in these catalogs contact the Alfred Publishing Company: Warner/Chappell Music Co., Inc., Belwin Mills Publishing Corp., Lawson-Gould Music Publishers.*	
ECS	ECS Publishing 615 Concord Street Framingham, MA 01702 Tel: 800.777.1919 Fax: 508.620.7401 E-mail: office@ecspublishing.com Web site: www.ecspublishing.com *Agent for E.C. Schirmer Music Company; Ione Press; Galaxy Music Corporation; and Highgate Press.*	
Editora Agusta	Editora Agusta Sao Paulo Brazil Fermata Int'l Melodies See Luck's for rental	
Elkan-Vogel	Elkan-Vogel, Inc. U.S. Agent: Presser	
EMI	EMI Music Publishing 27 Wrights Lane London W8 5SW United Kingdom Tel: +44 203 059 3059 Fax: +44 203 059 2059	EMI Music Publishing 550 Madison Avenue, 5th Floor New York, NY 10022 Tel: 212.833.7730 E-mail: mediauk@emimusicpub.com Web site: www.emimusicpub.com U.S. Agent: Schirmer

EMM	Ediciones Mexicanas de Música Avenida Juarez, 18; Desp. 206 Mexico D.F. Mexico U.S. Agent: Peer
EMR	Editions Marc Reift Case Postale 308-CH-3963 Crans-Montana, Switzerland E-mail: info@reift.ch Web site: www.reift.ch U.S. Agent: Solid Brass Music Co.
EMS	Educational Music Service 33 Elkay Drive Chester, NY 10918 Tel: 845.469.5790 Fax: 845.469.5817 E-mail: sales@emsmusic.com Web site: www.emsmusic.com
Eaton	Eaton Music Limited 14-15 Berners Street London, W1T 3LJ Tel: +20.7612.7400 Fax: +20.7836.4874 See Luck's for rental
Ernest Williams	Ernest Williams School of Music, 153 Ocean Ave., Brooklyn NY See Luck's for rental
Eschig	Durand-Salabert-Eschig (BMG) See: Durand U.S. Agent: Boosey (rental); Leonard (sales)
Eskola	Jari Eskola, Manager of services Music Finland (Finnish Music Information Centre) Lauttasaarentie 1 FIN-00200 Helsinki, Finland Tel. 011.358.(0).20.730.2230 E-mail: jari.eskola@gmail.com
Eulenburg	Edition Eulenburg U.S. Agent: EAM
Excelsior	Excelsior U.S. Agent: Presser

Faber	Faber Music Limited 74-77 Great Russell Street London WC1B 3DA England Tel: +44.(0).20.7908.5310 Fax: +44. (0).20.7908.5339 E-mail: information@fabermusic.com; hire@fabermusic.com Web site: www.fabermusic.com U.S. Agent: EAM
Famous	Famous Music Corporation 10635 Santa Monica Blvd., Ste. 300 Los Angeles, CA 90025 Tel: 310.441.1317 Fax: 310.441.4722 Web site: www.famousmusic.com U.S. Agent: Leonard (sales) *Famous Music is the music publishing arm of Paramount Pictures (a Viacom subsidiary).*
Feist	Leo Feist, Inc. U.S. Agent: CPP/Belwin Music
Filarmonika	Filarmonika Music Publishing PO Box 33554 Granada Hills, CA 91394 Tel: 817.995.9616 Fax: 866.789.5037 Web site: www.filarmonika.com
Fischer	Carl Fischer LLC Sales: 65 Bleeker Street New York, NY 10012 Tel: 800.762.2328; 212.777.0900 x209 Fax: 212.777.6996 E-mail: cf-info@carlfischer.com Web site: www.carlfischer.com U.S Agent: Presser (rentals)
Fleisher	Edwin A. Fleisher Collection of Orchestral Music at the Free Library of Philadelphia 1901 Vine St. Philadelphia, PA 19103 Tel: 215-686-5313 Fax: 215-563-3628 E-mail: Fleisher@freelibrary.org Web site: http://catalog.freelibrary.org *The Fleisher Collection is the largest lending library of orchestral performance material in the world.*
Fox	Sam Fox Publishing Company Inc. U.S. Agent: Alfred
Frank	Frank Music Corporation U.S. Agent: MTI (rental-partial); Leonard (sales)
Galaxy	Galaxy U.S. Agent: ECS Publishing

G&C	G&C Music Corporation U.S. Agent: Schirmer (rental)
GEA	Gould/European-American U.S. Agent: Schirmer (rental)
Glocken	Glocken Verlag, Ltd 12 - 14 Mortimer Street London W1N 8EL England U.S. Agent: EAM (rental); Leonard (sales)
Gold Horizon/ Golden Torch	Gold Horizon Music Corp and Golden Torch Music U.S. Agent: CPP/Belwin Music
Gomez	Alice Gomez Music Box 12004 San Antonio, TX 78212 Tel: 210.326 7646 Fax: 210.403 0918 E-mail: gomezmusiq@aol.com Web site: www.alicegomez.com
Goodmusic	Goodmusic Publishing (Roberton Publications) P.O. Box 100 Tewkesbury GL20 7YQ UK Tel: 011.44.1684.77.3883 Fax: 011.44.1684.77.3884 E-mail: sales@goodmusicpublishing.co.uk Web site: www.goodmusicpublishing.co.uk U.S. Agent: Presser *Sells the Oxford Contemporary Repertoire series on behalf of Oxford University Press.*
Grantwood Music	Grantwood Music Press Web site: www.jamesgrantmusic.com U.S. Agent: Wendel
GunMar	GunMar Music See Margun U.S. Agent: Schirmer
Hansen	Edition Wilhelm Hansen Tel: 011.45.33.11.7888 Fax: 011.45.33.14.8178 E-mail: ewh@ewh.dk Web site: www.ewh.dk U.S. Agent: Schirmer
Hansen House	Hansen House 1820 West Ave. Miami Beach, FL 33139 Tel: 800.357.7768; 305.532.5461 Fax: 305.672.8729 E-mail: info@hansenhousemusic.com Web site: www.hansenhousemusic.com

Harms	Harms, Inc. U.S. Agent: Alfred	
Helicon	Schott Helicon Music Corporation U.S. Agent: Leonard (sales); EAM (rental)	
Henle	G. Henle Verlag Forstenrieder Allee 122 81476 München Germany Tel: +49. (89).759.82 - 0 Fax: +49. (89).759.82 - 40 E-mail: info@henle.de (Germany) E-mail: info@henleusa.com (USA) Web site: www.henle.com	G. Henle USA P.O. Box 460127 St. Louis, MO 63146 Tel: 314.514.1791 Fax: 314.514.1269 E-mail: musicpubs@msn.com info@henleusa.com Web site: www.henleusa.com See: Bärenreiter (rentals) Breitkopf (sales in Europe)
	No U.S. Agent for orchestral materials. Leonard is sales agent for chamber music, study scores, and instrumental music sales.	
Heugel	Heugel & Cie. (A division of the Alphonse Leduc Group) U.S. Agent: King	
Highland/Etling	Highland/Etling Publishing U.S. Agent: Alfred (sales)	
Hinshaw	Hinshaw Music Inc. P.O. Box 470 Chapel Hill, NC 27514 Tel: 919.933.1691; Orders: 800.568.7805 Fax: 919.967.339 E-mail: does not accept orders by E-mail Web site: www.hinshawmusic.com	
Irving	Irving Music Inc. See Luck's for rental	
Janen	Janen Music 3113 West Burbank Boulevard Burbank, CA 91505 Tel: 877.77.janen; 818.563.2087 Fax: 818.563.2187 E-mail: smcrae@janenmusic.com; rentals@janenmusic.com Web site: www.janenmusic.com	
Jendras	Louis F. Jendras (Self publisher) See Luck's for rental	
Jobert	Societé des Editions Jobert 29 Boulevard Beaumarchais 75017 Paris France Tel: 011.56.68.8660 Fax: 011.56.68.9066 E-mail: info@jobert.fr Web site: www.jobert.fr Agent: Lemoine	

Kalmus	Edwin F. Kalmus LC P.O. Box 5011 Boca Raton, FL 33487-0811 Tel: 800.434.6340; 561.241.6340 Fax: 561.241.6347 E-mail: efkalmus@aol.com Web site: www.kalmus-music.com	Rentals: Edwin F. Kalmus LC 6403 W. Rodgers Circle Boca Raton, FL 33487 Tel: 800.434.6340 Tel: 561.241.6340 (rentals) Fax: 561.241.6347 E-mail: efkalmus@aol.com Web site: www.kalmus-music.com

Kane
JoAnn Kane Music Service
3526 Hayden Avenue
Culver City, CA 90232
Tel: 310.231.9733
Fax: 310.733.4126
E-mail: rentals@joannkanemusic.com
Web site: www.joannkanemusic.com
Agent for the Jerry Goldsmith and Henry Mancini Rental Libraries.

Kendor
Kendor Music, Inc.
21 Grove Street
PO Box 278
Delevan, New York 14042-0278
Phone: 716.492.1254
Fax: 716.492.5124
Web site: www.kendormusic.com
No direct orders. Order from your music dealer.

King
Robert King Music Sales, Inc. (A division of the Alphonse Leduc Group)
140 Main Street
North Easton, MA 02356-1499
Tel: 508.238.8118
Fax: 508.238.2571
E-mail: commerce@RKingMusic.com; rental@rkingmusic.com
Web site: www.rkingmusic.com
Rental agent for Heugel, Hamelle, and Leduc.

Kjos
Neil A. Kjos Music Company
4382 Jutland Dr.
P.O. Box 178270
San Diego, CA 92117
Tel: 858.270.9800
Fax: 858.270.3507
E-mail: email@kjos.com
Web site: www.kjos.com

Koff
Koff Music Company
c/o Mother Lode Music Services
P.O. Box 110
Jamestown, CA USA 95327
Tel: 209.984.0610
Fax: 209.984.0681
Web site: www.mlmusic-online.com

Kunzelmann	Edition Kunzelmann Grutstrasse 28, Postfach 1023 8134 Adliswil, Switzerland Tel: 011.41.44.710.3681 Fax: 011.41.44.710.3817 E-mail: edition@kunzelmann.com Web site: www.kunzelmann.ch U.S. Agent: Peters
Kuster	Kristin P. Kuster Earl V. Moore Building 1100 Baits Drive Ann Arbor MI 48109-2085 Tel: 917.674.7707 E-mail: kkuster@kristinkuster.com Web site: www.kristinkuster.com
Lagos	Editorial Lagos S.R.I. Talcahuano 638 - P.B. H Buenos Aires 1013, Argentina Tel: 011.54.11.4.371.3746 Fax: 011.54.11.4.374.5528 E-mail: editlagos@overnet.com.ar Web site: www.editoriallagos.com
Lakeview	Lakeview Music Publishing Company Ltd U.S. Agent: Music Sales
Lawdon	Lawdon Press 1008 Spruce St., #3F Philadelphia, PA 19107 Tel: 215.592.1847 Fax: 215.592.1095 E-mail: lawdonpress@aol.com Web site: www.jenniferhigdon.com
Lawson-Gould	Lawson-Gould Music Publishers, Inc. U.S. Agent: Alfred
LeDor	LeDor Group, Inc. 118 North Peters Rd., #330 Knoxville, TN 37923 Tel: 865.691.0428; 888.624.9094 Fax: 568.691.0448 E-mail: info@ledorgroup.com Web site: www.ledorgroup.com
Leduc	Editions Alphonse Leduc 175, rue Saint-Honoré 75040 Paris cedex 01 Tel: +33.01.42.96.8911 Fax: +33.01.42.86.0283 Web site: www.alphonseleduc.com U.S. Agent: King

Leeds	Leeds Music Corporation U.S. Agent: MCA
Lemoine	Henry Lemoine et Cie 27 Boulevard Beaumarchais F-75004 Paris France Tel: 011.33.01.56.68.8665 Fax: 011.33.01.56.68.9066 E-mail: orchestre@editions-lemoine.fr Web site: www.henry-lemoine.com
Lengnick	Alfred Lengnick & Company www.ricordi.co.uk/lengnick_catalogue/ US agent: Schirmer (rentals); Complete (sales)
Leonard	Hal Leonard Corporation 7777 W. Bluemound Rd. Milwaukee, WI 53213 Tel: 414.774.3630 Fax: 414.774.3259 E-mail: halinfo@halleonard.com www.laurenkeisermusic.com (rentals) Web site: www.halleonard.com *A list of some of the major publishers represented for print sales by Hal Leonard: G. Schirmer, AMP, and Music Sales Corp. and Shawnee. Leonard also administers rentals for the MJQ catalog.*
Leuckart	F.E.C. Leuckart Rheingoldstrasse 4 D-80639 Munich, Germany Tel: +49. (0).8917.3928 Fax: +49. (0).8917.6054 Web site: www.thomi-berg.de International Agent: See Thomi~Berg US agent: Peters (for North America)
Liben	Liben Music Publishers 1191 Eversole Road Cincinnati, OH 45230-3546 Tel: 513.232.6920 Fax: 513.232.1866 E-mail: info@liben.com Web site: www.liben.com
LKMP	Lauren Keiser Music Publishing 12685 Dorset Rd., #331 Maryland Heights, MO 63043-2100 USA Tel: 203-560-9436 Fax: 314-270-5305 E-mail: info@laurenkeisermusic.com Web site: www.laurenkeisermusic.com

Luck's	Luck's Music Library 32300 Edward P.O. Box 71397 Madison Heights, MI 48071 Tel: 800.348.8749 Fax: 248.583.1114 E-mail: sales@lucksmusic.net; helpdesk@lucksmusic.net Web site: www.lucksmusic.net
Ludwig	Ludwig Music Publishing Company Inc. U.S. Agent: LudwigMasters Publications
LudwigMasters	LudwigMasters Publications 6403 West Rogers Circle Boca Raton, FL 33487 Tel: 800.434.6340; 561.241.6169 Fax: 561.241.6347 Web site: www.masters-music.com
MAA	Music Associates of America 224 King Street or P.O. Box 671 Englewood, New Jersey 07631 Tel: 201.569.2898 Fax: 201.569.7023 E-mail: maasturm@sprynet.com Web site: www.musicassociatesofamerica.com
Mapleson	Mapleson Rental Library U.S. Agent: EMS
Margun	Margun Music U.S. Agent: Schirmer
Marks	Edward B. Marks Music Corp. c/o Carlin American Inc. 126 E. 38th Street New York, NY 10016 Tel: 212.779.7977 Fax: 212.779.7920 E-Mail: bkalban@carlinamerica.com Web site: www.ebmarks.com U.S. Agent: Presser (rental); Leonard (sales)
Masters	Masters Music Publications, Inc. U.S. Agent: LudwigMasters Publications
MBM	Manhattan Beach Music 1595 East 46th Street Brooklyn, NY 11234-3122 Tel: 800.978.4505 Fax: 718.338.1151 E-mail customerservice@manhattanbeachmusic.com Web site: www.ManhattanBeachMusic.com

MCA	MCA Music (Music Corporation of America/Universal Music Group) U.S. Agent: Alfred (rental); Leonard (sales)
Mercury	Mercury Music Corporation U.S. Agent: Presser (rental)
Merion	Merion Music, Inc. U.S. Agent: Presser
Miller	Miller Music Corporation See Luck's for rental
Mills	Mills Music, Inc. U.S. Agent: Schirmer (rentals); Alfred (sales)
Mitchell	Darren Mitchell 720 4th Ave. Suite 200 Kirkland, WA 98033 Tel: 919-645-8144 Fax: 425-822-3930 E-mails: dmitchell@catdaddy.com (office) dlmitchell64@comcast.net (home)
MJQ	MJQ Music Inc. 7777 West Bluemound Rd. Milwaukee, WI 53213 Tel: 414.774.3630 Fax: 414.774.3259 E-mail: permissions@halleonard.com Web site: http://www.mjqmusic.com/ U.S. Agent: Leonard (sales & licensing); LKMP (rentals)
MMB	U.S. Agent: LKMP
Morris	Edwin H. Morris & Co. U.S. Agent: MPL Communications; Leonard (sales)
MPA	Music Publishers' Association 243 5th Avenue, Suite 236 New York, NY 10016 Tel: 212.327.4044 E-mail: admin@mpa.org Web site: www.mpa.org
MPL	MPL Communications E-mail: info@mplcommunications.com. Web site: www.mplcommunications.com *MPL Communications, Inc. in New York and MPL Communications Ltd. in London were established upon the breakup of the Beatles. Paul McCartney founded MPL, which stands for McCartney Productions Ltd.*

MTI	Music Theatre International 421 West 54th Street, 2nd Floor New York, NY 10019 Tel: 212.541.4684 Fax: 212.397.4684 E-mail: Licensing@MTIshows.com Web site: www.mtimusicalworlds.com Web site: (Concert Library) www.mtishows.com/concerts.asp	
Musicians Pub.	Musicians Publications, Inc. 315 Great Bridge Blvd. Suite B Chesapeake VA 23320 Tel: 757.410.3111. Fax: 757.410.3127 E-mail: ehigh@billholcombe.com Web sites: www.musicianspublications.com www.myorchestrarentals.com	
Music Sales	Music Sales Group 8-9 Frith Street London W1D 3JB United Kingdom Tel: +44. (0).20.7434.0066 Fax: +44. (0).7287.6329	257 Park Avenue South, 20th Floor New York, NY 10010 Tel: 212.254.2100 Fax: 212.254.2013 Web site: www.musicsales.com U.S. Agent: Leonard (sales)
Naughtin	Matthew Naughtin 184 Funston Ave., #12 San Francisco, CA 94118 Tel: 415.831.8058 E-mail: mattmus@mindspring.com Web site: www.mattnaughtin.com	
New World	New World Music Company, Ltd. U.S. Agent: EAM (rental); Alfred (sales)	
Nordiska	AB Nordiska Musikforlaget U.S. Agent: Schirmer	
Northridge	Northridge Music Company C/O Universal Music Corporation 2100 Colorado Avenue Santa Monica, CA 90404 Telephone: 310.235.4700 Web site: www.umusicpub.com	
Novello	Novello & Co. See: Chester/Novello Web site: www.chesternovello.com U.S. Agent: Schirmer	

Oxford	Oxford University Press
Music Department
Great Clarendon Street
United Kingdom
Tel: +44.1865.35.5067; rent: +44. (0).1865.35.3323
Fax: +44.1865.35.5060; rent: +44. (0).1865.35.3767
E-mails: rentals@cfpeters-ny.com (USA, Mexico, Central and South America)
        Counterpoint_Musical@compuserve.com (Canada)
        music.hire.uk@oup.com (rest of world)
        music.enquiry.uk@oup.com
Web site: www.oup.co.uk/music

Music Department
198 Madison Avenue
New York, NY 10016
Tel: 212.726.6000
Fax: 212.726.6441
E-mail: music.us@oup.com
Web site: www.oup.com/us/music
U.S. Agent: Peters |
| **Pagani** | A. Pagani s.r.l. Edizioni Musicali e Discografiche
Via dei Gardanesi N°238
22030 Lipomo (Como) Italy
Tel: +39.031.55.3254
Fax: +39.031.55.3249
E-mail: info@apagani.it
Web site: www.apagani.it
No U.S. Agent |
| **PAR** | Parnassus Productions, Inc.
U.S. Agent: Schirmer (rental) |
| **Paumanok** | Paumanok Press Music Publishers
270 Madison Avenue, Suite 1501
New York, New York 10016
E-mail: info@michaelshapiro.com |
| **Pecktackular** | Pecktacular Music
3605 Brandywine Drive
Greensboro, NC 27410
Tel: 336.288.7034
Fax: 336.286.2940
E-mail: PeckMusic@RussellPeck.com
Web page: www.russellpeck.com |
| **Peer** | Peermusic Classical
810 Seventh Avenue
New York, NY 10019
Tel: 212.265.3910
Fax: 212.489.2465
Web site: www.peermusicclassical.com
U.S. Agent: Subito |
| **Pembroke** | Pembroke Music Co.
U.S. Agent: Fischer |

Pepper	J. W. Pepper & Son, Inc. 2480 Industrial Boulevard Paoli, PA 19301 Tel: 800.345.6296; 610.648.0500 Fax: 800.260.1482 Web site: www.peppermusic.com

Peters	C.F. Peters Musikverlag
	Kennedyallee 101
	D - 60596 Frankfurt/Main, Germany
	Tel: +49.(0).69.63.0099-0
	Fax: +49.(0).69.63.0099-54
	
	C. F. Peters Corporation, NY
	70-30 80th Street
	Glendale, NY 11385
	Tel: 718.416.7800; 718.416.7805 (rental)
	Fax: 718.416.7805
	E-mails: rentals@cfpeters-ny.com
	        sales@cfpeters-ny.com
	        rentals.us@editionpeters.com
	        info@edition-peters.de
	Web site: www.edition-peters.com

Piedmont	Piedmont Music Company US agent: EAM (rentals); Alfred (sales)
Presser	Theodore Presser Company 588 North Gulph Road King of Prussia, PA 19406 Tel: 610.592.1222 Fax: 610.592.1229 E-mail: rental@presser.com Web site: www.presser.com *Presser operates jointly with Fischer.*
PWM	Polskie Wydawnictwo Muzyczne SA Al. Krasińskiego 11a 31-111 Kraków, Poland Tel: +48.12.422.7044 Fax: +48.12.422.0174 E-mail: internet@pwm.com.pl Web site: www.pwm.com.pl U.S. Agent: Presser (rental); Boosey for Gorecki rental
RBC	RBC Publications P.O. Box 29128 San Antonio, Texas 78229 Tel: 800.548.0917 Fax: 210.736.2919 E-mail: sales@rbcmusic.com Web site: www.rbcmusic.com *Agents for Counterpoint Music, Wynn Music, Dorabet Music, Young World Publications, String Instrument Specialists, and Jerry Bilik Music.*

Regent	Regent Music Corporation 630 Ninth Avenue Suite 1004 New York NY 10036 Tel: 212.246.3333 Fax: 212.262.6299 Web site: www.arcmusic.com
Remick	Remick Music Corporation U.S, Agent: EAM (rental); Alfred (sales)
Ricordi	G. Ricordi & Co., S.p.A I-20121 Milano Italy Tel: +39.02.8881 Fax: +39.02.8881.2212 E-mail: promozione.ricordi@bmg.com Web site: www.ricordi.com U.S. Agent: Boosey (rental); Leonard (sales) Rentals: Casa Ricordi-BMG Ricordi Music Publishing S.p.A Music Rental Service Via Liguria 4 - fr. Sesto Ulteriano 20098 S. Giuliano Milanese (Mi), Italy Tel: +39.02.98813.4220 or 4302 Fax: +39.02.98813.4258 E-mail: rental.ricordi@bmg.com U.S. Agent: Boosey (rental)
Robbins	Robbins Music Corporation U.S. Agent: EMI Publishing
Robert King	Robert King Music See: King
Robinsdale	Robinsdale Music Co Inc 275 Central Park West New York, NY 10024-3015 Tel: 212.799.7169 Fax: 212.799.1674 E-mail: robinsdale@juno.com
R&H	Rodgers & Hammerstein Concert Library 229 West 28th Street, 11th Floor New York, NY 10001 Tel: 212.268.9300 Fax: 212.268.1245 E-mail: concert@rnh.com Web site: www.rnh.com_library/index.php The Rodgers and Hammerstein Organization 1065 Avenue of the Americas, Suite 2400 New York, NY 10018 Tel: 212.541.6600 Fax: 212.586.6155 Web site: www.rnh.com (For rental of musical shows)

Russian	G. Schirmer Russian (GSR)
	U.S. Agent: Schirmer (rental); Leonard (sales)
Salabert	Durand-Salabert-Eschig (BMG)
	See: Durand
	U.S. Agent: Boosey (rental); Leonard (sales)
Sam Fox	Sam Fox Publishing Company Inc.
	See: Fox
Saravah	Editions Saravah
	36 rue de l'Église 85500 Les Herbiers
	Paris, France
	Tel: +02.51.65.7231
	E-mail: info@saravah.fr
	See Luck's for rental
SBM	Solid Brass Music Co.
	71 Mt. Rainier Dr.
	San Rafael, CA 94903
	Tel: 415.479.1337
	E-mail: dick@sldbrass.com
	Web site: www.sldbrass.com
SC Gems	Screen Gems-EMI Music, Inc.
	U.S. Agent: EMI
Schirmer	Music Sales/G. Schirmer, Inc.
	Executive Offices
	257 Park Ave. South
	20th Floor
	New York, NY 10010
	Tel: 212.254.2100
	Fax: 212.254.2013
	U.S. Agent: Leonard (sales)

G. Schirmer, Inc.
Rental and Performance Department
445 Bellvale Road
Chester, NY 10918 USA
Tel: 845.469.4699
Fax: 845.469.7544
Web site: www.schirmer.com

Schott	Schott-Musik International GmbH
	Schott Music GmbH & Co. KG
	Weihergarten 5, Postfach 3640
	55116 Mainz, Germany
	Tel: +49.6131.246-0
	Fax: +49.6131.246-211
	E-mail: info@schott-musik.com
	Web site: www.Schott-Music.com
	U.S. Agent: EAM
Scott/Helena	Helena Music Corporation
	1501 Broadway
	Suite 1313
	New York NY 10036
	Tel: 212.764.1234
	Fax: 212.764.1197
	Imprints Held: Renleigh Music, Mitch Leigh Music, Kradar Music, Kamakura Music, Helena Music, and Andrew Scott Music.

Shawnee	Shawnee Press, Inc. 421 E. Iris, Ste. 202 Nashville, TN 37204 Tel: 800.962.8584; 615.320.5300 Fax: 800.971.4310; 615.320.7306 E-mail: shawnee-info@shawneepress.com shawnee-sales@shawneepress.com Web site: www.shawneepress.com U.S Agent: Leonard (sales); Schirmer (rental)
Sherwood	Ramsey Sherwood Press See Luck's for rental
Sikorski	Internationale Musikverlage Hans Sikorski Johnsalle 23, Postfach 13-2001 D-20148 Hamburg Germany Tel: +49.40.41.4100 – 0 Fax: +49.40.41.4100 – 41 E-mail: contact@sikorski.de Web site: www.sikorski.de U.S. Agent: Schirmer (rental); Leonard (sales)
Silva	Silva Screen Music America 555 8th Avenue, Suite 1803 New York, NY 10018 Tel: 212.564.8855; 866.564.8855 Fax: 212.564.8865 E-mail: info@fourquartersent.com Web site: www.silvascreen.co.uk
Simrock	N. Simrock Werderstraße 44 20144 Hamburg, Germany Tel: +49.040.45.1225 U.S. Agent: Boosey (rental); Leonard (sales)
SOD	Samuel Osler Douglas 522 Knollwood Drive Columbia, SC 29209 E-mail: sdouglas@mozart.sc.edu
SMC	Southern Music Publishing Co., Inc. 1248 Austin Highway, Ste. 212; PO Box 329 San Antonio, TX 78292 Tel: 210.226.8167; 800.284.5443 Fax: 210.223.4537 E-mail: info@smcpublications.com Web site: www.smcpublications.com US agent: LKMP

Sonzogno	Casa Musicale Sonzogno Via Bigli, 11 20121 Milano, Italy Tel: +39.02.76.00.00.65 Fax: +39.02.76.01.45.12 E-mail: sonzogno@sonzogno.it Web site: www.sonzogno.it US agent: Presser
Sorom	Sorom Editions c/o Susanna Moross Tarjan 8526 SW 94 St. Miami, FL 33156 Tel: 305.275.1790; 305.275.1774 E-mail: Smtarjan@aol.com
Spanka	Spanka Music Corporation See Luck's for rental
Stainer	Stainer & Bell Ltd. PO Box 110 Victoria House 23 Gruneisen Road London N3 1DZ United Kingdom Tel: +44.20.8343.2535 (or 3303 for sales) Fax: +44.20.8343.3024 E-mail: post@stainer.co.uk Web site: www.stainer.co.uk U.S. Agent: ECS
Stangland	Thomas C. Stangland Company 7804 S.W. 45th Ave., Suite 47 P.O. Box 19263 Portland, OR 97280-0263 Tel: 503.244.0634 Fax: 208.485.4393 E-mail: info@TomasSvoboda.com Web site: www.TomasSvoboda.com
Stephenson	Stephenson Music, Inc. 264 Park Ave. Lake Forest, IL 60045 Tel: 847.830.5882 E-mail: composerjim@gmail.com Website: www.stephensonmusic.com
Stokowski	Stokowski Collection Marjorie Hassen, Curator Otto E. Albrecht Music Library University of Pennsylvania Web site: www.library.upenn.edu/exhibits/rbm/stokowski/ U.S. Agent: Presser (rental)
Strouse	Charles Strouse U.S. Agent: MPL Communication; Leonard (sales)

Subito	Subito Music Corporation 60 Depot Street Verona, NY 07044 Tel: 973.857.3440 Fax: 973.857.3442 E-Mail: mail@subitomusic.com Web site: www.subitomusic.com *Publishers represented: Subito Music Publishing, Norevole Music Publishing, Seesaw Music, Treble Clef Music, Association for the Promotion of New Music, Dunsinane Music, Brassworks Music (Canadian Brass), Cambian Press, Columbia University Music Press, Ben Rena Music, Sorom Editions, Dunstan Press, Zimbel Press, Peermusic Classical.*
Sunbury	Sunbury Music Inc. See Luck's for rental
Supraphon	Editio Supraphon Palckeho 1 / 740 CS - 112 99 Praha 1 Czech Republic Tel: +420.221.966.600 Fax: +420.221.966.630 E-mail: info@supraphon.cz Web site: www.supraphon.cz US agent: EAM
Suvini	Edizioni Suvini Zerboni See: Zerboni
Tams-Witmark	Tams-Witmark 560 Lexington Avenue New York, NY 10022 Tel: 212.688.9191; 800.221.7196 Fax: 212.688.5656; 800.826.7121 Web site: www.tamswitmark.com *Complete musical shows only. No concert library.*
Templeton	Templeton Publishing Inc. U.S. Agent: Shawnee
Tempo	Tempo Music Resource 204 7th St. W., No.1 Northfield, MN 55057-2419 E-mail: inquire@tempomusicresource.org Web site: www.tempomusicresource.org
Tetra	Tetra/Continuo Music Group % Robert J. Bregman Co. Inc. 960 Park Ave., Apt. 10E New York, NY 10028 Tel: 212.628.0890 U.S. Agent: LudwigMasters

T&V	Themes and Variations 1255 Fairfield Beach Road Fairfield, CT 06824 Tel: 203.259.0401 Fax: 203.259.0405 E-mail: tnv@tnv.net Web site: www.tnv.net
Thomi~Berg	Thomi~Berg Verlag Pasinger Strasse 38a · Postfach 1736 D-82145 Planegg bei München, Germany Tel: +49.89.859.9944 Fax: +49.89.859.3323 E-mail: info@thomi-berg.de Web site: www.thomi-berg.de U.S. Agent: Peters (North America)
Thorpe	Thorpe Music Publishing Company U.S. Agent: Presser
Tonos	Tonos Musikverlags GmbH Lange Straße 89a 76530 Baden-Baden, Germany Tel: +49.7221.97370-0 Fax: +49.7221.97370-27 E-mail: mail@tonosmusic.com; administration@tonosmusic.com Web site: www.tonosmusic.com U.S. Agent: Alfred
TPO	Tempo Music Inc. U.S. Agent: Schirmer (rental)
Triple Star/Marjer/ Stage and Screen	Triple Star Music Inc. Marjer Music Pub, Inc Stage and Screen Music Inc. See Luck's for rental
Tritone	Tritone Press & Tenuto Publications E-mail: info@tritone-tenuto.com Web site: www.triton-tenuto.com U.S. Agent: Presser
TRO	The Richmond Organization U.S. Agent: Leonard
Turrin	Joseph Turrin 303 Harding Ave. Clifton, NJ 07011 USA Tel: 973.546.3088 Fax: 973.546.3466 E-mail: jturrin@josephturrin.com

UME	Unión Musical Ediciones S.L. C/Marqués de la Ensenada 4, 3o. Madrid, 28004 Spain Tel: +34.91.308.4040 Fax: +34.91.310.4429 U.S. Agent: AMP
United Artists	United Artists Music Co., Inc. New York NY See Luck's for rental
UMP	United Music Publishers 33 Lea Road, Waltham Abbey Essex EN9 1ES, UK Tel: +44.1992.703110 Fax: +44.1992.703189 E-mail: info@ump.co.uk Web site: www.ump.co.uk U.S. Agent: Presser
Universal	Universal Edition, Inc. Karlsplatz 6 A-1010 Vienna, Austria Tel: +43.1.337.23 – 0 Fax: +43.1.337.23 – 400 E-mail: office@universaledition.com Web site: www.universaledition.com 254 West 31st Street, Floor 15 New York, NY 10010 Tel: 212.461.6940 Fax: 212.810.4565 Web site: www.universaledition.com/usa U.S. Agents: EAM (rental); Fischer (sales)
Viola World	Viola World Publications Alan Arnold 2 Islander Road Saratoga Springs, NY 12866 Tel: 518.583.7022 E-mail: info@violaworldpublications.com Web site: www.violaworldpublications.com
Vogue	Vogue Music Inc. See Luck's for rental
Warner	Warner Bros. Publications; Warner/Chappell Web site: warnerchappell.com U.S. Agent: Alfred
Weintraub	Weintraub Music Company U.S. Agent: Schirmer (rental); Music Sales (sales)

Wendel	Robert Wendel Music 467 West 163rd Street, 3rd Floor New York City, NY 10032 Tel: 212.928.9094 Fax: 212.928.9094 E-mail: bobwen@pipeline.com Web site: www.wendelmusic.com
Williamson	Williamson Music 1065 Avenue of the Americas, Suite 2400 New York, NY 10018 Tel: 212.489.6637 Web site: www.williamsonmusic.com U.S. Agent: R&H Concert Library (rental); Leonard (sales)
Witmark	M. Witmark & Sons U.S. Agent: EAM (rental); Alfred (sales)
Wonderland	Wonderland Music Company U.S. Agent: Disney
Woodbury	Woodbury Music Company 33 Grassy Hill Road, P.O. Box 447 Woodbury, CT 06798 Tel: 203.263.0696 Fax: 203.263.5102 E-mail: info@woodburymusic.com Web site: www.leroy-anderson.com U.S. Agent: Presser (rental-partial); Wendel (rental-partial); Kalmus (sales)
Zanibon	Edizioni G. Zanibon U.S. Agent: Boosey (rental)
ZB	ZB Publishing Industries 1430 Bristol Terrace #104 Lawrence, KS 66049 Tel: 785.749.1110 E-mail: zbavel@ku.edu See Luck's for rental
Zerboni	Edizioni Suvini Zerboni Galleria del Corso 4 20122 Milan, Italy Tel: +39.02.77.07.0701 Fax: +39.02.77.07.0261 E-mail: suvini.zerboni@sugarmusic.com Web site: www.esz.it US agent: Boosey

ABOUT THE AUTHOR

This book is an outgrowth of **Lucy Manning's** doctoral dissertation and resulting first edition as she made the transition from violinist to conductor.

As a child of an avid amateur flute player, every summer began with the strains of her father revamping the piccolo solo in the *Stars and Stripes Forever.* Combined with his idolization of Arthur Fiedler, Lucy continues his interest with her enjoyment of well-rehearsed and inventive pops concerts.

Lucy recently retired as orchestra director and violin professor at Old Dominion University in Norfolk, Virginia.

She received a B.M. degree in violin from West Virginia University, an M.M. in violin from the University of Illinois, and a D.M.A in Orchestral Conducting from the University of South Carolina.